ONE WEEK LOAN

THE EVOLUTION OF EU LAW

Second Edition

EDITED BY

PAUL CRAIG

AND

GRÁINNE DE BÚRCA

OXFORD

UNIVERSITY PRESS

OXFORD
UNIVERSITY PRESS

Great Clarendon Street, Oxford OX2 6DP

Oxford University Press is a department of the University of Oxford.
It furthers the University's objective of excellence in research, scholarship,
and education by publishing worldwide in

Oxford New York

Auckland Cape Town Dar es Salaam Hong Kong Karachi
Kuala Lumpur Madrid Melbourne Mexico City Nairobi
New Delhi Shanghai Taipei Toronto

With offices in

Argentina Austria Brazil Chile Czech Republic France Greece
Guatemala Hungary Italy Japan Poland Portugal Singapore
South Korea Switzerland Thailand Turkey Ukraine Vietnam

Oxford is a registered trade mark of Oxford University Press
in the UK and in certain other countries

Published in the United States
by Oxford University Press Inc., New York

British Library Cataloguing in Publication Data
Data available

Library of Congress Cataloging in Publication Data
Data available

Typeset by SPI Publisher Services, Pondicherry, India
Printed in Great Britain on acid-free paper by
CPI Antony Rowe, Chippenham, Wiltshire

ISBN: 978–0–19–959297–5 (Hbk)
978–0–19–959296–8 (Pbk)

1 3 5 7 9 10 8 6 4 2

CONTENTS

TABLE OF CASES

Numerical

European Court of Justice

Alphabetical

European Court of Justice Opinions

TABLE OF TREATIES AND CONVENTIONS

National Legislation

BELGIUM

FRANCE

GERMANY

IRAQ

IRELAND

ITALY

LAOS

NETHERLANDS

NORTH KOREA

SAUDI ARABIA

SOUTH AFRICA

SPAIN

SWEDEN

1

INTRODUCTION

Paul Craig and Gráinne de Búrca

This is the second edition of a work that first appeared just over a decade ago in 1999. It seemed fitting for a book entitled the *Evolution of EU Law*, to see what had transpired in the decade between the first and second edition of this work. The inspiration and approach of the second edition remains the same as the first. We asked the contributors to stand back and to consider how their particular subject had evolved over time, to analyse the principal themes, and to assess the legal and political forces that shaped its development. The contributors have performed this task admirably, and we are grateful to them.[1] This book is not, therefore, a text, and the contributors have not been asked to give exhaustive treatment to every nuance or point of detail that pertains to their object of inquiry. They have free rein to tell the story of the evolution of their chosen area as they think fit. There are in any event many 'stories' that could be told about the evolution of the topics considered in this book.

Several significant changes have been made in this second edition as compared with the first. A number of new topics which seemed particularly prominent in EU law over the last decade—enlargement, the area of freedom, security and justice (including migration as well as civil and criminal law aspects), citizenship, human rights, regulation of financial services, free movement of capital, and cultural policy—have been added. A separate chapter on Agencies, which were previously treated within the chapter on Institutions, and a chapter on the institutional question of the 'legal basis' for EU action, have been included. For a variety of reasons, we have not been able to include updated versions of the chapters on the Regulation of the Single Market, the Free Movement of Goods, Regional Policy, or Education and Vocational Training. Several new contributors—Mark Bell, Kieran St Clair Bradley, Christophe Hillion, Pierre Larouche, Steve Peers, Jukka Snell, Alec Stone Sweet, Eva Storskrubb, and Takis Tridimas—have joined the team which wrote the first edition.

A wide range of forces has shaped and continues to shape the evolution of EU law. The most obvious legal novelty of the last decade has been Treaty reform, culminating

---

[1] We are also grateful to Kristina Schoenfeldt, who has provided excellent editorial assistance in preparing this book for publication.

in the Lisbon Treaty, which itself can only be understood in the light of the Constitutional Treaty, even though the latter never saw the light of legal day. The resulting Lisbon Treaty has impacted on all the topics studied in this book, although the degree of impact has, not surprisingly, varied depending on the nature of the subject matter. The very fact that we are now an EU with twenty-seven Member States is of real significance, both practical and symbolic, for EU law and politics. It is, however, clear from a reading of the chapters in this volume that many other forces apart from treaty reform have contributed to the evolution of the topics analysed in this work. The EU did not cease to function during the decade when reform was on the table. To the contrary, there was a significant volume of legislation and case law in all the areas studied. Thus the resulting evolution over the last decade has been the result of eclectic forces that have combined, albeit in different ways, to shape particular areas of the law. These forces include, in addition to Treaty reform and enlargement, incremental case law development, the gradual case by case change with which all lawyers are familiar, often characterized by more significant judgments that then shape the subsequent case law in that terrain. Lawyers—including academic lawyers—tend to 'like' case law more than legislation, but an important body of the latter has been in abundant supply during the last ten years, further contributing to the evolution of EU law. The pressures for the legislation are themselves varied, ranging from corrective exercises designed to cure problems revealed in earlier legislative initiatives, to responses to external events such as 9/11 and the banking crisis, and to changing social forces and economic conditions that generate new pressures for EU action. The preceding factors are apparent, albeit to differing degrees, in the contributions to this book.

In the next chapter Paul Craig addresses the rich literature that explores the rationale for EU integration. There are contending theories and the literature is, unsurprisingly, still evolving. The objective is to render accessible to lawyers the scholarship by those schooled in international relations and political science that has explored the dynamic of EU integration. It is also designed to reveal the assumptions and implications of particular integration theories for EU democracy. The chapter then directly considers the debates about EU democracy, the burgeoning literature concerned with the nature of EU democracy, the extent to which the EU suffers from a democratic deficit, and the ways in which it might be alleviated. It will be seen that there is divergence of opinion as to the factors that are regarded as important in assessing EU democracy, which then leads to differences of view as to particular aspects of the democratic deficit critique.

The third chapter of this work is concerned with the evolution of the Community and Union institutional framework, from the inception of the EEC to the Lisbon Treaty. It is a fascinating story, in which all the rationales for evolution adumbrated above played a part. Paul Craig divides the analysis into three periods, the first of which runs from the Rome Treaty to the Single European Act 1986 (SEA). The initial disposition of institutional power in the Rome Treaty was primarily divided between the Council and Commission, with the latter holding many of the 'legal' trump cards.

The underlying theme throughout this period was the way in which this institutional balance gradually shifted, such that Member State influence in the Council and European Council over the content of primary legislation, secondary legislation, and the overall direction of Community policy increased. The second period runs between the SEA and the Nice Treaty, and is marked by three themes, clarification, contestation, and complexity. The third period covers the decade between the Nice and Lisbon Treaties. Treaty reform is a continuation of politics by other means. It is not therefore surprising that institutional issues on the agenda in the previous decade dominated debates on more comprehensive Treaty reform, including the appropriate distribution of primary legislative power, authority over the making of secondary norms, and contestation as to the locus of executive power.

Kieran Bradley's chapter focuses on one particular and important institutional question which has occupied the Court of Justice on many occasions, namely the legal basis on which the EC/EU acts. He shows how the jurisprudence in this area reveals the ECJ undertaking three of the principal functions of a Constitutional Court in a federal-type polity: defining the division of powers between the centre and the Member States; regulating the inter-institutional balance of power; and impacting on the limits of the Court's own jurisdiction, as regards matters such as the categories of legal acts it may review, and the *locus standi* of those directly concerned by legal basis matters, such as the European Parliament. He charts the development of this jurisprudence over time, and reveals how the 'sites of contestation' have varied at different points in the Community's development.

Martin Shapiro addresses another important institutional issue, the ever-growing role of agencies in the EU. His discussion charts the growth in use of agencies in the EU and locates it within the broader debates as to the reasons why agencies have been favoured in other polities. The analysis reveals the variation in powers accorded to EU agencies, and the differing sense in which they are, and are not, independent. Shapiro's contribution details, moreover, the problems, legal and political, in assigning information-gathering, decision-making, regulatory, or quasi-regulatory tasks to such bodies, and the challenges of ensuring legal and political accountability.

Alec Stone Sweet focuses on the role of the Court, using important insights from political science scholarship to which he has contributed so much. He explicates the basic tenets of the principal/agent thesis as to why the Member States were willing to grant power to the ECJ, and elaborates a model of judicial agency and constitutional trusteeship that applies to review courts, including the ECJ. The basic idea is that the Member States established the ECJ to foster more credible commitments, in the face of problems associated with market and political integration. Alec Stone Sweet shows, however, the conceptual difficulties in conceiving of the relationship between Member States and the ECJ in any simple linear principal–agent fashion, insofar as that connotes the Member State principals being able to control the judicial agent, and the conceptual analysis is supported by extensive reference to empirical studies, which have examined the relationship between 'judicial agent' and 'political principal'. His chapter shows the significance of the ECJ's jurisprudence in shaping the very nature of the EU, through the development of doctrines such as direct effect, supremacy, pre-emption, state liability and the like, which have constitutionalized the EU legal order, and had a significant impact on the EU political order. Stone Sweet also forcefully demonstrates the ECJ's contribution to EU governance and market integration.

Deirdre Curtin and Ige Dekker consider the evolution of the EU from Maastricht to Lisbon, the focus being on institutional and legal unity. They recount the creation of the Pillar system in the Maastricht Treaty, and the fears that this would thereby lead to a Europe of 'bits and pieces'. The chapter picks up the story from their contribution to the first edition, in which they had concluded that the EU had in fact evolved into a legal system with a clear unitary character, albeit one that overarched different 'layers' of cooperation and integration. Curtin and Dekker reveal how this trend has continued in the ten years since the first edition of this work, showing how the replacement of the EC by the EU in the Lisbon Treaty reflected institutional reality, such that the formal provisions of the Lisbon Treaty had caught up with 'living' and sedimentary practices. This unitary character was further reinforced by the partial 'depillarization' evident in the Lisbon Treaty, and the application of 'general principles of the Community' to the whole legal framework of the Union, although they recognize the persistence of diverse elements within this overall structure. They situate their analysis within an 'institutional theory of law', which they regard as the best theoretical framework for analysing a complex modern legal system such as the EU. It is reinforced and supported by close consideration of the institutional ordering post-Lisbon, and the roles played by the European Council, High Representative, and the Council General Secretariat.

Christophe Hillion deals with enlargement, a topic that was not included in the first edition of this book. This was an omission that we are glad to have rectified, and that has become all the more pressing over the decade since the first edition was published. Hillion begins his contribution by stressing that enlargement is not just territorial expansion of EU membership rights and obligations to other European states and peoples. It triggers new policy demands on the EU, as well as altering its institutional functioning, and affects its legal corpus. Enlargement has also generated its own body of EU rules that govern how and when a third state becomes a Member State of the EU. The author shows how enlargement was originally conceived as a procedure whereby third states could become contracting parties to the founding treaties, but has now become a more wide-ranging and comprehensive policy, through which the EU engages with the applicants in their preparation for membership. Hillion, however, also demonstrates how the significant enlargement in the new millennium, coupled with further accession demands, has led at one and the same time to some 'enlarge-ment fatigue', and also some 'creeping (re)nationalization' of the procedure.

Marise Cremona considers the evolution of EU law and policy on external relations and external competence. This is a vast and daunting topic, in terms both of its scope and complexity, and we are grateful to Marise Cremona for providing a detailed and valuable overview. She examines three inter-connected themes which have emerged in the evolutionary development of the EU as an international actor. The first theme is concerned with the relationship between internal and external powers and policies, the extent to which the EU's external powers reflect internal competence, and the content of the policies pursued by the EU internally and externally. This theme necessarily has implications for the inter-institutional balance of power, and that between the EU and the Member States. The second theme in the chapter analyses how the classic approach to pre-emption has been modified, such that there is a wide acceptance of shared powers in external spheres of competence. Cremona's third theme is the emergent international identity of the EU and the factors that have shaped it, while being cognizant of the diverse patterns of decision-making and different power-structures between the actors involved, and the plethora of formal/informal instruments used in this area.

Steve Peers deals with an important topic that is new to this edition, the Area of Freedom, Security and Justice (AFSJ). It is a testimony to the mass of important legal and political initiatives in this area that it simply could not be omitted from the second edition of a book on the evolution of EU law, and Steve Peers navigates the non-civil law aspect of this complex terrain. He charts the institutional evolution in this area, showing the gradual shift from pure intergovernmentalism to the qualified triumph of the ordinary 'Community' method in the Lisbon Treaty. This is complemented by a rich analysis of the evolution of substantive EU law in areas such as asylum, immigration, and criminal law.

The scale and complexity of AFSJ law is the rationale for the separate chapter on those parts of the AFSJ dealing with the distinctive topic of civil justice. Eva Storskrubb shows the extent to which civil justice has become an integral part of EU law, a decade since its inception. She explores the background to EU involvement in this area, and the institutional and political dynamics that have shaped EU initiatives. Her analysis traverses the principal subject matter areas covered by EU civil justice, and points to the tensions and difficulties, as well as the benefits, from EU engagement in this field.

Bruno de Witte returns to the topic that he wrote on in the first edition, direct effect, supremacy, and the nature of the legal order. These issues have always been of seminal importance, and the topic is, as de Witte rightly states, an 'evergreen' in European legal studies. He skilfully traces the evolution of the doctrines of direct effect and supremacy over time, beginning with their invention by the ECJ almost fifty years ago. The basic tenets of the jurisprudence were laid during the founding period of the EEC, but they have continued to evolve since then, including in the period between the first and second edition of this work. Thus the case law on direct effect of directives has developed further in the first decade of the new millennium, the Lisbon Treaty has heralded change by de-pillarization, at least in relation to what was the Third Pillar, and there has been interesting case law on supremacy from the perspective of national courts, in part as a result of enlargement, and engagement by Constitutional Courts from the new accession states, and in part because the Lisbon Treaty has prompted decisions, such as that of the German Federal Constitutional Court, which contains new thinking on the relationship between the EU and the German state.

Tom de la Mare and Catherine Donnelly examine the preliminary ruling procedure, returning to the topic that Tom had addressed in the first edition of this work. The centrality of preliminary rulings, and the rationale for its being the jewel in the ECJ's jurisdictional crown, is well known. It has provided the vehicle through which the ECJ has been able to fashion the key doctrinal precepts of EU law, and operates as the focal point of contact with national courts. The preliminary ruling procedure has therefore been a prime tool of EU legal integration. Tom de la Mare and Catherine Donnelly explore the 'central integrative role played by preliminary rulings in the evolution of the EU', but question whether the demands placed on the procedure are sustainable. They argue that the procedure has been over-extended, and that although it has evolved in certain respects this has not alleviated the problems that beset the system. These problems are explicated in the course of the chapter and the dilemmas facing the procedure in the new millennium are revealed.

Michael Dougan brings his expertise to bear on the fertile ground of remedies, in relation to which there is always a plethora of challenging new decisions by the ECJ. The chapter on this subject in the first edition was written by Rachel Craufurd Smith. Dougan's chapter in this second edition adopts a slightly different approach by arguing that established 'stories' about the evolution of a particular body of law can be questioned. He sets out the 'core narrative' in this area, beginning with the basic challenge posed by national remedies and procedural rules to the effective and uniform application of EU law within the Member States, and the principles of equivalence and effectiveness established by the ECJ for dealing with the problem. He recounts the common understanding of how the case law developed over time, based on a division of the jurisprudence into three main periods: judicial restraint, judicial activism, and the balancing of competing interests. Dougan argues that while the core narrative has strengths, it does not, however, tell the whole story about the interaction between EU law and national remedies and procedural rules. His contribution identifies case law that bears little direct relationship to the original concerns about effectiveness and uniformity that informed the core scholarly narrative.

Carol Harlow returns to EU administrative law, the subject that she had written on in the first edition of this book. She relates a story of evolution in this area that is divided into three temporal periods. The first period runs till the end of the old millennium, and is characterized by the laying of the building blocks for EU administrative law, principally, albeit not exclusively, through the jurisprudence of the ECJ, which fashioned the doctrines of judicial review, reading them into the Treaty as general principles of law. The second phase of EU administrative law has been dominated by the need for administrative reform, the catalyst being the resignation of the Santer Commission as a result of the criticisms voiced by the Committee of Independent Experts. Her third period focuses on the current and future problems for EU administrative law, including the need to get to grips with the 'soft governance' that has assumed such importance in the EU, the normalization of the areas of competence transferred by the Third Pillar, the issues of accountability that surround the ever-increasing recourse to agencies, and finally the challenges presented by the inter-relationship between the EU and international law, as exemplified by the asset freezing cases. Carol Harlow argues that the multi-level system of governance calls for 'a networked, multi-dimensional response from administrative law', in order more especially to counter the proliferation of networks of 'governance outside the state'.

Gráinne de Búrca explores the evolution of EU human rights law, a subject not dealt with as a separate chapter in the first edition, but clearly meriting such treatment now. Her chapter does not, however, just recount the standard narrative of the development of EU human rights, a topic that has already been addressed in the extensive literature in this area. The main currents of this development are revealed in her analysis, but the chapter shows how the evolution story in a particular area can be markedly affected by the starting point. Thus Gráinne de Búrca begins her inquiry by reconsidering some of the very early steps of engagement with human rights protection in the process of European integration, drawing on unpublished archival material from the early 1950s. She focuses on the period in 1951–52 when the question of human rights protection featured prominently on the integration agenda, and reveals the differences in the constitutional framework for human rights envisaged by the drafters of the two exercises that took place during this period. The traditional narrative of the evolution of human rights protection within EU law normally begins with the silence of the EEC Treaty on human rights, the dominance of the economic, and the subsequent recognition of human rights as part of the legal and political order, this being viewed as a significant advance. If, however, we turn the clock back and begin the evolution story a few years earlier, a rather different picture emerges, one in which 'a robust and comprehensive' role for human rights protection within the new European construction was contemplated. The chapter reveals moreover the ways in which the role envisaged for human rights protection in the model constitutional framework of the early 1950s was different, in several respects, from that contained in the present EU constitutional framework.

Siofra O'Leary bravely tackles the huge and growing subject of the free movement of persons and services. Her analysis reveals the development of the law in this area over time, and the significant shifts that have occurred in the decade since the first edition of this work. The world of free movement of persons and services has become considerably more complex in the intervening period. Thus in the founding years the law governing services was generally treated by the ECJ as residual to workers and establishment, while its decisions in the 1990s revealed the extent to which the principles governing the fundamental freedoms central to the internal market were, in general, converging, 'as it became clear that even indistinctly applicable national measures restrictive of free movement could fall foul of the Treaty'. While this inter-relationship and convergence are still evident, there have nonetheless been significant changes in the regulatory and jurisprudential landscape. These changes have come in part from the ECJ's case law on citizenship, which, *inter alia*, decoupled free movement and non-discrimination from the exercise of an economic activity, in part from overhaul of the secondary legislation on the free movement of economically active Member State nationals adopted in the 1960s and early 1970s, and in further part from accession of ten new Member States, some of which have workforces wishing to use their free movement rights with consequential changes in EU migratory patterns. The realm of services has also been marked by increased litigation before the ECJ, including the much-discussed rulings in the Viking/Laval/Ruffert trilogy, and by the controversies surrounding passage of the Services Directive.

Jukka Snell studies free movement of capital, a subject that was not covered as a distinct chapter in the first edition. It fully warrants such treatment on this occasion, since it is both important in its own right, and also intimately linked with economic and monetary union. It can, moreover, impinge on sensitive aspects of statehood, namely national tax autonomy. The chapter reveals the differing forces that can shape the evolution story in a particular area, and the way in which their respective prominence can change over time. Thus Jukka Snell argues that in the early years of the Community the Member States were the driving force for the development of the law, but that since the mid-1990s the ECJ has played a more prominent role, more especially after the rewriting of the free movement of capital rules. He shows the ways in which the ECJ's case law up until 2006 posed significant challenges to the Member States, and the ways in which it has more recently been willing to moderate that jurisprudence.

Citizenship has become of greater significance in the EU, whether viewed from a legal, political, or symbolic perspective, and the inclusion of a separate chapter on this topic seems entirely appropriate for the second edition of this book. Jo Shaw explores the different ways in which citizenship has played a role in polity formation beyond the state, specifically in relation to the EU as an emergent non-state polity. She examines two dimensions of citizenship as it operates in the EU context. The first concerns the role of 'citizenship of the Union' as a legal status, as developed by the EU institutions, and more especially the ECJ, and the ways in which this has been increasingly applied separate from the direct confines of the single market. Jo Shaw also addresses a second dimension of citizenship, which concerns its actual and potential role in the EU as a polity, and considers whether it can acquire a 'distinct political dimension appropriate to a polity evolving beyond the state, albeit not without reference to the states which comprise its constituent partners'.

Mark Bell's subject is equal treatment, taking over from the chapter which was written in the first edition by Gillian More. He relates the initial role accorded to equal treatment, which was primarily economic in its orientation, designed to secure equality between the factors of production within the internal market. The concept therefore functioned instrumentally, to prevent impediment to market integration, whether in relation to goods or people. This rationale for equal treatment has, however, evolved over time, and alternative, 'more autonomous justifications for equal treatment began to emerge'. This was fuelled by judicial recognition of equal treatment as a general principle of law, and by judicial affirmation that non-discrimination on the ground of sex was part of 'fundamental personal human rights'. Development in this area has, moreover, been markedly affected by Treaty change, such as Article 13 EC, coupled with legislation made thereunder. Mark Bell's analysis concentrates on the evolution of equal treatment as a fundamental human right, which he explores through two trajectories, widening and deepening. He shows in relation to 'widening' the gap between equal treatment within anti-discrimination legislation and its articulation in other contexts, such as immigration and labour law, and this is reinforced by his analysis of 'deepening'.

Catherine Barnard returns to the topic of social policy, which she covered in the first edition. She presents three stories about this important area. The first concerns the historical evolution of social policy, with the principal staging posts being Treaty amendments. The second story focuses on the ECJ's contribution to the development of a distinct EU social policy, with detailed treatment given to the controversial decisions in *Viking* and *Laval*, and what they reveal about the ECJ's understanding of social issues. The third story concerns the reorientation of approach to regulating the labour market in the EU, which requires recourse to the myriad of documents on employment policy, many of which take the form of soft law.

Francis Snyder revisits economic and monetary union, tracing the legal and institutional controversies which have marked EMU since its origins, and identifying the 'dynamics, achievements and shortcomings of EMU and its role in European integration'. Francis Snyder's central thesis is that EMU is a unique conjunction of integration and differentiation, which was created mainly for political reasons, with its institutional and normative shape crystallizing 'conflicting views about the nature and purpose of European integration'. He considers the evolution of EMU from 1950 to the 2000 Nice Treaty, revealing how EMU reconfigured economic and monetary governance, and continues the story by examining the period between the Nice and Lisbon Treaties and the two contemporary challenges, the post-2007 financial crisis and the international stage.

Imelda Maher considers competition law, and more specifically the modernization reform process, which began in the late 1990s. She adopts an institutional perspective to examine changes in relation to governance of the two central concerns of competition law, restrictive agreements and the abuse of market dominance. Imelda Maher questions how far the recent changes can be explicated in evolutionary terms, given the extent to which they constitute a break from the past. To this end she reflects on the extent to which competition policy can be seen as a policy apart, and examines the very idea of evolution. This is followed by an overview of the development of competition law prior to modernization, and reflection on modernization in the evolution of the competition law regime.

Competition law is related to regulation of network industries and services of general economic interest, which is the focus of the chapter by Leigh Hancher and Pierre Larouche. The discussion highlights important trends in the evolution of EU law in this area, since publication of the first edition. Thus the authors argue that EU regulation of network industries reveals movement from one legal paradigm to another, which cannot be captured merely by thinking in terms of a shift from state to market, or from state to Community. They contend that the EU is moving away from the first paradigm, which is 'more traditional, static, formalistic and self-contained', with the hallmark being use of legal definitions and concepts to which consequences are attached. Leigh Hancher and Pierre Larouche maintain that the EU is moving towards a second paradigm, which is 'more dynamic, integrative and inter-disciplinary', the hallmark being use of general guidelines and principles drawn from economic concepts, in order thereby to assess specific situations in a wider sectoral setting.

EU financial regulation has become of increasing importance in the last decade, even before the recent banking crisis, and this explains the inclusion of a separate chapter on this subject. The evolutionary story related by Takis Tridimas is of a 'journey towards federalization' in this area. EU involvement in financial services assumed prominence at the end of the old millennium, as exemplified by the launch of the Commission's Financial Services Action Plan in 1999, and has since been one of the fastest growing areas of EU law. Takis Tridimas shows that while principles of mutual recognition and home country control constitute 'the pivotal integration paradigm' in this area, the trend is nonetheless towards uniformity rather than harmonization. The trend towards federalization has occurred through an increasing array of EU legislation governing capital markets law, by the shift from minimum to maximum harmonization and enhanced EU presence in relation to enforcement. The evolutionary story in this area includes recourse to novel regulatory techniques, such as the Lamfalussy process. Commission proposals from September 2009 take the process of federalization further, with plans for a 'new institutional architecture, more EU powers, and the regulation of areas previously left untouched by EU, and even national, law'.

Joanne Scott has contributed the chapter on environmental law, written in the previous edition by Damian Chalmers, who provided a valuable analysis of the evolution of EU environmental law that repays reading today. Joanne Scott has chosen to supplement that earlier chapter by focusing closely on climate change, which has been the most important preoccupation of EU environmental law in the last decade. She provides an overview of EU law and policy in relation to this area within the frame of multi-level governance, which is especially well-suited for analysis of this area. Joanne Scott notes key trends that inform this area, these being the move to a market-based approach to environmental protection, as exemplified by emissions trading, and the 'out-sourcing' of 'responsibility for achieving emission reductions on behalf of the EU and its Member States', with the backdrop to the area being the fact that EU policy is contingent on effective regulation of activities that are situated abroad. The more specific measures studied raise, moreover, important 'issues about the distribution of regulatory power in a system of multi-level governance and legal pluralism'.

Stephen Weatherill returns to the subject of consumer policy, on which he wrote in the first edition of this work. He details the evolution of this policy from the inception of the EEC, where there was no real focus on the 'consumer interest', the implication being that the consumer 'was expected to be the passive beneficiary of the restructuring of European markets', and no explicit legislative competence in the consumer field. It was the Maastricht Treaty that removed the 'constitutional inhibition on the elaboration of an autonomous consumer policy', but as Stephen Weatherill notes, the insertion of what is now Article 169 TFEU 'failed to resolve the question of whether there really is (or should be) a theoretical foundation to EC intervention designed to improve the position of the consumer'. The chapter reveals the way in which the evolution of consumer policy 'offers insights into how the judicial and legislative institutions of the EU are drawn into the task of elaborating regulatory policies in consequence of an inevitable dynamism whereby internal trade policy spreads beyond a one-dimensional concern for open borders'.

The final chapter of this work deals with the impact of EU law on culture. Rachael Craufurd Smith, who wrote in the first edition on the subject of remedies, now addresses the topic of culture and shows the various ways in which the EU has become an 'increasingly confident player in the cultural field', with its activities now firmly rooted in the EU Treaties. This was in stark contrast to the EEC Treaty, which contained 'scant reference to culture', primarily because of its economic focus, and wariness borne from failures of more ambitious attempts at political integration. Rachael Craufurd Smith reveals the duality with regard to culture for the EU, it being both problematic, but also having economic and political potential. Thus the EU has had to balance the desire to break down cultural barriers and open up peoples to foreign cultural influence through free movement provisions, while at the same time 'leaving sufficient space for domestic and EU intervention to support specific cultures at risk in the competitive environment thereby created'.

2

INTEGRATION, DEMOCRACY, AND LEGITIMACY

*Paul Craig**

The EEC, now the EU, has passed its half-century. The fifty plus years have witnessed development, change, and evolution that will be charted in the subsequent chapters of this book. This chapter seeks to lay the groundwork for later discussion by considering two related issues.

The first half of the chapter addresses the rich literature that explores the rationale for EU integration. There are contending theories and the literature is, unsurprisingly, still evolving.[1] The objective within this part of the discussion is to render accessible to lawyers the scholarship by those schooled in international relations and political science that has explored the dynamic of EU integration. It is also designed to reveal the assumptions and implications of particular integration theories for EU democracy.

The focus in the second half of the chapter shifts to democracy itself, and analysis of the burgeoning literature concerned with the nature of EU democracy, the extent to which the EU suffers from a democratic deficit, and the ways in which it can be alleviated. There is a significant measure of agreement as to the features that are or might be problematic within the EU from a democratic perspective. It will however be seen that the divergence between scholars turns on differences as to the factors that are regarded as important in assessing EU democracy, which then leads to differences of view as to particular aspects of the democratic deficit critique. The discussion will draw on insights from integration theory where relevant to the inquiry.

* Professor of English Law, St John's College, Oxford. The abbreviation 'TEU' used after a Treaty article refers to the Treaty on European Union in the version in force after 1 December 2009, while 'TFEU' refers to the Treaty on the Functioning of the European Union. 'EC' after a Treaty article refers to a provision of the European Community Treaty in the version in force until 30 November 2009. 'EU' refers to an article of the Treaty on European Union in the version in force until that date. 'CT' after a Treaty article signifies the Constitutional Treaty.

[1] D Chryssochoou, *Theorizing European Integration* (2nd edn, Routledge, 2009); A Wiener and T Diez (eds), *European Integration Theory* (2nd edn, Oxford University Press, 2009); M Pollack, 'Theorizing the European Union: Realist, Intergovernmentalist and Institutionalist Approaches' in E Jones, A Menon, and S Weatherill (eds), *The Oxford Handbook of the European Union* (Oxford University Press, 2011).

A. NEOFUNCTIONALISM, THE LEGITIMACY OF OUTCOMES AND THE LIMITS OF DEMOCRACY

1. NEOFUNCTIONALISM AND INTEGRATION

Neofunctionalism was the early ideology of Community integration,[2] embodying a pluralist theory of international politics:[3] the actions of a state were 'the outcome of a process in which political decision-makers were influenced by various pressures',[4] including bureaucratic actors, societal interest groups, and multinational corporations. These groups were expected to forge links with respective groups in other states. Neofunctionalists also believed that the Commission would be a decisive force in the integration process, even when this did not accord with the wishes of some Member States. The central tenet of neofunctionalism was the concept of 'spillover', which had both a functional and a political dimension.[5]

Functional spillover was a simple idea based on the interconnectedness of the economy. Integration in one sphere created pressure for integration in other areas. Thus, for example, removal of formal tariff barriers would generate a need to deal with non-tariff barriers, which could equally inhibit realization of a single market. The desire for a level playing field between the states would then lead to other matters being decided at Community level, in order to prevent states from giving advantages to their own industries, to remove more indirect barriers to intra-Community trade through harmonization measures, or to stop private actors from dividing the market through cartels.

Political spillover was equally important to neofunctionalism. It involved the 'build-up of political pressure in favour of further integration within the states involved'.[6] In integrated areas interest groups would be expected to concentrate their attention on the Community, consonant with the basic idea that 'you shoot where the ducks are' and apply pressure on those who have regulatory power. Such groups would also become mindful of the remaining barriers to interstate trade, which prevented them from reaping the full rewards from existing integration, thereby adding to the pressure for further integration. The Commission was to be a major player in this political spillover, since it would encourage the beliefs of the state players.

Neofunctionalism has however been challenged empirically and theoretically. The empirical challenge was based on its failure to explain the reality of the Community's development. The 1965 Luxembourg crisis had a profound impact, since Member State interests re-emerged with a vengeance. The resulting de facto unanimity principle signalled that Member States were not willing to allow Community development inconsistent with their vital interests. Decision-making for many years thereafter was conducted in

---

[2] E Haas, *The Uniting of Europe: Political, Social and Economic Forces 1950–1957* (Stanford University Press, 1958); L Lindberg, *The Political Dynamics of European Economic Integration* (Stanford University Press, 1963); L Lindberg and S Scheingold, *Europe's Would-Be Polity: Patterns of Change in the European Community* (Prentice-Hall, 1970); L Lindberg and S Scheingold, *Regional Integration* (Harvard University Press, 1970).

[3] S George, *Politics and Policy in the European Union* (3rd edn, Oxford University Press, 1996) 36.

[4] ibid 36.   [5] ibid 37.   [6] ibid 38.

the shadow of the veto. The Commission's role changed from emerging government for the Community to a more cautious bureaucracy.[7] Moreover, many of the predictions of political spillover were proving to be equally precarious at state level, since evidence of interest group pressure for greater integration was found to be equivocal or simply wanting.[8]

The theoretical challenge to neofunctionalism was both internal and external. The internal challenge stemmed from the empirical failure of neofunctionalism to accord with political reality, which led to modifications to the theory that rendered it increasingly complex and indeterminate.[9] The external challenge was based on neofunctionalism's failure to relate to general themes within international relations, which sought to explain why states engaged in international cooperation.

It would be wrong, notwithstanding these critiques, to conclude that neofunctionalism has no explanatory value for EC integration. It is arguable that functional spillover created impetus for further integration,[10] although it is difficult to determine causality in this context.[11]

2. NEOFUNCTIONALISM, LEGITIMACY, AND DEMOCRACY

In order to understand the normative vision of the Community which underpinned neofunctionalism it is necessary to consider the very foundations of integration and Monnet's vision of Europe.

Monnet's conception of Europe was strongly influenced by the role of technocrats trained in the French *Grandes Ecoles*. This serves to explain the structure of the European Coal and Steel Community (ECSC). The centrality of the High Authority was an expression of the technocratic approach. A corporatist style involving networks of interest groups was the other legacy of Monnet's experience with planning authorities in France.[12] This too was institutionalized in the ECSC in the form of the Consultative Committee. Integration was based on the combination of benevolent technocrats and economic interest groups, which would build transnational coalitions for European policy.[13] Monnet's strategy was thus for what has been termed elite-led gradualism.[14] The Assembly's powers within the ECSC were very limited. The same

---

[7] K Neunreither, 'Transformation of a Political Role: The Case of the Commission of the European Communities' (1971–72) 10 JCMS 233.

[8] George (n 3 above) 41–43.

[9] A Moravcsik, 'Preferences and Power in the European Community: A Liberal Intergovernmentalist Approach' (1993) 31 JCMS 473, 476.

[10] George (n 3 above) 40–41.

[11] 'Institutional Change in Europe in the 1980s' in R Keohane and S Hoffmann (eds), *The New European Community, Decisionmaking and Institutional Change* (Westview Press, 1991) 19, 20.

[12] K Featherstone, 'Jean Monnet and the "Democratic Deficit" in the European Union' (1994) 32 JCMS 149, 154–155.

[13] W Wallace, 'European Governance in Turbulent Times' (1993) 31 JCMS 300.

[14] W Wallace and J Smith, 'Democracy or Technocracy? European Integration and the Problem of Popular Consent' in J Hayward (ed), *The Crisis of Representation in Europe* (Frank Cass, 1995) 140.

general institutional structure was to be carried over to the EEC: 'enlightened admin-istration on behalf of uninformed publics, in cooperation with affected interests and subject to the approval of national governments, was therefore the compromise again struck in the Treaties of Rome'.[15] While Monnet favoured a democratic Community 'he saw the emergence of loyalties to the Community institutions developing as a *consequence* of elite agreements for the functional organization of Europe, not as an essential *prerequisite* to that organization'.[16]

Neofunctionalism was to be the vehicle through which Community integration, conceived of as technocratic, elite-led gradualism, combined with corporatist-style engagement of affected interests, was to be realized. Neofunctionalism fitted neatly with Monnet's perception of the Community. The idea of spillover reinforced the view that gradualism was a meaningful strategy for integration. The neofunctionalist view of the important players in the integration process at state and Community level aligned with Monnet's vision.

Monnet and neofunctionalists also shared the same sense of legitimacy and democracy. For Monnet and kindred spirits the legitimacy of the Community was to be secured through outcomes, peace and prosperity. The ECSC was estab-lished in part to prevent a third European war. The EEC was created in large part for the direct economic benefits of a common market. Peace and prosperity were potent benefits for the people in the 1950s. Democracy was, by way of contrast, a secondary consideration, since it was felt that the best way to secure peace and prosperity was by technocratic elite-led guidance. Moreover, the notion of democracy was not directed towards the role of normal democratic controls in the Community order, but on how EEC success would lead to acceptance of the Community institutions.

The same senses of legitimacy and democracy can be seen in neofunctionalism. Legitimacy was conceived in terms of outcomes, increased prosperity. Thus for Lindberg and Scheingold legitimacy was secured because of the very gains from technocracy, notwithstanding the diminution in the role of elected bodies.[17]

> The idea is that increasing affluence stoked by new technology and more aggressive business practices nurture a more benign environment, sublimating social cleavage in an increasingly successful quest for material goods and dissolving political conflict in a consensus of apathy. Control of the government ... is important only when a change of government portends significant changes in policies. In other words, they matter only when the parties perceive significant deprivations or rewards as the stakes of the political game. In pluralistic political systems ... social and political citizenship is assured and most significant groups can count on a slice of the expanding pie. Indeed, the major problem becomes one of maximising wealth—clearly a question for the experts, the technocrats.

---

[15] ibid 143.

[16] M Holland, *European Community Integration* (St Martin's Press, 1993) 16. Italics in the original.

[17] L Lindberg and S Scheingold, *Europe's Would-Be Polity, Patterns of Change in the European Community* (Prentice-Hall, 1970) 268–269.

The role to be accorded to democracy was strikingly similar to Monnet's vision. The neofunctionalist account dismissed the normal importance of democratic institutions because increased affluence rendered possible by technocracy would produce the 'consensus of apathy', which undermined active interest in the political process. The focus was directed towards the people's loyalty to the EEC, and to the requisite 'permissive consensus' to enable the technocratic elite to perform their tasks.[18]

B. LIBERAL INTERGOVERNMENTALISM, COLLECTIVE ACTION, AND THE LOGIC OF PUBLIC CHOICE

1. LIBERAL INTERGOVERNMENTALISM AND INTEGRATION

The limitations of neofunctionalism were apparent by the late 1960s. An alternative theory emerged known as liberal intergovernmentalism. Moravcsik produced the fullest and most elegant version of this theory.[19] His thesis is rooted in a branch of international relations theory, which is premised on assumptions derived from economics, public choice, and the logic of collective action. The central message is that states are the driving forces behind integration, that supranational actors are there largely at their behest, and that these actors as such have little independent impact on the pace of integration. The core of liberal intergovernmentalism is composed of three elements, 'the assumption of rational state behaviour, a liberal theory of national preference formation, and an intergovernmentalist analysis of interstate negotiation'.[20]

> The assumption of rational state behaviour provides a general framework of analysis, within which the costs and benefits of economic interdependence are the primary determinants of national preferences, while the relative intensity of national preferences, the existence of alternative coalitions, and the opportunity for issue linkages provide the basis for an intergovernmental analysis of the resolution of distributional conflicts among governments.[21]

The demand for integration is a function of domestic preference formation, which identifies the benefits of policy coordination at the European level. National foreign policy goals are a response to the shifting pressures of domestic groups, and these preferences are aggregated through their political institutions.[22] Thus liberal intergovernmentalists see the relationship between society and government as one of

---

[18] ibid ch 8.

[19] A Moravcsik, 'Preferences and Power in the European Community: A Liberal Intergovernmentalist Approach' (1993) 31 JCMS 473; A Moravcsik, *National Preference Formation and Interstate Bargaining in the European Community, 1955–86* (Harvard University Press, 1992); A Moravcsik, 'Negotiating the Single European Act: National Interests and Conventional Statecraft in the European Community' (1991) 45 International Organization 19.

[20] Moravcsik, 'Preferences and Power' (n 19 above) 480.

[21] ibid 480–481.   [22] ibid 481.

principal and agent, in which societal principals delegate power to government agents.[23] Liberal intergovernmentalism is not committed to particular motivations which might inhere in groups.[24] It none the less makes certain assumptions about why people might favour international policy coordination.[25]

> At the core of liberal theories of economic interdependence lies the claim that increasing transborder flows of goods, services, factors or pollutants create 'international policy externalities' among nations which in turn create incentives for policy co-ordination. International policy externalities arise where the policies of one government create costs and benefits for politically significant social groups outside its national jurisdiction. Where the achievement of domestic governmental goals depends on the policies of its foreign counterparts, national policies are interdependent and policy externalities arise.

The supply of integration is a function of interstate bargaining and strategic interaction. Domestic preferences define 'a "bargaining space" of potentially viable agreements, each of which generates gains for one or more participants'.[26] Governments must therefore choose one such agreement, normally through negotiation. Negotiations are not however cost free, and governments weigh the potential gains from collective action against the costs of negotiation and the diminution in the scope of autonomy entailed by an agreement.

Liberal intergovernmentalism also provides an explanation as to why such integration should be pursued through a supranational institution. The primary rationale is efficiency, by the reduction of transaction costs. Constructing individual *ad hoc* bargains between states can be costly.[27] This problem is obviated by a supranational structure such as the EC. Moravcsik also provides a rationale for the novel institutional features of the EC, such as qualified majority voting and delegation to semi-autonomous supranational institutions. The explanation is derived from public choice theory.[28]

> Following public choice analyses of domestic constitutional choice, intergovernmentalist theory views the decision to adopt qualified majority voting or delegation to common institutions as the result of a cost-benefit analysis of the stream of future substantive decisions expected to follow from alternative institutional designs. For individual Member States carrying out such a cost-benefit calculation, the decision to delegate or pool sovereignty signals the willingness of national governments to accept an increased risk of being outvoted or overruled on any individual issue in exchange for more efficient collective decision-making on average...Compared to unanimity voting, delegation

---

[23] ibid 483.   [24] ibid 484.

[25] ibid 485. There is no assumption that all groups in society will favour integration in order to remove such externalities. It is acknowledged that there will be distributional consequences of policy coordination which might disadvantage certain groups and hence generate opposition.

[26] ibid 497.

[27] R Keohane, *After Hegemony: Cooperation and Discord in the World Political Economy* (Princeton University Press, 1984); J Buchanan and G Tullock, *The Calculus of Consent: Logical Foundations of Constitutional Democracy* (University of Michigan Press, 1962).

[28] Moravcsik (n 20 above) 509–510.

and pooling of sovereignty are more efficient, but less controlled forms of collective decision-making. Of the two delegation involves greater political risk and more efficient decision-making, while pooling through qualified majority voting involves less risk, but correspondingly less efficiency.

The ECJ's powers are rationalized in a similar manner. Proper adjudicatory mechanisms at the supranational level prevent prisoner dilemma and free rider problems. This thereby diminishes the possibility that the system will be undermined by states seeking to reap the rewards of membership, while avoiding their obligations.[29]

2. LIBERAL INTERGOVERNMENTALISM AND DEMOCRACY

Liberal intergovernmentalism seeks to explain the rationale for integration and the distribution of political authority within the Community. It raises interesting questions as to the role of democracy within this schema, and the conception of democracy that flows from it.

(a) The role of the European Parliament

The existence of the European Parliament (EP) does not in reality sit easily with liberal intergovernmentalist theory. The theory assumes that states will engage in collective action and accept some loss of autonomy for the benefits gained, but their 'default position' is to maintain maximum collective control over subsequent events. The EP is however a potential constraint on state action at Community level, and reduces the degree of state control over the course of events, more especially through the EP's power under Article 251 EC.

It might be argued that national preferences that shape the demand for integration include a preference for some democratic organ at Community level, and that this is fed into the interstate bargains that structure the supply of integration and the conditions on which collective action will operate. It might alternatively be contended that the relevant national players themselves believe that when the EC has reached a certain degree of integration, there should then be some democratization at Community level. While such arguments might be put, they would still have to be consistent with the public choice cost–benefit analysis on which the theory is based: the states would have to decide that the loss of autonomy from the EP was worth the legitimacy gain.

This is however an impoverished way of thinking about democratic institutions. If we think that there are normative arguments for an empowered EP within the EU then we should press for this, irrespective of the outcome of the calculus which liberal intergovernmentalists would employ. The same is indeed true of broader issues of constitutionalism. Thus while the powers of the ECJ are rationalized in accord with the cost–benefit tenets of liberal intergovernmentalism, to conceive of the judicial

---

[29] ibid 512–514. Moravcsik accepts that the ECJ has extended its powers beyond those strictly necessary for the attainment of his theory, but does not regard this as undermining of his more general thesis.

role in this manner unduly limits the inquiry. It is part of the very essence of constitutionalism that there are sound normative arguments for judicial controls irrespective of whether the holders of political power might gain from the existence of a judiciary.

Liberal intergovernmentalists might respond by arguing that their claims were merely positive or descriptive, rather than normative, the object being to explicate the institutional structure of the EC in the light of their theory, without prejudice to normative foundations for the EP or constitutionalism. It is however questionable whether liberal intergovernmentalism is positive as opposed to normative. Insofar as it is, the content of any such normative argumentation would be constrained by, and have to be consistent with, the premises of the theory.

(b) Conceptions of democracy

It is therefore important to press further and consider which conception of democracy would most naturally be associated with liberal intergovernmentalism, more especially because there are, as is well known, numerous interpretations of democracy. We should therefore consider which vision of democracy follows most naturally given the intellectual foundations of liberal intergovernmentalism. It is premised, as we have seen, on economic analysis and more specifically on public choice theory. Space precludes detailed analysis of the descriptive or normative assumptions that underlie public choice theory. A brief explanation can nonetheless be given.

The intellectual ancestors of public choice are pluralists such as Bentley and Truman, who emphasized the group nature of politics and stressed that the public interest was nothing more than the outcome of the group exchange.[30] Public choice theorists applied economic analysis to explain behaviour in political markets, and agreed with many conclusions of the earlier pluralist writers.[31] Public choice theorists based their analysis on methodological individualism,[32] and while acknowledging that individuals could have selfish or altruistic preferences, they believed that there was no conception of the public interest separate from individual choice.[33] Individuals would engage in collective action where the benefits outweighed the transaction costs, combined with the costs flowing from a loss of autonomy. Public choice theorists believed that the role of the state should be narrowly confined because: private markets were better at

---

[30] A Bentley, *The Process of Government* (University of Chicago Press, 1908); D Truman, *The Governmental Process* (New York, 1951).

[31] J Buchanan and G Tullock, *The Calculus of Consent* (University of Michigan Press, 1962); J Buchanan, *The Limits of Liberty: Between Anarchy and Leviathan* (Chicago University Press, 1975); J Buchanan, *Freedom in Constitutional Contract* (Texas University Press, 1978); J Buchanan, *Liberty, Market and State: Political Economy in the 1980s* (New York University Press, 1986); G Brennan and J Buchanan, *The Reason of Rules* (Cambridge University Press, 1985). See also, I McLean, *Public Choice: An Introduction* (Oxford University Press, 1987); D Mueller, *Public Choice* (Cambridge University Press, 1979).

[32] Although they fully accepted that individuals would be likely to operate through pressure groups because of the gains in terms of power which individuals could attain by so grouping together, Buchanan and Tullock (n 31 above) 286–287.

[33] ibid 32, 122–124, 125–130, 209.

reaching optimal decisions than political markets; much legislation consisted of rent-seeking by interest groups; and because governmental intervention via redistributive policies was illegitimate, since it offended against individual entitlements.[34]

These descriptive and normative assumptions have been contested. In descriptive terms, it has, for example, been argued that there are important issues as to how market-place behaviour itself should be perceived and that the equation made between individual behaviour in the marketplace and the political arena is not self-evidently correct.[35] The normative aspect of public choice has also been contentious.[36] Thus it is, for example, highly debatable whether a vision of politics which seeks to legitimate legislation through group bargain is consistent in normative terms with the theory of justice postulated by public choice theorists themselves.

Liberal intergovernmentalists might be content with these implications of public choice. They might alternatively contend that they are not forced to adopt the entirety of public choice thought. If the latter course is taken then they must explain where they part company with the broader tenets of public choice theory. Liberal intergovernmentalism is a theory of integration, but one which is based upon intellectual foundations that have broader implications for the meaning of democracy.

C. MULTI-LEVEL GOVERNANCE, NEW INSTITUTIONALISM, AND THE COMPLEXITY OF DECISION-MAKING

1. MULTI-LEVEL GOVERNANCE, NEW INSTITUTIONALISM, AND INTEGRATION

Liberal intergovernmentalism was part of a broader state-centric view, which saw the Community not as a challenge to the nation state, but as a mechanism for strengthening state sovereignty. Supranational institutions enabled national executives to attain beneficial policy goals which could not be obtained by independent action.[37]

This state-centric view was challenged by those who saw the Community in terms of multi-level governance. This is, as the nomenclature suggests, a theory of governance, rather than a theory of integration, but it nonetheless has implications for integration.

---

[34] Brennan and Buchanan (n 31 above) chs 6–8; Buchanan (n 31 above) *Liberty, Market and State*, chs 12, 13, 15, 22, 23; Buchanan (n 31 above), *The Limits of Liberty*.

[35] M Kelman, 'On Democracy Bashing: A Skeptical Look at the Theoretical and Empirical Practice of the Public Choice Movement' 74 Va L Rev 199, 206 (1988).

[36] P Craig, *Public Law and Democracy in the United Kingdom and the United States of America* (Oxford University Press, 1990) 84–90.

[37] A Milward, *The European Rescue of the Nation State* (University of California Press, 1992); A Milward and V Sorensen, 'Independence or Integration? A National Choice' in A Milward, R Ranieri, F Romero, and V Sorensen (eds), *The Frontier of National Sovereignty: History and Theory, 1945–1992* (Routledge, 1993); P Taylor, 'The European Community and the State: Assumptions, Theories and Propositions' (1991) 17 Review of International Studies 109.

(a) Multi-level governance

Marks, Hooghe, and Blank argued that integration was a 'polity creating process in which authority and policy-making are shared across multiple levels of government—subnational, national and supranational'.[38] National governments are major players in this process, but do not have a monopoly of control. Decision-making competences 'are shared by actors at different levels rather than monopolized by state executives'.[39] Supranational institutions, including the Commission, the EP, and the ECJ, 'have independent influence in policy-making that cannot be derived from their role as agents of state executives'.[40] Political arenas are interconnected rather than nested. National arenas may be important for the formation of state preferences, but the 'multi-level model rejects the view that subnational actors are nested exclusively within them'.[41] Proponents of multi-level governance sustain the theory by a two-stage argument.

The first stage considers the circumstances under which national executives might lose their grip on power. A distinction is drawn between the state as an institution, and the state as the set of actors who happen to control that institution at a particular time. They argue that there is no reason why political actors whose tenure of office will be ephemeral should necessarily be committed to giving priority to the state as an institution. Government leaders may wish to transfer decision-making to the supranational level either because the political benefits outweigh the costs of the political control thereby foregone, or because of the benefits of shifting responsibility for unpopular decisions.[42] When competence over a certain subject matter has been transferred to Community level, proponents of multi-level governance contend that there are real limits to the degree of individual and collective state control over Community decisions.[43] Thus while Member States may play the decisive role in the Treaty-making process, they do not exert a monopoly of influence, and that the day to day control exercised by the states collectively is less than that postulated by state-centric theorists. Thus the ability of the 'principals', the Member States, to control the 'agents', the Commission and the ECJ, is limited by a range of factors, including the 'multiplicity of principals, the mistrust that exists among them, impediments to coherent principal action, informational asymmetries between principals and agents and by the unintended consequences of institutional change'.[44]

---

[38] G Marks, L Hooghe, and K Blank, 'European Integration from the 1980s: State-Centric v. Multiple-Level Governance' (1996) 34 JCMS 341, 342. See also, T Risse-Kappen, 'Exploring the Nature of the Beast: International Relations Theory and Comparative Policy Analysis Meet the European Union' (1996) 34 JCMS 53; J Golub, 'State Power and Institutional Influence in European Integration: Lessons from the Packaging Waste Directive' (1996) 34 JCMS 313; J Caporaso, 'The European Union and Forms of State: Westphalian, Regulatory or Post-Modern' (1996) 34 JCMS 29, 44–48; F Scharpf, 'The Problem Solving Capacity of Multi-Level Governance' (1997) 4 JEPP 520; G Marks, F Scharpf, P Schmitter, and W Streeck, *Governance in the European Union* (Sage, 1996).

[39] Marks, Hooghe, and Blank (n 38 above) 346.

[40] ibid 346.   [41] ibid 346.   [42] ibid 347–350.   [43] ibid 350–351.   [44] ibid 353–354.

The second stage of the argument considers whether policy-making is really dominated by Member States in the way posited by state-centric theorists, or whether it accords more closely with that postulated by multi-level governance. Thus in relation to policy initiation, they conclude that while the Council, the European Council, and the EP have circumscribed the Commission's formal monopoly of legislative initiative, 'none can claim that it has reduced the position of the Commission to that of an agent'.[45] They see agenda-setting as a shared and contested competence among the four Community institutions, rather than being monopolized by any one actor. The same pattern of mixed competence is seen in relation to the making of formal norms, more especially so in the areas covered by co-decision, which has transformed the legislative process from 'a simple Council-dominated process into a complex balancing act between Council, Parliament and Commission'.[46] A similar pattern of multi-level governance is perceived in relation to implementation, where the Commission, state technocrats, national bureaucracies, and interest groups all play a role.[47]

(b) New institutionalism

State-centric theories, such as liberal intergovernmentalism, have also been challenged by new institutionalism. Multi-level governance can indeed be seen as a manifestation of new institutionalist thinking as applied to the EC. The foundations for new institutionalism were laid by March and Olsen.[48] They posited a more independent role for political institutions than was common in the prevailing literature, and argued that such institutions served to 'define and defend values, norms, interests, identities, and beliefs' within society.[49] They were critical of the dominant themes in the literature of politics since the 1950s: contextualism, reductionism, utilitarianism, instrumentalism, and functionalism.[50]

Contextualism captured the idea that politics was not to be differentiated from the remainder of society. March and Olsen lamented the fact that whereas historically political scientists treated the state as an independent factor of importance to collective life, most modern political scientists did not do so.

Reductionism was expressive of the assumption that political phenomena were best understood as the aggregate consequences of individual behaviour, acting so as to maximize their exogenous preferences. This was by way of contrast to older modes of thinking which 'treated political institutions as determining, ordering, or modifying individual motives, and as acting autonomously in terms of institutional interests'.[51]

---

[45] ibid 358, 361.

[46] Marks, Hoohge, and Blank (n 38 above) 364. For similar views, M Westlake, *The Commission and the Parliament: Partners and Rivals in the European Policy Making Process* (Butterworths, 1994); P Craig, 'Democracy and Rule-Making within the EC: An Empirical and Normative Assessment' (1997) 3 ELJ 105.

[47] Marks, Hoohge, and Blank (n 38 above) 367–369. See also, J Weiler, U Haltern, and F Mayer, 'European Democracy and its Critique' in J Hayward (ed), *The Crisis of Representation in Europe* (Frank Cass, 1995) 32–33; W Sauter and E Vos, 'Harmonization under Community Law: The Comitology Issue' in P Craig and C Harlow (eds), *Lawmaking in the European Union* (Kluwer, 1998) ch 6.

[48] J March and J Olsen, *Rediscovering Institutions, The Organizational Basis of Politics* (Free Press, 1989).

[49] ibid 17.   [50] ibid 2–8.   [51] ibid 4.

Utilitarianism was indicative of the related inclination within modern political science to see action as stemming from calculated self-interest. This was contrasted with an historical tradition in which 'political behaviour was embedded in an institutional structure of rules, norms, expectations, and traditions that severely limited the free play of individual will and calculation'.[52]

Instrumentalism captured the primacy accorded to outcomes, expressed in terms of resource allocation, at the expense of the historical tradition which 'portrayed political decision making primarily as a process for developing a sense of purpose, direction, identity and belonging'.[53]

Functionalism signified the modern belief in the attainment of some equilibrium, or optimality, as opposed to the earlier approach that emphasized the singular within a particular historical context.

There was a resurgence of interest in institutionalism in numerous disciplines.[54] Not all who deploy the language of institutionalism subscribe to the same beliefs. It would be mistaken to assume that, for example, rational choice institutionalists are particularly close to the normative institutionalism of March and Olsen, or to historical institutionalism.

New institutionalism has been employed in relation to the EU. It has generated studies, which treat integration in less state-centred, monistic terms than liberal intergovernmentalists, and emphasize the importance of the supranational institutions for Community development.[55]

(c) Multi-level governance, institutionalism, and integration

Multi-level governance is not in itself a theory of integration. The assumptions underlying multi-level governance have however been supported by work on integration, which draws on new institutionalism. Stone Sweet and Sandholtz[56] advanced a theory of integration to rival the state-centric view posited by the intergovernmentalists.

They argued that there was a continuum between pure intergovernmental politics at one end of the spectrum and supranational politics at the other. Where pure intergovernmental politics operated the states were the central players, who would

---

[52] ibid 5.   [53] ibid 6.

[54] W Powell and P DiMaggio, *The New Institutionalism in Organizational Analysis* (University of Chicago Press, 1991) 1–41.

[55] S Bulmer, 'The Governance of the European Union: A New Institutionalist Approach' (1993) 13 JPP 351; T Risse-Kappen (n 38 above); D Wincott, 'Institutional Interaction and European Integration: Towards an Everyday Critique of Liberal Intergovernmentalism' (1995) 33 JCMS 597; D Wincott, 'Political Theory, Law, and European Union' in J Shaw and G More (eds), *New Legal Dynamics of European Union* (Clarendon Press, 1995) 293–311; K Armstrong, 'Regulating the Free Movement of Goods: Institutions and Institutional Change' ibid 165–191; M Jachtenfuchs, 'Theoretical Perspectives on European Governance' (1995) 1 ELJ 115; P Pierson, 'The Path to European Integration: A Historical Institutionalist Analysis' (1996) 29 Comparative Political Studies 123; K Armstrong, 'New Institutionalism in EU Legal Studies' in Craig and Harlow (n 47 above) ch 4.

[56] A Stone Sweet and W Sandholtz, 'European Integration and Supranational Governance' (1997) 4 JEPP 297.

bargain to reach commonly acceptable policies, and the EC would merely enhance the efficiency of such bargains. At the supranational end of the spectrum there were supranational institutions that could constrain the behaviour of all actors, including the Member States, within the relevant areas. Different areas of Community policy could therefore be located at different points along the spectrum.

The explanation for the shift along the spectrum is that non-state actors who transact across borders will often benefit from supranational governance in terms of common European rules, since in the absence thereof transaction costs will be higher. Governments can influence the pace of integration, but 'they do not drive the process or fully control it'.[57] Intergovernmental bargaining 'more often than not is responsive to the interests of a nascent, always developing, transnational society'.[58] The location of a policy area on the spectrum will be dependent on the levels of cross-border transactions, and the consequential need for supranational coordination within that area. It made sense therefore that the EC had moved furthest towards the supranational end of the spectrum with regard to the internal market.

This basic rationale for integration was reinforced by forces which institutionalized changes that had occurred.[59]

> Organizations produce and transmit the rules that guide social interaction. They structure access to policy processes, defining political power and privileging some parts of society more than others. As supranational organizations acquire and wield autonomy, they are able to shape not only specific policy outcomes but also the rules that channel policy-making behaviours. As supranational organizations and rules emerge and solidify, they constitute transnational society by establishing bases for interaction and access points for influence. As transnational society endures and expands, the organizations and rules that structure behaviours become more deeply rooted as 'givens', taken for granted as defining political life.

Thus the further one moved on the spectrum towards supranational politics, the greater was the ability of the supranational institutions to act autonomously. The greater also the capacity of transnational actors to choose whether to influence policy at the national or the Community level. Moreover, a shift towards supranational governance would often generate further movement in the same direction. This was in part because of neofunctionalist-type spillover,[60] and in part because supranational governance within certain areas institutionalized the process by which rules were created and shaped the perception of those subject to them of their own self-interest.[61]

2. MULTI-LEVEL GOVERNANCE, NEW INSTITUTIONALISM, AND DEMOCRACY

The literature on multi-level governance and new institutionalism does not lead inevitably to a particular theory of democracy or conception of legitimacy. These

---

[57] ibid 306.   [58] ibid 307.   [59] ibid 305.   [60] ibid 309.   [61] ibid 310–311.

approaches to integration do however have implications for democracy and legitimacy in the EC.

First, the literature on multi-level governance and new institutionalism is posited on the assumption that the 'players' in the policy-making process include states, supranational institutions, such as the Commission, EP and ECJ, subnational actors, and interest groups. This is significant when considering democracy and accountability in the EC. There is limited point in adapting democratic ideas to the Community if they are seriously at odds with the way in which it operates. A conception of democracy will affect the way in which we think that these players ought to interact, by indicating the nature of their respective participatory roles within the democratic process, and appropriate mechanisms for accountability.

Secondly, March and Olsen reject the view that preferences should be treated as given, arguing that it is more realistic to regard them as endogenous: to treat them as consistent, clear, or exogenous 'leads to predictive theories that are wrong and normative theories that are misleading'.[62] By way of contrast it was central to older theories of politics that 'the processes by which interests are created, nurtured, and transformed are a critical part of a political (or economic, or decision), process'.[63]

> Although there are exceptions, contemporary social welfare theorists in both political science and economics are inclined to define the problem of politics as one of aggregating prior and exogenous individual preferences into a collective choice. Individual interests are converted to collective decisions through bargaining, coalition formation, exchange and the exercise of power. Preferences (interests) are taken as given. The main thrust of the present chapter is that such a conception of politics and preferences leads to an incomplete understanding of power in a democracy, and consequently to an incomplete specification of the problems involved in designing democratic institutions.[64]

Many will doubtless continue to subscribe to the accepted orthodoxy of modern economics and political science, which forms the intellectual foundation for liberal intergovernmentalism. Yet March and Olsen remind us that there is another plausible view, with powerful historical antecedents, which can affect the way we think about democratic design.

D. RATIONAL CHOICE INSTITUTIONALISM, CONSTRUCTIVISM, AND THE CONTESTED DOMAIN

Integration theory developed further in the late 1990s and into the new millennium.[65] The principal strands in this development were as follows.

---

[62] March and Olsen (n 48 above) 154–155.
[63] ibid 155.   [64] ibid 156–157.   [65] Pollack (n 1 above).

1. MODIFIED LIBERAL INTERGOVERNMENTALISM AND RATIONAL CHOICE INSTITUTIONALISM

The late 1990s saw subtle, but important, modifications in liberal intergovernmental-ism. Most significantly Moravcsik modified his theory so as to acknowledge that supranational institutions might indeed have greater powers over agenda setting and the like outside of major Treaty negotiations.[66] Thus he accepted that such institutions could be influential within the ordinary legislative process. This was an important concession, since the interstate bargains struck within IGCs could often be incomplete, with the consequence that there could be considerable latitude as to the interpretation of the resulting Treaty amendments. Moravcsik also proffered thoughts as to why Member States chose to pool sovereignty and delegate power to supranational institutions, arguing that the best explanation was to enhance the credibility of their commitments.[67]

These modifications thereby reduced the difference between Moravcsik's thesis and rational choice institutionalism, and the latter now constitutes one of the two dominant theories of integration. The existence of different branches of institutionalism, rational choice, sociological, and historical,[68] was noted above.[69] Rational choice institutional-ism is, as the title would suggest, a derivative of rational choice theory. The latter is premised on methodological individualism, whereby individuals have exogenous preferences, and choose the course of action that is the optimal method of securing them.[70] Rational choice institutionalists were critical of liberal intergovernmentalism because of the minimal role that the latter accorded to EU institutions.[71] Proponents of rational choice institutionalism acknowledged that institutions were important. Insti-tutions constituted the rules of the game thereby enhancing equilibrium. They exem-plified principal/agent analysis. Member State 'principals' delegated to supranational 'agents' to enhance the credibility of their commitments, and to deal with incomplete contracting, since Treaty provisions are often open to a spectrum of possible interpret-ations. Principal/agent literature focuses on the *ex ante* and *ex post* controls that the principal might use to ensure that the agent does not deviate from the desired goals of the principal.[72]

---

[66] A Moravcsik, *The Choice for Europe: Social Purpose and State Power from Messina to Maastricht* (Cornell University Press, 1998) 8.

[67] ibid 9.

[68] P Hall and R Taylor, 'Political Science and the Three New Institutionalisms' (1996) 44 Political Studies 936.

[69] See, 26.

[70] J Jupille, J Caporaso, and J Checkel, 'Integrating Institutions: Rationalism, Constructivism, and the Study of the European Union' (2003) 36 Comparative Political Studies 7.

[71] M Pollack, 'International Relations Theory and European Integration' EUI Working Papers, RSC 2000/55; Pollack (n 1 above).

[72] M Pollack, *The Engines of European Integration: Delegation, Agency and Agenda Setting in the EU* (Oxford University Press, 2003); Pollack (n 71 above).

2. CONSTRUCTIVISM

Constructivists agree with rational choice institutionalists that institutions matter. They nonetheless dispute the foundations of much rational choice literature, more especially methodological individualism and exogenously determined preferences, which they regard as reductionist. Constructivists contend that the relevant environment in which preferences are formed is inescapably social.[73] This inevitably impacts on, and thus constitutes, a person's understandings of their own interests, which are endogenous. Institutions will embody social norms and will affect a person's interests and identity.

Thus whereas rational choice institutionalists regard institutions as rules of the game that provide incentives within which players pursue their exogenously given preferences, constructivists regard institutions more broadly to include 'informal rules and intersubjective understandings as well as formal rules, and posit a more important and fundamental role for institutions, which constitute actors and shape not simply their incentives but their preferences and identities as well'.[74]

There have been attempts to soften the divide between rational choice institutionalism and constructivism.[75] Thus, for example, many rational choice theorists accept that preferences may well be altruistic as opposed to egoistic, and that exogenous preferences may be constrained by social structure. There have moreover been moves to test the relative cogency of the two approaches through carefully crafted case studies.[76]

E. DEMOCRACY DEFICIT, PREMISE, AND ARGUMENT

1. 'DIFFERENT VIEWS OF THE CATHEDRAL'

The focus thus far has been upon theories of integration and their implications for democracy and legitimacy. We now shift the focus, and consider the burgeoning literature on democracy and legitimacy within the EU. Insights from integration theory will be relevant to this analysis. There is a veritable wealth of literature on democracy and legitimacy within the EU, which shows no sign of abating since the

---

[73] T Risse, 'Exploring the Nature of the Beast: International Relations Theory and Comparative Policy Analysis Meet the European Union' (1996) 34 JCMS 53; J Checkel, 'The Constructivist Turn in International Relations Theory' (1998) 50 World Politics 324; T Christiansen, K Jorgensen, and A Wiener, 'The Social Construction of Europe' (1999) 6 JEPP 528; March and Olsen (n 48 above).

[74] Pollack (n 71 above) 14–15.

[75] J Checkel, 'Bridging the Rational-Choice/Constructivist Gap? Theorizing Social Interaction in European Institutions' University of Oslo, ARENA Working Papers 00/11.

[76] See eg the essays in (2003) 36 Comparative Political Studies.

first edition of this book.[77] This chapter is not a literature review and there will therefore be no attempt to consider all aspects of this rich material. The approach will perforce be selective, but will it is hoped shed light on the differences of view that pervade the scholarly debate.

There is a metaphor used in academic discourse. It surfaces in diverse areas. It is framed in terms of 'different views of the cathedral'. The metaphor has no religious overtone, but rather captures the simple but significant truth that disagreement between academics on a particular topic is often explicable by the fact that they are looking at the same issue or structure, viz, the cathedral, from different perspectives, with the consequence that they describe and evaluate its characteristics differently.

This metaphor is pertinent to the rich literature on democracy and the EU. There is, as will be seen, a significant measure of agreement as to the features that are or might be problematic within the EU from a democratic perspective. The divergence between scholars turns on differences as to the factors that are regarded as important in assessing EU democracy, which then leads to differences of view as to particular aspects of the democratic deficit critique. This part of the chapter will therefore be structured so as to reveal this and to evaluate the resultant differences of view.

The discussion begins by elaborating the perceived democratic shortcomings of the existing regime. The analysis thereafter falls into two parts. It will be argued in the following section that a number of these alleged deficiencies are overstated, in the sense that insofar as there are problems within the EU these are no greater than in nation states, and that they would exist even if there were no EU. The focus then shifts in the section thereafter to the 'democratic features' that are prioritized by particular scholars when assessing EU democracy, and the consequences that follow from such prioritization.

---

[77] See, just in terms of books, S Garcia (ed), *European Identity and the Search for Legitimacy* (Pinter, 1993); Hayward (n 47 above); A Rosas and E Antola (eds), *A Citizens' Europe, In Search of a New Order* (Sage, 1995); R Bellamy, V Bufacchi, and D Castiglione (eds), *Democracy and Constitutional Culture in the Union of Europe* (Lothian Foundation Press, 1995); Andersen and Eliassen (n 81); R Bellamy and D Castiglione (eds), *Constitutionalism in Transformation: European and Theoretical Perspectives* (Blackwell, 1996); R Bellamy (ed), *Constitutionalism, Democracy and Sovereignty: American and European Perspectives* (Avebury, 1996); F Snyder (ed), *Constitutional Dimensions of European Economic Integration* (Kluwer, 1996); R Dehousse (ed), *Europe: The Impossible Status Quo* (1997); D Curtin, *Postnational Democracy, The European Union in Search of a Political Philosophy* (Kluwer, 1997); Craig and Harlow (n 47 above); J Weiler, *The Constitution of Europe* (Cambridge University Press, 1999); C Hoskyns and M Newman (eds), *Democratizing the European Union* (Manchester University Press, 2000); B Laffan, R O'Donnell, and M Smith, *Europe's Experimental Union: Rethinking Integration* (Routledge, 2000); F Mancini, *Democracy and Constitutionalism in the European Union* (Hart, 2000); K Neunreither and A Wiener (eds), *European Integration after Amsterdam, Institutional Dynamics and Prospects for Democracy* (Oxford University Press, 2000); R Prodi, *Europe As I See It* (Polity, 2000); K Nicolaidis and R Howse (eds), *The Federal Vision, Legitimacy and Levels of Governance in the United States and the European Union* (Oxford University Press, 2001); W van Gerven, *The European Union, A Polity of States and Peoples* (Hart, 2005).

2. THE DEMOCRATIC DEFICIT

While views undoubtedly differ as to the nature of the EU's democratic deficit, the following account, drawn from Weiler,[78] and Follesdal and Hix,[79] is reasonably representative. The phrase 'democratic deficit' encapsulates a number of different features.

A significant feature of the democracy deficit argument is the 'disjunction between power and electoral accountability'. It is axiomatic within national systems that the voters can express their dislike of the incumbent party through periodic elections. There may be limits to electoral accountability, but the bottom line is that governments can be changed if they incur electoral displeasure. In the EU, legislative power is divided between the Council, EP, and Commission, with the European Council playing a significant role in shaping the overall legislative agenda. The voters therefore have no direct way of signifying their desire for change in the legislative agenda. European elections can alter the complexion of the EP, but it is only one part of the legislative process. The Commission, Council, and European Council have input into the legislative agenda, but they cannot be voted out by the people.

Concern as to 'executive dominance' is arguably the second most important feature of the democracy deficit argument. Transfer of competence to the EU enhances executive power at the expense of national legislatures. This is because of the dominance of the Council and European Council in the decision-making process, and the difficulties faced by national legislatures in exercising control over EU decisions. It is argued that the EP alleviates, but does not remove, this problem, because its powers are limited, and due to lack of voter interest in European elections, and the absence of a developed party system within the EU.

A further critique is the 'by-passing of democracy argument'. This is applied to, for example, Comitology. Many important regulations are made by committees established pursuant to delegation of power to the Commission. Technocrats and national interest groups dominate this decision-making to the exclusion of more regular channels of democratic decision-making, such as the European Parliament.

Democracy is also felt to be diminished because of the 'distance issue'. The EU entails transfer of competence on many issues to Brussels and away from the nation state, with the consequence that matters are further removed from the citizen.

Concerns about democracy have also been raised relating to 'transparency and complexity'. Traditionally much EU decision-making has been behind closed doors. The complexity of the legislative procedures, combined with different voting rules, means that only experts can understand them.

---

[78] Weiler, Haltern, and Mayer (n 47 above); J Weiler, 'European Models: Polity, People and System' in Craig and Harlow (n 47 above) ch 1.

[79] A Follesdal and S Hix, 'Why there is a Democratic Deficit in the EU: A Response to Majone and Moravcsik' (2006) 44 JCMS 533, 534–537.

There is also the 'substantive imbalance issue'. It has been argued that the EU embodies an asymmetry between the economic and the social, such that the former is prioritized at the expense of the latter.[80]

F. EVALUATION, NATIONAL, AND INTERNATIONAL COMPARISON

We live by and through language. The very language of democratic deficit is powerful in its imagery. It speaks to some base point from which we are deviating. Democracy cannot however be measured in the same way as a budget. The deficit of democracy within the EU is normally judged by way of comparison with the position as it would be if matters were still dealt with at the national level. This requires us to examine the reality of decision-making within national polities, and to postulate what the locus of decision-making would be if there were no EU.

1. COMPARISON WITH NATIONAL POLITIES

There is undoubtedly force in the first aspect of the democracy critique. In national polities the people can vote the incumbent party out of office. In the EU the disjunction between power and electoral accountability means that this is not possible. The importance of this critique, and its consequences, will however be considered more fully in the following section.

The second critique of democracy in the EU, based on executive dominance, is important but less compelling, because executives tend to dominate most national polities. There is a prevailing tendency in the literature critical of the EU to make comparisons posited on some ideal version of national democracy. This is no basis for meaningful evaluation. The idea that parliaments really control national legislation no longer comports with reality in many Member States. The force of the 'executive dominance' critique of EU decision-making is weaker when viewed in this light.[81]

It is, moreover, not self-evident that the EP has less power over legislation than do national parliaments. Much Community legislation was subject to the co-decision procedure, which gave the EP close to co-equal status in the legislative process, and it had a pretty good strike rate at getting its amendments included in the final legislation.[82] Its contribution in this respect compared favourably with

---

[80] Caporaso (n 38 above) 48; F Scharpf, 'Economic Integration, Democracy and the Welfare State' (1997) 4 JEPP 18.

[81] S Andersen and T Burns, 'The European Union and the Erosion of Parliamentary Democracy: A Study of Post-Parliamentary Governance' in S Andersen and K Eliassen (eds), *The European Union: How Democratic Is It?* (Sage, 1996) ch 13.

[82] M Westlake, *The Commission and the Parliament: Partners and Rivals in the European Policy Making Process* (Butterworths, 1994) 39; S Boyron, 'The Co-decision Procedure: Rethinking the Constitutional Fundamentals' in Craig and Harlow (n 47 above) ch 8.

many national legislatures, which struggled to secure legislative amendments that were not supported by the executive. This point is further reinforced by changes made by the Lisbon Treaty.[83] It accords the EP co-equal status in the legislative process with the Council,[84] and the co-decision procedure, re-named the ordinary legislative procedure, has been extended to many new areas, including agriculture,[85] services,[86] asylum and immigration,[87] the structural and cohesion funds,[88] and the creation of specialized courts.[89]

The reality of national decision-making is also important when considering the Comitology problem and the 'bypassing of democracy'.[90] There is a problem here for the EU. We should, however, be mindful of the fact that the legitimation of secondary legislative norms is an endemic problem for all domestic polities. The UK, for example, has not satisfactorily resolved the need for the expeditious passage of secondary legislation and the need to ensure effective legislative oversight. Indeed, many norms of a legislative nature are not seen by the legislature at all.

2. COMPARISON WITH INTERNATIONAL POLITIES

The common assumption is that if the EU did not exist then the matters currently within its competence would return to the national level. Decisions would be made closer to the people, hence alleviating the 'distance problem' and parliaments would have greater control, hence mitigating the 'executive dominance' problem.

This reasoning is not sustainable, since if the EU did not exist there would still be pressures for international coordination. Liberal intergovernmentalism may be open to challenge, but correctly recognized that cross-border flows of goods created international policy externalities, which created incentives for policy coordination.[91] The same theme is present in the work of other scholars.[92] The key issue then becomes not whether states interact, but how. They can do so by *ad hoc* international agreements, which may be favoured for specific problems where Coasian bargaining can resolve differences. A more permanent forum for international cooperation may however be preferred when the parties and the range of issues increase. Thus, if the EU had never been created, it is fallacious to assume that all matters would be regulated at national level. There would either be

---

[83] P Craig, *The Lisbon Treaty, Law, Politics and Treaty Reform* (Oxford University Press, 2010) ch 2.

[84] Art 14 TEU.   [85] Art 43(2) TFEU.   [86] Art 56 TFEU.

[87] Arts 77–80 TFEU.   [88] Art 177 TFEU.   [89] Art 257 TFEU.

[90] Comitology is discussed in detail in Chapter 2.

[91] Moravcsik (n 20 above) 485.

[92] W Wessels, 'The Modern West-European State and the European Union: Democratic Erosion or a New Kind of Polity?' in Andersen and Eliassen (n 81 above) ch 4; G Majone, 'The European Community Between Social Policy and Social Regulation' (1993) 31 JCMS 153 and 'The Rise of the Regulatory State in Europe' (1994) WEP 1; Stone Sweet and Sandholtz (n 56 above); Follesdal and Hix (n 79 above).

incentives to create a body such as the EU, or there would be many bilateral/ multilateral agreements.

The real contrast is between how issues such as 'distance', 'executive dominance', and 'transparency' play out in these different forms of international coordination. There is little room for doubt here: the people fare less well when matters are regulated through *ad hoc* international agreements by comparison with the EU. International agreements normally include no forum such as the EP. Such agreements are made, run, and terminated by executives. The significance of any parliamentary power over ratification is diminished by executive control over the legislature. Parliamentary supervision thereafter will usually be interstitial and marginal, this problem being exacerbated by the large number of such agreements. The ordinary citizen normally plays no role in this arena.

G. EVALUATION, PRIORITIZATION, AND CONSEQUENCE

The discussion of EU democracy can be further sharpened by focusing on the views of particular commentators. It will be seen that disagreement about the EU and democracy turns on differences as to the factors that are regarded as important in assessing EU democracy, which then leads to different conclusions concerning the democratic critique outlined above.

1. LIMITS ON POWER, CHECKS AND BALANCES, AND DEMOCRACY

It is fitting to begin this section by considering Moravcsik's robust defence of the EU from the charge of democratic deficit.[93] He rightly notes that much of the literature critical of EU democracy is premised on comparison with some ideal-type plebiscitary or parliamentary democracy, as opposed to national democracies as they actually operate in the real world.[94] Moravcsik argues that this critique must be heavily qualified if reasonable criteria for judging democracy are used that comport with the reality of democracy with nation states. Viewed from this perspective he maintains that 'constitutional checks and balances, indirect democratic control via national governments, and the increasing powers of the European Parliament are sufficient to ensure that EU policy-making is, in nearly all cases, clean, transparent, effective and politically responsive to the demands of European citizens'.[95]

In more specific terms, Moravcsik analyses constraints that prevent the EU from becoming a despotic super-state. The EU only undertakes a 'modest subset of the substantive activities pursued by modern states';[96] implementation is, subject to

---

[93] A Moravcsik, 'In Defence of the "Democratic Deficit": Reassessing Legitimacy in the European Union' (2002) 40 JCMS 603.
[94] ibid 605, 621.   [95] ibid 605.   [96] ibid 606.

certain exceptions, decentralized, such that the powers of the 'EU to administer and implement are, in fact, exceptionally weak';[97] and the EU's ability to act 'is constrained by institutional checks and balances, notably the separation of powers, a multi-level structure of decision-making and a plural executive',[98] thereby rendering arbitrary action less likely.

Moravcsik then points to existing mechanisms for direct and indirect democratic accountability in the EU, via the EP and via the Council and European Council.[99] He moreover rightly notes that insofar as the EU makes decisions in certain areas that are insulated from direct political contestation the degree to which it does so, and the areas in which this occurs, bear close analogy to those in which analogous methods of decision-making are used in nation states.[100]

Moravcsik further maintains that there are impediments to increased participation in the EU, which explain in part at least the failure thus far to promote transnational political parties and European identity. He argues that the most significant impediment in this respect is that 'EU legislative and regulatory activity is inversely correlated with the salience of issues in the minds of European voters'.[101] They regard health care, education, law and order, pensions and social welfare, and tax as most important; the EU has limited competence in such areas, with the consequence that efforts to expand participation to overcome voter apathy are likely to be unsuccessful.[102]

Moravcsik's analysis is rich and thought-provoking. Numerous points could be made about aspects of the thesis. Thus, for example, the argument that EU enforcement is weak because it is decentralized is contestable, and the area over which the EU exercises some form of regulatory competence, albeit shared with Member States, is broader than is apparent from his argument.

It is however the 'particular view of the cathedral', which more generally underpins Moravcsik's argument, that is of interest here. For Moravcsik, the 'classic justification for democracy is to check and channel the arbitrary and potentially corrupt power of the state',[103] and the centrality of this theme to Moravcsik's argument is reflected in the fact that the starting point to his analysis focuses on constraints—substantive, administrative, and procedural—on the scope of EU power.

This proposition is however inherently ambiguous as to the more particular criteria by which one should judge the credentials of a particular polity. It is ambivalent as between input and output considerations that might prevent such 'arbitrary power' from becoming a reality. More important is the fact that the proposition is too narrow in its justification of democracy, which is not merely to prevent arbitrary or corrupt power, howsoever those terms are defined. The justification for democracy at its most fundamental is that it allows participatory input to determine the values on which people within that polity should live. Thus conceptions of democracy, for all their variety, are premised on input by those held entitled to vote, who then choose those who should govern for a period of time and make that choice in the light of policy

---

[97] ibid 608.   [98] ibid 609.   [99] ibid 609–610.   [100] ibid 613–614.
[101] ibid 615.   [102] ibid 615.   [103] ibid 606.

choices presented to them by rival political parties. Checks and balances are to be sure part of the standard fare of democratic polities, although the meaning ascribed to these terms will perforce vary depending on the nature of the political regime. This does not alter the force of the preceding point.

2. INPUT LEGITIMACY, ELECTORAL CONTESTATION, POLITICAL CHOICE, AND DEMOCRACY

Moravcsik's thesis has however been challenged. While writers such as Weiler, Bellamy,[104] and Follesdal and Hix agree with certain aspects of Moravcsik's thesis, it is clear that they disagree with other elements, the most important being the disjunction between power and electoral accountability, which, as we have seen, constitutes an important element of the democratic deficit critique of the EU. Their argument in this respect exemplifies the point made at the outset of the discussion concerning democracy in the EU, viz, that disagreement is often premised on the prioritization accorded to a particular feature of this critique.

Thus, for example, Follesdal and Hix contend that a democratic polity requires contestation for political leadership and over policy, this being an essential element of even the 'thinnest' theories of democracy, and that it is absent in the EU. They argue that democracy requires institutionally established procedures that regulate competition for control over political authority, on the basis of deliberation, where nearly all adult citizens are permitted to participate in an electoral mechanism where their expressed preferences over alternative candidates determine the outcome, in such ways that the government is responsive to the majority or to as many as possible.[105] They contend that these features are lacking in the EU since there is no institutionalized opposition, and scant opportunity to present an alternative set of policy outcomes to those currently espoused by the Commission, Council, and EP. Such electoral contests are moreover integral to the formation of voter preferences on policy issues.[106]

> Currently there are several constitution-like and institutional features that insulate the EU from political competition. Most fundamentally, there is no electoral contest for political leadership at the European level or the basic direction of the EU policy agenda. Representatives at the EU level are elected, and so can formally be 'thrown out'. However, the processes of electing national politicians and even the members of the European Parliament are not contests about the content or direction of EU policy. National elections are about domestic political issues, where the policies of different parties on issues on the EU agenda are rarely debated. Similarly, as discussed, European Parliament elections are not in fact about Europe, but are 'second-order national contests'. They are fought by national parties on the performance of national governments, with lower turnout than

---

[104] R Bellamy, 'Democracy without democracy? Can the EU's Democratic "Outputs" be Separated from the Democratic "Inputs" provided by Competitive Parties and Majority Rule?' (2010) 17 JEPP 2.
[105] Follesdal and Hix (n 79 above) 547.   [106] ibid 552.

national elections, and hence won by opposition and protest parties. At no point, then, do voters have the opportunity to choose between rival candidates for executive office at the European level, or to choose between rival policy agendas for EU action, or to throw out elected representatives for their policy positions or actions at the EU level.

Follesdal and Hix advocate certain changes to alleviate this malaise.[107] These include greater transparency in the Council, acknowledgement of the political contestability of Commission policy agendas, election, direct or indirect of the Commission President, and increase in the powers of the EP.

There is in my view force in this argument. It is the most important element in the range of arguments that constitute the critique of democracy in the EU. The problem has been alleviated but not cured by changes made by the Lisbon Treaty.[108] Council transparency has been improved. The European Parliament has been further empowered through the extension of what is now the ordinary legislative procedure to new areas, and it has greater control over the appointment of the Commission President than hitherto. Thus, while the European Council retains ultimate power over the choice of Commission President,[109] it is unlikely to attempt to force a candidate on the European Parliament that is of a radically different persuasion from the dominant party or coalition in the European Parliament. Insofar as the EU has been depicted as a polity in which policy is divorced from party politics, a formal linkage between the dominant party/coalition in the European Parliament and the appointment of the Commission President serves to strengthen the connection between policy and party politics. This will thereby alleviate the disjunction of power and responsibility that has underpinned previous critiques of the EU.

There are nonetheless obstacles that subsist to a closer link between policy and politics in the EU, even after the Lisbon Treaty reforms. The EU policy agenda is not exclusively in the hands of the European Parliament and/or Commission. The Council and the European Council have input both *de jure* and de facto. The extended Presidency of the European Council is likely to increase this tendency further. Thus even if the European Parliament and Commission President were very closely allied in terms of substantive policy for the EU, the policy that emerges will necessarily also bear the imprint of the political vision of the Council and European Council. Moreover while the President of the Commission may well be *primus inter pares*, he or she is still only one member of the Commission team. The other Commissioners will not necessarily be of the same political persuasion as the President or the dominant party in the European Parliament. The absence of a developed party system at the EU level is also important in this respect. EU elections have hitherto been fought by national political parties in which national political issues often predominate, with the result that there was little by way of a clear political agenda on EU issues that was proffered to the voters to choose from. This is unlikely to change in the near future.

---

[107] ibid 553–556.   [108] Craig (n 83 above) chs 2–3; Craig, Ch 3 below.   [109] See below, 79–80.

There are nonetheless tensions in relation to the preceding critique. Disposition of power in the EU is premised on the twin conceptions of legitimacy now embodied in Article 10 TEU: the people are represented through the European Parliament and the Member States in the Council and the European Council. This very division of power means that it is not possible for the people directly to vote out those in power and substitute a different party with different policies, since Member State representatives in the Council and European Council are not chosen in this manner. Given that this is so, there are then two tensions with the critique considered in this section.

First, we should be mindful of the institutional change that would be required truly to meet this critique. It would in theory be possible to have a regime in which the people voted directly for two constituent parts of the legislature, for the European Parliament and Council; and also for the President of the Commission and the President of the European Council. The political reality, as forcefully demonstrated by the deliberations on the Constitutional and Lisbon Treaties, is that radical change of this kind will not happen, and was not even on the political agenda. However even if it did it would still not ensure that the people could exercise electoral control over the direction of EU policy, since the European Council would still be populated by Heads of State, who would continue to have a marked influence over the policy agenda, and in addition members of the Commission, with diverse political views, would still be chosen by their Member States.

Secondly, if such institutional change did occur it could lead to the critique that the EU truly was becoming a super-state, in which Member State influence over the development of policy was diminished. While not inevitable, it is nonetheless likely that the inter-institutional disposition of power required to meet the version of the democratic deficit considered in this section would entail, in relative terms, diminution of state power in the Council and European Council. There would be questions as to Member State willingness to partake in a supranational polity in which their own influence over the policy agenda was thereby curtailed. There could moreover be considerable constitutional difficulties for those that predicate membership of such a polity on Member States being 'Masters of the Treaty'.[110]

3. OUTPUT LEGITIMACY, EFFECTIVENESS, SUPRANATIONALISM, AND DEMOCRACY

While commentators such as Weiler, and Follesdal and Hix, disagree with certain tenets of Moravcsik's argument, their view has in turn been challenged by Menon and Weatherill.[111] The basis of this disagreement reflects differences of view as to factors that should be prioritized when thinking about democracy and legitimacy in the EU.

---

[110] D Halberstam and C Mollers, 'The German Constitutional Court says "*Ja zu Deutschland!*"' (2009) 10 German Law Journal 1241.

[111] A Menon and S Weatherill, 'Democratic Politics in a Globalising World: Supranationalism and Legitimacy in the European Union' LSE, Law, Society and Economy Working Papers 13/2007.

Menon and Weatherill contend that using state paradigms to measure legitimacy in the EU is falsely to assume that the EU is seeking to become a state, and that insofar as there may be some virtue in drawing on state practice when thinking about the legitimacy of the EU this must be done fully cognizant of the failure of the state to live up to its own ideals.[112] They argue that the effectiveness of the EU is dependent on the Commission and ECJ acting as 'vigorous autonomous institutions'.[113] Output legitimacy is regarded as particularly important.[114] Effectiveness is a 'source of legitimacy'[115] and hence these institutions should not be tied to traditional ways of thinking about democratic accountability within nation states. This is to judge such institutions by the wrong standards and to undermine their autonomy. The supranational elements of the EU should not therefore be stripped out in the search for accountability analogous to that in the nation state. Menon and Weatherill contend moreover that supranationalism can provide a cure for democratic failings of nation states, through legally enforceable obligations that require the state to respect interests that would normally have little or no voice within national decision-making.[116] Thus the 'EC's market-making activities are legitimated by the effectiveness of their results and by their curative effect on flaws in the representative nature of national decisions in a context of transnational trade integration'.[117]

They are therefore sceptical about arguments designed to address the EU democracy deficit that are premised on analogy with nation states. Their scepticism in this regard embraces suggestions such as election of the Commission President, increase in control by the EP over the executive, and more generally initiatives designed to enhance the electoral accountability and mandate of the EU institutions in accord with voter preferences.[118] For Menon and Weatherill such suggestions miss the fact that the EU undertakes tasks, such as regulation of trans-border trade, that are not undertaken by states, and that other EU functions, such as regulation of competition, monetary policy, and risk regulation, are insulated from the full rigours of democratic scrutiny even within Member States.[119]

They accept that this still leaves a category of EU function that involves politically sensitive choices, which appear to demand electoral legitimation, akin to that in nation states.[120] Menon and Weatherill nonetheless 'caution against'[121] such importation. They contend that the EU is not a state; that the mechanisms for electoral accountability are often flawed within states; that the EU lacks European political parties and the like which are necessary to make input legitimacy a reality; and that EU democracy is implausible in the absence of a demos that is currently lacking.[122]

Menon and Weatherill conclude by drawing on multi-level constitutionalism. EU legitimacy should best be perceived in terms of output legitimacy, combined with mechanisms for the protection of interests that are often imperfectly protected

---

[112] ibid 2.   [113] ibid 2.   [114] ibid 6–9.   [115] ibid 3.   [116] ibid 3, 10–15.
[117] ibid 18.   [118] ibid 4–5.   [119] ibid 5, 18–19.   [120] ibid 5.   [121] ibid 20.
[122] ibid 20–22. For more detailed discussion of demos and democracy, Weiler, Haltern, and Mayer (n 47 above) 5; Weiler (n 78 above); J Weiler, 'Does Europe Need a Constitution? Demos, Telos and the German Maastricht Decision' (1995) 1 ELJ 217.

by nation states. Input legitimacy is provided in the Member States themselves and the control they exercise over the EU.[123]

Menon and Weatherill present their thesis clearly and vigorously. Their approach exemplifies the point noted at the outset of this discussion, that disagreement about the EU and democracy turns on differences as to the factors that are regarded as important in assessing EU democracy. For Menon and Weatherill output legitimacy, effectiveness and the virtues of supranationalism are central in this respect, and they are sceptical about the significance of input legitimacy, on both normative and pragmatic grounds. This thesis is nonetheless questionable on a number of related grounds.

The arguments presented against input democracy at the EU level are contestable. It can be readily accepted, as noted earlier,[124] that input democracy within nation states must be regarded from a realistic perspective, and that it should not be premised on some ideal that no longer comports with reality. It can be accepted also that there are impediments to the realization of input democracy within the EU, whether these flow from the absence of developed political parties, or the absence of some thick, constitutive sense of European demos. There is nonetheless a symbiotic connection between electoral accountability, development of voter preferences, understanding of EU issues, and construction of European identity, which are both articulated through and fostered by input democracy.[125]

Menon and Weatherill's contention that, because the EU is not a state, input democracy is therefore unnecessary or inappropriate is moreover unwarranted. The premise may be correct, but the conclusion is not. The EU may not be a state, but it nonetheless has political authority over a wide range of areas. The days when its sole focus was economic have long gone. It exercises significant power over political, social, and economic issues, ever more so with the increasing EU activity in relation to the Area of Freedom, Security and Justice. It is perforce more difficult to judge the efficacy of such initiatives purely in output terms, by way of comparison with market-making.

The legislative and executive initiatives undertaken by the EU in this and other areas have never been apolitical. This is true even in relation to core market-making activities, where the relevant Treaty provisions are set at a high level of generality, inviting and necessitating political choice as to the way in which they are fulfilled through Community legislation, the storm provoked by the Services Directive being merely a high profile example of this. The very balance between the political and the social within the EU has been contested. A glance at the Commission's detailed legislative agenda for any one year, or the longer term plans, reveals strikingly the political choices and value judgements that are inherent in EU decision-making. So too do the choices made by other institutional players, such as the European Council, when it decided to embark on, for example, the Lisbon agenda in 2000, or through its more frequent initiatives in deciding what issues to prioritize within the EU.

---

[123] ibid 24.   [124] 31–32.
[125] Follesdal and Hix (n 79 above); Curtin (n 77 above); J Habermas, *Between Facts and Norms: Contributions to a Discourse Theory of Law and Democracy* (Polity Press, 1996); J Habermas, 'Remarks on Dieter Grimm's "Does Europe Need a Constitution"' (1995) 1 ELJ 303.

It is undoubtedly true, as Menon and Weatherill state, that not all activities undertaken by nation states are subject to the full rigours of the democratic process, and indeed it is common to insulate some from the input of majoritarian politics. They rightly note that this is and should also be true for the EU. We should nonetheless tread carefully here. There are indeed arguments for insulating certain activities from the ordinary process of majoritarian politics, monetary policy being a prime example. The principles that should govern areas such as competition or risk regulation are however no more apolitical than any other area of the political agenda. There may well be good reasons why the application of such principles once chosen should be shielded from political meddling. The very choice of the governing principles is nonetheless a matter for the political domain.

Menon and Weatherill are also right to highlight the positive virtues of supra-nationalism and the way in which this has been fostered by the Commission and the Community courts. The conclusion that this thereby demands executive autonomy on the part of the Commission is more contestable, since much turns on the more particular meaning given to that term. Thus while it may justify Commission inde-pendence from Member State pressure, invocation of autonomy does not make the case for insulation of Commission initiatives from the political process, on the supposed ground that it is thereby neutrally applying dictates clearly specified in the empowering Treaties. The Commission is, it can be accepted, trying to fulfil the Treaty objectives, but this does not alter the fact that detailed determination as to what those objectives require when translated into specific legislation, and the priorities between the varying objectives, entails political choice and value judgement.

H. CONCLUSION

Central issues concerning the rationale for the development of the EU, and the legitimacy of the resulting entity, persist. Integration theory and democratic theory are both important in understanding the EU. They are moreover interconnected. Theories of integration are often premised on assumptions about human motivation and preferences, which have implications for democracy and legitimacy. Our very concerns with democracy and legitimacy cannot be considered in isolation from the integration forces that have shaped the Community. The debate about the nature of the EU will doubtless continue. The Lisbon Treaty is but one step in the overall evolution of the EU, and its implications for democracy and the inter-institutional distribution of power will be considered in the next chapter.

3

INSTITUTIONS, POWER, AND INSTITUTIONAL BALANCE

*Paul Craig**

The EU institutions have always been 'singular'. From the very inception of the EEC it has been difficult to fit the principal institutions within any neat ordering that corresponds to that within the traditional nation state. The very location of legislative and executive power in the Rome Treaty was problematic, and these problems were exacerbated over time as new institutions developed, often initially outside the strict letter of the Treaty, in response to a complex set of political pressures.

Institutional balance, as opposed to strict separation of powers, characterized the disposition of legislative and executive power in the EEC from the outset. The concept of institutional balance has a rich history. It was a central element in the republican conception of democratic ordering, embodying the ideal that the form of political ordering should encapsulate a balance between different interests, which represented different sections within civil society. This balance was perceived as necessary to ensure that decision-making served the public good rather than narrow sectional self-interest. The concept of institutional balance was an important part of republican discourse in the fifteenth and sixteenth centuries,[1] shaping the desired

---

* The abbreviation 'TEU' used after a Treaty article refers to the Treaty on European Union in the version in force after 1 December 2009, while 'TFEU' refers to the Treaty on the Functioning of the European Union. 'EC' after a Treaty article refers to a provision of the European Community Treaty in the version in force until 30 November 2009. 'EU' refers to an article of the Treaty on European Union in the version in force until that date. 'CT' after a Treaty article signifies the Constitutional Treaty.

[1] J Pocock, *The Machiavellian Moment: Florentine Political Thought and the Atlantic Republican Tradition* (Princeton, 1975) and *Virtue, Commerce and History* (Cambridge University Press, 1985); Q Skinner, *The Foundations of Modern Political Thought, Volume One, The Renaissance* (Cambridge University Press, 1978); R Bellamy, 'The Political Form of the Constitution: The Separation of Powers, Rights and Representative Democracy' in R Bellamy and D Castiglione (eds), *Constitutionalism in Transformation: European and Theoretical Perspectives* (Blackwell, 1996) 24–44.

structure of government in the Italian republics, exerting later influence in England[2] and the emergent United States.[3]

Institutional balance is not however self-executing. It presumes by its very nature a normative and political judgment as to which institutions should be able to partake of legislative and executive power, and it presumes also a view as to what constitutes the appropriate balance between them. These normative underpinnings have, not surprisingly, altered over time in the EU, and continue to do so. These changes will be charted throughout the subsequent analysis and form the underlying theme of the chapter, which is divided into three temporal periods.

The initial period runs between the Rome Treaty and the Single European Act 1986 (SEA). The discussion begins with the initial disposition of institutional power in the Rome Treaty, in which it was primarily divided between the Council and Commission, with the latter holding many of the 'legal' trump cards. The underlying theme throughout this period was the way in which the institutional balance between Council and Commission gradually shifted, such that Member State influence in the Council and European Council over the content of primary legislation, secondary legislation, and the overall direction of Community policy increased. The analysis includes the role played by the ECJ in the institutional ordering during this period, and the way in which integration through law inter-related with integration through the political process.

The second section covers the period between the SEA and the Nice Treaty. Three themes were evident during this time: clarification, contestation, and complexity. There was clarification of the principles governing Community administration and most importantly of the appropriate disposition of legislative power, with recognition that the European Parliament should properly have a role. The emerging consensus about the legislative process was not matched by agreement concerning the disposition of executive power. The period between the SEA and the Nice Treaty saw skirmishes as to the locus of executive authority, which played out in different ways in relation to Comitology, agencies, and the European Council. Institutional complexity was the third theme in this period, as exemplified by the variety of Community legislative procedures, the creation of new agencies, the Three Pillar structure, and emergence of new governance strategies. Thus viewed from the perspective of institutional balance there was growing consensus in normative terms as to the appropriate disposition of primary legislative power, but continuing contestation as to power over secondary rule-making and the locus of executive authority.

---

[2] J Harrington, 'The Commonwealth of Oceana' in J Pocock (ed), *The Political Works of James Harrington* (Cambridge University Press, 1977); Sir W Blackstone, *Commentaries on the Law of England* (16th edn, 1825) Vol I, Book 2, 146–161.

[3] B Bailyn, *The Ideological Origins of the American Revolution* (Harvard University Press, 1967); G Wood, *The Creation of the American Republic, 1776–1787* (University of North Carolina Press, 1969); C Sunstein, 'Interest Groups in American Public Law' (1985) 38 Stan L Rev 29 and 'Beyond the Republican Revival' (1988) 97 Yale LJ 1539; F Michelman, 'Foreword: Traces of Self-Government' (1986) 100 Harv L Rev 4.

These tensions were readily apparent in the third period, which covers the Constitutional Treaty and the Lisbon Treaty. Treaty reform is a continuation of politics by other means. It is not therefore surprising that institutional issues on the agenda in the previous decade dominated debates on more comprehensive Treaty reform, including in particular the appropriate distribution of legislative power, coupled with contestation as to the locus of executive power. These were the prominent themes in the debates on Treaty reform. It is clear that while most if not all protagonists in this debate believed in institutional balance, they nonetheless differed markedly as to what this should entail.

A. ROME TO THE SINGLE EUROPEAN ACT: INITIAL DISPOSITION, DEVELOPMENT AND CHANGE

Hindsight is a wonderful thing. It is tempting to view the current disposition of power between the major institutions as natural or inevitable. The reality is that the more particular nature of the 'institutional balance' within the EU has altered over time, and the current disposition was neither inevitable, nor necessarily foreseeable, at the inception of the EEC.

1. THE INITIAL DISPOSITION OF POWER: THE 'COMMISSION PROPOSES, THE COUNCIL DISPOSES'

It is important at the outset to appreciate the disposition of power in the original Rome Treaty. The Assembly was accorded limited power, and its only role in the legislative process was a right to be consulted where a particular Treaty article so specified. The principal institutional players were the Council and Commission, but in many respects the Rome Treaty placed the Commission in the driving seat in the development of Community policy. The Commission had the right of legislative initiative; it could alter a measure before the Council acted; its measurers could only be amended by unanimity in the Council;[4] it devised the overall legislative agenda; and it had a plethora of other executive, administrative, and judicial functions. The message was that, while the Council had to consent to proposed legislation, it was not easy for it to alter the Commission's proposal. The Commission might therefore have become something akin to a 'government' for the emerging Community.[5]

The Community's early years were however marked by tensions between an intergovernmental view of the Community, championed initially by President de Gaulle of France, but not necessarily shared by other Member States, and a more supranational perspective espoused initially by Walter Hallstein, the Commission President. There were de facto changes in the nature of Community decision-making.

[4] Art 250(1) EC.
[5] K Neunreither, 'Transformation of a Political Role: Reconsidering the Case of the Commission of the European Communities' (1971–72) 10 JCMS 233.

Limitations were placed on the supranational orientation of the Commission through institutional developments, often outside the strict letter of the Treaty, which allowed greater input for the intergovernmental interests of the Council. This does not mean that Council/Commission relations should be characterized in crudely intergovernmental/supranational terms. It does mean that Member State 'principals' placed greater controls over their supranational 'agents'[6] than envisaged by the original Rome Treaty, in response to the reality of decision-making in the newly emergent Community.

2. THE LUXEMBOURG ACCORDS: DECISION-MAKING
   IN THE SHADOW OF THE VETO

The tension between Commission and Council erupted into crisis in 1965, the catalyst being the shift under the transitional provisions of the Treaty from unanimity to qualified-majority voting in the Council. De Gaulle objected to a Commission proposal for institutional reform, which was combined with a proposal to resolve a conflict over agricultural policy, whereby the Community would raise its own resources from agricultural levies and external tariffs, rather than national contributions. He strenuously objected to the 'federalist logic' of the proposal[7] and, after a failure to reach a compromise in the Council, France refused to attend further Council meetings and adopted what became known as the 'empty-chair' policy. This lasted for seven months, from June 1965 until January 1966, after which a settlement was reached, known as the Luxembourg Compromise or the Luxembourg Accords.

These Accords were essentially an agreement to disagree over voting methods in the Council. The French asserted that even in cases governed by majority decision-making discussion should continue until unanimity was reached whenever important national interests were at stake, but the other Member States declared that in such circumstances the Council would 'endeavour, within a reasonable time, to reach solutions which can be adopted by all'.[8]

In practice, it seems that for many years the French view prevailed. Member States endeavoured to reach agreement in the Council, and the effect of pleading the 'very important interests' of a state was treated as a veto, which the other Member States would respect. Recourse to qualified-majority voting became the exception rather than the norm. The 'return to intergovernmentalism', with primacy being accorded to an individual Member State's wish even if it was opposed by the majority, affected decision-making in the following years, which was conducted under the shadow of the veto. Statistics on the number of occasions on which this power was actually used

---

[6] M Pollack, *The Engines of Integration, Delegation, Agency and Agenda Setting in the EU* (Oxford University Press, 2003).

[7] J Pinder, *The Building of the European Union* (3rd edn, Oxford University Press, 1998) 12.

[8] Bull EC 3-1966, 9.

are only part of the story, since the threat of the veto shaped the policies put forward by the Commission.[9]

3. COUNCIL INPUT INTO PRIMARY LEGISLATION: COREPER

The simple facts are the easiest to forget. The Member State representatives on the Council are just that, representatives with an important 'day job', most being ministers in their national governments. They attend a Council meeting for a day, two at most, and then fly home. If the Council was to understand, digest, and take a view on Commission legislative proposals it needed an institution in more 'permanent session' that could negotiate with the Commission on draft proposals and reconcile differences between the Member States themselves.

The framers of the Rome Treaty drew on experience from the ECSC Treaty, in which preparatory work was undertaken by a Commission for the Coordination of the Council of Ministers, 'Cocor'. Article 151 EEC allowed the Council's rules of procedure to provide for a committee of representatives of Member States, the competence of which would be decided by the Council. Such a committee was duly established at the inaugural meeting of the Council of Foreign Ministers in 1958; the first meeting of the Committee of Permanent Representatives, Coreper, took place the next day, and it has met more than 2,300 times since then. It was accorded more explicit recognition in the Maastricht Treaty, and was, prior to the Lisbon Treaty, governed by Article 207(1) EC.

Coreper is staffed by senior national officials and operates at two levels. Coreper II is the more important and consists of permanent representatives of ambassadorial rank. It deals with more contentious matters such as economic and financial affairs, and external relations, and liaises with national governments. Coreper I is composed of deputy permanent representatives and is responsible for issues such as the environment, social affairs, and the internal market.

While Coreper cannot take substantive decisions in its own right,[10] it has nonetheless evolved 'into a veritable decision-making factory'.[11] It will consider and digest draft legislative proposals from the Commission, and set the agenda for Council meetings.[12] The agenda is divided into Parts A and B: the former includes items which Coreper has agreed can be adopted by the Council without discussion; the latter will cover topics which do require further discussion. Approximately 85 per cent of Council decisions prepared by Coreper fall in Part A.[13] Many working parties—approximately

---

[9] Neunreither (n 5 above); P Dankert, 'The European Community—Past, Present and Future' in L Tsoukalis (ed), *The EC: Past, Present and Future* (Basil Blackwell, 1983) 7.

[10] Case C-25/94 *Commission v Council* [1996] ECR I-1469.

[11] J Lewis, 'National Interests, Coreper' in J Peterson and M Shackleton (eds), *The Institutions of the European Union* (2nd edn, Oxford University Press, 2006) ch 14.

[12] J Lewis, 'The Methods of Community in EU Decision-Making and Administrative Rivalry in the Council's Infrastructure' (2000) 7 JEPP 261; D Bostock, 'Coreper Revisited' (2002) 40 JCMS 215; Lewis (n 11 above) ch 14.

[13] F Hayes-Renshaw and H Wallace, *The Council of Ministers* (2nd edn, Palgrave, 2006) 77.

250—composed of national experts, feed into Coreper. They are the lifeblood of the Council. These groups will examine legislative proposals from the Commission, and report to Coreper or the Council. The Council also receives input from other specialist committees.[14]

It would be wrong to portray Coreper as exclusively intergovernmental in its orientation. Decision-making tends to be consensual, even where the formal voting rules specify qualified majority,[15] and Lewis notes that 'from a Janus-faced perspective, they act as both, and simultaneously, state agents and supranational entrepreneurs'.[16] This balanced perspective is important. It does not alter the fact that Coreper and the plethora of working groups were a 'necessary' development if the Council was to take an informed view of the meaning and merits of Commission proposals. The Council's ability for input and influence on primary legislation would have been severely limited without Coreper and the working parties, which redressed an otherwise significant informational and technical asymmetry between Council and Commission. This was more especially so given that the Council could only amend Commission proposals by unanimity. It was therefore even more important that Commission proposals were thoroughly digested before being formally presented to the Council.

4. COUNCIL INPUT INTO SECONDARY NORMS: COMITOLOGY

The Luxembourg Accords enabled the Member States to block measures that injuriously affected their vital interests. Coreper and the plethora of working parties allowed Council input into the making of primary legislation. It also rapidly became apparent that Member States sought influence over secondary norms and created an institutional mechanism to facilitate this.

It is common in democratic statal systems for primary legislation to be complemented by secondary norms, which flesh out the principles contained in the enabling statute. This is so for a number of reasons. The legislature may not be able to foresee all ramifications of primary legislation; it may have neither time, nor expertise, to address all issues in the original legislation; and measures consequential to the original statute may have to be passed expeditiously. The secondary norms may be individualized decisions. They will however commonly be legislative in nature: general rules applicable to all those falling within a certain factual situation. The method by which such measures are made varies in the Member States. The premise in some systems is that norms of a legislative nature should be legitimated through some degree of legislative oversight. This legitimation from the 'top' via the legislature may be complemented by legitimation from the 'bottom' through participation in rule-making by affected parties. The premise in other regimes is that the executive should have some autonomous power to make secondary norms, the principal check being judicial review. It is

---

[14] ibid ch 3.   [15] Lewis (n 11 above) ch 14.   [16] ibid 289.

important to dispel any illusion that the primary legislation captures all issues of principle, while secondary norms address insignificant points of detail. This does not represent reality. Secondary norms may address issues of principle or political choice that are just as controversial as those dealt with in the primary legislation.

This is especially so in the EU, which has been characterized as a regulatory state,[17] where secondary regulations will often deal with matters of principle or political contestation. This serves to explain the birth of the committee system known as Comitology.[18] The Commission has articulated a picture of the 'Community method' in which it sees itself as the Community executive with principal responsibility for the making of such secondary norms.[19] We shall return to this picture below. Suffice it to say for the present that the original Treaty was ambiguous in this respect.

The disposition of primary legislative power in the Rome Treaty was relatively clear; the maxim the 'Commission proposes, the Council disposes' held true for most areas. The disposition of power over secondary norms rules was less clear. The Commission's claim for authority over such norms was based on Article 155 EEC, which provided that in order to ensure the proper functioning and development of the common market the Commission should, *inter alia*, 'exercise the powers conferred on it by the Council for the implementation of the rules laid down by the latter'. This was however an uncertain foundation for the assertion of Commission authority. This was in part because, as the ECJ acknowledged,[20] Article 155 EEC was optional and became operative when the Council conferred power on the Commission. It was in part because of ambiguity as to the meaning of 'implementation'. The word could refer to the 'making' of secondary rules, or alternatively to the 'execution' of the primary regulation or directive, connoting the need for measures to ensure that the primary regulation or directive was properly applied.[21] We shall see that ambiguity in this regard persisted in later Treaty revisions. The reality was that the Rome Treaty provided little by way of definitive guidance on the making of secondary norms, or the conditions that could be attached to this process.

[17] G Majone, 'The Rise of the Regulatory State in Europe' (1994) 17 WEP 77; G Majone, *Regulating Europe* (Routledge, 1996); G Majone, 'Europe's "Democratic Deficit": The Question of Standards' (1998) 4 ELJ 5.

[18] R Pedler and GF Schaefer (eds), *Shaping European Law and Policy: The Role of Committees and Comitology in the Political Process* (European Institute of Public Administration, 1996); C Joerges, K-H Ladeur and E Vos (eds), *Integrating Scientific Expertise into Regulatory Decision-Making: National Traditions and European Innovations* (Nomos, 1997); C Joerges and E Vos (eds), *EU Committees: Social Regulation, Law and Politics* (Hart, 1999); E Vos, *Institutional Frameworks of Community Health and Safety Legislation: Committees, Agencies and Private Bodies* (Hart, 1999); M Andenas and A Turk (eds), *Delegated Legislation and the Role of Committees in the EC* (Kluwer Law International, 2000); C Bergstrom, *Comitology, Delegation of Powers in the European Union and the Committee System* (Oxford University Press, 2005).

[19] 63–65.

[20] Case 25/70 *Einfuhr- und Vorrasstelle fur Getreide und Futermittel v Koster, Berodt & Co* [1970] 2 ECR 1161, [9].

[21] Case 16/88 *Commission v Council* [1989] ECR 3457, [11]–[13].

Political reality is nonetheless often the catalyst for legal development. Comitology was born in the context of the Common Agricultural Policy (CAP).[22] It rapidly became clear that administration of the CAP required detailed rules in ever-changing market circumstances. Recourse to primary legislation was impracticable. The Member States were however wary of according the Commission a blank cheque over implementing rules, since power once delegated without encumbrance generated legally binding rules without the option for further Council oversight. This wariness was heightened by tensions between Council and Commission in the mid-1960s leading to the Luxembourg Accords. The creation of the committee system also facilitated interaction between national administrators and resolution of disagreement between the Member States, who might agree on the regulatory principles for an area, but disagree on the more detailed ramifications thereof.

The net result was the birth of the management committee procedure, embodied in early agricultural regulations. The committee, composed of national representatives with expertise in the relevant area, were involved with the Commission in the deliberations leading to the secondary regulations, which were immediately applicable, subject to the caveat that they could be returned to the Council if they were not in accord with the committee's opinion. The Council could then take a different decision by qualified majority within one month. The committee methodology rapidly became a standard feature of delegation of power to the Commission. It was not long before the more restrictive version, the regulatory committee procedure, was created: if the committee failed to deliver an opinion, or if it gave an opinion contrary to the recommended measure, the Commission would have to submit the proposal to the Council, which could then act by qualified majority. There was a safety net or *filet*, such that if the Council did not act within three months of the measure being submitted to it, then the proposed provisions could be adopted by the Commission. The desire for greater political control reached its apotheosis in the *contre-filet* version of the regulatory committee procedure: the normal regulatory committee procedure applied, subject to the caveat that the Council could by simple majority prevent the Commission from acting even after the expiry of the prescribed period.

The legitimacy of the management committee procedure was considered by the ECJ in *Koster*.[23] The German court asked whether the procedure was consistent with the institutional balance in the Treaty. If the ECJ had found against the legitimacy of the procedure it would have created serious problems, given the importance attached by the Council to input into the making of secondary norms. The ECJ avoided any such conflict by upholding the legitimacy of the management committee procedure. It reasoned that Article 155 EEC accorded the Council discretion to confer implementing powers on the Commission, and that therefore the Council could determine the rules to which the Commission was subject when exercising such powers. Moreover,

---

[22] C Bertram, 'Decision-Making in the EEC: The Management Committee Procedure' (1967–68) 5 CML Rev 246; P Schindler, 'The Problems of Decision-Making by Way of the Management Committee Procedure in the EEC' (1971) 8 CML Rev 184; Bergstrom (n 18 above) ch 2.

[23] Case 25/70 *Koster* (n 20 above).

because the committee could not take any decision, but merely served to send the matter back to the Council, the ECJ held that it did not distort the institutional balance within the EEC. Judicial support for the political status quo was evident once again in *Tedeschi*,[24] where the ECJ upheld the legality of the regulatory committee procedure.

Comitology has been much discussed by political scientists and lawyers. Rational choice institutionalists regard it as an exemplification of their principal/agent thesis. Member State principals delegate four functions to supranational agents: monitoring compliance; the resolution of incomplete contracts among principals; the adoption of regulations in areas where the principals would be biased or uninformed; and setting the legislative agenda so as to avoid the 'endless cycling' that would otherwise result if this power were exercised by the principals themselves.[25] The principals must however ensure insofar as possible that the agents do not stray from the preferences of the principals. Thus on this view Comitology constitutes a control mechanism whereby Member State principals exert control over supranational agents. The Member State principals recognized the need for delegation of power over secondary norms to the supranational agent, the Commission, but did not wish to give it a blank cheque, hence the creation of committees through which Member State preferences could be expressed, with the threat of recourse to the Council if agreement could not be reached with the Commission. It is assumed that the representatives on Comitology reflect their Member State exogenous preferences and bargain within the committees.[26] The variants of committee procedure reflect the Member States' ability to impose the degree of control that best suits their interests.

This view has been challenged by sociological institutionalists and constructivists. They contend that decision-making within Comitology is best viewed as a form of deliberative supranationalism.[27] Governments might be unaware of their preferences on particular issues. The national delegates on the committees will often regard themselves as a team dealing with a transnational problem, and become representatives of an inter-administrative discourse characterized by mutual learning. Comitology is portrayed as a network of European and national actors, with the Commission acting as coordinator. The national representatives in the deliberative process are willing to call their own preferences into question in searching for a Community solution.[28]

There have not surprisingly been empirical studies designed to test these rival hypotheses.[29] We shall return to this debate in due course. Suffice it to say for the

---

[24] Case 5/77 *Carlo Tedeschi v Denkavit Commerciale Srl* [1977] ECR 1555.   [25] Pollack (n 6 above) 6.

[26] ibid ch 2.

[27] C Joerges and J Neyer, 'From Intergovernmental Bargaining to Deliberative Political Processes: The Constitutionalization of Comitology' (1997) 3 ELJ 273; J Neyer, 'The Comitology Challenge to Analytical Integration Theory' in Joerges and Vos (n 18 above) ch 12; C Joerges, 'Good Governance through Comitology?' in Joerges and Vos (n 18 above) ch 17.

[28] Joerges and Neyer (n 27 above) 315.

[29] Pollack (n 6 above); F Franchino, 'Control of the Commission's Executive Functions: Uncertainty, Conflict and Decision Rules' (2000) 1 European Union Politics 63; M Pollack, 'Control Mechanism or Deliberative Democracy: Two Images of Comitology' (2003) 36 Comparative Political Studies 125.

present that there may be something to both hypotheses. Thus even if the creation of Comitology committees conforms to the rational choice hypothesis, this does not mean that the national representatives will necessarily always function in interstate bargaining mode. They might operate in a manner more akin to deliberative supranationalism. However whether they do so may depend on the subject matter, and conclusions reached in the context of, for example, food safety committees, may not be applicable in other areas.

5. MEMBER STATE INPUT INTO THE DIRECTION OF COMMUNITY POLICY: THE EUROPEAN COUNCIL

The period between the Rome Treaty and the SEA also saw the emergence of the European Council as a political actor.[30] The Rome Treaty gave no institutional role to the heads of state, but meetings between them were common from the early 1960s. The decision to institutionalize such meetings was taken in 1974 at the Paris Summit. The conclusion from the summit stated that such meetings would occur three times per year, normally outside the confines of the Council, but where necessary within the Council. These meetings continued to be held during the 1970s and 1980s, even though there was no formal remit until the SEA.

The rationale given for the institutionalization of the European Council at the 1974 Paris Summit was to ensure progress and consistency in the overall work of the Community. It has, as will be seen more fully below, grown into a major institutional player within the EU, such that nothing of real significance occurs without the imprimatur of the European Council. This is so notwithstanding the absence of Treaty foundation prior to 1986, and notwithstanding the brevity of legal mention of the European Council in the SEA.

For the purposes of the present analysis its significance in the early years was that it provided an institutionalized forum for the expression of Member State views at the highest level, which then shaped subsequent Community policy, despite the fact that European Council conclusions were not formally binding. Thus it allowed political leaders input into the overall Community agenda, operated as a forum for a Community response to external problems, and facilitated resolution of disagreements between Member States that could not be resolved through ordinary Council mechanisms.

---

[30] S Bulmer and W Wessels, *The European Council* (Macmillan, 1987); P de Schoutheete and H Wallace, *The European Council* (Notre Europe, 2002), available at <http://www.notre-europe.asso.fr>; P Ludlow, *The Making of the New Europe: The European Council in Brussels and Copenhagen 2002* (EuroComment, 2004); P de Schoutheete, 'The European Council' in Peterson and Shackleton (n 11 above) ch 3; Hayes-Renshaw and Wallace (n 13 above) ch 6; J Werts, *The European Council* (Harper, 2008).

6. THE ECJ: DECISIONAL AND NORMATIVE SUPRANATIONALISM

The discussion thus far has been concerned with the evolving institutional relationship of the Council and Commission between the Rome Treaty and the SEA. The ECJ was however also important during this period. Detailed treatment of direct effect and the general role of the Court will be provided in later chapters.[31] The present discussion focuses on the ECJ's role in shaping the Community's institutional balance in the period between Rome and the SEA.

The Rome Treaty was structured so as to lay down the principles governing core concepts such as free movement, with the express stipulation that regulations and directives should be enacted to make these principles a reality. Progress was made in this respect, and the quantity of legislation adopted in relation to negative integration should not be forgotten. There were, for example, approximately fifty such measures enacted from 1962–82, pursuant to the general programmes for the abolition of restrictions on freedom of establishment and the provision of services.

The passage of legislative initiatives nonetheless became increasingly difficult during the 1970s and early part of the 1980s. The Council rejected social measures, such as directives on co-determination and worker consultation, and many others were stalled, awaiting a Council decision. Progress was slow in relation to positive integration through Community harmonization, since Article 100 EEC required unanimity, and prior to the SEA Directives normally demanded Member State agreement on a detailed measure that was difficult to attain. There was growing concern that the Community's objectives were not being fulfilled. These difficulties led to what Middlemas termed a 'condition of immobility'.[32] The period from the early 1970s to the early 1980s was characterized as the 'dark ages' for the Community.[33] Dankert, the President of the European Parliament, bemoaned the jungle of half-implemented treaties, and neglected Treaty articles.[34] Wallace concluded that the Community had moved beyond other international regimes, but that it could drift back towards them as 'recession at home and uncertainty abroad progressively undermine its authority'.[35]

Attainment of Community objectives through the normal political process was therefore difficult, and in this sense 'decisional supranationalism' was at a low ebb during this period. This led, as Weiler argued,[36] to the growing significance of 'normative

---

[31] de Witte ch 12; Stone Sweet ch 6.

[32] K Middlemas, *Orchestrating Europe, The Informal Politics of the European Union 1973–1995* (Fontana, 1995) 90.

[33] J Caporaso and J Keeler, 'The European Union and Regional Integration Theory' in C Rhodes and S Mazey (eds), *The State of the European Union, Building a European Polity?* (Longman, 1995) 37; S George and I Bache, *Politics in the European Union* (Oxford University Press, 2001) ch 9.

[34] Dankert (n 9 above) 8.

[35] W Wallace, 'Europe as Confederation: The Community and the Nation State' in Tsoukalis (n 9 above) 68.

[36] J Weiler, 'The Community System: The Dual Character of Supranationalism' (1981) 1 YEL 267, and 'The Transformation of Europe' 100 Yale LJ 2403, 2412–2431 (1991); P Craig, 'Once Upon a Time in the West: Direct Effect and the Federalization of EEC Law' (1992) 12 OJLS 453.

supranationalism', whereby the ECJ, through doctrines of direct effect and supremacy, ensured the continued development of Community law, notwithstanding the difficulties of securing legislation through the political process. It is important to understand how this occurred.

Direct effect enabled individuals to assert rights derived from Treaty articles and Community legislation before national courts, and to argue that national action was inconsistent with Community law. The national courts referred to the ECJ issues of Community law that arose in such disputes. This provided the ECJ with the material through which to interpret the relevant Community provisions, and to do so in a way that ensured the continued vitality of those provisions notwithstanding infirmities in the political process.

Thus the ECJ made clear that it was willing to deploy direct effect to enforce important Treaty provisions, notwithstanding the fact that implementing legislation had not been enacted because of difficulties in the political process.[37] This can be exemplified by *Reyners*,[38] which was concerned with freedom of establishment. The Member States argued, *inter alia*, that Article 52 EEC did not fulfil the conditions for direct effect as laid down in *Van Gend* because further action at Community level, in the form of directives, had yet to be taken, which would then have to be implemented by the Member States. They claimed that it was not for the 'court to exercise a discretionary power reserved to the legislative institutions of the Community and the Member States'.[39] The ECJ rejected the argument. The Court accorded primacy to the principle of non-discrimination within Article 52, and treated the further legislation as a way of effectuating this goal.

The Community legislation had not been promulgated within the requisite period because of Member State unwillingness in the Council to make the necessary compromises. This was the period of legislative malaise in which getting things through the Council operating under the shadow of the veto was problematic. The ECJ signalled that it was not willing to allow Article 52 to atrophy. The Court would develop the principle through adjudication should the detailed legislation not be forthcoming. The decision therefore constitutes a prime example of normative supranationalism being used to overcome the deficiencies of decisional supranationalism.

The Commission responded with a Communication addressed to the Council in response to the *Reyners* decision.[40] It made clear to the Council that if it continued to delay passage of directives then recourse might be had to the ECJ, since such delaying tactics constituted derogation from the rule in Article 52. Directives designed solely to abolish restrictions based on nationality were unnecessary in the light of the *Reyners*

---

[37] Case 33/74 *Van Binsbergen v Bestuur van de Bedrijfsvereniging voor de Metaalnijverheid* [1974] ECR 1299; Case 43/75 *Defrenne v Société Anonyme Belge de Navigation Aérienne* [1976] ECR 455.

[38] Case 2/74 *Reyners v Belgian State* [1974] ECR 631.

[39] ibid [7].

[40] Commission Communication to the Council on the consequences of the judgment of the Court of Justice of June 21 1974, in Case 2/74 (Reyners and the Belgian State) on the proposals for Directives concerning the right of establishment and freedom to provide services at present before the Council, SEC (74) 4024 final.

case. The Council should, however, continue work on directives relating to Article 57 EEC and the mutual recognition of diplomas. The Commission therefore reinforced the Court's ruling. The principles in Article 52 could not be avoided, because of Member States' unwillingness to agree on implementing provisions. If the Member States continued to be tardy then the Court would fill out the more detailed meaning of this Article. The resulting norms might not be those which the Member States would have chosen in Community legislation. If the Member States delayed in promulgating these legislative norms to ensure that they accorded perfectly with their interests, they might then have little say in the rules developed by the Court.

Normative supranationalism also supplemented decisional supranationalism by shaping the very nature of the regulatory process within the Community, as exemplified by *Cassis de Dijon*.[41] The ECJ held that Article 30 EEC could apply to national trade rules that did not discriminate against imported products, but which nonetheless inhibited trade because they differed from those in the country of origin. When goods had been lawfully marketed in one Member State, they should be admitted into any other state, unless the state of import could successfully invoke a mandatory requirement. The judgment therefore encapsulated a principle of mutual recognition and had a marked impact on the scope of Article 30 EEC. It was also the catalyst for a major re-orientation of Community regulatory strategy. The difficulties of securing the passage of harmonization measures that were vital for positive integration were in part because of the unanimity requirement and in part because prior to *Cassis* such measures sought to regulate in considerable detail the relevant product. It was therefore unsurprising that progress was slow. The *Cassis* Decision however led the Commission to reconsider its regulatory strategy such that it would in general only try to regulate those issues that survived scrutiny under *Cassis*, these being national measures that were justified as mandatory requirements to protect public health, consumer safety and the like.

The rationale for, and role of, the Community courts has been debated more generally by political scientists, and more detailed treatment can be found in the chapter by Alec Stone Sweet. Rational choice institutionalists argue that the ECJ can be best explained in terms of principal/agent theory, the hypothesis being that Member State principals were willing to delegate authority to the ECJ in order to render their collective commitments under the Treaty more credible, and to enable the ECJ to complete the details of the incomplete contract that constituted the Treaty.[42] Some contend moreover that ECJ decisions were in accord with the preferences of the major Member States such as France and Germany,[43] although later literature offered a more nuanced picture.[44]

---

[41] Case 120/78 *Rewe-Zentrale AG v Bundesmonopolverwaltung für Branntwein* [1979] ECR 649.

[42] Pollack (n 6 above) ch 3.

[43] G Garrett, 'International Cooperation and Institutional Choice: The European Community's Internal Market' (1992) 46 International Organization 533.

[44] G Garrett, D Kelemen, and H Schulz, 'The European Court of Justice, National Governments and Legal Integration in the European Union' (1998) 52 International Organization 149.

The principal/agent view of the ECJ has however been vigorously challenged by those, such as Stone Sweet, who argue that the constitutionalization of the Treaties could not be explained by Member State preferences, but was rather driven by individual litigants who used the opportunities presented by direct effect and supremacy to contest national laws that interfered with Community rights and hindered free trade. This 'private enforcement' of Community law at the behest of individuals, in which national courts sent references to the ECJ and executed its rulings at national level, created the Community legal order; the ECJ exercised considerable autonomy in this respect and the results could not be captured by the principal/agent model.[45] This was more especially so given that Member States could only overrule ECJ decisions on Treaty interpretation through Treaty amendment.

We shall return to the role of the Court in due course. Suffice it to say for the present that the great majority of Community lawyers, while acknowledging the rationale for the ECJ cast in terms of credible commitments, would not accept the principal/agent hypothesis of the Court as some simple 'agent' carrying out Member State preferences. Its autonomy in this respect is manifest in all areas of Community law, and not just in relation to issues concerned with constitutionalization of the Treaties.

B. FROM THE SEA TO NICE: CLARIFICATION, CONTESTATION, AND COMPLEXITY

The Single European Act 1986 represents a watershed in Community inter-institutional relations for reasons that will become apparent below. The period between the SEA and the Nice Treaty witnessed a plethora of institutional changes, in which three themes were evident.

There was clarification of the principles governing Community administration and most importantly of the appropriate disposition of legislative power, with recognition that the EP should properly have a role. This was recognized initially in the SEA, and enhanced further by the Maastricht Treaty and the Amsterdam Treaty, most notably through creation and then extension of the co-decision procedure.

The emerging consensus about the legislative process was not matched by agreement concerning the disposition of executive power. The period between the SEA and the Nice Treaty saw contestation and skirmishes as to the locus of executive authority, which played out in different ways in relation to Comitology, agencies, and the European Council. In principal/agent terms, the Commission as 'supranational agent' chafed at restrictions imposed by Member State principals.

---

[45] A Stone Sweet and J Caporaso, 'From Free Trade to Supranational Polity: The European Court and Integration' in Wayne Sandholtz and Alec Stone Sweet (eds), *European Integration and Supranational Governance* (Oxford University Press, 1998); A Stone Sweet and T Brunell, 'Constructing a Supranational Constitution: Dispute Resolution and Governance in the European Community' (1998) 92 APSR 63.

Institutional complexity was the third theme in this period. The variety of Community legislative procedures, the creation of new agencies, the Three Pillar structure with different forms of legislation and a different disposition of authority, all served to render the EU difficult to comprehend even for the well-informed citizen. It is not therefore surprising that these three themes became central, as will be seen, to discussions of institutional reform in the Constitutional Treaty and the Lisbon Treaty.

1. EUROPEAN COUNCIL: DIRECTION OF EU POLICY

It is fitting to begin this section with reference to the ever-growing importance of the European Council. It was accorded Treaty recognition for the first time in the SEA, and assumed ever-greater importance for the overall direction of EU policy. There can be few major institutions where the lack of correlation between mention in the Treaties and the significance of its role is more marked. The paucity of Treaty references to the European Council[46] should not therefore lead one to doubt its importance. It increasingly played a central role in setting the pace and shape of EU policy, establishing the parameters within which the other institutions operated, and providing a forum at the highest level for resolution of tensions between the Member States.[47] This was reflected in lengthier conclusions that emerged from the European Council meetings, which would frequently contain detailed 'action points' for other institutional players, notably the Council and Commission. The fact that the European Council possessed no direct role in the legislative process did not therefore prevent it from shaping legislative priorities and the nature of legislative initiatives.

The European Council was central to Treaty reform, since the initiative for the establishment of an Inter-Governmental Conference would normally come from the European Council, which would also affirm or modify the conclusions reached in such negotiations. It was commonly the European Council that confirmed important changes in the institutional structure of the Community, such as the enlargement of the Parliament following German unification. It was the European Council once again that often provided the focal point for significant constitutional initiatives that affected the operation of the Community and Union, such as Inter-institutional Agreements between the three major institutions. The European Council regularly considered the state of the European economy, and proposed initiatives to combat unemployment, promote growth, and increase competitiveness.[48] It played a role in the initiation or development of particular policy strategies, dealing with matters as diverse as social policy, drugs, terrorism, asylum, and immigration. The European Council was in addition deeply involved in external relations, and determined the pace of new accessions to the EU.

---

[46] Art 4 EU.   [47] de Schoutheete (n 29).
[48] Lisbon European Council, Presidency Conclusions, 23–24 March 2000; Nice European Council, Presidency Conclusions, 7–9 December 2000; European Council, Presidency Conclusions, 22–23 March 2005.

The very fact that the chair of the European Council rotated every six months however did little to enhance continuity of policy, and provoked criticism. This led to reforms introduced by the Seville European Council 2002. It provided that the six Presidencies concerned, in consultation with the Commission, should draw up a joint proposal, which was submitted to the General Affairs and External Relations Council, GAERC, for adoption by the European Council in the form of a multi-annual strategic programme lasting three years. The first such programme was produced in 2003.[49] This three-year programme in turn led to annual operational programmes submitted by the two Presidencies to the GAERC, which would then finalize the programme.[50] This programme was itself influenced by the Commission programme, and by external events.[51]

2. COMMUNITY LEGISLATION: TRANSFORMATION AND INCLUSION

The SEA was primarily motivated by the desire to expedite completion of the internal market. It was nonetheless significant in institutional terms, notwithstanding Member State rejection of far-reaching proposals for Treaty reform advanced by the European Parliament. The Member States were however persuaded to accept some institutional reform, whereby the EP was given real power in the legislative process for the first time, through the creation of the cooperation procedure. The details of this procedure need not concern us here, but suffice it to say that it gave the European Parliament two readings for measures that came within its ambit, enabling it to propose amendments, and block legislation with the support of one Member State in the Council.[52] The advent of this procedure was all the more important given that it applied to harmonization measures enacted under the new Article 100a EEC, which was the provision used for the enactment of much of the single market legislation post-1986.

The cooperation procedure was largely overtaken by co-decision, discussed below. It was however the cooperation procedure that began the transformation of the primary legislative process. The previous reality encapsulated in the maxim that the 'Commission proposes, the Council disposes' changed. There were now three players in the game, with wide-ranging ramifications. The Commission recognized the need for increased inter-institutional cooperation. It had to draft proposals with an eye as to what would 'play' with Parliament as well as the Council.[53] Coreper, the gatekeeper for the Council, now had to consider the views of the EP, as well as the Council and Commission.[54] The EP's powers in the legislative process were

---

[49] POLGEN 76, 15047/03, Multi-annual Strategic Programme, Brussels 20 November 2003.

[50] Seville European Council, Annex II, Brussels 24 October 2002, 23–24.

[51] Hayes-Renshaw and Wallace (n 13 above) ch 6.

[52] R Corbett, 'Testing the New Procedures: The European Parliament's First Experience with its New "Single Act" Powers' (1989) 27 JCMS 4.

[53] M Westlake, *The Commission and the Parliament: Partners and Rivals in the European Policy-Making Process* (Butterworths, 1994) 37–39.

[54] Lewis (n 11 above).

'transformed from the weak and essentially unconstructive power of delay to a stronger and potentially constructive role in the drafting of legislation'.[55]

It was but a few years later that the Treaty on European Union, TEU, introduced the co-decision procedure, Article 251 EC. It was revised by the Treaty of Amsterdam, which strengthened further the role of the EP.[56] It became the method for making much important Community legislation, and areas previously governed by the cooperation procedure were upgraded to co-decision.[57]

The details of the co-decision procedure can be found elsewhere.[58] Suffice it to say for the present that it prevented a measure being adopted without approval of the Council and EP, and emphasized the reaching of a jointly approved text. The EP had two readings of a measure, the first of which occurred when it gave its opinion to the Council. There was no time limit for the first reading, either for the EP or the Council. The second reading took place on the assumption that the Council had not approved all the EP's first-reading amendments, or if it had other amendments of its own, which had to be passed unanimously in the Council. If this happened then the Council communicated its common position to the EP, which had the option at second reading to approve, reject, or propose amendments to the measure. The EP however limited the second reading amendments that it would propose.[59] If the EP suggested amendments, not all of which were acceptable to the Council, then the Conciliation Committee came into operation.[60] The EP and Council had to approve the joint text from the Conciliation Committee. The co-decision procedure could however be concluded at any of the earlier stages, provided that the EP and Council agreed. Thus during the Parliamentary session 1999–2004 115 co-decision dossiers (28 per cent) were concluded at first reading; 200 dossiers (50 per cent) at second reading; and 84 dossiers (22 per cent) through conciliation.[61]

The co-decision procedure was successful in practice, and accommodated the differing interests with a stake in the legislative process.[62] This was so notwithstanding disagreement about the 'power dynamics' within co-decision and about the relative power of the EP under co-decision and other legislative procedures.[63] The EP used its veto power under Article 251 EC sparingly, although decision-making still took place

---

[55] Westlake (n 53 above) 39.

[56] Joint Declaration on Practical Arrangements for the New Co-Decision Procedure [1999] OJ C148/1.

[57] <http://ec.europa.eu/codecision/index_en.htm>.

[58] P Craig and G de Búrca, *EU Law, Text, Cases and Materials* (4th edn, Oxford University Press, 2007) ch 4.

[59] European Parliament, *Conciliations and Co-decision, A Guide to how Parliament Co-legislates* (DV/547830EN.doc, 2004) 6.

[60] <http://www.europarl.eu.int/code/default_en.htm>.

[61] *Conciliations and Co-decision* (n 59 above) 7.

[62] A Dashwood, 'European Community Legislative Procedures after Amsterdam' (1998) 1 CYELS 25; Co-decision, An Analysis Prepared by the Co-decision Service of the Commission, <http://ec.europa.eu/codecision/institutional /analysis/index_en.htm>.

[63] G Garrett and G Tsebelis, 'Understanding Better the EU Legislative Process' (2001) 2 EUP 353; R Corbett, 'A Response to a Reply to a Reaction (I Hope Someone is Still Interested)' (2001) 2 EUP 361.

under its shadow. It is more difficult to generalize about the amendments secured by the EP. There is research indicating that EP amendments modified the Commission proposal, but did not significantly alter it.[64] This is to some extent unsurprising, since draft legislative proposals were discussed with the EP and Council/Coreper before Article 251 was initiated, thereby accommodating diverse opinion. Where this dialogic process still left major differences of view, the EP and Council could propose amendments, which forced the Commission to modify the measure significantly, as with the Services Directive.[65] The Commission also retained influence within co-decision: it could withdraw a proposed measure before it was adopted and/or submit a modified version; it routinely responded to proposed EP amendments, indicating those it could and could not accept; and where the Commission gave a negative opinion on EP second-reading amendments they could only be accepted by the Council if there was unanimity.

The co-decision procedure had a secure normative foundation. The EP had long pressed for a co-equal role in the legislative process with the Council, and the modifications to co-decision made by the Treaty of Amsterdam went a considerable way to achieving this. The attention placed on democracy and legitimacy in the 1990s helped to secure the EP this more equal role in the legislative process.[66] The co-decision procedure embodied an institutional balance in which the Commission, Council, and EP all played a role. It encouraged deliberative discourse between them, this being secured through the provisions of Article 251 that gave each player rights within this process. There were however concerns about the nature of this deliberative process, flowing from the institutionalization of trilogues.[67] They were originally meetings that preceded the Conciliation Committee, composed of representatives from the Council, EP, and Commission, to facilitate compromise. This is unobjectionable. The concern arose from the fact that such trilogues were moved earlier in the co-decision process, coinciding with the first reading of the measure, with the danger that compromises might be reached that inhibited contributions from those within the Council or the EP that were not party to the trilogue.[68]

The SEA and the TEU signalled acceptance of the EP in relation to the passage of Community primary legislation, and in that respect clarified the inter-institutional

---

[64] A Kreppel, 'Moving beyond Procedure: An Empirical Analysis of European Parliament Legislative Influence' (2002) 35 Comparative Political Studies 784; R Thomson and M Hosli, 'Who has Power in the EU? Council, Commission and Parliament in Legislative Decision-making' (2006) 44 JCMS 391.

[65] Proposal for a Directive of the European Parliament and of the Council, on services in the internal market, COM/2004/2 final/3; EP Committee on the Internal Market and Consumer Protection, A6-0409/2005, Rapporteur Evelyne Gebhardt; Amended Proposal for a Directive of the European Parliament and of the Council, on services in the internal market, COM(2006) 160 final.

[66] P Craig, 'Democracy and Rulemaking within the EC: An Empirical and Normative Assessment' (1997) 3 ELJ 105.

[67] Conciliations and Co-decision (n 59 above) 13–15; M Shackleton and T Raunio, 'Codecision since Amsterdam: A Laboratory for Institutional Innovation and Change' (2003) 10 JEPP 171, 177–179.

[68] D Curtin, 'The Council of Ministers: The Missing Link?' in L Verhey, P Kiiver, and S Loeffen (eds), Political Accountability and European Integration (Europa Law Publishing, 2009) ch 12.

disposition of power. The procedures for the passage of Community primary legislation nonetheless remained complex, because numerous procedures for the making of such legislation other than cooperation and co-decision continued to exist. The applicable procedure could only be divined by reference to the relevant Treaty article dealing with the making of Community legislation in that area.

3. COMMUNITY LEGISLATION: NATIONAL PARLIAMENTS AND SUBSIDIARITY

The discussion thus far has been primarily concerned with the balance of power between the EC institutions, and hence has a primarily 'horizontal' dimension. The early 1990s saw however increasing concern about the 'vertical' division of authority between the EC and the Member States. This provided the rationale for the inclusion of subsidiarity in the Maastricht Treaty, the basic idea being to limit the exercise of Community competence in accord with the criteria in Article 5 EC.

> The Community shall act within the limits of the powers conferred upon it by this Treaty and of the objectives assigned to it therein.
>
> In areas which do not fall within its exclusive competence, the Community shall take action, in accordance with the principle of subsidiarity, only if and in so far as the objectives of the proposed action cannot be sufficiently achieved by the Member States and can therefore, by reason of the scale or effects of the proposed action, be better achieved by the Community.
>
> Any action by the Community shall not go beyond what is necessary to achieve the objectives of this Treaty.

There were however real difficulties in making subsidiarity an effective limit on the exercise of Community power. Thus subsidiarity only had to be considered in relation to areas which did not fall within the EC's exclusive competence, but there was no ready agreement as to the scope of this competence, since the Treaty was not explicitly framed in such terms.[69]

The subsidiarity calculus was also problematic in those areas where it was considered.[70] It embraced three separate, albeit related, ideas: the Community was to take action only if the objectives of that action could not be sufficiently achieved by the Member States; the Community could better achieve the action, because of its scale or effects; if the Community did take action then this should not go beyond what was necessary to achieve the Treaty objectives. The first two parts of this formulation entailed a test of comparative efficiency, while the third embodied proportionality. The Amsterdam Treaty fleshed out this calculus in a Protocol on the Application of the Principles of Subsidiarity and Proportionality,[71] imposing obligations on the

---

[69] A Toth, 'A Legal Analysis of Subsidiarity' in D O'Keeffe and P Twomey (eds), *Legal Issues of the Maastricht Treaty* (Chancery, 1994) 39–40; J Steiner, 'Subsidiarity under the Maastricht Treaty' ibid 57–58.

[70] A Estella, *The EU Principle of Subsidiarity and its Critique* (Oxford University Press, 2002) 113–114.

[71] G de Búrca, 'Reappraising Subsidiarity's Significance after Amsterdam', Jean Monnet Working Paper 7/1999, <http://www.jeanmonnetprogram.org/>.

Commission to justify proposed legislation in terms of the subsidiarity principle through qualitative and quantitative indicators. It was nonetheless relatively easy for the Commission to provide some justification for action at Community level, more especially when it could point to divergence in national approach that could be said to hinder the realization of a single market.

It also became clear that while compliance with Article 5 was susceptible to judicial review, the ECJ used a relatively light touch review in cases that came before it. This was so irrespective of whether the challenge was to a procedural aspect of subsidiarity,[72] or whether it was cast in more substantive terms.[73] The light touch review left the ECJ open to the criticism that it effectively denuded the obligation in Article 5 of content. While the difficulties of more intensive review of a complex socio-economic calculus concerning the level of government for different regulatory tasks should not be underestimated, those difficulties would nonetheless have been alleviated if the ECJ had required more from the Commission in procedural terms. This would thereby have furnished the ECJ with more information as to the qualitative and quantitative data used by the Commission in reaching its conclusion, and hence have facilitated effective review.

4. UNION LEGISLATION: PILLARIZATION AND COMPLEXITY

The overall institutional framework was rendered more complex by the creation of the three-Pillar structure in the TEU,[74] which is considered in detail in later chapters.[75] The rationale for this development was considered in the previous chapter.[76] The Member States wished for some established mechanism for cooperation in the areas of Common Foreign and Security Policy (CFSP) and Justice and Home Affairs. Individual *ad hoc* meetings could be cumbersome, time consuming, and involve heavy 'transaction costs'. The Member States were however unwilling to accept the supranational mode of decision-making of the Community Pillar, with all that this entailed for the powers of the Commission, ECJ, and EP. They therefore devised a decision-making structure that was more intergovernmental, in which they retained power, with the other Community institutions having a diminished role by comparison with the Community Pillar. The legal acts that could be adopted within the Second and Third Pillar were also distinctive.

The predominance of Member State interests and the distinctiveness of the legal acts are apparent in relation to the CFSP.[77] Thus it was the European Council that defined

---

[72] Case C-233/94 *Germany v European Parliament and Council* [1997] ECR I-2405, [26]–[28].
[73] Case C-84/94 *United Kingdom v Council* [1996] ECR I-5755, [46]–[47], [55].
[74] E Denza, *The Intergovernmental Pillars of the European Union* (Oxford University Press, 2002); N Walker (ed), *Europe's Area of Freedom, Security and Justice* (Oxford University Press, 2004); S Peers, *EU Justice and Home Affairs Law* (2nd edn, Oxford University Press, 2006).
[75] Peers ch 10; Storskrubb ch 11.
[76] See above, 32–33.
[77] Arts 11–16 EU.

the principles of and general guidelines for the CFSP. It was the European Council once again that decided on common strategies for the EU, on the basis of recommendations made by the Council, where Member States have important interests in common. It was then for the Council to implement such common strategies through joint actions, which addressed specific situations where operational action by the Union was required, and common positions that defined the approach of the Union to a particular matter of a geographical or thematic nature. The Council could request that the Commission submit proposals in relation to the implementation of joint action. The reality was that the Commission had greater input into CFSP decision-making than was apparent from the face of the relevant Treaty provisions. This should not however mask the dominance of Member State interests in the decision-making process, and the general absence of legal controls, subject to the legal implications of the provision that nothing in the EU Treaty was to affect the Community Pillar.[78]

The centrality accorded to Member State interests, coupled with a distinctive range of legal acts, was also apparent in the Third Pillar. The original formulation of the Justice and Home Affairs Pillar governed policies such as asylum, immigration, 'third country' nationals, cooperation on international crime issues, and various forms of judicial, customs, and police cooperation. This was altered by the Treaty of Amsterdam, which moved asylum, immigration, and third country nationals to EC Title IV, and subjected the remaining Third Pillar provisions to institutional controls closer to those under the Community Pillar. The Third Pillar and Title IV EC were together labelled the Area of Freedom, Security and Justice (AFSJ).

The formal legal instruments and the disposition of power in the Third Pillar nonetheless remained distinctive. These could be adopted by the Council acting unanimously on the initiative of any Member State, or the Commission.[79] Thus the Council could adopt: common positions, which defined the EU's approach to a given matter; framework decisions for the approximation of Member State laws, these being similar to directives, but without direct effect; decisions for any purpose consistent with Third Pillar objectives, which were binding but did not have direct effect; and conventions. The EP had to be consulted on such measures, with the exception of common positions. The ECJ was given jurisdiction over the Third Pillar, but it was more limited than within the Community Pillar.[80]

The intergovernmental nature of the Third Pillar should not however be over-exaggerated. It is certainly true that the European Council set major policy strategies in this area,[81] the Justice and Home Affairs Council was an important institutional player,[82] and Coreper, together with working parties and other specialist committees, performed important gate-keeping and coordinating functions for the Member States.[83] The Commission was however important in this area. It was the principal

---

[78] Art 47 TEU.   [79] Art 34(2) EU.   [80] Art 35 EU.
[81] Tampere European Council, 15–16 October 1999; Brussels European Council, 4–5 November 2004, Hague Programme.
[82] Hayes-Renshaw and Wallace (n 13 above) 45.   [83] ibid 86–87.

source of legislative initiatives relating to the AFSJ,[84] and was charged by the Council with drawing up detailed plans to implement European Council initiatives such as the Hague programme.

It is nonetheless undeniable that the three-Pillar structure rendered decision-making more complex and more difficult to comprehend even for the well-informed EU citizen. This problem was exacerbated by the increasing tendency for policy initiatives to involve measures enacted under more than one Pillar,[85] the corollary being contestability as to the legal foundation for the Community or Union action.[86]

5. NEW GOVERNANCE: EXPERIMENTATION AND COMPLEXITY

The discussion thus far concerning legislation and policy-making has been primarily concerned with what has justly been termed the 'Classic Community Method':[87] the exercise of legislative power by the EC following the Commission's exclusive right of initiative, leading to the adoption of legislation by the Council and Parliament, resulting in a binding uniform rule which is subject to the jurisdiction of the Court of Justice. It is classic hierarchical governance, characterized by top-down decision-making by the central institutional actors leading to binding, uniform rules.[88]

An additional dimension to the inter-institutional landscape in the 1990s and the new millennium was the emergence and increased use of 'new methods of governance', analysis of which has grown exponentially in recent years, with commensurate growth in the size and complexity of the academic literature.[89] A core theme of new governance is the shift away from classic hierarchical governance, with its connotation of policy being delivered 'top-down', relatively complete and encapsulating binding legal norms backed by compulsory legal enforcement. The Classic Community Method is certainly still the norm, but there has been growing reliance on other kinds of governing mechanisms. In reality a multiplicity of new forms of governance are used in the EU, some of which exist alongside more classic hierarchical modes, others of which are employed instead of traditional methods of governance. It should also be acknowledged that within new modes of governance there is a spectrum. In some instances the obligations are voluntary, in other instances they are backed by direct or indirect legal sanction.

---

[84] Peers (n 74) 23.

[85] S Stetter, 'Cross-pillar Politics: Functional Unity and Institutional Fragmentation of EU Foreign Policies' (2004) 11 JEPP 720.

[86] Cases C-402 and C-415/05 P *Kadi v Council and Commission* [2008] ECR I-6351.

[87] J Scott and D Trubek, 'Mind the Gap: Law and New Approaches to Governance in the European Union' (2002) 8 ELJ 1.

[88] Craig and de Búrca (n 58) ch 5.

[89] C Kilpatrick and K Armstrong, 'Law, Governance and New Governance: The Changing Open Method of Coordination' (2007) 13 CJEL 649; N Walker and G de Búrca, 'Reconceiving Law and New Governance' (2007) 13 CJEL 519; C Sabel and J Zeitlin, 'Learning from Difference: The New Architecture of Experimentalist Governance in the European Union', European Governance Working Paper, EUROGOV No. C-07-02 / May 10, 2007.

New governance initiatives are apparent across the EU's terrain. Thus the 'new approach to harmonization', which came to prominence in the 1980s as part of the EC's single market programme, exemplifies aspects of the move away from hierarchy and towards greater flexibility. So too do some of the policy developments related to the search for 'better regulation', which reveal the influence of public management theories which resonate with aspects of new governance.

The best known example of new governance is however the Open Method of Coordination (OMC), which has generated a vast literature. While the OMC did not 'begin' with the Lisbon Summit in March 2000,[90] the meeting was nonetheless important, since the European Council gave its imprimatur to the OMC as an approach to be used more generally within EU governance. The European Council assessed the EU's strengths and weaknesses. The way forward was to be based on a new strategic goal for the coming decade, in which the EU was 'to become the most competitive and dynamic knowledge-based economy in the world, capable of sustainable economic growth with more and better jobs and greater social cohesion'.[91] The more particular aspects of this plan were in part economic, and in part social. The implementation of this overall strategy was to be by 'improving the existing processes, introducing a new open method of coordination at all levels, coupled with a stronger guiding and coordinating role for the European Council to ensure more coherent and strategic direction and effective monitoring of progress'.[92] The OMC was to be a decentralized process, and hence in accord with subsidiarity, and Member States, regional and local government, the social partners, and civil society would be actively involved.[93] The general features of OMC were said to be:[94] fixing guidelines for the Union combined with specific timetables for achieving the goals; establishing quantitative and qualitative indicators and benchmarks as a means of comparing best practice; translating European guidelines into national and regional policies by setting specific targets and adopting measures, taking into account national and regional differences; and periodic monitoring, evaluation, and peer review organized as mutual learning processes.

The OMC is used, albeit in different ways, in areas such as economic policy, employment policy, and combating social exclusion. It, and other new governance initiatives, reveal a willingness to experiment with ways of 'getting things done', more especially in areas, such as economic and employment policy, where there are limits to more traditional methods of EU governance.

6. SECONDARY COMMUNITY NORMS: CONTINUITY, CHANGE, AND CONTESTATION

The Community legislative process for the passage of primary legislation was, as we have seen, transformed post the SEA, the premise being that the three major

---

[90] Lisbon European Council, Presidency Conclusions, 23–24 March 2000.   [91] ibid [5].
[92] ibid [7].   [93] ibid [38].   [94] ibid [37].

institutional players all had a role to play. This premise was not shared in relation to the passage of secondary norms, and the period from the SEA to Nice and beyond saw continuing contestation as to power and authority over the making of such provisions.

Prior to the SEA, Comitology was, as we have seen, based on an admixture of legislative choice, backed by judicial approval. The SEA legitimated Comitology via the new third indent of Article 202 EC, which stipulated that the Council should confer on the Commission, in the acts adopted by the Council, powers for the implementation of the rules which the Council laid down, and that it could impose certain requirements in respect of the exercise of these powers. These procedures had to be consonant with principles and rules laid down in advance. The Council could also reserve the right, in specific cases, to exercise directly implementing powers itself. Article 202 EC demanded that the committee procedures should take place in accord with rules laid down in advance, and this was the catalyst for the first Comitology Decision in 1987.[95] It was certainly an improvement on the status quo ante, reducing the basic committee procedures to three: advisory, management, and regulatory, with two variants of both the management and regulatory committee procedures, plus safeguard committee procedures. The beneficial impact of the Decision was however qualified by the Council's insistence that it should not be taken to affect the plethora of procedures applicable to existing committees.

The Commission and the EP were however dissatisfied with the Comitology regime, albeit for different reasons. For the Commission the Treaty amendment to Article 202 was a 'plus', insofar as it embodied the general principle that the Council should confer implementing power on the Commission, unless the Council provided reasons why it should reserve implementing power to itself, although judicial review of this issue has not generally been searching or intensive.[96] It was nonetheless a defeat for more far-reaching Commission ambitions, since it entered the SEA negotiations hoping to secure amendment to Article 211 EC, whereby it would have implementing power without prior authorization from the Council, coupled with a strictly limited number of committee procedures, and a clear preference against regulatory committees.[97]

This aspiration was itself reflective of deeper Commission concerns about Comitology. The Commission's longstanding view was that the passage of 'implementing' provisions was part of the executive function, the authority for which should properly reside with the Commission. Thus while it was content to accept advisory committees it was unhappy with management and regulatory committees that cramped what it regarded as its proper sphere of executive autonomy. The political and normative foundation for this assumption is contestable to say the least. It is premised on the

---

[95] Council Decision 87/373/EEC of 13 July 1987 laying down the procedures for the exercise of implementing powers conferred on the Commission [1987] OJ L197/33.

[96] Case C-257/01 *Commission v Council* [2005] ECR I-345, [53]. The ECJ is also willing to review the choice as between management and regulatory procedures, Case C-378/00 *Commission v European Parliament and Council* [2003] ECR I-937.

[97] C-D Ehlermann, 'The Internal Market Following the Single European Act' (1987) 24 CML Rev 361.

argument that everything that occurs after the passage of the primary legislation should be regarded as part of the executive function. The reality is that while some secondary norms made pursuant to Comitology may simply be concerned with issues of technical detail, in many other instances the primary legislation may provide guidance but still leave issues of principle and political choice to be resolved through secondary norms that are legislative in nature. Given that this is so, the Commission's claim that such measures fall naturally within its sphere of 'executive' autonomy conceals more than it reveals.

The 1990s also saw increased opposition to Comitology by the EP. It expressed disquiet over Comitology from the very outset, but the EP's opposition grew commensurately with its increased status in the making of primary regulations and directives. The reason for this is not hard to divine. It had been on the side-lines of the legislative process for the first three decades of the Community's existence. This changed with the introduction of the cooperation and co-decision procedures. The significance of these gains was however undermined by the EP's exclusion from the making of secondary norms, which would often entail important issues of principle, practical detail, or political choice.

The EP fought the battle against Comitology on the legal and political front.[98] It argued that Article 202 could not be regarded as the basis for Comitology where the primary acts were adopted pursuant to co-decision, but only for those acts adopted by the Council alone. The Council rejected this view,[99] and drew comfort from the ECJ which held, albeit without detailed consideration, that acts of the Council covered those undertaken jointly with the EP pursuant to co-decision, as well as acts made by the Council alone.[100] The ECJ's jurisprudence moreover served to empower the Council and Commission at the expense of the EP by adopting a broad concept of implementation. Thus while the ECJ insisted that the primary regulation or directive must embody its 'essential elements', it interpreted this loosely, thereby allowing a broad range of implementing measures to be adopted through secondary regulations according to Comitology procedures from which the EP was effectively excluded.[101] The EP also contested the committee procedures through the political process.[102] The process of legislative attrition was wearing for all involved and hostilities were temporarily lessened through the *Modus Vivendi* in 1994:[103] the relevant committee of the

---

[98] K Bradley, 'Maintaining the Balance: The Role of the Court of Justice in Defining the Institutional Position of the European Parliament' (1987) 24 CML Rev 41; K Bradley, 'Comitology and the Law: Through a Glass Darkly' (1992) 29 CML Rev 693; K Bradley, 'The European Parliament and Comitology: On the Road to Nowhere?' (1997) 3 ELJ 230.

[99] J-P Jacque, 'Implementing Powers and Comitology' in Joerges and Vos (n 18 above) ch 4.

[100] Case C-259/95 *European Parliament v Council* [1997] ECR I-5303, [26]; Case C-378/00 (n 96 above) [40].

[101] Case C-156/93 *European Parliament v Commission* [1995] ECR I-2019, [18]–[22]; Case C-417/93 *European Parliament v Council* [1995] ECR I-1185, [30].

[102] R Corbett, *The European Parliament's Role in Closer EU Integration* (MacMillan, 1998) 347–348.

[103] *Modus Vivendi* of 20 December 1994 between the European Parliament, the Council and the Commission concerning the implementing measures for acts adopted in accordance with the procedure laid down in Article 189b of the EC Treaty [1996] OJ C102/1.

EP would be sent general draft implementing acts at the same time as the Comitology committee set up by the basic act.

The position of the EP was improved by the revised Comitology Decision, made pursuant to Declaration 31 of the Treaty of Amsterdam. Its passage was difficult,[104] and it was finally adopted in 1999.[105] The management and regulatory committee procedures were simplified to some degree. There were efforts to make the system more accessible to the public. The EP was accorded a greater role than hitherto. It was given power concerning rules made pursuant to the regulatory procedure, and the EP could now indicate by resolution that draft implementing measures, submitted to a committee pursuant to a primary act adopted by co-decision, would exceed the implementing powers in that act. The EP was also given a right to be informed by the Commission of committee proceedings, and to receive committee agendas, voting records, and draft measures submitted to the committees for implementation of primary law made under the co-decision procedure. In a subsequent agreement between the EP and the Commission,[106] the latter stated that it would also forward to the EP, at its request, specific draft measures for implementing basic instruments even if not adopted under co-decision, where they were of particular importance to the EP. The EP can moreover request access to minutes of committee meetings.[107]

The EP's position was further improved by the 2006 amendment to the 1999 Decision,[108] the catalyst for this being belated acceptance of the EP's objection to the 1999 Comitology Decision where co-decision applied.[109] It introduced a new 'regulatory procedure with scrutiny procedure', which gives the EP greater rights than hitherto. The legal and political significance of this reform will be considered more fully below, when discussing the fate of Comitology under the Lisbon Treaty.

7. AGENCIES: INNOVATION AND CONTESTATION

Agencies are a prominent feature of modern democratic polities.[110] They facilitate use of experts outside the normal bureaucratic structure; allow the parent department

---

[104] Bergstrom (n 18 above) 249–264.

[105] Council Decision 99/468/EC of 28 June 1999 laying down the procedures for the exercise of implementing powers conferred on the Commission [1999] OJ L184/23; K Lenaerts and A Verhoeven, 'Towards a Legal Framework for Executive Rule-Making in the EU? The Contribution of the New Comitology Decision' (2000) 37 CML Rev 645.

[106] Agreement between the European Parliament and the Commission on procedures for implementing Council Decision 99/468/EC of 28 June 1999 [2000] OJ L256/19, [2].

[107] Case T-188/97 *Rothmans v Commission* [1999] ECR II-2463.

[108] Council Decision 2006/512/EC of 17 July 2006 amending Decision 1999/468/EC laying down the procedures for the exercise of implementing powers by the Commission [2006] OJ L200/11.

[109] Proposal for a Council Decision Amending Decision 1999/468/EC laying down the procedures for the exercise of implementing powers conferred on the Commission, COM(2002) 719 final, 2.

[110] M Thatcher and A Stone Sweet, 'Theory and Practice of Delegation to Non-Majoritarian Institutions' (2002) 25 WEP 1.

to concentrate on strategic policy; and insulate technical regulatory issues from the vagaries of political change, thereby increasing the credibility of the choices thus made.

Agencies have become an important institutional feature of the EU,[111] and detailed treatment can be found in Martin Shapiro's chapter.[112] They deal with areas as diverse as air safety, medicines, border control, food safety, maritime safety, environment, trade marks, and fundamental rights,[113] and are also used in the Second[114] and Third Pillar.[115] The Commission's rationale for agency creation echoes that set out above—that agencies 'would make the executive more effective at European level in highly specialized technical areas requiring advanced expertise and continuity, credibility, and visibility of public action',[116] thereby enabling the Commission to focus on policy formation.[117] Majone stresses similar themes, in particular the credibility problem of traditional Community regulation, and the 'mismatch between highly complex regulatory tasks and available administrative instruments'.[118] Shapiro's view is more 'political':[119] if there are difficulties in direct routes to further political integration, then best proceed via small discrete technical units that have the added advantage of not being the Commission, and not being in Brussels.

The powers accorded to agencies vary.[120] Most have informational and coordinating functions, a few can take individualized decisions, and some have quasi-regulatory powers. None however are true 'regulatory' agencies as that term is normally understood. They do not have powers to make rules and adjudicate in the manner that is common for agencies in the USA. There are legal and political reasons for the limits on agency powers.

The principal legal constraint is the *Meroni* principle,[121] which stipulated that it was not possible to delegate power involving a wide margin of discretion, since it thereby transferred responsibility by replacing the choices of the delegator with those of the body to whom power was delegated.

The Commission provided the political rationale for limiting agency powers. It has been supportive of agencies, but nonetheless wished to adhere to the legal constraints for reasons that transcended the dictates of formal law. This was in order to preserve 'the unity and integrity of the executive function' and to ensure 'that it continues to be

---

[111] E Chiti, 'The Emergence of a Community Administration: The Case of European Agencies' (2000) 37 CML Rev 309.

[112] Shapiro ch 4.

[113] <http://europa.eu/agencies/community_agencies/index_en.htm>.

[114] <http://europa.eu/agencies/security_agencies/index_en.htm>.

[115] <http://europa.eu/agencies/pol_agencies/index_en.htm>.

[116] The Operating Framework for the European Regulatory Agencies, COM(2002) 718 final, 5.

[117] ibid 2.

[118] G Majone, 'Delegation of Regulatory Powers in a Mixed Polity' (2002) 8 ELJ 319, 329.

[119] M Shapiro, 'The Problems of Independent Agencies in the United States and the European Union' (1997) 4 JEPP 276.

[120] P Craig, *EU Administrative Law* (Oxford University Press, 2006) ch 5.

[121] Case 9/56 *Meroni & Co, Industrie Metallurgiche SpA v High Authority* [1958] ECR 133, 152.

vested in the chief of the Commission if the latter is to have the required responsibility vis-à-vis Europe's citizens, the Member States and the other institutions'.[122] The participation of agencies should therefore be 'organised in a way which is consistent and in balance with the unity and integrity of the executive function and the Commission's ensuing responsibilities'.[123] The Commission has therefore been reluctant to create real regulatory agencies exercising discretionary power through adjudication and rule-making, since if such power could be delegated then the Commission's sense of the unity of the executive function vested in it would be undermined. The emphasis placed on the unity and integrity of the executive function located in the President of the Commission was moreover not fortuitous given that the 2002 Communication was issued during the deliberations of the Convention on the Future of Europe, where the location of executive power was one of the most divisive issues.[124]

The Commission's concern as to the unity of the executive function played out not only in relation to the powers accorded to agencies, but also in relation to agency decision-making structure. The composition of agency boards has been crucial in this respect.[125] The Commission voiced concern in its 2002 Communication about the balance between its representation on agency boards and that of the Member States.[126] It drafted an Inter-institutional Agreement on agencies in 2005,[127] which enshrined its preferred position on composition of agency boards, but failed to secure the Agreement's passage and it was withdrawn in 2009.[128] It is nonetheless clear that the Commission adheres to the philosophy in the 2005 Draft Agreement,[129] and that it remains concerned about agency decision-making structure, stating that 'the degree of accountability of the Commission cannot exceed the degree of influence of the Commission on the agency's activities'.[130]

Institutional development will commonly throw into sharp relief the balance of power within a particular polity. The EU is no different in this respect. The Commission acknowledges the utility of agencies, but continues to be concerned about their impact on what the Commission perceives to be the unity and integrity of its executive function. Agencies constitute in this respect a site in which the locus of executive power remains contested.

---

[122] COM(2002) 718 (n 116) 1.

[123] ibid 1, 9.

[124] P Craig, 'European Governance: Executive and Administrative Powers under the New Constitutional Settlement' (2005) 3 I-CON 407.

[125] Craig (n 120 above).

[126] COM(2002) 718 (n 116) 9.

[127] Draft Interinstitutional Agreement on the Operating Framework for the European Regulatory Agencies, COM(2005) 59 final.

[128] [2009] OJ C71/17.

[129] European Agencies—The Way Forward, COM(2008) 135 final, 9.   [130] ibid 8.

8. COMMISSION REFORM: EXECUTIVE AGENCIES AND SHARED ADMINISTRATION

Institutional crisis is often the catalyst for institutional reform. While the word crisis should be used with care, the resignation of the Santer Commission, precipitated by the report of the Committee of Independent Experts,[131] did constitute a crisis for the Commission. The Committee's concluding paragraph, that it was 'becoming difficult to find anyone who has even the slightest sense of responsibility'[132] within the Commission, was widely reported. While the Commission was not blameless there was in reality scant evidence of nepotism, the principal difficulty being maintenance of control over those to whom power had been contracted-out.[133]

Romano Prodi, the new Commission President, rapidly introduced a new Code of Conduct for Commissioners,[134] and set up the Task Force for Administrative Reform (TFRA). The TFRA produced a White Paper,[135] which was heavily influenced by the important recommendations in the Second Report of the Committee of Independent Experts.[136] This in turn led to a new Financial Regulation, which established the constitutional architecture for Community administration.[137] It is premised on the divide between centralized and shared administration.

Centralized administration covers those instances where the Commission implements policy directly through its departments, or indirectly. The Commission is not however allowed to entrust its executive powers to third parties where they involve a large measure of discretion implying political choices. Within these limits the Commission has the option[138] of establishing one of the new breed of executive agency.[139] The objective is to foster flexible, accountable, and efficient management of tasks assigned to the Commission. Policy decisions remain with the Commission, implementation is assigned to the agency. Six executive agencies have been created thus far.[140] Such agencies are especially suited to the implementation of programmes involving multiple contracts, grants, or subsidies.

---

[131] Committee of Independent Experts, First Report on Allegations regarding Fraud, Mismanagement and Nepotism in the European Commission, 15 Mar. 1999, [1.4.2].

[132] ibid [9.4.25].

[133] P Craig, 'The Fall and Renewal of the Commission: Accountability, Contract and Administrative Organization' (2000) 6 ELJ 98.

[134] The Formation of the Commission, 12 July 1999.

[135] Reforming the Commission, COM(2000) 200.

[136] Committee of Independent Experts, Second Report on Reform of the Commission, Analysis of Current Practice and Proposals for Tackling Mismanagement, Irregularities and Fraud, 10 September 1999, available at <http://www.europarl.europa.eu/experts/default_en.htm>.

[137] Council Regulation (EC, Euratom) 1605/2002 of 25 June 2002 on the Financial Regulation applicable to the general budget of the European Communities [2002] OJ L248/1.

[138] It can also delegate tasks to national public-sector bodies, or bodies governed by private law with a public service mission guaranteed by the state.

[139] Council Regulation (EC) 58/2003 of 19 December 2002 laying down the statute for executive agencies to be entrusted with certain tasks in the management of Community programmes [2003] OJ L11/1.

[140] <http://europa.eu/agencies/executive_agencies/index_en.htm>.

Shared administration or mixed proceedings is nonetheless the most common method for the implementation of Community policy.[141] It connotes, as the nomenclature suggests, the situation in which both the Community and national administrations have obligations in law and fact, the correct performance of which is essential for the effective implementation of the relevant policy. It is this mode of administration that is used for areas such as the Common Agricultural Policy, Structural Funds, and the market liberalization in the context of utilities, such as gas, water, and telecommunications. The 2002 Financial Regulation established a number of important principles for shared administration, and these were strengthened by amendments in 2006 reinforcing the obligation on Member States to take all legislative, regulatory, and administrative or other measures necessary to protect the Communities' financial interests.[142]

The 2002 Financial Regulation produced a welcome clarification of the principles governing Community administration. The resulting picture was at the same time one of growing administrative complexity, with a plethora of modes of centralized administration and significant variety within shared administration.

9. COMMUNITY COURTS: NORMATIVE SUPRANATIONALISM, JUDICIAL REVIEW, AND INSTITUTIONAL BALANCE

Analysis of the period between the Rome Treaty and the SEA revealed the importance of the ECJ as an institutional actor in the disposition of power within the Community legal and political order. It was equally important in the period between the SEA and the Lisbon Treaty. Space precludes detailed assessment, but its significance in this respect was manifest in four ways.

First, normative supranationalism as made operational through direct effect and supremacy continued to exert a powerful force on integration and the attainment of the single market broadly conceived. Thus while this period saw the redefinition of Community competence in relation to goods,[143] and the limitation of Community regulatory competence,[144] the Court shifted its activism from free movement of

---

[141] E Schmidt-Aßmann, 'Verwaltungskooperation und Verwaltungskooperationsrecht in der Europäischen Gemeinschaft' (1996) Europarecht 270; E Chiti and C Franchini, *L'Integrazione Amministrativa Europea* (Il Mulino, 2003); S Cassese, 'European Administrative Proceedings' (2004) 68 LCP 21; Craig (n 120 above) ch 2.

[142] Council Regulation (EC, Euratom) 1995/2006 of 13 December 2006 amending Regulation (EC, Euratom) 1605/2002 on the Financial Regulation applicable to the general budget of the European Communities [2006] OJ L390/1.

[143] C-267 and C-268/91 *Criminal Proceedings against Keck and Mithouard* [1993] ECR I-6097.

[144] Case C-376/98 *Germany v European Parliament and Council* [2000] ECR I-8419. These limits were however undermined by subsequent case law, Case C-491/01 *The Queen v Secretary of State for Health, ex p British American Tobacco (Investments) Ltd and Imperial Tobacco Ltd* [2002] ECR I-11453; Case C-210/03 *R v Secretary of State for Health, ex p Swedish Match* [2004] ECR I-11893.

goods to the other freedoms,[145] such as establishment, services,[146] persons,[147] and citizenship.[148]

Secondly, the ECJ used the concept of institutional balance as a background principle to resolve inter-institutional disputes. The EP made frequent use of litigation in order to defend its role in the legislative process,[149] and to contest the choice of legislative procedure used for a particular measure.[150] The ECJ used inter-institutional balance to 'anticipate' and act as a 'catalyst' for future Treaty amendments. Thus it held, after some hesitation,[151] that the EP could be a plaintiff in annulment proceedings where its prerogatives had been infringed.[152] The Court also included the Parliament as a respondent in annulment proceedings, even though only the Council and the Commission were mentioned under what was Article 173 EEC at that time.[153] The various judicial developments were gradually incorporated into the relevant provisions of the EC Treaty following successive Treaty amendments. Thus, for example, Article 230 EC was amended to provide the EP with *locus standi* alongside the Commission, the Council, and the Member States to bring annulment proceedings. The CFI followed the same path. Thus Article 230 EC did not explicitly refer to agencies and other Community bodies as subject to judicial review. This formal deficiency was addressed by the Lisbon Treaty.[154] The CFI had however in effect already filled this gap in the *Sogelma* case,[155] concluding that it was not acceptable in a Community based on the rule of law for acts intended to produce legal effects vis-à-vis third parties to escape judicial review.

Thirdly, the Community courts tailored and refined the tools of judicial review in order to impose the degree of scrutiny that was felt warranted in different areas of EC law, with review for manifest error being one of the most important doctrinal tools in this regard.[156] The most searching application of manifest error review was in the

---

[145] M P Maduro, *We the Court, The European Court of Justice & the European Economic Constitution* (Hart, 1998) 100–102; E Johnson and D O' Keeffe, 'From Discrimination to Obstacles to Free Movement: Recent Developments Concerning the Free Movement of Workers 1989–1994' (1994) 31 CML Rev 1313.

[146] Case C-384/93 *Alpine Investments* [1995] ECR I-1141.

[147] Case C-415/93 *Bosman* [1995] ECR I-4921.

[148] Case C-184/99 *Rudy Grzelczyk v Centre Public D'Aide Sociale d'Ottignes-Louvain-la-Neuve (CPAS)* [2001] ECR I-6193, [31].

[149] Case 138/79 *Roquette Frères v Council* [1980] ECR 3333; Case 139/79 *Maizena v Council* [1980] ECR 3393.

[150] Case C-22/96 *European Parliament v Council (Telephonic Networks)* [1998] ECR I-3231; Case C-42/97 *European Parliament v Council (Linguistic Diversity)* [1999] ECR I-869; H Cullen and A Charlesworth, 'Diplomacy by Other Means: The Use of Legal Basis Litigation as a Political Strategy by the European Parliament and Member States' (1999) 36 CML Rev 1243; Bradley ch 5.

[151] Case 302/87 *Parliament v Council* (Comitology) [1988] ECR 5616.

[152] Case C-70/88 *Parliament v Council* (Chernobyl) [1990] ECR I-2041; Case C-187/93 *Parliament v Council* (Transfer of Waste) [1994] ECR I-2857.

[153] Case 294/83 *Parti Ecologiste 'Les Verts' v Parliament* [1986] ECR 1339, [23].

[154] Art 263(1) TFEU.

[155] Case T-411/06 *Sogelma—Societá generale lavori manutenzioni appalti Srl v European Agency for Reconstruction (AER)*, 8 October 2008, [37].

[156] Craig (n 120) ch 13.

context of competition and risk regulation. In the context of competition it was driven in part by criticisms voiced about the role of the Commission as prosecutor, judge, and jury, and thus more intensive review for manifest error was seen as a counterweight in this respect. In the context of risk regulation the Community judiciary recognized the controversy surrounding the precautionary principle that informed Community policy in this area, and intensive review of risk assessment and the like was designed to allay fears that the precautionary principle would be used as a disguised mode of arbitrary trade restriction. The Community courts looked closely at the discrete parts of the Commission reasoning process in order to see whether they made sense, considered the evidentiary foundations for its argument, and assessed the cogency of the Commission's overall conclusions in the light of this judicial scrutiny. Process rights were therefore used to facilitate substantive review.

Fourthly, the Community courts also regularly used judicial review as the medium through which to construe Community policy in a teleological manner so as to best attain its objectives. We naturally think of judicial review as a mechanism for challenging the legality of legislative or administrative acts, and so it is. Such cases however afford the courts with the opportunity to interpret the relevant acts in a manner best designed to achieve the underlying policy objectives. Viewed from this perspective if judicial review did not exist, the administration would naturally be desirous of some other method whereby recourse could be had to courts to facilitate such purposive construction. The significance of this judicial role is manifest across all areas of EC law, and is particularly marked in relation to Community policies, such as agriculture and the Structural Funds, where large sums of money are at stake and the regulatory regime is complex.[157]

C. THE CONSTITUTIONAL TREATY TO THE LISBON TREATY: LEGISLATIVE AND EXECUTIVE AUTHORITY

Treaty reform is a continuation of politics by other means. It is not therefore surprising that institutional issues on the agenda in the previous decade dominated debates on more comprehensive Treaty reform. Thus was it ever so. The prevalent themes in the 1990s were, as we have seen, increasing consensus as to the appropriate distribution of legislative power, coupled with contestation as to the locus of executive power.[158] These were the prominent themes in the debates on Treaty reform in the new millennium and the results embodied in the Lisbon Treaty will shape the inter-institutional distribution of power going forward.[159]

---

[157] ibid ch 3.

[158] D Curtin, *Executive Power in the European Union, Law, Practices and the Living Constitution* (Oxford University Press, 2009).

[159] For more detailed consideration of the issues in this section, P Craig, *The Lisbon Treaty, Law, Politics and Treaty Reform* (Oxford University Press, 2010).

1. THE ROAD FROM NICE TO LISBON

The first decade of the new millennium was dominated by attempts at reform, which began as soon as the ink on the Nice Treaty in 2000 had dried. The Nice Treaty left over certain issues, such as the division of competence between the EU and the Member States, and the status of the Charter of Rights, for determination at the next IGC, which would have been in 2004. However in 2001 there was a growing consensus among the key institutional players that such matters could not be divorced from broader issues concerning the EU, and that the legitimacy of such broad-ranging discussion would be enhanced if the decision-making process was more open and inclusive than the traditional IGC.

These sentiments were evident in the Laeken Declaration 2001,[160] which was the catalyst for the establishment of the Convention on the Future of Europe.[161] It was by no means pre-ordained that the Convention would produce a Constitutional Treaty,[162] and indeed such a possibility was mentioned only tentatively in the Laeken Declaration. A Constitutional Treaty, CT, nonetheless emerged from the Convention, and was agreed to by the Member States after some amendments.[163] It required ratification by each Member State, and was duly ratified by fifteen Member States, but the negative referenda in France and the Netherlands effectively sounded the death knell for the Constitutional Treaty.[164]

The European Council decided in 2005 that after these results there should be a 'period of reflection', and in 2006 it commissioned Germany, which held the Presidency of the European Council in the first half of 2007, to assess the possibilities of Treaty reform. The German Presidency sought agreement in the European Council in June 2007 on a revised version of the CT. The European Council set out the changes that should be made to the CT,[165] and this heralded the birth of the Reform Treaty.

Matters then moved rapidly. An Intergovernmental Conference (IGC) was convened to formulate the Reform Treaty, which was signed on 13 December 2007,[166] although the appellation was changed to the Lisbon Treaty (LT) in recognition of the place of signature. The 2007 IGC was power politics with a vengeance. The Lisbon Treaty was forged by the Member States and Community institutions, with scant time afforded for further deliberation. This was because the LT was the same in most

---

[160] Laeken European Council, 14–15 December 2001.

[161] <http://european-convention.eu.int>.

[162] P Norman, *The Accidental Constitution, The Making of Europe's Constitutional Treaty* (2nd edn, EuroComment, 2005).

[163] Treaty Establishing a Constitution for Europe [2004] OJ C310/1.

[164] R Dehousse, 'The Unmaking of a Constitution: Lessons from the European Referenda' (2006) 13 Constellations 151.

[165] Brussels European Council, 21–22 June 2007.

[166] Conference of the Representatives of the Governments of the Member States, Treaty of Lisbon Amending the Treaty on European Union and the Treaty Establishing the European Community, CIG 14/07, Brussels 3 December 2007, [2007] OJ C306/1; Consolidated Versions of Treaty on European Union and the Treaty on the Functioning of the European Union, Council 6655/08, Brussels 15 April 2008.

important respects as the CT. The issues had been debated in the Convention that produced the CT, and were considered again in the 2004 IGC. There was therefore little appetite to re-open Pandora's Box in the 2007 IGC. This justification could not however be pressed too explicitly by those in the 2007 IGC, since they would be open to the criticism that they were re-packaging provisions that had been rejected by voters in two Member States, regardless of the fact that the reasons for the negative votes in France and the Netherlands had relatively little to do with the new provisions in the CT. The LT however had to be ratified by all Member States, and on this occasion it was the Irish who voted no in a referendum, then reversing this decision in a second referendum in October 2009, after concessions had been made. The Czech Republic was the final state to ratify, with the Czech President reluctantly appending his signature in November 2009.

The Lisbon Treaty has seven articles, of which Articles 1 and 2 are the most important, plus numerous Protocols and Declarations. Article 1 LT contains the amendments to the Treaty on European Union (TEU). Article 2 LT amends the EC Treaty, which is renamed the Treaty on the Functioning of the European Union (TFEU). The EU is henceforth to be founded on the TEU and the TFEU, and the two Treaties have the same legal value.[167] The Union is to replace and succeed the EC.[168]

2. LEGISLATIVE ACTS: PARTICIPATION AND TYPOLOGY

The provisions of the Lisbon Treaty concerning the making of legislative acts largely replicate those in the Constitutional Treaty. The Commission retained its 'gold standard', the right of legislative initiative.[169] The EP and the Council both partake in the consideration of legislation and do so now on an increasingly equal footing. The EP and the Council are said to exercise legislative and budgetary functions jointly.[170] The co-decision procedure is deemed to be the ordinary legislative procedure,[171] and its reach has been extended to cover more areas than hitherto, including, for example, agriculture,[172] services,[173] asylum and immigration,[174] the structural and cohesion funds,[175] and the creation of specialized courts.[176]

This development is to be welcomed. The co-decision procedure has worked well, allowing input from the EP, representing directly the electorate, and from the Council, representing state interests. It provides a framework for deliberative dialogue between the EP, Council, and Commission. The extension of the ordinary legislative procedure to new areas is a natural development, building on earlier Treaty reform, and enhances the democratic legitimacy of Union legislation. This should however be read subject to the qualification as to the worrying development noted above, concerning the in-

---

[167] Art 1 para 3 TEU.   [168] Art 1 para 3 TEU.   [169] Art 17(2) TEU.
[170] Art 14(1) and Art 16(1) TEU.   [171] Arts 289 and 294 TFEU.   [172] Art 43(2) TFEU.
[173] Art 56 TFEU.   [174] Arts 77–80 TFEU.   [175] Art 177 TFEU.   [176] Art 257 TFEU.

creased use of trilogues at an early stage in the legislative process, thereby foreclosing more meaningful dialogue.[177]

The voting rules in the Council set out in the Lisbon Treaty also largely replicate those in the Constitutional Treaty. The requirements for a qualified majority have often been a battleground between the Member States. The Lisbon Treaty stipulates that the Council shall act by qualified majority, except where the Treaty provides otherwise.[178] The basic rule that operates from 1 November 2014 is that a qualified majority is defined as at least 55 per cent of the members of the Council, comprising at least fifteen of them and representing Member States comprising at least 65 per cent of the population of the Union.[179] A blocking minority must include at least four Council members, failing which the qualified majority shall be deemed attained. There are therefore three criteria to be taken into account for a qualified majority: a certain percentage of Member States in the Council; a certain number of Member States; and a certain percentage of the EU's population.

The Lisbon Treaty however differs from the Constitutional Treaty in relation to the typology of legal acts. The Constitutional Treaty introduced a hierarchy of norms, which distinguished between different categories of legal act, and used terms such as 'law', 'framework law' and the like.[180] The European Council of June 2007, which initiated the process leading to the LT, decided that the terms 'law', and 'framework law' should be dropped. The rationale given was that the Lisbon Treaty was not to have a 'constitutional character',[181] although it is not readily apparent why the terminology of 'law' or 'framework law' should be assumed to have a constitutional character.

It was decided to retain the existing terminology of regulations, directives, and decisions in the Lisbon Treaty.[182] A version of the hierarchy of norms is however preserved in the LT, which distinguishes between legislative acts, non-legislative acts of general application, and implementing acts.[183] Thus a legislative act is defined as one adopted in accord with a legislative procedure, either the ordinary legislative procedure, which is the successor to co-decision, or a special legislative procedure.[184] There are a number of difficulties with the interpretation of these provisions.[185]

3. LEGISLATIVE ACTS: SUBSIDIARITY AND NATIONAL PARLIAMENTS

The Lisbon Treaty modified the role played by national parliaments in relation to subsidiarity. The subsidiarity and proportionality principles are contained in Article 5 (3)–(4) TEU, which largely replicate Article 5 EC. The novelty of the new regime is to be found in the Protocol on the Application of the Principles of Subsidiarity and

---

[177] 57–58.   [178] Art 16(3) TEU LT.   [179] Art 16(4) TEU, Art 238 TFEU.
[180] Arts I-33-39 CT.   [181] Brussels European Council, 21–22 June 2007, Annex 1, para 3.
[182] Art 288 TFEU.   [183] Arts 289–291 TFEU.   [184] Art 289 TFEU.
[185] Craig (n 159 above) ch 7; B de Witte, 'Legal Instruments and Law-Making in the Lisbon Treaty' in S Griller and J Ziller (eds), *The Lisbon Treaty, EU Constitutionalism without a Constitutional Treaty?* (Springer, 2008) 79–108.

Proportionality, which should be read in tandem with the Protocol on the Role of National Parliaments in the EU.

The Subsidiarity Protocol imposes an obligation to consult widely before proposing legislative acts. The Commission must provide a detailed statement concerning proposed legislation so that compliance with subsidiarity can be appraised. The statement must contain some assessment of the financial impact of the proposals, and there should be qualitative and, wherever possible, quantitative indicators to substantiate the conclusion that the objective can be better attained at Union level. The ECJ has jurisdiction to consider infringement of subsidiarity under Article 263 TFEU, brought by the Member State, or 'notified by them in accordance with their legal order on behalf of their national Parliament or a chamber of it'.[186]

The most important innovation in the Protocol on Subsidiarity is the enhanced role accorded to national parliaments. The Commission must send all legislative proposals to the national parliaments at the same time as to the Union institutions.[187] A national parliament or chamber thereof, may, within eight weeks, send the Presidents of the Commission, EP, and Council a reasoned opinion as to why it considers that the proposal does not comply with subsidiarity.[188] The EP, Council, and Commission must take this opinion into account.[189] Where non-compliance with subsidiarity is expressed by national parliaments that represent one third of all the votes allocated to such parliaments, the Commission must review its proposal.[190] The Commission, after such review, may decide to maintain, amend, or withdraw the proposal, giving reasons for the decision.[191] Where a measure is made in accord with the ordinary legislative procedure, and at least a simple majority of votes given to national parliaments signal non-compliance with subsidiarity, then the proposal must once again be reviewed and although the Commission can decide not to amend it, the Commission must provide a reasoned opinion on the matter and this can, in effect, be overridden by the EP or the Council.[192]

It remains to be seen how subsidiarity operates in practice. There will continue to be many areas in which the comparative efficiency calculus in Article 5(3) TFEU favours Union action, more especially in an enlarged Union. Much will depend on the willingness of national parliaments to devote the requisite time and energy to the matter. The national parliament has to submit a reasoned opinion as to why it believes that the measure infringes subsidiarity. It will have to present reasoned argument as to why the Commission's comparative efficiency calculus is defective. This may not be easy. It will be even more difficult for the requisite number of national parliaments to present reasoned opinions in relation to the same Union measure so as to compel the Commission to review the proposal. The Commission is nonetheless likely to take

---

[186] Protocol (No 2) On the Application of the Principles of Subsidiarity and Proportionality, Art 8.
[187] ibid Art 4.   [188] ibid Art 6.   [189] ibid Art 7(1).
[190] ibid Art 7(2). This threshold is lowered to one quarter in certain cases concerning the area of freedom, justice, and security.
[191] ibid Art 7(2).   [192] ibid Art 7(3).

seriously any such reasoned opinion, particularly if it emanates from the parliament of a larger Member State.

It should moreover be noted that national parliaments are not given any role in relation to Article 5(4) TEU, which stipulates that the content and form of EU action shall not exceed what is necessary to achieve the EU's objectives. Thus while the Protocol imposes obligations on the Commission to ensure compliance with the principles of subsidiarity and proportionality, national parliaments are afforded a role only in relation to the former and not the latter, which is regrettable.[193]

4. DELEGATED ACTS: CONTROL AND POWER

The European Parliament certainly emerged as a winner in the Lisbon Treaty in relation to legislative acts. The inter-institutional implications of the provisions dealing with delegated acts are less clear. The schema in the Lisbon Treaty follows closely that in the Constitutional Treaty. It also, as will be seen, represents the continuation of battles over control of delegated acts that were evident hitherto.

Delegated acts are said to be non-legislative acts of general application, whereby power to adopt such acts is delegated to the Commission by a legislative act.[194] These non-legislative acts can supplement or amend certain non-essential elements of the legislative act, but the legislative act must define the objectives, content, scope, and duration of the delegation of power. The essential elements of an area cannot be delegated. The legislative act must specify the conditions to which the delegation is subject. Such conditions may allow the EP or the Council to revoke the delegation, and/or enable the EP or the Council to veto the delegated act within a specified period of time. The distinction between legislative and non-legislative acts is formal in the sense that legislative acts are defined as those enacted via a legislative procedure, either ordinary or special; non-legislative acts are those that are not enacted in this manner. Delegated acts will nonetheless often be legislative in nature, by laying down provisions of general application, and this is recognized in the Lisbon Treaty, which speaks of delegated acts having 'general application'.[195]

This new regime for delegated acts has had implications for the Comitology regime. There is a significant 'history' here. The Commission's primary goal has been to dismantle the established Comitology regime, at least insofar as it entails management and regulatory committees. It has supported the *ex ante* and *ex post* constraints on delegated acts in the hope that the Member States might then be persuaded to modify the existing Comitology oversight mechanisms for delegated regulations.[196] It is true

---

[193] S Weatherill, 'Better Competence Monitoring' (2005) 30 ELRev 23.

[194] Art 290 TFEU.   [195] ibid.

[196] European Governance, COM(2001) 428 final, [20]–[29]; Institutional Architecture, COM(2002) 728 final, [1.2], [1.3.4]; Proposal for a Council Decision Amending Decision 1999/468/EC laying down the procedures for the exercise of implementing powers conferred on the Commission, COM(2002) 719 final, 2; Final Report of Working Group IX on Simplification, CONV 424/02, Brussels 29 November 2002, 12.

that there is provision for Comitology-type controls over what are regarded as implementing acts in the Lisbon Treaty.[197] The divide between delegated acts and implementing acts is, however, fraught with difficulty and the reality is that Comitology hitherto operated in relation to what are now termed delegated acts. The Commission appears to have been successful in removing management and regulatory committees from the arena of delegated acts.[198] It remains to be seen whether the controls embodied over delegated acts will be effective if the Comitology regime is dismantled.[199] The problem for the Council is that unless it has some informational resource of the kind hitherto provided by Comitology then it will often not have the requisite expertise to decide whether to exercise its veto powers. The European Parliament's committees will also have to develop strategies to track draft delegated acts so as to be able to decide whether to exercise its veto power. It is equally important to recognize that control through a veto when the delegated act has been made is not the same as participation in the making of the delegated act itself.

5. EXECUTIVE POWER: CONTESTATION AND RESOLUTION

There was, as we have seen, contestation concerning the locus of executive power in the 1990s. The Presidency of the Union was the most contentious issue in the deliberations that led to the Constitutional Treaty,[200] and the 'resolution' of the issue was carried over unchanged into the Lisbon Treaty. There were two main positions.

The prominent version of the *single hat* view was that there should be one President for the Union as a whole; the office of President should be connected formally and substantively with the locus of executive power within the Union; and that the President of the Commission should hold this office. The Presidency of the European Council should continue to rotate on a six-monthly basis. The real 'head' of the Union would be the President of the Commission, whose legitimacy would be increased by his or her election.

The prominent version of the *separate hats* view was that there should be a President of the Commission and a President of the European Council, and that executive power would be exercised by both. It was central to this view that the Presidency of the European Council would be strengthened. It would no longer rotate between Member States on a six-monthly basis. It was felt that this would not work within an enlarged Union, and that greater continuity of policy would be required. This view was advocated by a number of the larger states, but was opposed by some of the smaller states, which felt that the Presidency of the European Council would be dominated by the larger Member States.

---

[197] Art 291(3) TFEU.
[198] Craig (n 159 above) ch 7.
[199] ibid; P Craig, 'The Role of the European Parliament under the Lisbon Treaty' in Griller and Ziller (n 185 above) 109–135.
[200] Craig (n 124).

The latter view prevailed. The Lisbon Treaty, following the Constitutional Treaty, provided that the European Council should elect a President, by qualified majority, for two and half years, renewable once; that the European Council should define the general political directions and priorities of the EU; and gave the President of the European Council increased powers within the Council itself.[201] The President of the Commission is nonetheless still central to this constitutional scheme. Thus it is the Commission that is accorded power to initiate annual and multi-annual programming with the aim of securing inter-institutional agreement, and the Commission President cooperates with the President of the European Council in ensuring the preparation and continuity of the work of the European Council.[202] The institutional inter-relation between the European Council, Council, and Commission is also personified in the High Representative of the Union for Foreign Affairs and Security Policy, who takes part in the European Council, chairs the Foreign Affairs Council, and is also a Vice President of the Commission.[203]

6. EXECUTIVE POWER: THE COMMISSION AND ITS INTERNAL ORGANIZATION

(a) The Commission President: Election and Legitimacy

The Commission had hitherto generally been opposed to the idea that its President should be elected, fearing the politicization that might result. Its attitude however changed by the time that the Convention deliberated. An important consideration inclining the Commission towards election was that this would enhance the legitimacy of the Commission President, thereby strengthening his claim to be President of the Union as a whole, or at the very least providing grounds for resisting the grant of far-reaching powers to the President of the European Council.[204]

The Commission's contribution to the debate concerning the emerging institutional architecture for the EU was timely, appearing in December 2002, just before the Convention discourse on institutions was set to begin in January 2003. Its vision for the method of choosing the Commission President featured prominently in this document.[205] The Commission argued that its responsibility for setting out the general interests of the Union meant that it must derive its political legitimacy from both the European Council and the European Parliament. It therefore recommended conferring on the European Council and the European Parliament equivalent rights both for the appointment and for monitoring the action of the Commission. The Commission proposed that the Commission President should be elected by the European Parliament, subject to approval by the European Council. The other members of the

---

[201] Art 15 TEU.   [202] Arts 16(6), 17(1) TEU.
[203] Arts 15(2), 16(9), 17(4)–(5) TEU.   [204] Norman (n 162) 120–121.
[205] CONV 448/02, For the European Union Peace, Freedom, Solidarity—Communication from the Commission on the Institutional Architecture, 5 December 2002, [2.3]; Peace, Freedom and Solidarity, COM(2002) 728 final.

Commission should be designated by the Council, acting by qualified majority in agreement with the Commission President, subject to approval of the full College of Commissioners by the European Parliament.

The European Parliament favoured an indirectly elected Commission President. It was however always doubtful whether the Member States would be willing to accept a regime in which they surrendered control over the Commission Presidency to the European Parliament. The Member States were, unsurprisingly, not willing to surrender this power.

The 'solution' in the Constitutional Treaty[206] was carried over directly into the Lisbon Treaty. Thus Article 14(1) TEU duly states that the European Parliament shall elect the President of the Commission. The retention of state power is however apparent in Article 17(7) TEU. The European Council, acting by qualified majority, after appropriate consultation,[207] and taking account of the elections to the European Parliament, puts forward to the European Parliament the European Council's candidate for Presidency of the Commission. This candidate shall then be elected by the European Parliament by a majority of its members. If the candidate does not get the requisite majority support, then the European Council puts forward a new candidate within one month, following the same procedure. Thus while there had been some limited support for the idea that the Commission President should be directly elected, the argument being that this would help to foster a European demos, the result is that the Commission President is indirectly elected.

It will be interesting to see the consequences of the new regime. There were some who felt that indirect election would not markedly affect the *modus operandi* of the Commission. It would be very much business as usual, except that the Commission would have added legitimacy from election of its President. There were others who accepted that election would significantly alter the character of the Commission. They acknowledged that election would lead to politicization, since an indirectly elected President would be likely to have a more prominent political platform or agenda than hitherto. They nonetheless regarded such a development with equanimity. They argued that the legislative and executive powers of the Commission inevitably entailed political choices. The exercise of these powers could not be politically neutral, any more than could such exercise in domestic polities. It was then better for this to be out in the open. This would moreover have the virtue of securing a greater link between power and responsibility than had been the case previously.

There is almost certainly something to be said for both sides of this argument. The very fact that the Commission President is indirectly elected means that in reality he or she will have to secure the support of the dominant grouping within the European Parliament. This means that the prospective incumbent will have to present some form of political platform or agenda for the term of office. The President of the

---

[206] Arts I-20(1), 27(1) CT.
[207] Declaration 11 LT emphasizes consultation between the European Council and European Parliament preceding choice of the candidate for Commission President.

Commission would moreover under the draft of the Constitutional Treaty presented to the IGC have exercised some real control over the choice of Commissioners, since it was for the President to choose from a list of three names presented by each Member State. He could therefore have fashioned a Commission that cohered with his political credo, and that of the dominant grouping within the European Parliament, while at the same time being mindful of the need to satisfy the different political groupings represented within the EU as a whole.[208]

There remain however real limits on the extent to which the voters will be able even indirectly to 'throw out' incumbents of political office they disliked. The voters' inability to do this at present is one aspect of the critique concerning the EU's democratic deficit. While the indirect election of the Commission President goes some way to alleviate this concern, it does not remove it.[209] The Commission President may be first among equals, but the other Commissioners will, under the Lisbon Treaty, be chosen by the Member States, albeit in common accord with the President-elect of the Commission.[210] They will have diverse political backgrounds/beliefs and Commission policy will have to be acceptable to the College of Commissioners as a whole. The Commission does not moreover have a monopoly over the direction of EU policy, with the European Council and Council both being important institutional players in this respect.

(b) Commission: Size and Appointment

There had been considerable debate, going back at least to the Nice Treaty 2000, concerning the overall size of the Commission, as to whether there should continue to be one Commissioner from each state, or whether there should be an upper limit combined with rotation. The composition and size of the Commission featured prominently in the Convention deliberations. It came to the fore because of the then pending enlargement. The issue was further complicated by the fact that mixed messages were forthcoming from the Commission itself.[211]

The Draft Constitution as it emerged from the Convention on the Future of Europe embodied a compromise. It provided that the Commission should consist of a College comprising the President, the Union Minister for Foreign Affairs, and thirteen Commissioners selected on the basis of a rotation system between the Member States.[212] These provisions reflected the view that there should be a small Commission, with a number of Commissioners that was less than that of the Member States. This was however undermined by the provision that the Commission President should appoint non-voting Commissioners from all the other Member States. This 'solution' was problematic, since it would have created a two-tier Commission, with voting and

---

[208] Art I-26(2) Draft CT.   [209] 36–37.   [210] Art 17(7) TEU.
[211] CONV 448/02 (n 205) [2.3.2]; Norman (n 162 above) 228–229.
[212] CONV 850/03, Draft Treaty Establishing a Constitution for Europe, Brussels 18 July 2003, Art I-25(3) Draft CT.

non-voting Commissioners. It was fiercely opposed by the Commission itself, which described the relevant provisions as 'complicated, muddled and inoperable'.[213]

The schema in the Draft Constitutional Treaty was altered by the IGC in December 2003. The result was embodied in the Constitutional Treaty[214] and taken over with some modification into the Lisbon Treaty. Thus the Commission will, until 31 October 2014, consist of one national from each Member State, including the President and the High Representative for Foreign Affairs.[215] After that date the Commission is to consist of members, including the President and the High Representative for Foreign Affairs, which correspond to two thirds of the number of Member States, unless the European Council, acting unanimously, decides to alter this number. Member States must be treated on a strictly equal footing as regards determination of the sequence of, and the time spent by their nationals as, members of the Commission, with the consequence that the difference between the total number of terms of office held by nationals of any given pair of Member States may never be more than one. Subject to the preceding point, each successive Commission must be composed so as to reflect satisfactorily the demographic and geographical range of all the Member States.[216] This system is to be established by the European Council.[217]

The basic position in the Lisbon Treaty is therefore that there will be a slimmed down Commission in the medium term, and all members thereof will have voting rights. It is however open to the European Council to modify the system that is intended to govern post-1 November 2014, by unanimously voting to alter the number of Commissioners.[218] The European Council could, for example, vote to retain one Commissioner per Member State post-2014, and it has indeed made such a commitment as part of the deal struck with Ireland prior to its second referendum.[219] Thus assuming that the requisite unanimity is forthcoming in the European Council we shall see a continuation of the status quo, with one Commissioner per Member State. This would then mark the 'end' of a long debate that has come full circle, with the new regime being the same as the old. It would not however preclude the European Council at some later date from voting unanimously for the slimmed down Commission that is the default position established by Article 17(5) TEU.

The method of choosing individual Commissioners has also been altered over the course of the deliberations on Treaty reform. The Convention proposed that the President-elect of the Commission would choose Commissioners from a list of three names put forward by each Member State, and that these would be approved by the European Parliament.[220] The President of the Commission would therefore have been in the driving seat as to the choice of the other Commissioners, subject to approval of the entire package by the European Parliament. Developments since then have

---

[213] A Constitution for the Union, Opinion of the Commission, pursuant to Article 48 of the Treaty on European Union, on the Conference of Representatives of the Member States' governments convened to revise the Treaties, COM(2003) 548 final, [2].

[214] Art I-26 CT.   [215] Art 17(4) TEU.   [216] Art 17(5) TEU, Art 244 TFEU.

[217] Art 17(7) TEU.   [218] Art 17(5) TEU.   [219] Brussels European Council, 10 July 2009, [I.2].

[220] Art I-26(2) Draft CT.

however 'ratcheted up' Member State input and control over choice of Commissioners. The Lisbon Treaty provides that Member States make suggestions for Commissioners, but it is now the Council, by common accord with the President-elect, that adopts the list of those who are to be Commissioners in accord with the two principles set out above. The body of Commissioners is then subject to a vote of approval by the European Parliament. However, the formal appointment of the Commission is made by the European Council, acting by qualified majority, albeit on the basis of the approval given by the European Parliament.[221]

7. EXECUTIVE POWER: THE HIGH REPRESENTATIVE

The Constitutional Treaty created the post of EU Minister for Foreign Affairs, who was to 'conduct' the Union's common foreign and security policy.[222] The idea that executive power within the Union was divided between the European Council and the Commission was personified in this post. The nomenclature changed in the Lisbon Treaty, but the substance remains the same. The rationale for the change was that some Member States were unhappy about the 'statist' connotations of the title 'EU Minister for Foreign Affairs',[223] and hence it was altered in the Lisbon Treaty to be High Representative of the Union for Foreign Affairs and Security Policy.[224]

The substance of the provisions concerning the High Representative in the Lisbon Treaty is however the same as that in the Constitutional Treaty. Thus the High Representative is appointed by the European Council by qualified majority, with the agreement of the Commission President.[225] The incumbent is one of the Vice-Presidents of the Commission, and is responsible for handling external relations and for coordinating other aspects of the Union's external action.[226] The holder of the office takes part in the work of the European Council,[227] chairs the Foreign Affairs Council,[228] and is also a Vice-President of the Commission. The High Representative therefore wears 'two hats', or perhaps three if one regards the role of chairing the Foreign Affairs Council as distinctive from the functions performed within the European Council and Commission.

D. CONCLUSION

There has been significant evolution in relation to the inter-institutional disposition of power over the last half century. Some changes have resulted from Treaty amendment, others from developments outside the Treaty that have later been incorporated into the Treaty, yet others from alteration in the political balance of power without modification of the formal Treaty rules.

---

[221] Art 17(5) TEU.   [222] Art I-28 CT.
[223] Brussels European Council, 21–22 June 2007, Annex 1, [3].   [224] Art 18 TEU.
[225] Art 18(1) TEU.   [226] Art 18(4) TEU.   [227] Art 15(2) TEU.   [228] Art 18(3) TEU.

Institutional balance has characterized the disposition of legislative and executive power from the outset. The changes reflect however shifting normative assumptions as to which institutions should be able to partake of legislative and executive power, and what constitutes the appropriate balance between them. The story of the last half-century reveals moreover that the devil is in the detail. Thus understanding of the contestation as to the locus of legislative and executive authority requires us to probe beyond the macro level. It requires more than abstract determination as to which institution partakes in, for example, executive authority. It necessitates detailed inquiry as to the type of executive authority wielded by a particular institution, and the constraints exercised by the other institutional players. It is these issues that have shaped debates about issues such as Comitology and agencies.

The Lisbon Treaty is part of this continuing story. The disposition of primary legislative power has become clearer and sharper, but the inter-institutional impact of the new provisions on delegated acts remains to be seen, and the same is true in relation to the High Representative for Foreign Affairs and Security Policy. The formal battles over the locus of executive authority have been 'settled' in favour of power being shared between the President of the Commission and President of the European Council, but the way in which they inter-relate will develop over time. The impact of the new rules relating to choice of the Commission President, and the extent to which this leads to more overt politicization of the Commission, will likewise only be apparent with the passage of time. Institutional balance may provide the background principle against which these and other issues are resolved, but it can never obviate the need for reasoned inquiry into the normative and political assumptions that shape the desired balance.

4

POWERS AND PROCEDURES IN THE EU CONSTITUTION: LEGAL BASES AND THE COURT

*Kieran St Clair Bradley**

A. INTRODUCTION: 'IT IS *A CONSTITUTION* WE ARE EXPOUNDING'[1]

1. THE CHOICE OF LEGAL BASIS IN THE EU SYSTEM OF GOVERNMENT

In December 2001, the Court of Justice grandly proclaimed, in its *Biosafety Protocol* Opinion, that '[the] choice of the appropriate legal basis has constitutional significance'.[2] That this is so may not be immediately obvious, given the procedural law context in which legal basis disputes tend to arise.[3] The Council agent in another *cause célèbre*, the so-called *Titanium dioxide* case, wondered aloud before the Court what the man in the Clapham omnibus, that omnipresent if shadowy figure in English legal

---

* Head of Unit in the Legal Service of the European Parliament. The views expressed are personal and should not be taken as representing those of the institution or any service thereof. Best thanks are due to the colleagues, too numerous to mention, who kindly read the text in draft; the responsibility for any errors is that of the author alone.

[1] Marshall C J delivering the judgment of the US Supreme Court in *McCulloch v Maryland* 17 US 316 (1819).

[2] Opinion 2/00 [2001] ECR I-9713, [5]. The timing of the Court's remark may not have been entirely coincidental; the Member States and institutions were then gearing up for the Union's first full Constitutional Convention.

[3] The context may account for the rather limited degree of academic interest in the concept of the legal basis as such, though certain individual judgments have generated large numbers of commentaries: see, generally, H Cullen and A Charlesworth, 'Diplomacy by other means: the use of legal basis litigation as a political strategy by the European Parliament and Member States' (1999) 36 CML Rev 1243, N Emiliou, 'Opening Pandora's box: the Legal Basis of Community measures before the Court of Justice' (1994) 19 ELRev 488, R Barents, 'The Internal Market Unlimited' (1993) 30 CML Rev 85, A Wachsmann, 'Le contentieux de la base juridique dans la jurisprudence de la Cour' (1993) Revue Europe 1, and K St C Bradley, 'The European Court and the Legal Basis of Community legislation' (1988) 13 ELRev 379.

writing, would make of the proceedings,[4] while an academic commentator noted that such disputes 'seem to be pettifogging 18th Century legal formalism run riot'.[5] In a large number of cases, it must appear to the Clapham commuter, should he stop to consider such matters, that the Council is arguing for the restriction of its own powers, and/or that the Commission is challenging legislation with which it is substantially in agreement.

The qualification 'constitutional' is none the less apt in the European Union's unique legal and political system. If the Union is founded on the principle of conferred or attributed powers,[6] it follows that every legally binding act must be based on a grant of power. The procedure for the adoption of every act determines the scope of the formal input of each of the principal institutional actors: Commission, Council, Parliament, and the individual Member States. The failure to respect that procedure violates the delicate balance of powers between the institutions, and/or that between the Union and the Member States, intended by the Treaty, while the failure to respect the limits of the competence derived from the particular legal basis infringes the principle of conferred powers.[7]

Treaty articles which serve as the legal basis for Union acts are either sectoral, being the enabling provision for a specific policy field, or functional, in that they may be used in different fields to pursue specified objectives.[8] The practice of the institutions in this regard is of course unmanageably vast. However, the Court's case law on legal bases disputes both reflects and guides that practice. Most disputes concern the choice between sectoral and functional legal bases; more occasionally, the choice is between two (or more) sectoral or functional provisions, between legal bases in different Treaties, or between Treaty and extra-Treaty powers.

Legal basis disputes may also concern the fulfilment of the conditions for recourse to the chosen legal basis, which goes to the competence of the adopting institutions,[9] and hence, in some cases, to that of the Community/Union. The substantive compatibility of resorting in a single act to different grants of power could give rise to litigation, given that each enabling provision is hedged about with substantive conditions, endowed with specific objectives and, in many cases, subject to possible derogations.[10] The old question of the respective competences of the Member States and the

---

[4] Case C-300/89 *Commission v Council* [1991] ECR I-2867; see K St C Bradley, 'The Fall and Rise of *Titanium dioxide*', in A Baas *et al* (eds), *Liber amicorum—le rôle de Johann Schoo dans la construction européenne* (Luxembourg, 2010).

[5] N March Hunnings, *The European Courts* (Cartermill, 1996) 152; he did not, of course, espouse this view.

[6] For the situation pre-Lisbon, see for example, Opinion 2/94 *ECHR Accession* [1996] ECR I-1759, [23]; see now Art 1, para 1, Art 3(6), and Art 4(1) TEU and, for the really inattentive reader, Art 5(1) and (2) TEU.

[7] See Opinion of AG Kokott in Case C-13/07 *Commission v Council (Vietnam WTO accession)*, withdrawn.

[8] Formerly Arts 95 and 308 EC, now Arts 114 and 352 TFEU respectively; see Parts C and D below.

[9] This includes the Commission acting under its limited autonomous law-making powers: see eg K St C Bradley (n 3 above) 385–388, though there have been numerous examples since, including in the areas of budget implementation and international relations (see respectively Case C-106/96 *United Kingdom v Commission* [1998] ECR I-2729 and Case C-327/91 *France v Commission* [1994] ECR I-3641).

[10] Compare the derogation provisions of Art 114(4) to (9) with those of Art 193 TFEU.

Community/Union in external relations[11] remains current, and will no doubt continue to flourish in the post-Lisbon Treaty era.

With admirable restraint, the Court of Justice noted in the *Erasmus* case that the attribution of powers to the Community institutions and the differences between legal bases was 'not always based on consistent criteria'.[12] Successive reforming Treaties both exacerbated and in some respects rationalized this state of affairs. The Lisbon Treaty has considerably reduced the procedural fragmentation of the Union's powers, particularly by generalizing the ordinary legislative procedure. It nonetheless leaves largely unchanged their substantive fragmentation, while possibly adding a further source of discord, by explicitly categorizing competences as exclusive, shared, or supplementary. The Treaty was not in force a month before a disagreement on the interpretation of two new provisions provoked annulment proceedings by Parliament challenging the legal basis of a Council act.[13]

2. POLITICAL AND LEGAL EVOLUTION

The evolution of the legal basis concept has taken place on two planes, through the application (or in some cases non-application) and revision of the Treaties, and as a result of the case law of the Court of Justice.[14] The EEC Treaty itself provided for the evolution of its enabling provisions by establishing a twelve-year transitional period during which ever more 'integrationist' procedural rules would come into operation. A good example is the procedure for the adoption of the agricultural policy, which went from that of a Commission proposal drawn up following an intergovernmental conference and Council unanimity (1958 to 1959), to a Commission proposal *simpliciter* and Council unanimity (1960 to 1965), to a Commission proposal and a qualified majority vote in the Council (from 1 January 1966).[15]

As is well known, this tidy little scheme was thrown out of kilter by the 'empty chair' crisis of June 1965, which arose, at least in part, from the passage to qualified majority voting for agricultural policy measures and the *états d'âme* of the French government in this regard.[16] Whatever the reasons, the result was the Luxembourg Compromise, and the near-universal practice the Council adopted of seeking consensus on proposed legislation, rather than moving to the vote. In evolutionary terms, this was an ugly mutation of the institutional scheme envisaged by the Treaty.

---

[11] See sections B.1 and B.2 below.

[12] Case 242/87 *Commission v Council* [1989] ECR 1425, [13].

[13] Case C-130/10, concerning Council Regulation (EU) 1286/2009, adopted on the basis of Art 215 TFEU rather than Art 75 TFEU, [2009] OJ L346/42; both provisions allow for the adoption of restrictive measures against individuals, such as the freezing of their economic resources, though under very different conditions.

[14] Given the constitutional character of the question, the Court of First Instance did not play a major role in this area, though the General Court may do so in the years to come.

[15] See Arts 43(1) and (2) EEC.

[16] See, for example, J Vanke, 'Charles de Gaulle's Uncertain Idea of Europe' in D Dinan (ed), *Origins and Evolution of the European Union* (Oxford University Press, 2006) 141, 157–159.

The next great leap forward was the adoption in 1986 of the Single European Act (SEA). Both at the time, and even now, the SEA might on first examination appear rather modest in scope. Compared to subsequent Treaty reforms, the number of legal bases it added—on economic and social cohesion, research, and technological development and environmental protection—was paltry; moreover, for the most part, these merely provided a specific foundation for activities already being carried out under functional legal bases, particularly Article 235 EEC. True, it added two new decision-making procedures to boost the influence of the European Parliament; however, they only applied in a small number of areas, and, in strictly formal terms, the increase in Parliament's formal role under the cooperation procedure was rather limited.[17]

The SEA also replaced the unanimity requirement for the adoption of legislation in a number of areas by qualified majority voting, in particular as regards internal market legislation. To ensure that this would not remain a dead letter, the Council amended its rules of procedure a fortnight after the SEA came into force to allow the Commission or any Member State to force a vote on proposed legislation, a procedural decision which only required a simple majority.[18] In all but political rhetoric, the Luxembourg Compromise was dead, though this did not prevent appeals to its continuing vitality for years to come, often from beleaguered prime ministers in their home parliament or at meetings of their peers, and the formal adoption of a successor instrument at Ioannina on the eve of the 1995 accessions.[19]

Most significantly of all, the SEA removed the taboo on formal Treaty amendment and kick-started a revision process which culminated in the Lisbon Treaty. The fact that the Member States, *qua* Masters of the Treaties, resumed their rightful role in adjusting the formal legal rules to the political necessities in turn had a marked impact on the Court's role in interpreting the enabling provisions of the Treaty. Each new Treaty brought new enabling provisions for the Court to interpret, and required both the Court and the political institutions to recalibrate, as it were, the relationship between potentially overlapping legal bases. It is more difficult to discern the full extent of the converse process. The prohibition on harmonization of legislation in various areas,[20] for example, might have been a reaction to the Court's generous interpretation of the legal bases for common/internal market legislation.

It is proposed to examine firstly the basic rules governing the determination of the legal basis (Part B), and then the evolution of the Court's interpretation of the two functional legal bases, that for internal market measures (Part C) and the fall-back

---

[17] *Titanium dioxide* case (n 44 above) [19].

[18] [1987] OJ L291/2.

[19] Council Decision 94/C 105/01 of 29 March 1994 concerning the taking of Decisions by qualified majority by the Council, [1994] OJ C105/1, as amended [1995] OJ C1/1. See now the so-called 'emergency brake' a Member State may apply to delay the adoption of legislation in certain areas (eg Articles 82(3) and 83(3) TFEU).

[20] Arts 166(4) TFEU, 167(5), first indent, TFEU, and 168(5) TFEU. Other, institutional, provisions were clearly inspired by Court judgments, such as Art 290 TFEU on delegated acts which uses the notion of 'non-essential elements' of an act, derived from Case 25/70 *Köster* [1970] ECR 1161, [6].

clause of Article 235 EEC/308 EC (Part D).[21] Some general observations on the evolution of the constitutional character of the notion of the legal basis may serve by way of conclusion (Part E).

B. LEGAL BASIS CASE LAW: FROM NEGLIGÉ TO STRAITJACKET

1. ON THE INTERPRETATION OF TREATY PROVISIONS

The Court's primary contribution in this area is through its interpretation of Treaty provisions which serve as the legal basis for Community, now Union, action. Before the EEC Treaty was even drafted, the Court had adopted a purposive approach to interpreting grants of power to the Coal and Steel Community. Explicitly drawing inspiration from both international and domestic law, it took the view that 'rules laid down by an international treaty or law presuppose the rules without which that treaty or law would have no meaning or could not be reasonably and usefully applied'.[22] In this case the Court held that, by virtue of the principle of the *effet utile* of a particular provision, the High Authority enjoyed implicit regulatory powers to achieve an explicit goal.[23]

In the *ERTA* case, the Court adopted a similar approach to the interpretation of the EEC Treaty where it held that the Community's authority to conclude international agreements in a given area 'arises not only from express conferment . . . but may equally flow from other provisions of the Treaty and from measures adopted . . . by the Community institutions'.[24] In ruling on the Commission's legislative competence in the *Financial transparency* case, the Court indicated that 'the limits of the powers of the [institutions] . . . are to be inferred . . . from an interpretation of the particular wording of the provision in question . . . analysed in the light of its purpose and place in the scheme of the Treaty'.[25] Where a Treaty provision imposes a duty on an institution without explicitly providing the necessary powers, it follows that 'if that provision is not to be rendered wholly ineffective . . . it confers on the [institution] necessarily and *per se* the powers which are indispensable in order to carry out that task'.[26]

Most controversially in the post-SEA era perhaps, the Court has on two occasions ruled that the Community was competent to require the Member States to impose

---

[21] The case law and legal writing on both sets of provisions are voluminous, and within the compass of the present chapter it is only possible to provide a brief overview of their evolution.

[22] Case 8/55 *Fédération Charbonnière de Belgique v High Authority* [1954]–[1956] ECR 292, 299–300.

[23] The ECSC Court was not always so accommodating (C J Mann, *The Function of Judicial Decision in European Economic Integration* (Martinus Nijhoff, 1972) 294–266, but at least the Member States were on notice as to the possibility of such an interpretation.

[24] Case 22/70 *Commission v Council* [1971] ECR 263, [16].

[25] Cases 188 to 190/80 *France, Italy and United Kingdom v Commission* [1982] ECR 2545, [6]; though the legislative powers at issue were those of the Commission, the same principle could be said to apply in respect of the other legislatures of the Union.

[26] Cases 282, 284–285, and 287/85 *Germany et al v Commission (Migration policy)* [1987] ECR 3203, [28].

criminal sanctions for particularly serious breaches of Community environmental law, where this was 'an essential measure' to achieve an essential objective.[27] It reached this conclusion notwithstanding the fact that the EC Treaty contained no explicit power to harmonize any aspect of criminal law, while the EU Treaty did provide some powers in this area.

2. LEGAL BASIS DISPUTES BEFORE THE SEA

Disputes on the choice between competing legal bases were few and far between in the pre-SEA epoch, and those which did arise between the institutions were rarely brought to Court. The sole major exception was the long-running disagreement on the scope and character of the Community's external relations powers which gave rise to the *ERTA* judgment and a number of Opinions on draft international agreements.[28] The Council's systematic recourse in certain areas to unanimous voting deprived the Member States, who presumptively agreed with the content of the legislation adopted, of any incentive to challenge its legal basis, while the Commission may have hesitated to jeopardize a hard-won, unanimous, political compromise in order to make a political point it could not realistically enforce.

With surprising *désinvolture*, in the *Massey-Ferguson* case the Court noted that different Treaty provisions either singly or in combination could have provided the necessary legal basis for the contested Regulation, concerning the valuation of goods for customs purposes. It held nonetheless that 'there is no reason why the Council could not legitimately consider that recourse to the procedure of Article 235 EEC was justified in the interest of legal certainty'.[29] Somewhat cryptically, the Court added that 'the rules of the Treaty on the forming of the Council's decision or on the division of powers between the institutions are not to be disregarded'.[30] It thereby identified two of the principal aspects of the legal basis issue, the voting rule in the Council and the participation of the European Parliament, which have recurred in most subsequent disputes. Here, the choice of Article 235 EEC meant that both the right of individual Member States to a veto and that of Parliament to the application of the consultation procedure were fully respected.

The Court was less concerned about Parliament's participation in the legislative process in the *Balkan Import* case a few months later.[31] There the Council had chosen the legal basis of a Regulation on imports of agricultural products with the sole purpose of avoiding the consultation of the European Parliament. The Court was quite clear that the Regulation was an agricultural policy measure, and that it could not in any case be qualified as the short-term economic policy measure the Regulation

---

[27] Case C-176/03 *Commission v Council (Environmental sanctions)* [2005] ECR I-7879, and Case C-440/05 *Commission v Council (Ship-source pollution)* [2007] ECR I-9097.

[28] The *ERTA* case (n 24 above) and Opinions 1/75, [1975] ECR 1355, 1/76 [1977] ECR 741, 1/78 [1979] ECR 2871, and Ruling 1/78 [1979] ECR 2151; see also Cases 3, 4, and 6/76 *Kramer* [1976] ECR 1279.

[29] Case 8/73 [1973] ECR 897, [4].   [30] *Loc cit.*

[31] Case 5/73 [1973] ECR 1091.

purported to be under its chosen legal basis. The Court nonetheless relied on the urgent and temporary character of the Regulation, the delay which would supposedly result from consulting Parliament, and the absence of any specific provision for the adoption of urgent agricultural policy measures, to conclude, somewhat lamely, that it was 'reasonable to suppose that the Council was justified in making interim use of [its] powers' regarding economic policy to uphold the Council's choice of legal basis.[32]

3. THE CHOICE OF THE LEGAL BASIS IN MODERN TIMES

The judgments in the *Massey-Ferguson* and *Balkan Import* cases have both been overruled, as regards the legality of the Council's conduct,[33] and the Court has since developed a fairly clear and comprehensive set of rules governing the choice of the legal basis for Community, and now Union, acts. Where the Union's regulatory power derives from overlapping Treaty provisions, the principle of conferred powers requires recourse to a double legal basis and the combination of their procedural provisions, which is indeed how the institutions have always proceeded in such cases. This was confirmed by the Court at the first opportunity; the Court also noted that the citation of an erroneous legal basis which did not affect the procedure followed was a 'purely formal defect which cannot make the measure void'.[34]

The choice of legal basis depends on objective factors which are amenable to judicial review.[35] Though now undisputed, there was a time when the Council argued that this matter fell within the margin of discretion enjoyed by the legislator (the Council).[36] For its part, the Commission took the view that, as regards the participation of the European Parliament, the legislature was obliged to follow the procedure dictated by the (Commission) proposal until the moment of the adoption of the act,[37] though this line of argument may have been motivated more by a desire that Parliament intervene in the case than any real concern for its institutional welfare. Parliament did in fact intervene, but contended that the Council was in no way so obliged; the Commission's argument was subsequently airbrushed entirely out of the picture, from the report for the hearing right through to the judgment.

The objective factors are primarily the aim and material content of the act,[38] a test the Court had already used in ruling on the Community's external relations competence.[39] The aim (or 'purpose' or 'objective') of a measure is normally deduced from the preamble and/or a statement to this effect in one of the substantive provisions, and

---

[32] ibid [15].

[33] See respectively Case 45/86 *Commission v Council (1986 GSP)* [1987] ECR 149 and Case 137/79 *Roquette Frères v Council (Isoglucose)* [1980] ECR 3333.

[34] Case 165/87 *Commission v Council (Customs nomenclature)* [1988] ECR 5545.

[35] *1986 GSP* (n 33 above) [11].

[36] Report for the hearing in Case 68/86 *United Kingdom v Council (Hormones)* [1988] ECR 855, 862.

[37] Application in *Titanium dioxide* (n 4 above) [1989] OJ C288/8.

[38] It is ironic that the Court should first establish this test in the *Titanium dioxide* case (n 4 above), where the legal basis was, exceptionally, determined by other factors.

[39] See, for example, Opinion 1/78 (n 28 above) [26].

the content from its substantive provisions considered together. In some cases, the content is essentially neutral as regards the choice of legal basis; the stated aims of the act thus tend to be given a great deal of importance. In the *Second Waste Regulation* case, for example, the Court relied on a recital in the preamble which had been proposed by the Commission and adopted unamended by Parliament and the Council.[40] The recital clearly identified environmental protection as the sole objective of the Regulation, a conclusion which the Commission then sought (unsuccessfully) to deny.

To date the Court has not found a clear mismatch between aim and content in a given instrument, though it has been suggested, on a purely hypothetical basis of course, that there is nothing to prevent a legislature which was so minded from drafting the preamble in function of its chosen legal basis, rather than to reflect the true content of the measure.[41] In the *Ireland Fund* case, following Parliament's (first-reading) opinion that the Regulation was a measure of economic and social cohesion, the Council had taken pains to add a recital affirming that the activities undertaken under the Regulation extended beyond the Community's policy on economic and social cohesion, a precaution which proved well justified in the result.[42]

As noted above, the principal problem which arises is the determination of the correct legal basis when a given act touches on different areas of regulation. If the measure pursues a twofold purpose of which one can be identified as the main or predominant purpose, whereas the other is merely incidental, the act must be based on a single legal basis. Exceptionally, if the act simultaneously pursues a number of objectives or has several components that are indissociably linked, without one being secondary and indirect in relation to the other, the act will have to be founded on the various corresponding legal bases.[43] Where it is not disputed that the act pursues one objective, a second legal basis is only required where the act pursues a second objective and contains components falling within another policy which are of such importance that the act ought to have a dual legal basis.[44]

The legal basis which derives from the aim and content may in certain circumstances be ousted for institutional reasons. This arises in particular when a double legal basis would result in the combination of incompatible procedures.[45] The exact extent of this exception, especially in the post-Lisbon Treaty era, remains unclear. While in one case the Court held explicitly that Treaty articles providing unanimity and a qualified majority vote in the Council could not be applied conjointly,[46] this ruling is

---

[40] Case C-411/06 *Commission v Parliament and Council, Second waste regulation* [2009] ECR I-7585, [51].

[41] Opinion of AG Saggio, Case C-269/97 *Commission v Council (Beef labelling)* [2000] ECR I-2257, [86].

[42] Case C-166/07 *Parliament v Council* [2009] ECR I-7135, [63]; during the debate on the legal basis, the Commission representative was unable to explain to Parliament's Committee on Legal Affairs in what respect the Regulation could exceed economic and social cohesion. In a sense, the honours were shared on this occasion, as the Court opted for a double legal basis which neither party had suggested, requiring both co-decision and unanimity.

[43] ibid [46]–[47] citing the *Titanium dioxide* case (n 4 above).

[44] ibid [48].

[45] *Titanium dioxide* (n 4 above).

[46] Case C-338/01 *Commission v Council* [2004] ECR I-4829, [58].

inconsistent with both previous and subsequent case law, to say nothing of the handful of Treaty provisions which provided precisely this combination. Recourse to a double legal basis was also excluded where an act fell at the same time within the Community Pillar and the Second or Third Pillar by Article 47 EU, a provision which in effect pre-empted the choice of legal basis in favour of the First Pillar provision.[47]

The practice of the legislature may neither derogate from the Treaty nor create a precedent as regards the choice of legal basis.[48] The legal basis of a given act depends on its specific characteristics, and the fact that it amends a previous act in the same area does not imply that the same legal basis should necessarily be used.[49] While the Court regularly repeats this finding, it appears to be unable to resist quoting past practice in its judgments where this happens to confirm its own analysis. Thus in the space of two paragraphs in the *Rotterdam Convention Decision* judgment, it held that previous practice was 'entirely irrelevant in the context of the present case', while noting with approval the Commission's citation of 'numerous Community measures' in support of its contended legal basis.[50] Even more remarkably, in the *Kadi* judgment the Court of Justice quoted a Council practice under a previous Treaty regime whose pertinence in the circumstances was, to say the least, a little tenuous,[51] given that 'Community measures must be adopted in accordance with the Treaty rules in force at the time of their adoption'.[52]

The Court has not been entirely consistent either as regards the relevance of the legislative context of the contested act. It is clear that the context is relevant for the legal basis of international agreements, in accordance with the 1969 Vienna Convention provisions on treaty interpretation.[53] As regards internal Community legislation, however, while the Court ruled rather sharply in the *Beef labelling* case that the context in which the measure was adopted was 'irrelevant', it corroborated its analysis of the legal basis in the *Second Waste Regulation* case by explicit reference to the legislative context.[54] The 'fact that an institution wishes to participate more fully in the adoption of a given measure' and the extent of its previous work in that area are also irrelevant for the choice of legal basis.[55]

As part of the statement of reasons justifying an act, the legal basis must be identifiable from the text, even if it is not necessary to refer to the precise Treaty provision, as the legislature almost invariably does.[56] The legislature may not therefore

---

[47] See most dramatically Case C-91/05 *Ireland v Parliament and Council (Small arms)* [2008] ECR I-3651, which was a sort of *Titanium dioxide* ruling for inter-Pillar disputes.

[48] *Hormones* (n 36 above) [24].

[49] Case C-187/93 *Parliament v Council (First Waste Regulation)* [1994] ECR I-2857, [28].

[50] Case C-94/03 *Commission v Parliament and Council* [2006] ECR I-1, [49]-[50].

[51] Joined Cases C-402/05 P and C-415/05 P *Kadi and Al Barakaat v Council* [2008] ECR I-6351, [215].

[52] *Beef labelling* (n 41 above) [45].

[53] Opinion 2/00 (n 1 above) [24].

[54] Respectively the *Beef labelling* case (n 41 above) [44], and the *Second Waste Regulation* case (n 40 above) [64].

[55] The *Beef labelling* case (n 41 above) [44].

[56] The *1986 GSP* case (n 33 above) [9].

simply 'disappear' the legal basis in order to hide an inconvenient truth, such as the Council's recourse to Article 235 EEC for measures which *prima facie* fell within the commercial policy. Also long undisputed, this obligation recently made a surprise reappearance in the roll of the Court when the Council decided that its official position on the extent of the Community's competence to protect endangered species could do without a legal basis.[57] The Court took the opportunity to add that the identification of the legal basis was also required in order to ensure respect for the principle of conferred powers, the prerogatives of the Community institutions concerned, and the division of powers between the Community and the Member States.

C. THE INTERNAL MARKET: NOT 'UNLIMITED'

1. THE USE AND EVOLUTION OF ARTICLE 100 EEC

The Treaty Articles governing Union action in respect of the common, and later internal, market provide a good example of provisions which have evolved through formal Treaty revision, influenced by and influencing the Court's legal basis case law.[58] In the beginning, there was Article 100 EEC, which allowed the unanimous Council to adopt directives 'for the approximation of such provisions . . . of the Member States as directly affect the establishment or functioning of the common market'. Parliamentary consultation applied, but only where the implementation of the directive would require the amendment of national legislation. The specific provisions which allowed, and still allow, the adoption of measures to ensure the free movement of persons, services, and capital,[59] often used in tandem with the general provision, do not require special treatment here.[60]

Starting in the mid-1960s, Article 100 EEC was widely employed as a legal basis for Community legislation, either alone or in combination with a variety of other Treaty articles. While many of the measures sought to implement the General Programme for the elimination of technical barriers to trade between the Member States, the Community also relied on Article 100 EEC to harmonize provisions, *inter alia*, on food safety, workers' rights, pharmaceutical products, environmental protection, customs law, tax law, agriculture, and public procurement. As the Luxembourg Compromise was in full swing at the time, the unanimity requirement was not of itself a meaningful obstacle using Article 100 EEC, though, as the Court noted in *Massey-Ferguson*, the

---

[57] Case C-370/07 *Commission v Council (CITES)*, [2009] ECR I-8917.

[58] Art 3(h) EEC; the 'common market' was not defined, while the 'internal market' is now defined in Art 26(2) TFEU. In its *Danish nitrates* judgment, the Court explicitly recognised the evolutionary character of the common/internal market legal bases: Case C-3/00 *Denmark v Commission* [2003] ECR I-2643, [56].

[59] See notably Arts 45, 49, 56, 62, and 64(2) TFEU.

[60] Arts 101 and 102 EEC, now Arts 116 and 117 TFEU, which are legal bases for other specific action in favour of the common or internal market, have been little used in practice and are also left out of account here.

restriction of the choice of legal instrument to the sole directive meant that in certain circumstances it did not provide 'a really adequate solution'.[61]

So successful was the Community's reliance on Article 100 EEC that it attracted the critical attention of the House of Lords. In a 1978 report, the Lords' Select Committee on the European Communities took the Community to task for adopting directives which were either not predominantly economic in purpose or which harmonized provisions whose effect on the functioning of the common market was not 'direct'.[62] Noting that this provision effected 'some transfer of legislative sovereignty from the Member States to the Community', and hence out of the direct control of the national legislatures, the committee considered it to be 'of the first importance that the limits of Article 100 powers should be strictly defined and that the Government should undertake to keep within them'.[63]

The Italian government took up the baton the following year, in defending itself in proceedings for failure to transpose a Directive on detergents.[64] It argued that 'combating pollution is not one of the tasks entrusted to the Community' and that hence the matter 'lies "on the fringe" of Community powers'.[65] The Court held that the Directive was properly based on Article 100 EEC as it eliminated a technical barrier to trade, and that in any case national health and environmental protection provisions could appreciably distort the conditions of competition.[66] As Member States could justify obstacles to the free movement of goods by relying on certain mandatory requirements, such as public health and environmental protection,[67] it followed that Article 100 EEC was a good legal basis for the harmonization of national provisions concerning environmental protection, with a view to maintaining the integrity of the common market.

The addition of a new 'internal market' legal basis, Article 100a EEC, was amongst the most important reforms of the SEA. At one fell swoop, it loosened the Council voting requirement to a qualified majority, brought Parliament more fully into the legislative process, allowed the adoption of regulations and decisions as well as directives, and replaced the requirement that the national provisions have a direct effect on the common market by one that the Community measure have as its object 'the establishment and functioning of the internal market'. True, Article 100a(1) EEC ostensibly applied 'by way of derogation from Article 100 and save where otherwise provided', but this proved to be no real hindrance to its use in practice. Article 100a

---

[61] Case 8/73 (n 29 above) [3].

[62] Session 1977–78, *Approximation of laws under Art 100 of the EEC Treaty*, 18 April 1978.

[63] Opinion 2/00 (n 1 above) [15].

[64] Case 91/79 *Commission v Italy* [1980] ECR 1099. A parallel case concerning a Directive on the sulphur content of liquid fuels is materially identical: Case 92/79 *Commission v Italy* [1980] ECR 1115.

[65] ibid [4].

[66] ibid [8].

[67] Respectively Case 120/78 *Rewe-Zentral AG* (*Cassis de Dijon*) [1979] ECR 649, Case 240/83 *ADBHU* [1985] ECR 531, and Case 302/86 *Commission v Denmark* (*Danish bottles*) [1988] ECR 4607; also Case C-2/90 *Commission v Belgium* (*Walloon waste*) [1992] ECR I-4431. On 'Art 30 case-law' generally, see M Poiares Maduro, *We the Court* (Hart, 1998).

was also subject to a number of restrictions, *ratione tempore* (Article 8a EEC, which Article 100a EEC was intended to implement, set a non-binding deadline of 31 December 1992, though this was forgotten long before then) and *ratione materiae*, Article 100a(2) EEC excluding the adoption of fiscal provisions and those concerning the free movement of persons and workers' rights.

Article 100a(3) EEC appeared to contemplate expressly that the Community could, on the basis of Article 100a(1) EEC, harmonize national provisions on health, safety, and environmental and consumer protection, by inviting the Commission to 'take as a base a high level of protection' in these areas. Mindful of the *Cassis de Dijon* case law, Article 100a(4) EEC allowed Member States a derogation on specified grounds to apply national provisions which differed from the harmonizing measure, subject to surveillance by the Commission and, as need be, the Court of Justice.[68] Harmonizing measures were, where appropriate, to include a safeguard clause authorizing Member States to adopt provisional measures to protect the interests protected by Article 36 EEC (now Article 36 TFEU).

Subsequent rounds of Treaty revision introduced the co-decision procedure for the adoption of harmonizing measures, required the legislature too to aim for a high level of environmental and consumer protection taking account of any relevant scientific developments, and allowed the Member States, under stricter conditions and a specific surveillance procedure, also to introduce derogatory national provisions 'based on new scientific evidence'. The Lisbon Treaty has removed the, by now faintly ridiculous, 1992 deadline, and abrogated the status as a derogation of the former Article 100a EEC, now re-numbered Article 114 TFEU.[69]

2. INTERNAL MARKET HARMONIZATION: INSTRUCTIONS FOR USE

Given the generally heightened interest in the choice of the legal basis caused by the SEA, it was inevitable that the Court would soon be called on to interpret the institutions' newest plaything, Article 100a EEC. As the SEA had also introduced a new specific legal basis for environmental protection measures, Article 130s EEC, without clearly distinguishing between their respective fields of application, it was almost as inevitable that the first major dispute to come to judgment would concern the relationship between these two provisions, as indeed the pundits had predicted. The case was C-300/89 *Commission v Council*, universally known as the *Titanium dioxide* case.[70] The contested Directive harmonized the national programmes for the reduction and eventual elimination of the pollution caused in the production of

---

[68] Art 100a(4) EEC was savaged by P Pescatore, 'Some critical remarks on the "Single European Act"' (1987) 24 CML Rev 9, but has often proved something of a damp squib in practice (see however the *Danish nitrates* judgment (n 58)).

[69] Art 100 EEC, latterly Art 94 EC, remains as Art 115 TFEU; it is to apply '[without] prejudice to Art 114' TFEU.

[70] More (n 4 above); see also K St C Bradley, 'L'arrêt dioxyde de titane: un jugement de Salomon?' (1992) XXVIII Cahiers Dr Euro 609.

titanium dioxide, a white pigment whose market price in each Member State depended to a large extent on the stringency of the applicable environmental protection provisions. The Commission (supported by Parliament) considered it to be an internal market measure; the Council adopted it as one of environmental protection.

The Court held that the Directive was, as regards its aim and content, 'concerned, indissociably, with both the protection of the environment and the elimination of disparities in conditions of competition'. As it displayed features of Community action under both Articles 100a and 130s EEC, the Directive should, in principle, have been based on both provisions. Having excluded this course on institutional grounds, the Court referred to the *Detergents* case and held that the 'approximation of national rules concerning production conditions in a given industrial sector with the aim of eliminating distortions of competition in that sector is conducive to the attainment of the internal market and thus falls within Article 100a'.[71] Moreover, Article 100a(3) EEC expressly indicated that Article 100a(1) was a proper legal basis for measures pursuing environmental protection objectives, while the 'integration clause' of Article 130s(2) EEC demonstrated that a measure should not be based on Article 130s(1) EEC on the sole ground that it pursued environmental protection objectives.

Remarkably, though urged upon it at least by the intervener, the Court omitted to refer to its *Greek Chernobyl* judgment the previous year, to the effect that 'Articles 130r and 130s [EEC]...leave intact the powers held by the Community under other provisions of the Treaty', notably Article 100a EEC.[72] A previous judgment had established that it was unnecessary to add a reference to the common market to the legal basis of an agricultural measure merely because it also pursued public health objectives.[73] While an analogy might have been drawn with the relationship between internal market and environmental protection measures, in the circumstances, however, the internal market component of the Titanium dioxide Directive was arguably too important to be ignored, and the Directive would by this token have been *ultra vires* Article 130s EEC alone.

The *Titanium dioxide* judgment was soon criticized as leaving the Community too free to harmonize national provisions on the mere ground that these distorted the conditions of competition. Subsequent judgments on measures which were said to pursue multiple objectives appeared to swing the balance in favour of legal bases which guaranteed the protection of the environment and/or public health (and, perhaps more importantly, unanimous voting in the Council) and against Article 100a EEC. In ruling on the merits of Parliament's *Chernobyl* case a few month later, the Court held that a Regulation fixing the maximum level of radioactive contamination in foodstuffs and feedingstuffs put on the market could be based on Article 31 Euratom, as its effects on the free movement of goods were only incidental.[74] A Directive on the management of waste and, somewhat less obviously, a Regulation on the movement of waste within the European Community were similarly held to have only incidental effects on the

---

[71] ibid [23].   [72] Case C-62/88 *Greece v Council* [1990] I-1527, [19].
[73] *Hormones* (n 36 above).   [74] Case C-70/88 *Parliament v Council* [1991] ECR I-4259, [17].

functioning of the internal market, and hence to have been properly based on Article 130s EEC.[75]

The most comprehensive interpretation of Article 100a EEC (by then Article 95 EC) was that in the Court's *First Tobacco Advertising* judgment.[76] The contested Directive prohibited, subject to a few minor exceptions, all forms of advertising of tobacco products and sponsorship of activities promoting such products. The institutions contended in particular that Article 100a EEC was 'not necessarily concerned with the liberalization of trade but rather with market regulation'.[77]

The Court's interpretation of Article 100a may be summarized as follows:

- the Community legislature does not enjoy a general power to regulate the internal market but only to improve the conditions for its establishment and functioning; the contrary view would infringe the principle of conferred powers and the wording of Article 100a;

- the mere finding of disparities between national rules and the abstract risk of obstacles to trade or of distortions of competition are not sufficient to justify recourse to Article 100a; otherwise the Court's review of the choice of legal basis would be rendered nugatory;

- for Article 100a to apply, the emergence of obstacles to the free movement of goods must be likely, and the harmonizing measure must be designed to prevent such obstacles arising; the Court will ensure these conditions are respected;

- the exclusion of harmonization of national provisions on public health does not preclude the adoption of internal market measures in which public health protection is a decisive factor, provided the conditions for recourse to Article 100a are fulfilled.

The Court was careful to verify 'whether the distortion of competition which the measure purports to eliminate is appreciable', noting that '[in] the absence of such a requirement, the powers of the Community legislature would be practically unlimited'.[78] It thereby responded to one of the strongest criticisms of its *Titanium dioxide* ruling; in fact, however, the requirement that any distortion of competition be 'appreciable' before the Community could act had already been laid down by the Court in the *Detergents* case in 1980, and repeated in the *Titanium dioxide* judgment.

On the facts of the case, the first Tobacco Advertising Directive was held to be too sweeping in its scope as regards the ban it imposed on advertising, except as regards that in print media. Such distortions of competition as had been identified, for example national prohibitions on sponsorship which could lead to the relocation of events, were not such as to justify the comprehensive ban on sponsorship laid down in the Directive. The judgment, the first in which a measure of primary legislation had

---

[75] Case C-155/91 *Commission v Council* [1993] ECR I-939 and the *First Waste Regulation* (n 49 above).
[76] Case C-376/98 *Germany v Parliament and Council* [2000] ECR I-8419.
[77] ibid [45].   [78] ibid [106]–[107].

been struck down as *ultra vires* its legal basis, was taken to be an important signal to the Constitutional Courts of the Member States, as well as the Community institutions, that the Court of Justice could be trusted to police the boundaries of the Community's competences.

The institutions appear to have taken the Court's strictures on respecting the conditions for employing Article 100A EEC closely to heart. Subsequent judgments upheld recourse to Article 95 EC as the legal basis for rules on the manufacture, labelling, and marketing of tobacco products, a prohibition on the manufacture or sale of 'snus' (a form of moist snuff which is kept in the mouth for long periods), and a second, more targeted, ban on tobacco advertising.[79] Without significantly amending it, the Court added a few nuances to its interpretation of Article 95 EC, such as the requirement that it may be used 'only where it is actually and objectively apparent from the legal act that its purpose is to improve the conditions of the establishment and functioning of the internal market'.[80] Responding to the argument that individual provisions of a measure did not contribute to the functioning of the internal market, the Court noted that 'what matters is that the measure...must actually be intended to improve' these conditions, not that it do so in every imaginable situation.[81]

3. SCOPE OF PERMITTED MEASURES

A wide variety of measures may be adopted in pursuit of the proper functioning of the internal market. This includes, for example, 'horizontal' harmonization, *in casu* by a set of general safety requirements for consumer products, combined with a mechanism for the adoption of Community measures to protect consumers from identified risks arising from individual products.[82] Article 100a EEC/95 EC was also at the time the correct legal basis for the harmonization of national laws on intellectual property, and for the creation of a supplementary protection certificate to prolong the protection afforded by certain types of patents, though the Treaty of Lisbon introduced a specific legal basis for this latter area.[83]

More generally, the legislature enjoys 'a discretion, depending on the general context and specific circumstances of the matter to be harmonized, as regards the harmonization technique most appropriate for achieving the desired result, in particular in fields which are characterised by complex technical features'. Thus, the

---

[79] Case C-491/01 *British American Tobacco* [2002] ECR I-11453, Case C-210/03 *Swedish Match* [2004] ECR I-11893, and Case C-380/03 *Germany v Parliament and Council* [2006] ERC I-11573.

[80] Case C-66/04 *United Kingdom v Parliament and Council (Smoke flavourings)* [2005] ECR I-10553 [44]; the *Vodafone* case illustrates the type of evidence of a threat to the internal market the Court will accept as justifying recourse to this legal basis (Case C-58/08 *Ex parte Vodafone and Others*, judgment of 8 June 2010, [38–48]).

[81] C-380/03 (n 79 above) [80].

[82] Case C-359/92 *Germany v Council* [1994] ECR I-3681.

[83] Respectively Case C-479/04 *Laserdisken* [2006] ECR I-8089, Case C-350/92 *Spain v Council* [1995] ECR I-1985, and Art 118 TFEU.

legislature may proceed in stages, that is, by adopting a basic regulation or directive and conferring on the Commission the power to adopt further harmonizing provisions by way of implementing measures.[84] Equally, it may establish an agency 'responsible for contributing to the implementation of a process of harmonization... where the adoption of non-binding supporting and framework measures seems appropriate'.[85]

D. THE LAST CHANCE SALOON: 'NECESSARY AND PROPER' POWERS

1. ARTICLE 235 EEC AND ITS SUCCESSORS

The grant to the European Community of a series of discrete powers to regulate different areas of activity has always been complemented by the possibility of resorting to a 'fall-back provision', equivalent in function to the 'necessary and proper clause' of Article I, section 8, subsection 18, of the United States Constitution. Article 235 EEC, latterly Article 308 EC (hereinafter 'Article 235/308'), empowered the Council to act where the Treaty had not provided the necessary powers elsewhere.[86] As befits a legal basis of last resort, Council unanimity was required, while Parliament's participation in the adoption of such measures had, until the advent of the Treaty of Lisbon, always been limited to simple consultation. While the text of this provision remained unchanged from 1958 to 2009, its interpretation and application have evolved substantially, as a result of both Treaty revision and the Court's case law.

Recourse to Article 235/308 was subject to both a negative condition, in that the existence of other legal bases precluded its use, and a positive condition, in that the Council measure had to seek to attain a Community objective within the operation of the common market. The positive condition rarely gave rise to problems, as the term 'common market' in the original version of the Treaty was treated as being essentially synonymous with 'Community'. Under the guise of defining the Community's 'task' (sic), Article 2 EEC/EC provided a number of Community objectives drafted in very general terms, while Article 3 EEC/EC provided a convenient, though not exhaustive, list of the Community's 'activities'. The addition of new objectives through successive rounds of Treaty reform expanded the potential ambit of Article 235/308, and hence rendered it easier to satisfy the positive condition; at the same time, the addition of

---

[84] *Smoke flavourings* (n 80 above).

[85] Case C-217/04 *United Kingdom v Parliament and Council* [2006] ECR I-3771, [44]. On this and the previous case, see K Gutman, case note, (2006) 13 CJEL 147, and K Bradley, 'Smoke flavourings, information security and the interpretation of Art 95 EC: the double whammy that wasn't' in C Pennera and J Schoo, *Au service du droit communautaire—Liber amicorum en l'honneur de Gregorio Garzón Clariana* (Luxembourg, 2006) 44.

[86] See generally R Schütze, 'Organised Change towards an "Ever Closer Union": Art 308 EC and the Limits to the Community's Legislative Competence' (2003) 22 YEL 79.

new specific legal bases for existing or new Community activities reduced its scope of application by widening that of the negative condition.

Moreover, the outer limit of the Council's competences under Article 235/308 was coterminous in practice with that of the Community itself. If the legal basis of last resort was not available, the only alternative for adopting a binding act required that the Treaty be amended first.

2. THE APPLICATION OF ARTICLE 235/308: THE NEGATIVE CONDITION

In the dark days of Euro-diffidence, not to say pessimism, which followed the adoption of the Luxembourg Compromise and the occurrence of various economic crises in the succeeding decades, the prospect of formally revising the Treaty seemed as elusive and evanescent as the Holy Grail. At the time, Article 235 EEC was considered a sort of magic portal to widen the scope of the Community's activities. Cautiously used at first, for example in the run-up to the creation of the customs union between the Member States, the European Council (as it then wasn't) of 19 and 20 October 1972 invited the institutions to rely on this provision more freely, in order to move the Community beyond the sphere of economic activity and improve the lot of the citizen as such.

Reliance on Article 235 was challenged in the *Massey-Ferguson* case, where, as noted above, the Court ratified its use in circumstances where the negative condition was *a priori* not fulfilled.[87] It is more probable than not that the Council relied on this judgment to justify recourse to Article 235 EEC in wide areas of policy-making, for example, in refusing to consider the annual regulations applying the generalized system of tariff preferences for developing countries (GSP) to be a matter of commercial policy, despite the Court's wide interpretation of the relevant Treaty provisions.[88] The Commission challenged this practice in the *1986 GSP* case, the first significant annulment proceedings it had initiated since the *ERTA* case in 1970.[89]

If the legal question and (some of) the Treaty provisions at issue were essentially the same as those in the *Massey-Ferguson* case, the constitutional context in which the Court was deciding had changed utterly, thanks to the SEA. In a brief judgment, which makes no mention of the earlier case, the Court relied on 'the very wording[90] of Article 235' to hold that 'its use as a legal basis ... is justified only where no other provision of the Treaty gives the Community institutions the necessary power to adopt the measure in question'.[91] As the development policy objectives of the Regulations were well within the scope of the Community's commercial policy, the Council was not justified in basing the measures on Article 235 EEC.

---

[87] Case 8/73 (n 29 above) [4].   [88] See in particular Opinion 1/78 (n 28 above).
[89] Case 22/70 (n 24 above).
[90] In the studiedly neutral language of the Court of Justice, the notion that an institution should have ignored the 'very wording' of a Treaty provision might be read as a substitute for sharp criticism, though here it may also serve as a *mea culpa*. The descriptive 'irrelevant' on occasion disguises a certain judicial irritation too.
[91] Case 45/86 (n 33 above) [13].

The Court has regularly been called upon thereafter to enforce the negative condition of recourse to Article 235/308 at the behest of the Commission or the European Parliament. It annulled further customs measures in the *Customs nomenclature* and *Containers* cases.[92] On the other hand, it held Article 235 EEC to be the correct legal basis for a Regulation on cooperation between national administrations *inter se* and with the Commission as regards the application of customs and agricultural law.[93] The 'aim and specific content' of the Regulation was held to be the fight against fraud, and hence the protection of the Community's financial interests, rather than the functioning of the internal market.

In the *Students' residence* case, the Court held that a Directive laying down rules for the application of the Treaty prohibition of discrimination on grounds of nationality should be adopted on the basis of Article 7(2) EEC, rather than Article 235 EEC.[94] Recourse to this provision was also barred in the case of a 1994 Council Decision on the interoperability of telematic networks for the collection of trade statistics.[95] The Council's defence was again dismissed on the basis of the 'very wording' of the more specific Treaty Article which provided for the adoption of 'measures...to ensure the interoperability of networks'. For the record, the Court also rejected the Commission's contention that the correct legal basis was Article 100a EEC, on the basis of the more specific character of Article 129d EEC and the Directive's 'merely ancillary' effects on the internal market.[96] Article 308 EC was, however, held to be the correct legal basis for a measure which creates a new industrial property right or a new legal form of company.[97]

Where the scope of the Community's action exceeds that of the specific legal basis, however, the addition of a reference to Article 235/308 is justified. The *Erasmus* Decision was found to be correctly classified as a measure of professional training, except in so far as it applied to scientific research activities other than those carried out by universities.[98] More recently, the Court held that, because of the Community's limited input in the decision-making procedures of the International Fund for Ireland, it (the Community) could not guarantee that its contribution to the Fund would be applied only to activities within the Community's policy on economic and social cohesion.[99]

---

[92] Case 165/87 *Commission v Council* [1988] ECR 5545 and Case 275/87 *Commission v Council* [1989] ECR 259.

[93] Case C-209/97 *Commission v Council* [1999] ECR I-8067.

[94] Case C-295/90 *Parliament v Council* [1992] ECR I-4193; the UK is reported as supporting the Council, though a judgment on the interpretation of Art 7 EEC delivered just before the hearing in the *Students' residence* case prompted a unique Pauline conversion by the UK to Parliament's cause at the hearing.

[95] Case C-271/94 *Parliament v Council (Edicom)* [1996] ECR I-1689; see also Case C-22/96 *Parliament v Council (IDA)* [1998] ECR I-3231.

[96] The *Edicom* case (preceding n) [32]–[33].

[97] Opinion 1/94 *WTO accession* [1994] ECR I-5267 and Case C-436/03 *Parliament v Council (European cooperative society)* [2006] ECR I-3733.

[98] Case 242/87 (n 12 above).

[99] Case C-166/07 (n 42 above).

The Council was therefore entitled to add a reference to Article 308 EC to the legal basis of the Decision governing that contribution.

3. THE INTERPRETATION OF ARTICLE 235/308: THE POSITIVE CONDITION

The Court is charged with enforcing the positive, as well as the negative, condition on recourse to Article 235/308. There was a time when it was fashionable to cast doubt on the Court's willingness to strike down Community legislation as *ultra vires* the Treaty, and it is true that the Court has to this day never struck down a Council measure based on Article 235/308 on the ground of 'lack of competence'.[100] This state of affairs may be due as much to a lack of opportunity as a lack of will on the Court's part. Its Opinion on the proposed accession of the Community to the European Convention on Human Rights (ECHR) nonetheless indicates the outer limits of Article 235/308.[101] Though acknowledging that 'respect for fundamental rights is a condition of the lawfulness of Community acts', the Court held that '[no] Treaty provision confers on the Community institutions any general power to enact rules on human rights or conclude international conventions in this field'. Article 235 EEC was recognized as being available to 'fill the gap' in the absence of a specific power, but it 'cannot serve as a basis for widening the scope of Community powers beyond the general framework created by the provisions of the Treaty as a whole ... [or to] amend the Treaty'. The change in the system of fundamental rights which accession to the ECHR would entail was 'of constitutional significance' and therefore exceeded the scope of Article 235 EEC.

The appeal judgment in the *Kadi* case adds a somewhat ambivalent postscript to the interpretation of this provision. The Court of First Instance had held that a Regulation on the freezing of funds of persons associated with Usama bin Laden *et al* had been correctly based on Article 308 EC, along with the more specific legal bases for such restrictive measures, Articles 60 EC and 301 EC. The latter two provisions read together were insufficient *ratione personae*, being restricted to measures against individuals associated with the government of a third state. While agreeing as to the scope of these two Articles, the Court of Justice held that the addition of Article 308 EC with a view to combating terrorism and terrorist financing would allow the adoption of Community measures in pursuit of non-Community (here, foreign policy) objectives, and hence widen the scope of the Community's powers. However, Articles 60 EC and 301 EC were said to express 'an implicit underlying objective, namely, that of making it possible to adopt [restrictive] measures through the efficient use of a Community

---

[100] J H H Weiler is correct that in the *Migration policy* case (n 26 above) the Court did not rule that cultural cooperation was *ultra vires* the Treaty; though this specific point was not extensively canvassed in the article cited: 'The Transformation of Europe' (1991) 100 Yale LJ 2403, 2448 fn 123. Ironically, a number of acts of the European Parliament have been annulled on this ground (see eg Case 294/83 *Les Verts v Parliament* [1986] ECR 1339).

[101] Opinion 2/94 [1996] ECR I-1759.

instrument', which was a Community objective for the purposes of Article 308 EC.[102] This much narrower objective justified the Council's choice of legal basis, while the impact of the restrictive measures on capital movements offered the necessary link to the operation of the common market.

4. LISBON PERSPECTIVES

The TFEU retains, at Article 352, the so-called 'flexibility clause', though the burdensome procedural requirements it fixes presage little flexibility as to its use. Council unanimity is maintained, Parliament's consent will be required, and the Commission is obliged to draw the attention of national parliaments to proposals based on this Article, lest they fail to apply the usual subsidiarity scrutiny. No harmonizing measure may be adopted on the basis of Article 352 TFEU where such harmonization is excluded elsewhere in the Treaties, that is, in the areas of vocational training policy, the flowering of cultures, and public health protection.[103] On the ground that Union action must now be necessary 'within the framework of the [Union's] policies' (excepting foreign policy), rather than pursuing a Community objective, the German *Bundesverfassungsgericht* has interpreted Article 352 TFEU as a relaxation of the principle of conferred powers which 'makes it possible to substantially amend [the] Treaty foundations of the European Union without the mandatory participation of [the] legislative bodies' of the Member States.[104] Future recourse to this provision will therefore also depend on a green light from the *Bundesrat* and *Bundestag*. The new formulation should, however, call off the chase for 'implicit underlying objectives' which might have resulted from the *Kadi* ruling.

E. CONCLUSIONS: THE JUDICIAL PROVINCE

In its legal basis case law, the Court performs two of the principal functions of a Constitutional Court in a federal-type polity, defining the division of powers between the centre and the component states, and regulating the balance of powers between the institutions or branches of government.[105] The seemingly technical, procedural context in which such disputes arise shields the Court to a certain extent from accusations of imposing a *gouvernement des juges* which plague Constitutional Courts from time to time.[106] Moreover, given the relatively open-ended character of the enabling

---

[102] Joined Cases C-402/05 P and C-415/05 P (n 51 above) [226].

[103] Arts 166(4) TFEU, 167(5), first indent, TFEU, and 168(5) TFEU.

[104] Judgment of the Second Senate of 30 June 2009, preliminary (English) version [327]–[328].

[105] Despite the passage of time, K Lenaerts, *Le juge et la constitution aux Etats-unis d'Amérique et dans l'ordre juridique européen* (Bruylant, 1988) is still well worth reading in this context. On the other hand, it is difficult to subscribe to the conception of the Court of Justice as an administrative court propagated so robustly by P Lindseth (see eg 'Democratic legitimacy and the administrative character of supranationalism: the example of the European Community' (1999) 99 Colum L Rev 628).

[106] Roosevelt's 'court packing' plan remains the paradigmatic extreme reaction to judicial decisions in a democracy; to the eternal credit of the US political system, the plan failed.

provisions of the Treaties, particularly the functional legal bases, the question of the Community/Union's power to act is rarely the stark matter of 'yes' or 'no', but 'who', 'how', and 'how much'?

The case law is 'constitutional' in a third sense, in that it has probed the limits of the Court's own jurisdiction, as regards the categories of legal acts it may review,[107] and the *locus standi* of those directly concerned by legal basis matters, especially the European Parliament.[108] The Court first explicitly compared the EEC Treaty to a 'constitution' in ruling on whether there was any legal basis for Parliament to disburse electoral campaign funding.[109] Over the objections of certain Member States, the Court has opened up the Opinion procedure under Article [218(11) TFEU] to legal basis questions,[110] and acknowledged in legal basis litigation that institutions may rely on a plea of illegality.[111] It even extended its power to preserve the legal effects of an act which has been annulled, which was at the time *prima facie* restricted to those of regulations, to those of directives and decisions annulled on grounds of a faulty legal basis.[112] In each case, the Court has risen to the challenge, in pursuit of its general duty under the Treaty 'to ensure . . . the law is observed',[113] which it interprets in effect as an injunction to avoid a denial of justice. Moreover, in the best functionalist tradition, the legal basis case law has on occasion spilt over to other areas of institutional law. The Court's finding in the *Hormones* case that the procedural rules by which the institutions take their decisions 'are not at the disposal of the Member States or of the institutions themselves'[114] has since been applied to decision-making generally.[115]

As befits a body of constitutional law, the Court has by and large been very consistent in its interpretation of the various legal bases in the post-SEA epoch. Differences in its judgments which some consider reflect 'confused reasoning' on its part, and the institutions' 'illogical and apparently random basis for the use of different kinds of procedure within different policy spheres',[116] are therefore usually a function of the material differences between the legislative acts at issue, rather than a volte-face by the Court in its understanding of the relevant Treaty articles. Thus the overwhelmingly environmental character of the *Waste Directive* explains why the Court reached a different result to that in the *Titanium dioxide* case two years before.[117] Equally, the

---

[107] See eg the *ERTA* and *Small arms* cases (nn 24 and 47 above).

[108] Actions by Parliament, see Case C-70/88 *Parliament v Council (EP Chernobyl)*—admissibility [1990] ECR I-2041; actions against Parliament, see Case 294/83 *Les Verts v Parliament* [1986] ECR 1339.

[109] *Les Verts* (n 108) [23].

[110] *Cartagena Protocol* (n 2 above).

[111] The *Small arms* case (n 47 above) [34], and see now Art 277 TFEU.

[112] See respectively the *Students' residence* case (n 94 above) [24] and Case C-360/93 *Parliament v Council (EC-US public procurement)* [1996] ECR I-1196, [35].

[113] Traditionally Art 164 EEC, latterly Art 220 EC; see now Art 19(1) para 1, 2nd sentence, TEU.

[114] *Hormones* case (n 36 above) [38].

[115] Case C-133/06 *Parliament v Council (Refugee reception procedure)* [2008] ECR I-3189, [54].

[116] G de Búrca, 'The institutional development of the EU: a Constitutional Analysis' in P Craig and G de Búrca (eds), *The Evolution of EU Law* (Oxford University Press, 1999) 55, 66.

[117] It is no accident that Parliament did not use its new-won *locus standi* before the Court to challenge the Waste Directive (n 4 above), but merely intervened to provide moral support for what looked like, and was, a lost cause.

institutions' choice of legal basis, if not always correct, is anything but 'random' or 'arbitrary'; the matter is examined attentively by each of the political institutions in turn before the act is adopted.[118] The number of acts whose legal basis give rise to litigation is but a tiny proportion of the total number of acts adopted; such disputes usually reflect considered differences of view on the interpretation of legal provisions, or on the content of legal acts, which are inevitable in any system for the institutional representation of interests.

In this regard, the interesting suggestion that the Member States and the European Parliament pursue anything so rational as a 'strategy' in regard to legal basis litigation remains unproven at best.[119] In the first place, the consistent pursuit of such a strategy would prove disruptive of the spirit of cooperation which generally informs relations between the political actors of the Union. Moreover, for the most part, Member States challenge Community acts they object to for policy rather than strategic reasons, using the legal basis argument as just another weapon; thus, for example, the first Hormones Directive came to grief, not on the choice of legal basis, but because the Council had failed to respect its own rules of procedure.[120] That said, the United Kingdom's twin actions in the *Smoke flavourings* and *ENISA* cases,[121] which raised in different forms the question of principle of what type of measures could be adopted by way of internal market harmonization, may be an exception disclosing the existence of a strategy, while a number of Member States appear to follow a strategy for ensuring that the Commission stays closely within the confines of its autonomous legislative powers.[122]

The European Parliament, on the other hand, tends to take annulment proceedings on a case by case basis for the same reason as individuals go to court, to pursue a claim to what it considers rightfully belongs to it—here, the application of a particular procedure. Contrary to popular belief, it is not particularly litigious; the number of annulment proceedings it has commenced in this area works out at less than one per year. Parliament has thus accepted, for political reasons, infinitely more measures with legal bases to which it objects than it has contested before the Court. One commentator has opined that the European Parliament chooses the legal basis in function of its institutional interests.[123] This comment rather overlooks the fact that, unlike both the Council and the Commission, Parliament does not adopt legislative acts on its own, and it may legitimately disagree with the other institutions on matters of legal interpretation, just as the other institutions may disagree with it.[124]

---

[118] See eg Rule 37 of the European Parliament's rules of procedure. Strangely, the Commission often fails properly to explain its choice of legal basis when submitting its legislative proposals.

[119] Cullen and Charlesworth (n 3 above).

[120] Case 68/86 (n 36 above).

[121] Cases C-66/04 and C-217/04 respectively (nn 80 and 85 above).

[122] See n 9 above.

[123] J P Jacqué, *Droit institutionnel de l'Union européenne* (3rd edn, Dalloz, 2004) 394. The intended slight was based on the personal opinion of a single MEP in a single parliamentary report; moreover, in this particular case, Parliament did not, in fact, challenge the Council's choice of legal basis.

[124] See also the text to nn 36, 37, and 95 above.

Perhaps the most controversial aspect of this case law[125] is the Court's consistently extensive interpretation of the enabling provisions of the Treaty. While the 'heroic' vision of the Court and its role in the constitutionalization of the Community/Union may have fallen out of favour in recent times,[126] the Court has held remarkably steady in attributing as *utile* an *effet* as possible to such provisions, presumably inspired by the dynamic character of the integration project reflected so eloquently in the preambles to the successive founding Treaties.

As the ultimate arbiter of the interpretation of those Treaties, however, the Court is also charged with enforcing the boundaries of the Union's powers; should it fail to do so with sufficient vigour, there is a clear and present danger that one or other national Constitutional Court will attempt to do so.[127] The Lisbon Treaty may also allow national parliaments and the Committee of the Regions in on the act. While their powers under the second Protocol are formally limited to ensuring respect for the principle of subsidiarity, the exercise of such powers may prompt a wider interest amongst the parliaments in other aspects of the application of the Union Constitution, including the choice of legal basis.[128]

When the Community was perceived as weak, facilitating the exercise of its powers may have seemed more important than enforcing their limits. The Court appears to have been on occasion excessively tender in this regard, notably as regards recourse to Article 235/308. In retrospect, its judgment in *Massey-Ferguson* was worse than result-oriented jurisprudence, it was a mistake. Not only did it pave the way for certain profligate legislative practices of the institutions, but it undermined the position of the Commission vis-à-vis the Council, and was taken as indicating to all concerned that the Court was not willing seriously to enforce one of the few legal limits on the Council's powers. The Court's thinking in this regard only evolved after the SEA had already come into force. Some two and a half rounds of Treaty reform later, the ill-fated first Directive on tobacco advertising gave the Court the opportunity to send a strong signal to the Member States and their national parliaments that it would enforce the limits of the internal market too.[129]

---

[125] Though the Court's interpretation of legislative acts, such as those at issue in the *Mangold* and *Metock* cases, often generates even more political heat (respectively Case C-144/04 [2005] ECR I-9981 and Case C-127/08 [2008] ECR I-624).

[126] J Hunt and J Shaw, 'Fairy tale of Luxembourg? Reflections on Law and Legal Scholarship in European Integration' in D Phinnemore and A Warleigh-Lack (eds), *Reflections on European Integration—50 Years of the Treaty of Rome* (Palgrave MacMillan, 2009) 93, 96. The question is a large one, well beyond the scope of the present chapter; see especially Weiler (n 100 above).

[127] On 2 March 2010, the German *Bundesverfassungsgericht* struck down the national measures transposing the Community Data Retention Directive, without commenting on the validity of the Directive as some had expected (joined cases BvR 256/08, 1 BvR 263/08, and 1 BvR 586/08; see also Case C-301/06 *Ireland v Parliament and Council* [2009] ECR I-593).

[128] Protocol (No 2) on the application of the principles of subsidiarity and proportionality, Art 8. In initiating proceedings under this provision, the governments are in no way limited to subsidiarity issues, and could raise legal basis matters, as did for example, the *Biotechnological Patents* case, which was taken at the behest of the Netherlands Parliament, Case C-377/98 *Netherlands v Parliament and Council* [2001] ECR I-7079, [4].

[129] Case C-376/98 (n 76 above).

But do the Court's legal basis judgments make any difference in practice? In certain circumstances, they clearly do; the addition of the then common market legal basis would simply have doomed the Hormones Directive,[130] while the only (possibly) viable alternative legal basis for the first tobacco advertising Directive would have required unanimity and would presumably have encountered a German veto. Equally, the rejection of Article 235 EEC as a legal basis blocked the Community's accession to the ECHR under the EC Treaty, and, incidentally, allowed opponents to impose extra obstacles to accession under the Lisbon Treaty regime, in compensation for creating both the power to accede and a *prima facie* obligation on the Union to do so.[131]

In other cases, the difference in content is barely visible to the naked eye. The 1993 Directive on the right of residence for students, for example, was not significantly different from that which it replaced;[132] on the other hand, this was the first legislative measure which sought to enforce the Treaty prohibition on discrimination on grounds of nationality,[133] and it has in turn been followed by, or perhaps even inspired, the inclusion in the Treaty of a new legal basis for legislation to prohibit discrimination on a variety of other grounds.[134] Equally, while the Directive on environmental sanctions is largely similar to the Framework Decision which was famously annulled,[135] the replacement Directive is a Community law measure subject to the entire panoply of provisions on judicial review, particularly as regards infringement proceedings, from which the Framework Decision was immune. More ambivalent is the tobacco advertising/products saga; the first judgment seems merely to have encouraged the institutions to redouble their efforts, especially as regards providing a plausible statement of reasons for the subsequent measures which have all survived legal challenge.[136]

Be that as it may, our Clapham passenger, now well informed of the Court's sterling service in the cause of procedural propriety, may be wondering why no acts of the Community legislature have ever been ruled *ultra vires* the Treaty. Surely in half a century the Council, or Parliament and the Council, must have overstepped the mark on at least a few occasions? Has the Court of Justice abdicated all responsibility in this regard, as the United States Supreme Court has been accused of doing in different periods of its history, or do the judicial safeguards of the Member States' competence simply not work?

The answer may lie in the Union's system of governance. Unlike those of the States of the Union in the United States of America, the governments of Member States participate fully, systematically, and directly in the Union's legislative process. It is not 'Brussels' which tells the national governments what to do, but the national

---

[130] And thereby saved the Community a great deal of WTO litigation; the *Hormones* case (n 36 above).

[131] Art 218(8), second sub-para, TFEU.

[132] Directives 93/96 [1996] OJ L371/59 and 90/366 [1990] OJ L180/30.

[133] S O'Leary, note on the *Students' residence* case, 30 CML Rev 639, 647.

[134] Latterly Art 13 EC; see now Art 19 TFEU.

[135] Directive 2008/99 [2008] OJ L328/28, Framework Decision 2003/80 [2003] OJ L29/55, and the *Environmental sanctions* case (n 27 above).

[136] See n 79 above.

governments which, along with the Commission and Parliament, make up 'Brussels'. In this regard, the wonder is less that the Court struck down the first Tobacco Advertising Directive, but that the Directive was adopted at all. In other words, not only did the Member States institute a system of 'political safeguards of federalism',[137] but these have worked to the almost entire satisfaction of the national governments, with legal safeguards available for those governments (and, possibly, their parliaments) and Union institutions which are unhappy with the result.[138]

The wave of legal basis disputes which has washed up at the Court reflects the greater juridification of relations between the institutions *inter se* and between the Community/Union and its Member States. While normally such a development might not be considered an unmitigated blessing,[139] it may very well have a salutary effect in the context of the European Union. Acting in the shadow of the robe,[140] as it were, should make the institutions more conscious of the potential scope and the limits of their powers. Without bringing the Court too directly into the political arena, the legal basis case law has gone a long way to improving the rule of law across the entire gamut of European Union policy-making. In that regard, the Court's ruling on the eve of the SEA's coming into force that the choice of legal basis was a matter of legal appreciation and not political volition was a 'constitutional moment' in the history of the European Union.[141] It is reminiscent of such a moment long ago, when another court declared that '[the] powers of the legislature are defined and limited; and that those limits may not be mistaken, or forgotten, the constitution is written'; in such circumstances, '[it] is emphatically the province and duty of the judicial department to say what the law is'.[142]

---

[137] K St C Bradley, 'Umpiring the system: States' rights and legal basis litigation' in L Brown-John (ed), *Federal-Type Solutions and European Integration* (University Press of America, 1995); see also G Bermann, 'The Role of Law in the Functioning of Federal Systems' in K Nicolaïdis and R Howse (eds), *The Federal Vision* (Oxford University Press, 2001) 191.

[138] While the Commission and Parliament have each more or less broken even in their legal bases disputes with the Council, the Member States have been strikingly unsuccessful before the Court; even the *First Tobacco Advertising* case (n 76 above) did not prevent the valid adoption of a second tobacco advertising Directive.

[139] For a warning on the repercussions of judicial empowerment, see R Hirschl, *Towards Juristocracy* (Harvard University Press, 2007), though his thesis may not necessarily apply in the context of the European Union.

[140] Weiler has suggested that with the SEA the Community moved from the shadow of the veto to the shadow of the vote (n 100 above) 2461.

[141] Case 45/86 (n 33 above) [11].

[142] Marshall C J delivering the judgment of the US Supreme Court case of *Marbury v Madison* (1803) 1 Cranch 137.

5

INDEPENDENT AGENCIES

*Martin Shapiro**

A survey of the world's polities would indicate that the word independent in independent agencies is highly problematic. From political system to political system how independent they are from whom and by what means varies enormously. The one really common feature appears to be that they are administrative agencies placed outside the organization chart of any cabinet ministry and thus outside the normal executive chain of command. In polities that profess a constitutional separation of powers, they necessarily constitute an anomaly that is rationalized by some legal fiction or device that allows them some independence while placing them within one of the constitutionally recognized branches of government.

In the European Union the independent agencies are independent in the sense that they are not placed within any of the directorates general of the Commission, but, by an opinion of the European Court of Justice,[1] they are dependencies of and report to the Commission or for some the Council as a whole. Established by European Union statute, there are over thirty of them.[2] Leaving aside the European Bank, which is better treated as one of the species central bank rather than thrown in with other independent agencies, and is not considered here, typically these agencies have a single head usually appointed by its executive board on nomination by the Commission—the executive board typically consisting of one member nominated by each of the Member States and expert in the relevant fields of knowledge, and a Commission representative and staff of technical experts who are members of the European Union civil service.

The subject matter specializations of the agencies vary enormously from environmental statistics to veterinary pharmacology, policing, and rail operations. Some of the agencies are, or claim to be, engaged solely in information-gathering and dissemination, others in information functions plus soft or indirect or advisory regulatory functions, others yet in what amounts to EU-wide standard-setting for or licensing of products.

---

* James W and Isabel Coffroth Professor of Law at UC Berkeley School of Law.

[1] Cases 9 and 10/56 *Meroni v High Authority* [1957/58] ECR 133.

[2] In general see D Geradin, R Munoz, and N Petit (eds), *Regulation Through Agencies in the EU* (Edward Elgar, 2005). Three new financial agencies have recently been added.

They have not had rule-making or delegated legislation authority, that is the power to make general legally binding rules with the same force as provisions of statutory law.

Each of the agencies appears to be developing its own procedures, a few with rather elaborate hearing opportunities with or without internal appeal mechanisms. Most provide access to their documents. Provisions for interest group participation some-times exist even in agencies that claim to be only information-gathering and/or advisory to the Commission. While certain overall administrative norms, such as giving reasons and the duty of good administration may apply, a style of administra-tive law seems to be emerging in which each agency is subject to procedures peculiar to itself and provided by the legislation creating it plus those developed by its own practices over time plus any emerging from judicial review.[3]

There was a first proliferation of independent agencies in the early 1990s and another about a decade later. At least those created in the first period claimed to be purely staff agencies gathering, collating, and disseminating information, and/or merely serving as sites and providing staff resources for Member State representatives meeting to coordinate policies and methods of operation without policy-making powers and thus raising no problem of democratic political accountability. In an age in which the politics of information has become central, these claims were always a bit pro forma. Over time, moreover, a number of the agencies have become major sources of Union soft law, issuing model sets of rules, procedures, standards, best practices, guidance documents, and consensus reports of coordination meetings. Even their reports systematizing scientific or other technical findings may point so irresistibly to government policy change as to have clear policy-making significance. Some of the agencies, particularly those engaged with transportation matters, come close to full regulatory powers. Others issue European-wide marketing authorizations that amount to the creation of legally enforceable intellectual property rights comparable to patents or copyrights.

There has been a tendency to move agencies into a more regulatory role, most markedly in the Aviation Safety Agency which is one of the few agencies whose procedures provide for extensive participation by non-governmental parties similar to US 'notice and comment' rule-making. Its safety and environmental certification of aircraft engines and parts is effectively binding on the industry, but its rule-making is in the form of recommendations to the Commission and/or Member States.[4] Similarly although the marketing authorizations for drugs issued by the Medicines Agency (EMEA) are only submissions to the Commission, which in turn submits them to Comitology, the agency's decisions are invariably confirmed. The EU itself lists eight agencies as 'regulatory'.[5] Independent agencies have become significant players in EU

---

[3] P Strauss, 'Rulemaking in the Age of Globalization and Information: What America Can Learn From Europe, and Vice Versa' (2006) 12 CJEL 645, 684–685.

[4] J Pierre and B Peters, 'From a Club to a Bureaucracy: JAA, EASA and European Aviation Regulation' (2009) 16 JEPP 337.

[5] P Strauss (n 3 above) op cit.

regulatory policy-making and implementation. Thus they raise important issues as to the nature of their independence and its relation to legal and political accountability.

We can begin to address these issues by looking at the intentions behind the creation of the independent agencies. Some of the causes of independent agency proliferation lie in the dynamics of the EU itself. The original group of agencies such as the Environmental Agency and many of the later ones performed staff functions for the Commission, mostly generating statistical data. There is no obvious or inherent reason that these functions could not have been performed within the Commission directorates. There was, however, growing public resentment of Brussels and the Eurocracy. By creating independent agencies the Commission could increase its staff resources without increasing its bulk, and the agencies could be distributed among major European cities so as not to further magnify the Brussels profile. The direct supervisory burden of the individual DGs was alleviated, as was any suspicion that the Commission was massaging technical and scientific data to favour its policy and/or institutional interests. Moreover the new agencies could be structured with executive boards consisting of representatives of every Member State, much stronger Member State participation than could be engineered into the directorate structure of the Commission. So might be achieved a bigger, better, more legitimate Commission without its looking bigger and more centralized.

EU-centric explanations are not sufficient, however, because the proliferation of EU independent agencies comes at the same time as European-wide proliferation in the Member States and must be seen as part of that more general phenomenon.[6] The general proliferation of what are, after all, new governmental bureaucracies, is, paradoxically, the result of the general withdrawal of public trust in government bureaucracies. At the most general level is the massive collapse of socialist ideology of both the Soviet and democratic varieties. No one any longer believes that government is likely to run things well. Privatization and deregulation became major banners on both sides of the Atlantic. The new public management with emphasis on services to clients, transparency to and participation of the public, and non-hierarchical organization became central public administration teaching and sometimes even practice. Command and control regulation was downplayed in favour of negotiated, consensual regulation and generally bringing the market back in.

Nevertheless, regulation and a lot of other government business had to get done. The end of socialism did not mean the end of the welfare state. Freer markets were soon seen as requiring more regulation. If the old cabinet ministry bureaucracies were not to be trusted, but much government work still had to be done, then the only answer was the creation of new bureaucracies independent of the old ministries.

All of these developments are episodes in the long-running struggle over whether public administration should be separated from or is necessarily a part of politics, and

---

[6] M Thatcher, 'Regulation After Delegation: Independent Regulatory Agencies in Europe' (2002) 9 JEPP 954; C Pollitt and C Talbot (eds), *Unfunded Government: A Critical Analysis of the Global Trend to Agencies, Quangoes and Contractualization* (Routledge, 2003).

particularly, election-oriented, partisan, party politics. In Europe, once proud of its non-partisan, neutral civil services, displeasure with bureaucracy has led to the increasing politicization of the senior levels of ministry executives.[7] At the same time, the fear that the intrusion of partisan politics will distort, particularly the more technological aspects of government administration, leads to the creation of 'non-majoritarian' agencies independent in the sense that they are designed to be beyond the reach of the political parties.[8] Politicized ministries and independent agencies are poles in the tension between the union and disjunction of politics and administration.

The US development of independent agencies from the Interstate Commerce Commission of 1889 onward has been one of the paradigms for the independent agency movement elsewhere. The ICC was a product of an American movement called Progressivism that was democratic, populist, and capitalist but sought a technocratic public administration shielded from party politics. Without hope of entirely escaping party politics, the ICC was structured as a commission, a multi-headed agency that usually would have a balance of commissioners from each of the two major political parties. Indeed the statutes creating some of the later commissions required such a party balance. If party politics could not entirely be avoided at least its pernicious effects could be weakened by creating countervailing partisan influences.[9]

In the EU the politics that represents a threat to bureaucratic neutrality is not party politics but national politics, that is the pursuit of selfish Member State interests at the expense of Union well being. Here too, however, Member State influence could hardly be entirely escaped even if such an escape were wholeheartedly desired. The EU independent agencies are staffed and headed by technical experts of the EU civil service. Most, however, also have executive boards consisting of technical experts nominated by the Member States or at least allowing for the appointment of members from a number of states.

Thus the EU independent agencies are doubly paradoxical. They are a new formation of bureaucrats engendered by distrust of bureaucracy, and, although supposedly independent of Member States and dedicated to the general Union interest, they are provided with a greater degree of Member State control than they would have been if they were units within the Commission directorates. They are not independent of, but are dependents of and report to, the Commission. They are independent in the sense that they lie outside the directorate structure and thus each is independent of any particular directorate general (DG) but responsible to the Commission as a whole. Some of the agencies are dependencies of the Council rather than the Commission. In contrast to US independent agencies they have had no power to make general rules having the force of law nor may they submit proposals for new legislation to the Council as US agencies may to Congress.[10]

---

[7] E Suleiman, *Dismantling Democratic States* (Princeton University Press, 2005).

[8] G Majone, 'Nonmajoritarian Institutions and the Limits of Democratic Government: A Political Trans-action-Cost Approach' (2001) JITE 157.

[9] See R Cushman, *The Independent Regulatory Commissions* (Oxford University Press, 1941).

[10] Although US independent regulatory agencies may not submit proposed legislation directly to Congress, they can almost always find some friendly member of Congress to do so for them.

The independent agencies have an extremely wide variety of functions. Some, such as the Plant Variety Office, the Medicines Agency, and the Office for Harmonization of the Internal Market grant licences, EU-wide marketing authorizations, or other rulings that effectively endow individuals or enterprises with property-like rights. Typically the statutes creating these agencies specify rather elaborate hearing, appeal, and other procedures and provide easy access to judicial review. They also tend to provide more open channels of access to interested non-governmental parties than do most of the other agencies.

Some of the agencies such as the Educational, Audiovisual, and Cultural Executive and Euratom Supply agencies and Eurojust administer rather narrow programmes or grants. Often they appear to have been created to signify the importance of their programmes, protect them against possible neglect if they had been placed within the Commission, and/or insure the influence of particular interest communities. Among these are the Agency for Fundamental Rights and the Data Protection Supervisor.

Leaving these two groups of agencies aside, a composite picture of the functions of the agencies is possible. First and foremost the agencies serve as a meeting point for experts from the Member States, typically senior national ministry officials. Their meetings serve to coordinate Member State policies and practices often producing more or less formal consensus documents. Some of these documents, while not technically having the force of law, are effectively binding on the Member States. Among these are the rail scheduling of the Railway Agency and the certification of aircraft, engines, and parts of the Aviation Safety Agency. They represent perhaps the clearest instances of a consensus among Member State ministry representatives giving norms to the national ministries they represent which are then happy to obey the Union norms to which their representatives have already agreed.

Beyond such relatively detailed and effectively binding pronouncements, the agencies produce a wide variety of soft law instruments. Some of these are statements of best practices or technical standards or model regulations that also come quite close to generating universal Member State compliance to relatively detailed Union norms. Others are more general reports or guidelines that point to the need for Member State action and can be taken home to motivate such action. Some agency activities and publications simply provide channels for production and exchange of information with more or less pointed policy implications. The Agency for Safety and Health at Work, and the Monitoring Centre for Drugs and Drug Addiction are examples of this latter activity. The agencies may propose legislation to the Commission and some like the Maritime Safety Agency and Fisheries Control Agency are specifically tasked with overseeing compliance with existing Union legislation and proposing new legislation.

Many of the agencies strenuously deny that they are policy-makers as such and only a few have engaged in, or come close to engaging in, legally binding regulation à la the US regulatory commissions. Yet the bodies of information that the Environmental Agency and others construct and disseminate often have very pointed policy implications. The best practices that Member State ministry people as representatives to the agencies construct and then recommend to themselves as ministry rule-makers often come close to Union-wide rules. The coordination of Member State activities which the agencies provide often comes close to legal harmonization. The independent agencies certainly play a significant role in Union policy-making.

The flourishing of the independent agencies can be viewed in parallel to that of pre-Lisbon Comitology. Indeed, much of the work of many of the agencies is done by committees composed of members of the agency staff and Member State ministry experts. Like Comitology the agencies augment the resources provided to the Commission and the technocratic legitimacy of EU governance but at the cost to any claim of democratic legitimacy given the agencies' many steps away from any electoral connection. Like Comitology the agencies increase opportunities for participation in governance for those with the technical resources and specific motivation to participate, particularly national ministry people, and thus provide some alleviation of the federal tensions between centre and Member States. In common with independent regulatory agencies everywhere, the EU agencies with regulatory and/or quasi-regulatory powers provide an even greater and more accessible target for interest groups' influence than the committees.

Like the committees too, by adding another layer of complexity, and a peculiarly complex one in itself, the over thirty agencies render the governance of the EU even more non-transparent—perhaps the better word is incomprehensible—to the citizenry. Unlike the committees, however, the agencies do provide some transparency through continuity and specificity of institutional structure. At least those who take the trouble to do so can find out who they are, where they are, and something of what they are doing.

Also like the committees the agencies present an acute problem that may be seen as one of delegation or one of coordination. To the extent that the agencies are seen as merely the expansion of staff resources for Council and Commission outside the directorate structure, principal–agent problems are relatively minor, consisting of whether the agencies are pursuing the research and analysis priorities most in demand by the policy-making organs. The agencies that are charged with the assignment of property-like rights, however, pose the danger of creating a property regime, particularly in the realm of transnational intellectual property, at odds with the one that might have been desired by Council-Commission if Council-Commission ever got around to desiring a specific one. To the extent that most of the agencies now generate soft law, some or much of that soft law might be at odds with Council-Commission present or potential desires. The more these agencies serve as loci for the various national ministry staffs to build what they deem to be technically correct, consensus policies isolated from both Council-Commission and national cabinet control, the greater the problems become whether defined in terms of delegation, coordination, or democratic accountability.

It certainly may be argued that no delegation problem arises precisely because the agencies are supposed to be independent rather than delegates of the Council-Commission, and that little or no law-making power has been delegated to them. Again to the extent that the independence only guarantees politically undistorted data analysis, such non-agency may be desirable. To the extent that the independent agencies are making independent policies through soft law or otherwise, certainly problems of coordination arise, problems endemic to independent agencies everywhere. If government speaks with many independent voices, some of the many things said may contradict one another. The felt need for single voiced strong political executives that has been vigorously expressed in many nations on both sides of the Atlantic, and certainly by the Lisbon initiatives, is in grave tension with the independent agencies movement. The independent agencies may alleviate federalism tensions by facilitating consensus-building among Member State technocrats out of reach of their national political superiors, but this relief is bought at the expense of potential cacophony in EU policy-making itself.

The Environmental Agency does seek to coordinate environmental concerns across policy areas. It may be argued that the cross-policy coordination problems generated by the agencies are offset by the coordination within each particular policy area between Member States and between Member States and the EU achieved by the agency devoted to that area. Moreover insertion of the agencies' functions into the appropriate DGs would only achieve greater cross-policy area coordination if the Commission itself were relatively successful in coordinating the work of the various DGs. In recent years the Environmental Agency has moved cautiously into a more policy-making role.[11]

The accountability or democratic deficit problem is almost too obvious to require comment. Independent means non-accountable at least to or through other EU organs. The typical agency executive boards, constructed to provide some Member State control, are supposed to be composed of relevant experts. Is an executive board consisting of German, French, etc safety engineers likely to pursue German, French, etc national interests or the common interests of the safety engineering profession? To the extent that the executive boards render the staffs of the independent agencies accountable, that accountability is far less likely to be to the Member States or the citizenry as a whole than to the epistemic community to which both the board members and the staff belong. A tendency to move from Member State representation to representation of shared expert values is most notable in the European Medicines Agency.[12] There is not space available here to lay out the whole litany of professional deformation, but, if the agencies are truly independent, they surely raise the spectre of the citizens of Europe having to obey the rules of child psychologists in raising their children and those of dieticians at their dinner tables. I can offer no more frightening examples of technocratic governors independent of popular accountability.

The agencies are accountable for their financial management to the Court of Auditors and/or other internal and external auditing bodies. The Court of Justice has extended judicial review even to many of the agencies for which it is not provided

---

[11] A Zito, 'European Agencies as Agencies of Governance and EU Learning' (2009) 16 JEPP 1224.
[12] B Hauray and P Urfalino, 'Mutual Transformation and the Development of European Policy Spaces. The Case of Medicines Licensing' (2009) 16 JEPP 431.

specifically by statute. The Parliament receives agency reports and holds hearings. However, particularly if we are content to substitute the substantive correctness of experts for majoritarian decision-making, it would seem unwise to leave the agency's decisions free of oversight as to their substantive correctness. To some extent judges enforcing a giving reasons requirement will look to substance. If the reasons must be good ones, they must be substantively persuasive ones. Given their lack of substantive expertise, judges necessarily are reluctant to challenge agency substantive expertise. The management boards have the expertise for substantive oversight but their meetings are short and periodic and their members preoccupied with the national ministries and agencies that employ them. Except when their own national ox is being gored they may be paying little attention. The members of parliamentary committees holding agency oversight hearings are less expert and likely to be equally quiescent absent particular Member State concerns.

Ultimately pre-Lisbon Comitology and the independent agencies exhibit the same yin and yang. They were designed to inject a high level of technological expertise into the EU policy-making process. They were also designed to inject a high level of Member State input. Both employ the device of technical experts designated by the Member States but dedicated to objectively correct technical judgment. The product of this yin and yang can be imagined as a perfectly balanced outcome, the deliberative decision-making of Joerges and Vos,[13] or it may be seen as a perfectly unstable contradiction in which either the particular, selfish interests of Member States will prevail through collective log rolling or the values will prevail of the epistemic community to which belong the particular set of engaged experts. Given that the setting and discourse of these deciding bodies, their basic *raison d'être*, and the values shared by the participants and defining their own professional success are technical rather than national, the best guess is probably that shared technical values are likely to dominate particular national interests.

Lisbon has now transformed the Comitology process. That the transformation occurred appears to indicate a lack of confidence that committee yin yang yields best or deliberative outcomes. The independent agencies do not appear to have undergone a Lisbon transformation. In part this may be because they are involved largely in soft law-making rather than the hard law of delegated legislation. In part it may be that Member State ministry people have found them sufficiently hospitable to national viewpoints. In part it may simply be that their limited number and fixed institutional forms render them inherently more transparent and accountable than were the myriad committees of transient existence, membership, and meeting times and places. Nevertheless for the agencies, the yin and yang of technological definition, discourse, and professional legitimacy *and* Member State interjection remains. The agencies may provide a successful locus at which Member State ministry experts can hammer out mutually agreed policies that they then go home to cheerfully implement. Yet the democratic deficit problem still lurks because of the suspicion that the civil servants are

---

[13] C Joerges and E Vos, *EU Committees: Social Regulation, Law and Politics* (Hart, 1999).

achieving results through EU agency collaborations that they might not have been able to sell on their own to their democratically chosen political masters at home.

The continuing appeal of agencies is largely due to their embodiment of a style of governance that is thought to be peculiarly suitable to the EU, perhaps particularly during its expansionary phase. The agencies act as loci for EU favoured networks[14] of Member State ministry experts, largely networks of government personnel sharing an expertise but engaged in formally institutionalized relationships rather than networks in the sense of informal communication channels among non-governmental actors who share a body of interests or knowledge. Taken as a whole the agencies allow fairly high levels of transparency, some level of outside participation, and some judicial review but very far from US-style interest group aggressiveness in lobbying and litigation. The agencies engage mostly in coordination of Member State administrations through consensually built soft law of many different kinds and degrees of hardness but considerable regulatory bite in some instances. Given their relationships to the Commission and Council, they provide a compromise between horizontal coordination among Member States and vertical integration through Union organs. They provide a useful ambiguity in which is encompassed technocratic legitimacy of rule by experts, Member State guardianship of national interests, and dedication to the general interests of the Union.

It is noteworthy that the Lisbon Accords precipitate a major reform of the Comitology process and the formalization of delegation of limited and controlled subsidiary law-making powers to the Commission, but do not appear to initiate formal changes in the structure or function of the agencies nor explicitly provide for delegation of law-making powers to them. Thus it appears that agencies have hit about the right note for the current stage of EU development.

The recent creation of the European Energy Agency (EEA)[15] provides a window into the continuing, indeed increasing, enthusiasm for independent agencies among the shapers of Union institutions. The agency's central jurisdiction is oversight of electricity and natural gas transmission systems. It is assigned a full array of soft law capacities: non-binding reports, opinions, best practices, guidelines and so on. It is to serve as the focal, coordinating point for a network composed of the relevant Member State regulatory agencies. In a most dramatic evolution of the mix of vertical and horizontal integration that marks most of the agencies, the new Council-Parliament Regulation appears to require that the Member States maintain or establish their own *independent* regulatory agencies to participate in this network.

What the EEA is to be independent of is made very clear: of direction by Member State governments, the governing organs of the EU and the industry, its suppliers and consumers. Yet clear provisions are made for representation of the Commission and Parliament, and there are specific and strong provisions for transparency and

---

[14] R Dehousse, 'Regulation by Networks in the European Community: The Role of European Agencies' (1997) 4 JEPP 246.

[15] Parliament-Council Regulation 713/2009/EEC, [2009] OJ L221/1.

non-government actor participation. There are particularly strong 'giving reasons' requirements specifically including one requiring the agency to explain why it has *not* acted in accord with particular outside submission, an 'any person' right of internal appeal to an independent appeals board within the agency, and very generous judicial review provisions. All this is particularly interesting in light of the debate about how far Union courts have moved toward a very expansive or 'synoptic' giving reasons requirement and concerns over the spread to Europe of American style 'adversarial legalism'.[16]

The agency is charged with monitoring Member State compliance with the Energy Regulations, authorized to make some kinds of legally binding decisions on such matters as 'exemptions' from some Energy Regulation provisions, and to issue 'opinions' to the Commission and the Member State regulatory agencies and in some instances to the Council and Parliament identifying failures of various actors to comply with the Energy Regulations. In limited instances the Agency may decide on regulatory issues that normally fall within the authority of national regulators.

The Energy Agency has an administrative board composed of two members appointed by the Commission, two by Parliament, and five by the Council whose appointments are to assure balanced Member State participation over time. The appointment of the agency's director is the joint product of the Commission, the Administrative Board, and the Board of Regulators with some oversight by the Parliament. The director should be an energy expert. The agency is to have an expert staff part of which is to be comprised of Member State agency staff seconded to the agency.

The heart of the agency with lead responsibly for most of its tasks is a Board of Regulators comprised of a senior staff representative from each of the Member State regulatory authorities and a non-voting representative of the Commission. The Board acts only by a two-thirds vote, one vote per Member State. Thus the Energy Agency preserves the familiar tension between independent pursuit of the Union general interest, Member State interests, and technological expertise.

---

[16] M Shapiro, 'The Giving Reasons Requirement' in M Shapiro and A Stone Sweet, *On Law, Politics and Judicialization* (Oxford University Press, 2002); H Nehl, *Principles of Administrative Procedure in EC Law* (Hart, 1999); A de Noriega, *El Control de la Administracion Comunitaris a Traves de la Motivacion* (Aranzadi, 2005).

6

THE EUROPEAN COURT
OF JUSTICE

*Alec Stone Sweet**

The Court of Justice of the European Union (CJEU) is today one of the most powerful high courts in the world. Its impact on the overall course of European integration has been deep and pervasive, and its rulings have exerted decisive influence on streams of outcomes, great and small, in diverse policy sectors. Tellingly, scholars have produced more intensive, cumulative, and inter-disciplinary research on the CJEU than on any other judicial body in the world, with the exception of the United States Supreme Court. Rightly, readers of this volume can now take for granted the Court's centrality within a multitude of projects that together comprise the dominion of EU law.

Martin Shapiro, in the version of this chapter written for the first edition of *The Evolution of EU Law*,[1] did not presume the CJEU's political success. Instead, he sought to explain it, primarily in terms of functional logics of delegation and commitment. Shapiro also insisted that we seek to understand the evolution of the CJEU with reference to broader historical processes, in particular, the global diffusion of constitutional judicial review in the aftermath of World War II, and the dynamics of European integration under the Treaty of Rome. The present chapter develops these themes, building on Shapiro's insights. In Part A, I elaborate a simple model of judicial agency and constitutional trusteeship that applies to review courts, including the CJEU. In Parts B and C, I focus on the impact of the Court on the legal, market, and political European integration, and on EU governance more generally.[2]

* Leitner Professor of Law, Politics, and International Studies at Yale Law School.

[1] M Shapiro, 'The European Court of Justice' in P Craig and G de Búrca (eds), *The Evolution of EU Law* (Oxford University Press, 1999) 321.

[2] In this chapter I assume basic knowledge about the CJEU and how it operates, and do not attempt to provide a comprehensive overview of the CJEU's activities. The present author and Thomas Brunell have compiled comprehensive data sets on litigating EU law under Arts 226, 230, and 234, making them freely available at the website of the Robert Schuman Centre, the European University Institute: <http://www.eu-newgov.org/datalists/deliverables_detail.asp?Project_ID=26>. The most recent versions were published online in 2008, along with accompanying codebooks, statistical analyses, and notes on using the data in

A. CONSTITUTIONAL JUDICIAL REVIEW

Prior to World War II, only a handful of high courts in the world had ever exercised the power of constitutional judicial review: the authority of a court to invalidate statutes and other acts of public authority found to be in conflict with a constitution. In the 1950s, Europe began to emerge as the epicentre of a 'new constitutionalism', a model of democracy and state legitimacy that rejects the dogmas of legislative sovereignty, prioritizes fundamental rights, and requires a mechanism of defending the normative superiority of the higher law in the form of review. With successive waves of democratization, this new constitutionalism spread across the Continent and, by the 1990s, the template had diffused globally. Of 106 national constitutions written since 1985,[3] all contained a charter of rights[4] and all but five established a mode of rights review.[5] Over these same decades, three Treaty regimes (the EU, the European Convention on Human Rights [ECHR], and the World Trade Organization) steadily developed features of internal hierarchy, including increasingly robust systems of review.[6] Those who once claimed to possess sovereignty in their respective legal systems—national lawmakers and States—now govern with judges, in the shadow of constitutional review.

The global expansion of constitutional review both within and above the nation state raises a crucial question, one that Shapiro emphasized throughout his chapter. Why would political actors choose to confer constitutional review authority upon a court, thereby ceding their capacity to control policy outcomes thereafter? The answer, Shapiro argued, is that courts comprise commitment devices that actors need if they are to realize their objectives, given certain dilemmas of collective action and governance. The Constitutional Court, in particular, comprises an elegant functional solution to fierce problems of constitutional governance in a pluralistic political system, most of which are associated with incomplete contracting.[7] Downstream, a court's effectiveness will be heavily conditioned by institutional structure, notably, the court's terms of

various types of research. The website also provides an introduction to litigating EU law under Arts 226, 230, and 234, with commentary on relevant scholarship, A Stone Sweet, C Harlow, and T Brunell, 'Litigating the Treaty of Rome: The European Court of Justice and Arts 226, 230, and 234'.

[3] The source is the *Data Set on Written Constitutions, Rights, and Constitutional Review since 1789,* completed by the author and Christine Andersen in 2007 (on file with the author). Today, of the 194 countries in the state system, 190 have written constitutions, and only four (Bhutan, Israel, New Zealand, and the United Kingdom) do not have fully codified, entrenched constitutions. Since 1985, 114 constitutions have entered into force, many of which did not last; though we were unable to obtain text of nine of these.

[4] The last constitution to leave out a charter of rights was the racist 1983 Constitution of South Africa, Stone Sweet and Andersen (n 3 above).

[5] The five are North Korea, Vietnam, Saudi Arabia, Laos, and Iraq (in its 1990 constitution, now abrogated), Stone Sweet and Andersen (n 3 above).

[6] Not everyone agrees that these three organizations are constitutional regimes. For a defence of the position that the courts of these regimes are Constitutional Courts, see A Stone Sweet, 'Constitutionalism, Legal Pluralism, and International Regimes' (2009) 16 Ind J Global Legal Studies 621.

[7] A Stone Sweet, 'Constitutional Courts and Parliamentary Democracy' (2002) 25 WEP 77.

jurisdiction and the decision rules that govern reversal of its decisions. As the system begins to operate, what will become crucial is the degree to which non-judicial officials tolerate the court's intrusion on their rule, and the extent to which they adapt their decision-making to the constitutional law, as it evolves under the court's tutelage. For the Constitutional Court to thrive, officials must consider such intrusions to be, more often than not, a reasonable tax to pay for the realization of their constitutional goals. And they must be willing to reinvest in the system as it evolves. The development of constitutional judicial review, not least within the confines of the Treaty of Rome, is in large measure an unfolding of these dynamics.

1. FUNCTIONAL LOGICS OF DELEGATION AND COMMITMENT

Although Shapiro did not dwell on the niceties of delegation theory, also known as principal–agent theory, he relied on core tenets of the framework in his discussion of the functional logics of successful experiments in constitutional judicial review. Simple variants of delegation theory began to appear in EU studies only in the 1990s.[8] Today, no other framework is used more widely by social scientists engaged in research on the Commission and the Court.[9] For this reason, I provide a short summary of the basics.[10]

By definition, *principals* are those actors who create *agents*, through a formal act in which the former confers upon the latter some authority to govern. The agent governs in so far as delegated authority is exercised in ways that impinge upon the distribution of values and resources in the relevant domain of the agent's competence. By assumption, the principals are initially in control, since they have unconstrained discretion to constitute (or not to constitute) the agent. Since the principals have chosen to assume the costs of delegation—which include expenditures of resources to design and sustain a new institution, and to monitor its activities—it is assumed that the principals expect the benefits of delegation to outweigh costs, over time. Put simply, delegation takes place insofar as it is functional for ('in the interest of') the principals. From the standpoint of the EU Treaty system, the Member States are principals in the sense that they designed the system at various *ex ante* moments; they are also principals in

---

[8] G Garrett and B Weingast, 'Ideas, Interests and Institutions: Constructing the EC's Internal Market' in J Goldstein and R Keohane (eds), *Ideas and Foreign Policy: Beliefs, Institutions, and Political Change* (Cornell University Press, 1993) 173; M Pollack, 'Delegation, Agency and Agenda Setting in the European Community' (1997) 51 International Organization 99; A Stone Sweet and J Caporaso, 'From Free Trade to Supranational Polity: The European Court and Integration' in W Sandholtz and A Stone Sweet (eds), *European Integration and Supranational Governance* (Oxford University Press, 1998) 92.

[9] M Pollack, *The Engines of Integration: Delegation, Agency, and Agency Setting in the European Union* (Oxford University Press, 2003); A Stone Sweet, *The Judicial Construction of Europe* (Oxford University Press, 2004); J Tallberg, 'The Anatomy of Autonomy: An Institutional Account of Variation in Supranational Influence' (2000) 38 JCMS 843; J Tallberg, 'Delegation to Supranational Institutions: Why, How, and with What Consequences?' (2002) 25 WEP 23.

[10] For a critical introduction to delegation theory, as it relates to governance in Europe, see the special issue of *West European Politics* devoted to the topic; M Thatcher and A Stone Sweet (eds), 'The Politics of Delegation: Non-Majoritarian Institutions in Europe' (2002) 25 WEP 1.

an ongoing sense, since they have the capacity to constitute themselves as a collective body for the purposes of revising the Treaty law. The principals are those who possess *constituent* power, the competence to make and amend the constitution.

The most common rationales for delegation are also functional.[11] Among others, principals constitute agents in order to help them: (1) resolve commitment problems: as when the agent is expected to work to enhance the credibility of promises made either between principals, or between principals and their constituents; (2) overcome information asymmetries in technical areas of governance: wherein the agent is expected to possess, develop, and employ expertise in the resolution of disputes and the formation of policy in a given policy domain; (3) enhance the efficiency of law-making: as when principals expect the agent to adapt law to situations (eg to complete incomplete contracts); (4) avoid taking blame for unpopular policies: as when the principals command their agent to pursue objectives that they know will be unpopular with important societal actors and groups. It should be obvious how these (often overlapping) logics apply to delegation in the EU, especially to the Commission and the Court.

To explain the broad expansion in constitutional judicial review, Shapiro focused on the attractiveness of courts as agents with innate capacities to guarantee the credibility of the commitments negotiated by the principals.[12] Certain types of constitutional bargains, the argument goes, generate functional demands for third party dispute resolution and judicialized governance. Shapiro focused on three such bargains—establishing federalism, horizontal division of powers, and fundamental rights—each of which pertains directly to the EU experience.

The logic of pre-commitment, or self-binding, has always lurked behind arguments for constitutional review within federal arrangements. As Shapiro emphasized, federations are cartels and, as such, they are unstable. A major rationale for federalism has been to build larger and more open markets. In the classic scenario, states form a cartel to liberalize trade across borders, and the cartel adopts rules to prohibit protectionism and other forms of discrimination against trade. The resulting situation is typically modelled as a prisoner's dilemma. Each member of the cartel knows that it can obtain advantage by ignoring its obligations, so long as the other members abide by them. The expected outcome, of course, is that no cartel member will comply fully with the agreement, and free trade will be stifled. One tested means of redressing the situation is to build institutions, in this case, a mechanism to monitor and enforce the cartel's rules. Courts provide such a mechanism. Indeed, it may be that market integration across state borders is all but impossible without the deployment of courts as commitment devices, that is, in the absence of judicial governance.[13]

---

[11] M Thatcher and A Stone Sweet, 'Theory and Practice of Delegation to Non-Majoritarian Institutions' (2002) 25 WEP 1.

[12] Shapiro (n 1 above) 321–322.

[13] W Mattli, *The Logic of Regional Integration: Europe and Beyond* (Cambridge University Press, 1999). D North famously argued that courts are basic to sustaining long-range, impersonal exchange within the nation state as well, see *Institutions, Institutional Change, and Economic Performance* (Cambridge University Press, 1990).

Shapiro argued further that federal systems, once subjected to judicial discipline, would evolve in ways that would centralize power at the federal level. The result hinges partly on the extent to which the court performs its assigned role: the more effective is federalism review, the more regulatory authority will migrate to the federal level. In part, the outcome depends on dynamics within the federation itself. If the joint gains of cooperation are important enough, each member of the cartel will have an interest in ensuring that all the other members obey the rules of the federation; each member will support the Court's activities, while expecting to lose important cases on occasion. The logics of long-range reciprocity will strengthen the arrangement, by undercutting incentives for any state to cheat its partners, reducing interstate concern about relative gains and losses, and insulating the Court from reprisal. On this account, which neatly fits the EU experience, judicialized governance is not primarily legitimized by the initial act of delegation; rather, legitimation flows from the tangible benefits that accrue as market integration proceeds.

Constitutions that distribute law-making competences among differentiated organs of government also beg for an umpire. As Shapiro put it: 'Division of powers within government itself necessarily [means] boundary conflicts among the divided power-holders, and thus resort to a standard resource for conflict resolution, a court.'[14] The more power is divided horizontally, and then further delegated to new or pre-existing agents, the greater the demand will be for dispute resolution, boundary-maintenance, and agency supervision. The EU has long featured one of the more complex (not to say convoluted) systems of government in the world. The competences and relative powers of its law-making institutions have shifted, over time and across the terms of legal basis and policy domain, kaleidoscopically as it were. Not surprisingly, the Court has been heavily implicated in resolving conflicts among the Parliament, the Commission, and the Council of Ministers. It is also true that the EU relies heavily on delegated rule-making and implementation (not least to and by the Member States, thus bringing federalism back into the mix). This style of governance is particularly conducive to judicialization.

A third bargain, the inclusion of a charter of fundamental rights in the constitution, all but necessitates review. Shapiro has long considered rights jurisdiction to be more dangerous than advantageous to the prospects of a review court.[15] I have always disagreed. The new constitutionalism, with its heavy emphasis on rights and review, emerged in reaction to the horrors of the Holocaust, the destruction of World War II, and American occupation. The new Federal Republic of Germany had firmly committed to protecting fundamental rights at the highest possible level, while the prestige of political parties and legislative authority was relatively low. As authoritarian regimes collapsed in Southern Europe in the 1970s, and then across Central and Eastern Europe and the Balkans in the 1990s, that situation was reproduced in key respects, and the German approach to constitutionalism was copied and extended. During these

[14] Shapiro (n 1 above) 321–322.
[15] Nonetheless, the case of post-Communist European States gave him pause, Shapiro (note 1 above) 322.

latter episodes, those who drafted new constitutions saw no contradiction between democracy and rights protection. On the contrary, a robust system of rights protection was viewed as a pre-condition for democratic rule. Today, even after the consolidation of stable party systems, European citizenries continue to support Constitutional Courts—which they equate with rights protection—far more than legislatures. Where an ideology of fundamental rights has congealed as a kind of civic religion,[16] rights jurisdiction may ground the legitimacy of constitutional review. In any event, as noted, virtually no one writes a constitution today without providing for rights protection.

If a charter of rights is meant to have the normative force of law, if it is meant to be effective as a constraint on the exercise of public authority, then a system of constitutional judicial review is positively required—yet another functional claim. Moreover, contemporary rights provisions embody dilemmas of incomplete contracting; indeed, rights are paradigmatic examples of incomplete norms. A Constitutional Court solves these dilemmas, providing a stable mechanism for interpreting and enforcing rights, in light of context and changing circumstances.

2. INCOMPLETE CONTRACTS, DISCRETION, AND CONSTITUTIONAL TRUSTEESHIP

All contracts, including constitutions and treaties, are 'incomplete' to the extent that meaningful uncertainty exists as to the precise nature of the contract's terms. Due to the impossibility of negotiating specific rules for all possible contingencies, and given that, as time passes, conditions will change and the interests of the parties to the agreement will evolve, most agreements of any complexity are generated by what organizational economists call 'relational contracting.'. The parties to an agreement seek to broadly 'frame' their relationship, by agreeing on a set of basic 'goals and objectives,' fixing outer limits on acceptable behaviour, and establishing procedures for 'completing' the contract over time.[17]

As we have seen, certain forms of constitutional contracting—the establishment of federalism, division of powers, and rights—imply a review court. Indeed, the more acute are the problems of imperfect commitment and incomplete contracting, the more discretion the principals will need to delegate to the review court, if they are to reach their goals. Relational contracting—the reliance on relatively imprecise constitutional provisions to express important objectives—can help the principals reach agreement in the first place. Yet, in the context of review, textual imprecision, if it is not to paralyse the review court *ex post*, must be understood to comprise a tacit,

---

[16] In common law countries, too, one finds this civic religion, Canada and South Africa being prominent examples.

[17] P Milgrom and J Roberts, *Economics, Organization and Management* (Prentice-Hall International, 1992) 127–133.

second-order, form of delegation to the agent.[18] The decision rules that govern constitutional amendment are also built into the delegation of discretion to the court: the harder it is for the principals to nullify the effects of the court's rulings through constitutional amendment, 'the more power to the court.'[19] Most European constitutions are far more difficult to amend than statutes, especially when it comes to rights, reflecting the fact that constitutions are themselves commitment devices. It should be obvious how these concepts apply to the EU Treaty system.

These points can be formalized in terms of a theoretical *zone of discretion*—the strategic environment—in which any court operates.[20] This zone is determined by (a) the sum of powers delegated to a court, or possessed as a result of a court's own accreted rulemaking, minus (b) the sum of control instruments available for use by non-judicial authorities to shape (constrain) or annul (reverse) outcomes resulting from the court's performance of its delegated tasks. It follows that the capacity of the principals to control judicial outcomes is inversely proportional to the size of the court's zone of discretion. The CJEU, a trustee court *par excellence*, operates in an unusually permissive strategic environment. When it interprets the treaties, for instance, its zone of discretion is virtually unlimited.

We now encounter a theoretical tension that inheres in the principal-agent framework, if it is to be applied to most European systems of constitutional judicial review. Delegation theory was developed to explain why a principal would constitute an agent to govern in its stead. In the paradigmatic case, the legislature creates, through a statutory grant of discretion, an administrative agency to govern activity in a particular domain. The legislature could have chosen to govern on its own, without deploying the agent; and, as the principal, it can alter the mandate of, and even destroy, its creation at any moment. For its part, the agent governs pursuant to a legal instrument that the principal directly controls—a statute. A Constitutional Court is a type of agent, but a peculiar one. In Europe, those who wrote post-World War II constitutions—the political parties—did so in the name of a fictitious principal: the Sovereign People. Once new constitutions entered into force, Constitutional Courts would possess the authority to control the activities of these same political officials, in their guise as legislators. But, unlike the legislature whose control over the agency is absolute, the political parties do not control the Constitutional Court; instead, they are subject to the court's control.

In the EU, the Member States established the CJEU to help them govern themselves, in the face of acute commitment problems associated with market and political integration. The Court is the authoritative interpreter of EU law, not the Member States. The Member States are principals when they are assembled as a constituent assembly. At most other times, each Member State is a subject of EU law on its own; and each has locked itself into a system of review whose dynamics it cannot easily

---

[18] 'The more general the text, the more discretion to the interpreter', Shapiro (n 1 above) 323.
[19] Shapiro (n 1 above) 323.
[20] For an application to the CJEU, see A Stone Sweet (n 9 above) 7–9.

control, given the Court's zone of discretion. Further, in the EU, constituent power is not unified in a single actor, but is held by a multiplicity of governments who will exhibit divergent interests with regard to important policy issues on which the Court has taken a position.

Not surprisingly, some scholars[21] began to question the applicability of standard delegation theory to the politics of delegation in the EU, in particular. Majone proposed a model of 'Trusteeship' to replace that of generic 'agency' in situations in which those who have delegated review powers have transferred, for all practical purposes, the relevant 'political property rights' to the EU's organs.[22] In my view, as applied to the CJEU, the concept of trusteeship is appropriate in so far as three criteria are met: (a) the Court possesses the authority to review the legality of, and to annul, acts taken by the EU's organs of governance and by the Member States in domains governed by EU law; (b) the Court's jurisdiction, with regard to the Member States, is compulsory; and (c) it is difficult, or impossible as a practical matter, for the Member States, as principals, to 'punish' the Court, by restricting its jurisdiction, or reversing its rulings. In this account, the Member States, as high contracting parties, made the CJEU a trustee of the values and principles that inhere in the Treaties. Drawing out the metaphor further, when the Court exercises review authority, it discharges a 'fiduciary' responsibility in the name of a fictitious entity designated by Article 1 TEU: 'the Peoples of Europe'.

3. CONSTITUTIONAL LAW-MAKING AND JUDICIALIZED GOVERNANCE

Functional perspectives provide useful, probably indispensable, theoretical materials for addressing first-order issues of institutional design and maintenance. Yet when it comes to less abstract questions of how courts actually operate, purely functional perspectives have proven to be woefully inadequate. Review courts have choices in how they resolve boundary conflicts and protect rights. But delegation theory tells us next to nothing about the interpretive methodologies a court will employ, or the type of constitutional jurisprudence it will construct, when it makes these choices. In the same way, mapping a court's zone of discretion does not tell us what judges will actually do with their review powers, or how other power-holders will react. The basic problem is that, in a world of constitutional trusteeship, the reference points internal to delegation theory—the preferences of those who delegated to the court in the first place and the details of institutional design—do not constrain Constitutional Courts in predictable ways. For this reason, no sophisticated approach to the evolution of effective systems of review relies exclusively, or even mainly, on functional analysis. Instead, functional insights are developed, and then given empirical content through a blend of doctrinal exegesis (of the court's case law) and 'process tracing' (case studies

---

[21] G Majone, 'Two Logics of Delegation: Agency and Fiduciary Relations in EU Governance' (2001) 2 European Union Politics 103; Stone Sweet and Caporaso (n 9 above).

[22] Majone (n 21 above).

of the impact of the court's case law). Most of the ambitious scholarship on the CJEU produced over the past two decades, and most of the contributions to this volume, do the same.

The proper role of any abstract theory, in my view, is to help to organize, but not to displace, more fine grained analysis of the output and impact of review courts. There also exists a middle-range level of analysis, in which one engages the findings of prior research to derive theoretical propositions that will be applied to a new case. In his chapter, Shapiro used this style of theorizing to focus our attention on the political prospects of review in Europe.[23] The Constitutional Court will seek to make the constitutional law effective, through judicial review; but success will mean increasing the likelihood that other power-holders in the system will resent review as an incursion. Shapiro argued that successful review courts manage this tension through exploiting advantages in the judicial repertoire.

Shapiro identified what are, in effect, tools that courts can deploy strategically to maximize compliance and reduce political backlash. The first is the control of temporal dynamics: 'No matter what the formal procedural rules, judicial review courts can nearly always choose the time . . . tempo [and significance] of their case-by-case policy interventions so as to at least partially avoid, finesse, and obfuscate policy conflict with other politically powerful actors.'[24] Second, governance through case by case law-making is, by definition, incremental, which gives courts 'certain . . . survival and growth advantages'.[25] Incrementalism is less likely to produce radical policy change, meaning that the challenge to other power-holders, too, is incremental; it is less likely to produce bad policy; and it tends to mitigate losses to the losing party, forcing outcomes to a comfortable middle ground. Over time, of course, minor adjustments can add up to major changes. In so far as societal actors adapt to the court's rulings along the way, power-holders will find it costly to roll back the court's law-making. Third, constitutional judges manage their environments, prospectively, through the development of precedent-based argumentation frameworks,[26] what Europeans call jurisprudence, and Americans call doctrine.[27] The propagation of argumentation frameworks enables courts to reduce the 'noise' of chaotic environments, to enhance predictability and coherence, and to attract other power-holders into a discourse that judicial review creates, thus legitimizing it. These factors overlap one another causally: stable constitutional doctrine facilitates incremental law-making, for example.

Shapiro also stressed the fact that law tends to constitute its own relatively autonomous discursive domain. In mature legal systems:

---

[23] Shapiro (n 1 above) 324–327.

[24] Shapiro (n 1 above) 324.

[25] ibid 325.

[26] R Alexy (N MacCormick, trans), *A Theory of Legal Argumentation: The Theory of Rational Discourse as Theory of Legal Justification* (Clarendon, 1989). A Stone Sweet (no 9 above) 4–5, 32–41.

[27] As Shapiro emphasizes, precedent does not necessarily imply *stare decisis* (n 1 above) 325.

[judicial] policy-making is successful in part because it is disguised, protected, and furthered by a powerful, quasi-autonomous lawyer community with strong ideological and material interests in protecting the judiciary. Precisely because a constitutional court creates an esoteric language to which prestige, power, and money are attracted, it creates an epistemic community that must support it in order to cultivate its own professional, economic, and political success.[28]

In the EU, as Cohen and Vauchez have jointly shown,[29] a nascent epistemic community came first, helping to create the CJEU and then pushing it to 'constitutionalize' the Treaty system. In a situation of trusteeship, all of these factors may combine to drive the system forward. 'Successful review courts,' Shapiro argued, 'turn constitutions into constitutional law,' as they 'convert a text enacted at a given historical moment into a continuous, collective stream of case law. In this way, they turn a general political discourse into a specifically legal one in which judges and their fellow lawyers are the most authoritative speakers.'[30]

A potentially explosive problem lurks behind these considerations: Constitutional Courts cannot perform their assigned tasks without making law. They do so through interpreting the constitution, and then applying these interpretations to resolve disputes that come before it. Of crucial importance is the fact that that law-making effects are typically registered on two levels, *simultaneously*. In resolving a specific policy dispute within the constitutional law, review courts will inevitably help to make that policy; at the same time, they will construct the constitutional law, clarifying, supplementing, or amending it outright. However obvious, this fact turns out to be profoundly important to how constitutional regimes, and the EU, evolve. Power-holders and private litigants cannot access the benefits of the constitution or review, to resolve a *pre-existing* dispute, without activating the court's *prospective* law-making capacity. In a system of constitutional trusteeship, the court will usually have the last word on a specific policy dispute; and, in resolving that dispute, it will typically generate normative guidance for future law-making in that domain. In this way, constitutional case law, as it unfolds, creates the conditions for the judicialization of policy-making.

The concept of 'effectiveness' has thus far been invoked to ground expectations about the impact of systems of constitutional judicial review on the greater political system of which it is a part. One can define the concept more explicitly, through identifying the conditions that are necessary for a review court to be politically 'successful' (Shapiro's term), or for its case law to provoke a 'judicialization' (my term) of the regime and modes of governance. The first necessary condition: a judge

---

[28] Shapiro (n 1 above) 325.

[29] A Cohen, 'Constitutionalism without a Constitution: Transnational Elites between Political Mobilization and Legal Expertise in the Making of a Constitution for Europe (1940s–1960s)' (2007) 32 Law & Social Inquiry 109; A Vauchez, 'How to Become a Transnational Elite: Lawyers' Politics at the Genesis of the European Communities (1950–1970)' in H Patersen, AL Kjaer, and H Krunke (eds), *Paradoxes of European Legal Integration* (Ashgate, 2008) 129.

[30] Shapiro (n 1 above) 326.

must have a case load. If actors, private and public, conspire not to activate review, judges will accrete no influence over the polity. Second, once activated, judges must resolve these disputes and give defensible reasons for their decisions. If they do, one output of judging will be the production of a case law, a formal record of how the law has been interpreted and applied. The third condition is that a minimally robust conception of precedent must develop within the system. Effectiveness varies across systems, and across time and policy domain within any given system, partly as a function of how, and to what extent, these conditions are fulfilled, in context. Constitutional Courts do not activate themselves, but must rely on those who would litigate; and they do not directly control how their decisions will be implemented. The implication is that effectiveness cannot be taken for granted. Instead, it can only be socially constructed, through interactions between the Constitutional Courts, litigants, and the other power-holders in the system. Those who are governed by the law must accept that legal meanings are (at least partly) constructed through judicial interpretation and law-making, and use or refer to relevant case law in their future decision-making.

B. THE COURT AND INTEGRATION

This section focuses on the *impact* of the CJEU and the legal system on (1) the scope of judicial authority within the EU, (2) market and political integration, and (3) discrete policy processes and outcomes. In the first edition of *The Evolution of EU Law*, Shapiro paid great attention to the relationship between the CJEU, as it steadily consolidated its status as a trustee court, and Member State governments, infirmed by their incapacity to react with unanimity.[31] In such a system, the Court's most audacious rulings would stick, giving them a chance to develop a jurisprudential life of their own, especially when supported by the Commission and powerful private actors pushing for more integration. The result was that legal system began to evolve along paths that could not be predicted from the constellation of Member State preferences at any given time. Since the early 1990s, a great deal of theory-driven research on the CJEU and its impact has been produced. I will focus here on those findings that are most relevant to these themes.

1. CONSTITUTIONALIZATION AND ITS EFFECTS

As a trustee court, the CJEU possesses the inherent capacity to alter the constitutional 'rules of the game' under which all other organs of governance, including the Member States, the EU's legislative institutions, and the courts interact. A trustee court also has the power to expand its own zone of discretion. The European Court has done so on a regular basis, with an eye toward enhancing the effectiveness of EU law and of judicial

[31] Shapiro (n 1 above) 329–331.

review. Most important, in announcing the doctrines of supremacy, direct effect, state liability, and related rules and principles,[32] the Court provoked processes that would famously 'transform' the Treaty of Rome,[33] 'constitutionalizing'[34] the regime in all but name. There may be good reasons to reject the 'constitutional' label and rhetoric. Nonetheless, it is indisputable that these doctrines, once institutionalized, radically expanded the Court's own zone of discretion and reconstituted the EU as a quasi-federal legal system, comparable to other federal systems.[35]

The 'constitutionalization' of the Treaty system is the single most coherent 'grand narrative' in the scholarly literature on European integration. Assuming that most readers will be familiar with the basics, a brief summary of the most important outcomes of this process will suffice.

The Treaty of Rome originally contained no supremacy clause, and the Member States did not provide for the direct effect of Treaty provisions or directives. The CJEU, in collaboration with national judges, secured both, rewriting the Treaty in fundamental ways. As a result, Article 267 TFEU developed into a decentralized mechanism for enforcing EU law; it connected those private actors with a stake in promoting integration and the development of European law to the CJEU, through the national courts; private litigants and national judges then generated a steady stream of cases alleging Member State non-compliance, which the Court used to construct a sophisticated, self-sustaining, jurisprudence. These developments comprise one of the most remarkable cases of systemic judicialization—through doctrinal innovation—on record, in that it steadily enhanced judicial authority vis-à-vis all other law-making organs. Once constructed as a kind of central nervous system for supranational, and multi-level, governance, the legal system also sustained an ongoing judicialization of policy-making within many important domains. The Court's rulings routinely required the Member States and the EU's legislative organs to produce new law which, in turn, generated more opportunities for individuals (under Article 267 TFEU) or the Commission (under Article 258 TFEU) to litigate anew, not least, in order to develop the legal system further. For their part, Member State governments did not re-contract their relationship with the Court although, in theory, they could have done so. Instead they adapted, if at times only grudgingly, ratifying the transformation over time.

In tracing the effects of supremacy, direct effect, and related doctrines on the national courts, one observes another set of outcomes, not all of which are coherent with one another. Legal integration, a federalizing process, steadily proceeded as courts across the EU accepted these doctrines, albeit on their own constitutional terms.[36] Supremacy required that judges refuse to apply those legal norms, including statutes,

---

[32] For a summary of the 'constitutional' doctrines announced by the CJEU, see Stone Sweet (n 9 above) 64–71.

[33] J Weiler, 'The Transformation of Europe' (1991) 100 Yale LJ 2403.

[34] E Stein, 'Lawyers, Judges, and the Making of a Transnational Constitution' (1981) 75 AJIL 1; F Mancini, 'The Making of a Constitution for Europe' (1989) 26 CML Rev 595.

[35] K Lenaerts, 'Constitutionalism and the Many Faces of Federalism' (1990) 38 AJCL 205.

[36] A-M Slaughter, A Stone Sweet, and J Weiler (eds), *The European Court and the National Courts— Doctrine and Jurisprudence: Legal Change in its Social Context* (Hart, 2008).

found to be in conflict with European norms. In embracing the doctrine, the courts in many national systems acquired new powers of judicial review, authority that had previously been denied them under national constitutional law. For its part, the CJEU acquired a steady caseload, which made it possible for the Court to give EU law a relevance to individuals, firms, and groups that it would not otherwise have had.

Although the process of legal integration was driven forward, in part, by inter-judicial cooperation and symbiotic empowerment, it has also been rife with friction. The CJEU does not sit at the apex of a unified system, yet the Court's commitment to promoting the effectiveness of EU law, within national legal orders, inevitably led it to behave as a federal supreme court. Further, the diffusion of judicial review threatened the position of national constitutional judges, who saw their capacities to control developments eroding. Some of the most important achievements of legal integration, including the progressive construction of a charter of rights for the EU, are rooted not in cooperation but in authority conflicts between the ECJ and national Constitutional Courts.[37] This 'jurisprudence of constitutional conflict',[38] an unintended consequence of the Court's supremacy doctrine, has become a permanent feature of the system.

2. THE DYNAMICS OF EUROPEAN INTEGRATION

In this section,[39] I discuss scholarship that purports to provide a holistic, macro-institutional account of the impact of constitutionalization on European integration. Since the early 1990s, with the appearance of seminal papers by Weiler, Garrett, and Burley and Mattli, scholars have sought to provide such accounts. More systematic data collection and research, aimed at developing and testing causal theory, subsequently appeared. Before reviewing this literature, several caveats are in order. As this volume demonstrates, there is no single dynamic to the evolution of EU law. Rather, there are multiple logics, driving differentiated processes that intersect in fluid, multi-dimensional ways. The most ambitious scholarship has given some theoretical order to this complexity, by seeking to explain a small number of important outcomes, rather than everything of importance. Here I give pride of place to such theory, and to the findings of those who have sought to test causal propositions derivable from it. My purpose is not to champion the methods and priorities of social science but, rather, to ground a discussion of how the legal system has evolved and operates.

Weiler's 'The Transformation of Europe' is, arguably, the most influential paper ever published in the field. It standardized the constitutionalization narrative, providing a subtle presentation of the Court's jurisprudence during the 'foundational' period; and it showed how the CJEU's (often conflictual) interactions with national judges subsequently served to allocate authority between the supranational and national legal

---

[37] A Stone Sweet, *The Judicial Construction of Europe* (Oxford University Press, 2004) 81–96.

[38] M Kumm, 'The Jurisprudence of Constitutional Conflict: Constitutional Supremacy in Europe before and after the Constitutional Treaty' (2005) 11 ELJ 262.

[39] This section is partly based on A Stone Sweet, 'Judicialization and EU Governance' in *Living Reviews in EU Governance* (forthcoming).

orders, while enhancing judicial power on both levels. Weiler also reflected normatively upon the steady expansion of the scope of the Community's jurisdiction. For
present purposes, the paper's most important contribution was a theory of how
constitutionalization had affected the EU's legislative system.[40] The EU had become,
in a juridical sense, more like a federal state than an international organization, yet the
Member States had resisted the move to supranationalism within legislative processes
(majority voting in the Council of Ministers to enact EU measures to complete the
common market). Weiler drew from this paradox the following hypothesis: 'The
"harder" the law in terms of its binding effect both on and within States, the less
willing States are to give up their prerogative to control the emergence of such law.'[41]
The governments of the Member States had accepted the legal transformation of the
regime, he claimed, only because each retained a veto over important new policy.

   If the political viability of constitutionalization rested on a specific equilibrium
between a *supranational* legal system and an *intergovernmental* legislative system,
then the Single Act (signed in February 1986) had 'shattered' that equilibrium.
Henceforth, every Member State would at times be required to enforce EU statutes
that its government had opposed in the Council of Ministers. A major crossroads had
been reached, but Weiler was unsure as to the direction the system would take. In the
post-Single Act EU, the constitutional settlement might unravel or, he speculated, the
Member States might leave it in place, having been 'socialized' by the system enough to
value its benefits.

   Garrett's 'International Cooperation and Institutional Choice: The European Community's Internal Market', rested on different premises. Although he had no use for
doctrinal niceties, Garrett stressed that the courts had been important to market
integration in the 1970s, and would be crucial to perfecting the internal market after
the Single Act. But why had the Member States allowed the courts to accrue so much
power? His response was twofold. First, the courts comprise commitment devices that
European States needed to help them build a common market. Second, the CJEU's
rulings generally 'accord with the interests of powerful States', especially those of
Germany and France.[42] If it were to be otherwise, these Member States would
punish the Court, and remake the legal system. Like Moravcsik,[43] Garrett offered an
account of integration that emphasized the primacy of state power, interests, and
intergovernmental bargaining, while denying the capacity of the EU's organs to
generate outcomes that might conflict with, or induce change in, the preferences of
powerful governments. In a follow-up piece, Garrett, focusing on the free movement of

---

[40] Although he employed Hirschman's (1970) 'exit-voice-loyalty' frame as a heuristic device, Weiler's own
theoretical offerings were a product of careful doctrinal analysis and a sophisticated understanding of EU
politics.

[41] Weiler (n 33 above) 2426.

[42] G Garrett, 'International Cooperation and Institutional Choice: The European Community's Internal
Market' (1992) 46 International Organization 533, 537, 556–569.

[43] A Moravcsik, 'Negotiating the Single European Act: National Interests and Conventional Statecraft in the
European Community' (1991) 45 International Organization 19.

goods domain, proposed that the Court would sometimes censure 'powerful Governments,' but only in 'unimportant sectors' of the economy, while 'accepting protectionist behavior' in more important sectors.[44]

Standing in stark contrast to Garrett's work is the paper by Burley (Slaughter) and Mattli, 'Europe before the Court: A Political Theory of Legal Integration'.[45] The paper's originality lies in how the authors translated the constitutionalization narrative into the neo-functionalist integration theory of Haas and his followers, thus melding the concerns of lawyers and social scientists. Most important, they demonstrated that the internal dynamics of EU *law*—of litigation, jurisprudence, and doctrinal discourse—have always been at the core of the *politics* of European integration. The theory highlighted the various ways in which the courts were responsive to the interests of those private actors who needed integration—such as large producers, traders, and other transnational actors—rather than those of any Member State. The authors also stressed that the legal system had developed as specific feedback loops were constituted, a process that neofunctionalists call 'spillover.' Constitutionalization enhanced the effectiveness of EU law, which attracted litigation brought by private actors; more litigation meant more preliminary references which, in turn, generated the context for a nuanced, intra-judicial dialogue between the ECJ and national judges on how best to accommodate, and empower, one another; and, as the domain of EC law, and of the ECJ's jurisprudence expanded, this dialogue intensified, socializing more into the system, encouraging more use. In contrast to Weiler's account, there is no theorized equilibrium: the legal system helps to organize integration which, in turn, shapes how the legal system evolves.

None of these papers sought to test their claims in any social scientific sense, though others would. To my knowledge, 'Constructing a Supranational Constitution: Dispute Resolution and Governance in the European Community', by Stone Sweet and Brunell, was the first paper to test hypotheses derived from any theory of integration against comprehensive data collected across the life of the EU. The theory models integration as an expansive, self-sustaining process driven by mechanisms of institutionalization (forms of spillover) that also feature in North, March and Olsen, and Haas.[46] Embedded in a project that modified and updated neofunctionalism,[47] it is broadly compatible with Burley-Mattli. The paper blended quantitative and qualitative methods, but it is the quantitative findings that generated the most follow-up work by others. Using econometric and other statistical methods, the authors demonstrated that, with constitutionalization, transnational economic activity and the development

---

[44] G Garrett, 'The Politics of Legal Integration in the European Union' (1995) 49 International Organization 171, 178–179.

[45] A-M Burley and W Mattli, 'Europe Before the Court: A Political Theory of Legal Integration' (1993) 47 International Organization 41.

[46] North (n 13 above); J March and J Olsen, *Rediscovering Institutions* (Free Press, 1989); E Haas, 'International Integration: The European and the Universal Process' (1961) 15 International Organization 366.

[47] Sandholtz and Stone Sweet (n 8 above); A Stone Sweet, N Fligstein, and W Sandholtz, *The Institutionalization of Europe* (Oxford University Press, 2001).

of the legal system had become causally connected to one another. As important, to the extent that the legal system actually removed national barriers to exchange within the EU (a process known as *negative integration*), it put pressure on governments to adopt EU Market Regulations (known as *positive integration*). With the completion of the internal market, the relationship between trade and litigation weakened, whereas the influence of the EU's developing regulatory structure on litigating EU law was growing. Subsequent testing efforts, using more sophisticated techniques and different measures, confirmed the major findings.[48]

In 'Constructing Markets and Polities: An Institutionalist Account of European Integration',[49] Fligstein and Stone Sweet pushed this project further, developing a macro-sociological theory of the reciprocal impact of legal, market, and political integration. The paper builds on Stone Sweet-Brunell, in that it models European integration as a series of feedback loops, and it made use of comprehensive data providing relatively direct measures of processes associated with integration. The analysis demonstrated that the activities of commercial actors, lobbyists, legislators, litigators, and judges had become connected to one another in specific ways (but not all ways). These linkages constituted an expansive, self-reinforcing system that has given the EU strength and resilience in the face of recurrent crises. The analysis also showed that two parameter shifts—whereby important qualitative events generated quantitatively significant transformations in the relationships among variables—had occurred. The first shift began roughly around 1970, the second in the mid-1980s. The EU's evolving legal system was implicated in both transitions, first, through the linked effects of constitutionalization and the entry into force of Treaty rules governing trade, and, then, through supervising Member State compliance with EU law, especially with regard to rules governing the common market.

Although I have emphasized relatively abstract arguments to this point, each of the papers discussed gave empirical content to the analysis with reference to how the development of the intra-EU trading system intersected with political struggles to complete the internal market. Shapiro, in his chapter for the first edition of this volume, also dwelt on this topic, the resolution of which he considered to be 'the central story of European integration'.[50] He also saw it as a properly constitutional one, illustrating the critical importance of effective judicial review to achieving market federalism. Scholars have, in fact, extensively documented the impact of adjudicating free movement of goods provisions, in particular Article 34 TFEU, on integration between 1970 (when Article 34 TFEU entered into force) and 1986 (when the Single European Act was signed by the Member States).

---

[48] See eg J-Y Pitarkis and G George, 'Joint Dynamics of Legal and Economic Integration in the European Union' (2003) 16 Eur J of L and Econ 357; C Carrubba and L Murrah, 'Legal Integration and Use of the Preliminary Ruling Process in the European Union' (2005) 59 International Organization 399.

[49] N Fligstein and A Stone Sweet, 'Constructing Markets and Polities: An Institutionalist Account of European Integration' (2002) 107 AJS 1206.

[50] Shapiro (n 1 above) 338.

Comprehensive data on the adjudication of free movement of goods provisions have been collected and analysed.[51] The data on Article 267 TFEU references show that litigation in the national courts disproportionately targeted larger national markets compared to smaller markets. As a lesson in basic political economy, or in neofunctionalist theory, the finding seems unsurprising: traders have a far greater interest in opening larger markets relative to smaller ones; and higher levels of cross-border trade, which are strongly correlated with larger markets, will generate relatively more trading disputes. Analysts then looked to see who won these cases: the trader-litigant or the Member State? In those decisions in which the CJEU clearly ruled on the question of whether a national rule or practice was in violation of Article 34 TFEU, traders won about half the time, but they had higher success rates in France, Germany, and Italy, than they did in the smaller states; and they enjoyed the best success rate in the courts of the largest market, Germany. Scholars also examined whether the CJEU's decisions followed from the Member State briefs ('observations') which comprise, in effect, revealed state preferences on how the Court should decide cases. German interventions were found to be particularly ineffectual in generating outcomes, whereas the Commission's observations 'predicted' the Court's decision about 85 per cent of the time. The evidence refuted Garret's various claims about the primacy of Member State power and interests on judicial process and outcomes. The policy preferences of powerful governments simply do not constrain the Court in any systematic way, in this area or any other in which systematic research has been undertaken.[52]

While useful for testing purposes, this kind of bean-counting should not obscure the importance of the Court's doctrinal approach to Article 34 TFEU, which it deployed to great success. As every reader knows, the *Dassonville-Cassis* framework is a highly intrusive one, potentially covering every nook and cranny of national law and administration; it is also maximally flexible, with proportionality-based balancing at its core. The framework facilitated the kinds of dynamics that Burley-Mattli and Stone Sweet-Brunell had stressed, with litigation steadily exposing layer upon layer of national regulation to the rigours of judicial review. Further, proportionality balancing is a mode of adjudication that the CJEU could use strategically, either to discipline the Member States, or to allow them more wiggle room, while maintaining doctrinal consistency. The framework positioned the courts as masters of negative integration which, in the context of a stalled harmonization process and a rising tide of litigation, produced a stream of decisions whose effect was to recast positive integration (spill-over).[53] The most salient occurred when the Court's views on 'mutual recognition', announced as dicta in *Cassis de Dijon*, were adapted by the Commission as part of a new push to complete the market.

---

[51] Stone Sweet (n 9 above) ch 3.

[52] Outcomes in the domains of sex equality and environmental protection are broadly congruent, see Stone Sweet (n 9 above) chs 4 and 5; R Cichowski, *The European Court and Civil Society: Litigation, Mobilization and Governance* (Cambridge University Press, 2007).

[53] M Van Empel, 'The 1992 Programme: Interaction Between Legislator And Judiciary' (1992) LIEI 1.

With mutual recognition, the Court had shown how states might retain their own national rules, capable of being applied within the domestic market, while prohibiting states from applying these same rules to goods originating elsewhere. For the Commission, reliance on mutual recognition would substantially reduce the resources required to complete the market through harmonization. Indeed, the Commission announced, it would henceforth focus its legislative efforts on those 'barriers to trade...which are admissible under the criteria set by the Court'.[54] Concurrently, the Commission began to use Article 258 TFEU aggressively (for the first time in its history) to ratchet-up pressure on the Member States. Prior to *Cassis*, the Court had produced only two rulings pursuant to infringement proceedings brought on the basis of alleged violations of Article 34 TFEU. From the date that *Cassis de Dijon* was rendered to the date the Single Act was signed, the Commission filed 82 such suits, leading to 46 final judgments by the Court. Member States lost 85 per cent of these cases (the other suits were settled and withdrawn by defendants anxious to avoid censure by the Court). In the end, the new strategy—mutual recognition, minimal harmonization, litigation of Article 34 TFEU—succeeded. Strongly supported by business elites across Europe, the Member States would ratify the Commission's move with the Single Act.

Maduro, in his important book, *We, the Court: The European Court of Justice and the European Economic Constitution*, focused squarely on the strategic aspects of the Court's Article 34 TFEU jurisprudence. Maduro examined every case decided under *Cassis de Dijon*, wherein the ECJ balances trading rights under Article 34 TFEU against derogations claimed by Member States under Article 36 TFEU. He found that the CJEU engaged, systematically, in what he called 'majoritarian activism'.[55] When the national measure under review is more unlike, than like, those equivalent measures in place in a majority of Member States, the CJEU invariably held the measure under review to be in violation of Article 34 TFEU (in the early 1980s, the Court began to ask the Commission to provide comparative information on regulation as a routine part of its fact-gathering). On the other hand, the Court typically upheld national measures in situations in which no dominant type of regulation exists, although there are important exceptions. Through majoritarian activism, Maduro demonstrated, the Court could pursue a 'judicial harmonization' process that steadily put pressure on the EU organs to re-regulate at the EU level. Thus, using different methods, Maduro observed the same feedback, or spillover, effects found in the quantitative analyses discussed above.

The literature on the sources of the Single European Act—which bundled together mutual recognition, a return to qualified majority voting, and the establishment of a binding timetable for harmonizing in the most important regulatory areas—has

---

[54] See Stone Sweet (n 9 above).

[55] 'Communication from the Commission concerning the Consequences of the Judgment Given by the Court of Justice on 20 February 1979 in Case 120/78 ("Cassis de Dijon")', online at: <http://ec.europa.eu/enterprise/policies/single-market-goods/files/goods/docs/mutrec/caasiscomm_en.pdf>.

sufficiently demonstrated the extent to which the Court, the Commission, and transnational business elites were ahead of governments in the process of 'relaunching' Europe.[56] Intergovernmental bargaining ensued, of course, producing a major Treaty revision that codified new solutions to problems the Member States had proved incapable of resolving on their own. But these solutions had emerged, in significant part, from the activities of transnational actors and the EU's supranational organizations, against the backdrop of ever-increasing demand for more, not less, harmonization. I do not mean to suggest that the process leading to the Single Act had only to do with linkages forged between transnational activity and supranational governance, though these were crucial. Also critical was the growing sense of crisis, the failure of go-it-alone policies to sustain economic growth, and an accumulation of legal precedents that empowered traders and the Commission, vis-à-vis recalcitrant Member State governments.

By the end of 1992, the legislative work necessary to complete the internal market had largely been concluded. However well-founded Weiler's fears were in theory, the constitutional foundations of supranationalism and federalism constructed by the courts did not, in fact, disintegrate. Rather, intergovernmentalism, as a mode of legislative decision-making, steadily declined, while supranational authority (eg majority voting and the powers of the Parliament) was upgraded. The Member States did not roll back the legal system, nor did the CJEU abandon its constitutional commitments and stage a retreat. Instead, as Keleman has shown,[57] with the completion of the internal market, the EU became even more rule-oriented, legalistic, procedurally complex, and adversarial (in an American sense), all factors that bolstered the centrality of the courts. The result, Keleman argued, was partly ordained by the multi-level structure of European market federalism, post-constitutionalization. Post-Single Act, the EU's legislative organs reinforced these features, notably, by delegating to the courts the charge of monitoring and enforcing EU Market Regulations, as they emerged.

I conclude this section with a remark on the relationship between theories of integration and empirical studies of the EU's legal system, which I realize is a topic that some readers may find wearisome.[58] Most strikingly, 'Intergovernmentalism,' as a

---

[56] A short list would include R Dehousse, *The European Court of Justice: The Politics of Judicial Integration* (St Martin's, 1998); J Weiler (n 33 above); W Sandholtz and J Zysman, '1992: Recasting the European Bargain' (1989) 42 World Politics 95. To my knowledge, only A Moravcsik disagrees, *The Choice for Europe: Social Purpose and State Power from Massina to Maastricht* (Cornell University Press, 1998).

[57] R D Keleman, 'Suing for Europe: Adversarial Legalism and European Governance' (2006) 39 Comparative Political Studies 101.

[58] It may be, as Craig and de Búrca claim, that readers now have little reason to be interested in the classic debates about constitutionalization, the relationship between intergovernmental and supranational modes of governance in the EU, or in the relative extent to which the Member States, national governments, or the EU's supranational organizations influence the course of integration or policy output. P Craig and G de Búrca, *EU Law: Text, Cases, and Materials* (4th edn, Oxford University Press, 1999) 2–3. In their view (incontestable), the EU today comprises a complex, multi-level, differentially networked system of law and governance. In my view, these features are an outcome that begs to be explained, and can be (by the expansionary dynamics of integration—the reciprocal impact of legal, market, and political integration—that the basic research has uncovered).

body of theorizing about integration and EU governance, has failed every serious empirical test (to my knowledge, there are no exceptions), while approaches possessing affinities with neofunctionalism, as modified in the 1990s, have thrived. In my view, this result flows from a kind of meta-theoretical congruence. Haas, a pioneer of institutionalist analysis, combined materials from (what we would now call) 'rational choice' and 'sociological-constructivist' perspectives, which allowed him to identify certain generic dynamics of how new systems of governance institutionalize as rule systems.[59] These dynamics turn out to be basic to all sophisticated accounts of how courts succeed in becoming important political actors.[60] In any event, what matters is not the rivalry between 'isms,' or theoretical labels, but what we learn from the results of theory-driven empirical research about the impact of judicial authority on integration.

3. DIVISION OF POWERS AND RIGHTS REVIEW

Let us now return to the broader themes developed in Section A, where it was suggested that the move to investing courts with powers of judicial review is typically embedded in one of three constitutional bargains. In his original chapter, Shapiro treated the EU, above all else, as an important instance of the success of *federalism* review, downplaying the significance of the CJEU's *division of powers* and *individual rights* jurisdiction. Nonetheless, the Court's activities in these areas, too, have also altered the course of integration in fundamental ways.

In the division of powers area, the Court resolves 'legal basis' disputes under Article 263 TFEU. These are inter-institutional conflicts between two or more of the EU's legislative organs—the Commission, the Council of Ministers, and the Parliament—concerning which decision rules are to be used to adopt secondary legislation. Legal basis disputes exploded into prominence after the entry into force of the Single Act in 1987. Without wading into the details, under the new Article 95 TEC, directives necessary to complete the internal market were to be adopted under qualified majority voting procedures in the Council of Ministers, whereas other classes of directives remained subject to a de facto unanimity requirement. For certain legislative purposes, more than one legal basis could arguably be used to adopt a directive, the choice of which would have huge consequences for the relative powers of the Commission and the Parliament vis-à-vis the Council of Ministers

---

[59] See especially Hass (n 44 above).

[60] I am not claiming that all important scholars in the field embrace a variant of neofunctionalism. Alter, for example, denies that she is a neofunctionalist, claiming that the theory was falsified in the 1970s. Since she chooses not to engage the imposing literature that revived the theory in the 1990s, while describing the dynamics of legal integration in compatible ways, it is difficult to evaluate her theoretical position. K Alter, *The European Court's Political Power: Selected Essays* (Oxford University Press, 2009) ch 1.

within the legislative process. In the 1987–99 period,[61] in particular, these conflicts were routinely transferred to the Court.

The adjudication of legal basis disputes is directly relevant to scholarly debates about the Court and integration. One group of scholars has forcefully claimed that neither the Court nor the Commission ever produces 'unintended consequences' from the perspective of those who designed and who maintain the system: Member State governments. Among the better known versions are the theories of Tsebelis and Garrett,[62] and Moravcsik, the latter going so far as to claim that supranational organizations have *never* generated outcomes that 'alter the terms under which governments negotiate new bargains' and legislate.[63] Both theories invoke logics of delegation, but they model the EU's organizations as relatively simple agents of Member States, at every point in time. A second group of scholars, and not only those associated with neofunctionalism, took an opposed position. To the extent that the Court could choose to exploit its trusteeship position in pursuit of a pro-integrative agenda, aligning itself with other actors and institutions when convenient or necessary, one would expect it to produce outcomes that would 'alter the terms under which governments' bargain on a regular basis. A trustee court, it bears repeating, possesses an inherent power to change the 'rules of the game,' through case by case constitutional law-making.

The legal basis cases provide an opportunity to *directly* test the rival claims just mentioned. If governments, acting in the Council of Ministers, *fail* to maintain intergovernmental modes of governance (eg unanimity voting) in those areas in which they prefer such modes, and *fail* to limit the extension of supranational modes of governance (eg majoritarian voting) to those domains in which they prefer intergovernmentalism, then the theories of Garrett, Garrett-Tsebelis, and Moravcsik are invalidated. The judicial politics of these disputes have, in fact, been the subject of high-quality, systematic research. Jupille[64] examined every such dispute brought to the Court after the entry into force of the Single Act. The Court, he found, showed itself 'dedicated throughout the period to the extension of "integration," defined as majoritarian decision-making in the Council, and the attendant increase in legislative output,' results that, in his words, 'strongly disconfirm' Garret-Tsebelis and others who claim that governments control the system's constitutional evolution.[65]

---

[61] The Maastricht Treaty on European Union (1993) and the Treaty of Amsterdam (1999) extended qualified majority voting and the 'co-decision' procedure to most classes of directives, which had the effect of expanding legislative production. Today, most secondary legislation is taken on the basis of one Treaty article, ex-Art 251.

[62] G Tsebelis and G Garrett, 'The Institutional Foundations of Intergovernmentalism and Supranationalism in the European Union' (2001) 55 International Organization 357.

[63] Moravcsik (n 54 above) 482–490.

[64] J Jupille, 'Power, Preferences, and Procedural Choice in the European Court of Justice', paper presented at the 2000 Annual Meeting of the American Political Science Association; J Jupille, *Procedural Politics: Influence and Institutional Choice in the European Union* (Cambridge University Press, 2004).

[65] Jupille, *Procedural Politics* (n 62 above) 14.

McCown[66] extended the analysis to all legal basis disputes, confirming Jupille's findings. The Court, she stressed, had also produced an intricate, precedent-based doctrinal framework which governments initially rejected but to which they gradually adapted, thereby legitimizing it. In her related study of what happens when the European Parliament 'litigates for constitutional change',[67] McCown found that the Court sustained the production of a 'pro-integrative' jurisprudence, even in 'highly politicized' areas. What is indisputable is that the adjudication of legal basis disputes routinely produced 'rules of the game' to which the Council of Ministers fiercely objected, and which governments would not have chosen on their own, given existing decision rules.[68]

With the Treaty on European Union (entry into force November 1993), the Member States established what became known as the 'three-Pillar structure.' The First Pillar was defined by the TEC, under which secondary legislation was to be proposed by the Commission and adopted by the Council of Ministers and the Parliament, according to various procedures, and the Court exercised legal basis review of EC acts pursuant to Article 263 TFEU. With the TEU, the Member States established formal EU competences in new areas, under the Second Pillar (Common Foreign and Security Policy) and Third Pillar (Justice and Home Affairs) but, as Craig and de Búrca stress, 'they were unwilling to subject these areas to the normal supranational methods of decision-making'[69] that characterized the First Pillar. Instead, the Council of Ministers could initiate and adopt legislation on its own, that is, neither the Commission nor the Parliament possessed veto authority. Further, the Member States excluded the Court from both Pillars. The Treaty of Amsterdam (entry into force 1 May 1999) added a new provision, Article 35 TEU which, among other things, gave to the Commission the authority to bring annulment actions under the Third Pillar. In a series of important cases, the Commission, supported by the Parliament, sued the Council under Article 35 TEU on the grounds that the acts in question should have been taken under the First Pillar. The Court annulled the legislation,[70] requiring that it be adopted under supranational (First Pillar) rather than intergovernmental (Third Pillar) decision rules. In another remarkable case, the Commission (presumably as an experiment) used Article 263 TFEU to challenge a Council act under the Second Pillar, leading to another invalidation.[71]

---

[66] M McCown, *Drafting the European Constitution Case by Case: Precedent and the Judicial Integration of the European Union* (Doctoral Dissertation, Oxford University, 2004).

[67] M McCown, 'The European Parliament before the Bench: ECJ Precedent and EP Litigation Strategies' (2003) 10 JEPP 974.

[68] See eg Case C-300/89 *Commission v Council (Titanium Dioxide)* [1991] ECR I-2687.

[69] Craig and de Búrca (n 56 above) 15.

[70] Case C-176/03 *Commission v Council* [2005] ECR I-7879; Case C-440/05 *Commission v Council* [2007] ECR I-9097.

[71] Case C-91/05 *Commission v Council* [2008] ECR I-3651.

4. RIGHTS REVIEW

In his original chapter, Shapiro had argued that rights protection was a much more problematic, even dangerous, task for courts in comparison to policing boundaries (federalism and division of powers review). With the American experience in mind, he also suggested that a rights-protecting court would be more likely to succeed, in the sense of gaining effectiveness, when building on a reservoir of legitimacy built up through performing one of the two other functions. The CJEU, in fact, constructed its 'constitutional' case law—of direct effect, supremacy, state liability, and so on—on the basis of rights rhetoric, though it had no codified charter of rights at its disposal. In the 1960s, the CJEU began to derive individual rights from Treaty provisions prohibiting Member State incursions on what came to be known as the four freedoms. Put differently, the CJEU leveraged its strong federalism review position to build a rights review position. Thus, federalism and economic rights review logics were connected from the beginning, as they were in the United States during the heyday of the 'dormant commerce clause' at the turn of the nineteenth century.[72] In the 1970s, the Court also worked to develop a right to be free from sex discrimination and, later, even broader notions of equality, from Article 157 TFEU, which guarantees only that women and men shall receive equal pay for equal work. Without this commitment to individual rights, Article 267 TFEU does not develop into a decentralized enforcement mechanism; the legal system does not organize the kinds of feedback effects that have given European integration its inherently expansionary character; the Single Act is not signed in 1987; the common market is not completed by 1992; and the social provisions of the Treaty of Rome may well have remained virtual dead letters, instead of evolving an extraordinary life of their own.

It is also true that the Court's commitment to supremacy threatened rights protection at the national level, in that supremacy would insulate EC legal norms from review systems. Indeed, in the *Simmenthal* saga,[73] the Court made it clear that even the most important procedural requirements of national rights protection may not hinder the effectiveness, and judicial enforcement, of EU law within national orders. The issue became impossible to ignore in the 1970s, a decade that saw Article 267 TFEU activity explode. As every reader knows, the German Federal Constitutional Court (*Solange I*, 1974) would announce that supremacy was unacceptable unless and until the EU 'possessed a catalogue of rights . . . of settled validity, which is adequate in comparison

---

[72] In 1901, the US Supreme Court summarized its position on the dormant commerce clause in ways that anyone familiar with *Cassis de Dijon* would immediately seem familiar: 'Now it is said that the defendant has a *right* under the Constitution of the United States to ship . . . from one State to another State. This will be conceded on all hands. But the defendant is not given by that instrument the right to introduce into a State, against its will, livestock affected by a . . . disease . . . The State, Congress not having assumed charge of the matter, may protect its people and their property against such dangers, taking care always that the means employed to that end do not go beyond the necessities of the case or unreasonably burden the exercise of privileges secured by the Constitution of the United States' *Reid v Colorado* 187 U.S. 137 (1902).

[73] See especially *Simmenthal II* ECJ 106/77 [1978] ECR 629.

with a catalogue of fundamental rights contained in the [German] constitution'.[74] The ECJ would respond by developing a jurisprudence which, under the rubric of unwritten 'general principles', amounted to incorporating fundamental rights into the Treaty on a case by case basis. Although the German court, and other high courts, would ultimately withdraw their objections to supremacy, the overall system of rights review, as it pertains to the judicial control of EU acts, remains highly unstable.[75]

Although they might have done so, constitutional conflicts over supremacy and rights did not paralyze broader integration processes. Instead, a process of inter-judicial dialogue emerged, producing accommodations that served to deepen legal integration, widen the Court's zone of discretion, and strengthen the supranational aspects of the Community. These are feedback effects that would ultimately be ratified by the Member States. Playing catch-up, the Member States, revised the Treaty, in the TEU, echoing the terms of the Court's seminal rulings in this area: '[T]he Union shall respect fundamental rights as guaranteed by the European Convention on Human Rights ... and as they result from the constitutional traditions common to the member states as general principles of Community law.'[76] In December 2000, the Member States produced a codified Charter of Rights, which finally entered into force with the Lisbon Treaty on December 1, 2009. In Craig and de Búrca's words, the Charter is 'a creative distillation of the rights contained in the various European and international agreements and national constitutions on which the ECJ had for some years already been drawing'.[77]

C. THE COURT AND EU GOVERNANCE

Wherever systems of constitutional judicial review are effective, high courts are heavily implicated in two generic functions of *governance*. The first is law-making, the progressive construction of legal norms, and the second is the enforcement of compliance with those norms. In practice, these two functions of governance overlap. Indeed, powerful Constitutional Courts expend a great deal of their time and resources monitoring and enforcing compliance with their own prior acts of law-making. The same is true of the European Court.

1. THE JUDICIALIZATION OF EU LAW-MAKING

One direct indicator of the 'political success,' or the 'effectiveness', of a court, is the extent to which its case law shapes, or organizes, the law-making of non-judicial officials and organs of governance (see section A.3). The more one finds such

---

[74] *Solange I*, BVerfGE [1974] 34, 269.
[75] See de Búrca in this volume.
[76] Case 4/73 *Nold v Commission* [1974] ECR 491.
[77] Craig and de Búrca (n 56 above) 413.

influence, the more we can say that a given system, or policy domain, has been 'judicialized'. As noted, the EU provides one of the most important examples of extensive judicialization ever documented, across a wide range of policy areas. Here I consider how and why this has happened, by breaking down the overall process into four discrete stages, and then showing how each can influence activity in the others. Each stage is defined by a different set of empirical questions. First, who activates the CJEU, and for what purposes? Second, what interests (or values) does the Court pursue when it adjudicates disputes? Third, what law-making techniques does the CJEU use to influence the future decision-making of non-judicial actors in the policy process, and future litigators? And, fourth, how do non-judicial power-holders respond to judicial law-making that imposes constraints on their decision-making? These questions can also be reformulated as a series of variables (or sub-processes) that drive the overall process. As will be shown, judicialization is spillover: it proceeds only to the extent that specific feedback loops—connecting judicial law-making to policy processes and back again—institutionalize as stable practices.

Why do actors, public and private, litigate EU law? Those who focus on a single case will have reason to focus on the activities of specific people. The tenacity of the labour lawyer, Elaine Vogel-Polsky, for example, is crucial to the process through which the ECJ recognized the direct effect of Article 157 TFEU,[78] which proclaims 'equal pay for equal work' for men and women.[79] But the story did not stop there. The Court's ruling generated a steady stream of cases which, as Cichowski shows,[80] catalyzed the development of a European social movement for women's rights. Once institutionalized as a significant NGO presence in Brussels, the movement helped workers and trade unions, at the national level, generate new litigation. It is through such feedback (spillover) that helps to sustain and deepen the scope of the judicialization process.

More generally, there are three basic motivations behind litigation that matter most to the evolution of EU law. First, in the negative integration area, transnational actors litigate in the hopes of removing national barriers to their activities. As discussed, transnational commercial activity, litigating free movement of goods provisions in the national courts, the Court's jurisprudence, and the evolution of the EU's market rules became connected to one another, through well-defined and understood feedback loops. Second, individuals and groups not directly engaged in cross-border exchange (eg those seeking to enhance women's rights) activate the courts in order to change national rules and practices in their favour, with reference to EU law. It is one of the basic driving forces of legal integration that those who lose in domestic politics have sought to Europeanize policy, through court actions. The best research has shown that how state structures and social interests are organized, and the resources potential

---

[78] Case 149/77 *Defrenne v SABENA* [1978] ECR 1365.
[79] S Mazey, 'The European Union and Women's Rights' (1998) 5 JEPP 131.
[80] Cichowski (n 50 above).

litigants command, can be crucial to success or failure.[81] Third, EU organs seeking to promote integration, like the Commission and the Parliament, may turn to the ECJ to undermine Member State claims of national regulatory autonomy, or the Council of Ministers' control of the policy process.

The most ambitious research in this area is Keleman's project on the emergence of a self-sustaining system of 'adversarial legalism' within the EU.[82] The seeds of this development were sown with constitutionalization, which generated a rights-based, court-centric system for monitoring and enforcing Member State compliance with EU law. But, Keleman, argues, the system did not fully emerge until after the completion of the single market. Simplifying a complex argument, adversarial legalism tends to develop and thrive in multi-level systems of fragmented authority. The EU governs primarily through rule-making, including establishing new procedures for further rule-making, and monitoring compliance with these rules. Keleman's major claim is that, post-1992, modes of litigating and modes of law-making have developed symbiotically, that is, their evolution is causally connected (feedback loops again). The claim is impressively supported with pertinent data and with case studies of the judicialization of diverse policy domains. If he is right, then the potential for the systematic judicialization of EU governance is very high—indeed, it may be inevitable.

A second set of issues concerns the motivations of the Court itself. There is, today, broad consensus on the following three assumptions. First, the CJEU will use its powers to promote integration (values that inhere in the treaties). Second, the Court has an interest in maximizing the coherence of its case law, in order to bolster its own political legitimacy. Third, the CJEU worries about the compliance of national judges, EU organs, and the Member States with its decisions, and will develop techniques to enhance compliance. The most sophisticated empirical research on the Court has shown these assumptions to be generally warranted. To the extent that the Court actually behaves in light of these expectations, of course, judicialization is likely to proceed.

Unfortunately, there is no sophisticated literature directly examining the attitudes and preferences of judges that have served on the Court. A major reason for this void is the fact that the CJEU does not publish its votes, and does not allow for dissenting opinions; judges are also precluded from commenting publicly on their work at the Court. One way to proceed, despite this limitation, would be to develop a theory of legal interpretation and precedent formation. Innovative scholarship on the Court's interpretive strategies exists,[83] showing, among other things, that the Court's influence on EU governance is partly a function of the structural coherence of its jurisprudence. The present author, too, developed a theory of precedent, conceived as a system of

---

[81] K Alter and J Vargas, 'Explaining Variation in the Use of European Litigation Strategies: EC Law and British Gender Equality' (2000) 33 Comparative Political Studies 452; Cichowski (n 53 above); L Conant, *Justice Contained: Law and Politics in the EU* (Cornell University Press, 2002); Cichowski (n 50 above).

[82] Keleman (n 55 above); R D Keleman, *Suing for Europe? The Rise of Adversarial Legalism in the European Union* (Harvard University Press, forthcoming).

[83] J Bengoetxea, *Legal Reasoning of the European Court of Justice* (Oxford University Press, 1993).

inter-locking 'argumentation frameworks' which the Court uses to legitimize its own law-making, to enhance compliance, and to help it socialize power-holders into judicialized governance.[84] Arguably, the most important research on the relationship between how the Court decides cases and the judicialization of EU governance is Maduro's book, *We the Court*. The Court's dominant strategy—to exploit the strategic benefits of 'majoritarian activism'—could not have succeeded had it not sustained its commitment to the *Dassonville-Cassis de Dijon* framework through 1992.

The third question relates to the capacity of the Court to alter the underlying 'rules of the game' that govern policy-making in any given field (Part B). A host of scholars, including those who do not primarily work on law and courts,[85] have identified mechanisms of institutional change that rely on litigation and judicial law-making. Certain types of decisions will provoke expansive judicialization, to the extent that they require the EU legislature to make new law. When the Court chooses to apply Treaty law to policy areas that were formerly assumed to be in the domain of national, not supranational, governance, it empowers the Commission and the courts, while undermining the authority of national officials. Important examples include the ECJ's decisions to subject the domains of telecommunications[86] and air transport to EU competition rules,[87] which helped break legislative deadlocks in the Council of Ministers. The ECJ may also interpret EU statutes as if certain provisions express values of a higher, 'constitutional' status. In doing so, the Court carves out substantive legal positions, or guiding principles for law-making. The most robust form of judicialization is triggered when the Court holds that specific policy dispositions are required by Treaty law. These techniques typically lead to the constitutional entrenchment of the Court's preferred policies. The Court's Trustee status makes such outcomes 'sticky'—difficult to reverse—except through subsequent rounds of adjudication.

The sex equality domain provides a well-documented illustration. Most spectacularly, the ECJ enacted, through interpreting Article 157 TFEU and the 1976 Equal Treatment Directive, the core of several proposed directives (eg pregnancy and occupational pensions) that had stalled in the Council of Ministers under the vetoes of France and the UK. In Curtin's telling phrase, the Court had 'scalped the legislator'.[88] In other areas (eg burden of proof and indirect discrimination), ECJ rulings all but required the production of new directives by the EU's legislative organs, empowering the Commission in the process. In this domain, constitutional law-making fundamentally altered the intergovernmental modes of governance that were in place, routinely producing outcomes that are, in fact, theoretical impossibilities

---

[84] Stone Sweet (n 9 above).

[85] A Héritier, *Explaining Institutional Change in Europe* (Oxford University Press, 2007); P Pierson, 'The Path to European Integration: A Historical-Institutionalist Analysis' in Sandholtz and Stone Sweet (n 8 above).

[86] W Sandholtz, 'The Emergence of a Supranational Telecommunications Regime' in Sandholtz and Stone Sweet (n 8 above); S Schmidt, 'Commission Activism: Subsuming telecommunications and electricity under European competition law' (1998) 5 JEPP 169.

[87] D O'Reilly and A Stone Sweet, 'The Liberalization and European Reregulation of Air Transport' in Sandholtz and Stone Sweet (n 8 above).

[88] D Curtin, 'Scalping the Community legislator: Occupational Pensions and "Barber", (1990) CML Rev 475–506.

under the theories of Moravcsik and Garrett-Tsebelis.[89] In this domain, as well, one observes another version of Maduro's 'majoritarian activism.' The Court, acting in the interest of a majority of the Member States, had no reason to fear reprisals on the part of the Member States.

The fourth stage of the process focuses attention on the impact of the Court's case law on subsequent policy-making, which has already been sufficiently covered (as spillover, or feedback). Rather than rehearse the findings of (literally) hundreds of research projects, a few summary points deserve emphasis. Most important, judicialization is registered *only* when the EU's legislative organs, or the Member States in Treaty revision processes, take decisions that, in effect, *implement* the Court's case law. Policy-makers may seek to limit the effects of the Court's law-making, of course, but these efforts will be countered by actors who wish to expand the Court's influence. Judicialization, as it proceeds, enhances the capacity of actors (individuals, firms, interest groups, national judges, and EU organs, as the case may be) to leverage the Court's jurisprudence for their own purposes.

If we know some important things about how the judicialization process works, there has been little or no research on the extent to which the depth and pace of judicialization varies across EU policy domains. In some domains, after all, harmonization efforts stalled for decades; the Court, for example, refused to take decisions that might have Europeanized regulation of the trucking industry. Integration in some important areas has progressed, but more slowly than, say, a neofunctionalist might expect; the market for services is, arguably, a good example.[90] A related issue concerns how we assess the impact of legal outcomes on the wider polity. Cichowski has shown that, in the domains of environmental protection and women's rights, litigating EU law and the development of social movements evolved in tandem.[91] Yet efforts to 'mainstream gender',[92] or 'green Europe',[93] may be thwarted as countervailing values and interests organize in opposition. Court rulings can help set agendas and restrict the menu of options available to legislative organs, but legislative resistance to judicialization should be the expected state of affairs, not the exception.[94] These points accepted, judicialized governance is today an institutional fact of EU politics.

---

[89] Stone Sweet (n 9 above) ch 4.

[90] S Schmidt, 'When Efficiency Results in Redistribution: The Conflict over the Single Services Market' (2009) 32 WEP 847.

[91] J Tallberg, 'Paths to Compliance: Enforcement, Management, and the European Union' (2002) 56 International Organization 609.

[92] M Pollack and E Hafner-Burton, 'Mainstreaming Gender in the European Union' (2000) 7 JEPP 432.

[93] H Temmink, 'From Danish Bottles to Danish Bees: The Dynamics of Free Movement of Goods and Environmental Protection' (2000) 1 YEEL 61.

[94] The study of judicial impact on policymaking raises fierce issues of measurement and interpretation. Two analysts, observing exactly the same politics and outcomes, might come to a very different evaluation of the Court's impact. One might consider to be significant *every* policy outcome that can be shown to be the result of the Court's impact on the policy process and outcomes (this is my view). Another, finding that non-judicial actors sought to dilute the Court's influence during the policy process, might reject the characterization that the process was meaningfully 'judicialized' at all, insofar as the 'political' actors organized resistance.

2. ENFORCING COMPLIANCE AND THE EUROPEANIZATION OF NATIONAL LAW

European integration and the steady expansion of EU law have impacted national legal orders in diverse ways, some of which directly implicate the CJEU. Here I will focus only on the Court's role in monitoring and enforcing Member State compliance with EU law under Articles 258 TFEU and 267 TFEU. Both procedures open a window onto national law and practices, through which the CJEU may reach to enhance the effectiveness of EU law within national legal orders. If it succeeds, then a measure of Europeanization is the result.

Tallberg provides the most succinct account of non-compliance as it relates to the EU's legal system.[95] He identifies two basic categories of non-compliance: (a) failure to transpose directives properly or on time; and (b) failure to properly apply the substantive terms of the directive once transposed. He also argues that non-compliance flows from two basic sources. The first can be expressed as a hypothesis: 'the greater the legal and behavioral adjustment required to conform' to new EU law, 'the less inclined . . . the Member States [will be] to comply'.[96] The more any new EU directive already 'fits' current legal and administrative arrangements and practices, the less costly it will be for the Member State to implement it. The second variable is a Member State's 'capacity' to implement secondary legislation. The more complex and inefficient are the legislative procedures for transposition, the more likely we will find delays in transposition. Because this account highlights system-level variables, it loses power at the sub-system level; it cannot, for example, explain variation *across* policy domains *within* a Member State. Börzel[97] and Panke[98] have elaborated a similar framework, but they also pay attention to how factors observed at a lower level of abstraction (state structures, party competition, interest group politics, and so on) vary. This complexity, of course, makes the tasks of the Commission and the Court (from fact gathering to the tailoring of rulings to specific contexts) difficult.

Under Article 258 TFEU, the Commission may sue a Member State for non-compliance with EC law; rounds of negotiation with the government then ensue; if these fail, the Commission may refer the matter to the Court for decision. The Commission is under no obligation to prosecute or to activate the Court; its discretion under Article 258 TFEU is absolute. While the courts were actively, spectacularly, building the legal system under Article 267 TFEU, the Commission adopted a passive stance on enforcement actions, to the point of negligence.[99] Only in the late-1970s did

---

[95] Tallberg (n 91 above).

[96] ibid 627.

[97] T Börzel, *States and Regions in the European Union. Institutional Adaptation in Germany and Spain* (Cambridge University Press, 2002).

[98] D Panke, 'The European Court of Justice as an Agent of Europeanization: Restoring compliance with EU law' (2007) 14 JEPP 847.

[99] In the 1970s, the ECJ strongly criticized the Commission for failing to bring Art 258 TFEU proceedings on several occasions, eg Case 149/77 *Defrenne v SABENA* [1978] ECR 1365.

the Commission begin to bring infringement proceedings more aggressively, in the service of its own legislative agenda, and in order to reinforce legal interpretations produced by the Court's preliminary rulings. After the Single Act, the Commission's enforcement actions exploded into prominence. Börzel[100] and Tallberg[101] have produced the most systematic research on the law and politics of Article 258 TFEU. Both found that the system works more effectively than many have claimed. Börzel, in particular, took pains to debunk the notion that there exists a 'compliance deficit' in the EU. Analysis of the data over the 1990–99 period shows, rather, that non-compliance has been 'rather modest and...stable over time', a non-trivial finding given that 'opportunities' and pressures for non-compliance steadily increased during this period, as the corpus of EU secondary legislation expanded under the Single Act regime.

Under Article 267 TFEU, national judges send questions—a *preliminary reference*—to the ECJ in order to obtain a formal interpretation of EU law when material to the resolution of a case at bar. The ECJ responds with a *preliminary ruling*, which the referring judge is expected to use to resolve the case. The provision was designed to promote the consistent application of EU law across jurisdictions. With the consolidation of supremacy, direct effect, state liability, and related constitutional doctrines, Article 267 TFEU evolved as a separate system for enforcing compliance. The process took place within the protective confines of Article 267 TFEU, gradually positioning national judges to act as important 'agents' of the CJEU, and of EU law, within national legal orders. They embraced their new roles with enough enthusiasm to sustain the process.

By any measure, constitutionalization comprises the most profound, and best understood, example of the Europeanization of state structures that we have. The first relatively systematic, comparative research on the reception of supremacy, *The European Court and the National Courts*,[102] focuses on both inter-judicial conflict and cooperation. The most intensive work in this vein, Alter's *Establishing the Supremacy of European Law*, traces how French and German judges reacted to the CJEU's supremacy moves, as legal integration progressed. Alter demonstrates that there are multiple, continuously evolving, factors that shape how national judges adopt, adapt, use, or ignore EU law.[103] In the other indispensable work on Europeanization, *Justice Contained*, Conant shows how difficult it is for the Court's rulings—including those that had meaningfully judicialized governance at the EU level—to gain traction in national systems. The CJEU's allies must compete for influence with those wedded

---

[100] T Börzel, 'Non-Compliance in the European Union: Pathology or Statistical Artefact?' (2001) 8 JEPP 803.

[101] Tallberg (n 91 above).

[102] Slaughter, Stone Sweet, and Weiler (n 36 above).

[103] It is unfortunate that comparable research has not been undertaken on all national systems, although a series of papers on the courts of new members is beginning to appear, eg M Bobek, 'Learning to Talk: Preliminary Rulings, the Courts of the New Member States and the Court of Justice' (2008) 45 CML Rev 1611. For the UK, see D Chalmers, 'The Positioning of EU Judicial Politics within the United Kingdom' (2000) 23 WEP 169.

to the *status quo*, and the forces favouring inertia often prevail. A court's case law may change legal norms, policy frames, and the incentive structures under which non-judicial actors make policy, but rulings are never self-implementing.

What is clear is that the impact of the CJEU's case law on national law and politics varies widely, as a function of myriad factors operating with different effects, at different places and times. Viewed in this way, the *Europeanization* of national law and courts may always appear 'patchwork', in Conant's terms, because the outcomes that matter are 'negotiated' between judges, organized interests, and elected officials. Yet such claims can be pushed too far. Similar situations arise routinely with respect to the implementation of federal law in other federal polities, such as Canada and the United States, as do intractable supremacy conflicts. Indeed, Goldstein has shown that national judges in Europe accommodated the supremacy of EC law (in the absence of a supremacy clause) faster and with less conflict than State judges accepted federal supremacy in the United States system, although the American Constitution possessed a supremacy clause.[104] In any event, there is no denying that the effectiveness of the decentralized system of monitoring and enforcement of EU law has been steadily upgraded since the big bang of the 1960s, as national judges invested in the system. In the most systematic research on Article 267 TFEU 'dialogues' to date, Nykios found judicial compliance with the Court's preliminary rulings to be well over 95 per cent, in part because national judges regularly signal the responses they want, and the CJEU regularly supplies them. Further, national judges today possess all of the authority necessary to provide effective remedies, alone and in conjunction with the ECJ.[105] These outcomes are a product of subtle inter-judicial dialogues, not master planning on the part of the Member States.

3. PROSPECTS

Shapiro concluded by reflecting on how the Court's major achievements would condition the future challenges that it would face. His argument, in a nutshell, was the following. Federalism review, if effective, will centralize law-making authority which, in turn, will lead the Court to become increasingly involved in reviewing the exercise of federal-level competences. This is precisely what happened in the EU. After the Single Act, division of powers review became more important, and annulment actions, brought by private plaintiffs, exploded. The Court then embarked on the laborious construction of an administrative law. Although this chapter has not stressed the point, the Article 263 TFEU annulment action has been central to the development of a European law of proper procedures, and to the ongoing judicialization of

---

[104] L Goldstein, *Constituting Federal Sovereignty: The European Union in Comparative Context* (Baltimore, 2001).

[105] See Dougan in this volume; A Ward, *Judicial Review and the Rights of Private Parties in EC Law* (Oxford University Press, 2000).

administrative governance.[106] I would quibble with this depiction only on the margins, giving more weight than Shapiro did to the Court's embracing of individual rights, and to the adoption of an overarching analytical procedure for rights adjudication—the proportionality framework.[107] Both moves were crucial to the Court's success in the 1960s and 1970s, and to the evolution of the EU legal system thereafter.

The entry into force of the Lisbon Treaty, on 1 December 2009,[108] provides another frame for assessing future prospects in light of this chapter's major themes. The new Treaty further strengthens the supranational features of the system: qualified majority voting and co-decision are now the presumptively 'normal' procedures for legislating, and the Parliament's powers have increased in other ways. The European Council, that most intergovernmental of institutions, is now a proper subject of EU law, rather than an external appendage to it. The Member States did not shrink the Court's zone of discretion. They tinkered with the rules governing Treaty revision, but the unanimity requirement remains in place for all important amendments. Further, the Member States extended the Court's 'normal' jurisdiction to matters that formerly constituted the 'Third Pillar'; and, on the road to Lisbon, they declared their acceptance of the Court's supremacy case law, for the first time.[109] The EU's administrative law system also appears ripe for renewed expansion: the TFEU now authorizes legislative delegation of considerable rule-making authority to the Commission, which will inevitably generate a great deal of administrative review.

The change with the greatest potential to shape the future evolution of the system is the promulgation of the Charter of Rights, which also enshrines the principle of proportionality. Lawyers and judges will be more comfortable working with a codified text than with unwritten general principles. They will generate more rights-oriented litigation and preliminary references, and they will plead and decide cases differently. The CJEU, for its part, will be able to find rights issues implied in almost any case in which it looks for them. Thus, there is every reason to expect that rights preoccupations will gradually infuse the exercise of *all* of the Court's competences, much like it does that of other national Constitutional Courts in Europe. On the immediate agenda, the Court will be forced to choose whether to maintain or alter its controversial

---

[106] Harlow and Shapiro in this volume; M Ruffert (ed), *The Transformation of Administrative Law in Europe* (Sellier, 2005). EU administrative law is now an autonomous field of research and teaching in its own right, with its own textbooks, eg P Craig, *EU Administrative Law* (Oxford University Press, 2006).

[107] A Stone Sweet and J Mathews, 'Proportionality Balancing and Global Constitutionalism' (2008) 47 Colum J Transn'l L 68, discussion of the EU at 137–145.

[108] I wrote this chapter a few weeks after the Lisbon Treaty entered into force, in December 2009. On a personal note, I have been teaching and doing research on the European Court and integration for more than two decades. I am unable to recall a single moment, going back to the 1960s, when the European project was not being characterized (by officials, scholars, and other commentators) as being mired in inter-institutional squabbles, and paralyzed by crises of governance and legitimacy. Nonetheless, integration proceeds, and the EU's supranational features continue to strengthen.

[109] Declaration 17—'Concerning Primacy.' *Declarations Annexed to the Final Act of the Intergovernmental Conference which Adopted the Treaty of Lisbon*, signed 13 December 2007, online at: <http://eur-lex.europa.eu/LexUriServ/LexUriServ.do?uri=OJ:C:2008:115:0335:0359:EN:PDF>.

jurisprudence on standing requirements for annulment actions under Article 263 TFEU. And it will have to decide how the Charter relates to the fundamental rights derived from its jurisprudence on general principles, which has important significance for its activity under Articles 258 TFEU and 267 TFEU. According to Article 51(1) Charter, Charter rights apply to the Member States 'only when they are implementing Union law', whereas the fundamental rights *qua* general principles apply to the Member States whenever they act 'within the scope of EU law'. The Court could close this gap by interpreting the notion of 'implementing Union law' broadly, thereby making it possible to fold its fundamental rights jurisprudence into its Charter rulings when desirable. But it could also choose to maintain its existing fundamental rights case law as a relatively autonomous corpus, which might allow for more flexibility and legitimacy when dealing with references from the national courts that concern sensitive Member State measures falling 'within the scope of EU law'. After all, the fundamental rights case law was developed through interactions with national courts, and it rests expressly on national traditions of rights protection.

As the authoritative interpreter of Charter rights, the CJEU's *bona fides* as a Constitutional Court have been secured. As a result, the Court will occupy a much grander place within the distinctive, pluralist architecture of rights-based constitutionalism in Europe. But this new status comes at a price. The Court now finds itself firmly locked into an inter-judicial structure—the triangle of national courts, the European Court of Human Rights, and the CJEU—which will generate its own, multi-dimensional, rights politics. These politics will force the CJEU to review the legality of EU acts much more robustly than it has to this point in time. National judges, through preliminary references that invoke the Charter, will routinely ask the Court to do so, as a pre-condition for enforcing EU law. Further, the Lisbon Treaty added Article 6(2) TEU, which commits the EU to accession to the European Convention on Human Rights (which is currently blocked by Russia's failure to ratify Protocol 14 ECHR). With accession, the position of the Strasbourg Court, as a de facto organ of EU governance, would be radically enhanced, not least, in that important elements of the CJEU's rights jurisprudence will be exposed to the direct supervision of the Strasbourg Court. Thus, the CJEU will find itself under increasing pressure from below (the national courts) and above (the European Court of Human Rights), and these pressures will require it to intrude ever more deeply into EU-level policy-making. More judicialization of EU governance will be the result.

7

THE EUROPEAN UNION FROM MAASTRICHT TO LISBON: INSTITUTIONAL AND LEGAL UNITY OUT OF THE SHADOWS

Deirdre M Curtin and Ige F Dekker*

A. INSTITUTIONAL SEDIMENTATION

The European Union is first and foremost a legal construct. As lawyers well know it was formally established in the Treaty of Maastricht that entered into force on 1 November 1993. Its aims were relatively modest: to associate two new sets of issue areas with the existing EC Treaties (respectively the CFSP and—at that time—the CJHA[1]) without replacing the existing Treaties as well as the more radical aim of creating an economic and monetary union. The two new sets of issue areas (Pillars) would exist side by side (with a few general overarching provisions). Lawyers and politicians were vehement that there would be little to no 'contamination' over and across. A Europe of 'bits and pieces' loomed[2] but did not in practice materialize in the manner expected. Our conclusion in the first edition of this book more than ten

---

* Deirdre Curtin is Professor in European Law, University of Amsterdam and Professor of Law and Governance of International and European Organizations, Utrecht University. Ige Dekker is Professor of International Institutional Law, Utrecht University. The authors are very grateful to Leonhard den Hertog, Angela Moisl, and Carlijn Ruers for their research and technical assistance.

[1] CFSP is the abbreviation for the 'Common Foreign and Security Policy' and is commonly known in shorthand as 'the Second Pillar' since the Treaty of Maastricht. The 'Third Pillar' was initially constituted by CJHA (Cooperation in Justice and Home Affairs) but after certain policy areas (in particular asylum and immigration) were moved to the 'First Pillar' (EC) in the Treaty of Amsterdam on 1 May 1999, the Third Pillar was reduced to PJCC (Police and Judicial Cooperation in Criminal Matters). CJHA acts adopted before 1 May 1999 remained in force insofar as they were not replaced by new EC acts. On 1 December 2009 PJCC was subsumed within the EU as a whole; here too PJCC acts adopted before 1 December 2009 remain in force insofar as they are not replaced by new EU acts.

[2] D M Curtin, 'The Constitutional Structure of the Union: A Europe of Bits and Pieces' (1993) 30 CML Rev 1, 17–69.

years ago (1999) was that already only five years later the Union had, in general terms, evolved as an international organization, into a legal system with a clear unitary character overarching many—and sometimes very different—'layers' of cooperation and integration. This conclusion was based on an analysis of the Treaty framework as amended by the Treaty of Amsterdam and the legal practices of the institutions of the Union since the Treaty of Maastricht.

In the past ten or more years, the evolution of the European Union has gone further, more or less along the lines we originally 'discovered' after five years of Treaty implementation and legal practices. More than fifteen years after the Treaty of Maastricht, the new Lisbon Treaty (2007) in Article 1 TEU ordains that the Union 'shall replace and succeed the European Community'. Article 1 TEU has not come out of the blue. It rather reflects institutional realities that had evolved and ripened to such an extent that the formal provisions of the Treaty of Lisbon caught up with 'living' and sedimentary practices. On the one hand, the unitary character of the Union seems to be reinforced in terms of, for instance, the partial 'depillarization' that has taken place as well as the application of 'general principles of the Community' to the whole legal framework of the Union. On the other hand, the trend of harbouring, within the outer shell of the Union, various autonomous and interlinked entities with their own specific roles and legal regimes has been continued. Rather than thinking in terms of 'layers' implying images of vertical and horizontal separation it may be more appropriate to think rather of a looser and less sharply defined 'marbling' effect.

Legal unity is in any event the order of the day and no longer 'in disguise'. The new Lisbon Treaty has the advantage that in one fell swoop it improves the systemic visibility and structural clarity of European integration processes. At the same time this catches up with social reality and the perception of citizens and third states already from the early days that the EU constitutes an organizational and legal unity.[3] The 'verdict' of both the Court of Justice in developing the 'living' constitution over time and the framers of *inter alia* the Treaty of Lisbon is that the legal system—and also the political system—of the European Union as such is developing as an institutional and legal unity. Such a unitary institutional legal system creates spaces for developing a variety of sub-legal systems not only within the Union itself, but also within the separate policy areas, a reality most recently consolidated in the Treaty of Lisbon.

We begin by outlining in some detail our theoretical starting point for the analysis of the development of the legal system of the European Union as such, namely the 'institutional theory of law' (section 2). This institutional approach still constitutes in our view the best possible theoretical framework for analysing a complex modern legal system such as that of the European Union. In applying the core concept of this theory—'legal institution'—to the Treaty on European Union, we defend the thesis that already in this Treaty and its legal system an international organization

---

[3] See further D M Curtin and I F Dekker, 'The EU as a "Layered" International Organization: Institutional Unity in Disguise?' in P Craig and G de Búrca (eds), *The Evolution of EU Law* (Oxford University Press, 1999) 83.

with a unitary but complex legal character was established in 1992. Whether this legal 'picture' presented by the provisions of the TEU itself is in fact operationalized in the institutional legal practices of the Union in the context of the CFSP, CJHA, and PJCC, is the focus of section 3. Finally we make some concluding observations on the nature and refinement of the 'marbling techniques' employed both in the Treaty provisions and in their (future) operationalization in practice.

B. THE EUROPEAN UNION AS AN INTERNATIONAL ORGANIZATION

1. UNDERSTANDING 'LEGAL INSTITUTIONS'

(a) Legal institutions

Before entering into the legal analysis of the European Union as an international organization one needs at least some understanding of the legal concept of international organization and what kind of social phenomena can be qualified as such. The problem is that, as far as matters of theory go, the law of international organizations is still somewhat immature.[4] We therefore tried in the earlier version of our contribution to frame a theoretical approach grounded in a general legal approach: the institutional legal theory.[5] In order to account for the plurality of legal phenomena, this theory conceives of the legal system as a system of so-called 'legal institutions'. In other words, legal institutions are the 'building blocks' of legal systems and are not to be seen as synonymous with organizations (or organs thereof) but are characterized as distinct legal systems governing specific forms of social conduct within an overall legal system from which they derive their validity. Ruiter defines a legal institution as 'a regime of legal norms purporting to effectuate a legal practice that can be interpreted as resulting from a common belief that the regime is an existent unity'.[6]

The element of legal 'unity' has institutional and substantive aspects. The institutional aspects refer to the fact that a legal institution is a system of rules and competences that originate—in the sense of validity—exclusively from, in the end, a single legal source.[7] It indicates that such an institution can be dealt with as a legally valid and more or less autonomous element within the overall legal system. Secondly,

---

[4] J Klabbers, *An Introduction to International Institutional Law* (2nd edn, Cambridge University Press, 2009) 3.

[5] See, also for further references: Curtin and Dekker (n 3 above) 83–136; I F Dekker and R A Wessel, 'Governance by International Organizations: Rethinking the Normative Force of International Decisions' in I F Dekker and W G Werner (eds), *Governance and International Legal Theory* (Martinus Nijhoff, 2004) 215–236.

[6] D W P Ruiter, *Institutional Legal Facts. Legal Powers and Their Effects* (Kluwer, 1993) 358.

[7] Legal institutions are to be distinguished from other systems of rules governing specific social action in the context of a comprehensive social order. See about these approaches, among others, D C North, *Institutions, Institutional Change, and Economic Performance* (Cambridge University Press, 1990); J G March and J P Olsen, *Rediscovering Institutions. The Organizational Basis of Politics* (MacMillan, 1989).

the unity of a legal institution implies that its legal system has to be 'coherent', meaning that the different parts of the legal regime of the institution are connected by common basic legal concepts uniting competing and sometimes even contradictory conceptions of such basic legal concepts used in the different sub-systems of the institution.[8]

Legal institutions, thus, refer to entities—subjects and objects—and to properties of these entities—qualities and status—and to connections between those entities. On the basis of these distinctions it is possible to develop logically a quite simple classification of seven legal institutions.[9] We will come back to some of them in relation to the phenomenon of international organizations. On this point suffice it to say that *if* the concept of international organizations can be conceived of as a legal institution, the question would be which kind of human linguistic activity could gain validity as part of the legal regime of that institution, and which legal 'facts' would therefore have to be taken seriously by the relevant legal community. According to the institutional legal theory, the legal 'facts' that can gain legal validity within legal institutions are far more shaded in their differentiation as acts than the classical distinction between duty-imposing and power-conferring rules. In this respect the theory (also) presents a classification of seven different categories.[10] In day-to-day language, such legal acts consist of (a) a declaration of a legal state of affairs; (b) a statement of purpose; (c) a command to perform; (d) a commitment to assume an obligation; (e) a recommendation of a course of conduct; (f) an assertion of a state of affairs; and (g) an expression of a state of mind. Examples of all of these norms and rules can be found in European Union law.[11] This approach makes it possible, regardless of the fact that the limits of the legal system are still defined by the criterion of validity, to account for a larger number of results stemming from human activity that qualify as legal acts. Besides legal obligations to follow a certain course of action, there are other elements of a legal regime—such as principles, inducements, and purposes—which are also institutional legal realities too and for that reason give rise to different expectations and different patterns of legitimization of conduct.

---

[8] See, in general on the concept of coherence in law, D W P Ruiter, *Legal Institutions* (Kluwer, 2001) 71–73; N MacCormick, 'Coherence in Legal Justification' in A Peczenik, L Lindahl, and G van Roermund (eds), *Theory of Legal Science, Proceedings of the Conference on Legal Theory and Philosophy of Science* (Reidel, 1984) 235–251; T M Franck, *Fairness in International Law and Institutions* (Clarendon, 1997) 38–41; E Christodoulidis and R Dukes, 'On the Unity of European Labour Law' in S Prechal and B van Roermund (eds), *The Coherence of EU Law. The Search for Unity in Divergent Concepts* (Oxford University Press, 2008) 399–403.

[9] See Ruiter (n 8 above) 102–115, who distinguishes the following legal institutions: *Legal persons* (subjects), *legal objects* (goods), *legal qualities* (property of subjects), *legal status* (property of objects), *personal legal relationships* (connection between subjects), *legal configurations* (connection between objects), and *objective legal relationships* (connection between subjects and objects).

[10] See Ruiter (n 6 above) 52–79, 90. Competence-conferring rules, determining the conditions under which rules of conduct are legally valid, are a special type of declarative legal acts.

[11] See Ruiter (n 6 above) 81–89; Dekker and Wessel (n 5 above) 225–226.

(b) Legal institutions and legal practices

The concept of legal institutions does not refer to an existent entity, but to a presentation of a phenomenon that ought to be made true in the form of social practices. Thus, legal institutions have their counterparts in social reality, often referred to as 'real' institutions, which reveal themselves in the form of recurrent and enduring legal and other practices.[12] Or as Ruiter puts it: 'a legal institution is in the first instance a fiction that is subsequently realised by people believing in it and acting upon this belief. It follows i) that human beings must be able to visualise legal institutions and ii) that the existence of legal institutions must be conceivable as inherent in human behaviour.'[13] Of course, legal institutions—as 'ideal' entities—can be studied separately from their real counterparts. However, as Weinberger claims, legal institutions are in the end only relevant in relation to real institutions.[14] There is a direct relation between legal rules and powers—as objective thoughts—and social reality. Rules and powers come to the fore in, for example, the fact that they exist in the realm of human consciousness, that they function as a motivational element in human behaviour, that they are related to the existence of social institutions, and that behaviour in conformity with or contrary to norms and rules gives rise to positive or negative social consequences.[15] Of course, a significant result of this view is that if one wants to analyse the meaning of positive law it is not enough to restrict this analysis to the content of valid enacted rules and competences, rather one must also examine whether these norms can be said to exist as social practices. However, Weinberger's theory at this point only partly solves the 'great' problem of legal positivism: the tension between the validity and efficacy of law. Weinberger's theory of action is one-sided, in the sense that it only explains the functional relationship between legal institutions and social practices and not the other way around. Thus, the institutional theory of law does not solve, in a theoretical sense, the problem of how and which social practices can influence the meaning of valid legal norms and rules.

This—not insignificant—limitation inherent in the (institutional) legal theory does not impede its use for the purposes of our analysis of the European Union as a legal system as such. As far as the practice is concerned, our analysis is limited to the 'legal practices' that have evolved in the legal system of the Union. 'Legal practices' are forms

---

[12] O Weinberger, *Law, Institution and Legal Practice. Fundamental Problems of Legal Theory and Social Philosophy* (Kluwer, 1991) 21–22; H Kenman, 'Approaches to the Analysis of Institutions' in B Steunenberg and F van Vught (eds), *Political Institutions and Public Policy* (Kluwer, 1997) 3.

[13] D W P Ruiter, 'A Basic Classification of Legal Institutions' (1991) 10 Ratio Iuris 4, 363; Ruiter (n 8 above) 71–99.

[14] Weinberger (n 12 above) 21–22: 'There does not appear to be a clearly drawn distinction which must not be infringed between normative institutions and institutions in the sense of structures and public utilities and both are functionally linked with each other.... As complexes of norms the legal institutions are linked to an actual whole on the strength of their connection with an existing factual sphere or one being constituted by these norms and they are institutionalized as social practices.'

[15] O Weinberger, 'The norm as thought and as reality' in N MacCormick and O Weinberger, *An Institutional Theory of Law* (Reidel, 1986) 40–41.

of legal action that are—explicitly or implicitly—employed in order to make a legal system an operational entity.[16] It can be said that all the elements of the legal regime of a legal institution have their counterparts in a legal practice. In other words legal practices could, for example, consist of acts of cooperation and negotiation between the participants in a legal institution, adherence to general principles, the establishment of decision-making or executive organs, of procedures followed in order to ensure compliance with legal norms, or in the appointment of agents for the implementation of certain regulations. Of course, such an analysis of legal practices cannot 'prove' the existence of a legal institution as a social institution. But developments in legal practices can be seen as *indicators* of whether social reality is attuning to the legal institution and its regime.[17]

(c) Legal institutions and international organizations

An international organization is a complex legal institution, in particular as a result of the special relationships between the organization and its Member States. The complexity is revealed by the fact that international organizations, in their legal set-up, have two 'faces'. They are, on the one hand, autonomous entities operating at the international and national level but, at the same time, they are for their legal birth and life—their existence—basically dependent on the consent of and cooperation between its members. This duality governs a lot of aspects of the legal regime of international organizations, such as their institutional structure, their decision-making processes, their functions and powers, and their responsibility and accountability.

In terms of institutional legal theory, these two 'faces' of international organizations can be identified as respectively an 'alliance' and as a 'legal person'.[18] An 'alliance' can be described as an enduring (multilateral) contractual legal relation between subjects—for example states—presenting a set of expectations about their reciprocal behaviour. In international law, such alliances are based on a treaty or some other international legal act between the 'participating' or better, 'contracting' parties and the obligations resulting from such 'contracts' have a multilateral, multi-sided character. This is only one side of the coin. International organizations have, at the same time, the institutional form of a 'legal person'. A 'legal person' is to be understood as an entity that has the capacity to act, through collective decision-making, both internally and externally. Within an international organization the original (multilateral) 'contractual' relationship between the states parties within the alliance is *supplemented* by a

---

[16] Compare P Morton, *An Institutional Theory of Law* (Clarendon, 1998) 38–43, 58–66.

[17] It is obvious that the concept 'legal practices' employed for the purposes of our chapter is, in fact, *broader* than the one used by the traditional theory of international law. The latter concept is restricted to those legal practices that are relevant for the interpretation and application of mandatory norms and rules of conduct and competences to adopt such norms and rules. The broader concept of legal norms and rules which we employ brings together a much wider range of legal practices which are relevant in getting a 'real' picture of an institutional legal system.

[18] D W P Ruiter, 'Types of Institutions as Pattern of Regulated Behaviour' (2004) 10 Res Publica 207, 214–216.

set of 'constitutional' relationships of each of the Member States with the established legal person. In order for the creation of a legal person to take place, the relationship between each of the Member States and the organization has to have some basic content, in particular the right of the members to participate—through their representatives—in the decision-making of the organs of the organization and the duty of the Member States to respect the autonomy of the organization through, *inter alia*, the recognition of their legal personality and their privileges and immunities. As a legal person, international organizations become the subject of the international legal system implying in principle the right to be treated on a par with other international legal subjects, including the capacity to perform international legal acts as well as to be accountable and responsible for their behaviour.[19]

It is important to realize that with the creation of an international organization the alliance between the Member States is *not* replaced by the legal person; were a complete transformation from the alliance into a legal person to have taken place the result would be a different kind of entity, a (federal) state or an entity *sui generis*. Instead, an international organization seems to be typically characterized by the two institutional legal forms—the alliance and the association—which exist legally side-by-side. The bottom line is that—even in the case of the most 'integrated' international organizations—the alliance of the Member States retains the power to change the constitutive instruments of the legal person and, in the end, can decide about its existence. This institutional legal structure explains to a great extent the complex legal nature of international organizations and some of the main legal issues, such as the legal status, the foundation and range of legal powers, the legal character of the acts, the decision-making processes, and the division of the responsibility between the organization and its members. To a large extent, this fundamental and inherent dual legal nature constantly threatens the unitary character of the Union, as will be illustrated in the next sub-sections.

2. THE EUROPEAN UNION AS A LEGAL INSTITUTION

(a) Diverging visions

In our earlier version of this chapter we discussed quite extensively the question of whether the European Union and its legal regime could be explained in legal institutional concepts other than as an international organization.[20] At that time, there was even a considerable reluctance, in particular in European legal circles, to acknowledge the European Union as a single legal entity, let alone an international organization in

---

[19] That is not to say that all international organizations will automatically have 'international legal personality', although being an international legal person this quality may be presumed. There is, of course, no such a presumption in case of a mere alliance, even if they are very influential in international relations ('G7' or 'G8'). Within alliances the states parties themselves are the decision-making entities and they are also themselves accountable for all the consequences of acts and omissions.

[20] Curtin and Dekker (n 3 above) 83–85, 93–97.

its own right.[21] In the view of some—mainly German—legal scholars, the Union, consisting of the European Communities and the cooperation in the Second and Third Pillars, was at best only an alliance—or, in German, a *Staatenverbund*—without a separate legal status under international law. According to them, the Union as such did not possess any legal capacity, internally or externally, and had no organs. The European Council and the Council of Ministers were in the framework of the Second and Third Pillars merely conferences of governments and their acts were not legal acts of the Union but multilateral agreements among governments. Also the description of the Union as a Greek temple—for many years a very popular metaphor for the Union—was basically (but often implicitly) picturing the Union as primarily an alliance.[22] Viewed from this perspective, the legal regime of the European Union brought together under one (thin) roof the different forms of intergovernmental cooperation previously existing among the Member States of the Communities.

On this understanding the Union's Second Pillar—the Common Foreign and Security Policy (CFSP)—was simply the continuation of the previously existing European Political Cooperation, which had started in the beginning of the seventies as a form of informal exchange of information and consultation on issues of foreign policy between the Member States, and which was for the first time formally codified in the Single European Act.[23] The Third Pillar of the Union—under the heading of, first, Co-operation in the fields of Justice and Home Affairs (CJHA) and, later, Police and Judicial Co-operation in Criminal Matters (PJCC)—structured and put on a *Treaty* basis the great variety of mainly intergovernmental fora in the field of home affairs and internal security existing at that time, such as, for example, the *Ad Hoc* Group on Immigration, TREVI, and the Group of Co-ordinators on the Free Movement of Persons.[24] The Union itself, it was held, only overarched the three Pillars by stating some general objectives and principles and some final provisions but certainly not as a legal entity that had the capacity to act on its own. This approach ignored what was already at that time the *double* institutional legal nature of the Union.

At that time, some authors took the opposite view, namely asserting that within the European Union a complete fusion has taken place between the European Communities and the Second and Third Pillars, constituting a single organization with legal

---

[21] This was—and still is?—most clearly and consistently held by two German legal scholars, Koenig and Pechstein. See C Koenig and M Pechstein, *Die Europäische Union* (Mohr Siebeck, 1995) and M Pechstein and C Koenig, *Die Europäische Union* (3rd edn, Mohr Siebeck, 2006).

[22] See, for example, U Everling, 'Reflections on the Structure of the European Union' (1992) 29 CML Rev 1053, 1063; Curtin (n 2 above) 17–70; J H H Weiler, 'Neither Unity Nor Three Pillars, The Trinity Structure of the Treaty on European Union' in J Monar *et al* (eds), *The Maastricht Treaty on European Union, Legal Complexity and Political Dynamic* (European Interuniversity, 1993) 49–62 and other sources cited in our chapter in the first edition of this volume.

[23] M Holland (ed), *The Future of European Political Cooperation* (MacMillan, 1991); S Nutall, *European Political Cooperation* (Clarendon, 1992).

[24] J de Zwaan, 'Institutional Problems and Free Movement of Persons. The Legal and Political Framework for Cooperation' in H G Schermers *et al* (eds), *Free Movement of Persons in Europe* (Asser Institute, 1991) 335–351.

personality and governed by one legal regime, including the legal Community principles of supremacy, direct applicability, and direct effect.[25] Also this assertion was—and, according to us, still is—difficult to reconcile with the legal system of the Union and the legal practices followed by the institutions because it overstretches the single legal entity character of the Union. Although the unitary character of the legal system of the European Union was to some extent already visible from the start, and certainly has been strengthened over the course of the past ten years, the two interrelated institutional forms of the Union's underlying legal nature are still in place.[26]

Our starting-point is, again, that the legal system of the European Union is most accurately analysed in terms of the institutional legal concept of an international organization, as explained above.[27] In the remainder of this sub-section we will substantiate this contention by way of a succinct analysis of the constitutive treaties in relation to, first, the two different institutional legal forms of the European Union and, secondly, the extent of its unitary character. In section 3 we will take this analysis further by identifying the legal practices, as defined above, in particular with regard to the unitary and dis-unitary nature of the political executive, in the front-stage as well as the backstage of the European Union.

(b) An alliance *and* a legal person

The European Union is obviously based on a treaty that regulates the mutual legal relationships between the now twenty-seven Member States. As is stated in Article 1 of the Treaty on European Union (TEU): 'By this treaty, the HIGH CONTRACTING PARTIES

---

[25] A von Bogdandy and M Nettesheim, 'Die Europäische Union: Ein einheitlicher Verband mit eigener Rechtsordnung' (1995) 30 Europarecht 3; this article is also published in English: A von Bogdandy and M Nettesheim, 'Ex Pluribus Unum: Fusion of the European Communities into the European Union' (1996) 2 ELJ 267; A von Bogdandy, 'The Legal Case for Unity: The European Union as a Single Organization with a Single Legal System' (1999) 36 CML Rev 887.

[26] This double institutional identity penetrates all parts of the Union, including the previous legal system of the EC. A good example is the Comitology system, as explained, with abundant empirical evidence, by G J Brandsma, *Backstage Europe, Comitology, Accountability and Democracy in the European Union* (Utrecht University Press, 2010).

[27] Compare the judgment of the German Constitutional Court on the Lisbon Treaty, delivered on 30 June 2009, in which the Court declared that the Lisbon Treaty is a treaty that improves, where necessary, the functioning of the European Union without changing its fundamental nature. According to the Court, the European Union: 'is designed as an association of sovereign national states (*Staatenverbund*) to which sovereign powers are transferred. The concept of *Verbund* covers a close long-term association of states which remain sovereign, an association which exercises public authority on the basis of a treaty, whose fundamental order, however, is subject to the disposal of the Member States alone and in which the peoples of their Member States, ie the citizens of the states, remain the subjects of democratic legitimisation. [...] The empowerment to transfer sovereign powers to the European Union or other intergovernmental institution permits a shift of political rule to international organizations. The empowerment to exercise supranational competences comes, however, from the Member States of such an institution. They therefore permanently remain the masters of the Treaties.' *Entscheidungen des Bundesverfassungsgerichts* [Federal Constitutional Court] 30 June 2009, Docket Nos. 2 BvE 2/08, 2 BvE 5/08, 2 BvR 1010/08, 2 BvR 1022/08, 2 BvR 1259/08, 2 BvR 182/0, paras 229 and 231; available at <http://www.bundesverfassungsgericht.de/entscheidungen/>. See further A Steinbach, 'The Lisbon Judgment of the German Federal Constitutional Court—New Guidance on the Limits of European Integration' (2010) 11 German Law Journal 367.

establish among themselves a European Union.' According to the same Article, the Union is founded on two Treaties, namely the Treaty on European Union and the Treaty on the Functioning of the European Union (TFEU)—the Treaties.[28] The *alliance* character of the Union is also revealed in other provisions, such as in the principle of conferral of competences, which is underlined several times, including in the—new—provision stating that the competences not conferred upon the Union in the Treaties remain with the Member States.[29] The TEU also prominently mentions the quite classic international law principle that the Union 'shall respect the equality of the Member States', 'their national identities', and 'their essential State functions, including ensuring the territorial integrity of the State, maintaining law and order and safeguarding national security'.[30] In some other respects the position of the Member States even seems to be strengthened, in particular by the increased role and competences of the European Council, which is of course an *organ* of the Union but one still resembling in many respects a 'conference' of the governments of the Members. It is not unimportant that the Member States remain the *'Herren der Verträge'* in that they are the parties who, ultimately, decide about the (important) changes of the Treaties, as laid down in the ordinary revision procedure.[31] This provision explicitly provides that such amendments can serve 'to reduce the competences conferred on the Union...'.[32] Last but not least, the alliance character of the Union seems to be strengthened by the new provision on the right of every Member to withdraw, at any moment, unilaterally from the Union.[33]

It is—and to a certain extent was from the beginning—equally clear that the European Union is a *legal person* too. The Lisbon Treaty also strengthens this institutional form more rather than less, not only in its external aspects but also with regard to the internal ones. As to the *internal* structure, the European Union is in the amended TEU more strongly presented than before as one, single legal entity. It states that the Union shall replace and succeed the European Community. In this respect, the 'fusion thesis'—the integration of Union and the EC in one legal person—seems to be realized, at least at Treaty level. The two Treaties do not—as was the case in the pre-Lisbon era—represent legal regimes of different legal entities. They rather constitute one legal entity: the Union. The distinction between the two Treaties

---

[28] See also Art 1(2) TFEU. The TEU covers mainly 'constitutional' and organizational matters, as well as the provisions on the Union's external relations, the Common Foreign and Security Policy (CFSP), including the Common Security and Defence Policy (CSDP). The TFEU is, in fact an adjusted replica of the former Treaty establishing the European Community, and deals, apart from some important additional institutional provisions—for instance, Arts 2–6 TFEU on the competences of the Union, Arts 258–268, 340 TFEU on enforcement actions, preliminary rulings, review of legality and actions for damages, Arts 288–292 TFEU on the categories and hierarchy of legal acts of the Union, and Art 312 TFEU on the principles of budgetary planning—with the *policies* of the Union, including the former Third Pillar on police and judicial cooperation on criminal matters.

[29] Art 4(1) TEU. See also Declarations nos 18 and 24, both attached to the Lisbon Treaty, on the delimitation of competences of the Union respectively the international legal personality of the Union.

[30] Art 4(2) TEU.   [31] Art 48 TEU.

[32] Art 48(2) TEU.   [33] Art 50 TEU.

follows, very roughly, the logic of the distinction between 'primary' and 'secondary' rules, in that the TEU concerns 'constitutional', including institutional, matters, whereas the TFEU covers the headlines of, and the competences to develop the policies of, the Union, although formally there is no ranking between them. This logic has led to the integration via the Lisbon Treaty of the substantive provisions of the former Third Pillar of the Union (PJCC), which have now been integrated in the 'Area of Freedom, Security and Justice' of the TFEU. A remarkable exception in this regard is the provisions on the former Second Pillar, the Common Foreign and Security Policy (CFSP), including the renewed and extended provisions on the Common Security and Defence Policy (CSDP). Not only the general and institutional provisions but also the substantive ones are (still) part of the TEU and are not, as far as policy matters are concerned, transferred to the TFEU.[34] This derogation from the general structure is probably still due to anxieties of some Member States for the 'communitarization' of the highly sensitive political issues involved in this area. However, this situation is without prejudice to the view that the Union has to be seen as one legal person with regard to *all* policy areas within its jurisdiction, whether regulated in the TEU or the TFEU. The real exception to this situation is the result of the fact that the Lisbon Treaty does not touch upon the legal status of the European Atomic Energy Community, which thus seems to have preserved, albeit within the Union, its existence as a separate legal person.[35]

The Union as a legal person is further expressed by the legal fact—which was disputed until now—that the Union itself has organs with decision-making capacity.[36] The Lisbon Treaty explicitly states that the Union 'shall have an institutional framework', consisting of seven main institutions.[37] Besides the traditional five institutions of the former European Communities—the European Parliament, the Council, the European Commission, the Court of Justice, and the Court of Auditors—the main institutions now also include the European Council and the European Central Bank. Through these institutions—and, of course, also through the extensive and complex structure of subsidiary organs and other bodies—the Union has the capacity to act vis-à-vis the Member States and its citizens. For the enactment of legal acts the European Union has at its disposal a rather wide range of types of 'legal instruments'. The triple set of instruments with legally binding force for the European Community—*regulations*, *directives*, and *decisions*—become post-Lisbon the main legal instruments of the Union.[38] There are new provisions in the Treaty on the Functioning of the European Union according to which these instruments can contain 'legislative acts', 'non-legislative acts of general application', or 'implementing acts', by which a certain

---

[34] An exception seems to be Art 222 TFEU on solidarity between the Member States in case of a terrorist attack or emergency situation.

[35] See Protocol No. 2 annexed to the Treaty of Lisbon on amending the Treaty on establishing the European Atomic Energy Community.

[36] See Curtin and Dekker (n 3 above) 98.

[37] Art 13 TEU.   [38] Art 288 TFEU (Art 249 EC).

hierarchy of the Union's legal acts is introduced.[39] Besides the formal legal instruments, the organs of the European Union made and continue to make use of a great variety of other, more informal legal instruments, some of them mentioned in the Treaties, others developed in practice, such as advisory opinions, recommendations, strategies, declarations, resolutions, white papers, and many other types of reports.[40]

For the Second and Third Pillars, there has always been a separate range of legal instruments, in particular *common strategies, common positions, joint actions, framework decisions, decisions, and conventions.*[41] With the Lisbon Treaty entering into force most of these instruments are replaced by one umbrella legal instrument: the *decision.* This will, from now on, be the only legal instrument for the CFSP.[42] However, this amendment is partly cosmetic and has not altered the explicitly stated competence of the Union to take decisions on 'general guidelines', 'operational action', and 'the approach of the Union',[43] ie formulations which pre-Lisbon were used to describe common strategies, joint actions, and common positions respectively, and to a large extent are maintained in the new Treaty on European Union. However, a clear distinction with other EU policy areas is that Article 24(1) TEU excludes 'the adoption of legislative acts' for CFSP matters, which in turn excludes the use of the legislative procedures (the 'Community method').[44] Apart from the continued exclusion of the European Parliament and the Commission in the decision-making phase, as well as the almost complete exclusion of the jurisdiction of the Court, this distinction will probably cause a continuation of the ongoing discussion on the legal force of CFSP decisions.[45] The language used by the relevant Treaty provisions nonetheless suggests that those legal acts, once adopted, limit the freedom of Member States in their individual policies.[46] In particular, CFSP joint actions 'shall commit the Member

---

[39] Arts 289 and 291 TFEU. See further Chapter 3 of this volume.

[40] See further, B de Witte, A Geelhoed, and J Inghleram, 'Legal Instruments, Decision-Making and EU Finances' in P J G Kapteyn, A M McDonnell, K J M Mortelmans, and C W A Timmermans (eds), *The Law of the European Union and the European Communities* (Kluwer, 2008) 273–419, 276; L A J Senden, 'Soft Law and its Implication for Institutional Balance' (2005) 1 Utrecht Law Review 79.

[41] See Arts 12–15 and 34 EU. The original provisions on the legal instruments of the Second and Third Pillar were heavily criticized for their obscure and ill-defined wording and, on that ground, substantially amended by the Treaty of Amsterdam. See Dekker and Curtin (n 3 above) 99.

[42] Art 25 TEU.

[43] See Arts 26(1), 28(1), and 29 TEU.

[44] See Art 289(1) TFEU.

[45] No interpretation could be expected from the Court of Justice given that Art 46 EU explicitly excludes Title V from its jurisdiction, as confirmed by eg Case T-201/99 *Royal Olympic Cruises Ltd and others v Council and Commission* [2000] ECR II-4005; Case T-228/02 *Organisation des Modjahedines du peuple d'Iran* [2006] ECR II-04665 [49]; Case C-354/04 P *Gestoras Pro Amnistía and Others v Council* [2007] ECR I-1579 [50]. The situation is different only with regard to the largely similarly worded instruments of Title VI EU.

[46] C Hillion and R A Wessel, 'Restraining External Competences of EU Member States under CFSP' in M Cremona and B de Witte (eds), *EU Foreign Relations Law, Constitutional Fundamentals* (Hart, 2008) 79, 82–86. On CFSP joint actions specifically, see A Dashwood, 'The Law and Practice of CFSP Joint Actions' in M Cremona and B de Witte (eds), *EU Foreign Relations Law, Constitutional Fundamentals* (Hart, 2008) 53–77; F Dehousse, 'Les caractéristiques fondamentales de la politique étrangère et de sécurité commune' in J V Louis and M Dony (eds), *Relations Extérieures: Commentaire J. Mégret: Le droit de la CE et de l'Union européenne*

States in the positions they adopt and in the conduct of their activity',[47] and with regard to CFSP Common Positions the Treaty on European Union stipulates that 'Member States shall ensure that their national policies conform to the common positions'.[48] The legally binding nature of these instruments can be further based on the 'loyalty' obligation, which with regard to the CFSP is certainly strengthened by the Lisbon Treaty.[49] Quite recently, the European Court of Justice also confirmed the binding nature of a Common Position in the *Segi* case.[50] Although the case primarily concerned the Third Pillar, it seems to be justified to transpose these findings to the field of the CFSP. After all, the Common Position in question could also be regarded as a CFSP decision since it was equally based on both a CFSP provision (Article 15 EU) and a PJCC provision (Article 34 EU). The *Segi* judgment, however, only partly helps in answering the question of the legal force of CFSP instruments, and in particular it does not settle the legal force of CFSP decisions in the national legal order of the Member States.

For the first time in the history of the Union the Treaty on European Union provides explicitly for the (international) legal personality of the Union.[51] As explained in the previous edition, the omission of such a provision did not prevent the Union, quite soon after its establishment, from acting externally, even by entering into legal relations with regard to third parties.[52] For that reason it was already concluded at that time that there were strong arguments for at least the presumption of its international legal personality and it seems undisputed that the practice of the Union in the last ten years has turned the presumption into a legal fact. This was certainly the case after the Union—and not the European Community and/or the Member States—without further ado from 2003 onwards concluded treaties with non-Member States and other international organizations.[53] Thus, one could certainly conclude that the new provision is a codification of a general and consistent legal practice. Following naturally from its personality, the TEU now provides expressly for

(Institut d'Etudes Européennes, 2005) 441, 475; P Koutrakos, *EU International Relations Law* (Hart, 2006) 399; L Münch, *Die gemeinsame Aktion als Mittel der Gemeinsamen Außen- und Sicherheitspolitik* (Duncker & Humblot, 1997) 60.

[47] Art 14(3) EU and Art 28(2) TEU.

[48] Art 15 EU and Art 29 TEU. In the same vein, EU Common Strategies, envisaged in Art 13 EU and Art 26 TEU, bind not only the EU institutions but also the Member States. See de Witte, Geelhoed, and Inghleram (n 40 above) 296.

[49] Art 24(3) TEU. See further below sub-section 2(c).

[50] Case C-355/04 P *Segi v Council* [2007] ECR I-1657, [52]: 'A common position requires the compliance of the Member States by virtue of the principle of the duty to cooperate in good faith, which means in particular that Member States are to take all appropriate measures, whether general or particular to ensure fulfilment of their obligations under European Union law.'

[51] Art 47 TEU. See also Declaration No 24, attached to the TEU.

[52] Curtin and Dekker (n 3 above) 105–106. See more extensively on this issue: R A Wessel, 'The International Legal Status of the European Union' (1997) 2 Eur Foreign Aff Rev 109; R A Wessel, 'Revisiting the International Legal Status of the EU' (2000) 5 Eur Foreign Aff Rev 507.

[53] R A Wessel, 'The European Union as a Party to International Agreements: Shared Competences, Mixed Responsibilities' in A Dashwood and M Maresceau (eds), *Law and Practice of the EU External Relations—Salient Features of a Changing Landscape* (Cambridge University Press, 2008) 145–180.

a *general* competence of the European Union to conclude treaties with third parties—
states and other international organizations—on all areas of the Union's external
action.[54] Thus, the Union's Treaty-making capacity is equal in all areas and they will
bind, also in CFSP matters, the institutions and the Member States of the Union.[55]

The codification of international legal personality of the Union has not resulted in
the external representation of the Union by one single agent. At least three agents of
the organization will have a role to play in the Union's external affairs: the newly
created position of President of the European Council, the High Representative of the
Union for Foreign Affairs and Security Policy (the High Representative), a function
introduced by the Treaty of Amsterdam, and, from the early days, the President and
other members of the Commission. According to the Treaties, these offices have
several external tasks in representing the Union but the Treaties are for the greater
part silent on the delimitation of their respective responsibilities. In particular, this can
cause problems in the relationship between the Council President and the High
Representative. Both are genuine offices of the Union, elected or appointed by the
European Council, for which a qualified majority will suffice, and have the capacity to
represent the Union in the area of the CFSP.[56] Initially the then rotating President
of the European Council had the lead in CFSP affairs, but the Lisbon Treaty has
certainly strengthened the position of the High Representative. She presides over the
most important decision-making institution on CFSP matters—the Foreign Affairs
Council—and is one of the Vice-Presidents of the Commission.[57] In that capacity
she will conduct and put into effect the Union's CFSP.[58] The only reference to the
delimitation of their respective tasks is to be found in the terms of a reference of the
President providing that he has to ensure the external representation of the Union
in the area of the CFSP 'without prejudice to the powers of the High Representative'.[59]
Time will tell whether a further refinement of the allocation of tasks is needed.

(c) A legal unity?

The fact that the European Union, as an international organization, displays two
institutional 'faces', does not, as such, need to be an obstacle to the unitary character
of its legal system. That holds true, in principle, for the formal and substantial sides of
the unity of the legal system. As to the formal side, international organizations are
generally based on *one* constituent Treaty, which is also the legal basis for the further
development of their legal system. The legal system of the European Union, however,
was, from its birth in 1992 onwards, based on two separate treaties raising the question
as to the existence of one single legal system encompassing the different legal systems
of the European Communities and the CFSP and CJHA/PJCC. As was pointed out in

---

[54] Art 37 TEU and—for the procedure for concluding international agreements—Art 216 TFEU. Compare
the former Art 24 TEU on the treaty-making capacity of the EU on CFSP and PJCC matters.
[55] Art 216(2) TFEU. This last addition was not included in the former Art 24 TEU. Compare the former Art
300(7) TEC regulating the legal force of treaties for institutions and Member States in relation to EC matters.
[56] See Arts 15(5) and 18(1)(2) TEU.   [57] Art 18(3)(4) TEU.
[58] Arts 18(2), 24(1), 26(3) TEU.   [59] Art 15(6) TEU.

the previous edition, it could be argued that, although the separate status of the two constituent Treaties could not be denied, they formed basically one legal system because of the firm formal ties between them, in particular the prescription of *one* amendment procedure for both Treaties and *one* accession procedure for Union and the Communities.[60] The Lisbon Treaty has not changed this situation principally—the Union is still legally based on two different Treaties, which from now on are of explicitly equal value, bound together by the said ties[61]—but the ties between them are even stronger because of the replacement and succession of the European Community by the Union,[62] and the new provision that a Member State can only withdraw from the Union as such.[63] Also the much discussed issue of the demarcation between the different policy areas of the Union—in particular in pursuance of the Small Arms or ECOWACS judgment of the European Court of Justice[64]—has been settled, post-Lisbon, in a far more balanced way.[65] The Treaty on European Union does not only stipulate that the implementation of the CFSP shall not affect the application of the procedures and the extent of the powers of the EU institutions in other EU policy areas, but also the other way round.[66]

A far more difficult question is whether or not the constituent Treaties in other respects are laying foundations for the unity of the legal system of the Union. Ten years ago we discerned, on the Treaty level, some stimulating conditions for the development of the legal unity of the Union.[67] In particular the common objectives and general principles on which the Union as a whole was based—such as its assertion of 'identity on the international scene' and the underlining of the 'principle of consistency' as a leading guideline—which had to be further developed by its 'single institutional framework', in particular by the European Council and the Council of Ministers. However, we also determined a lack of coherence in the legal system as shaped by the Treaties, mainly due to the 'institutional imbalance' between the

---

[60] See further Curtin and Dekker (n 3 above) 97–98; D M Curtin and I F Dekker, 'The Constitutional Structure of the European Union: Some Reflections on Vertical Unity-in-Diversity' in P Beaumont, C Lyons, and N Walker (eds), *Convergence and Divergence in European Public Law* (Hart, 2002) 59, 63–64. See also Ch Hermann, 'Much Ado about Pluto? The Unity of the Legal Order of the European Union Revisited' in M Cremona and B de Witte (eds), *EU Foreign Relations Law, Constitutional Fundamentals* (Hart, 2008) 19, 36–37.

[61] Arts 48, 49 TEU.

[62] Art 1 TEU.

[63] Art 50 TEU.

[64] Case C-91/05 *Commission v Council* [2008] ECR I-3651.

[65] A Dashwood, 'Article 47 TEU and the Relationship between First and Second Pillar Competences' in A Dashwood and M Maresceau (eds), *Law and Practice of the EU External Relations—Salient Features of a Changing Landscape* (Cambridge University Press, 2008) 70–103; R H van Ooik, 'Cross-Pillar Litigation Before the ECJ: Demarcation of Community and Union Competences' (2008) 4 ECL Rev 399; R A Wessel, 'The Dynamics of the European Union Legal Order: An Increasingly Coherent Framework of Action and Interpretation' (2009) 5 ECL Rev 117, 134–141; B van Vooren, 'EU-EC External Competences after the Small Arms Judgment' (2009) 14 Eur Foreign Aff Rev 7; ibid, 'The Small Arms Judgement in an Age of Constitutional Turmoil' (2009) 14 Eur Foreign Aff Rev 231; P Koutrakos, 'Legal Basis and Delimitation of Competence in EU External Realtions' in Cremona and de Witte (n 46 above) 171–198; Hermann (n 60 above) 27–33.

[66] Art 40 TEU. Compare Art 47 EU.

[67] Curtin and Dekker (n 3 above) 98–101.

different legal sub-systems of the Union, in particular between the 'core' of the European Communities and the 'supplementary' policy areas of the CFSP and CJHA/PJCC.[68] The common objectives and basic principles of the Union at that time were not only quite generally formulated but were also poorly translated into the Union's organizational structures and legal capacities. In particular, the Union's legal presence in the Second and Third Pillars was still relatively 'weak' in relation to the position of the Member States.

The question is whether or not the Lisbon Treaty has strengthened, on the level of the Treaties, the conditions for the development of the unity of the Union's legal regime as such—the horizontal legal unity—and of the unity of the relationship between the legal system of the Union and the national legal order of the Member States—the vertical legal unity. As to the *horizontal* legal unity, the least one can say is that through the amendments of the Lisbon Treaty the TEU expresses in a more encompassing and balanced way the values, objectives, and general principles of the Union.[69] One new element is the statement of the common values on which the Union is founded: respect for human dignity, freedom, democracy, equality, the rule of law, and respect for human rights—whereas the provisions on the elaboration of two of these values—respect for human rights and democracy—support more firmly than before the development of the unity of the legal system of the Union.[70] With regard to the *vertical* legal unity, the most important general provision concerns the principle of 'sincere cooperation' or 'loyalty', which the Lisbon Treaty—in more or less identical wording—has transferred from the EC Treaty to the TEU.[71] As we concluded elsewhere, this principle has evolved from a duty of cooperation on the part of the Member States to a multi-sided duty of loyalty and good faith in the vertical relationship between the Union and its Member States and also among the Member States themselves and among the Union institutions.[72]

The conditions for legal unity are enhanced too by the straightforward provisions on the institutional framework assigning to the institutions, *inter alia*, the obligation to

---

[68] Curtin and Dekker (n 3 above) 101–103.

[69] A von Bogdandy, 'Founding Principles of EU Law: A Theoretical and Doctrinal Sketch' (2010) 16 ELJ 95.

[70] Arts 2 and 6–12 TEU.

[71] Art 4(3) TEU: 'Pursuant to the principle of sincere cooperation, the Union and the Member States shall, in full mutual respect, assist each other in carrying out tasks which flow from the Treaties. The Member States shall take any appropriate measure, general or particular, to ensure fulfilment of the obligations arising out of the Treaties or resulting from the acts of the institutions of the Union. The Member States shall facilitate the achievement of the Union's tasks and refrain from any measure which could jeopardise the attainment of the Union's objectives.' See also Art 24(3) TEU: 'The Member States shall support the Union's external and security policy actively and unreservedly in a spirit of loyalty and mutual solidarity and shall comply with the Union's action in this area. The Member States shall work together to enhance and develop their mutual political solidarity. They shall refrain from any action which is contrary to the interests of the Union or likely to impair its effectiveness as a cohesive force in international relations.'

[72] Curtin and Dekker (n 60 above) 69–71. See also the interesting analysis of the loyalty obligation given by Hillion and Wessel (n 46 above) 91–96, 108–112, suggesting that the two principles of Arts 4(3) and 24(3) TEU are perhaps meant to operate differently.

ensure the consistency of the Union's policies and actions.[73] This principle is confirmed in the TFEU, stating: 'The Union shall ensure consistency between its policies and activities, taking all of its objectives into account and in accordance with the principle of conferral of powers.'[74] To achieve that end, the Lisbon Treaty strengthened the Union's institutional framework overall, in particular the competences of the European Council—which can now explicitly take 'decisions'—the European Parliament, and the Court of Justice. The different arrangements on enhanced cooperation of the former Three Pillars are under the new architecture brought together under one general provision in the TEU and one implementation arrangement in the TFEU.[75] Above all, the legal unity is enhanced by elimination of the separate status of the Third Pillar policies and actions, which are now merged with the provisions dealing with immigration, asylum, and civil law under the heading of the 'Area of Freedom, Security and Justice'.[76] This is an improvement especially in view of the unity of the Union's legal system because the acts taken in the field of judicial and police cooperation in criminal matters will, subject to several transitional provisions and exceptions, be governed by the general rules regarding the Union's legal acts and the adoption procedures for those acts,[77] by the well-known principles relating to the effects of the Union's legal acts in the legal orders of the Member States (direct applicability, direct effect, and supremacy), as well as by the full jurisdiction of the European Court of Justice.[78]

An improvement of the TEU from the perspective of a unitary legal system is the more comprehensive presentation of the objectives relating to the international relations of the Union.[79] The objectives focus on *all* the areas of the Union's external action and in that sense diminish the sharpness of the dividing lines between the external political and security policy, on the one hand, and the international economic, financial, and development policies on the other.[80] As far as the institutional framework is concerned, the 'up-grading' of the role of the High Representative of the Union for Foreign Affairs and Security Policy and especially her dual position as President of the Foreign Affairs Council and Vice-President of the Commission will enhance the possibilities for more coherence in the Union's external action. Another new element is that, in fulfilling her mandate, the High Representative will be assisted by a European External Action Service, consisting of officials from the General Secretariat of the Council, the Commission, and national diplomatic services of the Member States.[81] The unity of the Union's external action will also be promoted by the general

---

[73] Art 13(1) TEU.   [74] Art 7 TFEU.

[75] Art 20 TEU and Arts 326–334 TFEU.   [76] Title V TFEU.

[77] Arts 288–299 TFEU. See for certain exceptions in this regard, Art 76 TFEU (right of initiative of Member States), Arts 86(1), 87(3), 89 TFEU (adoption procedure), Arts 82(3) and 83(3) TFEU (suspension procedure).

[78] See for an exception to the full jurisdiction of the Court Arts 72 and 276 TFEU (maintenance of law and order and safeguarding of internal security).

[79] Arts 3(5), 8, 21 TEU.

[80] See also Art 212 TFEU requiring consistency of the Union's policies in the field of economic, financial, and technical cooperation *and* development cooperation.

[81] Art 27(3) TEU.

arrangement for the conclusion of Treaties with third parties, in principle, for all fields of activity within the Union's competence.[82] Besides, the TEU maintains the 'footbridge' provision stipulating that the administrative and operational expenditure to which the implementation of the CFSP give rise in principle will be charged to the budget of the Union.[83]

However, as stated before, the legal reality is that for the CFSP the Lisbon Treaty maintains a separate 'Pillar' within the Union's legal system. Not without grounds, the TEU provides that the CFSP 'is subject to specific rules and procedures'.[84] The most important distinct feature still lies in the fact that the authority to develop, define, and implement the common foreign and security policies, including 'the progressive framing of a common defence policy that might lead to a common defence',[85] is firmly vested with the European Council and the Council, acting unanimously, except where the Treaties provide otherwise.[86] The role of the European Parliament and the Commission in this area remains relatively marginal—also post-Lisbon.[87] The specific rules and procedures of the CFSP exclude the adoption of legislative acts, as well as the jurisdiction of the Court of Justice, except to monitor the demarcation of the Union's competences in this and other areas,[88] and the review of the legality of Council decisions imposing restrictive measures on natural or legal persons.[89] Whether CFSP decisions are directly applicable in the legal orders of the Member States and, if so, whether they can have direct effect and can set aside conflicting national legal measures was and still is a controversial issue.[90] The silence of the TEU on this point as such does not necessarily imply an answer in the negative—clauses to that effect were also absent in regard to the acts of the European Communities. The wording of Declaration no 17 concerning the primacy of Union law—annexed to the Final Act of the Lisbon conference—does not help very much either because it only generally refers to the conditions laid down by the case law of the Court of Justice. Although the case law of the Court with regard to the relationship between non-Community law and the national law of the Member States is very scarce—and above all is related to the former Third Pillar—it seems to support our arguments, put forward elsewhere,[91] for the recognition in principle of the unity of the Union's legal system also in this respect. In particular, the Court, in answering the question as to whether the principle of

---

[82] Art 37 TEU and Arts 216 and 218 TFEU. Art 219 TFEU provides for a specific procedure for agreements concluded under the Economic and Monetary Union.

[83] Art 41 TEU.

[84] Art 24(1) TEU.

[85] ibid.

[86] ibid.

[87] ibid. See, however, Art 30(1) TEU (Commission) and Art 36 (European Parliament). See also Curtin and Dekker (n 3 above) 98–100.

[88] Art 24(1) jo. 40 TEU.

[89] Art 24(1) TEU jo. Art 275 TFEU.

[90] M Cremona, 'A Constitutional Basis for External Action? An Assessment of the Provisions on EU External Action in the Constitutional Treaty', EUI Working Paper LAW No 2006/30.

[91] Curtin and Dekker (n 60 above) 65–69.

consistent interpretation also applies to legal instruments of the Third Pillar, found that such instruments could have 'similar effects' to those provided for by the EC Treaty, and rejected the argument that the 'principle of loyalty' did not exist with regard to the non-Community areas of cooperation.[92] This kind of reasoning seems to imply at least the *presumption* of the direct applicability and the primacy of the TEU as such and CFSP decisions in the legal order of the Member States.

The unity of the Union's legal system seems to be still fragile at least as far as the CFSP is concerned. However, one has to remember that for a long time the existence of separate legal sub-systems within the European Communities and—later—the European Union was not at all a rare phenomenon. The European Community, for its part, even sheltered legal persons with their own legal regimes, such as the Investment Bank and the European Central Bank. The Third Pillar had, under its roof, EUROPOL (the European Law Enforcement Agency), EURODAC (a Community-wide information technology system for the comparison of the fingerprints of asylum seekers), and others. And the former and amended Treaties provide for several forms of 'flexibility', including the Eurozone, and the forms of 'enhanced cooperation' which can be created by secondary legislation.[93] The existence of such legal sub-systems does not as such threaten the unity of the Union's legal system. Much depends on the extent to which the legal practices of the Union are governed by common EU concepts, objectives, and principles, in particular the principles of unity and consistency (or coherency).[94] These principles derive their legal significance from a certain fragmentation of the legal regime of the Union and become more than simply fairly self-evident guidelines governing the correct interpretation of the Treaties in a coherent fashion. The principles require rather that the policies and decisions taken under the different sub-systems of the Union's legal regime are attuned to each other especially in overlapping areas. Not without reason the TEU emphasizes particularly with regard to the external policy of the Union the obligation of the institutions and the Member States to take into account the principles of unity and consistency.[95]

Against the background of the legal unity, framed in the Treaties, we examine whether the legal practices of the European Union have strengthened the unitary character of the legal system of the Union as an international organization. In broadening the scope

---

[92] Case C-105/03 *Maria Pupino* [2005] ECR I-5285, [36] and [42]. See also the conclusion drawn by AG Kokott in this case, in particular [32] and [33].

[93] See Art 20 TEU and Arts 326–334 TFEU. See further also, I F Dekker and R A Wessel, 'The European Union and the Concept of Flexibility: Proliferation of Legal Systems Within International Organizations' in N M Blokker and H G Schermers (eds), *Proliferation of International Organizations* (Kluwer Law International, 2001) 381–414.

[94] The wording of the principle of consistency is not 'consistent' in the different language versions of the Treaty text. We follow the wording of the English version but in a meaning broader than only the absence of contradictions. See above, accompanying text by n 8.

[95] Art 21(3) TEU: 'The Union shall ensure consistency between the different areas of its external action and between these and its other policies. The Council and the Commission, assisted by the High Representative of the Union for Foreign Affairs and Security Policy, shall ensure that consistency and shall cooperate to that effect.' Art 26(2) TEU: 'The Council and the High Representative of the Union for Foreign Affairs and Security Policy shall ensure the unity, consistency and effectiveness of action by the Union.'

of our analysis in this fashion, we go further than existing literature on the subject and seek reinforcement for our overall thesis from the manner in which the Union legal order has been *operationalized* in practice.

C. INSTITUTIONAL LEGAL PRACTICES OF THE EUROPEAN UNION

1. AN EVOLVING TEMPLATE OF UNITY

In our original contribution published in 1999 we undertook a non-exhaustive analysis of the 'legal practices' of the EU. In doing so we stated that

> we have at times felt more like Sherlock Holmes and Dr. Watson—magnifying glasses in hand—looking behind the Treaty provisions to the actual decisions adopted and behind that again to the looser 'practices' of the institutions themselves which make the legal structure operational. All of this detective work has been to facilitate the piecing together of small fragments in order to produce a clearer picture, a core understanding, of complex and often hidden interactions.

It is important to recall that at that time we were exploring the real world legal and institutional realities of a novel entity (the EU) that had been formally framed, along with the intention of the framers, so as to have no 'contamination' between the separate Pillars. On the contrary, what we found was that the evolving legal practices even in a very limited time frame (1993–99) indicated that the legal system of the European Union as such was developing as an institutional unity. In line with our theoretical conception of unity as an overarching template of legal sub-systems, institutional sub-systems could continue to exist within the three respective 'Pillars'. In other words the existence of overall unity and specific differentiation were not contradictory but rather complementary phenomena undergirded by an overall notion of for example loyalty, coherence, fundamental rights etc.[96]

In 1999 we distinguished three different levels of analysis. First and quite logically at that time we explored the position that despite the fact that the EU had not been explicitly conferred with international legal personality, the legal practices of the Union, even in a very initial time frame, showed that in particular in its *external* relations with other subjects of international law, it could already be classified as an international legal person. The trend in legal practices that we discerned more than a decade ago has now been expressly consolidated and confirmed in the textual provisions of the Treaty of Lisbon (as already referred to in section 2 above). In addition we looked at elements of Council decisions and decision-making and the manner in which the international representation occurs for 'evidence' of unitary practices. Our second initial level of analysis focused on the legal practices regarding the *internal*

---

[96] Curtin and Dekker (n 3 and n 60 above).

structures of the Union, in particular its 'single' institutional structure. We answered affirmatively the question whether the institutions in their day-to-day operations in the field of the CFSP and CJHA (at that time) functioned (within the limits set by the TEU) as organs of the EU as such. Finally, we explored on a selective basis legal practices with an impact on the legal protection of individuals in particular and discovered that the Court of Justice in particular had a primordial role in ensuring that certain core fundamental principles were applied in different contexts.

With the entry into force of the Treaty of Lisbon at the end of 2009 there is no longer any added value to exploring the contribution that the legal practices of the institutions in their external relations with other legal persons had made to the unity of the system as a whole, since this was now expressly a given and is described in section 2 for the contribution made to the analysis of the EU as a unitary legal person. The other two levels of analysis remain pertinent but with some change of emphasis, given not only the changed constitutional context but also the extent to which certain subjects display differences, yet, at the same time, have a clear connection with a notion of overarching unity. Given the fact that the issue of the legal personality is now obsolete and that there is a separate chapter in the new volume on other aspects of external relations as well as specifically on human rights, we have decided to focus our discussion on the internal structure of the EU as revealing evidence of unitary framing and evolution, despite differences in policy areas.[97] We highlight the unitary nature or otherwise of the EU executive power both in its appearance of 'frontstage' actors as well as 'backstage' actors. With this topic there is a sense of the originally largely invisible becoming structurally more visible.

2. INSTITUTIONAL UNITY OF THE EXECUTIVE POWER

One general theme that was discussed in our chapter in the first edition of this book is that certain 'institutions' developed their own roles in the context of the CFSP and CJHA and that despite the very different normative context (in terms of Treaty provisions) in which they operate, they have been influenced to a considerable extent by their functions, roles, and practices in the context of the EC Treaties. In other words we perceived already a decade ago a growing institutional 'unity' across the Pillars, in particular in relation to the Council of Ministers, the Commission, and the European Parliament. It is not possible to provide an update of the evolving roles of these three institutions, which are also the specific subject of other chapters in this book. Instead we now focus on our perception of the intensification in some respects of a trend towards institutional unity and limit our analysis more to the *executive* level of decision-making. With the advent of the Treaty of Lisbon it is the reinforcement of the executive power of the EU that is most widespread and striking (although of course

---

[97] See also R A Wessel, 'The Constitutional Unity of the European Union: The Increasing Irrelevance of the Pillar Structure?' in J Wouters, L Verhey, and P Kiiver (eds), *European Constitutionalism beyond the EU Constitution* (Intersentia, 2009).

both the legislative power and the judicial power are reinforced, both of which are the focus of other specific chapters). That executive power is not unitary in the sense that it 'belongs' to only one institution (eg the Commission in its own self-perception), but is spread across several existing institutions and new actors. We perceive thus both elements of increasing 'unity' and elements of 'disunity', a theme to which we will return.

The two most important 'institutions', other than the Commission, with regard to EU-level executive power are: the European Council, recently described as 'the alpha and omega of executive power in the EU'[98] and the hierarchically inferior Council of Ministers, 'joined' and linked in concrete terms by the Council General Secretariat. The latter actor has incrementally acquired a more central role and a more influential position since the Treaty of Maastricht in particular. At the same time, the manner in which specific provisions of the Treaty of Lisbon are in the process of being implemented reveal the rationalization and centrality of its unique position, in particular as the key link in the coordination chain, among other actors and across all the various policy areas. At the same time it is not only a story of heightened coordination but also of some fragmentation existing side by side with the creation of more quasi-autonomous 'satellites' (agencies, new entities such as the European External Action Service; see below) with their own distinct roles and functions, especially in the field of foreign policy. This could arguably be seen as evidence of 'disunity', at the very least of fragmentation. On the other hand, the steady reinforcement over the years of other 'backstage' actors, such as Coreper,[99] provide the backbone that enables the Council to function as an institution, aided and abetted by often very powerful, (quasi-)autonomous committees such as the Political and Security Committee.[100]

(a) The front-stage: the European Council and its President

The 'ever mighty' European Council is authoritatively considered as the top-level 'leader' of the European Union as such.[101] It has seen its executive powers consolidated and even expanded in processes of incremental institutionalization, first in layers of legal and institutional practices and most recently in formal Treaty provisions in the Lisbon Treaty. The key—and general—agenda-setting role of the European Council is evident from Article 15(1) TEU in its Lisbon version: it 'shall provide the Union with the necessary impetus for its development and define the general political guidelines thereof'. Agenda setting is of course a crucial stage in the policy process for any

---

[98] D Curtin, *Executive Power of the European Union. Law, Practices and the Living Constitution* (Oxford University Press, 2009) 70.

[99] See further J de Zwaan, *The Permanent Representatives Committee: Its role in European Union Decision-Making* (Elsevier, 1995). See too D Bostock, 'COREPER revisited' (2002) 40 JCMS 215.

[100] A Juncos and Chr Reynolds, 'The Political and Security Committee: Governing in the Shadow' (2007) 12 Eur Foreign Aff Rev 127. See too, E Regelsberger, 'The EU as an Actor in Foreign and Security Policy: Some Key Features of CFSP in an Historical Perspective' (2007) 5 CFSP Forum 4, 1–8.

[101] Editorial Comments, 'An Ever Mighty European Council—Some Recent Institutional Developments' (2009) 46 CML Rev 1383.

political system.[102] But the European Council can also act as a type of 'court of appeal' in certain specified—and limited—circumstances (for example where a Member State has breached the core values of the EU).[103] And it takes (or will take) absolutely key decisions concerning the EU and its Member States outside of the legislative procedure as such.[104] In addition, through the medium of the conclusions of its summits, it steers the other decision-making institutions and more or less tells them what to do and where the priorities lie.[105]

These activities relate now to the full spectrum of EU activities. In a sense here we have an institution with an absolutely leading role, also in terms of Treaty provisions, which sees its role further 'normalized' and expanded in the formal provisions of the Lisbon Treaty across the spectrum of EU activities. Indeed, in the ruling by the German *Bundesverfassungsgericht* on the compatibility of the provisions of the Lisbon Treaty with the German Constitution, it held that the revision procedure under Article 48(6) TEU 'opens up to the European Council a broad scope of action for amendments of primary law'.[106] Moreover, numerous specific provisions of the Lisbon Treaty give the European Council the power to take by consensus, unanimity, or qualified majority voting decisions of a 'quasi-constitutional' or 'high political' nature, both on substance and procedure.[107] These decisions post-Lisbon apply to genuinely horizontal issues (composition, rotation, appointment etc. to various other institutions as well as external relations and the core values of the EU) as well as in more specific policy fields (eg in relation to a common defence policy and in the field of the integrated and normalized Area of Freedom, Security and Justice).

Since the entry into force of the Lisbon Treaty, a number of implementation 'practices' point to the further increase of the powers of the European Council, thus further altering the 'traditional' institutional balance foreseen by the Treaties (and guarded by the Court) until now. The European Council, the instant it became a formal EU-wide 'institution' (the day the Lisbon Treaty entered into force, 1 December 2009), adopted its own rules of procedure.[108] This regulates, as one might expect, the manner in which it adopts its 'decisions', where they are published (in the Official Journal, just like all other institutions), how and in what composition it votes, the fact that its meetings are not held in public (Article 4(3)) etc. Nothing is formally said about access to information or access to the minutes of its meetings etc. However, on

---

[102] See further B Guy Peters, 'Agenda-Setting in the European Community' (1994) 1 JEPP 9.

[103] See Art 7(2) TEU.

[104] See, for example, Art 7 TEU.

[105] For a clear recent example see Presidency Conclusions, Brussels European Council Summit, 11 and 12 December 2008, available at <http://www.consilium.europa.eu/ueDocs/cms_Data/docs/pressData/en/ec/104692.pdf>. See further, J Werts, The European Council (John Harper Publishing, 2008).

[106] See the judgment of the Second Senate of the *Bundesverfassungsgericht* of 30 June 2009 (n 27 above), 311.

[107] See for chapter and verse Editorial Comments (n 101 above).

[108] European Council Decision of 1 December 2009 adopting its own rules of procedure (2009/882/EU), OJ L315/51 (2 December 2009).

its new web page[109] under 'European Council meetings' there is a separate section on 'documents submitted to the European Council' with various—clickable—documents listed, including the annotated draft agenda (via the Council Register of documents). In its rules of procedure (Article 8), provision is made for the drawing up of draft minutes of each European Council meeting (prepared by the General Secretariat of the Council within 15 days), containing a (limited) amount of information rather than a verbatim account of the meetings. In any event it is not yet clear if these 'thin' minutes will be made public (via the Council Register of documents or the European Council website itself). The manner in which the European Council exercises its functions in public, and subject to the general EU-wide principle of the greatest possible access to information, will have to emerge in practice. In any event it seems that there is *prima facie* no reason why the fact that its decisions are explicitly said to be 'non-legislative' removes it in any way from the general obligation to be transparent in its functioning and activities, as applied to all other institutions and organs of the EU.

In one of the very first 'conclusions' issued by the European Council post-Lisbon,[110] it has agreed to a new EU-wide assessment function for itself to 'once a year, make an overall assessment of progress achieved' on the new European strategy of jobs and growth, including a strong external dimension. The President of the European Council is specifically given the task of establishing, in cooperation with the Commission, a special task force 'to reach the objective of an improved crisis resolution framework and better budgetary discipline, exploring all options to reinforce the legal framework'. In this way we see how the European Council leads in a manner that also maps the road to formal legal change.

In terms of democratic accountability, the rules of procedure, in line with the Lisbon Treaty, provide explicitly that the President of the European Council shall 'represent' the European Council before the European Parliament and present a report to the latter (Article 15). There was already an evolving relationship between the European Council and the European Parliament prior to the entry into force of the Lisbon Treaty.[111] Time will tell how the European Parliament in particular will try and steer what is now a formal and legally prescribed relationship with the European Council as a formal EU institution (also subject to the budgetary regime of the EU and its financial provisions). For Van Rompuy it is indeed much more important than for the previous semi-annual rotating Presidency to have a good working relationship with the European Parliament.[112] The sessions of the European Parliament with the President will become a repeated game in political science terms, increasing the power of soft sanctions. A negative judgment by the European Parliament in the future will

---

[109] Available at <http://www.european-council.europa.eu/home-page.aspx?lang=en>.

[110] Conclusions of the European Council of 25 and 26 March 2010, available at <http://www.consilium.europa.eu/uedocs/cms_Data/docs/pressdata/en/ec/113591.pdf>.

[111] See, for example, D Thym, 'Beyond Parliament's Reach? The Role of the European Parliament in the CFSP' (2006) 11 Eur Foreign Aff Rev 109.

[112] B Crum and J E Fossum, 'The Multi-level Parliamentary Field, A Framework for Theorizing Representative Democracy in the EU' (2009) 1 Eur Pol Science Rev 249.

have more consequences for the (semi-) permanent President than for the current rotating Presidencies whose incumbents are above all the heads of government in their respective Member States.[113] The expectation is that the tendency of the Presidency (and the future European Council President) to be more forthcoming in rendering account will continue and become more institutionalized. The European Parliament can in any event be expected to deepen its constitutional agenda setting in this regard, as it has done very successfully in the past with regard to the Commission and as it is beginning to do with its legislative partner, the Council of Ministers, across a greatly enhanced number of policy fields. The European Council's political accountability as a single institution at the level of the political system of the EU may be expected to evolve in an enhanced fashion in the coming years.[114]

(b) The backstage: the Council Secretariat General and autonomous satellite(s)

In our original contribution we emphasized the pivotal role of the Council in the field of CFSP and CJHA, as it then was. Evidence of the indivisibility of the Council as an institution was provided by certain cross-'Pillar' practices. In CFSP a cross-'Pillar' jurisdiction was already present in the post-Maastricht period where the General Council, for example, decided on any measure of external policy irrespective of its legal basis in either CFSP or CJHA. Another possible example of the indivisibility of the Council lay with the evolving decision-making and other roles of the Secretariat General of the Council, but at the time we wrote our first version the major institutional innovations that took place in 1999 had not yet occurred. Since then the 'success' of the Council Secretariat has been quite marked, continuing over the years and with it now operating as a type of parallel administration to that of the Commission. At the same time it is a somewhat 'janus-faced' actor: a highly distinct one, harbouring within its outer shell different—highly secretive—enclaves of defence and military cooperation. These 'new Eurocrats' socialize differently and may have different role conceptions to the original public 'Eurocrats'.[115] The example of the autonomous blacklisting of individuals and the role of the Council/Secretariat General therein provides further examples of the indivisibility of the Council across different policy areas and Pillars prior to the entry into force of the Treaty of Lisbon.[116]

In terms of formal legal provision the Council General Secretariat was not mentioned in the founding Treaties and was only formally introduced in a Treaty article (alongside Coreper) in the Maastricht Treaty in 1992. Article 151 of the then EEC Treaty (now Article 167 TFEU) provided the initial indirect legal basis for the

---

[113] See too, M van de Steeg, 'The European Council's evolving political accountability' in M Bovens, D M Curtin, and P 't Hart (eds), *The Real World of EU Accountability: What Deficit?* (Oxford University Press, 2010) 117–149.

[114] See too, Van de Steeg (n 113 above).

[115] See further K P Geuijen *et al*, *The New Eurocrats: National Civil Servants in EU Policy-making* (Amsterdam University Press, 2008).

[116] C Eckes, *EU Counter-Terrorist Policies and Fundamental Rights: The Case of Individual Sanctions* (Oxford University Press, 2010) 107–110, 376.

Secretariat General but said very little other than that the Council would be assisted by a General Secretariat under the direction of the Secretary General. But the General Secretariat has however always been referred to, albeit in cursory fashion, in the Council's own internal rules of procedure, and the changes over the years made to these internal rules reflect the gradually growing significance the Secretariat has had for the operation of the Council.[117] The fact, however, that this institution was initially set up without a clear set of formal rules governing its activities meant that the foundation was laid for 'unwritten rules, existing practices and bureaucratic reflexes to fill the normative vacuum'.[118] In other words, the formal legal rules traditionally tell little about the manner in which this institution has evolved in practice or its significance on a day-to-day basis across a wide range of policy fields. For example, the relative autonomy with which the Council Secretariat has exercised its functions in recent years is illustrated by the fact that a member of the General Secretariat actually holds the chair of a number of preparatory bodies of the Council (including the Security Committee and a number of Working Parties).[119]

The Council Secretariat has had a valuable role to play in supporting the Presidency of the day in organizing the work. All Presidencies rely—in different ways—on the Council Secretariat to advise them on procedures, to draw up minutes and other reports of meetings, and for functions such as arranging the production, translation, and circulation of Council documents. These are its standard tasks also within the context of EC activities. The central role of the Council in the context of CFSP decision-making implies a stronger role for the Council Secretariat. The Council Secretariat basically fills the political absence of the European Commission in the field of CFSP.[120] According to one author, 'there is a process of informal importation in the second pillar of the *Community method* and an almost mimetic reproduction of the role played by the Commission in the first pillar, which the Commission refuses to play in the second pillar, disapproving of its "intergovernmental structure"'.[121] Post-Lisbon the new High Representative 'imports' to some extent the Commission into the CFSP.

The tasks of the Secretariat include agenda setting, policy formulation, and implementation, especially in the fields of internal and external security. In addition, various external secretariats were effectively integrated into the Council Secretariat: those of the European Political Cooperation (EPC), the Schengen Convention, and the West European Union (WEU)—with a resulting considerable expansion of tasks and

---

[117] See further T Christiansen and S Vanhoonacker, 'At a Critical Juncture? Change and Continuity in the Institutional Development of the Council Secretariat' (2008) 31 WEP 751.

[118] ibid.

[119] See list included in the latest list of Council preparatory bodies (January 2009), available at <http://register.consilium.europa.eu/pdf/en/09/st05/st05433.en09.pdf>, 13 (Annex II).

[120] See further in detail, H Dijkstra, 'The Council Secretariat's Role in the Common Foreign and Security Policy' (2008) 13 Eur Foreign Aff Rev 149.

[121] M Mangenot, 'The Invention and Transformation of a Governmental Body: The Council Secretariat' in M Mangenot and J Rowell (eds), *A Political Sociology of the European Union. Reassessing Constructivism* (Manchester University Press, 2010) 12 (author's emphasis).

responsibilities. The growth was not only in terms of the numbers of staff working in the Council Secretariat, but also resulted in much greater diversity than hitherto in terms of the sectoral policies covered and expertise provided.

Whereas within the framework of the EC the Commission would perform logistical tasks (with regard to the management of data bases and 'implement' Action Plans etc) via its budgetary role and its power of initiative with regard to follow-up (legislative) action, these are tasks that are performed traditionally by the Council Secretariat in the framework of CFSP and CJHA (and later PJCC) activity. Specifically in the field of EU foreign policy there may even be some 'bureaucratic rivalry' between the Commission Secretariat and the Council Secretariat for the structural reason that the Council Secretariat challenges the Commission's political and informational role in the context of foreign policy.[122]

The executive-type tasks of the General Secretariat are particularly pronounced in what used to be termed European Security and Defence Policy (hereafter ESDP; post-Lisbon it is called 'the Common Security and Defence Policy'). The governance structure of ESDP was established during the Nice European Council[123] and has become operational through a range of civilian, military, and civil-military crisis management instruments and missions. The Secretariat plays an important and influential role in the preparation and implementation of civilian and military missions.[124] It draws up background documents and draft joint actions. Once the Member States have agreed upon the launching of a civilian or military operation, it prepares an operational plan, in cooperation with the Commission and the Presidency. Also during missions it fulfils certain implementing tasks. Through the so-called Athena mechanism, for instance, it administers the financing of the common costs of military operations.[125]

The role of the Council Secretariat is frequently underestimated if not completely ignored (by lawyers in any event). Besides its traditional supporting role there is an emerging political function.[126] This relatively new role began with the creation of the position of the High Representative and the Policy Unit and the fact that they have a voice of their own in order to do their own agenda setting. This more political role is accentuated with the implementation of the Lisbon Treaty, even though there is more counter-balance with the Commission than hitherto, both in certain aspects of CFSP and with regard to PJCC that is subsumed within the Union as a whole. At the same time, the fact that the new High Representative of the Union for Foreign Affairs and Security Policy is simultaneously to be a Vice-President of the Commission, will

---

[122] See further, H Dijkstra, 'Commission versus Council Secretariat: An Analysis of Bureaucratic Rivalry in European Foreign Policy' (2009) 14 Eur Foreign Aff Rev 431.

[123] See in general, S Duke and S Vanhoonacker, 'Administrative Governance in CFSP: Development and Practice' (2006) 11 Eur Foreign Aff Rev 163.

[124] See further Dijkstra (n 120 above).

[125] A Missiroli, 'Euros for ESDP: Financing EU Operations' Occasional Paper 45 (EU Institute for Security Studies Paris, 2003).

[126] Duke and Vanhoonacker (n 123 above).

profoundly impact both on the architecture of the Commission and of the Council/ European Council.

The relevant changes brought about by the Treaty of Lisbon include not only the altered and widened 'ordinary legislative procedure' in terms of policy and issue areas, but also the range of non-legislative powers of the Council in one or other of its permutations. In addition, the Treaty of Lisbon explicitly mentions the General Secretariat of the Council twice: first with regard to providing support for the Council of Ministers and second with regard to providing support for the European Council.[127] This exercise of formal 'catch-up' with what has long been reality in practice does not necessarily give an adequate picture of the manner in which, bit by bit and often quite invisibly, the position and tasks, and ultimately influence, of the General Secretariat have incrementally increased. At the same time it is also very much tied into the increase or alteration in the powers and practices of the Council itself as well as all its supporting instances and of course, increasingly, that of the European Council. The latter support role has been strengthened and consolidated by virtue of the further institutionalization of the European Council itself and in particular its new quasi-permanent President. This means, in practice, that post-Lisbon the Council Secretariat will 'service' *three* different Presidencies: the normal rotating Council President among the Member States (linked to the troika groups of three Member States),[128] the President of the Foreign Affairs Council (the High Representative of the Union for Foreign Affairs and Security Policy), and the President of the European Council. This means that there will de facto also be an important role for the Council Secretariat as the common denominator among these various actors and (Council) Presidencies in coordinating foreign policy with other policy areas. This power of coordination that has to some extent been present from earlier days[129] and sounds quite 'soft', has in fact been the backbone that has enabled the Council Secretariat to evolve into an 'autonomous administration'.[130] In addition, the fact is that the Council Presidency will still have some role in the management of external representation and a role is given too in this regard to the President of the European Council alongside that of the High Representative. For the former two actors the Council Secretariat will continue to play a coordinating and supportive role in spite of the creation of the EEAS (see further below).

The partial integration of CFSP in both the Council/European Council post-Lisbon as well as newly in the Commission has its own novelties and complications. One result has been to hive off much of the foreign policy that up until now had been dealt with by the Council Secretariat (including the staff of most of DGE, the Policy Unit, EUMS (The European Union Military Staff), CPCC (Civilian Planning and Conduct Capability), and JCS (Joint Situation Centre) and to put it in a quasi-autonomous new

---

[127] Arts 240(2) (ex 207 EC) and 235(4) TFEU, respectively.

[128] Declaration No 9 of the Lisbon Treaty: Declaration on Art 16(9) of the Treaty on European Union concerning the European Council Decision on the exercise of the Presidency of the Council.

[129] Mangenot (n 121 above).   [130] ibid.

European External Action Service (hereinafter EEAS) in accordance with Article 27(3) TEU. This represents the 'normalization' of the activities of the Council Secretariat (with foreign and security policy largely taken away from it)[131] in the sense that tasks originally acquired with regard to this exceptional and marginal policy area have now moved to the hard core of EU policy-making. In addition, a reinforcement has taken place in the role of the High Representative within the body of the Commission (with the line of political accountability to the European Parliament and not to the Member States).

The establishment of the EEAS clearly represents a significant step in EU foreign policy cooperation and has been likened to a foreign ministry of the Union.[132] This new institution[133] is separate both from the Council General Secretariat and from the Commission with its own legal capacity. It is explicitly stated in the Council Decision of 26 July 2010 that the EEAS is 'a functionally autonomous body of the Union' supporting the High Representative in fulfilling her mandates.[134] With the establishment of the EEAS outside the Council Secretariat and with an important representation of Commission officials, the Member States will create a body with the potential of becoming a powerful and influential actor in European foreign policy.[135] Officials in the EEAS will come from the Commission, the Council Secretariat, and the national diplomatic services of the Member States.

When discussing control over the new EEAS an important consideration is the manner of financing of the service. The draft Council Decision proposed initially by the High Representative is unequivocal: the operational costs for the EEAS are to be financed by a new budget line in the Union budget.[136] This choice, confirmed in the final Council Decision, gives the European Parliament an important means of influence and also of forcing the hand of the EEAS in the future in terms of giving some accountability for its actions directly to the European Parliament itself. This is due to the fact that any amendment of the Financial Regulation takes place after the entry into force of the Lisbon Treaty via the 'ordinary legislative procedure' which guarantees a full role for the European Parliament in this legislative amendment procedure. This is a space to be watched. We have seen how the European Parliament flexed its muscles with regard to the appointment of the Commission in February 2010 by insisting on a new inter-institutional agreement between the Commission and the

---

[131] Mangenot (n 121 above).

[132] L Rayner, *The EU Foreign Ministry and Union Embassies* (Foreign Policy Centre London, 2005).

[133] Formally the EEAS will not be an institution of the EU in the strict legal sense, but its establishment will lead to its operationalization in 'living' practice in the form of rules and procedures. In this looser sense it can be considered as the construction of a new institution, see further March and Olsen (n 7 above).

[134] Council Decision of 26 July 2010 establishing the organization and functioning of the European External Action Service, OJ L201/30, 3 August 2010.

[135] See S Vanhoonacker and N Reslow, 'The European External Action Service: Living Forwards by Understanding Backwards' (2010) 15 Eur Foreign Aff Rev 1, 1–18, at 14.

[136] See too, Proposal for a Regulation of the European Parliament and of the Council amending Council Regulation (EC, Euratom) No 1605/2002 on the Financial Regulation applicable to the general budget of the European Communities, as regards, the European external action service, COM(2010) 85 final, 24 March 2010.

European Parliament as to their ongoing relations, including several provisions that go far beyond the formal provisions of the Lisbon Treaty.[137] It has done the same with regard to getting more of a grip on quasi-independent agencies (regulatory and otherwise).[138] This is the manner in which the European Parliament has successfully and pro-actively pursued its own constitutional agenda over the years, exercising more control over various actors by using the power of the purse, the classic instrument for parliaments generally.

The new EEAS is deliberately constructed as a 'functionally autonomous body of the Union' and 'under the authority of the High Representative'.[139] At the same time it is embedded in a much broader vision and practice of institutional unity. First, the EEAS will also support those satellite bodies that will newly fall under the authority of the High Representative (viz the European Defence Agency, the European Union Satellite Centre, the European Union Institute for Security Studies, and the European Security and Defence College). Secondly, the EEAS is to be treated as an 'institution' within the meaning of the Staff Regulations. Thirdly, the EEAS is to be treated as an 'institution' within the meaning of the Financial Regulation. The latter qualification, as we have seen, gives the European Parliament an equal opportunity to force the EEAS—both initially and on an annual basis (by explicitly reviewing the administrative expenditure of the EEAS)—to account to it in a manner that the European Parliament wishes. This can potentially develop much further than the simple obligation to submit a 'report' on the functioning of the EEAS in 2012. Finally, the EEAS will be subject to the general rules of the EU on security, protection of classified information, and access to documents.

D. CONCLUSION

Our conclusion ten years ago was that the European Union, in general terms, has evolved, as an international organization, into a legal system with a unitary character overarching a lot of—sometimes very different—'layers' of cooperation and integration. At that time this unitary character was to a large extent hidden behind a complex pillar structure and could only be brought into the light on the basis of an analysis of the Treaty implementation and legal practices. Ever since, the legal unity of the Union has clearly come out of the shadows and has gained a far more solid and durable basis in its founding Treaties. The fact that the Union is still best qualified as an international organization does not deprive its framework rules of a unitary character. On

---

[137] Revised Framework Agreement on relations between the European Parliament and the Commission of 29 June 2010, to be found at http://register.consilium.europa.eu/pdf/en/10/st12/st12717.en10.pdf.

[138] See further, M Busuioc, *The Accountability of European Agencies: Legal Provisions and Ongoing Practices* (Eburon, 2010).

[139] Council Decision of 26 July 2010 establishing the organization and functioning of the European External Action Service, OJ L201/30, 3 August 2010.

the contrary, subsequent amendments of the Treaties culminating in the Lisbon Treaty have made more visible then ever before the unity of the organization in its constitutional architecture of a single international legal person that, at the same time, is based on a firm alliance of the Member States.

These Treaty-level developments were, to a large extent, the result of the ever-increasing legal practices in the field of the common foreign and security policy and the cooperation in the field of justice and home affairs, later reduced to police and judicial cooperation. By these legal practices not only were new legal regimes developed but they also largely contributed to the reforming of the European Union from a mainly socio-economic organization into a general one, more clearly dominated by political overtones. In that sense the Union has become a general political international organization with important functions in almost every field of public life. And this development has not stopped with the entry into force of the Treaty of Lisbon. What has emerged already quite clearly in the manner in which the Treaty of Lisbon is being implemented with regard to institutions and 'satellite' bodies is that the construction of new tasks for new actors is taking place within a vision of overall institutional unity (the 'single institutional framework' as the Treaty of Maastricht put it). One example is the de facto coordination role that the administrative 'backbone' of the Council will play in the future with regard to the various different 'Presidencies' as well as their respective external representation tasks.

Although it is clear that the influence of the legal practices in the Second and Third Pillars can hardly be underestimated it is equally clear that the evolution of the Union has not, as was feared in times of its establishment, in general undermined the separate, 'supranational' status of the legal system of the entity formerly known as the European Community. As we expected ten years ago, the Union has proven to be capable of integrating within its overarching legal structure sub-systems containing in certain respects more far-reaching principles and rules. In the context of that panorama it is not so surprising that Union law also harbours numerous possibilities for institutional variation but that this fact does not deprive the legal instruments of their character of belonging to a Union legal and political system. The European Union can still be categorized as a highly complex entity with diverse fragments but this complex structure of fragments—more reminiscent now of the capricious design of marble than of the old-fashioned Russian doll of a decade ago—exists within an overall institutional structure and legal and political systems. This remains the case even after the entry into force of the Treaty of Lisbon.

8

EU ENLARGEMENT

*Christophe Hillion**

Enlarging the European Union (EU) is more than the territorial expansion of EU membership rights and obligations to other European states and peoples. Enlargement also triggers new policy demands on the Union, alters its institutional functioning, and affects its legal corpus. Indeed, and this is the focus of this chapter, it sets in motion the application of a specific and evolving body of EU rules that govern the entire process through which a third state *becomes* a Member State of the Union. Based primarily on Treaty provisions, such rules have been incrementally produced and articulated, thanks notably to unique interactions between EU institutions and Member States. More than a reflection of the Union's own legal evolution, the development of the terms under which the EU admits an additional member—and whereby Member States co-opt another peer—also results from the specific needs of each expansion process.

The present chapter examines the main steps in the development of those EU enlargement rules. It is divided into three sections that roughly correspond to three consecutive and complementary phases in their evolution. Originally conceived as a procedure aimed at making it possible for third states to become contracting parties to the founding treaties (Part A), enlargement has become a comprehensive policy whereby the Union actively engages with the applicants' preparation for membership (Part B). The considerable EU expansion to central and eastern Europe, unabated accession demands from the south and further east of the continent, and perceived growing 'enlargement fatigue' within the EU, have however questioned the policy's sustainability, and led to significant adjustments to its application. Taking place at both EU and Member State levels, the ongoing rectification discloses a creeping (re)nationalization of the procedure, that sits uncomfortably with the Treaty rules and principles within which it is embedded (Part C).

* Universities of Leiden and Stockholm, Swedish Institute for European Policy Studies. I am grateful to Prof Steven Blockmans and Dr Anne Myrjord for all their valuable comments, and for the insightful discussions with officials from the European Commission, and from the Ministries for Foreign Affairs of several Member States. The usual disclaimer applies.

The developments identified under each sequence should not be understood as exclusive to the period to which they are related. In many ways, the features presented under the successive sections have been at work throughout the evolution of enlargement rules, albeit with different intensity. That they seemingly characterize a certain phase more specifically depends on various factors. In particular, the evolving state of EU integration and of its *acquis*, the number of states the Union comprises when it enlarges, their political and economic situation, evolving public opinion, and the views of elites on integration, all contribute to possible alterations of the enlargement methodology, and to the prominence of some particular features at any given time. Similarly, the profile of the applicant, its possible (historical) connections with the EU and perhaps more importantly with its Member States, willing (or not) to plea for its cause, as well as regional and global developments, equally colour the way in which enlargement rules are developed, interpreted, and practised.[1]

A. FIRST GENERATION OF EU ENLARGEMENT RULES: APPLYING AND CLARIFYING THE TREATY PROCEDURE

From the first Community's admission of new members to the 1993 European Council Decision to open the Union to countries from central and eastern Europe, enlargement has by and large been governed by the same basic rules. These primarily consisted of the Treaty requirements set out in Article 237 of the Treaty establishing the European Economic Community (EEC), as interpreted by the Member States.

In its foundational phase, enlargement was envisaged as a state-driven procedure. The state-centrism is enshrined in the Treaty (1) and has been inflated in practice (2)—ironically in the name of preserving the integration *acquis*.

1. OPTING FOR A MEMBER STATE DRIVEN PROCEDURE

The Schuman declaration foresaw that the European integration project would be 'open to the participation of the other countries of Europe'.[2] No substantive conditions of admission were envisaged, except that the applicant ought to be a 'European' country, 'willing to take part'. The original Community Treaties translated this principle into various procedures. Three enlargement models were envisaged based on different procedural arrangements, notably with respect to the roles allocated to the Member States, thereby reflecting varying conceptions of the nature of the integration process.

The first Community Treaty establishing the European Coal and Steel Community (ECSC) foresaw in its Article 98 that:

---

[1] Further: A Tatham, *Enlargement of the European Union* (Kluwer Law International, 2009).
[2] Available at: <http://europa.eu/abc/symbols/9-may/decl_en.htm>.

Any European State may apply to accede to this Treaty. It shall address its application to the Council, which shall act unanimously after obtaining the opinion of the High Authority; the Council shall also determine the terms of accession, likewise acting unanimously. Accession shall take effect on the day when the instrument of accession is received by the Government acting as depository of this Treaty.

Governing third European states' accession 'to this Treaty', the ECSC enlargement procedure was thus to be carried out by the organization itself, through the Council in cooperation with the then High Authority. No mention was made of the Member States as such, nor was there any reference to recourse to an international Accession Treaty. Instead, enlargement was to become effective once the 'instrument of accession', supposedly containing the 'terms of accession' worked out by the Council, would be received by the French government.

While any Member State's representative could block the process, given the unanimity requirement in the Council, the competence to open the 'Treaty' to other contracting parties thus seemed vested with the Coal and Steel Community, rather than with the Member States as such. Put differently, the ECSC had the exclusive competence to admit other contracting parties to the Treaty, a process envisaged as essentially technical, with no parliamentary supervision, whether at European or Member States level.

The procedure for enlarging the stillborn European Political Community built upon the above elements, but went further in filling the mechanism with supranational elements. Article 116(1) of the Treaty establishing the European Political Community thus stipulated that:

1. Accession to the Community shall be open to the Member States of the Council of Europe and to any other European State which guarantees the protection of human rights and fundamental freedoms mentioned in Article 3.

2. Any State desirous of acceding to the present Statute shall address its request to the European Executive Council. The latter shall inform the Council of National Ministers and the Parliament of the Community accordingly.

3. Accession shall form the subject of an instrument of accession which shall form a Protocol to the present Statute. This instrument, which shall contain the necessary amendments to the Statute, shall be drawn up by the European Executive Council with the concurrence of the Council of National Ministers. It shall be submitted to the Parliament of the Community for approval.

4. The instrument of accession shall come into force as soon as the European Executive Council has promulgated it, and the State concerned has deposited its instrument of ratification with the European Executive Council ... [3]

---

[3] Draft Treaty embodying the Statute of the European Community adopted by the Ad Hoc Assembly in Strasbourg on 10 March 1953 (Selection of texts concerning institutional matters of the Community from 1950 to 1982. Luxembourg: European Parliament—Committee on Institutional Affairs (1982) 58–75). In the same vein, the Resolutions adopted by the Study Committee for the European Constitution (Brussels, November 1952) included a section on enlargement that stipulated: '8. Any European State may apply to join the Community. The Parliament will decide on this request by a two-thirds majority of the votes given in each

Akin to Article 98 ECSC, the EPC enlargement procedure did not foresee any role for Member States as such. The Community institutions themselves, including this time the parliamentary organ, were asked to handle and approve of the admission of additional states, in consideration of the latter's compliance with substantive conditions.[4] In the same vein, the EPC provisions referred to accession 'to the Community' and not to 'the Treaty', a semantic shift that seemingly denoted a distinct approach to the nature of the organization in general, and of its enlargement process, in particular. On the whole, the procedure was getting closer to the federal logic of Article 4, section 3 of the US Constitution, according to which: '[n]ew States may be admitted by the Congress into this Union'.

The EPC procedure was never used in practice, and although the Coal and Steel Community was enlarged several times, it always was in the broader context of the expansion of the subsequent European Atomic Energy Community (EAEC) and the EEC, respectively established by the two Rome Treaties. Both constituent charters envisaged a similar procedure that differed from their predecessors, and which in effect became the standard enlargement mechanism, namely Article 237 EEC (and Article 205 EAEC):

> Any European State may apply to become a member of the Community. It shall address its application to the Council which, after obtaining the opinion of the Commission, shall act by means of a unanimous vote.
>
> The conditions of admission and the amendments to this Treaty necessitated thereby shall be the subject of an agreement between the Member States and the applicant State. Such agreement shall be submitted to all the contracting States for ratification in accordance with their respective constitutional rules.

The accession provisions of the Rome Treaties diverged from the ECSC procedure in at least two important respects. First, like the EPC Treaty, the EEC and EAEC Treaties referred to the notion of 'member[ship] of the Community'. They thus confirmed the move suggested by the ECP Treaty, and consolidated the notion that membership entailed a political commitment from the applicant state that was not conspicuous in the ECSC Treaty. As mentioned above, the latter merely referred to 'accession to this treaty' and its preamble did not contain the EEC's lyrical '[call] upon the other peoples of Europe who share their ideal to join in their efforts'.

Secondly, the role of the Member States was made far more significant in the procedures of Articles 237 EEC and 205 EAEC than in that of Article 98 ECSC.

---

of the two houses. Entrance into the Community becomes effective at the depositing of the formal acceptance in the hands of the President of the European Council. This entrance must be preceded by the conclusion of an agreement regulating the conditions of participation of the concerned State, and in particular its representation in the organs of the Community.' (Selection of texts concerning institutional matters of the Community from 1950 to 1982. Luxembourg: European Parliament—Committee on Institutional Affairs (1982) 80–93).

[4] Art 3 EPC, to which the EPC enlargement procedure refers, foresaw that 'The provisions of Part I of the Convention for the Protection of Human Rights and Fundamental Freedoms signed in Rome on 4 November 1950, together with those of the protocol signed in Paris on 20 March 1952, are an integral part of the present Statute'.

While the latter envisaged an accession based on an executive arrangement defined by the Council, the former foresaw that the terms of admission were to be negotiated and ratified by the Member States and the applicant. The process of accession to the Communities thus became imbued with state-centrism; all the more so that the Rome procedures disposed of the European Parliamentary control envisioned by the EPC Treaty.

While the founding Community Treaties were conceived as open Treaties, Member States thus became their gatekeepers. Not only have the early arrangements evolved to allow them to maintain control over the procedure, practice also displays that Member States have worked out additional preconditions which applicants would have to satisfy for being admitted. Despite the essentially procedural nature of the ECSC, EAEC, and the EEC enlargement provisions, Member States thus begun to articulate the preamble's '[call] upon the other peoples of Europe who share their ideal to join in their efforts'.

2. PRESERVING THE *ACQUIS* AND MEMBER STATES' CONTROL

The first episode of the enlargement saga shaped the way in which the European Communities and then the EU handled each and every subsequent wave of expansion. While the Rome procedure has been used as the standard mechanism, the enlargement to Denmark, Ireland, and the UK demonstrated that the Treaties provided only a basic procedure, upon which Member States would be able to build additional requirements. Two incidents exemplify this proposition.

First, the earliest endeavour to enlarge the Communities was stopped twice by a French veto, thereby glaringly demonstrating that the procedure could easily be held up by one single Member State. The event also epitomized that enlargement could be blocked for reasons that had more to do with crude domestic interests of a Member State, than with the applicant's inability to fulfil the meagre Treaty requirements.[5] The declaration made by the Council of Ministers that discussed the second British application typifies these points when noting that '*one Member State* considered the re-establishment of the British economy must be completed before Great Britain's request [for admission] can be considered' (emphasis added).[6] A state could thus invoke an unwritten argument (*in casu* the economic condition) to prevent an application being 'considered', regardless of the fact that the Commission had already provided its opinions, recommending the opening of negotiations.[7]

---

[5] Tatham (n 1 above) 7 *et seq.*

[6] J P Puissochet, *L'Elargissement des Communautés Européennes* (Editions Techniques et Economiques, 1974) 16; F Nicholson and R East, *From Six to Twelve. The Enlargement of the European Communities* (Longman, 1987) 56; C Preston, *Enlargement and Integration in the European Union* (Routledge, 1997) 31. More generally on UK accession to the EEC: D Hannay (ed), *Britain's Entry into the European Community* (Frank Cass Publishers, 2000).

[7] Avis de la Commision au Conseil concernant les demandes d'adhésion du Royaume Uni, de l'Irlande, du Danemark et de la Norvège; COM(1967) 750; Bull EC Supp 11–1967.

Secondly, the Council's abovementioned statement suggests that Member States could also elaborate the Treaty procedure, notably by invoking and thus establishing additional substantive conditions to which accession would be subject. The 1969 Hague Summit is a case in point. Having 'reaffirmed their agreement on the principle of the enlargement of the Community, as provided by Article 237 of the Treaty of Rome', the Heads of State or Government of the Member States pointed out that

> In so far as the applicant States *accept the Treaties and their political finality, the decisions taken since the entry into force of the Treaties and the options made in the sphere of development*, the Heads of State or Government have indicated their agreement to the opening of negotiations between the Community on the one hand and the applicant States on the other. They agreed that the essential preparatory work could be undertaken as soon as practically and conveniently possible; by common consent, the preparations would take place in a most positive spirit.[8] (emphasis added)

The candidate's commitment to accept the existing Community rules and objectives thereby became a precondition for the Member States to agree on the opening of negotiations 'between the Community... and the applicant states'. Each subsequent enlargement confirmed and strengthened the significance of this requirement, in particular by demanding that, more than 'shar[ing] their ideals' and accepting the Treaties and the decisions taken thereupon, the candidate should demonstrate that the *acquis* is not only translated in its own laws by the day of accession, but also properly implemented, through adequate administrative and judicial institutions.[9]

In correlation with this orthodoxy, Member States have always required that any practical difficulty for the applicant to adopt the *acquis* would have to be resolved through transitional derogatory measures, to be included in the Accession Treaty, instead of renegotiating the EU *acquis*, unless renegotiation would lead to further integration.[10] The 'adjustments of the Treaties which admission entails' referred to in the enlargement provisions, have thus been understood narrowly.[11]

The second veto to the British application also discloses the early intention of the Member States to stipulate the specific qualities of an eligible candidate. The Council's reference to the state of the UK economy exemplifies the notion that accession would be conditional upon the applicant's observance of various economic

---

[8] Final Communiqué of the Hague Summit, 2 December 1969. See L J Brinkhorst and M J Kuijper, 'The integration of the new Member States in the Community legal order' (1972) 9 CML Rev 364.

[9] See below Section B.1.

[10] Hence the Accession Treaty with Denmark, Ireland, (Norway), and the UK foresaw a Member States' transfer of competence in the field of fisheries (Ch 3 of Act of Accession, [1972] OJ L73); see Cases 3, 4, and 6/76 *Kramer* [1976] ECR 1279; Case 804/79 *Commission v United Kingdom* [1981] ECR I-1045.

[11] The rationale behind this approach is explained by Puissochet (n 6 above) 19–20. On adjustments to the treaties in Accession Treaties, and their limits, see Case C-413/04 *European Parliament v Council* [2006] ECR I-11221, and Case C-414/04 *European Parliament v Council* [2006] ECR I-11279; and annotation by K Inglis, (2009) 46 CML Rev 641.

and political principles that were articulated as the Community enlarged to southern Europe.[12]

While governed by Treaty provisions, enlargement rules have from their inception been subject to Member States' regular adjustment. Hence, the first generation of enlargement rules based on Article 237 EEC may be characterized as strongly *state-driven*. They are also *conservative* in view of their dogmatic emphasis on the candidate's acceptance of the *acquis*.[13] Finally, they can be regarded as *non-interventionist*, in that the EU leaves it almost entirely to the candidate to prepare itself for accession and fulfil the entry conditions.

B. SECOND GENERATION OF ENLARGEMENT RULES: FROM ENLARGEMENT PROCEDURE TO ENLARGEMENT POLICY

Consolidating the abovementioned conservative line, but nuancing state-centrism and moving away from a non-interventionist stance, the second generation of enlargement rules translates a vigorous EU engagement with the candidates' preparation for membership. Involving an elaborated normative basis (1), and an active role of EU institutions (2), an enlargement *policy* of the Union has progressively emerged as a comprehensive EU Member State-making policy. The political acknowledgment by the 1993 Copenhagen European Council that the post-communist central and eastern European countries had a vocation to become members of the Union sparks the beginning of that development.

1. ELABORATING THE NORMATIVE BASIS OF ENLARGEMENT

Building on the scarce substantive conditions evoked earlier, the EU developed the normative basis against which new admissions would be assessed, and in the light of which enlargement would be conducted. Initially conceived specifically for the accession of states from central and eastern Europe, the new rules have since become the standard framework for carrying out enlargement, eg towards candidates from the 'Western Balkans', Turkey or recently, Iceland.[14]

---

[12] See eg F Hoffmeister, 'Earlier enlargements' in A Ott and K Inglis (eds), *Handbook on European Enlargement* (TMC Asser Press, 2002) 90; C Hillion, 'The Copenhagen criteria and their progeny' in C Hillion (ed), *EU Enlargement: A Legal Approach* (Hart, 2004) 1, and literature mentioned.

[13] The Heads of State or Government meeting in The Hague also pointed out that: '[t]he European Communities remain the original nucleus from which European unity has been developed and intensified. The entry of other countries of this continent to the Communities—in accordance with the provisions of the Treaties of Rome—would undoubtedly help the Communities to grow to dimensions more in conformity with the present state of world economy and technology.'

[14] See EU-Western Balkans Summit—Declaration, Thessaloniki, 21 June 2003 (regarding the Western Balkans); Presidency Conclusions, European Council, Brussels, 16/17 December 2004 (Turkey); Commission Opinion on Iceland's application for membership of the European Union; COM(2010) 62 (Iceland). See also eg

To begin with, the basic accession conditions were further articulated and system-atized. In addition to the applicant's acceptance of the EU *acquis* (including for the first time the CFSP and JHA *acquis*), the candidates would have to fulfil the so-called 'Copenhagen criteria' set out by the European Council in 1993, and according to which membership requires that the candidate country has achieved:

- stability of institutions guaranteeing democracy, the rule of law, human rights and respect for and protection of minorities;

- the existence of a functioning market economy as well as the capacity to cope with competitive pressure and market forces within the Union; and

- demonstrated its ability to take on the obligations of membership including adherence to the aims of political, economic, and monetary union.[15]

The European Council thus established a consolidated list of the hitherto scattered accession conditions.[16] But the normative content of those established conditions was also progressively elaborated. For instance, the Madrid European Council of 1995 made clear that admission would entail more than the mere political commitment to accept the integration *acquis*, which the Heads of State or Government had required at the 1969 Hague Summit. It would equally involve specific structural reforms. In particular, the European Council emphasized that the candidate countries would have to adjust their administrative structures to guarantee effective implementation of EU rules.[17]

In codifying and elaborating accession conditions, the European Council also laid the grounds for what was to become a proactive and meticulous pre-membership policy: namely the 'pre-accession strategy'. Launched by the 1994 Essen European Council,[18] it finds its roots in the 1993 Copenhagen Summit:

> The European Council will continue to follow closely progress in each associated country towards fulfilling the conditions of accession to the Union and draw the appropriate conclusions.
>
> The European Council agreed that the future cooperation with the associated countries shall be geared to the objective of membership which has now been established.

While in the previous period, the candidate had been expected to fulfil the admission conditions by itself, the post-Copenhagen approach to enlargement has by contrast

---

K Inglis, 'EU Enlargement: Membership Conditions Applied to Future and Potential Member States' in S Blockmans and A Łazowski (eds), *The European Union and its Neighbours—A legal appraisal of the EU's policies of Stabilisation, partnership and integration* (TMC Asser Press, 2006) 61; on the Western Balkans, more specifically: S Blockmans, *Tough Love—The European Union's Relations with the Western Balkans* (TMC Asser Press, 2007) 282 *et seq.*

[15] Presidency Conclusions, Copenhagen European Council, 21–22 June 1993.

[16] M Cremona, 'Accession to the European Union: Membership conditionality and accession criteria' (2001) 25 Polish Yrbk Intl L 219; Hoffmeister (n 12 above); Hillion (n 12 above).

[17] Presidency Conclusions, Madrid European Council, 15–16 December 1995.

[18] Presidency Conclusions, Essen European Council, 9–10 December 1994.

entailed an EU pro-active engagement to steer and monitor the process whereby it prepares its accession. The Commission's subsequent opinions on the CEECs' applications for membership provided an opportunity for the institution to translate the Copenhagen criteria into various indicators for those countries to carry out the required reforms, as part of their accession preparation. For example, to assess the 'existence of a market economy', the Commission would look at whether the equilibrium between demand and supply is determined by the free interplay of market forces; whether prices as well as trade are liberalized, whether significant barriers to market entry (ie establishment of new firms) and exit (bankruptcies) remain; whether the legal system, including the regulation of property rights is in place; and whether laws and contracts may be enforced.[19]

On that basis, the 1997 Luxembourg European Council endorsed a Commission proposal to reinforce the so-called 'pre-accession strategy', involving the comprehensive and active projection of EU norms, with a view to their effective adoption *prior* to admission to the Union. Hence, the Copenhagen criteria were not only translated in several indicators, they were progressively spelled out into short, medium and long-term priorities, compiled in 'accession partnerships' adopted by the EU, and which the candidates would have to meet with a view, and as a condition, to their ultimate accession. The new strategy also entailed a system of close EU monitoring of the applicants' progress in carrying out the required adaptations and periodical reporting, which in turn would determine the candidates' advancement on the road to membership.[20]

The pre-accession adaptation was plugged into the broader and deeper process of political and economic transformation undertaken by CEECs. The EU and its Member States thus used the membership promise as a bargaining chip to influence, if not steer, the structural reforms with a view to ensuring that the newcomers would be as amenable to membership as possible. In becoming itself a key actor of the transformation process, the EU entered uncharted territories of liberal democratic and market economy state-building. In this process, it not only referred to its own norms viewed as a recipe for modernization, it also advocated other regional and international standards such as OSCE principles and Council of Europe rules, thus filling the broad Copenhagen political criteria with normative content that may have been lacking in view of the limited, if not non-existent relevant EU norms.[21] For instance, as regards

---

[19] Agenda 2000, 'The Challenge of Enlargement', Part II, COM(1997) 2000; see also the Commission's White Paper Preparation of the Associated Countries of Central and Eastern Europe for Integration into the Internal Market of the Union, COM(95) 163 final, 3 May 1995.

[20] On the pre-accession strategy, see eg M Maresceau, 'Pre-accession', and P Nicolaides, 'Preparing for Accession to the European Union: How to Establish Capacity for Effective and Credible Application of EU Rules' in M Cremona (ed), *The Enlargement of the European Union* (Oxford University Press, 2003) 9 and 43, respectively; K Smith, *The making of EU foreign policy: the case of Eastern Europe* (Palgrave, 1999) 122; Tatham (n 1 above) 287; C Hillion 'Enlargement: a legal analysis' in A Arnull and D Wincott (eds), *Accountability and Legitimacy in the European Union* (Oxford University Press, 2002) 403.

[21] H Grabbe, 'A Partnership for Accession? The Implications of EU Conditionality for the Central and East European Applicants' European University Institute Working Papers RSC No 99/12; A Albi, *EU Enlargement and the Constitutions of Central and Eastern Europe* (Cambridge University Press, 2005) 46 *et seq.*

the fulfilment of the Copenhagen criterion related to minority protection, EU institutions had to rely on the European Framework Convention on the Protection of National minorities and draw on the expertise of the OSCE High Commissioner for National Minorities to provide their own assessment of the candidates' progress.[22]

In other words, the post-Copenhagen normative basis of enlargement consisted not only of consolidated and systematized substantive conditions hitherto implicitly invoked by the Member States, and essentially geared towards the preservation of the EU *acquis*. It has also encompassed standards and norms of other European and international organizations whose EU promotion aimed at contributing and consolidating the candidates' broader political and economic restructuring. The pre-accession strategy turned enlargement into a policy with a transformative aim, thereby transforming the EU into a normative power in Europe. In that, enlargement has also had a self-identification dimension of constitutional significance. It has revealed what is required to be(come) a Member State of the Union, and signalled what the Union as an entity intends to be, or has been 'catapulted into' being.[23]

However, the pre-accession methodology has equally revealed a discrepancy between accession conditions and membership obligations because the norms the Union has promoted in the context of enlargement go well beyond the perimeter of the EU *acquis stricto sensu*. The inflated and evolving normative basis for enlargement has raised issues of double standards that have consequently undermined the credibility of the Union's commitments to the norms and values it has advocated vis-à-vis the applicants, questioned the legitimacy of its conditionality, and ultimately the effectiveness of the transformation agenda.[24] More worryingly, the discrepancy has led to a post-accession drop in the EU monitoring of new Member States,[25] and a setback in the protection of certain rights advocated in the pre-accession context.

---

[22] G Toggenburg (ed), *Minority Protection and The Enlarged European Union: The way forward* (LGI Books, 2004); P Van Elsuwege, 'Minority Protection in the EU—Challenges Ahead' in K Inglis and A Ott (eds), *The Constitution for Europe and an Enlarging Union: Unity in Diversity?* (Europa Law Publishers, 2005) 259; G Sasse, 'The Politics of Conditionality: The Norm of Minority Protection before and after EU Accession' (2008) 15 JEPP 842; O de Schutter, 'The Framework Convention on the Protection of National Minorities and the Law of the European Union' CRIDHO Working Paper 2006/01; C Hillion, 'The Framework Convention for the Protection of National Minorities and the European Union' (Council of Europe Report, 2008).

[23] See eg H Sjursen, 'Enlargement in perspective. The EU's quest for identity' Recon Online Working Paper 2007/15; K Smith, 'The conditional offer of membership as an instrument of EU foreign policy: reshaping Europe in the EU's image?' (2000) 8 Marmara Journal of European Studies 33, J Pelkmans and A Murphy, 'Catapulted into leadership: the community's trade and aid policies vis a vis Eastern Europe' (1991) 14 J European Integration 125.

[24] There is an abundant literature establishing the flaws of conditionality notably in the enlargement context; see for instance: A Albi, 'Ironies in Human Rights Protection in the EU: Pre-Accession Conditionality and Post-Accession Conundrums' (2009) 15 ELJ 46; D Kochenov, *EU Enlargement and the Failure of Conditionality* (Kluwer Law International, 2008) and the contributions in F Schimmelfennig and U Sedelmeier (eds), *The Europeanization of Central and Eastern Europe* (Cornell University Press, 2005).

[25] Except perhaps for Bulgaria and Romania, still formally under specific post-accession monitoring. Further: A Łazowski, 'And Then They Were Twenty-Seven . . . A Legal Appraisal of the Sixth Accession Treaty' (2007) 44 CML Rev 401.

While the gap may have been partly filled thanks to the Lisbon Treaty, full harmony between accession requirements and membership obligations remains unaccomplished.[26]

2. INVOLVING EU INSTITUTIONS TO MONITOR ACCESSION PREPARATION

The development of the pre-accession strategy, partly explained by the specific profile and thus adaptation needs of the candidates involved, also nuances the hitherto essentially intergovernmental nature of the process. EU institutions, and particularly the Commission were vested by the European Council with far-reaching powers to monitor the way candidates prepared their accession, and more generally to establish the pre-accession strategy.[27]

The development of arrangements involving the EU institutions started at the level of the *definition of the accession criteria*. As pointed out earlier, it was the European Council that set out the 'Copenhagen criteria', following earlier suggestions from the European Commission.[28] It supplemented the general Treaty provisions and refined the substantive rules for enlarging the European Union. But it also elaborated these conditions further, notably at its meetings in Madrid in 1995, at Helsinki in 1999, and regularly since.[29] Helped by the Commission,[30] the European Council thus established itself as the *pouvoir constituant* of the enlargement policy.

---

[26] See eg U Sedelmeier, 'After Conditionality: Post-accession compliance with EU law in East Central Europe' (2008) 15 JEPP 806; F Hoffmeister, 'Grundlagen und Vorgaben für den Schutz der Minderheiten im EU-Primärrecht' (2008) 68 ZaöRV 175; D Kochenov, 'A Summary of Contradictions: An Outline of the EU's Main Internal and External Approaches to Ethnic Minority Protection' (2008) 31 BC Int'l & Comp L Rev, 1; C Hillion, 'Enlargement of the European Union: The discrepancy between Accession conditionality and membership obligations' (2004) 27 Fordham Intl LJ 715.

[27] Note that the Commission was then reorganized so as to include a specific Directorate General for Enlargement.

[28] See Report by the Commission to the European Council, Edinburgh, 11–12 December 1992, *Towards a Closer Association with the Countries of Central and Eastern Europe*, SEC(92) 2301 final; Communication by the Commission to the Council, in view of the meeting of the European Council in Copenhagen, 21–22 June 1993, *Towards a closer association with the countries of central and eastern Europe*, SEC(93) 648 final. Further: A Mayhew, *Recreating Europe. The European Union's Policy towards Central and Eastern Europe* (Cambridge University Press, 1998); K Smith, 'The Evolution and Application of EU Membership Conditionality' in M Cremona (ed), *The Enlargement of the European Union* (Oxford University Press, 2003) 105, 113. M Maresceau, 'Quelques réflexions sur l'origine et l'application des principes fondamentaux dans la stratégie d'adhésion de l'UE' in *Le droit de l'Union européenne en principes—Liber Amicorum en l'honneur de Jean Raux* (Apogées, 2006) 69.

[29] Presidency Conclusions, Madrid European Council, 15–16 December 1995; Presidency Conclusions, Helsinki European Council, 10–11 December 1999. M Cremona, 'Accession to the European Union: membership conditionality and accession criteria' (2001) 25 Polish Yrbk Intl L 219; Hillion (n 12 above) 17. On the development of additional tailor-made accession conditions for the Western Balkans, see eg S Blockmans, 'Raising the Threshold for Further EU Enlargement: Process and Problems and Prospects' in A Ott and E Vos (eds), *50 Years of European Integration: Foundations and Perspectives* (TMC Asser Press, 2009) 203.

[30] Maresceau (n 28 above).

Following the formulation of the accession criteria, the European Council also endorsed the pre-accession strategy, based on the Commission's proposals.[31] This strategy entailed growing cooperation between the Commission, the Council and European Council in the definition of the enlargement policy and its management, notably in the form of a system of compliance control and sanctions.

A case in point is the management of the 'Accession Partnership' (AP) evoked earlier. On the basis of the framework AP Regulation adopted by the Council,[32] the Commission drafted individual accession partnerships containing the list of principles, priorities, intermediate objectives, and conditions on which the adaptation of the candidate should focus to meet the Copenhagen criteria. Such accession partnerships would then have to be adopted by the Council by qualified majority voting, before being presented to the candidates.[33]

On the request of the European Council,[34] the Commission also begun to produce detailed evaluation on each candidate's performance in implementing the APs, through the publication of annual reports, on the basis of which the Council would determine the pace of negotiations.[35] Indeed, the accession partnership established a system whereby the Council, on a proposal from the Commission, could *review* the EU financial assistance if progress in meeting the Copenhagen criteria were deemed insufficient. Acting well beyond its traditional role of 'guardian of the [EC] Treaty' vis-à-vis the Member States, the Commission thus acquired the pivotal function of promoting and controlling the progressive application of the wider EU *acquis* by future members. Indeed, in articulating *all* the Copenhagen accession criteria and monitoring the candidates' progress in meeting them,[36] it became intimately involved in defining the prototype of an

---

[31] Presidency Conclusions, Essen European Council, 9–10 December 1994; Communication from the Commission to the Council, *The Europe Agreements and Beyond: A Strategy to Prepare the Countries of Central and Eastern Europe For Accession*, COM(94) 320 final; Communication from the Commission to the Council, *Follow up to Commission Communication on 'The Europe Agreements and Beyond: A Strategy to Prepare the Countries of Central and Eastern Europe for Accession'*, COM(94) 361 final.

[32] Council Regulation 622/98 ([1998] OJ L85/1); for a recent example of an AP, see Council Decision 2008/157/EC of 18 February 2008 on the principles, priorities and conditions contained in the Accession Partnership with the Republic of Turkey and repealing Decision 2006/35/EC ([2008] OJ L51/4).

[33] Art 2 of Council Regulation 622/98 ([1998] OJ L85/1).

[34] The 1997 Luxembourg European Council decided that '[f]rom the end of 1998, the Commission will make regular reports to the Council, together with any necessary recommendations for opening bilateral intergovernmental conferences, reviewing the progress of each Central and Eastern European applicant State towards accession in the light of the Copenhagen criteria, in particular the rate at which it is adopting the Union *acquis*...The Commission's reports will serve as the basis for taking, in the Council context, the necessary decisions on the conduct of the accession negotiations or their extension to other applicants. In that context, the Commission will continue to follow the method adopted by Agenda 2000 in evaluating applicant States' ability to meet the economic criteria and fulfil the obligations deriving from accession' (Presidency Conclusions, Luxembourg European Council, 12–13 December 1997, 29).

[35] This periodical reporting on candidates' progress contrasted with previous accession procedures in which only *two* opinions were given by the Commission on any membership application.

[36] As regards more particularly the EU scrutiny of the political conditionality, see eg A Williams, 'Enlargement of the Union and human rights conditionality: a policy' (2000) 25 ELRev 601; K Smith, 'The evolution

EU Member State, both in political, economic, legal, administrative, and judicial terms.

The EU institutions' role in the enlargement policy also spilled over to *accession negotiations*. While Treaty provisions suggest that the process essentially involves the Member States, on the one hand, and the applicant state, on the other, in practice institutions became directly involved in the conduct of these negotiations.[37] For example, the Common Position presented by the Presidency in accession conferences would be first adopted by the General Affairs Council, on the basis of drafts prepared by the Commission on each of the chapters, for each of the candidates.

On the whole therefore, the post-Copenhagen enlargement of the Union is more than a mere Treaty procedure. A *droit constant*, enlargement was in practice turned into a policy governed by a set of elaborated substantive rules, encompassing new and evolving accession conditions and principles which include non-EU norms. Based on an *ad hoc* system, the EU has actively engaged in the preparation of the candidates with a view to transforming them into (super) Member States.[38] That evolution has nuanced the original intergovernmental character of the procedure in that it allowed for an increased role for the EU institutional framework. Having recognized the Eastern enlargement as 'political necessity and historic opportunity',[39] Member States were seemingly ready to hand over its daily preparation and management to the EU institutions, and particularly to the Commission.

Driven by institutional practice and based on soft law instruments,[40] in the form of eg bilateral accession partnerships and progress reports, enlargement could thus become a *common* policy of the *Union*, both substantively and institutionally integrated. In particular, the policy has not been determined by the constitutional differentiation characterizing the EU legal order. As the distinction between different policies and their specific modes of decision-making (CFSP v other EU policies) does not matter in the context of enlargement, bickering over the distribution of competences has been almost entirely absent. Indeed, the policy involves all facets and levels of EU governance. It engages the EU institutional framework, and its

---

and application of EU membership conditionality' in M Cremona (ed), *The enlargement of the European Union* (Oxford University Press, 2003) 105; E Tulmets, *La conditionnalité dans la politique d'élargissement de l'Union européenne à l'Est: un cadre d'apprentissages et de socialisation mutuelle?* (2005) PhD Thesis, Science-Po, Paris <http://ecoledoctorale.sciencespo.fr/theses/theses_en_ligne/tulmets_scpo_2005/tulmets_scpo_2005.pdf>.

[37] The institutions' role in the negotiations was already visible at the first enlargement of the EEC, as has been pointed out by Puissochet (n 6 above).

[38] Hillion (n 12 above).

[39] Presidency Conclusions, Madrid European Council, 15–16 December 2006.

[40] On these notions, see F Snyder, 'Soft law and institutional practice in the European Community' (1993) European University Institute Law Working Paper No 93/5; B van Vooren, 'A case study for soft law in EU external relations: The European Neighbourhood Policy' (2009) 34 ELR 696.

success ultimately depends on the cooperation between institutions and Member States,[41] a cooperation that has seemingly been decreasing recently.

C. THIRD GENERATION OF EU ENLARGEMENT RULES: PRESERVING THE INTEGRATION MOMENTUM?

Following the Union's expansion to the east, and against the backdrop of the rejection of the Constitutional Treaty, the EU and its Member States have adjusted their approach towards enlargement, rightly or wrongly presented as a factor of decreasing support for the Union.[42] Thus in its Enlargement Strategy of 2006, the Commission pointed out that the 'EU honours the commitments made to the countries already in the process, *but is cautious in assuming any new commitments*' (emphasis added).[43] In the garb of a better-prepared accession process and intentions to preserve the integration momentum, Member States have reasserted their control over the policy (1). At the same time, past *ad hoc* practices have been codified through Treaty revisions, further entrenching the procedure in the EU legal framework (2).

1. NATIONALIZING EU ENLARGEMENT?

The control regained by Member States over EU enlargement is conspicuous at various levels: in the extended use of conditionality throughout the procedure (a), through the multiplication of procedural steps in the application of Article 49(1) TEU (b), and by the Member States' unilaterally imposing new conditions for accession and enlargement (c).

(a) Extended use of conditionality
The adjustment of enlargement rules undertaken since 2006 corresponds to the growing anxiety that the pace of expansion ought to be 'carefully managed',[44] in the face of increased (perceived) domestic disenchantment in relation to the EU in general, and to its expansion in particular, captured in the almost proverbial 'enlargement fatigue'.

---

[41] The enlargement methodology has become a source of inspiration for other policies, such as the European Neighbourhood Policy; see eg J Kelley, 'New Wine in Old Wineskins: Policy Learning and Adaption in The new European Neighborhood Policy' (2006) 44 JCMS 29; A Magen, 'The Shadow of Enlargement: Can the European Neighbourhood Policy Achieve Compliance?' (2006) 12 CJEL 384; M Cremona and C Hillion, 'L'Union fait la force? Potential and limits of the European Neighbourhood Policy as an integrated EU foreign and security policy' European University Institute Law Working Paper No 39/2006.

[42] House of Lords, *The Further Enlargement of the EU: threat or opportunity?* European Union Committee, 53rd Report of Session 2005–06 (hereinafter 'House of Lords Report'); interview of former French Prime Minister Balladur, *Le Monde*, 27 September 2010.

[43] COM(2006) 649, 15.

[44] COM(2006) 649, 3.

A more restrictive approach to further expansion has been detectable since. Hence, the Commission's 2006 Enlargement Strategy, published just a few weeks before the accession of Bulgaria and Romania, displays an evolution in the EU discourse as regards admission of new states. While aiming at supporting countries on their way to membership, it also envisages 'ways to foster public support for further enlargement, to address the enlargement challenges and to ensure the EU's integration capacity [as] the basis for building a renewed consensus on enlargement'.[45] The document, subsequently endorsed by the European Council, notably envisages that 'rigorous and fair conditionality' ought to govern the EU enlargement policy and methodology.

One of the most noticeable methodological innovations in this respect lies in the introduction of conditionality in the accession *negotiations* phase. Thus, the Council defines 'benchmarks' on the basis of a Commission recommendation, which the candidate has to meet for the EU to open and/or close a particular negotiating chapter.[46] Non-fulfilment of such pre-defined benchmarks may be sanctioned by the suspension of negotiations in the form of a non-opening of the related negotiation chapter, or possibly in the reopening of the provisionally closed chapter. In this process, both the definition of the benchmarks and the assessment of their fulfilment are subject to the Council's (read: Member States') unanimous approval.

It is certainly the case that conditionality and negotiations had hitherto been connected, in that the *start* of accession negotiations has always been subject to the fulfilment of specific conditions, now enshrined in the Treaty. Yet, the new approach extends the use of such conditionality beyond the determination of whether accession negotiations should be started, to the entire enlargement procedure. The rationale behind the correlation between conditionality and negotiations is summarized in the Commission's notion that '[t]he pace of negotiations depends on the pace of reforms on the ground',[47] and that 'the negotiations offer countries the opportunity to demonstrate their ability to complete the necessary reforms and meet all membership requirements'.[48]

---

[45] COM(2006) 649, 3 *et seq.*

[46] According to the Commission 2006 document: 'Benchmarks are a new tool introduced as a result of lessons learnt from the fifth enlargement. Their purpose is to improve the quality of the negotiations, by providing incentives for the candidate countries to undertake necessary reforms at an early stage. Benchmarks are measurable and linked to key elements of the *acquis* chapter. In general, opening benchmarks concern key preparatory steps for future alignment (such as strategies or action plans), and the fulfilment of contractual obligations that mirror *acquis* requirements. Closing benchmarks primarily concern legislative measures, administrative or judicial bodies, and a track record of implementation of the *acquis*. For chapters in the economic field, they also include the criterion of being a functioning market economy.' It should be noted that the substance of such benchmarks, and *a fortiori* the evaluation of their fulfilment, is not public, contrary to earlier indications given by the Commission in the name of transparency (see Communication from the Commission to the European Parliament and the Council, Enlargement Strategy and Main Challenges 2006–2007, COM(2006) 649, 10).

[47] COM(2006) 649, 5.   [48] COM(2006) 649, 6.

In the same vein, candidate states' compliance with the foundational principles of the Union, namely the principles of liberty, democracy, respect for human rights and fundamental freedoms, as well as the rule of law, have become subject to *constant* monitoring, and a potential case for suspension of the negotiations process. Accession negotiations may be held up in case of 'serious and persistent breach...of the [political] principles...on which the Union is founded', to be established by qualified majority of the Member States.[49] In other words, fulfilment of what hitherto amounted to 'eligibility' requirements (ie conditions to trigger the procedure of Article 49 TEU), or 'admissibility' conditions (ie conditions to start accession negotiations—'Copenhagen political criteria') continues to be controlled throughout the process.

The more 'rigorous' pre-accession methodology has had various effects on the enlargement procedure. First, it may have increased the EU leverage on the candidate to deliver on reforms, and adapt to the requirements of membership, at least formally. Indeed, it has been argued that the broadening of conditionality and monitoring has not altered what has often amounted to a ticking-off exercise based on quantitative achievements, ie the number of laws adopted by the candidate,[50] rather than on an in-depth qualitative assessment of how entrenched the new norms have become in its system.

Secondly, the introduction of conditionality in accession negotiations, in the form of opening and closing benchmarks, has further reduced the negotiated aspects of accession envisioned in Article 49(2) TEU,[51] and ultimately the need to rely on temporary derogations. In other words, the generalization of conditionality tends to inflate the conservative nature of admission. At the same time, the introduction of conditions for opening and closing negotiation chapters increases candidates' expectations that once they are fulfilled, accession negotiations should proceed.

Thirdly, since the approval of benchmarks, and of the evaluation of their fulfilment, is the prerogative of Member States, the latter are offered additional opportunities to hold up the process, both because of concerns regarding the pace of reforms, and, as

---

[49] This mechanism is recalled in the Commission 2006 Strategy Document, and prominently in the Negotiating Framework for Turkey: 'In the case of a serious and persistent breach in Turkey of the principles of liberty, democracy, respect for human rights and fundamental freedoms and the rule of law on which the Union is founded, the Commission will, on its own initiative or on the request of one third of the Member States, recommend the suspension of negotiations and propose the conditions for eventual resumption. The Council will decide by qualified majority on such a recommendation, after having heard Turkey, whether to suspend the negotiations and on the conditions for their resumption. The Member States will act in the Intergovernmental Conference in accordance with the Council decision, without prejudice to the general requirement for unanimity in the Intergovernmental Conference. The European Parliament will be informed.' See pt 5 of the Negotiating Framework for Turkey, 3 October 2005; see also pt 17 of the Negotiating Framework for Iceland (both available on the Commission website).

[50] Indeed, it has been argued that the conditionality has had the effect of strengthening the executive-driven nature of the adaptation process, at the expense of parliamentary influence, see eg S Blockmans, 'EU Enlargement as a Peacebuilding Tool' in J Wouters, S Blockmans, and T Ruys (eds), *The European Union and Peacebuilding* (TMC Asser Press, 2009) 77, 91.

[51] Further Maresceau (n 20 above); S Duke and A Courtier, 'EU Peacebuilding: Concepts, players and instruments' in Wouters, Blockmans, and Ruys (n 50 above) 15.

practice shows, for reasons which do not always relate to compliance with accession criteria. For instance, in the negotiations with Croatia, Slovenia blocked the adoption of the Commission's benchmarks in relation to chapter 23 on judiciary and fundamental rights, because of the border dispute between the two countries. Similarly, chapter 31 of the accession negotiations, relating to Foreign, Security and Defence Policy could not be opened as Slovenia had been blocking the adoption of an EU Common Position for negotiation,[52] until the settlement of a border dispute between the two countries.[53] One may recall at this point that the list of negotiation chapters has grown since the fifth enlargement (from 30 originally to 35), and thus potentially the number of benchmarks to be fulfilled, and mechanically instances of possible suspension of the process.

Another illustration of the Member States' reasserted control over the procedure, by way of strengthened conditionality, is the increased emphasis put on the *absorption / integration capacity* discourse. Already on the occasion of the first expansion of the EEC, it was made clear that enlargement should not hamper the integration objectives. This has always been linked to, if not inherent in, the notion that any candidate should commit itself to respect the *acquis*.[54] However at Copenhagen, the European Council *explicitly* envisaged the absorption capacity as a prerequisite to further enlargement, by underlining that the latter would take place in consideration of 'the Union's capacity to absorb new members, while maintaining the momentum of European integration in the general interest of both the Union and the candidate countries'. What is sometimes referred to as the fourth Copenhagen criterion triggered a process whereby questioning the feasibility of an enlargement has been mainstreamed, and made increasingly significant if not determinant in the Member States' decision on whether or not to enlarge.[55]

The Member States thus made it plain that an institutional reform would indeed be required for the EU to admit central and eastern European states.[56] After the perceived failure of the Amsterdam Treaty on this account,[57] the Nice Treaty was considered to have provided the necessary reform, thus opening the way to

---

[52] See website of the Croatian Ministry of Foreign Affairs: <http://www.eu-pregovori.hr/files/100426-Progress-in-EU-Croatia-accession-negotiations-M.pdf>.

[53] On 6 June 2010, Slovenians agreed by referendum to settle the dispute through an international arbitration panel whose ruling will be binding for both countries; <http://euobserver.com/9/30222>.

[54] A Hassin, 'La capacité d'intégration de l'UE—prérequis politique ou alibi technique?' *Les Brefs de Notre Europe*, 2007/06.

[55] See in this respect, the Coalition Agreement of the current CDU-CSU-FDP German government: <http://www.cdu.de/doc/pdfc/091215-koalitionsvertrag-2009-2013-englisch.pdf> 167. Also: F Amtenbrink, 'On the European Union's Institutional Capacity to Cope with Further Enlargement' in S Blockmans and S Prechal (eds), *Reconciling 'Deepening' and 'Widening' of the European Union* (TMC Asser Press, 2008) 111; M Emerson, S Aydin, J De Clerck-Sachsse, and G Noutcheva, 'Just What is this "Absorption Capacity" of the European Union?' (2006) CEPS Policy Brief No 113.

[56] Presidency Conclusions, Corfu European Council, 24–25 June 1994.

[57] Presidency Conclusions, Luxembourg European Council, 12–13 December 1997.

enlargement.[58] The institutional argument came again to the fore in the context of the ratification of the Lisbon Treaty, when some Member States, and the institutions, maintained that enlargement could not proceed without the Lisbon Treaty. Institutional reform, as a means to ensure the Union's absorption capacity, thereby became a pre-condition to enlargement.[59] Thus Member States are both judge and party.

Indeed, the notion of absorption capacity has evolved since, to the effect that its constitutive elements have proliferated, while remaining chronically woolly. Hence, the European Council meeting in December 2004 considered that 'accession negotiations yet to be opened with candidates whose accession could have substantial financial consequences can only be concluded after the establishment of the Financial Framework for the period from 2014 together with possible consequential financial reforms'.[60] In the same vein, the 2005 negotiating framework for Turkey suggested that enlargement would be subject to the demonstration that the EU would continue to be in a position to pay for its policies.[61] Following the negative referenda in France and in the Netherlands, additional emphasis has also been put on public opinion and on the necessity, through communication, to increase public support for enlargement.[62] Requirements of democratic legitimacy and financial sustainability have therefore been added to the initial institutional component of the notion of absorption capacity.

At the behest of the European Council and following various reports from the European Parliament,[63] the Commission prepared a special report on the Union's capacity to integrate new Members, annexed to its 2006 Enlargement Strategy.[64] According to the document, the EU should not only be in a position to welcome new states, it should also ensure that their accession does not hamper its capacity to integrate:

> The EU's absorption capacity, or rather integration capacity, is determined by the development of the EU's policies and institutions, and by the transformation of applicants into well-prepared Member States . . . Integration capacity is about whether the EU can take in new members at a given moment or in a given period, without jeopardizing the political and policy objectives established by the Treaties. Hence, it is first and foremost a functional concept.

---

[58] See in particular, Protocol 10 on the Enlargement of the European Union and the Declaration on the Enlargement of the European Union, included in the Final Act of the Conference which adopted the Treaty of Nice.

[59] G Edwards, 'Reforming the Union's Institutional Framework: a new EU Obligation?' in Hillion (n 12 above) 23.

[60] Presidency Conclusions, European Council, Brussels, 16–17 December 2004.

[61] Negotiating Framework, 3 October 2005, pt 13.

[62] COM(2006) 649, 2–3, 5; Presidency Conclusions, European Council, 14–15 December 2006, pt 6.

[63] See eg the Stubb Report on the institutional aspects of the European Union's capacity to integrate new Member States, A6-0393/2006 (16.11.2006).

[64] COM(2006) 649; Annex 1: Special Report on the EU's capacity to integrate new members.

In the Commission's view, ensuring the capacity of the enlarging EU to maintain the integration momentum entails that institutions must continue to act effectively, that policies must meet their goals, and that the budget is commensurate with its objectives and with its financial resources. The European Council discussed that report at its subsequent meeting. Having recalled that '[t]he pace of enlargement *must* take into account the capacity of the Union to absorb new members' (emphasis added), it unimpressively concluded that '[a]s the Union enlarges, successful European integration requires that EU institutions function effectively and that EU policies are further developed and financed in a sustainable manner'.[65]

Whether the Report in general and the rebranding from 'absorption capacity' to 'integration capacity' have made the requirement more articulate is debatable. What is clear is that the notion is prone to abuse by some Member States wishing to slow down the enlargement process. It has indeed attracted criticism, notably from the House of Lords EU Select Committee, which has considered 'the debate about the absorption capacity... harmful since the term is inherently vague and is interpreted by many in the candidate countries as an excuse for closing the Union's doors'.[66]

(b) Multiplication of procedural steps

The vagueness and scarcity of Treaty enlargement rules have provided room for interpretation and elaboration. Despite its full jurisdiction over these rules, the European Court of Justice has played only a limited role in ensuring 'that in the interpretation and application of [these provisions] the law is observed'. Quizzed once on former Article 237 EEC, the Court considered that it establishes:

> a precise procedure encompassed within well-defined limits for the admission of new Member States, during which the conditions of accession are to be drawn up by the authorities indicated in the article itself. Thus *the legal conditions for such accession remain to be defined in the context of that procedure without it being possible to determine the content judicially in advance*... [Thus the Court cannot] give a ruling on the form or subject matter of the conditions which might be adopted. (Emphasis added)[67]

Interpreting the Treaty provisions on enlargement has thus been left to Member States and EU political institutions. In this exercise, political considerations and expediency have been more decisive than the quest for objectiveness, certainty, and effectiveness. For example, Article 49 TEU foresees that the candidate's application is to be sent to the Council, which decides by unanimity after the Commission has provided its Opinion and the EP its consent. While the procedure gives the impression that it only takes its decision once the other institutions have been consulted, in practice however, the Council decides at an early stage, and such decision(s) determines

---

[65] Presidency Conclusions, European Council, 14–15 December 2006, pts 6 and 9.

[66] Assuming that the debate is unlikely to go away, the Committee nevertheless suggested that 'it would be best if the term was deconstructed into its individual components and considered in that light', House of Lords Report (n 42 above).

[67] Case 93/78 *Mattheus v Doego* [1978] ECR 2203.

the fate of an application. A custom has thus developed according to which the Commission only prepares and gives its 'Opinion' on the application, once it has actually been *requested* to do so by the Council.[68]

A recent incident suggests that a Member State may actually block, or at least hold up the Council's move. Hence, the Commission's invitation to prepare an Opinion on Albania's application was withheld as a result of the German government's resolution first to consult its parliament on the matter, allegedly in application of the revised ratification law of the Treaty of Lisbon, adopted following the *Lisbon* judgment of the German Constitutional Court.[69] The procedure of Article 49 TEU could only be resumed after a German approval. Then, '[t]he Council *decided* to implement the procedure laid down in Article 49 of the Treaty on the European Union. Accordingly, the Commission *[was] invited* to submit its opinion' (emphasis added).[70]

This episode demonstrates that the Council does not automatically transmit the candidate's application to the Commission. Rather, it first has to '[decide] to implement the procedure' of Article 49 TEU. As a result, it (and thus, each of the Member States) acquires the power to assess the admissibility of the application, before the Commission and indeed the Parliament, both endowed with a power to give their views, actually have the chance to voice them.

It may be wondered whether this practice sits comfortably with the procedural requirements of Article 49(1) TEU which stipulate that the Council's formal decision on the application is to be taken *after* the Commission has formally presented its Opinion.[71] The duplication of the Council Decision weakens the role of the other EU political institutions and de facto changes the nature of the procedure of Article 49(1) TEU: in principle inter-institutional, in practice intergovernmental.

Indeed, the Council preliminary assessment is not restricted to ascertaining that the basic requirement set out in the Treaty is fulfilled, viz that the demand comes from a European state. The Council has also set conditions for its transmission of the application to the Commission. Hence the request for a Commission Opinion on the application of Serbia was held back awaiting the Advisory Opinion of the International Court of Justice (ICJ) on Kosovo's declaration of independence,[72] and importantly, awaiting the Serbian government's reaction to the ICJ's Opinion.[73] The Council has

---

[68] Cf Opinion on Iceland's application, 2.

[69] *Lissabon-Urteil*, judgment of 30 June 2009 (BVerfGE 123, 267). See further below.

[70] 16 November 2009; 15913/09 (Presse 328).

[71] Practice shows that a Commission's positive opinion may be ignored by the Council, as exemplified by the second British application.

[72] In accordance with International Law of the Unilateral Declaration of Independence by the Provisional Institutions of Self-Government of Kosovo (request for Advisory Opinion) <http://www.icj-cij.org/search/index.php?p2=2&str=international>.

[73] In view of the protracted controversy over the status of Kosovo, some Member States insisted that Serbia had to deal with the ICJ Opinion in 'an appropriate manner', before the Council could transmit its membership application to the Commission. The UN General Assembly Resolution (A/RES/64/298) adopted following the International Court's Opinion convinced some of these Member States that the precondition was met,

also shown that it may decide on the *expediency* of an application. In an unpreced-ented move, it 'stresse[d] that it [would] not be in a position to consider an application for membership by Bosnia and Herzegovina until the transition of the [Office of the High Representative] to a reinforced EU presence has been decided'.[74]

In addition to filling Article 49(1) with supplementary instances of unanimous decision-making, the EU has also set out a manifold ranking of third European states for the purpose of the accession procedure. A country seeking membership is *'eligible'* if it meets the basic conditions set out in the Treaty, or as 'agreed upon by the European Council'. A country meeting these basic conditions may apply, and become a *'potential candidate'* if the European Council considers that, in principle, the applicant state has the vocation to become a Member State, as was the case for the countries from south-east Europe.[75] A 'potential candidate' becomes an actual *'candidate'*, when the European Council so decides, after having received a positive opinion from the Commission, as foreseen in the Treaty. Accession negotiations may then begin. The state becomes an *acceding state*, once the Accession Treaty has been signed and put to ratification by the contracting parties, viz the Member States and applicant state(s).[76] The latter becomes a Member State once the ratification process has been successfully carried out by each Member State and by the applicant.[77]

Each of these labels corresponds to a particular stage in the accession process, that the candidate reaches through the fulfilment of various prerequisites, after a unani-mous decision in the (European) Council, and thus of the Member States. The specific contours of each category, and the conditions to be fulfilled for a country to move on to the next stage, are however not fully settled and continue to vary depending on the applicant concerned. Hence, having obtained a positive Opinion from the Commis-sion on its application,[78] Iceland was not immediately acknowledged as a 'candidate', as long as the Council had not decided to open accession negotiations; and was not considered as a 'potential candidate' either. At the same time, the former Yugoslav

---

though apparently not all, as the Commission was not immediately invited to produce an Opinion. Tellingly, the conclusions of the subsequent General Affairs Council briefly note that '[t]he Council briefly discussed recent developments with regard to Serbia'; 13 September 2010, Press Release, 13420/10 (Presse 236).

[74] General Affairs Council, Brussels, 7 December 2009, pt 39, Press Release, 17217/09 (Presse 370).

[75] See eg Presidency Conclusions, European Council, Santa Maria de Feira, 19–20 June 2000; Presidency Conclusions, European Council, Copenhagen, 12–13 December 2002, EU-Western Balkan Summit, Thessa-loniki 2003.

[76] The 'acceding state' status has some legal implications as pointed out by the Court in eg Case 413/04 *European Parliament v Council* (n 11 above), eg application of 'the principles of equality, good faith and solidarity' among current and future Member States [67]–[68].

[77] K Inglis, 'The Union's Fifth Accession Treaty: New Means to Make Enlargement Possible' (2004) 41 CML Rev 937; E Lannon, 'Le Traité d'Adhésion d'Athènes: Les négociations, les conditions de l'admission et les principales adaptations des Traités résultant de l'élargissement de l'UE à vingt-cinq Etats membres' (2004) 40 Cahiers Dr Euro 15; C Hillion, 'The European Union is dead. Long live the European Union... A Commentary on the Accession Treaty 2003' (2004) 29 ELRev 583; A Łazowski, 'And Then They Were Twenty-Seven... A Legal Appraisal of the Sixth Accession Treaty' (2007) 44 CML Rev 401.

[78] Commission Opinion on Iceland's application for membership of the European Union, COM(2010) 62.

Republic of Macedonia, whose application equally received a positive Opinion from the Commission,[79] but no Council approval to open accession negotiations, has been officially considered a 'candidate country' like Croatia and Turkey, which both started accession negotiations in October 2005. The acquisition by an applicant state of a particular status thus depends on political and fluctuating considerations more than on the objective fulfilment of pre-determined criteria.

The EU enlargement policy has thus been adjusted substantively and procedurally following the fifth enlargement, taking account of the lessons learned through it, and in its aftermath. Officially made so as to ensure better preparation to become Members, such adjustments have also been envisioned as ways to address domestic concerns, which in an enlarged Union have almost mechanically increased. Reconciling the need for better prepared candidates and Member States' interests has paradoxically resulted in increased unpredictability in the accession process,[80] as typified by the heavier reliance on the fuzzy notion of 'absorption/integration capacity'. Indeed, Member States have reasserted their influence not only on the conduct but also on the procedural aspects of the EU enlargement policy to the effect that it may be wondered whether the Treaty provisions are being emptied of their substance.

(c) Unilateral conditions for accession and enlargement

As if their control over the Treaty procedure was not sufficient, Member States have also strengthened their stranglehold on the Union's enlargement at *national* level, most notably by elaborating their 'constitutional requirements' for ratifying Accession Treaties.

For example, a new provision has been introduced in the French Constitution to the effect that future Accession Treaties have to be ratified by referendum. According to the first paragraph of new Article 88-5 (post-Lisbon):[81] 'Any Government Bill authorizing the ratification of a treaty pertaining to the accession of a state to the European Union shall be submitted to referendum by the President of the Republic.'

Article 88-5 is however not applicable to accessions that 'result from an Intergovernmental Conference whose meeting was decided by the European Council before July 1, 2004'.[82] Exposing the political expediency of the French constitutional amendment, the purpose of this limitation to the constitutional amendment was to ensure

---

[79] Commission Opinion on the application from the former Yugoslav Republic of Macedonia for membership of the European Union, COM(2005) 562.

[80] A point made by the Croatian negotiator, Mr Drobnjak, when underlining that changes to the accession process, in particular the introduction of benchmarking, had brought an added degree of insecurity for candidates; House of Lords Report (n 42 above) pt 200.

[81] This version of Art 88(5) has come into effect upon the coming into force of the Treaty of Lisbon, in accordance with Art 2 of Constitutional Act No 2008-103 of 4 February 2008 and Art 47 of Constitutional Act No 2008-724 of 23 July 2008.

[82] Art 47 of Constitutional Act No 2008-724 of 23 July 2008.

that it would not concern the Accession Treaty with Croatia, but would in any event apply to Turkey's and other subsequent admissions.

The second paragraph of Article 88-5 foresees a possible exception to the referendum requirement if the Parliament so decides, 'by passing a motion adopted in identical terms in each House by a three-fifths majority'. In this case, Parliament may authorize the passing of the Bill by the two chambers, convened in Congress. And to be approved, the Bill must be passed by a three-fifths majority of the votes cast.[83] The French Constitution thus exceptionally allows for parliamentary ratification of future Accession Treaties, but on the demanding condition that it is supported by a double qualified majority.

It is not clear how the new constitutional requirement would operate in case the Accession Treaty with Croatia were also to concern another state, such as Iceland. Like all other acceding states, save Croatia, Iceland's accession would result from an IGC whose meeting would be decided after 1 July 2004. In view of the Commission's Opinion on Iceland's application, and the country's degree of preparedness, Iceland could well conclude its accession negotiations at around the same time as Croatia. The EU could thus be tempted, as it has been in the past, to conclude one Accession Treaty for the two candidate states.[84] The French constitutional requirement would then have the effect of submitting the whole Accession Treaty, and thus Croatia's admission too, to referendum. In any event whether it is a referendum or specific parliamentary vote, the new French constitutional requirement for the purpose of Article 49 TEU,[85] undoubtedly affects the implementation of the EU enlargement procedure.[86]

Member States have also reasserted their control at other stages of the procedure. Following the *Bundesverfassungsgericht* judgment on the Lisbon Treaty, the amended German ratification law foresees an increased involvement of the *Bundestag* in EU

---

[83] According to Art 89(3), a government Bill is not submitted to referendum where the President of the Republic decides to submit it to Parliament convened in Congress, ie the meeting of the two chambers. To be approved, the Bill must be passed by a three-fifths majority of the votes cast.

[84] The only Accession Treaty that has been concluded with a single candidate is the one with Greece.

[85] On the initiative of its President, Mr Pompidou, France held a referendum on 23 April 1972 on the first enlargement of the European Communities: 68.32 per cent of the voters were in favour. The decision to hold a referendum was based essentially on internal political considerations: the centre right French President intended to divide the left. The communists voted against, and the socialist abstained.

[86] Other Member States are considering introducing specific constitutional requirements, notably for ratifying Accession Treaties, in the form of eg a 2/3 qualified majority in parliament (eg The Netherlands: Kamerstukken TK 30874, Nos 1–3). Some Member States have been inspired by the French precedent (eg Austria, see Government Programme 2007–2020 <http://www.austria.gv.at/DocView.axd?CobId=19542> at 8). Indeed, the European Union Bill discussed in the United Kingdom envisages a referendum requirement (or 'lock') for the UK ratification of future EU Treaties involving a transfer of power from the UK to the EU. The referendum lock could concern Accession Treaties if they were to include such a transfer (see Written Ministerial Statement on European Union Bill, by Minister for Europe David Lidington, 13 September 2010, <www.fco.gov. uk/en/news/latest-news/?view=PressS&id=22851533>) as did the 1972 Accession Treaty with Denmark, Ireland, (Norway), and the UK. It foresaw the Member States' transfer of competence in the field of fisheries (see Chapter 3 of Act of Accession, [1972] OJ L7; as confirmed by the European Court of Justice in Joined Cases 3, 4, and 6/76 *Kramer* [1976] ECR 1279; Case 804/79 *Commission v United Kingdom* [1981] ECR I-1045).

affairs.[87] In particular, the law explicitly requires that the German government seek the opinion of the parliament on the opening of membership negotiations.[88] This requirement has since then been invoked by the German government at various stages of the enlargement procedure, and not only for the specific decision to open accession negotiations. This is illustrated by the 'Albanian application' episode referred to above, in which the law was referred to prior to the decision to request the Commission's opinion on the applicant.[89] While the government is not bound by the *Bundestag*'s opinion, in the specific field of enlargement the two institutions are explicitly asked to seek a common position.[90] Were the German parliament to give a negative opinion on the matter, EU enlargement could be stalled. Incidentally such a requirement might increase Germany's bargaining power, which in turn could inspire other Member States to bring into play similar internal requirements.[91]

The creeping nationalization of enlargement, exemplified by these two legal developments, is also typified by the increasing impact of bilateral issues on the accession process. For instance, Croatia's accession process has been delayed as a result of the border dispute with Slovenia. Another case in point is the name issue between Greece and (the former Yugoslav Republic of) Macedonia, which has prevented the opening of accession negotiations with the latter, despite the favourable recommendation from the Commission. In the same vein, the start of accession negotiations with Iceland was stalled due to the ongoing Icesave dispute with the Netherlands and the UK. While various accession chapters could not be opened with Turkey, given its ongoing dispute with Cyprus.

Enlargement is thus being hijacked by some EU Member States using their relative power vis-à-vis candidate states to settle bilateral issues to their advantage.[92]

---

[87] *Gesetz über die Zusammenarbeit von Bundesregierung und Deutschem Bundestag in Angelegenheiten der Europäischen Union* (EuZBBG), available at <http://www.gesetze-im-internet.de/euzbbg/BJNR031100993.html> (amended on 22 September 2009). Prior to the judgment, the *Bundestag* had already proposed that the German government seek its approval before the start of new accession negotiations, as recalled in the House of Lords Report (above n 42) 20.

[88] § 3(1)2 EuZBBG.

[89] The impact of the new German law on the enlargement process has been all the more tangible in that the consultation of the *Bundestag* requires the translation of relevant background documents, notably the Commission reports, mostly written in English. It should however be noted that § 9(1) EuZBBG stipulates that the involvement of the *Bundestag* should not hold up the EU decision-making process.

[90] This is foreseen in § 10(2) EUZBBG, which also stipulates that the *Bundesregierung* has the right to take a decision that contradicts the position of the *Bundestag* for 'important reasons of foreign or integration policy'. Both institutions can turn to the *Bundesverfassungsgericht*, in case they consider that their rights are violated by the other institution ('*Organstreitverfahren*' laid down in detail in the *Bundesverfassungsgerichtsgesetz*, §§ 13 No 5 *et seq*). I am indebted to Thomas Ackermann and Jens-Uwe Franck for an explanation of these different points.

[91] See eg R Putnam, 'Diplomacy and Domestic Politics: The Logic of Two-Level Games' (1988) 42 International Organization 427.

[92] In its 2009 strategy paper, the Commission specifically referred to the tendency of bilateral issues hampering the enlargement process (see COM(2009) 533, 6). Unsurprisingly, the Member States did not follow up on this *problématique* as suggested by the conclusions of the ensuing General Affairs Council (17217/09, 7 December 2009) and of the European Council (Conclusions, 10–11 December 2009). The problem is not likely to go away, particularly in view of the progressive accession of the countries from the Western Balkans, many of which have unsettled disputes with their neighbours. For instance, Macedonia is, in 2010, the only state in the region with fully demarcated borders. The Commission has reiterated its concern in its 2010–2011 strategy paper (see COM(2010) 660, 11).

But perhaps more worryingly, the nationalization of the EU enlargement procedure has also been translated in Member States' tempering the fundamentals of integration with domestic concerns. A glaring illustration of this phenomenon can be found in the EU negotiating framework for Turkey.[93] It envisages that the Accession Treaty could include permanent safeguard clauses with respect notably to movement of persons, agricultural, and structural policies. As it has been suggested elsewhere, such clauses would put at risk the functioning of the internal market. More generally, they could strike at the 'very foundations' of the EU legal order,[94] and in particular at the principle of equality of EU citizens, and of states.[95]

What has hitherto developed into the most integrated EU policy is thus increasingly held hostage by Member States' domestic considerations. More generally, the trend exposes a tension between national behaviour and EU primary law, raising the question of preserving the latter's effectiveness against too much Member State encroachment.

2. CONSTITUTIONALIZING EU ENLARGEMENT?

While Member States have attempted to reassert their control over EU enlargement, they have also agreed *qua pouvoir constituant* of the Union to codify in primary law several *ad hoc* practices developed notably since Copenhagen (a). The legalization of past institutional practice strengthens the notion that the enlargement procedure is, despite its intergovernmental characteristics, an EU law-based procedure governed by the fundamental principles which underpin the EU legal order (b).

(a) Progressive codification of institutional practice

Recent Treaty reforms have included revisions of the enlargement provisions, mostly in the form of codification of past practices. For example, the additional accession criteria developed by the European Council have been partly translated in Treaty provisions. The consolidation started with the Treaty of Amsterdam, which introduced the explicit requirement that the applicant respect the principles set out in former Article 6(1) EU, viz liberty, democracy, respect for human rights and fundamental freedoms, and the rule of law.

The defunct Constitutional Treaty and the Treaty of Lisbon went further. According to Article 49 TEU, eligibility is now subject to the respect of 'the values referred to in Article 2' of the TEU, which contains a more elaborate list than former Article 6(1) TEU:

---

[93] Negotiating Framework, 3 October 2005.

[94] Joined Cases C-402/05 P and C-415/05 P *Kadi and Al Barakaat International Foundation v Council and Commission* [2008] ECR I-6351 at [282] and [304], Opinion 1/91 *EEA* [1991] ECR I-6079 at [35] and [71]. Further: C Hillion, 'Negotiating Turkey's membership to the European Union—Can Member States do as they please?' (2007) 3 ECL Rev 269.

[95] Case 231/78 *Commission v UK* [1979] ECR 1447, [9]. This principle of equality is enshrined in Art 4(2) TEU.

... respect for human dignity, freedom, democracy, equality, the rule of law and respect for human rights, including the rights of persons belonging to minorities.

These values are common to the Member States in a society in which pluralism, non-discrimination, tolerance, justice, solidarity and equality between women and men prevail.

Moreover, the Lisbon procedure foresees that the applicant is eligible if it is also *committed to promote* those values. That supplementary and somewhat ambiguous legal requirement points towards a close watch on the applicant's track-record in value promotion. Seemingly codifying the well-established EU monitoring of candidates' compliance with the fundamental principles underpinning the EU legal order, the new provisions of Article 49 TEU may also crystallize the Council's habit to pre-assess the expediency of an application by reference to a wide spectrum of principles, ie before the Commission and the Parliament have had a chance formally to expose their views.

At the same time, the Treaty of Lisbon codifies the European Council's ability to adjust the enlargement procedure. Revised Article 49 TEU stipulates that '[th]e conditions of eligibility agreed upon by the European Council shall be taken into account'. While some Member States intended simply to include a reference to the Copenhagen criteria, the Treaty's broad formulation instead opens up the possibility to modify the conditions of eligibility, and thus formally endows the European Council with a power to amend the Treaty procedure, ie a primary law-making power.

Short of a full codification of the post-Copenhagen substantive and procedural rules of enlargement,[96] the Lisbon version of Article 49 TEU thus goes a long way to consolidating past routines.[97] While, in itself, legalization should entail more object-iveness and predictability in the process, the codification has paradoxically increased the flexibility and adaptability of the procedure. Indeed, the codified power of the European Council to adjust at will the eligibility conditions, could lead to tightened entry conditions, thus entrenching the discrepancy between accession conditions and membership obligations. The question thus arises as to whether those constitutional developments denote an unfettered discretion for the authorities involved in the procedure.

(b) Embedding enlargement in the EU legal framework

As suggested earlier, the original conception of the enlargement procedure and its early implementation were imbued with state-centrism. Based essentially on intergov-ernmental mechanisms, entailing the conclusion of an international Treaty able to modify EU primary law, the procedure has often been located at the margins of the EU legal order, if not outside the reach of its rules and principles. The Court's restrained

---

[96] C Hillion, 'Enlargement of the European Union: The discrepancy between Accession conditionality and membership obligations' (2004) 27 Fordham Int'l LJ 715.

[97] The powers acquired by the Commission in the context of enlargement have also been legally endorsed. In the discussions regarding the new High Representative for Foreign Affairs and Security Policy and the External Action Service that she heads, it has been decided that the enlargement portfolio would remain part of the Commission remit, ie outside that of the HR and of the EEAS; see eg the Council Decision (2010/427/EU) establishing the organization and functioning of the European External Action Service (OJEU [2010] L201/30).

attitude towards the provisions on enlargement, suggested in *Mattheus v Doego*,[98] has indeed been presented as a judicial acknowledgement that enlargement is in essence a *political* process, within which decision-making authorities enjoy wide discretion in defining accession conditions. It has also been submitted that the ruling could be envisioned as an example of the Court's developing 'political question doctrine'.[99]

Without entering the debate on this point, suffice to mention briefly three elements that substantiate the notion that, despite its intergovernmental features, enlargement is embedded in the Union's legal framework, and as such governed by EU norms.

First, the use in Article 49 TEU of the phrase 'Member States' rather that 'High Contracting Parties', as in Article 1 TEU, indicates that in taking part in the Union's enlargement, the 27 states do not act as states in their own right, but in the context of the EU legal order.[100]

Secondly, the Court's *Mattheus* judgment could be read in a way that supports the proposition that the Member States and the institutions, acting in the context of the enlargement procedure, do not enjoy unfettered discretion. The Court's understanding of the enlargement provisions is that they establish 'a precise procedure *encompassed within well-defined limits* for the admission of new Member States' (emphasis added). While the Court did not specify what these limits are, the broad phraseology of the relevant part of the ruling suggests that they may be located in the enlargement procedure itself, but may also derive from other parts of EU primary law more generally.[101]

Thirdly, the Treaty acknowledgement of the Court's jurisdiction over the enlargement procedure intrinsically entails that the latter is not immune from the application of legal norms. That jurisdiction had been acknowledged already in the founding Communities treaties, without any particular explicit restriction. The establishment of

---

[98] Case 93/78 *Mattheus* (above n 67).

[99] H Rasmussen, *On Law and Policy in the European Court of Justice* (Martinus Nijhoff, 1986) 487–488; cf U Becker, 'EU-Enlargements and Limits to Amendments of the EC Treaty' (2001) 15 Jean Monnet Working Paper, available at <http://www.jeanmonnetprogram.org>, pt VI; and S Douglas-Scott, *Constitutional Law of the European Union* (Longman, 2002) 238.

[100] U Everling, 'Zur Stellung der Mitgliedstaaten der Europäischen Union als "Herren der Verträge"' in U Beyerlin *et al*, *Recht zwischen Umbruch und Bewahrung—Festschrift für Rudolf Bernhardt* (Springer, 1995) 1161, 1176.

[101] Hence, limits applying to the procedure could stem from the 'very foundations of the Community', which the Court of Justice emphasized in its *Kadi* judgment (Cases C-402/05 P and C-415/05 P *Kadi and Al Barakaat International Foundation v Council and Commission* [2008] ECR I-6351 [282] and [304] and in its first *EEA* Opinion (Opinion 1/91 [1991] ECR I-6079, [35] and [71], as well as from the General Principles of Union Law, eg equality, proportionality, protection of legitimate expectations (further on these: T Tridimas, *The General Principles of the EU Law* (Oxford University Press, 2006); P Craig, *EU Administrative Law* (Oxford University Press, 2006)). Moreover, such limits may derive from the rules of regional organizations such as the European Convention for the Protection of Human Rights and Fundamental Freedoms, notably once the Union has acceded to the Convention (as envisaged by Article 6(2) TEU), and from international law (eg the Vienna Convention on the Law of Treaties), particularly in view of the insistence, in the Treaty of Lisbon, on the Union's respect for the principles of the UN Charter and of international law (Art 21 TEU). See also: J L da Cruz Vilaça and N Piçarra, 'Y a-t-il des limites matérielles à la révision des traités instituant les Communautés européennes?'(1993) 29 Cahiers Dr Euro 3.

the multi-pillar EU by the Maastricht Treaty did nothing to change this. Article L EU made it clear that the Court had unrestricted jurisdiction over the final provisions of the Treaty, which included Article O EU. Under the Lisbon dispensation, Article 49 TEU is equally subject to the Court's jurisdiction as articulated in Article 19 TEU, and Article 275 TFEU. In principle therefore, the Court of Justice of the European Union is expected to ensure that in the interpretation and application of the provisions of Article 49 TEU, the law is observed.[102]

If, as it is suggested, the EU enlargement procedure is not immune from the application of rules and principles underpinning the EU legal order, and from the judicial control by the Court of Justice, it may be worth speculating briefly on the possible forms such a control would take. In particular, are there judicial means to address the creeping nationalization of the EU enlargement policy, and to preserve the integrity of the Treaty enlargement procedure?

Two avenues could be envisioned. First, the annulment of one of the many Council Decisions adopted in relation to enlargement could be sought on the basis of Article 263 TEU, in case of a violation of the 'well-defined limits' referred to by the Court in *Mattheus*. A Council decision could thus be challenged on the ground that one of the essential procedural requirements of Article 49 TEU has not been complied with. For instance, the European Parliament could be tempted to challenge the Council's refusal to consider an application from a European state, on the ground that the Treaty gives it the right to give its consent before the Council so decides. Indeed, delaying tactics in the Council to postpone indefinitely the invitation to start the procedure, as in the Albanian episode referred to above, could be addressed through an action to establish a failure to act, on the basis of Article 265 TFEU.

But the action for annulment could equally be triggered in case of violation of the substantive limits of Article 49 TEU, or other substantive requirements derived from the Treaty. For instance, if an agreement negotiated and concluded under Article 49 TEU were not to offer full membership to the acceding states, in view of permanent limitations to the application of fundamental freedoms it would contain, it could be argued that the Treaty does not qualify as an Accession Treaty, but amounts instead to an external agreement of an advanced form. The legal basis of the negotiation and conclusion of the agreement would thus have to be altered, and so would the procedure. Alternatively, the agreement would have to be renegotiated so as to ensure its compatibility with the substantive requirements of membership.

---

[102] On the Court's jurisdiction in relation to enlargement, see also the Opinion of AG Lenz in Joined Cases C-31 and 35/86 *LAISA et al v Council* [1988] ECR I-2285. Whether and how that jurisdiction would be exercised in practice remains to be seen. On this point, it may be noted that in *Coyle v Smith*, the US Supreme Court was asked to adjudicate on the terms of admission of a state (*in casu*, Oklahoma) to the Union. The jurisdiction of the Court was questioned on the ground that the power of Congress to admit new states is a political power uncontrollable by the courts. The Supreme Court was not moved by what smacked of the political question doctrine, and looked at the merits of the case; See *Coyle v Smith*, (1911) 221 US 559. Many thanks to Dr Jacco Bomhoff for the tip.

For example, if the Treaty of Accession with Turkey were to include permanent safeguard clauses in the field of movement of persons, regional, and agricultural policies, it could be argued that the Treaty in question would fall short of offering full membership to Turkey, and amounting instead to the 'privileged partnership' sought by several Member States.[103] The choice of legal basis for the conclusion of the agreement could thus not be Article 49 TEU, but eg Article 216 and/or Article 8 TEU (substantive legal basis) together with Article 218 TFEU (procedural legal basis). In that, the suggestion (sometimes made by some Member States' politicians) that the current negotiations with Turkey could lead to such a privileged partnership is based on the erroneous assumption that the procedure of Article 49 TEU can be used for this purpose.

Secondly, the Court might be asked, notably by the Commission, to ensure compliance, by the 'authorities indicated in ... Article [49 TEU]',[104] with their obligation of loyal cooperation enshrined in Article 4(3) TEU. In particular, the Court could be invited to sanction the actions or omissions of the Member States or institutions (eg the Council),[105] which would jeopardize the attainment of the Union's objective of enlarging to a state whose membership prospect has been acknowledged by the European Council, and with whom accession negotiations have begun. The effectiveness of the procedure to achieve that objective, ie Article 49 TEU, ought to be guaranteed, so that measures at EU or national levels that would make it impossible for those provisions to operate in practice would arguably endanger the attainment of the Union's objectives,[106] in infringement of Article 4(3) TEU.

D. CONCLUSION

Initially envisaged as a Member State-driven procedure, enlargement has become a 'Member State building' policy involving a significant role for the EU institutions, and notably the Commission. However, Member States have recently reasserted their control over the policy, perceived to have gone too far and too fast.[107] They have thus multiplied instances of unanimous decisions in the conduct of the procedure, and elaborated new legal requirements at national level. What is more, they have increasingly instrumentalized the accession prospect of third states to promote domestic interests.

---

[103] See Coalition Agreement (n 55 above) 166–167.

[104] Case 93/78 *Mattheus v Doego* (n 67 above).

[105] Art 13(1) and (2) TEU.

[106] Enlargement more generally appears to remain one of the Union's aims. The preamble of the TFEU still refers to the Member States' call to other peoples of Europe, while the specific procedure for enlargement has not been disposed of altogether. It could indeed be argued, using the Court's jurisprudence exposed at [226] of its *Kadi* judgment, that Article 49 TEU is the expression of an EU 'implicit underlying objective' of enlargement; see Joined Cases C-402/05 P and C-415/05 P *Kadi* (n 104 above).

[107] D Vaughan-Whitehead, 'L'élargissement de l'Union Européenne: une fuite en avant?' *Notre Europe* Policy Paper No 5, September 2003.

In contrast to most policies covered in this volume, the evolution of enlargement rules has not been shaped by judicial intervention. Although the Court of Justice's jurisdiction is acknowledged in the Treaty, EU accession provisions have hardly been touched upon in the case law, leaving their interpretation and implementation to political creativity. The ensuing freedom enjoyed by the Member States, if abused, could empty the EU procedure from much of its effectiveness, if not its raison d'être. In a Union based on the rule of law, such political discretion should therefore be tempered with judicial supervision, to ensure that *le fait du prince* does not prevail.

9

EXTERNAL RELATIONS AND EXTERNAL COMPETENCE OF THE EUROPEAN UNION: THE EMERGENCE OF AN INTEGRATED POLICY

*Marise Cremona**

A. INTRODUCTION[1]

The inter-relationship between the internal and external dimensions of the European Community's development emphasized by the European Court of Justice in *Commission v Council* (AETR) may be said to provide an overall perspective for this chapter:

> With regard to the implementation of the provisions of the Treaty, the system of internal Community measures may not therefore be separated from that of external relations.[2]

The objective here is not to provide a complete survey of the Union's external relations to date but rather to examine three inter-connected themes which have emerged in the evolutionary development of the Union as an international actor.

The first theme directly relates to the statement by the Court of Justice just quoted: the relationship between internal and external powers and policies. The degree to

---

* Professor of European Law, European University Institute, Florence.

[1] Treaty references: the abbreviation 'TEU' used after a Treaty article refers to the Treaty on European Union in the version in force after 1 December 2009, while 'TFEU' refers to the Treaty on the Functioning of the European Union. 'EC' after a Treaty article refers to a provision of the European Community Treaty in the version in force until 30 November 2009; similarly, 'EU' refers to an article of the Treaty on European Union in the version in force until that date.

[2] Case 22/70 *Commission v Council (AETR/ERTA)* [1971] ECR 263, [19].

which the Union's external powers reflect or mirror internal competence is not only a question of their extent; it extends to the objectives and content of the policies pursued by the Union internally and externally; the nature or fundamental legal characteristics of the external dimension to the Union legal order. To what extent are external powers an extension of internal powers and objectives? The expansion of the scope and extent of the Union's external powers (whether express or implied) has of course reflected not only the expansion of areas of activity internally but also the changing preoccupations of the Union, in particular as regards its place in the world. It is also true that external commitments and activity are having an increasing impact on the development of internal policies.

As always within the Community and Union systems, issues of competence are intimately connected with both the inter-institutional and the institution–Member State balance of power. The second theme of this chapter traces how the classic approach to pre-emption, whereby the occupation of a field of legislative activity by the Community legal order excludes concurrent Member State competence, has given way to a wide acceptance of shared powers in external and internal spheres of competence, as well as the legal principles and structural solutions by which shared competence is managed.

The emergent international identity of the Union and the factors that shape it form the third theme. A number of factors are at play here, including constitutional constraints on Union competence, the essential autonomy of the Union legal order within the wider context of international law and legal relations, the raised profile (and raised expectations) of the Union especially through the development of the Common Foreign and Security Policy, the complexity of relations between the 'Pillars' from 1993 and 2009 and the legacy of the Pillars present in the Union's constitutional structure following the Treaty of Lisbon.

The evolution of the Union as an effective international actor will depend on the balance between introspective concentration on (necessary) internal development and reform and a realistic confidence in its external relations, as the development of the external role of the Union depends on the emergence of sufficiently flexible and robust internal constitutional structures. The Court in the passage from *AETR* quoted at the start was of course positioning itself to make a bold claim about the extent of the Community's powers, but it was also making a fundamental point about the integrationist nature of the Community project. Amid the *angst* over policy fragmentation, the failure of the Constitutional Treaty, and the lack of institutional cohesion, it is possible to see a process of integration in the formation of an international identity for the Union. The terms 'integration' and 'identity' are not, however, intended to imply a monolithic structure. Highly diverse patterns of decision-making, different power-structures between the actors involved (Member States, Commission, Council, European Council, European Parliament), the wide variety of (formal and informal, binding and non-binding) instruments used, the connections between external policies and between internal and external aspects of policies, are all elements of a complex multi-dimensional construction.[3] The complexity and diversity are necessary but need to operate within a framework which manages to be both flexible and coherent, and this chapter will end by assessing some of the ways in which the most recent Treaty reform process responds to this need.[4]

B. INTERNAL POLICIES AND EXTERNAL POWERS

1. THE EMERGENCE OF IMPLIED POWERS

In the five decades of the Community's and then the Union's existence, periods of intense internal preoccupation have combined with periods of significant development in external activity. The initial transitional period lasting until the end of 1969 was dominated in legislative terms by the need to establish the customs union and put in place the fundamental elements of the Common Agricultural Policy and competition policy. External relationships were seen largely in terms of the need to achieve a common customs tariff at the external borders of the Community together with the earliest Regulations dealing with the valuation and origin of imports. The Court of Justice during this period was taking the first crucial steps towards the definition and constitutionalization of the Community legal order. It is in the confident assertions of the *Costa v ENEL* judgment that the first recognition of the Community's international legal personality is found, with the international legal capacity of the Community being explicitly linked to the transfer of powers from the Member States to the Community.[5]

It is the autonomy of the Community legal order (with its 'essential characteristics' of primacy and direct effect[6]) represented by this transfer of powers, which forms a legal basis for effective international action. In its *AETR* judgment of 1971 the Court builds on this statement of legal personality to conclude that the Community's external capacity extends over the 'whole extent of the field of the objectives defined in Part I' of the Treaty and its competence to enter into international agreements is not limited to those cases where there is express provision for action.[7] At this stage it is the independence of the Community's action, the fact that it is acting in its own right and not merely as a representative of the collective of Member States, which is more important than the scope of its powers.

---

[3] E Cannizzaro, 'Unity and Pluralism in the EU's Foreign Relations Power' in C Barnard (ed), *The Fundamentals of EU Law Revisited* (Oxford University Press, 2007).

[4] For an overall analysis and assessment of the Treaty of Lisbon provisions on external policy, see J Wouters, D Coppens, and B De Meester, 'The European Union's External Relations after the Lisbon Treaty' in S Griller and J Ziller (eds), *The Lisbon Treaty—EU Constitutionalism without a Constitutional Treaty?* (Springer, 2008).

[5] Case 6/64 *Costa v ENEL* [1964] ECR 585, 593.

[6] In Opinion 1/91 (Draft Agreement on a European Economic Area) [1991] ECR I-6079, the Court of Justice stated that 'the essential characteristics of the Community legal order which has thus been established are in particular its primacy over the law of the Member States and the direct effect of a whole series of provisions'.

[7] Case 22/70 *Commission v Council* (n 2 above).

However, the *AETR* case heralded a decade in which the Court of Justice delineated both the extent and the nature of external Community competence in a series of cases progressively developing the doctrines of implied powers and exclusivity in a characteristically incremental manner. The first step was taken in *AETR* itself, establishing the principle of implied external powers, and linking these to the existence of internal common policy measures in the relevant field (road transport):

> To determine in a particular case the Community's authority to enter into international agreements, regard must be had to the whole scheme of the treaty no less than to its substantive provisions. Such authority arises not only from an express conferment by the treaty... but may equally flow from other provisions of the treaty and from measures adopted, within the framework of those provisions, by the Community institutions. In particular, each time the Community, with a view to implementing a common policy envisaged by the treaty, adopts provisions laying down common rules, whatever form these may take, the Member States no longer have the right, acting individually or even collectively, to undertake obligations with third countries which affect those rules.[8]

In this decision, the Court puts some stress on the fact that at the time the contested decision was taken within the Council, a common policy on social aspects of road transport had been adopted. It was the adoption of internal rules which 'necessarily vested in the Community power to enter into any agreements with third countries relating to the subject-matter governed by that Regulation'.[9] Conversely, *before* the internal rules were adopted those powers remained with the Member States.[10]

A few years later, in the *Kramer* judgment, the Court of Justice took the next step in holding that Community competence may arise where, although the competence to adopt internal measures was explicit, this power had not yet been exercised. This was based on the argument that 'the only way to ensure the conservation of the biological resources of the sea both effectively and equitably' is through international agreements. Thus the 'very duties and powers' granted at the internal level give rise to the power to act externally.[11] In the following year the Court took the opportunity to summarize and confirm the emergent doctrine of implied powers. Opinion 1/76 concerned the compatibility with Community law of a draft agreement intended to regulate over-capacity on the Rhine and Moselle. The Court affirmed that the Community had the (exclusive) power to conclude the agreement, although it declared aspects of the institutional arrangements under the draft agreement to be incompatible with the Treaty.[12]

The concept of implied external powers is now well established, as illustrated not only by more recent case law (such as Opinion 2/91[13] and Opinion 1/2003[14]) but also by the preamble to the Council Decision concluding the WTO Agreements, which

---

[8] ibid [15]–[17].   [9] ibid [28].
[10] ibid [82].   [11] Cases 3, 4, and 6–76 *Cornelis Kramer and others* [1976] ECR 1279, [30]–[33].
[12] Opinion 1/76 (Rhine Navigation Agreement) [1977] ECR 741, [3]–[4].
[13] Opinion 2/91 (ILO Convention) [1993] ECR I-1061, [7].
[14] Opinion 1/03 (Lugano Convention) [2006] ECR I-1145.

reflects the wording of the Court's judgments.[15] In the cases since *AETR* we can trace two rationales for implied powers, both of which appear in the Court's summary of its case law in Opinion 1/03:

> The competence of the Community to conclude international agreements may arise not only from an express conferment by the Treaty but may equally flow implicitly from other provisions of the Treaty and from measures adopted, within the framework of those provisions, by the Community institutions (see *ERTA*, paragraph 16). The Court has also held that whenever Community law created for those institutions powers within its internal system for the purpose of attaining a specific objective, the Community had authority to undertake international commitments necessary for the attainment of that objective even in the absence of an express provision to that effect (Opinion 1/76, paragraph 3, and Opinion 2/91, paragraph 7). That competence of the Community may be exclusive or shared with the Member States.[16]

The Court here mentions the two traditional bases for implied powers: first, the existence of legislation, whether or not adopted within the framework of a common policy; and second, the existence of a Union objective for the attainment of which Treaty-based internal powers may be complemented by external powers. The first is founded on pre-emption, the occupation of the field by existing Union law (hence the equation in *AETR* between the existence of the competence and its exclusive nature); the second is based on the principle of *effet utile*, the implication of powers necessary to achieve an expressly defined objective. Both are founded on the close relationship between the internal and the external dimensions of EU policy-making: it is not sufficient to point to the existence of a general internal legislative power, such as the power to adopt measures to facilitate the provision of services within the Union, in order to justify the exercise of an external power.[17] In Opinion 1/03 itself the Court appears to derive the existence of an implied EU competence from the existence of internal Union legislation, viz the Regulations on jurisdiction and the recognition and enforcement of judgments in civil and commercial matters.[18] Questions as to the objective, scope, nature, and content (and future development) of those rules are regarded as relevant to the issue of exclusivity, not to the existence of competence.[19] In contrast, the alternative basis for implied powers (*effet utile*) does require attention to be paid to the nature and content of internal rules, including Treaty provisions, in order to identify the 'specific objective' for which internal powers have been granted but for which external powers may be necessary. The importance of that objective was

---

[15] 'Whereas the competence of the Community to conclude international agreements does not derive only from explicit conferral by the Treaty but may also derive from other provisions of the Treaty and from acts adopted pursuant to those provisions by Community institutions', preamble to Council Decision (EC) 94/800 [1994] OJ L336/1.

[16] Opinion 1/03 (n 14 above) [114]–[115].

[17] Opinion 1/94 [1994] ECR I-5267; C-476/98 *Commission v Germany* (open skies) [2002] ECR I-9855.

[18] Opinion 1/03 (n 14 above) [134].

[19] ibid, [126]–[127]; with one exception: where the Treaty base for the internal legislation excludes harmonization (for example, Art 168(5) TFEU on public health or Art 167(5) TFEU on culture) the Union will lack competence to conclude an international agreement encompassing harmonization (Opinion 1/03) [132].

underlined in Opinion 1/94.[20] In that ruling the Court defined the Treaty provisions on services as being essentially concerned with its internal market objective: the liberalization of services within the Union, rather than services liberalization *tout court*. This certainly appears to be consistent with Article 56 TFEU (ex-Article 49 EC) and explains why it was necessary to include express provision for international agreements on services within Article 207 TFEU (ex-Article 133 EC) insofar as those agreements seek (for example) to promote liberalization of services outside the internal market. In the case of some other internal market policies (intellectual property rights, taxation, establishment of companies, air transport services) a similar link to the completion or functioning of the internal market will be necessary. In other cases (capital movements for example) the EU Treaties specify external as well as internal objectives; or (energy policy, for example) the link between pursuing an external policy and its impact on the internal EU regime is so close that it is difficult to disentangle the two; in other cases (social policy for example) the extent of the Treaty objective is not so clear.

The emphasis on Treaty objectives is certainly a logical consequence of applying an *effet utile* principle. As we have seen Opinion 1/03 suggests that it does not play a central role where the basis for external competence is simply the existence of internal rules. The fact that Article 65 EC, the legal base for the internal rules in that instance, required measures to be 'necessary for the proper functioning of the internal market' was held to be irrelevant to determining the scope of implied external powers in the field.[21] The two alternative bases for implied powers may thus attach very different significance to the objectives of the relevant Treaty provisions, something which is implicit in the case law but not explicitly explained or justified. A justification may be found in the fact that where the external power is based on internal legislation, that legislation itself will reflect the objectives of its legal base. The result, in either case, is that implied external powers are inherently (and properly) limited and cannot provide the basis for developing an external policy independent of the needs and functioning of the internal regime. For that, under the current Treaty system, explicit powers are needed (such as are granted in fields such as trade in goods and services or environmental policy). This is coherent in terms of the balance between the necessary flexibility of an implied powers doctrine and the need to ensure compliance with the principle of conferred powers. It does, however, make it difficult to establish a coherent external dimension to the internal market regime as a whole.

The original Treaty of Rome, as had been pointed out by the Court in the *AETR* case, contained only two express treaty-making competences for the then EEC: trade agreements and Association Agreements. The acceptance of implied treaty-making

---

[20] See n 17 above.
[21] Opinion 1/03 (n 14 above) [131]. The Court here is referring to the exclusive nature of those powers, rather than their existence; however, it had already found external competence to be validly based on the internal rules and thus indirectly on Art 65 EC. Art 81 TFEU, which has replaced Art 65 EC, enables the EU to act 'particularly when necessary for the proper functioning of the internal market'.

power was therefore a crucial step in the evolution of the Community's external relations, enabling the development of an external dimension to policies that might otherwise have remained purely internal, broadening the possibilities for Community interaction with other international actors and allowing the Community to participate in international law-making.

During this period the Community also used the so-called 'flexibility clause' (now Article 352 TFEU) in particular as a basis for external agreements which included a cooperation dimension beyond the scope of trade.[22] In the period after the Maastricht Treaty, however, the Court of Justice has been careful to set limits to the use of the flexibility clause in an external context. Here the Court could be said to take a constitutional view against a background of debate over the legitimacy and autonomy of the Community legal order in relation to national constitutional legal systems.[23] Opinion 2/94 concerned the competence of the Community to accede to the European Convention for the Protection of Human Rights and Fundamental Freedoms (ECHR).[24] As far as implied powers are concerned, there are two aspects to the Court's Opinion which are significant. First, while reiterating the classic statement of implied powers the Court links this to the principle of conferred powers as explicitly stated in what was then Article 3b EC (and now in Article 5 TEU) and stresses the need for a clear internal power, created for the purpose of attaining a specific objective, to form the basis of an implied external power necessary to attain that objective.[25] In contrast to (for example) fisheries or transport, no general power to enact rules in the field of fundamental human rights was conferred on the institutions and there is therefore nothing from which to imply external powers. Fundamental human rights are recognized as general principles of Union law; however, an implied distinction is drawn between such underlying general principles and provisions which form a concrete basis for specific legislative competence. Respect for fundamental human rights may be 'a condition of the lawfulness of Community acts'[26] but general principles of law cannot themselves alone provide a legal basis for implied external Union action.

Secondly, the Court sets clear limits to the use of the flexibility clause (then Article 235 EC) as a basis for external competence. This Article might have seemed to provide

---

[22] For example see Council Decision 88/595/EEC concluding an agreement between the EEC and Hungary on trade and commercial and economic cooperation [1988] OJ L327/1, which was based on Arts 113 and 235 EEC.

[23] See the *'Maastricht'* decision of the German Federal Constitutional Court, judgment of 12 October 1993, 89 BVerfGE 155, English version [1994] 1 CMLR 57; N Reich, 'Judge-made "Europe a la carte": Some remarks on recent conflicts between European and German constitutional law provoked by the bananas litigation' (1996) 7 EJIL 103; J H H Weiler, 'Does Europe Need a Constitution? Demos, Telos and the German Maastricht Decision' (1995) 1 ELJ 219; G de Búrca, 'The Quest for Legitimacy in the European Union' (1996) 59 MLR 349.

[24] Opinion 2/94 [1996] ECR I-1759.

[25] Opinion 2/94 (n 24 above) [23]–[26]. Although Art 3b EC was introduced by the TEU, the principle of conferred powers is a familiar one within the Community legal order; see J H H Weiler, 'The Transformation of Europe' (1991) 100 Yale LJ 2431; A Dashwood, 'The Limits of European Community Powers' (1996) 21 ELRev 113, 115.

[26] Opinion 2/94 (n 24 above) [34]. See now also Joined Cases C-402/05 P and C-415/05 P *Yassin Abdullah Kadi and Al Barakaat International Foundation v Council and Commission* [2008] ECR I-06351, [284].

a solution to the lack of any Treaty article granting power to act if one can identify the protection of fundamental rights as one of the Union's objectives.[27] However, while it recognizes the gap-filling role of this provision, the Court nevertheless sets limits to its use in keeping with its earlier emphasis on conferred powers. Filling legislative gaps is one thing, writing new tasks and activities into the Treaty is another:

> Article 235, being an integral part of an institutional system based on the principle of conferred powers, cannot serve as a basis for widening the scope of Community powers beyond the general framework created by the provisions of the Treaty as a whole and, in particular, by those which define the tasks and activities of the Community.[28]

The Court then proceeds to argue that accession to the ECHR would entail 'a substantial change in the present Community system for the protection of human rights, in that it would entail the entry of the Community into a distinct international institutional system as well as integration of all the provisions of the Convention into the Community legal order'. Such a change would be of 'constitutional significance' and thus require Treaty amendment.[29] This Opinion can thus be seen as setting limits both to the doctrine of implied powers and to the use of the flexibility clause, in the sense that both are subject to the principle of conferred powers.

Successive Treaty reforms which have added to the Union's express internal competences in many cases also expressly referred to a new, or newly explicit, external power. Thus the Single European Act introduced a legal base for environment policy with its own external dimension; the TEU then introduced provisions on education and vocational training, development policy, culture, public health, and research and technological development; and the Treaty of Nice extended the common commercial policy to agreements covering trade in services and commercial aspects of intellectual property. As a result, implied powers became less necessary for the development of external competence into new areas. However, they did not lose their importance altogether; somewhat surprisingly, the new Title added by the Treaty of Amsterdam on visas, asylum, immigration, and other policies related to the free movement of

---

[27] Indeed, ex-Art 308 EC has been used as the legal basis for Council Regulation 1035/97 establishing a European Monitoring Centre for Racism and Xenophobia [1997] OJ L151/1. In its preamble the Regulation makes a clear reference to the language of Opinion 2/94. This Regulation, while reflecting the Community objective of protection of fundamental rights, does not 'entail a substantial change in the present Community system for the protection of human rights' or the integration of the Community system into a 'distinct international institutional system' (Opinion 2/94 (n 24 above) [34]); it can therefore properly be based on Art 308.

[28] Opinion 2/94 (n 24 above) [30].

[29] ibid [34]–[35]. Since the Opinion, Treaty amendment has indeed occurred: Art 6(2) TEU, as amended by the Treaty of Lisbon, provides that '[t]he Union shall accede to the European Convention for the Protection of Human Rights and Fundamental Freedoms'. In addition we may note the addition by the Treaty of Amsterdam of an explicit legal base for action to combat discrimination based on sex, racial or ethnic origin, religion or belief, disability, age, or sexual orientation (Art 13 EC, now Art 19 TFEU), which is capable of acting as an implied legal basis for external action: see for example Council Decision (EC) 2010/48 concerning the conclusion, by the European Community, of the UN Convention on the Rights of Persons with Disabilities [2010] OJ L23/35.

persons did not include any mention of external relations. The Union has nevertheless concluded a number of visa facilitation and readmission agreements, using powers implied from Articles 62(2)(b) and 63(3)(b) EC.[30] Likewise, the power to adopt measures in the field of judicial cooperation in civil matters having cross-border implications (Article 65 EC, now Article 81 TFEU) implies the power to enter into international agreements on the jurisdiction and enforcement of judgments.[31] Neither transport nor energy policy (the latter added to the TFEU by the Treaty of Lisbon) refer explicitly to external competence.

From this we may see that implied external powers are still a necessary complement to expressly granted internal powers. The Treaty of Lisbon inserts into the TFEU what amounts to a constitutionalization of the doctrine of implied powers, drawing for its formulation on the case law of the Court of Justice. Article 216(1) TFEU states:

> The Union may conclude an agreement with one or more third countries or international organisations where the Treaties so provide or where the conclusion of an agreement is necessary in order to achieve, within the framework of the Union's policies, one of the objectives referred to in the Treaties, or is provided for in a legally binding Union act or is likely to affect common rules or alter their scope.

The aim of this provision is to increase certainty and, by setting out the conditions under which non-explicit treaty-making powers arise, to achieve a clearer definition of competence. Difficulties emerge however in the attempt to reflect the case law on this issue. Three alternative conditions are included, alongside the express provision of competence. Let us briefly look at the first of these, which draws inspiration from the *effet utile* basis for implied powers: external powers exist 'where the conclusion of an agreement is necessary in order to achieve, within the framework of the Union's policies, one of the objectives referred to in the Treaties'. This seems on its face to establish a potentially wider basis for implied powers than hitherto. No longer is there a need for the agreement to be necessary to achieve an objective for which internal powers have been provided, and which is therefore likely though not inevitably to be internal in orientation; all that is needed is for the objective to be referred to in the Treaties, including the very widely drawn general external objectives of Article 21 TEU, and for the action to take place 'within the framework of the Union's policies'. It is not specified that the Union objective should be linked to the explicitly-stated objectives of that policy field. It might be wondered whether the general external policy objectives established in Article 21 TEU could, together with Article 216(1), provide a basis for action.

It is also worth noting in this context that the current version of the flexibility clause (Article 352 TFEU) also reflects this choice of wording, having removed the

---

[30] See for example Council Decision (EC) 2007/826 on the conclusion of a readmission agreement between the EC and Moldova, [2007] OJ L334/148; Council Decision (EC) 2007/827 on the conclusion of the visa facilitation agreement between the EC and Moldova, [2007] OJ L334/168. Under the Treaty of Lisbon, readmission agreements now have an explicit legal base, Art 79(3) TFEU.

[31] Opinion 1/03 (n 14 above).

requirement of a connection with the common market formerly in Article 308 EC.[32] Although Article 352(4) excludes the use of this provision 'for attaining objectives pertaining to the common foreign and security policy', it is not clear which of the general external objectives set out in Article 21 TEU are CFSP-specific, nor whether the phrase 'within the framework of the policies defined by the Treaties' in Article 352 TFEU could be said to refer to external policy generally or whether it would be necessary to argue that action was being taken within one of the more specific (non-CFSP) external or internal policy fields.[33] The Treaty of Lisbon has thus extended the possibilities for the use of both implied powers and the flexibility clause by loosening the link between internal objectives and external action.

2. DELIMITING COMPETENCES: THE EXAMPLE OF TRADE

As the number of Court Opinions and judgments during the 1970s might suggest, this decade witnessed a great burst of external activity especially in the commercial policy sphere. The customs union was complete, and the Community was participating in the Tokyo Round of GATT negotiations which succeeded not only in agreeing substantial tariff reductions but also in getting agreements on (among others) technical standards and government procurement. Alongside this general opening of markets, following the first wave of accessions (of Denmark, Ireland, and the United Kingdom) in 1973 the Community concluded free trade agreements with the seven remaining EFTA states (Sweden, Norway, Austria, Switzerland, Portugal, Iceland, Finland) which were designed to achieve free trade in industrial goods by (in most cases) July 1977. Preferential trading relations were consolidated with the southern Mediterranean countries: Malta, Cyprus, and the Mashreq (Egypt, Jordan, Lebanon, Syria) and Maghreb (Algeria, Morocco, Tunisia[34]) as well as with the African, Caribbean, and Pacific[35] and some Latin American

---

[32] Art 352 TFEU provides that action may be taken '[i]f action by the Union should prove necessary, within the framework of the policies defined by the Treaties, to attain one of the objectives set out in the Treaties, and the Treaties have not provided the necessary powers'.

[33] Art 308 EC required action to be 'necessary to attain, in the course of the operation of the common market, one of the objectives of the Community'. The sometimes strained link between external action and the operation of the common market will be less in evidence under Art 352 TFEU, containing as it does a reference to all substantive policy areas, including external action in Part V TFEU. It should be mentioned here, however, that in Opinion 2/94 the Court itself seemed to abandon the link to the common market: 'Art 235 [now Art 352 TFEU] is designed to fill the gap where no specific provisions of the Treaty confer on the Community institutions express or implied powers to act, if such powers appear none the less to be necessary to enable the Community to carry out its functions with a view to attaining one of the objectives laid down by the Treaty' (Opinion 2/94 (n 24 above) [29]).

[34] Morocco and Tunisia had already concluded Association Agreements in 1969: [1969] OJ L197; [1969] OJ L198; English version [1973] OJ L239. The Cooperation Agreements with Tunisia and Morocco concluded in 1976 replaced these early agreements and were part of a 'Global Mediterranean Policy' developed in the early 1970's. Turkey's Association Agreement was concluded in 1963.

[35] The second Yaounde Convention applied 1969–75; the first Lomé Convention (reflecting the UK's ties with its former colonies) came into force in 1975.

countries.[36] Alongside its case law on implied powers, the Court was having to respond to the institutional pressures arising from the elaboration and extension of international commercial relations and gave a series of judgments which both recognized the necessary evolution of the common commercial policy beyond preferential trade agreements and placed responsibility for its development onto the Community itself (not the Member States) and especially onto the Commission as the primary policy-maker and negotiator.[37]

By comparison, the 1980s were a period of consolidation for the external aspects of Community policy-making, a period in which the Community was occupied with 'internal' concerns, in particular of course the enormous legislative programme set in motion by the Commission's White Paper of 1985 and the Single European Act of 1986, designed to achieve the internal market by the end of 1992. It is surprising in retrospect that more attention was not paid earlier to the implications of the internal market for third country goods and services. The virtual absence of any discussion in the Commission's White Paper of the implications for the Community's external trading relations of the internal market programme is remarkable. It was not until 1988 that the Commission's draft Second Banking Directive and its proposed reciprocity rules led to accusations that the Community was busy building a protectionist 'fortress Europe' and prompted the Commission to attempt a refutation in a statement entitled 'Europe 1992: Europe World Partner'.[38] The under-developed nature of the external dimension of the internal market has been in part the cause of the controversy over Community competence in relation to parts of the Uruguay Round agreements. The reasons for this neglect are complex but certainly include an initial under-estimation of the significance of the external dimension—and especially the significance of the internal market for the Community's trading partners—as well as an unwillingness to be diverted from the primary goal by controversial questions of external relations. The concurrent progress of negotiations in the Uruguay Round was also an important factor: the Community was undoubtedly unwilling to compromise its negotiating position, and weaken its bargaining power, by making unilateral concessions which would pre-judge what Eeckhout has called the 'basic policy question' of Community preference: to what extent should the Community extend the benefits of internal market integration to third country suppliers of goods and services?[39] The conclusion of the Uruguay Round also required the resolution of a debate which had been simmering for some time over the extent of the Community's trade powers and more specifically

---

[36] For example Cooperation Agreement with Mexico [1975] OJ L247; Cooperation Agreement with Uruguay [1973] OJ L333.

[37] Opinion 1/75 (OECD Understanding) [1975] 1355; Opinion 1/78 (Natural Rubber Agreement) [1979] ECR 2871.

[38] Commission communication 'Europe 1992: Europe World Partner' Bulletin of the EC 10-1988, 10.

[39] P Eeckhout, *The European Internal Market and International Trade: A Legal Analysis* (Oxford University Press, 1994) 342.

whether Article 113 EC[40] covered trade in services and the trade-related aspects of intellectual property.

In Opinion 1/78 the Court had taken the view that the common commercial policy was not limited to traditional trade instruments: the fact that Article 113 required the development of a 'policy' based on 'uniform principles' suggested to the Court that it was intended to go beyond the administration of customs duties and quantitative restrictions and could be used as a basis for measures which are not traditional trade instruments.[41] During the 1980s and 1990s the Court consolidated its views on the scope of the Community's commercial policy, dealing with two further issues: first, the extent to which Article 113 EC extended beyond trade in goods to cover trade in services and intellectual property rights (IPR);[42] and secondly, the use of CCP powers for purposes which do not have a strictly trade-based rationale, including development, environmental, and even political object-ives. The first issue was tackled by the Court in Opinion 1/94, on the conclusion by the EC of the WTO agreements negotiated during the Uruguay Round. In addition to considering the possible application of implied powers, already referred to, the Court set limits to the use of Article 113 for agreements relating to services and IPR. Although it held that services could not 'as a matter of principle' be excluded from Article 113,[43] it adopted the distinction between different modes of supply of services used in the GATS and found that only one of them—cross-frontier provision of services by a supplier established in one country to a consumer residing in another—was sufficiently like trade in goods to be covered by Article 113.[44] Other modes of supply involving commercial presence or movement of either the service provider or the consumer fell outside the CCP as it was then constituted.[45] Similarly it was only to a very limited extent—border controls established to prevent trade in counterfeit goods—that IPR might fall within the CCP.[46] Since this decision, the commercial policy legal base has been amended three times, by the Treaties of Amsterdam, Nice, and most recently Lisbon, and its scope has incrementally but

---

[40] Art 113 was at that time the trade legal base; it was subsequently renumberd, with amendments, to Art 133, amended again by the Treaty of Nice, and is now Art 207 TFEU. In what follows the number in force at the time will be used in order to reflect the changing scope and content of the provision.

[41] Opinion 1/78 (n 37 above) [44]–[45].

[42] Opinion 1/94 (n 17 above); Opinion 2/92 (re OECD Decision on National Treatment) [1995] ECR I-521. For discussion of the debates over the scope of the CCP and its evolution, see M Maresceau, 'The Concept "Common Commercial Policy" and the difficult road to Maastricht' in M Maresceau (ed), *The EC's Commercial Policy after 1992: The Legal Dimension* (Kluwer, 1993); P Eeckhout, *External Relations of the European Union, Legal and Constitutional Foundations* (Oxford University Press, 2004) ch 2.

[43] Opinion 1/94 (n 17 above) [41].

[44] ibid at [44].

[45] The Court referred to the fact that other provisions of the Treaty are intended to deal with establishment, services, and the movement of people. Since the Court then went on to hold that these provisions did not have an inherently external dimension, this reasoning was not wholly convincing.

[46] Opinion 1/94 (n 17 above) [45].

substantially expanded.[47] As things stand now, Article 207(1) TFEU provides that the CCP is to include (non-exhaustively) 'changes in tariff rates, the conclusion of tariff and trade agreements relating to trade in goods and services, and the commercial aspects of intellectual property, foreign direct investment, the achievement of uniformity in measures of liberalisation, export policy and measures to protect trade such as those to be taken in the event of dumping or subsidies'. This is a welcome simplification in comparison to the complexity of the provision following the Treaty of Nice,[48] although questions still remain over the scope of 'services' and 'foreign direct investment'. Given its exclusive nature, the extension of the CCP to FDI is a matter of considerable significance for the Member States, the implications of which are currently under discussion.[49] What is clear is that the scope of the common commercial policy has evolved to reflect specifically external policy requirements, notably within the WTO; it does not simply present the external dimension of the internal market. This in turn implies the need to establish the relationship between CCP powers and those implied from other, predominantly internal, provisions including those relating to capital movements, establishment, energy, and environment; transport being expressly excluded from the CCP.[50] One aspect of this is policy coherence, reflected in Article 207(3) which requires CCP agreements to be 'compatible with internal Union policies and rules'. A second dimension is choice of legal base, and the approach to this question has been shaped by the long-standing practice of using commercial policy powers to adopt measures the objectives of which are not limited to trade.

In 1982 the Council agreed, after much debate (and in the absence of a UN Security Council Resolution) to use the CCP as the legal basis for a Community instrument imposing economic sanctions against the Soviet Union following the imposition of martial law in Poland.[51] The political reason is not mentioned explicitly in the Regulation, the preamble merely stating that 'the interests of the Community require that imports from the USSR be reduced'. Later in 1982, Article 113 EEC was again used to impose economic sanctions against Argentina following the invasion of the

---

[47] See for example, Opinion 1/08 (WTO - GATS), 30 November 2009; C-13/07 *Commission v Council (WTO—Vietnam accession)*, opinion of AG Kokott, 26 March 2009 (case withdrawn). M Krajewski, 'External Trade Law and the Constitution Treaty: Towards a Federal and More Democratic Common Commercial Policy?' (2005) CML Rev 91.

[48] H G Krenzler and C Pitschas, 'Progress or Stagnation? The Common Commercial Policy after Nice' (2001) Eur Foreign Affairs Rev 291; C Herrmann, 'Common Commercial Policy after Nice: Sisyphus Would Have Done a Better Job' (2002) CML Rev 7; M Cremona, 'A Policy of Bits and Pieces? The Common Commercial Policy After Nice' (2001) CYELS 61.

[49] M Krajewski (n 47 above); J Ceyssens, 'Towards a Common Foreign Investment Policy?—Foreign Investment in the European Constitution' (2005) 32 LIEI 259; A Dimopoulos, *Regulation of Foreign Investment in EU External Relations Law*, PhD thesis defended at the European University Institute, 2010; Commission Communication 'Towards a comprehensive European international investment policy', COM(2010) 343, 7 July 2010.

[50] Art 207(5) TFEU.

[51] Regulation (EEC) 596/82, [1982] OJ L72/15.

Falkland Islands.[52] Here for the first time, as well as mentioning consultation between the Member States pursuant to Article 224 (now Article 347 TFEU), there is a reference in the preamble to the UNSC Resolution and discussions in the framework of European Political Cooperation (EPC),[53] and this became standard practice. The political rationale is not regarded as detracting from the trade nature of the measure. Albeit in a different context, the Court had already held in Opinion 1/78, 'the fact that a product may have a political importance . . . is not a reason for excluding that product from the domain of the common commercial policy'.[54] In *Werner*, which concerned the export of dual-use goods, the Court said that 'a measure . . . whose effect is to prevent or restrict the export of certain products, cannot be treated as falling outside the scope of the common commercial policy on the ground that it has foreign policy and security objectives'.[55] The *Bosphorus* case also indicates that the Court did not regard the political objective of the sanctions as an obstacle to the use of Article 113.[56] This approach was confirmed the following year in *Centro-Com*, which concerned the implementation by the UK of a Regulation imposing sanctions against Serbia and Montenegro (the precursor of the Regulation at issue in *Bosphorus*), also based on Article 113.[57] In a well-known passage the Court describes the relationship between the foreign policy competence of the Member States acting through political cooperation (EPC) and the common commercial policy which is an exclusive Community competence: powers retained by the Member States, including foreign and security policy powers, must nevertheless respect Community law, including the proper scope of Community competence, *in casu* the CCP.[58] The use of commercial policy powers requires a genuine link to international trade. This point is clearly demonstrated in the most important recent consideration of the appropriate legal basis for economic sanctions, the *Kadi* case.[59]

The Treaty on European Union established a specific legal basis for economic sanctions. Under Articles 301 and 60 EC the Council, following a Common Position or joint action adopted under the Common Foreign and Security Policy (CFSP), may decide to interrupt or reduce, in part or completely, economic relations with one or

---

[52] Regulation (EEC) 877/82, [1982] OJ L102/1.

[53] The reference to the EPC is of interest also because at this time EPC had not been given a Treaty basis; this was to happen with the Single European Act in 1986.

[54] Opinion 1/78 (n 37 above) [39].

[55] Case C-70/94 *Fritz Werner Industrie-Ausrüstungen GmbH v Germany* [1995] ECR I-3189, [10]; see also C-83/94 *Criminal proceedings against Leifer, Krauskopf and Holzer* [1995] ECR I-3231.

[56] Case C-84/95 *Bosphorus v Ministry of Transport, Energy and Communications* [1996] ECR I-3953, [17].

[57] Council Regulation (EEC) 1432/92 prohibiting trade between the Community and Serbia and Montenegro, [1992] OJ L151/4. This Regulation followed an EPC decision and implemented UN Security Council Resolution 757 (1992) imposing an economic embargo on Serbia and Montenegro.

[58] Case C-124/95 *The Queen, ex p Centro-Com Srl v HM Treasury and Bank of England* [1997] ECR I-0081, [24]–[28].

[59] Cases C-402/05 P and C-415/05 P *Yassin Abdullah Kadi and Al Barakaat International Foundation v Council and Commission* [2008] ECR I-06351. On the competence issue see further M Cremona, 'EC Competence, "Smart Sanctions" and the *Kadi* Case' (2009) 28 YEL 559.

more third countries.[60] The new procedure was first used against Libya in late 1993 only a few weeks after the TEU entered into force,[61] and Article 133 (formerly Article 113) was no longer used as a legal basis for economic sanctions. However, since Article 301 referred to third countries it was unclear whether it provided a basis for so-called 'smart sanctions', those directed at groups or at individuals who are not members of a third country government or ruling regime, which have become more commonly used in the last decade, and especially by the UN Security Council since 1999 as part of its counter-terrorism policy.[62] These doubts had led the Council to base such measures not only on Articles 301 and 60 but also on the flexibility clause, Article 308 EC, but doubts remained as to whether Articles 301, 60, and 308 were the appropriate legal base, whether another legal base could be identified, and indeed whether the Union had competence to adopt such measures at all.

In *Kadi* the Court upheld the Council's actual choice of legal basis for the Regulation in question. In a complex line of reasoning which led to the conclusion that Article 308 EC was required alongside Articles 301 and 60, the Court held that financial sanctions directed at individuals are not covered by other possible EC Treaty provisions, and more specifically that they are outside the scope of the CCP. The Court argued that a measure falls within the common commercial policy 'only if it relates specifically to international trade in that it is essentially intended to promote, facilitate or govern trade and has direct and immediate effects on trade in the products concerned'.[63] In this case, the Regulation's 'essential purpose and object' is combating international terrorism through freezing the economic resources of individuals and entities; although trade effects might be the result, 'it is plainly not its purpose to give rise to direct and immediate effects of that nature'.[64] So although Article 113/133 EC might have been an adequate legal base for economic sanctions based on trade restrictions it could not provide a legal basis for sanctions directed at the financial assets of individuals, even where their trading activities—if they exist—are inevitably indirectly affected.[65] The ruling in *Kadi* on this point follows earlier case law dealing with the use of Article 133 for ulterior non-trade purposes. It is perfectly permissible to use trade instruments to promote other objectives, such as development[66]

---

[60] Art 301 EC (formerly Art 228a) was the general provision; Art 60 EC (formerly Art 73g) dealt specifically with restrictions on capital movements.

[61] Council Decision (CFSP) 93/614 of 22 November 1993 on a common position under Art J.2 TEU with regard to the reduction of economic relations with Libya, [1993] OJ L295/7; Council Regulation (EC) 3274/93 preventing the supply of certain goods and services to Libya, [1993] OJ L295/1; and Council Regulation (EC) 3275/93 prohibiting the satisfying of claims with regard to contracts and transactions the performance of which was affected by the UN Security Council Resolution 883 (1993) and related resolutions, [1993] OJ L295/4.

[62] See UN Doc S/RES/1267 (1999); UN Doc S/RES/1333 (2000); UN Doc S/Res/1368 (2001); UN Doc S/Res/1373 (2001).

[63] Cases C-402/05P and C-415/05P *Kadi* (n 59) [183].

[64] ibid [184]–[186].

[65] The Treaty of Lisbon has now expanded the scope of the provision on economic sanctions making it clear that measures against individuals and groups are included: Art 215 TFEU; see also Art 75 TFEU which covers asset freezing and other measures involving capital movements and payments aimed at combating terrorism.

[66] Opinion 1/78 (n 37 above); Case 45/86 *Commission v Council* (first GSP Case) [1987] ECR 1493.

or environmental protection,[67] as well as a broader Union policy agenda, such as the Lisbon Agenda.[68] But whatever the ulterior purpose, the immediate purpose must be to 'promote, facilitate or govern trade'.

The EU's trade, or common commercial policy, competence has had a special place in the evolution of its external relations. As one of the few explicit competences in existence from the inception of the EEC, it has helped to establish the Union from the start as a significant player in bilateral, multilateral, and regional trade relations. The Court supported this by refusing to restrict the scope of the CCP to the regulation of imports and exports and its justification in the earlier cases was the need to allow Community policy to adapt to changes in the regulation of international trade.[69] Even when setting limits to that policy as the Treaty then stood, in Opinion 1/94 the Court referred to its 'open' nature.[70] The exclusive nature of the Union's trade competence, established by the Court of Justice as long ago as 1975,[71] has never been questioned and is now enshrined in the EU Treaties.[72] Since trade was a field in which the Union held clearly established powers, it is not surprising that we see those powers being used to support the broader Union interest, thereby contributing to the characterization of the Union as an international actor relying on its economic power, using trade as a lever to gain political as well as economic objectives. Although the Union's powers are now much broader, encompassing even military power, it still points to its own trade-based regional integration as a model for economic and social development, political stability, and security.

3. INTERNATIONAL OBLIGATIONS AND THE COMMUNITY LEGAL ORDER

As the implied powers doctrine recognizes, Union objectives may be achieved by both internal and external action; it is also true of course that the Union's external commitments have an impact on the development of internal regulation and law-making. How do these internal and external instruments inter-relate? This section will examine the relation between international law and EU law largely through the evolution of the Court's approach. The relationship between international law and Union law is of increasing relevance and importance for a number of reasons. Increasingly we see that the system of multi-level governance (whether in matters of trade, environmental protection, energy, or anti-terrorism) is not limited to the Union

---

[67] See for example Opinion 2/00 [2001] ECR I-9713; Case C-178/03 *Commission v Parliament and Council* [2006] ECR I-107; C-94/03 *Commission v Council* [2006] ECR I-1; Case C-411/06 *Commission v European Parliament and Council*, 8 September 2009. For an example where the Court held that the trade objective was 'direct and immediate' whereas the environmental objective was 'indirect and distant', see Case C-281/01 *Commission v Council (Energy Star Agreement)* [2002] ECR I-12049, [41]. See generally P Koutrakos, 'Legal Base and Delimitation of Competence in EU External Relations' in M Cremona and B de Witte (eds), *EU Foreign Relations Law—Constitutional Fundamentals* (Hart, 2008).

[68] Commission communication 'Global Europe: competing in the world', COM(2006) 567.

[69] Opinion 1/78 (n 37 above) [43]–[45].   [70] Opinion 1/94 (n 17 above) [41].

[71] Opinion 1/75 (n 37 above).   [72] Art 3 TFEU.

and national levels but also includes the international level, by which is meant not only that different jurisdictions are dealing with the same problems, but further that those jurisdictions are becoming increasingly integrated.[73] It is not surprising that we are seeing an increasing number of cross-jurisdictional cases such as *Mox Plant*,[74] *Bosphorus*,[75] and *Kadi*,[76] not to mention the cases involving the enforcement of WTO norms within the EC legal order, and that the Court of Justice has to deal more often with international law issues.[77]

When one thinks of this question—the relationship between international law and the Union's legal order—the tendency is to focus on the effects of international law within the internal legal order. To what extent is the Union bound by international law? What effect do the international agreements which it concludes have within its legal order? Do they override Union legislation? Might they take precedence over the founding Treaties themselves? Can such agreements be directly enforced by the European courts, or by national courts? The EU Treaties merely provide (now in Article 216(2) TFEU) that international agreements concluded by the Union are binding on the Member States and on the Union institutions; an important principle but one which leaves many of these questions unanswered. In its earliest constitutional case law the Court of Justice was concerned to emphasize the distinctiveness of the Community legal order both from the international system and from the Member States. In *Van Gend en Loos*[78] the Court refers to the Community as 'a new legal order of international law': it is part 'of' the international legal order but has a distinct identity as a 'new legal order', one which is contrasted to international treaties which merely create mutual obligations between the contracting states. In *Costa v ENEL*[79] the Court again contrasts the EC Treaty with 'ordinary international treaties', and goes on to emphasize as a basis for the primacy of Community law the Community's legal personality, its own legal capacity, and capacity for representation on the international plane. The supranational character of the Community legal order, established in these early cases, implies its distinctness from both international law (it is more than an ordinary treaty) and from the Member States (it is a separate legal person with independent law-making powers). It is this autonomy which allows the Court to develop, on the basis of the Treaties and the constitutional traditions of the Member States, the Community's (and now the Union's) own distinctive constitutional

---

[73] D Bethlehem, 'International Law, European Community Law, National Law: Three Systems in Search of a Framework' in M Koskenniemi (ed), *International Law Aspects of the European Union* (Martinus Nijhoff, 1998); A Rosas, 'The European Court of Justice in Context: Forms and Patterns of Judicial Dialogue' (2007) Vol 1 EJLS 2 (online).

[74] C-459/03 *Commission v Ireland* (Mox Plant) [2006] ECR I-4635.

[75] Case C-84/95 *Bosphorus v Ministry of Transport, Energy and Communications* (n 56 above). ECHR *Bosphorus Airways v Ireland*, Application 45036/98, (2006) 42 EHRR 1.

[76] Cases C-402/05P and C-415/05P *Kadi* (n 59 above).

[77] Rosas (n 73 above).

[78] Case 26/62 *NV Algemene Transport- en Expeditie Onderneming van Gend & Loos v Netherlands Inland Revenue Administration* [1963] ECR 1.

[79] Case 6/64 *Costa* (n 5 above).

framework. Some of the broader implications of this will be developed in the final
section of this chapter.

It is from this standpoint that the Court has developed its position on international law and Union law, in particular the binding character and possible direct
effect of international agreements. To what extent might international agreements to
which the Union is a party take effect in the Union legal order and possess the
characteristics of 'Union law'? The Court has in fact been somewhat ambivalent over
the years with respect to this question. On the one hand, it has stated clearly that
the Union 'must respect international law in the exercise of its powers',[80] but on the
other hand it takes the role of gatekeeper establishing conditions under which
international law may take effect within the EU legal system—conditions which
are not always clear. In 1974 the Court held that Community agreements were 'an
integral part' of the Community legal order.[81] It did not however develop the full
implications of this statement, especially with respect to the issue of direct effect,
until the *Kupferberg* case in 1982.[82] As a part of Community law, the provisions of
agreements concluded by the Community are binding on both the Community
institutions and on the Member States: and the Member States, in implementing
these provisions, are fulfilling a Community law obligation. It is thus important that
the determination of the nature of the obligation—and specifically whether it can be
enforced by individuals before national courts—should be a matter of Community
law to be decided by the European Court, and not left to the national courts of
individual Member States.[83] It is thus clear that the Court is not merely discussing
the relationship between an international legal obligation and the Community
legal order: it is determining the relationship between an international agreement
(which has become part of the Community legal order) and the domestic legal orders
of the Member States. Furthermore, unless the agreement itself explicitly deals with
the question, the issue of direct effect—the relationship between legal orders—is a
matter for the Community legal order without reference to the position taken by
the other contracting party (or the Member State); the *bona fide* performance of the
agreement in international law terms does not predetermine the legal mechanisms
chosen by the parties to achieve its objectives. Thus as long as both parties perform
their obligations, it does not affect the reciprocity of the agreement if one does so by

---

[80] Case C-286/90 *Poulsen* [1992] ECR I-6048; Case C-162/96 *Racke GmbH & Co. v Hauptzollamt Mainz*
[1998] ECR I-3655.

[81] Case 181/73 *Haegeman v Belgium* [1974] ECR 449, [5]. This means, *inter alia*, that an agreement, via its
concluding act, is treated as an 'act of an institution' of the Union and liable to interpretation under Art 267
TFEU.

[82] Case 104/81 *Hauptzollamt Mainz v Kupferberg* [1982] ECR 3641. In 1976 the Court had held that a
provision of the Yaounde Convention was directly effective: Case 87/75 *Conceria Daniele Bresciani v Amministrazione delle Finanze Stato* [1976] ECR 129, but this was exceptional and in other cases the issue was side-
stepped or ignored: see for example Case 270/80 *Polydor Ltd and RSO Records Inc v Harlequin Record Shops
Ltd and Simons Records Ltd* [1982] ECR 329. G Bebr, 'Agreements Concluded by the Community and their
Possible Direct Effect: From International Fruit Company to Kupferberg' (1983) 20 CML Rev 35.

[83] Case 104/81 *Hauptzollamt Mainz v Kupferberg* (n 82 above) [13]-[14].

attributing direct effect to its provisions while the other does not.[84] In *Kupferberg* the Court examined first the 'nature and structure' of the agreement in question (the Free Trade Agreement with Portugal) and then the characteristics of the specific provision, concluding that the provision of the agreement which prohibited discriminatory internal taxation was 'capable of conferring upon individual traders rights which the Courts must protect'.[85] Later the Court was to summarize the position in relation to international agreements thus:

> A provision in an agreement concluded by the Community with non-member countries must be regarded as being directly applicable when, regard being had to its wording and the purpose and nature of the agreement itself, the provision contains a clear and precise obligation which is not subject, in its implementation or effects, to the adoption of any subsequent measure.[86]

It is even possible for decisions taken by institutions set up under international agreements to meet these criteria (for example an Association Council given the power to take binding decisions) and a considerable body of case law has built up in particular upon the decisions of the EU-Turkey Association Council.[87]

Despite declaring Community agreements to be an integral part of Community law, and granting direct effect to a variety of agreements during the 1980s and 1990s,[88] the Court resisted the idea that their specific provisions should be interpreted *mutatis mutandis* as if they were provisions of the EC Treaty. The specific—and different— objectives of the two legal instruments should be taken into account even where the wording of their provisions is very similar. In a case in which the Court refused to transpose onto a free trade agreement its case law on free movement of goods and exhaustion of rights in the context of copyright, the Court held that the two agreements had different objectives.[89] The difference between the two Treaties was a

---

[84] ibid [18]. This approach of the Court has been criticized by some commentators in the context of its refusal to grant direct effect to provisions of the GATT and then the WTO (see Cases 22–24/72 *International Fruit Company* [1972] ECR 1219; C-280/93 *Germany v Council* [1994] ECR I-4737; C-149/96 *Portugal v Council* [1999] ECR I-8395); see further discussion below.

[85] Case 104/81 *Hauptzollamt Mainz v Kupferberg* (n 82 above) [27].

[86] Case 12/86 *Demirel v Stadt Schwäbisch Gmünd* [1987] ECR 3719, [14]. Here, the Court held that Art 12 of the Association Agreement with Turkey, which set the freedom of movement of workers as an objective of the Association, together with Art 36 of the Protocol of 1970, were not directly effective as they 'essentially serve to set out a programme and are not sufficiently precise and unconditional to be capable of governing directly the movement of workers' [23].

[87] C-192/89 *Sevince v Staatssecretaris van Justitie* [1990] ECR I-3461.

[88] For examples of cases where provisions of Community agreements have been granted direct effect, see Case C-18/90 *ONEM v Kziber* [1991] ECR 199, on the Association Agreement with Morocco; Case C-432/92 *R v MAFF (ex p Anastasiou)* [1994] ECR I-3087, on a Protocol to the Association Agreement with Cyprus; Case T-115/94 *Opel Austria GmbH v Council* [1997] ECR II-0039, on the European Economic Area Agreement; C-257/99 *Barkoci and Malik* [2001] ECR I-6557 on a non-discrimination provision in the Association (Europe) Agreement with the Czech Republic; C-265/03 *Simutenkov* [2005] ECR I-2579 on the Partnership and Cooperation Agreement with Russia.

[89] Case 270/80 *Polydor Ltd and RSO Records Inc v Harlequin Record Shops Ltd and Simons Records Ltd* [1982] ECR 329.

matter not only of objectives and scope—the free trade Agreement being limited to 'negative' integration—but also the absence of legislative and judicial institutions with the task of reconciling the demands of the single market with intellectual property rights.[90]

In its first Opinion on the European Economic Area Agreement (EEA), the Court sets out this argument fully, in the context of a treaty which the parties expressly intended to be interpreted and applied 'homogeneously' with the EC Treaty. Having contrasted the EEA which 'merely' creates rights and obligations between the contracting parties and 'provides for no transfer of sovereign rights to the inter-governmental institutions which it sets up', with the EC Treaty which 'constitutes the constitutional charter of a Community based on the rule of law' and establishes a new legal order with the 'essential characteristics' of primacy and direct effect, the Court concludes that even identical wording does not (necessarily) secure homogeneity.[91] Even the provision of the EEA seeking to ensure that substantively identical provisions would be interpreted in the same way by 'incorporating' prior interpretative decisions of the European Court itself would not necessarily achieve this result since certain elements of that case law may be 'irreconcilable' with the characteristics of the EEA Agreement.[92] These cases indicate that we have to be careful, therefore, in viewing international agreements as an 'integral part' of Union law; they will not necessarily possess all the characteristics of an internal provision even where they appear to be substantively identical. This is the position still repeated by the Court of Justice when interpreting Union agreements but if we look at its more recent practice, the picture looks somewhat different.

Since 1990, in fact, attention has turned increasingly to the external dimension of the Community's activities. Out of a current total of 14 European Court of Justice Opinions under what is now Article 218(11) TFEU on the compatibility of an envisaged agreement with the EU Treaties, eleven have been handed down since 1990, a witness not only to the resurgence of activity in the last twenty years but also to the debate which has been taking place as to the extent and nature of the Union's external powers. Again, a number of factors are involved. The drawing to an end of the initial legislative phase of the internal market programme, a growing recognition that a true removal of internal frontiers requires common external frontiers, and a common external policy not merely for goods but for people as well, coincided with the conclusion of the WTO agreements and the need to determine the boundaries of Community and Member State competence especially in the 'new' areas of services and intellectual property rights. The Treaty on European Union of 1992 added a new and highly important dimension with the creation—building upon European Political Cooperation—of the Common Foreign and Security Policy

---

[90] ibid [20].

[91] Opinion 1/91 (Draft Agreement on a European Economic Area) [1991] ECR I-6079, [22].

[92] ibid [24]–[28]. It should be mentioned, however, that the Court of First Instance has had little difficulty in finding the EEA prohibition of charges of equivalent effect to customs duties to be directly effective and with the same scope as the equivalent prohibition in the EC Treaty, following the Court of Justice's case law in doing so: Case T-115/94 *Opel Austria GmbH v Council* (n 88 above).

(CFSP), and although the Court of Justice was not given jurisdiction over the CFSP as such, it was required to apply what was then Article 47 TEU governing the relationship between the CFSP and the EC Treaty. We will consider the inter-Pillar relationship and the changes resulting from the Treaty of Lisbon in the final section of this chapter.

These developments illustrate a fundamental aspect of the nature of Union competence. It is just not possible any longer—if it ever was—for the Union to pursue its own objectives solely within its own internal 'space'. This is not simply a matter of recognizing the external dimension of the internal market, nor simply of the need for Union legislation to conform to (external) international norms. The overlapping legal orders or 'meshing of international regimes'[93] means that Union policy emerges within an international context and increasingly that international context is helping to define the content of that policy, while Union policy and institutions contribute to the development of international norms and standards. This feature of the Union's external policies can be seen in their content as well as their scope. One very striking feature of cooperation and economic integration agreements over the last twenty years has been the extent to which the Union is engaged in exporting its norms and standards. Increasingly, and particularly where there is a development objective to the agreement, third state partners undertake to align key aspects of their economic law with that of the Union.[94] The Euro-Mediterranean Agreements (such as those with Tunisia, Jordan, and Israel), or the Partnership and Cooperation Agreements with Russia and other states of the former Soviet Union illustrate that it is not necessarily part of a pre-accession process. The EEA Agreement illustrates that this characteristic is not limited to agreements with developing countries or economies in transition: here the export of a broad and deep Union *acquis* is a condition of market access in the context of a fully reciprocal free trade agreement.

The EEA, signed in 1992, received its primary stimulus from the impetus of the internal market project and it lacks a foreign policy (CFSP) or explicit political dimension. This ambitious experiment in achieving a high level of economic integration without institutional integration was at one stage seen as a possible answer to the urgent questions facing the Union concerning the structure and priorities of its relations with its European partners—not only the EEA states of western Europe but also the emergent democracies of Central and Eastern Europe following the collapse of the Soviet Union. However it has proved to be neither: one EFTA state decided it could not accept the level of integration within the EEA;[95] three of the EFTA partners have since become members of the Union itself,[96] and only three remain on the EFTA 'side' of the EEA, one of which has also applied for membership of the EU.[97] The Central

---

[93] E U Petersmann, *The GATT/WTO Dispute Settlement System. International Law, International Organizations and Dispute Settlement* (Kluwer Law International, 1997) 22.

[94] The different agreements vary in terms of the areas and sectors covered, but may range from competition, indirect taxation, financial services, to technical standards, procurement and intellectual property law.

[95] Switzerland, which has instead concluded a number of bilateral sectoral agreements with the EU.

[96] Austria, Finland, Sweden.

[97] Liechtenstein, Norway, and Iceland, which has applied for membership.

and Eastern European states[98] and the states of the Western Balkans[99] have found, together with the Union, a different route in forming new types of relationship and eventual accession for some.[100]

There is clearly a sense in which this 'export' of the Union *acquis* is part of a wider dimension of conditionality, which makes respect for fundamental human rights and the rule of law an 'essential element' of cooperation and other agreements.[101] However, they also reflect the relation between the internal and external dimensions of Union policy. Harmonization or approximation of laws within the internal market has

---

[98] Partnership and Cooperation Agreements have been concluded with the states of the former Soviet Union, including Russia, Ukraine, Moldova, Georgia, Armenia, Azerbaijan, Kazakhstan, Kyrgyz Republic, Uzbekistan. The European Neighbourhood Policy (ENP) encompasses Ukraine, Moldova, Georgia, Armenia, Azerbaijan, together with the countries of the Euro-Mediterranean Partnership (Tunisia, Morocco, Jordan, Israel, Algeria, Egypt, Lebanon, Syria, and the Palestinian Authority for the West Bank and the Gaza Strip). See further E Philippart, 'The Euro-Mediterranean Partnership: A Critical Evaluation of an Ambitious Scheme' (2003) 8 Eur Foreign Aff Rev 201; S Pardo and L Zemer, 'Towards a New Euro-Mediterranean Neighbourhood Space' (2005) 10 Eur Foreign Aff Rev 39; S Blockmans and A Lazowski (eds), *The European Union and Its Neighbours: A Legal Appraisal of the EU's Policies of Stabilisation, Partnership and Integration* (Cambridge University Press, 2006); M Cremona, 'The European Neighbourhood Policy: More than a Partnership?' in M Cremona (ed), *Developments in EU External Relations Law* (Oxford University Press, 2008). Joint declaration of the Paris summit for the Mediterranean, Paris, 13 July 2008, Council doc 11887/08 (Presse 213); Final Statement of Union of the Mediterranean Ministers of Foreign Affairs, Marseille, 3–4 November 2008; Commission Communication on the Eastern Partnership, COM(2008) 823, 3 December 2008; European Council Conclusion and Declaration on the Eastern Partnership, 20 March 2009. Although the ENP remains as a framing policy structure, the launch in 2008–09 of both the Union for the Mediterranean and the Eastern Partnership demonstrate the need for differentiation between the two regional groupings covered by the ENP.

[99] The countries of the Western Balkans (Albania, Bosnia-Herzegovina, Croatia, the former Yugoslav Republic of Macedonia, Montenegro, Serbia, and Kosovo) are part of the Stabilisation and Association Process, founded on Stabilisation and Association Agreements and offering membership as a prospect subject to meeting the Union's conditions; of these Croatia and the former Yugoslav Republic of Macedonia are candidate states. The accession process is governed by the EU Treaty and having 'potential candidate' status does not of course commit the states concerned to apply for membership; it does however represent a political commitment on the part of the EU to assist the states concerned to prepare for accession. Commission Communication on the Western Balkans and European Integration, COM(2003) 285; Thessaloniki Agenda, External Relations Council 16 June 2003, European Council Conclusions, Thessaloniki 19–20 June 2003, and EU-Western Balkans Summit Declaration, Thessaloniki, 21 June 2003; Commission Communication 'The Western Balkans on the road to the EU: consolidating stability and raising prosperity', COM(2006) 27.

[100] In 2004 Estonia, Hungary, Czech Republic, Latvia, Lithuania, Poland, the Slovak Republic, and Slovenia joined the EU, together with Malta and Cyprus. Romania and Bulgaria followed in 2007.

[101] Commission Communication of 23 May 1995 on The Inclusion of Respect for Democratic Principles and Human Rights in Agreements Between the Community and Third Countries, COM(1995) 216. These now standard clauses emphasize respect for democratic principles and fundamental human rights, although they differ in the specific international and regional instruments to which reference might be made (Universal Declaration of Human Rights, Helsinki Final Act, Charter of Paris, European Convention on Human Rights) and they may also include other essential elements, such as minority rights and the principles of a market economy. For a discussion of their evolution, see M Cremona, 'Human Rights and Democracy Clauses in the EC's Trade Agreements' in N Emiliou and D O'Keeffe (eds), *The European Union and World Trade Law after the GATT Uruguay Round* (Wiley 1996); E Reidel and M Will, 'Human Rights Clauses in External Agreements of the EC' in P Alston (ed), *The EU and Human Rights* (Oxford University Press, 1999); E Fierro, *The EU's Approach to Human Rights Conditionality in Practice* (Martinus Nijhoff, 2003); L Bartels, *Human Rights Conditionality in the EU's International Agreements* (Oxford University Press, 2005).

been driven by the needs of market integration, and in particular the desire to remove barriers caused by non-discriminatory national regulation. Where, then, the Union embarks upon a wider process of economic integration—such as a free trade agreement—in a context where (as the Court of Justice pointed out in *Polydor*[102]) there is no formal institutional mechanism for legal approximation, an obligation to approximate relevant laws may be set out in the agreement itself.[103] In this context there is a need to remember the importance of the different objectives of integration in the internal and external dimensions of the 'Union project', a difference which is perhaps not always adequately recognized in the demands made in relation to approximation of laws. For example, the degree of harmonization required in the context of a highly integrative agreement (with highly developed economies) such as the EEA would not be appropriate in the context of an agreement where the approximation of laws has a predominantly developmental aim. EU competition policy, which was developed against a background of (more or less) sophisticated domestic systems and with an explicitly market-integrationist agenda in an interstate context, is not necessarily the appropriate model for an emerging market economy struggling to survive in a free-trade environment. Some of these issues have been to the fore in the debates over the six Economic Partnership Agreements (EPAs) being negotiated with groups of African, Caribbean, and Pacific countries in the framework of the Cotonou Convention.[104]

Since 2001 and especially since the adoption of the European Security Strategy in December 2003,[105] the limited form of political conditionality represented by the human rights essential elements clauses has extended beyond these fundamental values, importing into mixed Union agreements a broader CFSP agenda. Thus in

---

[102] Case 270/80 *Polydor* (n 89 above) [20].

[103] For example Art 52 of the Euro-Med Agreement with Tunisia COM(95) 235, states: 'Cooperation shall be aimed at helping Tunisia to bring its legislation closer to that of the Community in the areas covered by this Agreement.'

[104] EPAs are being negotiated with the Caribbean, West Africa, Central Africa, Eastern and Southern Africa, the SADC, and the Pacific, with a view to replacing the trade provisions in the Cotonou Convention with WTO-compatible agreements involving reciprocal although asymmetric trade liberalisation. The first of the EPAs to be agreed is with the CARIFORUM group of countries (Antigua and Barbuda, Bahamas, Barbados, Belize, Dominica, the Dominican Republic, Grenada, Guyana, Haiti, Jamaica, Saint Lucia, Saint Vincent and the Grenadines, St Kitts and Nevis, Suriname, and Trinidad and Tobago). Until full EPAs are negotiated with the other groups of ACP states, a number of interim EPAs have been agreed and are being provisionally applied and a Regulation on market access implementing these agreements has been adopted: Council Regulation (EC) 1528/2007 [2007] OJ L348/1. At the time of writing 36 of the 78 ACP states are covered by this Regulation; its operation will be extended as other ACP states conclude EPAs or interim EPAs with the EU; for those not covered by this Reg, the GSP Reg applies. See M G Desta, 'EC-ACP Economic Partnership Agreements and the Question of WTO Compatibility: An Experiment in North-South Regional Integration Agreements?' (2006) 43 CMLRev 1343; R Perez, 'Are Economic Partnership Agreements a First-Best Option for the ACP Countries?' (2006) 40(6) J of World Trade 999; K van Hoestenberghe and H Roelfsema, 'Economic Partnership Agreements between the EU and Groups of ACP Countries: Will they Promote Development?' UNU-CRIS Occasional Papers, 0-2006-27; G Thallinger, 'From Apology to Utopia: EU-ACP Economic Partnership Agreements Oscillating Between WTO Conformity and Sustainability' (2007) 12 Eur Foreign Aff Rev 499.

[105] J Solana, 'A Secure Europe in a Better World' adopted by the European Council in December 2003 as the European Union's Security Strategy.

2003 the Council agreed, as part of its policy to 'mainstream' non-proliferation policy into its wider external relations, to include a non-proliferation (WMD) clause in agreements with third countries.[106] The clause contains two elements. First is an obligation to comply with and implement *existing* commitments under international disarmament and non-proliferation treaties. Since this part of the clause is defined as an 'essential element' of the agreement it may lead to consultations and ultimately to suspension of the agreement if there is a serious failure to comply. Secondly, there is a commitment to cooperate in order to promote accession to and implementation of further instruments, and to strengthen export controls. It was agreed to include a WMD clause of this type in all future mixed agreements with third countries and to seek to include a clause where existing mixed agreements are renewed or revised, either in the agreement itself or in a separate legally binding instrument between the parties.[107] Examples of agreements including the new WMD clause are the Cotonou Convention,[108] the Stabilisation and Association Agreement (SAA) with Serbia,[109] and the SAA with Albania.[110] Similarly, in December 2008 the Council agreed to include a clause on small arms and light weapons (SALW) in all agreements with a CFSP dimension.[111] The Lisbon Treaty offers the possibility of including these clauses not only in mixed agreements but also in Union-only agreements, since international peace and security is clearly an objective of the Union and the Treaties appear to envisage the possibility of agreements covering both CFSP and non-CFSP matters.[112]

In cases concerning agreements forming part of this web of essentially bilateral relations, and despite its warnings in *Polydor* and Opinion 1/91, the Court of Justice has most often in practice both found their provisions to be directly effective and then proceeded to interpret them in line with existing case law on the EC Treaty.[113] The principle of effective judicial protection has also been extended to cover individuals exercising rights granted under the Europe Agreements, as a general principle which stems from the constitutional traditions common to the Member States and which is

---

[106] Council doc 14997/03. The Conclusions include a standard form of clause.

[107] For a recent assessment of the clause see Council Secretariat Note on the implementation of the WMD Clause, Council doc 5503/09, 19 January 2009.

[108] Partnership (Cotonou) Agreement between the members of the African, Caribbean and Pacific (ACP) States and the European Community and its Member States [2000] OJ L317/3, Art 11b.

[109] Proposal for a Decision on the conclusion of the Stabilisation and Association Agreement between the European Communities and their Member States and the Republic of Serbia, COM/2007/0743 final, Art 3.

[110] Stabilisation and Association Agreement between the European Communities and their Member States and the Republic of Albania, [2009] OJ L107/166, Art 8(3).

[111] Council doc 15506/08.

[112] See Art 218 TFEU.

[113] See for example Case C-257/99 *Barkoci and Malik* [2001] ECR I-6557; Case C-63/99 *Gloszczuk* [2001] ECR I-6369; C-235/99 *Kondova* [2001] ECR I-6427; Case C-268/99 *Jany and Others v Staatssecretaris van Justitie* [2001] ECR I-8615; Case C-162/00 *Land Nordrhein-Westfalen v Pokrzeptowicz-Meyer* [2002] ECR I-1049; Case C-438/00 *Deutscher Handballbund eV v Kolpak* [2003] ECR I-4135; Case C-265/03 *Simutenkov* [2005] ECR I-2579; Case C-228/06 *Soysal* [2009] ECR I-1031. F Jacobs, 'Direct Effect and Interpretation of International Agreements in the Recent Case Law of the European Court of Justice' in A Dashwood and M Maresceau, *Law and Practice of EU External Relations* (Cambridge University Press, 2008).

found in the European Convention on Human Rights,[114] and on the basis that the Europe Agreement has become an integral part of the Community legal order within which such general principles apply.[115] This does of course depend on the nature of the provisions of the specific agreement; in the case of the Agreement with Switzerland on Free Movement of Persons, for example, aspects of the right of establishment are limited to natural, and not legal, persons.[116] Further, and this point will be considered in more detail below, each of these cases concerned the application of the Union agreement in relation to the domestic law of a Member State.

We find a different approach to multilateral agreements of a regulatory or legislative character. Most striking in this context is the Court's refusal to accord direct effect to the GATT/WTO on the ground of its overall 'nature and structure'.[117] In the leading case on the WTO the Court based itself on a sequence of arguments: the continuing place for negotiation over compliance in WTO dispute settlement; the 'reciprocal and mutually advantageous' obligations at the heart of the WTO (as opposed to agreements establishing 'special relations of integration' which do not depend on reciprocity); the fact that 'some of the contracting parties, which are among the most important commercial partners' of the Union do not interpet the WTO as granting directly effective rights; and finally that '[t]o accept that the role of ensuring that those [WTO] rules comply with Community law devolves directly on the Community judicature would deprive the legislative or executive organs of the Community of the scope for manoeuvre enjoyed by their counterparts in the Community's trading partners'.[118] The argument is thus based in part on the Court's analysis of the nature of the WTO agreements—the centrality of reciprocity, in distinction to other EU agreements—and in part on the view that in this case compliance should be a matter for the political organs of the Union through negotiation and legislation, rather than its courts. The EU Council and Commission certainly share this view: the preamble to the decision concluding the WTO Agreements states that 'by its nature, the Agreement establishing the World Trade Organization, including the Annexes thereto, is not susceptible to being directly invoked in Community or Member State courts'.[119] It is of course the 'nature' of the WTO as a multilateral reciprocal regime which is at issue.

---

[114] Case C-327/02 *Panayotova* [2004] ECR I-11055, [27].

[115] Case C-23-25/04 *Sfakianakis* [2006] ECR I-01265, [28].

[116] Cases C-351/08 *Grimme*, judgment 12 November 2009; C-541/08 *Fokus Invest AG v Finanzierungsber-atung-Immobilientreuhand und Anlageberatung GmbH (FIAG)*, judgment 11 February 2010.

[117] C-149/96 *Portugal v Council* [1999] ECR I-8395. For comment see *inter alia* A von Bogdandy and T Makatsch, 'Collision, Co-existence or Co-operation? Prospects for the Relationship between WTO Law and European Union Law' in G de Búrca and J Scott (eds), *The EU and the WTO. Legal and Constitutional Issues* (Hart, 2001); P Eeckhout, 'Judicial Enforcement of WTO Law in the European Union—Some Further Reflections' (2002) 5 JIEL 91; F Snyder, 'The Gatekeepers: The European Courts and the WTO' (2003) 40 CML Rev 313; M Mendez, 'The Impact of WTO Rulings in the Community Legal Order' (2004) 29 ELRev 517; PJ Kuijper and M Bronckers, 'WTO Law in the European Court of Justice' (2005) 42 CML Rev 1313.

[118] Case C-149/96 *Portugal v Council*, (n 117 above) [42]–[46].

[119] Council Decision 94/800 [1994] OJ L336/1.

These cases, unlike most of those those involving the enforcement of bilateral agreements,[120] concern the possible incompatibility of Union legislation with the international agreement and the consequent invalidity of the former.[121] In *Intertanko* the Court adopted a similar approach with respect to the UN Convention on the Law of the Sea (UNCLOS). It held that the Court can examine the validity of Community legislation in the light of an international treaty only where the Community is bound by the rules in question,[122] where 'the nature and the broad logic of the latter do not preclude this and, in addition, the treaty's provisions appear, as regards their content, to be unconditional and sufficiently precise'.[123] The latter two conditions are essentially the criteria for direct effect and the Court seems here to be re-establishing these as the relevant criteria for the direct application of the agreement within the Union legal order. Indeed, the Court goes on to find that the 'nature and broad logic' of the UNCLOS is to establish a legal regime for seas and oceans, to balance interests of coastal and flag states, developing countries, and 'the interests and needs of mankind as a whole'; it is not, however (in the Court's view) intended to grant independent rights and freedoms to individuals. Consequently:

> UNCLOS does not establish rules intended to apply directly and immediately to individuals and to confer upon them rights or freedoms capable of being relied upon against States . . . It follows that the nature and the broad logic of UNCLOS prevent the Court from being able to assess the validity of a Community measure in the light of that Convention.[124]

The emphasis is not, as with the WTO, on reciprocity, the risk of 'disuniform application', and the need to give the political institutions room to manoeuvre in ensuring compliance. Nor, as in some other earlier cases, is the relevance of individual rights passed over or even denied.[125] Here the stress is specifically on the UNCLOS as establishing a general regulatory regime that does not 'directly and immediately' concern individuals. However it should be said that in the identification of individual rights it is not easy to distinguish clearly between (for example) the collective interests of airline passengers at issue in the *IATA* case, where judicial review was accepted,[126] and the 'interests and needs of mankind as a whole' identified as an objective of the UNCLOS, where it was not. It can also be argued that the link to individual rights

---

[120] An exception would be Case T-115/94 *Opel Austria GmbH v Council* (n 88 above).

[121] Or, as the Court put it in *Portugal v Council*, ensuring that the international rules comply with Union law: Case C-149/96 *Portugal v Council* (n 117 above) [46].

[122] This might seem to go without saying, but in Cases 21/72 to 24/72 *International Fruit Company and Others* (n 84 above) it had been held that in some special cases the Community might be bound by an agreement to which it was not a party, *in casu* the GATT; the conditions applied in this Case to the GATT did not apply, the Court held, to the Marpol 73/78 Convention on marine pollution from ships: Case C-308/06 *Intertanko* [2008] ECR I-4057, [47]–[52].

[123] Case C-308/06 *Intertanko* (n 122 above) [47]–[52].

[124] ibid [64]–[65].

[125] Case C-344/04 *R v Department of Transport ex parte IATA* [2006] ECR I-00403, [39]; Case C-377/98 *Netherlands v European Parliament and Council (biotechnology directive)* [2001] ECR I-7079, [53]–[54].

[126] Case C-344/04 *IATA* (n 125 above).

might be more appropriately directed at specific provisions of the agreement rather than its overall 'nature and broad logic', thereby excluding judicial review on the basis of the agreement as a whole as a matter of principle.

Apart from this focus on individual rights, other distinctions can be offered as possibly influencing the Court's attitude. First, as has already been pointed out, the Court seems more willing to countenance direct effect, and thus judicial review, in the case of agreements which establish an essentially bilateral preferential relationship between the Union (and its Member States) on the one hand and a third country on the other. In contrast, multilateral regulatory agreements have rarely been applied in this way. The is some hint of this in the Court's reasoning in *Portugal v Council* (on the WTO) and *Intertanko* (on UNCLOS). It relies on an appreciation of the structures and processes established by the agreement, the role played in them by the EU and its Member States, and the need to avoid fragmentation in the presentation of the Union interest in such international regulatory regimes.

A further distinction which is arguably relevant is that between cases where the Court was essentially concerned with ensuring compliance with the international agreement *by a Member State*, and those where a *Union measure* was at issue. It has been argued that this provides a convincing factual explanation, if not a normative rationale, of the case law.[127] Certainly the Court has been prepared to countenance enforcement actions against Member States, without requiring the *Intertanko* conditions, in relation to failures to comply with multilateral agreements, including the WTO and environmental agreements.[128] In performing a Union agreement, the Member States 'fulfil an obligation not only in relation to the non-member country concerned but also and above all in relation to the Community which has assumed responsibility for the due performance of the Agreement'.[129] Since the Union may be held responsible in international law where a Member State has failed to implement either a Union agreement or a mixed agreement, it is in the Union interest to ensure compliance: 'there is a Community interest in compliance by both the Community and its Member States with the commitments entered into'.[130] However, the distinction between compliance by Member States and compliance by the EU itself is hard to justify in terms of Article 216(2) TFEU which provides that international agreements concluded by the Union 'are binding upon the institutions of the Union and on its Member States'. One further point needs to be added here. Article 216(2) TFEU provides a basis for declaring invalid secondary Union law which is incompatible

---

[127] M Mendez, *The Legal Effect of Community Agreements: Lessons from the Court*, PhD thesis defended at the EUI, Florence, June 2009.

[128] Case C-61/94 *Commission v Germany* (International Dairy Arrangement) [1996] ECR I-3989; Case C-13/00 *Commission v Ireland* (EEA) [2002] ECR I-2943; Case C-239/03 *Commission v France* (Étang de Berre) [2004] ECR I-9325.

[129] Case C-104/81 *Hauptzollamt Mainz v Kupferberg* (n 82 above) [13].

[130] Case C-239/03 *Commission v France* (n 128 above) [23]. In this case the agreement was mixed and even though the alleged breach concerned an aspect of the agreement which was not actually covered by Community legislation, it was enough that the *field in general* was 'covered in large measure' by Community legislation.

with binding international law.[131] However, the logic of Article 216(2) does not apply to the EU Treaties themselves and this 'primacy' (the word used by the Court[132]) of the international agreement does not extend over primary Union law, including the Union's 'constitutional principles'.[133] In setting out this position, the Court refers to Article 218(11) TFEU which—by providing that a proposed treaty which is incompatible with the EU Treaties may not enter into force unless it is amended or the Treaties are revised—implies that the institutions may not validly (in terms of Union law) enter into international obligations which conflict with primary law.

C. EXCLUSIVE, SHARED AND COMPLEMENTARY COMPETENCE

1. PRE-EMPTION AND EXCLUSIVITY

Alongside debates as to the extent of Union external powers, an argument has continued as to the nature of that competence, and specifically over the extent to which its exercise (or even merely its existence) pre-empted Member States from acting in the field.[134] To what extent are Union external powers exclusive? In addition to the fact that the nature of that argument, and the institutions' response to it, has changed over the years, its true nature has been obscured. This is in part because a dispute as to the relative competencies of Union and Member States is often fought out as an inter-institutional battle over the scope of specific legal bases.[135] It is also due to the striking divergence until quite recently between theory and practice. Indeed it is possible to see the development of the theory over the last decade as a process of 'catching up' with existing practice. As we shall see, if we avoid what MacCormick has called a 'monocular view', what is emerging is a concept of overlapping and shared external competence involving the Union and its Member States, creating 'systems of rules, partly overlapping but capable of compatibility'.[136]

---

[131] In a recent example the Court declared a provision of national (German) law to be incompatible with a provision of the Association Agreement with Turkey; it was no defence that the national law merely implemented EU secondary legislation on visas: Case C-228/06 *Soysal*, 19 February 2009.

[132] Case C-459/03 *Commission v Ireland* (Mox Plant) (n 74 above).

[133] *Kadi* (n 59 above) [308-[309]. In an earlier decision, Case C-122/95 *Germany v Council* [1998] ECR 1973, the Court declared the Council decision concluding the Framework Agreement on Bananas invalid in so far as certain aspects of the Agreement were contrary to the fundamental Community law principle of non-discrimination. See K Lenaerts and E De Smijter, 'The European Union as an Actor under International Law' (1999–2000) 19 YEL 95, 102. Note that it is the decision concluding the agreement that is declared invalid; the validity in international law of the agreement itself is not affected.

[134] It should be noted that we are here referring to limits to Member States' powers imposed by and within the Union legal order; this does not necessarily imply a corresponding lack of capacity in the international law sense (which would be to deny the sovereignty of the Member States).

[135] Opinion 1/78 (n 37 above) is a good example of this.

[136] N MacCormick, 'Beyond the Sovereign State' (1993) 56 MLR 1; see also R Bieber, 'On The Mutual Completion of Overlapping Legal Systems: The Case of the European Communities and the National Legal Orders' (1988) 13 ELRev 147.

The period from 1970 to the late 1980s saw the development of the 'classic' form of pre-emption theory.[137] Community competence (internal or external) was either exclusive or shared. Shared competence at this stage meant distinct, discrete compartments for EC and Member States' competence and did not include the concept of complementary action by both EC and Member States in the same field (unless the Member States were acting under a form of authorization from the Community). On this view, once Community powers had been exercised (internally or externally), and the field 'occupied', Member States were pre-empted from acting alongside the Community. Unilateral action by individual Member States would undermine the unity of the market and the uniform application of Community law.[138] At this early stage (in the *AETR* case) the assertion of exclusivity is inextricably linked to the autonomy of the Community legal order vis-à-vis the Member States, and the Court links the very existence of implied powers with their exclusive nature.[139]

However over the next few years, the concept was refined and developed so that exclusive and non-exclusive implied powers emerge. We have already seen that in *Kramer* the Court found that the Community may possess implied powers even where there had not been any prior development of common rules.[140] However—in order to avoid a legislative vacuum—the Court recognized the continued (concurrent) existence of Member States' competence for as long as the Community competence had not yet been exercised. Exclusive Community competence was not compatible with the mere potential for Community action. This concurrent competence was transitional only and subject to the overall obligation to comply with Community rules found in what was then Article 5 of the EEC Treaty (now Article 4(3) TEU) and a more specific obligation to coordinate their actions then found in Article 116 EEC.

In Opinion 1/76 the European Court of Justice appeared to adopt an even stronger view, holding that exclusive external power could arise *on being exercised* without any prior exercise of internal powers, but this—it has subsequently appeared—was rather a special case where 'internal competence may be effectively exercised only at the same time as external competence..., the conclusion of the international agreement being thus necessary in order to attain objectives of the Treaty that cannot be attained by establishing autonomous rules'.[141] In more recent cases, the Court has made it clear that this case cannot be used as authority for saying that Community powers are exclusive any time they are exercised without prior internal legislation.[142] Internal legislation will generally be a pre-requisite for exclusivity of implied powers:

---

[137] M Waelbroeck, 'The Emergent Doctrine of Community Pre-emption—Consent and Re-Delegation' in T Sandalow and E Stein (eds), *Courts and Free Markets* (Oxford University Press, 1982); S Weatherill, 'Beyond Pre-emption? Shared Competence and Constitutional Change in the European Community' in D O'Keeffe and P Twomey (eds), *Legal Issues of the Maastricht Treaty* (Wiley Chancery, 1994).

[138] Case 22/70 *Commission v Council* (n 82 above) [17]–[18] and [31].

[139] Lachmann, 'International Legal Personality of the EC: Capacity and Competence' (1984) 1 LIEI 2.

[140] Cases 3, 4, and 6/76 *Kramer* (n 11 above) [30]–[33].

[141] Opinion 1/03 (n 14 above) [115].

[142] Opinion 1/94 (n 17 above); Opinion 2/92 (n 42 above).

[A]n internal power to harmonise which has not been exercised in a specific field cannot confer exclusive external competence in that field on the Community...Save where internal powers can only be effectively exercised at the same time as external powers (see *Opinion 1/76*...), internal competence can give rise to exclusive external competence only if it is exercised.[143]

As far as express powers were concerned, it was also during this period that the exclusivity of the Common Commercial Policy was established in cases such as Opinion 1/75[144] (in relation to the conclusion of international agreements) and *Donckerwolcke*[145] (in relation to autonomous legislative action). Since then this position has been firmly entrenched—since the Treaty of Lisbon it has been expressly stated in the EU Treaties—and the subsequent debate on the CCP has been over its extent. The rationale developed by the Court for the exclusivity of the CCP is of interest for the purposes of a comparison with the nature of pre-emption as applied to implied powers. It is based on (a) the threat which concurrent powers would pose to 'mutual trust within Community' and therefore to the coherence and effectiveness of the defence of Community commercial interests vis-à-vis third countries; and (b) the risks of distortions of competition within a single market brought about by the different commercial and trading policies (and different economic weight) of the Member States.[146] This reasoning is a characteristic mixture of pragmatism and (again) the link between external and internal trade policy. Although the amendment to Article 133 EC made by the Treaty of Nice introduced for a period the concept of non-exclusive CCP powers,[147] the Treaty of Lisbon has, while broadening its scope, returned to the idea that the CCP is by nature an exclusive competence—in other words, its exclusivity does not depend on prior legislative action or the operation of the Opinion 1/76 principle.[148]

However it is striking that, whatever the rhetoric, mixed agreements were in fact widely accepted. In fact, even at this time just about every external activity other than the CCP was in practice mixed, whether Association Agreements or development agreements, and even within the CCP the Court was prepared to sanction Member State and Community participation in the commodity agreements.[149] Although in theory the traditional doctrine of exclusivity is based on the principle of a 'separation of powers' between the Union and the Member States, when applied to international

---

[143] Opinion 1/94 (n 17 above) [88]–[89]. This interpretation of Opinion 1/76 is confirmed in Opinion 1/03 (n 14 above) although the case is better seen as referring to the existence of competence rather than its exclusivity: P Eeckhout, *External Relations of the European Union, Legal and Constitutional Foundations* (Oxford University Press, 2004) 68; A Dashwood and J Heliskoski, 'The Classic Authorities Revisited' in A Dashwood and C Hillion (eds), *The General Law of EC External Relations* (Sweet & Maxwell, 2000) 13–14.

[144] Opinion 1/75 (n 37 above).

[145] Case 41/76 *Criel, née Donckerwolcke et al v Procureur de la Republique* [1976] ECR 1921.

[146] Opinion 1/75 (n 37 above).

[147] Opinion 1/08 (n 47 above), in which the Court refused to interpret the sub-paragraphs of Art 133 EC requiring shared competence restrictively, demonstrates the effect of this amendment.

[148] Art 3(1) TFEU.   [149] Opinion 1/78 (n 37 above).

agreements the doctrine does not seem in practice to have discouraged the joint participation of the Union and the Member States in the negotiation and conclusion of agreements. Indeed, within the last two decades this tendency towards acceptance of non-exclusive competence has been marked. It is reflected both in Union/Member State practice and in the decisions of the Court. We can identify three linked strands to this development. The first is the approach of the Court of Justice to implied powers; the second is the decision of the Member States when amending the Treaty to categorize new express powers as explicitly non-exclusive—whether or not they are subject to pre-emption; the third is the way in which Article 4(3) TEU has been used to develop principles for managing shared competence.

2. IMPLIED POWERS AND PRE-EMPTION

Since 1990 the view adopted by the European Court towards shared competence and pre-emption in the context of implied powers has become considerably more nuanced, although its origins can yet again be traced back to the *AETR* case. Putting together the fact that the Treaty sets certain objectives (such as the adoption of a common transport policy) and the 'loyalty obligation' in Article 5 EEC (now Article 4(3) TFEU), the Court in *AETR* argued that '[i]t follows that to the extent to which Community rules are promulgated for the attainment of the objectives of the Treaty, the Member States cannot, outside the framework of the Community institutions, assume obligations which might affect those rules or alter their scope'.[150]

It can now be maintained that Member State competence is only excluded where its exercise would jeopardize Community objectives (not merely because the Community possesses competence, or has already acted, in particular areas) and it is not just assumed that any Member State action would necessarily have this effect—this will depend on the subject matter and nature of Community action.

The subject matter may be such that exclusive powers are necessary, such as fisheries conservation or commercial policy.[151] Or—in cases where there has been internal Union legislation—the nature of Union action may be such as to 'occupy the whole field' and pre-empt Member State action. In *AETR* the Court spoke in terms of the implementation of *common policies* but Opinion 2/91 makes it clear that the principle applies to all measures implementing Treaty objectives.[152] However, it is also clear that Union legislation is increasingly unlikely to occupy the field in this way. Flexibility, exceptions, and derogations built into directives, as well as the 'new approach' to harmonization and new modes of governance are a part of this story.

---

[150] Case 22/70 *Commission v Council* (n 82 above) [22].

[151] In Opinion 1/94 (n 17 above) [85]–[86] the Court also limits exclusivity in Opinion 1/76-type Cases (where there is no prior internal legislation) to situations where the Community objective *requires* the conclusion of agreements with third states: for example, conservation; in other cases external participation may not be essential for achieving EU objectives: for example, harmonization of intellectual property and freedom of establishment.

[152] Opinion 2/91 (n 13 above) [10]. See also C-45/07 *Commission v Greece*, 12 February 2009.

If Union action is of the nature of minimum harmonization so that competence is effectively shared internally, then shared external competence is possible. In the case of ILO Convention No 170 (concerning safety in the use of chemicals at work) considered in Opinion 2/91, some internal legislation had been adopted under social policy powers. The ILO Constitution itself is also drafted to allow for more stringent measures to be adopted by contracting parties. The Court held that there was no 'AETR effect' since it would always be possible to accommodate the adoption of higher standards.[153]

It is notable that Article 118a EC (now Article 153 TFEU), the legal base for the internal measures in this case, and from which the Court implied an external competence, was one which expressly preserves the power of the Member States to maintain or introduce 'more stringent protective measures compatible with the Treaties'. In this it is typical of provisions founding new Community competences introduced by both the Single European Act and the Treaty on European Union.[154]

Eighteen months later, the Court was again to declare that Community competence to conclude an agreement was shared with the Member States, in this case the agreements establishing the WTO, together with the revised GATT, and new GATS and TRIPS agreements. In Opinion 1/94 the Court held that (implied) Community competence to conclude GATS and TRIPS was not exclusive: although some harmonization of laws in the fields covered by the GATS and TRIPS had taken place it certainly did not cover all service sectors, and therefore international commitments would not 'affect' Community rules or distort competition. And although exclusive competence may arise from an explicit grant of powers to negotiate with non-member countries within secondary legislation in the field of services (such as under the Second Banking Directive, for example[155]), again, this did apply to the whole of the GATS.[156]

The Commission had argued that exclusive competence was necessary: internally, it was necessary for the cohesion of the internal market; externally it was necessary that the Community should not be inactive on the international scene: the WTO agreement represented a global approach to international trade, covering goods, services, and intellectual property. This was an argument clearly designed to reflect the Court's own reasoning in respect of the exclusivity of the common commercial policy.[157]

---

[153] Opinion 2/91(n 13 above) [18].

[154] Other earlier measures in the field of health and safety at work had been adopted under Art 100 EC, but also laid down minimum requirements and therefore in the view of the Court could not provide a foundation for *exclusive* Community competence externally: ibid [21].

[155] Council Directive (EEC) 89/646, [1989] OJ L386/1, Title III.

[156] Opinion 1/94 (n 17 above) [96]–[98]; see also [102]–[103] for similar reasoning in relation to TRIPS.

[157] Opinion 1/75 (n 37 above). It should also be remembered that in the context of the Inter-Governmental Conference which ultimately led to the Treaty on European Union, the Commission had argued for a re-drawing of the Community's external powers, including an extended 'external economic policy' within which Community competence would be exclusive. At one level, then, the Commission was seeking to persuade the Court to bring about judicially a result it had failed to achieve politically a few years before. As was seen above, following incremental amendment in the Treaties of Amstrerdam and Nice, exclusive Union competence over an extended CCP is now explicit as a result of the Treaty of Lisbon.

However, the Court suggests that further Community activity, especially in relation to third countries, would be the appropriate solution to any adverse effects or distortion.[158] So uniformity of external policy as between the Union and Member States in cases of implied powers depends on Union legislative activity rather than the *fiat* of the Court on the nature of implied powers—in marked contrast to the common commercial policy where the Court had stressed its exclusive character even where the common policy was manifestly incomplete.[159]

Two cases from the last decade illustrate the extent to which the Court sees it as necessary, in order to determine whether pre-emption has taken place, to investigate the detailed provisions of both the Union legislation and the international agreement in question; it is not enough merely to point to the existence of Union legislation in the field. In the *Open Skies* cases the conclusion was that although some aspects of the bilateral air services agreements concluded by Member States now fell within Union exclusive competence, other aspects did not, depending on the extent to which the relevant internal legislation regulated the position of third country service providers, and therefore would be 'affected' by Member State action in this respect.[160] The existence or not of a conflict between the agreement and the Union legislation was not itself a relevant factor: '[T]he failure of that Member State to fulfil its obligations lies in the fact that it was not authorised to enter into such a commitment on its own, even if the substance of that commitment does not conflict with Community law.'[161]

In both Opinion 1/94 and the *Open Skies* cases, the Court had not made a clear distinction between the existence of implied powers and their exclusive nature; some passages even appeared to imply that implied powers could only come into being under the conditions required for exclusivity.[162] However in its Opinion on the conclusion of the revised Lugano Convention, the Court confirmed that implied powers may indeed be either exclusive or shared with the Member States.[163] In order to determine exclusive competence a close examination of the agreement and its potential effects will be necessary:

> [T]he Community enjoys only conferred powers and that, accordingly, any competence, especially where it is exclusive and not expressly conferred by the Treaty, must have its basis in conclusions drawn from a specific analysis of the relationship between the agreement envisaged and the Community law in force and from which it is clear that the conclusion of such an agreement is capable of affecting the Community rules.[164]

This may require an examination not only of the scope but also of the nature and content of the rules laid down in the international agreement in the light not

---

[158] Opinion 1/94, (n 37 above) [79] and [90].

[159] See for example, Case 59/84 *Tezi-Textiel* [1986] ECR 887.

[160] C-476/98 *Commission v Germany* (n 17 above). R Holdgaard, 'The European Community's Implied External Competence After the Open Skies Cases' (2003) 28 ELRev 365.

[161] ibid 127.

[162] For example C-476/98 *Commission v Germany* (n 17 above) [120]–[121].

[163] Opinion 1/03 (n 17 above) [114]–[115].   [164] ibid [124].

only of the present state but also the future development of Union law 'insofar as that is foreseeable at the time of that analysis'.[165] In this case, the Union legislation (the Brussels Regulation on jurisdiction and enforcement of judgments in civil and commercial cases) established a 'unified and coherent system of rules on jurisdiction' and therefore an international agreement which establishes a similarly unified system will be capable of 'affecting' those rules.[166] And, the Court found, since the proposed Convention did indeed establish such a system, the Union's competence to conclude it was thereby rendered exclusive.

Setting aside the question of whether the Court did indeed accurately characterize the Union legislation and the Lugano Convention,[167] this case raises two points of interest to this discussion. First, the Convention in question was designed to replace an earlier Convention to which all Member States had been party. This was not a case of one or more Member States independently concluding bilateral agreements; the choice was rather between a collective participation of the Member States, or the exclusive participation of the Union (more like the WTO Agreements than *Open Skies*). In this sense the threat to uniformity was thus more theoretical than real; nevertheless this was sufficient to justify a finding of exclusivity. Secondly, the finding of exclusivity did not in fact prevent a threat to uniformity from a different source, that caused by the opt-out from this field of Union competence enjoyed by Denmark. When the Brussels Regulation was adopted, based on Title IV EC, the Brussels I Convention continued to apply between Denmark and the other Member States, who were bound by the new Regulation. In 2005 Denmark concluded a separate agreement with the Community with the aim of applying the Regulation in Denmark.[168] Denmark is thus not bound by the exclusive competence of the Union to conclude the revised Lugano Convention; instead, it concluded the Convention in its own right as a separate party, and rather than being bound *qua* EU Member State via Article 216(2) TFEU it is therefore bound in international law.[169] The agreement with Denmark provides for prior consultation and Union agreement before Denmark concludes any agreement with a third country which 'may affect' the Brussels Regulation.[170] So instead of exclusive competence pre-empting Member State action, here Denmark is circumscribed in its actions by its Union law (Article 4(3) TEU) obligations and its commitments under its agreement with the EU. In spite of the reasoning of the Court in Opinion 1/03 based on the unity

---

[165] ibid [126].   [166] ibid [151].

[167] J-J Kuipers, 'The Exclusive External Competence of the Union under Art 81 TFEU: Lugano Re-Opened?' in M Cremona, J Monar, and S Poli (eds), *The External Dimension Of The European Union's Area Of Freedom, Security And Justice* (forthcoming).

[168] Council Decision (EC) 2005/790 on the signing, on behalf of the Community, of the Agreement between the European Community and the Kingdom of Denmark on jurisdiction and the recognition and enforcement of judgments in civil and commercial matters, [2005] OJ L299/61.

[169] Thus on the one hand the Council Decision on the signing *by the EC* of the Lugano II Convention does not bind Denmark, while on the other hand the other signatories to this Convention are Iceland, Norway, Switzerland, and Denmark: see recitals 7 and 9 of the Decision approving the signing of the convention: Council Decision (EC) 2007/712 (?2007? OJ L339/1).

[170] Art 5 of the agreement with Denmark (n 168 above).

of the Union legal order, that unity is already breached by this differential legal basis for the application of the agreement, although one should add that the aim of all parties is that the Brussels Regulation and Lugano Convention should apply equally in all Member States.[171]

In Opinion 1/03 the Court justified the doctrine of pre-emption in terms of the unity of the common market, the uniform and consistent application of Union rules, and the 'proper functioning of the system they establish',[172] in other words in terms of the internal needs of the Union legal order. This internally oriented rationale may however produce effects not only on the ability of Member States to conclude a particular agreement but on their conduct in external fora. In *Commission v Greece*, for example, the Court found that Greece was in breach of its Treaty obligations by submitting a proposal to the International Maritime Organization (IMO) for monitoring compliance with international rules, the SOLAS Convention, and the International Ship and Port Facility Security Code (ISPS Code).[173] Although the Union is not a member of the IMO (which is open only to states) the rules in question had been incorporated into EU legislation and if the Greek proposal had been accepted the new rules would have had an effect on the EU Regulation. The *AETR* reasoning, the Court held, precluded Greece from setting in motion a process which might lead to the adoption of new rules requiring Union implementation. The absence of a Union common position on the issue did not—contrary to the argument put by Greece—legitimize national action. The existence of exclusive competence, based here on the pre-emptive effect of the EU Regulation, required the Member States to refrain from acting individually in the IMO; as far as this subject matter is concerned they must act jointly, via a common position, in the Union interest. This suggests that if there is no common position on a matter of exclusive competence, and no Union authorization, then no position can be taken by the Member States individually.

3. NEW NON-EXCLUSIVE COMPETENCES

In contrast to the silence of the original Treaty of Rome on the issue of exclusivity, the express external powers added to the Treaty by both the Single European Act and the Treaty on European Union envisage non-exclusive competence. This is of course true of the new explicit competencies added by those Treaties in general terms, not merely in the external sphere[174] and is linked to the developing concept of subsidiarity.

---

[171] According to Art 1(2) of the agreement with Denmark (n 168 above), '[i]t is the objective of the Contracting Parties to arrive at a uniform application and interpretation of the provisions of the Brussels I Regulation and its implementing measures in all Member States'.

[172] Opinion 1/03 (n 14 above) [122] and [128].

[173] C-45/07 *Commission v Greece* (n 152 above).

[174] See, for example, Art 169 TFEU on consumer protection which states that Union action is to 'support and supplement' Member State action, as well as safeguarding Member State rights to take Treaty-compatible measures which are more stringent than Union rules.

The external aspect of environmental policy is to be exercised by Union and Member States 'within their respective spheres of competence' and 'without prejudice' to the Member States' competence in the international arena.[175] This formula was also used when a specific provision on development cooperation policy was introduced by the TEU.[176] However, within development cooperation a significant new phraseology made its appearance. Union and Member State policy are to 'complement and reinforce' each other,[177] and this complementarity is to be achieved through coordination and consultation and the possibility of joint action.[178]

The reasons for this development are undoubtedly complex but among them is the legislative history of Community action in these areas. Prior to formal incorporation in the Treaty the Community had of course developed substantial environmental and development policies by means of a variety of measures (internal and external) and legal bases. The non-exclusive nature of Community competence in relation to both development aid and humanitarian aid had also been recognized by the Court of Justice.[179] It would have been difficult and unnecessary to argue for a new explicit exclusive competence against this background of incremental development. The Treaty of Amsterdam introduced a new non-exclusive external competence: economic, financial, and technical cooperation with third countries (now Article 212 TFEU), which provides a legal basis for non-development financial and technical assistance programmes[180] as well as agreements.[181] The Treaty of Lisbon continues the trend, with new express competences relating to humanitarian aid,[182] cooperation with third countries on asylum[183] and readmission agreements,[184] and other new competences such as civil protection, energy and tourism, which will have an external

---

[175] Art 191(4) TFEU.   [176] Now Art 208 TFEU.   [177] Art 208(1) TFEU.

[178] Art 210(1) TFEU. According to AG La Pergola, this provision for coordinated action helps to ensure that 'complementary competence, as defined in this sector, is thus able to operate in a manner fully compatible with the criterion of subsidiarity'; Case C-268/94 *Portuguese Republic v Council* [1996] ECR I-6177, Opinion of AG La Pergola [20].

[179] In Cases C-181/91 and C-248/91 *European Parliament v Council and Commission* [1993] ECR I-3685 (which concerned humanitarian aid to Bangladesh) the Court held at [16]: '[I]t should be pointed out that the Community does not have exclusive competence in the field of humanitarian aid, and that consequently the Member States are not precluded from exercising their competence in that regard collectively in the Council or outside it.' In Case C-316/91 *European Parliament v Council* [1994] ECR I-625 (which concerned financial assistance under the fourth Lomé Convention) the Court held at [26] 'The Community' s competence in that field [development aid] is not exclusive. The Member States are accordingly entitled to enter into commitments themselves vis-à-vis non-member States, either collectively or individually, or even jointly with the Community.' Characteristically, both these cases directly concerned the prerogatives of the European Parliament in the context of Community budgetary procedures. Issues of competence and legal base have frequently been fought out in the context of the inter-institutional balance of power. See generally L Bartels, 'Trade and Development Policy of the EU' in M Cremona (ed), *Developments in EU External Relations Law* (Oxford University Press, 2008).

[180] On the relationship with development cooperation in this respect, see Case C-155/07 *European Parliament v Council* [2008] ECR I-08103.

[181] Examples include the Partnership and Cooperation Agreements with the states of the former Soviet Union, which are now concluded under this legal base, and the UN Convention against Corruption.

[182] Art 214 TFEU; again, the EU and Member State actions are to 'complement and reinforce' each other.

[183] Art 78(2)(g) TFEU.   [184] Art 79(3) TFEU.

dimension. Indeed, the Treaty of Lisbon, in establishing and allocating competences to the different categories of exclusive, shared, and supporting, coordinating and supplementary, also makes explicit that the shared competences for development cooperation and humanitarian aid are a non-pre-emptive shared competence: '[T]he Union shall have competence to carry out activities and conduct a common policy; however, the exercise of that competence shall not result in Member States being prevented from exercising theirs.'[185]

A picture is thus emerging of shared and complementary competences, implying an overlapping of competence to make both policy and rules, but subject to the overriding obligation (derived from Article 3(4) TEU) that Member State action must be compatible with the Treaties and further the Union's objectives. What does this mean in practice? In the next section we will briefly outline some of the most important constraints on the Member States when acting within areas of shared competence.

4. MANAGING SHARED COMPETENCE

Although exclusivity and pre-emption are based on the need to safeguard the unity and interests of the Union, and are therefore ultimately founded on Article 4(3) TEU, shared competence is exercised in the framework of the duty of cooperation and in conformity with the principle of primacy of Union law, both of which are also based on Article 4(3) TEU. This section will illustrate that point with a few examples, certainly not exhaustive, which point to two distinct trends. On the one hand we can see some creative legislative ideas emerging for dealing with Member States' existing or future bilateral agreements, especially where competence is partly exclusive and partly shared. On the other hand, we can also see the Court developing an interpretation of the primacy of Union law and the duty of cooperation which is highly constraining, seeming at times to encroach on the existence and not only the exercise of competence.

In the aftermath of the *Open Skies* cases,[186] the Union was faced with two issues. On the one hand the ownership and control clauses in the Member States' bilateral air services agreements infringed Article 43 EC (now Article 49 TFEU) and there was therefore a need to renegotiate a large number of them. On the other hand the Court had decided that the agreements included elements of exclusive as well as shared competence. The solution involved a number of elements. Even where competence is shared, it may be more politically realistic for the Member States to negotiate collectively, especially if they need to persuade powerful third countries to extend the benefits of any agreement to all non-national EU service providers established in the contracting Member State. Despite the limited nature of EU exclusive competence in the field of air transport, the Council decided (after years of refusal) to grant the Commission a

---

[185] Art 4(4) TFEU.   [186] See n 17 above.

mandate to negotiate with third countries.[187] Second, and pending the negotiation of the Community agreements, the Council adopted a Regulation which attempts to give effect to the duty of cooperation in a field of shared competence where Member States are under an obligation to bring existing agreements into line with Community law.[188] The preamble to the Regulation refers to the duty of cooperation and confirms that the cooperation procedure established by the Regulation is 'without prejudice to the division of competences between the Community and Member States'.

The Regulation imposes two main types of obligation on the Member States, procedural and substantive. As far as procedural obligations are concerned, the Member States are to notify the Commission about the start, process, and conclusion of national negotiations, and the conclusion of the agreement is subject to authorization.[189] Substantively, Member States are to include in national negotiations relevant standard clauses developed jointly by the Commission and the Member States, and there are several obligations requiring equal treatment of all Union carriers. Thus the Regulation sets out in specific terms how the Member States' freedom to negotiate in an area of shared competence is constrained by the need to take into account not only compatibility with Community law but also the wider Community interest: the Commission will notify the Member States both if it sees a likely incompatibility and if it takes the view that the negotiations 'are likely to undermine the objectives of Community negotiations underway with the third country concerned'.[190] Even further, where the standard clauses are not incorporated into the agreement, authorization of its conclusion will depend on the terms of the agreement being found not to harm the object and purpose of EU transport policy.

The Member States have also agreed that the Union should negotiate, effectively on their behalf, amendments to their existing bilateral air transport agreements with third countries (so-called 'horizontal agreements').[191] Thus, in a field in which the standard international agreements fall partly but which are clearly not fully within exclusive competence, the primacy of Union law, the duty of cooperation, and the Union interest may be reflected in procedures designed to balance continuing Member State involvement and developing Union activity.

---

[187] Commission Communication on the consequences of the Court judgments of 5 November 2002 for European air transport policy, COM(2002) 649; Commission Communication on relations between the Community and third countries in the field of air transport, COM(2003) 94.

[188] Regulation (EC) 847/2004 on the Negotiation and Implementation of Air Service Agreements between Member States and Third Countries, [2004] OJ L/157/7; Recital 6 of the preamble states: 'All existing bilateral agreements between Member States and third countries that contain provisions contrary to Community law should be amended or replaced by new agreements that are wholly compatible with Community law.'

[189] ibid Art 1(2)–(4), Art 4.

[190] ibid Art 1(4).

[191] According to the Commission: 'Between June 2003 and August 2008, the method of separate bilateral negotiations has led to changes with 58 partner States, representing 118 bilateral agreements corrected. Under the second option, horizontal negotiations have led to changes with 36 partner states and one regional organisation with eight Member States, representing an additional 627 bilateral agreements. This approach has the advantages of simplicity, costs and speed', <http://ec.europa.eu/transport/air_portal/international/pillars/horizontal_agreements_en.htm>.

In a completely different sector, that of civil justice, we also find a creative legislative solution being found to practical difficulties following a ruling of exclusivity by the Court of Justice. In Opinion 1/03, as we have seen, the Court of Justice held that the Union possessed exclusive external competence in relation to matters affecting the Brussels I Regulation, that is, in relation to jurisdiction and the recognition and enforcement of judgments in civil and commercial matters. In the Commission's view, despite this exclusive competence there will not always be a Union interest in concluding agreements which contain provisions on jurisdiction and/or on recognition and enforcement of judgments.[192] Some of these agreements will be concerned with civil matters which fall essentially within Member State competence, such as family law. As a result two Regulations have recently been adopted relating to international agreements in the fields of (i) applicable law in relation to contractual and non-contractual obligations,[193] and (ii) jurisdiction, recognition, and enforcement of judgments and decisions in matrimonial matters, parental responsibility and maintenance obligations, and applicable law in matters relating to maintenance obligations.[194] The mechanism instituted by the Regulations both establishes a procedure for determining whether there is sufficient Union interest in the conclusion of a particular agreement by the Union, and if there is not, for authorizing the Member State to conclude the agreement itself. The two Regulations cover agreements falling wholly or partly within the scope of specific Community Regulations,[195] and which are 'sectoral', ie not horizontal agreements covering jurisdiction or recognition and enforcement generally, but only in relation to specific subject matters. The Commission argues that this procedure is better than either assuming that all agreements in these fields will be concluded by the EU, or trying to establish detailed rules for pre-authorization for each type of agreement. It preserves flexibility while providing a

---

[192] Regulation (EC) 44/2001 is of course not the only relevant legislation adopted in the field of civil justice which might give rise to exclusive competence; see also *inter alia* Council Regulation (EC) 2201/2003 concerning jurisdiction and the recognition and enforcement of judgments in matrimonial matters and matters of parental responsibility, [2003] OJ L338/1; Council Regulation (EC) 4/2009 on jurisdiction, applicable law, recognition and enforcement of decisions and cooperation in matters relating to maintenance obligations, [2009] OJ L7/1; European Parliament and Council Regulation (EC) 593/2008 on the law applicable to contractual obligations (Rome I), [2008] OJ L177/6; European Parliament and Council Regulation (EC) 864/2007 on the law applicable to non-contractual obligations (Rome II), [2007] OJ L199/40.

[193] Regulation (EC) 662/2009 establishing a procedure for the negotiation and conclusion of agreements between Member States and third countries on particular matters concerning the law applicable to contractual and non- contractual obligations, [2009] OJ L200/25.

[194] Council Regulation (EC) 664/2009 establishing a procedure for the negotiation and conclusion of agreements between Member States and third countries concerning jurisdiction, recognition and enforcement of judgments and decisions in matrimonial matters, matters of parental responsibility and matters relating to maintenance obligations, and the law applicable to matters relating to maintenance obligations, [2009] OJ L200/46.

[195] Regulation 662/2009 covers agreements concerning matters falling entirely or partly within the Rome I and Rome II Regulations (n 192 above); Regulation 664/2009 covers matters falling within the scope of Regulations 2201/2003 and 4/2009, 'to the extent that those matters fall within the exclusive competence of the Community' (n 192 above).

framework for taking the decision in each case. However little they might be used in practice,[196] these Regulations provide a striking example both of the implications of pre-emption for the Member States in fields of law hitherto their own, and of the possibility of devising practical legislative mechanisms to accommodate both the Union and the national interest.

A different type of mechanism, which allows Member States to take part in multilateral treaties which cover matters where there is a Union *acquis*, is the 'disconnection clause'. The clause, which has been used particularly in Conventions agreed within the Council of Europe framework, provides that as between EU Member States it will be EU law which will apply, rather than the international agreement; it is not intended to affect the position of the Member States with respect to other contracting parties. A recent example is found in the Council of Europe Convention on the Financing of Terrorism,[197] which provides in Article 52(4):

> Parties which are members of the European Union shall, in their mutual relations, apply Community and European Union rules in so far as there are Community or European Union rules governing the particular subject concerned and applicable to the specific case, without prejudice to the object and purpose of the present Convention and without prejudice to its full application with other Parties.

These clauses are not simple in their effects and there is no space to discuss them fully here.[198] They are intended to ensure the primacy of EU law for the Member States, to protect the autonomy of the EU legal order as far as the international obligations of its own Member States are concerned: when the Member States enter into an agreement which touches upon a field covered by EU law, they do so not only as contracting parties in their own right but also as Member States of the EU. Thus they are not merely entitled but are required to apply EU law 'in their mutual relations'. This example of 'EU exceptionalism' has attracted criticism both from the EU's negotiating partners and from commentators concerned about the fragmentation of international law.[199]

Although the UNCLOS does not contain a disconnection clause, the result in the *Mox Plant* case would have been more transparent to the other contracting parties had it done so.[200] The disconnection clause refers to the operation of substantive law, but

---

[196] J-J Kuipers, 'The Exclusive External Competence of the Union under Art 81 TFEU: Lugano Re-Opened?' in M Cremona, J Monar, and S Poli (eds), *The External Dimension of the European Union's Area Of Freedom, Security And Justice* (forthcoming).

[197] Council of Europe Convention on Laundering, Search, Seizure and Confiscation of the Proceeds from Crime and on the Financing of Terrorism, CETS No 198.

[198] See further M Cremona, 'Disconnection Clauses in EC Law and Practice' in C Hillion and P Koutrakos, *Mixed Agreements Revisited—The EU and its Member States in the World* (Hart, 2010).

[199] M Licková, 'European Exceptionalism in International Law' (2008) 19 EJIL 463. See also M Koskenniemi, *Fragmentation of International Law: Difficulties Arising from the Diversification and Expansion of International Law*, Report of the Study Group of the International Law Commission, doc A/CN.4/L.682, [289]–[294].

[200] C-459/03 *Commission v Ireland* (n 74 above).

what of the applicability between two EU Member States of international dispute settlement procedures under a mixed agreement? The establishment of a treaty regime external to the Union which involves dispute settlement mechanisms is not in itself controversial: the WTO would be an example of such a system. In such cases, the external dispute settlement body, court, or tribunal will interpret the provisions of an international agreement that is binding on the Union and such decisions, the Court has accepted, will be binding on the Community institutions, including the Court of Justice.[201] However, the Court has firmly resisted any suggestion that an external court might pronounce on Union law itself.[202] Under Article 344 TFEU (former Article 292 EC) the Court of Justice has exclusive jurisdiction over questions relating to 'the interpretation or application of the Treaties' and in the *Mox Plant* case the Court interpreted this to mean that a Member State was precluded from using the dispute settlement system set up by an international convention (UNCLOS) in a case against another Member State which dealt with provisions of the agreement that were within Community competence and thus raised questions of Community law. Since those provisions of the Convention form part of the Community legal order the Court has jurisdiction, and the agreement itself (by offering other forms of dispute settlement) cannot affect the autonomy of the Community legal order or its exclusive jurisdiction.[203] As we have already seen, compliance by the Member States with an international agreement entered into by the Union becomes a matter of Union law.[204] The Member States participate under shared competence in the environmental provisions of UNCLOS and this imposes constraints as to how they act within this multilateral Convention.

Let us look briefly at another recent case which raises the issue of Member State participation under shared competence in a multilateral convention—also an environmental convention. In *Commission v Sweden*,[205] the Court found that Sweden was in breach of its obligations under what was then Article 10 EC (now Article 4(3) TEU) as a result of having made a unilateral proposal within the framework of the Stockholm Convention on Persistent Organic Pollutants to add a chemical (perfluoroctane sulfonate, 'PFOS') to the list covered by the Convention. The Union and Member States are party to the Convention, whose provisions are implemented through Union legislation, and within the Union a committee procedure exists for deciding what submissions to make to the Convention regime for the inclusion of new substances.

---

[201] Opinion 1/91(n 91 above) [39]–[40]. This does not necessarily mean that they have direct effect: see, as far as rulings of the WTO Dispute Settlement Body are concerned, C-377/02 *Van Parys* [2005] ECR I-1465; T-69/00 *FIAMM v Council and Commission* [2005] ECR II-5393.

[202] It is worth noting the emphasis given by the Court in Opinion 2/94 (n 24 above) to the fact that by acceding to the ECHR the Community would be submitting itself to external adjudication; a decision to submit Union law to an external body would alter the Community legal system fundamentally and required explicit authority.

[203] Case C-459/03 *Commission v Ireland* (n 74 above) [121]–[123].

[204] See n 128 above.

[205] C-246/07 *Commission v Sweden*, 20 April 2010.

No agreement having been reached to submit PFOS within the EU's internal procedures, Sweden decided to put forward the proposal on its own account. There are clear
similarities here with *Commission v Greece* (IMO),[206] but it will be remembered that
that case involved an area of *exclusive* competence, whereas here we have a case of
shared competence, in a policy domain where the Treaties expressly protect the right
of Member States to introduce more stringent protective measures (and thus complete
uniformity is not the priority goal).[207] The Court in fact drew an analogy from two
previous cases where Germany and Luxembourg respectively had been found in
breach of Article 10 EC by concluding agreements with third countries in a situation
where a Community negotiating mandate had already been agreed.[208] Having found
that there was no exclusive Community competence, the Court had gone on to find
that the start of a 'concerted Community action at international level' requires 'if not a
duty of abstention on the part of the Member States, at the very least a duty of close
cooperation between the latter and the Community institutions in order to facilitate
the achievement of the Community tasks and to ensure the coherence and consistency
of the action and its international representation'.[209] In *Commission v Sweden*,
the Court cites these cases to argue that the duty of cooperation comes into play
once a Commission proposal or Council decision marks 'the point of departure for
concerted Community action'. Although here there had been no formal Council
decision the Court nevertheless denied that this was a 'decision-making vacuum',[210]
and identified a 'Community strategy' *not* to propose PFOS at that time:

> [I]t does not appear to be indispensable that a common position take a specific form for it
> to exist and to be taken into consideration in an action for failure to fulfil the obligation of
> cooperation in good faith, provided that the content of that position can be established to
> the requisite legal standard.[211]

In a case of exclusive competence, such as the *IMO* case, the Member States can only
act through a common position. That is not the case where competence is shared and
presumably in the absence of a common position Sweden could have acted; however
if—as in this case—the common position is not a formal act but is a strategy not to act,
identified from working party minutes and Council conclusions, the distinction is a
fine one.

Our final example concerns Member States' bilateral investment treaties (BITS).
The Commission was concerned that a number of these contain commitments to
ensure the transfer of payments relating to investment without including any safeguard clause or proviso which would allow the Member State to implement swiftly
restrictions on capital movements which might in the future be required as a result of

---

[206] See n 152 above.   [207] Art 193 TFEU.
[208] Case C-266/03 *Commission v Luxembourg* [2005] ECR I-4805; C-433/03 *Commission v Germany* [2005]
ECR I-6985.
[209] Case C-266/03 *Commission v Luxembourg* (n 208 above) [60].
[210] Case C-246/07 *Commission v Sweden* (n 205 above) [87].
[211] Case C-246/07 *Commission v Sweden* (n 205 above) [77].

restrictive measures adopted by the Union. Since such restrictive measures had not in fact been adopted in relation to the third countries in question, this was not a direct breach of any such act; rather, the Commission alleged a breach of Article 307 EC (now Article 351 TFEU) which requires Member States to eliminate any incompatibilities between their prior treaty commitments to third states and the EU Treaties.[212] The Court agreed with the Commission; in its view this was not merely a hypothetical future incompatibility, but a situation in which the *effet utile* of the power-conferring Treaty provisions was put in question:

> ...those powers of the Council, which consist in the unilateral adoption of restrictive measures with regard to third countries...reveal an incompatibility with that agreement where, first, the agreement does not contain a provision allowing the Member State concerned to exercise its rights and to fulfil its obligations as a member of the Community and, second, there is also no international-law mechanism which makes that possible.[213]

Having decided that the relevant international law mechanisms, such as *rebus sic stantibus,* were inadequate, the Court found the Member States to be in breach of Article 307(2) EC. There is obviously a question as to whether it is really possible to establish an incompatibility between a substantive treaty commitment (movement of capital in the BITS) and a power-conferring provision of the EU Treaties. If defensible at all, it must be on the grounds that the power in this special case (restrictive measures against capital flows) is effectively negated if it cannot be used with immediate effect.[214] Leaving this aside, Member States are now required to negotiate the amendment of their BITS at a time when a considerable part of their content has been brought by the Treaty of Lisbon within exclusive Union competence. Interestingly, in citing the injunction in Article 307(2) EC that the Member States are to assist each other in seeking to eliminate the incompatibilities, the Court directed the Commission 'to take any steps which may facilitate mutual assistance between the Member States concerned and their adoption of a common attitude'.[215] At the time of writing the outcome is not clear but it seems likely that since a large number of agreements are in issue a solution somewhat similar to that used in the *Open Skies* case will be found.[216]

As we have seen in these examples from a variety of fields of external policy, the Union and its Member States will very often be acting side by side and apart from the need to clarify the conditions under which pre-emption may take place (something that was attempted in Opinion 1/2003) there is a need to establish mechanisms and

---

[212] Case C-205/06 *Commission v Austria* (BITS), 3 March 2009; Case C-249/06 *Commission v Sweden* (BITS), 3 March 2009; Case C-118/07 *Commission v Finland* (BITS), 19 November 2009.

[213] Case C-205/06 *Commission v Austria* (n 212 above) [37].

[214] P Koutrakos, comment on Case C-205/06 *Commission v Austria* (BITS), 3 March 2009; Case C-249/06 *Commission v Sweden* (BITS), 3 March 2009, (2009) 46 CML Rev 2059.

[215] Case C-205/06 *Commission v Austria* (n 212 above) [44].

[216] See text at n 188 above; see the Commission proposal for a Regulation of the European Parliament and the Council establishing transitional arrangements for bilateral investment agreements between Member States and third countries, COM(2010) 344, 7 July 2010.

rules for managing these shared competences. On the one hand the Court has been prepared to use the loyalty clause to constrain the Member States' use of their own powers even where the Union has not yet decided to act, and on the other hand legislative mechanisms have allowed the Member States to act within a Union framework and, in some cases, under Union authorization. In all these cases, the priority has been to ensure the ability of the Union to act with unity, to avoid the fragmentation that would result from uncoordinated action, and to resolve (in favour of the Union) potential conflicts between the Member States' international and Union law obligations. The ability of the Union to be an effective international actor, whether in implementing economic sanctions or contributing to international environmental regulation, depends on the ability of the Union and its Member States to find ways of co-existing, of managing external policy so that the need for unity does not stifle action. Some of the cases we have considered (such as the PFOS case) may be said to fall the wrong side of that line.

D. THE EMERGENCE OF AN INTERNATIONAL IDENTITY FOR THE EU

The first edition of this chapter, written around the time of the Treaty of Amsterdam, posed a question about the international identity of the European Union which may still be asked: is it emerging from, and building upon, the undoubted international presence of the European Community, or is it still merely a poor relation, a rather ineffective mask for the very different national policies of the individual Member States? It identified an ambiguity in the attitude of the Member States to the European Union and a consequent imbalance between the Community and the Union of the time. The international capacity of the European Community was cited by the Court of Justice in *Costa v ENEL* as evidence to support the concept of a 'new legal order' with autonomous law-making institutions,[217] and the Community's legal personality, expressly declared in Article 210 EC, formed the basis for the development of its implied external powers.

From these beginnings the Community developed a formidable international identity. It is of course true in many instances, and particularly where regional policies are concerned, that Community policy has been driven by national policy interests and that reconciling these has not always been easy. The single negotiating voice of the Commission has sometimes struggled against dissenting national voices, even in areas of clear Community competence such as agriculture and transport. The need to hammer out a negotiating mandate or common position acceptable to all Member States and then to keep within it while retaining the flexibility essential to successful negotiation is certainly often difficult. Where a mixed agreement is being negotiated these tensions are accentuated. In spite of all this, there is no doubt that within its

---

[217] Case 6/64 *Costa* (n 5 above).

spheres of competence, and especially its 'core' external competence of trade policy, the Community has become a major international player. In the institutionalization of the world trading system through the establishment of the WTO the EC has played a key role and could even be said to have acted as a role model in some respects. Against this background the emerging international identity of the European Union was much more problematic.

A fundamental legal weakness in building the Union's role in the world until the Lisbon Treaty reform has been the ambiguity surrounding the legal personality of the Union itself,[218] the complication of retaining a separate international legal personality for the European Community, and the 'Pillar' structure, which was opaque to the outside world and posed complex challenges to coherence internally. Even the word 'identity' found in Article 2 EU, in which one of the Union's objectives was 'to assert its identity on the international scene', was a term carefully chosen to imply presence without mentioning legal personality. The Member States were trying to build up a sense of the Union as a significant actor 'on the international scene'. But they were trying to do this without transferring any external competences to the Union other than those that had already been transferred to the European Community. Although Article 24 EU, introduced by the Treaty of Amsterdam, and the practice that soon built up in concluding international agreements under this provision indicated that the Union possessed treaty-making powers, the absence of a clear statement of legal personality in the Treaty gave rise to confusion and a number of unanswered questions concerning international responsibility.[219] The kinds of contradictions to which this has led, including what Hill has called a 'capability–expectations gap', are well documented.[220] We appeared to have a gross imbalance between the European Community: an effective actor in limited economic-related technocratic fields; and the European Union: aspiring to greatness and with potentially wide fields of activity if Article 2 EU was to be taken seriously, but lacking legal and institutional mechanisms to make effective progress.

Has this changed over the last decade? What difference might the merger of the EC into the EU and the final resolution of the legal personality issue make? In the final section of this chapter, I should like to explore this question by looking at three concepts which are fundamental to an effective international identity—capacity, autonomy, and strategy—through the lens of one paradigmatic case, the *Kadi* case,[221] alongside some of

---

[218]   R A Wessel, 'The International Legal Status of the EU' (1997) 2 Eur Foreign Affairs Rev 109; N Neuwahl, 'A Partner with a Troubled Personality: EU Treaty-Making in Matters of CFSP and JHA after Amsterdam' (1998) 3 Eur Foreign Affairs Rev 177; R A Wessel, 'Revisiting the International Legal Status of the EU' (2000) 5 Eur Foreign Affairs Rev 507; R Gosalbo Bono, 'Some Reflections on the CFSP Legal Order' (2006) 43 CML Rev 354.

[219]   J Klabbers, 'Presumptive Personality: The European Union in International Law' in M Koskenniemi (ed), *International Law Aspects of the European Union* (Kluwer, 1998).

[220]   See eg C Hill, 'The Capability: Expectations Gap, or Conceptualizing Europe's International Role' [1993] 31 JCMS 305; E Regelsberger and W Wessels, 'The CFSP Institutions and Procedures: A Third Way for the Second Pillar' (1996) 1 Eur Foreign Affairs Rev 29.

[221]   Cases C-402/05 P and C-415/05 P *Kadi* (n 59 above).

the changes made by the Treaty of Lisbon. This case, which has prompted an avalanche of comment and reflection,[222] provides a fruitful perspective on the role of the Court of Justice in the development of the EU as an international actor. Of course this will be a very partial picture and each of these concepts deserves much fuller treatment, but it might help us to see the direction in which things are moving, and to appreciate the role of the Court of Justice in that process.

The international legal personality of the Union is now beyond doubt (Article 47 TEU) and it has 'replaced and succeeded' the European Community (Article 1 TEU). From the perspective of international action, capacity has two dimensions. In the first place, it requires recognition by the international community. The international community seems to have accepted the change from Community to Union without demur. In the Council of Europe's Treaty series, for example, we find the following note at the head of the explanatory reports for those Treaties open for signature by the European Community:

> The Treaty of Lisbon amending the Treaty on European Union and the Treaty establishing the European Community entered into force on 1 December 2009. As a consequence, as from that date, any reference to the European Community shall be read as the European Union.

However there are still limitations; the UN and its agencies[223] are open only to states and as a result the EU is in an ambiguous position with respect to the UN. In his judgment in the UK Supreme Court in the *Jabar Ahmed* case, Lord Hope said that the *Kadi* judgment 'is important and deserves close attention because of the way the ECJ dealt with the argument about the protection of fundamental rights'.[224] There are certainly signs that the UKSC was influenced by the *Kadi* approach.[225] However he also pointed out that 'caution must be exercised' by the Supreme Court in drawing conclusions from the case since 'the ECJ was not faced in *Kadi v Council of the European Union* with the problem that article 103 of the UN Charter gives rise to in member states in international law, as the institutions of the European Community are not party to the UN Charter'.[226]

---

[222] T Tridimas, 'Terrorism and the ECJ: Empowerment and Democracy in the EC Legal Order' (2009) 34 ELRev 103; Eeckhout (n 225 above); D Halberstam and E Stein, 'The United Nations, the European Union and the King of Sweden: Economic Sanctions and Individual Rights in a Plural World Order' (2009) 46 CML Rev 13; G de Búrca, 'The European Court of Justice and the International Legal Order after Kadi' (2010) 51 Harv Int'l LJ. More generally, see S Poli and M Tzanou, The Kadi Rulings: A Survey of the Literature (2009) 28 YEL 533.

[223] The FAO has changed its founding constitution to allow for EC (and now therefore EU) membership, but as we have seen this does not apply to other agencies such as the IMO (or IMF).

[224] *Her Majesty's Treasury v Mohammed Jabar Ahmed and others; Her Majesty's Treasury v Mohammed al-Ghabra; R (on the application of Hani El Sayed Sabaei Youssef) v Her Majesty's Treasury* [2010] UKSC 2, 27 January 2010, per Lord Hope [67].

[225] Particularly in finding the source of the fundamental right in domestic constitutional law; see P Eeckhout, 'Kadi and the EU as Instrument or Actor—Which Rule of Law for Counter-Terrorism?' in Cremona, Monar, and Poli (n 196 above).

[226] *Jabar Ahmed* (n 224 above) per Lord Hope [71].

The Court of Justice in *Kadi* did not follow the line taken by the CFI, which had argued that the EU was in any event bound by the UN Charter by analogy with the position taken by the Court in respect of the GATT in the *International Fruit Company* case.[227] It was able to distance itself from the problem that Article 103 of the UN Charter posed for EU Member States, saying that since it had no jurisdiction to pronounce on the validity of a UN Security Council Resolution, its judgment on the legality of the Union act 'would not entail any challenge to the primacy of that resolution in international law', and that in any event international law does not preclude judicial review of a domestic measure intended to implement a Security Council measure adopted under Chapter VII of the UN Charter.[228] Although it kept away from the issue of the binding nature of the UN Charter for the EU, the Court did however stress the need for the EU to 'observe the undertakings' given by its Member States in the context of the UN when enacting legislation on economic sanctions (arguing by analogy from the explicit provision with respect to development cooperation in Article 208(2) TFEU); to 'attach special importance' to the role of the UN Security Council; to 'take due account' of UNSC objectives in implementing the relevant Resolutions; and for the Court itself to refer to those objectives where necessary to interpret EU implementing legislation. We are left in no doubt, therefore, that the EU is acting in the framework of the UN system and making reference to it, even if it is not itself a member. The Treaty of Lisbon also indicates that the UN Charter has a special status for the EU: in both Articles 3(5) and 21 TEU, respect for the principles of the UN Charter is stated to be one of the basic principles guiding EU external policy. This careful wording in the Treaty itself,[229] then turns in Declaration 13 to the rather remarkable statement that:

> [The Conference] stresses that the European Union and its Member States will remain bound by the provisions of the Charter of the United Nations and, in particular, by the primary responsibility of the Security Council and of its Members for the maintenance of international peace and security.[230]

None of this alters the legal status of the EU towards the UN, of course; but given the increased role being played by the EU in support of UNSC resolutions (for example, the naval military operations to combat piracy off the coast of Somalia[231]) as unilateral declarations of intent they are nonetheless important.

---

[227] Case T-306/01 *Yusuf and Al Barakaat International Foundation* and Case T-315/01 *Kadi v Council and Commission* [2005] ECR II-03533; Cases 22–24/72 *International Fruit Company* (n 84 above).

[228] *Kadi* (n 59 above) [288] and [299].

[229] The reference to the principles of the Charter rather than simply the Charter reminds us of the formulation the Court habitually used to describe the ECHR.

[230] The central assertion in Declaration 13 is the continued competence and role of the Member States in respect of foreign policy, including diplomatic representation. Nevertheless it is interesting that the Declaration refers specifically to the *European Union* being (indeed 'remaining') bound by the UN Charter.

[231] Council Joint Action (CFSP) 2008/851 on a European Union military operation to contribute to the deterrence, prevention and repression of acts of piracy and armed robbery off the Somali coast, [2008] OJ L301/33; UNSC Resolutions 1814 (2008), 1816 (2008) and 1838 (2008).

The second dimension of the EU's international capacity is internal: the extent to which the EU may exercise its capacity to act is defined by the scope of the competences granted to it by its Member States. And of course the Court, with its formulation of implied powers and its willingness to take an open approach to the uses of trade policy powers, has been instrumental in shaping the capacity of the EC as an international actor. As we have already seen, although it was by no means clear that the EC had the competence to enact the regulation at issue in the *Kadi* case, the Court ultimately held that it did, discovering an 'implicit underlying objective' in the existing sanctions provisions—that objective being to make it possible to adopt restrictive measures of an economic nature through the efficient use of a Community instrument—thereby allowing the use of Article 308 EC to extend the Community's powers beyond those expressly granted in Articles 60 and 301 EC.[232] The Court's willingness to find a path to Community competence tells us something about its vision of the relationship between the Pillars and is in line with its recent case law on this point. In *Kadi* the Court insists that Article 308 EC cannot be used in order to achieve CFSP objectives (cf now Article 352(4) TFEU), but then defines *Community* objectives in such a way as to allow the use of a Community instrument for counter-terrorism purposes. In the *Small Arms* case the ECJ held that one effect of Article 47 EU was to require the use of an EC development instrument to achieve objectives that are security-based as much as they are development-based.[233] In both cases Community competence prevails and in both cases the Court stresses both the autonomy of the EC legal order with respect to the CFSP and the ability of the Community legal order to respond to new security challenges.

This takes us to the concept of autonomy, at the heart of the *Kadi* judgment but also underlying much of the case law discussed earlier in this chapter. This too has an internal and an external dimension. From an internal constitutional perspective, the Community legal order was, under the pre-Lisbon regime, protected not only from encroachment by the Member States through the doctrine of pre-emption, but also from possible encroachment by the CFSP. In the *Small Arms* case just mentioned the Court of Justice interpreted Article 47 EU as requiring that CFSP powers could not be used where EC powers were available.[234] Using its standard centre of gravity approach to legal base issues in order to distinguish between primary and incidental objectives, it then departed from that case law to hold that in the case of equally balanced CFSP and EC objectives, a joint legal base was not possible: Article 47 EU, in the ECJ's view, precluded that.[235] It thereby interpreted Article 47 EU as a delimitation rule, achieving

---

[232] Cases C-402/05 P and C-415/05 P *Kadi* (n 59 above) [226].

[233] Case C-91/05 *Commission v Council* (Small Arms) [2008] ECR I-03651.

[234] A Dashwood, 'Art 47 and the relationship between first and second pillar competences' in A Dashwood and M Maresceau (eds), *Law and Practice of EU External Relations—Salient Features of a Changing Landscape* (Cambridge University Press, 2008); C Hillion and R Wessel, 'Competence Distribution in EU External Relations After ECOWAS: Clarification or Continued Fuzziness?' (2009) 46 CML Rev 551.

[235] The standard legal base case law would permit a joint legal basis in such Cases (n 67 above). B Van Vooren, 'EU-EC External Competences after the Small Arms Judgment' (2009) 14 Eur Foreign Affairs Rev 7;

coherence via strict separation, rather than as a conflict rule, establishing priority in case of inconsistency but otherwise permitting some overlap of powers.[236] It was interesting in particular that this decision arose at the boundary of development and security powers, since, as we have seen, the Community's (and now Union's) development competence is complementary to the Member States. The Court itself has held that the Member States may choose to exercise their development competence individually or collectively, alongside the Community or jointly with it.[237] They could not, however, choose to exercise development powers through the CFSP; the Court expressly rejected the idea that the nature of EC development competence was of any relevance to Article 47 EU.[238] In *Kadi*, the Court of Justice also refused to countenance the use of Community powers for CFSP objectives, referring to 'the coexistence of the Union and the Community as integrated but separate legal orders, and the constitutional architecture of the pillars, as intended by the framers of the Treaties now in force'.[239] This last phrase reminds us that at the time of the *Kadi* judgment, although the fate of the Treaty of Lisbon was not yet known, its contents were. What is the position under the Treaties *now* in force?

The relationship between the TEU and TFEU is radically different; there is no reference in the TEU to building on the Community *acquis*; Article 1 of each Treaty proclaims their equal value, and Article 40 TEU significantly amends Article 47 EU. A distinction is still made between the CFSP and other powers—the shadow of the Pillars remains—but the need to protect non-CFSP powers from the CFSP is now matched by the need to protect the CFSP from non-CFSP. Community priority has disappeared. The provision is no longer phrased in terms of Treaty relationships but in terms of 'the application of the procedures and the extent of the powers of the institutions', in other words in terms of the standard legal base concerns of institutional balance.[240] Article 352(4) TFEU, in preventing the use of the flexibility clause to achieve CFSP objectives, echoes the Court in *Kadi* but in this case the aim is at least as much to ensure that the 'specific rules and procedures' of the CFSP[241] are not sidelined by use of the normal legislative procedure (with its co-legislator role for the European Parliament) via Article 352 TFEU: there is an explicit reference to Article 40(2) TEU. The 'specific rules and procedures' applied to the CFSP do not put into question the Union's single legal order; the chapter on the CFSP is included in the same Title as, and is subject to, the general principles governing the Union's external action: it is part of that external action and part of the

---

B Van Vooren, 'The Small Arms Judgment in an Age of Constitutional Turmoil' (2009) 14 Eur Foreign Affairs Rev 231.

[236] For further discussion see M Cremona, 'Coherence in EU Foreign Relations Law' in P Koutrakos (ed), *EU Foreign Policy—Legal and Political Perspectives* (forthcoming).

[237] See Cases C-181/91 and C-248/91 *European Parliament v Council and Commission* and Case C-316/91 *European Parliament v Council* (n 179 above).

[238] Case C-91/05 *Commission v Council* (n 233 above).

[239] Cases C-402/05 P and C-415/05 P *Kadi* (n 59 above) [202].

[240] J-P Jacqué, 'The Principle of Institutional Balance' (2004) 41 CML Rev 383.

[241] Art 24(1) TEU.

same legal system, albeit with a different institutional balance and decision-making procedure. Overall, then, there is no reason to interpret Article 40 TEU in the same way as Article 47 EU was interpreted (which is not to say that the Court might not do so). Autonomy, in fact, has become a defining characteristic of the EU legal order as a whole, not of the EC legal order set against the EU.

The autonomy of the EU legal order as a whole is defined in terms of its relation to its Member States (from which it derives its capacity to act), and to international law (of which it is a part). It is in relation to the second of these dimensions of autonomy that the Court of Justice in *Kadi* had significant points to make, athough the outcome of the case shows how inter-connected they are. Whereas both the CFI and AG Poiares Maduro framed their discussion—although with very different results—in terms of the relationship between EC law and international law, the ECJ's judgment is striking in the way that it does not start from that dichotomy, but instead frames the case in terms of what it calls the EC's own constitutional principles, in particular those governing judicial review. At the start of the relevant part of the judgment,[242] the Court reasserts the need for judicial review based on the rule of law, citing *Les Verts*,[243] and then goes on to affirm the autonomy of the Community legal order ensured by the exclusive jurisdiction of the Court (recalling the *Mox Plant* judgment). It makes the key claim that, when it comes to adjudicating on the lawfulness of Union acts, the constitutional principles of the Treaties must take precedence over the obligations flowing from an international agreement. International law takes effect within the Community legal order, not automatically, but through Treaty provisions especially Article 300(7) EC (now Article 216(2) TFEU) and specific implementing legislation, as had happened in this case. Since in *Kadi* the issue was not that the EU institutions had enacted secondary law allegedly in breach of international law, but rather that the institutions' desire to comply with international law brought about a breach with primary EC law, the Court was able to keep the UNSC Resolution in the background and to treat the case as an essentially 'internal affair': not EU law versus international law but secondary EU law versus primary EU law.

The ECJ therefore firmly situates the debate within the Community legal order and its constitutional principles. It emphasizes the autonomy of the Union legal order, but this is not just another way of saying that EU law is isolated from international law. The Court after all spends some time discussing the ways in which international law takes effect in the EU system, and the ways in which international norms interact with EU law are both complex and mutual.[244] Rather, autonomy is used by the Court to

---

[242] Cases C-402/05 P and C-415/05 P *Kadi* (n 59 above) [278] *et seq.*

[243] Case 294/83 *Les Verts v Parliament* [1986] ECR 1339.

[244] For a discussion of the ways in which international law both influences and is shaped by EU law and policy see M Cremona, 'Values in EU Foreign Policy' in M Evans and P Koutrakos (eds), *Beyond the Established Orders: Policy Interconnections between the EU and the Rest of the World* (forthcoming); J Wouters, A Nollkaemper, and E de Wet (eds), *The Europeanisation of International Law: The Status of International Law in the EU and its Member States* (TMC Asser Press, 2008); S Lucarelli and I Manners (eds), *Values and*

mean that it is a matter for EU law to determine the effect of international law in the EU legal order, to establish the conditions, as other constitutions do. The Court is claiming that the EU Treaties are not merely one treaty among many others whose inter-relations are determined by international law rules.[245] It is a constitutional order, which determines its own relationship to international law,[246] and also thereby influences the position of international law in the domestic legal orders of its own Member States,[247] and the Member States' ability to use international law in their own mutual relations.[248] From this perspective, the Court of Justice is helping to define the EU's international identity by insisting on its distinctiveness and its ability to define its relationship to international norms.

How does the Treaty of Lisbon respond to this position? It does not add anything specific to Article 216(2) TFEU, or anywhere else, which would confirm or otherwise the Court's view of the place of international norms in the EU legal order. However, it does reiterate more than once the Union's commitment to the observance and development of international law in general and the UN Charter, in particular Articles 3(5) and 21 TEU. These are of course 'virtuous' statements made at a sufficient level of generality not to answer the tough questions of the kind that *Kadi* posed. But they do tell us that the Union sees itself as an active participant in the evolving international system with a strategy that requires full engagement to 'uphold and promote its values and interests' and the capacity for autonomous action to carry this out. Article 3(5) TEU is the most fundamental statement of Union foreign relations strategy and here the Treaty refers to the 'development' of international law: the EU commits itself to participating in the formation of international norms as well as to multilateral cooperation (Article 21 TEU). An actor of that kind needs its autonomy, an ability to determine its strategy and policies. It can indeed be argued that the Treaty of Lisbon requires the Union to develop an overall foreign policy strategy and to maintain coherence to that stategy and constitutionalizes what that strategy might look like.[249] Institutionally, the European Council is given a crucial role: its strategy-defining responsibility is reiterated in general terms (Article 15(1) TEU), in the general provisions on external action (Article 22(1) TEU), and in the context of the CFSP

Principles in European Union Foreign Policy (Routledge, 2006); F Hoffmeister, 'The Contribution of EU Practice to International Law' in M Cremona (ed), *Developments in EU External Relations Law* (Oxford University Press, 2008).

[245] J Klabbers, *Treaty Conflict and the European Union* (Cambridge University Press, 2009).

[246] It is interesting that AG Maduro uses the phrase 'a municipal legal order of transnational dimensions' to describe the EU legal order: Cases C-402/05 P and C-415/05 P *Kadi* (n 59 above) Opinion of AG Maduro [21].

[247] S Besson, 'European Legal Pluralism after *Kadi*' (2009) 5 ECLRev 237.

[248] See, eg, Case C-459/03 *Commission v Ireland* (Mox Plant) (n 74 above); Case 10/61 *Commission v Italy* [1962] ECR 1.

[249] M Cremona and P Vennesson, 'Facing Global Challenges: the Lisbon Treaty and the European Union's External Relations', EUI Rev, Spring 2010, 13. A strategy in this sense is distinct from specific strategy documents, which are themselves becoming more common, such as the European Security Strategy, the strategies for Weapons of Mass Destruction and Small Arms and Light Weapons, and the European Consensus on Development.

(Article 26(1) TEU). Articles 3(5) and 21 TEU offer an indication of what that strategy's priorities should be and the principles on which it should be based: (among others) promoting values as well as interests, the rule of law, human rights and sustainable development, free and fair trade and support for global governance, and the development of international law. These are to inform not only all external policies but also the external aspects of its other policies. It is not easy to predict at this point what impact these principles and objectives will have; it will be interesting to see how much weight the Court might give them as constitutional principles which help to shape policy and which are certainly intended to define the international identity the EU wishes to project.

10

EU JUSTICE AND HOME AFFAIRS LAW (NON-CIVIL)

Steve Peers*

A. INTRODUCTION

Perhaps more than any other EU policy field, EU Justice and Home Affairs (JHA) law has been subject to a complex institutional evolution, culminating in the application (to a large degree) of the 'Community' approach to decision-making, legal instruments, and jurisdiction of the Court of Justice with the entry into force of the Treaty of Lisbon. The trade-off for this evolution has been (as with the creation of monetary union) an opt-out for those Member States with misgivings about applying a supranational institutional framework to this area.

The evolution of EU policy in this area has been less dramatic, although it is clear that to date, different models have been followed in different areas of JHA law (visas/ borders, asylum, irregular immigration, legal immigration, and criminal law), with some degree of evolution in the models followed, particularly as regards asylum and legal migration.[1] In particular, there are interesting points of comparison between this area and some of the principles underlying the development of the internal market.

B. INSTITUTIONAL EVOLUTION

1. PRIOR TO 1993

The EU's institutional framework for the adoption of JHA law has gone through several phases. First of all, there was a purely informal and intergovernmental phase, before the entry into force of the Maastricht Treaty in November 1993. During this phase, some international treaties (conventions) were concluded between Member States, largely within the framework of European Political Cooperation (EPC),

---

* Professor at the University of Essex.

[1] For reasons of space, the issue of EU policing law is not examined in depth.

mostly addressing criminal law issues.[2] Generally speaking, this approach to cooperation proved ineffective, as the Conventions concerned were not ratified, except for the Dublin Convention on responsibility for asylum requests, which took seven years to enter into force, and earlier civil law Conventions which were explicitly or implicitly linked to the EC legal order.[3] There was consistently no role given to the Community institutions as regards the negotiation of these Conventions, with the notable exception of jurisdiction for the Court of Justice to interpret the civil law Conventions—albeit subject to more restrictive jurisdictional rules than applied under the EEC Treaty.[4]

Outside the Community legal framework, but linked to the internal market project, the Schengen process among a small number of Member States—which entailed the adoption of treaties and implementing measures concerning the abolition of internal border controls and the parallel compensatory measures which were deemed necessary to increase security—started during this period, beginning with a short Agreement in 1985 and subsequently a longer Convention implementing the Schengen Agreement (the 'Schengen Convention') in 1990.[5] In light of the opposition of some Member States to the substance of the Convention (the UK, Ireland, and, at the time, Denmark), this approach proved more effective than intergovernmentalism among all Member States of the Community, as the implementing Schengen Convention was ratified in 1993, only three years after signature.

However, given the limited role of national parliaments and the European Parliament (EP) and the secrecy that attached to the negotiation of the Schengen Conventions and the negotiation and adoption of measures implementing them, the serious gaps in legitimacy began at this time.

2. 1993–1999

The next phase in this evolution could be described as formal intergovernmentalism, as applied during the Maastricht era (1993–99). The original TEU provided for specific rules relating to JHA (Title V of the original TEU, Articles K to K.9), but these rules nevertheless established an essentially intergovernmental process, specifying that the Council could adopt either Conventions or other acts, which were not clearly defined (Joint Actions, Joint Positions, and Common Positions). The original TEU established a distinct Treaty structure setting out a different institutional framework as regards the Community treaties (known in practice as the 'First Pillar', following the metaphor of

---

[2] For the texts of a number of these EPC conventions, see: <http://www.asser.nl/Default.aspx?site_id=8&level1=10785&level2=10846>.

[3] [1997] OJ C254 (Dublin Convention); [1998] OJ C27/1 (Brussels Convention) and [1998] OJ C27/34 (Rome Convention).

[4] See the Protocols to these Conventions (ibid).

[5] [2000] OJ L239. See generally D O'Keeffe, 'The Schengen Convention: A Suitable Model for European Integration?' (1991) 11 YEL 185, and J Schutte, 'Schengen: Its Meaning for the Free Movement of Persons in Europe' (1991) 28 CML Rev 549.

a Greek temple), Common Foreign and Security Policy (the Second Pillar), and JHA law (the Third Pillar).[6]

There was an official role for the EC institutions other than the Council, but it was very limited. The Court of Justice was not awarded any mandatory jurisdiction, but rather there was the case by case possibility of giving it jurisdiction over dispute settlement or references from national courts as regards each Third Pillar Convention.[7] In practice, the Court was given jurisdiction over two civil law Conventions concluded during this period, but Member States could not agree on a common approach as regards criminal law and policing Conventions. Instead, by way of compromise, they agreed on a multi-speed approach, by which Member States could opt to give the Court of Justice jurisdiction over references from all national courts, or from final courts only, or from no national courts at all.[8] As for the European Parliament, it did not even have the right to be consulted on individual measures (even Conventions), but only the right to be 'regularly inform[ed]' of discussions and 'consult[ed]' by the Member State holding the rotating Council Presidency on the 'principal aspects' of discussions.[9] The Commission was not only required to share the right of initiative with individual Member States, but was even refused this joint right of initiative in specified areas (essentially, policing and criminal law). By way of derogation, the Community method did apply to some specific issues relating to visas.[10]

While the intergovernmental approach certainly preserved maximum control for Member States' governments, it arguably imposed significant limits on the effectiveness of EU action. Of the eight policing and criminal law conventions agreed during the Maastricht period, only six entered in force—and it took between four and eleven years to ratify these measures.[11] The legal effect of measures other than Conventions was unclear, and soft law was widely used instead, in particular as regards immigration and asylum law (except for the Dublin Convention, which had been signed before the Maastricht Treaty anyway).

---

[6] See, *inter alia*, D Curtin, 'The Constitutional structure of the Union: A Europe of bits and pieces', (1993) 30 CML Rev 17; P Müller-Graff, 'The Legal Bases of the Third Pillar and its Position in the Framework of the Union Treaty' (1994) 29 CML Rev 493.

[7] Art K.3(2)(c), original TEU. No jurisdiction was possible as regards other Third Pillar measures.

[8] S Peers, 'Who's Judging the Watchmen?' The Judicial System of the Area of Freedom, Security and Justice' (2000) 18 YEL 337.

[9] Art K.6, original TEU.

[10] Arts 100c and 100d EC, subsequently repealed by the Treaty of Amsterdam, concerning visa lists and a common visa format. These provisions were subject to the Commission's right of initiative and the consultation of the EP, with QMV applicable to Council voting either immediately (as regards visa formats) or from the start of 1996 (as regards visa lists). On the scope of the visa list power, see Case C-170/96 *Commission v Council* [1998] ECR I-2763.

[11] The quickest ratification was the Europol Convention, [1995] OJ C316, ratified by 1999, while the Second Protocol to the Convention on the Protection of the EU's financial interests, [1997] OJ C221/12 was signed in 1997 and entered into force in 2009. The Conventions on extradition, [1995] OJ C78/1 and [1996] OJ C313/11, and driving disqualification [1998] OJ C216/1, never entered into force.

However, cooperation within the Schengen framework proved more effective during this period, despite sharing the intergovernmental approach, perhaps because it involved a more limited number of Member States which had agreed on the fundamental aspects of the cooperation concerned. The 1990 Schengen Convention was applied from March 1995, expanded to include more states, and implemented by means of a number of measures adopted by the Committee (the 'Executive Committee') established to that end by the Schengen Convention.[12] On the other hand, it became clear that the scope of cooperation established by the Convention exceeded the capacity of the Schengen institutional framework to deal with it—in particular in the absence of any dedicated administrative staff for the Schengen process.

3. 1999–2005

The next period, the initial 'Amsterdam era' (from the entry into force of the Treaty of Amsterdam to 2004–05), could best be described as 'modified intergovernmentalism', consisting as it did of retaining the key features of the intergovernmental approach with some modest concessions to the Community method. First of all, the Treaty of Amsterdam transferred the issues of immigration and asylum law to the First Pillar,[13] in order to make use of the Community legal order, but not without adopting special transitional rules as regards the application of traditional Community rules.[14] These rules were set out in a special Title IV of Part Three of the EC Treaty (known as 'Title IV'). While the legal instruments of EC law (ie regulations and directives) applied from the outset, for a five-year transitional period (ie until 1 May 2004), decision-making was subject not only to unanimity in the Council and consultation of the EP, but also the shared initiative of the Commission and the Member States.[15] The rule of the Court of Justice was curtailed as regards references from national courts, with only final courts in each Member State able to send questions to the Court. While there were no distinct rules regarding implementing measures, in practice the Council gave itself and even individual Member States powers to adopt implementing measures, and this unorthodox practice was even supported by the Court of Justice, in light of the transitional and historical context.[16] Taken as a whole, then, the issues transferred to the First Pillar were still subject in the *political* sense to an intergovernmental regime.

The issues remaining in the Third Pillar (policing and criminal law) were subjected to even fewer elements of the Community legal order. The Commission gained a purely joint right of initiative with Member States, and the EP gained consultation power over nearly every measure,[17] but in both cases this compared poorly with those

---

[12] Those implementing measures which were subsequently integrated into the EU legal order were also published in [2000] OJ L239.

[13] The Treaty also transferred civil law, the subject of Chapter 11 of this book, to the First Pillar.

[14] Arts 67 and 68 EC.

[15] There was a continued exception as regards visa lists and the visa format: Art 67(3) EC.

[16] Case C-257/01 *Commission v Council* [2005] ECR I-345.

[17] Arts 34 and 37, previous TEU.

institutions' role as regards EC law, in particular given that the Treaty of Amsterdam had also simplified (to the EP's benefit) and greatly expanded the scope of the co-decision process. The jurisdiction of the Court of Justice was now subject to standard rules, which in effect entrenched the 'variable geometry' approach already agreed as regards the Court's jurisdiction over Third Pillar Conventions, leaving it to each Member State to opt for full jurisdiction over references, no jurisdiction at all over references, or jurisdiction over references from top courts only.[18] But these standard rules applied not only to conventions, but also to nearly all Third Pillar measures adopted after the entry into force of the Treaty of Amsterdam, and moreover the Court gained jurisdiction over annulment actions and was subject to standard rules as regards jurisdiction over dispute settlement between Member States (or between Member States and the Commission).[19]

The drafters of the Treaty of Amsterdam were willing to agree greater changes as regards the legal instruments to be used in the remaining Third Pillar.[20] Conventions and common positions were retained, but there were two important new types of measure: framework decisions, to be used to approximate national law, with exactly the same definition as a directive, while ruling out direct effect; and decisions, to be used for any other purpose other than approximation of national law, while again ruling out direct effect. In practice, the Council was attracted to the greater efficiency offered by these measures, since they did not have to be ratified as such by national parliaments in order to take effect. To that end, the Council effectively phased out the use of conventions and protocols, with the last such instrument adopted in 2003; it is surely not coincidental that no new such measures were adopted after the huge EU enlargement of 2004, which promised even greater delays before conventions and protocols entered into force. This change in practice came despite an attempt by the drafters of the Treaty of Amsterdam to speed up ratification of conventions, by allowing them to enter into force for the Member States concerned once a majority of Member States had ratified them. Despite these amendments, it still took between three and seven years for those Conventions and Protocols which were signed after the Treaty of Amsterdam to enter into force.[21]

---

[18] In practice, by the end of the Amsterdam period nineteen Member States had given the Court jurisdiction (all except the UK, Ireland, and Denmark among the first fifteen Member States, and Poland, Estonia, Slovakia, Bulgaria, and Malta among the newer Member States, [2010] OJ L56/14. Only Spain restricted the Court's jurisdiction to final courts only.

[19] Art 35, previous TEU. Note that the Commission only had a dispute settlement role as regards Conventions, not any other form of Third Pillar act, and so lacked any equivalent authority to the First Pillar power to bring infringement proceedings. On the Court's jurisdiction over JHA in general under the Treaty of Amsterdam, see Peers (n 8 above).

[20] Art 34 TEU.

[21] These measures consisted of three further Protocols to the Europol Convention, [2000] OJ C358/1, [2002] OJ C312/2, and [2004] OJ C2/1, all in force in 2007; another Protocol to the Convention establishing the Customs Information System, [2003] OJ C139/1, in force 2007; and a Convention on mutual assistance in criminal matters, [2000] OJ C197), with a subsequent Protocol [2001] OJ C326, both in force in 2005. As of January 2011, some Member States had still not ratified the latter three measures.

Moreover, a number of pre-Amsterdam Joint Actions and conventions were replaced by framework decisions and decisions. The phasing out of new conventions and the replacement of prior Conventions meant that national parliaments no longer had a power of approval over the main Third Pillar acts, although in many cases national parliaments tried to maintain influence in this area by insisting on scrutiny reserves, which delayed the formal adoption of measures but did not appear to have any significant influence on the content of any measures.

Finally, the last significant changes introduced by the Treaty of Amsterdam both related to 'closer cooperation' (as it was then known) in this area between certain Member States. First of all, the Schengen *acquis* (ie the Schengen Conventions and the measures implementing them) was integrated into the EU and EC legal order, granting special status for the UK and Ireland (and, to a certain extent Denmark) but otherwise incorporating both the prior Schengen measures and future measures building upon the *acquis* into the EC and EU system. This brought an already established system of 'closer cooperation' (as it was then known) into the EC and EU framework, instead of leaving it outside.[22] Secondly, the UK, Ireland, and Denmark were given a more general power to opt out of all Title IV legislation, with capacity (in the case of the UK and Ireland) to opt in either at the initial stage of discussions, or after adoption of a measure. There was a clear link between these specific new provisions on closer cooperation and the institutional reform (limited as it was initially) as regards immigration and asylum law. Put simply, the UK, Ireland, and Denmark were willing to accept the expansion of the EC's role in this field if they could be exempted from the automatic application of it.

Finally, it should be noted that shortly after the entry into force of the Treaty of Amsterdam, the European Council began the process of adopting high-profile multi-year programmes offering political direction for the development of JHA law and policy. The first such programme was the Tampere programme, adopted in autumn 2009.

4. 2005–2009

At the mid-point in the Amsterdam period (which lasted from 1999–2009), in approximately 2004–05, a number of developments altered the institutional framework as regards EU JHA law, so that the remaining period might almost be considered a 'residual intergovernmental' period.

These changes were most obvious as regards immigration and asylum law,[23] where after the initial five-year transitional period ended on 1 May 2004, the Commission (pursuant to the Treaty) automatically gained its right of initiative, and the co-decision

---

[22] On the Schengen integration process, see generally D Thym, 'Schengen Law: A Challenge for Legal Accountability in the European Union' (2002) 8 ELJ 218; S Peers, '*Caveat Emptor*? Integrating the Schengen *Acquis* into the European Union Legal Order' (2000) 2 CYELS 87.

[23] There were also changes to decision-making as regards civil law, the subject of Chapter 11.

procedure (with QMV) applied to all visa legislation.[24] Although the further extension of co-decision (including QMV) and any change to the jurisdiction of the Court of Justice was dependent on a unanimous vote in the Council, it was soon agreed as part of the Hague Programme (the second multi-year programme for the development of EU JHA policy, agreed at the end of 2004)[25] that the Council would adopt a decision changing the rules to apply co-decision (with QMV) to all Title IV matters except legal migration (and family law), which remained subject to unanimity in Council and consultation of the EP, and visa lists and visa formats, which remained subject to QMV in Council with consultation of the EP.[26] This Decision took effect from 1 January 2005.[27]

Also, in the meantime, the Treaty of Nice, which entered into force on 1 February 2003, had amended the decision-making rules so that the decision-making rules on asylum matters (except for burden-sharing between Member States) would shift to QMV and co-decision as soon as the Council adopted EC measures 'defining the common rules and basic principles' on asylum issues.[28] The Treaty of Nice also added a Protocol to the EC Treaty which required the Council to act by QMV, consulting the EP, when adopting measures on administrative cooperation within the scope of Title IV.[29] These changes meant that the EP was able to have a significant influence on the adoption of visas and borders legislation in particular after this point, winning a number of battles in particular on procedural rights and data protection.[30] Even in the areas still subject to unanimous voting, there was some greater willingness by the Council to intervene at EU level. So although the first (far-reaching) attempt to adopt EC legislation on labour migration was unsuccessful in the early post-Amsterdam period,[31] the Council was nonetheless willing to adopt the 'Blue Card' Directive in 2009, encouraging the migration of highly skilled migrants to the EU.[32] The shift toward the traditional Community method is also

---

[24] Art 67(4) EC. There was an exception for legislation on visa lists and the visa format, which was still subject to adoption by QMV and consultation of the EP, pursuant to Art 67(3).

[25] [2005] OJ C53.

[26] Emergency measures (Art 64(2) EC) remained subject to QMV in Council with no EP involvement.

[27] [2004] OJ L396/45; S Peers, 'Transforming Decision-Making on EC Immigration and Asylum Law' (2005) 30 ELRev 283.

[28] Art 67(5). On the interpretation of this clause, see the judgment in Case C-133/06 *EP v Council* [2008] ECR I-3189, which implies that the rules changed at the latest from 1 December 2005, when the last of the basic EC asylum laws was adopted. The decision-making rules on asylum burden-sharing shifted separately to QMV and co-decision on 1 January 2005 (see ibid).

[29] Art 66 EC.

[30] The EP in particular played a notable role as regards negotiations on a Schengen Borders Code (Regulation 562/2006, [2006] OJ L105/1), the EU's visa code (Regulation 810/2009, [2009] OJ L243/1), the legislation establishing the second generation Schengen Information System, or 'SIS II' (Regulation 1987/2006, [2006] OJ L381/4), and (more controversially), the so-called 'Returns Directive' on the rules governing expulsion of third-country nationals who have stayed irregularly (Directive 2008/115, [2008] OJ L348/98).

[31] Proposed Directive (COM (2001) 386).

[32] Directive 2009/50, [2009] OJ L155/17. See further Section C.4 below.

evidenced by the replacement of nearly the entire Schengen *acquis* in this area between 2005 and 2009.[33]

On the other hand, no changes were made to the jurisdiction of the Court of Justice.[34] Nevertheless, beginning also in 2005, the Court began to receive references from national courts as regards EC immigration and asylum law. Although it only received eleven such references from 2005–09, the Court was nevertheless thereby able to begin to influence the implementation of EC legislation in practice, in a way which will be familiar to followers of the Court's jurisprudence in any other fields of EU law. In particular (treating joined cases as a single case), there was one reference in 2005 (the first on visas/borders issues),[35] one in 2007 (the first asylum law case),[36] five in 2008 (including the first reference on legal migration law),[37] and four in 2009 (including the first reference on irregular migration legislation).[38] The Commission also brought a large number of infringement actions against Member States.

The *quid pro quo* for these developments was the strengthening in practice of the British and Irish opt-outs from this field. In particular, those Member States now opted out of most irregular migration and asylum measures,[39] whereas they had generally opted into measures in these fields adopted up until 2004–05. This process was exacerbated, as regards measures building on the Schengen *acquis*, by rulings of the Court of Justice that required the Council to lock the UK and Ireland out of new measures which related to provisions of the Schengen *acquis* (ie external border control) which the UK and Ireland had not opted in to, even if the new measures did not amend that original *acquis*.[40]

As for the Third Pillar, from 2005–09 it still remained intergovernmental in principle, but Member States were in effect fighting a two-front war. On the one hand, aspects of EU criminal law and policing policy were shifting to the First Pillar, as regards in

---

[33] The prior measures were replaced by the Schengen Borders Code, the visa code, and the SIS II legislation (n 30 above), although the latter is not yet applied in practice.

[34] The Commission's proposal to this end was not adopted: COM(2006) 346.

[35] Case C-241/05 *Bot* [2006] ECR I-9627.

[36] Case C-465/07 *Elgafaji and Elgafaji* [2009] ECR I-921.

[37] Case C-19/08 *Petrosian* [2009] ECR I-495; Case C-139/08 *Kqiku* [2009] ECR I-2887; Case C-261/08 *Zurita Garcia* and Case C-348/08 *Choque Cabrera*, 22 Oct 2009; Cases C-175/08 to C-179/08 *Abdulla and others*, 2 Mar 2010; Case C-578/08 *Chakroun*, 4 Mar 2010.

[38] Case C-31/09 *Bolbol*, 17 June 2010; Cases C-57/09 and C-101/09 *B and D*, 9 Nov. 2010; Case C-247/09 *Xhymshiti*, 18 Nov. 2010; Case C-357/09 PPU *Kadzoev*, 30 Nov 2009.

[39] As regards irregular migration, both Member States opted out of the Returns Directive (n 30 above) and Directive 2009/52 on employment of irregular migrants ([2009] OJ L168/24). As regards asylum, the UK and Ireland both opted out of the proposed new Directives on qualification for international protection and international protection procedures (COM(2009) 551 and 554, 21 Oct 2009), whereas both Member States had opted in to the prior measures (Directive 2004/83, [2004] OJ L304/12 and Directive 2005/85, [2005] OJ L326/13). As regards legal migration, the UK opted into a Regulation on third country nationals' social security adopted in 2003 (Regulation 859/2003, [2003] OJ L124/1), but out of a proposal to replace that Regulation in 2007 (COM(2007) 439).

[40] Case C-77/05 *UK v Council* [2007] ECR I-11459; Case C-137/05 *UK v Council* [2007] ECR I-11459; see now Case C-482/08 *UK v Council*, 26 Oct. 2010.

particular Community competence to adopt criminal sanctions and rules on cooperation between law enforcement authorities and the private sector.[41] On the other hand,
First Pillar principles began to infiltrate the Third Pillar, in particular as regards
indirect effect, the scope of the Court's jurisdiction,[42] and the autonomous interpretation of Third Pillar measures.[43] The Court also endorsed the replacement of Conventions by the forms of legislative acts introduced by the Treaty of Amsterdam.[44]
There was a fairly steady number of cases referred to the Court of Justice from national
courts in this area. Leaving aside withdrawn cases, two cases were referred in 2001,[45]
two cases in 2003,[46] two cases in 2004,[47] five in 2005,[48] none in 2006, three in 2007,[49]
four in 2008,[50] and four in 2009.[51] It is striking, however, that these cases concerned
only three different Third Pillar measures.[52]

In spite of the increasing role played by the Court of Justice, there was no transformation of the role of the EP or the Commission, and as discussed below, the de
facto changes in the institutional framework had a limited impact on the evolution of
policy as regards the adoption of legislation.

---

[41] Case C-170/03 *Commission v Council* [2005] ECR I-7879; Case C-440/05 *Commission v Council* [2007]
ECR I-9097; Case C-301/06 *Ireland v EP and Council* [2009] ECR I-593; but see Cases C-317/04 and C-318/04
EP v Council and Commission [2006] ECR I-4721. In light of these rulings, the Council and EP adopted
legislation exercising the EC's criminal law competence: Directives 2008/99 on: environmental crime, [2008]
OJ L328/28; 2009/123 on shipping pollution, [2009] OJ L280/52; 2009/52 on employer sanctions for hiring
irregular migrants (n 39 above). On these developments, see: E Herlin-Karnell, 'Commission v Council: Some
Reflections on Criminal Law in the First Pillar' (2007) 13 EPL 69; S White, 'Harmonisation of Criminal Law
under the First Pillar' (2006) ELRev 81; S Peers, 'The Community's Criminal Law Competence: The Plot
Thickens' (2008) 33 ELRev 399.

[42] See respectively Case C-105/03 *Pupino* [2005] ECR I-5285 and Case C-355/04 P *SEGI* [2007] ECR I-1657,
and discussion in S Peers, 'Salvation outside the Church: Judicial Protection in the Third Pillar after the *Pupino*
and *SEGI* judgments' (2007) 44 CML Rev 883.

[43] Case C-66/08 *Koslowski* [2008] ECR I-6041; see earlier Joined Cases C-187/01 and C-345/01 *Gözütok
and Brugge* [2003] ECR I-1345, on the interpretation of provisions of the Schengen *acquis* after their
integration into the EU legal order.

[44] Case C-303/05 *Advocaten voor de Wereld* [2007] ECR I-3633. Following this judgment, the Council
replaced the Europol Convention and the Customs Information System Convention, and associated Protocols,
with Third Pillar Decisions, [2009] OJ L121/37 and [2009] OJ L323/20.

[45] *Gözütok and Brugge* (n 43 above).

[46] *Pupino* (n 42 above) and Case C-469/03 *Miraglia* [2005] ECR I-2009.

[47] Cases C-436/04 *van Esbroek* [2006] ECR I-2333 and C-467/04 *Gasparini* [2006] ECR I-9199.

[48] Cases C-150/05 *Van Straaten* [2006] ECR I-9327, C-288/05, *Kretzinger* [2007] ECR I-6441, C-303/05
Advocaten voor de Wereld [2007] ECR I-3633, C-367/05 *Kraaijenbrink* [2007] ECR I-6619, and C-467/05
Dell'Orto [2007] ECR I-5557.

[49] Case C-297/07 *Bourquain* [2008] ECR I-9425; Case C-491/07 *Turansky* [2008] ECR I-11039; Case
C-404/07 *Katz* [2008] ECR I-7607.

[50] Case C-66/08 *Koslowski* [2008] ECR I-6041; Case C-296/08 PPU *Santesteban Goicoechea* [2008] ECR
I-6307; Case C-388/08 PPU *Leymann and Pustovarov* [2008] ECR I-8993; Case C-123/08 *Wolzenburg* [2009]
ECR I-9621.

[51] Case C-205/09 Eredics, 21 Oct. 2010; Case C-261/09 Mantello, 16 Nov. 2010; Case C-306/09 I.B., 21 Oct.
2010; and Case C-483/09 *Gueye*, pending.

[52] More specifically, there were: ten cases on the Schengen Convention rules on double jeopardy (Arts 54–58 of
the Convention, n 5 above); seven cases on the Framework Decision establishing the European Arrest Warrant,
[2002] OJ L190/1; and five cases on the Framework Decision on crime victims' rights, [2001] OJ L82/1.

5. TREATY OF LISBON

Finally, with the Treaty of Lisbon we see, at least at first sight, the triumph of the Community method in this area, with QMV and the ordinary legislative procedure (ex-co-decision) extended to legal migration[53] and most criminal law and policing issues;[54] the ordinary legislative procedure applied to the issues of visa lists and visa formats; full jurisdiction for the Court of Justice in all JHA areas;[55] the application of the usual legal instruments (ie regulations and directives) to policing and criminal law matters; and the extensive revision of most competences in this area, particularly as regards immigration, asylum, and criminal law.[56] However, the application of the full Community method to policing and criminal law is limited by the continued possibility for a group of Member States to table initiatives to rival the Commission,[57] and the application of a five-year transitional period regarding the Court's jurisdiction over Third Pillar measures adopted before the entry into force of the Treaty of Lisbon.[58] The impact of expanding the Court's jurisdiction has also been modest in the first six months after the Treaty of Lisbon entered into force.[59]

Again, the Member States with misgivings about this change in the legal framework were bought off by opt-outs, this time extending to policing and criminal law matters.[60] The opt-out rules were also amended to address the situation if the UK or Ireland wished to opt out of an act amending a JHA act by which they were already bound, or (as regards the provisions of the Schengen *acquis* which applied to them) building upon the provisions of the Schengen *acquis*. The latter rules provided for the prospect, in certain circumstances, of terminating those Member States' participation in measures by which they were already bound. On the other hand, Denmark was conversely given the possibility to move *closer* to EU JHA policies, ie by applying a

[53] Arts 77–80 TFEU, in particular Art 79. Note however the requirement for unanimity and consultation of the EP as regards passports (Art 77(3) TFEU).

[54] Arts 82–89 TFEU. The exceptions concern the European Public Prosecutor (Art 86) and police operations (Arts 87(3) and 89). Note also the 'emergency brake' procedure for some other aspects of criminal law (Arts 82(2) and 83).

[55] Except for a limited restriction on jurisdiction as regards law enforcement issues: see Art 276 TFEU.

[56] Note in particular the limitation on the EU's immigration powers, as regards volumes of economic migrants coming from non-EU countries (Art 79(5) TFEU).

[57] Art 76 TFEU. In practice, this provision was applied several times in the first six months after the Treaty of Lisbon entered into force: see the Member States' initiatives for Directives on the right to interpretation and translation in the framework of criminal proceedings, [2010] OJ C69/1, on a European protection order, [2010] C69/5, and for a European investigation order, [2010] OJ C165/22.

[58] Art 10 of the transitional Protocol attached to the Treaty. For analysis, see S Peers, 'Finally "Fit for Purpose?" The Treaty of Lisbon and the end of the Third Pillar legal order' (2008) YEL 27, 47.

[59] Only five (non-civil law) JHA cases were referred to the Court: On immigration and asylum law: Case C-69/10 *Diouf*, pending, and Cases C-188/10 and C-189/10 *Melki and Abdeli*, 22 June 2010; on criminal law: Case C-1/10 *Salmeron Sanchez*, and Case C-264/10 *Kita*, both pending; and on both asylum law and criminal law: Case C-105/10 PPU *Gataev and Gataeva*, withdrawn. See also Case C-550/09 *E and F*, 29 June 2010, on the parallel issue of criminal prosecution for breach of EU anti-terrorist sanctions legislation.

[60] S Peers, 'In a world of their own? Justice and Home Affairs opt-outs and the Treaty of Lisbon' (2008–09) 10 CYELS 383.

version of the British and Irish opt-out in place of complete exclusion, subject to an initial extension of its opt-out to criminal law and policing. There are also rules providing for possible fast-track authorization of enhanced cooperation as regards several criminal law and policing matters.[61]

C. POLICY EVOLUTION

To what extent has EU JHA *policy* evolved over the years? This question will be assessed as regards five different policy areas in turn (visas/borders, asylum, irregular migration, legal migration, and criminal law), by examining main trends in the development of those particular policy areas throughout the time periods (pre-Maastricht, Maastricht, early Amsterdam, late Amsterdam, and post-Lisbon) discussed above.

1. VISAS AND BORDER CONTROLS

(a) Prior to 1993

During the pre-Maastricht period, the focus was on the negotiation of the original 1985 Schengen Agreement and the 1990 Convention implementing that Agreement. The relevant provisions of the Schengen Convention clearly follow a customs union model, as applied to the free movement of goods by the EU (*inter alia*), consisting of a set of common controls at the external borders,[62] abolition of internal frontiers (a concept borrowed from the EU's internal market, which in theory was being completed pursuant to the Single European Act at the time the original Schengen rules were being negotiated),[63] and freedom to travel for a three-month period between the participating states for those who are legally visiting or legally resident.[64] As a flanking measure, the Schengen Information System (SIS) was set up, *inter alia*, to establish a common list of persons who could not be granted visas or admitted at the borders because any single Member State considered them a threat.[65] Not all aspects of the relevant policies could be harmonized during the negotiations of the 1990 Convention, so there was provision for an Executive Committee made up of national civil servants to agree on further harmonization, in particular as regards a common visa list and common administrative instructions (the 'Common Consular Instructions' as

---

[61] See Arts 82(2), 83, 86, and 87(3) TFEU.

[62] Arts 3–8 of the Schengen Convention (n 5 above), complemented by Arts 9–17 regarding visa policy.

[63] Art 2 of the Convention (ibid).

[64] Arts 19–22 of the Convention (ibid), known in practice as 'freedom to travel'. Compare to the internal free circulation of third country goods in Art 29 TFEU (ex-Art 24 EC). See the comparison between the external and internal aspects of the various free movement regimes in S Peers, 'EU Borders and Globalisation' in Groenendijk, Guild, and Minderhoud (eds), *In Search of Europe's Borders* (Kluwer International Law, 2003) 45.

[65] Arts 92–119 of the Convention (ibid).

regards visas, and the 'Common Manual' for guards at the external borders).[66] Notably, this model was endorsed by the Court of Justice, which took the view that the checks at internal borders could not be abolished until, *inter alia*, common external border checks were established,[67] and that the simple rule of mutual recognition of other Member States' refusal decisions (established by the SIS) was acceptable, even (implicitly) without any harmonization of the grounds for issuing SIS alerts for the refusal of entry.[68]

(b) 1993–1999

In the Maastricht period, the main focus in this area was applying and implementing the Schengen rules, after the application of the Convention as from March 1995. There was limited EU activity, due to the resistance of the UK to participation in this area. The EU's initial visa (black)list legislation was based on the Schengen list, with certain Commonwealth states removed due to UK opposition,[69] and attempts to agree an External Borders Convention with the UK's participation founded mainly on arguments over the status of Gibraltar.[70]

(c) 1999–2009

Next, there was a modest uptake in activity during the early Amsterdam period, likely facilitated by the removal of Member States with objections to this policy from participation within it. The EU fully harmonized its visa lists as from 2001,[71] taking as a basis the high degree of Schengen harmonization accomplished by 1998 and beginning to develop a distinctive EU policy in this area, putting one state on the EU blacklist due to concerns about security and irregular migration,[72] but putting other states on the EU white list due to concerns about regional integration with EU neighbours, or in return for commitments relating to irregular migration.[73] At this point, the EU also began to develop a policy on visa reciprocity, ie expecting states on the white list to waive visa requirements for nationals of all Schengen states.[74]

---

[66] The Executive Committee Decisions which were still in force on 1 May 1999, were not then classified, and which were integrated into the EU legal order at that point (pursuant to the Treaty of Amsterdam) can be found, along with the 1985 Agreement and 1990 Convention, at [2000] OJ L239.

[67] Case C-378/97 *Wijsenbeek* [1999] ECR I-6207.

[68] Case C-503/03 *Commission v Spain* [2006] ECR I-1097. However, this judgment did establish limits as regards the application of the SIS where the free movement rights of EU citizens' third country national family members were concerned.

[69] Regulation 2317/95, [1995] OJ L234/1. See generally K Hailbronner, 'Visa Regulations and Third-Country Nationals in EC Law' (1994) 31 CML Rev 969.

[70] COM(93) 684, 10 Dec 1994, [1994] OJ C11/15. It is striking in hindsight that a British Conservative government was willing in principle at this time to sign up to a significant element of the Schengen rules.

[71] Reg 539/2001, [2001] OJ L81/1.

[72] Colombia, which had previously been the one State on the 'greylist', ie about which Schengen states could not agree.

[73] These states were Romania and Bulgaria, plus the entities of Hong Kong and Macao.

[74] See the original Art 1(4), Regulation 539/2001 (n 71 above).

Also during this period, the EU established rules for the amendment of the Schengen administrative instructions, and made some fairly modest amendments to those rules,[75] probably constrained by the unanimity requirement in the Council.

There were more significant changes during the late Amsterdam period, after the application of QMV and co-decision to this entire policy area in 2004–05. At this point, the Schengen rules concerning visas, border controls, and the SIS were entirely replaced by EU legislation,[76] which established streamlined rules with a clearer legal status, also enhancing (as noted above) procedural rights and data protection rights.[77] The Returns Directive implicitly provides for a degree of harmonization as regards alerts in the Schengen Information System, or the future SIS II.[78] An EC agency was created to assist Member States to manage the external borders (Frontex),[79] and a further agency has been proposed to manage the EU's JHA databases, including SIS II.[80] The legislation to establish the Visa Information System (VIS), a database containing information on all visa applicants for use in particular by national consulates, was adopted in 2008,[81] and the VIS is due to begin operations in 2011. The creation of the VIS is inextricably linked with further uniformity of visa policy.[82] Uniform EU rules on local border traffic treaties with neighbouring non-Member States were also drawn up.[83]

EU visa list legislation was also amended during this period to ensure greater uniformity as regards the exceptions from visa requirements and as regards quasi-British citizens.[84] In relation to external elements of the policy, the EU developed a policy of offering visa facilitation agreements (mostly) to neighbouring countries, in return for readmission agreements. These treaties reduce visa fees and simplify and speed up the issue of visas to the nationals of the countries concerned.[85] For Western Balkan States, and in future Russia and other Eastern neighbours, the EU has gone further and established visa liberalization roadmaps which offer visa abolition in return for extensive policy commitments as regards managing migration and internal

---

[75] See Regulations 789/2001 and 790/2001, [2001] OJ L116/2 and 5, upheld by the Court of Justice in Case C-257/01 (n 16 above).

[76] See the legislation establishing the Schengen Borders Code, the visa code, and SIS II (n 30 above). Note that in the *Bot* judgment (n 35 above), the Court of Justice stressed the importance of uniformity in this area.

[77] For example, individuals must be told about, and told the reason for, a refusal to issue a visa or a refusal to permit entry at the external border, and also have the right to information if they are listed in SIS II. They then have the right to appeal against such refusals or listings.

[78] See n 30 above.

[79] Regulation 2007/2004, [2004] OJ L349/1, as amended by Regulation 863/2007, [2007] OJ L199/30.

[80] See the proposed Regulation establishing an agency to manage VIS, SIS II, and Eurodac (COM(2009) 293; revised after the Treaty of Lisbon: COM(2010) 93.

[81] Regulation 767/2008, [2008] OJ L218/60.

[82] See, for instance, the amendments to the VIS Regulation (ibid) in the visa code (n 30 above), and the adoption of particular rules on taking biometric information from visa applicants and organizing consulates (Regulation 390/2009, [2009] OJ L131/1, now integrated into the visa code). See also the further harmonization of border procedures, as regards use of the VIS at the external borders (Regulation 81/2009, [2009] OJ L35/56).

[83] Regulation 1931/2006, [2006] OJ L405/1.

[84] Regulation 1932/2006, [2006] OJ L405/23.

[85] See, for instance, the agreement with Ukraine: [2007] OJ L332/66.

security.[86] Conversely, in order to liberalize visa requirements for EU citizens visiting third States, the EU's visa reciprocity rules were amended in 2005 to make them more effective at achieving this objective,[87] and the Commission has followed this up by placing pressure on the non-Member States concerned.[88] Ironically, in a mirror image of its own policies towards its poorer neighbours, the EU has had to act to enhance the security of its own citizens' passports in order to satisfy American concerns on this point.[89] The first visa waiver treaties were signed with a number of island states;[90] it was assumed the inhabitants of these states were unlikely to trade their tropical beaches for the delights of (say) some clandestine toilet cleaning during a Swedish winter.

In the early months after the entry into force of the Treaty of Lisbon, the basic trends regarding the development of policy in this area were reinforced by legislation extending the rules on freedom to travel to all holders of long-stays (but strengthening the obligation to check them in the SIS first),[91] and proposals to confer greater powers on Frontex,[92] to amend the EU's visa list,[93] and to conclude further visa liberalization and visa waiver treaties.[94] The Stockholm programme, the latest multi-year programme for the development of EU JHA policy, does not call for any fundamental changes in this area, besides the development of an entry-exit system (ie a system for registering the entry and exit of third-country nationals across the external borders), the parallel development of a registered traveller system (to allow EU citizens and certain third country nationals to cross borders more easily, in order to circumvent the delays which will result at border posts from fingerprinting third country nationals), and possibly an electronic system for prior checking of visitors not subject to visa requirements.[95]

Overall, the basic customs union model taken over from the Schengen framework has not been fundamentally altered, but rather further refined, in order to establish greater uniformity as regards the outside world (the visa list policy, treaties on visa waivers, visa liberalization, and border traffic) and further free circulation within the

---

[86] See Regulation 1244/2009 abolishing visa requirements as regards several Western Balkan States, [2009] OJ L336/1.

[87] Regulation 851/2005, [2005] OJ L141/3.

[88] See most recently COM(2009) 560.

[89] Regulation 2252/2004, [2004] OJ L385/1, as amended by Regulation 444/2009, [2009] OJ L142/1.

[90] Mauritius, Antigua/Barbuda, Barbados, Seychelles, St Kitts and Nevis, and the Bahamas, [2009] OJ L169.

[91] Regulation 265/2010, [2010] OJ L85/1. The adoption of this measure was facilitated by the abolition of the unanimity obligation as regards legal immigration (since the measure in part had a legal base concerning that issue). Previously a smaller group of long-stay visa holders had the freedom to travel: Regulation 1091/2001, [2001] OJ L150/4.

[92] COM(2010) 61.

[93] The amendments extended visa waivers to more Western Balkan States and to Taiwan (Regs. 1091/2010, [2010] OJ L 329/1 and 1211/2010, [2010] OJ L 339/6).

[94] See the proposed visa liberalization Treaty with Georgia (COM(2010) 197 and 198, and the two visa waiver treaties initialled at the July 2010 EU-Brazil summit: COM(2010) 419 and 420, 6 August 2010 (ordinary visas); COM(2010) 409 and 410, 6 August 2010 (diplomatic visas).

[95] [2010] OJ C115/1. On these issues, see the earlier Commission Communication (COM(2008) 69).

EU (by means of enlarging the Schengen area as well as the categories of people who benefit from freedom to travel). As with the common commercial policy, the external visa policy of the EU has become increasingly nuanced, with differentiation as regards more or less favoured third states (visa waiver, visa liberalization, visa obligations, more onerous visa obligations).[96] While elements of control have been stepped up, most notably as regards the introduction of the VIS, the creation of Frontex, the legislation on passport security, and the planned SIS II and entry–exit system, there are also elements of liberalization, in particular the gradual extension of the visa white list and the conclusion of visa liberalization treaties. There has also been a trend to establish and develop procedural rights in this area, whereas the original Schengen rules were silent on this point. The principle that a person should apply for a Schengen visa from only one Member State, determined by objective rules, has been clarified by the visa code and will be strengthened by the VIS, which aims to prevent 'visa shopping' between national consulates. On the other hand, despite the uniform controls at the external borders and the freedom to travel between Schengen States, it remains possible that individuals will be admitted to only one Member State in exceptional cases.[97]

2. ASYLUM

(a) Prior to 1999

During the initial intergovernmental period, the Member States focused on the issue of asylum responsibility, adopting the Dublin Convention on this issue and a small amount of soft law, starting with Resolutions of Member States on perceived abuse of asylum procedures,[98] and continuing (after the original TEU entered into force) with Council Resolutions or Joint Positions on aspects of asylum law.[99]

(b) 1999–2009

During the 'Amsterdam era', the orientation of EU asylum policy was changed significantly, first of all when the Tampere programme stipulated that the EU would establish a 'Common European Asylum System' (CEAS) in two phases.[100]

---

[96] The more onerous visa obligations take the form of advanced application of the VIS (see the Decision on early roll-out to the Middle East and North Africa, [2010] OJ L23/62), the application of an airport transit visa obligation (see Art 3 of the visa code, n 30 above), and the extra consultation or information requirements as regards certain third States (Arts 22 and 31 of the visa code, ibid).

[97] Art 5(4)(c) of the Borders Code (n 30 above) and Art 25 of the visa code (ibid).

[98] Unpublished in the OJ; see Bunyan, *Key Texts on Justice and Home Affairs in the European Union, Volume I* (SEMDOC, 1997) 64 and 66; E Guild and J Niessen, *The Emerging Immigration and Asylum Law of the European Union: Adopted Conventions, Resolutions, Recommendations, Decisions and Conclusions* (Kluwer International Law, 1996) 141, 161, and 177.

[99] Resolution on asylum procedures, [1996] OJ C274/13, and Joint Position on the definition of refugee, [1996] OJ L63/2.

[100] See generally H Battjes, *European Asylum Law and International Law* (Martinus Nijhoff, 2006).

The first phase of legislation to establish the CEAS was proposed from 2000 to 2001 and adopted, after great political difficulty, between 2003 and 2005, at which point the decision-making rules shifted entirely to QMV and co-decision.[101] These measures, which comprised in particular Directives on reception conditions for asylum-seekers, procedural rules in asylum cases, and the definition and content of refugee and subsidiary protection status,[102] in parallel with further measures on asylum responsibility (which did not alter the fundamental precepts of the Dublin Convention),[103] were widely criticized for setting low standards.[104] Nonetheless, in principle the legislation concerned covered most of the subject matter of asylum law.

The Hague programme, adopted in 2004, agreed that the second phase of the Common European Asylum System would be established by the end of 2010.[105] The Commission subsequently adopted an asylum policy plan,[106] which envisaged a wider scope for EU asylum legislation,[107] a greater degree of uniformity, significantly higher standards, and the creation of an asylum support agency. Proposals to this end were submitted before the entry into force of the Treaty of Lisbon, but despite the application of QMV and co-decision to this area from the outset of these second-phase proposals, agreement remained elusive except for the legislation to establish the European Asylum Support Office.[108] Equally, a proposal to facilitate the free movement of persons who obtain refugee and subsidiary protection status, by allowing them to obtain 'long-term resident' immigration status after five years' legal stay, was submitted by the Commission in 2007 but still not agreed by the entry into force of the Treaty of Lisbon.[109] The deadline to complete the second phase of the CEAS has been put back to 2012.[110]

---

[101] See Art 67(5) EC and Case C-133/06 (n 28 above).

[102] Directives 2003/9, [2003] OJ L31/18; 2005/85, [2005] OJ L326/13, and 2004/83, [2004] OJ L304/12. See also Directive 2001/55 on temporary protection, [2001] OJ L212/12, establishing an *ad hoc* system to be used in a crisis, which has not been used in practice.

[103] Regulation 343/2003, replacing the Dublin rules, [2003] OJ L50/1; the 'Dublin II Regulation'), and Regulation 2725/2000, [2000] OJ L 316/1, creating Eurodac, a system for the comparison of asylum-seekers' fingerprints, operational in 2003, [2003] OJ C5/2.

[104] See, for instance, the ECRE position papers, online at: <http://www.ecre.org/topics/ecre_agenda_for_europe>. It should be recalled that although EC legislation on asylum could at the time set only 'minimum standards', this did not mean that standards therefore had to be set at the lowest common denominator: see by analogy Case C-84/94 *UK v Council* [1996] ECR I-8755.

[105] See n 25 above.

[106] COM(2008) 360.

[107] In particular, the first-phase rules on asylum responsibility, reception conditions, and procedures only apply to persons applying for refugee status, not for the parallel 'subsidiary protection' status.

[108] Regulation 439/2010, [2010] OJ L132/11. The legislative proposals comprise COM(2008) 815 (reception conditions); COM(2008) 820 (responsibility rules); COM(2009) 342 (Eurodac); COM(2009) 551 (qualification and content of status); COM(2009) 554 (asylum procedures). See also COM(2009) 456 (resettlement), which is not controversial as regards its substance—the only dispute concerns the use of delegated powers or comitology to adopt implementing measures.

[109] COM(2007) 298. The proposal had a legal base relating to legal migration, and so remained subject to unanimous voting, unlike asylum legislation *per se*.

[110] See the 2008 immigration and asylum pact (Council doc 13440/08, 24 September 2008).

(c) After 2009

With the entry into force of the Treaty of Lisbon, there is a significant change in the EU's competence, providing now for the adopting of measures fully harmonizing the law and enshrining the Tampere principles (ie creation of a Common European Asylum System and a uniform status valid throughout the Union) into the binding text of the Treaty. So far, however, this change in the fundamental legal framework has not had any impact on the proposed legislation in this area, and the latest multi-year agenda for JHA measures, the Stockholm programme, devotes little attention to it.[111]

It is striking that although the initial model of an exclusive focus on asylum responsibility criteria was discarded in favour of a broader harmonization agenda, nevertheless the rationale of 'preventing secondary movements' (ie the movement of asylum-seekers between Member States) remained at least one rationale for the adoption of the harmonization measures, based on the assumption that one factor driving secondary movements was disparate treatment of asylum-seekers as regards substantive law, reception conditions, and procedural rules. The underlying logic of the policy development was therefore still connected to *movement between Member States*, albeit the objective was to *deter or reduce* such movement, rather than *facilitate* it, as is the case with the visa and borders policies, and the EU internal market generally. Needless to say, the objective of reducing such movements at the same time as abolishing border controls as between most Member States proved relatively futile, and the statistics showed only a modest increase in the low percentage of the asylum-seekers who were subject to the Dublin rules during the first phase of the CEAS.[112] The development of the Dublin rules was linked to the parallel strengthening of external border controls in that the Eurodac system requires Member States to take and transmit to the central database the fingerprints of all irregular migrants stopped at the external borders, because it is possible that such persons will subsequently apply for asylum in another Member State and the Dublin rules make the Member State which the person concerned entered irregularly responsible in most circumstances.[113] But the number of persons fingerprinted due to irregular border crossing was at first very low, although it has gradually risen.[114]

Although there is an implied mutual recognition of negative decisions related to asylum,[115] there is no required recognition of positive decisions, until and unless the proposal to amend the Long-term Residents' Directive is adopted. Even then persons with protection will have a long wait of five years' legal residence to obtain that status, and there are many constraints on long-term residents in general moving to another Member State.[116] Moreover, the protection status of the person concerned will not be

---

[111] See n 95 above.

[112] COM(2007) 299 and SEC(2007) 742.

[113] See Art 10, Regulation 343/2003 (n 103 above).

[114] See the annual reports on Eurodac: SEC(2004) 557 (for 2003); SEC(2005) 839 (for 2004); SEC(2006) 1170 (for 2005); SEC(2007) 1184 (for 2006); COM(2009) 13 (for 2007); COM(2009) 494 (for 2008).

[115] Art 25(1), Directive 2005/85 (n 39 above).

[116] See Section 3(d) below.

transferred with them if they move, and the Commission has proposed that the fingerprints of recognized refugees should also be available to other Member States pursuant to the Eurodac system (currently these fingerprints are blocked, ie stored but technically inaccessible), on the assumption that even recognized refugees might apply for refugee status in another Member State—and with the further assumption that this is undesirable, even though the Commission has proposed that recognized refugees should have the right to do this as long-term residents. Obviously, this situation falls a long way short of the rhetorical objective of having a status 'valid throughout the Union'. Among the Schengen states, there is a limited form of positive mutual recognition, since the grant of a residence permit to a person with protection status should in principle mean that they have the right to freedom to travel within the EU[117]—although in practice this depends on whether Member States notify the type of permit concerned as one which confers freedom to travel.[118]

Finally, it is striking to note that, by use of their opt-out, the UK and Ireland, having opted in to all or most of the first-phase legislation,[119] opted out of all of the substantive second-phase proposals,[120] except for those relating to asylum responsibility.[121] Effectively they aim to recreate for themselves the original position whereby the rules only concerned asylum responsibility, without any harmonization of law. To the extent that other Member States might then have higher standards than the UK and Ireland, in particular following the adoption of the second-phase legislation, this could deter secondary movements to the UK and Ireland, who might even be freed up from their obligations under the first-phase legislation as the second-phase legislation will repeal it.[122]

3. IRREGULAR MIGRATION

(a) Prior to 1999

During the initial intergovernmental period, the EU's measures in this area consisted almost entirely of soft law,[123] except for a few provisions of the Schengen Convention

---

[117] See Art 21 of the Schengen Convention (n 5 above). Directive 2004/83 (n 39 above) imposes an obligation to grant a residence permit to such persons after recognition of their status (Art 24). Also, the 2006 amendments to the visa list Regulation waive a visa requirement for a person with refugee status in *any* Member State (see Art 1(2) of Regulation 539/2001, as amended by Regulation 1932/2006, [2006] OJ L405/23).

[118] See Arts 2(15) and 34(1)(a) of the Schengen Borders Code (n 30 above).

[119] The only exception was the Irish opt-out from the Reception Conditions Directive (n 102 above).

[120] Namely the proposals on reception conditions, procedures, and the qualification and content of status (n 108 above). These states also opted in to the legislation on the Asylum Support Office and the resettlement proposal (both idem), and remain subject to the legislation establishing the European Refugee Fund, [2007] OJ L144/1.

[121] Namely the proposals on 'Dublin III' and Eurodac (n 108 above).

[122] On the process of rescinding the UK and Ireland's existing obligations under JHA legislation, see 'In a World of Their Own' (n 60 above).

[123] Recommendation of Immigration Ministers on 30 Nov/1 Dec 2002 on the main aspects of irregular migration policy (SN 4678/92, WGI 1266, 16 Nov 1992), published in Guild and Niessen and in Bunyan (ed) (n 98 above); Recommendation of Immigration Ministers on 1–2 June 2003 on in-country detection of

on carrier sanctions and facilitation of irregular entry and residence,[124] and a Decision on monitoring the implementation of some of the soft law.[125]

(b) 1999–2009

Originally, for the first few years following the entry into force of the Treaty of Amsterdam, the measures in this area were rather piecemeal. A first set of Directives building upon the Schengen *acquis* as regards carrier sanctions, facilitation of irregular entry and residence, and mutual recognition of expulsion Decisions were all adopted by the Council by 2001–02.[126] So was a Framework Decision on the criminal law aspects of trafficking in persons, replacing a pre-Amsterdam Joint Action on the same topic.[127] The Commission and Council then tried to elaborate a coherent policy in this field,[128] and subsequently adopted a number of specific measures, for instance concerning pre-entry control (a Regulation on a network of immigration liaison officers and a Directive on the exchange of passenger data);[129] control on the territory (a Directive on the legal status of victims of trafficking in persons);[130] aspects of expulsion (a Directive on assistance for expulsions via air transit,[131] a Decision on financing expulsion measures,[132] and a Decision on joint expulsion flights);[133] along with measures on administrative cooperation measures (a Decision establishing an information and coordination network for Member States' migration management services).[134] The development of the SIS and other border control and visas measures were also intended to contribute to the control of irregular migration.

On the external front, the EU also developed a policy of agreeing bilateral readmission agreements, both to clarify aspects of the process of identifying returning nationals

---

irregular migration and irregular employment (SN 3017/93, WGI 1516, 25 May 1993, published in idem; see also [1996] OJ C5/1 and [1996] OJ C304/1); Recommendations on expulsion, [1996] OJ C5/3, 5, and 7); Recommendations on a standard travel document (or laissez-passer) for use in individual expulsions, [1996] OJ C274/20; a standard bilateral readmission agreement, [1996] OJ C274/21; and principles to be included in protocols to readmission agreements, [1996] OJ C 274/25; and Council conclusions of 30 Nov 2004 on CIREFI, [1996] OJ C 274/50.

[124] Arts 23, 24, 26, and 27 of the Convention (n 5 above). Of course the provisions of the Convention dealing with borders, visas, and the SIS to some extent also aimed to prevent irregular migration.

[125] [1996] OJ L342/5.

[126] Directives 2001/51, [2001] OJ L187/45; 2002/90, [2002] OJ L328/17, along with a Framework Decision on the criminal law aspects: [2002] OJ L328/1; and 2001/40, [2001] OJ L149/34.

[127] [2002] OJ L203/1.

[128] Commission Communication on irregular migration (COM(2001) 672), followed by a Council action plan, [2002] OJ C142/23; Commission Green Paper on return policy (COM(2002) 175, followed by Communication on the same topic: COM(2002) 564), followed by a Council action plan (Council doc 14673/02, 25 Nov 2002). See also the subsequent reports on the development of the policy: COM(2003) 323; SEC(2004) 1349; SEC(2006) 1010; and SEC(2009) 320.

[129] Regulation 377/2004, [2004] OJ L64/1; and Directive 2004/82, [2004] OJ L261/24.

[130] Directive 2004/81, [2004] OJ L261/19.

[131] Directive 2003/110, [2003] OJ L321/26.

[132] [2004] OJ L60/55.

[133] [2004] OJ L261/28.

[134] [2005] OJ L83/48.

of the third states concerned, and in order to oblige each of those third states to take back persons who have merely transited through their territory.[135] The EU ran into difficulty incentivizing third states to sign agreements which were essentially solely in the EU's interest, but managed to overcome that difficulty in most cases by offering parallel visa facilitation agreements (with Balkan and ex-Soviet neighbours), visa waivers (for Hong Kong and Macao), anti-terrorist measures (for Sri Lanka), or money (for Pakistan). The EU also concluded Protocols to the UN Convention on organized crime, concerning smuggling and trafficking in persons.[136]

After 2005, the EU adopted fewer but more wide-ranging measures in this area, notably the Returns Directive (which addresses the issues of detention of irregular migrants, expulsion procedures, and treatment pending expulsion), and a Directive on employer sanctions for employment of irregular migrants, aiming to reduce the incentive (or 'pull') effect for irregular migrants to enter and stay in the EU.[137]

(c) After 2009

Since the Treaty of Lisbon made only limited changes to the EU's competence in this area and no change to the decision-making rules, it cannot be expected to impact on the development of policy much, although irregular migration falls within the scope of the more general power to develop a 'common immigration policy', set out in Article 79 TFEU. The Stockholm programme says little about this area, besides a long-term objective of codifying EU immigration law—although this process is meant to begin with legislation on *legal* migration.

As a whole, there is not a clearly discernible model for the development of EU legislation on irregular migration. It may make more sense to classify this policy as ancillary to other policies, in particular visas and border controls (as regards the prevention of irregular migration and the treatment of visa overstayers), legal migration, and asylum (as regards failed asylum-seekers). The adoption of the Returns Directive, which would presumably form the heart of a future codification initiative, points towards more ambitious objectives, but it is too early to tell how they will be pursued.

4. LEGAL MIGRATION

(a) Prior to 1999

During the initial intergovernmental period, only soft law was adopted on this topic, on the various categories of legal migrants (family reunion, employment,

---

[135] Agreements with: Hong Kong, [2004] OJ L17/23; Macao, [2004] OJ L143/97; Sri Lanka, [2005] OJ L124/43; Albania, [2005] OJ L124; Russia, [2007] OJ L129; Ukraine, Serbia, Montenegro, Bosnia, Macedonia, and Moldova, [2007] OJ L332 and 334; Pakistan ([2010] OJ L 339/6): and Georgia (COM(2010) 199 and 200). Negotiations have also been approved with Morocco, Algeria, Turkey, China, and Cape Verde.

[136] See 7.5.2 and 7.5.4 below.

[137] Directives 2008/115 and 2009/52 (nn 30 and 39 above). For the Court of Justice's interpretation of the former Dir, see *Kadzoev* (n 38 above).

self-employment, students) and on the status of long-term residents.[138] A Decision on follow-up was also adopted. However, a far-reaching proposal for a Convention on migration was not agreed by the Council.[139]

(b) 1999–2009

The Tampere programme set a broad agenda for harmonization of legal migration policy, and established a principle of 'fair' treatment of legally resident third country nationals, with equal treatment 'as far as possible'. However, it proved difficult to put these principles into practice during the initial period of EC competence (from 1999–2004), with key legislation proving difficult to negotiate and setting relatively low standards when agreed.[140] Moreover, it was entirely impossible to reach agreement on the issue of labour migration during this period.[141]

After 2005, even though there was no change to the decision-making rules applicable (ie unanimity still remained), it proved possible to relaunch attempts to adopt measures on labour migration,[142] with some degree of success as regards legislation on favoured categories of migrants (researchers and the highly-skilled, the latter being the subject of the well-known 'Blue Card' Directive).[143] But even here the degree of harmonization was limited, with Member States free to maintain or introduce parallel

[138] For the Ministers' Resolution on family reunion, see SN 2828/1/93, not published in the Official Journal; see Guild and Niessen (n 98 above) 250–257. For the other Resolutions, see [1996] OJ C274 and [1996] OJ C80/2. See also the Resolutions on marriages of convenience, [1997] OJ C382/1, and unaccompanied minors, [1997] OJ C221/23, and the Decision on monitoring implementation, [1997] OJ C11/1. The Council failed to agree on even a soft law measure concerning the admission of non-economic migrants other than students. For discussion, see M Hedemann-Robinson, 'Third-Country Nationals, European Union citizenship and free movement of persons: A time for bridges rather than divisions?' (1996) 16 YEL 321; S Peers, 'Building Fortress Europe: The Development of EU Migration Law' (1998) CML Rev 35, 1235.

[139] COM(97) 387; [1997] OJ C337/9. For more on the proposed Convention, see M Hedemann-Robinson, 'From Object to Subject? Non-EC Nationals and the Draft Proposal of the Commission for a Council Act Establishing the Rules for Admission of Third-Country Nationals to the Member States' (1998) 18 YEL 289.

[140] In particular, see Directive 2003/86 on family reunion, [2003] OJ L251/12, which was the subject of a challenge from the EP for setting standards that fell below minimum levels of human rights protection on several points (Case C-540/03 *EP v Council* [2006] ECR I-5769). See also Directive 2003/109 on long-term residents' rights, [2004] OJ L16/44, which omitted refugees and persons with subsidiary protection from its scope and left Member States many options to restrict the equal treatment of long-term residents or to limit their movement between Member States, and Directive 2004/114 on admission of students and other non-economic migrants, [2004] OJ L375/12, which is only optional for Member States as regards the three categories of persons other than students (school pupils, unpaid trainees, and volunteers). See also Regulations 1030/2002, [2002] OJ L157/1, on residence permit formats and 859/2003, [2003] OJ L124/1, on social security equality for third country nationals who move within the EU.

[141] The wide-ranging Commission proposal on this issue (COM(2001) 386) was only discussed a few times in the Council's working parties.

[142] See the Green Paper COM(2004) 811) and policy plan (COM(2005) 669) on labour migration.

[143] Directives 2005/71, [2005] OJ L289/15, and 2009/50, [2009] OJ L155/17, applicable from 19 June 2011. See also the Decisions on the European Migration Network, [2008] OJ L131/7; immigration policy information exchange, [2006] OJ L283/40; and the Integration Fund, [2008] OJ L168/18; and Regulations 330/2008 amending the Regulation on residence permit formats, [2008] OJ L115/1, and 862/2007 on immigration and asylum statistics, [2007] OJ L199/23.

regimes as regards the admission of highly skilled workers.[144] Also, it became clear in the limited number of cases reaching the Court of Justice that the Court was inclined to raise the standards in this legislation by means of its interpretation.[145]

On the other hand, the unanimity requirement still limited attempts to further develop EU policy in this field. In particular, before the entry into force of the Treaty of Lisbon, it was impossible to agree legislation on a single permit and equal treatment for third country national workers in general, or the extension of the long-term residents' legislation to include refugees and beneficiaries of subsidiary protection, or application of the new rules on social security to third country national workers.[146]

(c) After 2009

Following the entry into force of the Treaty of Lisbon, the shift to QMV, and the ordinary legislative procedure, as well as the redefinition of EU competence to include the development of a common migration policy, in principle suggests that there may be a transformation of EU policy in this area. To date, after the entry into force of the Treaty, the social security proposal has been adopted by the EU,[147] the talks on a single permit have been more successful,[148] and the discussions on the long-term residents' proposal have been revived.[149] Two post-Lisbon proposals, on seasonal workers and intra-corporate transferees, have greater chances of success.[150] However, it must still be kept in mind that the Treaty's exclusion of competence regarding volumes of labour migration of third country nationals coming from third states will make it impossible to have a fully common policy in this area.[151]

The model which would best describe developments in this area initially was the 'social policy' model, characterized by both a limited degree of harmonization of subject matter and by the setting of minimum standards only—although as compared to the social policy field, the EU was not *obliged* to set minimum standards only as regards legal immigration, and the standards which have been adopted are set at a lower level than the

---

[144] Art 3(4), Directive 2009/50 (ibid).

[145] In Case C-540/03 (n 140 above), the Court emphasized that Member States applying the impugned exceptions to the family reunion Directive could only apply those exceptions on a case by case basis, rather than rejecting all applications which fell within the scope of these exceptions automatically. In *Chakroun* (n 37 above), the Court interpreted the 'social assistance' condition for authorizing family reunion narrowly.

[146] See respectively: COM(2007) 638; COM(2007) 298; COM(2007) 439.

[147] Council doc 11160/10, 16 July 2010, the Council's first reading position, was approved by the EP. See Reg. 1231/2010 ([2010] OJ L 344/1).

[148] See Council doc 10708/10, 8 June 2010. In particular, the Council has agreed on a broad scope of the equal treatment rights (applicable to many third country nationals who are authorized to work, not just those admitted on the basis of a single work/residence permit). The text still has to be agreed with the EP.

[149] See Council doc 17758/10, 21 Dec. 2010, agreed by the Council and the EP. Note that this proposal had been blocked in 2008 by only one Member State.

[150] COM(2010) 378 and 379.

[151] Art 79(5). For interpretation of this exception, see S Peers, 'EU Immigration and Asylum Competence and Decision-Making in the Treaty of Lisbon' (2008) 10 EJML 219, 241–246.

social policy measures,[152] no doubt due to a combination of the unanimous voting requirement[153] and the fact that unlike employees (with home state nationality) and trade unions, third country nationals generally cannot vote or fund political parties. There is of course a degree of cross-over between the two subjects as regards their impact on the labour market,[154] in particular the consideration that differences in regulation of workers might lead to 'unfair competition' and a 'race to the bottom',[155] and both subjects are subject to an exclusion of EU competence for particularly sensitive topics.[156]

However, there are increasing signs of divergence between EU social policy and EU immigration law. First of all, the EU's immigration legislation has, in many cases, an explicit free movement element, setting out specific rules governing the secondary movement of the relevant categories of third country nationals between Member States.[157] Secondly, another point of diversion is the increasing tendency to confine Member States' power to set higher standards to only specific provisions of Immigration Directives;[158] this would be impossible as regards EU social law, since EU legislation in that area is limited to setting minimum standards only. Following the entry into force of the Treaty of Lisbon, this divergence is clearly understandable in light of the Treaty requirement to establish a 'common immigration policy'. Moreover, these two points are linked,[159] since from an internal market perspective, it is sometimes the case that the EU enables free movement between Member States based on

---

[152] It is tempting to speculate that if, say, the Working Time Directive had been an EU immigration measure, it would have set a limit of 168 hours a week working time—ie a 'minimum standard' so low that Member States could not possibly have provided for lower standards.

[153] By way of comparison, the EU has generally not adopted social policy measures subject to a unanimous voting requirement (see now Art 153(2) TFEU, previously Art 137(2) EC).

[154] In fact, there is a possible clash of legal bases as between Art 79 TFEU (as regards labour migration) and Art 153(1)(g) TFEU, as regards working conditions for third country nationals, given that the latter is still subject to unanimous voting with consultation of the EP only (see Art 153(2) TFEU). Also, the EU can only set minimum standards as regards social law (Art 153(4) TFEU, second indent), but is not subject to such a limit as regards immigration law.

[155] See point 9 in the preamble to the latest text of the 'single permit' Directive (n 148 above).

[156] Compare Art 79(5) to Art 153(5) TFEU, previously Art 137(5) EC. The obvious argument is that the former exclusion of competence must be interpreted narrowly, by analogy with the case law on the latter exclusions: see Case C-307/05 *Del Cerro Alonso* [2007] ECR I-7109 and Case C-268/06 *Impact* [2008] ECR I-2483.

[157] See Arts 14–23 of the Long-term Residents Directive (n 140 above); Arts 18–19 of the Blue Card Directive (n 32 above); Art 8 of the Students Directive (n 140 above); Art 13 of the Researchers Directive (n 143 above); and Art 16 of the proposed Directive on intra-corporate transferees (n 150 above).

[158] See Art 4(2) of the Blue Card Directive (ibid); Art 4(2) of the proposed Directive on intra-corporate transferees (ibid); and Art 4(2) of the proposed Directive on seasonal workers (n 150 above). These provisions, *a contrario*, mean that the rules on the *admission* of the persons concerned are (or would be) harmonized, although those rules permit some discretion for Member States: see Arts 5(2), 5(5), 8(2) to 8(5) and 9(3) of the Blue Card Directive, Arts 6(2) to (4) and 7(2) of the seasonal workers' proposal, Arts 6(3) and 7(2) of the intra-corporate transferees proposal.

[159] Note also that the rules on the cross-border movement of researchers and Blue Card holders also only apply to persons *admitted* pursuant to the relevant Directive (see n 157 above), while the rules on the cross-border movement of students require that the criteria for admission are met again as regards the second Member State (Art 8(1)(a) of the Students Directive, n 140 above).

common standards of regulation.[160] However, of course not all internal market legislation insists on such a strict approach, as sometimes compliance with minimum standards is sufficient to ensure free movement;[161] this method is followed in the earlier Long-term Residents' Directive, which does not regulate the initial admission of the persons concerned.[162]

Recent EU immigration legislation also consciously attempts to *facilitate* certain types of legal migration,[163] including by means of the adoption of more favourable rules waiving the more restrictive elements of the early EU immigration legislation for certain desired categories of migrants. Another measure aims to regulate legal migration with a view to *discouraging* irregular migration.[164] This approach shows clear signs of the development of a coherent policy, which has shifted from a minimum standards/social policy model to begin the gradual process of harmonizing national law more intensively. This trajectory is clearly set out in the Stockholm programme, which calls for possible further harmonization of national law in this field with a view to establishing a code on legal immigration—mirroring the development of visa and borders codes.[165]

5. CRIMINAL LAW

(a) Prior to 1999

Prior to the Treaty of Amsterdam, the field of criminal law had already been subject, first of all, to the agreement on a number of Conventions which had been agreed not ratified, during the informal intergovernmental period of JHA integration prior to 1993. There had been modest success agreeing measures on this subject within the Schengen framework as regards extradition, mutual assistance (concerning cooperation between criminal courts, in particular the movement of evidence), *ne bis in idem*

---

[160] For instance, see Chapter III of Directive 2005/36 on the mutual recognition of qualifications, [2005] OJ L255/22.

[161] See ibid, Chapter II.

[162] Art 13 of Directive 2003/109 (n 140 above), provides that Member States are free to set higher standards as regards qualification for long-term resident status, but the persons concerned will not qualify for free movement under the Directive. See the parallel with EU free movement law, as regards (for instance) the free movement of animals for slaughter: Case C-1/96 *CWF* [1998] ECR I-1251.

[163] Point 5 in the preamble to the Researchers Directive (n 143 above) states that 'this Directive is intended to contribute to achieving' the goal of increasing the number of researchers in the EU 'by fostering the admission and mobility for research purposes of third-country nationals... in order to make the Community more attractive to researchers from around the world and to boost its position as an international centre for research'. Point 3 in the preamble to the Blue Card Directive (n 32 above) links '[m]easures to attract and retain highly qualified third-country workers' to the 'broader context' of the Lisbon Strategy. Finally, point 3 in the preamble to the intra-corporate transferees' proposal (n 150 above), links rules 'to make it easier for third-country managers, specialists or graduate trainees to enter the Union in the framework of an intra-corporate transfer' with the 'broader context' of the 'Europe 2020' objectives. Compare with the blanket hostility to labour migration in the 1994 Resolution on the subject (n 138 above).

[164] See point 6 in the preamble to the proposed Directive on seasonal workers (n 150 above).

[165] See n 95 above.

(the cross-border 'double jeopardy' rule, preventing prosecution in a second Member State after a final judgment for the same acts in a first Member State), and the transfer of prisoners.[166]

During the formal intergovernmental period (1993–99), the Member States reached agreement on a limited number of conventions (concerning extradition, corruption, fraud, and driving disqualification), plus a few Joint Actions regarding substantive criminal law (as regards drug trafficking, racism, trafficking in persons and sexual exploitation, private corruption, and organized crime).[167] Overall, the results of this process were still modest, taking into account the delays in ratification of Conventions and the unclear legal effect of Joint Actions.

(b) 1999–2009

During the 'Amsterdam era', after the early adoption of a Convention and Protocol on mutual assistance, Conventions were eschewed in favour of Framework Decisions on criminal law matters, the use of which was ultimately bolstered by the Court of Justice as regards both their legal effect and their capacity to replace prior Conventions.[168] These measures had, as noted already, the advantage of earlier application within Member States. A Decision was used to establish Eurojust, the EU prosecutors' agency.[169]

As for the substance of measures in this area, the foundations were laid in 1999–2001 for the establishment of the principle of mutual recognition in criminal matters, enshrined in the Tampere programme as the central principle at the heart of EU criminal law.[170] Following the impetus of the September 11, 2001 terrorist attacks, the development of EU criminal law hit its high point between 2001–04, in particular as regards the agreement on Framework Decisions on the European Arrest Warrant (EAW) and terrorism within three months of the attacks.[171]

The EAW proved to be the template for the adoption of a number of other mutual recognition measures, each setting out the principle that Member States must recognize the decisions of another Member State's criminal authorities as regards a particular matter, subject to a limited number of grounds for refusal, detailed rules on

---

[166] Arts 48–69 of the Convention (n 5 above).

[167] See [1996] OJ L185/5 (racism); [1996] OJ L342/6 (drug trafficking); [1997] OJ L63/2 (trafficking in persons and sexual exploitation); [1997] OJ L167/1 (synthetic drugs); [1998] OJ L333/1 (money laundering); [1998] OJ L351/1 (organized crime); and [1998] OJ L358/2 (private corruption).

[168] *Pupino* and *Advocaten voor de Wereld* (nn 42 and 44 above).

[169] [2002] OJ L63, as amended by [2003] OJ L245/44 and by [2009] OJ L138/14. See also the Decision (re-)establishing the European Judicial Network: [2008] OJ L348/130.

[170] See the Council work programme on mutual recognition, [2001] OJ C12/10, the earlier Commission Communication on the issue (COM(2000) 495) and discussion of the development of the principle in S Peers, 'Mutual Recognition and Criminal Law in the European Union: Has the Council Got it Wrong?' (2004) 41 CML Rev 5, 7–10.

[171] The measures were formally adopted in 2002: [2002] OJ L190/1 and [2002] OJ L164/3. Contrary to a widespread 'Euromyth', neither measure was even under discussion before 11 September 2001; rather the Commission brought forward the release of its planned proposals on these matters to the end of September 2001. The agreement on these measures within ten weeks is therefore even more impressive.

procedures (such as time limits and standard forms), and vague provisions on human rights. Compared to the measures which they replaced (in most cases, existing Council of Europe Conventions), the EU measures contained fewer grounds for refusal, in particular obliging Member States to surrender their own nationals pursuant to an EAW (replacing the traditional possibility for Member States to refuse to extradite their own nationals, enshrined in many Member States' constitutions),[172] and abolishing, for a lengthy list of crimes, the principle of 'dual criminality', ie the principle that judicial cooperation could usually only take place where the act in question was criminal in both states concerned. It was followed in short order by Framework Decisions on the freezing of assets and evidence in 2003 and on the recognition of non-custodial criminal judgments in 2005.[173] However, the traditional reserve of Member States concerning these matters, in part as a consequence of national constitutional challenges to the EAW, was already reasserting itself: the second of these measures took longer to negotiate and then its adoption was subject to a lengthy delay due to national parliamentary scrutiny. And while the national implementation of the EAW in practice has been judged a success,[174] the implementation of these later two measures has been judged disappointing.[175]

This slowdown continued over the period from 2005–09, resulting in further lengthy negotiations and delays due to parliamentary scrutiny (and in many cases, extended transposition periods) as regards a further batch of mutual recognition measures: Framework Decisions on the recognition of confiscation orders,[176] the transfer of custodial sentences,[177] probation and parole,[178] the European evidence warrant,[179] and pre-trial supervision orders.[180] Member States also insisted on watering down the abolition of the dual criminality principle in many of these measures, and retaining a number of other grounds for refusal, resulting in a complex patchwork of legal requirements, although as regards one issue (the rules regarding *in absentia* trials) standard provisions were later agreed for all the relevant measures.[181] There were also closely connected measures on the recognition of other Member States' criminal convictions,[182] and the transfer of criminal records information between Member States.[183]

---

[172] E Guild and L Marin, *Still not resolved? Constitutional issues of the European Arrest Warrant* (Wolf, 2009).

[173] [2003] OJ L196/45 and [2005] OJ L76/16.

[174] COM(2007) 407 and SEC(2007) 979.

[175] COM(2008) 885; COM(2008) 888.

[176] [2006] OJ L328/59.

[177] [2008] OJ L327/27.

[178] [2008] OJ L337/102.

[179] [2008] OJ L350/72.

[180] [2009] OJ L294/20.

[181] Framework Decision, [2009] OJ L81/24.

[182] [2008] OJ L220/32. Also on this issue, see earlier the amendment to the Framework Decision on counterfeiting the Euro, [2001] OJ L329/3.

[183] See initially the Decision on this issue [2005] OJ L322/23, and subsequently the Framework Decision, [2009] OJ L93/23 and 33.

As regards the related issue of conflicts of jurisdiction, there was great difficulty agreeing on anything at all, with a failure to agree on proposed Framework Decisions updating the double jeopardy rules or regulating the transfer of criminal proceedings,[184] and adoption only of a very weak measure on information and consultation as regards possible conflicts of jurisdiction.[185] There was an even more profound failure to adopt any measures on the high-profile issue of suspects' rights, with a proposed Framework Decision failing to be adopted despite several years of effort.[186] However, as with the issue of labour migration, this topic was relaunched by means of an alternative strategy of tackling the issue piecemeal: a 'roadmap' for tackling the aspects of the issue on a case by case basis was adopted by the Council,[187] and agreement was soon reached on the first measure, concerning translation and interpretation rights for criminal suspects.[188]

On the other hand, it proved much easier to agree Framework Decisions on the more populist subject of crime victims' rights,[189] and on national confiscation proceedings (the latter linked to the mutual recognition measure on the same issue).[190] Moreover, despite the limits on the Court of Justice's jurisdiction in this area, the Court began to become engaged in the particular issues of double jeopardy, the EAW, and crime victims' rights.[191]

As regards substantive criminal law, the main focus of the EU's action was the review of pre-Amsterdam Joint Actions and their replacement by Framework Decisions.[192] A number of Framework Decisions were also adopted in new areas (besides terrorism): counterfeiting the Euro,[193] payment card fraud and counterfeiting,[194] the facilitation of illegal entry and residence;[195] and attacks on information systems;[196] the two adopted measures relating to environmental crime and shipping pollution were both annulled by the Court of Justice.[197] It must be pointed out that the Treaty framework only permitted the EU to establish minimum standards as regards substantive criminal law. Nevertheless, the Framework Decisions were an advance on the prior Joint Actions in particular due to their enhanced legal effect, clearer drafting,

---

[184] [2003] OJ C100/24 and [2009] OJ C219/7.   [185] Framework Decision [2009] OJ L328/42.

[186] COM(2004) 328.   [187] Resolution [2009] OJ C295/1.

[188] COM(2009) 338, 8 July 2009 (Commission proposal); Council doc 14792/09, 23 Oct 2009 (Council agreement). The measure was not adopted before the entry into force of the Treaty of Lisbon for procedural reasons.

[189] [2001] OJ L82/1.

[190] [2005] OJ L68/49.

[191] See the case law referred to at nn 42–51 above.

[192] See the Framework Decisions on money laundering, [2001] OJ L182/1; trafficking in humans [2002] OJ L203/1; corruption in the private sector, [2003] OJ L192/54; the sexual exploitation of children and child pornography, [2004] OJ L13/44; drug trafficking, [2004] OJ L335/8; organised crime, [2008] OJ L300/42; and racism and xenophobia, [2008] OJ L328/55.

[193] [2000] OJ L140/1.

[194] [2001] OJ L149/1.

[195] [2002] OJ L328/1. As noted above, however, this measure replaced the prior Art 27 of the Schengen Convention.

[196] [2005] OJ L69/67.   [197] See n 41 above.

and the rules on minimum penalties which Member States should impose. Towards the end of the Amsterdam era, further steps were taken, as regards amendments to the Framework Decision on terrorism (adding further crimes to reflect a Council of Europe Convention),[198] and as regards proposals to amend the Framework Decisions on trafficking in persons and sexual offences against children, which would have removed exceptions to the obligation to criminalize these acts, amended the rules on jurisdiction, and added a number of rules on victim protection.[199]

(c) After 2009

Following the entry into force of the Treaty of Lisbon, measures have been proposed regarding a new European Protection Order (to allow for the cross-border movement of victim protection orders) and a European Investigation Order (to replace existing measures concerning the cross-border movement of evidence).[200] As regards suspects' rights, the Council roadmap is being implemented in the form of an early agreement between the Council and the EP on a Directive on interpretation and translation rights, and a proposal on the right to information for criminal suspects.[201] In the field of substantive criminal law, the Commission has retabled its proposals for new measures on trafficking in persons and sexual offences against children, and has proposed a Directive (replacing the prior Framework Decision) on attacks on information systems;[202] the first of these has been agreed by the Council.[203] As for the future, the Stockholm programme includes the roadmap on suspects' rights and lists a number of measures in particular areas, but there is no systematic approach to the future development of EU criminal law.[204] It might be surmised, however, that with the abolition of vetoes (and, in effect of national parliamentary scrutiny reserves) it will be easier to reach agreement at a higher level of ambition—which the involvement of the EP will moreover bolster.

Overall, the mutual recognition model for the development of EU criminal law has shown in practice a profound tension between harmonization of law (both procedural and substantive) and the mutual recognition principle, along with battles over human rights issues, the institutional framework, and the constitutional protections of Member States.[205] The Treaty of Lisbon attempts to settle some of these issues but could prove a further forum for disputes, and the new opt-outs in this area raise the same issues as regards asylum, ie the UK could opt out of measures concerning suspects' rights, but into the mutual recognition measures which those suspects' rights measures aim to legitimize.

---

[198] [2008] OJ L330/21.

[199] COM(2009) 135 and 136. These proposals lapsed with the entry into force of the Treaty of Lisbon.

[200] See respectively [2010] OJ C69/5 and [2010] OJ C165/22.

[201] Respectively Directive 2010/64 ([2010] OJ L 280/1) and COM(2010) 392, 20 July 2010.

[202] COM(2010) 94, 95, and 517.

[203] Council doc 17751/10, 21 Dec. 2010, which has been agreed with the EP.

[204] See n 95 above.

[205] See, for instance, V Mitsilegas, *EU Criminal Law* (Hart, 2009).

D. CONCLUSIONS

As might be expected, the move toward the 'Community' model of supranational decision-making, legal instruments, and jurisdiction of the Court of Justice has had some influence on the evolution of policy in this area. The second-generation legislation on visas and borders issues would have been much more difficult to adopt without applying QMV in this area from 2004/05, and the development of EU immigration law and criminal law has already visibly been assisted by the removal of vetoes in these areas by the Treaty of Lisbon. But the change in decision-making rules has done little to assist the agreement on the second phase of EU asylum legislation, and the increased jurisdiction of the Court of Justice had no immediate impact on immigration and asylum cases in the first few months after the Treaty of Lisbon entered into force.

The most recognizable model for the development of EU JHA law has been the visas/borders model, which started out following the basic structure of the EU customs union (common external borders control, freedom of movement within), and has continued to develop along those lines, adding further degrees of harmonization as regards visa lists and conditions for visas, along with a highly nuanced external policy which has an increasing resemblance to the preferential aspects of the EU's common commercial policy. The EU's policy on legal immigration began with clear similarities to the minimum standards/partial harmonization approach familiar from EU social policy, but shows clear signs of moving toward a version of the internal market model, with enhanced possibilities of movement between Member States for those who satisfy the common standards on admission. EU asylum policy has been distorted by the bizarre premise that it should aim to *reduce* movements between Member States, not increase them, and has essentially failed to accomplish this objective—perhaps accounting for the inability to date of the EU to move forward on the second phase of legislative development. Finally, EU criminal law has based itself on the premise that it ought to facilitate the mutual recognition of judicial decisions between Member States without much harmonization of substantive law and with even less harmonization of procedural law—an approach which has avoided the frying pan of attempting extensive harmonization in these sensitive areas only to end up in the fire of national constitutional objections and political obstacles to the further development of this policy in practice, other than the flagship EAW. The cynicism of the EU legislators as regards JHA law can be summed up in the willingness to insist on a one-stop-shop principle for asylum-seekers and visa applicants but a refusal to apply the same principle to prosecutors.

11

CIVIL JUSTICE—A NEWCOMER AND AN UNSTOPPABLE WAVE?

*Eva Storskrubb**

A. INTRODUCTION[1]

> No longer is European law an incoming tide flowing up the estuaries of England. It is like a tidal wave bringing down our sea walls and flowing inland over our fields and houses—to the dismay of all.[2]

One of Lord Denning's immortal quotes introduces us to a relative newcomer on the EU policy scene. The policy area of 'judicial cooperation in civil matters' that will be called 'civil justice' in this chapter, could today, a decade since its inception, aptly be compared to a tidal wave. But what kind of wave is the policy area and should we indeed be dismayed? This chapter attempts to gauge the current stage of evolution of civil justice. First, its background influences are dealt with in Part B after which Parts C and D respectively present the institutional and legislative frameworks of the policy area and its phases. Thereafter, some of the constitutional, regulatory, and substantive themes that have arisen during the first decade of development of the policy area will be raised in Part E.

---

* Senior Attorney at Dittmar & Indrenius, Helsinki.

[1] Note that the abbreviation 'TEU' will be used in this chapter after a Treaty article that refers to the Treaty on European Union in the version in force after 1 December 2009, while 'TFEU' refers to the Treaty on the Functioning of the European Union. 'EC' after a Treaty article refers to a provision of the European Community Treaty in the version in force until 30 November 2009; similarly, 'EU' refers to an article of the Treaty on European Union in the version in force until that date. 'CT' after a Treaty article signifies the Constitutional Treaty.

[2] Denning LJ, 'Introduction' in G Smith, *The European Court of Justice: Judges or Policy Makers?* (Bruges Group, 1990).

B. BACKGROUND

1. INTRODUCTION: TRANSNATIONAL PROCEDURAL COOPERATION

Transnational procedural cooperation in cross-border civil cases regulating such questions as service or enforcement and based on bilateral or multilateral treaties is not a new phenomenon.[3] On a global level the Conventions since 1893 within the auspices of the Hague Conference on Private International Law stand as an example.[4] In addition, cooperation on the regional level such as that between the Benelux countries and the Nordic countries, as well as numerous bilateral treaties among states, have old roots.[5] Furthermore, the recent trends of liberalization of markets, transfrontier migrations, and globalization have occasioned a new evolution of international initiatives.[6]

2. OVERLAPPING INFLUENCES

Aside from transnational procedural cooperation as the obvious source of influence, various overlapping developments that relate to civil proceedings that have occurred on various regulatory levels have influenced the birth of civil justice in the EU and continue to interact with it. Reforms of domestic procedural rules in Europe have cut across the civil versus common law divide, through devices such as case management, managerial judges, and allocating resources and have enforced a mutual quest for procedural efficiency.[7] In addition, constitutional reforms on both the intergovernmental and national levels, in particular Article 6 of the European Convention on Human Rights and subsequent case law, have forged a mutual European standard for fair trial.[8] Various projects of the Council of Europe also support achieving speedy access to justice of litigants in practice.[9]

---

[3] See *inter alia* D McClean, International Co-operation in Civil and Criminal Matters (2nd edn, Oxford University Press, 2002).

[4] See <http://www.hcch.net/index_en.php?act=conventions.listing>.

[5] W A Kennett, 'Harmonization and the Judgments Convention: Historical Influences' (1993) 1 Euro Rev of Priv L 87, 104–106.

[6] B Hess, 'Le compétences externes de la Communauté européenne dans le cadre de l'Art 65 CE' in A Fuchs, H Muir Watt, and E Pataut (eds), *Les conflits de lois et le système juridique communautaire* (Dalloz-Sirey, 2004) 82–83.

[7] A A S Zuckerman, 'Justice in Crisis: Comparative Dimensions of Civil Procedure' in A A S Zuckerman (ed), *Civil Justice in Crisis—Comparative Perspectives of Civil Procedure* (Oxford University Press, 1999) 47–48; C H van Rhee, 'Introduction' in C H van Rhee (ed), *European Traditions in Civil Procedure* (Intersentia, 2005) 19–22; N Trocker and V Varano, 'Concluding Remarks' in N Trocker and V Varano (eds), *The Reforms of Civil Procedure in Comparative Perspective* (Giappichelli, 2005) 247–254.

[8] E Storskrubb and J Ziller, 'Access to Justice in European Comparative Law' in F Francioni (ed), *Access to Justice as a Human Right* (Oxford University Press, 2007) 178–179 and K Kerameus, 'Procedural Implications of Civil Law Unification' in A Hartkamp *et al* (eds), *Towards a European Civil Code*, (3rd edn, Kluwer International, 2004) 154–156.

[9] The Council of Europe has published Recommendations, R (81) 7 on Measures Facilitating Access to Justice (adopted on 14 May 1981) and R (84) on Principles of Civil Procedure Designed to Improve the

In parallel, aside from early limited sector specific rules,[10] the European Court of Justice (ECJ) has, in case law from 1976 onwards, imposed the requirements *of non-discrimination* and *efficiency* on national procedural rules because domestic enforcement of substantive EC rights relies on national procedural and remedial rules.[11] The Lisbon Treaty in Article 19(2) TEU is intended to embody these principles: 'the Member States shall provide remedies sufficient to ensure effective legal protection in the fields covered by Union law'. As a result of the case law of the ECJ it has been held that the EU has a combination of national procedural competence and European procedural primacy including an independent right of access to court.[12]

Following these developments two separate projects, (i) the Storme Report on harmonized European civil procedural rules in 1994,[13] and (ii) the ALI and UNIDROIT model civil procedure principles for transnational litigation in 2004,[14] have together with the ECJ case law raised a debate regarding the desirability and level of procedural regulation and potential harmonization. Common procedural rules are seen as a logical extension of market integration.[15] However, local legal culture, varied societal goals, subsidiarity, and diversity, are raised as arguments against harmonization or to emphasize its difficulty.[16] In addition, since harmonization can potentially

---

Functioning of Justice (adopted on 28 February 1984) both available at: <http://www.coe.int/t/dghl/cooperation/cepej/textes/ListeRecRes_en.asp>. In addition, its Commission for the Efficiency of Justice, CEPEJ, operates various projects; see homepages: <http://www.coe.int/t/dghl/cooperation/cepej/default_en.asp>.

[10] *Inter alia* in the sector of consumer law; Parliament and Council Directive (EC) 98/27 on injunctions for the protection of consumers' interest [1998] OJ L166/51, Council Resolution on a Community-wide network of national bodies for the extra-judicial settlement of consumer disputes [2000] OJ C155/1, see <http://ec.europa.eu/consumers/redress_cons/index_en.htm>. See also E Storskrubb, *Civil Procedure and EU Law—A Policy Area Uncovered* (Oxford University Press, 2008) 25–32.

[11] Case 33/76 *Rewe-Zentralfinanz eG and Rewe-Zentral AG v Landwirtschaftskammer für das Saarland* [1976] ECR 1989. For works regarding this case law see *inter alia* R Craufurd-Smith, 'Remedies for Breaches of EU Law in National Courts: Legal Variation and Selection' in P Craig and G de Búrca (eds), *The Evolution of EU Law* (Oxford University Press, 1999) 287–320; M Dougan, *National Remedies Before the Court of Justice, Issues of Harmonisation and Differentiation* (Hart, 2004) and Chapter 14 in this work, as well as J Engström, *The Europeanisation of Remedies and Procedures through Judge-made Law—Can a Trojan Horse Achieve Effectiveness?* PhD thesis EUI (2009). Note that most of the ECJ case law has developed in the context of administrative or public law but the importance for the private law field has been perceived as increasing; see Storskrubb (n 11 above) 16–17.

[12] J Delicostopoulos, 'Towards European Procedural Primacy in National Legal Systems', (2003) 9 ELJ 599; C N Kakouris, 'Do the Member States Possess Judicial Procedural "Autonomy"?' (1997) 34 CML Rev 1389–1390: W van Gerven, 'Of Rights, Remedies and Procedures' (2000) 37 CML Rev 501–502 and A Rosas, 'Oikeus kansalliseen oikeudenkäyntiin EU-oikeuden mukaan' in *Juhlajulkaisu Pekka Hallberg* (2004) 372.

[13] M Storme (ed), Approximation of Judiciary Law in the European Union (Nijhoff, 1994).

[14] See <http://www.unidroit.org/English/principles/civilprocedure/main.htm>.

[15] See *inter alia* A Schwarze, 'Enforcement of Private Law: The Missing Link in the Process of European Harmonisation' (2000) 8 Euro Rev Priv L 138–141.

[16] See *inter alia* S Prehal, 'Judge-made Harmonisation of National Procedural Rules: A Bridging Perspective' in J Wouters and J Stuyck (eds), *Principles of Proper Conduct for the Supranational, State and Private Actors in the European Union: Towards a Ius Commune* (Intersentia, 2001) 55–58, as well as P Mayer, 'L'utilité des règles transnationales de procédure civile: Une vue critique' and H Muir Watt, 'Quelle méthode?' both in P Fouchard (ed), *Vers un procès civil universel? Les règles transnationales de procédure civile de l'American Law Institute* (Pantheon-Assas, 2001) 24 and 40.

entail complexity and fragmentation as well as result in 'lowest common denominator' solutions there are also disincentives to harmonization.[17] Further, creating separate national and supranational procedural strands raise issues of scope, divergent interpretation, and discrimination.[18] A more decentralized and flexible development of common procedural rules and cooperation mechanisms has hence been favoured with simultaneous development of a common legal culture and discussion on fundamental principles.[19]

3. CONCLUSION

The background influences show that the modern themes of civil justice include access to justice, fair trial, and efficiency. These are *per se* complex to achieve but the regulatory debate also shows that any harmonization or creation of a supranational system must be fine-tuned. Whether the evolution of civil justice in the EU has so far succeeded will be considered in Part E after a review of the institutional (Part C) and legislative (Part D) developments.

C. INSTITUTIONAL AND POLITICAL EVOLUTION

1. INTRODUCTION: COMPETENCE AND IMPETUS

Within the European Union legislative competence and political impetus are necessary for the creation of legislation within a policy area. In this section the creation of the legal basis, its limitations as well as structural particularities will be presented together with the emergence and continuance of the necessary political impetus.

2. PRE-AMSTERDAM

The Treaty of Rome establishing the European Economic Community in 1957 already partly foresaw the need for civil justice. Article 220 EC (subsequently Article 293 EC) did not, however, allow for secondary Community law, but rather formed a basis for intergovernmental cooperation. As it was perceived that it would benefit the common market, the Member States enacted mutual jurisdiction and enforcement as well as contractual choice of law provisions in the Brussels and Rome Conventions of 1968

---

[17] See *inter alia* P H Lindblom, 'Harmony of the Legal Spheres, A Swedish View on the Construction of a Unified European Procedural Law' (1997) 5 Euro Rev Priv L 26 and T Andersson, 'Approximation of Procedural Law in Europe' in M Storme (ed), *Procedural Laws in Europe. Towards Harmonisation* (Maklu, 2003) 64.

[18] See *inter alia* M-L Niboyet, 'Quels litiges?' in Fouchard (n 17 above) 52–54.

[19] J Niemi-Kiesiläinen, 'International Cooperation and Approximation of Laws in the Field of Civil Procedure' in V Heiskanen and K Kulovesi (eds), *Function and Future of European Law* (Helsinki University Press, 1999) 254–256; P Biavati, 'Is Flexibility a Way to the Harmonization of Civil Procedural Law in Europe?' in F Carpi and M Lupoi (eds), *Essays on Transnational and Comparative Civil Procedure* (Giappichelli, 2001) 100–101.

and 1980 on this basis.[20] Other potential legal bases relating to the common market and to Union citizenship have been proposed by commentators, but none of these were used in the pre-Amsterdam era to introduce any further civil justice projects.[21] The Treaty of Maastricht in force in 1993 introduced the Third Pillar with Article K.1 EU specifically mentioning civil justice measures. However, the Third Pillar method was predominantly intergovernmental with inherent disadvantages including slowness, requirement of unanimity, absence of parliamentary control, and a cumbersome convention system.[22] The only two Conventions signed in the field of civil justice had not entered into force for slowness in transposition when the Treaty of Amsterdam entered into force.[23]

3. THE TREATY OF AMSTERDAM

(a) Community competence

Partly as a response to the structural deficiencies mentioned above, the Treaty of Amsterdam, which came into force in 1999, removed civil justice from the Third Pillar and placed it in the First Pillar. Thus, the EC Treaty for the first time in Article 65 EC contained a separate legal basis for civil justice including a list of themes for measures to be adopted.[24] The legal basis limited the competence to 'matters having cross-border implications' and 'insofar as necessary for the proper functioning of the internal market'. Commentators have argued for both a restrictive and an expansive interpretation of these competence limitations.[25] In practice, the Community institutions must take them into account and this is often confirmed in the preambles to the legislative measures. The cross-border limitation has occasioned an institutional competence debate in which the Commission has favoured and argued for an expansive interpretation.[26] The Member States in the Council, however, confirmed that the

---

[20] Pipkorn J, 'Les méthodes de rapprochement des législations a l'intérieur de la CEE' in P Bourel *et al*, *L'Influence des Communautés Européennes sur le Droit International Privé des Etats Membres* (Larcier, 1981) 40–42. Further attempts at intergovernmental projects failed, see A-M Rouchaud, 'Le renforcement de la coopération judiciaire' in Université Jean Moulin (ed), *Les effets des jugements nationaux dans les autres États membres de l'Union européenne* (Lyon, 2001) 20–21.

[21] Storskrubb (n 11 above) 35–38.

[22] G Barret, 'Cooperation in Justice and Home Affairs in the European Union—An Overview and a Critique' in G Barrett (ed), *Justice Cooperation in the EU, The Creation of a European Legal Space* (Institute of European Affairs, 1997) 17–38.

[23] Rouchaud (n 21 above) 22–23.

[24] H Labayle, 'Un espace de liberté, de sécurité et de justice' (1997) 4 RTDCiv 815–819 for an exposé of the Treaty negotiation process.

[25] C Kohler, 'Interrogations sur les sources du droit international privé européen après le traité d'Amsterdam' (1999) Revue Critique de Droit International Privé 1, 18–21; A-M Van den Bossche, 'L'espace européen de justice et le (rapprochement du) droit judiciaire' in G De Leval and M Storme (eds), *Le droit processuel et judiciaire européen* (La Carte, 2003) 1 ; P-E Partsch, *Le Droit International Privé Européen—De Rome à Nice* (Larcier, 2003) 310–312.

[26] See *inter alia* COM(2002) 746, Green Paper on a European order for payment procedure and on measures to simplify and speed up small claims litigation, 6–7, and COM(2004) 173 COM(2004) 17, Proposal for a Regulation of the European Parliament and of the Council creating a European order for payment procedure [2006] OJ C49/37.

cross-border limitation should be adhered to and reached a political compromise on the definition of cross-border matters. The competence issue, which has been called the constitutional conundrum, goes to the heart of whether the vision for the policy area is more restrictive or expansive.[27]

(b) Institutional and structural issues

An idiosyncratic legislative procedure was introduced in Article 67 EC that deviated from the co-decision procedure, the 'Community method'. First, the Commission shared the right to initiative with the Member States. Secondly, the European Parliament only had the right to be consulted. Thirdly, the Council had to adopt legislation by unanimity. In addition, the role of the ECJ was significantly limited in Article 68 EC, in that requests for preliminary rulings could only emanate from national courts of last resort, over whose decisions there was no appeal.[28] This contrasted not only with the normal powers of the ECJ in the Community system, but also with the prior system for the Brussels Convention.[29] A further derogation and complexity was added by enacting separate Protocols for the UK, Ireland, and Denmark in which they 'opted out' of civil justice and which introduced 'flexibility' or 'variable geometry'.[30] These Member States were hence not bound by Community legislation for civil justice but could 'opt in' by choice.[31]

Finally, a further structural consequence was Community external competence over civil justice. First, it entailed that the measures where relevant had to clarify the relationship with pre-existing international treaties.[32] Secondly, for new international projects the exact degree of competence, exclusive or shared with the Member Sates, had to be evaluated casuistically.[33] The ECJ has for example held the competence to be

---

[27] Storskrubb (n 11 above) 173, 185–186, 206–207, 272–273.

[28] On the interpretation of Art 68 see Case C-24/02 *Marseille Fret SA v Seatrano Shipping Company Ltd* [2002] ECR I-3383; Case C-555/03 *Magali Warbecq v Ryanair Ltd* [2004] ECR I-6041. In Case C-175/06 *Alessandro Tedesco v Tomasoni Fittings SrL and RWO Marine Equipment Ltd* (withdrawn after AG Opinion published) AG Kokott considered that a request for evidence under the Evidence Regulation might be the object of a referral for a preliminary ruling, because there was no appeal over the procedural decision and it constituted a decision in procedure separate from the main proceedings. The second derogation regarding the ECJ in Art 68 EC was a new procedural route for the Commission, Council, or Member States to request a ruling on the interpretation of Treaty provisions or secondary legislation. Such rulings would not apply to national court judgments which had become res judicata. There had been no request under this provision in relation to the civil justice when the Treaty of Lisbon entered into force and abolished this derogation.

[29] Partsch (n 26 above) 57–58.

[30] J Basedow, 'The Communitarization of the Conflict of Laws under the Treaty of Amsterdam' (2000) 37 CML Rev 695; J Monar, 'Justice and Home Affairs in the Treaty of Amsterdam: Reform at the Price of Fragmentation' (1998) 23 ELRev 332–335.

[31] Art 3 of Protocol 4, Art 7 of Protocol 5.

[32] I Thoma, 'La définition et l'exercice des compétences externes de la Communauté européenne au domaine de la coopération dans les matières civiles ayant une incidence transfrontière' (2002) 10 Euro Rev Priv L 408–413, analyses the Brussels I and II Regulations in this respect.

[33] The '*AETR* doctrine' will apply, ie Case 22/70 *Commission v Council (AETR or ERTA)* [1971] ECR 263 and subsequent case law. See M Cremona Chapter 9 in this work. See also in the civil justice context *inter alia* M Wilderspin and A-M Rouchaud-Joët, 'La competence externe de la Communauté européenne en droit international privé' (2004) Revue Critique de Droit International Privé 1, 7–10, and T Kruger, *Civil Jurisdiction Rules of the EU and their Impact on Third States* (Oxford University Press, 2008).

exclusive in the context of the project to revise the Lugano Convention.[34] When the competence is shared, the Community and the Member States are under an obligation to cooperate and find a uniform stance.[35] To clarify this cooperation two Regulations have been enacted to establish a procedure for the negotiation and conclusion of bilateral agreements for certain specific instruments.[36]

4. THE TREATY OF NICE AND OTHER POST-AMSTERDAM MEASURES

The Treaty of Nice, in force in 2003, amended Article 67 EC and introduced the normal legislative co-decision procedure for civil justice. However, family law measures specifically still remained within the derogation and required unanimity in the Council.[37] The Treaty of Nice did not address the derogation regarding the ECJ.[38] However, subsequently and apparently due to the unsuccessful ratification process for the Constitutional Treaty,[39] the Commission proposed a separate decision to adapt the provision relating to the ECJ.[40] However, this proposal was not accepted by the Council and remained an issue to be addressed in future Treaty reform. In relation to the Member State opt-out derogations, both the UK and Ireland opted in for several measures adopted in the policy area. Because the Danish opt-in was more

---

[34] Opinion 1/03 [2006] ECR I-1145. N Lavranos, Case Comment (2006) 43 CML Rev 1087-1110.

[35] For examples see W O'Brien, 'The Hague Convention on Jurisdiction and Judgments: The Way Forward' (2003) 66 MLR 491–492 and B Hess, 'Le compétences externes de la Communauté européenne dans le cadre de l'Art 65 CE' in A Fuchs, H Muir Watt, and E Pataut (eds), *Les conflits de lois et le système juridique communautaire* (Dalloz-Sirey, 2004) 90–95 and 98–99, and A Borrás, 'The Effect of the Adoption of Brussels I and Rome I on the External Competences of the EC and the Member States' in J Meeusen, M Pertegás, and G Straetmans (eds), *Enforcement of International Contracts in the European Union. Convergence and Divergence between Brussels I and Rome I* (Intersentia, 2004) 1107–1179.

[36] Council Regulation (EC) 662/2009 establishing a procedure for the negotiation and conclusion of agreements between Member States and third countries on particular matters concerning the law applicable to contractual and non-contractual obligations [2009] OJ L200/25; and Council Regulation (EC) 664/2009 establishing a procedure for the negotiation and conclusion of agreements between Member States and third countries concerning jurisdiction, recognition and enforcement of judgments and decisions in matrimonial matters, matters of parental responsibility and matters relating to maintenance obligations, and the law applicable to matters relating to maintenance obligations [2009] OJ L200/46.

[37] The Council could under amended Art 67 EC by unanimous decision decide to apply the co-decision legislative procedure for family law matters. However, this possibility or passerelle clause has never been used despite the proposal of the Commission to use it for matters relating to the maintenance obligations, calling on the Council to provide for measures relating to maintenance obligations taken under Art 65 of the Treaty establishing the European Community to be governed by the procedure laid down in Art 251 of that Treaty, COM(2005) 648.

[38] H Labayle, 'Les nouveaux domaines d'intervention de la Cour de justice: l'espace de liberté, de sécurité et de justice' in M Dony and E Bribosia (eds), *L'avenir du système juridictionnel de l'Union européenne* (Université de Bruxelles, 2002) 74–75, affirming that the Treaty of Nice did not reopen the matter even though it would have been possible.

[39] M Dougan, 'The Convention's Draft Constitutional Treaty: Bringing Europe Closer to its Lawyers?' (2003) 28 ELRev 792 and J-V Louis, 'La fonction juridictionnelle de Nice à Rome' (2003) JTDroit Eur 262, confirm that this was one of the successes of judicial reform proposed in the Draft Constitution.

[40] Adaptation of the provisions of Title IV of the Treaty establishing the European Community relating to the jurisdiction of the Court of Justice with a view to ensuring more effective judicial protection, COM(2006) 346.

cumbersome separate Conventions have been agreed including Denmark within the framework of two of the Regulations of the policy area from 2007.[41] The Conventions have been regarded as exceptional and transitional measures in anticipation of future Treaty reform.[42] Aside from these changes the framework for civil justice was not amended in the Nice era.

5. THE LISBON TREATY

(a) Union competence

Amendment to the legal basis for civil justice was already envisaged in the Constitutional Treaty signed in 2004.[43] The reform process has been completed with the Lisbon Treaty and most of the proposed amendments for civil justice are retained.[44] Article 81 TFEU replaces Article 65 EC. The first amendment in the new legal basis is the internal market limitation which has been changed from 'in so far as necessary' to 'particularly when necessary'. The limitation has therefore been turned into a mere impetus and hence the ambit of competence is extended. However, the more central cross-border limitation has, as expected, been retained, but whether or not it is still able to stem the dynamism of the policy area remains to be seen. The development of civil justice is specifically stated to be based on the principle of mutual recognition, which has been considered the cornerstone of the policy area. The exact implications of its addition to the legal basis also remain to be seen.

In addition, the new legal basis has extended the substantive list of themes to include alternative dispute resolution and judicial training. Such measures have already been proposed under the general theme 'measures eliminating obstacles to the good functioning of civil proceedings' already included in Article 65 EC. The new additions however provide more transparency, emphasize the importance of these procedural institutions, and may form a basis for more intrusive measures in these specific fields. The list of themes now also includes 'measures aiming to ensure effective access to justice'. It is not clear what kinds of additional measures are intended to fall within its scope. Significantly the ideology of efficiency is added to the traditional concept of 'access to justice'.[45] The new addition broadens the scope of the competence and

---

[41] Council Decision 2006/325/EC concerning the conclusion of the Agreement between the European Community and the Kingdom of Denmark on jurisdiction and the recognition and enforcement of judgments in civil and commercial matters [2006] OJ L120/22; Council Decision 2006/326/EC concerning the conclusion of the Agreement between the European Community and the Kingdom of Denmark on service of judicial and extrajudicial documents in civil and commercial matters [2006] OJ L120/23. Denmark ratified the agreements on 18 January 2007.

[42] Proposal for a Council Decision concerning the signing of the Agreement between the European Community and the Kingdom of Denmark extending to Denmark the provisions of Council Regulation (EC) 1348/2000 on the service in the Member States of judicial and extrajudicial documents in civil or commercial matters, COM(2005) 146, 2.

[43] Art III-269 CT, Constitutional Treaty [2004] OJ C310/1.

[44] [2007] OJ C306/1, consolidated version [2008] OJ C115/1. See G-R de Groot and J-J Kuipers, 'The New Provisions on Private International Law in the Treaty of Lisbon' (2008) 15 MJ 1, 109–114.

[45] See below Part E and Storskrubb (n 11 above) 279–284.

perhaps paves the way for more proactive measures, for example in relation to legal aid or execution proper. Its potential future interaction with Article 47 of the EU Charter of Fundamental Rights will be interesting and might lead to a higher or qualitative standard for civil justice.[46]

(b) Institutional and structural change

First, the restricted jurisdiction of the ECJ in relation to civil justice is removed. Hence, the ECJ has 'normal' jurisdiction over preliminary referrals. In relation to the legislative procedure, the ordinary procedure applies to the policy area. However, for family law matters the requirement of unanimity in the Council remains and the Parliament is only consulted. The scope of 'family law matters' is nevertheless relevant for the practical importance of the derogation.[47] A passerelle clause is included in Article 81(3) TFEU by which the Council may by unanimity after consulting the Parliament agree that certain family law matters may be enacted following the ordinary legislative procedure. However, in such cases the national parliaments shall be notified and if a national parliament objects within six months such a decision shall not be adopted. This clause, by which one national parliament might affect the legislative process, demonstrates the balance between the political desire to move forward in the area of family law and the politically sensitive nature of the area.[48] Finally, the position of Denmark is revised in relation to civil justice in Article 3 of the Annex to Protocol 22, which means that an opt-in by mere notification of participation is now also possible for Denmark.

6. FROM TAMPERE TO STOCKHOLM VIA THE HAGUE

In addition to the civil justice legal basis introduced in 1999 by the Treaty of Amsterdam the new policy vision of an Area of Freedom, Security and Justice (AFSJ) was enunciated in Article 2 EU. The new policy vision was rapidly followed by statements regarding its implementation as a response to the Treaty-set five-year deadline for the creation of the AFSJ.[49] From these early policy documents a new synergy and pressure for change is discernable in comparison to the very slow preceding intergovernmental method.[50] Of particular significance are the 2000 Conclusions of the Tampere European Council that fleshed out the specific aims and

---

[46] Storskrubb (n 11 above) 91. For an analysis of the role of the Charter of Fundamental Rights in the Treaty reform context see P Craig, 'The Community, Rights and the Charter' (2002) 14 ERPL 195 and 'The Treaty of Lisbon: Process, architecture and substance' (2008) 33 ELRev 137, 162–165.

[47] See *inter alia* Proposal for a Regulation on jurisdiction, applicable law, recognition and enforcement of decisions and authentic instruments in matters of succession and the creation of a European Certificate of Succession, COM(2009) 154, 3, in which the Commission considers that matters of succession fall outside the scope of the family law exception and are therefore subject to the ordinary legislative procedure.

[48] de Groot and Kuipers (n 45 above) 113–114 for examples of situations in which the passerelle might be used.

[49] Art 61 EC. Action Plan of Commission and Council [1999] OJ C19/1.

[50] W A Kennett, *Enforcement of Judgments in Europe* (Oxford University Press, 2000) 6.

objectives for the separate policy fields of AFSJ.[51] In 2004, after the first five years of implementing the AFSJ during which constant follow-up was undertaken,[52] a second phase was launched in the so-called Hague Programme of the European Council outlining a new five-year agenda.[53] At the end of 2009 a following five-year agenda has been launched by the European Council in the Stockholm Programme.[54]

After the first five years of legislative activity, the overall objective for civil justice in the Hague Programme was to strive towards effective access to justice by focusing on the enforcement of judgments and on the completion of the mutual recognition programme; and to build up confidence, mutual trust, and a European judicial culture through training and networking.[55] These aims demonstrated a new focus beyond merely creating legislation and in part echoed commentators' emphasis on the importance of simultaneously developing a common legal culture.

In the Stockholm Programme mutual recognition, the implementation and evaluation of enacted measures, as well as training and the creation of a mutual culture is still important.[56] In addition, the consolidation and streamlining of the measures is proposed to achieve coherent user-friendly instruments that ensure uniform application.[57] However, mention of e-Justice, electronic support tools for practitioners and citizens as well as networks, and the new Justice Forum as a means to achieve the desired goals, show an awareness of the holistic nature of the task ahead, as well as the need to get down to the grass-root level of implementation.[58] Finally, the Programme emphasizes perhaps more than before the role of fundamental rights albeit that efficiency is still also an underlying theme.[59] The Action Plan of the Commission that is intended to provide a road map for implementing the Stockholm Programme lists several measures that focus on follow-up, consolidation, and support tools for the measures already enacted.[60] However, the mention of future consultation on collective redress and on potential minimum standards for civil proceedings demonstrates that further substantive broadening and deepening of the policy area is envisaged for the years to come.[61]

[51] Council Conclusions No 200/1/99 available at: <http://www.consilium.europa.eu/ueDocs/cms_Data/docs/pressData/en/ec/00200-r1.en9.htm>.
[52] The Commission published biannual Scoreboards, see *inter alia* COM(2000) 167 and COM(2004) 401.
[53] The Hague Programme: Strengthening Freedom, Security and Justice in the European Union [2005] OJ C53/1.
[54] The Stockholm Programme—An open and secure Europe serving and protecting the citizens, 2 December 2009, Council Note 17024/09, 4–9.
[55] Hague Programme (n 54 above) 11, 13–14.
[56] Stockholm Programme (n 55 above) 4-9, 21–22, 24.
[57] ibid 4, 24.
[58] ibid 21, 26–27.
[59] ibid 11–12, 24, 31–32.
[60] Communication from the Commission to the European Parliament, the Council and the European Economic and Social Committee and the Committee of the Regions, delivering an area of freedom, security and justice for Europe's citizens, Action Plan Implementing the Stockholm Programme COM(2010) 171, 20–21, 23.
[61] ibid 19, 23.

7. CONCLUSION

The institutional evolution shows that civil justice has been formally subjected to the requirements relating to the conferral of power and institutional constraints that have in part stemmed its dynamism.[62] The most sensitive issues to arise in this evolution relate to the cross-border limitation, the requirement of unanimity in the Council for family law matters, and external competence. Nevertheless, use of Article 65 EC (now Article 81 TFEU) has been supported, and real legislative progress has been achieved in what was before perceived as a sovereignty-sensitive policy domain, as will be shown below in Part D that presents the legislative evolution.[63]

D. LEGISLATIVE FRAMEWORK

1. INTRODUCTION: TERMINOLOGY

The EU civil justice concept of 'judicial cooperation in civil matters' is a novel legal one and it was not defined in the Treaty of Amsterdam or any of the subsequent Treaty reforms. Neither of the legal concepts, private international law and international civil procedure, regardless of national variations in the scope of the concepts, encompasses the full breadth of the policy area, and it has been suggested that the study of the policy area is situated at the crossroads of procedural, private international, and European Community law.[64] The term has also been criticized for being inadequate as giving too narrow a title to a policy area and being potentially amorphous and unhelpful.[65] However, it is perhaps suitable that a new autonomous EU-wide umbrella concept has been created to encompass the panoply of measures that will be presented below under the following headings: procedural cooperation, applicable law, family law, substantive law, and overarching measures.

2. PROCEDURAL COOPERATION

Initially the judicial cooperation measures enacted in the policy dealt with traditional aspects of private transnational procedural cooperation: the 'Service Regulation'[66]

---

[62] J Meeusen, 'Fifteen Theses on Brussels I, Rome I and the European Union's Institutional Framework' in Meeusen, Pertegás, and Straetmans (n 36 above) 47.

[63] M Den Boer, 'An Area of Freedom, Security and Justice: Bogged Down by Compromise' in D O'Keeffe and P Twomey (eds), *Legal Issues of the Amsterdam Treaty* (Hart, 1999) 303.

[64] Storskrubb (note 11 above) 9–11 and D Lebeau and M-L Niboyet, 'Regards croisés du processualiste et de l'internationaliste sur le règlement CE du 28 mai 2001 relatif à l'obtention des preuves civiles à l'étranger' (2003) Gazette du Palais–Doctrine 221.

[65] Partsch (n 26 above) 295 and Storskrubb (n 11 above) 12.

[66] Council Regulation (EC) 1348/00 on the service in the Member States of judicial and extrajudicial documents in civil or commercial matters [2000] OJ L160/37, which has been replaced by Council and Parliament Regulation (EC) 1393/07 [2007] OJ L324/79. For a review of Regulation 1348/00 see Storskrubb (n 11 above) 98–113, and C Vanheukelen, 'Le règlement 1348/2000—Analyse et évaluation par un praticien du droit' in De Leval and Storme (n 26 above) 195–235.

regulating cross-border service of documents; the 'Evidence Regulation'[67] regulating cross-border taking of evidence; and the 'Brussels I Regulation'[68] regulating international jurisdiction and cross-border recognition and enforcement of judgments for civil and commercial matters excluding, however, *inter alia* family law matters.

In addition the 'Insolvency Regulation'[69] regulating jurisdiction, recognition, applicable law, and coordination of insolvency proceedings in several Member States; the 'Legal Aid Directive'[70] regulating legal aid applications and the scope of legal aid in cross-border cases; and the 'Enforcement Order Regulation'[71] regulating a simplified system of recognition and enforcement for uncontested claims that abolishes the exequatur procedure have been enacted. These are not novel procedural themes in the transnational procedural sense as such, but these measures are innovative due to the level and depth of regulation, and because of their specific substantive content.

Further, the 'Payment Order Regulation,'[72] the 'Small Claims Regulation',[73] and the 'ADR Directive'[74] have been enacted. These measures were all novel in the

---

[67] Council Regulation (EC) 1206/01 on cooperation between the courts of the Member States in the taking of evidence in civil or commercial matters [2001] OJ L174/1. For a review of Regulation 1206/01 see *inter alia* Storskrubb (n 11 above) 114–131 and Lebeau and Niboyet (n 65 above) 221–233.

[68] Council Regulation (EC) 44/01 on jurisdiction and the recognition and enforcement of judgments in civil and commercial matters [2001] OJ L12, 16/1. For a review of Regulation 1206/01 see *inter alia* Storskrubb (n 11 above) 133–152, W A Kennett, 'The Brussels I Regulation' (2001) 50 ICLQ 725–737.
The Commission has also published a Report on the application of Council Regulation 44/01, COM(2009) 174, and a Green Paper on the review of Council Regulation 44/01, COM(2009) 175. The Green Paper asked a number of questions for consultation on specific areas of potential reform, including *inter alia* (i) complete abolition of the exequatur procedure, (ii) the relationship to the international legal order and in particular defendants from third countries, (iii) parallel proceedings also in situation of choice of court agreements, and (iv) the effectiveness of arbitration agreements. At the time of writing no new legislative proposal has yet been published but according to the Action Plan (n 61 above) one is planned to be published in 2010. In addition, a group of experts has been appointed to deal with the interface between the regulation and arbitration, see <http://ec.europa.eu/home-affairs/tenders/docs/2010/tor_regulation_44_2001.pdf>.

[69] Council Regulation (EC) 1346/00 on insolvency proceedings [2006] OJ L160 /1. For a review of Regulation 1346/00 see *inter alia* J Israël, *European Cross-Border Insolvency* (Sweet & Maxwell, 2005).

[70] Council Directive 03/8/EC to improve access to justice in cross-border disputes by establishing minimum common rules relating to legal aid for such disputes [2003] OJ L26/4, corrigendum [2003] OJ L32/15. For a review of Council Directive 03/8 see *inter alia* E Leroy, 'L'aide juridique et judiciaire en droit européen' in De Leval and Storme (n 26 above) 295–327.

[71] Parliament and Council Regulation 805/04/EC creating a European Enforcement Order for uncontested claims [2004] OJ L143/15. For a review of Regulation 805/04 see *inter alia* C Crifò, 'First Steps towards the Harmonisation of Civil Procedure: the Regulation Creating a European Enforcement Order for Uncontested Claims' (2005) 24 CJQ 200–218, N Boschiero, 'The Forthcoming European Enforcement Order—Towards a European Law-Enforcement Area' (2003) Riv Dir Intern 2, 394–425, and Storskrubb (n 11 above) 153–168.

[72] Parliament and Council Regulation 1896/06/EC creating a European order for payment procedure [2006] OJ L399/1. For a review of Regulation 1896/06 see *inter alia* Storskrubb (n 11 above) 203–219, and J P Correa Delcasso, 'Le titre exécutoire européen et l'inversion du contentieux' (2001) RIDC 61–82.

[73] Parliament and Council Regulation 861/07/EC establishing a European Small Claims Procedure [2007] OJ L199/1. For a review of Regulation 861/07 see *inter alia* Storskrubb (n 11 above) 220–232, see G Haibach, 'The Commission Proposal for a Regulation Establishing a European Small Claims Procedure: An Analysis' (2005) 13 Euro Rev Priv L 593–601 and S De Greef, 'La procédure européenne pour des petits litiges: Un nouveau pas dans la convergence du droit judiciaire (2007–08) European Journal of Consumer Law 237–257.

[74] Parliament and Council Directive 08/52/EC on certain aspects of mediation in civil and commercial matters [2008] OJ L136/3. The date of transposition, 21 May 2011, has not yet expired at the time of writing. Before the

transnational procedural context. The Payment Order Regulation creates a new, uniform, and optional procedure for creditors to recover uncontested civil and commercial claims in cross-border matters.[75] The Small Claims Regulation creates a new, uniform, and optional procedure for civil and commercial claims, with certain specific exclusions, with a value of less than EUR 2,000 in cross-border matters.[76] Once a decision is obtained through either of these procedures, it may be enforced automatically in all European Member States without a formal recognition procedure.[77] The ADR Directive imposes an obligation on the Member States to encourage mediation in cross-border matters and aims *inter alia* to ensure enforceability of agreements resulting from mediation, the confidentiality of mediation, as well as to hinder that mediation is prevented because of concern for limitation or prescription periods.[78]

The measures clearly strive to move away from the intergovernmental style of transnational procedural cooperation with central authorities, towards a decentralized model with direct contact between the lowest courts.[79] In addition, the measures strive to achieve simplification, modernization, efficiency, and lower costs through streamlined standard forms, deadlines, as well as through mutual recognition with minimum standards and limited opportunities and grounds for rejection.[80] These aims are coupled and supported by the aim that litigants be able to avail themselves of these tools without counsel and by means of information technology.[81] A further feature is the obligation upon courts and Member States to cooperate and to provide information on procedures through the Internet, thereby attempting to support access to proper information for litigants.[82]

In addition to the already existing measures and in some cases pending reviews of them, further deepening of the policy area has been envisaged in two consultation papers: the more recent Green Paper on the transparency of debtors' assets[83] that followed the earlier Green Paper on attachment of bank accounts.[84] Both stem from the desire to speed up the proper enforcement of decisions and thus support the abolishment of the exequatur procedure. The enforcement or execution procedures

---

Directive was enacted an earlier soft law initiative, the European Code of Conduct for Mediators, was launched on 2 July 2004 by stakeholders and supported by the Commission. See: <http://www.europa.eu.int/comm/justice_home/ejn/adr/adr_ec_en.htm>. For a review of these measures, see *inter alia* Storskrubb (n 11 above) 181–202.

[75] *Inter alia* Regulation 1896/06 (n 73 above), Arts 1–3, 7(5), and recital 11.

[76] *Inter alia* Regulation 861/07 (n 74 above), Arts 1–3, 5.

[77] See *inter alia* Regulation 1896/06 (n 73 above), Arts 18–22 and Regulation 861/07 (n 74 above) Arts 20–23.

[78] Council Directive 08/52 (n 75 above), Arts 4–8.

[79] *Inter alia* Regulation 1393/07, Art 4.

[80] *Inter alia* Regulation 1393/07, Art 7, Regulation 1896/06, Art 1(a), 7(a), 12(1), and their Annexes, as well as Regulation 861/07, Art 20.

[81] *Inter alia* Regulation 861/07, recital 15, Art 10–12 and Regulation 1896/06, recital 11, Arts 7(5), 16(4).

[82] *Inter alia* Council Directive 08/52, Art 9 (n 75 above).

[83] COM(2008) 128, summary of responses available at: <http://ec.europa.eu/justice_home/news/ consulting_public/debtor_assets/docs/summary_en.pdf.>.

[84] COM(2006) 618, summary of responses available at: <http://ec.europa.eu/civiljustice/news/docs/summary_answers_com_2006_618_en.pdf>.

remain unregulated on the European level, but the ultimate success of all the enacted enforcement measures depends on effective execution.[85] However, since there is a great diversity between Member States' execution procedures, harmonization raises difficult issues of principle. A piecemeal approach has, therefore, been adopted and the consultations only deal with particular aspects of execution.[86] Recently, further activity has taken place in this field with a public hearing organized by the Commission on improving the enforcement of judgments and facilitating cross-border debt recovery and legislative proposals envisaged on both attachment of bank accounts and transparency of assets in the Action Plan.[87]

3. APPLICABLE LAW

In addition to harmonized international jurisdiction rules, mutual choice of law rules have in the EU been held to eliminate forum shopping. Hence, similarly to the Brussels jurisdiction regime, the Rome choice of law regime has been 'communitaurized' and further developed after lengthy negotiations. The Rome Convention on choice of law for contractual obligations of 1980 has been replaced and in part amended by the 'Rome I Regulation'[88] that has become applicable from 17 December 2009. However, before that the 'Rome II Regulation'[89] had already been adopted, creating for the first time mutual choice of law rules for non-contractual obligations. These Regulations do not, due to their nature, have the same tools for simplification and efficiency as the procedural cooperation measures. However, since they strive towards greater predictability and legal certainty, as well as the elimination of forum shopping, they fit in and are intended to enhance efficiency and support the policy area.

4. FAMILY LAW

In cross-border disputes relating to family law some of the abovementioned civil justice measures are considered applicable.[90] However, the regulations for jurisdiction and enforcement, enforcement orders, payment orders, small claims, and choice of law specifically excluded family law matters from their scope of application. In relation to family law matters the development of specific civil justice

---

[85] Towards greater efficiency in obtaining and enforcing judgments in the EU, COM(1997) 609.

[86] For the diversity of proceedings see P Kaye, *Methods of Execution of Orders and Judgments in Europe* (1995) and W A Kennett, 'Enforcement of Judgments—Chronique' (1997) 5 ERPL 321–427.

[87] See <http://ec.europa.eu/civiljustice/news/whatsnew_en.htm> and Action Plan (n 61 above) 24–25.

[88] Parliament and Council Regulation (EC) 593/08 on the law applicable to contractual obligations (Rome I) [2008] OJ L177/6. For a review of Regulation 593/08 see *inter alia* O Lando and P A Nielsen, 'The Rome I Regulation' (2008) 45 CML Rev 1688.

[89] Parliament and Council Regulation (EC) 864/07 on the law applicable to non-contractual obligations (Rome II) [2007] OJ L199/40. For reviews on Regulation 846/07 see *inter alia* S C Symeonides, 'Rome II and Tort Conflicts: A Missed Opportunity' (2008) 56 AJCL 173, and P J Kozyris, 'Rome II: Tort Conflicts on the Right Track! A Postscript to Symeon Symeonides' Missed Opportunity' [2008] 56 AJCL 471.

[90] See *inter alia* Regulation 1393/07, Art 1, and M Ekelmans, 'Le règlement 1348/2000 relatif à la signification et à la notification des actes judiciaires et extrajudiciaires' (2001) JdT 483.

measures has been piecemeal and gradual, the first measure being the 'Brussels II Regulation', later amended and thereafter called the 'Brussels II *bis* Regulation',[91] regulating international jurisdiction, and recognition and enforcement, for dissolution of marriage (divorces) and child custody matters. However, the Regulation does not deal with related matters that arise from divorce, such as maintenance and the division of matrimonial property, nor does it deal with applicable law. Hence these matters have been the subject of separate subsequent legislative projects.

First, for maintenance obligations, jurisdiction, recognition and enforcement as well as choice of law are specifically regulated in a recently enacted Regulation[92] that is not yet applicable.[93] The Regulation is closely linked to the 2007 Hague Protocol on the Law Applicable to Maintenance Obligations and the Hague Convention on the International Recovery of Child Support and other forms of Family Maintenance.[94]

Secondly, for divorce matters a separate legislative proposal to amend the Brussels II *bis* Regulation to include rules on applicable law, also called 'Rome III', was proposed in 2006, but not enacted apparently due to a political deadlock in the Council.[95] The deadlock has recently resulted in a new proposal for a Council decision to authorize enhanced cooperation in the field, together with a new substantive proposal for a Regulation implementing enhanced cooperation in the area of the law applicable to divorce and legal separation.[96] Thus, significantly some Member States wish to go ahead separately from the others in relation to this matter.

Thirdly, the Commission already in 2006 launched a Green Paper consultation on jurisdiction and applicable law in relation to matrimonial property regimes and

---

[91] Council Regulation (EC) 1347/00 on jurisdiction and the recognition and enforcement of judgments in matrimonial matters and in matters of parental responsibility for children of both spouses [2000] OJ L160/19 and Council Regulation (EC) 2201/03 concerning jurisdiction and the recognition and enforcement of judgments in matrimonial matters and in matters of parental responsibility repealing Regulation EC No 1347/2000 [2003] OJ L338/1. The Regulation deals with divorce and decisions on parental responsibility for the children of both spouses, if such decisions are taken at the time of the divorce. The substantive amendment in 2003 concerned the abolishment of the exequatur procedure for decisions concerning visiting rights.

[92] Council Regulation (EC) 4/09 on jurisdiction, applicable law, recognition and enforcement of decisions and cooperation in matters relating to maintenance obligations [2009] OJ L7/1. For a review of the legislative proposal for Regulation 4/09 see *inter alia* M Hellner, 'The Maintenance Regulation: A Critical Assessment of the Commission's Proposal' in K Boele-Woelke and T Svedrup (eds), *European Challenges in Contemporary Family Law* (Intersentia, 2008) 343–378.

[93] The substantive parts of the Regulation will according to Art 76 be applicable from 18 June 2011 subject to the 2007 Hague Protocol being applicable in the Community by that date. Failing that the Regulation shall apply from the date of application of the Protocol in the Community.

[94] The Commission has subsequent to the enactment of Regulation 4/09 and the consequent external competence of the Community proposed that the Community become a part to the Protocol and the Convention, see further Council Decision (EC) 2009/941EC on the conclusion by the European Community of the Hague Protocol of 23 November 2007 on the Law Applicable to Maintenance Obligations.

[95] COM(2006) 399, see also T M de Boer, 'The Second Revision of the Brussels II Regulation: Jurisdiction and Applicable Law' in Boele-Woelki and Svedrup (n 93 above) 321–341.

[96] COM(2010) 104 and COM(2010) 105.

following the renewed activity in the field of family law a future legislative proposal on applicable law also on this separate issue is envisaged in the Action Plan.[97]

Finally, the recently launched legislative proposal[98] on the jurisdiction, recognition, and enforcement as well as choice of law in matters of succession, and the creation of a European Certificate of Succession follows an aim already set out in several policy documents to pursue an instrument in relation to succession.[99]

These measures in general follow the philosophy of the generic procedural cooperation measures, but due to the specific public interest related to family matters there are discrete solutions in relation to, for example, jurisdictional grounds. However, the general characteristics of striving for efficiency by means of standard forms, regulated language requirements, and simplified enforcement procedures, including the abolition of exequatur, are visible in these measures too. However, the Maintenance Regulation also reintroduces the role of central authorities, which might be due to the influence of the Hague Conventions applicable in the field.[100] One might perhaps also discern an understanding of the fact that the decentralized system can be difficult to navigate for lay people. If there is a civil service Central Authority involved that has experience and knowledge to assist the maintenance creditors their access to justice might be more effective.

5. SUBSTANTIVE LAW

Aside from the procedural cooperation and choice of law measures the policy area of civil justice has also in practice been held by the institutions to encompass some other substantive law projects.[101] Among these measures is the 'Compensation to Crime Victims Directive'.[102] Its inclusion in the policy area is an anomaly, because the legal basis on which it was adopted was Article 308 EC not Article 65 EC, since the measure was considered applicable to both civil and criminal justice.[103] In addition, the Directive does not concern the rights and obligations between private parties, but

---

[97] COM(2006) 400. A summary of the responses are available at <http://ec.europa.eu/civiljustice/news/ docs/summary_answers_com_2006_400_en.pdf>. According to information obtained at <http://ec.europa.eu/ justice_home/news/consulting_public/news_consulting_public_en.htm> a public hearing was held on 28 September 2009 in Brussels on the issue as part of the ongoing consultation procedure. See also K Kroll, 'Unification of Conflict of laws in Europe—Matrimonial Property Regimes' in Boele-Woelki and Svedrup (n 93 above) 379–393. See also Action Plan (n 61 above) 19.

[98] COM(2009) 154 (n 48 above).

[99] COM(2009) 154, 2–3, see also *inter alia* Hague Programme (n 54 above) 13.

[100] Regulation 4/09 (n 93 above) Arts 49–63.

[101] See *inter alia* the Commission's civil justice webpage: <http://ec.europa.eu/justice_home/fsj/civil/fsj_ci-vil_intro_en.htm>.

[102] Council Directive 04/80/EC relating to compensation to crime victims [2004] OJ L651/15.

[103] Art 308 EC (now Art 352 TFEU) provides a fallback for measures considered necessary for the objectives of the Community, but where no specific legal basis exists. Note that because the legal basis does not include a 'cross-border' requirement compensation is to be available in national as well as in cross-border situations.

ensures adequate compensation from the Member States.[104] The measure is closely related to criminal proceedings,[105] but also to substantive civil law in that it sets out the limits of the obligation and the principles for determining the amount of compensation for the damage caused.[106] In addition, the Directive also creates a system for cooperation between national authorities regarding compensation applications in cross-border cases.[107] The cooperation system has standard forms and deadlines and in this respect resembles the civil justice measures and in particular the Legal Aid Directive albeit that courts are not the relevant actors.

In addition, projects regarding harmonization of contract law have been held to belong to civil justice. The EU has historically had a sector-specific approach to approximation of contract law with the elaboration of specific directives, for example in the field of consumer contract law.[108] However, academic experts have conducted two extensive general projects, with the aid of EU funding. The first of these resulted in the Principles on European Contract Law (PECL),[109] and the second in the Draft Common Frame of Reference (DCFR).[110] Neither of these projects has so far led to binding legislation. The aim of PECL is to provide a system of rules that can be adopted by parties, or applied by arbitrators operating as a contractual optional system. The aim of the later DCFR project is to provide fundamental principles, definitions, and model rules that can be used by the European institutions when revising existing legislation or devising new legislation. In parallel with these projects the policy debate on the focus of a European contract law[111] and the academic debate on the desirability of harmonization have been lively.[112]

---

[104] COM(2002) 562, 8–10. Other civil justice measures can assist crime victims in relation to compensation from the offender, eg the Brussels I Regulation provides that the victim may sue the offender for damages in the same court that deals with the criminal proceedings, if this is possible under national law. Crime victims can also enforce a judgment on damages in another Member State under the enforcement rules of the Brussels I Regulation.

[105] The Framework Decision on the standing of victims in criminal proceedings enacted within the Criminal Justice field provides that the victim shall have the right to seek civil damages in criminal proceedings, thus avoiding separate civil proceedings to obtain such damages. This goes one step further than the Brussels I Regulation.

[106] Council Directive 04/80 (n 104 above) Art 12.

[107] ibid Art 1-11.

[108] *Inter alia* in the field of consumer law Directive 05/29/EC concerning unfair business-to-consumer commercial practices in the internal market and amending Directives 84/450/EEC, 97/7/EC, 98/27/EC, and 2002/65/EC.

[109] O Lando and H Beale (eds), *Principles of European Contract Law, Parts I and II* (Kluwer Law International, 2000) and O Lando, E Clive, A Prüm, and R Zimmermann (eds), *Principles of European Contract Law, Part III* (Kluwer Law International, 2003).

[110] C von Bar and E Clive (eds), *Principles, Definitions and Model Rules of European Private Law, Draft Common Frame of Reference, Full Edition* (Sellier, 2009).

[111] A more coherent European contract law, COM(2003) 68; European contract law and the revision of the aquis: the way forward, COM(2004) 651.

[112] H Collins, 'European Private Law and the Cultural Identity of States' (1995) 3 Euro Rev Priv L 353; D Caruso, 'The Missing View of the Cathedral: The Private Law Paradigm of European Legal Integration' (1997) 3 ELJ 3. The debate includes in part the same themes and raises in part the same issues as the debate regarding civil procedural harmonization, see above Section B.5.

These projects have not originally been linked to the political vision of the AFSJ, but mutual or harmonized rules on contract law have the potential to lessen the importance of provisions on choice of law in relation to contracts, and thereby affect forum shopping and interact with civil justice. In addition, as the Commission has noted, the European judicial area should support economic activity and might do so by substantively facilitating contractual relations and standard contracts, and by providing a European optional legal framework, although following the DCFR the direction that any new EU contract law projects will take is still open.[113]

6. OVERARCHING MEASURES

Simultaneously with the various specific measures considered above, what have been called overarching instruments have evolved, which aim to support the application and implementation of civil justice.[114] Aside from funding initiatives,[115] the creation of the European Judicial Network (EJN) has so far been the most extensive of these measures.[116] It has since December 2002 organized meetings of national contact points and other involved parties, facilitated cooperation in actual cases, and launched a website.[117] A recent reform of the EJN entails the inclusion of the legal profession as a member and gives additional information duties to the Network.[118]

Aside from access to information it has been held that judicial training is imperative to support implementation and foster mutual trust.[119] The Lisbon Treaty mentions support for judicial training in Article 81 TFEU, but this occurred even under the prior Treaty rules.[120] However, most recently a Council Resolution of 2008 emphasizes that

---

[113] H Beale, 'From Draft Common Frame of Reference to Optional Instrument' (2009) 145 Tidskrift Utgiven av Juridiska Föreningen i Finland 3–4, 205. The Stockholm Programme (note 55 above) 32–33 reaffirms that the common frame of reference should be non-binding but also calls on the Commission to consider whether further measures need to be taken in the field of contract law. The Action Plan of the Commission envisages that a communication will be published in 2010 and a legislative proposal in 2011 (n 61 above) 24–25 but gives no further details,

[114] H Hartnell, 'EUstitia: Institutionalizing Justice in the European Union' [2002] 23 Northwest J Int'l L & Bus 65, for an early understanding of the importance of these measures.

[115] Council Regulation (EC) 743/02 establishing a general framework for Community activities to facilitate the implementation of judicial cooperation in civil matters [2002] OJ L115/1 and Decision (EC) 1149/07 establishing for the period 2007–2013 the Specific Programme Civil Justice as part of the General Programme Fundamental Rights and Justice [2007] OJ L257/16).

[116] Council Decision (EC) 470/01 establishing a European Judicial Network [2001] OJ L174/25 and Parliament and Council Decision (EC) 568/09 amending Council Decision 2001/470/EC establishing a European Judicial Network in civil and commercial matters [2009] OJ L168/35.

[117] On the tasks of the Networks see Decision 470/01, Art 5. See further the launched website: <http://ec.europa.eu/civiljustice/index_en.htm>, and COM(2006) 203, *Report on the functioning of the European Judicial Network*.

[118] Decision 568/09, Arts 2(1)(e), 3(2)(b), 5(2)(c), and 5(2)(f).

[119] COM(2006) 356, Communication on judicial training in the European Union.

[120] Initiative of the French Republic with [2001] OJ C18/9. See Storskrubb (n 11 above) 246–247.

the national training bodies remain the key vehicles and puts the Member States under an obligation to take certain actions in relation to judicial training within four years.[121] In the meantime the European Judicial Training Network (EJTN) has been set up as an external initiative.[122] Under its auspices judges can participate in training in other Member States or in an exchange programme.[123]

In addition, the Commission has set up a Justice Forum for discussing EU justice, policies, and practice.[124] The forum is intended to provide the Commission with a mechanism for consulting stakeholders, receiving feedback, and reviewing EU justice policies.[125] Finally, a multi-annual e-Justice Action Plan covering the period 2009–13 has been launched by the Council.[126] This will entail the first release of a new European e-Justice portal that is intended to be a more holistic tool than the existing tools.[127] The European e-Justice goals also include the promotion and creation of videoconferencing, automated translation tools, a database of legal translators and interpreters, and online application forms, and also secure electronic communications between courts and parties as well as between judicial authorities.[128]

7. CONCLUSION

The development of civil justice in the EU during its first decade created an astonishing wealth and breadth of measures reaching far beyond traditional forms of transnational procedural cooperation. Many of the enacted measures have however not been in force for long and some are still awaiting application. Others are awaiting reports on current implementation and futher possible revision. Therefore the full impact of the current civil justice measures has not yet been experienced. In addition, new measures that are still in the pipeline to be adopted may further transform the policy area, for example in relation to execution and various family law initiatives. It is nevertheless evident from the first decade of legislative evolution that the further the civil justice measures reach the more important become the regulatory issues that will be discussed below in Part E.

---

[121] Council meeting Justice and Home Affairs, 24 October 2008, PRESS/08/299.

[122] See <http://www.ejtn.net/www/en/html/index.htm>.

[123] G Charbonnier, 'Nouveaux défis pour la justice en Europe: Développement d'une culture judiciaire européenne' in W Heusel (ed), *The Future of Legal Europe: An emerging European judicial culture?* [2008] 9 ERA Forum, 114–117 regarding the future strategy and vision for the network.

[124] See <http://ec.europa.eu/justice_home/news/information_dossiers/justice_forum/index_en.htm>.

[125] COM(2008) 38, Communication on the creation of a Forum for discussing EU justice policies and practice.

[126] Council Note 15315/08 4 on a European e-Justice Action Plan that was preceded by Towards a European e-Justice Strategy, COM(2008) 329, and Parliament Report, T6-637/08.

[127] COM(2008) 329, 5–7, Council Note 15315/08, 4.

[128] COM(2008) 329, 8–9; T6-637/08 recommendation 2, pts 2, 6; as well as Council Note 15315/08, 7–9.

E. THEMES

1. INTRODUCTION

Perhaps due to the strong political impetus in the consecutive Tampere, Hague, and Stockholm programmes for the evolution of civil justice as one part of the AFSJ, a fully fledged regulatory debate regarding this tidal wave has yet to take place. Indeed, as one recent commentator notes 'the time has come for some reflection and re-evaluation'.[129] The reflection below will first focus on challenges in implementation and will thereafter deal with constitutional and regulatory challenges.

2. CHALLENGES OF IMPLEMENTATION

One of the main features of civil justice is its decentralized nature, which is linked to the principle of mutual recognition. The vision is that local domestic courts as the primary actors should cooperate with each other, and as long as certain minimum standards are fulfilled their decisions should be mutually recognizable across borders. The decentralized nature of the system has led to concerns of fragmentation in application due to a variety of factors, including resources and knowledge, with ensuing risk of discrimination between jurisdictions. In addition, the measures themselves have in part been considered unclear, and in part rely on national law with ensuing complexity.[130]

The reports regarding the functioning of certain of the first enacted measures confirm on a general level that there have been some improvements that support the aim of simplification, but also reveal variation in application and complexity.[131] According to one of the latest reports on the Compensation to Crime Victims Directive, claimants find the procedure complicated and time-consuming and language barriers form a major obstacle to facilitating the process.[132] The further consolidation and streamlining of measures should address the specific issues that have emerged and commentators have also emphasized the importance of expertise.[133] The new overarching measures,

---

[129] M Tulibacka, 'Europeanization of civil procedures: in search of a coherent approach' [2009] 46 CML Rev 1527.

[130] Storskrubb (n 11 above) 261–262; Tulibacka (n 131 above) 1544–1545.

[131] Report on the application of Council Regulation (EC) 1348/2000 on the service in the Member States of Judicial and Extrajudicial documents, COM(2004) 603; Report on the application of Council Decision 2001/470/EC establishing a European Judicial Network, COM(2006) 203; Report on the application of the Council Regulation (EC) 1206/2001 on cooperation between the courts of the Member States in the taking of evidence, COM(2007) 769; Report on the application of Council Directive 2004/80/EC relating to compensation to crime victims, COM(2009) 170; COM(2009) 174 (n 69 above). For the empirical studies commissioned by the Commission that underlie the reports see <http://ec.europa.eu/justice_home/doc_centre/civil/studies/doc_civil_studies_en.htm>.

[132] COM(2009) 170 (n 133 above) 10–11.

[133] Storskrubb (n 11 above) 305–306; Tulibacka (n 131 above) 1560–1561; Stockholm Programme (n 55 above) 24.

including e-Justice, the Justice Forum, and emphasis on judicial training, have the potential to counter diversity and fragmentation and support simplified cooperation and efficiency.[134] However, it is uncertain whether such measures will actually sufficiently impact on the relevant actors. In addition, the question of resources is one that remains at the will of domestic political actors.

Another concern has been that minimum standards introduced together with mutual recognition limit the possible mechanisms of the local court to review whether the rights of the defence have been protected, and in practice affect procedural standards such as the right to be heard.[135] In the absence so far of specific knowledge of cases on the EU level in which these matters have arisen, a debate and a critical review of the practice of the measures in light of guarantees of fundamental rights have been advocated.[136] The Justice Forum is charged with involving the Fundamental Rights Agency in the most appropriate way; it has the possibility to form sub-groups discussing fundamental rights issues and the Stockholm Programme emphasizes fundamental rights. These are positive developments, but must be carried through in practice.[137]

The question is also whether these promises will, together with increased mutual trust, be enough, or whether further harmonization of standards will have to be envisaged.[138] Criminal justice evolution in the EU with its debate on fundamental rights issues and with the current practical procedural proposals is a forerunner in this respect.[139] The fact that a report on the functioning of the whole current civil justice regime and a consultation on the need for minimum civil procedural standards are projected in the Action Plan shows that the institutions are already anticipating a discussion on further harmonization of standards.[140]

A further structural change that may in the long-term perspective counter fragmentation, and that will hopefully assist a fundamental rights debate, is the full right

---

[134] E Storskrubb, 'What Changes will European Harmonization Bring?' in J Walker and O G Chase (eds), *Common Law, Civil Law and the Future of Categories* (Lexis Nexis, 2010) 411–412, 417–418.

[135] Storskrubb (n 136 above) 416 and (n 11 above) *inter alia* 166–167, 217–218, 263 and the sources cited therein; G Cuniberti, 'The Recognition of Foreign Judgments Lacking Reasons In Europe: Access to Justice, Foreign Court Avoidance, and Efficiency' (2008) 57 ICLQ 48–52.

[136] E Storskrubb, 'Steering the Tide—The Mid-Term Perspective for Civil Justice' in D Frände *et al*, *In the Footsteps of Tampere—Justice in the European Union*, (Forum Iuris, 2006) 30–33; Storskrubb (n 11 above) 309–310.

[137] Stockholm Programme (n 60 above); COM(2008) 38 (n 127 above) [35]–[37].

[138] M Andenas, 'National Paradigms of Civil Enforcement: Mutual Recognition or Harmonization in Europe?' and T Andersson, 'Harmonization and Mutual Recognition: How to Handle Mutual Distrust' in M Andenas, B Hess, and P Oberhammer (eds), *Enforcement Agency Practice in Europe* (BIICL, 2005) 7 and 249–251.

[139] R Lööf, 'Shooting from the Hip—Proposed Minimum Rights in Criminal Proceedings' 12(3) (2006) ELJ 421; D Frände, 'Towards a Harmonized Criminal Justice System in the EU' in Frände (n 138 above) 49. For recent developments see also Proposal for a Council Framework Decision on the right to interpretation and to translation in criminal proceedings, COM(2009) 338, and information on agreement in the Council at <http://www.consilium.europa.eu/showFocus.aspx?id=1&focusId=413&lang=en>.

[140] Action Plan (n 61 above) 23.

for local courts to make requests for preliminary referral to the ECJ introduced in the Lisbon Treaty.[141] As procedural questions are not always appealed and since it might take several years for a matter to reach the ECJ via a court of last resort, there have been relatively few decisions from the ECJ during the first decade of civil justice. The change entails that the ECJ can forge a dialogue with all levels of local courts and can participate more actively in shaping the interpretation of the civil justice measures.

3. CONSTITUTIONAL AND REGULATORY CHALLENGES

Aside from striving towards consolidation and streamlining that relates more to the quality of current measures, the regulatory strategy for projected future development should be addressed in light of the experiences of civil justice so far, and in light of more overall developments in EU governance. The formation of a regulatory strategy is challenging for such a multifaceted policy area intended to protect parties as varied as large and small businesses, consumers, and family members. The ideology behind the measures is perceivably diverse including market integration, citizen rights of access to court, and fundamental rights.[142] Thus far market interests and efficiency have been most evident in EU civil justice.[143] However as commentators have noted a procedural system must also have a vision of justice.[144] Therefore, it is imperative going forward that fundamental rights and citizenship aspects be included in the EU civil justice vision that is evolving.

In addition, the level of regulatory action is also an important part of the strategy. So far in civil justice the level of regulation has centred on supranational top-down legislation mostly in the form of regulations. Due to the strong political impetus for civil justice the principles of subsidiarity and proportionality have not yet visibly played a strong role in its evolution and have arisen most broadly in relation to the ADR Directive.[145] However, the impact of these principles could be more central as evidenced by commentators critical of the subsidiarity and proportionality arguments in relation to the family law measures that have yet to be enacted.[146] Governance themes that are linked to regulation in the EU are also apposite here. Bench-marking and dialogue are governance themes that to some extent are already taking place in the context of the overarching measures of civil justice.[147] The existing efforts to increase

---

[141] See Sub-section C.5(b) above.

[142] Storskrubb (n 11 above) 77–91.

[143] ibid 278–279.

[144] Niemi-Kiesiläinen (n 20 above) 251; J Leubsdorf, 'The Myth of Civil Procedure Reform' in Zuckermann (n 8 above) 67.

[145] Storskrubb (n 11 above) 71–74, 188, 194–195, 275. For a discussion of the issue in the criminal justice context see E Herlin-Karnell, 'Subsidiarity in the Area of EU Justice and Home Affairs—A Lost Cause?' (2009) 15 ELJ 351.

[146] Hellner (n 93 above) 375–378; de Boer (n 97 above) 339–341.

[147] ibid 75–77.

dialogue should be further reinforced and governance themes such as softer regulation should also be actively considered where appropriate.

Finally, a recent resurgence of procedural measures in sectoral EU law including intellectual property, consumer, and competition law demonstrates that the EU procedural field is broader than the remit of civil justice.[148] The current civil justice measures are only intended to apply in cross-border matters, in which the relevant civil and commercial rights and obligations are mostly not derived from EU law, for example contractual business to business claims. However, in substantive EU law the pressure for enforcement of rights through procedural means can arise and domestic procedures coupled with the case law of the ECJ may not suffice in this respect.[149] The legal basis for the measures that are considered is unclear and the potential for extending Article 81 TFEU beyond the cross-border remit arises again.[150] Aside from the strict competence issue, commentators have stressed the importance of systematically coordinating any measures with civil justice and of carefully considering the regulatory options.[151]

F. CONCLUSION

The tidal wave of civil justice measures is unlikely to be stemmed, given the political impetus driving such measures. However, we might be able to steer it.[152] Civil justice is still in the relatively early stage of evolution, but we can nevertheless build on a decade of experience and implementation. The experience shows that the challenges are formidable and there are critical voices.[153] EU civil justice should never be an end in itself and the hope is therefore that interchanges and dialogue among relevant actors will foster a discursive process with genuine opportunity for input from the bottom up as to the vision of civil justice for the EU.[154]

---

[148] Tulibacka (n 131 above) 1529–1531 on the background and 1546—1553 on the recent measures. Regarding the background see also (n 11 above).

[149] J Stuyck, 'Class actions in Europe? To Opt-in or to Opt-out, that is the Question' (2009) 20 EBL Rev 492–497; C Hodges, 'Europeanisation of Civil Justice: Trends and Issues' (2006) CJQ 119–120.

[150] Stuyck (n 151 above) 498–502; Tulibacka (n 130 above) 1561–1564; S Peers, 'The European Community's criminal law competence: The plot thickens' (2008) 33 ELRev 399–410 for a review of the ECJ case law on the sectoral competence of the EC in relation to criminal procedure.

[151] Tulibacka (n 131 above) 1588–1560.

[152] Storskrubb (n 138 above).

[153] T C Hartley, 'The European Union and the Systematic Dismantling of the Common Law of Conflict of Laws' (2005) ICLQ 813–828.

[154] Storskrubb (n 136 above) 420. See also L Cadiet, 'Avenir des catégories, catégories de l'avenir, perspectives', in J Walker and O G Chase (eds), *Common Law, Civil Law and the Future of Categories* (Lexis Nexis, 2010) 651–655 for an interesting new model of cooperative procedure in the plural justice system as a new procedural model.

12

DIRECT EFFECT, PRIMACY, AND THE NATURE OF THE LEGAL ORDER

*Bruno de Witte**

The question of the legal status of norms of European Union law within the legal order of the Member States of the European Union is an evergreen in European legal studies. Each textbook of EU law devotes one or more chapters to this subject, and the main principles of the case law of the European Court of Justice on this question are widely known. In the spirit of this volume, the emphasis will be on the evolution through time, so that attention will be given, at the start, to the circumstances in which the doctrines of the direct effect and primacy of EC law were invented by the European Court of Justice almost fifty years ago. I will also draw attention to some less explored aspects of the evolution of the European Court's case law and devote ample space to the generally friendly, but also occasionally frosty, reception of those doctrines by their addressees, the national courts of the Member States.

Direct effect can be provisionally defined as the capacity of a norm of Union law to be applied in domestic court proceedings; whereas *primacy* (or *supremacy*)[1] denotes the capacity of that norm of Union law to overrule inconsistent norms of national law in domestic court proceedings. The two principles are therefore closely linked, and are habitually considered in conjunction. Yet, the principle of supremacy has a wider range of applications beyond its use by courts in setting aside national norms that are inconsistent with directly effective provisions of EU law. This internal judicial primacy is but the reflection of the primacy which, according to a long-established rule of international law, treaty norms possess over the national law of the contracting states in the relations between those states. Primacy, therefore, bears on all state authorities,

---

* Professor of European Union Law, Maastricht University.

[1] The two terms are used interchangeably in the English language literature, but the Court of Justice never uses the term 'supremacy'. I will therefore also use, in this chapter, the term 'primacy', but without attaching any particular significance to the use of that term rather than another.

including the legislator and the government, and not just the courts. This chapter will, however, mainly deal with primacy as a principle governing the activity of national *courts*.

Direct effect and primacy are not just frequently studied subjects of Union law among others; these principles are also taken to be defining characteristics of EU law. Those doctrines are therefore accompanied by meta-doctrines about the overall *nature of the European Union legal order*. This question has captured the attention of the more theoretically inclined Community law scholars since the 1960s, and will be briefly addressed in the final section of this chapter.

A. THE FOUNDATION YEARS

1. SUPREMACY AND DIRECT EFFECT PRIOR TO 1963–1964

If direct effect and supremacy are considered to be essential characteristics of EU law today, that was certainly not the case in the years prior to the European Court judgments of 1963 and 1964 in the cases *Van Gend en Loos* and *Costa*. None of the three Community Treaties that existed at the time mentioned those principles, and legal commentators by and large ignored the issue. At the time the European Community Treaties were signed, it was generally accepted that the status of international legal rules within the domestic legal order was determined by the constitutional rules of every single country.[2] Of course, *pacta sunt servanda* was already a well-established legal principle even then: Treaty obligations freely concluded by a state must be respected by that state. However, this principle merely implied that states could not invoke their national law as an excuse for failing to perform their Treaty obligations towards the other contracting parties. States were left to their own devices for finding the most appropriate domestic arrangements for fulfilling their international obligations. So, the *internal primacy* (as opposed to the international primacy) of Treaties and other aspects of their domestic status were a matter of national law.[3] The radically

---

[2] For a broad survey of the practice of domestic courts at the time the European Communities were created, see F Morgenstern, 'Judicial Practice and the Supremacy of International Law' (1950) 27 BYIL 42. A remarkable comparative study which also reflects the early national reception of EEC law is that by M Waelbroeck, *Traités internationaux et juridictions internes dans les pays du Marché commun* (Pedone, 1969). For a retrospective view of the pre-*Van Gend en Loos* and *Costa* situation, see M Claes, *The National Courts' Mandate in the European Constitution* (Hart, 2006) ch 2.

[3] Today, the position in international law has not changed: the effect of a treaty within the legal system of the participating states is determined by the constitutional law of each particular country. For a comprehensive study of the domestic effect of international treaties see T Buergenthal, 'Self-Executing and Non-Self-Executing Treaties in National and International Law' (1992-IV) 235 Hague Recueil 303. For a more recent collection of essays on this question, see J Nijman and A Nollkaemper (eds), *New Perspectives on the Divide between National and International Law* (Oxford University Press, 2007), in particular the chapter by A Peters. The European Convention on Human Rights (ECHR) has become a special case, with most national legal systems recognizing a more far-reaching domestic legal effect to it than to ordinary international treaties. On the reception of the ECHR in domestic law see the country reports in H Keller and A Stone Sweet (eds), *A Europe of Rights—The Impact of the ECHR on National Legal Systems* (Oxford University Press, 2008).

monist view (exposed, for instance, by Kelsen in some of his writings), that the national legal orders were 'creatures' of international law, never reflected the reality of state practice. The dualist views, as classically exposed in the early years of this century by Triepel and Anzilotti,[4] were rather more convincing where they showed that the national legal orders were separate legal orders, able to resist the penetration of international norms.

Monism and dualism become genuinely alternative doctrines when taken in a more narrow sense, ie when comparing the actual attitude taken towards international law within each constitutional system: dualist countries are those like the United Kingdom, Germany, and Italy where courts traditionally take the view that international treaties cannot, as such, display legal effects in the municipal sphere, so that their norms must be 'transplanted' into national law before they can become operational there. Monist countries (such as France, Spain, and the Benelux countries) are those where the view prevails that international legal norms are, upon their ratification and publication, 'received' within the national legal order while preserving their nature of international law.

What, now, were the consequences of those two different doctrines for the question of the direct effect (or 'self-executing character', to use the traditional expression in international law) and primacy of international treaties and of decisions by institutions created by such treaties? In dualist countries, international treaty norms are not enforceable *as international law*, but they may become, after transformation, enforceable by courts *as national law*; the wording of the norm may, or may not, have been changed, but the result will usually be achieved. As the EEC Treaty had been duly transformed into national law in the dualist Member States Germany and Italy, nothing could prevent their courts from applying some of the norms contained in that Treaty to individual cases brought before them. Indeed, the *Consiglio di Stato* already in 1962, that is, prior to *Van Gend en Loos*, had applied a provision of the EEC Treaty in an administrative law dispute.[5]

As for *primacy*, however, the attitude of dualist systems was certainly less favourable. In those systems, the relation between a norm of international origin and a purely national norm becomes, through the transformation of the former, a matter pertaining to the internal cohesion of the domestic legal order, and conflicts are to be solved according to the ordinary conflict rules applying within that order. As treaties are often transformed (if at all) by an act of the legislator, they will take precedence over conflicting administrative regulations and earlier legislative acts, but will be superseded in turn by later legislative acts according to the rule *lex posterior derogat priori*. This was the case in Germany and Italy at the time of signature of the EEC Treaty. The four other Member States belonged to the monist school. Only in the Netherlands and Luxembourg, however, was the primacy of international law an established practice.

---

[4] H Triepel, *Völkerrecht und Landesrecht* (1899); H Triepel, 'Les rapports entre le droit interne et le droit international' (1923) I Hague Recueil 77; D Anzilotti, *Il diritto internazionale nei giudizi interni* (1905).

[5] Judgment of 7 November 1962, (1963-III) Foro Italiano 143.

Although France, ever since the adoption of the Constitution of the Fourth Republic in 1946, had a very advanced constitutional provision recognizing the primacy of international treaty law over subsequent legislation, the courts continued to adhere to the traditional separation-of-powers view that 'no French court is entitled to question the popular will as expressed by the representative assembly'.[6] The prevailing opinion was that the constitutional provision was addressed solely to the legislator and not to the courts, who were not allowed to set aside French laws conflicting with an earlier treaty.

2. THE *VAN GEND EN LOOS* CASE

The constitutional background of this famous case[7] was formed by (what were then) the Articles 65 and 66 of the Dutch Constitution. Article 65 held: 'Provisions of agreements which, according to their terms, can be binding on anyone shall have such binding force after having been published'; and Article 66 added: 'Legislation in force within the Kingdom shall not apply if this application would be incompatible with provisions of agreements which are binding upon anyone and which have been entered into either before or after the enactment of such legislation.' The Dutch Supreme Court had, by a judgment of 18 May 1962, given its blessing to the first preliminary reference ever made under the EEC Treaty (by the Hague Court of Appeal in the *Bosch* case) by stating:[8] '[A]s is clear from Article 66, the question whether provisions of a Treaty bind the nationals of the Member States, is, at least for Dutch law, a question that can only be answered on the basis of interpretation of those treaty provisions.' The question of direct effect was therefore one which could properly be addressed by Dutch courts to the European Court of Justice. This newly recognized latitude to make preliminary references was used soon after by the *Tariefcommissie* (a specialized administrative court) in order to find out, in the course of a dispute about an import tax, whether Article 12 EEC (a standstill provision of the Treaty, in respect of import duties) had internal effect: 'in other words whether individuals can directly derive rights from the article that are enforceable by the judge'. Yet, what started as an appeal to the ECJ for help in the application of the Dutch Constitution became the occasion for the European Court to formulate its well-known doctrine on the internal effect of Community law which it addressed, beyond the obscure Dutch *Tariefcommissie*, to all courts in all Member States of the Community.

The governments of Belgium and the Netherlands intervened in *Van Gend en Loos* to challenge the jurisdiction of the Court of Justice 'on the ground that the reference relates not to the interpretation but to the application of the Treaty'.[9] In

---

[6] G Bermann, 'French Treaties and French Courts: Two Problems in Supremacy' (1979) ICLQ 458, 461.

[7] Case 26/62 *NV Algemene Transport en Expeditie Onderneming Van Gend en Loos v Nederlandse administratie der belastingen* [1963] ECR 1.

[8] Hoge Raad (Supreme Court), 18 May 1962, *De Geus en Uitenbogerd v Robert Bosch GmbH*, Nederlandse Jurisprudentie 1965, 115.

[9] *Van Gend en Loos* (n 7 above) 10–11.

their view, apparently, the states parties to the EEC Treaty had not intended to lay down any obligations as to the domestic effect of its provisions, so that this matter was left for determination by national authorities and courts according to their respective constitutional rules or judicial traditions. However, the Court of Justice decided that this matter could *not* be left to the national legal systems themselves, and that the *Tariefcommissie* should be told whether Article 12 of the EEC Treaty had direct effect or not. So, the major novelty of *Van Gend en Loos* is not the discovery that EEC law *could* have direct effect. For EEC *regulations*, that was indicated, implicitly but clearly, by the text of Article 189.[10] As for provisions of the *Treaty* itself, they could be perfectly suitable for judicial enforcement in the same way as other international agreements. The crucial contribution of the judgment was rather that the question whether specific provisions of the Treaty (or, later, secondary Community law) had direct effect was to be decided centrally by the Court of Justice, rather than by the various national courts according to their own views on the matter.

In addition, of course, the criteria used by the European Court for determining *which* provisions had direct effect proved to be very generous, both in *Van Gend en Loos* and in subsequent cases. In *Van Gend en Loos* itself, the Court's generosity can be seen both in its general hermeneutic approach and in its specific application to the case of Article 12 of the Treaty. At the *general* level, the Court did not openly contradict what was the received wisdom at the time, namely that the self-executing nature of treaty provisions had to be deduced from the intention of the contracting parties. Yet, the Court did not try to reconstruct the actual, subjective, intention of the drafters of the EEC Treaty, but rather chose to base itself on 'the spirit, the general scheme and the wording' of the EEC Treaty.[11] The result of this analysis was that Community law was intended to confer upon individuals rights which could be raised by them in domestic court proceedings. Turning then to the *specific* case of Article 12 of the EEC Treaty, which imposed a standstill obligation on the *Member States*, the Court held that the fact that this rule was addressed to the states did not prevent it from being invoked by *individuals*, the important thing being that Article 12 contained a negative obligation for whose implementation no legislative intervention on the part of the states was required.

---

[10] The stipulation in the EEC Treaty that regulations were to be directly applicable in the legal orders of the Member States, which was a major novelty at the time, would have made little sense if those regulations could not also be enforceable by the courts of the Member States, ie be given direct effect. The principled distinction I make here between *direct applicability* and *direct effect* was exposed most clearly by J Winter, 'Direct Applicability and Direct Effect—Two Distinct and Different Concepts in Community Law' (1972) 9 CML Rev 425. It remains a relevant distinction today; for example: international agreements of the EU are directly applicable within the EU legal order but often their provisions do not have direct effect. However, the term 'directly applicable' is also occasionally used as synonymous for 'having direct effect', both in the literature and in the case law of the ECJ.

[11] *Van Gend en Loos* (n 7 above) 12.

3. THE *COSTA V ENEL* CASE

Despite the close link between direct effect and primacy, the latter principle was not dealt with by the Court of Justice in *Van Gend en Loos*, because that question had not been put to it by the referring Dutch court. Indeed, under Dutch constitutional law at the time (and still today) if a treaty provision was self-executing, it would prevail over conflicting national law (Article 66 of the Dutch Constitution then, Article 94 today). In other words, primacy was unproblematic from the point of view of a Dutch court, whereas direct effect was a question on which it had to seek enlightenment from the European Court.

The occasion for the ECJ to affirm the principle of primacy was offered by a reference from a modest but recalcitrant judge from a dualist country, a *Pretore* in Milan, in the *Costa v ENEL* case.[12] Flaminio Costa refused to pay the bills of the newly created national electricity corporation ENEL, and argued that the Act of Parliament of 1962, by which the electricity industry had been nationalized, conflicted with the EEC Treaty. In another dispute about the payment of electricity bills between the same two parties, the local judge had decided to refer questions about the constitutionality of the Nationalization Act to the Italian Constitutional Court. That court, in its own *Costa v ENEL* judgment, which was handed down prior to the European Court's, took the view that the Italian Constitution, in its Article 11, allowed for limitations of sovereignty in favour of international organizations such as the EEC, but that this provision did not affect the domestic status of the European Treaties or the rules produced by the EC institutions. It held that the existing rules about the efficacy of international obligations should be applied in all dualist orthodoxy so that the EEC Treaty, which had been transformed into national law in 1957, could not prevail over the later Electricity Nationalization Act of 1962.[13]

With the fresh support offered by its Constitutional Court, the Italian government intervened before the European Court of Justice in *Costa v ENEL*, and submitted that the reference was 'absolutely inadmissible': as the Milan court had no power, under Italian law, to set aside the Electricity Act for breach of EEC law, its questions about the interpretation of EEC law could not serve a valid purpose. This open challenge to its jurisdiction encouraged the Court of Justice to formulate its doctrine of the primacy of Community law.

The ECJ's task in *Costa* was, in fact, more difficult than in *Van Gend en Loos*. Whereas the definition of the conditions of direct effect could easily be considered, under the canons of international law, as an inherent part of the interpretative function of the Court of Justice, the same could not be said about primacy. It was already then 'a generally accepted principle of international law that in the relations between powers who are contracting parties to a treaty, the provisions of municipal

---

[12] Case 6/64 *Costa v ENEL* [1964] ECR 585.
[13] Constitutional Court, judgment of 7 March 1964, No 14, (1964-I) Foro Italiano 465.

law cannot prevail over those of the treaty',[14] but that principle applied to 'relations between powers', that is, it merely implied that Community law prevailed over national law on the *international* plane. The *Costa* controversy, however, was about the *internal primacy* of EC law, that is, the duty of *national* courts to enforce EC rules when they conflict with national legislation. Such a duty had never been considered to be part of international law, although the failure of courts to enforce international treaty rules could, of course, be a contributory factor in the establishment of State responsibility under international law. The preliminary reference mechanism allowed the European Court, in *Costa*, to 'stop the clock'.[15] Instead of letting national judges commit what would be a breach of EC law, to be sanctioned under the infringement procedure of the then Articles 169 or 170 EEC Treaty, the European Court seized the occasion offered by the preliminary ruling procedure to order those judges to refrain from committing a breach and make Community law prevail over conflicting national norms. In order to arrive at that conclusion, the European Court used a vast array of arguments and particularly insisted on the need to distinguish the EEC Treaty from 'ordinary' international treaties. None of those arguments is particularly convincing by itself.[16] The most convincing argument for primacy, perhaps, was the simple *effet utile* argument: if states accept legal duties at the international level, they should be prepared to allow for the translation of those duties into daily practice, by means of judicial and other instruments. The dualist attitude, which consists in first ratifying a treaty and then wondering whether one should adapt one's domestic rules to the treaty, was perhaps justifiable at a time when signature and ratification of treaties was a governmental competence from which parliaments were excluded, but could seem logically flawed in relation to a treaty such as the EEC Treaty which had amply been debated by all national parliaments. But more importantly, unlike other and equally 'worthy' international treaties, the EEC Treaty provided for the ingenious judicial mechanism which allowed the Court of Justice to state its primacy doctrine and to request national courts to follow suit.

B. EVOLUTION OF THE DIRECT EFFECT DOCTRINE

1. THE NATURE OF DIRECT EFFECT: A 'SIMPLE' OBLIGATION TO APPLY THE EUROPEAN NORM?

The provision declared to have direct effect in *Van Gend en Loos*, Article 12 EEC Treaty, was a standstill provision containing, as the Court noted, a clear and unconditional prohibition addressed to the Member States, which was not qualified by the need for any national or Community implementing measures. It could seem, after that

---

[14] Permanent Court of International Justice, *Greek and Bulgarian Communities*, Series B, No 17, 32.

[15] This metaphor was aptly used by D Wyatt, 'New Legal Order, or Old?' (1982) 7 ELRev 147, 153.

[16] See, for an analysis of the Court's reasoning, B De Witte, 'Retour à Costa. La primauté du droit communautaire à la lumière du droit international' (1984) RTD eur 425.

judgment, that only very few Treaty provisions would pass the direct effect test. But soon the European Court, while insisting on the clarity and unconditionality criteria, started to extend the benefit of direct effect to a growing range of Treaty articles dealing with the common market, even those that *did* seem to require national or Community implementing acts and even those granting to the Member States a power to derogate. Those judgments of the early 1970s, in cases like *Reyners* and *Defrenne*, may well have been inspired by the will to react to the political inertia of the Council which was unable, in those years, to implement the integration programme formulated by the Treaty.[17] Later, the direct effect doctrine continued, with a momentum of its own, to become ever broader in its scope. The European Court specified that the fact that a norm of Community law leaves some latitude or discretion to the Member States does not preclude judicial review, by national courts, of the question whether the national authorities exceeded the limits of that discretion. Today, although the criteria used by the Court still vaguely echo those in *Van Gend en Loos*, the only thing required is that a national court, with the possible preliminary help of the ECJ, is able to apply the provision so as to determine the outcome of the case in hand.

Originally, direct effect was often defined, not least by the Court of Justice itself, as the creation of *rights* for individuals which the national courts must protect. That expression was gradually superseded by what the French call *invocabilité*, namely the capacity of the norm to be invoked by individuals in national courts which are bound to apply them. The reason for this shift was the gradual realization that many norms of Community law, particularly norms contained in directives, though not having as their object the attribution of a benefit to individuals, may very well serve as a standard for reviewing the legality of Member State action when individuals can show a sufficient interest in the outcome of such a review. Thus, the Court of Justice has repeatedly accepted that individuals could invoke provisions of a directive which merely sets out procedural obligations for the Member States, in order to oppose measures adopted in breach of those obligations. This happened, for instance, with the obligation of prior notification of technical standards under Directive 83/189[18] and with the obligation to make an environmental impact assessment under Directive 85/337.[19] A standard formula used by the Court in such cases is that:

> where the Community authorities have [...] imposed on Member States an obligation to
> pursue a particular course of conduct, the effectiveness of such an act would be diminished
> if individuals were prevented from relying on it in legal proceedings and if national courts

---

[17] This point is elaborated, within the context of a careful analysis of the expansion of the direct effect doctrine, by P Craig, 'Once upon a Time in the West: Direct Effect and the Federalization of EEC Law' (1992) OJLS 453, 463–470.

[18] Case C-194/94 *CIA Security International SA v Signalson SA and Securitel SPRL* [1996] ECR I-02201.

[19] Case C-72/95 *Aannemersbedrijf P.K. Kraaijeveld BV and others v Gedeputeerde Staten van Zuid-Holland* [1996] ECR I-5403; Case C-287/98 *Luxembourg v Berthe Linster* [2000] ECR I-6917; and, in relation to another environmental directive, Case C-127/02 *Landelijke Vereniging tot Behoud van de Waddenzee* [2004] ECR I-7405.

were prevented from taking it into consideration [...] in determining whether the national legislature [...] had kept within the limits of its discretion [...].[20]

EU law norms can therefore be used by parties in a national court case both as a sword (that is, as a source of new rights) and as a shield (that is, as a protection against conflicting national norms).[21] In the former case, EU law has a 'substitution effect', taking the place of a national norm that would otherwise be applicable; in the latter case, EU law has an 'exclusionary effect': it merely excludes the application of a conflicting national norm, but is not itself a source of new rights. The question whether the former or the latter of these effects occurs depends, to a large extent, on the pre-existing state of national law rather than on any inherent characteristic of the EU norm. The Court of Justice, rather wisely it seems, has not so far drawn sharp distinctions between these two situations; it covers them both by using the same general terminology.[22] The terms most frequently used by the Court are the 'capacity to invoke' or 'to rely on' a provision of EU law, but the Court has occasionally specified that this is, indeed, what 'direct effect' nowadays means.[23] The Court's terminology is not entirely satisfactory, because the verbs 'to invoke' and 'to rely on' are rather vague. In a state liability case, for instance, the claimant also 'invokes' a Community norm; yet, this happens not in order to have that norm applied to the case, but rather in order to establish a sufficiently serious breach by the national authorities which may give rise to compensation.[24]

Therefore, direct effect really boils down, as far as courts are concerned, to a test of justiciability: is the norm 'sufficiently operational in itself to be applied by a court'[25] in a given case. In a similar vein, Prechal offers the following definition: 'Direct effect is the obligation of a court or another authority to apply the relevant provision of Community law, either as a norm which governs the case or as a standard for legal review.'[26] This may seem a rather trivial definition which does not appear to say anything specific about Union law which cannot be said about norms of national law as well. This was precisely Judge Pescatore's expectation when he affirmed in 1983 that

---

[20] *Linster* (n 19 above) [32].

[21] The 'sword and shield' metaphor is commonly used in the literature on direct effect; see eg C Hilson and A Downes, 'Making Sense of Rights: Community Rights in EC Law' (1999) 24 ELRev 121.

[22] One example among many: Case C-430/04 *Feuerbestattungsverein Halle* [2006] ECR I-4999, [28]: '[I]t is settled case-law that unconditional and sufficiently precise provisions of a directive may [...] be relied on by private individuals against any national provision which is incompatible with the directive or in so far as they define rights which individuals are able to assert against the State ... '

[23] See for example Case C-226/07 *Flughafen Köln/Bonn* [2008] ECR I-5999, [39]: and operational part of the judgment: '[A]rt 14 (1)(a) of Directive 2003/96 ... *has direct effect in the sense that it may be relied upon by an individual before national courts* ... in a dispute, such as that in the main proceedings, between that individual and the customs authorities of that State, for the purpose of having national legislation which is incompatible with that provision disapplied ... ' (emphasis added).

[24] S Prechal, *Directives in EC Law* (2nd edn, Oxford University Press, 2005) 231.

[25] This is the often quoted expression used by AG Van Gerven in the *Banks* Case [1994] ECR I-1209, [27] of the Opinion.

[26] Prechal (n 24 above) 241.

direct effect is 'nothing but the ordinary state of the law' and that the direct effect discussion was just an 'infant disease' soon to be overcome.[27] One may note, in this regard, that when a national court does not pose a separate direct effect question, the Court sometimes 'forgets' the assessment of the norm's direct effect and proceeds immediately to the question of compatibility of national law with EU law. A recent example is *Michaeler*,[28] in which the Court was requested to interpret Clause 5 of the EC Directive on part-time work which states that 'Member States, following consultations with the social partners in accordance with national law or practice, should identify and review obstacles of a legal or administrative nature which may limit the opportunities for part-time work and, where appropriate, eliminate them'. The Court did not discuss the clear and precise nature of this provision (which seems rather doubtful) but immediately went on to conclude that an Italian regulation which required employers to notify all part-time employment contracts to the labour inspection was contrary to Clause 5 and must be set aside by the national court. When reading such judgments, and when observing the loose language of the Court of Justice when it is asked about the direct effect of an EU law norm, one might indeed be tempted think that the doctrine of direct effect was an 'infant disease', that it has no explanatory value any more in a mature EU legal order, and that one could therefore better drop it altogether and let national judges apply EU law in exactly the same manner as they would apply their national law.[29]

Yet, despite its undeniable dilution over the years, the concept of direct effect is not about to disappear entirely, in my view. The continued existence of a doctrine of direct effect of EU law is justified by the fact that the judicial enforcement of European Union norms is still different from that of national norms in certain respects. *First*, because the existence of direct effect is a matter of interpretation of EU law to be settled by the European Court of Justice, rather than by the national courts separately, and national courts still regularly ask the Court to Justice to decide on the direct effect of a norm of EU law in terms of 'whether or not'.[30] *Secondly*, because there are special categories of Union law (directives and external agreements) containing norms that, taken by themselves, seem sufficiently operational but which may not be enforced by national courts for other reasons, as we will discuss below. There is a *third* distinctive, and rather odd, characteristic, of direct effect in EU law, namely the fact that it was defined

---

[27] P Pescatore, 'The Doctrine of Direct Effect: An Infant Disease of Community Law' (1983) ELRev 155, 177 (first quote) and title of the Art (second quote).

[28] Cases C-55/07 and C-56/07 *Othmar Michaeler and others* [2008] ECR I-3135.

[29] See the views exposed by S Prechal in a number of writings: S Prechal, 'Does Direct Effect Still Matter?' (2000) 37 CML Rev 1047; S Prechal, 'Direct Effect Reconsidered, Redefined and Rejected' in J M Prinssen and A Schrauwen (eds), *Direct Effect—Rethinking a Classic of EC Legal Doctrine* (Europa Law, 2002) 15, 22: 'Why should we not accept that national courts should handle Community law provisions in the same way as national law, ie without making this formalistic and obsolete preliminary inquiry into unconditionality and sufficient precision?'

[30] See for example Cases C-471/07 and C-472/07 *Association générale de l'industrie du médicament and Others*, 14 January 2010. The Court's answer in this case was that a particular provision of a directive lacked direct effect for not being sufficiently precise [25]–[29].

by the Court of Justice as an obligation for a national court or 'another authority' (see Prechal's definition, mentioned above). Indeed, the Court of Justice stated in *Costanzo* that 'when the conditions under which the Court has held that individuals may rely on the provisions of a directive before the national courts are met, all organs of the administration, including decentralized authorities such as municipalities, are obliged to apply those provisions'.[31] In domestic law, executive authorities are normally subordinate to the legislator and cannot set aside, of their own motion, legislative norms conflicting with the constitution; only the appropriate (constitutional) courts can do so, if at all. In the EU context however, administrative authorities are put under a duty to enforce directly effective norms of EU law, and to set aside conflicting national legislation, even though they cannot use the mechanism of Article 177 EC Treaty to ask the Court of Justice for guidance on whether the EU norm has direct effect and on whether there is a conflict with national law; therefore, those authorities are liable to apply EU law in the wrong way. This *Costanzo* obligation seems, therefore, rather curious. Few national courts have adopted it,[32] and there is little evidence that administrative authorities actually abide by it.[33] Recently, a German court referred a preliminary question to the ECJ inviting it to reconsider its *Costanzo* doctrine, but the Court, disappointingly, refused to answer the question as not being strictly relevant for the solution of the case.[34]

2. VARIATIONS OF DIRECT EFFECT ACROSS THE CATEGORIES OF EU NORMS

In addition to the general conditions of direct effect, discussed above, there is an important additional variable which relates to the formal *source of law* in which the EU law norm is contained. It makes a difference whether the norm is part of the founding Treaties, or whether it is included in a regulation, a directive, an external agreement, or a framework decision, or whether it is an unwritten principle.

---

[31] Case 103/88 *Costanzo* [1989] ECR 1839, [30]–[32]. The ECJ repeated this duty in several later judgments, so that it can be considered as its established doctrine; see eg Case C-224/97 *Ciola* [1999] ECR I-2517, [30]; Case C-198/01 *Consorzio Industrie Fiammiferi (CIF)* [2003] ECR I-8055, [49].

[32] The French *Conseil d'Etat*, for one, has adopted this mandate, instructing French administrative authorities to take individual measures for the application of EU law even if this implies disregard for a conflicting legislative norm. See its Decision No 281629 of 27 July 2006, *Association Avenir de la langue française*, with comment by P Cassia in (2006) Europe—Juris-Classeur, October Issue, 12. For a comparative discussion of the application of the *Costanzo* doctrine, see M Verhoeven, 'The "Costanzo Obligation" of National Administrative Authorities in the Light of the Principle of Legality: Prodigy or Problem Child?' (2009) 5 Croatian Yearbook of European Law and Policy 65.

[33] For a recent criticism of the *Costanzo* doctrine, see T Bombois, 'L'administration "juge" de la légalité communautaire—Réflexions autour des arrêts *Fratelli Costanzo* et *Abna* de la Cour de Justice de Luxembourg' (2009) 128 JdT 169.

[34] Cases C-171/07 and C-172/07 *Apothekerkammer des Saarlandes and others*, judgment of 19 May 2009, [15]–[62]. The facts of this judgment show how an overenthusiastic administrative authority (a ministry of Saarland) had got it wrong by disapplying a German federal statute for alleged contrast with EU law, whereas the ECJ, in this judgment, found that there was no such contrast after all.

(a) The founding Treaties

As regards the founding Treaties, now called the Treaty on European Union and the Treaty on the Functioning of the European Union, it is possible to make a fairly complete list of those provisions that have direct effect and those that have not, although each of the Treaty revisions since the Single European Act has introduced new substantive provisions which may raise new direct effect queries. Thus, after the introduction in 1993 of a Citizenship chapter in the EC Treaty, the question arose as to the direct effect of the new Treaty provision that '[e]very citizen of the Union shall have the right to move and reside freely within the territory of the Member States, subject to the limitations and conditions laid down in this Treaty and by the measures adopted to give it effect'.[35] Following the line taken in its earlier case law about the common market freedoms, the ECJ held in *Baumbast* that the reference to the 'limitations and conditions' did not prevent citizens from relying on their right to mobility and residence before national courts.[36]

A curiously unresolved question is the extent to which TEU and TFEU provisions that have direct effect are also capable of having *horizontal* direct effect in relations between private parties. Whether horizontal effect is appropriate depends on the specific objective of each Treaty provision and its place in the overall scheme of the Treaty.[37] Some Treaty articles are clearly meant to be applied in relations between private parties, and their direct effect unavoidably means horizontal direct effect: see, for instance, Articles 101 and 102 TFEU dealing with anticompetitive behaviour of firms. The common market freedoms, by contrast, involve duties for the state authorities and should therefore not display horizontal direct effect, except in the case of collective 'state-like' regulation by private organizations such as a sports federation (as in the *Walrave* and *Bosman* cases). Normally, the Treaty rules on the free movement of goods, and on other freedoms, may not be relied upon against private parties. However, the Court did admit the horizontal application of the Treaty provision on free movement of workers in *Angonese*,[38] and it admitted the horizontal application of the Treaty provisions on freedom of establishment and freedom to provide services in *Laval* and *Viking*.[39] The Court did so without much explanation, and yet one may wonder why a private bank (as in *Angonese*) or a trade union (as in *Laval* and *Viking*) should be exposed to the obligation to respect the free trade or free movement rights of other private parties, when the legitimate reasons that can justify restrictions to trade and mobility are entirely framed in terms of the *public* interest and therefore leave private parties empty handed in trying to justify their behaviour.[40]

---

[35] Art 18(1) EC Treaty (now formulated somewhat differently in Art 20(2) TFEU).

[36] Case C-413/99 *Baumbast* [2002] ECR I-7091, [80 *et seq*].

[37] D Wyatt and A Dashwood, *European Union Law* (5th edn, Sweet & Maxwell, 2006) 154.

[38] Case C-281/98 *Roman Angonese* [2000] ECR I-4139, [35]–[36].

[39] Case C-438/05 *Viking* [2007] ECR I-10779, [35]–[37]; Case C-341/05 *Laval* [2007] ECR I-11767 [98]–[100].

[40] For discussion of the horizontal direct effect of the Treaty freedoms, see A Dashwood, '*Viking* and *Laval*: Issues of Horizontal Direct Effect' (2007–08) 10 CYELS 525.

(b) Regulations and directives

Turning then to the direct effect of secondary EC law, it is a well-known fact that provisions of a *regulation* will often but not always have direct effect, depending on their formulation,[41] and that provisions of a *directive* are supposed not to have direct effect,[42] though there are many occasions on which they do have such effect, namely when their clear ('precise and unconditional') provisions are not adequately implemented at the national level.[43] The vexed question of the *horizontal* effect of directives has exercised the minds of many academics and many an Advocate General. The European Court of Justice still insists on the principled position that directives do not have horizontal direct effect. Thus, in the *Carp* case, it held:

> [A]ccording to settled case-law, a directive cannot of itself impose obligations on an individual and cannot therefore be relied upon as such against an individual. It follows that even a clear, precise and unconditional provision of a directive seeking to confer rights or impose obligations on individuals cannot of itself apply in proceedings exclusively between private parties.[44]

But it seems that the Court's doctrine turns rather narrowly on the words 'of itself'. In cases where a directive does not apply 'of itself', but is 'merely' used to exclude the application of a national legal rule, then there is no problem, even when that disapplication adversely affects the legal position of a private party:

> [M]ere adverse repercussions on the rights of third parties, even if the repercussions are certain, do not justify preventing an individual from relying on the provisions of a directive against the Member States concerned [...].[45]

---

[41] For a case in which the ECJ found that a provision of a regulation lacked direct effect, see Case C-403/98 *Monte Arcosu* [2001] ECR I-103.

[42] Rather, the substantive norms contained in a directive are supposed to be turned into national law. If the transposition process happens as it should, then those norms will be applied as national law, and the question of the direct effect of *European Union law* will not arise. But, of course, things are different when the transposition does not take place in due time, and when national law is inconsistent with the directive after the latter's transposition.

[43] For a synthetic discussion of the evolution of the case law and doctrinal reflection about the direct effect of directives, see Prechal (n 24 above) ch 9.

[44] Case C-80/06 *Carp* [2007] ECR I-4473, [20]. Other recent judgments in which the Court confirmed its principled position in this matter include: Cases C-397/01 to C-403/01 *Pfeiffer and Others*, [2004] ECR I-8835, [108] and Cases C-37/06 and C-58/06 *Viamex Agrar und Zuchtvieh-Kontor* [2008] ECR I-69, [27].

[45] Cases C-152/07 to C-154/07 *Arcor* [2008] ECR I-5959, [36]. Famous instances of judgments in which the Court admitted such 'indirect' or 'triangular' horizontal effect are: Case C-194/94 *CIA Security International SA v Signalson SA and Securitel SPRL* (n 18 above) in which the European Court of Justice held that individuals may rely on the 'notification directive' 83/189 in order to oppose the application of a non-notified national measure, even in a situation—like in the case at hand—where such application was requested by a private individual in a civil lawsuit; and Case C-201/02 *Wells* [2004] ECR I-723, in which an individual was allowed to rely on the failure of public authorities to conduct a proper environmental impact assessment prior to delivering an authorization to exploit a quarry, even though this had a clearly detrimental impact on the legal position of the private owner of the quarry. For a synthetic discussion of those 'indirect horizontal effect cases' see A Dashwood, 'From *Van Duyn* to *Mangold* via *Marshall*: Reducing Direct Effect to Absurdity?' (2006–07) 9 CYELS 81, 94 *et seq*.

Thus, in many of its judgments the Court of Justice has allowed provisions of directives to affect the position of private parties in domestic litigation. Many writers have tried to make sense of the ECJ's meandering case law and, where they could not make sense of it, have challenged both the soundness of allowing for the vertical but not the horizontal direct effect of directives, and the consistency of the Court's attitude to horizontal effect.[46]

(c) International agreements of the European Union

The question of the direct effect of *international agreements* (and decisions adopted by bodies set up under such agreements) is a separate domain, whose practical importance is rapidly increasing with the growth of the number and scope of agreements concluded by the Community and the Union. The European Court of Justice has adopted a 'monist' attitude to international treaties, considering that they form, upon their ratification by the EU, an 'integral part' of the EU legal order.[47] This does not imply that all their provisions have direct effect. In fact, the Court has, globally speaking, taken a somewhat less generous view on the conditions for their direct effect within the Community and national legal orders than the view it takes, and seeks to impose, with regard to internal Community acts. The usual criterion of the sufficiently precise character of the single norm is subject to the prior qualification that the agreement, taken as a whole, should be suitable for producing direct effects. This area of EU law continues to be marked by a dichotomy which originated in the 1970s between some agreements (most prominently the WTO Agreement), to which the ECJ denies direct effect within the legal orders of the EU and its Member States, and most of the other international agreements, which the ECJ is quite ready to use as a standard for the review of EC secondary law and for the protection of individual rights.[48] An

---

[46] For an early critical view, see W Van Gerven, 'The Horizontal Direct Effect of Directive Provisions Revisited: The Reality of Catchwords' in D Curtin and T Heukels (eds), *The Institutional Dynamics of European Integration. Liber Amicorum Henry G. Schermers* (Dordrecht, 1994). A recent and comprehensive criticism of the Court's case law in this area is offered by P Craig, 'The Legal Effect of Directives: Policy, Rules and Exceptions' (2009) 34 ELRev 349; see also, among many others: T Tridimas, 'Black, Whites and Shades of Grey: Horizontality of Directives Revisited' (2002) 21 YEL 327. For a critical argument going in the opposite direction, namely stating that the Court should have more firmly and systematically limited the effect of directives in relations between individuals, see Dashwood (n 45 above). Most authors agree that the case law is not easily understandable; according to one author, 'the search for a theoretically respectable, watertight descriptive account of the fractured, fumbling case law on the direct effect of directives is a task fit only for masochists.' (M Dougan, 'When Worlds Collide! Competing Visions of the Relationship between Direct Effect and Supremacy' (2007) 44 CML Rev 931, 963.) See however, for an interesting attempt by a member of the Court of Justice to offer a coherent view of the case law, C Timmermans, 'Un nouveau chapitre sur l'invocabilité des directives' in *Mélanges en l'honneur de Jean-Pierre Puissochet—L'Etat souverain dans le monde d'aujourd'hui* (Pedone, 2008) 291.

[47] For a recent confirmation of this monist doctrine, see Case C-301/08 *Irène Bogiatzi*, 22 October 2009, [23].

[48] There is a very rich literature dealing with the effects of international agreements in the EU legal order, including the issue of the direct effect of the provisions of such agreements, and of decisions of international bodies. See among others: A Rosas, 'The European Court of Justice and Public International Law' in J Wouters, A Nollkaemper, and E de Wet (eds), *The Europeanisation of International Law—The Status of International*

extension of the 'restrictive' limb of the Court's case law recently occurred in *Intertanko* in relation, this time, to the UN Convention on the Law of the Sea, but there also continue to be rather spectacular examples of the more 'generous' approach, as for instance in *Soysal*[49] where the Court, by recognizing the direct effect of an obscure standstill provision in a Protocol to the 1963 Association Agreement with Turkey, precludes the application of the 'Schengen' visa requirement to Turkish service providers entering Germany, thereby disrupting a major piece of the Union's harmonized immigration control regime. The internal effect of international treaty law and international decisions is, however, always subject to the requirement that it should be compatible with primary EU law, ie the text of the Treaty and the general principles of Union law, as the ECJ recently repeated in its *Kadi* judgment:[50] on this point, we find a remarkable similarity between the conditional openness of the ECJ towards international law, and the conditional openness displayed by national Constitutional Courts towards EU law itself (on which, see below).

(d) Decisions and framework decisions in the former 'Third Pillar'

Partly in order to avoid the complications, discussed above, in relation to the direct effect of directives, the Member State governments had decided, when adopting the Treaty of Amsterdam, to exclude the direct effect of decisions and framework decisions, the new legal instruments they created for action under the Third Pillar (former Article 34 EU Treaty). In its *Pupino* judgment of 2005,[51] the ECJ held that this exclusion was no obstacle against imposing on national courts the usual *duty of interpretation* with regard to framework decisions (and therefore a right for domestic litigants to invoke the text of a framework decision for this purpose). This seems perfectly justified, if one considers that even dualist countries recognize a duty for courts to interpret national law in accordance with international treaties which have not been transformed into national law and therefore cannot, by definition, be self-executing. The Court of Justice went no further than this, but some authors have suggested that the ECJ might also recognize a right for individuals to rely on clear and precise provisions of a framework decision in order to set aside a conflicting rule of national law, thereby recognizing an 'exclusionary effect' to framework decisions.[52] In order to defend this view despite the clear Treaty

---

Law in the EU and its Member States (Cambridge University Press, 2008) 71; C Kaddous, 'Effects of International Agreements in the EU Legal Order' in M Cremona and B De Witte (eds), *EU Foreign Relations Law—Constitutional Fundamentals* (Hart, 2008) 291; J Klabbers, 'International Law in Community Law: The Law and Politics of Direct Effect' (2002) 21 YEL 263; P Koutrakos, *EU International Relations Law* (Hart, 2006) chs 6 and 7; N Lavranos, *Decisions of International Organisations in the European and Domestic Legal Orders of Selected EU Member States* (Europa Law, 2004); R Holdgaard, *External Relations Law of the European Community: Legal Reasoning and Legal Discourse* (Kluwer, 2008). See also, for consideration of this question, the chapter by M Cremona in this volume.

[49] Case C-228/06 *Soysal and Savatli* [2009] ECR I-1031.

[50] Cases C-402/05 P and C-415/05 P *Kadi and Al Barakaat v Council and Commission* [2008] I-6351 [306]–[308].

[51] Case C-105/03 *Pupino* (2005) ECR I-5285.

[52] See in particular K Lenaerts and T Corthaut, 'Of Birds and Hedges: The Role of Primacy in Invoking Norms of EU Law' (2006) 32 ELRev 287, 301.

prohibition of direct effect of decisions and framework decisions, those authors proposed a narrow definition of *direct effect* (as implying only 'substitution effect', ie situations in which EU law itself grants precisely defined rights to individuals), to be distinguished from a broader notion of *invocability* which simply requires the existence, in front of a national court, of a conflict between a norm of national law and a norm of EU law. The basis for the national court's role (and duty) is then the principle of *primacy* rather than that of *direct effect*. Contrary to that view, it seems preferable to assume that, when the Member States excluded direct effect for Third Pillar acts, they excluded *both* ways of invoking EU law norms before national courts;[53] as was argued above, the Court of Justice does not sharply distinguish between the substitution and the exclusionary effect and, indeed, uses the notion of 'direct effect' to describe both of them. It rightly does so, because the question whether an EU law norm is called to simply exclude the application of a national norm, or to replace it, is often not straightforward; it depends on the existing state of national law and may therefore vary from one country to the other.[54] It would not make good sense if framework decisions were enforceable by national courts in one Member State, and not in another, depending on differences in the way their domestic law is arranged. Anyway, this problem will now gradually be phased out. The Lisbon Treaty has abolished framework decisions as special legal instruments for the harmonization of criminal law and procedure, but the existing framework decisions will continue to display their particular legal effects for some years to come, until they are amended or replaced by directives.

(e) General principles of Union law

Finally, there is a source of law for which the direct effect question was seldom debated until recently, namely the *general principles of Union law* (previously better known as the general principles of *Community* law, since they operated mainly, if not exclusively, within the domain of the 'First Pillar'). Those principles are far from 'precise', but they are certainly 'unconditional', in the sense of not requiring further measures by EU or national institutions. Indeed, general principles serve primarily for use in adjudication, and one could therefore say that they have direct effect by their nature. This is most evident for the general principle of access to a (national) court for the enforcement of EU rights, as first formulated by the European Court in *Johnston* and *Heylens*[55] and often repeated since, but it also applies to the many other principles 'discovered' by the Court of Justice over the course of the years. National courts must review national measures, whenever they come within the scope of Union law,[56] in the

---

[53] The position defended here is developed in greater detail by A Hinarejos, 'On the Legal Effect of Framework Decisions and Decisions: Directly Applicable, Directly Effective, Self-executing, Supreme?' (2008) 14 ELJ 620. See also Timmermans (n 46 above) 296.

[54] See, on this point, Dougan (n 46 above) 938–940.

[55] Case 222/84 *Johnston v Chief Constable of the Royal Ulster Constabulary* [1986] ECR 1651; Case 222/86 *UNECTEF v Heylens* [1987] ECR 4097.

[56] The question when national measures come within the scope of Community law is notoriously controversial; see P Craig and G de Búrca, *EU Law—Text, Cases and Materials* (4th edn, Oxford University Press, 2008) 395–402.

light of fundamental rights but also of such ubiquitous principles of administrative law as proportionality, equality, legal certainty, and protection of legitimate expectations.[57]

Despite this long-established line of cases, the question of the horizontal direct effect of general principles of Community law became suddenly controversial in 2005, in the wake of the *Mangold* judgment. In that case, the ECJ held that the principle of non-discrimination on the ground of age, being part of the principle of equality, was a general principle of Community law and that, consequently, national courts had a duty to set aside domestic employment laws that were in breach of that principle.[58] So, what was different and, for many commentators, disturbing about *Mangold*? First, the fact that the ECJ resorted to the general principle of equality in a case where a directive, containing a more specific prohibition on discrimination, was not yet applicable to the facts of the case; and secondly the fact that, unlike in other cases, the national court was instructed to apply the general principle to the detriment of a private party (rather than against the state). Indeed, this case raised the question whether it is appropriate that general principles of Union law, being Court-made norms with an often very vague meaning, be used by national courts in litigation between private parties. In the constitutional law of many countries, general principles and even written fundamental rights are not directly enforceable by courts against private parties but require implementation or specification by the legislator.[59] The Court of Justice has not yet clearly addressed this problematic question, which will probably arise again in the context of the application, by national courts, of the EU Charter of Rights to disputes between private persons.

3. THE USEFUL EFFECT OF DIRECT EFFECT[60]

The function of direct effect is that EU law is to be considered by national courts as a *source of law* to be applied to individual cases and controversies. But the substantive law flowing from this source is filtered through fifteen different national procedural systems.

---

[57] Among the many instances in which national courts were called by the ECJ to apply the principles of legitimate expectations and legal certainty, see Case C-376/02 *Stichting 'Goed Wonen'* [2005] I-3445, [32], and Cases C-181/04 to 183/04 *Elmeka* [2006] I-8167 [31]. For an example of the application of the principle of equality, see Case C-442/00 *Rodriguez Caballero* [2002] ECR I-11915, [42]–[43].

[58] Case C-144/04 *Mangold* [75]–[76]. See, among the many comments of the judgment, E Muir, 'Establishing the Effects of Community Law on National Employment Policies: The Mangold Case' (2006) 31 ELRev 879. *Mangold* was more recently confirmed, on this same point, by a Grand Chamber judgment in Case C-555/07 *Seda Kücükdeveci*, 19 January 2010, [51].

[59] For a comparative law study of the horizontal effect of fundamental rights, see D Oliver and J Fedtke (eds), *Human Rights and the Private Sphere—A Comparative Study* (Routledge, 2007). It is true that EU anti-discrimination law applies to relations between private persons but this was done either on the basis of Treaty provisions or of EU legislation that expressly defined its scope of application as including horizontal situations; see B De Witte, 'The Crumbling Public/Private Divide: Horizontality in European Anti-Discrimination Law' (2009) 13 Citizenship Studies 515.

[60] The expression '*l'effet utile de l'effet direct*' probably stems from former ECJ judge Mertens de Wilmars in his Article 'L'efficacité des différentes techniques nationales de protection juridique contre les violations du droit communautaire par les autorités nationales' (1981) Cahiers Dr Euro 379.

The ability to invoke the Union norm might thus be rendered ineffective by national procedural or remedial rules. Therefore, the Court of Justice has imposed limits on the procedural autonomy of the Member States through the application of a standard formula, which it first adopted in *Rewe* in 1976, and which it repeatedly confirmed since. In the *Peterbroeck* judgment of 1995, the formula was stated as follows:

> [I]t is for the Member States to ensure the legal protection which individuals derive from the direct effect of Community law. In the absence of Community rules governing a matter, it is for the domestic legal system of each Member State to designate the courts having jurisdiction and to lay down the detailed procedural rules governing actions for safeguarding rights which individuals derive from the direct effect of Community law. However, such rules must not be less favourable than those governing similar domestic actions nor render virtually impossible or excessively difficult the exercise of rights conferred by Community law...[61]

The Court of Justice did in fact decide, in a well-known string of cases, that certain procedural or remedial rules had to be available so as not to make the exercise of Community rights 'excessively difficult'. This idea of the useful effect of direct effect was emphasized, in different ways, in cases such as *Heylens, Johnston, Borelli, Emmott, Factortame,* and *Francovich* with its progeny. They need no detailed consideration here, as they are examined in another chapter in this volume.[62] Since these obligations for national courts go beyond the requirement of granting direct effect to EU law, they have sometimes been considered as a dimension of the primacy principle (so-called 'structural primacy', on which see the next section). One may note that the Court's doctrine applies, according to its own formulation, only 'in the absence of Community rules governing a matter'. It is interesting to observe that there is a growing number of rules of secondary EU law 'governing' procedure and remedies, that are usually adopted to accompany substantive rules of EU law in a particular sector.[63]

C. EVOLUTION OF THE PRIMACY DOCTRINE

1. THE NATURE OF PRIMACY

(a) A 'mere' duty to disapply the conflicting norm of national law
The primacy of Union law entails duties for the various national authorities. For the national legislator, it implies a prohibition to adopt laws that are inconsistent with binding rules of Union law, and a duty to modify the laws that prove to be inconsistent

---

[61] Case C-312/93 *Peterbroeck, Van Campenhout & Cie SCS v Belgian State* [1995] ECR I-4599, 4621. The words quoted are followed by references to a large number of earlier judgments in which the same, or a similar, formula had been used by the Court, and similar language has been used in many judgments given after *Peterbroeck*.

[62] See the chapter by M Dougan in this volume.

[63] Areas of EU law in which this has occurred include public procurement, anti-discrimination, and consumer protection.

with EU law obligations. For national courts, the primary focus of analysis here, respecting the principle of primacy means that, when an EU rule applies in a given case, any conflicting national norm should be *set aside*. This is often called a duty to *disapply* national law. The mature formula, elaborated in the *Simmenthal* judgment, was rendered as follows in a later judgment of 1991:

> [A] national court which is called upon, within the limits of its jurisdiction, to apply provisions of Community law is under a duty to give full effect to those provisions, if necessary by refusing of its own motion to apply any conflicting provision of national legislation, and it is not necessary for the court to request or await the prior setting aside of such provision by legislative or other constitutional means.[64]

As the operation of setting aside conflicting national law has to be repeated by the same court, and by other courts, in all similar individual cases, the result in practical terms is close to the invalidation of the rule. But there remains a distinction (which is more heavily emphasized in continental legal systems than in Britain) between *invalidity* and *non-application*, and the Court of Justice only requires non-application of the inconsistent national rule.[65] A national rule, which is set aside for being inconsistent with Union law, is inoperative only to the extent of this inconsistency; the rule may continue to be applied to cases where it is not inconsistent, or to cases which are not covered by the EU norm, and it may fully apply again if and when the EU norm ceases to exist. Things are different only when EU law is intended to harmonize national legislation; then, inconsistencies must be removed by repealing or modifying national laws to the extent required by the harmonizing act. In this case, the possible disapplication of the inconsistent national norm by the courts cannot be an excuse for the legislator's failure to change the law.[66]

Yet, disapplication is only a minimum requirement. Whether national courts can, and must, go beyond this and offer a more incisive remedy depends on domestic law and on the particular configuration of each case. Thus, national courts will usually *annul* individual administrative measures based on a national statute conflicting with EU law, whereas the statute itself is not subject to annulment (although that might perhaps be desirable for the sake of legal certainty).

More generally, the Court's traditional view of primacy has been a rather pragmatic one: it is certainly radical in its intended effects (it makes *any* norm of EC law prevail

---

[64] Case C-184/89 *Nimz v City of Hamburg* [1991] ECR I-297, 321. The first part of the phrase was affirmed already in *Costa v ENEL*, the latter part (starting with 'and it is not necessary') is the result of *Simmenthal*.

[65] This view was reaffirmed by the Court of Justice in Case C-314/08 *Krzysztof Filipiak*, 19 November 2009 [82]: 'Pursuant to the principle of the primacy of Community law, a conflict between a provision of national law and a directly applicable provision of the Treaty is to be resolved by a national court applying Community law, if necessary by refusing to apply the conflicting national provision, and not by a declaration that the national provision is invalid, the powers of authorities, courts and tribunals in that regard being a matter to be determined by each Member States.' See also, earlier on, Cases C-10/97 to C-22/97 *Ministero delle Finanze v IN.CO.GE '90 Srl and others* [1998] ECR 6307, [20]–[21].

[66] For the rule that national authorities have a duty to eliminate conflicting national norms quite apart from the disapplication of those norms by the courts, see Case C-197/96 *Commission v France* [1997] ECR I-1489, [14].

over *any* norm of national law, see below) but it comes into play only when there is an actual conflict between two norms that are both capable of being applied to the facts of a case:

> [T]he issue as to whether an instrument is capable of having direct effect is logically prior to that of its status relative to national law. In other words, a provision must first be cognisable by Member State courts, before there can be any conflict with the applicable national rules, which might lead to the disapplication of the latter.[67]

A striking characteristic of primacy is its absolute nature: 'even the most minor piece of technical Community legislation ranks above the most cherished constitutional norm'.[68] Already in the *Costa* case, the Court held that Community law 'cannot be overridden by domestic legal provisions, however framed'.[69] The classic assertion of the full supremacy of Community law came in the *Internationale Handelsgesellschaft* case in 1970. Faced with a challenge to the validity of a Community Regulation for violation of the German Basic Law, the Court of Justice held that 'the validity of a Community measure or its effect within a Member State cannot be affected by allegations that it runs counter to either fundamental rights as formulated by the constitution of that state or the principles of a national constitutional structure'.[70] The main reason offered by the Court was that the unity and efficacy of Community law would be gravely affected if one allowed a review of its validity on the basis of particular national legal standards. In several later cases, the Court of Justice confirmed that EU law had to be given precedence over national law even where the relevant national norm had a constitutional character.[71]

Primacy attaches to both primary and secondary EU law. For the latter category, an obvious condition for primacy is that the acts should be validly adopted as a matter of EU law. *Ultra vires* acts of Union law cannot prevail over national law, and the preliminary reference procedure allows national courts to express doubts as to whether an EU act is valid and may justifiably claim to overrule contrary national norms.

(b) Structural supremacy: 'disapplying' rules on procedures and remedies

The Court of Justice used its disapplication terminology even in a case like *Factortame-I*,[72] suggesting that the national courts could simply 'set aside' constitutional norms defining their jurisdiction or their powers in relation to other state

---

[67] A Dashwood, 'The Law and Practice of CFSP Joint Actions' in M Cremona and B De Witte (eds), *EU Foreign Relations Law—Constitutional Fundamentals* (Hart, 2008) 53, 55. See for example the formula used by the Court in *Krzysztof Filipiak* (n 65 above) referring to 'a directly applicable provision'.

[68] S Weatherill, *Law and Integration in the European Union* (Oxford University Press, 1995) 106.

[69] The French text of the judgment is even clearer: Community law 'ne peut se voir opposer de norme interne *quelle qu'elle soit*' (*Recueil* 1964, 1141).

[70] Case 11/70 *Internationale Handelsgesellschaft* [1970] ECR 1125, 1134.

[71] See for example Case C-285/98 *Tanja Kreil* [2000] ECR I-69, and Case C-213/07 *Michaniki* [2008] I-9999. In both these cases, the existence of a conflict with a norm of constitutional law is clear from the Court's presentation of the facts, but does not explicitly appear in the Court's own reasoning.

[72] Case C-213/89 *The Queen v Secretary of State for Transport, ex p Factortame and Others* [1990] ECR I-2433, 2474.

authorities. In fact, the national courts in this case were invited to assume new jurisdictional powers and therefore *create* new law rather than simply *choose* between two applicable norms. This effect was even clearer in the state liability cases, particularly in *Brasserie du Pêcheur/Factortame*, where the Court of Justice held that there should be provision for state liability also where the national legislature was responsible for the breach of EC law, whereas such liability for legislative acts was unknown to many national legal systems.[73] Those cases make clear that the partial harmonization of legal remedies imposed by the Court of Justice requires national courts to do more than just 'set aside' national laws. How then to understand this development of a European standard with respect to judicial remedies? Are they a new branch of the principle of primacy (which might perhaps be called 'procedural' or 'structural' primacy)[74] or should one avoid stretching the concept of supremacy and rather consider that the Court of Justice has gradually been developing a new principle of *effectiveness*, alongside direct effect and primacy, or even encompassing direct effect and primacy?[75] Legal doctrine is in a state of flux here. However, the language used by the Court seems to point to an approach in terms of primacy: it holds that EU law may *preclude the application* of national rules on actions for damages or on remedies, when these rules do not offer an 'effective and equivalent' remedy for infringements of EU law. An example of this approach is *Lucchini* in which the Court of Justice held that:

> Community law precludes the application of a provision of national law, such as Article 2909 of the Italian Civil Code, which seeks to lay down the principle of *res judicata* in so far as the application of that provision prevents the recovery of state aid granted in breach of Community law which has been found to be incompatible with the common market in a decision of the Commission of the European Communities which has become final.[76]

2. THE SCOPE OF PRIMACY: EXTENSION FROM EC LAW TO EU LAW IN THE LISBON TREATY

The Treaty of Maastricht incorporated the European Community into a wider organization, the European Union, whose other parts (the 'Second Pillar' dealing with common foreign policy and the 'Third Pillar' dealing with justice and home affairs) did not share many of the supranational characteristics of the Community, in terms of

---

[73] Cases C-46/93 and C-48/93 *Brasserie du Pêcheur v Germany and The Queen v Secretary of State for Transport, ex p Factortame* [1996] ECR I-1029, 1141–1145.

[74] This was the prevailing approach in the French language literature; see eg D Simon, 'Les exigences de la primauté du droit communautaire: continuité ou métamorphoses?' in *L'Europe et le droit. Mélanges en hommage de Jean Boulouis* (1991) 481; and R Dehousse, *La Cour de Justice des Communautés européennes* (1995) 50.

[75] See Weatherill (n 68 above) 116: 'Direct effect and supremacy have become part of a bolder and more ambitious notion of "effectiveness". Effectiveness encapsulates the notion that Community law shall confer rights plus remedies that make real the practical enjoyment of those rights.'

[76] Case C-119/05 *Lucchini* [2007] ECR I-6199 [63]. Similar 'precluding the application' language is used, this time in respect of a Spanish rule on actions for damages against the state, in Case C-118/08 *Transportes Urbanos y Servicios Generales*, 26 January 2010, [46].

decision-making and legal instruments. Since that time, it became a matter of specu-
lation whether the principle of primacy, which the Court of Justice had developed with
respect to *Community* law, would also extend more broadly to *Union* law as a whole.
In the *Costa v ENEL* judgment, it may be recalled, the Court had heavily insisted on the
special characteristics of the EEC Treaty in order to conclude on its necessary primacy
within the national legal orders. The Second and Third Pillar parts of the EU Treaty
did not share many of these special supranational characteristics of the EC Treaty, so
that one could doubt whether their primacy over national law should be recognized by
national courts. In the many years since the entry into force of the Maastricht Treaty,
the Court of Justice never had the opportunity to pronounce itself on the question
whether the EU Treaty creates, like the EC Treaty, a specific legal order whose norms
must have precedence over conflicting national norms,[77] but the various judgments of
national Constitutional Courts dealing with the domestic measures for the implementation of the European Arrest Warrant (which is a Framework Decision adopted
within the Third Pillar) did not show great willingness of those courts to recognize
the internal primacy of Third Pillar law.[78] However, with the entry into force of the
Lisbon Treaty, Community law has disappeared and is absorbed by EU law, so that the
question of the scope of the primacy principle in brought into a new light.

This new post-Lisbon situation must be considered in the perspective of a curious
sequence of events that occurred between 2002 and 2007 in relation to the possible
codification of the primacy principle. In the framework of the Convention on the
Future of the Union, which operated in 2002–03, a consensus was reached fairly
quickly and without much controversy on incorporating the principle of primacy
into the Treaty text—as part of the Convention's general aim of 'simplifying' EU law
by enhancing the visibility of its basic norms for the citizens. The relevant provision
was incorporated in the opening part of the Treaty establishing a Constitution for
Europe of 2004, as its Article I-6:

> The Constitution and law adopted by the institutions of the Union in exercising compe-
> tences conferred on it shall have primacy over the law of the Member States.

However, in the course of the Intergovernmental Conference leading up to the
Treaty, the codification of primacy had become controversial in the domestic debate
of the United Kingdom, and Article I-6 was accompanied by a reassuring Declaration

---

[77] For an argument in favour of such primacy, see K Lenaerts and T Corthaut (n 52 above) 287. More
dubitatively: M Claes (n 2 above) 586–590. An intermediate position was proposed by S Prechal, 'Direct Effect,
Indirect Effect, Supremacy and the Evolving Constitution of the European Union' in C Barnard (ed), *The
Fundamentals of EU Law Revisited—Assessing the Impact of the Constitutional Debate* (Oxford University
Press, 2007) 35, 60 *et seq*.

[78] See, for comparative studies of the national constitutional case law dealing with the Arrest Warrant:
E Guild (ed), *Constitutional Challenges to the European Arrest Warrant* (Wolf Legal, 2006); E Guild and
L Marin (eds), *Still not Resolved? Constitutional Issues of the European Arrest Warrant* (Centre for European
Policy Studies, 2009); J Komarek, 'European Constitutionalism and the European Arrest Warrant: In Search of
Limits of "Contrapunctual Principles"' (2007) 44 CML Rev 9.

in which the Conference noted 'that Article I-6 reflects existing case-law of the Court of Justice of the European Communities and of the Court of First Instance' and did not, therefore, cause any additional limitations of state sovereignty.[79] In their Decisions of late 2004 dealing with the compatibility of the Constitutional Treaty with their own national constitution, the Constitutional Courts of France and Spain agreed that the new primacy clause did not bring any changes to the existing relationship between EU law and national law.[80]

Three years later, the European Council of June 2007, when deciding to turn the Constitutional Treaty into a de-constitutionalized 'Reform Treaty' considered that a deletion of the primacy article would fit in its attempt to visualize the differences between the Constitutional Treaty and its more modest avatar. The principle of primacy was removed again from the text of the founding Treaties, and instead a new and much longer Declaration was adopted and attached to the Treaty of Lisbon, which sounds as follows:

> The Conference recalls that, in accordance with well settled case law of the Court of Justice of the European Union, the Treaties and the law adopted by the Union on the basis of the Treaties have primacy over the law of Member States, under the conditions laid down by the said case law.
>
> The Conference has also decided to attach as an Annex to this Final Act the Opinion of the Council Legal Service on the primacy of EC law as set out in 11197/07 (JUR 260):
>
> Opinion of the Council Legal Service of 22 June 2007
>
> It results from the case-law of the Court of Justice that primacy of EC law is a cornerstone principle of Community law. According to the Court, this principle is inherent to the specific nature of the European Community. At the time of the first judgment of this established case law (Costa/ENEL, 15 July 1964, Case 6/64) there was no mention of primacy in the treaty. It is still the case today. The fact that the principle of primacy will not be included in the future treaty shall not in any way change the existence of the principle and the existing case-law of the Court of Justice.[81]

So, according to this Declaration, the entry into force of the Lisbon Treaty 'shall not in any way change' the current position as regards to primacy. Is this a credible statement? Not entirely, it seems.

First, it is difficult to pretend that 'nothing has happened', and to ignore the effect of the backtracking that occurred between 2004 and 2007. One may well wonder whether removal of the express primacy clause will weaken the authority of EU law and, in particular, encourage national courts to preserve and strengthen their reservations to primacy.[82]

---

[79] Declaration on Art I-6, attached to the Final Act of the Constitutional Treaty.

[80] See discussion in M Kumm and V Ferreres Comella, 'The Primacy Clause of the Constitutional Treaty and the Future of Constitutional Conflict in the European Union' (2005) 3 ICON 473. Those national court decisions are also discussed further below.

[81] Declaration (No 17) concerning primacy, attached to the Final Act of the Treaty of Lisbon, [2008] OJ C115/344.

[82] M Dougan, 'The Treaty of Lisbon 2007: Winning Minds not Hearts' (2008) 45 CML Rev 617, 700.

Secondly, the Council's legal opinion relates to *Community law* whereas there simply is no settled case law (contrary to what the Lisbon Declaration states) regarding *Union law as a whole* (ie including Second and Third Pillar law). The disappearance of Community law, through the Lisbon Treaty, and its absorption within the new and broader regime of EU law will create new questions about the scope of the principle of primacy. There will no longer be any principled reason to deny the primacy of any part of EU law, although in relation to common foreign and security law the severe limits to the ECJ's jurisdiction will possibly not allow the ECJ to discuss the extension of the primacy doctrine to that area. As for the current Third Pillar, primacy will clearly apply there, with a possible temporary limit deriving from the complicated transitional provisions.[83]

D. THE RECEPTION OF THE DOCTRINES AT THE NATIONAL LEVEL

In its report submitted in 1995 to the Intergovernmental Conference on the revision of the Treaties, the Court of Justice stated that

> the success of Community law in embedding itself so thoroughly in the legal life of the Member States is due to its having been perceived, interpreted and applied by the nationals, the administrations and the courts and tribunals of all the Member States as a uniform body of rules upon which individuals may rely in their national courts.[84]

Thus, the European Court indicated, quite rightly, that the crucial element for the effective application of the principles of primacy and direct effect is the attitude of *national* courts and authorities. It is not enough for the Court of Justice to proclaim that EU law rules should have direct effect and should prevail over national law: '[T]o put it bluntly, the ECJ can say whatever it wants, the real question is why anyone should heed it.'[85] There is therefore a second dimension to the matter, which is decisive for determining whether the Court's doctrines have an impact on legal reality: the attitude of national courts and other institutions.

One could offer one simple reason why national courts should heed the European Court's doctrines, namely that those doctrines were formulated in the context of preliminary rulings given on request of national courts. Preliminary rulings are binding for the referring courts and, indirectly, also for the other courts in the EU faced with similar questions. But, on the other hand, the ECJ's authority is restricted to

---

[83] Lisbon Treaty, Art 9 of the Protocol on Transitional Provisions. This Article provides that the pre-existing Third Pillar measures shall retain their legal effect after the entry into force of the Lisbon Treaty until they are repealed, annulled, or amended by later acts. This must probably be read as also preserving the lack of direct effect (and hence the lack of effective primacy) of existing decisions and framework decisions adopted under the pre-Lisbon Third Pillar (on this point, see S Peers, 'Finally "Fit for Purpose"? The Treaty of Lisbon and the End of the Third Pillar Legal Order' (2008) 27 YEL 47, 63).

[84] Report of the Court of Justice on Certain Aspects of the Application of the Treaty on European Union, May 1995, 2.

[85] K J Alter, 'The European Court's Political Power' (1996) 19 WEP 458, 459.

the interpretation and application of the Treaties. National courts or governments could therefore be tempted to refuse elements of the doctrines of direct effect and supremacy with the argument that they are not really about the interpretation of EU law but about matters of national constitutional law which are not within the European Court's province. Also, to base the binding character of the ECJ's rulings about primacy on the Treaty Article mentioning the preliminary reference mechanism introduces an element of circularity, because it is precisely the primacy of that Treaty which the ECJ is seeking to establish. Thus, the legal parameters for controversies on the legitimacy and appropriateness of the European Court's doctrines did exist. Yet, as the following pages will help to show, the reception of those doctrines at the national level has been rather successful, on the whole.

1. THE ABSENCE OF REACTION BY POLITICAL INSTITUTIONS

Perhaps the most surprising thing, when looking back at the almost fifty years of existence of the supremacy and direct effect doctrines is that they still have the status of *unwritten principles of law*. As mentioned above, the principles have not been squarely incorporated in the Treaties at any of the several occasions on which those Treaties were revised, except for the failed attempt at codification of primacy in the Constitutional Treaty. Conversely, there have been few (surprisingly few?) attempts by national governments or parliaments either to positively incorporate the principles into the national constitutions or, conversely, to curb the scope of those principles unilaterally. It seems that the political institutions of the Member States have taken little interest in those arcane lawyers' doctrines, and have been happy to let their domestic courts grapple with their implications.[86]

2. THE EASY ACCEPTANCE OF THE DIRECT EFFECT DOCTRINE

The initial resistance displayed by the intervening governments in *Van Gend en Loos* was not mirrored by the attitude of national courts in the following years. Indeed, it is remarkable how easily they followed the basic principle established by the Court of Justice, namely that it could tell national courts which EC law norms had, or did not have, direct effect. But perhaps that should not come as a surprise. Indeed, the constitutional doctrines followed by national courts in relation to the self-executing nature of international treaty obligations (to the extent that the sparse occasions prior to 1963 allowed for the development of true doctrines) often took as the decisive criterion the intention of the contracting parties towards the Treaty. It was, therefore, a matter of interpretation of the relevant Treaty. Now, the EEC Treaty provided precisely for a novel mechanism in Article 177, which allowed national courts to

---

[86] For further discussion of this question, see K J Alter, *Establishing the Supremacy of European Law—The Making of an International Rule of Law in Europe* (Oxford University Press, 2001) ch 5.

refer such matters of interpretation to a common and well-qualified body, the Euro-pean Court of Justice. Following the lead of that Court was therefore no clean break with their past habits, even though the generous way in which the ECJ attributed the direct effect label to EC law provisions may have contrasted with their own previously more hesitant attitude towards international treaty norms.

Still, there have been some isolated pockets of resistance to the European Court's direct effect doctrine. Apart from an early and short-lived 'rebellion' by the German Financial Supreme Court in the 1960s,[87] the principle itself that Community law *can* have direct effect has not been contested anywhere. The further principle established by *Van Gend en Loos*, namely that the European Court of Justice has sole authority to decide *which* provisions of Community law have direct effect, has been contested with respect to one particular category of Community acts, namely directives. In its famous *Cohn Bendit* Decision of 1978, the French *Conseil d'Etat* held that individuals may not invoke a directive as a ground for the annulment of an individual administrative act.[88] *Cohn Bendit* was only very recently formally overruled by the *Conseil d'Etat*,[89] although its scope had been gradually reduced in the course of time. Yet, the misgiv-ings expressed by national courts may well have led the European Court of Justice to exercise moderation in its later rulings on the direct effect of directives; its refusal to recognize the horizontal direct effect of directives might be explained in this way.[90]

3. THE SLOW AND DIFFICULT ACCEPTANCE OF THE PRINCIPLE OF PRIMACY

The reception of the principle of primacy gave rise to many more difficulties than that of the doctrine of direct effect. One may usefully distinguish, here, between the original six Member States, for which the *Costa v Enel* judgment may have come as a surprise, and the states joining later, at a time when primacy was a firmly established and widely publicized characteristic of the Community legal order.

Among the original Six, no special efforts were required from the courts in the Netherlands and Luxembourg, where the primacy of international treaty provisions over national legislation was accepted prior to 1957. Of the other four countries, the courts in Belgium reacted most promptly and loyally to the European Court's injunctions. A model of what national courts can achieve in the absence of clear constitutional guidelines is the 1971 judgment of the Belgian *Cour de Cassation* in

---

[87] See the first edition of this volume (Oxford University Press, 1997) 195.

[88] *Conseil d'Etat*, 22 December 1978, *Ministère de l'Intérieur c. Sieur Cohn-Bendit* (and conclusions Genevois), (1979) Revue trimestrielle de droit européen 157, with note by L Dubouis, (1980) 1 CML Rev 543.

[89] *Conseil d'Etat*, 30 October 2009 *Mme Perreux* (and conclusions Guyomar), (2009) Revue française de droit administratif 1125, with note by P Cassia.

[90] See, for instance, the argument by Weatherill that the European Court, in its *Marshall* judgment, 'set a boundary to the spread of direct effect. In return for such clarification and such restraint it hoped to gain from the national courts an acceptance of the more restricted notion of direct effect—against the state alone. The tactic seems largely to have worked' (n 68 above) 124.

the *Franco-Suisse Le Ski* case.[91] Although the Belgian Constitution was silent on the domestic effect of international or European law (or precisely because of this absence of written rules) the Supreme Court adopted the principle of primacy as it had been formulated in *Costa,* and based it on the nature of international law and (*a fortiori*) of EC law. The other Belgian courts soon followed the same line. In France, although the text of Article 55 of the Constitution recognized the priority of international treaties even over later French laws, the courts were surprisingly slow to accept that this constitutional provision could actually be used as a conflict rule in real cases and controversies. The *Cour de Cassation,* taking the lead in relation to all ordinary courts, decided to cross the Rubicon in the 1975 *Cafés Jacques Vabre* judgment.[92] The *Conseil d'Etat* (and the administrative courts subject to its authority) followed suit much later, with the *Nicolo* Decision (1989), after what must have been a very painful revision of established truths.[93] One may note that one of the arguments used by the *commissaire* Frydman, when advising the *Conseil* in *Nicolò* to change its views on the primacy of EC law, was that the supreme courts of surrounding countries (even those with ingrained dualist traditions) had long recognized this primacy.

In Italy and Germany, the actual duties imposed on national courts by *Costa* went well beyond what the mainstream constitutional doctrine, at that time, was prepared to accept in terms of the domestic force of international treaty law. Yet, the European Court suggested, by cleverly distinguishing EEC law from 'ordinary' international law, that the German and Italian courts might, with some creativity, find the constitutional resources needed for recognizing the primacy of Community law. The message, in *Costa,* was primarily addressed to the Italian Constitutional Court. This court has indeed gradually come to recognize the primacy of Community law over national legislation, on the basis of its special nature which distinguishes it from other international treaties. A similar evolution took place in Germany.[94]

For the twenty-one countries that joined the European Community (or the European Union) after *Costa,* the situation was rather different. For them, unlike for the original Six, primacy did not require *ex post* constitutional creativity but was a matter of voluntary acceptance as part of the *acquis communautaire.* As Lord Bridge put it in his speech in *Factortame (No 2):* '[I]f the supremacy within the European Community of Community law over the national law of Member States was not always inherent in the EEC Treaty it was certainly well established in the jurisprudence of the Court of

---

[91] *Cour de Cassation* (Belgium), 27 May 1971, *S.A. Fromagerie franco-suisse "Le Ski"* (1971) RTD eur 495.

[92] *Cour de Cassation* (France), *Jacques Vabre,* 23 May 1975 (with conclusions Touffait), (1975) Revue trimestrielle de droit européen 336.

[93] *Conseil d'Etat, Nicolo,* 20 October 1989 (with conclusions Frydman), (1989) Revue trimestrielle de droit européen 771, note by G Isaac.

[94] For further references to the doctrinal and judicial evolution in those two countries, see B De Witte, 'Sovereignty and European Integration: The Weight of Legal Tradition' (1995) MJ 145, 156-158, and Claes (n 2 above) 596-625.

Justice long before the United Kingdom joined the Community.'[95] One would therefore expect the principle of primacy to be part of the terms of accession, and
recognition of primacy to be part of constitutional preparations for membership. On
both these points, however, the practice of states was rather ambiguous. Indeed, none
of the Accession Treaties explicitly mentions primacy (or direct effect). It seems rather
that primacy was an *implicit* part of the *acquis communautaire* which all new Members accepted.

By and large, 'ordinary' primacy of Union law, that is, primacy over national
legislation and sources of national law lower in rank than legislation, seems now
firmly anchored in the national legal orders of all Member States, although with
some important exceptions. In Denmark and Sweden, in particular, there is no other
basis for the application of EU law than the statute which confers domestic effect on
EU law, and EU law remains therefore at the mercy of a later, conflicting, statute, so
that primacy remains a logical problem in those countries even if conflicts have been
avoided in practice.[96] Also in the United Kingdom, the doctrine of the sovereignty of
parliament, cannot easily—because of its unwritten nature—be changed, and the
discussion is therefore still open as to whether the UK Parliament could adopt a
statute expressly overruling its European Communities Act which forms the basis of
the primacy of EU law in the UK legal order.[97]

Primacy over national *constitutional* law is quite another matter, on which there is
no similar quasi-consensus across all EU states; because of its theoretical importance,
and the considerable attention given to it in the legal literature, this question will be
considered separately in the next section.

E. CONSTITUTIONAL RESERVATIONS

1. THE CONSTITUTION AS FOUNDATION OF THE INTERNAL EFFECT OF EU LAW

The position of the European Court of Justice was that the direct effect and primacy of
EC law was based on the nature of Community law itself, and that same view may now,
after the Lisbon Treaty, be extended to European Union law as a whole. One could
interpret this position in two ways. A benign interpretation is that national courts
must necessarily find a way to recognize those principles and to achieve the result
imposed by the European Court on them. A stronger interpretation would be that
national courts have no choice and that they simply cannot resist the authority of EU
law. The latter reading implies that national courts, when acting on the duties imposed

---

[95] [1991] 1 AC 603, 658.

[96] See the analysis by C Lebeck, 'Supranational Law in a Cold Climate: European Law in Scandinavia' (2010)
STALS Research Papers No 4.

[97] See the discussion by P Craig, 'Britain in the European Union' in J Jowell and D Oliver (eds), *The
Changing Constitution* (7th edn, Oxford University Press, 2007) 84.

on them by the European Court, are exercising a jurisdiction attributed to them directly by Union law, and not a jurisdiction given to them by their own constitution. This view was adopted by many European Community law scholars, particularly those of France and the Benelux countries,[98] but there is hardly any evidence of national courts adopting this radical approach. National courts rather see themselves as organs of their state, and try to fit their European mandate within the framework of the powers attributed to them by their national legal system. For them (and, indeed, for most constitutional law scholars throughout Europe), the idea that EU law can claim its primacy within the national legal orders on the basis of its own authority seems as implausible as Baron von Munchhausen's claim that he had lifted himself from the quicksand by pulling on his bootstraps. The national courts (with the possible exception of those of the Netherlands)[99] see EU law as rooted in their constitution, and seek a foundation for the primacy and direct effect of EU law in that constitution.

This is often not an easy task, as most national constitutions fail to deal explicitly with the internal effect of EU law (or international law in general). In the absence of such explicit provisions, recourse may be had to the constitutional clauses allowing for EU membership or, more generally, allowing for the attribution of state powers to organizations like the European Union. Such provisions *do* occur in all the (written) constitutions of the Member States, except that of Finland;[100] although their wording is different, they serve broadly the same purpose of enabling membership of advanced international organizations such as the European Union. In some countries they have been given an additional significance as the basis for the domestic effect of EU law. One could argue, though, that attributing state powers to international institutions is one thing, and deciding upon the domestic effect of rules adopted by such institutions (*and* rules contained in the Treaty creating the institutions) is quite a different thing. Certainly, when the 'attribution of powers' clauses were inserted in the post-fascist constitutions of Germany and Italy, the European Community did not exist, and nobody thought those clauses could affect the enforcement of international law (or of a future European law) by national courts. And yet, perhaps for lack of a better foundation, some of the countries lacking an explicit primacy and direct effect clause have sought a constitutional anchorage for those doctrines in the 'attribution of powers' clauses.

---

[98] For powerful statements of this view, see R Kovar, 'La contribution de la Cour de justice à l'édification de l'ordre juridique communautaire' in (1995) *IV Collected Courses of the Academy of European Law*, Book 1, 15, 47–59, and R Barents, *The Autonomy of Community Law* (Kluwer International Law, 2004).

[99] Art 94 of the Constitution of the Netherlands recognizes the priority of (self-executing) treaty provisions over any source of national law, and forms therefore a perfect basis for the recognition of the primacy of EU law. Yet, the majority of legal writers defends the view that the constitutional provision only deals with 'ordinary' international treaties, whereas EU law, due to its special supranational character, prevails over national law by its own authority and not due to any constitutional provision. In practice, though, the Dutch courts prefer to recognize the primacy of EU law without specifying where they find its foundation, whether in EU law or in the constitution.

[100] For a comparative analysis of those provisions, see M Claes, 'Constitutionalizing Europe at its Source: The "European Clauses" in the National Constitutions: Evolution and Typology' (2005) 24 YEL 81; and J V Louis and T Ronse, *L'ordre juridique de l'Union européenne* (Pedone, 2005) 334 *et seq.*

Thus, in Italy, Article 11 became the constitutional peg on which to hang the primacy of Community law, or, to quote another frequently used metaphor, the instrument piercing the barrier of dualism and allowing Community law to have full effect within the Italian legal order. The reasoning could perhaps be spelled out as follows: one of the 'limitations of sovereignty' allowed by the terms of Article 11 is that the parliament could accept, when ratifying the EEC Treaty, that its statutes would no longer be enforceable by the Italian courts when found incompatible with Community obligations. In the interpretation of Article 24 of the German Constitution adopted by the Constitutional Court since the late 1960s, that Article had come to play exactly the same role as Article 11 of the Italian Constitution. Its explicit and primary function was to allow for membership of international organizations with such incisive powers as those of the European Communities; but its implicit and secondary function had become to serve as the constitutional 'bridge' allowing Community law to enter the German legal order carrying its flags of primacy and direct effect. In the aftermath of the Maastricht Treaty, a new Article 23 was introduced in the German Constitution, dealing specifically with the European Union, and replacing henceforth the former Article 24 as the constitutional basis for the primacy and direct effect of EU law. More recently, the French and Spanish Constitutional Court have similarly come to identify the 'attribution of powers' clause of their Constitution as the basis from which the primacy and direct effect of EU law flows.

2. THE PROTECTION OF NATIONAL CONSTITUTIONAL VALUES

The thesis defended by the Court of Justice that Union law has absolute primacy, even over national constitutional provisions, is generally not accepted by national constitutional and supreme courts. Indeed, as was mentioned before, those courts recognize the privileged position of EU law, not by virtue of the inherent nature of that law, as the Court of Justice would have it, but by grace of their own constitutional system. This does not matter too much for the relation between EU law and ordinary legislation, because all national courts have found the legal resources to ensure, by and large, the supremacy of EU law in those cases. The theoretical basis matters more when it comes to decide a conflict between EU law and a norm of constitutional rank. If the national courts (and other national authorities) think that European law ultimately derives its validity in the domestic legal order from the authority of the constitution, then they are unlikely to recognize that EU law might simply prevail over the very foundation from which its legal force derives. In most countries, the constitutional provision allowing for the transfer of powers to international organizations (or to the European Union specifically) is seen as implicitly permitting adaptations of the institutional provisions of the constitution, but not as allowing alterations to its basic principles. The essential question then is where to draw the line between minor adaptations and essential changes, and, consequently, where to set the limits of the penetration of EU law into the domestic constitutional order.

The Italian Constitutional Court has consistently held, ever since its *Frontini* judgment of 1973, that EU law may derogate from 'ordinary' rules of constitutional law, but not from certain fundamental principles or inalienable rights of persons. The latter are, in Italian legal parlance, 'counter-limits' (*controlimiti*) to the limitations of sovereignty allowed by Article 11 of the constitution: when *State* institutions exercise sovereign powers, they must respect the fundamental values and principles of the constitution; one cannot accept a complete renunciation of those values and principles when powers are attributed to the *European* institutions. In its *Fragd* ruling of 1989, the Italian Court went so far as to state that it could control the consistency of *individual* rules of EC law with the fundamental principles of the Italian Constitution, particularly (but not only) in the field of human rights.[101] The Court has not actually used this review power so far, but it is clear that there is no place, in this scheme of thought, for the recognition of an absolute primacy of Union law.

German constitutional case law presents a similar picture, as is well known. The German Constitutional Court held, in its *Solange I* and *Solange II* judgments of 1974 and 1986, with express reference to the doctrine of its Italian counterpart, that Article 24 of the *Grundgesetz* 'does not confer a power to surrender by way of ceding sovereign rights to international institutions the identity of the prevailing constitutional order of the Federal Republic by breaking into its basic framework, that is, into the structure that makes it up'.[102] The exact extent of this limitation was controversial. It was thought that the words 'identity of the prevailing constitutional order' referred to Article 79(3) of the *Grundgesetz* which prohibits any constitutional amendments affecting the principles of democracy, protection of fundamental rights, and federalism. In the *Maastricht* judgment of 1993, however, the Constitutional Court made clear that it would also review the respect, by European institutions, of the Treaty-based limits to their powers, and that this review may be exercised even with respect to individual EU acts. In its *Lisbon* judgment of 2009, the Constitutional Court insisted once more on its power to undertake an 'identity review' of EU acts, ie to check whether measures adopted by the European institutions threaten German constitutional identity.[103] The revival of this 'identity review' may be linked to the fact that the Lisbon Treaty itself introduces a duty for the EU institutions to respect the national constitutional identity of the Member States (see below). However, the German

---

[101] Judgment of 21 April 1989, No 232, *S.p.a. Fragd v Amministrazione delle Finanze* (1990-I) Foro Italiano 1855 (English text in A Oppenheimer (ed), *The Relationship between European Community Law and National Law—The Cases* (Cambridge University Press, 1994), 653). On the gradual construction of the Italian Court's case law about the limits to the primacy of EU law, see M Cartabia, 'The Italian Constitutional Court and the Relationship Between the Italian Legal System and the European Union' in A M Slaughter, A Stone Sweet, and J Weiler (eds), *The European Court and National Courts. Doctrine and Jurisprudence* (Hart, 1997) 133.

[102] German Constitutional Court, judgment of 22 October 1986 (*Solange II*), passage as translated in (1987) 3 CML Rev 225, 257.

[103] German Constitutional Court, judgment of 30 June 2009, 2 BvE 2/08, published in (2009) 62 Neue Juristische Wochenschrift 2267. An unofficial translation of the judgment is available on the Court's website . The relevant passages, dealing with the limits to the primacy of EU law and the newly formulated identity review, are [240], [248]–[250], and [331]–[343].

Constitutional Court affirms clearly that the power to define the constitutional identity of Germany is not a matter of EU law, to be interpreted by the European Court of Justice, but a matter of national law, which the *Bundesverfassungsgericht* alone has the power to determine.

Thus, the constitutional clauses about limitation of sovereignty have been given by the Italian and German Constitutional courts a closely similar interpretation in the context of European integration. Those clauses have been used in a double capacity. On the one hand, they allow for the smooth integration of EU law into the national legal system, discarding dualist doctrine for the exclusive benefit of EU law and ensuring the direct effect and primacy of EU law in all 'normal' situations. On the other hand, the sovereignty clauses allow the Constitutional Courts of those two countries to protect what they consider to be the core of the constitution against any encroachments of Union law; in this way, those courts continue to assume what they conceive to be their function, that of being the guardian of the constitution against both internal and external threats.

The situation in Spain, despite its monist tradition, is not that different from Italy and Germany. Primacy of Union law is based on the 'attribution of powers' clause of Article 93 and is also subject to constitutional limitations. In its judgment of December 2004 dealing with the compatibility of the Constitutional Treaty with the Spanish Constitution, the Spanish Constitutional Tribunal operated a distinction between the *primacía* of EU law and the *supremacía* of the Spanish Constitution: whereas the 'primacy' of EU law allows it in principle to override conflicting norms of national law, the Constitution claims 'supremacy' both in the sense of being the source from which EU law's primacy in the domestic legal order stems, and of containing some core values and principles that cannot be overridden by EU law.[104]

The position in French law is also similar in that all the main courts of the country have affirmed the prevalence of the constitution over EU law. The *Conseil constitutionnel*, in its Decision of 2004 on the European Constitutional Treaty took a position which was very similar to that of its Spanish counterpart one month earlier, affirming that the inclusion of a written primacy rule in the Constitutional Treaty (which was later deleted in the Lisbon Treaty; see above) did not affect the position of the national constitution at the apex of the internal legal order.[105] A few years later, it specified that EU law prevailed over national law except where it is in conflict with France's

---

[104] *Tribunal Constitucional*, Opinion 1/2004 of 13 December 2004, on the Treaty establishing a Constitution for Europe (summarized and commented in English by F Castillo de la Torre in (2005) 42 CML Rev 1169, especially, as regards the primacy/supremacy distinction, at 1186 *et seq*. Some authors have criticized this conceptual distinction between primacy and supremacy (which is not made in the case law of the ECJ nor in most of the literature on the subject) as creating confusion: R Alonso García, 'The Spanish Constitution and the European Constitution: The Script for a Virtual Collision and Other Observations on the Principle of Primacy' (2005) 6 German Law Journal 1001. Generally, on the evolution of the Spanish Court's position, R Alonso García, *Justicia constitucional y Unión europea* (2005).

[105] *Conseil constitutionnel*, Decision 2004-505 DC of 19 November 2004, *Traité établissant une Constitution pour l'Europe*. See a case summary and comment in English by L Azoulai and F Ronkes Agerbeek in (2005) 42 CML Rev 871.

'constitutional identity',[106] a notion which was invented by the *Conseil* on this occasion but clearly echoes the new reference in the EU Treaty (added by the Constitutional Treaty as confirmed by the Lisbon Treaty) to the respect owed by EU law to the national constitutional identity of the Member States. It is not clear what is covered by the nebulous notion of 'French constitutional identity',[107] but it would seem to be narrower than constitutional law as a whole, and in this sense the position adopted by the *Conseil* seems somewhat more pro-European than that of the *Cour de Cassation* and the *Conseil d'Etat* which seemed, in earlier judgments, to give precedence to *all* norms of French constitutional law.[108]

Indeed, if the constitution is seen as the basis for recognizing the primacy of Union law, then absolute primacy of the type postulated by the European Court in *Internationale Handelsgesellschaft* is only possible by way of an 'auto-limitation' clause in the Constitution. The Netherlands offers a good example of this. Article 120 of the Dutch Constitution expressly prohibits national courts from reviewing the constitutionality of Treaty provisions and of decisions of international organizations, and thereby ensures the absolute supremacy of Treaties once they have been properly ratified. The Irish Constitution also seems to provide immunity to EU law from any constitutional challenge, since each Treaty revision leads (by means of one of Irish infamous referendums!) to a specific amendment of the Irish Constitution stating that nothing in that constitution impedes the application of EU law. Yet, this constitutional provision possibly does not prevent the Irish legislator from adopting statutes that deliberately contrast with EU law, nor does it form a protection against later changes of the Irish Constitution that would openly contradict EU law.[109]

In the first edition of this volume, it was argued that the reluctance of national courts to recognize the absolute primacy of EU law (which the ECJ requires) was not an attitude to be found only in Germany (with the famous *Maastricht* judgment of 1993) or in Italy, but in fact the default position in most countries, even where no clear Constitutional Court decisions existed to confirm this. Ten years later, we do indeed find a number of new Constitutional Court judgments, in both old and new Member States, which confirm a general convergence around the Italian-German position of the 1990s, namely that Union law may prevail over conflicting national legislation, and possibly even over conflicting detailed rules of the national constitution, but not over

---

[106] Conseil constitutionnel, Decision 2600-540 DC of 27 July 2006, Loi transposant la directive sur le droit d'auteur.

[107] See C Charpy, 'The Status of (Secondary) Community Law in the French Internal Order: the Recent Case-Law of the *Conseil Constitutionnel* and the *Conseil d'Etat*' (2007) 3 ECLRev 436, 445.

[108] *Conseil d'Etat*, Decision of 3 December 2001, Syndicat national de l'industrie pharmaceutique, in (2002) Revue française de droit administratif 166; *Cour de Cassation*, judgment of 2 June 2000, Pauline Fraisse, (2000) RTDCiv 672.

[109] See the discussion of this question by W Phelan, 'Can Ireland Legislate Contrary to EC Law?' (2008) 33 ELRev 530. The constitutional provision on the domestic effect of EU law is currently, after the ratification of the Treaty of Lisbon, in Art 29.4.6 of the Constitution.

the fundamental provisions of the constitution.[110] Everywhere, the national constitution remains at the apex of the hierarchy of legal norms, and EU law is allowed to
trump national law only under the conditions, and within the limits, set by the
national constitution. In particular, the 2004 rulings of the French and Spanish
Constitutional Courts relating to the Constitutional Treaty gave those courts an
occasion to join the 'counterlimits' consensus. The 'domino effect' of the counter-
limits doctrine is also visible in the newer Member States of Central and Eastern
Europe, although with some interesting variations.[111] In Poland and Lithuania, the
Constitutional Courts have affirmed the supremacy of *all* constitutional provisions
(not just of the constitutional core) over EU law;[112] and in Estonia, the constitution—
as interpreted by the supreme court—operated a self-limitation which leaves room for
the absolute primacy of EU law for as long as the constitution is not modified on this
point.[113]

The consequence of the fact that practically all national legal systems find the source
of EU primacy (and direct effect) in their own constitution, is that the current legal
situation is subject to 'decentralized' change: it remains possible for the Member States
to introduce new constitutional provisions, or for their Constitutional Courts to adopt
new interpretations of the constitution, that will affect, positively or negatively, the
domestic legal status of EU law.

In the light of this two-dimensional reality, whereby both the EU legal order, as
interpreted by the Court of Justice, and the constitutional orders of the Member States,
as interpreted by their highest courts, claim ultimate supremacy for themselves in the
case of a conflict on 'important matters', a current in the legal literature has proposed
to adopt a 'pluralist' reading of the relation between EU law and national law, which
accepts that there are inherently different viewpoints and that the search for a perfect
hierarchical ordering between legal norms and across legal systems may therefore be
futile; and that one should accept that the relationship between the EU and national

---

[110] For a general view of this constitutional case law, see J Baquero Cruz, 'The Legacy of the Maastricht-
Urteil and the Pluralist Movement' (2008) 14 ELJ 389; J V Louis and T Ronse (n 100 above) 346 *et seq*;
C Grabenwarter, 'National Constitutional Law Relating to the European Union' in A von Bogdandy and J Bast
(eds), *Principles of European Constitutional Law* (2nd edn, Hart, 2010) 83, 84–94; F C Mayer, 'Multilevel
Constitutional Jurisdiction' in von Bogdandy and Bast (cited above) 399, 407–421; Claes (n 2 above) chs 16
and 19.

[111] With special reference to the Constitutional Courts of the new Member States of Central and Eastern
Europe, see W Sadurski, 'Solange, Chapter 3: Constitutional Courts in Central Europe—Democracy—European Union' (2008) 14 ELJ 1; A Albi, 'Supremacy of EC Law in the New Member States. Bringing Parliaments
into the Equation of Co-operative Constitutionalism' (2007) 3 ECLRev 25.

[112] Constitutional Court of Poland, *Accession Treaty*, judgment of 11 May 2005, [13] of the English
translation of the summary: 'a collision would occur in the event that an irreconcilable inconsistency appeared
between a constitutional norm and a Community norm...Such a collision may in no event be resolved by
assuming the supremacy of a Community norm over a constitutional norm.' Constitutional Court of
Lithuania, Joined Cases No 17/02, 24/02, 06/03, and 22/04, judgment of 14 March 2006 [9.4].

[113] Constitutional Review Chamber of the Estonian Supreme Court, *On the Interpretation of the Constitution*, Opinion of 11 May 2006, Case No 3-4-1-3-06.

legal orders is, and remains, a heterarchical one.[114] Therefore, those authors insist on the need for an open attitude both on the side of the European Court (and the EU law doctrine) and on that of national Constitutional Courts (and constitutional law doctrine), whereby the values and interests of the 'other side' are taken seriously, and are seen to be taken seriously. In order to do this, those courts should engage in a structural dialogue, whereby national supreme and Constitutional Courts are prepared to submit controversial issues to the ECJ rather than solve them solely according to their own preferences, and whereby the European Court of Justice, in turn, shows willingness to listen to the constitutional concerns of its national interlocutors.[115] As Miguel Poiares Maduro put it: '[A]ny judicial body (national or European) would be obliged to reason and justify its decisions in the context of a coherent and integrated EU legal order.'[116] In particular, the European Court of Justice ought to recognize a greater role for national courts and national constitutions in the interpretation and application of EU law. The ECJ missed a few opportunities, recently, to recognize the special role and importance of national constitutional law in the EU legal order, despite invitations by its Advocate General to do so,[117] but national constitutional law is likely to play a growing role in the ECJ's case law after the entry into force of the Lisbon Treaty which has introduced in Article 4(2) TEU a reference to national constitutional law which can be understood as an 'implicit limit' to the primacy of EU law:

> The Union shall respect the equality of Member States before the Treaties as well as their national identities, inherent in their fundamental structures, political and constitutional, inclusive of regional and local self-government. It shall respect their essential State functions, including ensuring the territorial integrity of the State, maintaining law and order and safeguarding national security. In particular, national security remains the sole responsibility of each Member State.

---

[114] Among the leading contributors to this conception of a new 'legal pluralism' in Europe are N Walker, 'Late Sovereignty in the European Union' in N Walker (ed), *Sovereignty in Transition* (Hart, 2003) 3; M Poiares Maduro, 'Contrapunctual Law: Europe's Constitutional Pluralism in Action' in N Walker (ibid) 501; M Kumm, 'The Jurisprudence of Constitutional Conflict: Constitutional Supremacy in Europe before and after the Constitutional Treaty' (2005) 11 ELJ 262.

[115] Pleadings for an enhanced dialogue rather than the mutual affirmation of hierarchical principles can be found in a number of recent scholarly contributions (in addition to the authors cited in the previous footnote): M Cartabia, 'Europe and Rights: Taking Dialogue Seriously' (2009) 5 ECLRev 5; A Torres Pérez, *Conflicts of Rights in the European Union—A Theory of Supranational Adjudication* (Oxford University Press, 2009); D Ritleng, 'De l'utilité du principe de primauté du droit de l'Union' (2009) RTD eur 677, 689 *et seq*; F Fontanelli, G Martinico, and P Carrozza (eds), *Shaping Rule of Law through Dialogue. International and Supranational Experiences* (Europa Law, 2009).

[116] Maduro (n 114 above) 533.

[117] Case C-213/07 *Michaniki* (n 71 above), Opinion of AG Poiares Maduro [31]–[33], but no reference to national constitutional law in the judgment of 16 December 2008; see the case comment by V Kosta, (2009) 5 ECLRev 501. And Case C-127/07 *Arcelor* [2008] ECR I-9895, Opinion of AG Poiares Maduro [15]–[17], but no reference to national constitutional law in the Court's judgment of 16 December 2008. In referring the latter case to the ECJ, the French *Conseil d'Etat* seemed keen to engage in a dialogue with the Court of Justice on how to organize the multi-level protection of fundamental rights; see on this aspect of the case, M P Granger, 'France is "Already" Back in Europe: The Europeanization of French Courts and the Influence of France in the EU' (2008) 14 EPL 335, 367.

F. THE ROLE OF PRIMACY AND DIRECT EFFECT IN THE EUROPEAN INTEGRATION PROCESS

1. A CENTRAL ROLE FOR THE INDIVIDUAL

The virtual reality question put by a former president of the European Court of Justice, Robert Lecourt: '*Quel eut été le droit des Communautés sans les arrêts de 1963 et 1964?*'[118] is difficult to answer. But it is safe to say that those judgments (in *Van Gend en Loos* and *Costa*) and their progeny have helped to put the individual person, and her rights and interests, at the heart of European law. In the self-analysis which the Court of Justice wrote prior to the Intergovernmental Conference that would adopt the Treaty of Amsterdam, it stated: 'Even before there was the idea of citizenship of the Union, the Court had inferred from the Treaties the concept of a new legal order applying to individuals and had in many cases ensured that those individuals could exercise effectively the rights conferred upon them.'[119] In contrast with other regimes of international cooperation, where individuals are mainly looking from the sidelines at the action taken on their behalf by governments and international institutions, the individual has been made a direct participant in the European integration process thanks, in large part, to the principles of primacy and direct effect. It is not easy, though, to assess the practical difference which primacy and direct effect have made in the life of individual citizens (and, of course, of business firms, which have been particularly active 'individuals' on the judicial scene). There could seem to be a contrast between the core importance attributed to those doctrines by the ECJ and by legal scholars, and the relatively small number of cases in which national courts expressly address the question of the direct effect or primacy of European Union law. Of course, leading court cases are reverberating through the entire national judiciary and may determine the routine activity of lower courts, and furthermore, leading court cases may have a preventive effect on choices made by governments and administrations when confronted with EU norms.

However, even the undiluted acceptance of the 'mandate for national courts' as defined by the ECJ cannot guarantee a genuinely uniform application of EC law. The procedural autonomy of the Member States, although indented by the European Court's requirements of equivalence and effectiveness, is still meaningful. The European Union norm is therefore unavoidably distorted by judicial preconceptions and styles of judgment, and by the pre-existing structure of each national legal system. This distortion may be rendered by the well-worn metaphor of EU law as a source of law which is filtered through the national judicial procedures and styles. Or one may resort to another liquid metaphor proposed by Jolowicz some time ago:

---

[118] In the Article with that title, in *L'Europe et le droit. Mélanges en hommage à Jean Boulouis* (Dalloz, 1991) 349.

[119] See n 84 above, 4.

It is not to be expected that the insertion into different legal systems of a single text will produce identical or even similar results in all those systems any more than it is to be expected that the addition of a litre of green paint to four litres of yellow will give us the same colour as the addition of the same quantity of the same paint to four litres of red.[120]

Furthermore, it should be kept in mind that the legal position of individuals is not only determined by the judicial enforcement of EU law by national courts. The direct enforcement by the European Court of Justice of Member State duties towards individuals, through the procedure of Articles 258 to 260 TFEU, is an important alternative route through which individual interests are advanced, also (and above all) where the infringement action does not lead to an actual judgment by the ECJ but is resolved at the pre-litigation stage. In addition, of course, judicial enforcement is only one element of the broader picture of the effectiveness of, and compliance with, EU law. In many situations, EU norms will be violated with little or no likelihood of sanctions being imposed or litigation being brought.

The prominent role given to individual persons and firms by the doctrines of primacy and direct effect has not only modified their own legal status. Already in *Van Gend en Loos*, the European Court referred, in a famous phrase, to the beneficial impact of its new direct effect doctrine on the European integration process as a whole: 'The vigilance of individuals concerned to protect their rights amounts to an effective supervision in addition to the supervision entrusted by Articles 169 and 170 to the diligence of the Commission and of the Member States.'[121] Indeed, in the first decades after the *Van Gend en Loos* and *Costa* judgments, one of their main consequences was to transform state duties in the economic sphere into individual rights, thus allowing private parties to drive forward the process of market integration.

It has often been observed that this produced an imbalance between market integration and policy integration (or, to use another pair of notions, 'negative' and 'positive' integration). Whereas market integration has been pushed forward by the Court's bold interpretation of the rules requiring states to abstain from interfering with free trade and free movement of persons, policy integration could not be brought about by judicial fiat but needed the active involvement of the political institutions of the Union. Yet, today, that imbalance is no longer obvious. Once policy integration is put into place in a certain field, in the form of regulations or directives, then primacy and direct effect will make it stick. Today, unlike in the 1960s, policy integration norms are certainly more often invoked by individuals before national courts than market integration norms. That may justify the claim that EU law has become a charter, not just of economic rights but also of consumer rights, social rights, ecological rights, and citizenship rights.[122]

---

[120] J A Jolowicz, 'New Perspectives of a Common Law of Europe: Some Practical Aspects and the Case for Applied Comparative Law' in M Cappelletti (ed), *New Perspectives for a Common Law of Europe* (Springer, 1978) 237, 244.

[121] *Van Gend en Loos* (n 7 above) 13. The then Arts 169 and 170 EEC are now Arts 258 and 259 TFEU.

[122] N Reich, 'A European Constitution for Citizens: Reflections on the Rethinking of Union and Community Law' (1997) 3 ELJ 131.

2. INSTITUTIONAL CONSEQUENCES

The European Court of Justice itself has never discussed the various institutional consequences of its invention of direct effect and primacy, either with respect to its own position in the institutional balance between EU institutions or with respect to the relations between national courts and other national constitutional organs. Yet, the two doctrines have caused changes, particularly at that second level. The mandate formulated by the Court of Justice has modified the constitutional status of the national judicial authorities. On the basis of the principle of primacy, all national courts now exercise the power of judicial review of national legislative acts, whereas in non-EU cases, such power is either denied to all courts (Netherlands), or limited in its effects to a declaration of invalidity (United Kingdom), or reserved to one single Constitutional Court (Germany, Italy, Spain and, indeed, most other EU countries). Where the judicial review power is not centralized but is given to all courts, it must be exercised by them with extreme caution (Sweden, Greece). In matters of EU law, however, such judicial review should be exercised by all courts not as an exceptional occurrence but as a routine matter. EU law has thus had a decentralizing impact on national systems of judicial review.[123] This 'empowerment' of ordinary courts was seen by some commentators as a major explanation for those courts' easy acceptance of primacy.[124] Conversely, the *capitis diminutio* suffered by Constitutional Courts is perhaps a further reason why those courts have proved more hesitant to recognize the full force of Community law.

A further institutional consequence of primacy which is sometimes drawn is that 'the more weakly legitimated law is supposed to overrule the better legitimated one'.[125] That statement was truer at a time when secondary Community law was effectively the result of 'executive law-making' and was, nevertheless, claimed to have priority over laws enacted by directly elected national parliaments. But even the increasing role of the European Parliament in Union legislation has not entirely cured this weakness, as *all* binding acts of EU law are endowed with primacy, whether or not the European Parliament played a major role in their adoption. Primacy also extends to acts adopted by the Commission, which certainly is executive law-making *par excellence*. The paradoxical result is that, while the doctrines of direct effect and primacy are often hailed as core elements of the 'constitutionalization' of European law, they also mean that rules may be imposed on persons who did not participate, through their representatives, in the making of those rules, and this is at odds with a traditional principle of European constitutionalism. In that sense, the principle of direct effect and primacy are a powerful reminder of the need to ensure that European Union law is enacted with as much democratic participation and transparency as possible.

---

[123] See Claes (n 2 above) ch 9; and V Ferreres Comella, *Constitutional Courts and Democratic Values—A European Perspective* (Yale University Press, 2009) ch 11.

[124] Alter (n 86 above) ch 2.

[125] F W Scharpf, 'Democratic Policy in Europe' (1996) 2 ELJ 136, 149.

G. THE NATURE OF THE LEGAL ORDER

The invention in the 1960s, by the European Court of Justice, of the principles of direct effect and primacy was accompanied by sweeping statements about the special nature of the European Community treaties as compared with other international agreements. Some of those arguments may have been overstated, and were needed more to convince the national judicial interlocutors of the Court than to justify the formulation of the principles themselves. But the sweeping discourse used by the European Court in those judgments of the 1960s has left its mark on doctrinal writing and, indeed, on the way national courts have come to view EC law.

The argument linking primacy/direct effect and the nature of EC law has gradually acquired an element of circularity. At first, primacy and direct effect were to be recognized *because* the EC Treaty was unlike other international treaties, a theory which proved to be particularly successful in those countries where the domestic status of (other) international treaties was modest, like Italy, Germany, the UK and Ireland, and the Scandinavian countries. But now that these principles have been accepted everywhere, at least for most practical purposes, the direction of the argument is often reversed: EU law is now often presented as being unique *because* it is endowed with direct effect and primacy. It is this latter claim which I want to examine briefly: given the fact that direct effect and primacy are established doctrines of Union law, what do they tell us about the nature of the EU legal order?

To start with direct effect: the fact that provisions of an international treaty, and of decisions made by the institutions of an international organization, are enforceable by national courts is not exceptional. What is special is that the ECJ held that the EC Treaty itself contains directions, albeit unwritten, as to its domestic application. This is rather more unusual, but not incompatible with the nature of international treaties.[126] Nor does the principle of primacy, in its present state, justify the claim that EU law has ceased to be international law. The claim made by the European Court of Justice that Community law should have unfettered primacy over national law before domestic courts may well be unprecedented but it is not unrelated to the age-old rule *pacta sunt servanda*. It is undisputable that the EEC Treaty was a treaty with some strongly innovative features, and one of them was the preliminary reference mechanism which allowed the ECJ to courageously articulate a duty for national courts which may have been (and still is) implicitly contained in other international treaties as well—but there is no court for saying so.

The view that the principle of primacy does not set EU law completely apart from the general body of international law finds additional support in the continuing two-dimensional character of primacy: it is a legal reality only to the extent that national

---

[126] See the Permanent Court of Justice in the *Jurisdiction of the Courts of Danzig* case (PCIJ Series B, N 15, 17): 'the very object of an international agreement, according to the intention of the contracting Parties, may be the adoption by the Parties of some definite rules creating individual rights and obligations and enforceable by the national courts.'

courts accept the role allocated to them by the ECJ, and the practice shows that this acceptance, so far, is selective and generally based on the national courts' own constitutional terms. The latter fact continues to distinguish EU primacy from analogous federal principles. In federal states, the relation between central and Member State law is a matter for federal constitutional law. All courts in the country will uphold the supremacy of federal law on the basis of an express clause in the federal constitution, of which famous examples can be found in the US Constitution and the German *Grundgesetz*. Curiously though, these supremacy clauses play a much less prominent role in the judicial practice of those states than the comparable doctrine of EU law. In a federal system, federal laws may be contested with the argument that they are *ultra vires*, and federal Constitutional Courts play a more or less active role in guarding this boundary between federal and Member State powers, but the precedence of a validly adopted federal law over Member State laws is beyond dispute. The reason for this is the uncontested prevalence of the federal constitution which allocates the powers between the two levels. In contrast, the claim of the autonomous validity of European Union law is not widely accepted by national courts, and the European Treaties are not granted supreme legal authority by the courts and political institutions of the Member States. Most of them continue to consider their national constitution as the *fons et origo* of all law applicable on the national territory.

Writing in 1950 on the domestic status of international treaties, Morgenstern stated:

> Only the full integration of international society, by giving international law the means of enforcing its authority directly within the state, can establish the supremacy of international law in its fullest sense.[127]

EU law is only half way on the road traced by Morgenstern. The principles of direct effect and supremacy, as presently formulated and accepted, continue to confirm the nature of EU law as that of a branch of international law, albeit a branch with some unusual, quasi-federal, blossoms.

---

[127] Morgenstern (n 2 above) 91.

13

PRELIMINARY RULINGS AND EU LEGAL INTEGRATION: EVOLUTION AND STASIS

Thomas de la Mare and Catherine Donnelly*

A. INTRODUCTION

In a narrow, legal sense the case law on preliminary rulings, whether before the Court of Justice (CJEU) or national courts, has a critical impact upon the way in which the national and EU legal systems interact and communicate. On a wider level, the development of the preliminary ruling jurisprudence over the years can be seen as an historical record of legal integration. For instance, preliminary ruling procedures have provided a platform for the CJEU to deliver seminal constitutional decisions that define the relationship between the EU and the Member States, decisions such as *Van Gend en Loos*, *Costa v ENEL*, *Van Duyn*, *Gravier*, *Marshall*, *Factortame II*, or *Pupino*.[1] As the primary interface between national law and EU law, preliminary rulings provide perspectives on shifting national or EU legal reasoning, judicial attitudes, and evolution in internal constitutional thinking. In short, the preliminary ruling procedure—newly located in Article 267 TFEU and having undergone diversification and consolidation over the last decade—has been pivotal to EU legal integration.

This chapter seeks to both explore the central integrative role played by preliminary rulings in the evolution of the EU, and thinking ahead to future evolution, to examine

---

* T de la Mare is a Barrister at Blackstone Chambers, London. C Donnelly is a Barrister at Blackstone Chambers, London, and Law Library, Dublin, and Lecturer in Law at Trinity College Dublin.

[1] Case 26/62 *Van Gend en Loos v Nederlandse Administratie der Berlastingen* [1963] ECR 1; Case 6/64 *Costa v ENEL* [1964] ECR 585; Case 41/74 *Van Duyn v Home Office* [1974] ECR 1337; Case 293/83 *Gravier v City of Liège* [1985] ECR I-593; Case 152/84 *Marshall v Southampton and South West Area Health Authority (No 1)* [1986] ECR 737; Cases C-46 and C-48/93 *Brasserie du Pêcheur SA v Germany; R v Secretary of State for Transport, ex p Factortame Ltd* [1996] ECR I-1029; Case C-105/03 *Criminal Proceedings against Pupino* [2005] ECR I-5285.

whether the demands currently placed on the preliminary ruling procedure are sustainable. It will be argued that the procedure has been over-extended—under pressure from both national courts and the CJEU—in ways which, if left unchecked, may ultimately undermine its usefulness in future EU evolution. From the perspective of the evolution of EU law to date, this is a disappointing conclusion as, over a decade on from the publication of the first edition of this book, many of the concerns raised then about the functioning of the preliminary ruling procedure must be repeated here. Indeed, not only that, but, as will be seen, if anything, those concerns have intensified over the years, such that problems only predicted then have actually started to manifest themselves now. What is also notable is that the CJEU appears to have no interest in engaging in serious reform of the preliminary ruling procedure, and the same is true of Member States, with Lisbon Treaty reform more likely to exacerbate than ameliorate current problems. As such, although the preliminary ruling procedure has been evolving in many respects, that evolution has not assisted it in addressing the problems it faces. Consequently, overall, it seems that the procedure is in a state of stasis.

Structurally, this chapter will be divided into four main Parts. In Part B, a very brief descriptive overview of the expansion and variation of preliminary ruling procedures, as well as the impact of the Lisbon Treaty, will be presented. Part C will undertake an analysis of what are described as 'valve' factors. To understand how the preliminary ruling procedure functions, it is necessary to appreciate the gateways that combine to render the making of a reference more or less likely; together these gateways act as a crude 'valve' which regulates the procedure's potential for use by national courts. Study of the 'valve factors' is revealing for a variety of reasons. First, taken together the valve factors reveal in broad terms the overall potential for use of preliminary references or 'reference potential'. Secondly, the way in which the CJEU attempts to regulate this pressure illuminates the way in which the CJEU seeks to define its relationship with the national courts. Thirdly, analysis of valve factors can lead to important insights into the national courts' self-perceived role in the EU and their views of the role of the CJEU. Fourthly, investigation of the valve factors facilitates study of the procedural dynamic that underpins EU law's substantive developments. In brief, scrutiny of the valve factors can demonstrate a more general EU 'integration differential'.

Turning to Part D of this chapter, review of a number of perspectives on the role of preliminary rulings in the EU will highlight the multi-faceted way in which preliminary references promote EU legal integration, as well as demonstrate the onerous burden currently being placed on this procedure. Finally, in Part E, the challenges created by the current stasis in the preliminary ruling procedure will be examined. Throughout the chapter, reference will be made where relevant to the empirical data provided in the accompanying tables and figures.[2]

---

[2] Most of the figures and tables have been compiled using information published in the CJEU's annual reports. For the remainder, we are extremely grateful to Niamh Cleary for research assistance.

B. DIVERSIFICATION AND CONSOLIDATION

Prior to Lisbon Treaty consolidation, the preliminary ruling procedure had developed three different forms: Article 234 EC (now Article 267 TFEU), the 'gold standard' procedure;[3] the restricted procedures of Article 68 EC (repealed) applying to Visas, Asylum, Immigration and Other Policies Concerning the Free Movement of Persons; and Article 35 TEU (repealed), applying in the context of Police and Judicial Co-operation in Criminal Matters. Pursuant to Article 35 TEU, the CJEU only had jurisdiction to give preliminary rulings if the Member State accepted the CJEU's jurisdiction by making a declaration and only in relation to framework decisions, decisions, and conventions. In accepting jurisdiction, the Member State could also limit the availability of preliminary rulings to final instance courts. Meanwhile, Article 68 EC stated that a preliminary ruling could only be sought by a national court or tribunal against whose decisions there was no judicial remedy in national law.

Following Lisbon Treaty consolidation, a restriction on use of preliminary references remains to preclude the CJEU from reviewing the validity or proportionality of operations carried out by the police or other law-enforcement services of a Member State, or the exercise of the responsibilities incumbent upon Member States with regard to the maintenance of law and order and the safeguarding of internal security.[4] Reflecting concerns about the efficiency of preliminary ruling procedures,[5] Article 267 TFEU also provides that if the question raised by the national court relates to a person in custody, the CJEU must act with the minimum of delay. For present purposes though, the most important aspect of the Lisbon Treaty reforms is that the availability of the preliminary ruling procedure has been significantly extended.

C. THE VALVE ANALOGY

Article 267 TFEU, like its predecessor Article 234 EC, provides that the CJEU shall have jurisdiction to give preliminary rulings in a variety of situations, the most important of which are those concerning questions of interpretation of the Treaty or alternatively those concerning the validity and interpretation of the acts of the institutions of the Union. Where such a question is 'raised' before any court or tribunal of a Member State, that court *may* refer the question to the CJEU;[6] however, where there is no judicial appeal or remedy from the court or tribunal where the EU point is raised, that court or tribunal *must* refer the issue.[7] From these questions, a range of 'valve factors' emerge, namely: (1) raising a question of EU law in a national court; (2) the types of questions which are referable; (3) the types of bodies which can refer;

---

[3] A Arnull, 'Me and My Shadow: The European Court of Justice and the Disintegration of European Union Law' (2008) 31 Fordham Int'l LJ 1174, 1197.

[4] Art 276 TFEU.   [5] See text to nn 88–93 below.

[6] Art 234(2) EC; Art 267(2) TFEU.   [7] Art 234(3) EC; Art 267(3) TFEU.

(4) the appropriateness of a reference; (5) the obligation to make a reference; and (6) the costs of a reference. By way of preliminary comment, for each factor, it is convenient to assume three potential ways in which it can be modulated, namely by the CJEU itself, the national courts, or by residual non-judicial forces, such as litigants, economic forces and political pressure. Thus, at the risk of stating the obvious, it is important to recall that the 'reference potential' is different from Member State to Member State and indeed, from time to time.

1. RAISING A QUESTION OF EU LAW IN A NATIONAL COURT

To be able to raise an EU law point capable of being referred, one has to be able to gain access to national courts in the first instance and to mechanisms by which to argue EU law points. Therefore, national procedural rules, such as rules of standing, are in themselves a significant gateway, only partially regulated by EU law according to the well-known principles of equivalence and effectiveness.[8] Thus, for example, if national standing rules are not receptive to interest group or public interest litigation, such litigants have restricted access to the CJEU via Article 267 TFEU; their options may be confined to funding actions brought by private applicants.[9]

That said, the CJEU's influence has been increasingly perceptible here. Relying on the Member State's duty of fidelity in former Article 10 EC (now as amended, Article 4 TEU), the CJEU has indicated that national courts may be required to re-open final administrative decisions if concerned about misinterpretation of EU law where there has been no preliminary reference.[10] In addition, it is not incumbent on the litigant to raise the EU law point; rather national courts 'are *obliged* to raise *of their own motion* points of law based on binding EU rules where, under national law, they must or may do so in relation to a binding rule of national law'.[11] The duty is qualified where legal certainty may be jeopardized.[12] In the context of consumer protection, the CJEU has gone further and the emphasis has not been on equivalence of the duty to raise EU law points and national points, but rather on the effectiveness of EU law. The CJEU has explained that what exists is not a 'mere power' on the part of national courts to raise the EU consumer protection point, but an obligation,[13] as effective consumer

---

[8] Case 33/76 *Rewe-Zentralfinanz eG and others v Landwirtschaftskammer für das Saarland* [1976] ECR 1989; Case 158/80 *Rewe-Handelsgesellschaft Nord mbH v Hauptzollampt Kiel* [1981] ECR 1805; Joined Cases C-430/93 and C-431/93 *Van Schijndel and van Veen* [1995] ECR I-4705, [17]; and Case C-129/00 *Commission v Italy* [2003] ECR I-14637, [25].

[9] Direct interest group litigation, rather than a funded individual's actions, is typically used precisely because of the lack of any particular effect upon an individual of the rules in question. In such cases funding an individual's test case is not an option.

[10] Case C-453/00 *Kühne & Heitz NV v Produktschap voor Pluimvee en Eieren* [2004] ECR I-837, [27]–[28].

[11] Case C-2/06 *Willy Kempter KG v Hauptzollamt Hamburg-Jonas* [2008] ECR I-411, [45] (emphasis added).

[12] Case C-455/06 *Heemskerk BV and Firma Schaap v Productschap Vee en Vlees* [2008] ECR I-8763 [47].

[13] Case C-243/08 *Pannon GSM Zrt v Erzsébet Sustikné Gyrfi* [2009] ECR I-4713, [32] and [35]; Case C-240/98 *Océano Grupo Editorial SA v Roció Murciano Quintero* [2000] ECR I-4941, [39]; Case C-473/00 *Cofidis SA v Jean-Louis Fredout* [2002] ECR I-10875, [33]; and Case C-168/05 *Mostaza Claro v Centro Móvil Milenium SL* [2006] ECR I-10421, [28].

protection would not be achieved if the consumer were himself obliged to raise the point.[14] In the absence of a problem of equivalence, this duty has not been extended beyond the consumer protection context as yet.[15] However, its consequence is to pressurize national courts to raise EU law points, with a corresponding potential to maximize access to the preliminary ruling procedure.

2. THE TYPES OF QUESTIONS THAT ARE REFERABLE

To date the CJEU has approached the question of substantive referability in the widest of fashions. The concept of 'act of an institution' has been extended to include various *sui generis* measures,[16] including international agreements insofar as they are acts of the Council,[17] even where the international agreement concerned was not in any way 'an act of an institution'.[18] The EU acts examined need not be ones with automatic or necessary legal effects; hence, in the case of *Grimaldi* the CJEU found itself able to rule on the interpretation of recommendations, notwithstanding the fact that such acts were not reviewable pursuant to a direct action.[19] Similarly, in *Gestoras pro Amnestia*,[20] the CJEU reasoned that it would run counter to the overarching objective of the preliminary ruling procedure to guarantee 'observance of the law' to interpret Article 35(1) TEU (repealed) narrowly. Thus, although Article 35 TEU did not grant the court jurisdiction to review common positions, the CJEU held that it treated as acts capable of being the subject of a reference all measures intended to produce legal effects in relation to third parties—including Common Positions.[21] Similarly, in *Advocaten voor de Wereld*, the CJEU held that Article 35(1) TEU 'necessarily implie[d]' that the Court could, even if there was no express power to that effect, be called upon to interpret provisions of primary law, such as Article 34(2)(b) TEU (repealed), where the Court was being asked to examine whether a framework decision had been properly adopted on the basis of that latter provision.[22]

Perhaps a more striking example of the expansive approach taken to substantive referability is found in the use of preliminary references to rule upon the compatibility of national rules and legislation with EU law. Such a direct determination of compatibility is always strenuously denied by the CJEU—which has insisted on there being a

---

[14] *Océano Grupo* (n 13 above) [26]; *Cofidis* (n 13 above) [33]; *Mostaza Claro* (n 13 above) [28].

[15] Case C-225/05 *van der Weerd v Minister van Landouw, Natuur en Voedselkwaliteit* [2007] ECR I-4233, [41].

[16] D Anderson and M Demetriou, *References to the European Court* (2nd edn, Sweet & Maxwell, 2002) 3–25.

[17] ibid 3–43.

[18] See eg, Cases 267–269/81 *Amministrazione delle Finanze dello Stato v SPI SpA* [1983] ECR 801, [14].

[19] Case 322/88 *Grimaldi v Fonds des Maladies Professionelles* [1989] ECR 4407. See also Case T-109/06 *Vodafone España SA v Commission* [2007] ECR II-5151, [102].

[20] Case C-354/04 P *Gestoras Pro Amnistía and Others v Council* [2007] ECR I-1579; Case C-355/04 P *Segi v Council* [2007] ECR I-1657, [53].

[21] *Gestoras pro Amnestia* (n 20 above) [53].

[22] Case C-303/05 *Advocaten Voor De Wereld VZW v Leden Van De Ministerraad* [2007] ECR I-3633, [17]-[18].

'clear separation of functions between the national court' and it[23]—yet often in reality, the CJEU's interpretation of EU law in the context presented by the national court is to determine the validity of national legislation.[24] On occasion, the question has been reformulated so as to present the issue in non-fact-specific terms—although the essence of the question answered and its consequential effect as a compatibility decision remain unchanged.[25] On other occasions, however, the CJEU has deliberately framed its role more broadly, in one case, accepting that it was for the national court to determine whether objective justification for discrimination existed, but adding that it, the CJEU, could 'provide guidance based on the documents in the file and on the written and oral observations which have been submitted to it, in order to enable the national court to give judgment'.[26] Sometimes, the CJEU will even provide the national court with all the elements of interpretation of EU law which may be of use for deciding the case before it, whether or not that court has referred to them in the wording of its question.[27]

Consideration of national law by the CJEU also arises from the line of cases starting with *Thomasdünger*[28] and *Dzodzi*.[29] These cases establish that even where the EU rules to be interpreted are only of relevance because of a national choice to replicate the EU provisions to deal with purely internal situations (a so-called renvoi) the CJEU nevertheless has jurisdiction to rule upon the meaning of these EU provisions. The CJEU has simply asserted that it is 'clearly in the Community interest that . . . provisions or concepts taken from Community law should be interpreted uniformly, irrespective of the circumstances in which they are to apply'.[30] This has meant that the CJEU has accepted references relating to purely internal situations on the basis

---

[23] Case C-419/04 *Conseil général de la Vienne v Directeur général des douanes et droits indirects* [2006] ECR I-5645, [19].

[24] See Case C-294/97 *Eurowings* [1999] ECR I-7447, [46]: discussed in M Broberg, 'Acte Clair Revisited: Adapting the Acte Clair Criteria to the Demands of the Times' (2008) 45 CML Rev 1383, 1385. See also Case C-147/04 *Société de Groot en Slot Allium BV v Minister for the Economy, Finance and Industry* [2006] ECR I-245 (noted in R Errera, 'ECJ—Preliminary Ruling under Art. 234 EC' [2007] PL 385).

[25] Examples of such reformulation include: C-250/95 *Futura Participation v Administration des Contributions* [1997] ECR I-2471; Case C-329/95 *VAG Sverige AB* [1997] ECR I-2675; Case C-470/04 *N v Inspecteur Van de Belastingdienst Oost/Kantoor Almelo* [2006] ECR I-7409. See also R Voss, 'The National Perception of the Court of First Instance and the European Court of Justice' (1993) 30 CML Rev 1119, 1123.

[26] Case C-77/02 *Steinicke v Bundesanstalt für Arbeit* [2003] ECR I-9027, [59]; Case C-187/00 *Kutz-Bauer v Freie und Hansestadt Hamburg* [2003] ECR I-2741, [52].

[27] Case C-275/06 *Productores de Musica de Espana (Promusicae) v Telefonica de Espana SAU* [2008] ECR I-271, [42].

[28] Case 166/84 *Thomasdünger GmbH v Oberfinanzdirektion Frankfurt am Main* [1985] ECR 3001; Case C-197/89 *Dzodzi v Belgium* [1990] ECR I-3763; Case C-231/89 *Gmurzynska-Bscher v Oberfinanzdirektion Köln* [1990] ECR I-4003.

[29] See also Case C-28/95 *Leur-Bloem v Inspecteur der Belastingdienst/Ondernemingen Amsterdam 2* [1997] ECR I-4161, distinguishing the earlier Brussels Convention case of Case C-346/93 *Kleinwort Benson Ltd v City of Glasgow District Council* [1995] ECR I-615.

[30] Case C-280/06 *Autorità Garante della Concorrenza e del Mercato v Ente Tabacchi Italiani—ETI SpA* [2007] ECR I-10893, [21]; Case C-267/99 *Adam v Administarion de l'enregistrement et des domains* [2001] ECR I-7467, [27].

that 'a reply *might be* useful to' the referring court,[31] or, in what could arguably be considered to be an inappropriate reverse onus of proof in this context, because it was 'not obvious that the interpretation of Community law requested [was] not necessary for the national court'.[32] Earlier restraint on the basis that renvoi should be 'direct and unconditional' in order for the CJEU to have a role[33] appears to have been abandoned more recently.[34] For example, in the *BIAO* case, the CJEU accepted that the provisions of national law 'did not reproduce' the EU law provisions,[35] but answered the reference on the sole basis that the interpretation given would be regarded as binding by the national court.[36] The dangers in such an approach are evident, most obviously where the original EU measure is replicated in a subtly different national context, and the renvoi case law has created confusion for national courts.[37] Indeed, if the paramount strength of the EU is to adopt an EU legal perspective, it is strange for the CJEU to commit itself to answering questions that often require a peculiarly national viewpoint.[38]

Interestingly, perhaps the only context in which the CJEU has exhibited restraint on substantive referability has been in what Bobek has described as its 'chilling welcome' for 2004 accession states, where, departing from earlier jurisprudence, it refused to accept references from new accession states if the facts in the dispute arose prior to the date of accession.[39] Overall though, the CJEU appears only to refuse preliminary references on the basis of substantive referability objections 'when the subject-matter of the dispute is not connected *in any way* with any of the situations contemplated by the treaties'.[40]

---

[31] Case C-448/98 *Guimont* [2000] ECR I-10663, [23] (emphasis added); see also Case C-363/93 *Lancry* [1994] ECR I-3957; Case C-72/03 *Carbonati Apuani Srl v Comune di Carrara* [2004] ECR I-8027; Case C-515/99 *Reisch* [2002] ECR I-2157; and Case C-6/01 *Associação Nacional de Operadores de Máquinas Recreativas (Anomar) and Others v Estado português* [2003] ECR I-8621.

[32] eg *Guimont* (n 31 above) [23].

[33] eg *Kleinwort Benson* (n 29 above) [16].

[34] There is no mention of this requirement in *Autorità Garante* (n 30 above). See also Case C-306/99 *Banque Internationale pour l'Afrique Occidentale v Finanzamt für Großunternehmen in Hamburg* ('*BIAO*') [2002] ECR I-1, [83]; Case C-281/98 *Angonese v Cassa di Risparmio di Bolzano SpA* [2000] ECR I-4139.

[35] *BIAO* (n 34 above) [92].

[36] ibid.

[37] eg *Gingi v Secretary of State for Work and Pensions* [2001] EWCA Civ 1685, [2002] 1 CMLR 20 discussed in S Lefevre, 'The Interpretation of Community Law by the Court of Justice in Areas of National Competence' (2004) 29 ELRev 3.

[38] For extensive criticism of the CJEU's renvoi jurisprudence, see: Lefevre (n 37 above); see also C Ritter, 'Purely Internal Situations, Reverse Discrimination, *Guimont*, *Dzodzi* and Art 234' (2006) 31 ELRev 690; T Tridimas, 'Knocking on Heaven's Door: Fragmentation, Efficiency and Defiance in the Preliminary Reference Procedure' (2003) 40 CML Rev 9, 34–37. This jurisprudence may also constitute an illegitimate extension of the CJEU's jurisdiction: see Lefevre, 509–513.

[39] Case C-302/04 *Ynos kft v János Varga* [2006] ECR I-371. This involved a departure from the CJEU's previous accession case law: M Bobek, 'Learning to Talk: Preliminary Rulings, the Courts of the New Member States and the Court of Justice' (2008) 45 CML Rev 1611, 1616–1617. See also N Półtorak, '*Ratione Temporis* Application of the Preliminary Rulings Procedure' (2008) 45 CML Rev 1357.

[40] Case C-328/04 *Vajnai* [2005] ECR I-8577, [13] (emphasis added) (refusing to consider whether a prohibition on wearing a red-pointed star was compatible with former Art 6 TEU and the principles of freedom of expression and non-discrimination).

To a significant extent, substantive referability is a question which is within the CJEU's control, subject to the qualification that it is the national referring courts that push the limits (as in *Dzodzi*) of what might be referable,[41] often as a result of national jurisdictional disputes.[42] For a recent example, the case of *Kovalsky* concerned a Slovak law pursuant to which electrical installations could be placed on private land without the owners being entitled to compensation. A regional Slovak court had made two unsuccessful references to the Slovak Constitutional Court on the issue of the legislation's constitutionality, and promptly on Slovakia's accession to the EU, made a preliminary reference.[43] The CJEU found the subject matter of the dispute not 'connected in any way' with the Treaties; however, the case provides an interesting illustration of the complicity of national courts in pushing the boundaries of use of preliminary rulings.[44] Thus, any radicalism on the part of the CJEU may in some respects be merely confirmatory.

3. THE TYPES OF BODIES WHICH CAN REFER

This is a factor largely within the CJEU's control, subject, again, to the vision of national actors in pushing the potential boundaries of the definition. While the Court has consistently refused to accept references from arbitration tribunals[45] or administrative authorities not determining legal disputes,[46] otherwise, the Court has set the valve fairly wide open by taking a broad, purposive view of what a court is.[47]

4. THE APPROPRIATENESS OF A DISCRETIONARY REFERENCE

(a) The Treaty and the CJEU

Empowerment of national courts to refer is largely a question of Treaty definition. As was outlined above, this power was exercised through limitations on use of the preliminary reference procedure prior to the Lisbon Treaty. Now, post-Lisbon and as was the case with Article 234 EC, if the national court in question is one from which there is 'no judicial remedy under national law', it has an obligation to refer[48] and for

---

[41] See also discussion of *Van Gend en Loos* (n 1 above) in text to n 123 below.

[42] K Alter, 'Explaining National Court Acceptance of European Court Jurisprudence: A Critical Evaluation of Theories of Legal Integration' (1995) EUI Working Paper RSC No 95/27; D Nicol, 'Disapplying with Relish? The Industrial Tribunals and Acts of Parliament' [1996] PL 579.

[43] This case is discussed in Bobek (n 39 above) 1613.

[44] See also Tridimas (n 38 above) 37.

[45] Case C-125/04 *Denuit v Transorient Mosaique Voyages and Culture SA* [2005] ECR I-923, [13].

[46] Case C-14/08 *Roda Golf & Beach Resort* [2009] ECR I-5439, [35]. See also Case C-53/03 *Synetairismos Farmakopoion Aitolias & Akarnanias (Syfait) and Others v GlaxoSmithKline plc* [2005] ECR I-4609.

[47] See also Anderson and Demetriou (n 16 above) ch 2.

[48] Art 267(3) TFEU.

the remainder of 'courts' and 'tribunals', referral is largely discretionary though conditional upon the reference being necessary to enable the 'referring Court to give judgment'.

The enabling of national courts to refer is evidently a modulating factor heavily in the control of Member States and as the CJEU has observed repeatedly, this aspect of referral is '*solely* for the national court'[49] and 'depends *entirely* on the national court's assessment as to whether a reference is appropriate and necessary'.[50] While the CJEU has followed the Treaty text by holding that the decision to refer is an 'entitlement',[51] which 'cannot...be transformed into an obligation',[52] it has always encouraged references by insisting on a general 'rule of non-enquiry', pursuant to which it has created only minimal protective rules in 'exceptional' circumstances[53] against manufactured, hypothetical, and moot questions,[54] manifestly irrelevant questions,[55] incomprehensible or unintelligible references,[56] and references which lack an adequate factual or legal basis.[57] The CJEU will however endeavour to answer the reference unless these deficiencies are blatant: for instance, in the *Pedro IV Servicios* case, the CJEU accepted that the reference lacked 'certain information relevant to the outcome of the case', but concluded that it could answer the reference nonetheless.[58] A presumption operates in favour of answering the reference, such that if it is 'not obvious' that the reference bears no relation to the facts of the main action, the CJEU will deal with the reference and, indeed, reformulate questions in order to assist.[59] Moreover, the CJEU has also refused to decline to deal with a reference even where the answers are clear from existing well-established EU and national case law.[60]

---

[49] Case C-260/07 *Pedro IV Servicios SL v Total España SA* [2009] ECR I-2437, [28] (emphasis added).

[50] *Kempter* (n 11 above) [42].

[51] Case C-555/07 *Seda Kücükdeveci v Swedex GmbH & Co KG*, 19 January 2010, [56].

[52] ibid [54]. The discretion to refer cannot be transformed into an obligation where national law does not allow the court to disapply a provision unless the provision has first been declared unconstitutional by the national Constitutional Court; rather the principle of effectiveness of EU law requires the national court to decline to apply the incompatible national provision: [53]. See also n 130 below.

[53] *Conseil général de la Vienne* (n 23 above), [20].

[54] Starting with the cases of Case 104/79 *Foglia v Novello* [1980] ECR 745 and Case 244/80 *Foglia v Novello (No 2)* [1981] ECR 3045.

[55] For example, Case C-343/90 *Lourenço Dias v Director da Alfândega do Porto* [1992] ECR I-4673; Case C-11/07 *Eckelkamp v Belgium* [2008] ECR I-6845, [25]. Every reference will also enjoy a 'presumption of relevance': Case C-333/07 *Société Régie Networks v Direction de Contrôle Fiscal Rhône-Alpes Bourgogne* [2008] ECR I-10807, [46].

[56] Case C-318/00 *Bacardi-Martini SAS and Cellier des Dauphins v Newcastle United Football Club* [2003] ECR I-905. For a stricter application, see: Case C-116/00 *Laguillaumie* [2000] ECR I-4979.

[57] Case C-250/06 *United Pan-Europe Communications Belgium SA v Belgium* [2007] ECR I-11135, [19]–[21]; *Information Note on References from National Courts for a Preliminary Ruling* [2005] OJ C143/1, [18].

[58] *Pedro IV Servicios* (n 49 above) [30].

[59] C-429/05 *Rampion v Franfinance SA* [2007] ECR I-8017, [25] and [27].

[60] *Pedro IV Servicios* (n 49 above) [31].

(b) The response of the national courts

By its general rule of non-enquiry, the CJEU has set this valve factor wide open; and it is for the national courts to fix their own guidelines to regulate the discretionary decision to refer and thus determine varying degrees of 'reference liberalism'. For the national court itself, there is no cost, in the sense of resource implications at least, in making a reference—costs are borne by the parties and the CJEU.[61] As such, this factor can provide a very useful illustration of evolving national court attitudes to the CJEU.

To take an example: for a long time, the UK courts adhered to the restrictive approach to referral adopted by Lord Denning MR in *Bulmer v Bollinger* to the effect that '[u]nless the point is really difficult and important, it would seem better for the English judge to decide it himself'.[62] This was followed by a period of liberalization, as exhibited in such authorities as *Samex*[63] and *ex parte Else*,[64] pursuant to which it was considered that the appropriate course for a court would be ordinarily to refer the issue to the CJEU unless the national court could with complete confidence resolve the issue itself. More recently however, caution has again been suggested and 'the court must observe some measure of self-restraint; lest the Court of Justice become over-whelmed'.[65] This is a significant statement, which will be considered further below; for present purposes, it implies a further transition in UK judicial attitudes to the CJEU. Increasing familiarity of UK courts with EU law is now advocated as a factor operating against a reference[66] and caution should be exercised where there is an established body of case law; or where the question turns on a narrow point considered in the light of a very specific set of facts and the ruling is unlikely to have any application beyond the instant case.[67] By contrast, it will be appropriate to make a reference 'where the question is one of general importance and where the ruling is likely to promote the uniform application of the law throughout the European Union'.[68] Interestingly, however, even though the guidance provided by the UK courts seems designed to encourage restraint in the making of references, UK courts actually referred at their highest ever rate in 2009, totalling 28 references.[69]

---

[61] G Tridimas and T Tridimas, 'National Courts and the European Court of Justice: A Public Choice Analysis of the Preliminary Reference Procedure' (2004) 24 Intl Rev Law & Econ 125, 136.

[62] *Bulmer v Bollinger* [1974] Ch 401, CA.

[63] *Customs and Excise Commissioners v Samex* [1983] 1 All ER 1042, QBD.

[64] *R v International Stock Exchange of the United Kingdom and the Republic of Ireland Ltd, ex p Else Ltd* [1993] QB 534, 545 (per Sir Thomas Bingham MR).

[65] *Prudential Assurance Co v Prudential Insurance Co* [2003] EWCA Civ 327, [2003] 1 WLR 2295, [50] (Chadwick LJ declining to make a reference where determination of the point would not have been decisive). See also *Trinity Mirror Plc (formerly Mirror Group Newspapers Ltd) v Commissioners of Customs and Excise* [2001] EWCA Civ 65, [2001] 2 CMLR 33, [51]–[55]; *Professional Contractors Group v Commissioners for Inland Revenue* [2002] 1 CMLR 46, CA, [91] (per Walker LJ).

[66] *Professional Contractors' Group* (n 65 above) [91].

[67] *Trinity Mirror* (n 65) [52]. See also Case C-338/95 *Wiener v SI GmbH v Hauptzollamt Emmerich* [1997] ECR I-6495, Opinion of AG Jacobs [20].

[68] *Wiener* (n 67 above) [20].

[69] See Table 13.2.

(c) The absence of CJEU guidance

The guidance given by the UK courts is reasonable (if not guaranteed to produce fewer references); and what is signally absent from the CJEU's jurisprudence, despite the encouragement of AG Jacobs in the *Wiener* case, is any attempt to give similar guidance to national courts regarding their referral decisions. Whilst the historic absence of guidelines on the appropriateness of or necessity for a reference may be explicable by an initial urge to maximize the number of rulings—and thus the coverage of subject matter, the detailed exposition of EU law, and the frequency of cooperation with national courts—such an *ad hoc* solution has been unsatisfactory for a long time now. Indeed, the recent references of the UK courts to an 'overwhelmed' CJEU demonstrate the unsatisfactory nature of the CJEU not exercising greater control over its docket. As is well known, docket control is often a key feature of a Supreme or Constitutional Court, whether by a system of petitions, leave, certiorari, or guidelines for appeal or referral; yet at present the CJEU does not even formulate specific guidelines as to the need for future references in sectors which are heavily litigated. Instead, where confronted with reference overload on a particular subject the CJEU often uses the technique of reiterating principles of law and then stating that it is for the national court to make a determination in light of the interpretative guidance given.[70] Such a restatement may often contain no answer to the question in a form expected by a CJEU-illiterate national court; and yet that is deliberate, either because the CJEU considers that the answer already exists in the case law or because it feels that the question is actually a request to apply the case law to the facts, a task reserved for the national court. In short, the case was not an appropriate one for referral. Such an oblique deterrent to future referral is often insufficient, especially for infrequent interlocutors with the CJEU.

5. THE OBLIGATION TO REFER

At least at the outset, this would appear to be a factor determined exclusively by the Treaty. Yet over time the CJEU has significantly added to it.[71] First, and most obviously, the CJEU is the ultimate arbiter of what exactly is meant by a court from which there is 'no judicial remedy under national law' and thus which courts are obliged to refer.[72] Secondly, the CJEU's case law has explicitly supplemented the obligation to refer imposed by the Treaty. Whenever any national court is minded to find that an EU regulation or directive is invalid it must refer that question for final determination by the CJEU;[73] otherwise, according to the CJEU, the consequences for uniform application of EU law would be unpalatable.[74]

---

[70] The post-*Keck* free movement of goods cases are good examples.

[71] B H ter Kuile, 'To Refer or not to Refer: About the Last Paragraph of Art 177 of the EC Treaty' in D Curtin and T Heukels, *Institutional Dynamics of European Integration: Vol II* (1995) 381.

[72] See now Case C-99/00 *Lyckeskog* [2002] ECR I-4839.

[73] Case 314/85 *Firma Foto-Frost v Hauptzollamt Lübeck-Ost* [1987] ECR 4199.

[74] Case C-344/04 R *(IATA and European Low Fares Airline Association) v Department of Transport* [2006] ECR I-403, [30].

Thirdly, by its doctrines of *acte éclairé* and *acte clair* the CJEU has created judicial exceptions to the rules on the obligation to refer.[75] As is well known, a national court falling within Article 267(3) TFEU (ex Article 234(3) EC) is not obliged to refer where the answer to the EU point is 'so obvious as to leave no scope for any reasonable doubt', and the court is 'convinced' (having had regard to different language versions) that the matter is 'equally obvious to the courts of the other Member States and to the Court of Justice'.[76] In practice, it seems that final national courts have sometimes seized upon the doctrines of *acte éclairé* and *acte clair* to avoid making references,[77] even where a 'dogmatic' interpretation of the *CILFIT* criteria appears not to have been fully complied with.[78]

Perhaps, given that Member State courts do not comply with the strict rigours of *CILFIT*, it is unsurprising that despite being invited to do so, and despite calls by Advocates General to do so,[79] the CJEU has declined to relax the *CILFIT* requirements.[80] Quite the opposite, the CJEU has actually strengthened the obligation of national courts of last instance to refer through the introduction of the *Köbler* damages doctrine.[81] As will be recalled, pursuant to *Köbler*, damages are available in respect of manifest infringements of EU law by courts of last instance.[82] This doctrine not only encourages references by courts of last instance, but also by lower courts: given that the individual will normally be bringing proceedings for *Köbler* damages in an inferior court to the court whose judgment is under scrutiny, that inferior court will be more likely to refer than to decide the issue itself.[83] Indeed, in *Köbler* itself, Advocate

---

[75] See Cases 28/62 to 30/62 *Da Costa en Schaake NV and others v Nederlandse Belastingadministratie* [1963] ECR 31 for the genesis of the former doctrine and Case 283/81 *CILFIT and Lanificio di Gavardo SpA v Ministry of Health* [1982] ECR 3415 for the latter.

[76] *CILFIT* (n 75 above) [16]–[18].

[77] A Arnull, 'The Use and Abuse of Art 177 EEC' (1989) 52 MLR 622. Tridimas (n 38 above) 42–44. The House of Lords does not generally consider each of the CILFIT criteria, but asks if the answer is 'clear beyond the bounds of reasonable argument': *R (Countryside Alliance) v Attorney General* [2007] UKHL 52, [2009] 1 AC 719, [31]; *O'Byrne v Aventis Pasteur* [2008] UKHL 34, [2008] 3 CMLR 10 [23]–[24].

[78] Bobek (n 39 above) 1631–1632.

[79] eg AG Jacobs, *Wiener* (n 67 above); AG Tizzano, *Lyckeskog* (n 72 above); AG Colomer, Case C-461/03 *Gaston Schul Douane-expediteur BV v Minister van Landbouw, Natuur en Voedselkwaliteit* [2005] ECR I-10513.

[80] eg *Gaston Schul* (n 79 above); Case T-47/02 *Danzer and Danzer v Council* [2006] ECR II-1779, [36]–[37]. See also *Lyckeskog* (n 72 above) [15]; Case C-495/03 *Intermodal Transports BV v Staatssecretaris van Financiën* [2005] ECR I-8151, [39]. It is worth noting that in *Lyckeskog*, the CJEU did not dismiss the possibility of altering the *CILFIT* criteria; it evaded answering a question on the issue (noting that the referring court was not a court of last instance).

[81] Case C-224/01 *Köbler v Austria* [2003] ECR I-10239. See also Case C-173/03 *Traghetti del Mediterraneo SpA in liquidation v Repubblica Italiana* [2006] ECR 5177. Much has been written about these cases, see: G Bertolino, 'The Traghetti Case: A New CJEU Decision on State Liability for Judicial Acts-National Legislations under Examination' (2008) 27 CJQ 448; H Scott and NW Barber, 'State Liability under Francovich for Decisions of National Courts' (2004) 120 LQR 403; A A S Zuckerman, '"Appeal" to the High Court against House of Lords Decisions on the Interpretation of Community Law—Damages for Judicial Error' (2004) 23 CJQ 8.

[82] *Köbler* (n 81 above) [33]–[36] and [53].

[83] J Komárek, 'Federal Elements in the Community Judicial System: Building Coherence in the Community Legal Order' (2005) CML Rev 9, 14.

General Léger urged the national court to refer '[i]n order to dispel any reasonable doubt as to its impartiality'.[84]

6. THE COSTS OF REFERRAL

The financial and temporal costs of a preliminary reference represent a significant barrier to CJEU access. Starting with the position on financial costs, it has been the CJEU's consistent stance that the costs of a preliminary reference are a matter for decision by the national referring court,[85] although EU-based legal aid is available under the CJEU's Rules of Procedure to a party unable to bear all or part of the costs of proceedings.[86]

The upshot of this rule is to put individual litigants at the mercy of individual national cost rules. This can have interesting and variable 'access to justice' consequences. In a Member State with traditionally low (in some sectors at least) and tightly regulated fees, such as in German social security or employment cases, the barriers to litigation are low. In England by contrast, with its high professional costs, the barriers are much more extensive unless legal aid is available, especially in the light of the usual rule of 'costs following the event'. Heavy potential costs exposure is a significant deterrent to litigation, especially where the sum at stake is small, however important the principle. In such Member States, one might expect a higher reliance upon public interest litigation.

The time factor is clearly relevant too. Delays in processing references, whether at national level[87] or at EU level can present an irremediable barrier to referrals. The temporal costs of referral have received extensive attention in recent years, with the time taken to deal with a reference increasing until 2004 and decreasing thereafter, resulting, in 2008, in a time period of 16.8 months.[88] The CJEU has indicated that the 2008 figure is the shortest time identified in the entire period for which reliable data exists;[89] but closer scrutiny of the figures has revealed a more negative analysis. The reduction has been attributed to the welcoming on to the court of new judges from the acceding Member States, during a period in which the rate of reference from these Member States has been low; and it has been shown that proportionately, the rate of dealing with references is actually slowing.[90] That the 16.8-month figure may have been unsustainable is suggested by the 2009 average time period, which was 17.1 months with the average rate of references per Member State at its highest since 2003.[91]

---

[84] Opinion of the AG, *Köbler* (n 81 above) [111].

[85] Case C-472/99 *Clean Car Autoservice GmbH v Stadt Wien* [2001] ECR I-9687.

[86] *Rules of Procedure of the Court of Justice*, Art 76. For an explanation of the practice see T Kennedy, 'Paying the Piper: Legal Aid in Proceedings before the Court of Justice' (1998) 25 CML Rev 559.

[87] D Vaughan, 'The Advocate's View' in M Andenas (ed), *Article 177 References to the European Court— Policy and Practice* (Butterworths, 1994) 55 for English examples.

[88] Court of Justice, *Annual Report 2008*.

[89] ibid 3–4.

[90] Bobek (n 39 above) 1642.

[91] Court of Justice, *Annual Report 2009*, 94.

Whilst in many cases one party will try to use the threat of delay for tactical advantage, there exist cases where the standard delay of at least 17.1 months for an answer to a reference (in addition to the time taken to list and relist national proceedings) is unacceptable to both parties.[92] Temporal delays need to be addressed if Member State engagement with the preliminary reference process is to be sustained, given that there is evidence that the delay has become a disincentive to making a reference at all.[93]

D. PERSPECTIVES ON A MULTI-FUNCTIONING PROCEDURE

A review of the different 'valve' factors in the preliminary reference procedure indicates that, over the years, 'reference potential' has not stabilized, but rather, is ever-increasing, whether due to the efforts of the CJEU or the national courts or, more recently, Treaty amendment. Explaining this maximalist approach is not straightforward, but it would appear that it can be at least partially attributed to the multiple, and indeed ever-increasing, functions performed by the preliminary reference procedure within the EU legal order. As can be seen from Table 13.12 and Figures 13.1 and 13.1.1, preliminary rulings generally constitute over 50 per cent of the workload of the CJEU. This is unsurprising, as, viewed from different perspectives, preliminary rulings can be seen to fulfil a number of highly significant functions: first, and most obviously, they frame the relationship between national courts and the CJEU; secondly, and less obviously, they provide a mechanism for discourse between Member States, the CJEU, and the Union institutions; thirdly, they can offer an attractive form of litigation for private interests; fourthly, a function emphasized in recent case law, they constitute the cornerstone of compliance with the principle of effective judicial protection within the EU legal order; and fifthly, and allied to all these functions, they facilitate deeper integration of the EU legal order.

1. RELATIONSHIP BETWEEN THE NATIONAL COURTS AND THE CJEU

Black letter or legalistic interpretations of the preliminary reference process show a procedure symptomatic of early ideas of cooperative federalism, premised on notions of separate but equal realms of authority. In Craig and de Búrca's terminology, the textual provision for preliminary references—including in the Lisbon Treaty—reveals an allocation of roles that is both 'horizontal' and 'bilateral'.[94] The CJEU constantly emphasizes that the reference is an 'instrument of co-operation between the Court of

---

[92] See *R v Minister of Agriculture, Fisheries and Food, ex p Portman Agrochemicals Limited* [1994] 3 CMLR 18, QB, where the delay was an explicit factor that both parties agreed was material in persuading the court not to refer.

[93] eg, Tridimas (n 38 above) 17; O Due, 'Danish Preliminary References' in D O'Keeffe and A Bavasso, *Judicial Review in European Union Law* (Kluwer Law International, 2001) 363.

[94] P Craig and G de Búrca, *EU Law: Text, Cases and Materials* (4th edn, Oxford University Press, 2008) 461.

Justice and the national courts'.[95] Yet, in practice, the CJEU has had a mixed relationship with the black letter implications of textual drafting. On the one hand, reliance on the horizontal implications of the text may explain the CJEU's reluctance to adopt anything other than very minimal filtering controls on references. On the other hand, the CJEU regularly ignores the Treaty text. The striking examples of *Gestoras* and *Advocaten van der Wereld* have already been discussed. Likewise, the Treaty obligation on courts of final instance to refer has been amended through the *acte clair* doctrine, while, in a large number of cases, it is difficult to find a strict allocation of functions between the CJEU and the national court where what is really at issue is detailed factual evaluation,[96] or where the answer to the preliminary ruling effectively determines the issue, leaving no role for the national court.[97]

Moreover, for some time, it has not been strictly correct to describe the relationship between the CJEU and the national courts as based solely on cooperation. The initial choice of a cooperation model by the Treaty's framers was realistic and non-confrontational, in short classic neofunctionalism. Over the years, however, the role of preliminary references has shifted from the cooperational to the coordinational; yet this is only minimally reflected by the express wording of the case law which still seeks to identify '*national courts as partners, not inferiors*', and is not reflected at all in the Treaty language.[98] The most notable amendment to the system of cooperation envisaged by the Treaty has been introduced by the *Köbler* judgment. As Auby notes, *Köbler* 'donne au système, non pas un caractère hiérarchique, mais une plus grande verticalité';[99] the case creates an 'indirect possibility to appeal, and reach the Court of Justice' for disappointed litigants.[100] That the CJEU is at the apex of the hierarchy is insinuated in the definition of 'sufficiently serious breach', which entails a 'manifest breach of the *case law of the Court* in the matter'[101]—albeit that the CJEU has adopted a very 'benevolent' interpretation of what might constitute a 'manifest breach' by a court.[102]

It is probably fair to say that the CJEU's continued use[103] of the language of cooperation—thereby adhering to the textual intention—may be of fluctuating sincerity. On one entirely cynical level it can be pointed out that continued usage of the language of cooperation is aimed at sweetening the bitter pill of the CJEU's own repositioning of itself by pointing out the important role of national courts. At the other

---

[95] Case C-445/06 *Danske Slagterier v Bundesrepublik Deutschland* [2009] ECR I-2119, [65].

[96] For instance, see the Common Customs Tariff classification cases discussed in AG Jacobs' Opinion in *Wiener* (n 67 above).

[97] See text to nn 24–26.

[98] Komárek (n 83 above) 34.

[99] J B Auby, 'Physionomie du contentieux administratif européen' in *What's New in European Administration Law*, EUI Working Paper Law, 2005/10, 15–18; B Beutler, 'State Liability for Breaches of Community Law by National Courts: Is the Requirement of a Manifest Infringement of the Applicable Law an Insurmountable Obstacle?' (2009) 46 CML Rev 773. Even if this is the case, the doctrine has created uncertainty: P J Wattel, '*Köbler, Cilfit* and *Welthgrove*: we can't go on meeting like this' (2004) 41 CML Rev 177, 190.

[100] Komárek (n 83 above) 14. See also Opinion of AG Léger in *Köbler* (n 81 above) [111].

[101] *Köbler* (n 81 above) [56] (emphasis added). See also Komárek (n 83 above) 14–16.

[102] Komárek (n 83 above) 17.

[103] eg *Pedro IV Servicios* (n 49 above) [28]; *Danske Slagterier* (n 95 above) [65].

end of the spectrum, the language of cooperation is entirely sincere as it recognizes that the functioning of EU legal integration is entirely dependent upon national courts acting in good faith to implement EU law. Direct effect and the 'privatized Attorney-Generals'[104] that it creates are to no avail without the 'sincere cooperation' of the national courts. It is perhaps unsurprising therefore that the CJEU, while subtly re-positioning itself, strives to ensure positive relationships with national courts. For instance, in the infringement proceedings, *Commission v Italy*,[105] in which the Commission placed stress on the fault of the *Corte suprema di cassazione*,[106] the CJEU was careful to reason the case in such a way as to find that the ultimate fault was with the legislature.[107] Thus, although the evolution of the preliminary reference procedure has promoted an increasingly 'vertical' relationship between the national courts and the CJEU,[108] this promotion has been cautious.

2. EU DISCOURSE

Generating EU discourse is a central feature of the preliminary ruling process. The term 'discourse' is more appropriate here than 'dialogue' for a number of reasons. First, given systematic intervention before the CJEU by third party Member States, the Commission, and other interested parties, it is mistaken to take a purely bilateral perspective of the procedure. Secondly, the term 'discourse' connotes binding out-comes attained through multilateral involvement in procedure, and again, is reflective of actual preliminary ruling practice,[109] which provides for a very interesting and novel form of legal discourse.

Taking the attributes of that discourse in turn: first, there is equality of access from any 'court or tribunal' of a Member State. Secondly, the Member States, the Commission and the Council all have the exclusive right to make observations.[110] Unlike the case with direct actions, no observations from other interested private parties are possible. Thus, preliminary reference participants (and those tending to be bound by

---

[104] P Craig, 'Once Upon a Time in the West: Direct Effect and the Federalization of EEC law' (1992) 12 OJLS 453.

[105] Case C-129/00 [2003] ECR I-14637.

[106] ibid [11]–[16].

[107] ibid [33], [41]. For discussion, see Komárek (n 83 above) 42.

[108] Craig and de Búrca (n 94 above) 461.

[109] Discourse theory, which has its origins in political theory, has been recently applied to legal processes and reasoning, most notably by R Alexy. Introductory reading can be found in R Alexy, *A Theory of Legal Argumentation* (Clarendon, 1989); see also R Alexy, 'Justification and Application of Norms' (1993) 6 Ratio Juris 157. See also J Habermas, *Between Facts and Norms* (Polity Press, 1996). There is not sufficient space here to set out the basic tenets of discourse theory. However, it has for present purposes the following key features: first it is initially polysupremacist or polynormative, a fact stemming from the equal importance and respect accorded to all interlocutors. Secondly, its procedural results are normatively binding on those interlocutors. Thirdly, the results are always reviewable, since factual reality and the imperfections inherent in legal discourse make them essentially contestable.

[110] EEC Statute of the Court of Justice, Art 20; Rules of Procedure of the Court of Justice, Art 104.

it) are limited to Member States, EU institutions, and those private parties that have prompted the domestic litigation; as such there is a heavy state emphasis in the discourse. Thirdly, whilst the results of the discourse, namely the answers given to the questions referred, are normatively binding, they are contingent and can be reopened by any request for reconsideration and refinement of the issue. This further adds to the cyclical nature of the interaction between national courts and the CJEU. Fourthly, there is an often overlooked value in having national courts ask a question by the reference procedure. The very fact that it has been put implies both that it is a legitimate question to ask and that the national court in question intends to implement the answer it receives. The national court is therefore bound in by its participation.[111] Similarly, less active forms of participation, such as intervention by observations, also serve to legitimize the result. On occasion, the CJEU may itself seek to promote discussion of an important issue, and thereby bind participants to its determination of that issue, by expressly addressing questions to Member State authorities, usually in the form of a request for information.

The preliminary reference procedure also facilitates different types of discourse. For example, there is what one might call the 'supremacy' or 'constitutional' discourse, in which high-level values are posited against and located within EU law. The classic example of such a discourse is the creation of the CJEU's fundamental human rights jurisprudence which gradually developed as a result of the interaction of the German national courts with the CJEU.[112] A lower level of discourse, which one can call 'public law' discourse, also exists, concerning the development of lower level but nonetheless general principles of EU administrative law, for instance the nature of proportionality or the extent of the duty to purposively construe legislation. A third level concerns the development of individual or specific notions within particular branches of EU law.

As a further rough and ready distinction, questions referred by national courts can be broken down into two types, namely weak or inquisitive discourse and strong or confrontational discourse. The former, by far and away the most common, is really no more than an adjunct to the coordinational and hierarchical nature of EU law. In this form of discourse, the questions asked in references may be posed in order to comply with supremacy rules[113] or explore the ramifications of hierarchical law, for instance in a discussion of effective remedies. The question often takes the basic shape of, 'this is how we do it here, does EU law do it like this?' or simply 'what does EU law require in this situation?' This is to be contrasted with confrontational or strong discourse. Here the question is more of the sort, 'this is how we do it, and you do it like this as well, don't you?' Confrontational discourse also arises in what Tridimas has described as 'protest

---

[111] J C Cohen, 'The European Preliminary Reference and U.S. Supreme Court Review of State Court Judgments: A Study in Comparative Judicial Federalism' (1996) 44 AJCL 421, 427, and especially 461.

[112] See J Kokott, 'Report on Germany' in A-M Slaughter, A Stone Sweet et al, *The European Courts and National Courts: Doctrine and Jurisprudence* (Hart, 1998) 177.

[113] It is important to note that in this context, supremacy rules, such as the *Foto-Frost* (n 73 above) obligation to refer take on a more procedural and less substantive aspect. They ensure that important questions have the maximum discursive input before resolution.

through co-operation', where national courts, if they disagree with CJEU rulings, will refer again the same or similar questions, thereby asking the CJEU to re-consider.[114]

Participation in the discourse can arise in two principal forms: the number of references and the number of observations submitted by that state.[115] The number of references can be dependent upon varied factors, such as: institutional practice; the level of EU compliance; active and educated interest groups; (paradoxically) resistance to developments in EU law (as in the German human rights saga); and deficiencies or less advantageous remedies in national law.[116] As can be seen from Table 13.2 and Figure 13.2.1, Germany has always had a very high referral rate, reaching a peak in 2006. Figure 13.2.3 illustrates that Austria, Sweden, and Finland have also been quite active since their accession; while Figure 13.2.4 demonstrates the incremental rise in references from 2004 Accession Member States. Regardless of its cause, a high referral rate offers the opportunity for national legal values to be tested, explored, incorporated, refined, or rejected in the preliminary ruling discursive process; in short, national courts can influence the substantive evolution of EU law by participating in the preliminary ruling process.

In addition to references, each Member State's patterns of intervention are records of the importance attached to participating in debate.[117] This is a form of secondary or substituted input, particularly important from a political perspective as it represents a decision to intervene from a purely policy perspective. There is no compulsion to be a party, merely perceived interest in affecting the result.[118] The Commission's policy of intervention in every case is precisely such a policy, born from the desire for influence. Likewise, governments, realizing the central integrative role of CJEU case law, wish to participate in its formulation; they may also wish to contribute to obtaining a finding of invalidity of an EU act, having unsuccessfully opposed it in Council, but without the litigation effort involved in direct action.[119]

Table 13.3.1 and Figure 13.3.1 contain data on the observations statistics for the big four of France, Germany, Italy, and the UK for cases coming from their own courts.

---

[114] Tridimas (n 38 above) 39 (and discussing a number of references from Greek courts in a number of company law cases: 39–40).

[115] For an early study see C A Crisham and K Mortelmans, 'Observations of Member States in the Preliminary Rulings Procedure before the Court of Justice of the European Communities' in D O'Keeffe and H G Schermers (eds), *Essays in European Law and Integration* (Brill, 1982).

[116] There are different theories to explain national rates of referral: A-M Slaughter, Stone Sweet *et al* (n 112 above). Emphasis has been placed recently on Member State size, ratio of EU trade to GDP, and litigation rates, as well as the existence of abstract or specialist judicial review and monism: M Vink, M Claes, and C Arnold, 'Explaining the Use of Preliminary References by Domestic Courts in EU Member States: A Mixed-Method Comparative Analysis', paper presented at the 11th Biennial Conference of the European Union Studies Association, 24 April 2009, 'Judicial Politics in the EU and Beyond', 11th Biennial Conference of the European Union Studies Association.

[117] The contributions to H G Schermers, C W A Timmermans and others (eds), *Article 177 EEC: Experiences and Problems* (North-Holland Publishers, 1987), particularly those of the Commission and the UK, strongly reflect the policy perspective inherent in observation strategies.

[118] An active policy of intervention can be likened to a maximization of 'voice' in a situation where 'exit' is not a viable option: see Weiler's use of these terms invented by Hirschmann in J H H Weiler, 'The Transformation of Europe' (1991) 100 Yale LJ 2403.

[119] Vink, Claes, and Arnold (n 116 above).

Table 13.4.1 and Figure 13.4.1 exhibit the number of interventions made by those Member States in cases coming from other Member States. Certain patterns emerge. For instance, over the years, the UK has always been an active intervenor, submitting observations in roughly thirty to forty cases per year from other Member States. The submission of observations thus increases the UK input to preliminary references. France pre-*Nicolo* had a moderate rate of observations, both in its own cases and in those of other Member States. Since that date its observation rate has literally shot up, and since then, France has demonstrated a steady rate of participation in the preliminary ruling procedure. Meanwhile, Germany, which remains the leading state in terms of references, is comparatively relaxed about its observation policy. Germany now intervenes in about 50 per cent of its own cases and about 20 other cases per year. Italy, which has a modest number of judgments per year, had a historically higher rate of intervention in its own cases but this has tailed off as the rate of references increased. However, its rates of intervention in cases from other Member States has increased very significantly in recent years, peaking at 76 in 2008. Perhaps what is particularly interesting though is the speed with which 2004 Accession Member States seized upon the possibility of participation through preliminary rulings. As illustrated by Tables 13.3.2 and 13.4.2, Hungary, the Czech Republic, and particularly Poland, have made a significant number of observations and interventions. There is also evidence to suggest that many Member States actually make the greater proportion of their observations in cases from other Member States rather than from their own;[120] and that such is the importance of making observations, government agents will sometimes coordinate in respect of their observations.[121]

The discourse perspective illustrates, in a striking way, the pivotal role of the preliminary reference procedure in embedding loyalty within EU law: results mediated through the participatory preliminary reference procedure are more likely to have a normative pull. It is the synthetic and participatory nature of the resulting norms (for instance fundamental human rights based on common constitutional traditions that are recognizable in part to every participant or general principles that borrow from a blend of traditions) that is one of the strengths of EU law.

3. INSTITUTIONS AND INTERESTS

Following from these comments on participation in the discourse, it is also clear that national courts can use preliminary references to promote values in their own legal culture, whether derived from substantive areas of the law, legal institutions such as the judiciary or bar, or procedural rules and techniques. The institutional culture of both national courts and the CJEU is central to the way in which questions are referred, handled, framed, and answered. Equally, given that private actors are the

---

[120] M-P F Granger, 'When Governments go to Luxembourg ... the Influence of Governments on the Court of Justice' (2004) 29 ELRev 3, 15.
[121] ibid 22.

driving force behind references, in that it is their litigation that gives rise to the
questions of EU law referred, an interest-based perspective on preliminary rulings is
also pertinent.

(a) Institutional culture

The legal culture of each Member State has always had a marked effect upon the
approach judges take towards preliminary references. A simple example should
suffice, namely the role of Dutch courts in the early preliminary references. Dutch
courts referred eight out of the first ten preliminary rulings considered by the Court;[122]
one of the other two references came from Luxembourg. This is a revealing statistic,
showing in part the importance of Dutch legal internationalism, the experience
obtained under the Benelux Court system and a peculiarly Dutch approach to legal
problem solving that reached its apotheosis is *Van Gend*. It has been convincingly
argued by de Witte and Claes that the truly radical party in *Van Gend* was not the
CJEU but the Dutch national court that referred the questions in the first place, which
itself used and introduced the terminology of direct effect, already well known in
Dutch law.[123] The phrasing of these questions, they have argued, was a product of
Dutch legal culture.

By contrast, it is noticeable that specialist Constitutional Courts may avoid making
references. Mayer for instance has reviewed the reluctance of a number of specialist
Constitutional Courts to make references, such as, the German *Bundesverfassungsgericht*, the Italian *Corte Costituzionale*, the Spanish *Tribunal Constitucional*, and the
Portuguese *Tribunal Constitucional*.[124] Generalist civil courts often accept supremacy
much earlier, and indeed have much to gain over their public law rivals by accepting
the resulting judicial review powers. This is a pattern which is also in evidence in the
2004 Accession Member States.[125]

To take two further examples, Germany and the UK, Germany has a sophisticated,
transparent constitution allied with a strong, rights-based legal culture designed to
guarantee fundamental democratic values.[126] Similar principles, whilst no doubt

---

[122] From Case 13/61 *Kledingverkoopbedrijf de Geus en Uitdenbogerd v Robert Bosch GmbH and Others*
[1962] ECR 45 to Case 6/64 *Costa v ENEL* [1964] ECR 585.

[123] See B De Witte and M Claes, 'Report on the Netherlands' in A-M Slaughter, Stone Sweet *et al* (n 112
above) 171. The first question referred was 'Whether Article 12 of the EEC Treaty has direct application within
the territory of a Member State, in other words, whether nationals of such a State can, on the basis of the Article
in question, lay claim to individual rights which courts protect': see *Van Gend* (n 1 above) 3.

[124] F Mayer, 'The European Constitution and the Courts: Adjudicating European Constitutional Law in a
Multilevel System', Jean Monnet Working Paper No 9/03, 9–10; F Fontanelli and G Martinico, 'Between
procedural impermeability and constitutional openness: the Italian Constitutional Court and preliminary
references to the European Court of Justice' (2010) 16 ELJ 345 (discussing the Italian Constitutional Court's
decision in *Presidente del Consiglio dei Ministri v Regione Sardegna* in April 2008 to make its first preliminary
reference to the CJEU).

[125] See the discussion of the *Kovalsky* case in text to nn 43–44 above.

[126] eg the German Constitutional Court's judgment on the Lisbon Treaty, 30 June 2009.

existing in the common law, do so in a residual and weaker form.[127] Simply put, without clear, detailed, and entrenched 'constitutional armoury' the opportunity for constitutional conflict and thus discourse of a constitutional nature is thus greatly limited in the UK by comparison with Germany. That is reflected by the near complete absence of any 'kompetenz kompetenz' debate in the UK.[128] At a less glorified level, suppose a contentious EU directive disturbed or modified specific legislative provisions in one Member State whilst interacting with general and vague provisions of codified or common law in another. Strong debate may be triggered in the former because of the difficulty of accommodation of new and different rules whereas the latter state may accept the new and potentially quite different EU position with less difficulty or in the form of weak discourse.

(b) Interests

Quite apart from the nature of the national courts that make the references, one must look carefully at those using such courts and their incentive for doing so.[129] The actual use of preliminary rulings by private and public parties can be understood when one considers the opportunities for what may be described as 'circumvention' of other forms of public interest litigation. Circumvention takes three forms: attack upon and trumping of national laws, whether seeking declarations of inapplicability or constructive reinterpretation; circumvention of procedural disadvantages or shortcomings inherent in other EU procedures; and circumvention of EU institutions, notably the Commission.

Review for compatibility with EU law supplements national review powers, whether by increasing their scope or the number of courts to which they are available,[130] and in some Member States introduces unparalleled powers of legislative review.[131] So EU law,

---

[127] eg the ease with which strict Diceyan orthodoxy was abandoned by the House of Lords in *R v Secretary of State for Transport, ex p Factortame (No 2)* [1991] 1 AC 603 (HL) as explained in P Craig, 'Sovereignty of the United Kingdom Parliament after Factortame' (1991) 11 YEL 221. See also *Thoburn v Sunderland District Council* [2002] EWHC 195, [2003] QB 151 (departing from the principle of implied repeal for the purposes of the European Communities Act 1972, described by Laws J as a 'constitutional statute').

[128] The nearest to it is *R v Secretary of State for Foreign and Commonwealth Affairs, ex p Rees-Mogg* [1994] QB 552 (QBD DC) in which the Divisional Court committed itself to acceptance of the Maastricht Treaty on the basis of a certain interpretation of the Social Chapter. Arguably, if that interpretation had subsequently been departed from by the CJEU a competence issue might have arisen.

[129] See, by way of sample only, R Rawlings, 'The Eurolaw Game: Some Deductions from a Saga' (1993) 20 JL & Soc'y 309; C Harlow, 'A Community of Interests? Making the Most of European Law' (1992) 55 MLR 331; C Harlow and R Rawlings, *Pressure through Law* (Routledge, 1992). The insights of M Galanter, 'Why the "Haves" Come out Ahead: Speculations on the Limits of Legal Change' (1974) 9 Law and Society Review 95 have been much applied, especially his useful distinction between those interested parties who are 'repeat players' and 'one shotters'.

[130] Case 106/77 *Amministrazione delle Finanze dello Stato v Simmenthal SpA* [1978] 3 CMLR 263 emphasizes the general availability of EU law-based judicial review to all national courts. See also *Seda Kücükdeveci* (n 51 above) [54].

[131] The French Republic constitution contained no powers of private, concrete, such review powers being concentrated in the *Conseil Constitutionnel*: see L N Brown and J S Bell, *French Administrative Law* (5th edn, Clarendon, 1998). In the UK there existed no power of legislative review at all until *Factortame* (n 127 above).

as mediated via preliminary rulings, can offer unique or at least alternative opportunities to those wishing to attack national rules. Moreover, EU law contains a parallel system of administrative law, with differing general principles, standards, and intensities of review. The preliminary ruling is the mechanism by which parties wishing to invoke such standards, which may improve by comparison with the case under purely national law, can do so. Turning to circumvention of alternative procedures, whatever the reasons for the Court's narrow interpretation of the availability of direct actions, it has led to the situation whereby cases that cannot be brought using the direct action procedure by private parties, are raised as issues before national courts. A noteworthy example is found in the *British American Tobacco* case, in which a directive, which had not yet been implemented into national law, was challenged via a preliminary ruling.[132] The third form of circumvention aims to exclude the involvement of certain EU institutions, especially the Commission. This is particularly relevant where, for example, the Commission has shown itself unwilling to intervene and the matter may instead be raised before the CJEU through a preliminary reference.[133]

These circumvention opportunities have been seized upon by a number of EU law 'repeat players': namely, Member State governments, activist courts,[134] and interest or pressure groups such as trading associations or unions.[135] Various well-documented 'sagas' of repeat-player-generated, concerted attacks (often by group action) upon national laws have resulted: see for instance the first Sunday Trading cases.[136] Of course, a directly effective right offers the easiest route for interest group litigation. Where EU law is operating in a context not of individual rights but of more general public interest regulation, pressure group action is harder. For example, the doctrine of direct effect has diminished relevance in the context of environmental law making interest group litigation more difficult as access to courts using individual test cases is prevented and one is thrown back on national rules of standing.[137] As a result, national standing rules are perhaps the crucial valve factor from the perspective of repeat-player-based litigation. To give an example, following liberalization of English standing rules in the 1994 *Greenpeace* case,[138] over the years, a significant number of

---

[132] Case C-491/01 *R v Secretary of State ex p British American Tobacco* [2002] ECR I-11453.

[133] Case C-379/87 *Groener v Minister of Education* [1989] ECR 3967 (the Commission had opened and then discontinued infraction proceedings about the rules in question).

[134] Alter (n 42 above). Alter's theory of court competition is a useful variant of neofunctionalist theories of integration; it would appear to work best in explaining interactions between rival specialist courts or lower specialist and higher generalist courts where the tendency for one to see the other as having got it wrong is strongest. See also D Nicol, 'Disapplying with Relish? The Industrial Tribunals and Acts of Parliament' [1996] PL 579 for a study of court empowerment in action.

[135] For instance, *British Steel* or *BA* who have proved adept in using the state aid and competition rules; or the drugs manufacturers and parallel importers whose repeat playing litigation has shaped the courts' free movement and intellectual property case law.

[136] See Rawlings (n 129 above); C Barnard, 'Sunday Trading: A Drama in Five Acts' (1994) 57 MLR 449.

[137] See A Ward, 'The Right to an Effective Remedy in European Community Law and Environmental Protection: A Case Study of United Kingdom Judicial Decisions Concerning the Environmental Assessment Directive' (1993) 5 JEL 221, 232.

[138] *R v Inspectorate of Pollution and another, ex p Greenpeace Ltd (No 2)* [1994] 4 All ER 329.

preliminary references from the UK (set out in Table 13.5) can be seen to have arisen out of challenges brought by interest groups. Leading recent examples include the well-known *Heyday* case.[139]

4. EFFECTIVE JUDICIAL PROTECTION

The preliminary ruling system is also perceived as an aspect of the EU legal order's ability to deliver effective judicial protection of rights. The CJEU's restrictive standing test in the direct action procedure[140] has resulted in pressure on preliminary rulings to ensure a 'complete system of legal remedies and procedures designed to ensure judicial review of the legality of acts of the institutions'.[141] The preliminary reference procedure has also been considered by the European Court of Human Rights (the ECtHR) in assessing whether the EU system provides 'equivalence' of human rights protection to the Strasbourg system,[142] and the duration of preliminary reference proceedings has arisen, although it has not been scrutinized closely, before the ECtHR.[143] The CJEU's willingness to accept preliminary references challenging validity of EU measures in the absence of national implementing measures appears to have been motivated partially by the restrictions it, itself, has drawn around the availability of the direct action procedure.

The weight placed on preliminary rulings as a mechanism to review the lawfulness of Union law has been criticized by Advocate General Jacobs in *UPA*,[144] the General Court in *Jégo-Quéré*,[145] and others,[146] for a number of reasons, including that the national courts are not competent (as noted above) to declare EU law invalid;[147] the applicant has no right to decide whether a reference is made;[148] and it may be necessary for an applicant to breach the measures implementing EU law in order to challenge the resulting sanctions or in the absence of implementing measures, to breach EU law and then assert its illegality in proceedings against it—both of which are highly unsatisfactory.[149] The delays involved in challenging an EU measure via a preliminary ruling also undermine legal certainty.[150]

---

[139] Case C-388/07 *R (Incorporated Trustees of the National Council on Ageing (Age Concern England)) v Secretary of State for Business, Enterprise and Regulatory Reform* [2009] ECR I-1569.

[140] Case T-177/01 *Jégo-Quéré* [2002] ECR II-2365; Case C-50/00 *Unión d Pequeños Agricultores v Council* ('*UPA*') [2002] ECR I-6677, Opinion of AG Jacobs.

[141] *UPA* (n 140 above) [40].

[142] *Bosphorus Hava Yollari Turizm Ve Ticaret Anonim Sirketi v Ireland* (2006) 42 EHRR 1, [164] (the majority judgment of the court mischaracterized the preliminary ruling procedure as follows: 'The parties to the domestic proceedings have the right to put their case to the CJEU during the Art. 267 process').

[143] *Pafitis v Greece* (1999) 27 EHRR 566, [95].

[144] Note 140 above.   [145] ibid.

[146] See E Berry and S Boyes, 'Access to Justice in Community Courts: a Limited Right?' (2005) 24 CJQ 224.

[147] AG Jacobs, *UPA* (n 140 above) [41].   [148] ibid [42].

[149] *Jégo-Quéré* (n 140 above) [45]; AG Jacobs, *UPA* (n 140 above) [43]. See also L Heffernan, 'Effective Judicial Remedies: The Limits of Direct and Indirect Access to the European Community Courts' (2006) 5 LPICT 285, 288–289.

[150] AG Jacobs, *UPA* (n 140 above) [44].

Of course, it remains to be seen whether this particular pressure on the preliminary ruling process may be alleviated with the introduction of a new and more generous definition of standing in Article 263(4) TFEU (ex Article 230 EC, as amended). Nonetheless, at least while the parameters of Article 263(4) TFEU are explored in the case law, the preliminary reference procedure will remain pivotal to the EU's claim to provide effective judicial protection.

5. LEGALLY FEDERALIST/INTEGRATIONIST

What is understood here by a legally federalist or integrationist focus is tendencies in the preliminary reference procedure towards a classically federalist, vertical understanding of the relationship between the CJEU and national courts.[151] The deeply integrating impetus of preliminary rulings has been visible throughout this analysis: whether in the emerging hierarchy between the CJEU and the national courts; the discourse which seeks to encourage participation by Member States and national courts in CJEU law-making in a way which may, in turn, encourage compliance with the resultant EU norms; the incentives for national courts and interest groups to challenge national rules through using the preliminary ruling procedure; or the promotion of preliminary rulings as part of the EU's system of remedies. It may be argued that the integrationist focus is also evident in the favouring of preliminary references over direct actions,[152] as to a greater extent, the former procedure facilitates the repositioning of the CJEU vis-à-vis the national court.

To these integrating effects must also be added the doctrines of uniformity and effectiveness; in particular, concerns for uniformity weigh heavily in the CJEU's thinking on the preliminary ruling procedure.[153] The CJEU has explained on numerous occasions that the

> obligation to refer imposed by the third paragraph of Article 234 EC [now Article 267 TFEU] is based on cooperation, *established with a view to ensuring the proper application and uniform interpretation of [EU] law in all the Member States*, between national courts, in their capacity as courts responsible for the application of [EU] law, and the Court of Justice (see, inter alia, *Cilfit and Others*, paragraph 7, Case C-337/95 *Parfums Christian Dior* [1997] ECR I-6013, paragraph 25, and *Gomes Valente*, cited above, paragraph 17).[154]

---

[151] J H H Weiler, 'The Community System: the Dual Character of Supranationalism' (1981) 1 YEL 267 is a classic account of the development of legal or normative supranationalism.

[152] H Rasmussen, 'Why is Art 173 Interpreted against Private Plaintiffs?' (1980) 5 ELRev 112; see for a more nuanced view C Harding, 'The Private Interest in Challenging Community Action' (1981) 6 ELRev 354. See also the interesting analysis of access to justice problems in C Harlow, 'Towards a Theory of Access for the European Court of Justice' (1992) 12 YEL 213.

[153] There are many examples. For relatively recent illustrations, see eg Case C-495/03 *Intermodal Transports BV v Staatssecretaris van Financiën* [2005] ECR I-8151, [38]; Case C-458/06 *Skatteverket v Gourmet Classic Ltd* [2008] ECR I-4207, [23] and [32]; and *Pedro IV Servicios* (n 49 above) [32].

[154] *Intermodal Transports BV* (n 153 above) [38] (emphasis added).

Superficially, an integrationist focus demands maximum uniformity and thus maximum control through maximal valve settings, tempered only by pragmatic constraints. To a large extent this reflects the current reality. Whether it is the wide definition of 'court or tribunal', the broad approach taken to substantive referability, or the minimum control on the content of references, the result is maximum referral and thus in theory maximum central control and uniformity. Indeed, it has been argued persuasively that in the case of *CILFIT*, the intention was actually to spur, rather than deter references.[155] As will be explored further below however, if legal integration is the CJEU's objective, its emphasis on uniformity and maximal 'reference potential' may prove to be counter-productive.

E. CONSEQUENCES OF THE CURRENT SCHEME OF PRELIMINARY RULINGS

As was shown in Part C of this chapter, the 'valve' factor in the preliminary ruling mechanism has been set at maximal through the actions of the CJEU and national courts. Part D then explored the multiple functional demands placed on the preliminary ruling process within the EU project. This maximizing of the 'valve' factor and over-tasking of the process has created a number of notable consequences. The primary and most-discussed consequence has been in respect of the CJEU's docket, and in recent years, docket reform has been at the core of commentary and thinking about the CJEU. Delays in dealing with preliminary references have even required the indulgence of the ECtHR in not counting the period taken to obtain a ruling in calculating whether there has been an unreasonable delay in proceedings in breach of Article 6(1) of the European Convention on Human Rights.[156] Delays are not, however, the only challenge created by an overburdened docket. Two further consequences must be considered, namely, the impact of the current situation on the continued effective functioning of the preliminary ruling procedure, and how the CJEU's concern for uniformity and effectiveness of EU law, which, as has been noted, underpins its approach to preliminary rulings, reflects on the nature of EU law more generally.

1. DEALING WITH THE DOCKET

Over the years, the range of reform proposals that has been made has been diverse, ranging from: constraining the ability of lower national courts to make a reference;[157] introducing a filtering or certiorari mechanism based on the complexity or importance of the question, thereby enabling the CJEU 'to concentrate wholly upon questions

---

[155] See H Rasmussen, 'The European Court's acte clair Strategy in CILFIT' (1984) 9 ELRev 242.

[156] *Pafitis* (n 143) [95].

[157] J Komárek, 'In the Court(s) We Trust? On the Need for Hierarchy and Differentiation in the Preliminary Ruling Procedure' (2007) 32 ELRev 467, 471; A Arnull, 'Judicial Architecture or Judicial Folly? The Challenge Facing the European Union' (1999) 24 ELRev 516.

which are fundamental from the point of view of the uniformity and development of Community law';[158] encouraging national courts to provide suggested answers to the questions;[159] introduction of an appellate regime;[160] creation of decentralized specialist preliminary reference tribunals;[161] and enhancing the role of the General Court.

Of the reforms that have been adopted, what has been striking is that most of the measures have focused primarily upon expediting procedures before the CJEU, rather than entrusting greater discretion to national courts or the General Court. While Article 256(3) TFEU—as did Article 225(1) EC—accords jurisdiction to the General Court to give preliminary rulings in specific areas set down by Statute, this provision has not been implemented. Meanwhile, the option of entrusting the national courts with application of EU law to a greater extent appears to have been expressly rejected. For example, the Due Report in January 2000 before Nice IGC proposed that the *acte clair* doctrine be revised slightly and incorporated into the Treaty text; yet the report of the CJEU and the General Court, which followed, on the future judicial architecture of the EU did not discuss this option.[162] Instead, the types of measures adopted have focused on CJEU procedures, such as increased recourse to chambers;[163] issuing of practice directions;[164] dispensing with oral hearings in certain cases;[165] and drawing up of timetables for preliminary references.[166] Expedition of procedures has been central: whether through Article 20 of the Statute, the simplified procedure; the accelerated procedure pursuant to Article 104a of the Statute;[167] or the urgent procedure pursuant to Article 104b of the Statute. For example, according to Article 20 of the Statute, the Court may determine cases without an Opinion of the Advocate General where they do not raise any new point of law. As shown in Table 13.6 and Figure 13.6 (which refer to all judgments and not just preliminary rulings), in 2007, 43 per cent of the CJEU's judgments were delivered without an Opinion, while in 2008, the figure was 41 per cent.

Pursuant to Article 104(3)—the simplified procedure—a reasoned order can be used where

---

[158] The European Court of Justice and the Court of First Instance, *The Future of the Judicial System of the European Union (Proposals and Reflections)* (May 1999) 25; *Wiener* (n 67 above) AG Jacobs. See also L Heffernan, 'Reform of the Community Courts Post-Nice: A European *Certiorari* Revisited' (2003) 52 ICLQ 907.

[159] *The Future of the Judicial System* (n 158 above) 25–26; *Report by the Working Party on the Future of the European Communities' Court System* ('the Due Report'), 18 January 2000.

[160] *The Future of the Judicial System* (n 158 above) 26.

[161] J P Jacqué and J Weiler, 'On the Road to European Union—a New Judicial Architecture: An Agenda for the Intergovernmental Conference' (1990) 27 CML Rev 185.

[162] See n 158 above.

[163] See also generally Heffernan (n 149 above) 297; F G Jacobs, 'Recent and Ongoing Measures to Improve the Efficiency of the European Court of Justice' (2004) 29 ELRev 823; A Johnston, 'Judicial Reform and the Treaty of Nice' (2001) 38 CML Rev 499.

[164] Rules of Procedure, Art 125a.

[165] Rules of Procedure, Art 104(3).

[166] Jacobs (n 163 above) 829–830.

[167] For commentary, see E B de la Serre, 'Accelerated and Expedited Procedures before the EC Courts: A Review of the Practice' (2006) 43 CML Rev 783.

[a] question referred to the Court for a preliminary ruling is identical to a question on which the Court has already ruled, where the answer to such a question may be clearly deduced from existing case-law or where the answer to the question admits of no reasonable doubt.[168]

Table 13.7 and Figure 13.7 indicate that use of the simplified procedure has fluctuated; however, it reached its highest point in 2008, accounting for 13 per cent of the total number of preliminary rulings given.

Article 104a, which came into force in 2000, deals with the accelerated procedure,[169] the request for which must be made by the national court, followed by a decision of the President of the CJEU on whether the case is a matter of 'exceptional urgency'. Once a decision has been made that the accelerated procedure is appropriate, a case can be dealt with in a matter of weeks.[170] Gaining access to the accelerated procedure has, however, been very difficult,[171] and it only seems to be available where important human rights are at risk.[172] Meanwhile, the urgent procedure was established by Article 104b, and was made available where the reference raised queries pursuant to Title VI of the EU Treaty or Title IV of Part Three of the EC Treaty[173]—this provision for urgency is now reflected in the text of the Article 267 TFEU itself. A number of decisions have been taken pursuant to this mechanism,[174] with the time taken extremely short.[175]

Although there have therefore been significant reforms aimed at controlling docket pressures, it is not clear that these reforms will be adequate after the Lisbon Treaty expansion in availability of preliminary references. Additionally, as noted above, and as is evident from Table 13.2, the new Member States could be considered to be going through a 'familiarization' process at present; the extent of any increase in the rate of their usage of the preliminary ruling procedure is uncertain. Other challenges that are raising concerns include the Services Directive, described as a 'case-monger';[176] while of course the Charter of Fundamental Rights may also require extensive elucidation through references for preliminary rulings.

2. THE EFFECTIVE FUNCTIONING OF THE PRELIMINARY RULING PROCEDURE

In the previous edition of this book, the concern was raised that failure to reduce the docket may have a worse effect than lack of uniformity, either through diluting

---

[168] This was introduced in its current form in July 2000.

[169] Amendments of the Rules of Procedure (ROP) of the CJ ([2000] OJ L122 43) entered into force on 1 July 2000.

[170] See eg Case C-189/01 *Jippes and Others* [2001] ECR I-5689.

[171] For discussion, see N Cambien, 'Case C-127/08 *Blaise Baheten Metock and Others v Minister for Justice, Equality and Law Reform*' (2009) 15 CJEL 321.

[172] Case C-127/08 *Order of the President of the Court*, CJEU, 17 April 2008, [16].

[173] See C Kumar, 'A Fast-track to Europe: The Urgent Procedure for Preliminary Rulings' (2008) IFL 180.

[174] Case C-195/08 PPU *Inga Rinau* [2008] ECR I-5271; Case C-296/08 PPU *Goicoechea*, [2008] ECR I-6307.

[175] ibid *Inga Rinau* (two months); *Goicoechea* (six weeks).

[176] H Rasmussen, 'Present and Future European Judicial Problems after Enlargement and the Post-2005 Ideological Revolt' (2007) 44 CML Rev 1661.

or degrading the manner in which each case is handled[177] or by increasing the damage caused by delay. As has been demonstrated by the revised UK guidance on when to exercise discretion to make a preliminary ruling,[178] the question of delay also affects the approach of national courts in deciding whether to refer questions to the CJEU.

Aside from the concerns about delay highlighted above, with regard to the CJEU's responses to preliminary rulings, there are signs that other problems may be emerging. Attention has been drawn by commentators to the increasingly 'magisterial' reasoning of the CJEU,[179] to failures to deal adequately with arguments opposing the position adopted by the Court (which has the further consequence of undermining the important preliminary ruling discourse),[180] and to failures to always fully explain conclusions.[181] One apparently particularly dissatisfied national judge has commented that '[d]iscerning shifts of emphasis in successive decisions of the [CJEU] sometimes resembles the finer points of Kremlinology at the height of the Cold War'.[182]

A number of regrettable examples present themselves. In the notable case of *O'Byrne v Aventis Pasteur*,[183] the House of Lords could not find it 'beyond doubt'[184] that a particular interpretation of the Product Liability Directive had been intended by the CJEU's answer to a preliminary reference. It was concluded, therefore, that a second reference was required, even though this was 'particularly unfortunate for the claimant in this case, who has been trying for over seven years to litigate the question of whether he is entitled to any compensation'.[185] This experience has even been repeated recently in *Test Claimants in the FII Litigation v HMRC*,[186] in which the Court of Appeal decided to refer an issue back to the CJEU so that it could clarify a ruling given on an earlier reference in the same proceedings. At first instance, Henderson J observed that he could not 'escape the impression that at this critical point the CJEU must have misunderstood the argument being advanced for the UK government'.[187] Although a majority of the Court of Appeal did not share this analysis, there was sufficient doubt to persuade the Court to make a second reference. It is not just in UK courts that concerns have arisen: in Case *X Holdings BV v Staatssecretaris van Financiën*[188] when the reference went back to the Netherlands

---

[177] See Jacqué and Weiler (n 161 above).

[178] See text to nn 65–68 above. See also *Portman Agrochemicals* (n 92 above); and see *ex p Else* (n 64 above). Some delay is attributable to national procedures: see D Vaughan, 'The Advocate's View' in M Andenas (n 87 above) 55 for an account of recent UK procedural reforms designed to eliminate such delays.

[179] Bobek (n 39 above) 1639.

[180] Komárek (n 157 above) 482–483.

[181] Bobek (n 39 above) 1640.

[182] *Livewire Telecom Ltd v Revenue and Customs Commissioners* [2009] EWHC 15 (Ch), [40] (Lewison J).

[183] [2008] UKHL 34, [2008] 3 CMLR 10.

[184] ibid [27].   [185] ibid [21].

[186] [2010] EWCA Civ 103.   [187] [2008] EWHC 2893 (Ch) [59].

[188] C-337/08, 25 February 2010, CJEU; discussed in 'What if the ECJ Gets National Law Wrong?' (2010) 9 H&I 28.

referring court, the Advocate General in the Hoge Raad indicated that the CJEU had misunderstood the applicable Netherlands law.

While well-drafted and well-reasoned responses to preliminary references are always imperative, the need for such responses will arguably become even more acute with the Lisbon reforms, as the issues involved (for example, criminal law and asylum) will 'intrude regularly into areas of acute national sensitivity'.[189] These 'extreme examples'[190] of unsatisfactory responses to preliminary references cannot become more prevalent if engagement with the preliminary ruling procedure is to be sustained.

3. THE EU LEGAL ORDER

Insofar as preliminary rulings provide a perspective on EU legal integration, the current state of the preliminary ruling procedure reflects a certain stasis on the part of EU law—perhaps unsurprising from a general perspective, in an era in which a Constitutional Treaty was rejected and institutional reform ratified with difficulty. Specific to the preliminary ruling procedure, the CJEU's emphasis on the function of preliminary rulings as a mechanism to ensure uniformity in the application of EU law is strong.[191] While the CJEU's emphasis on maximum uniformity through the preliminary ruling procedure superficially promotes legal integration, at a deeper level, it has the potential to undermine legal integration in a number of ways.

First, the CJEU's continued insistence on accepting references undermines the role of national courts as a network of EU courts; the condition so far for their participation has been strict oversight by the CJEU. In the first edition of this book, it was suggested that with greater maturity of the EU legal order, there may well follow scope for greater off-loading of judicial work without the same degree of oversight. However, national EU courts continue to be handled with a degree of what one might call 'supremacist supervision'; in blunt terms, national courts may not have been fully trusted properly to implement EU law. In the past such a stance may have been justified given rumbling supremacy worries, or fear of bad faith or 'rebellion', which did arise on occasion. Now however, the greatest factor in the CJEU's close supervision appears to be a fear of error on the part of national courts. Without doubt, national courts make mistakes; however, it does not seem that the solution to this is for the CJEU, itself, to attempt to eliminate every possibility of error. Nonetheless, the CJEU's attachment to the goal of total uniformity still seems to be relatively absolute and that this goal underpins the preliminary reference procedure is never questioned.[192]

Secondly, the CJEU's attachment to uniformity runs strongly against any claim that may be made by the EU to be evolving into a more mature legal order. In any developed legal system a play-off is always made between the urge for uniformity

---

[189] Chalmers, 'The Dynamics of Judicial Authority and the Constitutional Treaty', Jean Monnet Working Paper, 5/04.

[190] Bobek (n 39 above) 1640.   [191] eg, *Pedro IV Servicios* (n 49 above) [32].

[192] See cases in n 153 above.

and competing desires for legal certainty, speed, pragmatic delegation, and exercise of authority.

To illustrate the point anecdotally: it is a fairly common experience in any case-law system for differing strands of reasoning and precedent on one legal issue to co-exist and interact, even conflict, without there necessarily being an immediate or even any ultimate decision that reconciles them. A variety of incomplete internal controls exist, such as appeal, re-litigation with different parties, legislation and so on to attempt to control such flaws; but their existence is taken as read. The imperfection of such a system is the inevitable consequence of an appellate system with limited resources which takes decisions in an acceptable amount of time.

To illustrate the point by more concrete comparison, for US federal courts, the need for uniformity in the application of federal law—although articulated on occasion[193]— has never really succeeded in gaining predominance[194] and is now, perhaps more than ever, generally considered unappealing.[195] In *United States v Kimbell Foods*[196] the Supreme Court deemed application of a federal rule unnecessary where there had been mere 'generalized pleas for uniformity', which did not provide 'concrete evidence that adopting state law would adversely affect administration of the federal programs'.[197] US federal courts have exhibited a preference for 'synergistic, symbiotic, and dynamic interaction' with states.[198]

Thus, while superficially, an emphasis on uniformity may promote integration, there has been increasing concern that the CJEU's attachment to uniformity is not facilitating, but rather jeopardizing and undermining legal integration.[199] To explain, it has become of increasing concern that preliminary rulings 'symbolize and embody the alienation of the [EU's] legal system from the national legal systems'; they constitute, as Allott suggested, 'another infant disease' of EU law, alongside direct effect.[200] While uniformity is 'mostly taken for granted' in national legal systems— even if this is not always the case—the CJEU is still fighting for these presumptions to be applied to EU law.[201] It has also been noted that the CJEU's core concern is not always uniformity, but:

---

[193] *Martin v Hunter's Lessee* 14 US (1 Wheat) 304, 348 (1816).

[194] P R Dubinsky, 'The Essential Function of Federal Courts: The European Union and the United States Compared' (1994) 42 AJCL 295, 324.

[195] P J Weiser, 'Federal Common Law, Cooperative Federalism, and the Enforcement of the Telecom Act' (2001) 76 NYUL Rev 1692, 1706.

[196] 440 US 715 (1979).

[197] ibid 730.

[198] M H Redish, 'Reassessing the Allocation of Judicial Business between State and Federal Courts: Federal Jurisdiction and "the Martian Chronicles"' (1992) 78 Va L Rev 1769, 1773. See also S D O'Connor, 'Proceedings of the Middle Atlantic State-Federal Judicial Relationships Conference' (1994) 162 Fed Rules Dec 173, 181–182.

[199] See eg Chalmers (n 189 above).

[200] P Allott, 'Preliminary Rulings—Another Infant Disease' (2000) 25 ELRev 538, 542.

[201] Komárek (n 157 above) 471.

[t]he Court rather fears that EU law would not be applied at all. The strong (and unrealistic) strive for uniformity serves as a justification for the Court of Justice's involvement in cases of minor importance for EU legal order as a whole, where an ordinary supreme court in a mature system of law would never intervene.[202]

The *Köbler* judgment illustrates effectively the CJEU's unwillingness to trust national courts with the application of EU law.

Despite alternative perspectives on the relevance of uniformity,[203] the CJEU has persisted with this account of the role of the preliminary ruling procedure. Of course, the CJEU's eagerness to encourage engagement with national courts is understandable to some extent: there are still Member State courts that demonstrate reluctance to make preliminary references at all.[204] However, as can been seen from Table 13.2, at this stage in the evolution of the EU, most Member State courts are now engaging actively with the CJEU. Ultimately, therefore, if there is to be evolution, the compromise between legal certainty and substantive justice visible in national law is one that has to replicated with the same conviction at the EU level; as yet, the balance seems to be heavily in favour of determination of the substantive point by the CJEU— also at the expense of the General Court however unpalatable the consequences.

F. EVOLVING OUT OF STASIS

All the reforms to the preliminary ruling procedure have been entirely directed at *managing* the volume of references, rather than *curtailing* the number of references received. While generally welcomed, it is not clear that the reforms will adequately address the docket problem. It is also not apparent that the reforms will promote the important interest of fully-reasoned responses to preliminary rulings: the increasing recourse to dispensing with an Advocate General's opinion, for example, detracts from the deliberative nature of the process. What has been eschewed is any attempt to indicate what type of question is appropriately referred to the CJEU; rather the CJEU prefers to invoke the need for legal uniformity to answer all questions itself. What is needed are mechanisms to filter the referral of questions such that those questions that genuinely require the assistance of the CJEU are addressed by the CJEU, while those questions which have already been answered in repeat referrals or which are on the margin of the CJEU's jurisdiction are resolved through other means.

The decision of the CJEU to attempt to answer all questions itself is revealing of a dilemma that goes beyond the preliminary ruling procedure. Despite significant

---

[202] ibid 472.

[203] See more generally M Dougan, *National Remedies before the Court of Justice: Issues of Harmonisation and Differentiation* (Hart, 2004).

[204] See discussion in E Fahey, *Practice and Procedure in Preliminary References in Europe: 30 Years of Article 234 E C Caselaw from the Irish Courts* (Firstlaw, 2007), 142–143 (noting in 2007 that Irish 'lower courts have yet to begin a sustained dialogue with the Court of Justice of any kind').

institutional reform in the Lisbon Treaty, evolution to something more akin to a system of a federal court, as has been proposed in the past by Jacqué and Weiler amongst others,[205] has not been pursued by the Member States, and given the difficulties of ratifying the Lisbon Treaty, Treaty reform of the preliminary ruling procedure is unlikely to be on the agenda for quite some time. When the opportunity for institutional reform arises again, it may be that radical innovations are necessary, such as, for example, mechanisms to involve Advocates General (or some equivalent office providing expert EU law input on an *amicus* basis) in *national* proceedings, thereby obviating the need for references where unnecessary and forcing or at least encouraging references where necessary. Perhaps modified versions of the reference procedures currently used by the Commission in the context of state aid and competition law could be adopted:[206] these procedures produce results relatively quickly and while not legally binding on the national court (which can still opt to make a reference to the CJEU), they do provide useful assistance for the national court. Rather than allowing for a referral to the Commission, it may be that a referral could be made to an Advocate General, for a speedy response, which would assist the national court in either resolving the matter itself or determining whether to seek a preliminary ruling.

However, even without institutional reform—and in the absence of any move to sharing the burden with the General Court—there are options available to the CJEU to reduce the number of cases, such as refusing jurisdiction in marginal cases, including renvoi; or more importantly trusting national courts to a greater extent, by giving them clear guidance on the appropriateness of making a reference.[207] It might be argued that giving guidance on the appropriateness of references would also have some (though lesser) federal implications, by entrenching the CJEU's position as being at the apex of an EU hierarchy of courts. However, after the dramatic re-positioning of itself entailed in *Köbler*, it has to be highly doubtful whether more robust control of its docket would make a significant further impact on the CJEU's position vis-à-vis the national courts. Moreover, this concern could be addressed by asking the national courts to apply an EU interest filter, which could be set out and explained in a CJEU Practice Direction. This should stress that references must be reserved for difficult and important points of EU law and address the interaction of reference and fact finding, reference and appeal, and reference and *acte clair*. Indeed, the criteria proposed by the English courts may be regarded as a reasonable and useful starting point.[208] Moreover, the danger in such an approach is limited; national courts already control the factors guiding the discretionary decision to refer with their own informal guidance cases.

---

[205] Jacqué and Weiler (n 161 above).

[206] See eg Commission notice on the enforcement of State aid law by national courts [2009] OJ C85/1, paras 89–98; Council Regulation (EC) No 1/2003 of 16 December 2002 on the implementation of the rules on competition laid down in Articles 81 and 82 of the Treaty (Text with EEA relevance) [2003] OJ L1/1, Art 15(1).

[207] See eg, T Kennedy, 'First steps towards a European certiorari' (1993) 18 ELRev 121.

[208] See text to nn 65–68.

Ultimately, the preliminary ruling procedure is very largely dependent upon the good faith of the referring court.

It is not denied that the CJEU's position is difficult: the contribution of national courts to expanding the pressure on preliminary rulings has been noted here and is significant; and national courts notice when requests for references are refused.[209] However, as long as such an absolute value is attached to uniformity with valve settings set to maximum as a result, the Court's docket will continue to grow. If ongoing stasis is to be avoided, our view is that—at least pending institutional reform of a structural nature going beyond measures expediting how references are handled within the CJEU and failing engagement with the General Court—the CJEU simply must modulate the reference valve. Wider structural reform in the medium term looks increasingly necessary if the CJEU is to remain both a persuasive and effective partner to national courts in the development of EU law in the challenges that are to come.

Table 13.1 Actions pending before the CJEU

Year	Direct Action	Appeal	Special	Opinion	Prelim Ref	Total	% Prelim Ref
1992	405	31	1	2	230	669	34.4
1993	109	36	3	1	240	389	61.7
1994	134	29	4	3	259	429	60.4
1995	148	58	3	0	299	508	58.9
1996	166	59	5	0	382	612	62.4
1997[1]	225	61	2	0	395	683	57.8
1998	236	95	4	0	413	748	55.2
1999	309	110	1	0	476	896	53.1
2000	326	111	2	2	432	873	49.5
2001	334	120	1	1	487	943	51.6
2002	323	117	5	0	462	907	50.9
2003	407	121	6	1	439	974	45.1
2004	327	85	1	1	426	840	50.7
2005	243	102	1	1	393	740	53.1
2006	232	120	1	0	378	731	51.7
2007	213	117	4	0	408	742	55.1
2008	242	126	4	1	395	768	51.5
2009	170	128	4	1	395	741	53.3

[1] The figures for 1997 onwards are gross, ie they represent the total number of cases, without account being taken of the joinder of cases on the grounds of similarity.

[209] Bobek (n 39 above) 161–169, discussing the response of the Czech Supreme Court to *Ynos* (n 39 above).

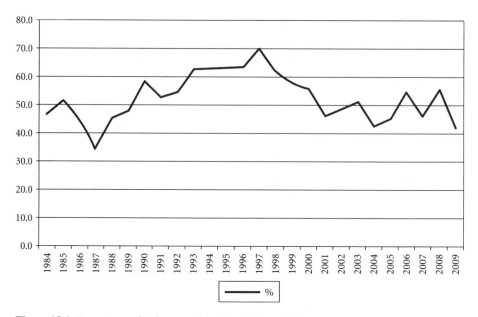

Figure 13.1 Percentage of Judgments from Preliminary References

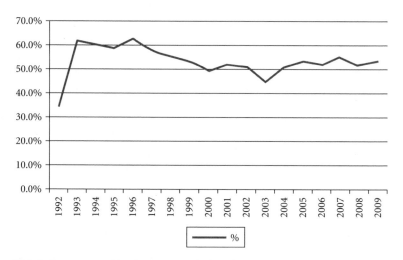

Figure 13.1.1 Percentage of Pending Actions before the CJEU that are Preliminary References

Table 13.2 Preliminary References per year per Member State

YEAR	BE	BG	CZ	DK	DE	EE	EL	ES	FR	IRL	IT	CY	LV	LT	LU	HU	MT	NL	AT	PL	PT	RO	SI	SK	FI	SE	UK	Total	MS Av
1973	8			0	37				4	0	5				1			6									0	61	**6.8**
1974	5			0	15				6	0	5				0			7									1	39	**4.3**
1975	7			1	26				15	0	14				1			4									1	69	**7.7**
1976	11			0	28				8	1	12				0			14									1	75	**8.3**
1977	16			1	30				14	2	7				0			9									5	84	**9.3**
1978	7			3	46				12	1	11				0			38									5	123	**13.7**
1979	13			1	33				18	2	19				1			11									8	106	**11.8**
1980	14			2	24				14	3	19				0			17									6	99	**11.0**
1981	12			1	41		0		17	0	11				4			17									5	108	**10.8**
1982	10			1	36		0		39	0	18				0			21									4	129	**12.9**
1983	9			4	36		0		15	2	7				0			19									6	98	**9.8**
1984	13			2	38		0		34	1	10				0			22									9	129	**12.9**
1985	13			0	40		0		45	2	11				6			14									8	139	**13.9**
1986	13			4	18		2	1	19	4	5				1			16									8	91	**7.6**
1987	15			5	32		17	1	36	2	5				3			19									9	144	**12.0**
1988	30			4	34		0	1	38	0	28				2			26									16	179	**14.9**
1989	13			2	47		2	2	28	1	10				1			18			1						14	139	**11.6**
1990	17			5	34		2	6	21	4	25				4			9			2						12	141	**11.8**
1991	19			2	54		3	5	29	2	36				2			17			3						14	186	**15.5**
1992	16			3	62		1	5	15	0	22				1			18			1						18	162	**13.5**

(*continued*)

Year																								n	%
1993	22		7		57		5	7	22	1	24					1	43						3	12	204	**17.0**
1994	19		4		44		0	13	36	2	46					1	13						1	24	203	**16.9**
1995	14		8		51		10	10	43	3	58					2	19	2	5			6		20	251	**16.7**
1996	30		4		66		4	6	24	0	70					2	10	6	6		3	4		21	256	**17.1**
1997	19		7		46		2	9	10	1	50					3	24	35	2		6	7		18	239	**15.9**
1998	12		7		49		5	55	16	3	39					2	21	16	7		2	6		24	264	**17.6**
1999	13		3		49		3	4	17	2	43					4	23	56	7		4	5		22	255	**17.0**
2000	15		3		47		3	5	12	2	50					0	12	31	8		5	4		26	224²	**14.9**
2001	10		5		53		4	4	15	1	40					2	14	57	4		3	4		21	237	**15.8**
2002	18		8		59		7	3	8	0	37					4	12	31	3		7	5		14	216	**14.4**
2003	18		3		43		4	8	9	2	45					4	28	15	1		4	4		22	210	**14.0**
2004	24		4		50		18	8	21	1	48				1	2	28	12	1		4	5		22	249	**10.0**
2005	21	1	4		51		11	10	17	2	18				2	3	36	15	2		4	11		12	221	**8.8**
2006	17		3		77		14	17	24	1	34			1	1	4	20	12	3		5	2		10	251	**10.0**
2007	22	1	2		59	2	8	14	26	2	43			1	0	2	19	20	7	1	5	6		16	265	**9.8**
2008	24	1	6		71	2	9	17	12	1	39			3	3	4	34	25	3		4	7		14	288	**10.7**
2009	35	8	5	3	59	2	11	11	28		29	1	4	3	3	10	24	15	10	3	2	5		28	301	**11.6**

² One reference was from Benelux, Case C-265/00 *Campina Melkuine*.

Figure 13.2 Three yearly Rate of Reference by Member State.

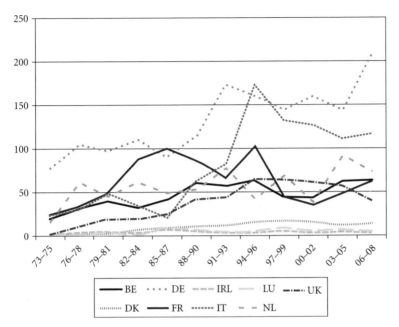

Figure 13.2.1 1973–2008 (Belgium, Denmark, Germany, France, Ireland, Italy, Luxembourg, The Netherlands, United Kingdom)

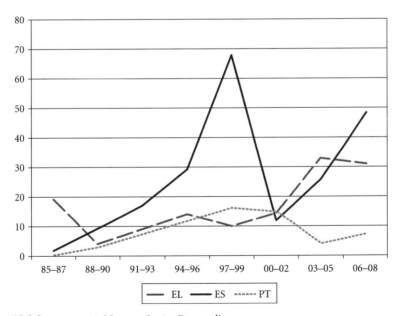

Figure 13.2.2 1986–2008 (Greece, Spain, Portugal)

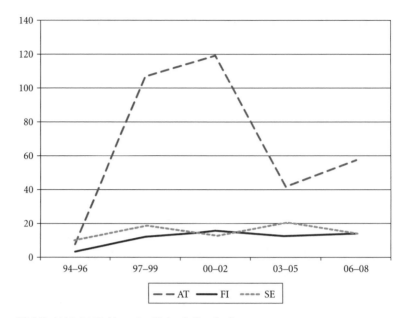

Figure 13.2.3 1995–2008 (Austria, Finland, Sweden)

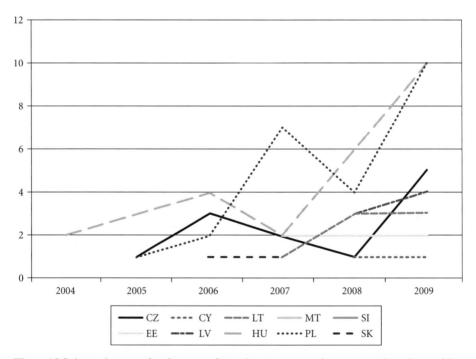

Figure 13.2.4 Yearly Rate of References of Member States Acceding in 2004 (Czech Republic, Estonia, Cyprus, Latvia, Lithuania, Hungary, Malta, Poland, Slovenia, Slovakia)

Table 13.3.1 Percentage of big four Member State Observations in References from that same Member State

Year	FRANCE	GERMANY	ITALY	UK
73-75	52.9	27.9	73.3	100.0
76-78	33.3	25.3	75.0	55.6
79-81	61.8	23.6	82.8	73.3
82-84	50.0	27.0	81.8	84.6
84-87	59.0	13.3	85.7	72.0
88-90	80.5	24.3	54.0	90.5
91-93	63.6	48.0	67.1	97.7
94-96	90.3	54.7	44.8	92.3
97-99	75.3	55.6	92.5	100.0
00-02	90.7	41.9	57.4	89.0
03-05	100.0	59.3	69.3	88.3
06-08	96.3	62.4	78.3	85.1

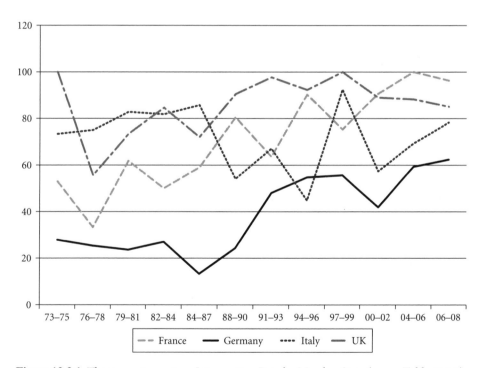

Figure 13.3.1 Three year percentage Intervention Rate by Member State (as per Table 13.3.1)

Table 13.4.1 Number of Observations by the Big Four in other Member States' References

Year	FRANCE	GERMANY	ITALY	UK
1973	1	2	2	4
1974	1	5	5	7
1975	1	0	11	0
1976	5	4	6	12
1977	1	2	4	6
1978	1	2	7	9
1979	3	3	8	5
1980	7	6	6	13
1981	9	5	5	10
1982	15	2	11	14
1983	7	2	8	6
1984	7	6	19	14
1985	3	3	11	10
1986	9	9	17	19
1987	8	7	17	22
1988	7	6	16	22
1989	9	8	13	32
1990	10	9	8	21
1991	5	22	12	20
1992	7	18	9	26
1993	28	23	10	35
1994	42	19	14	42
1995	50	18	21	32
1996	60	26	10	43
1997	22	13	11	30
1998	57	14	11	39
1999	39	17	13	32
2000	52	20	21	32
2001	40	19	12	26
2002	19	13	8	21
2003	31	15	29	36
2004	29	12	22	34
2005	29	22	10	21
2006	28	27	33	40
2007	30	20	48	40
2008	15	19	76	41

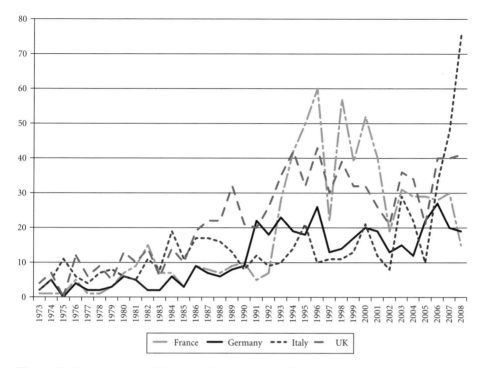

Figure 13.4.1 Percentage of Big Four Member State's Observations in other Member State's References

Table 13.4.2 Percentage of larger 2004 Accession Member State Observations in References from that same Member State

Year	Hungary	Czech Republic	Poland
2006	100%		
2007	100%	100%	100%
2008	100%		100%

Table 13.4.3 Number of Observations by Larger 2004 Accession Member States in other Member States' References

Year	Hungary	Czech Republic	Poland
2006	5	10	22
2007	2	9	22
2008	4	11	32

Table 13.5 Interest Group References[3]

Year	Case No.	Party	Status	Type of Action
1986	C-77/86	National Dried Fruit Trade Association	A	JR
1987	C-266/87	Association of Pharmaceutical Importers	A	JR
1988	C-301/88	Fish Producers' Organisation Ltd	A	JR
		Grimsby Fish Producers' Organisation Ltd	A	
1988	C-331/88	FEDESA	A	JR
1991	C-9/91	EOC	A	JR
1991	C-328/91	EOC	A	SSA
1994	C-38/94	Country Landowners Association	A	JR
1994	C-44/94	Federation of Highlands and Islands	A	JR
		Fishermen	A	
		National Federation of Fishermen's Organisations		
1995	C-44/95	RSPB	A	JR
1995	C-354/95	National Farmers Union	A	JR
1996	C-1/96	RSPCA	A	JR
		Compassion in World Farming	A	
1996	C-4/96	Northern Irish Fish Producer's Organisation Ltd	A	Other
		Northern Ireland Fishermen's Federation	A	
1996	C-82/96	The Consumers' Association	A	JR
		Which(?) Ltd	A	
1996	C-100/96	British Agrochemicals Association Ltd	A	JR
1996	C-157/96	National Farmers Union	A	JR
		British Association of Sheep Exporters	IP	
1999	C-173/99	Broadcasting, Entertainment, Cinematographic and Theatre Union (BECTU)	A	JR
2003	C-535/03	North Sea Fishermen's Organisation	A	JR
2004	C-344/04	International Air Transport Association	A	JR
		European Low Fares Airline Association	A	
2004	C-388/04	South Western Fish Producers' Organisation Ltd		
2007	C-388/07	The Incorporated Trustees of the National Council for Ageing (Age Concern England)	A	JR

[3] A = action, IP = intervening party, JR = judicial review, SSA = social security appeal.

Table 13.6 Determination of Cases without an Opinion of an Advocate General

YEAR	Percentage of Judgments Issued without an Advocate Generals Opinion
2004	30%
2005	35%
2006	33%
2007	43%
2008	41%

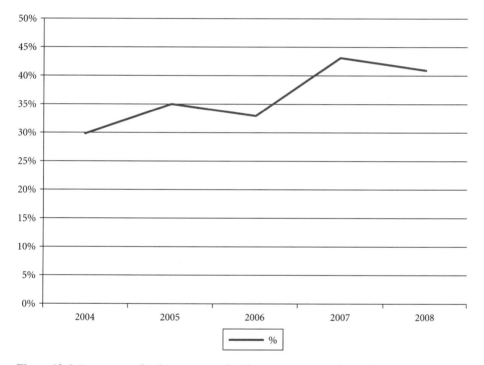

Figure 13.6 Percentage of Judgments issued without an Opinion of an Advocate General

Table 13.7 Use of simplified Procedure in Preliminary Reference Judgments

Year	Total preliminary reference judgments[d]	Number of simplified procedure	% simplified procedure
2001	182	12	6.6%
2002	241	12	5%
2003	233	11	4.7%
2004	262	22	8.4%
2005	254	29	11.4%
2006	266	21	7.9%
2007	235	18	7.7%
2008	301	39	13%

[d] These figures represent the total gross number of cases, ie the total number of cases, without account being taken of the joinder of cases on the grounds of similarity. Percentages of cases using the simplified procedure are calculated on the basis of these gross totals.

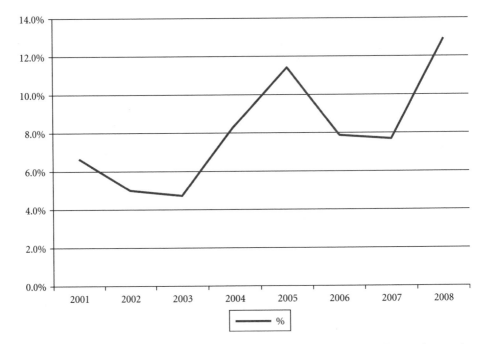

Figure 13.7 Percentage of Preliminary References using the simplified Procedure under Article 104(3) of the Rules of Procedure

14

THE VICISSITUDES OF LIFE AT THE COALFACE: REMEDIES AND PROCEDURES FOR ENFORCING UNION LAW BEFORE THE NATIONAL COURTS

*Michael Dougan**

A. INTRODUCTION

This chapter deals with the evolution of Community (now Union) law concerning the national remedies and procedural rules involved in the decentralized enforcement of rights and obligations derived from the Treaties.[1] Since readers can already find excellent accounts of the development of the relevant jurisprudence elsewhere in the literature,[2] this contribution seeks to offer something a little different, by combining its exposition of the essential case law with certain observations about how one might read the accompanying scholarship on effective judicial protection.

Part B will explain how the scholarship has constructed a 'core narrative' which (first) describes the basic challenge posed by national remedies and procedural rules, to the effective and uniform application of Union law within the Member States; (secondly) identifies the framework of principles involved in addressing

* Liverpool Law School. I am very grateful to participants at the EUI *Evolution of EU Law* conference in April 2009 for their comments. I am also indebted to Eleanor Spaventa, Paul Craig, and Gráinne de Búrca for their invaluable suggestions.

[1] We are here referring to 'Community law' as previously contained in the EC Treaty; and to 'Union law' as now contained primarily (though not exclusively) in the TFEU.

[2] See eg R Craufurd Smith, 'Remedies for Breaches of EU Law in National Courts: Legal Variation and Selection' in P Craig and G de Búrca (eds), *The Evolution of EU Law* (Oxford University Press, 1999); P Craig and G de Búrca, *EU Law: Text, Cases & Materials* (4th edn, Oxford University Press, 2007) ch 9.

that challenge, based on the twin requirements of equivalence and effectiveness originally established by the Court of Justice in *Rewe* and *Comet*;[3] and (thirdly) articulates a common understanding of how the relevant case law has developed over time, based on a division of the jurisprudence into three main periods, characterized initially by severe judicial restraint, followed by robust judicial activism, and finally giving way to a more judicious balancing of competing interests. Part C will then highlight how that 'core narrative'—whatever its many strengths—does not represent the whole story of the interaction between Union law and national remedies and procedural rules. The case law continues to identify and explore new facets to the *Rewe/Comet* jurisprudence—though these often bear little relationship to the original concerns about effectiveness and uniformity associated with the core scholarly narrative. Moreover, a fuller understanding of this field requires us to consider certain additional principles recognized by the Court, various conceptual knots which remain unresolved in the case law and literature, and the growing importance of the contribution made by the Union legislature. Part D will conclude by suggesting that this branch of Union law, once possessed of a central organizing model of analysis and an accepted linear explanation for the evolution of the case law, has now grown into a much more disparate legal framework.

B. THE 'CORE NARRATIVE' ON NATIONAL REMEDIES

By the mid-1990s, two decades of scholarship had produced an identifiable academic consensus on the analytical framework through which to examine the interaction between Community law and the domestic systems of judicial protection.[4] That 'core narrative', which remains the touchstone for both an historical understanding and any contemporary analysis of national remedies under Community/Union law, is constructed from three main elements: first, the proposition that Member State remedies and procedural rules pose a challenge to the effectiveness and uniform application of the Treaty; secondly, the establishment by the Court of Justice of a basic doctrinal formula for addressing that challenge in its 1976 *Rewe* and *Comet* rulings; and thirdly, the manner in which the detailed application and implications of that formula have unfolded over three relatively distinct periods of time.

---

[3] Case 33/76 *Rewe-Zentralfinanz v Landwirtschaftskammer für das Saarland* [1976] ECR 1989; Case 45/76 *Comet BV v Produktschap voor Siergewassen* [1976] ECR 2043.

[4] See, further, M Dougan, *National Remedies Before the Court of Justice: Issues of Harmonisation and Differentiation* (Hart, 2004); T Tridimas, *The General Principles of EC Law* (2nd edn, Oxford University Press, 2006); A Ward, *Individual Rights and Private Party Judicial Review in the EU* (2nd edn, Oxford University Press, 2007). Also: J Lonbay and A Biondi (eds), *Remedies for Breach of EC Law* (Wiley, 1997); C Kilpatrick, T Novitz, and P Skidmore (eds), *The Future of Remedies in Europe* (Hart, 2000).

1. SECURING THE EFFECTIVENESS AND UNIFORMITY OF COMMUNITY/UNION LAW

In certain situations, it is possible that specific national remedies and procedural rules may fall directly within the scope of application of the primary Treaty provisions in fields such as free movement[5] or competition law.[6] But cases where the domestic systems of judicial protection are found, in themselves and autonomously, to be incompatible with substantive Union policies are relatively uncommon.[7] Of far greater importance are the 'second order' issues which arise from the general role performed by national remedies and procedural rules in the system for enforcing Union law within the Member States.

De Witte's chapter in this collection provides a critical account of the key 'creation story' in EU law: the transformation of the Treaty of Rome from a traditional international agreement into the 'new legal order' of *van Gend en Loos* and *Costa v Enel*, whereby provisions of Community law were in principle to be recognized as a valid and indeed superior source of law within the national legal systems.[8] In that 'creation story', the Court's concern to secure the effectiveness of Community law within each Member State, as well as the uniform application of Community law across all the Member States, provided not only the essential rationale for establishing the principles of direct effect and supremacy in the first place, but also the key conceptual drivers for pressing ahead with the task of constructing a fully-fledged system for the decentralized enforcement of Community law before the domestic courts, which was to include the role performed by national remedies and procedural rules.

In fact, during the first disputes to reach the Court in the 1960s and early 1970s, seeking clarification of the nature of judicial protection that national courts should provide in respect of Community law rights, the Court seems to have either considered the issue to be non-existent, or believed it to be undeserving of close attention: its answer was invariably to leave each dispute to be determined in accordance with the applicable domestic law.[9] Nevertheless, as the 1970s progressed—a time when direct effect was developing apace through rulings such as *van Duyn* and *Defrenne v Sabena*,[10] and the implications of supremacy were being hammered out in cases like *Internationale Handelsgesellschaft* and *Simmenthal*[11]—the distinct challenges posed by

---

[5] See eg Case C-398/92 *Mund and Fester* [1994] ECR I-467; Case C-43/95 *Data Delecta* [1996] ECR I-4661; Case C-29/95 *Pastoors* [1997] ECR I-285; Case C-274/96 *Bickel and Franz* [1998] ECR I-7637.

[6] See eg Case T-111/96 *Promedia* [1998] ECR II-2937.

[7] Recently, eg Case C-224/00 *Commission v Italy* [2002] ECR I-2965; Case C-167/01 *Inspire Art* [2003] ECR I-10155; Case C-255/04 *Commission v France* [2006] ECR I-5251.

[8] Case 26/62 *van Gend en Loos* [1963] ECR 1; Case 6/64 *Costa v ENEL* [1964] ECR 585. See Chapter 12 in this collection.

[9] See eg Case 28/67 *Molkerei-Zentrale* [1968] ECR 143; Case 34/67 *Lück* [1968] ECR 245; Case 13/68 *Salgoil* [1968] ECR 661; Case 35/74 *Mutualités Chrétiennes v Rzepa* [1974] ECR 1241.

[10] Case 41/74 *van Duyn* [1974] ECR 1337; Case 43/75 *Defrenne v Sabena* [1976] ECR 455.

[11] Case 11/70 *Internationale Handelsgesellschaft* [1970] ECR 1125; Case 106/77 *Simmenthal* [1978] ECR 629.

national remedies and procedural rules began to surface more clearly. Securing the status of Community law as an autonomous and supreme source of rights and obligations within the Member States was a necessary but not sufficient achievement. Weaknesses in the domestic standards of judicial protection as regards matters such as the availability of interim relief or compensation, or concerning rules of evidence or the imposition of limitation periods, could *in themselves* endanger the effectiveness of substantive Community rules within any given country. In any case, significant differences in the national approaches to such issues across the Member States could *in themselves* undermine the uniform application of the Treaty.[12]

Identifying the problem was one matter; supplying a solution proved quite another. In the first place, it was of course unsurprising that the Treaty of Rome itself lacked any express mandate or legal basis for legislative intervention in the national systems of judicial protection; given that the attentions of the Commission and Council were in any event devoted to substantive policy-making (or deadlock), there was never, during this period, any serious prospect of the Community drawing up a programme for the harmonization of national remedies and procedural rules. In the second place, the alternative strategy of judicial intervention led by the ECJ implied significant challenges and limitations: for example, concerns that attempting to rewrite the rules of judicial procedure on a case by case basis would suffer from all the usual drawbacks, in terms of legal uncertainty, of law-making through process of litigation; and fears that certain national courts would resist or even openly rebel against such blatant 'judicial activism', particularly at a time when the principles of direct effect and supremacy were still deeply contested in several countries.[13]

Other factors must also have played an important role in these early debates about what to do with national remedies. It was perfectly possible that certain domestic procedural rules should (for reasons of historical accident or deliberate obstructionism) be considered plainly inadequate to the task of enforcing Community law. But in most cases, even if aspects of the national systems of judicial protection could somehow prejudice the effective and/or uniform application of Community law, such rules nevertheless served some entirely rational and indeed valuable purpose, and not merely of a technical nature of interest only to lawyers and court administrators, but often of a constitutional stature directly or indirectly reflecting fundamental conceptions about relations between state and citizen, or between private citizens themselves, or concerning appropriate standards of fairness in the administration of justice. Furthermore, it is obvious that such constitutional conceptions are often bound up with the specific political, social, and cultural features of each Member State—such that it is both inevitable and entirely appropriate to find significant

---

[12] For (relatively) early analyses: T Hartley, 'The Effects in National Law of Judgments of the European Court' (1980) 5 ELRev 366; J Bridge, 'Procedural Aspects of the Enforcement of European Community Law through the Legal Systems of the Member States' (1984) 9 ELRev 28.

[13] Notably in Italy and Germany: further, eg P Craig and G de Búrca (n 2 above) ch 10.

divergences in the overall design and detailed operation of each country's own system of remedies and procedural rules.

Against that background, solving the 'problem' of national remedies emerges as no mere mechanical exercise. According to our 'core narrative', the underlying challenge posed by this field of EU law consists in the need to strike a balance between (on the one hand) legitimate Union concerns about its own legal effectiveness and uniformity and (on the other hand) equally legitimate, and legitimately different, national conceptions about the organization and functioning of the administration of justice.

2. THE BASIC *REWE/COMET* MODEL

Equally central to our 'core narrative' is the proposition that the main breakthrough in the ECJ's case law came in 1976, with the twin rulings in *Rewe-Zentralfinanz eG and Rewe-Zentral AG v Landwirtschaftskammer für das Saarland* and *Comet BV v Produktschap voor Siergewassen*.[14] Those judgments established the basic framework that (with certain modifications) has consistently served the Court ever since when addressing issues relating to the decentralized enforcement of Community/Union law. In the absence of Community legislation, the enforcement of Treaty-based rights and obligations is presumed to take place in accordance with existing national remedies and procedural rules, subject to two requirements imposed by Community law: the rules applicable to Treaty-based actions (first) cannot be less favourable than those relating to similar domestic actions and (secondly) cannot in any case make it impossible in practice to exercise rights derived from Community law. Those requirements have since become known as the principles of equivalence and effectiveness (respectively).[15]

Since 1976, an enormous body of jurisprudence has built up within the framework provided by *Rewe/Comet*, though it goes without saying that the Court has not followed any clear or consistent plan or pathway. That is true partly because the case law has indeed displayed all the usual characteristics of law-making through litigation. Yet even if one must therefore guard against falsely attributing to the Court some 'grand design' for national remedies,[16] there is surely far more to the disjointed evolution of the *Rewe/Comet* case law than the natural vicissitudes of litigation alone: as befits a field whose underlying challenge consists in a confrontation of fundamental values between the Union and national legal orders, much of the development of the case law can be attributed to the fluctuating policy preferences of the ECJ, and indeed, to the changing constitutional environment and political dynamic of the broader process of European integration.

---

[14] Case 33/76 and Case 45/76 (n 3 above).

[15] The terms 'equivalence' and 'effectiveness' first emerged into common usage during 1997: eg Case C-261/95 *Palmisani* [1997] ECR I-4025; Case C-188/95 *Fantask* [1997] ECR I-6783.

[16] Craufurd Smith (n 2 above).

3. THE 'THREE-PERIOD' FRAMEWORK FOR ANALYSIS

To make sense of that case law, our 'core narrative' offers a model for analysis divided into three main historical periods, though in each case the centre of attention consists firmly in the tension between the presumption of national autonomy and the principle of effectiveness.

(a) Early period: until the mid-1980s

The early period of the Court's case law can be summarized quite simply: domestic standards of judicial protection remained the rule; despite the creation of new tools for scrutinizing national remedies and procedural rules in *Rewe/Comet*, Community interference actually proved to be an ill-defined and rarely practised exception. For example, the Court held in *Rewe/Comet* themselves that domestic limitation periods regulating the initiation of proceedings before the national courts may also apply to Community cases. In order to satisfy the principle of effectiveness, the relevant time-limit must be reasonable in duration; a 30-day limitation period in respect of actions for the recovery of unlawfully levied charges passed that test.[17] Moreover, in the *Butter Buying Cruises* case, it was bluntly stated that the Treaty was not intended to create any new forms of relief not already available under national law.[18] Thus, for example, the ruling in *Russo* held that the availability of compensatory damages against a Member State for its breach of Community law was to be determined by domestic rules;[19] while the judgment in *Roquette Frères* established that the Member States were entitled to apply their own rules regarding the payment of statutory interest in cases concerning the reimbursement of unlawfully levied charges.[20]

The 'core narrative' has sought to explain such judicial restraint by various means: for example, the possibility that the ECJ was mindful of its own institutional limitations and therefore hesitant about further alienating those national courts which (as mentioned before) were still encountering difficulties with the principles of direct effect and supremacy, let alone any more developed system of decentralized enforcement;[21] and perhaps also an assumption on the part of the Court that what was good for the national goose must be good enough too for the Community gander, so that the brunt of Community scrutiny could be carried by the principle of equivalence, whilst reserving intervention on grounds of the principle of effectiveness for those rare occasions when ordinary national remedies might indeed prove to be patently deficient.[22] Nevertheless, it might be worth noting that, even in this early period in the Court's case law, there were already some signs of the

---

[17] Case 33/76 and Case 45/76 (n 3 above).
[18] Case 158/80 *Rewe-Handelsgesellschaft Nord v Hauptzollamt Kiel* [1981] ECR 1805.
[19] Case 60/75 *Russo* [1976] ECR 45.
[20] Case 26/74 *Roquette Frères* [1976] ECR 677.
[21] Consider eg Case 265/78 *Ferwerda* [1980] ECR 617; Case 130/79 *Express Dairy Foods* [1980] ECR 1887; Case 54/81 *Fromme* [1982] ECR 1449; Cases 205–215/82 *Deutsches Milchkontor* [1983] ECR 2633.
[22] Consider eg Case 811/79 *Ariete* [1980] ECR 2545; Case 826/79 *MIRECO* [1980] ECR 2559.

potential for a more interventionist approach. Consider, for example, the Court's insistence that, where the Member State has levied charges contrary to Community law, the payer must in principle be entitled to seek reimbursement through the national courts.[23] Similarly, consider the finding in *Simmenthal* that any domestic judge must be in a position to disapply a provision of national legislation in breach of the Treaty, without having to refer the dispute to some higher tribunal—a ruling with significant implications for the procedural conduct of cases, and indeed, for the distribution of jurisdiction within certain Member States.[24] It is thus an interesting if idle diversion to speculate whether the Court's early period case law was the product, less of judicial content or conscious restraint, than of limited opportunity and/or pretext to implement some more ambitious vision for the decentralized enforcement of Community law.[25]

(b) Middle period: until 1993

In any event, the Court's middle period jurisprudence was, by contrast, dominated by the increasing frequency and vitality of Community intervention in the national systems of judicial protection, a process achieved almost entirely through a renewed conception and application of the principle of effectiveness. That renewed conception can be seen in the changing language of the Court: to the idea in *Rewe/Comet* that national rules cannot render the exercise of Community rights 'virtually impossible...' was added the appreciably lower threshold of scrutiny '...or excessively difficult';[26] the language of negative scrutiny was then supplemented by a more positive obligation upon the national courts to guarantee the 'effective protection' of rights derived from Community law.[27]

As for the renewed application of the principle of effectiveness, that is borne witness to in a series of rulings which rank among the best known in the whole of EU law. For example, the Court held in *Emmott* that, even if a domestic limitation period complies with the requirement of reasonableness set out in *Rewe/Comet*, it must nevertheless be set aside in cases where the Member State has failed correctly to implement a Community directive within the prescribed deadline, and the individual would otherwise be deprived of the opportunity to rely on rights based on that directive.[28] Moreover, despite the *Butter Buying Cruises* ruling, the judgment in *Factortame* established that national courts must be able to offer interim protection to claimants seeking to assert their Community rights by judicial process—even if such relief is not ordinarily available under domestic rules.[29] Similarly, despite the

---

[23] Case 177/78 *Pigs and Bacon Commission v McCarren* [1979] ECR 2161.

[24] Case 106/77 *Simmenthal* (n 11 above).

[25] Further: C N Kakouris, 'Do the Member States Possess Judicial Procedural "Autonomy"?' (1997) 34 CML Rev 1389.

[26] Case 199/82 *San Giorgio* [1983] ECR 3595.

[27] Case 179/84 *Bozzetti* [1985] ECR 2301.

[28] Case C-208/90 *Emmott* [1991] ECR I-4269.

[29] Case C-213/89 *Factortame* [1990] ECR I-2433.

Russo case, the Court in *Francovich* held that it is inherent in the system of the Treaty that individuals are entitled to seek compensation in respect of losses suffered through a Member State's breach of their intended Treaty rights—and went on to specify the substantive conditions that must be fulfilled in order to exercise that right to reparation.[30] Another good illustration is *Marshall II*, which established that where the Member State chooses to protect victims of discriminatory dismissal from employment, contrary to the provisions of the Equal Treatment Directive,[31] through the award of compensation, such compensation should be full; notwithstanding the judgment in *Roquette Frères*, full compensation must include the payment of interest to represent losses suffered through the effluxion of time.[32] Against that background, many commentators speculated that the Court had embarked upon a strategy virtually amounting to the 'positive harmonization' of national remedies and procedural rules.[33]

This change in judicial policy has been attributed to a number of factors.[34] First, confidence in the legal fundamentals of the system of decentralized enforcement had increased, as the principles of direct effect and supremacy became less controversial with previously sceptical national courts.[35] Secondly, it was clear that, if the Court had indeed placed its faith in the underlying adequacy (and therefore equivalent application) of domestic rules, that faith had been overly optimistic: in fact, as disputes such as *San Giorgio* on the recovery of unlawful levied charges,[36] *von Colson* on compensation to the victims of sex discrimination,[37] and *Factortame* on interim relief for the protection of Community rights all demonstrated, national law often offered less than satisfactory levels of protection. Thirdly, there was a growing feeling that such challenges to the effectiveness and uniform application of Community law were indeed a serious problem and deserved to be treated as such. In particular, the renewed impetus towards the creation of an internal market following the ruling in *Cassis de Dijon*,[38] and especially after the Single European Act,[39] fuelled concerns that, without

---

[30] Cases C-6 and 9/90 *Francovich* [1991] ECR I-5357.

[31] Directive 76/207, [1976] OJ L39/40. See now Directive 2006/54, [2006] OJ L204/23.

[32] Case C-271/91 *Marshall II* [1993] ECR I-4367. Cf Case 14/83 *von Colson* [1984] ECR 1891; Case C-177/88 *Dekker* [1990] ECR I-3941.

[33] See eg D Curtin and K Mortelmans, 'Application and Enforcement of Community Law by the Member States: Actors in Search of a Third Generation Script' in D Curtin and T Heukels (eds), *Institutional Dynamics of European Integration* (Nijhoff, 1994). Further: R Caranta, 'Judicial Protection Against Member States: A New *Jus Commune* Takes Shape' (1995) 32 CML Rev 703; S Weatherill, 'Beyond "EC Law Rights, National Remedies"' in A Caiger and D A Floudas (eds), *1996 Onwards: Lowering the Barriers Further* (Chancery Law, 1996).

[34] A Ward, 'Effective Sanctions in EC Law: A Moving Boundary in the Division of Competence' (1995) 1 ELJ 205.

[35] Consider the judgment of the German Federal Constitutional Court known as *Solange II* [1987] 3 CMLR 225.

[36] Case 199/82 *San Giorgio* (n 26 above).

[37] Case 14/83 *von Colson* (n 32 above).

[38] Case 120/78 '*Cassis de Dijon*' [1979] ECR 649.

[39] [1987] OJ L169.

greater Community intervention, the benefits of closer economic integration would be dissipated as the rules on free movement and fair competition were filtered through the national systems of judicial protection.[40] Fourthly, the character of the challenge to effectiveness and uniformity was itself changing significantly. The Court of Justice was increasingly being called upon not only by big business to assist in enforcing the rules of the common market, but also by ordinary citizens asserting their right to enjoy the social benefits of Community membership (for example) as consumers or workers. Bearing in mind the initiatives launched by the European Council in the 1970s to forge a 'Europe with a human face',[41] this change may well have increased the Court's inclination to bolster the levels of judicial protection guaranteed by Community law.[42] Finally, repeated requests for legislative intervention by the political institutions to address the problems posed by national remedies had gone largely unheeded.[43] The initiative for action therefore lay firmly with the judiciary.

However, the Court's newfound confidence in scrutinizing the effectiveness of the national systems of judicial protection, and increasingly in substituting its own solutions for those of the Member States, also drew growing criticism. First, there were concerns about the practical effects of the Court's case law on values such as legal certainty, and for the financial interests of the Member States. In particular, it was argued that the Court's creative but also unpredictable application of the principle of effectiveness was making it increasingly difficult for legal practitioners to advise their clients, and conduct their cases, when no one really knew whether the relevant domestic limitation period, or rules on evidence, or limits on damages, would remain in place. For their part, the Member States were evidently increasingly alarmed at the newfound costs of failing to comply with their obligations under Community law: rulings such as *Emmott*, *Marshall II*, and *Francovich* seemed to be systematically dismantling the safeguards against 'excessive liability' built into the domestic systems of judicial protection. Secondly, such practical concerns were accompanied by consti-tutional reservations about what many commentators felt to be blatant judicial law-making. The ruling in *Francovich*, for example, was seen in certain quarters as little more than legislation without a legislature, motivated by woolly concerns about effectiveness with an almost limitless potential to justify (or rather excuse) the exercise of judicial power. Those constitutional concerns should be read against the broader context of the negotiations culminating in the signing of the Maastricht Treaty: not only the increasing emphasis on the principle that the Union was an organization of

---

[40] M Bronckers, 'Private Enforcement of 1992: Do Trade and Industry stand a chance against the Member States?' (1989) 26 CML Rev 513; D Curtin, 'Directives: The Effectiveness of Judicial Protection of Individual Rights' (1990) 27 CML Rev 709.

[41] eg Declaration by the Heads of Government of the Member States meeting at Paris on 19–20 October 1972 (EC Bull 10-1972); Reports from the *ad hoc* Committee on 'A People's Europe' (EC Bull Supp 7/85).

[42] See further: AP Tash, 'Remedies for European Community Law Claims in Member State Courts: Toward a European Standard' (1993) 31 Colum J Transnat'l L 377; E Szyszczak, 'Making Europe More Relevant to Its Citizens: Effective Judicial Process' (1996) 21 ELRev 351.

[43] See further Sub-section C.2(c) (below).

strictly attributed powers,[44] but also the introduction of more robust enforcement structures which seemed to undermine the case for a judge-led solution to the problem of recalcitrant Member States.[45] Moreover, the adoption of a directive specifically addressing the question of remedies in the field of public procurement raised the prospect of a more considered intervention in the field of judicial protection by the Community legislature—thus putting the Court under further pressure to defer to the competent political institutions.[46]

Thirdly, although the ECJ remains adamant that, by virtue of the principle of equivalence, Union rights may not suffer a lesser level of protection than that enjoyed by comparable national rights,[47] it has long tolerated reverse discrimination, whereby citizens relying on national rights are treated less favourably than those relying on comparable Treaty provisions.[48] The gradual but partial 'Europeanization' of national remedies and procedural rules therefore implied the creation of a dual system of judicial protection within each Member State, attracting the criticism that this contradicts basic values such as equality between citizens, and also undermines the internal coherence of the national legal system.[49] It is true that Member States may resolve such problems for themselves, by permitting Union standards of judicial protection to 'spill over' into wholly internal structures.[50] But such spillover, which in any event is far from guaranteed, merely magnifies another range of concerns: for example, that Union law is interfering with the local political, social, and cultural preferences embodied in the national systems of judicial protection, which command greater legitimacy than choices made by the Court of Justice, and should not be reduced to the status of mere obstacles to the greater effectiveness and uniform application of the Treaty.[51] Finally, the Court's case law began to draw accusations of a double standard in the treatment of the Member States and Community institutions as regards the levels of judicial protection offered to individuals. Particularly after the ruling in *Francovich*, there were concerns that the Member States were now being forced to provide more effective remedies for breaching the Treaty than were the Community institutions themselves: for example,

---

[44] As now enshrined in Arts 4(1) and 5(2) TEU.

[45] Especially the power to fine Member States under (what is now) Art 260 TFEU.

[46] Dir 89/665 [1989] OJ L395/33.

[47] See eg Case C-261/95 *Palmisani* (n 15 above); Case C-326/96 *Levez* [1998] ECR I-7835; Case C-78/98 *Preston* [2000] ECR I-3201.

[48] Cf Case 355/85 *Driancourt v Michel Cognet* [1986] ECR 3231; Cases C-64-65/96 *Uecker and Jacquet* [1997] ECR I-3171; Case C-148/02 *Garcia Avello* [2003] ECR I-11613.

[49] Caranta (n 33 above); and 'Learning from our Neighbours: Public Law Remedies, Homogenisation from Bottom Up' (1997) 4 MJ 220.

[50] eg the English House of Lords in *M v Home Office* [1994] 1 AC 377 (in the light of Case C-213/89 *Factortame* (n 29 above)); and in *Woolwich Building Society v IRC* [1993] AC 70 (in the light of Case 199/82 *San Giorgio* (n 26 above)).

[51] C Harlow, '*Francovich* and the Problem of the Disobedient State' (1996) 2 ELJ 199; C Harlow, 'A Common European Law of Remedies?' in C Kilpatrick, T Novitz, and P Skidmore (n 4 above); C Harlow 'Voices of Difference in a Pluralist Community' in P Beaumont, C Lyons, and N Walker (eds), *Convergence and Divergence in European Public Law* (Hart, 2002).

the conditions for imposing non-contractual liability upon the Community pursuant to (what are now) Articles 268 and 340 TFEU were notoriously difficult to fulfil, contrasting starkly with the more lenient approach to Member State liability suggested by the ruling in *Francovich* itself.[52]

(c) Later period: since 1993

By the early 1990s, the case law on effective judicial protection had therefore both accumulated a considerable following and provoked a significant body of critical reaction. Against that background, during the course of 1993, the ECJ seems to have suffered a genuine crisis of confidence—what Ward memorably referred to as the Court's 'hasty retreat'.[53]

By way of illustration, consider perhaps the most high-profile casualty of that 'hasty retreat': the ruling in *Emmott* concerning the national court's obligation to set aside even reasonable limitation periods where the dispute involved the Member State's failure properly to implement a Community directive—an approach which seemed to have particularly serious consequences for legal certainty, evidential reliability, and Member State budgets. In October 1993, the Court held in *Steenhorst-Neerings* that that obligation did not apply in the case of national rules limiting back claims for the payment of wrongly withheld social security benefits—even though the rationale for extending the *Emmott* ruling to such analogous disputes seemed entirely applicable.[54] Then, in December 1994, the Court stated in *Johnson II* that, even as regards limitation periods for the commencement of proceedings, the ruling in *Emmott* had been justified by the particular circumstances of that dispute, whereby the competent Irish ministry had actively dissuaded the claimant from enforcing her Community rights within the relevant limitation period.[55] Subsequent rulings confirm that *Emmott* has indeed been distinguished down to a much narrower principle: where one party misleads another as to the latter's rights under Union law, thus causing him/her to exceed the applicable domestic time-limit, the national court should (exceptionally) disapply that procedural rule and permit the action to proceed.[56]

It is unclear how far the immediate causes of the Court's 'hasty retreat' in 1993 lay in the specific concerns (discussed above) stemming from increased Community intervention in the national systems of judicial protection; or should instead be attributed to the considerably more far-reaching 'systemic shock' suffered by the entire process of

---

[52] W Van Gerven, 'Non-Contractual Liability of Member States, Community Institutions and Individuals for Breaches of Community Law with a View to a Common Law for Europe' (1994) 1 MJ 6. See now the rulings in Cases C-46 and 48/93 *Brasserie du Pêcheur* and *Factortame III* [1996] ECR I-1029 and Case C-352/98 P *Bergaderm* [2000] ECR I-5291.

[53] Ward (n 34 above).

[54] Case C-338/91 *Steenhorst-Neerings* [1993] ECR I-5475.

[55] Case C-410/92 *Johnston II* [1994] ECR I-5483.

[56] See eg Case C-188/95 *Fantask* (n 15 above); Case C-445/06 *Danske Slagterier* (judgment of 24 March 2009). In similar vein, consider Case C-326/96 *Levez* (n 47 above); Case C-327/00 *Santex* [2003] ECR I-1877; Case C-241/06 *Lämmerzahl* [2007] ECR I-8415.

European integration during the tortured ratification of the Maastricht Treaty, and especially as a result of the TEU's rejection by the Danes, and its only very narrow approval by the French, in their respective referenda. If the latter explanation is true, then rulings such as *Steenhorst-Neerings*—and indeed, the changing dynamic of the entire case law on effective judicial protection—should be classed alongside major developments in other areas of Community law (particularly the judgment in *Keck and Mithouard* as regards the free movement of goods)[57] where the Court was perceived to have reined in its previous case law in order to show greater deference towards the policy competences of the Member States.[58]

Whatever the immediate causes of the ECJ's 'hasty retreat' in 1993, the case law soon regained its own internal dynamic and the next few years clearly demonstrated that the Court had no intention of abandoning, merely of refining, its commitment to the effective judicial protection of Community rights, by seeking to strike a better balance—better at least than it had achieved in the previous two periods of its case law—between the Community's legitimate concerns about effectiveness and uniformity and respect for each Member State's choices concerning the administration of justice.

Again, the case law on limitation periods provides an instructive case-study. Just as the Court was engineering the demise of its own broad and bothersome *Emmott* ruling, the case law witnessed the growth of other important dimensions to the principle of effectiveness insofar as it applies to national time-limits. For example, the Court used its previous rulings in *Bruno Barra* and *Deville* to build on the idea that Member States cannot reduce the duration of their limitation periods so as specifically to disadvantage the exercise of Treaty rights which have been the subject of proceedings before the ECJ;[59] while also establishing that Member States cannot in any case shorten the duration of the limitation period applicable to the exercise of a Community right in a manner which has retroactive effects, without including adequate transitional provisions respecting the principle of legitimate expectations.[60] Meanwhile, in judgments such as *Preston*, the Court considerably strengthened its once laissez-faire scrutiny of domestic time-limits under the original *Rewe/Comet* rulings, by finding that the 'reasonableness' of a limitation period should be examined not merely in the abstract but within its specific legal and factual context, including by reference to the particular circumstances of each individual dispute.[61]

---

[57] Cases C-267–268/91 *Keck and Mithouard* [1993] ECR I-6097.

[58] See, further, N Reich, 'The "November Revolution" of the European Court of Justice: *Keck, Meng* and *Audi* Revisited' (1994) 31 CML Rev 459.

[59] Case 309/85 *Bruno Barra* [1988] ECR 355; Case 240/87 *Deville* [1988] ECR 3513. eg Case C-228/96 *Aprile* [1998] ECR I-7141; Case C-343/96 *Dilexport* [1999] ECR I-579.

[60] See eg Case C-228/96 *Aprile* (n 59 above); Case C-343/96 *Dilexport* (n 59 above); Case C-62/00 *Marks & Spencer* [2002] ECR I-6325; Case C-255/00 *Grundig Italiana* [2002] ECR I-8003.

[61] Case C-78/98 *Preston* (n 47 above). Consider also: Case C-481/99 *Heininger* [2001] ECR I-9945; Case C-125/01 *Pflücke* [2003] ECR I-9375; Cases C-295-298/04 *Manfredi* [2006] ECR I-6619; Case C-69/08 *Visciano*, 16 July 2009; Case C-63/08 *Pontin*, 29 October 2009.

Indeed, it is now common to regard the ECJ's approach to questions of national judicial protection as akin to a form of 'objective justification', not dissimilar to that developed in other Community law contexts such as free movement or equal treatment: national procedural rules which restrict the exercise of Community rights must be analysed by reference to their purpose within the domestic legal order, and an appropriate balance must be struck against the extent of their restrictive effects upon the full application of Community law.[62] This idea of applying the principle of effectiveness in a more contextual manner was most famously (if rather obtusely) expressed by the Court in *Peterbroeck*:

> Each case which raises the question whether a national procedural provision renders application of Community law impossible or excessively difficult must be analysed by reference to the role of that provision in the procedure, its progress and its special features, viewed as a whole, before the various national instances. In the light of that analysis the basic principles of the domestic judicial system, such as protection of the rights of the defence, the principle of legal certainty and the proper conduct of procedure, must, where appropriate, be taken into consideration.[63]

Moreover, the ECJ now applies the principle of effectiveness in not only a contextual but also an *ad hoc* manner, wary of setting out generic rules, and keen to stress the factors at work in specific disputes. As was stated in *Cofidis*, judgments on national remedies and procedures are 'merely the result of assessments on a case by case basis, taking account of each case's own factual and legal context as a whole, which cannot be applied mechanically in fields other than those in which they were made'.[64]

So, now that the dust has settled since 1993, it appears that the overall thrust of the Court's approach to questions about decentralized enforcement is merely to establish certain minimum standards of effective judicial protection, but otherwise leave much to the discretion of each Member State to design their own national remedies and procedural rules. The scholarly reaction to this development has been largely positive: the pragmatic goal of striking a fair balance between Union interests and Member State competences is generally viewed as preferable to the previous extremes of either neglecting altogether to safeguard the effectiveness and uniform application of Union law or riding roughshod over domestic concerns such as legal certainty and coherence of the judicial system.[65]

But there have still been voices of dissent. On the Union side, some commentators have expressed concerns about whether the Court's contextual and *ad hoc* case law is really sufficient to guarantee the effectiveness of the Treaty against the restrictions and

---

[62] S Prechal, 'Community Law in National Courts: The Lessons From *Van Schijndel*' (1998) 35 CML Rev 681.

[63] Case C-312/93 *Peterbroeck* [1995] ECR I-4599 [14]. Also: Cases C-430-431/93 *Van Schijndel* [1995] ECR I-4705 [18].

[64] Case C-473/00 *Cofidis* [2002] ECR I-10875 [37].

[65] For a recent example of the ECJ giving 'due weight' to considerations of national procedural economy, consider Case C-19/08 *Petrosian*, 29 January 2009.

dilutions which result from the dependence of Union law upon national remedies and procedural rules.[66] In particular, it has been suggested that the Court needs to define more precisely the 'margin of discretion' left to Member States for the purposes of balancing the legitimate role performed by any given national requirement against its adverse impact upon the full application of Union law—perhaps moving away from the relatively lax approach suggested by the 'virtually impossible or excessively difficult' test and towards a more rigorous assessment based on a strict reading of the principle of proportionality.[67] Other commentators have focused less on the imperative of effectiveness and more on promoting the uniform application of Union law, arguing that the Court's current approach of establishing only minimum (and sometimes merely minimal) standards of judicial protection has all but sacrificed the Treaty's fundamental goals of equalizing the conditions of competition for economic actors and promoting common standards of social rights for the Union's own citizens;[68] though that analysis has not gone uncontested among those who believe that the EU's increasing political heterogeneity and regulatory differentiation actually renders many traditional concerns about the uniform application of Union law more rhetorical than real.[69]

On the Member State side, too, the Court's post-1993 case law has hardly received unanimous praise. National courts and tribunals may often appear to be enthusiastic accomplices, even procurers, in the ECJ's case law on effective judicial protection; but if anything, practical concerns about the adverse implications of legal certainty for litigants, and intellectual reservations about preserving the coherence of the national legal systems, seem to have increased.[70] It would certainly be fair to admit that the Court's contextual and *ad hoc* approach to the principle of effectiveness has sometimes given rise to serious difficulties of predictability and consistency—a point well illustrated if one were to explore the case law following *Marshall II* 'clarifying' how far the principle of effectiveness requires the payment of statutory interest.[71] Such uncertainty and confusion has provided the basis for certain more far-reaching criticisms of the Court's contemporary approach to decentralized enforcement. In particular, it has been argued that the ECJ surely spends a disproportionate amount of its scarce judicial energy delving into the nitty-gritty of the national legal systems, in a way unbefitting what is (in effect) a federal constitutional court surrounded by more pressing legal

---

[66] B Fitzpatrick and E Szyszczak, 'Remedies and Effective Judicial Protection in Community Law' (1994) 57 MLR 434.

[67] W van Gerven, 'Of Rights, Remedies and Procedures' (2000) 37 CML Rev 501.

[68] M P Chiti, 'Towards a Unified Judicial Protection in Europe (?)' (1997) 9 ERPL 553; C Himsworth, 'Things Fall Apart: The Harmonisation of Community Judicial Procedural Protection Revisited' (1997) 22 ELRev 291.

[69] Dougan (n 4 above).

[70] M Hoskins, 'Tilting the Balance: Supremacy and National Procedural Rules' (1996) 21 ELRev 365; Himsworth (n 68 above); A Biondi, 'The European Court of Justice and Certain National Procedural Limitations: Not Such a Tough Relationship' (1999) 36 CML Rev 1271.

[71] Consider: Case C-66/95 *Sutton* [1997] ECR I-2163; Cases C-397 and 410/98 *Metallgesellschaft* [2001] ECR I-1727; Case C-63/01 *Evans* [2003] ECR I-14447; Case C-470/04 *N* [2006] ECR I-7409.

issues to resolve, and with few tangible benefits in terms of improving the effectiveness or uniform application of Union law to show for all its trouble. Thus, by contrast with those commentators who fear the Court has become too neglectful in its scrutiny of the domestic standards of judicial protection, others have called for the delivery in this field of some sort of 'remedies equivalent' to the *Keck* judgment as regards the free movement of goods,[72] so that the great majority of national remedies and procedural rules are simply acknowledged not to endanger any fundamental Union interest, or at least not to do so in any fundamental way, and are therefore pushed outside the scope of Union law altogether.[73]

C. BEYOND AND BESIDES THE 'CORE NARRATIVE' ON NATIONAL REMEDIES

The 'core narrative' on national remedies and procedural rules thus provides a compelling account of the historical development of the Court's case law as it has descended from its source in the *Rewe/Comet* rulings.

1. THE MORE RECENT EVOLUTION OF THE *REWE/COMET* CASE LAW: STILL FAR FROM THE 'END OF HISTORY'

However, there are certain risks in too perfunctory a reading of that 'core narrative'. In particular, its neat division of the case law into three distinct periods—of which the first and second are defined by two virtually polar extremes of judicial practice, while the third practises compromise born of experience and pragmatism through the smile of reason—could tempt the naïve observer into believing that the ECJ has somehow ushered in the 'end of history' for its own jurisprudence on effective judicial protection. Having succeeded in striking a fairer balance between the competing interests of the Union and competences of the Member States, based on its contextual and *ad hoc* interpretation of the needs of effectiveness, the case law might appear to have settled into a rather bourgeois conceptual equilibrium: eager not to offend, yet stale and undynamic. True, there will always be new factual contexts that challenge the Court to consider affirming or instead distinguishing its existing case law; and there seems to be an inexhaustible supply of new procedural rules, hidden in the nooks and crannies of every national legal system, the ability of which to render the exercise of some Union right 'virtually impossible or excessively difficult' can be tested for the first time.[74] But if such disputes merely provide an

---

[72] Cases C-267-268/91 *Keck and Mithouard* (n 57 above).   [73] Biondi (n 70 above).

[74] Consider eg Case C-336/94 *Dafeki* [1997] ECR I-6761; Case C-132/95 *Jensen and Korn* [1998] ECR I-2975; Case C-472/99 *Clean Car Autoservice* [2001] ECR I-9687; Case C-276/01 *Steffensen* [2003] ECR I-3735; Case C-443/03 *Leffler* [2005] ECR I-9611; Case C-526/04 *Laboratoires Boiron* [2006] ECR I-7529; Case C-300/04 *Eman and Sevinger* [2006] ECR I-8055; Case C-421/05 *City Motors Groep* [2007] ECR I-653; Case C-55/06 *Arcor* [2008] ECR I-2931; Case C-478/07 *Budějovický Budvar*, 8 September 2009.

excuse to re-enact old arguments about effectiveness and uniformity versus national autonomy and local preferences, or about how far the 'modern' principle of effectiveness lacks a clear hermeneutic framework and confers significant discretion upon the ECJ, then it would indeed be tempting to conclude that we have reached the 'end of history' for this field of Union law.

Such a perfunctory reading would, however, be naïve indeed: the remedies case law, even in its mature 'third period', has obviously continued to drive forward along legal and intellectual paths that call for further investigation in their own right. In particular, this section will illustrate how the Court has identified new facets to the principles of equivalence and effectiveness—though it must be admitted that those facets often bear little relationship to the original concerns about effectiveness and uniformity associated with the core scholarly narrative, but instead illuminate novel problems and explore fresh issues thrown up by the evolution of the *Rewe/Comet* framework.

(a) The principle of equivalence

Consider first the principle of equivalence. Upon reflection, it might feel as if the 'three-period' model identified by our 'core narrative' reveals certain limits when applied to the principle of equivalence. Whilst it is true that the waxing and waning of the principle of effectiveness has periodically thrust equivalence (by default) out of and back into the academic limelight, the latter principle has in itself enjoyed a much more stable evolution, experiencing none of the great dramas or reversals of fortune associated with its more tempestuous sibling; it is also striking that the legal nature of equivalence has been more fully explored according to a very different time frame from that of effectiveness, since the great majority of significant rulings here only date from around 1997 onwards.[75] Moreover, the forces which have acted upon the development of the principle of equivalence appear to derive less from the underlying policy dialectic postulated by our 'core narrative', than from the internal logic of a legal test which is essentially a manifestation of the general principle of equal treatment.[76] Indeed, the case law on equivalence is perhaps better interpreted as clarifying the three main limbs involved in *any* anti-discrimination analysis: establishing comparability between the two subjects; identifying the existence of less favourable treatment to the detriment of the protected subject; and determining whether such less favourable treatment might nevertheless be objectively justified.

Thus, as regards the existence of comparability, the Court held in rulings such as *Palmisani* that the national court should take into account the purpose and cause, as well as the essential characteristics, of the relevant Community and national actions.[77] For example, an action for the recovery of charges levied by a Member State in breach of Union law should be compared to a claim for the refund of taxes wrongly collected

---

[75] Beginning with Case C-261/95 *Palmisani* (n 15 above). For an earlier example of equivalence, see Case 54/81 *Fromme* (n 21 above).

[76] See Case C-34/02 *Pasquini* [2003] ECR I-6515.

[77] Case C-261/95 *Palmisani* (n 15 above).

by the public authorities (not to an action for restitution in respect of monies wrongly held by a private individual).[78] As regards the existence of less favourable treatment, the Court clarified in *Levez* that the national judges should consider the place of the disputed rules within the relevant procedures as a whole and taking into account their special features.[79] On that basis, less favourable treatment can arise not only from patent differences (for example) in the availability of punitive damages as between comparable Union and national actions,[80] but also from less obvious factors such as the degree of formality involved in bringing proceedings, which might cause the Union claim to be more expensive and less convenient to pursue than its domestic comparator.[81] Finally, as regards the objective justification of less favourable treatment, the Court is prepared to accept that differences in the regulation of comparable claims may in fact be attributable to factors unrelated to their Union or domestic provenance.[82]

No doubt because the principle of effectiveness has been more virile and volatile, there has been rather less academic interest in analysing the principle of equivalence: the main point of comment usually concerns how detailed an assessment of the various elements of equivalence the ECJ is prepared undertake; as such, equivalence becomes as much an aspect of judicial relations within the preliminary reference system as an integral part of Union law on effective judicial protection.[83] But some commentators have noted that the principle of equivalence does in fact possess hidden depths. Indeed, Tridimas has commented that equivalence is in some ways more onerous a requirement for Member States than that of effectiveness, and together the two principles 'unveil the inter-relationship of national remedies, and unearth inconsistencies hidden in the evolution of national legal systems'.[84] It is certainly true that the principle of equivalence carries significant integrative potential, not only for the purposes of embedding Union rights into the domestic legal orders on an equal basis with national rights, but also in questioning the overall coherence of national choices about remedies and procedural rules: particularly where a given Union claim might be compared to several distinct national actions, each of which attracts rather different standards of judicial protection, the equivalence assessment can challenge each Member State to revisit the inherited but possibly rather incoherent structures of its own legal system. Moreover, the ECJ's 2007 ruling in *Paquay* has opened up another dimension to this integrative potential: the principle of equivalence requires that the Member State guarantee equal treatment in the remedies and procedural rules

---

[78] See eg Case C-231/96 *Edis* [1998] ECR I-4951; Case C-88/99 *Roquette Frères* [2000] ECR I-10465.

[79] Case C-326/96 *Levez* (n 47 above).

[80] See eg Cases C-295-298/04 *Manfredi* (n 61 above).

[81] Also eg Case C-78/98 *Preston* (n 47 above).

[82] Consider, eg Case C-132/95 *Jensen and Korn* (n 74 above).

[83] For examples of relatively detailed guidance: Case C-34/02 *Pasquini* (n 76 above); Cases C-392 and 422/04 *i-21 Germany* [2006] ECR I-8559; Case C-63/08 *Pontin* (n 61 above).

[84] T Tridimas, 'Liability for Breach of Community Law: Growing Up and Mellowing Down?' (2001) 38 CML Rev 301, 321.

applicable not only to comparable Union and national actions, but also to Union rights *inter se* where the latter are of similar nature and importance.[85] Nevertheless, it remains as true today as it ever was before, that the Court's mission to promote a more rational approach towards judicial protection reaches its limit when the unjustified discrimination in question works against rights derived from purely national law.[86]

(b) Effectiveness for and against the individual

Just as the emergence of a new equilibrium in the case law following the high water mark and 'hasty retreat' of 1993 allowed neglected issues such as the legal content of the principle of equivalence to be explored by the Court in greater detail, so too it encouraged the scholarship to engage more closely with certain doctrinal and conceptual issues underpinning the principle of effectiveness itself. For example, there is evidence in the recent jurisprudence that the ECJ believes certain categories of citizens to be deserving of more effective judicial protection than others: consider the imposition on national judges of a duty to raise of their own motion unfair terms in consumer contracts, which surely goes further than the standard of effectiveness applicable to the *ex officio* application of Union law in other contexts.[87] The unfair terms case law is motivated by the Court's concern over the particularly vulnerable position of consumers, and the importance attached to the protection of their economic interests by the Union legislature—a line of reasoning which could readily extend to other categories of consumer disputes,[88] and thereby provide the basis for a distinct sectoral conception of the principle of effectiveness in that policy field.[89]

However, not only does the case law reveal increasingly diffuse understandings of effectiveness in different sectors of Union law; it also invites a more critical interrogation into whose interests the principle of effectiveness is actually articulating and protecting. According to its standard formulation, the principle of effectiveness protects the individual beneficiary of Union law against national remedies and procedural rules that would render the exercise of his/her Treaty-based rights virtually impossible or excessively difficult. That formulation seems to equate the concept of effectiveness

---

[85] Case C-460/06 *Paquay* [2007] ECR I-8511.

[86] See eg Case C-432/05 *Unibet* [2007] ECR I-2271.

[87] Contrast Cases C-240-4/98 *Océano Grupo Editorial* [2000] ECR I-4941, Case C-473/00 *Cofidis* (n 64 above), and Case C-243/08 *Pannon*, 4 June 2009; with Cases C-430–431/93 *Van Schijndel* (n 63 above), Cases C-222–225/05 *van der Weerd* [2007] ECR I-4233 and Case C-455/06 *Heemskerk*, 25 November 2008. See also Case C-168/05 *Mostaza Claro* [2006] ECR I-10421 and Case C-40/08 *Asturcom*, 6 October 2009 on the principle of equivalence; cf Case C-126/97 *EcoSwiss v Benetton* [1999] ECR I-3055.

[88] Consider Case C-429/05 *Rampion and Godard* [2007] ECR I-8017.

[89] Consider Case C-481/99 *Heininger* [2001] ECR I-9945; Case C-168/00 *Leitner* [2002] ECR I-2631; though cf Case C-412/06 *Hamilton* [2008] ECR I-2383. Note also decisions concerning vulnerable employees, eg Case C-185/97 *Coote v Granada Hospitality* [1998] ECR I-5199; Case C-306/07 *Ruben Andersen*, 18 December 2008; Case C-63/08 *Pontin* (n 61 above).

with the interests of the individual citizen.[90] However, many commentators have increasingly adopted the view that the concept of effectiveness refers primarily to the enforcement of Union law *per se*, protecting the individual's rights (if at all) only incidentally or instrumentally.[91]

Consider (for example) whether one undertaking should be permitted to seek an injunction from the national courts so as to restrain a rival company from selling agricultural goods in breach of the applicable Union quality standards (despite the fact that national law reserves exclusive enforcement powers to the competent public authorities);[92] or whether one party to an agreement deemed anti-competitive under Article 101 TFEU should nevertheless be permitted to seek damages from its co-contractor for losses incurred as a result of that breach of Union law (despite the fact that no such action for compensation would ordinarily be admissible under the domestic legal system).[93] Each such scenario raises difficult conceptual questions about whether promoting the effectiveness of Union law by scrutinizing the available national sanctions merely coincides with, or rather actively reinforces, or indeed creates *de novo*, rights for the individual claimant—and thus important substantive questions about whether securing the effective enforcement of a given Union policy by rewriting the applicable domestic procedural rules really justifies the appreciable enhancement of one party's legal position to the detriment of another.

Such tensions escalate into outright conflict in those situations where promoting the effectiveness of Union law requires the Member State to act directly contrary to the individual's interests through the imposition of effective and dissuasive public penalties. That obligation was first recognized as such by the ECJ in its famous *Greek Maize* ruling from 1989,[94] which can easily be classed alongside cases such as *Emmott*, *Factortame*, *Marshall II*, and *Francovich* as yet another manifestation of the Court's judicial activism during its middle period case law;[95] though it is worth noting that the case law on the imposition of public penalties against individuals has witnessed neither the splendours nor the miseries of the case law on effective judicial protection for

---

[90] Particularly when read in the light of the Art 13 ECHR right to an effective remedy specifically for violations of the substantive rights and freedoms guaranteed by the Convention; now taken up but significantly extended in scope by the Charter of Fundamental Rights as the Art 47 right to an effective remedy for any violation of Union law. Further: A Ward, 'National and EC Remedies Under the EU Treaty: Limits and the Role of the ECHR' in C Barnard and O Odudu (eds), *The Outer Limits of European Union Law* (Hart, 2009).

[91] A Komninos, 'New Prospects for Private Enforcement of EC Competition Law: *Courage v Crehan* and the Community Right to Damages' (2002) 39 CML Rev 447; Dougan (n 4 above); P Nebbia, 'The Double Life of Effectiveness' (2007/8) 10 CYELS 287.

[92] Case C-253/00 *Muñoz* [2002] ECR I-7289.

[93] Case C-453/99 *Courage v Crehan* [2001] ECR I-6297.

[94] Case 68/88 *Commission v Greece* [1989] ECR 2965. Note that certain earlier rulings (eg Case 14/83 *von Colson* (n 32 above)) referring to the need for effective and dissuasive penalties are better seen as manifestations of the case law on judicial protection of individual rights rather than part of the *Greek Maize* case law on the imposition of public sanctions. Similarly with certain more recent rulings, eg Case C-212/04 *Adeneler* [2006] ECR I-6057; Cases C-378–380/07 *Angelidaki*, 23 April 2009.

[95] Just as the relevant rulings pre-*Greek Maize* can be seen as an integral part of the Court's early period case law, eg Case 50/76 *Amsterdam Bulb* [1977] ECR 137.

individual right-holders, enjoying instead a rather sleepy existence, characterized by a relatively hands-off approach by the ECJ and a wide margin of discretion for the Member States when it comes to applying the criteria of effective and dissuasive sanctions.[96] In fact, judicial oversight in *Greek Maize* disputes is as much concerned with guaranteeing respect for the principle of proportionality, so as to restrain the Member State from imposing penalties that would make Union law *too* effective; such scrutiny has nothing to do with the *Rewe/Comet* case law or indeed its underlying policy dialectic, and derives instead from the binding administrative law standards embodied in the general principles of Union law, which apply to all situations falling within the scope of the Treaty, including those where a Member State is implementing Union law.[97] In any case, the *Greek Maize* jurisprudence surely demonstrates how conceptualizing the requirement of effectiveness solely in terms of 'protecting individual rights' becomes unconvincing or even untenable.[98]

(c) The development of the 'autonomous Union actions'

Another area of the *Rewe/Comet* case law the recent and continuing development of which seems difficult to explain by reference to our 'core narrative' alone concerns the so-called 'autonomous Union actions'. The latter refer to certain causes of action or specific forms of remedy—including the right to interim relief for the protection of putative Union law rights, the right to the recovery of unlawfully levied charges, and the right to reparation against Member States under *Francovich*—the legal origin of which is deemed by the Court to derive from the Treaty itself, inherently and directly, without being initially mediated through the *Rewe/Comet* presumption of national remedial autonomy subject to the principles of equivalence and effectiveness.

Historically, it seems fair to describe these autonomous Union actions as 'left-overs', or (more picturesquely) as 'mesas': having largely been established by the Court during its confident middle period case law, they were perhaps deemed too fundamental to the functioning of the system of decentralized enforcement to be treated as reversible, and have as such survived (almost) intact the subsequent judicial retrenchment after 1993. Yet far from being mere walking dinosaurs, the autonomous Union actions positively defy any caricature of the more recent case law as a period of mere judicial restraint and deference: these lines of jurisprudence continue to provide the source for many of the most important and controversial developments in the

---

[96] See eg Case C-7/90 *Vandevenne* [1991] ECR I-4371; C-352/92 *Milchwerke Köln* [1994] ECR I-3385; Case C-230/01 *Penycoed Framing Partnership* [2004] ECR I-937; Case C-315/05 *Lidl Italia* [2006] ECR I-11181.

[97] See eg Case C-326/88 *Hansen* [1990] ECR I-2911; Case C-177/95 *Ebony Maritime* [1997] ECR I-1111; Case C-262/99 *Louloudakis* [2001] ECR I-5547; Case C-156/04 *Commission v Greece* [2007] ECR I-4129.

[98] Consider also the case law on decentralized enforcement of the state aids rules, where the ECJ often adopts an aggressive approach towards the rectification of procedurally/substantively flawed domestic subsidies, eg Case C-24/95 *Alcan Deutschland* [1997] ECR I-1591; Case C-119/05 *Lucchini* [2007] ECR I-6199; Case C-199/06 *CELF* [2008] ECR I-469. Cf case law on the recovery of wrongly paid Community monies, eg Case 26/74 *Roquette Frères* (n 20 above); Cases 205–215/82 *Deutsches Milchkontor* (n 21 above); Case C-366/95 *Steff-Houlberg* [1998] ECR I-2661; Case C-298/96 *Oelmühle Hamburg* [1998] ECR I-4767; Case C-336/00 *Huber* [2002] ECR I-7699.

field of effective judicial protection. In this context, their particular juridical basis makes the autonomous Union actions not only quantitatively but qualitatively different from the principle of effectiveness in its narrow *Rewe/Comet* sense; they represent independent manifestations of some broader concept of effectiveness which justifies its own specific Union interventions in the system of decentralized enforcement. Moreover, when it comes to explaining the continuing evolution of these highly specialized bodies of case law, the underlying policy framework and accepted historical analysis underpinning the 'core narrative' seem inadequate or at least incomplete, as compared to the insights which can be garnered from a detailed examination of the internal dynamics driving each specific remedy. The Union actions are thus 'autonomous' not only to the extent that they stem directly from the Treaty; but also in the sense that, having originally been born from our 'core narrative', much of their subsequent development has nonetheless been determined by their own particular doctrinal logic and needs.

And indeed, the development of each autonomous Union action has proved highly distinctive. Consider, for example, interim relief. As regards national rules allegedly in breach of the Treaty, the Court held in *Factortame* that interim relief is a Union right in principle;[99] but clarified in *Unibet* that the substantive conditions under which such interim relief is to be granted by the national courts are to be determined within the *Rewe/Comet* framework.[100] By contrast, as regards Union rules alleged to infringe a higher Treaty norm, judgments such as *Zuckerfabrik* and *Atlanta* established that interim relief is a Union right the substantive conditions of which are also exhaustively determined by Union law, drawing upon the criteria by which the Union courts themselves grant interim relief pursuant to Articles 278–279 TFEU.[101] The latter more centralized approach was justified on the grounds of protecting the uniform application of Union legislation from being distorted by national courts reaching very different assessments of the necessity and appropriateness of granting interim relief. As such, the rulings in *Zuckerfabrik* and *Atlanta* perhaps have less in common with *Factortame* and *Unibet* than they do with the broader case law on challenging the validity of Union acts via the national courts, where the latter's jurisdiction is carefully delimited,[102] and other national procedural rules (such as those on limitation periods) are subject to additional constraints as compared to those generally imposed under *Rewe/Comet* alone.[103]

---

[99] Case C-213/89 *Factortame* (n 29 above). Cf Case C-1/99 *Kofisa Italia* [2001] ECR I-207; Case C-226/99 *Siples* [2001] ECR I-277.

[100] Case C-432/05 *Unibet* (n 86 above).

[101] Cases C-143/88 and C-92/89 *Zuckerfabrik Süderdithmarshen* [1991] ECR I-415; Case C-465/93 *Atlanta* [1995] ECR I-3761.

[102] In particular: Case 314/85 *Firma Foto-Frost* [1987] ECR 4199. Cf Case C-461/03 *Gaston Schul Douane-expediteur BV* [2005] ECR I-10513; Case C-344/04 *European Low Fares Airline Association* [2006] ECR I-403.

[103] See eg Case C-188/92 *TWD* [1994] ECR I-833; Case C-178/95 *Wiljo* [1997] ECR I-585; Case C-241/01 *National Farmers' Union* [2002] ECR I-9079.

Consider also the recovery of unlawfully levied charges. As we have seen, the ECJ recognized this right relatively early in its case law,[104] and has consistently confirmed it to be an autonomous Union action.[105] In theory, like interim relief against allegedly invalid national acts, the conditions under which the Union right to recovery must be exercised are governed by the *Rewe/Comet* framework. However, the degree of Union scrutiny exercised through the principle of effectiveness has reached such an extent that the Court now controls in an almost exhaustive manner the circumstances in which Member States may legitimately resist claims for reimbursement.[106] For example, the Court established in cases like *FMC* and *Fantask* that liability to repay arises from the illegality *per se* and may not be subject to additional (fault-based) requirements.[107] In fact, the only defence to an action for reimbursement still left open to Member States is that of passing on and unjust enrichment;[108] but even here, a long line of case law strictly controls allocation of the burden of proof and closely regulates any obligation on the claimant to cooperate with the national authorities.[109] In practice, therefore, the right to recovery perhaps lies closer to the template of *Zuckerfabrik* and *Atlanta* than to that of *Factorame* and *Unibet*.

As for *Francovich*, it presents yet another model. The right to reparation is an autonomous Union cause of action, directly exercised in accordance with the substantive conditions definitively enumerated by the ECJ in *Brasserie de Pêcheur* and *Dillenkofer*.[110] However, unlike the right to interim relief against allegedly invalid Union acts, the substantive criteria for *Francovich* actions have not been exhaustively harmonized at Union level: the requirement of a direct causal link between the Member State's breach of the Treaty and the losses suffered by the claimant falls to be determined by national law subject to the principles of equivalence and effectiveness;[111] in any case, the Member States remain free to provide for reparation to be

---

[104] Case 177/78 *Pigs and Bacon Commission v McCarren* (n 23 above).

[105] More recently Case C-343/96 *Dilexport* (n 59 above); Cases C-397/98 and C-410/98 *Metallgesellschaft* (n 71 above); Case C-62/00 *Marks & Spencer* (n 60 above); Case C-309/06 *Marks & Spencer* [2008] ECR I-2283.

[106] M Dougan, 'Cutting Your Losses in the Enforcement Deficit: A Community Right to the Recovery of Unlawfully Levied Charges?' (1998) 1 CYELS 233.

[107] Case C-212/94 *FMC* [1996] ECR I-389; Case C-188/95 *Fantask* (n 15 above).

[108] See eg Case 68/79 *Hans Just* [1980] ECR 501; Case 811/79 *Ariete* (n 22 above); Cases 142–143/80 *Essevi and Salengo* [1981] ECR 1413.

[109] Case 199/82 *San Giorgio* (n 26 above). Also, eg Cases 331, 376 and 378/85 *Bianco* [1988] ECR 1099; Cases C-192–218/95 *Comateb* [1997] ECR I-165; Case C-343/96 *Dilexport* (n 59 above); Cases C-441-2/98 *Mikhailidis* [2000] ECR I-7145; Cases C-397 and C-410/98 *Metallgesellschaft* (n 71 above); Case C-147/01 *Weber's Wine World* [2003] ECR I-11365; Case C-129/00 *Commission v Italy* [2003] ECR I-14637; Case C-309/06 *Marks & Spencer* (n 105 above).

[110] Cases C-46 and 48/93 *Brasserie du Pêcheur* and *Factortame III* (n 52 above); Cases C-178–179 and 188-190/94 *Dillenkofer* [1996] ECR I-4845.

[111] Cases C-46 and 48/93 *Brasserie du Pêcheur* and *Factortame III* (n 52 above) [65]. The ECJ does occasionally give relatively detailed instructions to national courts on the issue of causation: consider Case C-319/96 *Brinkmann* [1998] ECR I-5255; Case C-140/97 *Rechberger* [1999] ECR I-3499; Case C-470/03 *AGM-COS.MET* [2007] ECR I-2749.

provided under terms more generous towards the individual than those applicable under Union law itself.[112]

Moreover, the *Francovich* case law is a good illustration of the limitations of our 'core narrative' in providing a comprehensive explanation for the remedies case law. It is true that *Francovich* fits neatly into our 'three-period' historical analysis: the early *Russo* ruling stated that the question of Member State liability for breaching Community law was a matter for national law alone;[113] *Francovich* itself established the right to reparation and appeared to suggest that the substantive criteria for incurring liability were to be relatively generous towards the individual;[114] then *Brasserie de Pêcheur* clarified that the conditions for reparation (based on the 'sufficiently serious breach' requirement) were after all going to be significantly more protective towards the Member State.[115] But that is where the explanative power of our 'core narrative' reaches its limit. After *Brasserie*, we have to look elsewhere to answer the major questions which now populate the *Francovich* case law: for example, how to identify which rules of Union law are intended to confer rights on individuals;[116] what precise standard of culpability should be required to trigger liability on the part of the Member State;[117] exactly what range and extent of losses should be considered recoverable under *Francovich*;[118] how far claimants can be expected to mitigate their own losses through the exhaustion of adequate alternative remedies;[119] and the range of bodies whose acts can be attributed to the Member State for the purposes of imposing *Francovich* liability.[120] In answering such questions, one should look less to our 'core narrative', and more at the very nature of the right to reparation itself, as an administrative tort in respect of the Member State's infringement of its public law obligations under the Treaty, which should provide Court and commentators alike with a wealth of national and comparative experience, as well as theoretical discourse, for inspiration.[121]

---

[112] See eg Cases C-46 and 48/93 *Brasserie du Pêcheur* and *Factortame III* (n 52 above) [66].

[113] Case 60/75 *Russo* (n 19 above).

[114] P Craig, '*Francovich*, Remedies and the Scope of Damages Liability' (1993) 109 LQR 595; M Ross, 'Beyond *Francovich*' (1993) 56 MLR 55.

[115] P Craig, 'Once More Unto the Breach: The Community, the State and Damages Liability' (1997) 113 LQR 67; E Deards, 'Curiouser and Curiouser? The Development of Member State Liability in the Court of Justice' (1997) 3 EPL 117.

[116] See eg Case C-222/02 *Peter Paul* [2004] ECR I-9425; Case C-445/06 *Danske Slagterier* (n 56 above).

[117] See eg Case C-392/93 *ex p British Telecommunications* [1996] ECR I-1631; Case C-127/95 *Norbrook* [1998] ECR I-1531; Case C-424/97 *Haim* [2000] ECR I-5123; Case C-150/99 *Stockholm Lindöpark* [2001] ECR I-493; Case C-118/00 *Larsy* [2001] ECR I-5063; Case C-278/05 *Robins* [2007] ECR I-1059; Case C-452/06 *Synthon*, 16 October 2008.

[118] See eg Cases C-94-5/95 *Bonifaci* [1997] ECR I-3969; Case C-373/95 *Maso* [1997] ECR I-4051; Case C-470/03 *AGM-COS.MET* (n 111 above).

[119] See eg Cases C-397 and 410/98 *Metallgesellschaft* (n 71 above); Case C-445/06 *Danske Slagterier* (n 56 above).

[120] See eg Case C-302/97 *Konle* [1999] ECR I-3099; Case C-424/97 *Haim* (n 117 above); Case C-224/01 *Köbler* [2003] ECR I-10239; Case C-173/03 *Traghetti del Mediterraneo* [2006] ECR I-5177; Case C-470/03 *AGM-COS.MET* (n 111 above).

[121] M Dougan, 'What is the Point of Francovich?' in T Tridimas and P Nebbia (eds), *European Union Law for the Twenty-First Century: Rethinking the New Legal Order*, Vol 1 (Hart, 2004).

One issue which has aroused considerable interest over recent years is the possibility that the Court might manufacture a 'private *Francovich*': a Treaty-based right to reparation in respect of individual (or better still: private law) infringements of directly effective Union obligations. Even 'middle period' rulings such as *Marshall II* had continued to recognize the Member State's margin of discretion in choosing the most appropriate form of relief in contexts such as anti-discrimination law.[122] Things changed when Advocate General van Gerven in *Banks* famously proposed the idea of promoting the effective and uniform application of the Treaty through the introduction of an autonomous Union action for damages against private parties.[123] The Court's initial response in the key *Courage v Crehan* case from 2000 was ambiguous to say the least.[124] That ruling stressed the importance played by damages actions in securing the effective enforcement of Union competition policy, yet shied away from stating unequivocally that such a right to damages exists as a matter of Union law, or must be exercised in accordance with substantive criteria harmonized at the Union level, or should be available in other fields of Union law where enforceable obligations are imposed upon private parties (such as equal treatment for migrant workers under Article 45 TFEU).[125] Subsequent rulings, such as *Manfredi* and *City Motors*, have affirmed the existence in principle of a Union right to compensation, to be exercised under defined conditions, at least as regards competition law;[126] though there seems no inherent reason to confine such an autonomous Union action for private law damages to Articles 101 and 102 TFEU, even if the substantive conditions set out in the *Courage* case law as regards competition law will not necessarily prove transposable to other policy contexts.[127] In any case, the *Courage* case law provides an interesting case-study of the gradual transition of one important element of judicial protection, from being governed by the ordinary *Rewe/Comet* principle of effectiveness, into some form of autonomous Union action—a development which has taken place almost entirely within the 'third period' of the case law and therefore illustrates that the remedies jurisprudence is very far from any having settled into any kind of 'end of history'.

2. OTHER NARRATIVE STRANDS IN THE NATIONAL REMEDIES STORY

It should by now be apparent that, whatever its many strengths, the 'core narrative' on national remedies and procedural rules does not represent the only or the whole story of the interaction between Union law and the national systems of judicial protection.

---

[122] Case C-271/91 *Marshall II* (n 32 above). Also: Case 14/83 *von Colson* (n 32 above); Case 248/83 *Commission v Germany* [1985] ECR 1459; Case C-180/95 *Draehmpaehl* [1997] ECR I-2195; Case C-460/06 *Paquay* (n 85 above); Case C-94/07 *Raccanelli* [2008] ECR I-5939; Case C-63/08 *Pontin* (n 61 above).

[123] Case C-128/92 *Banks* [1994] ECR I-1209.

[124] Case C-453/99 *Courage v Crehan* (n 93 above).

[125] Case C-281/98 *Angonese* [2000] ECR I-4131.

[126] Cases C-295-298/04 *Manfredi* (n 61 above); Case C-421/05 *City Motors Groep* (n 74 above).

[127] Komninos (n 91 above); W van Gerven, 'Harmonization of Private Law: Do We Need It?' (2004) 41 CML Rev 505; S Drake, 'Scope of *Courage* and the Principle of "Individual Liability" for Damages' (2006) 31 ELRev 841.

This section will briefly examine a series of additional topics which co-exist alongside rather than forming part of the legal framework established in *Rewe/Comet*, stand apart from rather than share in the evolutionary pattern presented by the 'three-period' analysis, and in many respects do not respond to the basic policy concern of promoting the effectiveness and uniform application of Union law which underpins the 'core narrative'.

(a) The fundamental right of access to judicial process

Article 6 ECHR provides that, in the determination of his/her civil rights and obligations or of any criminal charge against him/her, everyone is entitled to a fair and public hearing within a reasonable time by an independent and impartial tribunal established by law. As the ECJ first recognized in *Johnson*, this fundamental right of access to judicial process forms part of the general principles of Union law binding upon the Member States when acting within the scope of the Treaty, and thus applies for the benefit of all individuals whose Union rights are implemented through the national systems of judicial protection.[128] The *Johnson* ruling is now reflected in Article 47 of the Charter of Fundamental Rights,[129] the indirect legal status of which had already been recognized by the ECJ in judgments such as *Unibet*,[130] even before it became directly legally binding (with the entry into force of the Lisbon Treaty) in accordance with Article 6(1) TEU.[131]

The *Johnson* fundamental right of access to judicial process is conceptually and legally distinct from the *Rewe/Comet* framework for addressing issues surrounding national remedies and procedural rules. Conceptually, *Johnson* should be specifically distinguished from the policy framework of the 'core narrative', and indeed from scholarly debate about the 'concealed' nature of the principle of effectiveness: the protection afforded by Article 6 ECHR through the general principles of Union law is not merely instrumental to the Union's interests in promoting the effectiveness and uniform application of the Treaty, but instead fulfils the Union's binding obligation to safeguard respect for human rights on behalf of those individuals who derive legal entitlements from the Treaty. Legally, *Johnson* should be seen as a distinct Union right in and of itself (albeit one ultimately derived from the existence of another substantive Treaty right); even though aspects of its implementation are necessarily governed by the presumption of national autonomy, its content still consists of an irreducible core of protection which must be determined in accordance with the minimum standards imposed by Article 6 ECHR.[132]

---

[128] Case 222/84 *Johnston* [1986] ECR 1651. Affirmed on many occasions since, eg Case C-228/98 *Dounias* [2000] ECR I-577; Case C-7/98 *Krombach* [2000] ECR I-1935; Case C-426/05 *Tele2* [2008] ECR I-685; Case C-55/06 *Arcor* [2008] ECR I-2931.

[129] [2000] OJ C364/1.

[130] Case C-432/05 *Unibet* (n 86 above).

[131] Note the revised version of the Charter accompanying the Lisbon Treaty: [2007] OJ C303/1.

[132] The ECJ itself sometimes fails to distinguish clearly between the fundamental right of access to judicial process and the ordinary principle of effectiveness: contrast Case C-34/02 *Pasquini* (n 76 above) with Case C-63/01 *Evans* (n 71 above).

Such interaction between *Johnson* and *Rewe/Comet* has occasionally presented the Court with certain difficult questions. Consider, for example, the balance between guaranteeing the fundamental right of access to judicial process (on the one hand) and respecting the Member State's competence to designate the courts and tribunals having jurisdiction over particular categories of action (on the other hand).[133] Where a Member State entirely fails to exercise that competence, and the resulting gap in jurisdiction cannot be resolved through reliance on other legal tools such as the duty of consistent interpretation, the Court is effectively forced to acknowledge that the individual's only recourse lies in an action for reparation against the Member State under *Francovich*.[134] Conversely, as demonstrated by the *Impact* ruling, even if the Member State's allocation of jurisdiction between various national tribunals is adequate enough to satisfy the minimum standards expected under *Johnson*, the detailed operation of/interaction between those jurisdictions might still prove sufficiently complex, costly, and inconvenient as to render the exercise of the claimant's substantive Union rights excessively difficult under the principle of effectiveness.[135]

Otherwise, the case law following *Johnson* has been largely preoccupied with addressing familiar questions about the detailed application of the fundamental right of access to judicial process: for example, concerning when particular rules of evidence or procedure might render a trial unfair for the purposes of Article 6 ECHR;[136] when courts of first instance and/or appeal can be said to exercise full jurisdiction over a dispute so as to guarantee an adequate level of judicial scrutiny;[137] the circumstances in which provisional acts adopted by the national authorities must also be subject to judicial review;[138] and which bodies satisfy the institutional requirements required to exercise independent and impartial judicial scrutiny in the first place.[139] However, the *Johnson* case law is not merely a mirror image of the protection individuals would in any case be entitled to expect under the ECHR; the Union's fundamental right of access to judicial process also offers certain specific advantages. For example, *Johnson* applies to the exercise of *all* rights derived from Union law, including those of a purely administrative character, which would not ordinarily fall within the scope of Article 6

---

[133] See eg Case 179/84 *Bozzetti* (n 27 above); Case C-446/93 *SEIM* [1996] ECR I-73; Cases C-10–22/97 *IN. CO.GE.'90* [1998] ECR I-6307.

[134] See eg Case C-54/96 *Dorsch Consult* [1997] ECR I-4961; Case C-111/97 *EvoBus Austria* [1998] ECR I-5411; Case C-258/97 *Hospital Ingenieure* [1999] ECR I-1405. Cf Case C-462/99 *Connect Austria* [2003] ECR I-5197; Case C-15/04 *Koppensteiner* [2005] ECR I-4855.

[135] Case C-268/06 *Impact* [2008] ECR I-2483.

[136] See eg Case C-276/01 *Steffensen* (n 74 above); Case C-105/03 *Pupino* [2005] ECR I-5285; Case C-450/06 *Varec* [2008] ECR I-581.

[137] See eg Case 222/84 *Johnston* (n 128 above); Case C-92/00 *Hospital Ingenieure* [2002] ECR I-5553; Case C-120/97 *Upjohn* [1999] ECR I-223.

[138] See eg Case C-97/91 *Borelli* [1992] ECR I-6313; Cases C-286, C-340, and C-401/95 and C-47/96 *Garage Molenheide* [1997] ECR I-7281; Case C-269/99 *Kühne* [2001] ECR I-9517.

[139] See eg Case C-424/99 *Commission v Austria* [2001] ECR I-9285; Case C-506/04 *Wilson* [2006] ECR I-8613.

ECHR *per se*.[140] Furthermore, the Court has divined from *Johnson* certain supplementary rights, intended to safeguard the practical effects of Article 6 ECHR within the Union legal order: for example, a right to know the reasoning behind adverse administrative decisions of a final character;[141] and a degree of protection against harassment or retribution intended to deter individuals from exercising their Treaty rights.[142]

(b) Ascertaining the boundaries of 'national remedies'

Another distinct strand in the remedies story—though one which raises issues altogether less clear and more controversial than the *Johnson* case law—concerns the question: what exactly counts as a 'remedial' or 'procedural' issue which properly falls within the purview of the *Rewe/Comet* framework, to be resolved through the presumption of national autonomy and the principles of equivalence and effectiveness?

Consider, for example, the obligations imposed by Community law upon public authorities. The ECJ in rulings such as *Fratelli Costanzo* and *Erich Ciola* clarified that the principles of direct effect and supremacy are binding not only on the Member State's judicial but also its administrative bodies.[143] That raised the question: how far might the *Rewe/Comet* principles also extend beyond the sphere of judicial protection so as to govern the structures of administrative procedure and redress? In rulings such as *Kühne & Heitz*, the Court was asked to assess the compatibility with Union law of domestic rules conferring finality upon administrative decisions which had been adopted in breach of the Treaty.[144] Such judgments suggest that the Court uses both legal tools and substantive standards of review, extrapolated from the duty of loyal cooperation under (what is now) Article 4(3) TEU, quite different from those it would employ when addressing the equivalence and effectiveness of national rules implementing the (analogous) principle of *res judicata* in the context of the judicial function.[145] However, other recent rulings, concerning various aspects of national administrative procedures and redress, have indeed stressed that public authorities are obliged to respect the *Rewe/Comet* requirements in all situations where the exercise of their powers impinges upon rights derived from the Treaty.[146] Indeed, the ECJ held in

---

[140] See Art 47 Charter of Fundamental Rights.

[141] See eg Case 222/86 *Heylens* [1987] ECR 4097; Case C-340/89 *Vlassopoulou* [1991] ECR I-2357; Case C-75/08 *Mellor*, 30 April 2009. Cf other rulings linking the transparency of national procedures to effective judicial review, eg Case C-157/99 *Smits and Peerbooms* [2001] ECR I-5473; Case C-138/02 *Collins* [2004] ECR I-2703.

[142] See eg Case C-185/97 *Coote* [1998] ECR I-5199.

[143] Case 103/88 *Fratelli Costanzo* [1989] ECR 1839; Case C-224/97 *Erich Ciola* [1999] ECR I-2517. Further: M Claes, *The National Courts' Mandate in the European Constitution* (Hart, 2006) ch 10.

[144] Case C-453/00 *Kühne & Heitz* [2004] ECR I-837.

[145] See eg Case C-234/04 *Kapferer* [2006] ECR I-2585; Cases C-392 and 422/04 *i-21 Germany* [2006] ECR I-8559; Case C-2/08 *Fallimento Olimpiclub*, 3 September 2009; Case C-40/08 *Asturcom*, 6 October 2009.

[146] See eg Case C-34/02 *Pasquini* (n 76 above); Case C-224/02 *Pusa* [2004] ECR I-5763; Case C-245/03 *Merck, Sharp & Dohme* [2005] ECR I-637; Case C-296/03 *GlaxoSmithKline* [2005] ECR I-669; Case C-244/05 *Bund Naturschutz in Bayern* [2006] ECR I-8445; Case C-120/05 *Heinrich Schulze* [2006] ECR I-10745; Case C-426/05 *Tele2* (n 128 above).

Kempter that, whereas national rules conferring finality upon administrative decisions in the interests of legal certainty are governed by the criteria set out in *Kühne & Heitz*, in order to determine whether the administrative time-limit for challenging such decisions complies with Union law, the need for legal certainty is to be calculated according to the standards laid down in *Rewe/Comet*.[147] It thus appears that what we have traditionally thought of as the principles of effective *judicial* protection are in the course of being adopted—and surely also adapted—so as to establish minimum standards of good *administrative* process in cases involving Union law.[148]

Similarly, commentators have long pointed out that dividing 'substantive Union law' from 'national procedural autonomy' is a far from simple exercise.[149] Such 'boundary disputes' arise acutely over the issue of standing, that is, the task of determining precisely which range of individuals should be considered as enjoying legal capacity to bring an action before the national courts for the purposes of enforcing any given provision of Union law. There is significant academic support for the proposition that, whereas subsequent questions concerning the available range of remedies or at least the applicable forms of procedure can be left to national law within the framework of Community supervision provided for under *Rewe/Comet*, the prior task of identifying who can rely on a given provision of Union law in the first place is simply not an issue of effective judicial protection at all, but rather a matter of interpreting the content of the relevant Treaty provisions and, in particular, of determining their inherent personal scope—a responsibility which must fall within the exclusive competence of Union law itself, as exercised through the hermeneutic monopoly of the ECJ.[150]

It is indeed true that, in many cases, the Court treats questions about standing to enforce Union law as an integral aspect of Treaty interpretation which must be undertaken directly by the Court itself and should result in a common approach across all the Member States: consider, for example, case law defining the scope of persons other than migrant workers entitled to rely upon the direct effect of Article 45 TFEU;[151] or the range of individuals entitled to enforce various instruments of Union environmental policy.[152] But that is not always the case. In other rulings, the ECJ has indeed considered the issue of standing to enforce Union law as an aspect of effective judicial protection which should be dealt with using the more complex legal tools provided by the *Rewe/Comet* framework and thus amenable to (potentially consider-

---

[147] Case C-2/06 *Kempter* [2008] ECR I-411. Cf Case C-291/03 *MyTravel* [2005] ECR I-8477.

[148] Consider Case C-194/04 *Nevedi* [2005] ECR I-10423.

[149] Consider Case C-8/08 *T-Mobile Netherlands*, 4 June 2009: rules governing the burden of proof for the purposes of determining the existence of a concerted practice under Art 101 TFEU form part of substantive Community competition law (and are therefore not to be treated as a procedural issue governed by *Rewe/Comet*).

[150] T Eilmansberger, 'The Relationship Between Rights and Remedies in EC Law: In Search of the Missing Link' (2004) 41 CML Rev 1199.

[151] See eg Case C-350/96 *Clean Car Autoservice* (n 74 above); Case C-208/05 *ITC Innovative Technology Centre* [2007] ECR I-181.

[152] See eg Case C-72/95 *Kraaijeveld* [1996] ECR I-5403; Case C-201/02 *Delena Wells* [2004] ECR I-723; Case C-237/07 *Janecek* [2008] ECR I-6221. Also: Case C-97/96 *Daihatsu Deutschland* [1997] ECR I-6843; Case C-253/00 *Muñoz* (n 92 above).

able) variation across the Member States:[153] consider, for example, case law concerning the range of persons able to enforce the principle of equal treatment on grounds of sex as regards the national social security systems;[154] or the categories of party entitled to invoke the prohibition on giving effect to state aid measures as contained in Article 108(3) TFEU.[155] Developing a coherent conceptual and doctrinal approach to resolving this fundamental uncertainty evidently poses a significant challenge for the future.[156]

(c) Union legislation on national remedies and procedures

According to our 'core narrative', the legislative harmonization of national remedies and procedural rules represents the ultimate and indeed preferred solution to the problems of effectiveness and uniformity posed by decentralized enforcement. After all, the ECJ itself in *Rewe/Comet* seemed to envisage that its framework of national autonomy, equivalence, and effectiveness provided only a temporary or default approach to Union control over the national systems of judicial protection, and specifically suggested the use of legal bases such as (what are now) Articles 115 and 352 TFEU for the purpose of removing distortions of competition and other obstacles to the proper functioning of the common market attributable to differences in the Member State's remedies and procedural rules.[157]

In practice, the Union legislature has responded to the Court's call to reinforce the effectiveness and uniform application of Union law—whether for the benefit of the internal market,[158] or for the sake of any other substantive Treaty policy[159]—only occasionally and often through relatively marginal intrusions into the presumption of national autonomy.[160] To be sure, there are a small number of secondary measures which address the decentralized enforcement of Union law in significant detail for specific sectors: the Public Procurement Remedies Directive has given rise to a considerable jurisprudence in its own right;[161] consider also measures such as those dealing with the burden of proof in sex discrimination cases,[162] injunctions in consumer disputes,[163]

---

[153] Van Gerven (n 67 above).

[154] See eg Cases C-87-89/09 *Verholen* [1991] ECR I-3757.

[155] See eg Case C-174/02 *Streekgewest Westelijk Noord-Brabant* [2005] ECR I-85. Consider also Case C-13/01 *Safalero* [2003] ECR I-8679; Case C-432/05 *Unibet* (n 86 above).

[156] Other recent rulings include Case C-216/02 *Österreichischer Zuchtverband für Ponys, Kleinpferde und Spezialrassen* [2004] ECR I-10683; Case C-12/08 *Mono Car Styling*, 16 July 2009; Case C-263/08 *Djurgården-Lilla Värtans Miljöskyddsförening*, 15 October 2009. See M Dougan, 'Who Exactly Benefits from the Treaties? The Murky Interaction Between Union and National Competence over the Capacity to Enforce EU Law?' (2010) 12 CYELS 73.

[157] Case 33/76 and Case 45/76 (n 3 above) [5] and [14] (respectively).

[158] See eg under Art 95 EC (now Art 114 TFEU).

[159] See eg under Art 137 EC on social policy or Art 175 EC on environmental policy (now Arts 153 and 192 TFEU respectively).

[160] T Heukels and J Tib, 'Towards Homogeneity in the Field of Legal Remedies: Convergence and Divergence' in P Beaumont, C Lyons, and N Walker (n 51 above).

[161] Council Directive 89/665, [1989] OJ L395/33.

[162] Directive 97/80, [1998] OJ L14/6; now Directive 2006/54, [2006] OJ L204/23.

[163] Council Directive 98/27, [1998] OJ L166/51; now Directive 2009/22, [2009] OJ L110/30.

implementation of the Århus Convention on access to justice in environmental matters,[164] environmental liability with regard to the prevention and remedying of environmental damage,[165] and the enforcement of intellectual property rights.[166] But for the
most part, the Union legislature has confined itself either to tinkering with limited
procedural issues,[167] or including general clauses about enforcement which do no more
than codify or recall the Member States' existing obligations under the *Rewe/Comet*
case law.[168] Any systematic programme for the harmonization of the national systems
of judicial protection in cases involving the enforcement of substantive Treaty rules has
yet to emerge, despite the considerable effort devoted to the issue through projects such
as the *Storme Report*.[169] For their part, the Member States, in their capacity as 'masters
of the Treaties', appear basically content with the status quo: Article 19(1) TEU now states
merely that Member States shall provide remedies sufficient to ensure effective legal
protection in the fields covered by Union law.[170]

However, in the period since the Treaty on European Union, and especially following
the Treaty of Amsterdam, the interest of the Union legislature in issues concerning judicial
enforcement within the Member States has been kindled in a manner neither envisaged
nor accounted for by our 'core narrative' and, in particular, for reasons distinct from the
latter's concerns about securing the effectiveness and uniform application of substantive
Treaty rules. That interest is attributable rather to the goal of developing the Union into an
Area of Freedom, Security and Justice.[171] Through the legal bases previously provided for
under Title IV, Part Three EC (which included judicial cooperation in civil matters) and
Title VI EU (which covered judicial cooperation in criminal matters)—now to be found
all together in Title V, Part Three TFEU—the Union legislature has adopted a series of
measures which impact upon national remedies, sanctions, and procedural rules in a
variety of ways: sometimes pursuant to the objective of facilitating mutual recognition in
certain fields of civil and criminal law;[172] also through the straightforward approximation
of selected substantive and procedural rules.[173]

---

[164] Council Directive 2003/35, [2003] OJ L156/17.

[165] Council Directive 2004/35, [2004] OJ L143/56.

[166] Council Directive 2004/48, [2004] OJ L157/45.

[167] Consider: Council Directive 85/374, [1985] OJ L210/29; Directive 93/13, [1993] OJ L95/29; Directive
99/44, [1999] OJ L171/12; Regulation 1/2003, [2003] OJ L1/1.

[168] Consider: Council Directives 91/533, [1991] OJ L288/32; 92/85, [1992] OJ L348/1; 94/33, [1994] OJ
L216/12; 98/59, [1998] OJ L225/16; 2001/23, [2001] OJ L82/16.

[169] M Storme (ed), *Approximation of Judiciary Law in the European Union* (Kluwer Law International,
1994).

[170] Similarly, the introduction of Art 83(2) TFEU on the Union's competence to impose criminal sanctions
in areas already subject to harmonization measures builds on the existing position under Case C-176/03
Commission v Council [2005] ECR I-7879 and Case C-440/05 *Commission v Council* [2007] ECR I-9097.

[171] See Chapters 11 and 10 in this collection by Storskrubb and Peers (respectively).

[172] On civil law, eg Regulation 44/2001, [2001] OJ L12/1; Regulation 2201/2003, [2003] OJ L338/1. On
criminal law, eg Framework Decision 2002/584, [2002] OJ L190/1; Framework Decision 2008/909, [2008] OJ
L327/27.

[173] See eg Framework Decision 2001/220, [2001] OJ L82/1; Framework Decision 2002/475, [2002] OJ L164/
3; Directive 2003/8, [2003] OJ L26/41; Directive 2008/99, [2008] OJ L328/28.

Building the AFSJ has thereby resulted in significant interventions into the ordinary functioning of the domestic legal systems—often with controversial results. For example, the Union's considerable efforts at approximating the type and level of criminal sanctions which Member States should impose for a wide range of offences, some of which are primarily intended to bolster the effective enforcement of particular substantive Community policies,[174] while others are considered necessary for the purposes of facilitating closer cross-border police and judicial cooperation within the specific context of the AFSJ,[175] have led to accusations that the EU is promoting excessive resort to the criminal justice system and encouraging reliance upon repressive punishments such as incarceration.[176] Again, however, the products of this new-found legislative activity remain, for the time being, too targeted in scope and limited in content to presage the construction of a unified system of judicial protection in Europe. Reform of the primary law governing the AFSJ as contained in the Lisbon Treaty does not in itself signal any significant change in this regard; indeed, if the warnings contained in the judgment of the German Federal Constitutional Court concerning ratification of the Lisbon Treaty are taken seriously, Union action, particularly in the field of criminal law and procedure, should if anything become more targeted and restrained.[177] In any case, the coordination/approximation of national remedies and procedural rules for the purposes of the AFSJ is evidently a very different pattern of legislative activity from that originally envisaged by the ECJ in *Rewe/Comet*, bearing as it does no inherent connection to either the policy framework or the allocation of institutional tasks contemplated by our 'core narrative'.

D. CONCLUDING REMARKS

Union law on national remedies and procedural rules has traditionally been dominated by a particular scholarly narrative characterized by the mutually reinforcing combination of a particular understanding of the relevant policy challenges, a specific doctrinal model within which those challenges should be addressed, and an agreed historical framework for analysing the relevant case law. This chapter has suggested that that triptych served us extraordinarily well for many years, but more recently, its elements have jointly as well as severally lost their ability to provide a comprehensive picture of Union activity in the field of effective judicial protection. Additional legal tools possessed of their own specific conceptual framework and particular doctrinal

---

[174] See eg Framework Decision 2001/500, [2001] OJ L182/1; Framework Decision 2002/946, [2002] OJ L328/1; Directive 2008/99, [2008] OJ L328/28.

[175] See eg Framework Decision 2002/475, [2002] OJ L164/3; Framework Decision 2004/757, [2004] OJ L335/8; Framework Decision 2008/841, [2008] OJ L300/42; Framework Decision 2008/913, [2008] OJ L328/55.

[176] P Asp, 'Harmonisation and Cooperation Within the Third Pillar: Built In Risks' (2001) 4 CYELS 15; E Herlin-Karnell, '*Commission v Council:* Some Reflections on Criminal Law in the First Pillar' (2007) 13 EPL 69.

[177] German Constitutional Court, *Lisbon Decision*, 2 BvE 2/08, 2 BvE 5/08, 2 BvR 1010/08, 2 BvR 1022/08, 2 BvR 1259/08 and 2 BvR 182/09 (judgment of 30 June 2009).

concerns, lines of case law and legislative activity displaying their own distinct evolutionary experiences, and a more critical approach towards the nature and importance of the core imperatives of effectiveness and uniformity, have all exploded the range of legal and policy issues at stake in the decentralized enforcement of Union law.

Altogether, one senses that the fuel which fired the 'core narrative' across several decades, giving the case law its turbulence and the scholarship its excitement, all within a nevertheless coherent overarching picture, has now been largely spent. Of course, the rich body of academic discourse which blossomed alongside the unfolding case law during its two formative decades after 1976 should still be valued as an indispensable source of historical and contextual understanding for the present law. But absent another dramatic volte-face by the ECJ, to expect that 'core narrative' to continue providing the primary critical framework for analysing the more recent (or future) case law risks becoming trapped in something of an academic cul-de-sac in which the potential for novel insights becomes all but exhausted. That said, even if the terms of the policy debate may seem less confidently drawn, and the legal landscape appears ever more fragmented and specialized, the contemporary jurisprudence on effective judicial protection still offers a host of neglected issues and emerging novelties which should provide the basis for a new and equally rich programme of research into the future.

15

THREE PHASES IN THE EVOLUTION OF EU ADMINISTRATIVE LAW

*Carol Harlow**

A. INTRODUCTION

Administrative law is generally understood to be that branch of public law which regulates the administration, the assumption being also that it relates to state or government. Thus Shapiro sees public administration as 'bounded' or 'billeted' or 'nested' in a constitution of a particular kind where the administrator owes a dual duty to 'faithfully implement' the laws and regulations produced by the legislator and to citizens 'to whom administrators owe legally correct procedural and substantive action'.[1] Outside this framework, Shapiro believes that the control function seen by him as the core of administrative law is difficult or impossible to achieve. The problems of this classical style of definition for a transnational legal order like that of the European Union, where citizenship has always been an essentially contested concept[2] and where, at the genesis of administrative law, no democratic legislature of the type envisaged by Shapiro yet existed, are self-evident. This is probably one reason why the European Court of Justice[3] found it helpful in laying the foundations of a system of European administrative law to 'billet' it inside the framework of a supposed 'constitution' based on the Treaties, conceptualizing the new dual-level system much like a federal system of administrative law. Inside this framework, as explained in Section B, general principles of a European administrative law, founded on concepts familiar inside national systems, were laid down by the ECJ.

---

* Emeritus Professor of Law at the London School of Economics.
[1] M Shapiro, 'Administrative Law Unbounded' (2001) 8 Ind J Global Legal Studies 369.
[2] J Shaw, 'The Interpretation of European Citizenship' (1998) 61 MLR 293.
[3] Formally the Court of Justice of the European Union, hereinafter always ECJ. The Court of First Instance is correctly the General Court but the abbreviation CFI is used throughout. The term 'Community Courts' here refers only to the ECJ and CFI.

I shall argue in Section C, however, that rigid adherence to this framework has left the ECJ with problems that it must now face up to and overcome.

Public law space is then broadly speaking shared between constitutional law, which prescribes the institutions of government and administrative law, which governs their operation, though definitions of constitutional or administrative law and distinctions drawn between them tend to be both arbitrary and 'based on the convenience of the particular writer'.[4] There is certainly considerable overlap; Taggart, for example, sees the general principles of administrative and constitutional law as covering much the same ground.[5] This is an important point in considering the jurisprudence of the ECJ which, in exercising its Treaty responsibility for ensuring that the law is observed in the interpretation and application of the Treaties (TEC Article 220 ex 164) has come to see itself as a Constitutional Court. This undoubtedly encouraged an integrationist tendency that has led the ECJ from the earliest days to treat the general principles that form the building blocks of the European system of administrative law as constitutional principles. This then encouraged a further temptation to 'constitutionalize' the principles and pass them vertically downwards into the administrative law of the Member States. Although in giving way to this temptation, the ECJ is following a path trodden by most transnational and Constitutional Courts, I shall argue that it is not an appropriate way forward in the third, post-Lisbon phase of development.

Constitutional and administrative law have in common the overarching objective of establishing the rule of law by overseeing the legality of administrative action and this is clearly the fundamental principle of European administrative law as derived from the Treaties and conceived by the ECJ. In EU administrative law, as in most modern administrative law systems, two further elements derived from classical administrative law theory share the space. On the one hand, we find an emphasis on control of administration and the protection of private and individual rights with the central role accorded to courts, a bias very evident in academic commentaries and notably the pioneering work of Jürgen Schwarze.[6] A second and equally important role for administrative law lies, however, in establishing the rules for the operation of the administrative process, a secondary framework inside which the administration operates. Thus a classical definition from a French treatise describes administrative law as concerned with 'all the special rules relative to the functioning of the public services'[7], allocating the primary role to administration and law-maker.

---

[4] J Griffith and H Street, *Principles of Administrative Law* (5th edn, Pitman, 1973) 3.

[5] M Taggart, 'The Province of Administrative Law Determined' in M Taggart (ed), *The Province of Administrative Law* (Hart, 1997) 4.

[6] See, eg, J Schwarze, 'Sources of European Administrative Law in S Martin (ed), *The Construction of Europe, Essays in Honour of Emile Noel* (Kluwer, 1994); idem, 'Towards a Common European Public Law' (1995) 1 EPL 227; J Schwarze, *European Administrative Law* (Sweet & Maxwell, 1992).

[7] C Harlow, 'European Administrative Law and the Global Challenge' in P Craig and G de Búrca (eds), *The European Union in Perspective* (Oxford University Press, 1999) citing C Eisenmann, *Cours de droit administratif* (LGDJ, 1982) Vol 1, 17.

Administrative law, then, regulates the ways in which executive and administration carry out their policies and exercise their functions. It structures and confines the use of administrative discretion—a primary target for twentieth-century administrative law—both by the use of rules and retrospectively through judicial decision-making. It is also responsible for putting in place a body of administrative procedures. Both types of operation contribute to the control of public power and afford protection for the rights of private parties. Developed systems of judicial review have today become the norm with the functions of establishing the legality of administrative action, proscribing misuse of power, and protecting the rights of private parties. It would seem to follow that, without a developed judicial review system, the rule of law in the European Communities would have been in doubt and its Court would have lacked standing. It was therefore incumbent on the ECJ to create or spell one out of the Treaties[8] and this, as we shall see in Section B, is precisely what it did.

Understandings of administrative law may, however, change and recently a wider agenda has been set for administrative law. As already indicated, the general principles of administrative law originated in constitutional or administrative law: the familiar due process rules, for example, have long been part of administrative law, overlapping with the rights of the defence in criminal procedure. In EU law, new or newly formulated principles such as the right of 'access to the court' and 'effective judicial remedy' have emerged as constitutional rights. Alternatively, general principles may originate inside public administration, borrowed from fashionable 'good governance' principles such as transparency, accountability, and participation, adopted for the EU by the European Commission in 2001.[9] These too have taken hold, as described in Section B.

The tendency to lift rights to constitutional level where they could operate as 'trump cards' has been greatly accentuated by the spread of the human rights movement. Accordingly, the concept of due process was gradually absorbed into the catalogue of fundamental human rights and began to be globalized as a 'universal human right'.[10] This is a direction in which European administrative law is currently being pushed, as Section D suggests.

These and similar pressures are sometimes seen as a 'global challenge' to administrative law generally.[11] In the EU system they are however accentuated by the emerging style of governance. As initially envisaged, the European Commission, although described in the Treaties as the European administration (TEC Article 211), was more

---

[8] See the view of M Lagrange, 'La Cour de Justice des Communautés Européennes: du plan Schuman à l'union européene' (1978) RTD eur 1.

[9] European Commission, White Paper on European Governance (hereinafter White Paper), COM(2001) 428 final, [2001] OJ C287, 1, 10.

[10] C Harlow, 'Global Administrative Law: The Quest for Principles and Values' (2006) 17 EJIL 187; R Teitel, 'New Approaches to Comparative Law: Comparativism and International Governance', (2004) 117 Harv L Rev 2570.

[11] A Aman, 'Administrative Law for a New Century' in Taggart (n 5 above) and *The Democracy Deficit* (New York University Press, 2004).

like an autonomous regulatory agency than the central administration of a nation state.[12] Its role has always transcended the duty of 'faithful implementation' described by Shapiro.[13] The Commission possesses a formal power to initiate legislation and even today, when the Lisbon Treaty has established Council and Parliament co-decision as the 'ordinary legislative procedure' for the EU (TFEU Articles 289 and 29), the Commission remains an unusually influential participant in the law-making procedure.[14] In short, the institutional arrangements have never followed the classical separation of powers model and argument has always raged over the nature and characteristics of the regime:[15] on one side, a journey to integration, statehood, and federation; on the other, a confederation of sovereign national states.[16] Integrationism was the dominant ethos and ultimate goal of those engaged in shaping the future of Europe. As Weiler observed, lawyers during the foundational period were likely to say that the Community was becoming 'more and more like a federal (or at least pre-federal) state',[17] the actual picture being one of 'integration by stealth' in which, as is well known, law fulfilled a central function and lawyers were key actors. The infant Community was weak while the Commission and Court of Justice (ECJ), 'founding fathers' of the Community administrative law system, were strong and self-confident. The two institutions set about laying the foundation stones for a European administrative law. Section B of this chapter deals with the early days.

Two key events mark the opening of a new phase of administrative law in the EU, briefly described in Section C. The first was the Treaty of Maastricht in 1992, which created the EU and also for the first time formally extended its ambit into areas of justice and home affairs, which had previously fallen squarely within the competence of the Member States. This created new challenges for administrative law, while at the same time seriously diminishing the ability of the two key institutions to respond. It is perhaps surprising that the ECJ should have so easily established its credentials as 'constitution-maker' and shown itself able to enforce its seminal constitutional decisions[18] in the face of considerable antagonism from Member State governments[19]

---

[12] G Majone, 'The rise of the regulatory state in Europe' (1994) 17 WEP 77.

[13] K Lenaerts, 'Some Reflections on the Separation of Powers in the European Community' (1991) 28 CML Rev 11.

[14] TFEU Arts 289, 293(1) and (2). It also gains powers of delegated legislation (Art 290).

[15] This is not the place for a literature survey: see for general discussion, B Rosamond, *Theories of European Integration* (Palgrave Macmillan, 2000).

[16] See the debates between F Mancini, 'Europe: The Case for Statehood' (1998) 4 ELJ 29 and J Weiler, 'Europe: The Case against the Case for Statehood' (1998) 4 ELJ 43 and between G Majone, *Dilemmas of European Integration: The Ambiguities and Pitfalls of Integration by Stealth* (Oxford University Press, 2005) and M Dougan, '"And some fell on stony ground"...' (2006) 31 ELRev 865.

[17] J Weiler, *The Constitution of Europe* (Cambridge University Press, 1999) 16.

[18] Case 26/62 *Van Gend en Loos v Nederlandse Administratie Belastingen* [1963] ECR 1; Case 6/64 *Costa v ENEL* [1964] ECR 585; Case 35/76 *Simmenthal v Amministrazione delle Finanze dello Stato* [1976] ECR 1871.

[19] K Alter, 'Who are the Masters of the Treaty? European Governments and the ECJ' (1998) 52 IO 121; R Dehousse, *The European Court of Justice* (Macmillan, 1998) 165–168.

and occasional rebellion by national courts.[20] Whatever the explanation, some of the resentment undoubtedly found its way into the Maastricht Treaty, which dismantled for the area of Justice and Home Affairs (JHA) the judicial safeguards that had allowed for the building of a European system of judicial review.[21] Ironically, in the so-called 'area of security, freedom and justice', the Commission was replaced as executive power by the Council and its key committees[22] while the ECJ did not acquire the powers of strong judicial review that it possessed in the Community Pillar.

The second key event for administrative law was the fall of the disgraced Santer Commission in 1999, leading directly to changes in the role and position of the Commission. For President-elect Prodi, the Commission had to do less but do it rather better. Some of the reforms introduced in response are considered in Section C. Alongside, however, new systems of governance were beginning, almost unnoticed, to develop. The Community was at first perceived as a two-level system. The traditional way to analyse its administration was triadic: there was *direct administration*, as with EC competition law; *indirect administration*, where implementation of EU policy was 'downloaded' to national administrative systems; and *cooperative or shared administration*, where the two levels worked together. But as Rhodes noted, the EU system of government was changing radically. The role of the Commission (doing less) was more that of a 'coordinator of networks' than of a classical public administration responsible for service delivery.[23] A multi-level system of 'governance' began to emerge based on informal, cooperative practices: the 'open method of coordination', 'new governance', and 'governance by networks'. Chiti pointed to 'bottom-up' mechanisms of integration, where an EU objective is carried out through mutual cooperation between Member States and 'top-down' mechanisms, where the EU operates through 'autonomous' bodies such as agencies, which exchange information and monitor collaboration.[24] Cassese talks of transnational 'networks' of national and supranational actors acting in 'regulatory concert' to carry out jointly agreed policies by diverse means.[25] European agencies and networks of agencies began to proliferate. What the various forms of new governance have in common is that all avoid the methodology of administrative law and depend more on administrative practice. These changes and their implications for European administrative law are considered at the end of Section C.

Section D of this chapter is largely speculative. I shall argue that a transformative moment has been reached. In the wake of the Lisbon Treaty, EU administrative law faces several further challenges. The first is the extension of the rule of law and

---

[20] See the country studies in A M Slaughter *et al* (eds), *The European Courts and National Courts—Doctrine and Jurisprudence* (Hart, 1998).

[21] See Art 35 EU, which allowed Member States to opt in to preliminary reference procedure in JHA matters and restricted the courts that could refer. But see now Art 276 TFEU.

[22] D Curtin, *The Executive Power of the European Union* (Oxford University Press, 2009).

[23] R Rhodes, 'What is New about Governance and Why does it Matter?' in Hayward and A Menon (eds), *Governing Europe* (Oxford University Press, 2003).

[24] E Chiti, 'The Administrative Implementation of European Union Law: A Taxonomy and its Implications' in H Hofmann and A Turk (eds), *Legal Challenges in EU Administrative Law* (Edward Elgar, 2009).

[25] S Cassese, 'European Administrative Proceedings' (2004) 68 LCP 21, 22.

principle of legality to the areas of justice, home affairs, and immigration where they have been notoriously absent. This entails an enhanced concern for human rights. The second challenge comes from the hiving off of governmental functions to agencies and networks. The third comes from globalization, which increasingly impinges on the EU, challenging its defensive autonomy. In my conclusions, I shall argue that only a pluralist approach, in which diversity is valued and the concept of subsidiarity respected, can adequately resolve these problems.

B. PHASE I: BUILDING BLOCKS

The infant Community administrative law emerged against a rapidly changing institutional backdrop of a Europe of 'bits and pieces' in which neither the political priorities nor the desired constitutional structure were, or ever have been, adequately agreed or formulated. Commission and Court (ECJ), the two principal actors, shared a generally integrationist mentality and the ECJ in particular tended to deal with the issues as they arose in classical public law terms. It improvised a constitutional framework by reading the Treaties as a constitutional document ('constitutionalizing' the Treaties), developing the doctrines of 'Community method' and 'institutional balance' as a substitute for separation of powers doctrine.[26] Cautiously, it dealt with the problem that Community institutions could not operate within the territory of the Member States but had to operate through national institutions, by developing quasi-federalist doctrines. Grounded in the constitutional premise of the primacy of Community law,[27] these included the idea of shared competence: the ECJ would be responsible for developing general principles of administrative law governing Community action and acts undertaken on behalf of the Community by Member States; otherwise national administrative and procedural law would remain in place. The Court treated the Commission as the Community executive, as the Treaties authorized it to do. In practice, however, the Commission did not operate like a national executive; it steered but did not row. There was some decision-making in competition law but the Commission was never (and is not now) responsible for general service delivery, typically carried out on its behalf by national administrations.

The Treaties provided the overarching notion of a Community based on the rule of law. This was concretized by the ECJ, which drew on the jurisprudence of the Strasbourg Court of Human Rights to install the right of access to justice as a general principle of EC constitutional law The Treaties provided a second fundamental principle—very much in advance of the times—that all acts and decisions of the institutions must be *reasoned* (Article 253, ex 190 EC). Both the ECJ and, later, the CFI, treated and continue to treat reasons as a fundamental general principle of

---

[26] K Lenaerts, 'Some Reflections on the Separation of Powers in the European Community' (1991) 28 CML Rev 11.

[27] Case 26/62 *Van Gend en Loos v Nederlandse Administratie Belastingen* [1963] ECR 1.

EC law, taking every opportunity to reiterate the motives for reasoned decision-making: reasons are no mere formality but are designed 'to give an opportunity to the parties of defending their rights, to the Court of exercising its supervisory functions and to Member-states and to all interested nationals of ascertaining the circumstances in which the Commission has applied the Treaty'.[28]

The Treaty provided that acts and decisions of and failure or refusal to act by the Community institutions could be challenged through an action for annulment (Articles 230, 232 EC). An important breakthrough was made when the ECJ ruled in *Les Verts*, with a generous interpretation of the provisions, that any measure intended to produce legal effects in respect of third parties was subject to review by the Court for legality.[29] In the same case, the Court ruled that review by the European Court of Auditors (ECA), which monitors the financial legality of EU accounts, was insufficient to extinguish the need for wider review by the ECJ, covering 'legality of the basic measure'. This was a significant step on the road to establishing the primacy of the ECJ over other administrative law machinery for control. In the name of the rule of law, later cases make the same point in respect of the European Ombudsman.[30]

The EC Treaty was almost silent on the grounds for judicial review,[31] leaving the ECJ free to develop general principles. Schwarze, doyen of administrative law studies in the Community, suggests that initially the main interest lay in the construction of a system of administrative law *for* the Community; in other words, in a system applicable to Community institutions and Community administrative procedures.[32] This is, however, contestable; many would agree with Shapiro that the first priority was the 'taming' of the Member States.[33] However this may be, the ECJ drew on Article 288 (ex 215) EC, which provided that the non-contractual liability of the Community should be based on the 'general principles common to the laws of the Member States', to explore this fertile source of general principles. Thus the proportionality principle, which would ultimately emerge as the central principle of European judicial review, was derived from German law, where it is best developed and recognized as a general principle of constitutional law.[34] In the field of administrative procedure on the other

---

[28] Case 24/62 *Germany v Commission* [1963] ECR 69; Case 37/83 *Rewe-Zentrale AG v Direktor der Landwirtschaftskammer Rheinland* [1984] ECR 1229.

[29] Case 294/83 *Parti Ecologiste 'Les Verts' v European Parliament* [1986] ECR 1339. The action was directed at the bureau of the EP in allocating resources to political parties.

[30] Case T-209/00 *Lamberts v Commission* [2002] ECR II-2203; Case T-412/05 *M v Mediateur* (unreported judgment of 24 September 2008).

[31] Art 230 EC states only that the Court may annul on grounds of lack of competence, infringement of an essential procedural requirement, infringement of this Treaty or of any rule of law relating to its application, or misuse of powers.

[32] J Schwarze (ed), *Administrative Law under European Influence* (Sweet & Maxwell/Nomos, 1996) 14–16.

[33] M Shapiro, 'The European Court of Justice' in P Craig and G de Búrca, *Evolution of EU Law* (Oxford University Press, 1999).

[34] See E Emiliou, *The Principle of Proportionality in European Law: A Comparative Study* (Kluwer Law International, 1996); J Schwarze, 'The Role of General Principles of Administrative Law in the Process of Europeanization of National Law: The Case of Proportionality' in L Ortega (ed), *Studies on European Public Law* (Lex Nova, 2005).

hand the ECJ drew the central principle of due process from English principles of natural justice.[35]

Again, Schwarze sees the Court as successful in 'integrat[ing] different principles into the Community's legal order and...particularly successful in finding an appropriate synthesis between common law and continental European standards'[36] though he admits that the Court's choice usually fell on the principle most compatible with the legal order of Community law and with the closest correspondence with 'the functional capacity and the goals of the Community'.[37] This did not seem to disturb Schwarze unduly; he argued indeed that responsibility for the development of principles and procedures should 'stay in the court's hands and not be turned over to legislation, at least not in the sense of a fully-fledged codification of administrative law',[38] a view not universally shared. In any event, by the end of the first phase, the impetus had passed to the Commission, which was rapidly transforming the Community administrative processes into sector-specific rules and regulations.[39] Competition procedure had, for example, from early on been governed by a Council Regulation.[40] This had the effect of moving Community administrative law away from its previous court-based orientation towards an administrative law based on rule-making.

In practice, the administrative law of the Community was developing in several discrete areas:

(i) Following French usage, administrative law regulated the terms and conditions of employment of the institutions' staff. Since 2005, appeals in staff cases have been handled by a staff tribunal but in the early days they went to the ECJ; they thus became an important source of the law on due process in administrative proceedings.

(ii) In competition proceedings, where the Commission was faced with determined and powerful opponents with access to lawyers well-versed in American anti-trust law and due process requirements, who forced the pace of development. The response of the ECJ was to lay down procedural requirements strongly reminiscent of Anglo-American administrative law (above) and of the Commission to fill in gaps by procedural codification.[41] In this way, the foundation of due process requirements, a central preoccupation of every administrative law system, were taken into Community administrative law.

---

[35] Case 17/74 *Transocean Marine Paint v Commission* [1974] ECR 1063.

[36] J Schwarze, 'Developing Principles of European Administrative Law' [1993] PL 229, 238.

[37] J Schwarze, 'Introduction' in J Schwarze (ed), *Administrative Law under European Influence* (Sweet & Maxwell/Nomos, 1996) 14–16.

[38] ibid.

[39] C Harlow and R Rawlings, 'National Administrative Procedures in a European Perspective: Pathways to a Slow Convergence?' (forthcoming).

[40] See Council Regulation No 17/62; Commission Regulation 2842/98 OJ L354/18; Council Regulation 1/2003.

[41] K Lenaerts and L Vanhamme, 'Procedural Rights of Private Parties in the Community Administrative Process' (1997) CML Rev 523.

(iii) As already indicated, the Commission took steps from the early 1970s to regulate administrative procedure on a sector-specific basis. The importance of public procurement for the single market led, for example, to early attempts at codification, procedural as well as substantive.[42] A technique began to emerge which would be developed in the second phase of a gentle, permissive start to a harmonizing regime with 'very much of a framework character', which later moved 'markedly away from its framework character in the direction of a system of common rules'.[43] In the so-called Remedies Directives[44] in particular, the Commission attempted to provide a common system of judicial remedies available to private parties in national courts. This, though not always successful in practice, was a more ambitious approach than could be undertaken by the ECJ in its case law on judicial remedies. Although the Commission was the major player, it had to work with the ECJ, which did not stop short at interpreting the regulations but introduced of its own volition new principles in often controversial case law, frequently implying *additional* obligations when no explicit rules existed.[45]

(iv) Through preliminary references under Article 234 of the Treaty, where the ECJ was able to make its voice heard by monitoring enforcement of EC law at national level through actions by private parties, consciously built up by the ECJ into a system of 'judicial liability'.[46] As indicated earlier, the ECJ did not always resist the temptation to 'constitutionalize'. In the seminal *Johnston* decision,[47] for example, the ECJ ruled that a ministerial certificate ousting the jurisdiction of an employment tribunal, at the time a perfectly proper if undesirable UK practice, offended against the principle of access to the court. In the *Heylens* case,[48] the same principle was extended to administrative proceedings, blurring a long-established distinction in French administrative law between administrative proceedings, where the rights of the defence were applicable, and criminal-type proceedings, where they were not.

Much had been achieved by the end of the first phase. The ECJ had set significant general principles of constitutional and administrative law in place, adding to the constitutional doctrine of primacy, the principles of effectiveness of EC law, and the duty of mutual cooperation imposed on institutions and Member States by Article 10

---

[42] Commission Green Paper, Public Procurement in the European Union: Exploring the Way Forward, COM(96) 583 and Commission White Paper, Completing the Internal Market, COM(85) 310 were followed by a raft of Directives: 89/665 (Compliance), 92/13 (Utilities Remedies), 93/38 (Utilities), 93/37 (Works), 93/96 (Supplies), 92/50 (Services). This phase of law-making is now superseded.

[43] S Arrowsmith, 'The Past and Future Evolution of EC Procurement Law: From Framework to Common Code?' (2006) 35 Pub Cont LJ 337.

[44] Council Directive 2007/66/EC amending Council Directives 89/665/EEC and 92/13/EEC with regard to improving the effectiveness of review procedures concerning the award of public contracts. And see J Golding and P Henty, 'The New Remedies Directive of the EC: Standstill and Ineffectiveness' [2008] PPLR 146.

[45] Arrowsmith (n 43 above) 354.

[46] F Snyder, The Effectiveness of European Community Law: Institutions, Processes, Tools and Techniques' (1993) 56 MLR 19.

[47] Case 222/84 *Johnston v Royal Ulster Constabulary* [1986] ECR 1651.

[48] Case 222/86 *UNECTEF v Heylens* [1987] ECR 4097. The applicant in this case had asked for his Belgian qualification to be recognized in France.

(ex 5) EC. It had established the fundamental principles of administrative procedure and by the end of this period, the Commission and legislator had also taken a leading role in procedural matters. This was an important development. Rule-making is a more transparent way of regulating procedures. It affords the basis for wider input by 'stakeholders' than the standing rules of the ECJ permit (see below) and allows for public discussion of what the procedures should be.[49]

Much had also been achieved by way of institution-building. The first European Ombudsman (EO) was appointed in 1995 and quickly began to make a mark with 'own initiative investigations'[50] and a commitment to promoting good administration. The CFI had come into being in 1988 with competence to deal with claims by 'individuals' (in practice largely transnational commercial enterprises and their in-house lawyers, which played a significant and aggressive role in the development of Community administrative procedures). It was now forging a role for itself as the Community's administrative law court. The CFI took its role in relieving the ECJ from the burden of 'time-consuming factually highly complex matters' very seriously, developing a style of intensive scrutiny of administrative fact-finding and administrative procedures stylistically comparable to the Court's performance of the 'hard look review' used in the same period by American courts.[51] As Nehl put it, it 'soon became clear—as it was actually intended—that the CFI, as compared to the ECJ, would shift to a more active and thorough fact finding and evaluation'.[52] The CFI was also prepared to experiment: it tried, for example, to develop the idea of a Commission 'duty of care' to handle cases with 'due diligence'[53] and has played a significant role in developing adequate procedures for handling access to information requests.[54]

Three distinct modes of administration had been recognized, which received differential treatment from the ECJ. *Direct administration* was covered by a new system of Community administrative law, based on principles developed by the ECJ, though often drawn from the law of the Member States and on rules promulgated by the Community legislator. *Indirect administration,* where a national administration or

---

[49] This is the celebrated argument of K C Davis in *Discretionary Justice: A Preliminary Inquiry* (Louisiana State University Press, 1969) discussed by C Harlow and R Rawlings, *Law and Administration* (3rd edn, Cambridge University Press, 2009) ch 5.

[50] Notably the Special Report and Decision by the EO following the Own-Initiative Inquiry into Public Access to Documents held by Community Institutions and Bodies (December 1997).

[51] Notable examples are Case T-7/89 *Hercules Chemicals v Commission* [1991] ECR II-171; Case T-13//99 *Pfizer* [2002] ECR II-3305; Case T-70//99 *Alpharma v Council* [2002] ELR II-3475. For other examples, see H-P Nehl, *Principles of Administrative Procedure in EC Law* (Hart, 1998).

[52] Nehl (n 51 above) at 8.

[53] Case T-54/99 *Max.mobil Telekommunikation Service GmbH v Commission* [2002] II-0313 [47]–[63]. Supported by AG Maduro, the novelty was crushed by the ECJ on appeal: Case C-141/02P *Commission v T-Mobile Austria GmbH* [2005] ECR I-1283.

[54] Cf Case T-194/94 *Carvel and Guardian Newspapers v Council* [1995] ECR II-2769 with Case C-68/94 *Netherlands v Council* [1996] ECR I-2169. See Case T-174/95 *Svenska Journalistforbundet v Council* [1998] ECR II-2289. Later the courts' roles were to be reversed: see Case T-84/03, *Maurizio Turco v Council* [2004] ECR II-4061; Cases C-39/05 and C-52/05 *Sweden and Turco v Council* [2008] ECR I-4723, noted Arnull (2009) 46 CML Rev 1219.

agency implemented Community policies on behalf of the Commission, was chal-
lengeable in national courts and governed by the principle of procedural autonomy,
subject to the proviso that effective and non-discriminatory legal remedies for violations of EC law must be available in the national legal order.[55] As already indicated,
the ECJ found the opportunity to make its voice heard through the preliminary
reference procedure. It was here that serious potential for impact on national administrative law systems existed, leading to clashes. The Court's centralizing mentality
began to attract criticism that it was pushing the Community's competence boundaries
too far and penetrating too deeply into national legal systems;[56] it was, in other words,
ignoring its self-imposed limits on intervention in national legal orders. In *Watts*,[57] for
example, a UK resident sought to use medical services in France and charge the cost to
the British National Health Service. The ECJ ruled that the necessity for prior
authorization on which the NHS insisted would be lawful only if the system were
'based on a procedural system which is easily accessible and capable of ensuring that a
request for authorisation will be dealt with objectively and impartially within a
reasonable time'. To this requirement of transparency the ECJ added that refusals
to grant authorization must also 'be capable of being challenged in judicial or quasi-
judicial proceedings'. Nor did the ECJ baulk at creating 'new' administrative law
remedies and imposing them on national legal orders, such as new doctrines of state
liability[58] or the power to order interim measures against the state.[59] A further
allegation was that the ECJ was not neutral; it treated the Commission too favourably,
often condoning vestigial statements of reasons and blatant breaches of due process
principles, which would not have been tolerated if committed by a Member State.[60]
Some credence was lent to this impression by the Commission's habit of appearing
regularly as *amicus curiae* in preliminary references, a strategy designed to enhance its
position next to the Court.[61]

---

[55] Case 33/76 *Rewe-Zentralfinanz eG and Rewe-Zentral AG v Land Wirtschaftskammer für das Saarland*
[1976] ECR 1989. See R Crauford Smith, 'Remedies for Breaches of EU Law in National Courts: Legal
Variation and Selection' in P Craig and G de Búrca, *Evolution of EU Law* (n 33 above) and, for recent
developments, Dougan in this volume.

[56] See especially the debate that followed publication of the controversial attack on the ECJ by
H Rasmussen, *On Law and Policy in the Court of Justice* (Martinus Nijhoff, 1986); Weiler, (1987) 24 MLR
556; Cappelletti, (1987) 12 ELRev 3; Shapiro, (1987) 81 AJIL 1007. And see T Hartley, 'The European Court,
Judicial Objectivity and the Constitution of the European Union' (1996) 112 LQR 95.

[57] Case C-372/04 *R (Yvonne Watts) v Bedford Primary Care Trust and Secretary of State for Health* [2006]
ECR I-4325 [116]. A stronger expression of these views is found in AG Geelhoed's Opinion at [86].

[58] Cases C-6 and 9/90 *Francovich and Bonafaci v Italy* [1991] ECR I-5357; Case C-224/01 *Köbler v Austria*
[2003] ELR I-10239.

[59] Case C-213/89 *R v Secretary of State for Transport ex p Factortame* [1990] ECR I-2433.

[60] D Slater, S Thomas, and D Waelbroeck, 'Competition Law Proceedings before the European Commission
and the Right to a Fair Trial: No Need for Reform?' [2009] Comp Law 97; A Forrester, 'Due Process in EC
Competition Cases: A Distinguished Institution with Flawed Procedures' (2009) 34 ELRev 817.

[61] H Schermers *et al* (eds), *Article 177 of the EEC: Experiences and Problems* (North Holland, 1987). The
Commission still maintains this practice.

In areas of *shared administration*, where the two administrative levels worked in tandem, the emergent multi-level system of administration was beginning to throw up novel problems for European administrative law, creating 'accountability gaps', which the Community Courts found difficulty in filling. Indeed, the split-level, dual competence solutions devised by the ECJ were arguably inadequate to deal with the problems and the ECJ was slow to face up to them. The Community administration was evolving into an 'administrative space' or 'governance system' for which the dualist system of administrative law that had come into being was patently insufficient. The gaps were beginning to show. At the very end of the first phase came the seminal *Munich University* case[62] in which for the first time the ECJ attempted an answer. The University wished to import a telescope without submitting to unduly heavy import duties imposed by the Community but was frustrated by the actions of the national customs service acting in concert with the Commission. The split-level decision-making process was analysed by the ECJ as a 'composite' or 'multi-step' procedure[63] for which it was able to fashion an appropriate administrative procedure based on the due process principles that it had already established. This was a step in the direction of assuming control over multi-level administrative processes.

The ECJ has, however, shown itself much less inventive in handling the controversial question of individual standing to sue. It is unnecessary to describe in detail the well-known difficulty for parties other than Member States and Community institutions to bring an annulment action to the Community Courts.[64] As Advocate General Jacobs emphasized in the important case of *Unión de Pequeños Agricultores*,[65] this acts as a serious barrier to challenging illegal Community regulations in the Community Courts. Recognizing that an unduly strict interpretation of the Treaty provisions on standing left many of those adversely affected by Community regulations without effective judicial protection, both Advocate General Jacobs and the CFI favoured relaxing the restrictive case law.[66] The ECJ remained unmoved.

C. PHASE 2: CONSOLIDATION AND CHANGE

The second phase of European administrative law has been dominated by a perceived need for administrative reform dictated by scandal that rocked the Commission

---

[62] Case C-269/90 *Hauptzollamt München-Mitte v Technische Universitat München* [1991] ECR I-5469.

[63] See H Hofmann, 'Composite decision making procedures in EU administrative law' in Hofmann and Turk (n 23 above).

[64] Art 230 EC. There is a copious literature collected in C Koch, 'Locus Standi of Private Applicants under the EU Constitution: Preserving Gaps in the Protection of Individuals' Right to an Effective Remedy' (2005) 30 ELRev 511. Art 263 TFEU eases the problem by substituting: 'Any natural or legal person may...institute proceedings against...a regulatory act which is of direct concern to them and does not entail implementing measures.'

[65] Case C-50/00 *Unión de Pequenos Agricultores v Council* [2002] ECR II-2365.

[66] Case T-177/01 *Jégo-Quéré et Cie SA v Commission* [2002] ECR II-2365; Case C-263/02P *Commission v Jégo-Quéré et Cie SA* [2004] ECR I-3425.

during 1999. Inside the Commission, change was motored by highly unfavourable reports on Commission performance from a Committee of Independent Experts appointed by the EP.[67] The Commission headed by President Santer duly resigned in the face of a vote of no confidence and the incoming Prodi Commission came into power vowing to do less and to do things better.[68] Prodi focused on fostering a more collegiate spirit in the Commission, assuming greater control of the Commissioners, applying principles of cabinet responsibility, and attacking the nationalistic ethos with which the Commission was riddled. These reforms did something to restore Commission credibility, though it never regained the authority and central position of its early years.[69] They undoubtedly helped, however, to get Vice-President Kinnock's ambitious reform programme, designed to improve the management and financial skills of the Commission, off the ground.

To meet the Experts' shocked condemnation of the 'growing reluctance among the members of the hierarchy to acknowledge their responsibility',[70] a raft of new measures was put in place. Financial controls within the Commission were reorganized and more efficient audit methods introduced.[71] A new financial Regulation specified the circumstances in which management could be devolved, decentralized, shared, or outsourced.[72] By 2003, the European Court of Auditors (ECA), which had regularly refused to sign off the Commission accounts, reported that the Commission was working hard at improving its administrative and control practices; by 2008, they withdrew their qualifications, though still reporting 'much error' in specific programmes.[73] There was more oversight and more transparency. OLAF, the new Commission unit introduced to pursue fraud on Community funds was, for example, made (at least in principle)[74] accountable to a surveillance committee, responsible for the 'regular monitoring of the discharge by the Office of its investigative function' with composition and powers laid down by the Community

---

[67] Committee of Independent Experts, First Report on Allegations regarding fraud, mismanagement and nepotism in the European Commission (Brussels, 15 March 1999) and Second Report on Reform of the Commission—analysis of current practice and proposals for tackling mismanagement, irregularities and fraud (Brussels, 10 September 1999).

[68] D Dimitrakopolous (ed), *The Changing European Commission* (Manchester University Press, 2004) 5.

[69] J Peterson, 'The Prodi Commission: Fresh Start or Free Fall?' in Dimitrakopolous (n 68 above) 30.

[70] *First Report* [9.4.25].

[71] Reforming the Commission, COM(2000) 200; H Kassim, 'The Prodi Commission and Administrative Reform' in Dimitrakopolous (above n 68) 50–51.

[72] Council Regulation 1605/2002 on the financial regulation applicable to the general budget of the European Communities [2002] OJ L248/1, noted P Craig, 'The Constitutionalisation of Community Administration' (2003) 28 ELRev 840.

[73] Kassim (n 71 above) 57. The level of error in agriculture and natural resources was estimated at between 2 and 5 per cent and in cohesion policies at least 11 per cent: ECA, Annual Report for 2008.

[74] See events surrounding the shocking case of Hans Tillack: Case T-193/04R *Tillack v Commission* [2004] ECR II-3575; Case C-521/04 *Tillack v Commission* [2005] ECR I-3103; Case T-193/04R *Tillack v Commission* [2006] ECR II-3995; EO case 1840/2002/GG; EO Case 3446/2004/GG; ECHR, Application 20477/05 *Tillack v Belgium* (Judgment of 27 November 2007).

legislature.[75] Its investigatory and notification procedures were moreover accessible online.[76]

Not without protest, the Commission underwent reforms of the type associated elsewhere with 'new public management'. Much-needed reforms were made to the staff regulations[77] and efforts made to introduce a new management ethos.[78] The EO, acting as external monitor, introduced a code of principles of good administrative behaviour and sought through his investigations to impress its tenets on the administration, an effort approved by the EP[79] that would culminate in Article 41 of the Charter of Fundamental Rights, which creates a right, admittedly strictly limited, to good administration. By 2009, when 'star cases' were regularly highlighted in the Annual Reports to serve as examples of best practice in reacting to complaints, the EO was noting a change in mentality in the EU administration, which, he reported, 'already adhere[d] to a high standard of administrative practice': in 56 per cent of the cases closed in 2009, the institution concerned accepted a friendly solution or settled the matter, an increase from 36 per cent in 2008.

The White Paper on European Governance[80] on which these reforms were premised promised new relations with the European public. At the level of principle, 'good governance principles' were developed in conjunction with the OECD; openness, participation, accountability, effectiveness, and coherence were singled out as the hallmarks of good governance appropriate for a public-service oriented European administration. The Scandinavian version of administrative law was making its influence felt not only with the introduction of an ombudsman[81] but also through a northern commitment to open government first manifested in Declaration 17 of the Maastricht Treaty. In time the self-regulatory institutional codes of conduct (soft law) that followed found their way into a general regulation (hard law).[82] This restrictive

---

[75] Commission Decision of 28 April 1999 establishing the European Anti-Fraud Office (OLAF), [1999] OJ L136.

[76] eg Regulation 1073/99 of the EP and Council of 25 May 1999 concerning investigations by the European Anti-Fraud Office (OLAF), [1999] OJ L136; Inter-institutional Agreement of 25 May 1999 between the EP, Council and Commission concerning internal investigations by the European Anti-fraud Office (OLAF); 'Requirement to notify irregularities: Practical arrangements' 19° CoCoLaF, 11/04/2002.

[77] See European Commission, Reforming the Commission, COM (2000) 200; European Commission, New Staff Policy, IP/01/283, Brussels (28 February 2000). A raft of amendments to the basic Reg No 31 (EEC), 11 (EAEC) laying down the Staff Regulations of Officials and the Conditions of Employment of Other Servants of the European Economic Community and the European Atomic Energy Community OJ P45, 14 June 1962, 1385) followed between 2000 and 2004.

[78] L Metcalfe, 'Reforming the Commission: Will Organizational Efficiency Produce Effective Governance?' (2000) 38 JCMS 817 and 'Reforming the European Governance: Old Problems or New Principles?' (2001) 67 International Review of Administrative Sciences 415.

[79] EP, Code of Good Administrative Behaviour approved by resolution of the European Parliament 6 September 2001.

[80] See n 9 above.

[81] See P Leino, 'The Wind is in the North' (2004) EPL 333.

[82] Council Decision 93/731/EC, [1993] OJ L340, 41 and Code of Conduct, 43; Commission Decision 94/90, [1994] OJ L46, 58; EP access rules [1997] OJ L263/27, replaced by Regulation EC 1049/2001 of the EP and Council regarding public access to EP, Council and Commission Documents, [2001] OJ L145/43.

piece of legislation has, however, never satisfied whole-hearted supporters of open government, though reform is currently deadlocked by inter-institutional squabbling and disagreement between the Member States.[83]

Commission discretion, unavoidable in the early years, was increasingly structured and confined. The standard infringement procedures (Article 226 EC) had, for example, been treated by the ECJ as the epitome of discretionary procedure for which virtually no accountability was imposed.[84] They were not immune to the cold winds of reform. In line with 'NPM' methodology, the Commission introduced and published a set of enforcement priorities[85] and, after it brought into use Article 228 EC, providing fines in cases of Member State violations, guidelines were again issued on use of the new powers.[86] Again, no clear procedures had previously been in place to deal with complaints from members of the public, on which the Commission largely relied for knowledge of infringements. Complaints might be registered and acknowledged but the complainant had no right of access to documentation; was not usually permitted to make observations; could not see either the 'reasoned opinion' from the Commission, which formally opened infringement proceedings or the Member State's response; and might not even be notified that the procedure had been discontinued. At the EO's insistence, the Commission was forced to introduce new, user-friendly procedures to regulate relationships with complainants. Opening an Own Initiative Inquiry into Article 226 procedure, the EO obtained the significant concession that complainants should receive notice of closure of a non-compliance file with a reasoned decision.[87] Today, infringement procedure is the subject of a 'soft law' Communication in which the Commission undertakes to take all complaints seriously, to 'take action as appropriate', and to try for a final decision within twelve months.[88] Systems are in place for automatically recording

---

[83] See for criticism of the existing regime and performance of the Community Courts, J Heliskosi and P Leino, 'Darkness at the Break of Noon: The Case Law on Reg No 1049/2001 on Access to Documents' (2006) 43 CML Rev 735 and on reform, I Harden, 'The Revision of Reg 1049/2001 on Public Access to Documents (2009) 15 EPL 239. The European Commission, Proposal for a Regulation of the European Parliament and of the Council regarding public access to European Parliament, Council and Commission documents, COM (2008) 229 final 2008/0090 is comprehensively critiqued by *Statewatch* on the *Statewatch* website. And see House of Lords European Union Committee, Access to EU Documents (HL 108, 2008/9).

[84] Case 247/87 *Star Fruit v Commission* [1989] ECR 291; Case C-87/89 *Sonito v Commission* [1990] ECR I-1981; F Snyder, 'The Effectiveness of European Community Law: Institutions, Processes, Tools and Techniques' (1993) 56 MLR 19. Later case law imposes the rights of the defence on the Commission's dealing with Member States: see C Harlow and R Rawlings, 'Accountability and Law Enforcement: The Centralised EU Infringement Procedure' (2006) 31 ELRev 447. Arts 226, 228 EC are now Arts 258–260 TFEU, with slight changes to the wording.

[85] White Paper, 25f, elaborated in Better Monitoring of the Application of Community Law, COM(2002) 725 final/4, 11–12.

[86] Communication 96/C 242/07 on applying Art 228 of the Treaty, [1996] OJ C242/6; Communication 97/C 63/02 on the method of calculating the penalty payments provided for pursuant to Art 228 of the EC Treaty, [1997] OJ C63/2. And see Case C-304/02 *Commission v France* [2005] ECR I-6263.

[87] EO, Decision in the own initiative inquiry 303/97/PD, AR 1997, 270.

[88] Communication to the EP and EO on relations with the complainant in respect of infringements of Community law, COM (2002) 141 final.

and acknowledging complaints, the Commission puts out a standard complaint form on its website, and relations with complainants are conducted in accordance with the EO's *Code of good administrative behaviour* (above).[89] Where appropriate, 'useful practical advice' on alternative means of redress for complainants is also offered.[90] The process, previously confined to a European elite, was in short being opened up and forced to become more transparent and user-friendly.

Using the techniques of modern public administration and administrative law, an old-fashioned bureaucracy with wide discretionary executive power was being gradually re-modelled as a European administration. Regulation was increasingly a more significant contributor to the growing body of administrative law than sporadic judicial review, though this did not mean a decrease in the volume of litigation. New administrative law institutions had been introduced and, in the case of the ECA, substantially strengthened. Surprisingly quickly, the EO had made his mark.[91] The watchdog was being watched and perhaps more importantly, was learning to watch itself and was becoming more accessible. Good use was made of information technology. Green and White Papers are now published on the website and public consultation is a routine procedure. Measures were taken to regulate the 'Comitology', an intricate network of committees originally set in place by the Council to monitor the Commission's use of implementing rule-making powers.[92] Using its budgetary powers to good effect, the EP insisted that information about the Comitology and its procedures should appear openly on the Europa website, making the committees more accountable and accessible and facilitating public participation.[93]

The Commission's main tools for coordinating and harmonizing action across increasingly ambitious EU programmes were recording, notification, report back, and monitoring. The Commission receives data from national administrations, which have a duty to report and notify the Commission of proposed policy changes in areas ranging (eg) from food safety measures to proscription of dangerous chemicals and regulating emissions trading. Data on transposition and implementation of European Union law is studiously compiled by the Commission. This information enables the Commission to react through 'soft governance' methods of negotiation, training, and advice, as it has done in providing assistance to help Member States deal

---

[89] White Paper 'Better Monitoring' (n 85 above) 13.

[90] ibid. And see C Harlow and R Rawlings, 'Accountability and Law Enforcement: The Centralised EU Infringement Procedure' (2006) 31 ELRev 447.

[91] See B Laffan, 'Becoming a 'Living Institution': The Evolution of the European Court of Auditors' (1999) 37 JCMS 251 and 'Auditing and Accountability in the EU' (2003) 10 JEPP 762.

[92] For an account of comitology, see E Vos, '50 Years of European Integration, 45 Years of Comitology' 3 *Maastricht Online Working Papers* (2009) and for the Commission's post-Lisbon position, Proposal for a Regulation of the EP and Council laying down the rules and general principles concerning mechanisms for control by Member States of the Commission's exercise of implementing powers, COM(2010) 83 final 2010/0051.

[93] G J Brandsma et al, 'How Transparent Are EU Committees in Practice?' (2008) 14 ELJ 19.

quickly with cases of 'benign non-compliance', in the case of new Member States often caused by unfamiliarity with the Community *acquis*.[94]

D. PHASE 3: POST-LISBON CHALLENGES

Those who watched with anxiety the struggle for ratification of the Lisbon Treaty may be forgiven for feeling a sense of relief. Ratification brought a (temporary) measure of certainty over the institutional arrangements for the EU, now reconstructed under a single roof. In its post-Lisbon phase, however, EU administrative law is left with significant problems. These start with the need to come to grips with the 'soft governance' modalities described below. The Commission must also deal urgently with normalization of the areas of competence transferred by the Third Pillar and grapple with the rapidly growing phenomenon of 'agencification', while the ECJ has to come to terms with the idea of the EU as an actor in an increasingly globalized world.

The EU is joining the wider post-modern process of transition from 'government' to 'governance', which caused Shapiro such unease[95] and the classical, split-level model of quasi-federal government to which in the early days the institutions apparently aspired is being superseded by new models of 'composite decision making'. In these, the Commission might exercise coordinating, regulatory, and supervisory functions, leaving execution to national and sub-national administrations, as it largely does in the field of regional structural funds. It might collapse the public/private border, as exemplified by extensive private participation in overseas aid and regional programmes. The Commission has become a coordinator of networks. In competition, for example, the paradigm of direct administration, the Commission now forms the central node of a network of competition regulators.[96] Its small size and the post-1999 reforms had led to experiments with 'cooperative administration', a process of working towards EU objectives through cooperation between administrations of Member States, between autonomous bodies in the banking sector, and, increasingly, through networks of agencies through which information was exchanged, collaboration promoted, and implementation monitored.

Experience of soft governance gained in periods when the Commission found itself blocked at the political level[97] proved useful when economic union (EMU) made it necessary for the Commission to cooperate with a network of financial institutions designed to be at least semi-autonomous. The 'open method of coordination' (OMC) introduced by the Commission was based on joint information sharing

---

[94] See 21st Annual Report on monitoring the application of Community law, COM(2004) 839.

[95] Shapiro (n 1 above). And see C Harlow, 'Deconstructing Governance' (2004) 23 YEL 57.

[96] Notice on cooperation within the Network of Competition Authorities [2004] OJ C101/43; H Hofmann, 'Negotiated and Non-negotiated Administrative Rule-making: The Example of EC Competition Policy' (2006) 43 CML Rev 153.

[97] G della Cananea, 'Administration by Guidelines: The Policy Guidelines of the Commission in the Field of State Aids' in *Trierer Schriftenreihe der Europaischen Rechtsakademie* (1993).

and cooperative action.[98] More structured experiments with 'soft governance' followed the Lisbon European Council. The central feature of the new style is a process of consensus-forming. Its core characteristics include: public/private participation; acceptance of diversity and pluralism; 'approximation' of laws and administrative practice; process constraints (such as consultation requirements) during implementation; setting of targets with benchmarks and performance indicators tailored to specific actors or sectors; reliance on soft law rather than formal rule-making by the Community method; law-making by framework directive; and enforcement through monitoring, report back, peer review, and evaluation.[99]

More significant is the practice of delegating rule-making powers to the private sector, as is the case with the 'social dialogue' arrangements authorized by the Agreement on social policy.[100] This cooperative procedure in which the Commission essentially rubber-stamps decisions agreed by the 'social partners' requires the Commission to consult management and labour at Community level and 'take measures to facilitate their dialogue' by ensuring 'balanced support' for the parties. In the *UEAPME* case, this association of small businesses had been consulted at an earlier, informal stage of the two-stage proceedings but was not a formal signatory to the final text of a Framework Directive on parental leave by which it claimed to be disproportionately affected. In a legal challenge, UEAPME came up against the intractable problem of standing when the CFI concluded that it was not 'individually' affected; it was not 'distinguished from all other organisations of management and labour consulted by the Commission which were not signatories to the framework agreement'.[101]

This is just one among many examples of obstacles standing in the way of those falling outside the charmed circle of participants who wish to challenge the EU policy- and law-making process. Admittedly, codes of conduct are now in place to govern Commission relations with lobby groups and civil society organizations and a register of CSOs is published on the website but these leave the Commission firmly in charge of choosing its 'stakeholders' and contain no guarantees as to representativity.[102] Significant efforts are necessary if the EU is to move into the 'third generation of participation rights' in European law.[103]

---

[98] D Hodson and I Maher, 'The Open Method as a New Mode of Governance' (2001) 39 JCMS 719.

[99] White Paper, 'Better Monitoring' (n 85 above) 21.

[100] L Betten, 'The Democratic Deficit of Participatory Democracy in Community Social Policy' (1998) 23 ELRev 20; S Fredman, 'Social Law in the European Union: The Impact of the Lawmaking Process' in P Craig and C Harlow (eds), *Lawmaking in the European Union* (Kluwer International, 1998).

[101] Case T-135/96 *UEAPME v Council* [1998] ECR II-2335, now partly ameliorated by Art 263 TFEU: see (n 64 above).

[102] See now European Transparency Initiative: A framework for relations with interest representatives by the Commission (Register and Code of Conduct), COM(2008) 323 final. See D Curtin, 'Private Interest *Representation* or Civil Society *Deliberation*? A Contemporary Dilemma for European Union Governance' (2003) 12 Social & Legal Studies 56; D Obradovic and J Vizcarino, 'Good Governance Requirements Concerning the Participation of Interest Groups on EU Consultation' (2006) 43 CML Rev 1049.

[103] F Bignami, 'Three Generations of Participation Rights before the European Commission' (2004) 68 LCP 61.

Scott and Trubek, in their introduction to a collection of conference papers in 2002, described the moves to 'soft governance' as a threat to the 'traditional conception of law within the Community'.[104] It is true that a second stage of 'hard administrative law' can follow, as it does when the Commission resorts to infringement proceedings, which have been used aggressively by the ECJ to punish recalcitrant Member States by the imposition of heavy fines.[105] Similarly, soft law may often be no more than a stage on the way to regulation. Scott and Trubek, however, direct particular criticism at the two Community Courts for their failure to come to grips with the phenomenon of new governance. Only very occasionally, the authors suggest, have the courts engaged seriously with the new phenomena; usually they have acted to thwart, ignore, or distort it. In the *UEAPME* case, for example, the CFI showed some understanding of the participatory rule-making procedures, making reference to democracy and under-lining the importance of the duty laid on both Commission and Council to 'verify the representativity' of the signatories of legislative texts made under Agreement proced-ure. Ultimately, however, the case failed to pass the admissibility threshold, as in the *Jégo-Quéré* and *UPA* cases discussed earlier, where it was suggested that the ECJ entirely failed to engage with the problems of multi-level decision-making.

Turning to the former 'Third Pillar' area of 'freedom, security and justice', there is unquestionably a long and complex agenda. The Tampere 'milestones',[106] as far-reaching as the Single European Act, allowed the Council to embark with minimal publicity on an ambitious new programme, the advantage for policy-makers being that the new competences operated outside the administrative law protections painfully built up within the First Pillar. Recently, the Commission has shown signs of wishing to embark on normalization; whether the Council will allow this to happen is another question altogether.

The Third Pillar operated through techniques of 'soft governance': Member States were to 'inform and consult one another...with a view to co-ordinating their action'. The Commission lost power to the Council, Coreper, and the powerful Political and Security Committee, an underground presence that, as Curtin observes, has 'seen its role expanded with every new mission and new policy [until] it now covers virtually every aspect of foreign policy', yet about which little was known.[107] Crucial areas of civil liberties and human rights—very much the core concern of modern administra-tive law—were involved, yet the jurisdiction of the ECJ was restricted.[108] As with

---

[104] J Scott and D Trubek, 'Mind the Gap: Law and New Approaches to Governance in the European Union' (2002) 8 ELJ 1.

[105] The starting-point is Case C-304/02, *Commission v France* [2005] ECR I-6263, where the ECJ estab-lished its mastery over the procedure and Case C-494/01 *Commission v Ireland* [2005] ECR-I 3331, where the procedure was applied to non-specific, recurrent infringements: see Harlow and Rawlings (n 90 above); P Wenneras, 'A New Dawn for Commission Enforcement under Articles 226 and 228 EC: General and Persistent (GAP) Infringements, Lump Sums and Penalty Payments' (2006) 43 CML Rev 31.

[106] Tamperere Presidency Conclusions, 15/16 October 1999.

[107] D Curtin, *The Executive Power of the European Union*, (Oxford University Press, 2009) 89.

[108] Art 35 TEU, replaced by Art 276 TFEU, which retains restrictions in respect of policing, law and order, and security in Member States.

comitology procedure, rule-making by 'common position' and 'framework decision' minimized the EP's role, an omission that was certainly intentional, as the following example suggests.

Article 67 EC left the Council with a choice of legislative procedures in asylum matters: unanimity in the Council plus consultation with the EP or co-decision. In drawing up a Directive on minimum standards for asylum procedures, however, the Council could not agree a common list of safe third countries. It therefore sought to hold the question back for later resolution, specifying in its Directive a 'secondary legal base' involving QMV in the Council and consultation with the EP—a clear dilution of control. Not only did the ECJ annul the Directive but it laid down the important general principle that the Treaty provisions were exhaustive; no inherent power to delegate legislative powers existed.[109] What followed nicely illustrates the difficulties that the Commission may in practice face. Its proposal for a new directive does indeed re-work the procedural standards, with valuable provisions on personal interviews, legal advice, translation, etc. But it does not deal with the vexed question of safe third countries; listing is returned to the Member States.[110]

Third Pillar procedures enabled Member States to authorize trans-European data bases to be established, often based on cooperation arrangements between a handful of the Member States. This manoeuvre enabled the participants to pre-empt not only Community law-making procedure but even the softer Third Pillar requirements. Responsibility for establishing and maintaining the Schengen computerized data systems (SIS I and II), which allow for input, access, and analysis of data provided by Member States, and make the databank accessible to their authorities, was entrusted to Europol; Eurojust was given similar powers in 'the fight against serious organized crime', a category that was steadily extended.[111] The Prüm Convention[112] provided for the establishment of DNA profile and fingerprint databases, again with access for partner countries, which they may access on request for the general purpose of prosecution and prevention of 'criminal activity, political demonstrations and other mass events'. Data protection became an issue, which the Council dealt with by a Framework Decision. The proposals emanated from its multi-disciplinary group on organized crime, were not submitted to the EP, and were the subject of three largely unfavourable opinions from the European Data Protection Authorities, which acts as the accountability forum in this field. As enacted, the Decision provides only minimal

---

[109] Case C133/06 *Parliament v Council* [2008] ECR I-3189 noted P Craig, (2009) 46 CML Rev 193. Art 290 TFEU now contains a Commission power of delegated legislation.

[110] Commission Proposal for a Directive on minimum standards on procedures in Member States for granting and withdrawing international protection, COM(2009) 554/4, Art 33 (ex 30).

[111] Council Decision of 16 December 2008 on the strengthening of Eurojust and amending Decision 2002/187/JHA setting up Eurojust with a view to reinforcing the fight against serious crime [2008] OJ L138/14; Art 85 TFEU.

[112] Convention on the stepping up of cross border cooperation, particularly in combating terrorism, cross border crime and illegal migration, signed by Austria, the Benelux countries, France, Germany and Spain: see Council Note 10900/05, Brussels (7 July 2005). And see T Balzacq *et al*, *Security and the Two-Level Game: The Treaty of Prüm, the EU and the Management of Threats*, CEPS WP No 234 (2006).

standards of data protection, leaving the area largely to regulation by the Member States.[113] Significantly, the preamble to the new Europol Decision speaks of the necessity of providing:

> [e]nhanced control over Europol by the European Parliament in order to ensure that Europol remains a fully accountable and transparent organisation, due account being taken of the need to safeguard the confidentiality of operational information.[114]

The Stockholm Programme, which now governs JHA policy-making, follows Tampere in notionally taking a softer line, focusing 'on the interests and needs of citizens' and 'ensuring respect for fundamental freedoms and integrity while guaranteeing security in Europe'. A process of 'mutual trust between authorities and services in the different Member States' should develop.[115] Yet there are hints in the Stockholm Programme of a more integrationist agenda: the area of freedom, security and justice must 'above all be a single area' and 'the achievement of a European area of justice must be consolidated so as to move beyond the current fragmentation'. It is important that the Community courts work with the Commission to incorporate into future policy-making the procedural protections painfully established in the Community Pillar, together with a greatly enhanced judicial respect for human rights.[116]

The third challenge to administrative law lies in the proliferation of European agencies set up in recent years. When European agencies first appeared on the scene they were limited to information-gathering and advisory functions, the belief being that further development would be restricted by the *Meroni* decision, which outlawed the delegation of discretionary power.[117] The justification for agencies was initially technocratic: the small and generalist Commission required specialist advice, but would remain in charge of policy. Gradually, however, the Commission found its role reduced across every area of scientific, technical expertise to that of commissioner in the sense of someone who commissions reports from experts. In the *Munich University* case,[118] for example, the ECJ noted that the Commission 'always followed the opinions of the group of experts because it has no other sources of information concerning the apparatus being considered'. Consequently, it imposed an obligation to

---

[113] Council Framework Decision 2008/977/JHA of 27 November 2008 on the protection of personal data processed in the framework of police and judicial cooperation in criminal matters. On the need for action, see M Nino, 'The Protection of Personal Data in the Fight Against Terrorism: New Perspectives of PNR European Union Instruments in the Light of the Treaty of Lisbon' (2010) 6 Utrecht Law Review No 1.

[114] Preamble [20] of Council Decision (2009/371/JHA).

[115] The Stockholm Programme—An open and secure Europe serving and protecting the citizens for the next five years of reform, 16484/09 JAI 866 (16 October 2009, as amended 25 November 2009).

[116] S Douglas-Scott, 'The Rule of Law in the European Union—Putting the Security into the Area of "Freedom, Security and Justice"', (2004) 29 ELRev 219.

[117] Case 9/56 *Meroni v High Authority* [1957/8] ECR 133.

[118] Case C-269/90 *Hauptzollamt München-Mitte v Technische Universitat München* [1991] ECR I-5469 [21]–[22].

seek out the best technical and scientific advice from properly qualified advisers. This ruling, reinforced by introduction of the precautionary principle in environmental matters (Article 174 EC, now Article 191(2) TFEU) became the guiding principle in risk regulation, a central area of the Commission's work,[119] strengthening the case for committee and agency expertise.

At first the Commission seemed to favour agencies, stating that they 'should be granted the power to take individual decisions in application of regulatory measures', while arguing also for some standardization: 'limits of their activities and powers, their responsibilities and requirements for openness' should be set out in each agency-creating regulation.[120] A rather bland operating framework was later agreed and set out in a Commission communication, which classified existing agencies by function with a view to establishing 'a coherent approach to creating future regulatory agencies' and ensuring that 'the unity and integrity of the executive function at Community level is safeguarded'.[121] But agencies were fast acquiring powers that were more than purely technocratic. The Commission classification showed that, of the twenty-nine listed 'regulatory' agencies, three CFSP, and three JHA agencies with an annual budget of €1,100 million, three agencies acted directly on the public and, of those engaged in information-gathering, several had interesting 'networking' functions.[122] The European Food and Safety Agency (EFSA), classified as offering technical and scientific advice, possesses powers to cooperate closely with 'competent bodies' in the Member States; to commission scientific studies; to assign tasks to organizations in the Member States; to promote and coordinate the development of uniform risk assessment methodologies in the fields falling within its mission; and to establish a system of networks of organizations operating in the fields within its mission and be responsible for their operation.[123] The Fundamental Rights Agency (EFRA) is mandated to collaborate with the Council of Europe and promote dialogue with non-governmental organizations and with institutions of civil society active in the field of fundamental rights. It should set up a cooperation network called the 'Fundamental Rights Platform'

---

[119] The foundational cases are Case T-13/99 *Pfizer* [2002] ECR II-3305; Case T-70/99 *Alpharma v Council* [2002] ELR II-3475. See V Heyvaert, 'Facing the Consequences of the Precautionary Principle in EC Law' (2006) 31 ELR 186; E Fisher, 'Opening Pandora's Box: Contextualising the Precautionary Principle in The European Union' in E Vos *et al* (eds), *Uncertain Risks Regulated: National, EU and International Regulatory Models Compared* (Cavendish Publishing, 2008).

[120] White Paper on European Governance, COM(2001) 428, 24.

[121] The operating framework for the European regulatory agencies, COM(2002) 728 final. See generally D Geradin, R Muñoz, and N Petit (eds), *Regulation Through Agencies in the EU. A New Paradigm for European Governance,* (Edward Elgar, 2005).

[122] European Agencies—the way forward, COM(2008) 135 final, 7.

[123] Regulation (EC) 178/2002 of the European Parliament and of the Council of 28 January 2002 laying down the general principles and requirements of food law, establishing the European Food Safety Authority and laying down procedures in matters of food safety. And see R Fischer, 'European governance still technocratic? New modes of governance for food safety Regulation in the European Union', European Integration online papers (2008).

with a view to creating a structured and fruitful dialogue and close cooperation with all relevant stakeholders.[124]

Six agencies already possess operational powers. These include Frontex, the borders agency, and Europol and Eurojust, established by interstate Convention in the Third Pillar where accountability was poor, illustrating a point made in the Commission Communication that the 'establishment of agencies can make possible a pooling of powers at EU level which would be resisted if centred on the institutions'.[125] Not only does Europol possess powers to liaise directly with national police forces but also to conclude agreements with third states. Significantly, the new governing statute provides that 'further simplification and improvement of Europol's functioning can be achieved through measures aimed at widening the possibilities for Europol's assisting and supporting the competent law enforcement authorities of the Member States, *without providing for executive powers for Europol staff*'.[126] The Community Fisheries Control Agency (CFCA) crossed another barrier: its governing statute provides not only for the 'operational coordination of fisheries control and inspection' but also authorizes inspection: CFCA shall '*carry out* on behalf of Member States tasks under international fisheries agreements to which the Community is a party'.[127]

When the Commission, clearly concerned, returned to the topic in 2008, it recommended:

> The mechanisms in place to ensure accountability for the actions of regulatory agencies should be clear to both the agencies and the Institutions. This should include reporting and auditing requirements, relations with stakeholders, and responses to parliamentary questions. The management of the agencies must also respect basic standards of good stewardship to mitigate possible risks. There should also be coherent rules for evaluation of the agencies.[128]

Deprecating lack of progress, the Commission had nonetheless to withdraw its proposal, with the proviso that no new regulatory agencies be created until its 'work of evaluation' was complete.[129] Barely a month later the Commission announced additions: a European Asylum Support Office was under consideration.[130] In June 2009, under the pressure of financial crisis, a formal proposal for a Europe Banking

---

[124] Council Regulation EC 168/2007 of 15 February 2007 establishing a European Union Agency for Fundamental Rights.

[125] COM(2008) 135 final.

[126] Established by the Europol Convention, [1995] OJ C316/2. Europol is now regulated by Council Decision of 6 April 2009 establishing the European Police Office (2009/371/JHA). See Art 23 and preamble [7] (emphasis mine).

[127] Arts 1 and 4 of Council Regulation 768/2005 of 26 April 2005 establishing a Community Fisheries Control Agency and amending Regulation 2847/93 establishing a control system applicable to the common fisheries policy (emphasis mine).

[128] COM(2008) 135 final, 7.

[129] ibid 8–9.

[130] Press Release 18 April 2009; Proposal to establish a European Asylum Support Office, COD/2009/0027, awaiting 1st reading in the Council.

Authority, an Insurance Authority, and Securities Authority was agreed.[131] This major growth area raises a serious question. Agencies are the newest form of 'governance', born inside national systems and translated to the EU; are they on course to emerge as a new and threatening form of regime outside the control of either?[132]

Finally, the challenges of a new era of global politics have recently moved up the agenda, challenging the autonomy of the European Union legal order in several ways.[133] Cases flooded courts after fund-freezing measures dictated by the UN were imposed on individuals listed as suspected of terrorism. Acting as the Constitutional Court of the European Union, the ECJ confirmed that:

> [t]he obligations imposed by an international agreement cannot have the effect of prejudicing the constitutional principles of the EC Treaty, which include the principle that all Community acts must respect fundamental rights, that respect constituting a condition of their lawfulness which it is for the Court to review in the framework of the complete system of legal remedies established by the Treaty.[134]

It was left to the CFI as the EU administrative court to flesh out the implications for administrative procedure, which it did in original fashion in the *OMPI* cases[135] brought to counter the 'cat-and-mouse' game played out by certain Member States of repeated listings, de-listings, and re-listings. Making specific reference to listing as 'a multi-level procedure, taking place at Community and national level', the CFI underlined the need for a fair hearing in decisions to freeze funds.[136] It went on to spell out the duties at *every* level, making particular reference to the duty of loyal cooperation imposed by Article 10 EC. In a second decision, the CFI looked closely at proceedings in the national institutions, including the specialist UK tribunal, POAC. The CFI treated this 'first decision of a competent judicial authority ruling on the lawfulness, in the light of the domestic law applicable, of the [national authority's] refusal to withdraw the order', as 'of considerable importance'. POAC had described the Home Secretary's refusal to lift the applicant's proscription as 'unreasonable' and 'perverse'; the Council had not taken this into consideration, preferring to rely on the

---

[131] Proposal for a Regulation of the EP and Council establishing a European Banking Authority, COM (2009) 501 final 2009/0142.

[132] M Everson, 'Agencies: the "dark hour" of the executive?' in *Legal Challenges in EU Administrative Law*, (n 24 above).

[133] See on enforceability Case C-149/96 *Portugal v Council* [1999] ECR I-8395; P Eeckhout, 'Judicial Enforcement of WTO Law in the European Union-Some Further Reflections' (2002) 5 JIEL 91; and on liability, Case C-93/02 *Biret International SA v Council* [2002] ECR I-10497 noted A Thies, 'Biret and Beyond: The Status of WTO Rulings in EC Law' (2004) 41 CML Rev 1661.

[134] Case C-402/05 *Kadi v Council and Commission* [2008] ECR I-6351 [285] overruling Case T-315/01 *Yassin Abdullah Kadi v Council and Commission* [2005] ECR II-3649.

[135] Case T-256/07 *Organisation des Modjahedines des peuples d'Iran v Council* [2008] ECR II-2019 and Case T-284/08 *Organisation des Mojahedines des peuples d'Iran v Council* [2009] ECR II-161.

[136] [2006] ECR II-4665 [117].

fact that an appeal had been lodged.[137] The CFI annulled the Council decision to re-list on the classical ground of insufficient reasons.[138] Global space is becoming crowded, complicating delicate relationships. Tactful inter-court cooperation and communication will prove essential if EU courts are to face up to the growing complexities of a web of national and transnational courts.

E. CONCLUSIONS: TOWARDS PLURALISM?

Two divergent approaches to problems of EU governance emerge marking the first phases of EU administrative law. The first, successfully adopted throughout the first, building phase, is a process of 'integration by stealth'; the second, favoured *faute de mieux* by the Commission, is more pluralist and more accepting of diversity. The Community legal order drew its principles from legal systems that could loosely be grouped into four legal families[139] and, although administrative law operated in different constitutional contexts and in systems of public administration with different administrative cultures, there was also a relatively high degree of commonality. The advent of 27 different systems radically changed the picture, changed again by the advent of European agencies.

Only rarely have the Community courts taken subsidiarity seriously, though the CFI did so in a recent case where it annulled an attempt by the Commission to standardize criteria on emissions in an area of joint competence. Unusually, the CFI made explicit reference to the 'principle of subsidiarity enshrined in the second paragraph of Article 5 EC...which binds the Community institutions in the exercise of their legislative functions and which is deemed to have been complied with in respect of the adoption of [this] Directive'.[140] Elsewhere 'subjects plainly reserved as such to the states have been regularly transformed into a Community matter to whatever extent the federal policy branches find that the cross-border mobility of goods (or, by parallel reasoning, workers, services, or capital) would be advanced by bringing the various national rules on the subject into closer alignment with each other'.[141]

Integrationism may yet prove to be, in the colourful metaphor of an eminent judge, 'a genetic code transmitted to the court by the founding fathers'.[142] But neither the Lisbon Treaty with its general provisions on subsidiarity (TEU Article 5(1)(3)(4)),

---

[137] In *Secretary of State for Home Affairs v Lord Alton and others* [2008] EWCA Civ 443 (7 May 2008) the Home Secretary's appeal was dismissed. She withdrew the listing on the grounds that OMPI was still listed in the EU.

[138] Case T-256/07 [183]–[185]. An appeal is pending.

[139] J Bell, 'Mechanisms for Cross-fertilisation of Administrative Law in Europe' in J Beatson and T Tridimas (eds), *New Directions in European Public Law* (Hart, 1998).

[140] Cases T-183/07 *Poland v European Commission*, T-263/07 *Estonia v Commission* [59] citing Case T-374/04 *Germany v Commission* [2007] ECR II-4431. The case has been appealed.

[141] G Bermann, 'Taking Subsidiarity Seriously: Federalism in the European Community and US' 94 Colum L Rev 331 (1994) 356.

[142] F Mancini and D Keeling, 'Democracy and the European Court of Justice' (1994) 57 MLR 175, 186.

constant references to subsidiarity and provisions for a 'subsidiarity-watch' by national parliaments (TEU Protocols 1 and 2), nor the events surrounding its ratification provide a mandate for this approach. The Lisbon Treaty invites the second, more pluralist approach. This involves recognizing diversity as a strength rather than a sign of weakness in EU law.[143] The objective would be a gradual convergence inside a common 'European administrative space' achieved through the methodology of 'soft governance'.

This approach, however, calls for a trust in national accountability systems that may be misplaced. It also fails to grapple adequately with problems of composite decision-making. In a joint article with Richard Rawlings[144] I have argued that multi-level systems of governance call for a networked, multi-dimensional response from administrative law. 'Accountability networks', formed of existing accountability actors, are necessary to counter the proliferating networks of 'governance outside the state'. Thus European auditors are mandated by the Treaties to work 'in liaison' and 'cooperate in a spirit of trust'.[145] The *OMPI* case law in the CFI provides a first tentative example of courts working collaboratively to transfer the traditional control function of administrative law to a multi-level administrative process. The European Network of Ombudsmen, an information-sharing and advisory network managed by the EO's Office, brings together on a voluntary basis national and regional ombudsmen and similar institutions and meets regularly to discuss problem cases. New powers to undertake joint investigations could see the network transformed into a true accountability network. National parliaments are also preparing for their new responsibilities under the Lisbon Treaty (Article 5(1), (3), (4) and Protocols 1 and 2 TFEU), exchanging documents, holding joint meetings, and maintaining a joint (IPEX) website.[146] If the central control function of classical administrative law is to retain its potency outside the framework of a nation state, networking must surely be the shape of things to come.

---

[143] C Harlow, 'Voices of Difference in a Plural Community' 50 AJCL 339 (2002).

[144] C Harlow and R Rawlings, 'Promoting Accountability in Multi-Level Governance: A Network Approach' in D Curtin and A Wille (eds), *Meaning and Practice of Accountability in the EU Multi-Level Context* (CONNEX Report Series No 07 (2008)).

[145] Art 287(3) TFEU, replicating earlier provisions. And see AR for 2008.

[146] House of Lords European Union Committee, AR for 2009, HL 168 (2008-9) [58]–[63].

16

THE EVOLUTION OF EU HUMAN RIGHTS LAW

*Gráinne de Búrca**

A. INTRODUCTION

The subject of the European Union's human rights law and policy was not included in the first edition of this book in 1999. Although there was a constitutionally significant line of case law of the European Court of Justice on the subject,[1] human rights issues did not feature prominently in EU law at the time, and despite scattered human rights activity across the field of external relations and in the area of gender discrimination, the EU did not, to quote the views of leading commentators in 1998, have a human rights policy.[2] Just over ten years later, the picture is a very different one, and the absence of a chapter on human rights would be a notable omission from a book on the evolution of EU law. There is now an emergent EU constitutional regime for human rights protection, and there is a rich scholarly literature on EU human rights law.

This chapter does not attempt to provide an overview of developments in this field or to summarize the analyses contained in the extensive literature.[3] Instead, it aims to add a new dimension to existing understandings of the evolution of human rights law

* I am grateful to the participants at the preparatory workshop for this book which took place at the European University Institute, Florence, in April 2009 for their comments and input. Thanks are also due to the Academy of European Law at the EUI for its generosity both in supporting the workshop, as well as in providing additional funding to facilitate the archival work on which parts of this chapter are based. Finally, warm thanks are due to Jasper Pauw and also to Katharina Hermann for their excellent research assistance.

[1] B De Witte, 'The Past and Future Role of the European Court of Justice in the Protection of Human Rights' in P Alston and J H H Weiler (eds), *The EU and Human Rights* (Oxford University Press, 1999) ch 28.

[2] P Alston and J H H Weiler, 'An Ever Closer Union in Need of a Human Rights Policy' (1998) 9 EJIL 658–723, and more generally their introduction to and annex to their edited volume, *The EU and Human Rights* (n 1 above).

[3] For some early seminal accounts see M Dauses, 'The Protection of Fundamental Rights in the Community Legal Order' (1985) 10 ELRev 398; P Pescatore, 'The Context and Significance of Fundamental Rights in the Law of the European Communities' (1981) 2 HRLJ 295; U Scheuner, 'Fundamental Rights in European Community Law and in National Constitutional Law' (1975) 12 CML Rev 171; A Clapham, 'A Human Rights Policy for the European Community' (1990) 10 YEL 309.

and policy in the EU by returning to reconsider some of the earliest steps of engagement with the issue of human rights protection in the process of European integration, drawing on largely unknown archival material from the early 1950s. To that end the chapter focuses closely on the brief but intense period in 1951–52 when the question of human rights protection was prominent on the agenda of those promoting the process of integration, before its abrupt disappearance from the agenda of the new European Communities in 1957. Two significant drafting exercises took place during this time. The first resulted in the draft articles produced by the *Comité d'études sur une constitution européene* (CECE) in 1952, and the second the relevant provisions of the draft Treaty on a European Political Community (EPC) in 1952–53. Little or no attention has been given in the EU legal literature on human rights so far to these early attempts to define a role for the emerging European entity in the field of human rights protection. The reason for this neglect is at one level evident and understandable, since neither attempt ultimately bore fruit. As is well known by students of EU law, the failure of the European Defence Treaty in the early 1950s led to a significant scaling back of ambitions for European integration and for the very idea of a European political community. One of the consequences of this scaling back was that, following the European Coal and Steel Community Treaty, neither the Euratom Treaty nor the EEC Treaty of 1957 made any mention of a role for the EU in relation to human rights, and the earlier drafting attempts of the 1950s were consigned to history.

The intention of the chapter however is to rescue this interesting piece of drafting history from obscurity and to use it to shed light on the evolution of EU human rights law and policy. A comparative analysis of the constitutional framework for human rights protection envisaged by those drafting in 1952–53 and the constitutional framework for human rights protection which exists in the EU, following the adoption of the Lisbon Treaty, provides fresh and interesting material for reflection on how understandings of the appropriate role of the European polity in the area of human rights, and the vision underpinning the proposed constitutional framework, have changed and evolved since the early stages of the European integration project. I will suggest that there are three notable lines of difference between the constitutional framework for human rights protection drafted in the early 1950s and that which has emerged over the last decade and a half in the EU.

The first is that the 1950s model envisaged a strong monitoring, intervention, and review role for the European Community with regard to human rights protection within the Member States, while the existing constitutional framework significantly limits and seeks to restrain the possibility of EU monitoring or review of human rights within Member States. Secondly, the 1950s constitutional model envisaged a closely entwined constitutional relationship between the European Community and the European Convention on Human Rights and their respective courts, and between the EC and the regional and international human rights systems more generally. By comparison, despite the imminent prospect of EU accession to the ECHR, significant emphasis is placed in today's constitutional framework on the autonomy and separateness of the

EU's own human rights regime. Thirdly, the model constitutional framework of the early 1950s was both outwardly and inwardly focused, aiming to promote human rights and to protect against human rights abuses equally in internal and external Community policies and relations. The existing post-Lisbon constitutional framework on the other hand, with the exception of anti-discrimination law, assigns a more circumscribed role to human rights within the context of internally focused EU policies, and the dominant focus is external, empowering and even obliging the EU to promote human rights actively in its international policies.

For the purposes of the analysis, I have divided the stages of evolution of EU human rights law and policy into three broad periods. The first is the period prior to the creation of the European Communities when the human rights provisions of the draft European Political Community Treaty and the Resolutions of the *Comité d'études sur une constitution européene* were drawn up in the early 1950s. The second covers the period from the banishment of human rights matters from European Community discourse with the adoption of the EEC and Euratom Treaties in 1957 until their re-emergence through the 1970s and 1980s in judicial and political discourse. The third and final stage brings us up to the present-day framework, covering the period from the adoption of the Maastricht Treaty in 1992 until the adoption of the Lisbon Treaty in late 2009.

B. PHASE 1: THE BACKGROUND AND DRAFTING OF THE EUROPEAN POLITICAL COMMUNITY TREATY 1952–1953

The *Comité d'études pour la constitution européenne* (CECE) was set up in 1952 by members of the Mouvement europeén, a European movement—or rather a collection of movements—which had formally been established in 1948 to promote the cause of European unity and integration.[4] The CECE, which was officially labelled a 'study group' (*comité d'études*), was set up specifically with a view to contributing to the process of drafting a constitution ('statute') for a European political community. The CECE was established some time before the Ad Hoc Assembly which was tasked with actually drafting the European Political Community Treaty had been formally constituted,[5] but the membership and aims of the study group and the subsequent

---

[4] For information about the history and founding of the European Movement, see <http://www.europeanmovement.eu/index.php?id=6024>.

[5] For an early account of the drafting of the EPC, see B Karp, 'The Draft Constitution for a European Political Community' (1954) 8 IO 181–202, A H Robertson, 'The European Political Community' (1952) XXIX BYIL 383 and more recently the book length treatment by R T Griffiths, *Europe's First Constitution: The European Political Community 1952–54* (London, The Federal Trust, 2005). See also A Cohen, 'Constitutionalism Without Constitution: Transnational Elites Between Political Mobilization and Legal Expertise in the Making of a Constitution for Europe (1940s–1960s)' (2007) 32 Law & Social Inquiry 109–135.

Ad Hoc Assembly overlapped.[6] Notably, the CECE was chaired by Paul Henri Spaak, who had also been the first President of the Council of Europe, and who subsequently became chairman of the Ad Hoc Assembly. One of the consequences of the close relationship between the two bodies was that the draft articles and resolutions produced by the CECE were used by the Ad Hoc Assembly and its Constitutional Committee as a basis for drawing up the provisions of the draft European Political Community Treaty.

In addition to Paul Henri Spaak and Altiero Spinelli, the membership of the CECE was composed of a select group of legal experts including international legal academics and national parliamentarians.[7] The membership of the subsequent Ad Hoc Assembly was more broadly drawn from the newly formed Assembly of the European Coal and Steel Community, and supplemented with a number of additional members coopted from France, Italy, and Germany, to serve as a pre-constituent body for the European Political Community, at the same time as the European Defence Community Treaty was being drawn up. The Ad Hoc Assembly, under Spaak's chairmanship, established a 26-member Constitutional Committee chaired by a German representative, Heinrich von Brentano, with a smaller working group and four sub-committees to undertake the task of drafting.[8]

1. THE WORK OF THE COMITE D'ETUDES POUR LA CONSTITUTION EUROPEENNE (CECE) ON HUMAN RIGHTS

The CECE began work early in 1952, and—perhaps unsurprisingly, given the number of prominent lawyers on the committee—the question of the place of human rights in the proposed new European polity seems to have been raised quite soon. In the third session of the *Comité* on 24 May, Altiero Spinelli seems to have been the first person to remark that the committee should give attention to 'les droits de l'homme et des libertés fondamentales'.[9] Other members however, and in particular one of the influential German parliamentarians, Max Becker, countered that the issue of fundamental rights protection was better left to the nation states.

Despite these basic differences of view about the role of human rights in the new European construction, '*Droits de l'homme*' were assigned a separate chapter by the committee. Fernand Dehousse, the CECE rapporteur, raised a number of questions in this regard. He asked first what the source of inspiration for human rights protection in the proposed European Constitution should be: whether the Universal Declaration of Human Rights, the European Convention on Human Rights, or a synthesis of the

---

[6] For a discussion of this see Cohen, (n 5 above) at 120–123 and D Preda, 'The Debate over the European Constituent Assembly: a Story of Drafts, Desires and Disappointments' (2003) 1 The Federalist 12–30.

[7] Cohen (n 5 above) 120–122.

[8] These were the subcommittees on powers and competences, on political institutions, on judicial institutions, and on liaison with other states and international organizations.

[9] See Projet de Statut de la Communauté Politique Europeénne: Travaux Preparatoires, (Brussels : European Movement, 1952) 18.

national constitutional provisions; and secondly he asked whether it was necessary for these rights to be mentioned in the European Constitution itself, as opposed to being contained in the constitutions of the separate Member States.[10] Ultimately, there was least resistance amongst the members of the *Comité* to relying on the ECHR as a source of human rights protection in the proposed European Constitution, despite the fact that the ECHR had not yet been ratified by the six Member States of the European Coal and Steel Community. The likelihood that using the ECHR would facilitate the accession of other countries in the future was mentioned.[11] Max Becker raised questions about the risk of divergent interpretations as between the Member States and asked a question which has continued to dominate debates today, namely who should be the final arbiter of those different interpretations—whether the European Court of Human Rights, the 'Supreme Court' of the proposed new European Community, or even the International Court of Justice.[12] The other—by now very familiar—question of possible clashes of jurisdiction in the field of human rights protection between the European Community Court and the European Court of Human Rights, despite the fact that at the time the latter had not yet begun to function, was also raised.[13] It was proposed by Fernand Dehousse that there be a separate chamber for dealing with human rights within the proposed European Community Court.[14] Finally, the possibility of Community accession to the ECHR was also raised.[15]

Ultimately, in the first of nine Resolutions which were adopted by the CECE as the product of its drafting work, the solution chosen was to declare 'protection of fundamental freedoms' to be one of the aims of the new Community, and to oblige the Member States of the Community to respect human rights as defined in the European Convention on Human Rights. The first of the nine Resolutions declared that a new and indissoluble European Community was to be created, with

> the aim, through establishing a closer bond between the [peoples of the Member States], of guaranteeing the common well-being, existence and external security of the Member States and of protecting the constitutional order, democratic institutions and fundamental freedoms.

In other words, protection of fundamental freedoms within the new Community was to be one of its central aims. The recent experience of the Second World War seems clear also in the references to the protection of constitutional order and democratic institutions. From this perspective, the interest of the new Europe in human rights protection was concentrated on the need to tame the potential excesses of Member States. Paragraph 7 of the first CECE Resolution went on to outline a very specific and substantial crisis-intervention role for the proposed European Community in relation to the protection of human rights.

---

[10] ibid 24. See also 31–32.   [11] ibid 46.   [12] ibid 33.
[13] See ibid 46, for the committee's discussion of the relevant report of Henry Frenay who had been Chairman of the European Union of Federalists.
[14] ibid 125–127.   [15] ibid 207.

7. Each Member State is held to respect human rights as they are defined in the Convention on Defence of Human Rights and Fundamental Liberties, signed in Rome on November, 4th, 1950 as well as in the supplementary Protocol signed in Paris on March, 20th, 1952.

Should the Community be so requested by the constitutional authorities of a Member State, it will assist the latter with a view to maintaining the constitutional order, democratic institutions or man's fundamental liberties.

Should the Community Government establish that, in one Member State, the constitutional order, democratic institutions or man's fundamental liberties have been seriously violated, without the constitutional authorities of this State being able or wishing to re-establish these, the Community may intervene in place of these authorities until such time as the situation is brought under control. In such a case, the measures taken by the Community Government would be submitted without delay for the approval of the Community Parliament.

Several aspects of the approach adopted here are worthy of note. The first is the unequivocal assumption—despite the objection of the German member noted above—of the desirability of a central role for the European Community in protecting and preserving human rights *within* the Member States, even though the Member States themselves were clearly expected to take primary responsibility for this task. Secondly, the objects of suspicion from the point of view of human rights protection were the Member States rather than the Community, since apart from the fact that the Community was assigned the general aim of protecting fundamental freedoms, only the Member States and not the Community institutions were specifically placed under an obligation to respect human rights. Thirdly, the source of the rights the Member States were held to respect was the European Convention on Human Rights, and express reference was not made to Member State constitutions. Fourthly, the role of the Community was envisaged as a kind of strong-arm back-stop in the event of a serious failure on the part of a Member State in protecting human rights and fundamental freedoms. To that extent, section 7 paragraph 3 of the first Resolution bears a slight resemblance to the provision now contained in Article 7 of the Treaty on European Union,[16] albeit with a much more extensive enforcement role envisaged for the Community at the time. Coming not long after the end of the war and the experience of the Holocaust, and a time of dictatorship in Spain and Portugal, the primary concern from the point of view of human rights seems to have been the fear of totalitarianism or similar abuses by European Member States, and the wish to confer power on the new Community to intervene in the event of such serious violations. Section 7 paragraph 2 of the Resolution provided a softer option than this direct intervention, under which a Member State's constitutional authorities could request the Community for assistance to maintain democratic institutions or fundamental liberties if these were threatened within the state.

---

[16] Art 7 TEU provides for a set of procedures whereby the Council may ultimately suspend the voting rights of a Member State where the European Council has determined the existence of a serious and persistent breach by that state of the values of respect for human dignity, freedom, democracy, equality, the rule of law, and respect for human rights, including the rights of persons belonging to minorities.

In the CECE's Resolution 4, which dealt with the judicial power of the proposed European constitutional framework, no express jurisdiction was to be conferred on the new court over human rights issues, but it was specified that the new Community Supreme Court would be both a Constitutional Court and a Court of Appeal.[17] There was a clause similar to that which is currently contained in Article 19 TEU[18] which provided that the Court was to ensure that 'in the interpretation and application of the [Statute] and laws of the Community the law is observed', and perhaps most significantly, individual citizens were to be given a right to take action before the Court in cases of alleged conflict between the new Treaty and acts of the Community institutions or of the Member States.

In short, the draft articles produced by the CECE envisaged a European Community with a strong role in the field of human rights protection, with the emphasis on human rights protection within the European Community, and with a view to guarding against totalitarianism or other kinds of repression within Member States. While the job of protecting human rights was to be the first-line responsibility of the Member States, the Community would have a powerful back-up role of what might nowadays be called humanitarian intervention, either with or without the consent of the Member State in question, in the case of serious violation of fundamental rights and freedoms within or by a Member State. The European Convention on Human Rights was envisaged as the formal legal source for the rights to be protected, and—despite the lack of explicit provision for this—the new Community Court would apparently have had jurisdiction to entertain actions brought by individuals for violation of the fundamental rights guaranteed by the new Treaty.

---

[17] The relevant parts of the Fourth Resolution on the Community Judicial Power set out principles which provided:

1. The juridical functions of the Community are performed by a Supreme Court and by other Courts established by law.
2. The Supreme Court ensures that in the interpretation and application of the Statute and laws of the Community the law is observed.

It is at the same time a Constitutional Court and a Court of Appeal.

3. Consequently it is competent:
(a) in cases of conflict between the Statute and the laws or public acts of the Community;
(b) in cases of conflict between the Statute and the laws or public acts of the Member States;
(c) in cases of disputes between the Member States or disputes to which the Community is a party;
(d) in cases of violations of diplomatic prerogatives or immunities;
(e) it is finally competent in areas of civil, penal, and public law coming within the competence of the Community which are entrusted to it by law.

The Community Parliament will regulate by law the right to take action before the Court.
In cases (a) and (b), this right will be open to any injured citizen, Member State and Community organ or to a determined fraction of each of these.

[18] Art 19 TEU provides that 'the Court of Justice of the European Union...shall ensure that in the interpretation and application of the Treaties the law is observed'.

2. THE WORK OF THE *AD HOC* ASSEMBLY AND ITS CONSTITUTIONAL COMMITTEE IN DRAFTING THE EPC TREATY

As explained above, at the same time that plans for a European Defence Community (EDC) were being developed, the idea of establishing a European Political Community was simultaneously promoted as a way of providing political leadership and a democratic basis for the defence community. After the Treaty establishing the EDC was signed in May 1952, the Consultative Assembly of the Council of Europe asked the six governments to give the Common Assembly of the European Coal and Steel Community (ECSC) the responsibility for drawing up a plan for a European Political Community. In this way the Ad Hoc Assembly was formally created by the Special Council of Ministers of the ECSC to draft the statute for a European Political Community.

The human rights provisions eventually included in the EPC Treaty draft were different in several respects from those in the relevant CECE Resolutions. In common with the CECE Resolutions, Article 2 of the EPC Treaty declared that the Community would have the general aim of contributing towards the protection of human rights and fundamental freedoms in the Member States. Unlike in the earlier Resolutions however, the EPC Treaty stipulated that the provisions of the European Convention on Human Rights were to become an integral part of the new Community Constitution (or Statute, as it was then called).[19]

A second difference is that the drafting committees of the Ad Hoc Assembly were focused explicitly on the risk of the Community itself becoming a potential violator of human rights. In other words, unlike the CECE, which seemed to conceive of the role of the Community primarily as a watchdog and enforcer which would intervene where Member States seriously failed to protect human rights, the drafting committees of the Ad Hoc Assembly expressly contemplated the prospect of the new Community itself being responsible for human rights violations. The Constitutional Committee of the Ad Hoc Assembly was concerned about this prospect, and discussed various possible ways of ensuring European Court of Human Rights jurisdiction over Community acts, including accession by the Community to the ECHR.[20] Even at this early stage, problems were envisaged in seeking to amend the Rome Convention establishing the European Convention on Human Rights. The Constitutional Committee however recommended that EC Member States could be requested by the Community to bring proceedings against another Member State before the ECHR where a violation was taking place; and further recommended that the statute of the Council of Europe be amended to permit the EC to take a Member State directly before the ECHR.[21]

The eventual outcome of these discussions within the Constitutional Committee is to be found in the provisions of the draft Treaty in Article 45 concerning the role of the

---

[19] Art 3 provides: 'The provisions of Part I of the Convention for the Protection of Human Rights and Fundamental Freedoms signed in Rome on 4 November 1950, together with those of the protocol signed in Paris on 20 March 1952, are an integral part of the present Statute.'

[20] See document AH 162, Historical Archives of the European Union (Florence, European University Institute).

[21] ibid.

new Community Court. Article 45 explicitly envisaged that any dispute arising from action taken by one of the Community institutions which affected the rights guaranteed in the European Convention on Human Rights was to be referred to the Community Court, and such cases could be brought by natural or legal persons. In other words, the draft EPC Treaty provided for a right of action before the Community Court by individuals against the Community institutions for violation of the ECHR.

Article 45 also contains interesting provisions—even if they are not altogether clear—on the relationship between the European Community Court when adjudicating on alleged violations of the ECHR (which was incorporated by Article 3 of the EPC Treaty) and the European Court of Human Rights.[22] These provisions reflect something of the extensive debates which took place during the process of drafting the EPC, in which the drafters considered not only the technical problems associated with the fact that the Community was not and could not easily become party to the Convention on Human Rights, but also the potential problems of conflicts between the two courts and the impact that rulings of the Community Court on the meaning of the ECHR could have on other states party to the ECHR but not party to the European Political Community Treaty. In essence, Article 45 provided for the Community Court to exercise jurisdiction but to 'relinquish' it to the European Court of Human Rights (once that Court began operating) in any case involving a question of principle of relevance to all the parties to the ECHR. This is an interesting and fairly nuanced position falling somewhere between that of those who felt that only the ECtHR should properly have jurisdiction over such disputes[23] and those who would have given full jurisdiction to the Community Court. The compromise is that Article 45 of the EPC

---

[22] The relevant provisions of Art 45 provide:

1. Any dispute arising from a decision or measure taken by one of the Institutions of the Community, which affects the rights recognized in the Convention for the Protection of Human Rights and Fundamental Freedoms, shall be referred to the Court.
2. If an appeal is lodged with the Court under the conditions mentioned in the preceding paragraph by a natural or legal person, such appeal shall be deemed to be lodged in accordance with the terms of Art 26 of the Convention for the Protection of Human Rights and Fundamental Freedoms.
3. After the establishment of the legal machinery for which provision is made in the Convention for the Protection of Human Rights and Fundamental Freedoms, should any dispute arise which involves a question of principle as to the interpretation or extent of the obligations resulting from the said Convention and which consequently affects all the Parties thereto, the Court shall renounce judgment, if necessary, until the question of principle has been settled by the judicial organs for which provision is made in the Convention.

[23] For example Max Becker, one of the German members of the Constitutional Committee, expressed his concern about the broad and imprecise way in which the Community Court's jurisdiction over matters 'interior' to the Community, between Member States of the Community or between a Member State and the EC, to which the ECHR was applicable, was defined. He took the view that this was impinging on the jurisdiction of the European Court of Human Rights. He considered that it was inappropriate to make it compulsory for a dispute concerning human rights between EPC Member States to be submitted first to the Community Court, and thought this was properly the job of the European Court of Human Rights. However, the constitutional committee seemed to see the Community Court rather as a 'domestic tribunal' for the purposes of exhaustion of domestic remedies for the ECtHR, and envisaged that a dispute on which the Community Court ruled could be subsequently brought, by another means, before the ECtHR.

Treaty provides for initial jurisdiction, subject to relinquishment to the ECtHR under the conditions mentioned above.

Finally, like the CECE's Resolution 7, Article 104 of the EPC Treaty provided for the possibility of intervention by the Community to maintain 'constitutional order and democratic institutions' within the territory of a Member State. Unlike the CECE Resolution, however, which would have enabled the Community to intervene in the absence of a request and where a Member State was unwilling to act, Article 104 provided for such intervention only where the Member State in question requested such assistance.[24]

The various differences between the approach of the CECE drafters and that of the eventual EPC Treaty drafters to the problem of potential violations by the Community of human rights are interesting. The primary concern at the time the CECE Resolutions were drafted appears to have been to restrain potential human rights violations by the Member States, and to empower the European Community to intervene in the case of such violations. The drafters of the EPC Treaty on the other hand—which was a larger body and included many more national parliamentarians—adopted a more restrained approach to the Community, addressing the possibility that the Community institutions themselves could encroach through the exercise of their powers on human rights.[25] The draft EPC Treaty also clearly accorded a key role to the institutions of the ECHR in adjudicating on human rights violations, even while confronting the legal complexities of the fact that the Community could not itself become a party to the Convention on Human Rights.

Ultimately, the draft Treaty on a European Political Community prepared by the Constitutional Committee, which included these provisions on human rights protection, was accepted without difficulty by the Ad Hoc Assembly. However, at the Intergovernmental Conference which followed in 1953, not all of the national delegations were happy with the content of the new draft Treaty. The French delegation in particular raised objections, and argued for a significantly less 'supranational' approach. Eventually, as is well known, the draft European Political Community Treaty was abandoned when the prospects for ratification of the European Defence Community Treaty collapsed.[26] It was at this point that the ambitious early attempts to promote European political integration were abandoned in favour of a significantly

---

[24] Art 104 EPC provided: 'Member States may request the European Executive Council for assistance in maintaining constitutional order and democratic institutions within their territory. The European Executive Council, with the unanimous concurrence of the Council of National Ministers, shall lay down the conditions under which the Community shall be empowered to intervene on its own initiative. The relevant provisions shall take the form of a bill to be submitted to Parliament for approval within one year from the date of the coming into being of the Peoples' Chamber. They shall be enacted as legislation of the Community.'

[25] It was also proposed that the Community should be subject to the explicit requirement, along with the individual Member States, to respect human rights and fundamental freedoms, but such an obligation did not appear in these terms in the final text. The subcommittee on powers and competences of the constitutional committee of the Ad Hoc Assembly had proposed an article whereby the Community as well as the Member States would guarantee to everyone within their jurisdiction the rights and freedoms in the ECHR. See Document AH 114, Historical Archives of the European Union (n 20 above).

[26] For an interesting account see R Dwan, 'Jean Monnet and the European Defence Community, 1950–54' (2001) Cold War History 141.

more restrained and pragmatic strategy in the shape of the European Economic and Atomic Energy Communities established in 1957. And with the abandonment of these political integration plans, the lively debates and various blueprints for an ambitious European Community human rights system also vanished.

C. PHASE 2: FROM THE ROME TREATY TO THE MAASTRICHT TREATY: THE DISAPPEARANCE OF HUMAN RIGHTS FROM THE EC TREATY FRAMEWORK AND THEIR RETURN

1. THE SILENCE OF THE 1957 EC TREATY FRAMEWORK ON HUMAN RIGHTS

The silence of the European Economic Community Treaty and the accompanying European Atomic Energy Treaty in 1957 on the subject of human rights has often been noted and its implications discussed. There seems to be no evidence of an explicit decision being taken to exclude all references to human rights, or to rule out any role for human rights protection, in the two Treaties establishing the new Communities. On the contrary, much was made at the time of establishing the 1957 Communities of the fact that they were intended to serve a 'human ideal of brotherhood' shared by the six Member States.[27] Nevertheless, what occurred in the aftermath of the failure of the European Defence Community was that a decision was taken, following the mandate of the Messina conference which led to the establishment of the European Economic Community,[28] to hew very closely to the terms of that mandate and to exclude discussion of any issues which were not expressly mentioned there. Paul Henri Spaak, by now the Belgian Minister for Foreign Affairs, once again chaired the relevant committee (the Intergovernmental Committee on European Integration) and prepared the report which led ultimately to the drafting of the EEC Treaty.[29] Spaak insisted strongly on this strategy of adhering closely to the Messina mandate and avoiding any subjects which were not expressly mentioned in the foreign ministers' Resolution, as a way of avoiding the many controversial and political issues which

[27] See P-H Spaak, Discourse (Rome, 25 March 1957), Historical Archives of the Council of the European Union, Brussels, Rue de la Loi 175, Negotiations of the treaties instituting the EEC and the CECA (1955–57), CM3, Conference of the foreign ministers and signature of the treaties of the EEC and the CECA, (Rome, 25 March 1957) CM3/NEGO/098, available at <http://www.ena.lu/discours-paul-henri-spaak-occasion-signature-traites-rome-rome-25-mars-1957-010000644.html>.

[28] See the so-called Messina Resolution, ie the Resolution adopted by the Foreign Ministers of the ECSC Member States (Messina, 1–3 June 1955) to revive the process of European integration by focusing on economic integration and the establishment of a common market. See also the earlier Benelux Memorandum of 18 May 1955, adopted by the foreign ministers of the three countries, making a similar proposal.

[29] Now simply known as the Spaak Report, this was formally entitled *The Brussels Report on the General Common Market*, and was adopted in June 1956.

arguably led to the downfall of the EDC and EPC Treaties.[30] It is at least in part in this context that the silence of the 1957 Treaties on the subject of human rights protection can be understood.

This is not to say that the topic of the possible impact of the new Communities on human rights protection was not raised at all during the drafting process. On the contrary, it seems that an attempt was made by the German delegation during the drafting of the EEC Treaty to have a kind of human rights 'reservation clause' (*Verfassungsvorbehalt*), similar to that contained in Article 3 of the European Defence Community Treaty, inserted into the new EEC Treaty. Article 3 of the EDC Treaty had begun with an articulation of the subsidiarity principle, and continued by indicating that the Defence Community would not take measures impinging on protected human rights and freedoms.[31] In other words, in the EDC Treaty reservation-clause, the fundamental human rights of the individual were posited as a notional bulwark against the exercise of power by the new Community and a constraint on the way in which the conferred powers were to be exercised. The German proposal for a similar clause in the EEC Treaty was however rejected by other delegations, apparently because of a perceived risk that Member States might misuse a reservation clause of that kind to undermine Community goals, and that it would be difficult or impossible for the new Community to pay attention to all of the different sets of rights protected under the various Member State constitutions without subordinating Community laws and goals to these multiple and varying requirements.[32]

In other words, what we see by the time of the drafting of the Euratom and European Economic Community Treaties is that the vision of the new European system as one which would have a substantial political role involving the protection of human rights against abuse by or within the Member States or even on the part of its own new institutions, and working alongside the Council of Europe and European Convention system in order to assure this, had disappeared. The ambitions of the new Communities were to be strictly determined by the common market mandate outlined in the Messina Resolution, and the issue of human rights protection was remitted once again primarily to the realm of the national constitutional systems.

The German delegation's attempt to introduce this kind of liberal restraint on Community power, expressed in terms which included the fundamental rights of the individual, was rejected, but more because of the perceived risk of Member State

[30] P-H Spaak, *The Continuing Battle: Memoirs of a European 1936–1966* (Weidenfeld and Nicholson, 1971). The *travaux préparatoires* also make this strategy evident.

[31] The express language of Art 3(1) of the EDC Treaty (translated into English) provide: 'The Community shall accomplish the goals assigned to it by employing the least burdensome and most efficient methods. It shall intervene only to the extent necessary for the fulfillment of its mission and with due respect to public liberties and the fundamental rights of the individual.'

[32] M Zuleeg, 'Fundamental Rights and the Law of the European Communities' (1971) 8 CML Rev 446, citing E Wohlfarth, U Everling, H Glaesner, and R Sprung, *Die Europäische Wirtschaftsgemeinschaft, Kommentar zum Vertrag* (Berlin/Frankfurt, 1960).

abuse of such a clause than because of any generally expressed objection to a human rights role for the new Community. However, it is evident that although this German vision of human rights as a negative constraint on the integration process, and a residual core requiring protection against the institutions of the new Community just as against any institutions of government, may have been temporarily dismissed, it returned to shape the way in which the question of EU human rights protection re-emerged over a decade later through judicial challenges before the European Court of Justice.

2. THE RETURN OF HUMAN RIGHTS INTO EUROPEAN COMMUNITY LAW AND DISCOURSE

The next part of the story is the most familiar one, in which repeated challenges from economic actors in Germany, premised on this understanding of domestically pro-tected economic and liberty rights as a limitation on the regulatory powers of the Community, forced the issue which had been dismissed during the drafting process back onto the agenda, most notably onto the agenda of the Court of Justice. In *Stork*,[33] in which a coal wholesaler complained of a Decision of the High Authority of the Economic Coal and Steel Community governing the sale of coal, the ECJ refused to consider the argument that the Decision breached basic rights which were protected under German law. The ECJ, echoing the refusal of other Member State delegations to entertain the proposal of the German delegation for a human-rights reservation clause in the original EEC Treaty, ruled that 'the High Authority is not empowered to examine a ground of complaint which maintains that, when it adopted its decision, it infringed principles of German constitutional law'.[34] Subsequently in *Geitling*,[35] another case concerning a challenge by coal wholesalers to a High Authority Decision which prevented them from selling coal directly, the Court not only rejected the relevance of a fundamental right in German constitutional law, but also dismissed the argument that Community law might independently protect such a right.[36] And in *Sgarlata*,[37] some five years later, the ECJ stated that it could not allow the express provisions of the Treaty to be overridden by a plea founded upon other principles, even if those were fundamental principles which were common to the legal systems of all the Member States.[38] Thus not only was the specific German vision of domestically

---

[33] Case 1/ 58 *Stork v High Authority* [1959] ECR, [17].
[34] ibid [4].
[35] Cases 36, 37, 38, and 40/59 *Geitling v High Authority* [1960] ECR 423.
[36] ibid 438.
[37] Case 40/64 *Sgarlata and others v Commission* [1965] ECR 215, [1966] CMLR 314.
[38] Note, however, that the Court did not deny the existence in Community law of any general principles of law other than those written in the Treaty: see Case 35/67 *Van Eick v Commission* [1968] ECR 329, 342, where the Court held that the Disciplinary Board under the Community staff regulations was bound to exercise its powers in accordance with 'the fundamental principles of the law of procedure'. However, unlike in the case of *Sgarlata*, there was no question of these general principles overriding specific Treaty provisions.

protected fundamental rights as a constraint on Community powers rejected by the Court, but also the vision of human rights as general principles of European law which should guide and shape the interpretation of the EEC Treaty.

Yet the persistence of the German vision, and the determination of litigants based in Germany to question the regulatory powers of the Community from the perspective of domestically protected constitutional rights, led eventually to a softening of the Court's approach and an adjustment seen initially in the *Stauder* case,[39] and elaborated upon in the cases of *Internationale Handelsgesellschaft*[40] and *Nold*.[41] As is well known, this triptych of cases produced a new constitutional account by the ECJ of the role of human rights in the EC legal order. No longer were they to be treated as irrelevant or entirely peripheral to the common market project, but instead respect for fundamental rights—inspired by the common constitutional traditions of the Member States and international human rights treaties on which they collaborated—was declared to be part of the general principles of Community law, and the Court would henceforth entertain claims that such rights had been adversely affected by Community acts and policies.

In this way a position close to that which was rejected during the drafting of the EEC Treaty eventually came to be accepted by the ECJ, even without the existence of an express reservation clause in the Treaty. Fundamental human rights would constitute a brake on Community policies, and if a Community act encroached on a protected right, the Court would ensure protection for the latter. The reason for the volte-face of the Court is widely accepted to be its concern to maintain the autonomy and supremacy of EC law, and to avoid claims that Community law must be subordinate to national constitutional rights. The difference between a reservation clause of the kind argued for in 1956 and the approach eventually adopted by the ECJ is that the Court of Justice insisted on the autonomous nature and source of the rights which were to be recognized and protected, so that they would be understood as genuinely European and not domestic in their origin.

The famous judicial about-turn in *Stauder* and *Nold* did not, of course, come out of the blue, but was preceded by heated political and legal debates in various European arenas about the implications of the doctrine of supremacy of EC law which the Court had pronounced shortly beforehand in *Costa v ENEL*,[42] and more specifically about the consequent risk of subordinating or undermining human rights protected in domestic constitutions.[43] In this context, already some years before the ECJ's decision in *Stauder*, the President of the Commission had been arguing openly for

---

[39] Case 29/69 *Stauder v City of Ulm* [1969] ECR 419.

[40] Case 11/70 *Internationale Handelsgesellschaft v Einfuhr und Vorratsstelle für Getreide und Futtermittel* [1970] ECR 1125.

[41] Case 4/73 *Nold v Commission* [1974] ECR 491.

[42] Case 6/64 *Flaminio Costa v ENEL* [1964] ECR 585.

[43] Report by Fernand Dehousse, who was by then a Belgian member of the European Parliament: *Report on the Supremacy of EC Law over National Law of the Member States*, EP Doc 43 (1965/66) JO 2923, 14.

an understanding of fundamental human rights as part of the 'general principles' of EC law, which although autonomous in source from national constitutions, nevertheless took into account the common legal conceptions of the Member States.[44] We might say that once this account of the place of fundamental rights in the EC legal order was confirmed and validated by the ECJ in its trio of cases, the period of silence of the EC constitutional framework from 1957 until 1969, and the legal vacuum on the subject of human rights came to an end.[45] From this time on, the terms of the debate had changed and the question shifted from whether the European Community should concern itself at all with fundamental human rights protection to what exactly its role should be in this regard.

A growing concern with the external role and perception of the EU in the world at the same time, following the inauguration of 'European Political Cooperation' on foreign policy in 1970, led to the declaration by the European Council on European identity in 1973. This Declaration announced that respect for human rights—along with social justice, representative democracy, and the rule of law—was a fundamental element of EU identity.[46] The 1978 Copenhagen Declaration first articulated the so-called political criteria for EU accession,[47] including respect for human rights as a condition of European Union membership. And the 1977 Joint Declaration of the European Parliament, Council, and Commission on fundamental rights affirmed the earlier case law of the Court of Justice and asserted that the EC Treaties were based on respect for the general principles of law, including fundamental rights as recognized in the constitutions of the Member States and under the ECHR, and that the institutions of the EC would respect these rights in the exercise of their powers.[48] Although a declaration has little practical effect and is not a legally binding instrument, the joint statement of the three political institutions had symbolic importance in indicating that these institutions supported the Court's 'derivation' of rights from the ECHR and from Member States' constitutional principles, and that they were willing in principle to respect these rights in the exercise of their powers. From this time on, the case law of the Court of Justice addressing human rights issues expanded, and various legal and political initiatives were taken to develop

---

[44] W Hallstein, *Discussions on the Dehousse Report*, 79 Proceedings of the European Parliament (French Edition, 1965) 218–222.

[45] There had also been a number of notable earlier attempts to bring human-rights related issues within the remit of the new Communities. These include the Bonn Conference and the Fouchet Plan of 1961, the 1968 Commission Declaration on completion of the customs union, and the 1970 Davignon report.

[46] For an analysis of the symbolic significance of this move, see A Williams, *EU Human Rights Policies: A Study in Irony* (Oxford University Press, 2004), especially chs 6–7.

[47] This may have been the first official and operational articulation of human rights and democracy conditions for accession to the European Community, but it was not the first attempt, since Art 116 of the abandoned European Political Community Treaty had specified that 'accession to the Community shall be open to the Member States of the Council of Europe and to any other European State which guarantees the protection of human rights and fundamental freedoms mentioned in Art 3.

[48] Joint Declaration of the Parliament, Council and Commission of the European Communities [1977] OJ C103/1.

a more active role for human rights within EU law and policy.[49] But it was not until the early 1990s that the first distinct contours of a European Union constitutional framework for human rights protection began to emerge.

D. PHASE 3: FROM THE MAASTRICHT TO THE LISBON TREATY: THE EMERGENCE OF AN EU CONSTITUTIONAL FRAMEWORK FOR HUMAN RIGHTS PROTECTION

It was in the Maastricht Treaty on European Union 1992 that formal Treaty recognition was finally given to human rights as part of EU law.[50] This was followed in 1997 by the grant of Treaty status to the 'Copenhagen criteria' for EU accession in the Treaty of Amsterdam,[51] and the insertion of Article 13 in the EC Treaty which conferred power on the EU to adopt legislation to combat discrimination across a range of grounds within the fields of existing EC competences.[52] At the same time, the Amsterdam Treaty introduced the 'suspension of rights' mechanism for any EU Member State which was found responsible for serious and persistent violation of human rights, and this was amended by the Nice Treaty a few years later—following the Haider affair[53]—to cover situations involving a risk rather than actual violation of rights.[54] Not long after the adoption of the Amsterdam Treaty, the EU Charter of Fundamental Rights and Freedoms was drafted and proclaimed in 2000. Following the adoption but non-ratification of the Treaty Establishing a Constitution for Europe in

---

[49] Amongst the institutional attempts to articulate a role for the EC in the area of human rights around this time and thereafter are the 1974 Paris Summit and the 1976 Tindemans Report, the 1976 Commission Report on Human Rights, the 1978 Declaration of the Council on Democracy in Copenhagen, the 1984 Adonnino Committee on a People's Europe, the 1984 European Parliament draft Treaty on a European Union and Spinelli Report, the Single European Act of 1986, the 1989 European Parliament Declaration on Fundamental Rights and Freedoms, and the 1989 Community Charter of Fundamental Social Rights of Workers.

[50] The preamble to the Single European Act in 1987 had made mention of human rights in the following terms: 'Determined to work together to promote democracy on the basis of fundamental rights recognized in the constitutions and laws of the Member States, in the Convention for the Protection of Human Rights and Fundamental Freedoms, and the European Social Charter, notably freedom, equality and social justice.'

[51] Art 49 TEU now provides: 'Any European State which respects the values referred to in Art 2 and is committed to promoting them may apply to become a member of the Union' and Art 2 provides: 'The Union is founded on the values of respect for human dignity, freedom, democracy, equality, the rule of law and respect for human rights, including the rights of persons belonging to minorities.'

[52] Art 13 EC is now Art 19 TFEU. On the drafting of Art 13 EC, see M Bell, *Anti-discrimination Law and the European Union* (Oxford University Press, 2002).

[53] See eg M Merlingen, C Mudde, and U Sedelmeier, 'The Right and the Righteous?: European Norms, Domestic Politics and the Sanctions against Austria' (2001) 39 JCMS 59; C Leconte, 'The Fragility of the EU as a "Community of Values": Lessons from the Haider Affair' (2005) 28 WEP 620.

[54] See Art 7 TEU.

2004–05,[55] the Charter was eventually given binding legal status by the Lisbon Treaty in 2009.[56] At the same time, the Lisbon Treaty introduced an obligation for the EU to accede to the European Convention on Human Rights.[57] This period of major constitutional change in the field of human rights also saw a number of other interesting institutional developments take place, such as the establishments of a network of experts on fundamental rights, a Personal Representative on human rights to advise the High Representative for Foreign and Security Policy and Council Secretary General, and finally the EU Fundamental Rights Agency[58] which replaced the previous Vienna Monitoring Centre against Racism and Xenophobia.

These moves formally marked the constitutional coming-of-age of human rights within the EU legal and constitutional framework. They gave official affirmation to the case law of the Court of Justice which declared fundamental rights, as derived from domestic constitutional traditions and from the ECHR, to be part of EU law, and they asserted that fundamental human rights were part of the values on which the EU was founded. They established compliance with human rights as a condition for EU membership and set up an ex-post membership mechanism for suspension of the rights of a Member State which was found to be violating such rights in a serious and persistent way. They saw the enactment of the EU's own Charter of Rights, and the establishment of a set of institutions to support and develop the EU's human rights policies. Such policies include the expansion of anti-discrimination law, the regular use of various forms of human rights conditionality and assistance in EU external relations,[59] and more generally a declared commitment by the EU to 'mainstream' human rights concerns throughout the field of external policies.[60] At the same time, the case law of the Court of Justice and the Court of First Instance touching on human rights matters has expanded and grown, not only in number but also in the range of subject matter areas in which such claims are arising. It is no longer the case that human rights claims before EU courts are concerned mainly with staff complaints or with procedural rights in EU competition cases. Instead, a variety of human rights claims are

[55] For information on the drafting and attempted ratification of the Treaty Establishing a Constitution for Europe, see <http://european-convention.eu.int/DraftTreaty.asp?lang=EN> and <http://www.consilium. europa.eu/cms3_applications/Applications/igc/doc_register.asp?content=DOC&lang=EN&cmsid=754>.

[56] See Art 6(1) TEU. The full text of the Charter, which was originally adopted in 2000 and in slightly amended form in 2007 following the changes proposed in the unratified Constitutional treaty and the subsequent Lisbon Treaty, can be found in [2007] OJ C303/01.

[57] Art 6(2) TEU.

[58] Council Regulation (EC) 168/2007 of 15 February 2007 establishing a European Union Agency for Fundamental Rights, see [2007] OJ L53/1.

[59] eg L Bartels, *Human Rights Conditionality in the EU's External Agreements* (Oxford University Press, 2005) and E Fierro, *The EU's Approach to Human Rights Conditionality in Practice* (Kluwer, 2003). For a broader appraisal, see U Khaliq, *Ethical Dimensions of the Foreign Policy of the EU: A Legal Analysis* (Cambridge University Press, 2008).

[60] See for an early statement the Council's Annual Report on Human Rights for 2001, <http://www. consilium.europa.eu/uedocs/cmsUpload/HR2001EN.pdf> and more recently its Annual Report for 2008. See also Document 10076/06 of the Political and Security Committee of the Council on 'Mainstreaming human rights across CFSP and other EU Policies', of 7 June 2006.

regularly invoked in all kinds of subject matter fields from criminal justice[61] to data privacy[62] to family reunification[63] and anti-terrorist asset-freezing.[64] A significant body of scholarship analysing these developments has also appeared, with extensive commentary on the Charter of Fundamental Rights,[65] the relationship between the EU and the ECHR systems,[66] the suspension mechanism of Article 7 TEU,[67] and most recently the Fundamental Rights Agency.[68] Last but not least, the growing case law of the Court of Justice touching on fundamental rights issues continues to attract scholarly interest.[69]

[61] For discussion, see O De Schutter, 'The Promotion of Fundamental Rights by the Union as a contribution to the European Legal Space: Mutual Recognition and Mutual Trust in the Establishment of the Area of Freedom, Security and Justice' RefGov Working Paper, available online at <http://refgovcpdr.ucl.ac.be/?go=publications&dc=f4d3720606c3fb7b34f3d9d56e17267cd8ee6805>.

[62] See eg Case C-301/06 *Ireland v Council* ERC [2009] Page I-00593.

[63] See eg Case C-540/03 *European Parliament v Council* [2006] ECR I-5769.

[64] The case law in this field is now voluminous. For discussion, see T Tridimas, 'Terrorism and the ECJ: Empowerment and Democracy in the EC Legal Order', Queen Mary School of Law Legal Studies Research Paper No 12/2009.

[65] For some of the collections of writing on the Charter, see (2001) 8(1); E Eriksen, JE Fossum, and A Menéndez (eds), *The Chartering of Europe* (Arena Report No 8/2001); K Feus (ed), *An EU Charter of Fundamental Rights: Text and Commentaries* (Federal Trust, 2000); EU Network of Independent Experts on Fundamental Rights, *Commentary on the Charter* (June, 2006); J Schönlau, *Drafting the EU Charter: Rights, Legitimacy and Process* (Palgrave MacMillan, 2005). For some individual essays on the Charter, see S Douglas Scott, 'The Charter of Fundamental Rights as a Constitutional Document' (2004) EHRLR 37; T Goldsmith, 'A Charter of Rights, Freedoms and Principles' (2001) 38 CML Rev 1201; K Lenaerts and E De Smijter, 'A Bill of Rights for the EU' (2001) 38 CML Rev 273; F Rubio Llorente, 'A Charter of Dubious Utility' (2003) 1 ICON 3, 405; A Young, 'The Charter, Constitution and Human Rights: Is this the Beginning or the End for Human Rights Protections by Community Law' (2005) 11 EPL 219.

[66] See eg K Kuhnert, 'Bosphorus—Double standards in European human rights protection?' (2006) 2 Utrecht Law Review 177, and for a more approving assessment, see C Costello, 'The Bosphorus Ruling of the ECtHR: Fundamental Rights and Blurred Boundaries in Europe' (2006) 6 HRL Rev 87; L Besselink, 'The EU and the European Convention of Human Rights after Lisbon: From 'Bosphorus' Sovereign Immunity to Full Scrutiny?' at <http://papers.ssrn.com/sol3/papers.cfm?abstract_id=1132788>, and more generally S Greer and A Williams, 'Human Rights in the Council of Europe and the EU: Towards "Individual", "Constitutional" or "Institutional" Justice?'; C Salignat, 'The Impact of the Emergence of the European Union as a Human Rights Actor on the Council of Europe' (2004) 4 Baltic Yearbook of International Law 55; O De Schutter, 'The Two Europes of Human Rights: The Emerging Division of Tasks Between the Council of Europe and the European Union in Promoting Human Rights in Europe' (2008) 14 CJEL 509; F Van den Berghe, 'The EU and Issues of Human Rights Protection: Same Solutions to More Acute Problems?' (2010) 16 ELJ 112.

[67] See eg M Merlingen, C Muddle, and U Sedelmeier, 'The Right and the Righteous?: European Norms, Domestic Politics and the Sanctions against Austria' (2001) 39 JCMS 59; A Williams, 'The Indifferent Gesture: Art 7 TEU, the Fundamental Rights Agency and the UK's invasion of Iraq' (2006) 31 ELRev 3; W Sadurski 'Adding a Bite to a Bark: A Story of Art 7, the EU Enlargement and Jörg Haider', U of Sydney Working Paper No 10/01, at <http://ssrn.com/abstract=1531393>.

[68] See O De Schutter and V Van Goethem, 'The Fundamental Rights Agency: towards an Active Fundamental Rights Policy of the Union' (2006) 7 ERA Forum 587; and A von Bogdandy and J von Bernstorff, 'The EU Fundamental Rights Agency in the European and international human rights architecture' (2009) 46 CML Rev 1035; G von Toggenburg, 'The Role of the New EU Fundamental Rights Agency: Debating the Sex of Angels or Improving Europe's Human Rights Performance?' (2008) ELRev 385; A Arnull, 'Does Europe Need a Fundamental Rights Agency?' (2007) 32 ELRev 285. For a comprehensive survey of human rights monitoring in the EU see P Alston and O De Schutter (eds), *Monitoring Fundamental Rights in the EU* (Hart, 2005).

[69] See eg A Hinarejos, 'Recent Human Rights Developments in the EU Courts: The Charter of Fundamental Rights' (2007) 7 HRL Rev 793.

In short, the topic of human rights protection and promotion has come to occupy a significant place in EU law and policy over the past decade and a half, and the EU unquestionably now has a constitutional framework of kinds concerning human rights protection. The following section of the chapter examines the ways in which this framework differs from the constitutional framework for human rights protection envisaged in the 1950s, when the CECE and the Ad Hoc Committee were drafting proposals for the European Political Community.

E. COMPARING THE EU CONSTITUTIONAL FRAMEWORK FOR HUMAN RIGHTS PROTECTION AS DRAFTED IN THE 1950s AND TODAY

I suggest that there are three main differences to be seen between the constitutional framework for human rights envisaged by the drafters of the CECE Resolutions and the EPC Treaty. The first concerns the EU's role in monitoring Member States' human rights practices, the second whether the EU human rights regime is conceived of as an integral part of the regional and international human rights system or as an autonomous constitutional system, and the third concerns the nature of the role envisaged for human rights in internal as well as external EU activities.

1. HUMAN RIGHTS MONITORING OF EU MEMBER STATES

We have seen above how the CECE Resolutions envisaged a robust and interventionist role for the new European Community in monitoring Member State compliance with fundamental human rights. Even the draft EPC Treaty which followed, although its provisions acknowledged the possibility that the new Community itself could be a source of abuse, outlined a central role for the European Community in monitoring human rights protection within the Member States. The first of the aims of the Community listed in Article 2 of the EPC Treaty was 'to contribute towards the protection of human rights and fundamental freedoms in Member States'[70] and Article 3 made the provisions of the ECHR an integral part of the EPC Treaty. Article 41 declared that the Court of Justice would have jurisdiction over any dispute arising between the Community and the Member States in relation to the application or interpretation of the Treaty itself.[71] In other words, the draft EPC Treaty clearly envisaged that protection of human rights by the Member States would be a core concern of the Community, both through the provision for intervention in Article 104

---

[70] Complementing this provision, Art 55 of the draft EPC Treaty provided that '[t]he Community may make proposals to the Member States with the object of attaining the general aims defined in Art 2'.

[71] See Art 41 of the draft EPC Treaty: '1. The Court shall in its own right take cognizance of disputes arising out of the application or interpretation of the present Statute or of a law of the Community, to which the parties are either Member States among themselves or one or more Member States and the Community.'

and by allowing questions of compliance by Member States with the ECHR to be brought before the Community Court.

Under the current EU Treaty framework, however, despite the regular invocation of human rights in official discourse and documents, there is great reluctance to specify any clear role for the EU in relation to the actions of Member States as far as human rights compliance is concerned. Despite the broad statement in Article 2 TEU that the Union is founded on respect for human rights, and more importantly the provision in Article 6 giving legal force to the Charter of Fundamental Rights, the fine print makes clear the continuing and determined resistance of the Member States to any role for the EU in scrutinizing or regulating their activities. Article 51 of the Charter famously limits its scope of application by providing that it is addressed to the institutions of the European Union, but to the Member States only when they are implementing EU law.[72] Even the clear potential of Article 7 TEU to become the basis for a serious monitoring mechanism for human rights compliance by EU Member States has been dampened. When Article 7 TEU was first included by the Amsterdam Treaty and subsequently revised in the Nice Treaty, it seemed that perhaps the resistance of Member States to a monitoring role for the EU in relation to human rights within the territories of the Member States themselves had finally been overcome.[73] In what appears to have been a gesture prompted by the imminent future enlargement of the Union to include up to ten states from Central and Eastern Europe, the existing Member States decided that there should be a provision in Article 7 TEU for the suspension (though not expulsion) of the rights of a Member State found to be seriously and persistently violating human rights or democratic principles.[74]

However, it was the subsequent 'Haider Affair' in Austria, during which fourteen of the then fifteen EU Member States adopted diplomatic sanctions against Austria following the entry into coalition government of the far-right Freedom Party (the FPÖ), which revealed the clear interest of the EU in the existence of threats—whether current or future—to human rights and freedoms within its already existing Member States. The Haider affair led to Article 7 TEU being amended to provide a mechanism for intervention in the case of a risk and not only in the case of actual occurrence of serious human rights violations.[75] Shortly afterwards, at the European Parliament's proposal,[76] a Network of Experts on Fundamental Rights was established which began

---

[72] For a discussion of the drafting of Art 51 of the Charter, see G de Búrca, 'The Drafting of the EU Charter of Fundamental Rights' (2001) 26 ELRev 214–228.

[73] See G de Búrca, 'Beyond the Charter: How Enlargement has Enlarged the Human Rights Policy of the EU' (2004) 27 Fordham Int'l LJ 679, and see also A Williams, 'The Indifferent Gesture: Art 7 TEU, the Fundamental Rights Agency and the UK's invasion of Iraq' (2006) 31 ELRev 3, and W Sadurski, 'Adding a Bite to a Bark: A Story of Art 7, the EU Enlargement and Jörg Haider' (n 67 above).

[74] For a suggestion that some of the Member States of Central and Eastern Europe had to downgrade their protection for certain human rights in the wake of accession to the EU, see A Albi, 'Ironies in Human Rights Protection in the EU: Pre-accession Conditionality and Post-accession Conundrums' (2009) 15 ELJ 46.

[75] See n 63 above.

[76] This suggestion was made in 2001 in the European Parliament Report on the Situation as regards Fundamental Rights in the European Union (2000), A-5 2223 /2001.

regular monitoring of compliance with human rights in the EU Member States, with a view to making the Article 7 mechanism operative.[77]

Yet although the Network produced excellent annual reports on human rights protection in the Member States, as well as a number of interesting thematic reports and opinions, it was replaced, when the Fundamental Rights Agency was established in 2007, by a similar network (FRALEX) which was prohibited from doing exactly what the earlier network had been established to do. In other words, the FRALEX network has no role in relation to Article 7 TEU,[78] and hence no role in monitoring the Member States in relation to human rights issues.[79] The mandate of the Agency instead is to 'provide assistance and expertise relating to fundamental rights to the relevant Community institutions and its Member States when implementing Community law', to collect, publish and disseminate data and research, to provide relevant analysis and advice to the EU and the Member States, to raise public awareness and cooperate with civil society. Further, Article 3 of the Regulation establishing the Agency which defines the scope of its mandate contains a sentence similar to that in Article 51 of the Charter of Fundamental Rights, restricting the Agency's remit to: 'fundamental rights issues in the European Union and in its Member States when implementing Union law', in another attempt to restrict the extent to which the Agency and its actors can concern themselves with human rights issues internal to the Member States.[80]

To conclude, what is evident in the current EU constitutional framework for human rights protection is an insistent emphasis by Member States on restricting the extent to which the EU and its institutions can scrutinize or monitor the policies of the Member States. Some of the clearest examples of this are in the provisions of the Charter of Fundamental Rights and the Fundamental Rights Agency which seek to restrict their respective scope of application and mandate to actions of the European Union, and to Member States only when 'implementing EU law'. It is of course possible that these restrictive provisions may ultimately prove unsuccessful in their attempt to screen the actions of the states from EU scrutiny, given the various other activities of the Fundamental Rights Agency in cooperating with civil society actors and promoting

---

[77] See <http://ec.europa.eu/justice_home/cfr_cdf/index_en.htm>.

[78] The Council of Ministers did however issue a declaration to the effect that it may 'seek the assistance of the Agency as an independent person if it finds it useful during a possible procedure under Art 7 TEU. The Agency will however not carry out systematic and permanent monitoring of Member State for the purposes of Art 7 TEU.'

[79] Controversially, the mandate of the Fundamental Rights Agency was also restricted so that it had no role in relation to what was formerly the 'Third Pillar' of the EU, ie the areas of police and judicial cooperation in criminal matters, unless it was so requested by the EU or the Member States. Following the integration of the Third Pillar by the Lisbon Treaty, the FRA mandate may be extended to cover also police and criminal cooperation, if indeed any formal extension is necessary after the dissolution of the Third Pillar: See <http://www.bmeia.gvat/en/foreign-ministry/foreign-policy/human-rights/eu-human-rights-policy/fundamental-rights-agency.html>. Finally, the Agency's role does not include examination of individual complaints, regulatory decision-making, or consideration of compliance by Member State with the Treaties.

[80] Council Regulation 168/2007/EC ([2007] OJ L53/1).

human rights within the Union more generally, and given the potential of the Charter to be used by civil society actors and others as part of broader strategies of human rights promotion. Nevertheless, the contrast between the current emphasis on minimizing the EU's role in monitoring or promoting human rights within the Member States, and the clear expectation during the drafting processes of the 1950s that the European Community would have a central role in monitoring the activities of Member States in this field, is stark.

2. THE AUTONOMY OF THE EU HUMAN RIGHTS REGIME

A recurrent concern of the drafters in the 1950s was, as we have seen, the relationship between the new European Community and the European Convention on Human Rights. There was no suggestion that the European Community should have its own Charter of Rights, distinct from that of the new regional human rights system or the international human rights system. Nor was European Community human rights law to be founded on the human rights provisions of Member State constitutions. Instead it was relatively quickly agreed that the ECHR would be the authoritative source for the new European Political Community's human rights system, and the provisions of the ECHR were incorporated by Article 3 of the EPC Treaty as an integral part of that Treaty. Further, both the CECE drafters and the EPC Treaty drafters contemplated the possibility of Community accession to the ECHR, but took the view that the requirement of amending the relevant Council of Europe statute complicated this option excessively at the time. Instead it was decided that a procedure would be established under the EPC Treaty whereby the European Community Court would relinquish jurisdiction to the European Court of Human Rights in human rights cases brought against the Community which raised a point of principle for all ECHR Member States. In other words, the EU human rights system designed in the 1950s would have been integrally connected to the European Convention on Human Rights system with a formal relationship being established between the two Courts.

Under today's constitutional framework, by comparison, despite the fact that the European Convention on Human Rights is mentioned in Article 6(3) TEU and treated by the Court of Justice as a source of 'special significance' for EU human rights law,[81] and despite the likelihood that the EU will shortly accede to the ECHR,[82] the

---

[81] For an argument that the ECHR should be understood as already formally binding on the EU, as a matter of EU law, even prior to EU accession to the ECHR, see B De Witte, 'Human Rights' in P Koutrakos (ed), *Beyond the Established Orders: Policy Interconnections Between the EU and the Rest of the World* (forthcoming). He argues similarly that the EU has made the Geneva Convention Relating to the Status of Refugees binding upon itself in the context of its own asylum policy, via Art 78(1) TFEU.

[82] Accession has been made legally possible following the enactment by the Lisbon Treaty of Art 6(2) TEU to overcome the obstacle created by the Court of Justice in its *Opinion 2/94 on EC Accession to the ECHR* [1996] ECR I-1759, and following the ratification of Protocol 14 to the ECHR by all Member States of the Council of Europe. Art 17 of Protocol 14 declares that the ECHR is to be amended to provide that '[t]he European Union may accede to this Convention'.

willingness to establish a formal institutional link between the two Courts is much less evident than it was in the 1950s.[83] Currently the European Court of Human Rights exercises a kind of indirect jurisdiction over acts of the EU in certain circumstances, displaying great deference via a presumption that acts of the EU are in conformity with the ECHR.[84] But even if the EU becomes a party to the ECHR and the Court of Human Rights thereby gains jurisdiction to rule directly on whether the EU has violated provisions of the ECHR, such membership is currently envisaged as an external system of EU accountability to the regional human rights system. More specifically, it has repeatedly been said that EU accession to the ECHR will not affect the autonomy of the European Court of Justice, and will not formally subordinate the ECJ to the rulings of the European Court of Human Rights.[85] Thus it seems likely that the extent to which judgments of the European Court of Human Rights will be binding on the ECJ, either in cases dealing with the EU or in other cases involving relevant legal principles, will remain to be worked out by the EU institutions themselves.[86] The direct mechanism envisaged in Article 45 of the EPC Treaty, on the other hand, was clearly intended to place the ECJ in the position of having to comply directly with rulings of the European Court of Human Rights in cases arising before the Community Court concerning a claim of a human rights violation against the European Community.

Today's emphasis on the formal autonomy of the ECJ from the ECHR may seem a relatively minor point in practice, given that the European Court of Justice seems inclined to follow most of the case law of the Court of Human Rights, at least in cases in which the result comports well with EU law.[87] Nonetheless, it is an interesting symbolic change from the system envisaged in the 1950s, and it could well prove to be of practical significance if cases arise in which—as is increasingly likely given the extension of the

---

[83] For a recent argument even against the need for EU accession to the ECHR, see F Jacobs, former AG of the ECJ, 'The European Convention on Human Rights, the EU Charter of Fundamental Rights and the European Court of Justice', available online at <http://www.ecln.net/elements/conferences/book_berlin/jacobs. pdf>. Compare the contrary argument of F Van den Berghe 'The EU and issues of human rights protection: same solutions to more acute problems?' (2010) 16 ELJ 112.

[84] *Bosphorus v Ireland*, Application 45036/98, (2006) 42 EHRR 1 (Grand Chamber).

[85] For a recent pronouncement to this effect see the Draft Report of the Committee on Institutional Affairs of the European Parliament on 'Institutional Aspects of Accession of the EU to the European Convention on Human Rights', 2009/2241(INI): '[A]ccession will not in any way call into question the principle of the autonomy of Union law, as the Court of Justice will remain the sole supreme court adjudicating on issues relating to EU law and the validity of the Union's acts, as the Court of Human Rights must be regarded not as a higher court but rather as having special jurisdiction in exercising external supervision over the Union's compliance with obligations under international law arising from its accession to the ECHR.'

[86] The ECJ did suggest, in *Opinion 1/91 concerning the European Economic Area Agreement* [1991] ECR I-6079 that where an international agreement establishes a court with jurisdiction to settle disputes between parties to the Agreement, that the ECJ would be bound also by the decisions of that court, and this has been taken by some to mean that the ECJ will be bound by judgments of the ECtHR after accession of the EU to the ECtHR: see T Lock, 'The ECJ and the ECtHR: The Future Relationship between the Two European Courts' (2009) 8 LPICT 375. Others, however, including A Rosas who is currently judge on the European Court of Justice, have cast doubt on whether the ECJ in Opinion 1/91 can really have meant this: see A Rosas, 'The European Court of Justice in Context: Forms and Patterns of Judicial Dialogue' (2007) 1 EJLS 43-44 and text.

[87] On the interactions between the two courts, see J Callewaert, 'The European Convention on Human Rights and European Union Law: A Long Way to Harmony' (2009) 6 EHRLR 768.

powers and competences of the EU—the interpretation given by the ECtHR to provisions of the ECHR would prejudice the application of a provision of EU law.

It seems clear that the decision to maintain and underscore the autonomy of the ECJ is a deliberate and conscious one. The debate which took place during the drafting of Article 52(3) of the EU Charter on Fundamental Rights, concerning the relationship between the Court of Justice and the Court of Human Rights, revealed a clear unwillingness to place the European Court of Justice in any kind of formally subordinate position vis-à-vis the ECtHR.[88] Ultimately, while Article 52(3) declares that the rights in the EU Charter of Rights which correspond to rights guaranteed by the ECHR are to have the same meaning and scope of as those laid down by the European Convention, no reference to the case law of Court of Human Rights is to be found in the provisions of the Charter.[89] The idea of a bridging mechanism between the two Courts such as that provided for in Article 45 of the EPC Treaty draft has not met with support in more recent times.[90]

The EU preference clearly remains for an informal and mutually respectful arrangement such as exists at present between the two Courts. This arrangement has been described as a kind of 'common supranational diplomacy',[91] but one which nonetheless clearly maintains the autonomy and primacy of the European Court of Justice within the EU realm.

This emphasis on the autonomy and primacy of the EU's system of human rights protection is clear not only in the political and legal discussions on the implications of EU accession to the ECHR, or in debates on the drafting of the EU Charter of Rights, but also in the recent case law of the European Court of Justice itself. The autonomy of the EU's human rights system was perhaps most famously emphasized in the *Kadi* case in which the Court of Justice ruled that certain EC Regulations implementing Security Council resolutions, which had been adopted under Chapter

---

[88] J Lüsberg, 'Does the EU Charter of Fundamental Rights Threaten The Supremacy of Community Law', Jean Monnet Working Paper No 4 of 2001, who states that 'the drafting history...shows that several Member States strongly objected to any reference to the case law of the European Court of Human Rights in Art 53 or Art 52(3)'.

[89] A reference was later made in the explanations to Art 52(3) of the Charter which were subsequently prepared by the Charter's legal secretariat and given legal relevance by Art 52(7) of the Charter. See [2007] OJ C303/33.

[90] See the comments of the constitutional affairs committee of the European Parliament in its draft Report on Institutional Aspects of EU Accession to the ECHR (n 81 above) that it '[c]onsiders that it would be unwise to formalize relations between the Court of Justice and the European Court of Human Rights by establishing a preliminary ruling procedure before the latter or by creating a body or panel which would take decisions when one of the two courts intended to adopt an interpretation of the ECHR which differed from that adopted by the other; recalls in this context Declaration No 2 concerning Art 6(2) of the Treaty on European Union, which notes the existence of a regular dialogue between the Court of Justice and the European Court of Human Rights, which should be reinforced when the Union accedes to the ECHR'.

[91] L Scheeck, 'The Supranational Diplomacy of the European Courts: A Mutually Reinforcing Relationship?' in G Martinico and F Fontanelli (eds), *The ECJ Under Siege: New Constitutional Challenges for the ECJ* (Icfai University Press, 2009) 172–193. See also, G Harpaz, 'The European Court of Justice and its Relations with the European Court of Human Rights: The Quest for Enhanced Reliance, Coherence and Legitimacy' (2009) 46 CML Rev 105.

VII of the UN Charter, violated fundamental rights protected under the European Community legal order.[92] The Court ruled that the provisions of the UN Charter themselves could not have primacy over fundamental rights which were part of EC law, and repeatedly emphasized the autonomy of the EU's constitutional framework for human rights protection: 'the review by the Court of the validity of any Community measure in the light of fundamental rights must be considered to be the expression, in a community based on the rule of law, of a constitutional guarantee stemming from the EC Treaty as an autonomous legal system which is not to be prejudiced by an international agreement'.[93] Less dramatically, but also notably, the ECJ in the case of *Elgafaji* was asked by the referring Dutch court for guidance on the meaning of subsidiary protection within Article 15(c) of the EU Asylum Qualification Directive as compared with Article 3 of the ECHR as interpreted by the European Court of Human Rights in its case law.[94] While affirming that the right contained in Article 3 ECHR 'forms part of the general principles of Community law, observance of which is ensured by the Court, and while the case-law of the European Court of Human Rights is taken into consideration in interpreting the scope of that right in the Community legal order' the ECJ ruled that the particular sub-section of the provision of the Directive which was at issue in the case did not (unlike the preceding subsection) correspond directly with Article 3 ECHR. As a consequence, the interpretation of Article 15(c) had to be carried out 'independently . . . although with due regard for fundamental rights, as they are guaranteed under the ECHR'.[95] This insistence on the formal autonomy of the ECJ to interpret provisions of EU law, even while paying due regard to the ECHR and to the relevant case law of the ECtHR, is notable.

None of this is to suggest that the EU ignores or snubs international or regional human rights law, nor that the EU system is fundamentally disconnected from the regional and international systems.[96] Clearly that is not the case, as the EU continues to assert its commitment to the principles contained in the ECHR as well as in some other human rights treaties, and was a negotiator and signatory recently of the UN Disability Convention. On the other hand, the ECJ has been notoriously reluctant to cite and to rely on other international and regional human rights treaties apart from the ECHR, and the EU is not—with the exception of the mechanism set up by the UN Disability Convention to which the EU is party—subject to regional

---

[92] Cases C-402/05 P and C-415/05 P, *Kadi and Al Barakaat International Foundation v Commission and Council* [2008] ECR I-6351.

[93] ibid [316].

[94] Case C-465/07 *Elgafaji v Staatssecretaris van Justitie* [2009] WLR (D) 59.

[95] ibid [28].

[96] See eg B De Witte 'Human Rights', especially section 3, in P Koutrakos (ed), *Beyond the Established Orders: Policy Interconnections Between the EU and the Rest of the World* (forthcoming) who looks beyond the question of judicial relations to the way EU human rights laws and policies are related to those of other regional and international systems. Nevertheless, he also concludes his chapter by cautioning the EU against moving to a 'splendid isolation' in the human rights field.

or international human rights monitoring at present.[97] This has led senior commentators to argue that the European Court of Justice, by focusing almost exclusively on the ECHR, is 'ignoring the range of other human rights treaties', and that the EU is 'estranged from the universal human rights regimes established under the UN as well as other regional instruments'.[98] It is not that the EU dismisses sources of human rights law deriving from outside the EU itself, but rather that the EU and the ECJ at best draw sporadically and inconsistently on such international human rights sources, and insist on the ECJ as the final and authoritative arbiter of their meaning and impact within the EU. To conclude, this insistence on the constitutional autonomy and separateness of the EU human rights system is striking, and contrasts with the constitutional vision of the 1950s in which the Community was to be integrally connected to the emerging regional and international human rights system.

3. THE EXTERNAL FOCUS OF THE EU HUMAN RIGHTS REGIME TODAY

The third significant difference between the constitutional framework for EU human rights protection drafted in the 1950s and that existing today is that while the 1950s framework was oriented as much towards internal as external spheres of EU activity, the dominant emphasis of the current EU constitutional framework for human rights protection is on external policies.

We have seen above how in the early 1950s the task of monitoring the human rights practices of Member States was envisaged as a central part of the new European Political Community's role. Further, protection of human rights within the Member States was explicitly declared to be one of the aims of the Community in both the CECE Resolutions and in Article 2 of the EPC Treaty, and the Community under Article 55 was given the power to make proposals to further the aims of Article 2. In other words, protection of human rights within the Community and within the Member States was to be a core part of the Community's concern. At the same time, the EPC also outlined a significant external role for the new Community in which human rights had an important place. In the first place, Article 116 of the draft EPC Treaty articulated what are now known as the Copenhagen criteria for prospective Member States, providing that 'accession to the Community shall be open to the Member States of the Council of Europe and to any other European State which guarantees the protection of human rights and fundamental freedoms mentioned in Article 3'. Secondly, Article 90 of the EPC Treaty provided that the Community could conclude Association Agreements 'with such third States as guarantee the protection of the human rights and fundamental freedoms mentioned in Article 3'. More

---

[97] O De Schutter and I De Jesus Butler, 'Binding the EU to International Human Rights Law' (2008) 27 YEL 277.
[98] ibid.

generally, Article 2 as well as Chapter III of the EPC Treaty clearly envisaged an active role in international relations for the new European Political Community.[99]

The major emphasis of the EU's constitutional regime of human rights protection today, however, is externally focused, setting up a distinct difference between external and internal policies. This is evident not just in the reluctance on the part of Member States to submit themselves to human rights monitoring by the EU, as discussed above, but more specifically in the contrast between the active assertion of human rights protection as a goal of EU foreign policy and the unwillingness to declare human rights protection to be a general goal or a cross-cutting objective of internal EU policies. On the contrary, any legal or constitutional discussion of human rights issues in the European Union today is invariably accompanied by assertions on the part of the Council and the Member States of the limited competences of the EU, and a narrow view is taken of the legitimate scope of human rights law and policy within the EU. This phenomenon of double standards,[100] or rather of a clear difference between the importance accorded to human rights in EU external relations as compared with internal relations, was first clearly identified in a collective research project on human rights in the EU in 1999,[101] but the 'bifurcated'[102] approach seems to have survived the enactment of the Charter of Fundamental Rights and to be retained in the new constitutional framework.

A first indication of the distinction drawn between the role of human rights in the internal and the external policy realms can be seen in the comparison between Article 3(3) TEU, dealing with human rights within internal EU policies, and Article 3(5) dealing with human rights in external relations. Article 2 TEU declares that the EU is 'founded on' the value of respect for human rights and Article 3 declares that the Union's aims include the promotion of its values. Article 3(3) is then more specific in naming the major internal EU policy fields which are considered to implicate human rights-related objectives.[103] Article 3(3) declares that the Union 'shall combat social exclusion and discrimination, and shall promote social justice and protection, equality between women and men, solidarity between generations and protection of the rights

---

[99] Following the protection of human rights, the second and third aims of the European Community listed in Art 2 EPC were 'to co-operate with the other free nations in ensuring the security of Member States against all aggression' and 'to ensure the co-ordination of the foreign policy of Member States in questions likely to involve the existence, the security or the prosperity of the Community'.

[100] F Van den Berghe, 'The EU and the Protection of Minorities: How Real is the Alleged Double Standard?' (2003) 22 YEL 155.

[101] See the 'Leading by Example' Report of the Comité des Sages and P Alston and J H H Weiler, 'An Ever Closer Union in Need of a Human Rights Policy: the European Union and Human Rights' in P Alston and J H H Weiler (eds), *The EU and Human Rights* (Oxford University Press, 1999).

[102] This is the term used by A Williams, *EU Human Rights Policies: A Study in Irony* (Oxford University Press, 2004) ch 4.

[103] See the listing on the EU's website of those areas of internal EU policy which are considered to implicate human rights (or 'fundamental rights', in EU discourse): <http://europa.eu/legislation_summaries/human_rights/fundamental_rights_within_european_union/index_en.htm>.

of the child'. By comparison, Article 3(5) on external relations is broader and more general, and specifically identifies the protection of human rights worldwide as a goal:

> In its relations with the wider world, the Union shall uphold and promote its values and interests and contribute to the protection of its citizens. It shall contribute to peace, security, the sustainable development of the Earth, solidarity and mutual respect among peoples, free and fair trade, eradication of poverty and the protection of human rights, in particular the rights of the child, as well as to the strict observance and the development of international law, including respect for the principles of the United Nations Charter.

In other words, while the protection of human rights is asserted as an overarching objective in all EU external relations, in its internal policies the EU treats the proper sphere of human rights policy as being limited to those areas of EU power or competence which directly promote human rights—ie mainly anti-discrimination and social inclusion policy.[104] Thus the strategy has been to identify the fields of EU internal policy in which human rights concerns are considered relevant by reference to the precise scope of the EU's powers in fields such as social inclusion or anti-discrimination.[105] This strategy is not however used in the external domain, in which human rights protection is treated as a cross-cutting goal relevant to all domains of EU external action.

Within the borders of the EU, the most important and expansive area of human rights activity is the EU regime of anti-discrimination law, which has been developed substantially since the adoption of Article 13 EC (now Article 18 TFEU) by the Amsterdam Treaty. The two Discrimination Directives adopted in 2000[106] have been supplemented by several pieces of gender equality legislation,[107] and most recently by a proposal to expand the legislation prohibiting discrimination on grounds of

---

[104] Protection of the rights of the child is an interesting exception, since it has been asserted as an objective of internal EU policy even though the EU has no other expressly enumerated competence in the field of children's rights. The Commission began in 2006 to identify protection of children's rights as a major concern of the EU, publishing a paper 'Towards an EU Strategy on the Rights of the Child'. On its website the Commission declares 'The EU Charter of Fundamental Rights provides a clear political mandate for action on children's rights even if it does not establish any new powers or tasks for the Community.' See <http://ec.europa.eu/justice_home/fsj/children/fsj_children_intro_en.htm>.

[105] For a similar criticism in relation to the EU's unwillingness to accede to human rights treaties other than in policy areas specifically covered by EU competences, see de Schutter and de Jesus Butler (n 97 above) 277–320: 'Accession of the EU [to human rights treaties] should not be limited to treaties which have a direct overlap with areas of EU competence. Human rights obligations affect the exercise of all public power since it is through the exercise of their authority that states or other entities violate or uphold human rights. In this sense human rights cut across all areas of EU competence.'

[106] Council Directive 2000/43/EC of 29 June 2000 implementing the principle of equal treatment between persons irrespective of racial or ethnic origin, [2000] OJ L180/22–26 and Council Directive 2000/78/EC of 27 November 2000 establishing a general framework for equal treatment in employment and occupation, [2000] OJ L303/16–22.

[107] Council Directive 2006/54/EC of the European Parliament and of the Council of 5 July 2006 on the implementation of the principle of equal opportunities and equal treatment of men and women in matters of employment and occupation (recast) [2006] OJ L204, and Council Directive 2004/113/EC of 13 December 2004 implementing the principle of equal treatment between women and men in the access to and supply of goods and services, [2004] OJ L373.

age, disability, religion, and sexual orientation to cover similar ground to the Race Discrimination Directive of 2000,[108] as well as by a series of action programmes. In a notable move giving Treaty status to the expanding anti-discrimination regime, Article 10 TFEU was added by the Lisbon Treaty to declare that 'in defining and implementing its policies and activities, the Union shall aim to combat discrimination based on sex, racial or ethnic origin, religion or belief, disability, age or sexual orientation'.

However, apart from the thriving field of anti-discrimination law and policy, the growing area of data protection,[109] and a number of funding initiatives such as the Daphne[110] and Progress[111] programmes concerning gender and child-related violence and social inclusion policies, human rights concerns do not figure significantly in internal EU laws or policies. Within important policy fields such the area of freedom, security, and justice, including civil as well as criminal cooperation, activity is mostly focused on mutual recognition, aligning or coordinating laws to avoid obstacles, and not on questions of the impact on human rights. Similarly in the fields of asylum and immigration, issues such as securing borders and managing migration rather than human rights protection have been given priority,[112] and EU policies in these fields have been argued to have regressive effects on human rights.[113]

Even the enactment of the Charter of Fundamental Rights, whose existence would seem to refute the argument that human rights issues are relevant only to particular fields of internal EU power, is hedged about with restrictive clauses seeking to limit its influence on EU policy. Apart from the Lisbon Treaty Protocols dealing with the UK, Poland, and the Czech Republic,[114] Article 51(2) declares that the Charter does not 'modify powers and tasks as defined in the Treaties', and both Article 51 of the Charter and Article 6 TEU repeat that the provisions of the Charter shall not extend the

---

[108] COM(2008) 426, Commission Proposal for a Council Directive on implementing the principle of equal treatment between persons irrespective of religion or belief, disability, age or sexual orientation.

[109] See Council Directive 95/46 on the protection of individuals with regard to the processing of personal data and on the free movement of such data, [1995] OJ L281/31–50, and the Report of the Fundamental Rights Agency 'Data Protection in the EU: the role of National Data Protection Authorities—Strengthening the fundamental rights architecture in the EU II' 2010, <http://fra.europa.eu/fraWebsite/attachments/Data-protection_en.pdf>.

[110] <http://ec.europa.eu/justice_home/funding/2004_2007/daphne/funding_daphne_en.htm>.

[111] <http://ec.europa.eu/social/main.jsp?catId=327&langId=en>.

[112] See eg J Pirjola, 'European Asylum Policy: Inclusions and Exclusions under the Surface of Universal Human Rights Language' (2009) 11 EJML 347; S H Krieg, 'Trafficking in Human Beings: The EU Approach between Border Control, Law Enforcement and Human Rights' (2009) 15 ELJ 775.

[113] See eg Amnesty International, 'Human Rights Dissolving at the Borders? Counter-Terrorism and EU Criminal Law', 2005; C Teitgen-Colly, 'The European Union and Asylum: An Illusion of Protection' (2006) 43 CML Rev 1503. For a critique of the limited jurisdiction of the ECJ over the field of justice and home affairs, and its human rights implications, see S Carruthers, 'The Treaty of Lisbon and the Reformed Jurisdictional Powers of the European Court of Justice in the Field of Justice and Home Affairs' (2009) 6 EHRLR 784.

[114] The Protocol on the application of the Charter of Fundamental Rights of the EU to Poland and to the UK, [2007] OJ C306/156, and the Protocol on the application of the Charter of Fundamental Rights of the EU to the Czech Republic attempt to limit aspects of the application of the Charter to the UK, Poland, and the Czech Republic.

competences, tasks, or field of action of the EU in any way. One development which has the potential to challenge these consistent moves by Member States to enshrine a restricted role for internally-focused human rights protection within the EU constitutional framework, however, is the move by the Commission to develop some kind of meaningful human rights impact assessment by reference to the Charter.[115] The unfolding of this tension between the clear determination of the Member States when drafting the EU Treaties, the Charter of Fundamental Rights, and new institutions like the Fundamental Rights Agency, to limit the internal focus of EU human rights policies and powers on the one hand, and the practice of the Commission, the FRA, and national human rights institutions and organizations on the other in mobilizing the potential of the Charter within the EU on the other hand, will be interesting to observe in the coming years.[116]

Contrasting with the official reluctance to prescribe an unambiguous role for human rights protection in internal EU policies, the aim of promoting human rights figures openly and prominently in external EU policies and activities, even if in ways that are not always consistent or that may be politically strategic.[117] The EU unquestionably attempts to influence the conduct of many third states and regions as regards human rights protection. Human rights concerns feature centrally in EU development policy and in external trade, and are promoted through instruments such as political dialogue, human rights clauses in bilateral agreements,[118] trade preferences,[119] in multilateral settings,[120] in EU neighbourhood policies,[121] and in its human rights and democratization programmes.[122] Needless to say, the prominence of human rights in EU external policies does not mean that these policies have not been criticized.[123]

---

[115] See Commission Report COM(2009) 205 'Report on the Practical Operation of the Methodology for a Systematic and Rigorous Monitoring of Compliance with the Charter of Fundamental Rights' and its earlier communication COM(2005) 172, together with the Voggenhuber Report and Resolution of the European Parliament (A6-0034/2007).

[116] For an account of the EU human rights regime that is premised on the second, expansive vision of the role of human rights within the EU polity, see O de Schutter 'Fundamental Rights and the Transformation of Governance in the European Union' RefGov Working Paper FR-13, available online at <http://refgovcpdr.ucl. ac.be/?go=publications&dc=92c9c54b49130598ec9900bad0b18ca85d19dd15>.

[117] U Khaliq, *Ethical Dimensions of the Foreign Policy of the European Union: An Appraisal* (Cambridge University Press, 2008).

[118] See n 59 above.

[119] In 2010 the EU suspended trade preferences with Sri Lanka, citing human rights concerns. See also J Orbie and L Tortell, 'The New GSP+Beneficiaries: Ticking the Box or Truly Consistent with ILO Findings?' (2009) European Foreign Affairs Review 663–681. For a more general analysis of the legality of the EU's GSP system, see L Bartels, 'The WTO Legality of the EU's GSP Arrangement' (2007) 10 EJIL 869.

[120] For an appraisal, see K Smith, 'Speaking with One Voice? European Union Coordination on Human Rights Issues at the United Nations' (2006) JCMS 113.

[121] See the Commission's European Neighbourhood Policy Strategy Paper COM(2004) 373.

[122] See <http://ec.europa.eu/europeaid/how/finance/eidhr_en.htm>.

[123] For a summary of some of the criticisms see P Craig and G de Búrca, *EU Law: Text Cases and Materials* (4th edn, Oxford University Press, 2008) ch 11. For a powerful critical overview of the EU's engagement with human rights, with particular emphasis on the bifurcation between external and internal policies, see A Williams, *EU Human Rights Policies: A Study in Irony* (Oxford University Press, 2004).

Criticisms include the claim that the EU's interest in human rights protection is primarily about promoting its own influence and strategic advantage internationally, that it has failed to show real leadership in addressing human rights violations internationally,[124] and that it lacks the political will to address many pressing human rights problems.[125]

Nonetheless, despite the shortcomings of the EU's external human rights policies in practice, the constitutional framework established by the Treaties and developed in secondary EU instruments and policies clearly make human rights protection a prominent dimension of the external activities of the EU, contrasting with the officially circumscribed role for human rights within internal EU activities and policies.

F. CONCLUSION

Human rights protection and promotion have come to represent an important part of the European Union's identity today. Values, including the promotion of democracy, human rights, and the rule of law, have been allocated a central place in the constitutional framework and legal discourse of the EU following the Lisbon Treaty. While the claim that the EU can be understood as a human rights organization remains untenable,[126] human rights certainly feature prominently both in the constitutional self-understanding of the EU and in its international self-representation.

The traditional narrative of the evolution of human rights protection within EU law generally begins with the silence of the EEC Treaty on the subject and the subsequently dominant economic focus of the Communities, and therefore presents the current situation as a very significant advance, in human rights terms, on those origins. I have suggested, however, that a look back just a few years, prior to the adoption of the EEC Treaty at the efforts of drafting a constitutional framework for the new European Communities, reveals that a robust and comprehensive role for human rights protection within the new European construction was contemplated then. Further, the role envisaged for human rights protection and promotion in this model constitutional framework of the early 1950s was quite different, in several key respects, from that which is outlined in today's EU constitutional framework.

Three key differences have been identified in this chapter. The first is that the early 1950s framework assumed that monitoring and responding to human rights abuses by

---

[124] See eg the European Council on Foreign Relations reports for 2008 and 2009 by R Gowan and F Brantner, 'A Global Force for Human Rights? An Audit of EU Power at the UN' (2008), and 'The EU and Human Rights at the UN: 2009 Review' available online at <http://ecfr.3cdn.net/c85a326a9956fc4ded_qhm6vaacc.pdf> and <http://ecfr.3cdn.net/30b67f149cd7aaa888_3xm6bq7ff.pdf>. See also K Roth, 'Filling the Leadership Void: Where is the European Union?' (Human Rights Watch World Report, 2007).

[125] Amnesty International, 'The EU and Human Rights: Making the Impact on People Count' 2009, <http://www.amnesty.org/en/library/asset/IOR61/004/2009/en/64787ed1-83dd-49dd-bd27-c96e773f5ec1/ior610042009eng.pdf>.

[126] A von Bogdandy, 'The European Union as a Human Rights Organization? Human Rights and the Core of the European Union' (2000) 37 CML Rev 1307–1338.

or within Member States would be a core task of the European Community, while the current constitutional framework resists and seeks to limit any role for the EU in monitoring human rights within the Member States. The second is that the early 1950s framework envisaged a European Community system which would be integrally linked to the regional human rights system, with a formal relationship existing between the Community Court and the European Court of Human Rights. In contrast, the current constitutional framework, even with the prospect of EU accession to the ECHR, emphasizes the autonomy and separateness of the EU's human rights system. It envisions the ECHR as an external system of accountability, and pays little attention to the international human rights regime. The third difference lies in the fact the 1950s constitutional framework envisaged human rights protection as being equally central to internal and external EU policies and activities, while the role outlined for human rights within today's constitutional framework remains predominantly focused on the external relations of the EU.

As in many other areas of EU law and policy, however, the formal constitutional framework established in the Treaties and in primary legislation represents a particular vision of the European Union which is conceived and promulgated by the Member States, but which is often at odds with the evolving practices of European governance.[127] Thus the attempt by the Member States through the Treaties, the Charter, and the mandate of the Fundamental Rights Agency, to restrict or limit any EU monitoring of Member State activities in the field of human rights is at odds with the developing practices of the EU anti-discrimination regime, and more generally with the activities of the network of national human rights bodies and civil society actors which interact with the new Fundamental Rights Agency. Similarly the official emphasis on the autonomy and distinctiveness of the EU's human rights regime is challenged by the existence of what has been described as a de facto 'overlapping consensus' and by the informal mutual monitoring of various national, regional, and international human rights regimes.[128] Thirdly, the official resistance to identifying human rights protection and promotion as a cross-cutting objective of internal EU policy, as compared with external policies, is likely to be undercut by the Commission's moves to develop a genuine practice of impact assessment based on the Charter of Fundamental Rights.[129]

Nevertheless, the 'Masters of the Treaties'[130] continue firmly to resist such a conception of the EU, and to deny such a robust role for human rights protection and

---

[127] G de Búrca, 'Beyond the Charter: How Enlargement has Enlarged the Human Rights Policy of the EU' (n 73 above).

[128] C Sabel and O Gerstenberg, 'Constitutionalising an Overlapping Consensus: The ECJ and the Emergence of a Coordinate Constitutional Order' 16 ELJ (forthcoming). On the possibility that EU practices could be monitored by international human rights organizations and treaty bodies even when the EU is not a signatory or member of the latter, see O de Schutter and I de Jesus Butler (n 97 above).

[129] See n 115 above.

[130] This ('Herren der Verträge') is the iconic term which was used by the German *Bundesverfassungsgericht* in its famous *Maastricht* judgment of 12 October 1993, 89 BVerfGE 155, 190 to describe the Member States' ongoing control over the EU constitutional process, and specifically over the process of Treaty amendment.

promotion within EU law and policy. Instead, they seek to define a European Union whose engagement with human rights is deliberately qualified and limited in various ways, with the aim of ensuring that the Member States are as far as possible free from EU monitoring and scrutiny, that the EU's human rights activities are predominantly outwardly and not inwardly focused, and that the autonomy of the EU itself is not excessively constrained by external institutions and norms. In these ways, the formal constitutional framework for human rights in the EU today stands in marked contrast with the overt embrace by the drafters of the early 1950s of the European Community as an organization committed to human rights protection and promotion in all of its spheres of action, both internal and external, which would be properly engaged in monitoring and scrutiny of its Member States, and which would be an integral part of the emerging regional and international network of human rights regimes.

17

FREE MOVEMENT OF PERSONS AND SERVICES

Siofra O'Leary*

A. INTRODUCTION

Ten years ago, when the *Evolution of EU Law* was first published, a chapter devoted to the free movement of workers, establishment, and services made perfect sense.[1] Although the legislative and judicial development of these fundamental freedoms may have differed somewhat and the Court of Justice regarded them as mutually exclusive, their interrelationship had always been clear, with services treated as residual to the other two. The Court emphasized from the outset that the relevant provisions of the EEC and EC Treaties were based on the twin principles of free movement and the prohibition of all discrimination on grounds of nationality.[2] Its decisions in the 1990s further revealed the extent to which the principles governing the fundamental freedoms central to the internal market were, with one notable exception, converging, as it became clear that even indistinctly applicable national measures restrictive of free movement could fall foul of the Treaty.[3] This development provided and continues to provide fertile ground for academics and practitioners to analyse the difficulties provoked by the Court's sometimes incoherent case law on directly and indirectly discriminatory measures, indistinctly applicable restrictions, and the correct

* Référendaire at the Court of Justice of the European Union, Visiting Professor at the College of Europe, Bruges.

[1] The free movement of workers, establishment, and services was governed by Arts 48 to 66 EEC, subsequently renumbered as Arts 39 to 55 EC. Arts 45 (workers), 49 (establishment), and 56 and 57 (services) of the Treaty on the functioning of the European Union (TFEU) are the principal provisions of the TFEU now governing these fields.

[2] See eg Case 48/75 *Royer* [1976] ECR 497, [12] and Case 118/75 *Watson and Belmann* [1976] ECR 1185, [9].

[3] See Case C-76/90 *Säger* [1991] ECR I-4221 (services); Case C-55/94 *Gebhard* [1995] ECR I-4165 (establishment), and Case C-413/95 *Bosman* [1995] ECR I-4921 (workers). For the notable exception, concerning the free movement of goods, see Joined Cases C-267/91 and C-268/91 *Keck and Mithouard* [1993] ECR I-6097, [16]. On the subject of convergence see, for example, P Oliver and W H Roth, 'The Internal Market and the Four Freedoms' (2004) 41 CML Rev 407.

application of express Treaty derogations and judicially developed public interest justifications.[4]

Ten years on, although both this interrelationship and convergence remain patent, the regulatory and jurisprudential landscape in which the free movement of persons and services must now be located differs significantly from that examined in the previous edition. For before the latter was even hot off the presses, the Court handed down its first decision of significance on Union citizenship, a status conferred on Member State nationals a few years previously by the Maastricht Treaty. The Decision in that case—*Martínez Sala*—was a milestone in the interpretation of the scope and application of the provisions of EU law on the free movement of persons.[5] First, it exploded the notion that the introduction of Union citizenship was little more than a cosmetic exercise which left essentially unaltered the existing legal framework governing the free movement of persons. Secondly, it decoupled the application of the aforementioned principles of free movement and non-discrimination from the need to exercise an economic activity. Thirdly, and regardless of the Court's protestations to the contrary, *Martínez Sala* indicated that Union citizenship could have a significant impact on the material scope of application of EU law or, at the very least, on what situations were henceforth to be deemed to be governed by EU law and therefore falling within the material scope of the latter. The Court has since had to busy itself answering preliminary reference questions seeking to work out the import and consequences of this new citizenship status. The judicial turbulence which has characterized this line of case law is symptomatic of the unsettling effect which the establishment of Union citizenship has had on EU law on the free movement of persons generally.[6]

Meanwhile, there has been a complete overhaul of secondary legislation on the free movement of economically active Member State nationals adopted in the 1960s and early 1970s.[7] Early signs from the case law suggest that Directive 2004/38 may prove a source of tension between the requirements flowing from the Treaty provisions as previously interpreted by the Court and as identified by the EU legislature when

---

[4] An examination of this case law, which is beyond the scope of this chapter, continues to lack the clear characterization identified as necessary in the first edition of G de Búrca and P Craig (eds), *The Evolution of EU Law* (Oxford University Press, 1999). For further analysis see C Barnard and J Scott (eds), *The Law of the Single European Market* (Hart, 2002) or, specifically in the context of the free movement of persons, E Spaventa, *Free Movement of Persons in the European Union* (Kluwer Law International, 2007).

[5] Case C-85/96 *Martínez Sala* [1998] ECR I-2691, [63] in which the Court held that a Union citizen lawfully resident in the territory of a host Member State can rely on Art 18 TFEU (ex Art 12 EC) in all situations which fall within the scope *ratione materiae* of EU law. See further J Shaw and S Fries, 'Citizenship of the Union: First Steps in the European Court of Justice' (1998) EPL 533; S O'Leary, 'Putting Flesh on the Bones of European Union Citizenship' (1999) 24 ELRev 68, and J Shaw, Chapter 19.

[6] See below section F.2 on the rights of entry and residence of family members and sub-section D.3(a) on the scope of the rights of students and job-seekers to equal treatment.

[7] Directive 2004/38/EC of the European Parliament and of the Council on the right of citizens of the Union and their family members to move and reside freely within the territory of the Member States amending Regulation 1612/68/EEC and repealing Directives 64/221/EEC, 68/360/EEC, 72/194/EEC, 73/148/EEC, 75/34/EEC, 75/35/EEC, 90/364/EEC, 90/365/EEC, and 93/96/EEC [2004] OJ L158/77.

codifying. Furthermore, the accession of ten new Member States, some of which had and have workforces ready and willing to avail of their free movement rights seems to have signalled a notable change in EU migratory patterns. Finally, the last decade has seen the provisions on the free movement of persons take their place in the wider and under-defined context of an area of freedom, security, and justice. Some of the Court's more polemic recent decisions on Articles 45, 49, and 56 TFEU suggest that now that physical borders to free movement have been lifted and EU competence as regards the control of external EU borders has been extended, very different visions of the imperatives underpinning the free movement of persons may come to the fore. The objectives which have until now prevailed may be strained as future decisions of the Court revisit concepts such as public policy, residence, or the principle of non-discrimination on grounds of nationality in highly sensitive criminal and family law contexts which may make the decisions concerning the *Rutilis, Sagulos*, and *Boucher-aus* of the past look parochial.[8]

As regards the free provision of services, significant changes in the scope, character, and volume of services in the EU have seen a marked increase in litigation before the Court;[9] an increase further heightened by the aforementioned change in the thrust of its case law on services since the 1990s. A proposal for the adoption of a comprehensive, horizontal directive on services was presented by the Commission in 2004.[10] One of its central components—a country of origin principle which would have allowed service providers to operate under the rules and regulations applicable in their Member State of origin—proved so controversial, particularly in the context of an enlarged EU, that it could be credited, certainly in part, with the demise of the Draft Constitutional Treaty. A greatly reduced text, omitting the country of origin principle, was finally adopted in 2006.[11] As if timing was not everything, the Court then found itself confronted with a series of cases in which the exercise, in particular, of the freedom to provide services was pitted against the general interest objectives of protecting workers and preventing social dumping. The Court's decisions could be

---

[8] See, for example, the issues raised in the context of recent accelerated, urgent, and normal preliminary reference procedures on secondary legislation and framework decisions adopted pursuant to Title VI TEU and Title IV EC—Case C-66/08 *Kozlowski* [2008] ECR I-6041; Case C-123/08 *Wolzenburg* [2009] ECR I-9621; Case C-195/08 PPU *Rinau* [2008] ECR I-5271; Case C-388/08 PPU *Leymann and Pustovarov* [2008] ECR I-8993.

[9] See further European Commission, *The State of the Internal Market for Services*, COM(2002) 441 final. As regards increased litigation and the jurisprudential cycles which have characterized the latter, see A Biondi, 'Recurring Cycles in the Internal Market: Some Reflections on the Free Movement of Services' in A Arnull (ed), *Continuity and Change in EU Law. Essays in Honour of Sir Francis Jacobs* (Oxford University Press, 2008) 228, and V Hatzopolous and T Uyen Do, 'The Case-law of the ECJ Concerning the Free Provision of Services: 2000–2005' (2006) 43 CML Rev 923.

[10] COM(2004) 2 final/3, commonly referred to as the Bolkestein draft Directive after the then Internal Market commissioner. See further B De Witte, 'Setting the Scene: How Did Services get to Bolkestein and Why?' 3/2007 *Mitchell Working Paper Series* (Edinburgh Europa Institute).

[11] Directive 2006/123/EC of the European Parliament and of the Council on services in the internal market [2006] OJ L376/36.

regarded as having partly resurrected the very principle which the legislature had abandoned and whose application to posted workers had, in any event, barely been intended.[12]

In short, over the past decade, the contours, content, and scope of the law relating to the free movement of persons and services in the EU have changed considerably. It would now make more sense to address the free movement of persons, encompassing the economically active and inactive, in one chapter, and the freedom of establishment and the free provision of services in another. Separating economically inactive migrants from their economically active counterparts results in a highly truncated analysis of the free movement of persons. Such a division is no longer tenable precisely because the Court's case law, and now secondary legislation, have meshed the foundations and treatment of the free movement and non-discrimination rights of the two categories. The complexity of the changes which have already taken shape as regards the free movement of persons and constraints of time and space mean that those solely or primarily interested in establishment and services risk being sorely disappointed. Treatment of the free provision of services is, of necessity, selective, concentrating on the legislative and judicial highs and lows of the past decade, while freedom of establishment is relegated to the status of poor relation. This chapter cannot therefore pretend to be a comprehensive review of the free movement of persons and services since the ratification of the Treaty of Rome but instead, ten years after the first edition of *The Evolution of EU Law*, seeks to provide a series of snapshots capturing the progressive slide of EU law on the free movement of persons and services into middle age.

B. CHANGING PATTERNS OF EU MIGRATION

Two important preconditions for labour migration are the existence of workers willing to migrate and host states willing to alter or adjust their immigration rules in order to receive them. The elimination of obstacles to the free movement of employed and self-employed persons in the EEC Treaty sought to harmonize the latter to the extent necessary to facilitate the effective functioning of the common market. However, additional push and pull factors are necessary for migration to occur. In general, the labour market conditions in an exporting state have to provide the incentive for workers to leave (high unemployment, low wages) and the conditions in the host

---

[12] As regards the free provision of services, Case C-341/05 *Laval* [2007] ECR I-11767; Case C-346/06 *Rüffert* [2008] ECR I-1989; Case C-319/06 *Commission v Luxembourg* [2008] ECR I-4323; as regards freedom of establishment, Case C-438/05 *Viking* [2007] ECR I-10779, discussed further in Part C and sub-section D.3(b), and by C Barnard, Chapter 21. As regards the exclusion of posted workers from the proposed country of origin principle see Arts 17 and 24 of the Bolkestein draft Directive. On the relationship between the Services Directive (n 11 above) and secondary legislation on posted workers see Case C-319/06 *Commission v Luxembourg* ibid [23].

state must be such as to render leaving behind one's country of origin sufficiently attractive (high demand for labour, higher wages, better social protection).[13]

The Spaak Report envisaged that the elimination of obstacles to the free movement of the factors of production would stimulate labour movements from Member States of low productivity to those industrial regions and economic sectors where productivity and demand for labour were highest. This would, over time, produce an ever more efficient allocation of the labour force.[14] Initially, of the six original Member States, Italy, the one founding Member State guaranteed to export workers to the regions and sectors in question, was the sole negotiating partner in favour of the inclusion in the EEC Treaty of provisions on the free movement of persons. The negotiation of that Treaty revealed to what extent the Member States most likely to import workers feared uncontrolled migration flows.[15] That fear has subsequently resurfaced on almost every occasion when new Member States have acceded to the EEC, EC, and subsequently the EU, reaching its apogee prior to the accession of ten new Member States between 2004 and 2007.

An examination in the first edition of *The Evolution of EU Law* of the number, composition, and origins of migrant workers in the EEC before and after the elimination of obstacles to free movement revealed that, contrary to the expectations of the founding fathers, the creation of a common market for labour did not promote wholesale movement of workers among the Member States. The movement which did take place in the early years seemed to have occurred prescinding from and not because of the establishment of the common market.[16] One important conclusion which did emerge from early studies of intra-Community migration patterns was that by restricting the free movement of workers to Member State nationals,[17] the recruitment of third country nationals had been rendered more attractive to employers,

---

[13] See, generally, S A W Goedings, *Labour Migration in an Integrating Europe* (SDU, 2005); W R Böhning, *The Migration of Workers in the United Kingdom and the European Community* (Springer, 1972); T Straubhaar, 'International Labour Migration within a Common Market: Some Aspects of EC Experience' (1988) 27 JCMS 45; W Molle and A Van Mourik, 'International Movements of Labour under Conditions of Economic Integration: The Case of Western Europe' (1988) 26 JMCS 317; F Romero, 'Cross-border Population Movements' in W Wallace (ed), *The Dynamics of European Integration* (Palgrave, 1990) 171–191; H Werner, 'Free Movement of Labour in the Single European Market' (1990) 25 Intereconomics 77; chs by K Groenendijk and E Guild in P Minderhoud and N Trimikliniotis (eds), *Rethinking the Free Movement of Workers* (University of Nijmegen, 2009) 11–24 and 25–38, respectively.

[14] See the Rapport des Chefs de Délégations aux Ministres des Affaires Etrangères (Brussels, 1956).

[15] See further Goedings (n 13 above).

[16] See the discussion of statistics in Straubhaar (n 13 above) 49–55, and the analysis of figures for each individual founding Member State in Böhning (n 13 above). The intra-Community share of the total number of migrants working in the original six Member States decreased from 44 per cent before the establishment of the common market to 32 per cent in 1968 and 20 per cent in 1974, remaining constant at that level throughout the 1980s.

[17] This limitation, to be found in Art 1 of Directives 64/221, 68/360, and Regulation 1612/68, is of fundamental importance as Art 45 TFEU referred simply to workers, without reference to a nationality requirement.

further contributing to low levels of intra-Community migration.[18] Thus, contrary to the fears of some of the founding Member States, the establishment of the common labour market did not induce a strong movement of workers migrating from low-income to higher-income Member States. The removal of obstacles to free movement in the EEC and then EC was not sufficient to offset the disincentives to migration—uncertainty and lack of information about the level of income in the host Member State, problems of assimilation, cultural, social and linguistic difficulties, housing availability and cost, education, and job security—despite significant differences in living standards and social protection between some of the Member States. The anticipated major influx of migrant workers into more northern Member States following the subsequent accession of Greece, Portugal, and Spain also failed to materialize and transitional arrangements seeking to stem or temper flows of workers from the latter two Member States were even abandoned before schedule.[19]

Did the accession to the EU of ten new Member States from mainly Central and Eastern Europe stimulate the type of migration feared by Member States since obstacles to the free movement of labour were first eliminated? Certainly the conditions which should favour reallocation of labour were and still are present in at least some of these states, with average wages and levels of social protection far lower than in existing Member States. With these differences in mind, recurrent fears about a mass influx of workers following further enlargement led the majority of established Member States to avail of the possibility of imposing transitional restrictions on the free movement of workers from accession states.[20] Eurostat statistics report a significant increase in migration in the EU in the last decade and the transformation during the economic boom of some states which traditionally exported labour, not least Ireland and Spain, into importing states. Between 2002 and 2006, for example, the number of EU nationals migrating to Member States other than their Member State of origin increased by 10 per cent.[21] Nevertheless, even during this period, non-EU migrants continued to outnumber migrant EU nationals. Many of these EU migrants

---

[18] By 1994, of the 369 million people living in the EU, only 5.5 million EU nationals were living in a Member State other than their Member State of origin. This compared to 11.7 million legally resident non-EU nationals. See Eurostat, *Statistics in Focus. Population and Social Conditions*, 2/1996. See R Plender, 'An Incipient Form of European Citizenship' in F G Jacobs (ed), *European Law and the Individual* (North-Holland Publishers, 1976) 39–55, 40.

[19] See Council Regulation 2194/91/EEC on the transitional period for freedom of movement of workers between Spain and Portugal, on the one hand, and the other Member States, on the other hand [1991] OJ L206/1.

[20] There were no transitional limits as regards the free movement of workers from Malta and Cyprus and the United Kingdom, Ireland, and Sweden declined to impose such limits on workers from the other accession states. See further European Commission, Report on the Functioning of the Transitional Arrangements set out in the 2003 Accession Treaty (period 1 May 2004–30 April 2006), COM(2006) 48 final; M Dougan, 'A Spectre is Haunting Europe: Free Movement of Persons and the Eastern Enlargement' in C Hillion (ed), *EU Enlargement: A Legal Approach* (Hart, 2004) 111–141; E Guild, 'Free Movement of Workers: From Third Country National to Citizen of the Union' in Minderhoud and Guild (n 13 above) 25–38, 34–37.

[21] Eurostat, Population and Social Conditions, 98/2008. See also European Commission, Fifth Report on Citizenship of the Union, COM(2008) 85 final, which estimated that on 1 January 2006, 8.2 million EU nationals were exercising their right to reside in another Member State.

came from some of the most populous new Member States and those where living and working conditions were comparatively worse. Although perhaps too early to tell, particularly given transitional restrictions, some country-specific reports suggest that although the influx of newly acceded EU nationals into the Member States which posed no or few restrictions was considerable, around half of those who migrated have since returned, the employment rate amongst the group has tended to be very high, and the percentage of 'post-accession' migrants seeking state benefits has been low.[22] The spectre of the Central and Eastern European benefit tourist which had haunted some Member States prior to accession in 2004 has not, it seems, materialized. Decreased labour demand as a result of the recent economic recession combined with improved living and working conditions in some of these new exporting Member States have certainly contributed to both a decrease in the numbers of those migrating and an increase in the numbers of those returning to their Member States of origin. It may have taken the transformation of the common market into an internal market serving a greatly enlarged EU of 27 Member States to realize the type of labour migration expected by the founding fathers.[23]

C. THE OBJECTIVES OF EU LAW ON THE FREE MOVEMENT OF PERSONS AND SERVICES

It is commonplace that the provisions on the free movement of persons were intended to facilitate the pursuit by EU nationals of occupational activities of all kinds throughout the Union and to preclude measures which might place them at a disadvantage when they wish to pursue an economic activity in the territory of another Member State.[24] The economic imperatives which underpinned the creation of the common market continue to resonate in the case law of the Court.[25]

However, it is equally well known that the case law on the free movement of persons and services is replete with decisions whose reasoning derives as much from a desire to protect and respect the social and human consequences or demands of migration as it does from the aforementioned economic objectives. The Court stressed from very early on that a restrictive interpretation of Article 45 TFEU (ex Article 39 EC) 'would reduce

---

[22] See Institute for Public Policy Research, *Floodgates or turnstiles? Post-EU enlargement migration flows to (and from) the UK* (2008).

[23] The 'Ryanair effect' should not perhaps be underestimated in this context! Given that social, cultural, and linguistic barriers are recognized as important deterrents to migration, the much maligned low-cost airlines which have proliferated in the past decade have provided mobile workers with easy and cheap access to the labour markets of host Member States and the possibility of easy, cheap and frequent return to their Member States of origin.

[24] See, for example, Case 143/87 *Stanton v INASTI* [1988] ECR I-3877, [13], and C-413/95 *Bosman* [1995] ECR I-4921, [94].

[25] See further G More, 'The Principle of Equal Treatment: From Market Unifier to Fundamental Right?' in de Búrca and Craig (n 4 above) 517–553; M Streit and W Mussler, 'The Economic Constitution of the European Community—From Rome to Maastricht' (1995) 1 ELJ 5.

free movement to a mere instrument of economic integration and would be contrary to its broader objective of creating an area in which Community citizens enjoy freedom of movement'.[26] Long before the establishment of Union citizenship and the transform- ation of free movement rights which that status instigated, or at the very least consoli- dated, numerous decisions of the Court reflected this shift from the conferral of rights by virtue of the exercise of an economic activity and in order to facilitate that exercise, to the conferral of rights on EU nationals *qua* individuals falling, for reasons increasingly detached from economic integration, within the scope of application of the Treaties.[27] The Court may be regarded as having at times overstretched, or even contradicted, the terms of the Treaty provisions on the free movement of persons and services and secondary legislation adopted to give them effect.[28] However, it is important not to lose sight of the objectives of the law in this field as articulated in the preambles and articles of successive Treaties and secondary legislation.[29] If the Court has refused to regard labour simply as a commodity it is because, as one Advocate General reminded us, the relevant provisions of secondary legislation notably gave precedence to the fundamental rights of workers over satisfying the requirements of the economies of Member States.[30] Since the Treaty of Rome, the objective has not simply been to raise the employment and living standards of those who move but generally to improve those standards throughout the Community and, subsequently, the Union. It was assumed that those who availed of their free movement rights would do so to better their position. It should not be forgotten either that nationals of host Member States were not meant to suffer the unfavourable consequences which might result in EU nationals from other Member States accepting conditions of employment or remuneration less advantageous

---

[26] Case 66/85 *Lawrie-Blum* [1986] ECR 2121, [12].

[27] See, for example, Case 59/85 *Netherlands v Reed* [1986] ECR 1283 (the right to be joined by one's unmarried partner in a host Member State qualified as a social advantage pursuant to Council Regulation 1612/68/EEC on freedom of movement for workers within the Community [1968] OJ Spec ed, 475)) Case 186/ 87 *Cowan v Le Trésor public* [1989] ECR 195 (the right of a recipient of services to have equal access to a criminal compensation scheme in a Member State where services are, briefly, provided); or Case 293/83 *Gravier* [1985] ECR 593 (the right of Member State nationals not to be discriminated against on grounds of nationality as regards access to vocational training). The Court's adoption of the citizenship denomination prior to the Maastricht Treaty was in itself indicative of this trend.

[28] See, for an early example, Case 293/83 *Gravier* (n 27 above) as regards equal access to vocational training or, more recently, the interpretation of secondary legislation on the rights of residence of economically inactive EU nationals in Case C-184/99 *Grzelczyk* [2001] ECR I-6193 and Case C-209/03 *Bidar* [2005] ECR I-2119.

[29] The objective of attaining an ever closer union between the peoples of Europe has been ever present in the EEC and EC Treaties and the provision of a higher standard of living and working conditions was identified at the outset as the Member States' essential objective (see now recitals 1 and 3 of the preamble to the TFEU). Regulation 1612/68 (n 27 above) referred to the fundamental right of migrant workers and their families to free movement and the exercise of this right in freedom and dignity (recitals 4 and 8). See also the Charter of Fundamental Rights of the European Union, [2007] OJ C303/1, Art 1, and Case C-377/98 *Netherlands v European Parliament and Council* [2001] ECR I-7079, [70]–[77]. As regards Union citizenship, its establish- ment was intended to strengthen the rights and interests of EU nationals (Art 2 TEU as amended by the Treaty of Amsterdam).

[30] See the Opinion in Case 344/87 *Bettray* [1988] ECR 1621, [29], referring to the preamble of Regulation 1612/68 (n 27 below). See further section F.2 as regards case law on the right to respect for family life.

than those obtaining under the national law of that state.[31] The establishment and gradual constitutionalization of Union citizenship further confirms this recognition of free movement rights as individual rights worthy of protection not simply when exercised in the pursuit of economic integration but in their own right, as benefits conferred on Member State nationals in the context of the creation of an ever closer union.[32]

The pursuance of competing social and economic objectives in the provisions of the Treaty and secondary legislation is hardly unique to the free movement of persons. In the field of social policy, the Court's identification in *Defrenne II* of the dual economic and social aims underpinning the principle of equal pay for male and female workers in Article 157 TFEU (ex Article 119 EEC) is legendary.[33] As regards the freedom of establishment and the freedom to provide services, these dual economic and social aims were brought to the fore in the *Viking* and *Laval* cases. The economic objectives underpinning these fundamental freedoms must be balanced against the objectives pursued by social policy, including improved living and working conditions, proper social protection, and dialogue between the social partners.[34] In those cases, as discussed further below, the Court recognized the legitimacy of collective action and characterized the taking of such action in the defence of workers' rights and interests as a fundamental right. Nevertheless, when it came to balancing the fundamental right to collective action with the fundamental freedom to provide services, the former had to be relied on defensively and was subject to a strict proportionality test, unmitigated by any reference to the margin of appreciation of those semi-regulatory bodies exercising the fundamental right in question or of those Member States which had, in accordance with national law, sanctioned that exercise.

The parity between the economic and social aims underpinning Article 157 TFEU was discarded in 2000, with the Court declaring that, in light of the fact that the right not to be discriminated against on grounds of sex is a fundamental human right, the economic aim pursued by that provision must be regarded as secondary to its social aims.[35] It remains to be seen whether, in time, a similar reordering of the social and economic objectives fuelling the fundamental freedoms consecrated in Articles 45, 49, and 56 TFEU will also take place.[36] The fact that the secondary legislation at issue in

---

[31] See Case 167/73 *Commission v France* [1974] ECR 359, [44]–[45].

[32] As illustrated, for example, in Case C-413/99 *Baumbast* [2002] ECR I-7091. See further recital 2 of the preamble to the Charter of Fundamental Rights of the European Union: '[The Union] places the individual at the heart of its activities, by establishing the citizenship of the Union and by creating an area of freedom, security and justice'. See further the discussion of Union citizenship by Shaw, Chapter 20, and Dougan (n 20 above) 116.

[33] Case 43/75 *Defrenne II* [1976] ECR 455, [8]–[12].

[34] See, for example, Case C-341/05 *Laval* (n 12 above) [104].

[35] As regards the general principle of equality, this readjustment of priorities finds further expression in the Court's far-reaching endorsement of this principle in Case C-555/07 *Kücükdeveci*, 19 January 2010.

[36] Subsequent applications of *Laval* (n 12 above) have, surprisingly, failed to mention the economic/social equilibrium on which these fundamental freedoms are allegedly based. See, for example, Case C-346/06 *Rüffert* (n 12 above) or Case C-319/06 *Commission v Luxembourg* (n 12 above).

Laval was adopted on the basis of an exclusively internal market legal basis may have contributed to the balance struck by the Court in the aforementioned cases. If so, when future disputes arise within the scope of application of the Services Directive touching on where and how the balance should be struck between the EU's economic and social objectives, the fact that the legal basis of that Directive is rooted exclusively in the internal market may equally prove relevant.[37]

D. LEGISLATIVE TRANSFORMATION

1. FREE MOVEMENT OF EMPLOYED AND SELF-EMPLOYED PERSONS

For several decades, the provisions of secondary legislation dealing with the free movement of employed and self-employed persons were so unchanged they appeared immutable. Directives and regulations adopted in the 1960s and early 1970s detailed the rights of entry and residence of workers and self-employed persons as well as their right in certain circumstances to remain, facilitated the application of the derogations from free movement permitted by the Treaty, and developed the scope of the right of migrant workers to equal treatment when they settled in a host Member State.[38] In accordance with the essentially economic underpinnings of the then common market, the rights of free movement and residence conferred on Member State nationals were conceived and originally applied in terms allowing them to take up economic activities as employed and self-employed persons in the territory of another Member State.[39] Initially, derogations from these rights were limited to the grounds now reproduced in Articles 45(3) and (4) and 51 and 52 TFEU—namely public policy, security, or health as well as limited exceptions as regards employment in the public administration or the exercise of official authority. With the Court's extension of the remit of Articles 45 and 49 TFEU to cover indistinctly applicable restrictions of free movement, a number of judicially created imperative requirements were added to this limited list of permissible grounds with

---

[37] Both the Posted Workers Directive (Directive 96/71/EC of the European Parliament and of the Council, of 16 December 1996, concerning the posting of workers in the framework of the provision of services [1996] OJ L18/1) and the Services Directive (n 11 above) are based on Arts 47(2) and 55 EC. See further sections D.2 and D.3.

[38] See, principally, Council Directive 64/221/EEC of 25 February 1964, on the co-ordination of special measures concerning the movement and residence of foreign nationals which are justified on grounds of public policy, public security and public health [1963–1964] OJ Spec ed, 117; Council Directive 68/360/EEC of 15 October 1968 on the abolition of restrictions on movement and residence within the Community for workers of Member States and their families [1968] OJ L257/13; Council Directive 73/148/EEC of 21 May 1973 on the abolition of restrictions on movement and residence within the Community for nationals of Member States with regard to establishment and the provision of services [1973] OJ L172/14; Council Directive 75/34/EEC of 17 December 1974 concerning the right of nationals of a Member State to remain in the territory of another Member State after having pursued therein an activity in a self-employed capacity [1975] OJ L14/10; Regulation 1612/68 (n 27 above) and Commission Regulation (EEC) 1251/70 of 29 June 1970 on the right of workers to remain in the territory of a Member State after having been employed in that State [1970] OJ L142/24.

[39] Arts 45(3) TFEU, 2 of Directive 68/360 and 1 of Regulation 1612/68, (n 27 above).

reference to which a Member State could derogate from the provisions on free movement.[40] This legislation and the case law it engendered were the bread and butter of generations of EEC and EC free movement specialists. Through the Court's interpretation of this legislation, in the light of the relevant provisions of the EEC and EC Treaties, the key parameters and content of the law in this field were established.

The principle of non-discrimination on grounds of nationality which finds general expression in Article 18 TFEU and more specific expression in Article 45(2) TFEU permeated Regulation 1612/68. Migrant workers and, to a certain extent, members of their families were entitled to equal treatment as regards employment conditions, access to vocational training, and social and tax advantages. The Court's case law with reference specifically to Article 7 of the 1968 Regulation proved instrumental in pushing the boundaries of the free movement of workers and transforming its very character. A status originally viewed in almost purely economic terms soon enabled its beneficiaries to invoke, in the widest and most varied contexts, the principle of non-discrimination on grounds of nationality by declaring effectively, in the inimitable words of one Advocate General, *civis europeus sum*.[41] The provisions of secondary legislation governing the freedom of establishment and services lacked a guarantee of equal treatment similar to Article 7 of Regulation 1612/68 but comparable protection was carved by the Court from the provisions of Articles 49 and 56 TFEU.[42] In addition, while the Treaty had been silent on the rights of free movement and residence of family members, Regulation 1612/68 provided for rights of entry and residence as well as the right to pursue an activity as an employed or self-employed person and, in the case of children, to be admitted to general educational and vocational courses.[43] The Court's role in developing and extending the protection afforded the beneficiaries of these free movement provisions and, in the process, creating what some authors referred to, years before the advent

[40] See, for example, the general interest justifications advanced in Case C-18/95 *Terhoeve* [1999] ECR I-345, [44]–[47]; Case C-224/01 *Köbler* [2003] ECR I-10239, [82]–[87]; Case C-208/05 *ITC* [2007] ECR I-181, [44], or Case C-269/07 *Commission v Germany* [2009] ECR I-7811, [60] and [63].

[41] See the Opinion in Case C-168/91 *Konstantinidis* [1993] ECR I-1191 [46]. The Court in that case preferred a market access approach to the fundamental rights approach expounded by its AG but many previous and subsequent decisions applying the principle of non-discrimination on grounds of nationality confirm the ethos of that Opinion. Travel reductions for large families (Case 32/75 *Cristini* [1975] ECR 1085), social security allowances for handicapped dependent adults (Case 63/76 *Inzirillo* [1976] ECR 2057), state pensions guaranteed to old persons (Case 261/83 *Castelli* [1984] ECR 3199), unemployment benefit (Case 94/84 *Deak* [1985] ECR 1873), minimum subsistence allowances (Case 249/83 *Hoeckx* [1985] ECR 973), maintenance grants and tuition fees (Case 39/86 *Lair* [1988] ECR 3161), study finance (Case C-337/97 *Meeusen* [1999] ECR I-3289), child-raising allowances (Joined Cases C-245/94 and C-312/94 *Hoever and Zachow* [1996] ECR I-4895), and state-subsidised childbirth loans to low income families (Case 65/81 *Reina* [1982] ECR 33), to name but a few, all constitute social advantages to which migrant workers and their family members are entitled, pursuant to Art 7(2) of Regulation 1612/68 (n 27 above), subject to the same conditions as nationals of the host Member State.

[42] See, for example, Case 197/84 *Steinhauser* [1985] ECR 1819; Case 305/87 *Commission v Greece* [1989] ECR 1461; Case C-111/91 *Commission v Luxembourg* [1993] ECR I-817; Case C-45/93 *Commission v Spain* [1994] ECR I-911, Case C-274/96 *Bickel and Franz* [1998] ECR I-7637.

[43] eg G Barrett, 'Family Matters: European Community Law and Third-country Family Members' (2003) 40 CML Rev 369.

of Union citizenship, as an incipient form of European citizenship,[44] cannot be under-estimated. Nevertheless, as indicated above, the seeds for this transformation had been at least partly sown by the Member States themselves, who framed secondary legislation not simply in economic but also in humanitarian terms.

Following the introduction in 1990 of secondary legislation regulating the right of residence of the economically inactive[45] and the establishment of Union citizen-ship in 1992 and in the light of the development of the Court's case law as regards both traditional free movement and the free movement of this new category of economically inactive Union citizens, the existing legislative framework governing free movement was fundamentally changed in 2004. Most of the Free Movement Directives were repealed, Regulations No 1612/68 and No 1408/71 being the only and, in the case of the former, partial, survivors of this process of codification and review.[46]

Directive 2004/38 provides that all Union citizens, and their family members, have the right to enter another Member State and reside there for up to three months on the basis of a valid identity card or passport.[47] The definition of family members has been extended to cover registered partnerships, albeit recognition of such partnerships appears to apply only in those host Member States which treat the latter as equivalent to marriage.[48] A right of residence for more than three months depends on the fulfilment of certain conditions. The Union citizen in question must be engaged in an economic activity, or have sufficient resources and sickness insurance to ensure not becoming a burden on the social assistance system of the host Member State, or be enrolled at a private or public educational establishment for the principal purpose of following a course of study, or be a family member of a Union citizen who falls into one of the above categories.[49] Union citizens may, in certain circumstances, and in certain cases for a limited period only, retain the status of worker or self-employed person even though they are no longer economically active.[50] The death of the Union citizen, his or her departure from the host Member State, divorce, annulment of marriage, or termination of a registered partnership does not affect the right of family members who are not themselves Union citizens to continue to reside in the host

---

[44] See, for example, Plender (n 18 above) or A C Evans, 'European Citizenship' (1982) 45 MLR 497–515.
[45] Council Directive 90/366/EEC on the right of residence for students ([1990] OJ L180/30), replaced by Council Directive 93/96 [1993] OJ L317/59; Council Directive 90/365/EEC on the right of residence for employees and self-employed persons who have ceased their occupational activity [1990] OJ L180/28, and Council Directive 90/364/EEC on the right of residence [1990] OJ L180/26 (hereafter referred to collectively as the 1990 Residence Directives).
[46] For an overview of the changes introduced by Council Directive 2004/38 (n 7 above) see, for example, J-Y Carlier and E Guild (eds), *The Future of the Free Movement of Persons in the EU* (Bruylant, 2006).
[47] Arts 5 and 6 of Council Directive 2004/38 (n 7 above).
[48] ibid Art 2(2)(b).
[49] See, in particular, ibid Art 7(1), which reproduces the residence requirements for economically inactive Union citizens first established in the 1990 Residence Directives (n 45 above). A more limited category of family member can join a Union citizen whose right of residence is based on a period of study in the host Member State.
[50] ibid Art 7(3).

Member State, provided certain conditions are fulfilled.[51] An unconditional right of permanent residence in the host Member State is conferred on Union citizens and their family members after a period of five years' uninterrupted legal residence.[52] All Union citizens residing on the basis of Directive 2004/38 in the territory of the host Member State shall enjoy equal treatment with the nationals of that Member State within the scope of the Treaty.[53] The benefit of this right to equal treatment is extended to family members, including third country nationals who have a right of permanent residence. Important derogations from the principle of equal treatment are set out in the second paragraph of Article 24 of the Directive for certain economically inactive Union citizens as regards access to social assistance and maintenance aid. Member States are not obliged to accord equal treatment as regards social assistance during the first three months of residence or, where appropriate, the longer period permitted to job-seekers genuinely seeking employment.[54] Member States are not obliged, prior to the acquisition of the right of permanent residence, to grant maintenance aid for studies to persons other than workers, self-employed persons, persons who retain such status, and members of their families.[55]

2. FREEDOM TO PROVIDE SERVICES

Prior to the adoption of the Services Directive, the Community legislature had taken a piecemeal, sectoral approach to harmonization in the related fields of establishment and services. Numerous directives had been adopted to regulate, amongst others, the mutual recognition of diplomas and professional qualifications, financial services, television, telecommunications, energy, transport, or postal services.[56] Given the particular difficulties presented by the temporary posting of both EU and non-EU workers by service providers not established in the host Member State, the Posted Workers Directive was adopted in their regard. To a very great extent, however, the

---

[51] ibid Art 12. This provision seeks to relieve the precarious legal position in which third country national spouses might find themselves following divorce. See previously Case 267/83 *Diatta* [1985] ECR 567, and Case C-370/90 *Singh* [1992] ECR I-4265.

[52] ibid Art 16. Continuity of residence is not affected by absences of a certain length or for certain reasons (Art 16(3)). Consecutive absence of over two years from the host Member State may result in loss of the permanent right of residence (Art 16(4)). A permanent right of residence may also be granted before five years have elapsed to certain categories of EU nationals (Art 17).

[53] ibid Art 24(1) is subject to specific provisions as are expressly provided for in the Treaty and secondary legislation, not least Arts 18 and 45(2) TFEU and, presumably, Art 7(2) of Regulation 1612/68 (n 27 above). See further sub-section D.3(a).

[54] ibid Arts 14(4)(b) and 24(2). The latter seeks to codify Case C-292/89 *Antonissen* [1991] ECR I-745. The job-seeker in question must have a genuine chance of being engaged for the basic three-month right of residence to be extended.

[55] ibid Art 24(2). Maintenance aid for studies is defined as student grants or student loans.

[56] For a broad outline of the regulatory framework in these fields see V Hatzopoulos, *Le principe communautaire d'équivalence et de reconnaissance mutuelle dans la libre prestation de services* (Bruylant, 1999), or N Maydell, 'The Services Directive and Existing Community Law' in F Breuss, G Fink, and S Griller (eds), *Services Liberalisation in the Internal Market* (Springer, 2008) 21–124.

free provision of services was regulated with reference to the principles enunciated in the case law of the Court and derived directly from what the Court interpreted the relevant provisions of successive Treaties as requiring. The Court's market access approach to obstacles and restrictions liable to hinder or render less attractive the exercise of this fundamental freedom meant that a wide array of national measures had to be scrutinized for their compatibility with the provisions on services and assessed with reference to objective justification and proportionality tests. Such scrutiny depended, however, on interested individuals, economic operators and, pursuant to Article 258 TFEU, the Commission, challenging *ex post* such obstacles and restrictions before national and EU courts.

Directive 2006/123 represents a fundamental departure in the field of establishment and services in that it seeks to regulate the provision of services horizontally, albeit subject to numerous and important exceptions to its scope of application.[57] The new Directive, like the provisions of the EC Treaty and now the TFEU and the case law of the Court of Justice before it, seeks to remove barriers to the establishment in host Member States of service providers and to the temporary provision of services between Member States. The latter are now required to simplify the administrative procedures applicable to service providers, provide points of single contact at which such a provider may complete the necessary formalities and enhance the right to information of providers and recipients of services. Chapter III is devoted to freedom of establishment for service providers and requires Member States to verify that their authorization schemes are non-discriminatory, objectively justified, and proportionate.[58] Chapter III also provides a list of requirements and conditions which a Member State of establishment might apply to service providers and distinguishes between those which are blacklisted and others which are suspect and open to evaluation, effectively reproducing the case law of the Court on Article 56 TFEU.[59] Chapter IV contains more controversial provisions concerning the freedom to provide services on a temporary basis. The country of origin principle has been replaced by a commonplace statement to the effect that Member States shall respect the right of service providers to provide services in a Member State other than their Member State of establishment. However, while restrictions on establishment can be justified by a wide range of overriding reasons or requirements in the public interest, restrictions on temporary service providers can only be saved with reference to a very narrowly defined category of justification.[60] Article 16 refers simply to public policy, public security, and public health as well as the protection of the environment and Member State rules on employment conditions, including those laid down in collective agreements. When transposing the Services Directive, Member States have had to identify

---

[57] For a comprehensive analysis of the Services Directives see FIDE, *The New Services Directive of the European Union* (Nomos, 2008); C Barnard, 'Unravelling the Services Directive'(2008) 45 CML Rev 323; Breuss, Fink, and Griller (eds) (n 56 above).

[58] Arts 9–13 and 39(1) of Council Directive 2006/123 (n 11 above).

[59] ibid Arts 14 and 15, respectively.   [60] ibid Art 16.

and assess all requirements affecting the establishment of service providers and those providing services on a more temporary basis. The purpose of this exercise is to simplify these requirements or abolish those that are discriminatory, unjustified, or disproportionate. In addition, Member States must evaluate the compatibility of national authorization schemes, obligations, and legal requirements applicable to those who wish to establish themselves on the territory of the host Member State in order to provide services there and provide temporary service providers with free access to the service activity and the freedom to exercise it in the territory of the Member State in question. Instead of service providers having to rely *ex post* on the principles developed by the Court to counteract restrictions of Article 56 TFEU, national authorities are subject to obligations *ex ante* to avoid or remove such restrictions.

3. PONDERING THE EFFECTS OF CODIFICATION FOR THE FREE MOVEMENT OF PERSONS AND SERVICES

When the Union legislature and hence the Member States seek to codify existing legislation and incorporate principles deriving from or identified in the Court's case law they generally explain the exercise in terms of the need for clarification and simplification of the applicable laws. As regards legislation affecting Union citizens, a further justification is inexorably found in the desire or need to strengthen their rights, the very leitmotif for the establishment of Union citizenship. The aforementioned legislation on the free movement of persons and services fails to disappoint in this respect.[61]

Any codification exercise carries a risk, however, that the principles which it is sought to codify may be altered or distorted. After all, EU codifying legislation, even if adopted on the basis of a qualified majority, has to survive the Byzantine complexity of the Union's legislative procedures and suffer the legal and political compromises necessary to secure consensus. If the codified case law was mandated and founded upon an interpretation of the provisions of primary law, it is difficult, unless the Treaty itself has in the meantime been amended, to see how a codifying measure which alters the tenor or effect of the Court's interpretation of primary law can be valid.[62] This is not to deny the evolutionary nature of the Treaties or the need, particularly as regards regulation of something as complex as the internal market, for implementing legislation. The Court is no legislator and it is clearly unable to fill in the numerous gaps left by the loosely framed language of the Treaties or the political compromises which tend to dictate the scope and terms of controversial secondary legislation. Furthermore, the fact that the Court has no control over its docket and that its jurisprudence is

---

[61] See recital 3 of Council Directive 2004/38 (n 7 above) and 1 of Council Directive 2006/123 (n 11 above).

[62] If the codification process clarifies case law interpreting provisions of secondary legislation and those provisions are themselves altered, there may be no particular problem as regards respect for the hierarchy of norms.

constructed on a case by case basis as a result of a haphazard flow of preliminary references and infringement actions further diminishes its regulatory impact. The purpose of the general and specific legal basis provided by the Treaties is precisely to allow the Union's legislator to adopt legislation which has as its object the improvement of the conditions for the establishing and functioning of the internal market. Harmonized legislation, as Weatherill points out, picks up the pace of market integration when judicially applied Treaty prohibitions appear powerless in the face of resistant and diverse national measures and practices which impede integration.[63] Nevertheless, for the *acquis communautaire*, including its jurisprudential component and the hierarchy of norms to be respected, secondary legislation must comply with primary law. If it is left for years to the judicial branch to clarify what the requirements of primary law are, problems may ensue when a comprehensive set of rules seeks to review and codify those requirements. What is gained in terms of legal certainty if the provisions of the codifying legislation are as woolly as those of primary law or if they are interpreted differently from Treaty provisions which have been the subject of established case law? How many years and how much litigation will it take to clarify the relationship between the two?

With very little legislative activity for decades regulating the free movement of workers and the freedom of establishment, the Court of Justice was, to a very large extent, left to fill in the gaps in primary law and what secondary law existed.[64] As regards the free provision of services, in the absence of a comprehensive, detailed regulatory framework, the essential parameters governing the law in this field were also largely constructed and developed by the Court's case law.[65] Indeed, by declaring the provisions of the Treaty on workers, establishment, and services to be vertically and, subsequently, horizontally directly effective, the Court guaranteed the primacy of its interpretation of these provisions, engaged directly in a dialogue with national courts and legislatures and, to a certain degree, side-stepped the law-making process at EU level.[66] What followed from the 1970s through to the 1990s was the creation of a rich, complex tapestry of case law.[67] The establishment of Union citizenship did not

---

[63] S Weatherill, 'Promoting the Consumer Interest in an Integrated Services Market', *Mitchell Working Paper Series* (Europa Institute Edinburgh, 1/2007).

[64] A classic example is the regulation of the free movement and residence rights of job-seekers in *Antonissen* (n 54 above).

[65] See, for example, on professional qualifications, Case C-340/89 *Vlassopoulou* [1991] ECR I-2357; on the regulation of financial services, Case 205/84 *Commission v Germany* [1986] ECR 3755, or on the posting of workers, Case C-113/89 *Rush Portuguesa* [1990] ECR I-1417.

[66] See in this respect as regards the Court's role in the field of social policy S Fredman, 'Social Law in the European Union: The Impact of the Law-making Process' in P Craig and C Harlow (eds), *Lawmaking in the European Union* (Hart, 1998) 386–411, 398.

[67] See, *inter alia*, the case law on directly effective rights of free movement and residence (eg Case 2/74 *Reyners* [1974] ECR 631, [32] and Case 33/74 *Van Binsbergen* [1974] ECR 1299, [27]); mutual recognition (eg Case 279/88 *Webb* [1989] ECR 3305); application of the principle of non-discrimination on grounds of nationality to situations or social benefits unspecified in the aforementioned legislative texts (see n 42 above); rights of family members (see below section F.2); recognition of academic and professional qualifications (eg Case 136/78 *Auer* [1979] ECR 437; Case C-340/89 *Vlassopoulou* (n 65 above) or Case C-19/92 *Kraus* [1993] ECR

mark an end to the Court's industry but simply provided the opportunity for the further judicial transposition of principles and rights developed with reference to freely moving economically active Member State nationals and their families to freely moving economically inactive Union citizens and their families.

(a) Free movement of persons

It is clear that the rationalization of the various instruments regulating free movement and codification of aspects of the Court's case law in the form of Directive 2004/38 has simplified the procedures applicable to EU nationals who wish to avail themselves of their rights to free movement and residence. A number of decisions handed down by the Court thus far call into question whether, in contrast, their rights can be said to have been strengthened.

In the *Förster* case, the Court indirectly tested the validity of the five-year residence condition which Member States can impose as a precondition for economically inactive Union citizens to be entitled to equal treatment when claiming certain social benefits or social assistance.[68] The Court concluded that this residence requirement does not go beyond what is necessary to attain the objective of ensuring that students from other Member States who claim maintenance aid are to a certain degree integrated into the society of the host Member State.[69] Its conclusion on the conformity of the national residence requirement at issue in that case indirectly saved the validity of Article 24(2) of Directive 2004/38. However, the reasoning in *Förster* contrasts starkly with the Court's previous insistence, pursuant to Articles 18 and 21 TFEU, on a case by case assessment by the competent authorities of the host Member State of the circumstances of the Union citizen claiming entitlement to the social benefit in question. To the extent that they could demonstrate a real or effective link with the host Member State and that requiring the latter to pay the benefit in question did not create an unreasonable burden for public funds, Union citizens had been found to be entitled, on the basis of those provisions of the Treaty, to equal treatment. The Court had explicitly rejected the imposition of blanket requirements by host Member States that might favour an element which is not necessarily representative of the degree of connection between the benefit claimant and the Member State concerned to the exclusion of other representative elements.[70] The right of Member

---

I-1663); rights of posted workers and the position of the Member States which temporarily host them and their service provider employers (eg Case C-113/89 *Rush Portuguesa*, (n 65 above) or Case C-43/93 *Van der Elst* [1994] ECR I-3803).

[68] Case C-158/07 *Förster* [2008] ECR I-8507. The provisions of Art 24(2) of Directive 2004/38 (n 7 above) did not apply *ratione temporis* to the facts of the case but the host Member State legislation had been adopted to replicate the five-year residence condition for entitlement to maintenance aid contained in that provision.

[69] See Case C-158/07 *Förster* (n 68 above), [51]–[58], and the comment by S O'Leary (2009) 34 ELRev 612.

[70] These principles were established in decisions on Union citizenship which post-dated the adoption of Directive 2004/38 (n 7 above) and which even contradicted the terms of the latter on the basis of the primacy of the requirements of Arts 18 and 21 TFEU. See, for example, Case C-184/99 *Grzelczyk* (n 28 above); Case C-224/98 *D'Hoop* [2002] ECR I-6191, and Case C-209/03 *Bidar* (n 28 above). A case by case assessment of whether the Union citizen constitutes an unreasonable burden seems also, in accordance with the

State nationals to reside in another Member State is conferred directly by Article 18 EC.[71] Their right to equal treatment, which derives from their lawful residence in the host Member State, stems from Article 18 TFEU.[72] A directive—particularly one whose legal basis includes Articles 18 and 21 TFEU—should not detract from the requirements flowing from those provisions of the Treaty.[73] In *Förster*, the Court used Directive 2004/38 to confirm that a five-year residence requirement is not disproportionate when it could have been expected to question whether the imposition of such a requirement by national law and, by extension, the authorization of such a requirement by Directive 2004/38, was compatible with Articles 18 and 21 TFEU in the light of its own case law.[74]

The Court's position in *Förster* is surprising not simply because it suggests that a directive can renege on or restrict the jurisprudential *acquis* established with reference to the Treaty, but also because it contradicts the Court's initial assessment of the relationship between Directive 2004/38 and the existing *acquis*. In a decision postdating the adoption of that Directive but prior to its transposition, the Court had already referred to the limitation of the principle of non-discrimination in Article 24 of Directive 2004/38. In *Bidar*, the Court overturned previous case law on the free movement of persons, concluding that student loans and grants intended to cover maintenance costs come within the scope of application of EU law and are therefore subject to Article 18 TFEU. It relied on Article 24(1) of the Directive in support of this conclusion.[75] The limitation of the principle of non-discrimination in the second paragraph of Article 24 was relied on as further confirmation of this development of the material scope of application induced by the establishment of Union citizenship. In addition, just a few months prior to the decision in *Förster*, emphasizing the fact that Directive 2004/38 sought to strengthen the rights of Union

---

aforementioned case law, to be required by the terms of Directive 2004/38 (see recital 16 and Art 14(3)). Another question entirely is whether the Court's previous interpretations of the terms of the 1990 Residence Directives (n 45 above) and Directive 2004/38 (n 7 above) in *Grzelczyk* and *Bidar* withstand legal scrutiny. On the consequences of long-established case law on the free movement of persons for the limits placed by the 1990 Residence Directives on the rights of residence of EU nationals see the comment by S O'Leary on Case C-295/90 *European Parliament v Council* [1992] ECR I-4193, (1993) 30 CML Rev 639.

[71] See Case C-413/99 *Baumbast* (n 32 above), [84]–[86] and [93]. As such, it is surprising that no mention is made in Case C-158/07 *Förster* (n 68 above), [40]–[43], of this decision when determining whether the right of residence of the applicant derived from Art 21 TFEU or the Students' Residence Directive (n 45 above). While migrant students may have derived their rights originally from Arts 7 and 128 EEC, it is difficult to contest that the transformation of Art 21 TFEU in the Court's case law strengthened the basis for their rights of residence and contingent rights.

[72] Case C-85/96 *Martínez Sala* (n 5 above).

[73] See also the Opinion in Case C-209/03 *Bidar* (n 28 above) [64].

[74] The Court has, in the past, relied on secondary legislation which was not yet in force to validate a particular interpretation of EU primary law (see, for example, Case C-342/93 *Gillespie* [1996] ECR I-475, as regards equal pay and Article 157 TFEU). In Case C-158/07 *Förster* (n 68 above), in contrast, Council Directive 2004/38 (n 7 above) was relied on to support an interpretation of provisions of the Treaty at odds with the Court's previous interpretations of those same provisions.

[75] Case C-209/03 *Bidar* (n 28 above) [42]–[43], overturning Case 39/86 *Lair* (n 41 above) [15], and Case 197/86 *Brown* [1988] ECR 3205 [18].

citizens, the Court had held that those citizens cannot derive fewer rights from Directive 2004/38 than from the instruments of secondary legislation which it amends or repeals.[76] It would seem to follow logically that Union citizens cannot derive fewer rights from Directive 2004/38 than from the Treaty provisions on which that piece of secondary legislation is based.

The assessment of the right of job-seekers to equal treatment pursuant to Directive 2004/38 has been somewhat more reassuring. Having recognized that job-seekers enjoy a right of residence when genuinely in search of work, the Court had initially limited their right to equal treatment to Articles 2 and 5 of Regulation 1612/68, to the exclusion of social and tax advantages under Article 7(2).[77] Once again, following the introduction of Union citizenship, the Court had revised its case law, qualifying job-seekers as workers and holding that this limitation of their right to equal treatment was no longer tenable. It held in *Collins* that the interpretation of the scope of the principle of equal treatment in relation to access to employment must reflect the developments resulting from the establishment of Union citizenship and the case law developed thereunder. Overruling *Lebon*, it recognized the right of job-seekers to equal treatment pursuant to Article 45(2) TFEU and therefore to a job-seeker's allowance intended to facilitate access to employment.[78] The applicants in *Vatsouras* were job-seekers who, after a certain period of employment in the host Member State, had lost their jobs and applied for social assistance.[79] As in *Förster*, the Court concluded in this case that the derogation from the entitlement of Union citizens to equal treatment in Article 24(2) of Directive 2004/38 was valid in so far as it related to the right of job-seekers to enjoy equal access to social assistance. It reached this conclusion, however, by interpreting the Directive in conformity with its previous case law and Article 45 TFEU, albeit limiting somewhat the terms in which *Collins* had overruled *Lebon*.[80] Nevertheless, the contrast between the interpretation of Directive 2004/38 in *Förster* and *Vatsouras* is striking.

The provisions of Directive 2004/38 suggest that there will be plenty of opportunity to test the Court's mettle further as several of those provisions appear problematic

---

[76] Case C-127/08 *Metock* [2008] ECR I-6241, [59], discussed further below at section F.2. See also, Case C-480/08 *Teixeira*, 23 February 2010, [60] and Case C-310/08 *Ibrahim*, 23 February 2010, [49].

[77] Case 316/85 *Lebon* [1987] ECR 2811.

[78] Case C-138/02 *Collins* [2004] ECR I-2703, [63]–[64].

[79] Joined Cases C-22/08 and C-23/08 *Vatsouras* [2009] ECR I-4585. The Court directed the national court at the outset to check whether, as former migrant workers seeking work afresh, the applicants did not benefit from equal treatment pursuant to Art 7(3)(c) of Directive 2004/38 (n 7 above). A similar instruction as regards the applicant's possible status as a migrant worker was absent from Case C-158/07 *Förster* (n 68 above).

[80] Case C-138/02 *Collins* (n 78 above) [63]–[64] could be interpreted as having extended to job-seekers on the basis of Art 45(2) TFEU a general right to equal treatment within the scope of application of EU law, including equal treatment as regards social advantages. This interpretation is supported by Case C-258/04 *Ioannidis* [2005] ECR I-8275, [23]–[34], which concerned a social assistance measure which the Court qualified also as a social advantage within the meaning of Regulation 1612/68 (n 27 above). Cases C-22/08 and C-23/08 *Vatsouras* (n 79 above), consecrate a right to equal treatment for job-seekers of, arguably, a more limited scope. The application of Art 24(2) of Directive 2004/38 (n 7 above) instead of Art 45(2) TFEU will depend on whether the benefit in question can be said to facilitate access to employment.

when compared with established principles relating to the free movement of persons. For example, the rights of Member State nationals to enter the territory of another Member State and reside there for the purposes intended by the Treaty provisions on free movement are rights directly conferred by the Treaty.[81] Articles 1, 7, 14, 16, and 24(1) of Directive 2004/38 either ignore this case law or have not been drafted in a sufficiently sympathetic way to reflect it. The definition of family members who derive rights from Union citizens has been extended to include those in registered partnerships. However, those partnerships must be recognized as equivalent to marriage in the host Member State. In the *Reed* case, the Court characterized the right to be accompanied in the host Member State by one's unmarried partner as a social advantage and an advantage, therefore, to which migrant workers are entitled on an equal basis. Since Article 7(2) of Regulation 1612/68 survives the adoption of Directive 2004/38, the more generous terms of the *Reed* decision, free of difficult questions regarding the equivalence of the civil status of marriage and registered partnerships, should presumably survive. More generally, Directive 2004/38 refers to social assistance while Regulation 1612/68 refers to social advantages. Are similar or identical categories of benefits intended? How will the Court decide on which expression of the principle of non-discrimination it will rely when determining a Union citizen's right to equal treatment?[82] As *Förster, Vatsouras*, and the terms of Article 24(2) of Directive 2004/38 foretell, one of the most sensitive problems concerning Union citizens who are economically inactive is the extent of their entitlement to equal treatment in the context of social welfare and assistance programmes. In accordance with the Court's case law, Directive 2004/38 directs Member States to eschew expulsion as the automatic consequence of reliance on social assistance. However, it does nothing to clarify when a Member State can consider that a drip of benefit claimants turns into an unreasonable flood. It is not clear either from the individual assessment of the claimant's circumstances required by the Court's case law, and indeed by some of the provisions of Directive 2004/38, whether such a global assessment of unreasonableness would be permissible.

However the Court resolves these questions, the fact remains that the relationship between the rights conferred by Articles 18, 21, and 45 TFEU as interpreted by the Court and their regulation by secondary legislation risks becoming more rather than less complicated in the aftermath of this codification and review. The Court's jurisprudential *acquis* is a legacy which the legislature could not ignore when adopting Directive 2004/38 and which the Court cannot ignore when interpreting it. Yet the codifying legislation, like the case law on which it is partly based, reflects an unreconciled conflict between the rights of the economically active and inactive. In the

---

[81] Case 48/75 *Royer* (n 2 above) [31]; Case C-215/03 *Oulane* [2005] ECR I-1215 [17]–[21], and Case C-413/98 *Baumbast* (n 32 above) [84].

[82] Arts 18, 45, 49, and 56 TFEU or Arts 24 and 7 of Directive 2004/38 (n 7 above) and Regulation 1612/68 (n 27 above), respectively. Presumably the answer depends, as before, on the status of the claimant. Case C-158/07 *Förster* (n 68 above), and Cases C-22/08 and C-23/08 *Vatsouras* (n 79 above) suggest that deciding who qualifies as what is not without difficulty.

absence of a larger body of case law interpreting Directive 2004/38 it is impossible at this stage to predict whether the Court will adopt the restrictive bent it did in *Förster*, whether it will more faithfully refer back to the interpretations of primary law already consecrated in its case law, or whether its degree of faith with that case law will depend on the facts of a particular case, the rights at stake, or the particular category of Union citizen with which it is dealing.[83]

(b) Free provision of services

The date for the transposition of the Services Directive has barely passed and its provisions remain untested. Given its origins, scope, and complexity, as well as the volume of services litigation, one can expect a further steady increase in preliminary references relating to the provision of services. The Court will be forced to unravel some of the convoluted provisions of Directive 2006/123 and confront them with the principles governing establishment and services previously developed by the Court itself with reference to the relevant provisions of the Treaty. Although the Directive refers to the definition of services in Article 57 TFEU,[84] the Court may have to test further the limits of the Directive and the scope of application of EU law on the provision of services with reference to the public or private nature of funding or examine the definition of what constitutes a 'requirement' in the light of the Court's existing case law on restrictions.[85] A requirement is defined as any obligation, prohibition, condition, or limit provided for in the laws, regulation, or administrative provisions of the Member States or in consequence of case law, administrative practice, the rules of professional bodies, or the collective rules of professional associations or other professional organizations, adopted in the exercise of their legal autonomy, bar rules laid down by collective agreements. How does this definition of a requirement compare with the Court's definition of the scope and object of Article 56 TFEU in *Van Binsbergen*?[86] This precise and less expansive definition has been credited with sheltering services from the difficulties which afflicted goods as a result of the all-embracing *Dassonville* formula.[87] The attempt in some recitals to clarify the limits of the concept of requirement may prove unsuccessful given that some of the rules which are said not to constitute requirements for the purposes of the Services Directive have been assessed by the Court and found wanting as regards their

---

[83] A comparison of Case C-128/07 *Metock* (n 76 above) (right of worker to family reunification), and C-158/07 *Förster* (n 68 above) (right of Union citizen to maintenance aid for studies) suggests both that the category of Union citizen continues to be of importance and that some rights are more fundamental than others.

[84] Art 4(1) of Directive 2006/123 (n 11 above) defines a service as 'any self-employed economic activity, normally provided for remuneration, as referred to in Art [57 TFEU]'.

[85] ibid Art 4(7).

[86] See the identification of the restrictions of services caught by Art 56 TFEU in Case 33/74 *Van Binsbergen* (n 67 above) [10]–[11].

[87] Case 8/74 *Dassonville* [1974] ECR 837. See Barnard (n 57 above) [336] and D Edward and N Nic Shuibhne, 'Continuity and Change in the Law Relating to Services' in Arnull *et al* (eds), (n 9 above) 254 on difficulties with the breadth of the concept of requirement.

compliance with at least one of the fundamental freedoms already.[88] The scope and effects of the extensive list of exceptions and derogations which pepper that Directive will also need to be clarified. Recital 34, for example, refers to the Court's case law on the absence of the essential characteristics of remuneration in services provided, for no consideration, by or on behalf of the state in the context of its duties in the educational field. It concludes that such services are not covered by Article 57 TFEU and fall outside the scope of the Services Directive. While the ring-fencing of public educational services may be understandable, it sits uneasily with the Court's case law on the right of Union citizens to non-discriminatory access to such services as well as their right to financial support in certain circumstances while studies are being pursued.

It is a well-established principle of EU free movement law that the retention by Member States of competence in a particular field does not prevent the exercise of that competence falling foul of the free movement provisions. The Court has tempered the expansive scope of application of the free movement rules which has resulted with reference to the express derogations provided by the Treaty and by crafting a category of overriding reasons in the public interest. Express derogations and those crafted by the Court in its case law are both defined as overriding reasons in Article 4(8) of Directive 2006/123 despite the fact that, traditionally, only one category can be relied on to justify discriminatory obstacles and restrictions. More importantly, it remains to be seen how the Court will assess the legislator's decision in the Services Directive to reject certain justifications outright, admit others for evaluation and, as regards the temporary provision of services, provide for narrower categories of justification than those permitted by the case law. Barnard suggests that whether the assessment of overriding requirements takes places under the auspices of the Services Directive or with reference to Articles 49 and 56 TFEU, the outcome will not be very different.[89] Given that the Services Directive is rooted firmly within the Treaty's internal market objectives while the fundamental freedoms in the Treaty are part of a broader and much more complex whole and in the light of the Court's interpretation of the Posted Workers Directive, such an outcome cannot be guaranteed.

The Services Directive recognizes at the outset that there is a considerable body of EU law on services and states that the Directive builds on this and seeks to complement the Union *acquis*.[90] In addition, Member States are enjoined by Article 3(3) of the Services Directive to apply the provisions of the Directive in compliance with the rules of the Treaty on the right of establishment and the free provision movement of services. The real question in coming years will be whether the Court will ensure that the EU's *acquis* regarding those two fundamental freedoms is not (unduly) altered or

---

[88] As regards, for example, rules on land use and town and country planning, see recital 9 and Art 14(5) of Council Directive 2006/123 (n 11 above). See also decisions of the Court, albeit in the context of the free movement of capital, concerning planning restrictions on the construction of second homes in Austria—eg Case C-302/97 *Konle* [1999] ECR I-3099.

[89] Barnard (n 57 above) [358] and [367].

[90] Recital 30 of Directive 2006/123 (n 11 above).

distorted by the provisions of the Directive. If too much deference is paid to the intention of the Union legislature when adopting the Directive without sufficient reference to the other essential aspects of teleological review (the Treaty and regulatory context into which the Directive fits, the jurisprudential *acquis*, the objectives and aims of the Directive itself and, where appropriate, the social and economic aims underpinning the internal market), it will be difficult to see how this harmonization and codification exercise will have built upon and strengthened the rights of service providers and recipients and the existing *acquis*.

The problems and tensions stemming from codification will not be confined to those matters covered by the Services Directive but will undoubtedly extend to the numerous exclusions from its scope of application. The excluded services and sectors will continue to be governed by the relevant provisions of the Treaty or by those provisions in conjunction with specific pieces of secondary legislation adopted to give them effect. One sector which will likely present problems in the future is that relating to healthcare services and cross-border patient mobility. The Court held over two decades ago that medical services constitute services within the meaning of Article 59 TFEU.[91] *Luisi and Carbone* sowed the seeds for patient mobility within the EU and Regulation (EEC) No 1408/71 quickly proved an insufficient framework within which to manage and accommodate the legal problems which ensued.[92] According to the case law, national systems of prior authorization imposed on patients wishing to receive medical treatment in another Member State and seeking reimbursement in their Member State of origin are regarded, in principle, as restrictive of the free provision of services.[93] Healthcare services provided in the context of national social security schemes are subject to Article 56 TFEU, albeit the Court made clear that the possible risk of seriously undermining a social security system's financial balance may constitute an overriding reason in the general interest capable of justifying a barrier to the free provision of services. Subsequent decisions have clarified to what extent and in what way restrictions resulting from systems based on refunds, benefits-in-kind or forming part of a general, nationalized health system can fall foul of Article 56 TFEU.[94] The Court has made clear that, for the purposes of that provision, there is no need to distinguish between hospital care and care provided outside a hospital environment, albeit the general interest justifications which may be relied on with reference to different types of care may differ and prior authorization for hospital care may be

---

[91] Joined Cases C-286/82 and C-26/83 *Luisi and Carbone* [1984] ECR 377.

[92] Case C-158/96 *Kohll* [1998] ECR I-1931, [25] or Case C-372/04 *Watts* [2006] ECR I-4325, [47] on the relationship between Regulation 1408/71 and Art 56 TFEU.

[93] See eg Case C-158/96 *Kohll* (n 92 above) [35]–[36].

[94] See further Case C-368/98 *Vanbraekel* [2001] ECR I-5363; Case C-157/99 *Smits and Peerbooms* [2001] ECR I-5473; Case C-385/99 *Müller-Fauré and Van Riet* [2003] ECR I-4509, all of which concerned systems offering benefits in kind; Case C-158/96 *Kohll* (n 92 above) and Case C-56/01 *Inizan* [2003] ECR I-12403 which concerned national health insurance systems offering refunds; and Case C-372/04 *Watts*, (n 92 above), which concerned a national health system offering benefits in kind through public funds and public infrastructure.

required if justified and proportionate.[95] Considerable criticism has centred on the further judicial incursion which this case law represents into a particularly sensitive area of national competence involving complex, costly, and important political and social choices.[96] However one assesses the Court's treatment of these cases, the fact remains that, in this field as in others, the Court was left to sketch the basic components of a regulatory framework on cross-border healthcare services.[97] It should have been obvious in the aftermath of *Luisi and Carbone* that further regulation might or would at some stage prove necessary. Confronted with requests for interpretations of the provisions of EU primary and secondary law in the context of preliminary references which it was obliged to answer, the Court was arguably forced to fill a legal vacuum.

The Bolkestein draft Directive included healthcare services within its horizontal framework. It was decided to exclude this sector from the Services Directive, the sensitivity involved in the regulation of services in this field and the implications for public funds proving too much for the European Parliament and the Council.[98] In 2008, the Commission adopted a proposal for a directive on the application of patients' rights in cross-border healthcare aiming to ensure that there is a clear framework for cross-border healthcare within the EU.[99] In its explanatory notes, the Commission draws attention to the *ad hoc* nature in which EU law as regards healthcare services has developed, dependent on the introduction of cases by individual EU nationals and resulting from a case by case assessment by the Court of the requirements of the Treaty in the context of those preliminary references. The proposed Directive applies to the provision of healthcare regardless of how it is organized, delivered, and financed or whether it is public or private. It seeks to clarify the rights of patients to reimbursement for healthcare provided in Member States other than their Member State of residence or establishment. The Member State of affiliation may impose on a patient seeking healthcare provided in another Member State the same conditions, criteria of eligibility, and regulatory and administrative

---

[95] See eg Case C-368/98 *Vanbraekel* (n 94 above) [41]; Case C-157/99 *Smits and Peerbooms* (n 94 above) [53]; Case C-385/99 *Müller-Fauré and van Riet* (n 94 above) [38]; and Case C-372/04 *Watts* (n 92 above) [86].

[96] On the ill-suited nature of the Court as a forum for resolving social policy issues, not least because of the case by case nature in which law and policy are formed, see Fredman (n 66 above) [402]–[403].

[97] See also Biondi (n 9 above) [233]–[234]. See, further, as regards the Court's case law on Art 56 TFEU and cross-border healthcare services, V Hatzopoulos, 'Killing National Health and Insurance Systems but Healing Patients' (2002) 39 CML Rev 683; P Van Nuffel, 'Patients' Free Movement Rights and Cross-Border Access to Healthcare' (2005) 12 MJ 253; C Newdick, 'Citizenship, Free Movement and Healthcare: Cementing Individual Rights by Corroding Social Solidarity' (2006) 43 CML Rev 1645.

[98] Art 17 of Council Directive 2006/123 (n 11 above) provides that Art 16 shall not apply to matters covered by Regulation 1408/71. See also ibid recital 22 and Art 2(2)(f) as regards the exclusion of healthcare (and possibly pharmaceutical services, excluded by the recital but not the terms of Art 2) from the scope of that Directive.

[99] COM(2008) 414 final. Note that the definition of healthcare in this proposed Healthcare Directive differs from that under the Services Directive (n 11 above). For an analysis of the Commission's proposed Healthcare Directive see W Sauter, 'The Proposed Patients' Rights Directive and the Reform of (cross-border) Healthcare in the European Union' (2009) 36 LIEI 109.

formalities for receiving healthcare and reimbursement of healthcare costs as it would impose if the same or similar healthcare was provided in its territory, in so far as they are neither discriminatory nor an obstacle to freedom of movement of persons. Given the Court's case law on restrictions, what type of criterion, condition, or formality will fall outside of this notion and therefore be free of the objective justification and proportionality assessment required by the Court's case law on Article 56 TFEU? Even though the proposed Directive may seek to establish a general framework for patients' rights in cross-border healthcare beyond the piecemeal approach which necessarily results from individual preliminary references, the fact remains that, at its heart, a case by case analysis seems nevertheless to be required of national authorities. Nowhere in the proposed Directive is there the reminder which was included in the Services Directive that when applying the former's provisions, Member States must act in compliance with the requirements of the Treaty as regards the free provision of services. Such a reminder may seem facile until one remembers that the draft Directive, if adopted, will be adopted by the Member States which have, with understandable force and in great numbers, intervened in the preliminary references in which the aforementioned principles on cross-border healthcare services were developed by the Court with reference to the provisions of the Treaty. Indeed the reluctance or resistance of many Member States to implement this case law was one of the Commission's primary justifications for the proposed Directive.[100]

Leaving aside prospective problems, for an instructive example of how the Court has already resolved the relationship between the requirements of primary law on the free provision of services with the provisions of secondary law—albeit the Directive in question is not a classic codification directive—one need look no further than the case law on posted workers. In a series of cases dating back to the 1990s, the Court had indicated that the application of a host Member State's social and employment legislation and standards to workers employed by an undertaking established elsewhere but temporarily posted to that state for the duration of the services provision constitutes a restriction on the undertaking's freedom to provide services contrary to Article 56 TFEU. Provided that they comply with the principle of proportionality, such restrictions can be justified, however, by overriding reasons relating to the public interest, not least the protection of workers and the need to avoid social dumping.[101] As the Court fine-tuned this jurisprudence, it instructed national courts to balance the administrative and economic burdens that the rules of the host Member State impose on the provider of services against the increased social protection that they confer on

---

[100] This opposition is further illustrated by Case C-211/08 *Commission v Spain* ([2008] OJ C197/12), and Case C-512/08 *Commission v France* [2009] OJ C44/29, regarding disputed aspects of the Court's healthcare case law pursuant to Art 56 TFEU and their interaction with Regulation 1408/71.

[101] See eg Joined Cases C-369/96 *Arblade* [1999] ECR I-8453, [36]; Case C-165/98 *Mazzoleni* [2001] ECR I-2189, [27], and Case C-244/04 *Commission v Germany* [2006] ECR I-885 [61]. The Court vacillates between the more general need to protect workers, which presumably means both host Member State and posted workers, and the specific need to protect the latter when in the host Member State—see Cases C-49/98, 50/98, C-52/98 to C-54/98, and C-68/98 to C-71/98 *Finalarte Sociedade de Construção Civil Lda e.a.* [2001] ECR I-7831, [33] (workers) and [41] and [52] (posted workers).

workers compared with that guaranteed by the law of the home Member State. For the host Member State to apply its social and employment legislation, the posted workers on its territory must not already enjoy the same protection or essentially comparable protection by virtue of obligations to which their employer is already subject in the Member State in which he is established.[102] The host Member State's legislation or collective agreements must contribute in a significant manner to the posted workers social protection.[103] The Court was asked in one particular case about the compatibility with Article 56 TFEU of host Member State legislation requiring that workers, both national and posted, be entitled to more favourable protection than the minimum standard required by an EU Employment Directive. It held that it is for each Member State to determine the employment protection standard which is necessary in the public interest. Since the Member State in question had determined that a specific number of days of paid leave was necessary for the social protection of construction workers, the provisions of the Treaty on services did not, in principle, prevent that Member State from extending this level of protection to posted workers, regardless of the fact that that protection exceeded the required EU minimum.[104]

It was to be expected that when, for the first time, the Court had to interpret Directive 96/71, it would remain sensitive, if not loyal, to its interpretation of what the provisions of the Treaty dictated as regards service providers, posted workers, and imperative requirements which could be relied on by the host Member State in defence of its social and employment rules. Some commentators have regarded the *Viking* and *Laval* decisions as confounding this expectation.[105] The facts of the *Laval* case, which concerned the provision of construction services in Sweden by an undertaking established in Latvia using manpower subject to a Latvian collective agreement, do not need to be rehearsed in full. Crucially, in the construction sector, Swedish collective agreements transposing the Posted Workers Directive were not universally or generally applicable nor did they provide for a minimum wage but stipulated negotiation of wages between unions and service providers for each construction project. As such, at least as regards wage costs, they lacked the type of predictability and transparency which a service provider would deem desirable. Two important aspects of the Court's decision should be singled out in the context of a discussion of the relationship between primary and secondary EU law regarding the free provision of services. Article 3(7) of Directive 96/71 is the classic statement to be found in almost all Social Policy Directives to the effect that Member States may provide for more favourable

---

[102] Case C-445/03 *Commission v Luxembourg* [2004] ECR I-10191, [29], and Case C-272/94 *Guiot* [1996] ECR I-1905.

[103] See eg Case C-165/98 *Mazzoleni* (n 101 above).

[104] See Cases C-49/98 *Finalarte* (n 101 above) [58], as regards German legislation imposing a requirement to provide construction workers with a number of weeks paid annual leave above the four-week minimum established in Council Directive 93/104/EC concerning certain aspects of the organisation of working time [1993] OJ L 307/18.

[105] See, for example, the analysis of posted workers case law pre and post-*Laval* by C Kilpatrick, 'The ECJ and Labour Law: A 2008 Retrospective' (2009) 38 ILJ 180–208.

protection than that established in the Directive in question.[106] Firstly, the Court held that that guarantee cannot be interpreted as allowing host Member States to make the provision of services in its territory conditional on the observance of terms and conditions of employment which go beyond the mandatory rules for minimum protection laid down by the Posted Workers Directive.[107] The latter, according to the Court, establishes the *degree* of protection for posted workers in the host Member State and the reference in Article 3(7) of that Directive to more favourable protection must be understood as referring to protection afforded by collective agreements and legislation in the Member State where the service provider is established.[108] This interpretation converts a minimum requirement regarding protection of workers into a maximum ceiling. It also confounds the Court's previous case law on posted workers under Article 56 TFEU, regarding the determination by the host Member State of the degree of protection afforded workers in that state and the legitimacy of extending to posted workers more favourable protection, in accordance with the public interest, than that provided by EU minimum requirements legislation.[109] Secondly, the Court proceeded to use its restrictive interpretation of the terms of Directive 96/71 to limit the scope of application of Article 56 TFEU. It recognized the legitimacy, in principle, for the purposes of justifying restrictions of services, of objectives relating to the protection of workers or the need to prevent social dumping. However, since Directive 96/71 required undertakings posting workers to observe only a nucleus of mandatory rules for minimum protection in the host Member State—Article 3(7) having been deprived of its essential relevance as regards the latter—those overriding reasons could not be invoked to justify restrictions resulting from the rules applicable in a host Member State which sought to go beyond that nucleus.[110]

Laval could be dismissed as a decision engendered by a national system which was particularly impenetrable for foreign service providers. That would be to miss the point as regards how the Court's reasoning with reference to secondary legislation paid such little regard to a substantial body of case law directly based on the Treaty provisions relating to services.[111] In addition, the reasoning in *Laval* has

---

[106] A general statement to this effect is also to be found in Art 153(4) TFEU.

[107] See Case C-341/05 *Laval* (n 12 above) [80]. Contrast with the terms of Art 3(7) of the Posted Workers Directive (n 37 above): 'Paragraphs 1 to 6 [of Art 3] shall not prevent application of terms and conditions of employment which are more favourable to workers' and recital 17: 'Whereas the mandatory rules for minimum protection in force in the host country must not prevent the application of terms and conditions of employment which are more favourable to workers.'

[108] Case C-341/05 *Laval* (n 12 above) [80]–[81].

[109] Compare this conclusion in Case C-341/05 *Laval* (n 12 above), with that reached in Joined Cases C-49/98 *Finalarte* (n 101 above). See P Davies, 'Posted Workers: Single Market or Protection of National Labour Law Systems' (1997) 34 CML Rev 571 for his prescient identification of the various and conflicting objectives which could be said to underpin the Posted Workers Directive (n 37 above).

[110] Case C-341/05 *Laval* (n 12 above) [108].

[111] As regards the relationship between the terms of the Posted Workers Directive (n 37 above) and Art 56 TFEU, it is worth contrasting the Opinion of the AG with the reasoning of the Court.

been reiterated, indeed entrenched, in two subsequent cases involving host Member States whose legislation did not suffer from the lack of transparency which the Court felt characterized the Swedish system.[112]

E. WHO'S WHO?—DELIMITING THE PARAMETERS OF THE FREE MOVEMENT OF PERSONS AND SERVICES

Prior to the introduction of Union citizenship, the Court's jurisprudence recognized the right of Member State nationals to enter and reside in the territory of other Member States, but only for the purposes intended by the Treaty—in other words those specified in Articles 45, 49, and 56 TFEU.[113] Migrant workers, the self-employed, providers and, over time, recipients of services, students and job-seekers were all declared to come within the personal scope of Community, now Union, law and were thus the beneficiaries of rights to free movement and protected from discrimination on grounds of nationality within the material scope of application of EU law. The rights of those Member State nationals falling within what could be regarded as peripheral categories—family members, job-seekers, the retired, students—tended to be subject to temporal or other limitations which did not apply to the economically active.[114] The breadth of the rights afforded by the classification of a Member State national as a worker, a self-employed person, a provider or recipient of services; the absence of almost any limitations and conditions on the exercise of the rights which they derived from the Treaty; and their ability to confer rights on family members who would not otherwise come within the scope of application of EU law rendered the definitions of these categories of paramount importance.[115]

1. WORKERS

In the specific context of Article 45 TFEU, the Court has been vehement that the concepts of worker and employed person, which define the field of application of this fundamental freedom, must receive an autonomous, Union definition and not a

---

[112] See Case C-346/06 *Rüffert* and Case C-319/06 *Commission v Luxembourg* (n 12 above).

[113] See, variously, Case 43/75 *Royer* (n 2 above) [31], or Case C-363/89 *Roux* [1991] ECR 273 [9].

[114] See, as regards job-seekers, the approval of temporal limitations in Case C-292/89 *Antonissen* (n 54 above) [21] or, before the introduction of Union citizenship, their limited right to rely on the principle of non-discrimination on grounds of nationality to gain access to substantive benefits available to workers: Case 316/85 *Lebon* (n 77 above). See, as regards students, recognition of a right of residence to pursue vocational studies subject, however, to the legitimate interests of the Member States: Case C-357/98 *Raulin* [1992] ECR I-1027, [39]. See, as regards the derived nature of the rights of family members, Case 267/83 *Diatta* (n 51 above).

[115] For a detailed account of the case law on the personal scope of Arts 45, 49, and 56 TFEU, see A Van der Mei, *Free Movement of Persons within the European Community* (Hart, 2003); R White, *Workers, Establishment and Services in the European Union* (Oxford University Press, 2004); Minderhoud and Trimikliniotis (n 13 above), and C Barnard, *The Substantive Law of the EU. The Four Freedoms* (2nd edn, Oxford University Press, 2004).

restrictive one at that.[116] The rules on the free movement of workers cover the pursuit of effective and genuine activities, to the exclusion of activities on such a small scale as to be regarded as purely marginal and ancillary. As long as their work is genuine and effective, even part-time workers and those who claim financial assistance payable out of the public funds of the host Member State in order to supplement their income, cannot be excluded from the personal scope of the free movement provisions,[117] nor should they, in principle, be denied the material benefits accruing thereunder.[118] The existence of an employment relationship must be determined in accordance with objective criteria, the essential feature being that for a certain period of time a person performs services for and under the direction of another person in return for which he receives remuneration.[119] In this context, the Court very quickly demonstrated that it was attuned to the changing structure and demands of the labour market and resulting changes in the nature of employment relationships. In general, the fact that a worker is employed on a fixed-term contract, works part-time, is employed as part of an overall training programme, performs very limited numbers of hours work per week or month, or earns limited remuneration, have not inhibited their qualification as workers within the meaning of Article 45 TFEU, provided they comply with the *Levin* and *Lawrie-Blum* criteria outlined above.[120] National judges are entitled, when assessing the real and effective character of the professional activity exercised by someone claiming to qualify as a worker, to take into consideration the irregular character of that activity or its limited duration. However, these factors do not as such disqualify the individual from qualifying as a worker.

Although the definition of migrant worker is an autonomous Union definition, the fact that its application falls to national judges implies that differences will inevitably emerge between Member States or within a single Member State. A worker qualified by one national judge as coming within the scope of Article 45 TFEU might not prove so fortunate before the courts of a different Member State or even before a different national judge. This is the inevitable consequence of leaving the factual appreciation of

[116] Unilateral definitions of the concept of worker with reference to national provisions on minimum wages or minimum working hours have been rejected both under Arts 45 and 157 TFEU and secondary legislation adopted thereunder: see, for example, Case 75/63 *Hoekstra* [1964] ECR 347, [184], and Case C-317/93 *Nolte* [1995] ECR I-4625, [19].

[117] See, for example, Case 53/81 *Levin* [1982] ECR 1035, [12]–[17]; Case 139/85 *Kempf* [1986] ECR 1741, [14]–[15]; Case C-10/05 *Mattern and Citokic* [2006] ECR I-3145, [18]–[23], and Case C-413/01 *Ninni-Orasche* [2003] ECR I-13187, [27].

[118] See, however, Case C-213/05 *Geven* [2007] ECR I-6347, discussed below in section F.1.

[119] See Case 66/85 *Lawrie-Blum* (n 26 above).

[120] See, generally, Case C-27/91 *Hostellerie Le Manoir* [1991] ECR I-5531; Case C-357/89 *Raulin* (n 114 above) [14]; Case C-3/90 *Bernini* [1992] ECR I-1071; Case C-413/01 *Ninni-Orasche* (n 117 above); Case C-109/04 *Kranemann* [2005] ECR I-2421, [17]; Case C-213/05 *Geven* (n 118 above), and Case C-94/07 *Raccanelli v Max-Planck-Gesellschaft zur Förderung der Wissenschaft eV* [2008] ECR I-5939. Exceptions to the inclusiveness of the Court's definition of worker can be found in Cases 344/87 *Bettray* (n 30 above), and C-456/02 *Trojani* [2004] ECR I-7543, [21] as regards social employment schemes. Contrast with Case C-287/05 *Hendrix* [2007] ECR I-6909, where it was not contested that the applicant was a worker for the purposes of Art 45 TFEU despite being employed in specially adapted work due to a slight mental disability and receiving remuneration subsidized by the state.

the individual's situation to the national judge and of the absence of a minimum threshold as regards the number of hours which must be worked or the minimum pay necessary to guarantee qualification as a worker.[121] However, since that qualification is the gateway for entitlement to a whole range of social benefits with reference to the principle of non-discrimination on grounds of nationality in Articles 18 and 45(2) TFEU, one can only wonder whether the relative strictness or generosity with which the criteria established by the Court's case law is applied at national level relate to the consequences of the qualification rather than the intrinsic nature of the activity performed.

The introduction of Union citizenship has not been without consequences as regards the parameters of free movement law set by the definition of worker, establishment, and services. Since the right of Union citizens to move and reside freely within the territory of the Member States finds specific expression in Articles 45, 49, and 56 TFEU, the Court in its early Union citizenship case law deferred to the latter provisions whenever possible.[122] Its practice has since become more variable. In some cases, despite the fact that there has been a clear dispute at national level regarding whether or not the applicant qualified as a worker, the Court has ignored the question of the application of Article 45 TFEU and moved straight to Article 21 TFEU read, more often than not, in conjunction with Article 18 TFEU.[123] In other cases, despite the fact that the national court asked about Article 21 TFEU, the Court proffered a response based on Article 45 TFEU.[124] While it seems to have privileged the provisions on Union citizenship where its interpretation of those provisions is sympathetic to the position of the applicant,[125] that has not always been the case.[126] All EU nationals are Union citizens but the extent to which they enjoy certain rights or are protected against discrimination on grounds of nationality continues to depend on the category of Union citizen to which they belong.

2. ESTABLISHMENT

The Court classifies any economic activity which a person performs outside a relationship of subordination with respect to the conditions of work or remuneration and under his own personal responsibility as an activity pursued in a self-employed capacity for the

---

[121] See Case C-14/09 *Genc*, 4 February 2010, where the referring court sought to establish some sort of minimum threshold for qualification as a worker with reference to pay and working time, something which the Court implicitly rejected.

[122] See, for example, Case C-193/94 *Skanavi* [1996] ECR I-929; Case C-348/96 *Calfa* [1999] ECR I-11; Case C-100/01 *Olazabal* [2002] ECR I-10981.

[123] Case C-128/07 *Förster* (n 68 above).

[124] Case C-258/04 *Ioannidis* (n 80 above). The job-seeker in question derived his right to the disputed social advantage from Art 45 TFEU and not from the more general provisions relating to Union citizenship.

[125] Thus, in Case C-184/99 *Grzelczyk* (n 28 above), where the applicant had worked and studied at the same time but where there was no connection between his studies and his occupational activity, the Court answered the national court exclusively in terms of Arts 18 and 21 TFEU, despite the fact that the national court had also questioned the import of Art 45 TFEU in that case.

[126] Cases C-22/08 and C-23/08 *Vatsouras* (n 79 above), where the Court's judgment simply contained a series of indices for the national judge to consider.

purposes of Article 49 TFEU.[127] The concept of establishment involves the actual pursuit of an economic activity through a fixed establishment in another Member State for an indefinite period. It is the permanence of establishment compared to the generally more temporary nature of the provision of services which explains the lighter regulatory touch expected of the host Member State as regards the latter. The difficulties encountered as regards delimiting establishment and distinguishing it from services relates to the fact that clear blue water often fails to divide the two, since they may involve the same type of economic activities performed in a different manner. One of the Court's clearest attempts to explain the distinction between establishment and services remains the *Gebhard* case. In that case the Court held that the concept of establishment within the meaning of the Treaty is a very broad one, allowing an EU national to participate, on a stable and continuous basis, in the economic life of a Member State other than his State of origin and to profit therefrom, so contributing to economic and social interpenetration within the Union in the sphere of activities as self-employed persons.[128] The Court noted at that time that the provisions of the chapter on services are subordinate to those in the chapter on the right of establishment, and that the latter covered all types of self-employed activity to be taken up and pursued on the territory of any other Member State, undertakings to be formed and operated, and agencies, branches, or subsidiaries to be set up. The temporary nature of the service activities in question had to be determined in the light, not only of the duration of the provision of the service but also of its regularity, periodicity, or continuity. As the next section on services suggests, the traditional subordination of services to the free movement of workers and the freedom of establishment could be said to be changing not merely because of the increased volume of services in the EU and fundamental changes in their character, but also because of resulting changes in the definition of what constitutes a service for the purpose of Articles 56 and 57 TFEU.

3. SERVICES

Article 57 TFEU provides that services shall be considered to be services within the meaning of the Treaties where they are normally provided for remuneration, in so far as they are not governed by the provisions relating to freedom of movement for goods, capital, and persons. The Services Directive equally defines services with reference to this provision of the Treaty.[129] While the Member States saw no need in the TFEU to update, extend, or remove the non-exhaustive but outmoded list of examples of services provided in the EEC and EC Treaties, Directive 2006/123 is more progressive.[130] Although it seems that the service being provided must be legal, that does not

---

[127] See, for example, Case C-268/99 *Jany* [2001] ECR I-8615, [34]–[37] and [38]; Cases C-151/04 and C-152/04 *Nadin* [2005] ECR I-11203, [30]–[31]. It is for the national court, to determine whether or not the relevant element of subordination is absent or present.

[128] Case C-55/94 *Gebhard* (n 3 above) [25].

[129] Art 4(1) of Council Directive 2006/123 (n 11 above).

[130] See the examples provided in ibid recital 33.

mean that all Member States should regard it as such in order for it to constitute a service within the meaning of Articles 56 and 57 TFEU. In *Grogan*, perhaps the most infamous example, the medical termination of pregnancy performed in accordance with the law of the state in which it was carried out was described as a service, despite abortion being considered illegal in the Member State of the potential recipients of services where it was advertised. The Court refused to substitute its own assessment of morality for that of a Member State where a service is legally provided.[131]

The Court defines remuneration in the context of Article 57 TFEU as financial consideration for the service performed, normally fixed by agreement between the person providing the service and its recipients.[132] The requirement that the service be 'normally' provided for remuneration has excluded gratuitous services or services where an insufficient economic link exists between the provider and the ultimate recipient of the service from the scope of application of the Treaty.[133] The requirement of consideration in return for the services provided has, over time, been interpreted flexibly. In *Steymann* the Court qualified as a service work performed by a member of a religious community in return for basic food and accommodation. In so far as the work, which aimed to ensure a measure of self-sufficiency for the religious community, constituted an essential part of participation in that community, the services which the latter provided to its members were regarded as being an indirect *quid pro quo* for their work.[134] To qualify as a service there need not necessarily be a direct legal relationship translated into monetary terms between the provider of a service and its recipient. The Court's case law admits of the possibility that revenue to pay for the service might be generated from a third source, such as, for example, in the form of advertising. In *Bond van Adverteerders*, the Court accepted that Article 57 TFEU does not require that a service be paid for directly by its beneficiaries.[135] It follows that if the abortion clinics whose services were the subject of the preliminary reference in *Grogan* had paid the students' union a nominal fee for the information they distributed the Court would have found it more difficult to dodge the thorny constitutional questions which the case presented.

The Court's case law is less sure-footed as regards what is meant by services 'normally' provided for remuneration and the implications of this definition of

---

[131] See also Case C-275/92 *Schindler* [1994] ECR I-1039 (lotteries) and Case C-268/99 *Jany*, (n 127 above) (prostitution). See, however, Case C-137/09 *Josemans*, judgment of 16 December 2010, on the prohibition of access of non-residents to Dutch coffee shops where the sale and consumption of illegal drugs is tolerated.

[132] See Case 263/86 *Humbel* [1988] ECR 5635, [17], or Case C-157/99 *Smits and Peerbooms* (n 94 above) [58].

[133] Case C-159/90 *Grogan* [1991] ECR I-4685.

[134] Case 196/87 *Steymann* [1988] ECR 6159. Compare the more restrictive treatment pursuant to Art 45 TFEU of an applicant engaged in the activities of a charitable, religious organization in Case C-456/02 *Trojani* (n 120 above).

[135] Case 352/85 *Bond van Adverteerders* [1988] ECR 2085, [16]. See also Cases C-51/96 and C-191/97 *Deliège* [2000] ECR I-2549, [56] or Case C-157/99 *Smits and Peerbooms* (n 94 above), [57]. Contrast the Court's definition of services in the field of VAT, which require reciprocal performance and remuneration corresponding to the value of the service received—see, for example, Case C-246/08 *Commission v Finland* [2009] ECR I-10605, [44].

services for those which are publicly rather than privately funded.[136] Article 57 TFEU suggests that public services, provided by the state, funded essentially by the taxpayer, and provided free to the recipient of services at the point of delivery, or available at a reduced cost or subject to reimbursement, should fall outside the scope of the Treaty provisions on services. As regards publicly funded education, the Court emphasized in *Humbel* that the essential characteristic of remuneration lies in the fact that it constitutes consideration for the service in question, and is normally agreed upon between the provider and the recipient of the service. This essential characteristic was said to be absent as regards courses provided in the context of a national educational system. In establishing and maintaining such a system the state was not seeking to engage in gainful activity, but was simply fulfilling its duties towards its own population in the social, cultural, and educational fields. In addition, such a system is, as a general rule, funded by the public purse and not by pupils (the direct recipients of the service in question) or their parents. The Court also held that the nature of the activity was not affected either by the fact that pupils or their parents must sometimes pay teaching or enrolment fees in order to make a certain contribution to the operating expenses of the system.[137] This reasoning was confirmed in *Wirth* as regards courses given in an institute of higher education which is financed essentially out of public funds.[138] In contrast, where courses are given in private establishments which are financed essentially out of private funds, in particular by students or their parents, and which seek to make an economic profit, the Court held that they become services within the meaning of Article 57 TFEU since the provider is offering the services in question in return for remuneration.[139]

It is clear from sub-section D.3(b), however, that the Court's treatment of publicly funded educational and healthcare services for the purposes of Article 56 TFEU contrasts sharply.[140] The fact that, even prior to the establishment of Union citizenship, access to vocational training was held to come within the scope of application of EU law and EU nationals were declared to have a right of equal access to such training underlines further a degree of artificiality in the exclusion of educational services from

---

[136] Edward and NicShuibhne (n 87 above) [251]–[252] on unanswered questions in this regard.

[137] Case 263/86 *Humbel* (n 9 above), [17]–[18].

[138] Case C-109/92 *Wirth* [1993] ECR I-6447, [15]–[16].

[139] ibid. In addition, services provided on a secondary basis by natural persons called upon by public universities to help them fulfil their mission may constitute services within the meaning of Art 57 TFEU even if, were the services to be provided directly by the full-time staff of those publicly funded institutions, they would fall outwith that provision—see Case C-281/06 *Jundt* [2007] ECR I-12231, [31].

[140] The contrast between the treatment of educational and healthcare services is best illustrated in Case C-372/04 *Watts* (n 92 above), where the patient whose payment for services in another Member State had to be reimbursed pursuant to Art 56 TFEU would, in her own Member State, have had those services provided by a wholly publicly funded, nationalized health service. In that case, the Court reasoned that it did not have to determine whether the provision of hospital treatment in the context of a national health service such as the NHS was in itself a service within the meaning of the Treaty provisions on services. It was sufficient to activate those provisions that a person whose state of health necessitates hospital treatment goes to another Member State and there receives the treatment in question.

the Treaty provisions on services.[141] The establishment of the status of citizenship has served to emphasize this further in two distinct ways. On the one hand, the combined effect of that status and Articles 18 and 21 TFEU has been to reinforce the right of equal access to vocational training by providing Union citizens additionally with a right to equal treatment as regards related financial benefits such as favourable student loans and maintenance grants.[142] Union citizens have a right to access educational services on an equal basis with the host state's nationals and, where they can demonstrate a genuine link with that state, a right to access publicly funded benefits while they do so. On the other hand, the case law of the Court demonstrates that resort can be had to the provisions on Union citizenship if the public nature of the funding of an educational establishment makes recourse to Article 56 TFEU impossible.[143] Thus, the provisions on Union citizenship further subvert the ring-fencing of public educational services in the Court's case law on Articles 56 and 57 TFEU.

If one combines the right of access to vocational training established in *Gravier*, with the ever-evolving rights of Union citizens and the established principle that, even if Member States remain competent in the field of education, they are obliged when exercising that competence to respect the provisions of EU law, there seems to be little reason to continue in such an *ad hoc* manner to intrude on the provision of educational services outside of the ambit of Articles 56 and 57 TFEU. The controversy which has surrounded the Court's trespass into the regulation of cross-border healthcare may of course be relied on to justify the line that has been taken on the exclusion of publicly funded educational services pursuant to these provisions. It is worth asking, however, whether it is preferable to continue to allow restrictions on free movement resulting from the organization and functioning of publicly funded educational services to be policed with reference to vague objectives relating to the encouragement of student and teacher mobility, the provisions of Article 166 TFEU on vocational training, the provisions on Union citizenship, and the amorphous genuine link developed in the Court's case law with respect to that status. Reference to the somewhat more sophisticated justification and proportionality tools developed by the Court pursuant to Article 56 TFEU in the field of healthcare might be more respectful of Member State competence in the field of education and the complex socio-political issues at stake, the latter being the rationale for the exclusion of educational services from the provisions of Article 56 TFEU.[144]

---

[141] See Case 293/83 *Gravier* (n 27 above); Case 24/86 *Blaizot* [1988] ECR 379; Case C-147/03 *Commission v Austria* [2005] ECR I-5969.

[142] See Case C-184/99 *Grzelczyk*, or Case C-209/03 *Bidar* (n 28 above). Subject now to the effects of Art 24(2) of Council Directive 2004/38 (n 7 above) as interpreted in Case C-158/07 *Förster* (n 68 above).

[143] See eg Case C-76/05 *Schwarz and Gootjes-Schwarz* [2007] ECR I-6849.

[144] See, for example, Cases C-11/06 and C-12/06 *Morgan and Bucher* [2007] ECR I-9161, where objective justification is essentially assessed through the prism of the rights of the applicant Union citizen. To date, the distinction between healthcare and education pursuant to Article 56 TFEU has been used to justify not extending the imperative reasons developed with reference to the former to the latter—see the Opinion in Case C-147/03 *Commission v Austria* (n 141 above) [31]–[46], albeit the AG proposed the revision of this distinction in the event that students' rights to equal treatment were extended to maintenance grants.

It is now well-established that it is not necessary for the provider or recipient of services to physically move in order for Article 56 TFEU to apply. The Court has made clear that the mere existence of cross-border recipients of services suffices to bring a case within the scope of application of Article 56 TFEU.[145] In *Carpenter*, the existence of virtual recipients of services located in another Member State sufficed to bring a case concerning the right to reside of a third country national spouse of a self-employed British national, residing in the UK, within the scope of application of Article 56 TFEU.[146] There must, however, be the intention to provide services and the material possibility to provide them. Purely hypothetical receipt of services does not suffice.[147] One of the most important developments regarding Article 56 TFEU over the last decade has been the gradual erosion of the subordinate or residual status of the freedom to provide services, regardless of the continued assertion of the Treaty in this regard. Although in *Gebhard* the Court had made clear that a provider of services could remain within the scope of Article 56 TFEU even if he availed of some sort of infrastructure in the host Member State,[148] it continued to insist on largely temporal criteria to delimit this fundamental freedom. National courts were directed to examine the duration, regularity, periodicity, or continuity of the economic activity in question in order to ascertain whether the provisions on establishment or services applied. Hatzopoulos and others identify a conceptual shift in the Court's qualification of services in recent years and a new reliance on economic as distinct from temporal criteria for this purpose. Thus, in *Schnitzer*, the Court has indicated that services within the meaning of Article 56 and 57 TFEU can vary widely in nature and can include services provided over an extended period, even over several years.[149] This case law clearly calls into question the categorization of the provision of services as being residual or subsidiary to the other fundamental freedoms but it should also raise questions about the lighter regulatory touch which host Member States are meant to reserve for service providers precisely because of the temporary nature of the economic activity in question. In addition, the emergence of Union citizenship as a fifth freedom, offering an alternative source of rights should the services provisions prove inapplicable, further undermines the traditional residual status of Articles 56 and 57 TFEU.

---

[145] Case C-384/93 *Alpine Investments* [1995] ECR I-1141.

[146] Case C-60/00 *Carpenter* [2002] ECR I-6279. See further Section F.2 below.

[147] Compare Case C-215/03 *Oulane* (n 81 above), and Case C-274/96 *Bickel and Franz* (n 42 above).

[148] Case C-55/94 *Gebhard* (n 3 above) [27].

[149] Case C-215/01 [2003] ECR I-14847, [30]. See further Case C-171/02 *Commission v Portugal* [2004] ECR I-5645, [25], and generally V Hatzopoulos, 'The Case-law of the ECJ Concerning the Free Provision of Services: 2000–2005' (2006) 43 CML Rev 923, 927, and Edward and NicShuibhne (n 9 above) 249.

F. REASSESSING THE PLACE AND SCOPE OF THE PROVISIONS ON THE FREE MOVEMENT OF PERSONS

1. FREE MOVEMENT OF PERSONS AND UNION CITIZENSHIP: A TALE OF TWO (UN)HAPPY BEDFELLOWS?

The case law of the Court and Directive 2004/38 reveal to what extent Union citizenship has been constructed on the foundations already laid by established jurisprudence on the free movement of persons. The terminology of the Court in *Cowan*, to the effect that those in situations governed by EU law are entitled not to be discriminated against on grounds of nationality, has been imported into the Union citizenship case law and the provisions on citizenship have in turn expanded what situations can be considered as being governed by that law.[150]

Article 21 TFEU confers directly upon Union citizens the right to move and reside freely across Member States. The exercise, as distinct from the existence, of this right of free movement and residence is subject to the limitations and conditions to which that provision refers in general terms. The latter range from derogations on grounds of public policy to fulfilment of the conditions for residence established first in the 1990 Residence Directives and now in Directive 2004/38.[151] However, in accordance with the Court's case law on Article 21 TFEU, these limitations and conditions must be applied by Member States in accordance with the general principles of EU law, not least, respect for fundamental rights and the principle of proportionality. Withdrawal of a residence permit or refusal to renew one should not be the automatic consequence of a Union citizen having recourse to social benefits in a host Member State.[152] Thus, Member State nationals may, by virtue of their status as Union citizens, have a *prima facie* entitlement to residence and/or equal treatment with respect to a whole range of social benefits but it is legitimate for the Member State from which a benefit is being sought to demand proof, at least as regards indirectly discriminatory conditions for or restrictions of entitlement to welfare provision, of a real, effective, or genuine link with the territory in which the social benefit in question is being claimed. The objective behind the requirement of a real or genuine link is to ensure that the obligation of

---

[150] The denial of any consequence for the material scope of EU law of the introduction of Union citizenship in, for example, Joined Cases C-64/96 and C-65/96 *Uecker and Jacquet* [1997] ECR I-317, [23] is contradicted by the conclusion reached by the Court in Case C-209/03 *Bidar* (n 28 above) [31] and [39]–[40], and Case C-138/02 *Collins* (n 78 above) [63]. Furthermore, the status of Union citizenship continues to push the boundaries as regards what may be considered purely internal situations—see, for example, Case C-135/08 *Rottmann*, 2 March 2010, where the nature and consequences of a Member State decision which would lead to the loss of the status of Union citizenship and the enjoyment of the rights attached thereto led the Court to regard the situation as not a purely internal one.

[151] See the 1990 Residence Directives (n 45 above) and Arts 7 and 8 of Council Directive 2004/38 (n 7 above).

[152] See further Case C-184/99 *Grzelczyk* (n 28 above) [44], and Case C-413/98 *Baumbast* (n 32 above) [92]–[93]. On the implications of the *Baumbast* proportionality test see M Dougan, 'The Constitutional Dimension of the Case Law on Union Citizenship' (2006) 31 ELRev 613.

financial solidarity towards Union citizens is not, from the host state's point of view, stretched beyond acceptable limits.[153]

Where commentators have mainly expressed concern about the Court's case law on Union citizenship it has tended to be with regard to its actual or potential effect on the provision of social welfare in the Member States. The overall focus of these commentaries is on whether the Court's case law in this field, and its extension of social solidarity between Union citizens on the basis of Articles 18, 20, and 21 TFEU, may have a negative impact on the national provision of social welfare, on the organization of national social welfare schemes, and on the bonds of solidarity on which those schemes are traditionally based.[154] Few have questioned whether the case law on Union citizenship may also be having a restrictive impact on established principles of EU law relating to the free movement of persons. It emerges, however, from recent decisions of the Court on the free movement of workers that concepts designed specifically with reference to freely moving, economically inactive Union citizens are being transposed to those economically active EU nationals whose rights predate the establishment of Union citizenship, derive from the original Treaty of Rome, and have been safeguarded to date by an abundant and seemingly unassailable line of jurisprudence.

The requirement of a genuine or real link originated in cases where economically inactive Union citizens were seeking access to social benefits on the basis of a combination of Articles 18, 20, and 21 TFEU and, when necessary or relevant, Regulation 1612/68. Requiring such a link is seen as a legitimate means for Member States to justify any differential treatment of or restrictions on EU citizens claiming benefits, its purpose being essentially to counteract the possibility of abuse and benefit tourism. Such a requirement would seem inappropriate as regards economically active Union citizens precisely because their performance of or involvement in an economic activity presupposes or provides proof of the existence of such a link. In the past, where social benefits were denied such free movers it was because they did not come within the personal scope of application of the free movement provisions, because the benefit in question was held not to constitute a social advantage, or because it did not profit the migrant worker.[155] The genuine link has now emerged as a requirement which Member States can also justifiably impose on migrant workers claiming indirect discrimination or restrictions as regards access to benefits either in their Member State of residence or, in the case of frontier workers, in their Member State of employment.

---

[153] On the suitability or sufficiency of the requirement of a genuine link even for economically active Union citizens see K Hailbronner, 'Union Citizenship and Access to Social Benefits' (2005) 42 CML Rev 1245 or C O'Brien, 'Real Links, Abstract Rights and False Alarms: The Relationship Between the ECJ's "Real Link" Case-law and National Solidarity' (2008) 33 ELRev 643.

[154] eg S Giubboni, 'Free Movement of Persons and Social Solidarity' (2007) 13 ELJ 360 or M Dougan and E Spaventa, '"Wish you Weren't Here"... New Models of Social Solidarity in the European Union' in M Dougan and E Spaventa (eds), *Social Welfare and EU Law* (Hart, 2005) 180–218.

[155] See eg Case C-43/99 *Leclere* [2001] ECR I-4265, [59]–[61]; Case 207/88 *Even* [1979] ECR 2019, [23]–[24], or Case 316/85 *Lebon* (n 77 above) [12]–[13].

In two cases involving frontier workers, both of whom qualified as workers within the meaning of Article 45 TFEU, the Court instructed the national court to verify whether the Member State of employment's refusal to grant these workers child-raising allowances was objectively justified, due to the fact that, although employed in that Member State, they were not resident. The latter argued that a residence condition was objectively justified as it constituted proof of the establishment of a real link with the society of that Member State.[156] The Court accepted as a general principle that the entitlement of a worker to a social benefit could be made dependant on demonstration of the existence of a genuine link between the Member State providing the benefit and the worker seeking it. In *Hartmann*, a case involving a German frontier working, married and resident in Austria, the Court rejected the residence requirement as a valid means of demonstrating a connecting link with the Member State of employment. The existence of other connecting factors permitted by the impugned national legislation—such as a substantial contribution to the national labour market—indicated that residence was not the only valid factor of integration into the society of the Member State of employment justifying entitlement on an equal basis to the child-raising allowance.[157] Imposing a residence requirement on some workers when others could avoid it due to their substantial contribution to the labour market thus lacked coherence and consistency. In *Geven*, however, it accepted that a substantial contribution to the national labour market could be regarded as a valid requirement demonstrating integration into the society of the Member State of employment. The fact that a migrant worker worked full-time or part-time had never previously been considered relevant when it came to consideration of their entitlement not to be discriminated against as regards receipt of social advantages. While the applicant qualified as a migrant worker, the Court imported into its case law on workers, via the requirement of a genuine link, a limitation on the type of social benefit to which this status could give her access.

Hartmann and *Geven* could perhaps be restricted to the particular circumstances of the frontier workers involved and specifically to the part-time nature of the work of one of the applicants. However, those decisions contrast with previous decisions concerning frontier workers where the question of residence conditions and the exportability of social advantages were examined by the Court with reference to more traditional objective justification and proportionality conditions.[158] Under the influence, perhaps indirect and inadvertent, of Union citizenship, this established approach to objective justification and proportionality as regards restrictions to the rights of the economically active EU nationals may no longer hold sway. Other decisions of the Court on the free movement of persons also suggest that one of the consequences of the 'mainstreaming' of the provisions on Union citizenship may be a reversal or, at the very least, an alteration, of the traditional scale of values regarding

---

[156] Case C-212/05 *Hartmann* [2007] ECR I-6303, [32]–[33].

[157] Case C-212/05 *Hartmann* (n 156 above) [36], and Case C-213/05 *Geven* (n 118 above) [25]–[26].

[158] See, for example, Cases C-57/96 *Meints* [1997] ECR I-6689, and C-237/97 *Meeusen* (n 41 above).

economically active and inactive migrants and their families. Job-seekers, who qualify as workers within the meaning of Article 45 TFEU, have equally been subject, when claiming indirect discrimination on grounds of nationality as regards access to social benefits, to the genuine link test.[159] The family of a deceased migrant worker has been refused the right to remain in the host Member State because of the failure of the migrant worker to comply, prior to his death, with a residence condition imposed by secondary legislation on the right to remain.[160] Interpreting that residence condition with a strictness at odds with other decisions on the rights of family members, the Court held that the residence condition in question was intended to establish a significant connection between, on the one hand, the host Member State, and on the other hand, the migrant worker and his family, and to ensure a certain level of integration in the society of that state.[161] In another case involving a frontier worker, this time a Dutch national, resident in Belgium, but claiming a social advantage in a Member State which was both that of his origin and his employment, the Advocate General, referring almost exclusively to case law on Union citizenship, affirmed that the entitlement of a migrant worker to a social benefit can, as a matter of principle, be subject to the requirement of a link or attachment to the host Member State.[162] For its part, the Court held that Article 45 TFEU, 7 of Regulation 1612/68 and the relevant provisions of Regulation 1408/71 do not preclude legislation which grants a social benefit such as that at issue in the case only to persons resident on the national territory.[163] According to the Court, the benefit in question is closely linked to the socio-economic situation in the host Member State, since it is based on the minimum wage and the national standard of living.[164]

The Court's initial eagerness to confirm Union citizenship as the fundamental status of the nationals of the Member States was soon tempered by case law reigning in the potentially far-reaching consequences which the potent combination of Articles 18, 20,

---

[159] See also, as regards job-seekers, whose rights fall to be determined with reference to Art 45 TFEU and not Art 21 TFEU in conjunction with Art 18 TFEU, Case C-138/02 *Collins* (n 78 above) [67], and Case C-258/04 *Ioannidis* (n 80 above) [30]–[33], and above sub-section D.3(b).

[160] Case C-257/00 *Givane* [2003] ECR I-345. The Court interpreted the reference in Regulation 1251/70 (n 38 above) as requiring the migrant worker to have resided in the host Member State continuously in the period of two years immediately preceding his death.

[161] Case C-257/00 *Givane* (n 160 above) [46].

[162] See the Opinion of AG Kokott in Case C-287/05 *Hendrix* (n 120 above) [63]–[64]. Compare with the Opinion of the same AG in Case C-286/03 *Hosse* [2006] ECR I-1771, [112], where the employed person's tax contributions were deemed a sufficient basis for the Member State in question to extend its solidarity and indeed to be obliged to do so.

[163] Given that the benefit in Case C-287/05 *Hendrix* (n 120 above), was a special non-contributory benefit and, as such, was not exportable under the provisions of Regulation 1408/71, the Court's decision to examine Art 7(2) of Regulation 1612/68 (n 38 above) is, in any event, unusual, if not incorrect. Having concluded that it was a non-exportable benefit under the first Regulation all that remained for it to do was to examine the validity of that non-exportability with reference to the provisions of Art 45 TFEU.

[164] See also the sufficiently close connection discussed in Case C-269/07 *Commission v Germany* (n 40 above) [60], involving frontier workers and in Case C-123/08 *Wolzenburg* (n 8 above) [66]–[68], regarding the need to establish a sufficient connection with the Member State of execution of a European Arrest Warrant which would justify its refusal to execute such a warrant.

and 21 TFEU might have in the field of social welfare.[165] It is not clear at this point whether the adoption of Directive 2004/38 will further restrict or expand the rights of Union citizens as existing case law on that Directive points in different directions. That being said, the Court's recent case law can appear surprisingly restrictive with reference to claims brought pursuant to Article 45 TFEU and Regulation 1612/68.[166] What we are witnessing is a general blurring of the distinction between the economically active and inactive without the provision of a coherent framework within which to deal with the claims of either in the future. It is no doubt a good thing that the Court has begun to come to grips with the meaning and scope of the Union citizenship provisions, but it seems odd that the development of that status is at the expense of established case law on the free movement of persons.

2. FREE MOVEMENT OF PERSONS IN AN AREA OF FREEDOM, SECURITY, AND JUSTICE

The creation by Member States of a common market in which the free movement of persons was authorized across national borders pursuant to harmonized supranational rules clearly constituted an incursion on national powers to control immigration. Extending the right of free movement to family members of EEC nationals, regardless of their nationality of origin, eroded that competence further by widening the pool of those who fell outside the scope of application of national immigration rules and whose entry and residence was determined not by national law but additionally, if not exclusively, by EEC and now EU law.

There has been a tendency to view a series of cases which came before the Court in the past decade on the free movement rights of family members as highlighting, essentially for the first time, the conflict between the application by Member States of their normal immigration rules and their obligations under EU free movement rules.[167] This is to ignore, first, the basic but very fundamental changes to national immigration competence which the creation of a common and then internal labour market mandated from the outset; secondly, the import of long-standing secondary legislation adopted to regulate the free movement of EU nationals and their family members, and, thirdly, a long line of cases interpreting both secondary legislation and primary law with a view to clarifying the rights of those persons.

In the absence of express provision in the early Treaties, provisions of secondary legislation on the free movement of persons provided family members of economically

---

[165] Contrast the decisions in Case C-85/96 *Martínez Sala* (n 5 above); Case C-184/99 *Grzelczyk* and Case C-209/03 *Bidar* (n 28 above), with those in Case C-138/02 *Collins* (n 78 above); Case C-406/04 *De Cuyper* [2006] ECR I-6947, or Case C-208/07 *von Chamier-Glisczinki* [2009] ECR I-6095.

[166] See further D Martin, 'De Martínez Sala à Bidar. Les paradoxes de la jurisprudence sur la libre circulation des citoyens' in Guild and Carlier (n 46 above) 160–170, and Giubboni (n 154 above) 370.

[167] See, for example, the terms of the Opinion of AG Geelhoed in Case C-109/01 *Akrich* [2003] ECR I-9607 or, in academic literature, C Dauticourt, 'Citoyenneté de l'Union et politique migratoire' (2008) Revue du Droit de l'Union européenne 858.

active EU nationals, regardless of their nationality of origin, with a right to enter and reside in host Member States equivalent to that granted to those nationals themselves.[168] An examination of the case law to which the early provisions of secondary legislation gave rise indicates that many if not most of the claims relating, for example, to Articles 10 to 12 of Regulation 1612/68 involved third country national family members. They sought, where necessary, to rely on rights of entry and residence which they could derive from EU national spouses and family members where those rights were more favourable when compared with the rights available to them in the given host Member State pursuant to national immigration rules.[169]

Both the Treaty and secondary legislation were silent on the rights of entry and residence of family members on the return of economically active EU nationals to their Member State of origin following the exercise of their free movement rights. The Court held that, for the free movement rights of an EU national to be fully effective, when such a national avails himself of those rights and then returns to his Member State of origin, his spouse and family members must enjoy at least the same rights of entry and residence as would be granted to him under EU law if his spouse chose to enter and reside in another Member State.[170] The rights of returning EU nationals— employed and self-employed—and the derived rights of their family members, are based on Articles 45 and 49 TFEU.[171] Rights of residence for family members of service providers in the provider's Member State of origin have also been located in the Treaty provisions on services. The Court has held that the deportation from that state of the third country national spouse of a service provider would be detrimental to their family life and therefore to the conditions pursuant to which the service provider exercised a fundamental freedom. While Member States might invoke reasons of public interest to justify such a deportation decision, the latter had to be compatible with the fundamental rights whose observance the Court ensures, including the service provider's right to respect for his family life.[172] It appeared to follow from these

---

[168] See Art 10 of Regulation 1612/68 (n 27 above), Arts 1 and 4 of Council Directive 68/360 and Arts 1(c) and 4 of Council Directive 73/148 (n 38 above). Council Directive 2004/38 (n 7 above) now confirms that all Union citizens, regardless of their exercise of an economic activity, albeit more stringent limitations and conditions apply to the family members of those who do not, may now be joined by their family members in the host Member State. See further ibid Arts 2(2), 3(1), 5, 6(2), 7(2), and 16.

[169] See, for example, Joined Cases 35 and 36/82 *Morson and Jhanjan* [1982] ECR I-3723; Case 131/85 *Gül* [1986] ECR I-1573; Case 267/83 *Diatta* (n 51 above); Cases C-297/88 and C-197/89 *Dzodzi* [1990] ECR I-3763; Case C-257/00 *Givane* (n 160 above); Case C-356/98 *Kaba* [2000] ECR I-2623; Case C-413/99 *Baumbast* (n 32 above).

[170] Case C-370/90 *Singh* (n 51 above) [19]–[23].

[171] ibid [21]–[23].

[172] Case C-60/00 *Carpenter* (n 146 above) [39]–[45]. Although the third country spouse in that case had entered the United Kingdom lawfully, she had overstayed her leave to enter and was thus illegally resident when she married the EU national in question. For other cases on the entry and residence rights of third country national family members, including those who have entered the territory of the host Member State unlawfully, see Case C-459/99 *MRAX* [2002] ECR I-6591, [53] and Case C-157/03 *Commission v Spain* [2005] ECR I-2911 [26], where the Court once again interpreted the requirements of EU law with reference to the importance attached by the Union legislature to the protection of family life.

decisions that the illegal status of a third country national prior to their marriage to an EU national was irrelevant as regards the acquisition of EU rights to enter and reside. In addition, the decisions of the Court in those cases were taken with a clear understanding of the concerns expressed forcibly by Member States about the breach which such a conclusion might create in the application of national immigration rules and the risks presented by sham marriages and illegitimate reliance on EU rules to evade national immigration controls. The Court in both *Singh* and *Carpenter* re-assured Member States that it was not only impossible to rely on EU law in order to evade the application of national law but that Member States could take measures to prevent such abuse.

These decisions were followed by the decision of the Court in *Akrich*. In that case, the Court interpreted its previous case law and the provisions of the Treaty and secondary legislation as being limited to freedom of movement within the EU, leaving to Member States the competence to regulate a third country national's first entry into the EU and the first establishment of lawful residence therein. In order to benefit from the rights granted by Article 10 of Regulation 1612/68, the third country national spouse of an EU migrant worker must have been lawfully resident in a Member State when he or she moved to another Member State to which the EU national was migrating or had migrated.[173] Prior lawful residence of a third country national in a Member State was thus a precondition to the exercise of rights to enter and reside *qua* family member of an EU national. The Court reconciled this finding with its previous case law by identifying the objective of the provisions seeking to secure freedom of movement for workers and persons as being to ensure that the migrant worker and his family were not penalized as a result of exercising their Treaty rights. If a family member had not previously resided lawfully in a Member State before seeking to rely in another Member State on a right to reside derived from EU law, migrant workers could not claim to be dissuaded from exercising their free movement rights when refused a right which they and their family member had not in any event previously enjoyed.[174]

The scope of the *Akrich* decision was initially quietly limited by the Court before being categorically overruled. The Court first held that the condition of prior lawful residence in another Member State as formulated in that decision could not be applied to a third country national family member who had lawfully entered the territory of the Member State in which a right of residence *qua* family member was being requested.[175] It then departed from the strict interpretation in *Akrich* of what can be regarded as constituting a deterrent effect restrictive of free movement, holding that barriers to family reunification in themselves, regardless of the performance of an economic activity in the Member State to which the EU national returns, are liable to

---

[173] Case C-109/01 *Akrich* (n 167 above) [50].

[174] On the unclear scope of the Court's decision in ibid. See further E Spaventa, (2005) 42 CML Rev 225, and R Plender, 'Quo vadis? Nouvelle orientation des règles sur la libre circulation des personnes suivant l'affaire Akrich' (2004) Cahiers Dr Euro 261.

[175] Case C-1/05 *Jia* [2007] ECR I-1, [31]–[33].

undermine the right to free movement of EU nationals.[176] Express reconsideration of the *Akrich* thesis came in *Metock*, a case in which the referring court sought to ascertain principally whether Directive 2004/38 precluded a Member State from imposing on third country family members the previous lawful residence condition identified by the Court in the former case.[177] The Court held that no such condition was to be found in the Directive.[178] Its decision to reconsider *Akrich* and the requirement of previous lawful residence was based clearly on previous case law which contradicted the essence of the reasoning in the *Akrich* case.[179] In much more explicit terms than it had employed in *Singh* and *Carpenter*, the Court rejected Member State arguments based on their competence in the field of immigration. The latter did not retain exclusive competence to regulate the first access to the EU of third country national family members regardless of a context typified, according to the intervening Member States, by strong pressure of migration. Directive 2004/38 was but an instrument adopted by the Member States pursuant to Articles 21, 46, and 50 TFEU with a view to achieving the objectives of the Treaty as regards the freedom of movement of Union citizens. The refusal of a Member State to grant a right of entry and residence to third country national family members of EU nationals discourages those EU nationals from availing of their free movement rights even if those family members have not previously resided in a Member State, even if marriage has been contracted after the exercise by the EU nationals of their free movement rights and even if the third country national is illegally resident in the host Member State when marriage is contracted and a derived right of residence is sought.[180] The Court sought

[176] Case C-291/05 *Eind* [2007] ECR I-10719, [36]–[37]. In rejecting Member States' arguments to the effect that, for a third country family member to enjoy a right of residence on the return of an EU national to his Member State of origin, that family member must have been lawfully resident in that Member State before the exercise of free movement rights elsewhere, the Court held that such an interpretation ran counter to the express provisions of EU law and to its objectives, principally the importance of ensuring protection for the family life of EU nationals in order to eliminate obstacles to the exercise of the fundamental freedoms (Case C-291/05 *Eind* [43]–[44]).

[177] Case C-127/08 *Metock* (n 76 above). A report by the European Commission to the European Parliament and the Council on the transposition of Directive 2004/38 confirmed that Denmark, Finland, and the United Kingdom had incorporated the *Akrich* condition in their transposing legislation and that seven other Member States had interpreted the Directive as incorporating the same condition in their administrative guidelines (COM(2008) 840/3).

[178] Case C-127/08 *Metock* (n 76 above) [49]–[57].

[179] See, in particular, Case C-459/99 *MRAX* (n 172 above) [59] and [62]: '[T]he right of a third country national married to a Member State national to enter the territory of the Member States derives under Community law from the family ties alone [. . .]', and Case C-503/03 *Commission v Spain* [2006] ECR I-1097, [28].

[180] Case C-127/08 *Metock* (n 76 above) [87]–[93]. The paucity of the Court's reasoning in *Metock* and its failure to justify or explain why Case C-109/01 *Akrich* (n 167 above), was being overruled has been criticized— see S Currie, 'Accelerated Justice or a Step Too Far? Residence Rights of Non-EU Family Members and the Court's Ruling in Metock' (2009) 34 ELRev 310. This is somewhat surprising given that the reasoning of the Court in the case—particularly the examination of the legal status and content of Council Directive 2004/38 (n 7 above) and the relationship of *Akrich* with the body of the Court's case law on the rights of family members—is considerably clearer and more extensive than many of its other decisions in the series of cases reviewed in this section, not least *Akrich*, Case C-1/05 *Jia* (n 175 above), and C-60/00 *Carpenter* (n 146 above).

to assuage Member State fears regarding the possible consequences of such an interpretation of EU free movement law with reference to the controls which Member States may exercise pursuant to the terms of Directive 2004/38 and EU law generally to deal with marriages of convenience and other abuses of immigration controls.[181]

The *Akrich* decision could be regarded merely as another judicial anomaly; a prime example of a bad case making bad law and the consequence of the tendency of the Court in recent years to indulge in a case by case assessment of preliminary references, sometimes resulting in a loss of clarity and consistency and the obfuscation of principle, all of which would seem anathema to the success of that procedure. Although such an analysis may be partly correct, it fails to explore if and why the Court's reasoning in that case clashed with existing jurisprudence. The Court in *Akrich* had emphasized that its interpretation of Regulation 1612/68 was consistent with the structure and purpose of EU provisions on the free movement of persons. While it examined the rights of free movement of EU nationals with reference to Article 45 TFEU—in accordance with *Singh*, *Carpenter*, and *MRAX*—it framed its answer as regards the derived rights of the third country national spouse exclusively in terms of Regulation 1612/68. With reference to Directive 2004/38, the Court in *Metock* demolished this sequence of reasoning by underlining that that Directive was merely an instrument of secondary legislation designed to implement the free movement rights guaranteed by primary law. While the rights of family members may be regulated by secondary legislation they ultimately derive from the Treaty itself. The conflict with previous case law was clearly identified by the Court in *Metock*.[182]

Perhaps the best explanation for the *Akrich* decision can be gleaned from the Opinion of the Advocate General, who characterized the case as a head-on collision between the competence of Member States to regulate immigration and the competence of the EU to regulate the free movement of persons. He concluded that the case was not about free movement within the EU but about Member States' competence to subject a third country national's first entry to the EU to an individual assessment in accordance with their increasingly stringent immigration rules.[183] In his view, application of those rules in circumstances such as those presented to the Court in the *Akrich* case, albeit restrictive of the EU national's free movement rights, constituted an overriding public interest justification. Although the Opinion in *Akrich* overplays the novelty of the clash between national immigration rules and the rules on free movement, it did identify something new in the political and legal zeitgeist. The case law prior to *Akrich* had been decided with reference purely to the dynamics of internal free movement and it was partly if not

---

[181] See, in particular, Art 27 of Directive 2004/38 (n 7 above) on restrictions on free movement on grounds of public policy and Art 35 on abuse of rights.

[182] The Court's reference in Case C-127/8 *Metock* (n 76 above) to previous case law could, however, have been more extensive, stretching back for decades to case law which quite simply disavowed the statement made in Case C-109/01 *Akrich* (n 167 above) to the effect that Regulation 1612/68 (n 27 above) was silent as to the rights of a third country national, married to an EU national, in regard to access to the territory of the EU. See the case law cited in n 169 above.

[183] See the Opinion in Case C-109/01 *Akrich* (n 167 above) [130]–[148].

principally based on the increasing importance accorded to the protection of the right to respect for family life as an independent right of EU nationals and as itself an objective of the free movement rules. These cases were vivid examples of the transformation of the EEC and EC's objectives in the field of free movement from purely or principally economic objectives to ones influenced by social and humanitarian concerns. The Advocate General, however, located *Akrich* within a wider and more complex legal and political context—that of a nascent area of freedom, security, and justice where 'internal' free movement rules were only part of a complex division of competence between the EU and Member States as regards migration into and inside the EU generally.

The decision in *Metock* reasserted the terms of the traditional equation of internal free movement bolstered by the humanitarian concerns outlined above. However, although that decision may have extinguished the specific restrictive condition established in *Akrich*, it is unlikely to stifle the debate on the consequences for internal EU free movement rules of the extension of EU competence in the wider field of justice and home affairs. Concepts such as residence or public policy, which have been interpreted and applied by the Court for years within the more limited confines of Articles 45, 49, and 56 TFEU, have now been extended not simply to economically inactive freely moving Union citizens, but now fall to be applied in the context of framework decisions and regulations on subjects entirely new to the EU, not least the European Arrest Warrant or issues relating to child custody.[184] In the wider context of an area of freedom, security, and justice, principles such as that prohibiting discrimination on grounds of nationality, which have proved a fertile source of protection for EU nationals, whether economically active or inactive, may acquire a somewhat different complexion.[185] The political reaction to the *Metock* judgment further confirms that although the judicial anomaly which was *Akrich* has now been remedied, the wider legislative and political forces which may have contributed to that departure from previous case law have far from disappeared.[186] An area of freedom, security, and justice was established to facilitate the free movement of persons but also to ensure the safety and security of EU nationals.[187] In a world subject to, or perceived to be subject

[184] See, for example, the terms of Framework Decision 2002/584/JHA of 13 June 2002 on the European Arrest Warrant and the surrender procedures between Member States [2002] OJ L190/1 as interpreted in Case C-66/08 *Kozlowski* (n 8 above) and the case law cited in n 8 above.

[185] Once again, in the context of the framework decision on the European Arrest Warrant, see the judgment in Case C-123/08 *Wolzenburg* (n 8 above) [74]. In the case of a national of another Member State having a right of residence on the basis of Art 21(1) TFEU, the refusal to execute the Arrest Warrant was subject to a condition imposed by national law that the person in question had lawfully resided for a continuous period of five years in the Member State of execution. The Court held that Art 18 TFEU did not preclude such a difference in treatment. The five-year condition imposed by Council Directive 2004/38 (n 7 above) for the acquisition of a permanent right of residence for Union citizens was used to justify this difference in treatment.

[186] See, for example, the discussions at the Justice and Home Affairs Council, Brussels, 25 September 2008 where several Member States, some more vociferously than others, expressed concern that the judgment in Case C-127/08 *Metock* (n 76 above), would have serious implications for Member States' efforts to tackle marriages of convenience and provide greater opportunities for trafficking and smuggling.

[187] See 10th recital of the preamble to the TEU, inserted by the Treaty of Amsterdam. See, even more forcefully, Art 3(2) TEU, as amended by the Treaty of Lisbon.

to, far greater security threats than in the past, the potential for friction between these two objectives may present a considerable challenge to the values which have traditionally underpinned EU law on the free movement of persons as identified in Part C. In *Metock*, the Court was able to rely on the fact that the legislature, when adopting Directive 2004/38, did not choose to codify the *Akrich* precondition. Admittedly, that was but one, and not necessarily the strongest, of the reasons it advanced for the reconsideration of that judgment. However, what if that Directive had included that precondition for the enjoyment by third country national family members of a right to enter and reside? Would the Court, despite the clear contradiction between *Akrich* and previous case law derived from Article 45 TFEU, nevertheless have asserted with such vigour the primacy of the requirements of that primary law? The terms of *Metock* suggest that it could have done so. Other decisions examined in the context of recent codification exercises render such an outcome less certain.

G. CONCLUSIONS

Two factors which have dominated the evolution of EU law on the free movement of persons and services over the last decade look set to influence its development in the next. On the one hand, although it took several years, Union citizenship has, over the last decade, demonstrated that it has real teeth. The development of that status, with reference to and indeed on the basis of the principles developed previously as regards the free movement of economically active Member State nationals, has had an unsettling effect on those established principles. Union citizenship has influenced not only those who can be considered to be in a situation governed by EU law but also the material scope of that law and consequently the scope of application of the principle of non-discrimination on grounds of nationality in its various general and specific forms of expression. The coming years will bring further clarification of the scope and limits of the status of Union citizenship and the consequences of the creation of this fifth fundamental freedom for the established four. Many questions remain to be answered, not least the effect of this status for the free movement of persons in an area of freedom, security, and justice or in the context of a reassessment of the scope of and rationale for the Court's traditional exclusion of purely internal situations from the scope of application of EU law.[188] The decision of the Court in *Rottmann* on the relationship between Member State nationality and Union citizenship and the effect of the loss of the former on the exercise of the rights derived from the latter suggest that what can be regarded as being purely internal may have to be fundamentally reassessed in the future.

---

[188] See, in this respect, the Opinion in Case C-212/06 *Government of the French Community and Walloon Government v Flemish Government* [2008] ECR I-1683, [134]–[157] and, generally, S O'Leary, 'The Past, Present and Future of the Purely Internal Rule' forthcoming [2010] *Irish Jurist*.

On the other hand, the review and codification of secondary legislation governing the free movement of persons and services has played a vital role in reshaping and clarifying the applicable provisions. It is likely that what will characterize this field in the coming years is the interaction between principles developed, in the absence of comprehensive secondary legislation, directly on the basis of the Treaty provisions and this expanded or revised secondary legislation. The integration of this new, codified legislation into the body of EU law may occur seamlessly. Where, however, the codified legislation is in tension with principles established previously with reference to the provisions of primary law, it will be interesting to see how the Court will reconcile the requirements of the existing *acquis* with the provisions of this new generation of secondary legislation.

18

FREE MOVEMENT OF CAPITAL: EVOLUTION AS A NON-LINEAR PROCESS

*Jukka Snell**

Free movement of capital was described as the last of the freedoms by the Spaak Report,[1] and so it has proven in practice. The freedom developed more slowly than the others and has arguably still not reached full maturity. Yet the current formulation of the free movement of capital in the Treaty gives it pride of place. Alone among the four freedoms its effects are not limited to the intra-EU context, but also relate to movements of capital between the Member States and third countries. It is not only a part of the internal market, but also a critical aspect of the economic and monetary union. It has the potential to impinge significantly on one of the most sensitive and fundamental aspects of statehood, namely national tax autonomy, and the liberalization of capital movements may have important consequences for national varieties of capitalism. It also provides a new frontier for the European Court of Justice to explore, whether as an agent of the Member States faithfully enforcing the bargains struck by them, or as a significant player in its own right shaping the law in accordance with its own agenda.

The chapter will begin by offering a broad macro-level overview of the evolution of the free movement of capital, focusing in particular on the interplay between the various actors in the political and legal system of the Union. It will then zoom to a more micro-level, investigating how the Court's approach to the concept of restriction has developed in the last fifteen years or so, and analysing the tension that has emerged

* I wish to thank Mads Andenas, Catherine Barnard, and Volker Röben for their helpful comments. The abbreviation 'TFEU' used after a Treaty article refers to the Treaty on the Functioning of the European Union. 'EC' after a Treaty article refers to a provision of the European Community Treaty in the version in force until 30 November 2009, while 'EEC' refers to the European Economic Community Treaty. Where possible, the new numbering has been used.

[1] Report of the Heads of Delegations to the Foreign Ministers at the Messina Conference, 21 April 1956. The report envisaged safeguard clauses on movements of capital beyond the transitional period, due to the national autonomy in budgetary, financial, and social fields, and the lack of a single currency.

between regulatory and tax matters. Finally, it will seek to examine the likeliest source of significant future developments in the field, namely the application of the freedom to capital movements between the EU and third countries. It will be argued that in the early years of the Community the Member States were the driving force for the development of the law. Since the mid-1990s, the Court has come to play a more prominent part, following the rewriting of the free movement of capital rules. However, while the Court's case law up until 2006 posed a significant challenge to the Member States, more recently it has shown a willingness to moderate its jurisprudence in key respects. Nevertheless, it is clear that the evolution of this area of law has not yet come to an end.[2]

A. THE DEVELOPMENT OF THE FREEDOM

The free movement of capital has undergone perhaps the most dramatic metamorphosis of all the freedoms. From humble beginnings as a weakly worded Treaty Article with little legal or practical significance, it has developed into a powerful liberalizing force both within and outside the EU. Interestingly, while the European Court of Justice and the Commission have played a part in this evolution, the contribution of the Member States has been more significant, in particular in the early years. After the Maastricht Treaty the Court took a more prominent role, something that the Member States have partially sought to curtail in the Lisbon Treaty. A study of the developments therefore not only reveals interesting insights into European economic law, but also into the more general institutional dynamics in the EU.

The original EEC Treaty treated the free movement of capital differently from the other freedoms. While goods, persons, and services were dealt with by provisions that contained prohibitions of restrictions, those on capital were more subdued. Article 67 (1) EEC provided that:

> [d]uring the transitional period and to the extent necessary to ensure the proper functioning of the common market, Member States shall progressively abolish between themselves all restrictions on the movement of capital belonging to persons resident in Member States and any discrimination based on the nationality or on the place of residence of the parties or on the place where such capital is invested.

Critically, capital movements were therefore only to be liberalized 'to the extent necessary'. Article 69 EEC authorized the Council to issue directives to achieve the progressive liberalization, while the stand-still provision Article 71 EEC exhorted the Member States to refrain from adopting new restrictions.

The Court was called to interpret Article 67 EEC in *Casati* in 1981,[3] well after it had delivered seminal judgments such as *Dassonville*, *Cassis de Dijon*, *Reyners*, and *Van*

---

[2] See J Usher, 'The Evolution of the Free Movement of Capital' (2008) 31 Fordham Int'l LJ 1533 for another recent treatment of the free movement of capital from an evolutionary perspective.

[3] Case 203/80 *Casati* [1981] ECR 2595.

Binsbergen on other freedoms.[4] Mr Casati, an Italian national living in Germany, was caught leaving Italy with 24,000 Deutschmarks. He explained that he had brought them to Italy in order to buy some equipment for his business in Germany, but was now taking them back as the factory at which he had intended to make the purchases was closed for holidays. He was prosecuted for violating a 1976 Italian law that prohibited the unauthorized export of currency. The Court, following Advocate General Capotorti, ruled that Community law did not prevent the prosecution. Article 67(1) EEC did not abolish the restrictions on the exportation of bank notes and the stand-still provision in Article 71 EEC lacked direct effect, as it only declared that Member States would 'endeavour to avoid introducing' new restrictions.

The ruling in *Casati* differed fundamentally from those delivered in the fields of goods, persons, and services. There the Court had been prepared to rely directly on the Treaty provisions to achieve liberalization even in the absence of secondary legislation. This had in no way been the inevitable conclusion from the wording of the Treaty. It would have been equally possible to see these Treaty Articles as programmatic commands aimed at the Community legislature, rather than as directly applicable rules of law.[5] Yet the Court chose to remedy the inaction of the Member States in the Council and push for the common market. Why the difference? After all, as the Court itself pointed out in the judgment, all the relevant rules were part of the foundations of the Community, could be characterized as fundamental freedoms, and were in practice interconnected. It seems that three issues were decisive. First, as pointed out above, the wording of the Treaty on capital was less categorical than for the other freedoms. This may not have been sufficient on its own, however. In numerous decisions the Court has shown a willingness to ignore the nuances of wording in favour of a more contextual teleological understanding of the law,[6] a course of action proposed in *Casati* by the German government, which argued that the language of the provision did not introduce a condition for abolition of restrictions but simply limited its scope.[7] Secondly, the Court explicitly pointed out the political sensitivity of the matter, in particular at a time of unrest on the currency markets,[8] and its intimate connection to policy areas where the Member States retained full competence at the relevant time.[9] It should be noted here that the liberalization of capital movements entails a significant

---

[4] Case 8/74 *Dassonville* [1974] ECR 837; Case 120/78 *Rewe-Zentral AG v Bundesmonopolverwaltung für Branntwein* [1979] ECR 649; Case 2/74 *Reyners* [1974] ECR 631; Case 33/74 *Van Binsbergen* [1974] ECR 1299.

[5] V Skouris, 'Fundamental Rights and Fundamental Freedoms: The Challenge of Striking a Delicate Balance' (2006) 17 EBL Rev 225, 227.

[6] See generally eg P Craig and G de Búrca, *EU Law: Text, Cases, and Materials* (4th edn, Oxford University Press, 2007) 72–76.

[7] *Casati* (n 3 above) 2603.

[8] A F P Bakker, *The Liberalization of Capital Movements in Europe: The Monetary Committee and Financial Integration 1958–1994* (Kluwer, 1996) 47.

[9] See M Andenas, 'Who is Going to Supervise Europe's Financial Markets' in M Andenas and Y Avgerinos (eds), *Financial Markets in Europe: Towards a Single Regulator?* (Kluwer Law International, 2003) xvi–xviii on the rationale for capital controls, and more generally W Molle, *The Economics of European Integration: Theory, Practice, Policy* (5th edn, Ashgate, 2006) 120–123.

reduction in the national exchange and interest rate autonomy. Essentially, capital movements will either require the exchange rate to adjust to in- and outflows, or interest rates will have to be used to defend the exchange rate.[10] Again this may not have been decisive; the Court has in general not shown reticence in intervening in areas such as direct taxation and healthcare where Member State competence is similarly paramount, although admittedly the majority of these judgments are of more recent vintage.[11] Finally, this was not a field where the Council had failed to act, as in the case of establishment and services at the time of the key judgments in *Reyners* and *Van Binsbergen*.[12] Instead, the Council had adopted Directives defining its stance on the matter, and had expressly decided not to liberalize the physical exportation of financial assets. In general, the Court has tended to show deference towards the Union legislature that Member States would not enjoy.[13] The end result of *Casati* was that the Court refused to take a leadership role in the area of the free movement of capital, despite the fact that it had been willing to embrace this position in respect of the other freedoms. Instead, it showed deference towards Member State sensitivities and the decisions of those states in the Council.

The role of the Commission was unusual as well. In the early years, it had pushed for liberalization, successfully proposing the First and Second Capital Directives, which were adopted in 1960 and 1962,[14] but failing to secure agreement in the Council for a Third Directive.[15] However, it completely reversed its course in the 1970s, successfully putting forward a Directive that required Member States to develop instruments to stop undesirable capital flows,[16] and tolerating national safeguard measures of unlimited duration, thus stepping back from the earlier liberalization and institutionalizing restrictions on capital movements in the Community. In the early 1980s, it resisted proposals for liberalization that had been put forward by the Netherlands with British and German support, and was only gradually brought to the cause of free movement.[17]

---

[10] The impossibility of having at the same time a fixed exchange rate, an independent monetary policy, and free capital movements is known in international economics as the impossible trinity. See eg A El-Agraa, 'The theory of monetary integration' in A M El-Agraa (ed), *The European Union: Economics and Policies* (8th edn, Cambridge University Press, 2007) 205.

[11] But not all, see in particular Case 270/83 *Commission v France* [1986] ECR 273.

[12] See cases in n 4 above.

[13] M Poiares Maduro, *We The Court: The European Court of Justice and the European Economic Constitution* (Hart, 1998) 76–78; J Snell, 'Who's Got the Power? Free Movement and Allocation of Competences in EC Law' (2003) 22 YEL 323, 345–350.

[14] First Council Directive 60/921 (EEC) for the implementation of Art 67 of the Treaty [1959–1962] OJ Spec Ed 49 and Second Council Directive 63/21 (EEC) adding to and amending the First Directive for the implementation of Art 67 of the Treaty [1963–1964] OJ Spec Ed 5. See P Oliver and J-P Baché, 'Free Movement of Capital Between the Member States: Recent Developments' (1989) 26 CML Rev 61, 73–81 on the case law under the Directives, which they describe as 'timid'.

[15] COM(64) 128.

[16] Council Directive 72/156 (EEC) on regulating international capital flows and neutralizing their undesirable effects on domestic liquidity [1972] OJ L91/13.

[17] Bakker (n 8 above) 154–156.

Instead of the European institutions, the driving force was the Member States. In the early 1960s the Directives that were successfully adopted largely served to consolidate the unilateral measures of the states.[18] The attempt to push beyond these was unsuccessful, and when the Member States resorted to capital controls at the end of the 1960s and the beginning of the 1970s, the Commission provided them with support. Only when a number of key countries liberalized their policies in the early 1980s, and in particular following the change of heart in France,[19] did the Commission once again emerge as a supporter of the free movement of capital.[20]

The decisive breakthrough for the free movement of capital took place in the late 1980s. The Commission 1985 White Paper on Completing the Internal Market portrayed capital as a vital ingredient of the single market,[21] and this was confirmed by the definition of the internal market in the Single European Act 1986, if not yet by the substantive provisions of the Treaty. It was only in 1990 that the actual liberalization took place, following the adoption of a new Directive in 1988,[22] and coinciding with the start of the first stage of the economic and monetary union. The liberalization was finally written into the EC Treaty at Maastricht in 1991,[23] although the provisions only entered fully into force in 1994 when the second stage of the EMU commenced.[24] The timing underlined the fact that the free movement of capital not only constituted an element of the internal market but was also an essential aspect of the EMU.

The provisions adopted in the Maastricht Treaty are still in force today. They enshrine the free movement of capital, but also contain potentially significant exceptions. Article 63 TFEU is framed in uncompromising terms, prohibiting 'all restrictions on the movement of capital between Member States and between Member States and third countries'. Remarkably and uniquely, the freedom therefore applies both to intra- and extra-EU situations. However, Articles 64 and 66 TFEU offer the Member States or the Council opportunities to restrict the free movement of capital to or from third countries, and Article 65 TFEU contains a number of derogations allowing the Member States to limit capital movements generally. Particularly interestingly, Article 65(1)(a) TFEU permits Member States 'to apply the relevant provisions of their tax law which distinguish between taxpayers who are not in the same situation with regard to their place of residence or with regard to the place where their capital is invested',[25] while Article 65(1)(b) TFEU allows them *inter alia* 'to take all requisite measures to prevent infringements of national law and regulations, in particular in the field of

---

[18] ibid 88 and 93.   [19] ibid 153–154.

[20] In the mid- and late 1980s the Commission pushed liberalization strongly forward. However, in the context of the 1993 currency crisis it again toyed with the idea of capital controls, only to be discouraged in this by the more liberal instincts displayed by Germany and the UK. See ibid 239.

[21] COM(85) 310 final, 32–34.

[22] Council Directive 88/361 (EEC) for the implementation of Art 67 of the Treaty [1988] OJ L178/5.

[23] Art 73b EC.

[24] Arts 73h and 109e EC.

[25] Declaration on Art 73d of the Treaty establishing the European Community [1992] OJ C191 confined it to laws in effect at the end of 1993 in the case of intra-EU capital movements.

taxation and the prudential supervision of financial institutions'. The Treaty was thus sending slightly mixed messages: the Member States wanted both free movement of capital and national tax autonomy. Following the general move towards more market-oriented economic policies and the aim of EMU, they were content to see the liberalization of capital movements, but did not wish their tax policies to be interfered with.

The Court now assumed the leadership position that it had been accustomed to in the context of the other freedoms. It found that Article 63 TFEU was directly effective. It adopted a wide understanding of what amounts to a restriction, opting for language that focused on the dissuading or deterring effects of national measures, rather than on their disparate impact.[26] Significantly, it also limited the exceptions contained in Article 65 TFEU. In *Veerkoijen* the Full Court, following Advocate General La Pergola and contrary to the submissions of all the intervening governments, reasoned that rather than being a new invention, Article 65(1)(a) TFEU was merely a codification of its earlier case law in the fields of services and workers,[27] and in any event was subject to the third paragraph of the same Article, which prohibits arbitrary discrimination and disguised restrictions.[28] As a result, the Court went on to apply its normal rule of reason test, in particular rejecting purely economic considerations, finding that tax cohesion arguments failed on the facts due to the lack of a direct link between the tax advantage and the offsetting levy, and that unfavourable tax treatment could not be justified by the existence of other tax advantages. A similar approach was taken by the Grand Chamber four years later in *Manninen*.[29] In other words, Article 65(1) (a) TFEU made no difference whatsoever to the rulings. The Court proceeded just as it would have done in its absence. The inclusion of the exception in the Treaty was superfluous.[30]

The Member States reacted to the jurisprudence with some alarm. In particular, the application of the full force of the internal market law in the field of taxation caused disquiet. There is a basic tension between the idea of a single market and the territorially based national tax systems. This manifests for example in the traditional starting point of the free movement law that differential treatment of residents and non-residents constitutes indirect discrimination on grounds of nationality,[31] unless justified, and the basic premise of national tax systems, which typically tax residents on the basis of their worldwide income and non-residents on the basis of their income earned in the state in question. In other words, residence is a highly suspect

---

[26] Discussed fully in Part B below.

[27] See in particular Case C-204/90 *Bachmann* [1992] ECR I-249; Case C-279/93 *Schumacker* [1995] ECR I-225.

[28] Case C-35/98 *Verkooijen* [2000] ECR I-4071. See in the context of Art 65(1)(b) TFEU Case C-478/98 *Commission v Belgium* [2000] ECR I-7587, [37]–[47]; J Usher, *The Law of Money and Financial Services in the EC* (2nd edn, Oxford University Press, 2000) 33–37.

[29] Case C-319/02 *Manninen* [2004] ECR I-7477.

[30] For criticism, S Peers, 'Free movement of capital: learning lessons or slipping on spilt milk?' in C Barnard and J Scott (eds), *The Law of the Single European Market* (Hart, 2002) 348–349.

[31] See, eg, *Schumacker* (n 27 above) [28].

distinguishing criterion in Union law, but the generally accepted distinguishing criterion in national and international tax law.[32] The Member States perceived the danger of a significant erosion of their tax bases and made strong interventions, sometimes with warnings of revenue losses of cataclysmic proportions.[33] The international tax law community provided some support for the states with many critical analyses of the Court's case law.[34] The Court may have proven receptive to the concerns of the Member States. It altered the course of its jurisprudence, in particular toning down the language of restrictions in the tax context.[35] Member States that had essentially lost all the tax cases in the Court started winning again.[36]

However, at the same time the Member States sought to wrestle even more of the initiative into their hands. The Treaty of Lisbon inserted a new Article 65(4) TFEU,[37] which provides that:

[i]n the absence of measures pursuant to Article 64(3) [which allows the Council to restrict the free movement of capital to and from third countries], the Commission or, in the absence of a Commission decision within three months from the request of the Member State concerned, the Council, may adopt a decision stating that restrictive tax measures adopted by a Member State concerning one or more third countries are to be considered compatible with the Treaties in so far as they are justified by one of the objectives of the Union and compatible with the proper functioning of the internal market. The Council shall act unanimously on application by a Member State.

The provision bears a certain resemblance to the controversial[38] Article 108(2)(3) TFEU which allows the Council to declare certain state aids compatible with the internal market 'if justified by exceptional circumstances'.

Article 65(4) TFEU is remarkable in that it places the Member States in the Council in the position to rule on the legality of national measures, something that is normally reserved for the Court. In this it goes even further than Article 108(2)(3) TFEU, which merely replaces a decision of the Commission. The criteria employed—justification by one of the objectives of the EU and compatibility with functioning of the internal market—are extremely wide, and do not in practice curtail the discretion of the Council much. It can be anticipated that Member States may seek to use the procedure to shield themselves against potential litigation. Apart from the difficulties private parties will face regarding *locus standi* if they seek to proceed under Article 263

---

[32] See generally BJM Terra and PJ Wattel, *European Tax Law* (5th edn, Kluwer Law International, 2008) 715–720.

[33] See eg Case C-446/04 *FII Group Litigation* [2006] ECR I-11753, [222] and Case C-292/04 *Meilicke* [2007] ECR I-1835, [61] of the Opinion of AG Stix-Hackl.

[34] See P J Wattel, 'Red Herrings in Direct Tax Cases Before the ECJ' (2004) 31 LIEI 81 for a particularly scathing example.

[35] See Part B below.

[36] S Kingston, 'A Light in the Darkness: Recent Developments in the ECJ's Direct Tax Jurisprudence' (2007) 44 CML Rev 1321, 1335–1336.

[37] The provision made its first appearance as an amendment to the Draft Constitutional Treaty by the IGC in 2004.

[38] See eg the Opinion of AG Jacobs in Case C-110/02 *Commission v Council* [2004] ECR I-6333, [22].

TFEU,[39] the wide discretion granted to the Council will make the judicial review of its decisions difficult. From a wider perspective, the inclusion of the Article in the Lisbon Treaty clearly demonstrates a distrust of the Court on the part of the Member States when it comes to deciding on tax matters and their willingness to curtail the free movement of capital to and from third countries.[40] The Court, for its own part, seems to have received the message sent by the Member States, and has chosen to tread lightly in the third country context.[41]

Altogether, the story of the historical development of the free movement of capital differs significantly from the stories told about the other freedoms. Instead of a determined Court and an enlightened Commission providing leadership for the reluctant Member States, in the early period the Member States were very much in the driving seat, with the Court silent and the Commission at times even an outright opponent of liberalization. Only when a sufficient number of states had unilaterally decided to relax their capital controls did the European institutions spring into action. After the Maastricht Treaty the Court in particular did seek to assume a leadership role, but in the end had to curtail some of its expansionist case law in the face of the resistance of the Member States, who also inserted a new clause to the Treaty at Lisbon to ensure their control of certain key decisions. From the perspective of the theoretical accounts of European integration,[42] the free movement of capital thus displays features of liberal intergovernmentalism, which is not the framework the four freedoms have traditionally been associated with.[43]

B. THE NOTION OF RESTRICTION

The most important and the most contested issue in the development of the case law is how the notion of a restriction is to be defined. As is well known, the answers given by the European Court of Justice to this question have varied both in time and among the freedoms.[44] It is less often remarked that there is also a significant tension within the freedoms, a matter that is particularly visible in the case of the free movement of

---

[39] Case 25/62 *Plaumann* [1963] ECR 95 on individual concern and Case T-69/99 *DSTV v Commission* [2000] ECR II-4039 on direct concern, although Art 263(4) TFEU does relax the standing rules when compared with Art 230(4) EC.

[40] See also M O'Brien, 'Taxation and the Third Country Dimension of Free Movement of Capital in EU Law: The ECJ's Rulings and Unresolved Issues' [2008] BTR 628, 661–662.

[41] See Part C below.

[42] See generally eg A Wiener and T Diez (eds), *European Integration Theory* (2nd edn, Oxford University Press, 2009).

[43] See eg A Stone Sweet, *Governing with Judges: Constitutional Politics in Europe* (Oxford University Press, 2000) 178–183, and 190–193; MA Pollack, *The Engines of European Integration: Delegation, Agency, and Agenda Setting in the EU* (Oxford University Press, 2003) 299–322.

[44] See eg J Snell, 'And then there were two: products and citizens in Community law' in T Tridimas and P Nebbia (eds), *European Union Law for the Twenty-first Century: Rethinking the New Legal Order. Vol II* (Hart, 2004).

capital.[45] This tension relates to the different treatment given to regulatory and fiscal rules.[46]

The approach of the Court towards national regulatory measures has been expansive,[47] in line with the approach adopted for the free movement of persons and services. After confirming the direct effect of the 1988 Capital Directive[48] and Article 63 TFEU,[49] it began using language that made it clear that the free movement of capital was not only concerned with discriminatory rules but had a much wider scope. For example, in *Trummer and Mayer* the Court found that the relevant Austrian law, which only permitted the registration of a mortgage if it was denominated in Austrian schillings, constituted a restriction as it was 'liable to dissuade the parties concerned from denominating a debt in the currency of another Member State' and 'may well cause the contracting parties to incur additional costs'.[50]

The broad scope given to the concept of restriction can be best seen in the case law on golden shares. In *Commission v UK*[51] the Full Court condemned the arrangements flowing out of the privatization of the British Airports Authority BAA. Although the BAA had been converted to a limited company, the government had retained a special share which according to the articles of association allowed it to veto certain key decisions, such as disposing of airports, and also to prevent anybody from acquiring more than 15 per cent of the voting rights in the company. The UK government argued that the Treaty freedoms were not violated as there was no discrimination and market access was not restricted. While Advocate General Ruiz-Jarabo Colomer described the arguments as very persuasive,[52] the Court was not impressed. It reasoned that Article 63 TFEU goes beyond the mere elimination of discrimination and that the UK rules 'affect the position of a person acquiring a shareholding as such and are thus liable to deter investors from other Member States from making such investments and, consequently, affect access to the market'.[53] The First Chamber of the Court made even more far-reaching statements in *Commission v Netherlands*[54] in relation to golden shares held by the Dutch government that allowed it to veto certain critical decisions, such as significant investments and mergers. In particular, the Court held that the golden shares:

---

[45] See generally also C Barnard, *The Substantive Law of the EU: The Four Freedoms* (3rd edn, Oxford University Press, 2010) 571–580.

[46] See generally K Banks, 'The Application of the Fundamental Freedoms to Member State Tax Measures: Guarding Against Protectionism or Second-Guessing National Policy Choices?' (2008) 33 ELRev 482; J Snell, 'Non-discriminatory Tax Obstacles in Community Law' (2007) 56 ICLQ 339.

[47] See also, L Flynn, 'Coming of Age: The Free Movement of Capital Case Law 1993–2002' (2002) 39 CML Rev 773, 778–785.

[48] Council Directive 88/361 (n 22 above).

[49] Case C-358/93 *Bordessa* [1995] ECR I-361; Case C-163/94 *Sanz de Lera* [1995] ECR I-4821.

[50] Case C-222/97 *Trummer and Mayer* [1999] ECR I-1661 [26]–[27].

[51] Case C-98/01 *Commission v United Kingdom* [2003] ECR I-4641.

[52] ibid [49].   [53] ibid [47].

[54] Cases C-282–283/04 *Commission v Netherlands* [2006] ECR I-9141.

may have a deterrent effect on portfolio investments... A possible refusal by the Netherlands State to approve an important decision, proposed by the organs of the company concerned as being in the company's interests, would be capable of depressing the (stock market) value of the shares of that company and thus reduces the attractiveness of an investment in such shares.[55]

This time the concept of market access was not referred to,[56] and the scope of Article 63 TFEU was extended significantly, with the Court indicating that measures which may reduce the stock market value of a company amount to restrictions. Taken at face value, this would open most national rules to challenge under the free movement of capital, as any interference with economic freedom is likely to depress the share prices in some companies.[57]

On the level of facts, it could perhaps still be argued that golden share schemes have a disparate impact on foreign interests.[58] Giving a national (public) shareholder the ultimate control over the key decisions of a company might be seen as discriminatory,[59] due to national control being maintained and foreign control prevented.[60] However, far-going decisions have been handed down in other contexts as well. For instance, in *Burtscher*[61] the Third Chamber of the Court considered the legality of a non-discriminatory Austrian rule that obliged the purchaser of land to make a declaration to the relevant local authority, in particular stating whether or not the property was acquired for holiday purposes. This informed the authorities of the purpose of the transaction and allowed them to monitor land use. The purchase could not be entered in the land register before the declaration was made, and in the absence of a declaration within some two years of the conclusion of the contract the transaction would become retroactively invalid. The Court held, following Advocate General Jacobs, that the declaration system, 'even though it does not affect the actual carrying out of the transaction, constitutes nevertheless a mandatory formality prior to legal registration of the contract of sale in the land register, which alone can guarantee the effectiveness of that contract'[62] and that the very purpose of the system was therefore to restrict the free movement of capital. As the result, the rule was disapplied as a

---

[55] ibid [27]. See also AG Mengozzi in Case C-171/08 *Commission v Portugal* [2010] ECR I-0000, [69].

[56] Although the Court did briefly dismiss the argument that the restrictive effects were too uncertain or indirect at [29]–[30].

[57] See also Case C-112/05 *Commission v Germany* [2007] ECR I-8995; Cases C-463–464/04 *Federconsumatori* [2007] ECR I-10419; W-G Ringe, 'Company Law and Free Movement of Capital: Nothing Escapes the ECJ?', University of Oxford Legal Research Paper 42/2008, who warns that the Court may end up exercising 'quality control' over national company laws.

[58] See also, the Opinion of AG Ruiz-Jarabo Colomer in Case C-98/01 *Commission v UK* (n 51 above) [50]–[51].

[59] The schemes often also involve the approval of share transfers by governmental authorities. This may in practice operate in a discriminatory manner, with foreign investors being more likely to be rebuffed. See E Szyszczak, 'Golden Shares and Market Governance' (2002) 29 LIEI 255, 271 who argues that in fact 'many privatizations favour domestic investors, providing a means of "paying back" political favours'.

[60] The fact that other domestic shareholders are also deprived of the possibility of controlling the undertaking is immaterial. See Case C-21/88 *Du Pont de Nemours* [1990] ECR I-889.

[61] Case C-213/04 *Burtscher v Stauderer* [2005] ECR I-10309.   [62] ibid [42].

disproportionate restriction on Article 63 TFEU. In *Burtscher* the Court again cast the net of the free movement of capital very wide, essentially enabling it to consider the proportionality of many non-discriminatory registration formalities and the penalties attached to any non-compliance. As such registration requirements are very common and often long-standing, and as consequences of variable severity attach to non-compliance, this represents a significant extension of the Court's reach. In sum: in the context of national regulatory measures, the concept of restriction is a very wide one and does not require any disparate effect to the detriment of cross-border capital movements.[63]

In the tax context, the Court has on occasion taken a similarly broad view of the notion of restriction. In 1999 in *Sandoz*[64] the Sixth Chamber of the Court considered an Austrian rule that applied a stamp duty of 0.8 per cent to loans obtained by residents. The same stamp duty was applicable irrespective of where the lender was established. The Court, following Advocate General Léger, found that the imposition of the stamp duty on loans contracted abroad amounted to a restriction on free movement of capital, as it 'deprives residents of a Member State of the possibility of benefiting from the absence of taxation which may be associated with loans obtained outside the national territory. Accordingly, such a measure is likely to deter such residents from obtaining loans from persons established in other Member States.'[65] The Court then examined the justification of the measure and found that it stopped Austrian residents from evading domestic taxes and was therefore essential to prevent the infringement of national tax law within the meaning of Article 65(1)(b) TFEU, thus ultimately upholding it.

According to *Sandoz* the mere imposition of a tax on 'imported' loans amounted to a restriction on the free movement of capital, despite the absence of discrimination. This fitted well with the obstacle-oriented general case law on Article 63 TFEU, but ran counter to the general case law on indirect taxes under Article 110 TFEU, where the aim has been the achievement of fiscal neutrality between domestic goods and imports, not the preservation of any possible tax advantages of foreign products.[66] However, it is important to note that the Court's treatment of justifications was extremely generous and would permit essentially all equally applicable national tax rules. Accordingly, the case deserves to be treated with considerable caution.

In hindsight, the high-water mark of the tax case law came a few years later in *Manninen*,[67] which concerned the Finnish imputation system that granted tax credits to shareholders if they received dividends from domestic companies, but excluded dividends from companies established in other Member States. The reason for the tax credits was that the Finnish companies had already paid corporate tax in Finland, while the foreign companies had not done so. In other words, the legislation sought to

---

[63] For criticism, see Peers (n 30 above) 340–346.
[64] Case C-439/97 *Sandoz* [1999] ECR I-7041.
[65] ibid [19].
[66] See generally P Farmer and R Lyal, *EC Tax Law* (Oxford University Press, 1994) 56–76.
[67] See *Manninen* (n 29 above).

avoid a situation where Finland would tax the same income twice. The Grand
Chamber of the Court condemned the system,[68] following Advocate General Kokott
who argued that even in the context of direct taxation,

> [a]ny measure that makes the cross-border transfer of capital more difficult or less
> attractive and is thus liable to deter the investor constitutes a restriction on the free
> movement of capital. In this respect the concept of a restriction of capital movements
> corresponds to the concept of a restriction that the Court has developed with regard to the
> other fundamental freedoms.[69]

Yet within two years the Court changed its approach decisively. The key case in the
series was *Kerckhaert*,[70] which concerned the vexed question of international double
taxation. In issue was a Belgian tax of 25 per cent that was imposed on all dividends,
whatever their source. Mr and Mrs Kerckhaert-Morres, who resided in Belgium, had
received dividends from a French company. The dividends had already been subject to
a 15 per cent withholding levy in France. Now the Belgian tax was applied as well. Mr
and Mrs Kerckhaert-Morres objected, arguing that the tax violated the free movement
of capital, as it did not provide for the possibility of setting off the French tax, with the
result that the dividends from the French company were taxed twice, while dividends
from a Belgian company would only have been subject to the single tax of 25 per cent.

The Grand Chamber of the Court followed Advocate General Geelhoed[71] and found
that Article 63 TFEU had not been breached. The Court proceeded in three stages.
First it distinguished cases such as *Manninen*,[72] where it had held that a Member State
granting a tax benefit to domestic dividends had to grant the same advantage to
foreign source dividends. The Court reasoned that in these cases the national law
had made a distinction between domestic and foreign dividends, while the Belgian tax
in issue at the present case treated all dividends in the same manner. Secondly, it dealt
with the argument that this similar treatment of all dividends was discriminatory as
the situation of the shareholders whose dividends had already been taxed was dissimilar to those whose dividends had not been taxed. The Court accepted that in principle
the application of the same rule to different circumstances could amount to prohibited
discrimination, but then stated that:

> in respect of the tax legislation of his State of residence, the position of a shareholder
> receiving dividends is not necessarily altered, in terms of [earlier] case-law, merely by the
> fact that he receives those dividends from a company established in another Member State,

---

[68] For criticism, see D Weber, 'Community report' in X L Xenopoulos (ed), *Direct Tax Rules and the EU Fundamental Freedoms: Origin and Scope of the Problem* (Theopress, 2006) 454 and 460–461.

[69] *Manninen* (n 29 above) [28].

[70] Case C-513/04 *Kerckhaert* [2006] ECR I-10967.

[71] To be more precise, AG Geelhoed had argued at [25]–[26] that the tax should stand as, on the facts, taking into account the French imputation tax credit, there was no less favourable treatment. However, in his additional remarks at [27]–[36] he argued that in principle international double taxation was not contrary to the Treaty. The Court followed these additional remarks.

[72] *Manninen* (n 29 above).

which, in exercising its fiscal sovereignty, makes those dividends subject to a deduction at source by way of income tax.[73]

Finally, it pointed out that any adverse consequences to the taxpayers were the result of the parallel exercise of fiscal sovereignty by two Member States. The Treaty envisaged that the negative effects of the coexistence of national tax systems be dealt with by Conventions under Article 293 EC (repealed at Lisbon),[74] but apart from some isolated measures such Community legislation had not been adopted. Consequently, the matter of apportioning fiscal sovereignty was left entirely to the Member States and the Court ruled that the Belgian tax did not violate Article 63 TFEU.

The judgment in *Kerckhaert* was a clear statement of principle. International double taxation is not contrary to the Treaty free movement rules. A country can apply an even-handed tax to all income, regardless of the fact that the same income has already been taxed in another Member State. In this, the Court totally departed from its case law on double regulation, where in a consistent line of rulings stemming from the late 1970s the Court has held that an attempt by a Member State to regulate subject matter that has already complied with the rules of another Member State amounts to a restriction on free movement rights.[75] There is widespread approval of this case law and it is considered that the single market could not become a reality without such a legal stance.[76] Yet, in the field of tax barriers a different approach now prevails, despite that fact that double taxation 'is the most serious obstacle there can be to people and their capital crossing internal borders'.[77]

The Court also adopted a narrower view than the US case law.[78] The US Supreme Court has interpreted the free movement rule of the US Constitution, the Dormant Commerce Clause,[79] as prohibiting cumulative tax burdens that would expose businesses active in interstate trade to a higher tax burden than those operating in a single state. This was established in the case of *Western Live Stock* where Justice Stone wrote for the Court that state taxes are invalidated when they place

> on the commerce burdens of such a nature as to be capable in point of substance, of being imposed ... or added to ... with equal right by every state which the commerce touches,

---

[73] *Kerhaert* (n 70 above) [19].

[74] The impact of the repeal is likely to prove negligible, L Hinnekens, 'The Uneasy Case and Fate of Article 293 Second Indent EC' (2009) 37 Intertax 602, 606–607.

[75] The best known example is *Cassis de Dijon* (n 4 above). The same applies *inter alia* to social security contributions. See eg Joined Cases 62 and 63/81 *Seco* [1982] ECR 223. See J Snell, 'Free Movement of Services and the Services Directive: The Legitimacy of the Case Law' in J Van de Gronden (ed), *The EU and WTO Law on Services* (Kluwer Law International, 2009) 40–49 for a discussion of the legitimacy of this jurisprudence in the context of services.

[76] For discussion, see S Weatherill, 'Pre-emption, Harmonisation and the Distribution of Competence to Regulate the Internal Market' in Barnard and Scott (n 30 above) 42–51.

[77] AG Ruiz-Jarabo Colomer in Case C-376/03 *D* [2005] ECR I-5821, [85].

[78] See also G W Kofler and R Mason, 'Double Taxation: A European "Switch in Time?"' (2007) 14 CJEL 63, 91–94.

[79] Art I, section 8.

merely because interstate commerce is being done, so that without the protection of commerce clause it would bear cumulative burdens not imposed on local commerce.[80]

He feared that the multiplication of state taxes burdening the same activity 'would spell the destruction of interstate commerce'.[81] Under the modern *Complete Auto Transit*[82] approach, double taxation has been tackled under the requirement of fair apportionment[83] and sometimes cumulative tax burdens have also been viewed as discriminatory.[84]

While *Kerckhaert* represents an important change of course, the reasons given by the European Court of Justice in the ruling were not compelling. The course correction was not forced upon it by an inevitable Cartesian logic. First, the distinction it drew between the present case and earlier decisions is not sound. It can be argued that the rulings the Court cites require that a Member State recognize the tax system of another Member State, something that *Kerckhaert* emphatically denies. For example, in *Manninen*,[85] the Court held that a country granting shareholders receiving dividends a tax credit which corresponds to the national corporate tax paid on the profits must extend that tax credit to dividends received from abroad. In effect, this entails the mutual recognition of a foreign tax for the purpose of granting a tax credit.[86] It is not clear from the reasoning of the Court why, as a matter of policy,[87] mutual recognition applies when a Member State grants a tax advantage but does not apply when it imposes a tax.

The second criticism of the Court's reasoning in *Kerckhaert* concerns the treatment of the concept of discrimination.[88] It was argued that it is discriminatory to impose the same tax both on income that has not been taxed and on income that has already been subject to a withholding levy. The argument was entirely credible, as the Court has repeatedly held that the application of the same rule to different situations can be

---

[80] *Western Live Stock v Bureau of Revenue* 303 US 250 (1938) 255–256.

[81] ibid 256.

[82] *Complete Auto Transit, Inc v Brady* 430 US 274 (1977).

[83] See eg W Hellerstein, 'State Taxation and the Supreme Court' [1989] Sup Ct Rev 223, 234; L H Tribe, *American Constitutional Law, Vol 1* (3rd edn, Foundation Press, 2000) 1132–1133.

[84] See eg *American Trucking Associations, Inc v Scheiner* 483 US 266 (1987).

[85] *Manninen* (n 29 above).

[86] See also the discussion in F Vanistendael, 'Cohesion: The Phoenix Rises from his Ashes' [2005] EC Tax Review 208, 217–222.

[87] On a formal level *Kerkhaert* does differ from the previous judgments. The Finnish system in *Manninen* where a tax credit was granted if the dividends originated in Finland, but not if they originated in Sweden, entailed a differential treatment depending on whether the situation was internal or cross-border. By contrast, in the case of multiple taxation, the state treats both internal and cross-border situations in the same way. K Lenaerts and L Bernardeau, 'L'encadrement communautaire de la fiscalité directe' (2007) 43 Cahiers Dr Euro 19, 62–63 refer to the distinction between the allocation and exercise of tax powers.

[88] On the various meanings that can be attached to the notion of discrimination, and the 'labyrinth of impossibility' that an overly broad concept can create, see M J Graetz and A C Warren, 'Income Tax Discrimination and the Political and Economic Integration of Europe' (2006) 115 Yale LJ 1186, 1215–1223, and more generally G Davies, *Nationality Discrimination in the European Internal Market* (Kluwer Law International, 2003).

discriminatory.[89] The imposition of double taxation obviously has a disparate impact to the detriment of cross-border situations, and was condemned as discriminatory by the European Court of Justice in the context of the common system of VAT in *Gaston Schul*[90] and by the US Supreme Court in the context of the Dormant Commerce Clause. It may be said that there is a sin of omission, namely a failure by one state to take into account the distinct situation of a product or person that is also subject to a tax in another Member State.[91] Yet in its reasoning the Court simply asserts that the position of the shareholder is not necessarily altered in the meaning of its earlier case law by the fact that the income has already been taxed in another Member State.

Thirdly, the statements that any adverse consequences for the plaintiffs arise from the parallel exercise of fiscal sovereignty by two states and that in the absence of Union measures its apportionment is purely a matter for the Member States are highly significant expressions of principle.[92] However, they were not entirely free of doubt,[93] and once again the Court's reasoning was not as full as might be hoped for, given that Article 293 EC (repealed at Lisbon) did not necessitate such a conclusion, in other areas of Union law the Court had allocated regulatory powers on the basis of free movement rules, and the US Supreme Court had managed the task in the tax context without overstepping the judicial role.

The Treaty recognized the problem of double taxation in Article 293 EC (repealed at Lisbon), which provided that Member States were to enter into negotiations with each other, to the extent necessary, to abolish double taxation. Although, at first sight this could be interpreted, *a contrario*, as indicating that the Treaty had not solved the problem and additional conventions were needed to deal with the issue, this interpretation was not necessary. Already in *Reyners*[94] in 1974 the Court had held that the failure of the political institutions to agree on Directives envisaged in the Treaty Chapter on the right of establishment did not deprive Article 49 TFEU of its effect. Rather, the Directives could serve to facilitate the exercise of the right of establishment, but the right itself arose directly from the Treaty. This reasoning was transposed to Article 293 EC (repealed at Lisbon) by the Full Court in *Überseering*.[95] For double

---

[89] Cases 13/63 *Commission v Italy* [1963] ECR 165 and *Schumacker* (n 27 above) [30]. Further, the premise of Art 65(1)(a) TFEU is that the place where capital is invested may render otherwise identical situations different.

[90] Case 15/81 *Gaston Schul* [1982] ECR 1409, but see Case 142/77 *Larsen and Kjerulff* [1978] ECR 1543.

[91] Because of this, any distinction between (unlawful) discrimination caused by a single jurisdiction and (lawful) difficulties arising out of the existence of different legal system may be logically difficult to maintain. It can be argued that a state is at fault for failing to consider the effects of the rules of another state.

[92] See more recently eg Case C-128/08 *Damseaux* [2009] ECR I-6823 and generally on the implications Terra and Wattel (n 32 above) 724–733.

[93] Compare eg P J Wattel, 'Corporate Tax Jurisdiction in the EU with Respect to Branches and Subsidiaries; Dislocation Distinguished from Discrimination and Disparity; A Plea for Territoriality' [2003] EC Tax Review 194, 199 and J Englisch, 'The European Treaties' Implications for Direct Taxes' (2005) 33 Intertax 310, 324–325.

[94] *Reyners* (n 4 above).

[95] Case C-208/00 *Überseering* [2002] ECR I-9919.

taxation this means that Article 293 EC (repealed at Lisbon) could not automatically exclude the issue from the scope of the free movement rules.[96]

Further, the Court has not been reticent in allocating regulatory competences in its general free movement law to avoid double regulatory burdens. It was possible to argue that cases such as *Keck*, *Groenveld*, and *Alpine Investments*[97] served to confer the power to regulate a product and its production to the home state, while the competence to regulate selling arrangements had been given to the host state,[98] although in its more recent decisions the Court has admittedly been narrowing the regulatory autonomy of the Member States.[99] Allocation of tax competences would have been politically more contentious,[100] but not a fundamentally different exercise.[101]

Finally, the European Court of Justice could have drawn lessons from the case law of the US Supreme Court, which insists that each state tax only that portion of revenues from interstate activity which reasonably reflects the in-state component of the activity. The Supreme Court has not imposed any specific apportionment formula on the states, giving them a margin of discretion, but if the income attributed by a state to itself is out of all proportion to the business transacted in that state or if the attribution leads to a grossly distorted result, the tax will be struck down.[102] The approach does not ensure the abolition of all double taxation. Sometimes the application of fair but different formulas by the states involved may result in multiple taxation, but at least the spectre of unfettered double taxation has been avoided without the Supreme Court overstepping the judicial role.[103]

The ruling in *Kerckhaert* did not prove to be an isolated example of unusual leniency but a part of a new trend,[104] and was confirmed in *Columbus Container*.[105] For example, in *ACT Group Litigation*[106] the Grand Chamber of the Court, following

---

[96] Indeed, the Court in Case C-336/96 *Gilly* [1998] ECR I-2793 [16] drew from Art 293 EC the conclusion that the abolition of double taxation was included within the objectives of the Treaty.

[97] Cases C-267–268/91 *Keck* [1993] ECR I-6097; Case 15/79 *Groenveld* [1979] ECR 3409; Case C-384/93 *Alpine Investments* [1995] ECR I-1141.

[98] N Bernard, 'La libre circulation des merchandises, des personnes et des services dans la Traité CE sous l'angle de la compétence' (1998) 34 Cahier Dr Euro 11, 33–35 ; J Snell and M Andenas, 'Exploring the Outer Limits: Restrictions on the Free Movement of Goods and Services' (1999) 10 EBL Rev 252, 264–267.

[99] Case C-110/05 *Commission v Italy* [2009] ECR I-519; Case C-205/07 *Gysbrechts* [2008] ECR I-9947. See generally J Snell, 'The Notion of Market Access: A Concept or a Slogan?' (2010) 47 CMLRev 437.

[100] Allocation can also be contentious in other contexts, as shown by European Parliament and Council Directive (EC) 2006/123 on services in the internal market [2006] OJ L376/36, discussed in J Snell, 'Freedom to Provide Services in the Case Law and in the Services Directive: Problems, Solutions, and Institutions' in U Neergaard, R Nielsen, and L M Roseberry (eds), *The Services Directive: Consequences for the Welfare State and the European Social Model* (DJOF Publishing, 2008).

[101] Terra and Wattel (n 32 above) 722–723 propose holding both the home and the host state responsible and requiring both countries to apply worldwide taxation.

[102] Tribe (n 83 above) 1136.

[103] See *Moorman Manufacturing Co v Bair* 437 US 267 (1978) 277–281.

[104] See also Kingston (n 36 above) 1339–1343.

[105] Case C-298/05 *Columbus Container Services* [2007] ECR I-10451. See also eg *Damseaux* (n 92 above).

[106] Case C-374/04 *ACT Group Litigation* [2006] ECR I-11673. The ruling was based on the free movement of capital, together with the right of establishment.

Advocate General Geelhoed, decided that a source Member State granting relief for economic double taxation in case of profits distributed to residents did not have to extend the same relief to shareholders in other Member States. In other words, the home state is free to impose a second tax regardless of what the source state has done, and the source state is not obliged to provide relief in cross-border situations, even if it does grant such relief internally.[107] The impact of the trend could also be seen in practice: after some years where the Member States had lost virtually all tax cases, they started winning again.[108]

The result of *Kerckhaert* was that the biggest open question relating to the application of the free movement rules to direct taxes was answered: international double taxation is not contrary to the Treaty. Member States may exercise their fiscal sovereignty in parallel, and its apportionment is a matter for them. The answer is totally different from the one the Court had given in the context of double regulation. The Court is prepared to accommodate Member States in the field of taxation to a far greater degree than in the field of regulation.[109]

To sum up, after the Maastricht Treaty the Court applied the free movement of capital with vigour, equating the concept of restriction with that found for the other freedoms. However, in the field of taxation the initial advance had to be halted and reversed. Thus, a strong tension emerged between the approach to regulatory and fiscal barriers, with the latter receiving a much more understanding treatment than the former.[110] The reasons for the difference have never been articulated by the Court and remain unclear. From the perspective of the evolution of the law, the developments described above show that we are not concerned with a linear process. Free movement has branched into two subspecies. The split contains seeds for further developments. It is easy to ask what the justification for the different approaches is, and argue that the deference shown to national tax autonomy should also be extended to the regulatory autonomy of Member States.[111]

---

[107] Formally the ruling is in line with Case C-319/02 *Manninen* (n 29 above) which involved the obligations of a home state, while *ACT Group Litigation* concerned a source state. However, the Court's basic approach appears rather different and the way the cases are distinguished is not particularly convincing. The statement at [59] that if the source state had to extend the relief to non-residents, it would be obliged to abandon its right to tax profits generated in its territory, can be countered with the observation that the state would be free to adopt a neutral method by for example not granting relief to anyone. Further, the same line of reasoning, *mutatis mutandis*, could have been adopted in *Manninen*, but the Court declined to do so. Finally, it is not clear what the relevance of the ability to pay argument at [60] is in the present context.

[108] Terra and Wattel (n 32 above) 725–726.

[109] Kofler and Mason (n 78 above) describe this as rewarding the inactivity of Member States, which have failed to adopt Union legislation to deal with the matter.

[110] While a similar tension exists also for the other freedoms, it is particularly salient in the context of capital, given the importance of tax restrictions in this context.

[111] Banks (n 46 above) 505–506.

C. THE EXTERNAL DIMENSION

A largely unanswered, but nevertheless extremely important question remains: how should the law treat third country situations? Article 63 TFEU, alone among the freedoms, applies to capital movements both within and to or from the EU, although a number of additional exceptions are available for the extra-Union situations. The extension makes sense for a number of reasons. First, the free movement of capital between Member States would in any event undermine capital controls towards third countries, as investors would simply enter (or exit) the EU via the most liberal jurisdiction to access (or leave) the target state.[112] Secondly, the credibility of the single currency is bolstered by the liberalization. In particular, overseas investments in euros are facilitated by a legal regime that guarantees the free repatriation of those investments without capital export controls.[113] Thirdly, it can be argued that the *erga omnes* effect contributes to the principle of an open market economy expressed in Article 119 TFEU,[114] although from this perspective it is not clear why the extension was limited to just capital among the four freedoms. Finally, the aim of 'maintaining financial centres with a world-wide dimension within the Member States' has been mentioned by the Court,[115] but unfortunately it failed to explain why the matter needed to be tackled by the Treaty, as liberalization by individual Member States would seem sufficient to achieve it. Be that as it may, the key issue is whether the law should treat both extra- and intra-EU situations in the same way, subject only to the explicit exceptions, or whether the approaches should differ. A simple textual analysis would suggest an identical approach: the command to liberalize has been phrased identically for both situations in the same Treaty Article. Yet a number of arguments to the contrary can be put forward.[116]

First, the Court has in practice sometimes given different interpretations to identically worded provisions, depending on the context. For example, in *Polydor*[117] the Court had to interpret a free trade agreement with Portugal which contained provisions identical to Articles 34 and 36 TFEU. Nevertheless, the Court adopted a radically different reading, citing the objective of the Union to 'unite national markets into a single market having characteristics of a domestic market'.[118] The more limited purpose of the free trade agreement resulted in a narrower interpretation. The emphasis on different aims could potentially also prove important for Article 63

---

[112] This was recognized already in the Spaak Report (n 1 above).

[113] Case C-101/05 *Skatteverket v A* [2007] ECR I-11531, [31].

[114] S Hindelang, *The Free Movement of Capital and Foreign Direct Investment: The Scope of Protection in EU Law* (Oxford University Press, 2009) 27–28.

[115] Case C-101/05 *Skatteverket v A* (n 113 above), [31]. By contrast, S Mohamed, *European Community Law on the Free Movement of Capital and the EMU* (Kluwer Law International, 1999) 216 finds the reasons for the unilateral opening of the EU capital markets difficult to comprehend.

[116] See also the detailed discussion in Hindelang (n 114 above) 170–183.

[117] Case 270/80 *Polydor* [1982] ECR 329.   [118] ibid [16].

TFEU. It could be argued that the lack of internal market and EMU aims in the third country context could justify a less expansive approach.

Secondly, the Court's case law on the effects of the WTO Agreement has been sensitive to the lack of reciprocity and the reduction in the political organs' freedom of manoeuvre that a rigorous enforcement of WTO obligations in the EU might entail.[119] In the same vein, it could be argued that a far-going interpretation of the free movement of capital in the third country context would tie the hands of the political institutions and might well not be reciprocated, although the third country specific exceptions in Article 64 TFEU limit the strength of the argument.

Finally, the preconditions for far-going liberalization may not be met in the third country context. For a state to enter the EU it must fulfil a number of preconditions such as having a functioning market economy, implementation of the *acquis*, and compliance with the basic principles and values of the Union.[120] This results in legal systems that are partially harmonized and may also engender mutual trust. Further, any difficulties resulting from liberalization can be corrected relatively easily by measures of the Union legislature. By contrast, in third country situations there can be no such reliance on mutual trust or legal approximation.

In *Ospelt* Advocate General Geelhoed emphasized the connection between the free movement of capital and the EMU, and stated that 'although Article [63 TFEU] draws no distinction between the movement of capital within the European Union and the movement of capital to and from third countries outside, that does not mean that the prohibition of restrictions has the same effect on both situations'.[121] He repeated this view in *FII Group Litigation* arguing that 'in analysing whether... restrictions are justified (whether under Article [65(1) TFEU] or under the discrimination analysis of Article [63 TFEU]), different considerations may apply than is the case with purely intra-[Union] restrictions'.[122] Similarly Advocate General Kokott suggested in *Manninen* that the principles developed in the intra-EU context might not apply when third countries were concerned.[123] In *FII Group Litigation* the Court laconically held that 'it may be that a Member State will be able to demonstrate that a restriction on capital movements to or from non-member countries is justified for a particular reason in circumstances where that reason would not constitute a valid justification for a restriction on capital movements between Member States',[124] but did not need to explore the matter in any depth on the facts.

The Court's first real encounter with third country situations took place in *Skatteverket v A*.[125] The case concerned a Swedish law that exempted dividend payments in the form of shares in a subsidiary company from taxation, but only if

---

[119] See Case C-149/96 *Portugal v Council* [1999] ECR I-8395, in particular [45]–[46].

[120] See generally eg U Sedelmeier, 'Enlargement: From Rules for Accession to a Policy Towards Europe' in H Wallace, M A Pollack, and A R Young (eds), *Policy-Making in the European Union* (6th edn, Oxford University Press, 2010).

[121] Case C-452/01 *Ospelt* [2003] ECR I-9743, [40].

[122] *FII Group Litigation* (n 33 above) [121].

[123] *Manninen* (n 29 above) [79].   [124] ibid [171].   [125] *Skatteverket v A* (n 113 above).

the parent company was established within the EEA or in a country with which Sweden had a qualifying tax convention. On the facts, a company based in Switzerland was considering distributing shares in one of its subsidiaries, and a question arose as to whether the imposition of the Swedish income tax would amount to a restriction on the free movement of capital between Sweden and Switzerland. The Grand Chamber, following Advocate General Bot, found that there was an obstacle to free movement of capital, but that it could quite possibly be justified, although ultimately the application of the law was left for the referring national court.

The judgment proceeded in a number of stages. First, the Court confronted arguments put forward by a number of Member States that the concept of restriction needed to be given a different meaning in the external context. This was rejected by the Court, which noted that the authors of the Treaty had chosen to use the same terms for intra- and extra-Union situations. It also drew attention to the specific safeguard clauses and derogations, and reasoned that these served to deal with differences in the objectives and the context. However, it also acknowledged that the different legal contexts might in some cases result in different outcomes. This could occur because the advanced level of legal integration within the EU renders intra- and extra-Union situations non-comparable. Furthermore, the Court repeated the statement in *FII Group Litigation* that a measure which would breach the Treaty if the capital movement occurred between Member States might be justified in the case of movement to or from a third country. As a result, the Court concluded that the less favourable tax treatment in the Swedish legislation discouraged investment in companies established outside the EEA and amounted to a restriction on Article 63 TFEU. Next the Court turned to the issue of justification. A number of governments had argued that the Swedish rules were justified by the needs of fiscal supervision, in particular as the EU legislation mandating cooperation between national tax authorities[126] could not be applied. The Court accepted that this could in principle justify a restriction, and then turned to the issue of proportionality. Here A and the Commission both argued that even if the Swedish authorities were unable to rely on the cooperation of the Swiss authorities, they could simply request that the company in question supply the relevant information and proof, something which the Court had accepted in intra-EU situations.[127] However, the Court proved reluctant to extend this case law, given the differing legal contexts. First, there was no framework of mutual cooperation between authorities in the case of third countries, and secondly, the documentary evidence which the taxpayer could be required to provide might not correspond to that mandated by the Union harmonization measures on company accounts. As a result, the Court was in principle prepared to accept the Swedish rules, although it left the final application of the law to the referring national court.

---

[126] Council Directive (EEC) 77/799 concerning mutual assistance by the competent authorities of the Member States in the field of direct and indirect taxation [1977] OJ L336/15, as amended.

[127] *Bachmann* (n 27 above) [20].

In *Skatteverket v A* the Court maximized the freedom of manoeuvre it enjoys. On the one hand, it maintained the same general concept of restriction it uses when the facts concern transactions between Member States, ensuring that it has the jurisdiction to inspect the detail of numerous national measures. On the other hand, it signalled that it is not bound by the results of its intra-Union decisions, due to the differences in the legal context.[128] The Court demonstrated this also on the facts. The outcome of the case was determined by the lack of harmonizing legislation, which allowed the justification of fiscal supervision to be pleaded successfully. In the tax context, this may well result in national laws being upheld in a substantial number of cases.[129] More intriguingly, the Court signalled its readiness to entertain arguments that are based on grounds of justification not accepted in the intra-Union context. In particular economic justifications have traditionally been condemned for all four freedoms,[130] but might not always fail in the third country situations.[131] In *Orange European Smallcap Fund* this argument was run by the Dutch government,[132] which claimed that the objective of combating the reduction of tax revenue could justify a restriction in the third country context. The Court did not reject the argument out-of-hand, but instead reasoned that even if it were correct, it could not be relied upon in the circumstances of the case as the restriction in question impacted both on intra- and extra-Union situations without distinction.[133] On a related note, while regulatory and tax arbitrage and the resulting jurisdictional competition are undoubtedly inherent in the concept of the internal market,[134] they may not be equally desirable in the third country context, in particular given the existence of off-shore tax havens. As a result, Article 65(1) TFEU, or the doctrine of abuse of rights,[135] could find a broad application in the extra-EU situations. Further, it might be argued that while cases such as *Manninen*[136] have insisted that one Member State must take cognizance of a tax that has been levied in another Member State and grant a tax credit even though the result will be a reduction in tax revenue, the same cannot be extended to extra-EU situations.[137] The solidarity and reciprocity that exist within

---

[128] See also Case C-182/08 *Glaxo Wellcome v Finanzamt München II* [2009] ECR I-8591, where AG Bot expressly limited his Opinion to the intra-EU situations [90].

[129] Most recently Case C-540/07 *Commission v Italy* [2009] ECR I-10983. See also Case C-318/07 *Persche* [2009] ECR I-359, [70] and O'Brien (n 40 above) 663–664.

[130] See J Snell, 'Economic Aims as Justification for Restrictions on Free Movement' in A Schrauwen (ed), *Rule of Reason: Rethinking another Classic of European Legal Doctrine* (Europa Law, 2005).

[131] A Cordewener, G W Kofler, and C P Schindler, 'Free Movement of Capital, Third Country Relationships and National Tax Law: An Emerging Issue before the ECJ' [2007] ET 107, 116–117.

[132] Case C-194/06 *Orange European Smallcap Fund* [2008] ECR I-3747, [93].

[133] See also the treatment of the same argument by AG Geelhoed in *FII Group Litigation* (n 33 above) [122].

[134] Case C-212/97 *Centros* [1999] ECR I-1459 [27] and Case C-196/04 *Cadbury Schweppes* [2006] ECR I-7995, [36].

[135] See generally R de la Feria and S Vogenauer (eds), *Prohibition of Abuse of Law: A New General Principle of EU Law* (Hart, forthcoming).

[136] *Manninen* (n 29 above).

[137] The issue was left open by AG Kokott, ibid [79]. See also R Lyal, 'Free Movement of Capital and Non-member Countries—Consequences for Direct Taxation' in D Weber (ed), *The Influence of European Law on Direct Taxation* (Kluwer Law International, 2007) 24.

the EU where the Member States know that they all have to play by the same internal market rules do not extend to the extra-Union context. In the EU, fiscal cohesion has been 'shifted to another level, that of the reciprocity of the rules applicable in the Contracting States',[138] with every Member State knowing that it will win some and lose some.

The third country case law gives rise to a question whether there is also scope for a graduated approach within the intra-Union context. Not all EU countries have entered into the third stage of the EMU and adopted the single currency. As a result, there is deeper policy coordination and even unification among some Member States than others. The Treaty recognizes this difference and allows for safeguard measures in cases of balance of payments difficulties for countries outside the Euro, while the same measures are no longer available for Member States that have joined the Eurozone. Given that the Court has shown a willingness to adopt a differential approach to the same Treaty provision due to the different legal contexts in the case of extra- and intra-EU situations, it is not inconceivable that we could come to see some differentiation also for intra- and extra-Eurozone cases.[139]

The third country issue has also forced the Court to clarify the borderline between capital and the other freedoms.[140] Some of the earlier cases on intra-Union situations had taken a fairly haphazard approach to distinguishing between the competing free movement provisions,[141] probably because nothing much depended on whether the rules on capital or, say, establishment or services were applied. For example when it comes to the borderline between capital and services, the Court had referred to both freedoms in cases such as *Svensson and Gustavsson*,[142] examined only Article 63 TFEU in *Sandoz*,[143] but resorted to Article 56 TFEU in *Safir*[144] without ruling out the applicability of the free movement of capital. A lack of principle had also reigned in respect of the borderline between capital and establishment.[145] However, in the third country context the choice of the relevant freedom is obviously of decisive importance and in the more recent jurisprudence the Court has sought to spell out more clearly how it is to be made. At the same time, the Court has significantly reduced the remit of the free movement of capital. While the earlier case law had countenanced the parallel

---

[138] Case C-80/94 *Wielockx* [1995] ECR I-2493, [24] known as macro-cohesion.

[139] This may be implicit in the Opinion of AG Geelhoed in *Ospelt* (n 121 above) [37]. For further differentiation, see the Opinion of AG Jääskinen in Case C-72/09 *Rimbaud* (pending) in relation to EEA countries.

[140] The Court's usual starting point for defining capital has been the nomenclature annexed to Directive 88/361 (n 22 above).

[141] See Flynn (n 47 above) 804, who writes that 'it is quite unsettling not to be certain in a relatively significant number of cases as to what is the correct starting point of analysis'. See Case C-279/00 *Commission v Italy* [2002] ECR I-1425 for an example of a more principled approach.

[142] Case C-484/93 *Svensson and Gustavsson* [1995] ECR I-3955.

[143] See n 64 above. The national court had framed its question in the terms of the free movement of capital, despite the fact that services were affected as well.

[144] Case C-118/96 *Safir* [1998] ECR I-1897.   [145] See eg Peers (n 30 above) 339.

application of a number of freedoms, implying that Article 63 TFEU could be of relevance for a large number of extra-EU situations, the more recent case law has moved towards exclusive application of just one freedom, which often may not turn out to be the free movement of capital.

Fidium Finanz[146] concerned a Swiss company that provided small loans to customers in Germany via the Internet without the requisite authorization by the relevant authorities. The company argued that the authorization requirement violated the free movement of capital between Switzerland and the EU. The Grand Chamber, contrary to the Opinion of Advocate General Stix-Hackl, ruled that Article 63 TFEU was not applicable, and instead held that the case related to the free movement of services, which does not extend its effects to extra-EU situations. The ruling came as a great surprise, not least since Article 57 TFEU provides that activities qualify as 'services' only 'in so far as they are not governed by the provisions relating to freedom of movement for goods, capital and persons'. Additionally, as the Advocate General had pointed out, apart from an isolated ruling in *Bachmann*,[147] the Court had in practice not excluded the application of the capital provisions. The reasoning of the Court proceeded in a number of stages. First, it denied that services were a residual category, holding that the wording of Article 57 TFEU only goes to the definition of services and does not establish any order of priority between the freedoms. Secondly, it stated that when the national rules relate simultaneously both to services and capital, the Court would consider the extent of the effects on each of them. If in the circumstances of the case one was entirely secondary, the Court would only examine the primary freedom. Thirdly, the Court went on to investigate whether one of the freedoms prevailed on the facts. It found that the provision of loans constituted a service and also involved capital movements. However, it then noted that the relevant German rule formed a part of the legislation on the supervision of banks and financial service providers. The purpose of these rules was to regulate services and their effect was to restrict or even negate the freedom. By contrast, the reduction of cross-border capital flows was seen merely as an unavoidable consequence of the restrictions on services, and therefore it was unnecessary to consider whether Article 63 TFEU was violated. As a result, the Swiss undertaking was denied the protection of EU law.

In the same vein, the Grand Chamber of the Court held in *Thin Cap Group Litigation*[148] that the free movement of capital was inapplicable, following Advocate General Geelhoed. The national rules concerned interest payments by subsidiaries to parent or intermediate group companies. In all situations covered by the relevant law, there was a relationship of control and definite influence between the companies. Previous case law had deemed this a hallmark of the freedom of

---

[146] Case C-452/04 *Fidium Finanz* [2006] ECR I-9521 confirmed eg in Case C-42/07 *Liga Portuguesa* [2009] ECR I-7633, [47].

[147] *Bachmann* (n 27 above).

[148] Case C-524/04 *Thin Cap Group Litigation* [2007] ECR I-2107, confirmed eg in Case C-492/04 *Lasertec* [2007] ECR I-3775.

establishment.[149] As a result, the Court stated that the legislation affected primarily Article 49 TFEU. Any possible restrictive effects on capital were irrelevant, as they were an unavoidable consequence of the restriction on the right of establishment.

By contrast, in the Grand Chamber judgment in *FII Group Litigation*[150] the relevant national legislation was examined both under Articles 49 and 63 TFEU, as it could in principle affect both situations where there was a definite influence and situations where such influence was lacking. However, it appears that if the litigant in question did fall under the freedom of establishment, the provisions on the free movement of capital should not be applied, as the Court specifically stated that the reason it examined the free movement of capital at all was that some parties might not be in the possession of holdings giving them a definite influence.[151] This appears to be the logical corollary of the decision in *Thin Cap Group Litigation*. If a litigant with a definite influence cannot benefit from Article 63 TFEU in cases where the national rule only ever applies to such parties, it is difficult to see why the situation should change merely because other types of parties could in theory be affected by the rule.[152] Conversely, if a litigant with a definite influence could in principle invoke the free movement of capital, why would a national rule applying solely to these parties be governed exclusively by Article 49 TFEU? However, some doubt was cast on this finding by the judgment of the Fourth Chamber, delivered without the Opinion of an Advocate General, in *Holböck*.[153] On the facts, Mr Holböck, an Austrian resident, had a definite influence in the Swiss company in question. Yet the Court did not dismiss the case out of hand, but stated that:

> even if a Member State national who holds two thirds of the share capital of a company established in a non-member country were justified in invoking the prohibition of restrictions on the movement of capital between Member States and non-member countries... that legislation is caught by the exception laid down in Article [64(1) TFEU].

In other words, the Court did not challenge *FII Group Litigation*, but neither did it endorse it. Nevertheless, in *Burda*[154] the same Chamber, following Advocate General Mengozzi, relied exclusively on Article 49 TFEU in an intra-EU situation due to the definite influence of the defendant, despite the fact that the national law applied irrespective of the size of the shareholding, and the same approach was adopted by

---

[149] According to Case C-251/98 *Baars* [2000] ECR I-2787, [22] 'a national of a Member State who has a holding in the capital of a company established in another Member State which gives him definite influence over the company's decisions and allows him to determine its activities is exercising his right of establishment.'

[150] See n 33 above.

[151] ibid [38] and Opinion of AG Geelhoed (n 139 above) [31].

[152] Of course, the Court may still decide to pronounce on the free movement of capital, for example to assist the national court in dealing with different fact configurations.

[153] Case C-157/05 *Holböck* [2007] ECR I-4051. See M O'Brien, 'Case note on *Commission v Italy*' (2010) 47 CML Rev 245, 258 on confusion in national courts.

[154] Case C-284/06 *Burda* [2008] ECR I-4571.

the First Chamber, which followed Advocate General Mazák, in *Aberdeen Property* and by the Third Chamber in *SGI*.[155]

The rulings put forward a set of principles that are rather restrictive from the point of view of extra-EU situations. First, even if the national legislation potentially concerns two freedoms, the Court will only apply one of them provided that, having regard to the purpose of the national law, the other can be deemed secondary. Secondly, if the national legislation can only ever be applied in circumstances of definite influence, the matter falls exclusively within the remit of the right of establishment and the free movement of capital gives way. Thirdly, even if the law can in principle apply both where there is a definite influence and where it is lacking, a plaintiff can only rely on the free movement of capital if, on the facts, his or her holdings do not confer such influence. However, somewhat illogically, the first principle trumps the third one. Even if there is a definite influence on the facts, the capital rules may apply if the right of establishment is deemed secondary due to the purpose of the national law.[156]

The principles detailed above represent a move towards exclusivity. Increasingly only one freedom is to be applied,[157] rather than two in parallel. This prevents the extension of all the internal market freedoms to third country situations via the back door of the free movement of capital and therefore corresponds to the wishes of the Member States. It also allows them to regulate freely investments that would result in third country investors obtaining a definite influence in a domestic company, a matter that is of some political sensitivity in particular in the context of acquisitions by foreign state-controlled entities.[158]

Unfortunately, the exclusive approach is not without problems. First, the wording of the Treaty anticipates a parallel rather than an exclusive application of different freedoms, in particular by subjecting the right of establishment to the rules on capital in Article 49(2) TFEU, and conversely exempting justified restrictions on establishment from the free movement of capital in Article 65(2) TFEU. Under an exclusive approach these reciprocal cross-references are superfluous. Further, Article 64 TFEU offers a possibility to derogate from Article 63 TFEU in respect of third country capital movements involving direct investment, establishment, and the provision of financial services. Yet the exclusive approach recently favoured by the Court typically denies any application of Article 63 TFEU in these contexts,[159] making the derogation unnecessary. Therefore, a more natural interpretation of the wording of the Treaty would be that in principle every freedom that is restricted applies, which in the extra-EU context would translate to the applicability of the free movement of capital, as the

[155] Case C-303/07 *Aberdeen Property* [2009] ECR I-5145 and Case C-311/08 *SGI* [2010] ECR I-0000. Similarly AG Kokott in Case C-222/07 *UTECA* [2009] ECR I-1407 at fn 62.

[156] *Glaxo Wellcome* (n 128 above). See also AG Mengozzi in Case C-569/07 *HSBC Holdings and Vidacos Nominees* [2009] ECR I-9047, [57].

[157] But not always, see eg Cases C-155 and 157/08 *X and EHA Passenheim-van Schoot* [2009] ECR I-5093.

[158] Hindelang (n 114 above) 3–7.

[159] Cordewener, Kofler, and Schindler (n 131 above) 113–114.

other freedoms lack an *erga omnes* effect. Secondly, even if the exclusive approach were the correct one, should not the free movement of capital be considered the primary freedom in third country situations? Finding, as the Court does, that a national law primarily affects an inapplicable freedom requires considerable mental agility. Thirdly, there is something odd about deciding the relevant freedom on the basis of the purpose of the national law.[160] Why is the purpose considered at all? Should not the applicable freedom be determined exclusively by the effects of the Member State rules?[161] For example, why does it matter that the aim of a national law is to regulate financial services if there is a restrictive impact on capital movements? Further, the reliance on purpose may give rise to manipulation. At least to the extent that the objective of a law is determined with reference to *travaux préparatoires* or the national equivalent of recitals, there is a danger that Member States may seek to evade Article 63 TFEU through judicious drafting that emphasizes aspects other than capital. Fourthly, how feasible is it really to draw a line between the primary and the secondary freedoms?[162] In the words of Advocate General Stix-Hackl, any criteria based on directness or 'principal aspect' may prove insufficiently 'clear-cut and too vague'.[163] Finally, the exclusive approach serves to undermine the protection of direct investment, one of the classic types of capital movement. Direct, as opposed to portfolio, investment in a company involves *inter alia* the '[e]stablishment and extension of branches or new undertakings belonging solely to the person providing the capital, and the acquisition in full of existing undertaking',[164] or effective participation in the management of a company or in its control.[165] This largely coincides with the definition of establishment, which requires a 'definite influence over a company's decisions'.[166] If the situations of definite influence are exclusively dealt with under Article 49 TFEU, extra-EU restrictions on direct investment will to a significant degree evade the free movement of capital, and rather fine and difficult-to-apply distinctions need to be drawn between the different influence levels.[167] As a result, the larger the investment of a third country investor, the less legal protection he or she will have.[168]

---

[160] See also Hindelang (n 114 above) 99–100.

[161] AG Stix-Hackl in *Fidium Finanz* (n 146 above) [72].

[162] See eg the disagreement between AG Ruiz-Jarabo Colomer and the Court in *Commission v UK* (n 51 above) and the subsequent refinement of the Court's position in Case C-326/07 *Commission v Italy* [2009] ECR I-2291, and the disagreement between AG Bot and the Court in Case C-531/06 *Commission v Italy* [2009] ECR I-4103.

[163] *Fidium Finanz* (n 146 above) [62]. Hindelang (n 114 above) 99 uses words 'vague and fuzzy'. *Contra*, eg AG Alber in *Baars* (n 149 above) [26].

[164] Council Directive 88/361 (n 22 above) Annex I.

[165] Explanatory Note to Council Directive 88/361 ibid.

[166] *Baars* (n 149 above) [22].

[167] As suggested by AG Geelhoed in *FII Group Litigation* (n 33 above) [119]. In *Commission v Italy* (n 162 above) [38] the Court suggests that in a company with a large number of small shareholders 5 per cent of voting rights might give rise to a position of definite influence. See also the discussion in Usher (n 2 above) 1545–1549.

[168] See AG Alber in *Baars* (n 149 above) [50].

Altogether, the case law on third country situations is characterized by caution. The Court is not seeking to apply the full force of its intra-EU jurisprudence. Its efforts to define more clearly the applicable freedom often result in the free movement of capital giving way to establishment or services, which do not apply outside the EU. It is difficult to avoid the conclusion that the Court has received the message the Member States sent when they inserted a new clause to the Constitutional Treaty in 2004, later carrying it to the Lisbon Treaty as Article 65(4) TFEU, which allows the Council to pronounce on the legality of restrictive tax measures adopted by Member States concerning third countries.[169] However, it should be added that while the Member States may have sought to reduce the influence of the Court, the influence of the EU has not been diminished. Article 207(1) TFEU now brings foreign direct investment fully within the scope of the Common Commercial Policy, where the EU enjoys exclusive powers.[170] The role of the EU political institutions is set to grow.

D. CONCLUSION

The evolution of the free movement of capital has been a non-linear process. After a promising start with two liberalizing Directives in the early 1960s, the gains were reversed with a 1972 Directive that institutionalized restrictions on capital movements and with a tolerant approach to national safeguard measures of unlimited duration. Liberalization advanced again in the context of the internal market and the economic and monetary union in the late 1980s and early 1990s. The European Court of Justice took the new more strongly worded provisions on the free movement of capital seriously in its jurisprudence, giving Article 63 TFEU direct effect, and interpreting the notion of restriction broadly and the exception in Article 65(1)(a) TFEU narrowly. Yet it soon backtracked in its tax case law, adopted a permissive approach to justifications in the third country context, and moved towards an exclusive approach in respect of the application of the freedoms, with the result that the rules on establishment or services often take precedence over those concerning capital. At the same time, Member States wrote a new exception to the Treaty to reduce the role of the judicature. Altogether, the law has split into a number of distinct subspecies, with different approaches for regulatory and tax rules and for intra- and extra-Union situations.

The evolution will undoubtedly continue.[171] The tension between the law on regulatory and tax restrictions will give ample ammunition to parties wishing to challenge the status quo. The ruling that the answers provided in the intra-EU context may not apply for capital movements to or from third countries provides fertile

---

[169] Discussed in Part A above.

[170] Art 3 TFEU.

[171] The impact of the financial crisis that began in 2007 is another source of evolutionary pressure. In particular, the stricter regulation of financial institutions may create new restrictions. For the most recent developments, see N Tait, 'EU financial services reform passes final hurdle' *Financial Times* 22 September 2010 on the creation of the European System of Financial Supervision.

ground for litigation. Altogether, the extra-EU aspect of the free movement of capital remains the least explored area of the four freedoms, and may well result in significant tensions, even with the Court's current comparatively cautious attitude and the new Article 65(4) TFEU.

Ultimately it is impossible to know for certain the reasons for the relatively restrained approach the Court has taken towards certain aspects of the free movement of capital, as it has never sought to explain the variations. The resistance of the Member States, in particular when coupled with the sometimes fierce criticism from the international tax law community, may have influenced the Court. The complexity of the field and the lack of judicial expertise, together with the political sensitivity and the potentially substantial financial consequences of the decisions are also likely to have played a major part.[172] After all, a rational response to a high probability of costly errors is caution. Further, some of the basic tools of the internal market law simply do not work well in this context. For example, nearly all national tax laws have been adopted for economic reasons and are liable to dissuade cross-border movement. The traditional approach of the Court would therefore strike them all down as unjustified restrictions. The logic of mutual recognition that underpins much of the case law also reaches its limits here. While consumer protection measures adopted by the home country may also protect the consumers in the host country, revenue collection by one state in no way protects the fiscal interests of another.

The Spaak Report that laid the foundations for the original EEC Treaty saw the free movement of capital as the last of the freedoms, to be achieved after the others had been completed. This has proven correct. However, while the liberalization of capital movements has been slow, its effects may yet prove to be profound. The free movement of capital is a part of deep integration. It does not merely relate to movement of tradable products, but affects the way production is organized in various countries. The issue is no longer simply competition between products, but methods of production are affected directly. As such, the free movement of capital is likely to create challenges to coordinated market economies that have traditionally relied on patient capital and have therefore been able to promote production strategies that forgo immediate profits in favour of more long-term success. The free movement of capital, together with the free movement of companies under the right of establishment, has the capacity to affect fundamentally how capital is provided and organized within the EU. Market-based coordination mechanisms familiar from liberal market economies may become more important, upsetting the structures and institutions that coordinated market economies have relied upon. But that, as they say, is another story.[173]

---

[172] See M J Graetz and A C Warren Jr, 'Dividend Taxation in Europe: When the ECJ Makes Tax Policy' (2007) 44 CML Rev 1577 for a taste of the complexity just in the area of dividend taxation.

[173] See generally P A Hall and D Soskice, 'An Introduction to Varieties of Capitalism' in P A Hall and D Soskice (eds), *Varieties of Capitalism: The Institutional Foundations of Comparative Advantage* (Oxford University Press, 2001); M Höpner and A Schäfer, 'A New Phase of European Integration: Organized Capitalisms in Post-Ricardian Europe' MPIfG Discussion Paper 07/4; J Snell, 'Economic Integration, Varieties of Capitalism, and the Lisbon Treaty', a paper presented at the University of Leeds, 4 September 2009.

19

CITIZENSHIP: CONTRASTING DYNAMICS AT THE INTERFACE OF INTEGRATION AND CONSTITUTIONALISM

*Jo Shaw**

A. INTRODUCTION

This chapter explores the different ways in which citizenship, both as a resonant political ideal and as a legal status attached to individuals, has played a role in polity formation beyond the state, specifically in relation to the EU as an emergent non-state polity. It explores two dimensions of citizenship as it operates in the Union context. The first concerns the role of 'citizenship of the Union' as a legal status, viewed in relation to the function of EU law as a framework for integration based on Treaties agreed between the Member States, but endowed with institutions which operate autonomously—in particular a Court of Justice. Studying this dimension of citizenship in the EU context has traditionally implied a primary focus on the transnational character of most Union citizenship rights as enumerated in the Treaties and interpreted by the Court of Justice. However, as we shall see—as in other fields of EU law— the Court of Justice is now tentatively exploring the terrain of citizenship beyond or, perhaps better, outwith the immediate confines of the single market, deploying the symbolic capital of citizenship-related arguments in ways which seem more and more remote from the immediate practices of the single market. The second dimension of citizenship under the microscope concerns the actual and potential role of citizenship *in* (not *of*) the Union as a polity. Can citizenship be about more than individual rights (and duties?), and can it acquire a distinct political dimension appropriate to a polity evolving beyond the state, albeit not without reference to the states which comprise its constituent partners. This is the task of identifying the putative constitutional

* Salvesen Chair of European Institutions at the University of Edinburgh.

character of citizenship in the European Union. Part B explains in more detail the approach adopted by the chapter, and Parts C and D explore those two dimensions with a view, in particular, to understanding the relationship between them. As these sections will show, the dual character of the Union's constitutional nature makes it harder to develop a secure understanding of how citizenship fits into the framework of the Union.

Before moving on, however, a word of introduction is needed to delimit the scope of this chapter in order to put the argument into its proper context. It is important to draw a distinction between the study of citizenship in the context of a state and its study in the context of the European Union. Citizenship *of* the Union, as introduced by the Treaty of Maastricht in 1993, has often been mocked as a form of 'citizenship-lite', or as a purely symbolic status, redolent of rights without identity, and of access without belonging.[1] When the Court of Justice asserted in *Grzelczyk* that citizenship of the Union was 'destined to be the fundamental status of the nationals of the Member States',[2] it was outlining an aspiration and not claiming that this was presently the case. It is also a rather confusing statement, given that—as a *status*—citizenship of the Union is dependent upon the differing approaches to citizenship definition of the Member States,[3] as only the nationals of the Member States are citizens of the Union (Article 20(1) TFEU). Whether it becomes the fundamental basis on which such persons hold *rights* is another matter entirely. Presently the list of rights ascribed to *mobile* EU citizens under the Treaties themselves is rather limited and the impact of EU citizenship on nationals of the Member States who do not exercise their free movement rights is even less clear. It could be argued that the Court itself acknowledges that point because it went on in *Grzelczyk* to say that Union citizenship enables 'those who find themselves in the same situation to enjoy the same treatment in law irrespective of their nationality, subject to such exceptions as are expressly provided for'.[4] In other words, at that point the Court was expressly recognizing that the basis of Union citizenship in law at the present has been as an equal treatment law. This has been evident since its initial case law on the interpretation of Union citizenship in the late 1990s, and on that view the case law since that time has largely been focused on finding the limits of that equal treatment principle, with the Court of Justice not always being entirely consistent in its approach.[5] The non-discrimination approach remains in large measure the defining characteristic of most EU citizenship case law into the

---

[1] W Maas, 'Unrespected, Unequal, Hollow ? Contingent Citizenship and Reversible Rights in the European Union' (2009) 15 CJEL 265.

[2] Case C-184/99 *Grzelczyk v Centre public d'aide sociale d'Ottignies-Louvain-La-Neuve* [2001] ECR-I 6193, [31].

[3] For details on this question, see the country profile sections of the EUDO-Citizenship Observatory: <http://www.eudo-citizenship.eu>. See further D Kochenov, '*Ius Tractum* of Many Faces: European Citizenship and the Difficult Relationship between Status and Rights' (2009) 15 CJEL 169.

[4] Grzelczyk (n 2 above) [31].

[5] See for example the analysis of S O'Leary, 'Equal Treatment and EU Citizens: A New Chapter on Cross Border Educational Mobility and Access to Student Financial Assistance' (2009) 34 ELRev 612.

second decade of the twenty-first century, although—as we shall see below—the Court has taken some steps towards asserting pro-actively how EU citizenship could be seen as constraining the scope and boundaries of national citizenship.

It is clear that the concept of citizenship as it operates in relation to a state still remains a much more rounded creature than citizenship of the Union. Subject to the strictures of international law[6] and EU law,[7] states act as their own gatekeepers in terms of determining the body of the citizenry. Moreover, at the national level, citizenship is invested with an intensity of political significance and substance, and a connection to the body politic in the broadest sense. The same cannot be said in the case of the EU, which is a polity whose 'own' elections (ie elections of members of the European Parliament) tend to be fought on the basis of national political platforms by national political parties fielding national candidates, despite the existence of electoral rights for EU citizens under Articles 22(2)(b) and 23 TFEU. In practice, most of the legal regulations governing European Parliament elections are national, not European in character.[8]

Even so, to adopt a phrase coined by Niamh Nic Shuibhne, the EU appears to be a 'citizenship-capable polity', from a normative perspective.[9] That is, it is a polity which displays the types of constitutional features where one might also expect to find some sort of concept of membership in operation as a means of distinguishing between groups of included and excluded persons, and rules setting out the boundaries and contents of rights and duties. Thus it is a polity based on a constitutional framework underpinned by the rule of law, respect for fundamental rights and principles of accountability, including (limited) electoral accountability, but also accountability through judicial review and a variety of other mechanisms, such as the right to complain to the Ombudsman, to petition the European Parliament and to seek access to documents. We should expect therefore to find some evidence of citizenship-related practices *in* the context of the EU's development as a polity. 'Citizenship-capability' thus seems a reasonable intuition with which to begin the discussion, although no one could deny that there are many challenges to such a notion, not least because both the process and structures of European integration remain highly contested and because the idea of the EU undertaking 'citizenship-type' tasks and activities struggles to attain a legitimate status in the eyes of many citizens of the Member States. It is hard, for example, to imagine the EU in its present stage of development acquiring the 'obligations' dimension of the citizenship concept, given the limitations upon its legal competences as well as limited recognition of its political capacity. Hence even with

---

[6] *Liechtenstein v Guatemala (Nottebohm)* 1955 ICJ 4.

[7] Case C-369/90 *Micheletti v Delegacion del Gobierno en Cantabria* [1992] ECR I-4239; Case C-135/08 *Rottmann v Freistaat Bayern* [2010] All ER 52.

[8] This point was recognized by the Court of Justice in Case C-145/04 *Spain v United Kingdom* [2006] ECR I-07917.

[9] N Nic Shuibhne, 'The Outer Limits of EU Citizenship; Displacing Economic Free Movement Rights?' in C Barnard and O Odudu (eds), *The Outer Limits of European Union Law* (Hart, 2009) 167–195, 168; the idea is discussed in more detail in N Nic Shuibhne, 'The Resilience of EU Market Citizenship', (2010) 47 Common Market Law Review 1597–1628.

such soft intuitions, caution should be exercised. All in all, if a good working definition of citizenship combines elements of rights, access, and belonging,[10] then the value-added of citizenship at the EU level is strongest in relation to the rights to which it gives rise, but much weaker in relation to questions of access and belonging. One task of this chapter will be to consider to what extent this is changing, and if so, in what ways and with what consequences.

B. KEY QUESTIONS IN (EU) CITIZENSHIP STUDIES

The key to understanding citizenship's role within the European Union is to avoid thinking about Union citizenship and citizenship of the Member States as two separate and unrelated phenomena, even though they are different in character. The two concepts are not linked just because one (national citizenship) gives access to the other (Union citizenship), or because the Treaties have always reinforced their complementary character. On the contrary, the complex relationship between the two can only be effectively understood by deploying a composite concept of citizenship which links together the different levels and different spheres in which individuals claim citizenship rights, carry out citizenship duties, and act out citizenship practices. In other words, we should focus on citizenship *in* the EU context, not specifically and solely on citizenship *of* the Union. For those who live in complex polities which exhibit shifting and evolving vertical and horizontal relationships between different levels and spheres of political authority, citizenship itself is best understood multi-perspectively. The concept of citizenship operating in Europe today is both multi-level and composite in character. It comprises a range of different legal statuses at the international, supranational, national, and subnational level—as well as at the level of individual and group identity—with various normative systems cutting across each other and, from time to time, coming into conflict. In important respects, however, these different elements are mutually constitutive. Samantha Besson and André Utzinger[11] explain the evolution of a composite 'European' citizenship in an interesting way. They argue that changes have not occurred:

> by supplanting national citizenships and replacing them with an overarching supranational citizenship of the Union... Rather, citizenship remains strongly anchored at the national level in Europe albeit in a different way. The change is both quantitative and qualitative. First, citizenship in Europe has become multi-levelled as European citizens are members of

---

[10] See A Wiener, 'From *Special* to *Specialized* Rights: The Politics of Citizenship and Identity in the European Union' in M Hanagan and C Tilly (eds), *Extending Citizenship, Reconfiguring States*, (Rowman and Littlefield, 1999) 200–201.

[11] S Besson and A Utzinger, 'Towards European Citizenship' (2008) JSP 185, 196; see also L Besselink, 'Case Notes on *Gibraltar, Aruba, and Sevinger and Eman v The Netherlands*' (2008) 45 CML Rev 787, 801 arguing that the composite constitutional arrangement underpinning the Euro-polity is not a 'monolithic European concept of citizenship'.

different polities both horizontally across Europe (other Member States) and vertically (European transnational, international and supranational institutions). Second, national citizenship in and of itself has changed in quality and has been made more inclusive in its scope and mode of functioning. Union citizenship adds a European dimension to each national *demos* and, to a certain extent, alters national citizenship in reconceiving it in a complementary relation to other Member States' citizenships.

Their argument reinforces the point that engaging in citizenship practices in the context of the Euro-polity—ie in relation to the EU and its Member States viewed as a composite and conjoined polity—does not involve a zero-sum game. Indeed, as has been articulated in the EU Treaties since the Treaty of Amsterdam, Union citizenship and national citizenship are complementary in character and the former, in particular, is not supposed to supplant or replace the latter, but rather to be additional to it (Article 20(1) TFEU). A similar approach is suggested by Christoph Schönberger, who argues in favour of thinking about citizenship in the Union from a federal perspective, which means we must 'free ourselves from the unitary state-centred categories and consider the possibility of *tiered, nested citizenships in federal systems*'.[12] Coming at the issue from the point of view of international law, the approach here shares much in common with the dual track approach to democratic legitimation within the context of the constitutionalization of international law, adopted by Anne Peters in her joint work with Jan Klabbers and Geir Ulfstein.[13] As Peters argues, a democratized world order depends for its legitimacy both upon democracy *within* states and within *international institutions and processes*.

Against that backdrop, this chapter seeks answers to four central questions about the role of these composite concepts of citizenship in the evolution of the Union as a polity:

- At the highest level of generality, what role has citizenship played in the 'constitutionalization' of the European Union and thus in the process of polity-formation beyond the state?

- How has the concept of citizenship—specifically the concept of citizenship of the Union, but also more generally the idea of the Union being 'citizenship-capable'—been used within and/or affected by the evolution of the law/integration/disintegration narrative? What difference has citizenship made to the evolution of the law governing free movement and the principle of non-discrimination which together underpin the (market) integration project of the EU?

- What more, if anything, is there to citizenship of the Union outwith the integration or market citizenship dynamic, specifically in the context of the role of citizens in the democratic legitimation of policies and institutions?

---

[12] Emphasis in the original. C Schönberger, 'European Citizenship as Federal Citizenship: Some Citizenship Lessons of Comparative Federalism' (2007) 19 Rev Eur Dr Pub 61.

[13] See J Klabbers, A Peters, and G Ulfstein, *The Constitutionalization of International Law* (Oxford University Press, 2009) ch 6.

- Drawing a distinction between 'old' constitutionalism (the 'constitutionalization' of the Treaties) and 'new' constitutionalism (the search for a 'refounding' of the Union on the basis of a single 'constitutional' text), can we discern any differences in how the concepts of citizenship *of* and *in* the Union have been understood and used by the key actors in the processes of legal and institutional change?

The aim is to complement existing literatures which have adopted other related 'evolutionary' perspectives upon citizenship questions. There have already been numerous descriptive and analytical surveys of the evolution and entrenchment of a concept of citizenship into the political and legal framework of the European Union, starting from the inception of the EEC Treaty and focusing on the roles of the European Parliament, the European Commission, the Court of Justice, and latterly the Member States at the intergovernmental conferences which led to the Treaty of Maastricht. There has been work which has made use of both politico-legal[14] and political science/international relations perspectives,[15] as well as more recent attempts to explain the subsequent evolution of the Court of Justice's case law.[16] More adventurous work has addressed these questions via the dynamics of institutional change using various tools drawn from political science,[17] or on the basis of rights theories of legal philosophers such as Ronald Dworkin and Robert Alexy.[18] The precise character of Union citizenship has come under scrutiny from multiple angles including normative political philosophy,[19] political science,[20] political sociology,[21] as well as the obvious reference point of legal scholarship. From time to time, the specific relationship between

---

[14] J Shaw, 'Citizenship of the Union: Towards Post-national Membership?' in Academy of European Law (ed), *Collected Courses of the Academy of European Law*, Vol VI, Book 1, (Kluwer Law International, 1998) 237–347; J Shaw, 'The Interpretation of European Union Citizenship' (1998) 61 MLR 293; M Elmore and P Starup, 'Union Citizenship—Background, Jurisprudence, and Perspective: the Past, Present, and Future of Law and Policy' (2007) 26 YEL 57.

[15] A Wiener, *'European' Citizenship Practice. Building Institutions of a Non-State* (Westview Press, 1998); W Maas, *Creating European Citizens* (Rowman and Littlefield, 2007); id, 'The Genesis of European Rights' (2005) 43 JCMS 1009; E Olsen, 'The Origins of European Citizenship in the First Two Decades of European Integration' (2008) 15 JEPP 40.

[16] Especially by current and former members of the Court of Justice: eg F Jacobs, 'Citizenship of the European Union—A Legal Analysis' (2007) 13 ELJ 591; J Kokott, *EU citizenship—citoyens sans frontières?* Annual Lecture of the Durham European Law Institute, 2005.

[17] D Kostakopoulou, 'Ideas, Norms and European Citizenship: Explaining Institutional Change' (2005) 68 MLR 233.

[18] Y Borgmann-Prebil, 'The Rule of Reason in European Citizenship' (2008) 14 ELJ 328.

[19] R Bellamy, 'Evaluating Union Citizenship: Belonging, Rights and Participation within the EU' (2008) 12 Citizenship Studies, 597–611; R Bellamy, 'The "Right to Have Rights": Citizenship Practice and the Political Constitution of the EU' in R Bellamy and A Warleigh (eds), *Citizenship and Governance in the European Union* (Continuum, 2001) 41–70; R Bauböck, 'Why European Citizenship? Normative Approaches to Supranational Union' (2007) 8 Theo Inq L 452; D Kostakopoulou, 'European Union Citizenship: Writing the Future' (2007) 13 ELJ 623; Besson and Utzinger (n 11 above).

[20] W Maas, 'Migrants, States, and EU Citizenship's Unfulfilled Promise' (2008) 12 Citizenship Studies 583; K Eder and B Giesen (eds), *European Citizenship. National Legacies and Transnational Projects* (Oxford University Press, 2001).

[21] G Delanty, 'European Citizenship: A Critical Reassessment' (2007) 11 Citizenship Studies 63.

citizenship of the Union and the citizenship laws of the Member States has been closely examined, with sharply differing conclusions amongst scholars as to the residual significance of national citizenship law in an era of Europeanization and, indeed, globalization.[22] Finally, in my own work, I focused on exploring in detail the developmental character of citizenship as currently constituted in the EU through a case study of the electoral rights guaranteed under the EU Treaties.[23]

Rather than simply add to this substantial corpus of material, the approach chosen here is a little different. It will, inevitably, cover some of the same ground, and indeed it must do so, because it remains important to chart both the emergence of a concept of citizenship and its instantiation in the Treaties, legislative measures, and case law as well as in certain broader social and political practices which constitute 'European' politics, so far as it exists. This is a story which 'can be seen as a microcosm of some of the key variables at play within the story of EU integration more generally'.[24] But this ground will be covered with a specific purpose in mind, which is to show that there are two distinct and quite different discourses on citizenship operating within the framework of the European Union, and that there is—perhaps surprisingly—relatively little interaction between the two. On the one hand, we can see that in relation to the principles of free movement and non-discrimination which represent the central pillars of the EU's single market and legal integration project, citizenship has become—since the late 1990s—an important factor in legal and policy development. The 'legacy of market citizenship',[25] predicted by Michele Everson in the early 1990s, has proved to be even more durable than might have been expected, and in many respects it has been the activism of the Court of Justice which has contributed to this. In comparison, in relation to the further development of treaty-based reform since the heady days of the early 1990s when the Member States first appeared to subscribe to the Commission's much vaunted manifesto of creating 'special rights' for Union citizens,[26] there have been noticeably fewer changes and a general failure to harness the resonance of citizenship as a political and legal concept. It is possible to explain why this is so, and these issues will be explored in full in Part D.

There is, of course, a well worn argument that the Court of Justice has been and remains the main engine of European integration. This argument retains some traction even today, not least for the purposes of offsetting the continuing widespread ignorance about what the Court of Justice does, which is still to be found amongst

---

[22] C Closa, 'Citizenship of the Union and Nationality of the Member States' (1995) 32 CML Rev 487; G-R De Groot, 'Towards a European Nationality Law' EJCL Vol 8.3 (October 2004), at <http://www.ejcl.org/>; D Kochenov, *Rounding up the Circle: The Mutation of Member States' Nationalities under Pressure from EU Citizenship*, EUDO-Citizenship Working Paper (2010, forthcoming) <http://www.eudo-citizenship.eu>; G Davies, '"Any Place I Hang My Hat?" or: Residence is the New Nationality' (2005) 11 ELJ 43.

[23] J Shaw, *The Transformation of Citizenship in the European Union. Electoral Rights and the Restructuring of Political Space* (Cambridge University Press, 2007).

[24] Shaw (n 23 above) 93.

[25] M Everson, 'The Legacy of the Market Citizen' in J Shaw and G More (eds), *New Legal Dynamics of European Union* (Oxford University Press, 1995) 73–90.

[26] Wiener (n 15 above) especially chs 5 and 8.

many scholars of European integration; but it is an argument that must in truth be treated with caution as it would tend to 'overstate the integrative capacity of law and posit a view of the case law as progressing ineluctably to a particular constitutional *finalité*.[27] More precisely, the point of the comparison here is to draw attention to the contrast between how the powerful notion of citizenship is regularly used in a symbolic manner by the Court of Justice, sometimes in conjunction with human rights arguments,[28] in order to justify some of its most daring judgments on free movement and single market questions since the end of the 1990s onwards, and the more sporadic and less effective invocation of citizenship questions in political debates about EU constitutionalism. Since the grandiose 'establishment' of Union citizenship in the Treaty structure through the Treaty of Maastricht, there have been few institutional developments of note aimed at reconstructing the position of the individual citizen as a political subject, as opposed to invoking the collective name of 'citizens', as the basis for a claim to be constructing 'a Europe for its citizens', which is 'close to its citizens'.[29] The relative poverty of the political rhetoric and action in this field has not, of course, silenced other voices, especially those of scholars, who have picked up on the inevitable centrality of concepts of citizenship in the context of polity-building,[30] but much of the academic debate has stalled around the fundamental demos/no demos debate. For some,[31] debating European citizenship is a futile exercise, as there cannot be a European people for there European state, and thus in the absence of a common identity based on a 'story of peoplehood',[32] there cannot be a 'European' citizenship. Such a notion could only ever be artifice. For others, the telos of European integration demands a strong concept of citizenship and although it is acknowledged that at present it is in a state of becoming, rather than the finished article, its construction none the less remains the central normative challenge for the Union, the Member States, and political elites.[33] A 'middle way' focuses on the articulation of the EU as a

---

[27] See J Hunt and J Shaw, 'Fairy Tale of Luxembourg? Reflections on Law and Legal Scholarship in European Integration' in D Phinnemore and A Warleigh-Lack (eds), *Reflections on European Integration. 50 Years of the Treaty of Rome* (Palgrave Macmillan, 2009) 93–108, 111.

[28] This has been particularly visible in cases where there is a family reunion element involved, where the Court has often been ready to invoke Art 8 ECHR to support its arguments. See for example Case C-200/02 *Chen v Secretary of State for the Home Department* [2004] ECR I-9925 and Case C-127/08 *Metock and Others v Minister for Justice, Equality and Law Reform* [2008] ECR I-06241.

[29] The best example of such rhetoric is the Laeken Declaration, Presidency Conclusions of the European Council meeting of 14 and 15 December 2001, available on the European Convention website at <http://european-convention.eu.int/pdf/LKNEN.pdf>. This is discussed in more detail below.

[30] N Walker, 'Denizenship and Deterritorialisation in the European Union' in H Lindahl (ed), *A Right to Inclusion and Exclusion*, (Hart, 2009) 261–272.

[31] See, most recently, a return to the *demos*/no *demos* arguments under the shadow of the German Federal Constitutional Court's decision on the constitutionality of the Treaty of Lisbon: D Grimm, 'Comments on the German Constitutional Court's Decision on the Lisbon Treaty. Defending Sovereign Statehood against Transforming the European Union into a State' (2010) 5 ECL Rev 353.

[32] R Smith, *Stories of Peoplehood. The Politics and Morals of Political Membership* (Cambridge University Press, 2003).

[33] M Aziz, 'Implementation as the Test Case of Union Citizenship' (2009) 15 CJEL 281.

'demoi-cracy', not a democracy, where it is the interplay between the still largely national spheres of democratic practice, rather than the attempt to create a single holistic democratic sphere at the EU level, which is the central normative challenge.[34] In that sense, the debate in the EU context has reflected in certain respects a broader debate about whether citizenship at the *state* level is withering away in the face of the effects of globalization and the widespread invocation of international law as the root of many human rights claims. Citizenship, on this reading, is transformed into a multivalent form of postnational membership.[35]

This paper does not seek to add further enlightenment to these important scholarly and political debates, but rather it is an attempt to identify and analyse relevant institutional practices which incrementally constitute the Union's emergence as a polity which is more than simply an international organization grounded on treaties between sovereign states. The focus here is on how citizenship concepts have been used in legal and constitutional contexts and on the contestations and debates which have occurred around such use. The aim is to draw out some of the patterns and exchanges between key actors, with a view to understanding how these key ideas have developed. If there is a political conclusion to be drawn, then it is this: citizenship still has an uncertain 'constitutional' role in the European Union and this can be attributed at least in part to the uneasy shift which has occurred between 'old' and 'incremental' versions of European constitutionalism based on the classic law/integration interface and the 'newer' more formalized ones, epitomized by the grand and ultimately misplaced 'dreams' of a 'Constitution for Europe's citizens' trailed in the Laeken Declaration of December 2001. This was a dream which went on to dominate the Convention on the Future of Europe and even the intergovernmental conference which finalized the draft produced by the Convention into a formal treaty text, until it turned into a nightmare with the negative referenda on the Treaty establishing a Constitution for Europe in France and the Netherlands in Spring 2005. At that moment, it became clear that whatever Europe's citizens expected of the Union, it was not reasonable for elites to expect citizens to offer an easy acceptance of a ready-made 'European constitution', perceived as having been imposed with minimum consultation and little democratic legitimacy. Thus, in contrast to some scholars, I do not see the different practices of the EU institutions (judicial, legislative, executive) as capable of being subsumed under a single normative argument about the fundamental character of EU citizenship.[36]

---

[34] S Besson, 'Deliberative demoi-cracy in the European Union: Towards the Deterritorialization of Democracy' in S Besson and JL Marti (eds), *Deliberative Democracy and its Discontents: National and Post-National Challenges* (Ashgate, 2006) 181–214; K Nicolaïdes, 'We, the Peoples of Europe...' (2004) 83 Foreign Affairs 97; Besson and Utzinger (n 11 above).

[35] For a somewhat partial review of the debates see R Hansen, 'The Poverty of Postnationalism: Citizenship, Immigration, and the New Europe' (2009) 38 Theory and Society 1; see also C Joppke, 'The Vulnerability of Non-citizens' (2009) 39 Perspectives on Europe 18; C Joppke, 'Transformation of Citizenship: Status, Rights, Identity' (2007) 11 Citizenship Studies 37.

[36] See D Kostakopoulou, 'European Union Citizenship: Writing the Future' (2007) 13 ELJ 623.

C. CITIZENSHIP, FREE MOVEMENT, AND THE 'OLD' CONSTITUTIONALISM OF THE EUROPEAN UNION

1. 'OLD' AND 'NEW' CONSTITUTIONALISM

The narrative of citizenship in the context of European integration predates by some distance the rather protracted and ultimately fruitless post-Laeken debates about formulating a single 'constitutional' text for the Union. (EU) citizenship, in its origins, belongs to an earlier perhaps more optimistic era, before the expectations and later anxieties of the 2000s about the fading promise of codifying a constitutional text for the Union. Indeed, from the 1970s onwards, drawing on what one might call the 'proto-citizenship' case law of the Court of Justice,[37] some lawyers were talking of an 'incipient form' of European citizenship.[38] 'Citizenship', in this sense, has long been linked to the manner in which the Court of Justice has interpreted the provisions of the Treaty governing the free movement and non-discrimination rights of individuals, and in particular its willingness—even in advance of legislative[39] and later Treaty developments[40]—to extend the categories of protected persons beyond the traditional groups of economically active persons protected by the EEC Treaties (workers, self-employed, service-providers) and to put in place strict scrutiny of national restrictions on free movement and practices discriminating against EU citizens, subject to the application of a proportionality test. Interestingly enough, some of the main beneficiaries of this case law were students, some of whom have gone on to comment positively upon the interface between free movement, non-discrimination, and citizenship in an academic capacity.[41]

---

[37] See eg Case 293/87 *Gravier v City of Liège* [1985] ECR 593; Case 186/87 *Cowan v Le Trésor public* [1989] ECR 195.

[38] See W Böhning, *The Migration of Workers in the United Kingdom and the European Community*, (Oxford University Press, 1972), cited in B Wilkinson, 'Towards European Citizenship? Nationality, Discrimination and Free Movement of Workers in the European Union' (1995) 1 EPL 417, 418; R Plender, 'An Incipient Form of European Citizenship' in F Jacobs (ed), *European Law and the Individual* (North Holland, 1976) 39–52; A Evans, 'European Citizenship: A Novel Concept in EEC Law' (1984) AJCL 679; G Ress, 'Free Movement of Persons, Services and Capital' in Commission of the European Communities (ed), *Thirty Years of Community Law*, Luxembourg: OOPEC, 1981, 302, has a section entitled 'Are we on the way towards creating European citizenship?'

[39] See the three Council Directives introduced in 1990 and 1993 (now repealed and replaced by European Parliament and Council Directive 2004/38 on Citizens' Rights, [2004] OJ L158/77) which provided for the free movement of students, those of independent means, and retired persons.

[40] Treaty developments focus on what was Art 8A EC, immediately after the entry into force of the Treaty of Maastricht, which is now Art 20(2)(a) TFEU. This guarantees the right of citizens to move and reside freely within the territory of the Member States.

[41] If a note of personal 'evolution' may be permitted, I would observe that I belong to the pre-*Gravier* era of free moving students, having studied at the Institut des Etudes Européennes of the Université Libre de Bruxelles at a time when the *minerval* (or fee) imposed on foreign students and outlawed by *Gravier* (n 37 above) was still collected.

Citizenship, in this sense, is also a part of what I would term the 'old' constitutionalism of the European Union.[42] This is a form of constitutionalism which, whilst 'old' in the sense of being rooted in the early days of the evolution of the EU legal order, remains as central as ever to understanding whether, how, and why we can regard the EU today as a constitutionalized polity, not least since the Member States—in formulating the negotiating brief for the 'Reform Treaty' (ie what became the Treaty of Lisbon)—self-consciously disavowed the 'constitutional' mandate of the Laeken Declaration as well as the symbols and mottos of the Constitutional Treaty.[43] Thus 'old' constitutionalism persists, alongside the 'reforms' of the Treaty of Lisbon, which retain a paradoxical relationship with the 'new' constitutionalism of the failed Constitutional Treaty. Much of the text is the same—but the constitutional vocation and mandate was stripped out and 'abandoned'.[44] Meanwhile 'old' constitutionalism continues, comprising not only the rules governing the relationship between the EU and the national legal orders (supremacy, direct effect, etc), the parallel principles of respect for limited competences and of implied powers, and the rule of law and judicial protection, combined with respect for fundamental rights, but also the core animating principles of the single market without which the EU legal order would, from the outset, have largely lacked a *raison d'être*. 'Old' constitutionalism thus brings (transnational) citizenship into the legal framework as a quasi-single market practice through the connection to free movement law, but citizenship in turn brings a human development angle which adds resonance to the effects of the legal order and in particular to the historic focus on *economic* integration from the neofunctionalist perspective which many scholars have argued underpinned the original European Economic Community Treaty.

The connection between citizenship and 'old' constitutionalism in this sense was reinforced at the moment when citizenship was included in the EU Treaties. The main rights which were formally attached to the concept were precisely those transnational rights which are triggered when an individual exercises his or her free movement rights, and is resident in a Member State other than the one of which he or she is a national or, less commonly, when he or she returns to the home state after exercising free movement rights and faces obstacles to accessing, for example, welfare or educational benefits, as a result of having exercised free movement rights. The right to move and reside freely in the territory of the Member States is the centrepiece of the Treaty rights (Articles 20(2)(a) and 21 TFEU), along with the right to vote and stand in local and European Parliament elections on the basis of residence, not citizenship, and under the same conditions as nationals (Articles 20(2)(b) and 22 TFEU). In addition, there are rights to diplomatic protection

---

[42] See generally J Shaw, 'One or Many Constitutions? The Constitutional Future of the European Union in the 2000s from a Legal Perspective' (2007) 52 Scandinavian Stud L 393.

[43] Presidency Conclusions, Council Document 11177/1/07, Rev 1, Concl 2, 20 July 2007, Annex 1, IGC Mandate.

[44] ibid point 1 of the Mandate.

when outwith the territory of the Union, and rights concerned with transparency and access to the institutions, although these latter are not exclusive to citizens but are also given to legal and natural persons *resident* in the Member States.

The link between these main citizenship rights and the right to non-discrimination on grounds of nationality (now Article 18 TFEU) is now, post-Lisbon, more evident than ever, as these two cornerstones of the EU legal order are included in the same part of the Treaty on the Functioning of the Union, headed 'Non-Discrimination and Citizenship'. Moreover, the Court of Justice has linked them together in its case law, focusing on what was previously Article 17(2) EC, a freestanding statement that '[c]itizens of the Union shall enjoy the rights conferred by this Treaty and shall be subject to the duties imposed thereby', and emphasizing that the right to non-discrimination is central to the 'rights enjoyed'. It did this first in the groundbreaking case of *Martínez Sala*,[45] when it chose to adopt an approach to protecting the rights of a long-standing and apparently well integrated member of German society who none the less retained Spanish citizenship which cut across its previous case law on migrant workers and workseekers, and it has continued to do so ever since even though its case law has not always been entirely internally consistent. In fact, setting aside the right of residence, which is specifically articulated within the citizenship provisions but has required creative judicial interpretation to render it directly effective,[46] the only 'right conferred by this Treaty' other than non-discrimination which the Court of Justice has invoked within the framework of a citizenship case is the general right to equal treatment. This came in its judgment in a reference for a preliminary ruling from a Dutch court concerning the right of Netherlands nationals (ie EU citizens) to vote in European Parliament elections when resident in Aruba—a non-European and quasi-autonomous territory of the Kingdom of the Netherlands.[47]

All of the above reinforces the argument that the most obvious quality of citizenship *of* the Union is above all its *transnational*, not its *postnational* character, an argument which fits well with much scholarship which has addressed the increasingly porous boundaries of *national* citizenships in the context of globalization and Europeanization.[48] This is precisely what led Paul Magnette to use the term 'isopolity', drawn from the Greek traditions of city states, to describe the current basis of EU citizenship, and to deduce certain political conclusions from the choices made by the 'masters' of the Treaty:

> The fact that the authors of the treaty have developed this horizontal dimension of citizenship, rather than the vertical bonds between the citizens and the Union, confirms

---

[45] Case C-85/96 *Martínez Sala v Freistaat Bayern* [1998] ECR-I 2691.

[46] In Case C-413/99 *Baumbast and R* [2002] ECR I-7091 the Court concluded that the right of residence as expressed in the EC Treaty was directly effective, thus allowing the Court to scrutinize the reasonableness and proportionality of the restrictions placed upon the right of free movement, in accordance with the text of the Treaty: Art 18 EC and now Art 21 TFEU; see also Case C-200/02 *Chen v Secretary of State for the Home Department* [2004] ECR I-9925.

[47] Case C-300/04 *Eman and Sevinger v College van burgemeester en wethouders van Den Haag* (Aruba) [2006] ECR I-8055.

[48] See eg J Fox, 'Unpacking "Transnational Citizenship"' (2005) 8 Annual Review of Political Science 171.

that they intended to build a 'federation of states' rather than a 'European state'. In the EU, as in the ancient leagues of Greek cities, the *isopoliteia* is more developed than the *sympoliteia*.[49]

Because of the weakness of the vertical bonds, the 'static' European citizen, in contrast to the mobile transnational one, does not seem to derive many benefits from the institution of citizenship as a fundamental building block of the European Union. We shall focus on this question in the next section and see whether or not Magnette's proposition still holds true to the same extent.

2. CITIZENSHIP, FREE MOVEMENT, AND NON-DISCRIMINATION

We should now explore in more detail the extent to which the formalization of a concept of citizenship has had an impact upon the evolution of free movement and non-discrimination law, in order to identify the significance of the citizenship/'old' constitutionalism interaction. This is an area where the Court of Justice has led the way, but where it is increasingly important also to have regard to the role of the legislature, especially when its work is viewed in combination with the Court of Justice. We can, for example, anticipate that there is likely to be an increasing body of case law on the interpretation of the Citizens' Rights Directive of 2004,[50] not least because the implementation of this Directive at the national level has been a particular cause of concern for the Commission.[51] In its early case law on the Directive, there has been some uncertainty about the Court's approach. On the one hand, it has given a broad interpretation of the rights of mobile EU citizens to be joined by their third country national family members,[52] and it has declined to allow the restrictions on the conditions placed on the right of residence in Directive 2004/38 to prevent it using the earlier Regulation No 1612/68, which is still in force, to find a right of residence for non-self-sufficient non-national carers of EU citizen children in full-time education in the host state.[53] On the other hand, it has taken a more equivocal and uneven approach to the challenge of working out the relationship between the restrictions which Member States may place on access to welfare benefits by mobile EU citizens, the derogations from the equal treatment principle permitted in the Directive (notably Article 24(2)), and the Court's own pre-existing case law on the relationship between

---

[49] P Magnette, *Citizenship: The History of an Idea* (ECPR, 2005) 177.

[50] European Parliament and Council Directive 2004/38 on Citizens' Rights, [2004] OJ L158/77.

[51] See for details of the Citizens' Rights Directive (n 39 above); on the role of the Commission in transposition and implementation see Commission Communication, on Guidance for better transposition and application of Directive 2004/38/EC on the right of citizens and their family members to move and reside freely within the territory of the Member States, COM(2009) 313, building on an earlier report of 2008 (COM (2008) 840).

[52] Case C-127/08 *Metock and Others v Minister for Justice, Equality and Law Reform* [2008] ECR I-6241.

[53] See Case C-480/08 *Teixeira v London Borough of Lambeth*, 23 February 2010; Case C-310/08 *London Borough of Harrow v Ibrahim*, 23 February 2010.

what were—pre-Lisbon—Articles 12 and 18 EC (non-discrimination and the right of free movement).[54]

However, the central point here is to highlight the enthusiasm with which the Court of Justice, egged on at least initially by its Advocates General,[55] has embraced the possibilities of using the concept of citizenship of the Union in order to push its case law in directions which hardly seemed likely when these cases were 'merely' matters concerning the law on free movement and non-discrimination on grounds of nationality. It is true that even prior to the Treaty of Maastricht, in order to deal with cases where the putative beneficiaries of free movement and non-discrimination rights fell into marginal categories such as students, children, other persons not in the labour market such as carers and retired persons, and tourists, the Court already chose to deploy a teleological interpretation which pushed at the limits of the law. This was particularly visible in *Gravier*, where the Court put together the principle of non-discrimination on grounds of nationality along with an outline competence granted to the (then) European Economic Community in the field of vocational training (Article 128 EEC) in order to conclude that 'migrant' students had free movement rights within the territory of the Member States and were granted equal treatment with domestic students. But in the era of citizenship, the Court can add extra weight to its conclusions precisely by invoking this concept when it has to deal with the 'marginal' categories, who fall outwith the group of core economic actors. In so doing, the Court is simply making use of the extra tools put at its disposal. Thus, in recent years, the Court has overruled some of the conclusions which it reached in the era of 'mere' free movement. Overall, the Court has often reached conclusions which place greater weight on the value of free movement than they do on states' choices about the distribution of educational benefits or other public goods.[56] Thus the logic of the case law has carried the Court a long way away from its original and more modest pre-citizenship case law, even if a continuum of development can be seen.

In *Bidar*,[57] a case on educational benefits for students concerning the closeness of the connection to the host state which students needed to show before they could be entitled to subsidised loans and grants, it reversed its earlier ruling in *Brown*[58] on the

---

[54] See Case C-11/06 *Morgan v Bezirksregierung Köln* and Case C-12/06 *Bucher v Landrat des Kreises Düren* [2007] ECR I-9161 and, taking a somewhat different approach, Case C-158/07 *Förster v Hoofddirectie van de Informatie Beheer* [2008] ECR I-08507; see Cases C-22/08 and C-23/08 *Vatsouras and Koupatantze*, 4 June 2009. See generally O'Leary (n 5 above).

[55] N Burrows and R Greaves, *The Advocate General and EC Law* (Oxford University Press, 2007) ch 10.

[56] A Menéndez, 'European Citizenship after *Martínez Sala* and *Baumbast*: Has European Law Become More Human but Less Social' in M Maduro and L Azoulai (eds), *The Past and Future of EU Law; The Classics of EU Law Revisited on the 50th Anniversary of the Rome Treaty* (Hart, 2010) 363–393, and M Dougan, 'Expanding the Frontiers of Union Citizenship by Dismantling the Territorial Boundaries of the National Welfare States?' in Barnard and Odudo (n 9 above) 119–165.

[57] Case C-209/03 *R v London Borough of Ealing, ex p Bidar* [2005] ECR I-2119. On workseekers see Case C-138/02 *Collins v Secretary of State for Work and Pensions* [2004] ECR I-2703, as discussed in S O'Leary, Developing an Ever Closer Union between the Peoples of Europe, Edinburgh Mitchell Working Paper 6/2008, 15.

[58] Case 197/86 *Brown v Secretary of State for Scotland* [1988] ECR 3205.

grounds of the added value provided by the introduction of the citizenship provisions. Its treatment of the scope and effects of Article 7(2) of Regulation No 1612/68 in *Martínez Sala*[59] is hard to square with earlier case law on the extent to which persons not active in the labour market could receive the benefit of the non-discrimination principle such as *Lebon*.[60] Its approach to the differing rules on the formulation of surnames which exist in the Member States has seen a significant change of emphasis. In the era of *Konstantinidis*,[61] the Court preferred to ground its judgment on the existence of an economic link (however tenuous) between the rule under challenge (German rules on the transliteration of Greek names) and the presence of the applicant on the territory of the host Member States (as a self-employed masseur resident and working in Germany). Thus it opted for an approach based entirely on the risk of confusion in the market-place faced by a person exercising their freedom of establishment under Article 49 TFEU, rather than choosing the broad-based citizenship and fundamental rights approaches advocated by Advocate General Jacobs who urged the Court to allow nationals of the Member States to assert their rights by stating '*civis europeus sum*'. In the post-citizenship era, the issue in *Garcia Avello*[62] was the 'right to a name', in that case the right of dual Belgian-Spanish national children to use, when in Belgium, the Spanish version of their surnames, incorporating elements of the mother's and the father's name, notwithstanding Belgian rules on the 'unity' of the family surname. In this case, the applicants themselves were born and had resided throughout their lives in Belgium. In approach, if not in outcome, *Garcia Avello* effectively reversed *Konstantinidis*.[63] In other words, there is something in the Court's approach that involves more than the casual repetition of the 'destined to be the fundamental status' mantra,[64] and constitutes a real willingness to reconsider the (in some cases) long-standing boundaries of free movement law and to accept an ever remoter link to the actual exercise of free movement rights.

Thus in these cases concerned with the civil law status and recognition of individuals and their names we can note the dropping of the economic link. Accordingly the Court has been asked on a number of occasions to make dispositions about matters of national civil law (eg rules on names) which fall beyond the scope of EU law in ordinary circumstances, but which are caught by the principle that the Member States must exercise *their* competences in compatibility with their duties under EU law. When combined with the Court's willingness to impose a low threshold for triggering the applicability of EU law, by requiring the Member States to take care not to place obstacles in the way of exercising free movement rights, this generates a huge

---

[59] See n 45 above.

[60] Case 316/85 *Lebon* [1987] ECR 2811.

[61] Case C-168/91 *Konstantinides v Stadt Altensteig* [1993] ECR I-1191.

[62] Case C-148/02 *Garcia Avello v Belgian State* [2003] ECR I-11613; see also Case C-353/08 *Grunkin and Paul v Grunkin-Paul and Standesamt Stadt Niebüll* [2008] I-07639.

[63] For a more general discussion of the citizenship case law see J Shaw, 'A View of the Citizenship Classics: *Martínez Sala* and Subsequent Cases on Citizenship of the Union' in Maduro and Azoulai (n 56 above) 356–362.

[64] See n 2 above.

potential for the Court to intrude substantially into areas which are matters for national law (and also into the realm of private law as well as in distributional matters). In its approach to surnames, it could be said that the Court is riding roughshod over some Member States' hesitancy about dual nationality. More seriously, as Agustin Menéndez has commented, the Court's activism in the field of social, welfare, and educational benefits already raises doubts, because it has the capacity to disturb solidaristic bargains *within* (welfare) states, in the interests of promoting the development of human capital *between* them.[65] The justification given in cases such as *Grzelczyk*[66] to the effect that it is reasonable to expect a certain degree of solidarity *between* states, when it comes to balancing out the consequences of the mobility of students can simply ring hollow, especially in an era of straitened public finances. More striking has been the Court's willingness to use an integration test as the basis for determining the proportionality of national rules which, for example, use a residence test in order to substitute for traditional tests based on nationality. Here the Court has indicated that a certain length of residence as an indication of a genuine link with the host state is a reasonable restriction for Member States to impose.[67] The intrusiveness of the Court is also particularly striking where the case law has allowed citizens to export benefits which could only previously be enjoyed within the territory of the state, as it has in cases such as *Tas Hagen*[68] and *Morgan*.[69] In those cases, the national restrictions on export have failed the test of proportionality imposed by the Court of Justice. On the other hand, it is of interest that Síofra O'Leary discerns something of a 'spillback' effect from the citizenship case law into cases which otherwise were 'orthodox' migrant workers' cases, with the Court taking a more lenient approach to the proportionality of the national restriction than might otherwise have been expected, and indicating—where this had not previously been required—that a genuine link test might be allowable where previously the very fact of employment was sufficient.[70]

The embrace of citizenship rhetoric has not, moreover, always been confined to what one might call the classic citizenship cases. Several Advocates General have put forward arguments grounded in the logic of citizenship in order to test the boundaries of free movement law more generally, including in relation to the free movement of goods and services.[71] This is often used in the service of an argument in favour of

---

[65] See Menéndez (n 56 above).   [66] See n 2 above.

[67] See *Bidar* (n 57 above) and Case C-138/02 *Collins v Secretary of State for Work and Pensions* [2004] ECR I-2703.

[68] Case C-192/05 *Tas-Hagen* I-10451.

[69] Case C-11/06 *Morgan v Bezirksregierung Köln* [2007] ECR I-9161.

[70] O'Leary (n 57 above) 16–24.

[71] The logic of citizenship also infuses the Opinion of Advocate General Bot in a case on the interpretation of the Framework Decision on the European Arrest Warrant, but is noticeably absent from the Court's judgment which permits Member States to engage in differential treatment of their own citizens and resident non-national EU citizens in respect of certain penal matters: Case C-123/08 *Wolzenburg*, judgment of 6 October 2009.

the convergence of the different 'heads' of free movement law, *inter alia*, as an attack upon the restrictive interpretation of Article 28 EC on the free movement of goods and the requirement of direct or indirect discrimination, under the *Keck* principle.[72] The backdrop to the argument could be seen as the claim made by Jukka Snell that the Court has taken a different line with free movement rights involving citizens' rights compared to those 'merely' involving products.[73] Thus arguments that link citizenship to *all* of the freedoms rather than just those involving obvious signs of human movement or human capital development can be seen as focused specifically at attacking certain restrictions placed on the free movement of goods.[74] A classic linkage statement can be found in the Opinion of Advocate General Maduro in the *Alfa Vita Vassilopoulos* case:

> [S]uch a harmonisation of the systems of free movement seems...to be essential in the light of the requirements of a genuine Union citizenship. It would be desirable for the same system to be applied to all the citizens of the Union wishing to use their freedom of movement or freedom to move services, goods or capital as well as their freedom to reside or to set up the seat of their activities in the Community.[75]

Here, therefore, we have a clear normative statement from a member of the Court. According to Maduro, there is a link between market citizenship and 'genuine' Union citizenship, and that could be constituted via the means of a convergence of market freedoms. This would occur, presumably, around the norm that offers most opportunities to the market citizen and places most restraints on the autonomy of the Member States. However, this is terrain, as we shall see below, that the Court of Justice should be hesitant about entering, as few can agree about what constitute the appropriate limits to Union citizenship.

3. CITIZENSHIP'S LIMITS?

One could speculate as to how far the process of extending rights to migrant EU citizens based on having achieved integration into the host state might in future be taken, especially once the conundrum is reformulated as follows: citizens of the Union should not be deprived of rights which they could otherwise exercise or benefit from

---

[72] Case C-145/88 *Criminal Proceedings against Keck* [1993] ECR I-6097.

[73] J Snell, 'And Then There Were Two: Products and Citizens in Community Law' in T Tridimas and P Nebbia (eds), *European Union Law for the Twenty-first Century. Rethinking the New Legal Order*, Vol 2 (Hart, 2004) 49–72.

[74] See also Case C-72/03 *Carbonati Apuani Srl v Comune di Carrara* [2004] ECR I-08027, for a further invocation of citizenship by AG Maduro in a case concerning the free movement of goods. For a more general discussion of these questions see A Tryfonidou, 'Further Steps on the Road to Convergence among the Market Freedoms' (2010) 35 ELRev 36.

[75] Cases C-158 and C-159/04 *Alfa Vita Vassilopoulos AE v Greece* [2006] ECR I-8135, [51]. See also the manner in which AG Sharpston buttresses her argument about so-called 'wholly internal situations' and thus the scenario of reverse discrimination in Case C-212/06 *Government of the French Community and Walloon Government v Flemish Government* [2008] ECR I-1683, [133 *et seq*] by reference to the concept of citizenship.

just because they have exercised their free movement rights and moved to another Member State. Dimitry Kochenov has recently gone so far as to suggest that this argument could be applied to the scenario where nationals of the Member States lose the right to vote in any parliamentary elections when they exercise their right of free movement, because there are very restricted rights to vote for non-nationals at the national level and patchy coverage of expatriate/external voting rights.[76] Such restrictions might also in future be subjected to a proportionality test, taking the decision about whether to allow external voting out of the hands of the national legislature, and giving it—in effect—to the judges of the Court of Justice (or the national court applying EU law).

Of course, the classic answer to the loss of political participation rights experienced by any person who migrates across national boundaries is to point to the possibility of naturalization—which automatically allows the migrant to join the political community through the ultimate act of integration. Here again, some remarks could be made. First, it is arguable that the exercise of EU free movement rights differs from the classic immigration scenario where a person moves from country A to country B (with or without his or her family) and integrates in the latter state, acquiring along the way full membership of the polity through naturalization. Regardless of whether such a scenario accurately reflects much contemporary international migration which is often circular in character, it is certainly a poor fit with the ideology of free movement in the contemporary European Union. This would be much better expressed in terms of a series of moves involving lifestyle choices: for educational purposes; for love; for caring responsibilities; for economic reasons; for retirement; for leisure. On that scenario, it is arguable that there will be a net loss of political engagement amongst European citizens if Member States do not take care that the 11 million persons who are resident outside their home state (who represent 2.5 per cent of the population of the Member States and one third of the total foreign resident population[77]) can vote in what remains at present the 'gold standard' of political participation, namely the election of national parliamentarians, which leads in turn to the formation of the governments of the Member States (who in turn constitute the Council of Ministers in the European Union). Secondly, if this were to be regarded as a barrier to free movement, then a number of routes exist to eliminating what might be regarded as an anomaly, via universal expatriate voting, automatic naturalization,[78] or perhaps some form of mutual recognition amongst the Member States.[79] And indeed *if* it is a barrier to free movement, then that might imply that the EU has some power to regulate in order to harmonize national laws or to remove the barrier. However, it is not clear how this would be possible under the Treaties at present, and to suggest that a

---

[76] D Kochenov, 'Free Movement and Participation in the Parliamentary Elections in the Member State of Nationality: An Ignored Link?' (2009) 16 MJ 197.

[77] Eurostat Statistics in Focus, 94/2009, Citizens of European countries account for the majority of the foreign population in EU-27 in 2008.

[78] See the discussion and possibilities canvassed in Kochenov (n 22 above).

[79] See Shaw (n 23 above) 189–208.

Treaty change comparable to the introduction of the local and European Parliamentary electoral rights in the form of Article 19 EC (now Article 22 TFEU) is likely in the foreseeable future seems to depart radically from current political realities.

Similar arguments could, of course, be made about the differing requirements that the Member States currently impose in respect of naturalization, with only a minority presently imposing different—more lenient—rules in respect of nationals of other Member States compared to their general rules.[80] Perhaps it is indeed the obstacles to acquiring national citizenship, combined with the rights which are denied to non-nationals such as voting rights in national elections, which account—notwithstanding the best efforts of the European institutions to ensure that Union citizens really are treated as privileged non-nationals in the host state—for the persistently low level of intra-EU migration, when compared to the United States, where a migrant American automatically takes on the citizenship of the state in which he or she is resident[81] and where cross-state mobility is generally thought to be a great deal more common.[82] On the other hand, no one should disregard the cultural and language barriers which present disincentives to mobility, nor indeed the likelihood of loss of professional status and the persistent low-level xenophobia which is prevalent in many Member States, evidenced by an insistence in the UK, for example, on calling Polish or Lithuanian workers in the UK 'A8 nationals' six years after the accession which gave them the prefix 'A', even in a report of the Equality and Human Rights Commission.[83]

In any event, it would suggest a significant development in the Court's approach hitherto to examining national rules on the acquisition and loss of nationality for it to subject these to a proportionality test, simply because there were differences between Member States which might impinge upon individual decision-making in relation to the mobility of human capital, or because they impact upon EU citizenship *per se*. In the case of *Rottmann*,[84] however, it is arguable that the Court has made precisely this step change in its treatment of Union citizenship.

In *Micheletti*,[85] even before the introduction of Union citizenship, the Court confirmed that while Member States remain competent alone to define the scope of their citizenship laws in order to determine who are their citizens, when the host state is faced with a person who has the nationality of a Member State and also the nationality of a third state, it is obliged to recognize that part of a person's dual (or multiple)

---

[80] See Kochenov (n 22 above). For further details see the extensive national reports available at <http://www.eudo-citizenship.eu>.

[81] See the Citizenship Clause of the Fourteenth Amendment to the US Constitution.

[82] The situation, almost inevitably, is a good deal more complicated when a close comparison is made: see P Ester and H Krieger, 'Comparing Labour Mobility in Europe and the US: Facts and Pitfalls' (2008) Tijdschrift van het Steunpunt WSE 3-4/2008, 94–98.

[83] M Sumption and W Somerville, *The UK's New Europeans. Progress and Challenges Five Years after Accession*, Equality and Human Rights Commission Policy Report, 2009; however, to be fair, for the most part this paper does refer to this group of migrants as 'European citizens'.

[84] Case C-135/08 *Rottmann v Freistaat Bayern*, 2 March 2010.

[85] Case C-369/90 *Micheletti v Delegacion del Gobierno en Cantabria* [1992] ECR I-4239.

nationality which gives them access to free movement and non-discrimination rights. Post-Maastricht this means that Member States must recognize the Union citizenship of nationals of other Member States also holding the nationality of a third state. In his generally cautious Opinion in the case of *Rottmann*,[86] Advocate General Maduro acknowledged that Member States are obliged to apply their nationality laws in ways which comply with the requirements of EU law and envisaged a number of scenarios where problems could arise. First, there could be actions which are in some way directly related to the free movement rules, such as arbitrary removal of nationality of a naturalized former citizen of another Member State on the grounds of political activities or membership of a trades union. Alternatively, there could be actions which breached the Article 4 TEU duty of sincere cooperation, such as collective naturalizations of third country nationals which would have impacts on other Member States through the effects of the free movement rules and which could be said to subvert their immigration policies.

However, the Court's judgment in *Rottmann* seems a good deal bolder than the Opinion, and suggests that we may soon need a new way of thinking about the reach and effects of Union citizenship vis-à-vis national law, especially national rules on the acquisition and loss of citizenship, depending both upon how the Court applies the principles it appears to have announced in *Rottmann* in the future and upon how national courts take up the challenge which they have been given in this case.

In *Rottmann*, the complainant was threatened with the withdrawal of the citizenship of Germany which he gained through naturalization, on the grounds that he committed a fraud during the application process because he failed to disclose criminal proceedings brought against him in Austria, his state of origin. On naturalization in Germany, however, Rottmann had, by operation of law, lost his Austrian citizenship, and as things stood he would not automatically regain his Austrian citizenship just because he lost his German citizenship. He risked, therefore, the loss of his EU citizenship, because he would no longer hold any citizenship which gave him access to EU citizenship and its associated rights.

In its judgment the Court rejected the contention that the case concerned a 'wholly internal situation', as it involved a decision of a German administrative authority about a German citizenship. It noted that it is for each Member State to lay down the conditions for the acquisition and loss of nationality, but they must do so 'having due regard to Community law'[87] in 'situations covered by European Union law'.[88] Where the essence of Advocate General Maduro's Opinion was that loss of citizenship was not related to the exercise of free movement rights in such a way as to render it subject to scrutiny under EU law, the Court in contrast made a very strong statement about the 'reach' of Union citizenship and consequently the capacity of Member States to withdraw national citizenship where that results in the loss of Union citizenship:

---

[86] Case C-135/08 *Rottmann* (n 83 above) Opinion of AG Maduro, 30 September 2009.
[87] ibid [39].   [88] ibid [41].

It is clear that the situation of a citizen of the Union who, like the applicant in the main proceedings, is faced with a decision withdrawing his naturalisation, adopted by the authorities of one Member State, and placing him, after he has lost the nationality of another Member State that he originally possessed, in a position capable of causing him to lose the status conferred by Article 17 EC [i.e. Union citizenship] and the rights attaching thereto falls, *by reason of its nature and its consequences*, within the ambit of European Union law.[89]

In *Rottmann* the connection which the Court draws between EU law and national law is the simple fact that by losing national citizenship a person will also lose EU citizenship rights. This seems to be a step beyond the approach in *Micheletti* where the Court formulated the issue thus:

[I]t is not permissible for the legislation of a Member State to restrict the effects of the grant of the nationality of another Member State by imposing an additional condition for recognition of that nationality *with a view to the exercise* of the fundamental freedoms provided for in the Treaty.[90]

The *Rottmann* formulation is justified by reference to the oft-repeated statement that 'citizenship of the Union is intended[91] to be the fundamental status of nationals of the Member States',[92] but significantly the Court omitted the second part of this quotation which refers to the equal treatment principle.[93] Later on, the Court emphasized again 'the importance which primary law attaches to the status of citizen of the Union'.[94] It will be interesting to see how far the Court's reasoning can be stretched and what its impact upon national rules on the acquisition and loss of citizenship might be. Could it result, for example, in the scrutiny of the German nationality law which requires a person who has acquired German nationality by birth in the territory as the child of a legally resident non-national to opt, within five years of reaching the age of eighteen, for either German nationality or the nationality acquired by descent? This rule only applies to those who hold dual German/third country national citizenship, since Germany does not object to citizens of other Member States continuing to hold dual citizenship. Not renouncing the nationality acquired by descent in such circumstances means losing EU citizenship. Is this an issue falling 'by reason of its nature and its consequences' within the ambit of EU law? What about refusals to grant naturalization—which is often a wholly discretionary act under national law? In order to permit judicial review, is it now necessary that such national decisions must *always* be reasoned? It is intriguing that the Court reached this conclusion even though it wanted to assure the Member States that taking action in such a case of false representations in the context of naturalization does correspond 'to a reason relating to the public interest. In this regard, it is legitimate for a Member

---

[89] Emphasis added; ibid [42].   [90] *Micheletti* (n 7 above) [10].
[91] Note the slight change of language from 'destined' to 'intended'.
[92] *Rottmann* (n 84 above) [43].
[93] See n 4 above.   [94] *Rottmann* (n 84 above) [56].

State to wish to protect the special relationship of solidarity and good faith between it and its nationals and also the reciprocity of rights and duties, which form the bedrock of the bond of nationality.'[95] In practice, it may prove very hard for Member States to resist substantial encroachment into their national sovereignty in this field, and this could open the door to large numbers of challenges to nationality law.

The second important dimension of the *Rottmann* case was the Court's conclusion that the appropriate standard of review is a test of proportionality. It is for the national court

> to ascertain whether the withdrawal decision at issue in the main proceedings observes the principle of proportionality so far as concerns the consequences it entails for the situation of the person concerned in the light of European Union law.[96]

This is an explicit invitation to national courts to weigh considerations relating to the national interest (ie the severity of the deception, for example) against the significance of losing EU citizenship (loss of free movement rights and other Union citizenship rights; possible impact upon family members, etc).

To conclude, it would appear that while the link between citizenship and the free movement and non-discrimination foundations of the EU has been a dynamic motor of legal development, it may be that the Court has opened the door in *Rottmann* to a new phase in its case law. *Rottmann* is arguably the logical conclusion of a line of case law in which the Court has countenanced ever more remote links with the putative exercise of free movement rights as justifying scrutiny and control of national laws and policies. However, the suggestion that the Court may scrutinize national citizenship rules for their impact on the putative exercise of free movement rights may have the effect of further hollowing out national citizenship. But it still leaves open the question as to precisely what the content of citizenship at the Union level may be, not least because questions about solidarity remain so contested, such that many judgments do not find ready acceptance at national level.[97] Questions persist about the legitimacy of the way in which the Court has privileged individual human capital development over collective decision-making in relation to the (relatively) scarce resources of the welfare state.[98] The dominant focus on transnationalism moreover leaves a huge question mark, as many have commented, in relation to the so-called 'wholly internal situations'. As has often been said, what—in truth—is an 'internal situation' within an evolving single market where the elimination of national frontiers and barriers to free movement is sought? For the reverse side of the coin of the 'wholly internal situation', which is unrelated to the application of EU law, is that it would appear that Member States can apply different, and stricter, standards to nationals who do not exercise their free movement rights than to those who do not. Many have observed that this

---

[95] *Rottmann* (n 84 above) [51].   [96] ibid [54].

[97] Reactions to *Metock* (n 52 above), and to *Ibrahim* and *Teixeira* (n 53 above) are good cases in point. On this issue see A Lansbergen, 'Metock, Implementation of the Citizens' Rights Directive and Lessons for EU Citizenship' (2009) 31 JSWFL 285.

[98] Menéndez (n 56 above).

situation seems unjust, and it seems even more challenging in circumstances, such as those at issue in *Carpenter*,[99] where the connection between the EU citizen seeking to assert a right to family reunification (in order to remove a threat to deport his third country national spouse) and free movement rights (sometimes acting as a service provider in another Member State) seems tenuous at best.

So long as the Court of Justice declines, however, to leave the safe haven of its 'wholly internal situation' case law,[100] and tackle the challenge of reverse discrimination, it remains important to consider how this concept of market citizenship could be relevant for the vast majority of citizens of the Member States who are 'static' and who do not take advantage—other than for temporary travel mainly for leisure or business—of their free movement rights. On that reading, for a fuller and more politically rounded concept of citizenship to evolve there is a wider challenge which goes beyond the development of the free movement-oriented provisions introduced by the Treaty of Maastricht and tenderly husbanded since then by the Court of Justice, with some assistance from the Commission and the Union's legislature. If the Union is to have a citizenship which extends a meaningful experience of membership to all residents on its territory, then this must—by definition—have a stronger political character than can be deduced from a picture of busy transnational citizens relying upon their EU-derived rights in order to better their personal situation or to enhance their human capital. We must turn, therefore, to the 'new' constitutional travails of the Union. And there, as was suggested at the beginning of the chapter, we see a very different conjunction of institutional interests and a much greater reluctance to take advantage of the political symbolism of citizenship, other than as a tool of political rhetoric.

D. CITIZENSHIP: LOST IN TRANSITION FROM 'OLD' TO 'NEW' CONSTITUTIONALISM

This section shows how citizenship—so easy to develop as a creature of the basic transnational character of the EU, where it operates in a positive relation with the EU's old legal constitutionalism—has not found a secure and comfortable position in debates about a 'new' constitutionalism for the Union. One of the key reference points in what follows is provided by the changes to the Treaty framework introduced by the Treaty of Lisbon, understood as a compromise document, but the evidence can be drawn from throughout the uneasy period that followed the conclusion of the Treaty of Nice in 2000. While an effective—albeit largely non-political—concept of citizenship is strongly anchored in the EU's 'old' constitutionalism of the single market and the supranational legal order, in particular through the connection to transnational

---

[99] Case C-60/00 *Carpenter v Secretary of State for the Home Department* [2002] ECR I-6279.

[100] For the standard recitation of the 'no factor linking the case to any of the situations envisaged by Community (sic) law' formula, see *Government of the French Community and Walloon Government* [33], n 75 above.

market and quasi-market practices, there has not been a similar breakthrough to find a comfortable understanding of what it means, in political terms, to be a citizen of a euro-polity founded on a formal constitutional framework. Does it mean the same as being a citizen of a 'national' polity, but simply writ large? Or do we need some sort of new vocabulary with which to address such questions of belonging which breaks the bonds of citizenship's binary divides of inclusion and exclusion?[101] And, above all, how do concepts of democracy and democratic legitimation, as key citizenship practices, translate in the context of the plural and multi-level character of euro-polity, with its demand, as we noted in Part B, for multiple and linked approaches to questions of accountability to stakeholders, including citizens, at the supranational, national, and indeed the subnational level.[102]

After a brief discussion of what might be thought of as a semantic change in how the EU Treaties express the relationship between national citizenship and citizenship of the Union, the main part of the discussion proceeds by looking more closely at political citizenship in the Union. Here we can consider the two cases in which the Court of Justice has so far had an opportunity to engage with the right to vote in European Parliament elections. These are reviewed in the light of some further changes to the terminology of the Treaty on European Union, instituted by the Treaty of Lisbon. A related question concerns the significance of the fact that the Treaty of Lisbon, unlike the Constitutional Treaty before it, does not refer to the 'will' of the citizens in relation to the establishment of the Union. Finally we turn to some substantive reforms in the area of democratic procedures introduced by the Treaty of Lisbon.

Inevitably, in what follows, there is some assessment of these changes, and in particular of differences between the Treaty of Lisbon and the Constitutional Treaty, on the one hand, and between the Treaty of Lisbon and the earlier Treaties of Maastricht and Amsterdam on the other hand. However, that is not the main objective of the presentation which is to present, as explained above, how these issues have emerged from the debates amongst key actors, and to highlight the differences between how citizenship is constructed under conditions of classic 'old' constitutionalism and how it fares under the mixed new/old regime of the Treaty of Lisbon.

1. THE DIFFERENCE WHICH (UNION) CITIZENSHIP MAKES: COMPLEMENTARITY OR ADDITIONALITY?

In both the pre- and post-Lisbon Treaty texts, it is made clear that EU citizenship does not *replace* national citizenship; this wording was introduced by the Treaty of Amsterdam partly as a result of the Danish negative referendum on the Treaty of Maastricht which delayed its ratification, and in view of the European Council conclusions which

---

[101] See eg Walker (n 30 above).   [102] See n 12 above.

followed at a summit in Edinburgh in December 1992.[103] However, after the Treaty of Lisbon, the Treaties provide that Union citizenship is *additional* to national citizenship (Article 20(1) TFEU), replacing the earlier expression that it is *complementary* (Article 17(1) EC). Is this change purely semantic, or does it have some deeper meaning?

Expressing Union citizenship as *additional* to national citizenship was insisted upon by the Member States, in order to reinforce the point that EU citizenship can only *add* rights, and cannot *detract* from national citizenship. It reflects the earlier Edinburgh Agreement. Andrew Duff suggests it was done 'cleverly, to mollify conservative eurosceptic opinion'.[104]

For Duff and other parliamentarians, a bigger threat was posed to the essence of Union citizenship by the possibility that citizenship might not be mentioned in the Treaty on European Union at all. However, in its final version signed in December 2007, Article 9 TEU provides:

> In all its activities, the Union shall observe the principle of the equality of its citizens, who shall receive equal attention from its institutions, bodies, offices and agencies. Every national of a Member State shall be a citizen of the Union. Citizenship of the Union shall be additional to national citizenship and shall not replace it.

The final two sentences, drawn from the text of Article 20(1) TFEU, were included in the Treaty of Lisbon at the behest of the European Parliament representatives in the IGC.[105] The parliamentarians had adopted citizenship of the Union as a political priority because of its symbolic importance.[106] It is obviously clumsy to have such textual repetition between the TEU and the TFEU, but it was unavoidable in this particular context given what the parliamentarians saw as a severe threat to the status of citizenship if it was not mentioned in terms in the TEU itself.

Legally speaking, additionality, reinforcing the duality between national and EU citizenship as legal statuses, seems to be a more accurate delineation of the relationship between the two, and avoids any unfortunate implications that there is somehow a notion that one status should bend to the will of the other, in order to achieve the sought after 'complementarity'.[107] Conceptually speaking, it makes the point that the development of different layers of citizenship entitlements is not a zero sum game, in which rights given at one level must necessarily detract from those given at another level. In that sense, it is not so far from—but avoids the negative connotations of—the

---

[103] The text of the Agreement can be found on a Danish Parliament website dealing with Danish opt-outs: <http://www.eu-oplysningen.dk/emner_en/forbehold/edinburgh/>.

[104] A Duff, *The Struggle for Europe's Constitution* (Federal Trust, 2005) 56.

[105] See the interviews with two of the European Parliament representatives at the 2007 IGC (Enrique Baron Crespo and Elmar Brok) for the website of the Young European Federalists, available at <http://www.taurillon. org/IGC-on-the-Reform-Treaty-Interview-with-MEPs>.

[106] See also the emphasis placed on citizenship by A Duff, the third of the 2007 European Parliament IGC representatives, in his book on the Constitutional Treaty: *The Struggle for Europe's Constitution* (n 103 above).

[107] For a strong normative defence of complementarity which—it can be assumed—would not be opposed to the principle of 'additionality' see Bellamy, 'Evaluating Union Citizenship' (n 19 above).

controversial wording contained in the first draft of Part One of the Constitutional Treaty prepared by the Praesidium to the Convention on the Future of Europe. This referred to citizens having 'dual' citizenship: EU and national, and being 'free to use either, as he or she chooses'.[108] Gràinne de Búrca subjected this wording to some trenchant criticism back in 2003:[109]

> The notion of a dual citizenship is an unfortunate way of describing the co-existence of national and EU citizenship. If it is intended as a description of the currently existing relationship between EU and national citizenship it is misleading, and if it is intended to define these categories in a new way for the future, under the basic Constitutional Treaty, then it is a regrettable move. The concept of dual citizenship suggests full and competing loyalties/relationships to two different and entirely separate polities, each of which makes similar claims of allegiance on the individual.

Perhaps these criticisms were heard, because in subsequent versions of Part One of the Constitutional Treaty it was the additionality formula which prevailed. Annette Schrauwen takes a positive view, suggesting that this formula represents one step towards a 'more autonomous development of Union citizenship'.[110]

Despite these comments, the shift from complementarity to additionality seems unlikely to make a substantial difference to the political trajectory of EU citizenship. Thus far, at least until *Rottmann*, the cases in which the Court of Justice has placed weight upon the status of EU citizenship, from *Martínez Sala* onwards, have not truly detracted from the *status* and *legal boundaries* of national citizenship, except in terms of undermining its exclusivity by, for example, extending the territorial boundaries of the welfare state or in relation to the capacity of the national legislature to set rules on matters such as surnames. But again, it should be reinforced that these have hitherto been cases involving migrant citizens. Whether and how additionality might play out as Union citizenship gradually becomes more significant within rather than solely across the boundaries of the Member States is as yet unclear.

2. THE NATURE OF EU POLITICAL RIGHTS

The provisions governing the nature of the European Parliament in the amended Treaty on European Union refer post-Lisbon to 'citizens', where previously the analogous provisions in the EC Treaty referred to the 'people'. Article 14(2) TEU provides that: '[t]he European Parliament shall be composed of representatives of the Union's citizens . . .'; Article 10(2) TEU states that 'citizens are directly represented at the Union level in the European Parliament'; and Article 10(3) TEU states that '[e]very citizen shall have the right to participate in the democratic life of the Union'. The text

---

[108] See Convention 360/02 of 28 October 2002, 9.

[109] G de Búrca, 'Fundamental Rights and Citizenship' in B De Witte (ed), *Ten Reflections of the Constitutional Treaty for Europe* (European University Institute, 2003) 11, 13.

[110] See A Schrauwen, 'European Union Citizenship in the Treaty of Lisbon: Any Change at all?' (2008) 15 MJ 55–64, 59–60.

of Article I-19(2) of the Constitutional Treaty[111] providing for the European Parliament to be elected 'by direct universal suffrage of European citizens in free and secret ballot' is not in the post-Lisbon TEU, but the reference to universal suffrage in connection with the European Parliament does appear in Article 39 of the Charter of Fundamental Rights.[112] The Charter is recognized under Article 6(1) TEU post-Lisbon as a legal source of equal standing to the Treaties.

In any event, the status of the principle of universal suffrage under EU law (whether by virtue of the Charter, or by virtue of Article 3 of Protocol No 1 of the ECHR) had already been clarified even before the Treaty of Lisbon, as a result of the judgments of the Court of Justice in the *Gibraltar* and *Aruba* cases.[113] It is implicit in the Court's important judgments in these politically sensitive cases about the scope of voting rights in European Parliament elections that European citizens have a right, as a matter of democratic principle, to vote for 'their' parliament. This emerges especially clearly from the *Aruba* case concerned with the right of EU citizens resident in Aruba (a dependent territory of the Kingdom of the Netherlands which is not part of the European Union) to vote in European Parliament elections. The provisions of both Article 19 EC and Article 22 TFEU only provide explicitly for an *equal treatment* right, whereby nationals of the Member States resident in *other* Member States have the right to vote in the European Parliament under the *same conditions* as nationals. There has, hitherto, never been a text in the EU Treaties which states, in terms, that 'the citizens of the Union shall elect the members of the European Parliament'. However, an important conclusion can be drawn, in particular from the *Aruba* case, that citizens of the Union cannot be deprived of their right to vote in European Parliament elections, if the national legislation which excludes them from the franchise fails a basic rationality test because, as in this case, the Arubans could gain a right to vote in European Parliament elections not only by moving to the Netherlands proper, but also by moving to a third country and taking advantage of Netherlands external voting rights. This amounts to recognizing the right to vote in European Parliament elections as a normal incident of EU citizenship, even if this is not explicitly stated in the Treaties. In fact, the Advocate General explicitly made this point in his joint Opinion on the two cases and he argued that the right to vote in European Parliament elections is *the most important* EU citizenship right.[114]

The shift from the language of 'people' to that of 'citizens' in relation to the European Parliament raises important questions about the allocation of seats. The

---

[111] See [2004] OJ C310/1.

[112] See the Charter as adapted post-Lisbon: [2007] OJ C303/1.

[113] Case C-145/04 *Spain v United Kingdom (Gibraltar)* [2006] ECR I-7917; Case C-300/04 *Eman and Sevinger v College van burgemeester en wethouders van Den Haag (Aruba)* [2006] ECR I-8055. For an extended discussion of these cases see J Shaw, 'The Political Representation of Europe's Citizens: Developments' (2008) 4 ECLRev 162. See also Besselink (n 11 above).

[114] Opinion of AG Tizzano of 6 April 2006 [67]: '[I]t can be directly inferred from Community principles and legislation as a whole, thus overriding any indications to the contrary within national legislation, that there is an obligation to grant the voting rights [in European elections] to citizens of the Member States and, consequently, to citizens of the Union.'

principle of 'degressive proportionality' was enshrined in Article 14(2) TEU, and its application already caused some difficulty with respect to the allocation of seats to Italy during the 2007 IGC. This led to the establishment of the 'fudge' whereby the European Parliament will constitute 750 members, plus one—the President—in order to accommodate one extra MEP for Italy. Hitherto the calculation base for Member State populations, both for EP purposes and for purposes of QMV in the Council of Ministers, has been that of the number of residents rather than the number of nationals. This avoids difficult questions about the divergences in national laws on citizenship acquisition. For example, if a Member State has national rules which make acquisition of national citizenship so hard that this artificially deflates the number of national citizens, should this be taken into account when assessing the relevant numbers for purposes of calculating MEPs or QMV weightings?[115] There are also more advanced statistical methods available for estimating the number of residents present on the territory between the dates of comprehensive national censuses than there are for calculating the number of national citizens. Even so, Italy was successful in raising a specific issue about numbers of citizens abroad as part of the array of arguments it used to lay claim to the same number of MEPs in the 2009–14 Parliament as the UK, where the principle of degressive proportionality seemed to demand that it should have one less. It remains to be seen whether any future reforms of the European Parliament electoral procedures, such as are currently under review before the Committee on Constitutional Affairs,[116] might take on board this shift from 'people' to 'citizens'. In his presentation of these matters for the Committee in a preliminary paper, Duff made it rather clear where his own preferences lay:

> [D]o we follow James Madison's belief that, in the republic, parliamentary representation is more of a birthright than a civic privilege? The Madisonian approach suggests that the European Parliament represents not only de jure EU citizens (as formally established by the EU Treaty), but that it also represents, and has a duty of care towards, anyone else who abides in the territory of the Union, including minors and denizens. That being the case, the traditional method of distributing seats in the Parliament on the basis of total population—to say nothing of counting votes in the Council—is the right one and should not be amended.[117]

Finally, the question arises as to whether the rewording in the Treaty of Lisbon would make any difference if the issues such as those which arose in the *Gibraltar* case came before the Court of Justice once again. In that case, the Court of Justice was faced with a challenge by Spain to the UK's policy of including Commonwealth citizens in its normal franchise for European Parliament elections. The particular scenario at issue concerned Gibraltar, which was only first included in European Parliament elections

---

[115] See the discussion by A Duff in a Working Document for the European Parliament Committee on Constitutional Affairs on the Election of the European Parliament (III), PE400.478v01-00, 18 January 2008 at 2–3.

[116] See the papers prepared by Duff (n 115 above) in that context.

[117] Duff (n 115 above) 3.

in 2004, following a case brought by Gibraltarians before the European Court of Human Rights contesting their prior exclusion from the framework of European Parliament elections in the United Kingdom.[118] The proceedings before the Court of Justice encompassed an interesting discussion by Advocate General Tizzano of the provisions of the EC Treaty on the European Parliament. He concluded that the reference to 'peoples' of the Member States in Articles 189 and 190 EC should be treated as largely coterminous with the citizens or nationals of the Member States (thus avoiding alternative 'ethnic' rather than 'civic' connotations of the term 'peoples'), which would suggest that it makes little difference that the TEU post-Lisbon now explicitly refers to citizens. On the other hand, he denied that the people/citizens, so defined, and the electorate for the European Parliament should not be treated as automatically coextensive, an argument which the Court of Justice also accepted. The Court concluded that there was nothing in the text of the Treaties as they were at the time, in their pre-Lisbon format which is now essentially unchanged, to suggest that it was not reasonable for Member States, which had such a constitutional tradition, as the UK does in relation to Commonwealth citizens, to extend the right to vote in such elections to persons with a close connection to the territory, recognized in national law. The Court noted that other EU 'citizenship' rights are non-exclusive in character, such as the right to apply to the Ombudsman, or to petition the European Parliament, which can be exercised by natural and legal persons resident in the Union.[119] Such an argument, which focuses on the civic connotations of 'people' as used in the previous version of the EC Treaty, pre-empts rather effectively the possibility of relying upon the shift, in Article 10 TEU, from 'people' to 'citizens' as a significant change in terminology, since the non-exclusivity of these key participatory citizenship rights is maintained. The Advocate General doubted, in any event, whether the expression 'peoples of the States brought together in the Community' in Article 190(1) EC was intended to have a 'precise legal meaning'.[120]

3. THE 'WILL' OF CITIZENS

Article I-1 of the Constitutional Treaty, which sought to 'establish' the refounded European Union under the Constitutional Treaty, purported in that context to reflect 'the will of the citizens and the States of Europe to build a common future'. One of the most prominent dimensions of the transition from the Constitutional Treaty to the Treaty of Lisbon was the so-called 'abandonment' of the constitutional idea, formalized in the detailed mandate for reform rather than refoundation, agreed at the June 2007 European Council.[121] Unsurprisingly, the Madisonian ideal of constitutive self-government expressed in Article I-1 CT was excised from the more modest provisions

---

[118] *Matthews v UK* Application 24833/94 [1999] 28 EHHR 361.
[119] See Arts 227 and 228 TFEU.
[120] Opinion AG Tizzano (n 114 above) [80].
[121] Presidency Conclusions, Council Document 11177/1/07, Rev 1, Conclusion 2, 20 July 2007.

of the Treaty of Lisbon as part of that 'abandonment'. In that it joined other elements such as the reference to the primacy of Union law, the flag, the symbols, and the motto.

The Treaty of Lisbon, not least in the manner in which it was negotiated via the detailed mandate prepared under the German Presidency and the perfunctory IGC held under the Portuguese Presidency, not to mention the marked preference for parliamentary ratification insisted upon in every Member State apart from Ireland, seemed to offer the authoritative reassertion of the principle that the Member States are the ultimate masters of the Treaties. At the same time, those elites thought that by dropping the blatant state-like symbols they were appeasing some of the anxieties expressed in the 2005 Dutch and French referendums. The Irish referendum vote seems, at least in part, to suggest that matters are not as simple as that. While this chapter has already reflected upon two different sources of constitutional change in the Union, namely Treaty amendments and judicial activism, the Irish Referendum reminds us that there is still the issue of popular consent to be taken into consideration. It is clear that one strand of argument which objects, on democratic and participatory grounds rather than eurosceptic grounds, to the denial of referendums in other states played at least a minor theme in the Irish referendum campaign. Whatever the political elites of the European Union and at least some of its Member States might wish, it is clear that the question of the proper role of popular consent in relation to the further development of European integration is not an issue which is simply going to dissipate on the back of a set of assurances to national parliaments that Treaty amendments are a good thing.[122] It may of course be the case that the concerns that citizens have too little influence over the direction and content may gradually ebb away if and when European Parliament elections come to be perceived as significant moments of 'European' democracy (as opposed to being second-order national elections with ever lower participation rates as is generally the case at present), but it is ironic that had the Irish referendum not been controversially repeated with a different result, after assurances to the Irish government, the failure of the Treaty of Lisbon to enter into force would have retarded that very trend.

Overall though, it is tempting to argue that the story of the Laeken Declaration, the Convention, the Constitutional Treaty, the reflection period, the negotiation and signature of the Treaty of Lisbon, and now the laborious process whereby the Lisbon Treaty was eventually ratified, including grandstanding by the Czech President and interventions from two Constitutional Courts (German and Czech) shows how the political elites which have most influence over the content of both EU treaties and the focus of EU policies have failed to break out of a vicious circle in which the more they think they are doing to increase the democratic legitimacy of the EU polity and its treaty basis, the more they are perceived within the confines of national politics as illegitimately meddling in the arena of national (popular and parliamentary) sovereignty.

---

[122] See J Habermas, 'The search for Europe's future', *Spiegel Online International*, 18 June 2008, <http://www.spiegel.de/international/europe/0,1518,560549,00.html>.

This bleak assessment is upheld by opinion surveys on citizenship issues. A Euro-barometer survey published in February 2008[123] highlighted (continuing) widespread ignorance about the details of citizens' rights under EU law, especially in the new Member States, even though a substantial 78 per cent of those questioned across the Member States did claim some familiarity with the term. In practice, they were often unable to identify correctly which rights attach specifically to Union citizens and/or did not know that they automatically were Union citizens by virtue of their national citizenship. However, an earlier Eurobarometer survey published in May 2006 on the topic of the Future of Europe,[124] which contained some questions on citizenship, revealed an interesting trend. When respondents were asked what would be the best ways to strengthen European citizenship, rather large numbers of them *spontaneously* replied that they did not wish to be a European citizen. The figure stood at 8 per cent across the EU as a whole, but was a daunting 25 per cent in the United Kingdom. This suggests a modest approach remains necessary when discussing such matters, espe-cially, but not solely, in the UK. It also suggests that citizenship of the Union has—for most people—a Cinderella status. This point needs to be borne in mind as the analysis in this paper proceeds. While it is often said that citizenship of the Union, in its current Treaty form, is a vapid and impoverished version of the membership concept which has been central to liberal democratic and constitutionally based (national) polities, there does not seem to be any obvious popular legitimacy driving the argument that EU citizenship *should* be developed in more substantial ways than it is at present. It is to the specific challenge of the Union citizen as an actor in the context of structures for democratic participation that we therefore now turn to see whether there is anything in the Treaty of Lisbon that can overcome the doubts expressed here.

4. THE DEMOCRATIC LIFE OF THE UNION

Where the Constitutional Treaty grandiosely referred to 'the democratic life of the Union', the TEU post-Lisbon contains merely a title on 'democratic principles', although the basic provisions are the same. This title fleshes out somewhat the notion of the citizen as a political actor within the EU, without fully embracing a concept of democratic citizenship. Speaking to the provisions of the Constitutional Treaty on democratic engagement, but with clear resonance for the Lisbon Treaty provisions also, Closa warned that:

> The conception of citizenship that emanates from these provisions privileges a vision of citizens as bearers of rights that provide them protection from public authorities, grant them some reduced scope of participation in the policy process but, by and large, it does not establish a solid connection between the citizens and the exercise of their political rights and the 'democratic life of the Union'.[125]

---

[123] Flash Eurobarometer, 213.   [124] Special Eurobarometer, 251.
[125] C Closa, 'Constitutional Prospects of European Citizenship and New Forms of Democracy' in G Amato, H Bribosia, and B De Witte (eds), *Genesis and Destiny of the European Constitution* (Bruylant, 2007) 1037, 1052.

The provisions on democracy, which could be criticized for lacking a central focus, address consecutively concepts of representative, direct, and participatory democracy, without giving the impression of how these might be linked in a coherent way. The provision with the greatest capacity to capture headlines is the one on citizens' initiatives, where an important link to citizenship of the Union is made through the location of the relevant legal basis. Article 24 TFEU, within the citizenship provisions, contains a legislative power, permitting the European Parliament and Council, acting by co-decision, to adopt the provisions necessary to implement the new 'citizens' initiatives'.

Article 11(4) TEU provides:

> Not less than one million citizens who are nationals of a significant number of Member States may take the initiative of inviting the European Commission, within the framework of its powers, to submit any appropriate proposal on matters where citizens consider that a legal act of the Union is required for the purpose of implementing the Treaties.

This new opportunity for a European Citizens' Initiative (ECI) to direct the input of a minimum of one million signatures into the legislative process is intended to harness citizen power, especially via the Internet, enabling it to be channelled towards seeking specific legislative initiatives to be put forward by the Commission. Citizens' initiatives, well known in other national and—especially—subnational contexts, were originally included in the Constitutional Treaty (allegedly at the behest of Giscard d'Estaing himself), and they were retained in the TEU provisions on 'democratic principles' (Article 11(4) TEU). Under the TFEU, the European Parliament and the Council must together define what constitutes a 'significant number of Member States', for the purposes of determining the minimum standard of cross-EU representativity for any citizens' initiative which is to be taken up in legislative format. These initiatives could develop into interesting cases of *transnational* popular democratic pressure, without as such detracting from the powers of national parliaments. In a commentary on the Constitutional Treaty, Jean-Claude Piris described the ECI provision as 'very innovative and symbolic'.[126] He notes that while 'the Commission will not be legally obliged to follow up on any such initiative, the political weight of it will, in practice, force the Commission to engage in serious work following the result of an initiative'.

Ever since they were first mooted in the Convention on the Future of Europe, citizens' initiatives have received quite substantial attention on the part of NGOs and think tanks specifically engaged with campaigning on the issue[127] as well as more

---

[126] J C Piris, *The Constitution for Europe* (Cambridge University Press, 2006) 119.
[127] See, for example, the Initiative for the European Citizens' Initiative, <http://www.citizens-initiative.eu/>; Democracy International, <http://www.democracy-international.org/eci.html>; Initiative and Referendum Institute Europe, <http://www.iri-europe.org/>.

general civil society organizations,[128] academics (especially those coming from traditions of direct democracy such as Switzerland[129]), and governmental bodies especially the European Commission and the European Parliament.[130] Informally, quite a number of such initiatives have been launched since the conclusion of the Constitutional Treaty, although largely on matters which are outside the competence of the Union as such or on matters which the Commission could simply not take up as legislative proposals such as the so-called 'One Seat' campaign to see the European Parliament located only in Brussels.[131] Already, Internet sites have sprung up offering the software capabilities for collecting the requisite number of signatures in a sufficiently secure way,[132] under the aegis of the European Commission funded eParticipation preparatory action.[133] The Commission has not been idle, bringing out a Green Paper on the ECI, and organizing a public consultation process and public hearing on the matter.[134] Even before the Treaty of Lisbon came into force, the European Parliament adopted a resolution requesting the Commission to come forward with a proposal for the necessary legislation to implement the ECI,[135] expressing a concern, for example, that the Commission should not propose to set the bar too high in respect of the minimum number of Member States from which the persons supporting the initiative must come. A particular concern lies with the transparency of those organizing the initiative, and the Parliament suggested that it should be a requirement that the proposers should produce a report stating where the sources of funding for organizing the initiative and the collection of signatures had been drawn from, which must be submitted before the Commission began to examine the issues raised by any successful initiative. The fear is, of course, that citizens' initiatives— whatever their inspiration—may be captured by the same interests, often of a corporate nature, which crowd around the legislative process within the EU already. Such initiatives could end up damaging the representative process itself, for example, by inflating

[128] See, for example, Permanent Forum for European Civil Society, <http://en.forum-civil-society.org/spip.php?rubrique37>.

[129] See for example A Auer, 'European Citizens' Initiative' (2005) 1 ECLRev 79; some papers written during the 'constitutional interregnum' after the rejection of the Constitutional Treaty and before the Treaty of Lisbon was brought forward addressed whether there are other means to bring the ECI into effect: M Elfer, *European Citizens' Initiative. Legal options for implementation below the constitutional level*, December 2006.

[130] It has also attracted the attention of non-core public bodies such as the Assembly of European Regions, which debated the ECI on 12 February 2010: <http://www.aer.eu/news/2010/2010021201.html>.

[131] Details of the initiatives thus far can be found in C Berg *et al* (eds), *Initiative for Europe. Handbook 2008. The Guide to Transnational Democracy* (Marburg: Initiative and Referendum Institute Europe, 2007) <http://www.iri-europe.org/fileadmin/user_upload/media/IRI-Handbook2008.pdf>.

[132] <http://www.europetition.eu/>.

[133] <http://ec.europa.eu/information_society/activities/egovernment/implementation/prep_action/index_en.htm>.

[134] See Commission Green Paper on a European Citizens' Initiative, COM(2009) 622; for more on citizens' initiatives see the Commission's dedicated Internet page at <http://ec.europa.eu/dgs/secretariat_general/citizens_initiative/index_en.htm>.

[135] European Parliament resolution of 7 May 2009 requesting the Commission to submit a proposal for a regulation of the European Parliament and of the Council on the implementation of the citizens' initiative.

minority views or compressing complex decisions into simple binary choices in favour of or against the initiative.[136] They are not, on that view, a panacea for the evil of falling popular participation in elections, or a simple means by which the EU can find the elusive popular legitimacy and 'closeness' to the citizen so often cited in official documents and elite rhetoric on the Union's institutional practices. The ECI will, however, undoubtedly be established, given the provisions of the TEU and the TFEU and the level of momentum from the political institutions and organized civil society behind the idea. Its impact on the challenge of constructing an effective political citizenship *in* and *of* the Union seems, at this stage, much less clear.

E. CITIZENSHIP'S FUTURE: INTEGRATIVE OR CONSTITUTIVE?

The objective of this chapter was, it should be recalled, not to plead for any specific model of citizenship, but rather to identify the conditions under which polity-building occurs and to highlight the diffuse and incremental changes which are occurring in the formal and informal arrangements which contribute to the construction of membership norms and membership practices. The chapter has thus attempted to explore the multiple dimensions of 'citizenship' as a membership status and set of practices, as it operates in the EU context. The conscious intention was to go beyond a focus on the legal institution of citizenship *of* the Union and to see how citizenship has contributed to wider constitutional debate in the EU context. It has identified a bifurcation between the integrationist and constitutionalist dimensions in citizenship hitherto. While citizenship as a thin transnational concept sits comfortably within the 'old' constitutional norms of the constitutionalized legal order based on the Treaties as interpreted by the Court of Justice, it has not been taken forward in a coherent manner in the context of the various processes of constitution-building (Charters, Conventions, Treaties, and ratification processes) of the 2000s.[137] On the contrary, 'citizenship' has rather been invoked to contest rather than to confirm the legitimacy of the EU, through rejectionist referendums in particular. Inevitably—in declaring that Citizenship of the Union is destined to be the fundamental status of the nationals of the Member States—the Court has not paid equal attention to the construction of a defensible and legitimate concept of citizenship at the EU level as it has to hollowing out, sometimes at an alarming rate, national competences which ostensibly exist in relation to citizenship rights (eg welfare issues) and—most recently—citizenship status

---

[136] For a review of the arguments for and against citizens' initiatives (in the context presented to the UK Parliament), see House of Commons Library Standard Note, *Citizens' Initiatives*, SN/PC/04483, 1 May 2008.

[137] D Castiglione, 'We the Citizens? Representation and Participation in EU Constitutional Politics' in R Bellamy, D Castiglione, and J Shaw (eds), *Making European Citizens. Civic Inclusion in a Transnational Context* (Palgrave Macmillan, 2006) 75–95.

definition (in the *Rottmann* case). Thus, in most respects, citizenship has had integrative rather than constitutive effects, despite the symbolic power of the membership concept. But this is a dangerous and unsustainable status quo, not least because it demands, as the Court has itself recognized, a 'certain degree of solidarity between the Member States'. And while the Treaty of Lisbon does slowly begin to invest more political content into the citizenship provisions, the challenge of simultaneously thinking about what kind of membership is appropriate for a polity emerging *beyond* but not *without* the state has yet to be taken up.

20

THE PRINCIPLE OF EQUAL TREATMENT: WIDENING AND DEEPENING

*Mark Bell**

A. INTRODUCTION

Writing in the first edition of this book, Gillian More traced how the principle of equal treatment had developed since the founding Treaties.[1] There were various provisions in those Treaties which sought to establish equal treatment between the factors of production within the internal market.[2] The role of equal treatment in this context was instrumental; free movement and the integration of markets within the EU would be hindered if discrimination against imports, foreign companies, and migrant workers was allowed to persist. Over time, the principle of equal treatment evolved from this market integration rationale and alternative, more autonomous justifications for equal treatment began to emerge. The Court recognized equal treatment as one of its general principles of law,[3] and accordingly treats it as a potential ground for judicial review. More boldly, in 1978, the Court deemed non-discrimination on the ground of sex to form part of the 'fundamental personal human rights' which it protects.[4] Gillian More recognized that a process of constitutionalization was underway and she

---

* Professor, Centre for European Law and Integration, School of Law, University of Leicester. The abbreviation 'TEU' used after a Treaty article refers to the Treaty on European Union in the version in force after 1 December 2009, while 'TFEU' refers to the Treaty on the Functioning of the European Union. 'EC' after a Treaty article refers to a provision of the European Community Treaty in the version in force until 30 November 2009; similarly, 'EU' refers to an article of the Treaty on European Union in the version in force until that date.

[1] G More, 'The principle of equal treatment: from market unifier to fundamental right' in P Craig and G de Búrca (eds), *The Evolution of EU Law* (Oxford University Press, 1999) 517.

[2] See eg EC Treaty, Art 31(1) (goods), Art 39(2) (workers).

[3] See eg Cases 117/76 and 16/77 *Ruckdeschel & Co and Hansa-Lagerhaus Ströh & Co v Hauptzollamt Hamburg-St Annen* [1977] ECR 1753, [16]–[17].

[4] Case 149/77 *Defrenne v SABENA (III)* [1978] ECR 1365, [26]–[27].

identified the potential for further evolution in this direction, both in relation to the equal treatment of EU citizens and following the insertion of Article 13 into the EC Treaty.[5] The latter expanded EC legal competence to address a wider range of discrimination grounds, namely 'sex, racial or ethnic origin, religion or belief, disability, age or sexual orientation'.

Approaching this topic a decade later, there can be little doubt that the principle of equal treatment is now accepted as an autonomous area of EU law and policy. Although the extensive body of anti-discrimination legislation built in recent years is consistent with the objective of facilitating free movement, its contents stretch well beyond the minimum intervention required by a pure market integration rationale.[6] Instead of revisiting the role of equal treatment in the regulation of the internal market, this chapter focuses on the evolution which Gillian More anticipated. It will concentrate on equal treatment as a fundamental human right and consequently it is concerned with the regulation of relations between natural persons, rather than products or companies.

Compared to the situation in 1999, two trajectories can be identified in the evolution of the principle of equal treatment: widening and deepening. These will serve as two central themes for the organization of this chapter. It aims to demonstrate how the principle of equal treatment within EU law has changed, as well as considering whether there is any tension between the simultaneous widening and deepening processes.

B. WIDENING THE PRINCIPLE OF EQUAL TREATMENT

Prior to 1999, equal treatment was primarily limited to questions of sex and nationality. The addition of Article 13 to the EC Treaty reconfigured these parameters,[7] rapidly leading to the adoption of a suite of new anti-discrimination Directives. While this has received substantial focus in EU law and policy, as well as within academic commentary,[8] two other strands can also be identified. Following the creation of a new competence for immigration and asylum law in the EC Treaty (also in 1999), a variety of Directives were adopted which address the equal treatment of third country nationals based on their immigration status. In addition, EU labour law has seen the completion of a package of Directives on 'atypical' work. These introduced the equal treatment principle in respect of part-time, fixed-term, and agency workers. This section of the chapter will consider each of these new strands to EU law on equal

---

[5] More (n 1 above) 548.

[6] L Waddington, 'The expanding role of the equality principle in European Union law' Policy Papers (Series on Constitutional Reform of the EU) 2003/04 (European University Institute, 2003) 11.

[7] Now Art 19 TFEU.

[8] H Meenan (ed), *Equality Law in an Enlarged European Union —Understanding the Art 13 Directives* (Cambridge University Press, 2007).

treatment, but it commences with a brief overview of the starting point of the law on nationality and sex discrimination.

1. WHERE IT ALL BEGAN: NATIONALITY AND SEX DISCRIMINATION

(a) Discrimination on the ground of nationality

The strongest evidence of equal treatment as a principle within the founding Treaties related to nationality. Article 6 EEC provided a general prohibition of 'any discrimination on grounds of nationality'.[9] Although this is phrased in open-ended terms, its articulation over the years has reflected the straightjacket of a market integration rationale. A human rights rationale would imply that EU law is concerned with any unjustified differential treatment based on nationality, akin to Article 14 of the European Convention of Human Rights.[10] In reality, subsequent legislation and case law revealed that EU law mainly intervenes where there is a connection between nationality discrimination and the exercise of free movement rights.[11] A classic illustration of this point is the restraint of EU law when faced with 'purely internal' situations, that is, where a Member State discriminates on the ground of nationality against its own nationals. EU law is not applicable to these situations, unless the national can find a link to the exercise of free movement rights.[12] In a similar vein, the Treaty-based protection from nationality discrimination has not been applied to third country nationals.[13] This limitation was not spelt out in the original text of the EEC Treaty, but Article 1(1) of Regulation 1612/68 limited free movement for employment to 'any national of a Member State'.[14] Once third country nationals were excluded from the right to free movement, they fell outside the market integration rationale motivating the prohibition of nationality discrimination. Directive 2004/38 clarifies the contemporary legal situation.[15] Union citizens are entitled to equal treatment with the nationals of the host state, as well as any family members who have the right to reside with them, regardless of nationality.[16] Again this reinforces the underlying need for some connection to the exercise of free movement rights in order to trigger the EU law prohibition of nationality discrimination.

The instrumental nature of EU law on nationality discrimination tends to detach it from the familiar concepts of anti-discrimination law. In both the Treaties and in

---

[9] Now Art 18 TFEU.

[10] eg *Gaygusuz v Austria* (1997) 23 EHRR 364.

[11] See Chapter 17 by Siofra O'Leary.

[12] eg EU citizens returning to their Member State after exercising free movement rights have been able to invoke the principle of equal treatment: Case C-224/98 *D'Hoop v Office national de l'emploi* [2002] ECR I-6191.

[13] For a detailed analysis and argument in favour of applying Art 18 TFEU (ex Art 12 EC) to third country nationals, see C Hublet, 'The Scope of Art 12 of the Treaty of the European Communities *vis-à-vis* Third-country Nationals: Evolution at Last?' (2009) 15 ELJ 757.

[14] [1968] OJ Spec Ed (II) 475.

[15] Council Directive (EC) 2004/38 on the right of citizens of the Union and their family members to move and reside freely within the territory of the Member States [2004] OJ L158/77.

[16] Art 24(1).

Directive 2004/38, the principle of equal treatment lacks any further definition or elaboration. This contrasts starkly with the EU legislation on other forms of discrimination, such as sex and ethnic origin, where discrimination is sub-divided into more detailed categories of direct and indirect discrimination, harassment, and instruction to discriminate. Those Directives also accompany the detailed definition of discrimination with measures to support victims who seek to bring a complaint, such as a duty on Member States to create institutions to assist victims.[17] Although the prohibition of nationality discrimination lacks this level of specificity, it has been robustly substantiated by the case law of the Court of Justice. Equality between the citizens of the Union has assumed a constitutional character subject to strict judicial scrutiny.[18] The Court's case law on Union citizenship is examined in more depth elsewhere in this collection of essays,[19] but it does include recognition that nationality discrimination can be both direct and indirect.[20] Nevertheless, there is no sense that the wider panoply of anti-discrimination law, such as shifting the burden of proof or positive action, is applicable or considered relevant to EU law on nationality discrimination. One explanation for this lies in the original motivation for the law. EU law on racial discrimination, for example, stems from an acknowledgement that racist and xenophobic prejudice exists within the Member States and that this results in socio-economic inequalities for ethnic minority communities. In contrast, EU law on nationality discrimination is driven by removing obstacles to free movement and there does not appear to be any underpinning assumption that EU citizen migrants constitute a disadvantaged group in society. The impact of the EU enlargements of 2004 and 2007 calls into question whether the functional nature of EU law on nationality discrimination continues to be adequate. Some of the post-enlargement migration has been accompanied by discrimination and violence against new EU citizens, ranging from Romanians in Italy to Polish communities in Northern Ireland. Such situations suggest that the Court may have to consider whether discrimination between EU citizens can also overlap with the scope of discrimination on the ground of ethnic origin. This could permit EU citizen migrants to benefit from the wider range of anti-discrimination instruments found within the Racial Equality Directive.[21]

(b) Discrimination on the ground of sex

There was no general commitment to equal treatment for women and men in the founding Treaties, but Article 119 EEC (now Article 157 TFEU) provided for equal

---

[17] eg Articles 19 and 20, Council Directive (EC) 2006/54 on the implementation of the principle of equal opportunities and equal treatment of men and women in matters of employment and occupation (recast) [2006] OJ L204/23.

[18] D Kostakopoulou, 'Ideas, norms and European citizenship: explaining institutional change' (2005) 68 MLR 233.

[19] See Chapter 19 by Jo Shaw.

[20] eg Case C-237/94 *O'Flynn v Adjudication Officer* [1996] ECR I-2617.

[21] Council Directive (EC) 2000/43 implementing the principle of equal treatment between persons irrespective of racial or ethnic origin [2000] OJ L180/22.

pay. As with the prohibition of nationality discrimination, this was grounded in an economic rationale, namely, the concern that certain Member States could gain a competitive advantage through cheap female labour.[22] During the 1970s, this bare Treaty provision was transformed into a corpus of law on equal treatment of women and men in employment and social security. On one side, the Court issued a series of vanguard judgments in which it recognized that Article 119 EEC was capable of enforcement by individuals within their national courts through the principle of direct effect.[23] Moreover, it began the process of recasting EU gender equality law as a question of fundamental human rights, and not merely an economic expedient.[24] On the other side, legislation was adopted expanding the material scope of the prohibition of sex discrimination beyond the specific issue of equal pay. Most notably, Directive 76/207 addressed equal treatment in matters relating to employment (other than pay),[25] whilst Directive 79/7 extended equal treatment to the sphere of social security, albeit subject to limitations.[26]

The initial burst of legislative activity during the 1970s slowed during the subsequent decades, and the Court became a key engine for innovation in the law.[27] Judgments fleshed out the meaning of concepts such as indirect discrimination[28] and often focused on the effectiveness of the law, for example, through permitting a shift in the burden of proof from complainant to respondent,[29] or excluding any prior fixing of an upper limit on compensation.[30] The Court also pushed the boundaries of the material scope of the law, holding that contracted-out occupational pensions were subject to Article 119 EEC.[31]

As will be examined below, a significant extension in EU anti-discrimination law occurred in 2000 with the adoption of Directives addressing discrimination on grounds other than sex. These instruments had the perhaps unanticipated effect of stimulating a revival of legislative innovation in relation to gender equality. In 2002,

---

[22] D Hoskyns, *Integrating Gender—Women, Law and Politics in the European Union* (Verso, 1996) 49.

[23] Case 80/70 *Defrenne v Belgian State (No 1)* [1971] ECR 445; Case 43/75 *Defrenne v SABENA (No 2)* [1976] ECR 455.

[24] '... this provision forms part of the social objectives of the Community, which is not merely an economic union, but is at the same time intended, by common action, to ensure social progress...', Case 43/75 *Defrenne v SABENA (No 2)*, ibid [10]. Also, Case 149/77 *Defrenne v SABENA (No 3)*, (n 4 above).

[25] Council Directive (EEC) 76/207 on the implementation of the principle of equal treatment for men and women as regards access to employment, vocational training and promotion and working conditions [1976] OJ L39/40.

[26] eg the Directive allows Member States to exclude pensionable age from its scope: Art 7, Council Directive (EEC) 79/7 on the progressive implementation of the principle of equal treatment for men and women in matters of social security [1979] OJ L6/24.

[27] T Hervey, 'Thirty Years of EU Sex Equality Law: Looking Backwards, Looking Forwards' (2005) 12 MJ 307.

[28] eg Case 170/84 *Bilka-Kaufhaus GmbH v Weber Von Hartz* [1986] ECR 1607.

[29] eg Case C-127/92 *Enderby v Frenchay Health Authority* [1993] ECR I-5535.

[30] Case C-271/91 *Marshall v Southampton and South-West Hants Area Health Authority (No 2)* [1993] ECR I-4367.

[31] Case C-262/88 *Barber v Guardian Royal Exchange Assurance Group* [1990] ECR I-1889.

significant amendments were made to Directive 76/207.[32] These borrowed from and built upon the Directives of 2000 with the result that the rather general norms found in the 1976 Directive were replaced with a more detailed set of rules. For instance, a specific prohibition of sexual harassment was added. In 2004, a further Directive was adopted which extended the principle of equal treatment into the area of goods and services.[33] This was the first major extension in the material scope of gender equality legislation since the 1979 Social Security Directive. It is notable that the preamble situates this Directive in the context of human rights protection. Reference is made to a wide range of international and European human rights instruments, as well as the EU Charter of Fundamental Rights.[34] A similar linkage of sex discrimination legislation with broader human rights principles can be found in the most recent intervention, the 'Recast' Directive, which consolidated a variety of gender equality Directives in the field of employment.[35]

On the surface, it seems as if the main shift in gender equality law has been the expansion in the material scope of the legislation, combined with a thickening in the substance of the obligations. At the same time, the Court has been faced with periodic challenges as regards the boundaries of non-discrimination on the ground of 'sex'. The first set of cases relate to pregnancy and maternity. In *Dekker*, the Court held that a decision not to appoint a woman due to her pregnancy constituted direct discrimination, following the logic that 'only women can be refused employment on grounds of pregnancy'.[36] In *Mayr*, the Court of Justice extended this line of case law, holding that dismissal of a woman 'at an advanced stage of in vitro fertilisation treatment' constitutes sex discrimination, even though the woman was not deemed to be pregnant at this stage.[37] The Court's rationale was that the medical treatment in question directly affected only women.[38] While this seems logical, it sits uneasily with other decisions concerning pregnancy-related illness. The Court maintains that dismissal due to a pregnancy-related illness which arises *after* maternity leave has ended does not constitute sex discrimination:

> Male and female workers are equally exposed to illness. Although certain disorders are, it is true, specific to one or other sex, the only question is whether a woman is dismissed on account of absence due to illness in the same circumstances as a man; if that is the case, then there is no direct discrimination on grounds of sex.[39]

---

[32] European Parliament and Council Directive (EC) 2002/73 amending Directive (EEC) 76/207 on the implementation of the principle of equal treatment for men and women as regards access to employment, vocational training and promotion, and working conditions [2002] OJ L 269/15.

[33] Council Directive (EC) 2004/113 implementing the principle of equal treatment between men and women in the access to and supply of goods and services [2004] OJ L373/37.

[34] Recitals 1, 2, and 4.

[35] Council Directive 2006/54 (n 17 above) recitals 2 and 5.

[36] Case C-177/88 *Dekker v Stichting Vormingscentrum voor Jong Volwassenen* [1990] ECR I-3941, [12].

[37] Case C-506/06 *Mayr v Bäckerei und Konditorei Gerhard Flöckner OHG* [2008] ECR I-1017, [52]. On the facts, *in vitro* fertilized ova existed but they had not been transferred to the woman's uterus, ibid [53].

[38] ibid [50].

[39] Case C-179/88 *Handels- og Kontorfunktionærernes Forbund i Danmark v Dansk Arbejdsgiverforening* [1990] ECR I-3979, [17]; E Caracciolo di Torella and A Masselot, 'Pregnancy, Maternity and the Organisation of Family Life: An Attempt to Classify the Case-law of the Court of Justice' (2001) 26 ELRev 239.

In the wake of *Mayr*, it seems that the Court distinguishes between differential treatment based on a sex-specific medical treatment which will constitute sex discrimination, and differential treatment due to a sex-specific illness which will not constitute sex discrimination. This seems a fragile and tenuous boundary, not least because sex-specific illnesses may give rise to sex-specific medical treatment.[40]

Another area where the Court has wrestled with the meaning of 'sex' discrimination is sexual orientation and gender identity. Beginning in *P v S and Cornwall County Council*,[41] the Court has held on several occasions that discrimination related to 'gender reassignment' constitutes sex discrimination.[42] In *P*, the Court expressly linked its decision to upholding respect for human dignity,[43] whilst later decisions have referred to judgments from the European Court of Human Rights regarding transgender people.[44] The undertone of these decisions is a concept of gender equality infused by human rights protection. The value-based reasoning in these cases stands in contrast to the strict comparator test applied in *Grant*.[45] This concerned a workplace policy which provided travel concessions to married or unmarried opposite-sex partners of workers. Borrowing from the Court's language in *P*, it was argued that this was 'essentially if not exclusively' discrimination on the ground of sex; Lisa Grant was treated less favourably than a male worker because her partner was a woman rather than a man. The Court rejected this approach and instead opted for a narrow concept of formal equal treatment:

> [S]ince the condition imposed by the undertaking's regulations applies in the same way to female and male workers, it cannot be regarded as constituting discrimination directly based on sex.[46]

The inconsistencies in the Court's approach to the scope of 'sex' discrimination suggest uncertainty about the compass to be followed when legislative ambiguity leaves discretion for judicial interpretation. There seems to be a qualitative difference between the reasoning in *P* and that subsequently applied in *Grant*. In retrospect, the gender reassignment cases provide examples of how the Court can move beyond a narrow reading of the law by taking into account contextual principles of human rights. Given the reference to human rights in the preambles of the Gender Recast and Goods and Services Directives, the Court may feel emboldened to pursue further this approach to interpretation in the future. This is unlikely to reopen the question of sexual orientation discrimination, which is now

---

[40] eg questions arise as to whether treatment for prostate cancer would be regarded as sex-specific.

[41] Case C-13/94 *P v S and Cornwall County Council* [1996] ECR I-2143.

[42] Case C-117/01 *KB v NHS Trust Pensions Agency* [2004] ECR I-541; Case C-423/04 *Richards v Secretary of State for Work and Pensions* [2006] ECR I-3585.

[43] *P* (n 41 above) [22].

[44] *KB* (n 42 above) [33]–[36].

[45] Case C-249/96 *Grant v South-West Trains* [1998] ECR I-621. Waddington argues that the reasoning of the Court in *P* is also constrained when a comparison is made with the Opinion of the AG in that case, who relied more explicitly on fundamental human rights (n 6 above) 20.

[46] ibid [28].

dealt with in separate legislation (at least in respect of employment). It could, though, assist the Court in dealing with other instances of discrimination related to sex. Notably, the Court has so far considered only 'gender reassignment'. Although this concerns one aspect of the transgender umbrella, there are a wider range of situations where gender identity and gender expression can give rise to discrimination without any connection to the individual undergoing a medical process of gender reassignment.[47]

2. THE NEXT GENERATION: EU ANTI-DISCRIMINATION LAW

The EU's focus on nationality discrimination and gender equality was a remarkably stable feature of this area of law until 1999. Although pressure had been growing from civil society and the European Parliament for EU action on a wider range of discrimination grounds, especially ethnic origin and disability, such calls were typically rebuffed by the supposed lack of legal competence of the Union for other forms of discrimination.[48] Those campaigns eventually proved fruitful and the Treaty of Amsterdam amended the EC Treaty in order to extend the legal competence. This is now found in Article 19(1) TFEU, which states:

> Without prejudice to the other provisions of the Treaties and within the limits of the powers conferred by them upon the Union, the Council, acting unanimously in accordance with a special legislative procedure and after obtaining the consent of the European Parliament, may take appropriate action to combat discrimination based on sex, racial or ethnic origin, religion or belief, disability, age or sexual orientation.[49]

Unlike the original Article 119 EEC, this provision was evidently permissive in nature and accordingly did not confer rights that were capable of bearing direct effect. In addition, the requirement of unanimity naturally raised doubts as to whether the Member States would be able to find consensus on issues that tend to provoke considerable social and political controversy, such as the rights of religious minorities or same-sex couples. By an unusual twist of political fate, the potential political pitfalls fell by the wayside. As is well documented,[50] the entry of an extreme right-wing party into the Austrian government in February 2000 sparked a clamour for a reaction from the EU and part of that response was the fast-tracking of the Commission's proposal for a Directive on discrimination on grounds of racial or ethnic origin. Having adopted the

---

[47] S Whittle, 'Gender Identity Discrimination', Paper presented at the European Commission conference 'Legal seminar on the implementation of EU law on equal opportunities and anti-discrimination', Brussels, 6 October 2009.

[48] For a more detailed history, see M Bell, *Anti-discrimination Law and the European Union* (Oxford University Press, 2002).

[49] Art 19(2) TFEU applies the ordinary legislative procedure, but only for adopting 'basic principles of Union incentive measures, excluding any harmonization of the laws and regulations of the Member States'.

[50] G de Búrca, 'The Drafting of the European Union Charter of Fundamental Rights' (2001) 26 ELRev 126, 136.

Racial Equality Directive in June 2000,[51] the Member States moved swiftly to complement this with the Employment Equality Directive,[52] which extended the prohibition of discrimination to the grounds of religion or belief, disability, age, and sexual orientation.

The two Directives share a very similar approach to the construction of discrimination. They prohibit direct and indirect discrimination, as well as harassment and instructions to discriminate.[53] Member States may permit positive action, but this is not obligatory.[54] They are both based on a paradigm of complaints-based enforcement by individuals. To this end, both Directives include measures to facilitate individual litigation. Borrowing from gender equality law, there is provision for a shift in the burden of proof from the complainant to the respondent.[55] Individual litigants are protected from victimization[56] and sanctions have to be effective, proportionate, and dissuasive.[57] Associations are entitled to engage in legal proceedings under the Directive either on behalf or in support of the complainant.[58] Notwithstanding the high degree of overlap between the Directives, there are three principal differences.

First, the material scope of the Racial Equality Directive is much wider than that of the Employment Equality Directive. Whereas the latter mainly covers employment and vocational training,[59] the former extends to social protection (including social security and healthcare); social advantages; education; goods and services (including housing).[60] Indeed, the Racial Equality Directive has a broader legal scope than EU gender equality legislation, which does not cover social advantages, education, or those aspects of social protection falling outside the material scope of the 1979 Social Security Directive.[61] Secondly, the Racial Equality Directive, and the subsequent gender equality Directives, require Member States to establish a body or bodies for the promotion of equal treatment.[62] These must include within their mandates the provision of independent assistance to victims of discrimination. No such obligation exists within the Employment Equality Directive. Thirdly, the exceptions to the prohibition of discrimination are notably wider in the Employment Equality Directive when compared to those found within the Racial Equality Directive.[63] This is also true

---

[51] Council Directive 2000/43 (n 21 above).

[52] Council Directive (EC) 2000/78 establishing a general framework for equal treatment in employment and occupation [2000] OJ L303/16.

[53] Art 2, Council Directive 2000/43; Art 2, Council Directive 2000/78.

[54] Art 5, Council Directive 2000/43; Art 7, Council Directive 2000/78.

[55] Art 8, Council Directive 2000/43; Art 10, Council Directive 2000/78.

[56] Art 9, Council Directive 2000/43; Art 11, Council Directive 2000/78.

[57] Art 15, Council Directive 2000/43; Art 17, Council Directive 2000/78.

[58] Art 7(2), Council Directive; Art 9(2), Council Directive 2000/78.

[59] Art 3, Council Directive 2000/78.

[60] Art 3, Council Directive 2000/43.

[61] E Ellis, *EU Anti-Discrimination Law* (Oxford University Press, 2006) 350–362.

[62] Art 13, Council Directive 2000/43; Art 12, Council Directive 2004/113 (n 33 above); Art 20, Council Directive 2006/54, (n 17 above).

[63] D Schiek, 'A new framework on equal treatment of persons in EC law?' (2002) 8 ELJ 290, 301–302.

if a comparison is made between the Racial Equality Directive and the Gender Goods and Services Directive.[64]

The disparities between the Directives have been a long-running bone of contention. In academic literature, there has been a debate around whether this constitutes a 'hierarchy of equalities', and, if so, whether or not this is justified.[65] Unsurprisingly, civil society associations and the European Parliament have demanded additional legislation to prohibit discrimination on grounds of religion or belief, disability, age, and sexual orientation in areas outside the labour market. This culminated in the Commission's proposal of a new anti-discrimination Directive in 2008.[66] In relation to material scope, this would level up protection from discrimination for these grounds to replicate the material scope of the Racial Equality Directive. At the time of writing, negotiations in the Council were ongoing, but it seems that many Member States are reluctant to accept the broad-brush approach to material scope which was assumed in the rushed negotiation of the Racial Equality Directive. Ten years later, it appears that Member States desire a more nuanced and circumscribed regulation of the extent to which EU anti-discrimination legislation can impact upon domestic law in relation to health, education, and social protection.[67] Consequently, it seems inevitable that differences in the material scope of the prohibition of discrimination will continue to exist between the various grounds, even if the proposed Directive is adopted.

3. FRAGMENTING EQUAL TREATMENT AND THIRD COUNTRY NATIONALS

Although there have been rapid advances in EU anti-discrimination law, the picture is less healthy when considering equal treatment in relation to third country nationals. The traditional justification for the non-application of the principle of equal treatment resided in the market integration rationale; equal treatment was designed to facilitate free movement, but third country nationals did not possess autonomous free movement rights. This logic for the exclusion of third country nationals has become more tenuous over time. There have been tentative steps to open free movement rights to certain third country nationals. Specifically, those with long-term resident status or holding the EU 'Blue Card' are entitled to reside in another Member State, subject to certain provisos.[68] Moreover, a blanket denial of equal treatment to third country

---

[64] E Caracciolo di Torella, 'The Principle of Gender Equality, the Goods and Services Directive and Insurance: a Conceptual Analysis' (2006) 13 MJ 339.

[65] See, eg, Schiek (n 63 above) 308; M Bell and L Waddington, 'Reflecting on inequalities in European equality law' (2003) 28 ELRev 349; E Howard, 'The Case for a Considered Hierarchy of Discrimination Grounds in EU law' (2006) 13 MJ 443.

[66] Commission, 'Proposal for a Council Directive on implementing the principle of equal treatment between persons irrespective of religion or belief, disability, age or sexual orientation' COM(2008) 426.

[67] Council, Document 16594/08 ADD 1, 9 December 2008, 15–16.

[68] Art 14, Council Directive (EC) 2003/109 concerning the status of third-country nationals who are long-term residents [2004] OJ L16/44; Art 18, Council Directive (EC) 2009/50 on the conditions of entry and residence of third-country nationals for the purposes of highly qualified employment [2009] OJ L155/17.

nationals seems increasingly hard to reconcile with the Union's rhetorical commitments to promoting migrant integration[69] and the fight against racism and xenophobia.[70] Nevertheless, old habits seem hard to break. The Racial Equality Directive specifically excludes difference of treatment based on nationality,[71] and nationality was omitted from the list of grounds mentioned in the general non-discrimination guarantee within the Charter of Fundamental Rights.[72]

One area where signs of change are emerging is immigration legislation. Following the insertion of competences for immigration and asylum into the EC Treaty in 1999, there has been a rolling programme of legislation designed to construct an EU *acquis* in these fields. Many of these instruments have touched upon the question of equal treatment of third country nationals. The most comprehensive approach is found within the Long-Term Residents Directive. Equal treatment with (domestic) nationals is to be provided in the areas of employment; education and vocational training, including recognition of qualifications; social security, social assistance, and social protection; tax benefits; access to goods and services, including procedures for obtaining housing; freedom of association and participation in employer, employee, or professional organizations; and free access to the entire territory of the Member State.[73] The impressive length of this list has to be read alongside various qualifications and exceptions.[74] Member States are entitled to retain existing restrictions which limit access to employment or self-employment to EU/EEA citizens.[75] Equal treatment in social assistance and social protection can be restricted to 'core benefits'.[76] Equal access to employment is not applicable where there is 'even occasional involvement in the exercise of public authority'.[77] These significant qualifications must be combined with the rather limited concept of long-term resident. This is based on five years of legal and continuous residence, but subject to broad exceptions such as residence for the purpose of study or training.[78]

---

[69] The Council adopted 'Common Basic Principles for Immigrant Integration Policy in the European Union' in 2004: Council, 'Press Release: 2618th Council Meeting Justice and Home Affairs' 14615/04 (Press 321), 19 November 2004, 15.

[70] European Council Declaration on the 50th anniversary of signing the EEC Treaty: <http://www.eu2007.de/de/News/download_docs/Maerz/0324-RAA/English.pdf>; Hublet (n 13 above) 765.

[71] Art 3(2). For a detailed critique, see S Benedí Lahuerta, 'Race Equality and TCNs, or How to Fight Discrimination with a Discriminatory Law' (2009) 15 ELJ 738.

[72] Art 21(1). Discrimination on the ground of nationality is dealt with separately in Art 21(2), but in terms that echo Art 18 TFEU, which has been traditionally applied only to differences in treatment between EU citizens.

[73] Art 11, Council Directive 2003/109 (n 68 above).

[74] L Halleskov, 'The Long-Term Residents Directive: A Fulfilment of the Tampere Objective of Near-equality?' (2005) 7 EJML 181.

[75] Art 11(3)(a).

[76] Art 11(4) and recital 13.

[77] Art 11(1)(a).

[78] Art 3(2). A more detailed analysis is provided in: S Peers, 'Implementing equality? The Directive on long-term resident third-country nationals' (2004) 29 ELRev 437; S Boelaert-Suominen, 'Non-EU Nationals and Council Directive 2003/109/EC on the Status of Third Country Nationals who are Long-term Residents: Five Paces Forward and Possibly Three Paces Back' (2005) 42 CML Rev 1011.

A more searching critique of the Directive is the absence of any guidance on what the principle of equal treatment might entail in this context. Equal treatment is an isolated norm within a broader legislative instrument and in this respect it appears much thinner than the approach to equal treatment found within the anti-discrimination Directives. As with EU law on nationality discrimination vis-à-vis EU citizens, there is no reference to concepts such as indirect discrimination or positive action. No procedural mechanisms are established to assist victims of discrimination. Furthermore, the Long-Term Residents Directive is not truly concerned with discrimination on the ground of nationality; rather it is focused on discrimination based on a particular immigration status. Given the threshold for acquisition of long-term resident status, many third country nationals will fall outside the scope of the Directive. Beyond the privileged status of long-term resident, a range of legislation has accumulated dealing with other migration categories, such as family members, researchers, students, refugees, asylum applicants, or those benefiting from subsidiary or temporary protection.[79] There is little consistency in the manner in which each of these Directives deals with the principle of equal treatment. For example, researchers are entitled to equal treatment in working conditions, including pay and dismissal, whereas there are no provisions regarding equal treatment of students who engage in employment (even though the relevant Directive permits them to work 10 hours per week).[80] The resulting picture is one where the principle of equal treatment has been fragmented and attached to immigration status rather than nationality. The EU legislator appears to reward economically attractive forms of migration with better rights to equal treatment than those provided for less-desired categories such as asylum applicants. This is manifest in the Directive on highly qualified employment (the EU 'Blue Card'), which aims to make the EU more attractive in the global market for highly qualified workers.[81] These sought-after individuals receive equal treatment rights which are similar in their extent to those of long-term residents,[82] but they are entitled to exercise free movement rights after eighteen months, placing them in a more privileged position than long-term residents.[83]

The variable geometry applied to the principle of equal treatment in respect of third country nationals arguably reflects the failure of the Union to embed its legislative framework in a human rights perspective. The treatment of nationality discrimination by EU law stands in contrast to the European Convention on Human Rights. Article 14 of the Convention prohibits nationality discrimination in respect of all persons; it is not apportioned according to immigration status.

---

[79] A more detailed analysis of the equal treatment rights of each of these categories is available in M Bell, 'Civic Citizenship and Migrant Integration' (2007) 13 EPL 311, 325–326.
[80] ibid.   [81] Recital 7, Council Directive 2009/50 (n 68 above).
[82] ibid Art 14.   [83] ibid Art 18.

4. STRETCHING THE EQUAL TREATMENT PRINCIPLE: ATYPICAL WORKERS

The final issue to consider in the 'widening' section of this chapter is the application of the principle of equal treatment to atypical workers. Since 1997, the Union has extended equal treatment rights to certain categories of worker based on contractual status. In this respect, there is a parallel with equal treatment according to immigration status; individuals are receiving equal treatment rights based on a legal category rather than a personal attribute. This is somewhat distinct from equal treatment by reference to the grounds found in Article 19 TFEU; the protected personal characteristics found therein may not be immutable, but they do stem from individuals' innate attributes. In contrast, the type of employment contract an individual works under is considerably more likely to fluctuate over time and reflects the work rather than the worker.

For several decades, the Member States had been debating what, if any, legislative response the EU should adopt to the diversification of employment contracts. The legislative breakthrough emerged from the social dialogue process between European trade unions and employer organizations. Two Framework Agreements were reached, on part-time and fixed-term work, and each was given binding force of law through the subsequent adoption of a Directive.[84] Choosing the principle of equal treatment as the method for regulating part-time work resonates well with sex discrimination law given that women are substantially over-represented in part-time work and EU case law on indirect sex discrimination has often addressed less favourable treatment of part-time workers.[85] The rationale for recourse to the principle of equal treatment is less obvious in relation to fixed-term work, where there is no settled pattern linking fixed-term contracts and gender across the Member States.[86] The most recent piece in the legislative jigsaw was the Temporary Agency Work Directive adopted in 2008.[87]

Although the Directives are not purely concerned with the principle of equal treatment,[88] this lies at their heart. They adopt an asymmetrical approach to equal treatment, so the rights are conferred only on the protected category; in other words, full-time workers have no corresponding protection from being treated less favourably than part-time workers. In the Directives on part-time and fixed-term work, equal treatment is tightly defined by reference to a comparable full-time or permanent worker:

---

[84] Council Directive (EC) 97/81 concerning the framework agreement on part-time work concluded by UNICE, CEEP and the ETUC [1998] OJ L14/9; Council Directive (EC) 1999/70 concerning the framework agreement on fixed-term work concluded by ETUC, UNICE and CEEP [1999] OJ L175/43.

[85] Ellis (n 61 above) 91–93.

[86] O Hardarson, 'Men and women employed on fixed-term contracts involuntarily' Statistics in focus: population and social conditions, 98/2007 (Eurostat, 2007).

[87] Council Directive (EC) 2008/104 on temporary agency work [2009] OJ L327/9.

[88] eg the Framework Agreement on Fixed-Term Work aims to prevent abuse arising from the successive use of fixed-term contracts (cl 5).

[I]n respect of employment conditions, part-time workers shall not be treated in a less favourable manner than comparable full-time workers solely because they work part-time unless different treatment is justified on objective grounds.[89]

This implies that part-time or fixed-term workers need to be able to find a comparable worker in order to assert their rights to equal treatment. The Directives also indicate that this comparator needs to be in the same employment, unless otherwise provided in national law or collective agreement. This hurdle creates the risk that workers will struggle to locate an appropriate comparator, especially if the employer concentrates part-time or fixed-term workers into certain parts of the enterprise, or alternatively if the workforce is fragmented through contracting-out. There are obvious echoes here of the difficulties encountered in EU equal pay law where an actual comparator needs to be identified and pay must be attributed to a single source.[90] In contrast, the Agency Work Directive permits a hypothetical comparator:

The basic working and employment conditions of temporary agency workers shall be, for the duration of their assignment at a user undertaking, at least those that would apply if they had been recruited directly by that undertaking to occupy the same job.[91]

The centrality of the principle of equal treatment within the atypical work Directives evokes EU anti-discrimination legislation, but the parallels do not extend far. Rather like the situation with nationality discrimination law, the atypical work Directives do not contain reference to concepts such as direct and indirect discrimination, or positive action.[92] Furthermore, the atypical work Directives are underpinned by a careful balancing of equal treatment with labour market flexibility. Less favourable treatment of part-time or fixed-term workers is open to justification on objective grounds. Although the Court of Justice has clarified the need for such justification to pursue a genuine need which is appropriate and necessary,[93] the possibility to justify direct discrimination is not a feature of most EU anti-discrimination legislation.[94] While objective justification is not referred to in the Agency Work Directive, it provides flexibility through several broad possibilities to derogate from the principle of equal treatment.[95]

---

[89] Cl 4(1), Framework Agreement on Part-Time Work. Equivalent text is found in clause 4 of the Framework Agreement on Fixed-Term Work.

[90] Case C-256/01 *Allonby v Accrington & Rossendale College* [2004] ECR I-873; S Fredman, 'Marginalising Equal Pay Laws' (2004) 33 ILJ 281.

[91] Art 5(1), Council Directive 2008/104 (n 87 above).

[92] It has been suggested that the use of the word 'solely' in clause 4 in the Part-Time and Fixed-Term Work Framework Agreements may exclude their application to situations of indirect discrimination: C Vigneau, 'The principle of equal treatment of temporary and permanent workers' in C Vigneau, K Ahlberg, B Bercusson, and N Bruun (eds), *Fixed-term Work in the EU: A European Agreement against Discrimination and Abuse* (National Institute for Working Life, Stockholm, 1999) 135, 145.

[93] Case C-307/05 *Del Cerro Alonso v Osakidetza-Servicio Vasco de Salud* [2007] ECR I-7109, [58].

[94] The exception is age: Art 6, Council Directive 2000/78 (n 52 above).

[95] eg Member States may impose a qualifying period prior to which the principle of equal treatment will not apply; Art 5(4), Council Directive 2008/104 (n 87 above).

Standing back from the atypical work Directives, they appear to be less rooted in the protection of fundamental rights than the anti-discrimination Directives. Each Directive states that it is designed to improve the quality of part-time/fixed-term/agency work.[96] This portrays a more instrumental image of equal treatment as a tool in labour market management. This seems qualitatively different to the anti-discrimination Directives, which draw a connection between their aims and those of international human rights treaties.[97]

5. CONCLUSION

Taking an overview, a gap emerges between the approach adopted in respect of the grounds found in Article 19 TFEU and other manifestations of the principle of equal treatment between persons. The former can be collected together under the heading 'EU anti-discrimination law'. This body of legislation has converged around a common template. Relatively consistent definitions of discrimination have been coupled with a shared menu of procedures and standards relating to the enforcement of the law. Although there is not a complete harmony in the approach adopted in respect of each discrimination ground, there is a tendency to dovetail law and policy on these grounds, and this trajectory has arguably increased in the past decade. Outside this inner circle, there is less coherence in the way in which the principle of equal treatment is articulated. At one level, it is easy to explain why the approach adopted differs between immigrant researchers and students, or between fixed-term and agency workers; each has been subject to the vagaries of the legislative process and the *ad hoc* striking of political bargains. Yet underneath it reveals the absence of a shared vision concerning what equal treatment means within these instruments or why it should be applied to these categories. Whereas anti-discrimination legislation has, to some extent, been anchored in a framework of human rights protection, equal treatment within immigration law or labour law lacks this ethical compass.

C. DEEPENING THE PRINCIPLE OF EQUAL TREATMENT

As mentioned in the introduction, Gillian More observed that a process of constitutionalization was occurring in relation to the principle of equal treatment.[98] For current purposes, this can be summarized as a process where the norm is entrenched and accorded a higher legal status. This implies that it is more deeply rooted in the

---

[96] Clause 1, Framework Agreement on Part-Time Work; Clause 1, Framework Agreement on Fixed-Term Work; Art 2, Council Directive 2008/104, ibid.

[97] Recitals 2 and 3, Council Directive 2000/43 (n 21 above); Recitals 1 and 4, Council Directive 2000/78 (n 52 above); Recitals 1 and 2, Council Directive 2004/113 (n 33 above).

[98] More (n 1 above) 548.

legal system in the sense that it is less vulnerable to change or repeal, and that where conflicts of legal norms arise, those which are constitutionalized will be attributed with a greater weight. More broadly, Shaw refers to the 'undoubtedly foundational character of constitutional law and discourse for any polity'.[99] She argues that constitutional texts become a defining frame of reference. Consequently, the extent to which issues such as equality are present or absent in constitutional texts is of wider significance than a doctrinal focus on the precise interpretation of any rights thereby conferred. In considering the extent to which there has been a deepening of the principle of equal treatment, this section of the chapter will begin with a brief review of the case law of the Court of Justice, which identified equal treatment as one of the general principles of EU law. It will then turn to consider the subsequent reforms to the founding Treaties and the evidence of embedding equal treatment within these constitutional documents. In the light of this evidence, it will consider how this process affects the interpretation given to the principle of equal treatment.

1. EQUAL TREATMENT AS A GENERAL PRINCIPLE OF EU LAW

A key part of the Court's constitutional architecture is the notion of 'general principles' of law. Respect for these higher legal norms is a condition for the legality of EU legislation or other acts of the EU institutions; breach of the general principles forms a ground for judicial review. The Treaties contain no definitive catalogue of general principles, but the Court's case law has consistently recognized that equal treatment falls therein. As a general principle of law, equal treatment is a loose principle that amounts to little more than a general standard of fairness and rationality.[100] A standard formula is the following: '[T]he principle of equal treatment is breached when two categories of persons whose factual and legal circumstances disclose no essential difference are treated differently or where situations which are different are treated in an identical manner.'[101] This can be applied to a wide diversity of situations, ranging from differences in the treatment of agricultural products through to differences of treatment between natural persons, the latter being the focus of this chapter. Alongside the general principle of equal treatment, another strand of the Court's general principles is respect for fundamental rights. Equal treatment for natural persons arguably occupies a special place as it straddles both the general principle of equal treatment and that of respect for fundamental rights.[102] For example, in *Defrenne (No 3)*, the Court states:

---

[99] J Shaw, 'The European Union and Gender Mainstreaming: Constitutionally Embedded or Comprehensively Marginalized?' (2002) 10 Feminist Legal Studies 213, 215.

[100] C McCrudden and H Kountouris, 'Human rights and European equality law' in H Meenan (ed), *Equality Law in an Enlarged European Union—Understanding the Art 13 Directives* (Cambridge University Press, 2007) 73, 75.

[101] Case T-10/93 *A v Commission* [1994] ECR II-179, [42].

[102] D Schiek, 'The ECJ Decision in *Mangold*: A Further Twist on Effects of Directives and Constitutional Relevance of Community Equality Legislation' (2006) 35 ILJ 329, 333.

[R]espect for fundamental personal human rights is one of the general principles of Community law, the observance of which it has a duty to ensure. There can be no doubt that the elimination of discrimination based on sex forms part of those fundamental rights.[103]

Locating equal treatment of persons within a context of constitutionally protected principles has provided the Court with a point of reference when considering how to exercise its discretion in interpreting anti-discrimination legislation. For example, in *P* (discussed earlier), the Court reiterates the above quotation from *Defrenne (No 3)* in support of its broader reading of what constitutes sex discrimination.[104] Similarly, in *Schröder*, the Court relies on general principles in rejecting arguments for the curtailment of retrospective equal pay where this could place the Member State concerned at a competitive disadvantage:

> [I]t must be concluded that the economic aim pursued by Article 119 of the Treaty, namely the elimination of distortions of competition between undertakings established in different Member States, is secondary to the social aim pursued by the same provision, which constitutes the expression of a fundamental human right.[105]

Although the Court has demonstrated its willingness to rely on general principles as a means of bolstering its interpretation of anti-discrimination legislation, its approach to the discrimination grounds added via Article 13 EC is more difficult to read. Having invoked general principles of human rights in *P*, in *Grant v South-West Trains* the Court rejected the argument that general principles could be relied upon to include sexual orientation within the scope of sex discrimination.[106] In contrast to the Court's conservatism in *Grant*, a much bolder approach was adopted in *Mangold*.[107] In this case, the Court was confronted with a provision of German law permitting fixed-term contracts for workers over the age of 52 without the normal requirement of objective justification for employment under a temporary contract. The facts arose between two private parties and during the extended period granted to Germany for transposition of the age provisions of the Employment Equality Directive, so recourse to the doctrine of direct effect was apparently obstructed. The Court circumvented this barrier by an extensive interpretation of its general principles case law. The domestic legislation in question fell within the scope of the Fixed-Term Work Directive and the Court requires Member States to respect the general principles of EU law when implementing EU legislation.[108] The Court held that those general principles include non-discrimination on the ground of age, therefore, the German legislation had to be set

---

[103] Case 149/77 *Defrenne v SABENA (No 3)* [1978] ECR 1365, [26]–[27].

[104] *P v S and Cornwall County Council* (n 41 above) [19].

[105] Case C-50/96 *Deutsche Telekom AG v Schröder* [2000] ECR I-743, [57].

[106] *Grant v South-West Trains*, (n 45 above) [45]; C Favilli, *La non discriminazione nell'Unione europea* (Il Mulino, Bologna, 2008) 196.

[107] Case C-144/04 *Mangold v Helm* [2005] ECR I-9981.

[108] Opinion of AG Sharpston, Case C-427/06 *Bartsch v Bosch und Siemens Hausgeräte Altersfürsorge GmbH* [2008] ECR I-7245, [69].

aside insofar as it was inconsistent with that principle. Strikingly, the Court embodies the 'general principle of equal treatment' with the detailed contents of the Employment Equality Directive, stating that the general principle entailed an obligation to ensure 'appropriate legal remedies, the burden of proof, protection against victimization, social dialogue, affirmative action'.[109]

The decision in *Mangold* provoked a lively debate amongst academics and Advocates General.[110] Some of this comment contended that the Court had overstretched the elastic boundaries of the general principle of equal treatment; this might explain the prudent silence in subsequent case law where the Court omitted to elaborate on *Mangold*.[111] The Court has, though, returned to the fray with its decision in *Kücükdeveci*.[112] This case concerned a rule that when calculating length of employment, periods of service prior to the age of 25 were not counted. This impacted negatively on the claimant in respect of the length of notice to which she was entitled from her employer upon dismissal. Unsurprisingly, the Court held that this constituted direct age discrimination that lacked justification.[113] Although the time limit for implementation of the Employment Equality Directive had expired, the problem raised by the national court was that the dispute was between two private parties. This horizontal relationship apparently excluded the doctrine of direct effect and the national court felt that there was no possibility to reinterpret the national legislation in a manner compatible with the Directive as it was unambiguous.[114] In its judgment, the Court places great emphasis on the general principle of equal treatment, rather than the Directive. Indeed, it argued that 'Directive 2000/78 merely gives expression to, but does not lay down, the principle of equal treatment in employment'.[115] Moreover, the Court underlined the significance in the legal order of the general principle of equal treatment by linking it to the right to non-discrimination in the Charter of Fundamental Rights.[116] Consequently, the national court was *obliged* to decline to apply national legislation that was incompatible with the principle of equal treatment.[117]

The decisions in *Mangold* and *Kücükdeveci* provide a good indication of the way in which the Court has constitutionalized anti-discrimination legislation by embedding it in higher legal norms and then drawing upon these as a justification for an extensive interpretation of the legislation. As discussed below, the legal context is altered by the Treaty of Lisbon and the attribution of binding legal status to the Charter of Fundamental Rights. Arguably, this provides a more authoritative foundation than the general principles. The unwritten nature of the latter means that their content is inevitably contentious. It might have been expected that the Court would shift its focus to the Charter following the Treaty of Lisbon, but the reasoning in *Kücükdeveci*

---

[109] *Mangold* (n 107 above) [76].
[110] For an overview, see the Opinion of AG Sharpston (n 108 above) [31]–[41].
[111] Favilli (n 106 above) 201.
[112] Case C-555/07 *Kücükdeveci v Swedex GmbH & Co. KG* [2010] OJ C63/4.
[113] ibid [39]–[42].   [114] ibid [16].   [115] ibid [50].
[116] ibid [22].   [117] ibid [53].

suggests a more nuanced approach whereby the Court will weave together the Charter and the general principles as a combined source of authority for constitutionalizing equal treatment.

2. ENTRENCHING THE PRINCIPLE OF EQUAL TREATMENT WITHIN THE TREATIES

The founding Treaties have always contained some references to the principle of equal treatment, such as the provisions on nationality discrimination and equal pay. Over time, the Treaties have gradually been adjusted to uncouple the link between equal treatment and the construction of the internal market.[118] This was already apparent in the changes made through the Treaty of Amsterdam,[119] but it is firmly resolved in the post-Lisbon era. The Treaty on European Union entrenches equality as one of the central missions and activities of the Union. Article 2 TEU sets out the values on which the Union is founded. These include 'equality' and 'the rights of persons belonging to minorities'. Article 3 TEU on the Union's aims includes combating discrimination, equality between women and men, and respecting cultural and linguistic diversity. In terms of the legal competences for combating discrimination, the Treaty of Lisbon made minor changes, mainly concerned with legislative procedure.[120] Nevertheless, two substantive changes in the Treaties will affect this field: the Charter of Fundamental Rights and the extended provisions on 'mainstreaming'.

Article 6(1) TEU resolves the debate surrounding the legal status of the Charter by declaring that it 'shall have the same legal value as the Treaties'. Although the Court had already begun to refer to the Charter as one of a variety of sources for the interpretation of its general principle of respect for fundamental rights, it seems reasonable to expect that it will accord much greater weight to this instrument now that it has been attributed with Treaty status. In relation to equality, the Charter offers considerable potential. The specific chapter on equality is composed of three types of provisions. First, Article 20 provides that 'everyone is equal before the law'. This seems to echo the general principle of equal treatment and as such may be invoked to challenge any arbitrary differential treatment of persons.[121] Secondly, Article 21(1) contains a prohibition on discrimination:

> Any discrimination based on any ground such as sex, race, colour, ethnic or social origin, genetic features, language, religion or belief, political or any other opinion, membership of a national minority, property, birth, disability, age or sexual orientation shall be prohibited.

---

[118] Waddington (n 6 above) 11.

[119] eg former Art 13 EC.

[120] Art 19 TFEU enhances the role for the European Parliament in anti-discrimination legislation. The pre-existing consultation procedure is replaced with a requirement for the Council to obtain the Parliament's consent for such legislation.

[121] Favilli notes that Art 20 was cited by the Court in a challenge to the legality of the European Arrest Warrant (n 106 above) 188.

Thirdly, several provisions address specific forms of discrimination and inequality. These vary in their substantive content; Shaw describes this as 'a veritable "pot pourri" of rights, some of a traditional justiciable and constitutional type, some of a more aspirational nature'.[122] For example, Article 22 is an open-textured obligation to 'respect cultural, religious and linguistic diversity'. In contrast, Article 23 reiterates some established tenets of EU gender equality law, such as the legality of positive action measures.

Although it is too early to predict the full impact of the Charter on this area of law, it evidently reinforces the trend towards the constitutionalization of the principle of equal treatment.[123] The central space occupied by equality within the Charter underscores the Treaty provisions that place equality within the core values and aims of the Union. Perhaps the greatest significance of the Charter lies in its approach to equality. It combines a common threshold of non-discrimination that extends to all grounds (Article 21), with a pluralistic vision in the 'strand-specific' provisions (Articles 22–26). The subtle differences in the wording of each of these provisions imply a recognition that equality is not a 'one-size fits all' concept. Waddington suggests that the Charter leads towards a view that 'vulnerable groups need targeted and diverse approaches to achieve the goal of equality'.[124] The call in Article 22 for respect of diversity no doubt responds to the challenges arising within Europe's multicultural social reality. Alternatively, Article 25 on the rights of the elderly refers to the right to 'lead a life of dignity and independence', which reflects contemporary debates around the way Europe caters for its ageing population, especially in areas such as social and health care. Critics of the Charter could rightly point to the rather woolly language used in these provisions and the difficulty of translating these principles into operational legal standards. This may, though, miss the value of the Charter as a point of reference for the Court in steering its interpretation of anti-discrimination legislation.

As well as assisting the Court, the Charter should inform the work of the EU institutions. Indeed, the Commission has already adopted the practice of monitoring legislative proposals for compliance with the Charter.[125] This complements the idea of mainstreaming:[126] mobilizing all areas of law and policy for the promotion of equality. The Treaty of Amsterdam already embarked along this path by inserting a commitment to gender mainstreaming in the EC Treaty. Article 8 TFEU (ex Article 3(2) EC) states: '[I]n all its activities, the Union shall aim to eliminate inequalities, and to promote equality, between women and men.' Following the Lisbon amendments, this is now complemented by Article 10 TFEU: '[I] n defining and implementing its policies and activities, the Union shall aim to combat discrimination based on sex, racial or ethnic origin, religion or belief, disability, age or sexual orientation.' The experience with Article 8 TFEU suggests

---

[122] Shaw (n 99 above) 218.   [123] ibid.   [124] Waddington (n 6 above) 23.

[125] Commission, 'Compliance with the Charter of Fundamental Rights in Commission legislative proposals—methodology for systematic and rigorous monitoring' COM(2005) 172.

[126] Waddington (n 6 above) 15.

that these duties have potential, but they will not, by themselves, bring about significant change in institutional behaviour. Notwithstanding its Treaty status, Beveridge concludes that Article 8 TFEU has operated more 'as a political than a legal obligation'.[127] Indeed, Shaw found little evidence that it had been actively taken on board by the Court of Justice.[128] The importance of the Treaty mandate for mainstreaming lies in the foundation it provides for further steps to put this into practice. In this respect, it would have been productive if the general mainstreaming obligations had been combined with (for example) a protocol or a declaration placing more flesh on the bare bones found in the Treaty.

The equality mainstreaming duties do not exist in a vacuum. They are nested within a set of largely new or reorganized provisions at the beginning of the TFEU that pursue a similar goal to mainstreaming, in other words, seeking to have a particular objective taken into account across EU law and policy.[129] These duties address topics such as environmental protection, consumer protection, and animal welfare.[130] There is also a new, omnibus duty to take into account in all policies 'the promotion of a high level of employment, the guarantee of adequate social protection, the fight against social exclusion, and a high level of education, training and protection of human health'.[131] There are undoubtedly good reasons to support the integration of all of these diverse objectives throughout the policy-making process. The logic that underpins equality mainstreaming can be easily transposed to other issues.[132] The risk is that the proliferation of such duties will dilute effectiveness. Policy-makers may feel submerged amongst these different duties and there is no obvious path for the resolution of conflicts between mainstreaming duties. For example, a shortage of housing may cause Roma communities to settle on land without planning authorization. Permitting such settlements might be acceptable from the perspective of combating socio-economic inequalities, but it could conflict with environmental protection objectives. Of course, the Treaties are not the place to attempt to resolve complex public policy problems. The duties serve to remind policy-makers of the myriad of interweaving interests that need to be juggled. Yet the capacity of this framework to enhance public decision-making will depend greatly on how these new obligations are brought to life.

---

[127] F Beveridge, 'Building against the Past: The Impact of Mainstreaming on EU Gender Law and Policy' (2007) 32 ELRev 193, 208.

[128] Shaw (n 99 above) 223.

[129] J Shaw, 'Mainstreaming Equality and Diversity in European Union Law and Policy' in J Holder and C O'Cinneide (eds), *Current Legal Problems 2005, Vol 58* (Oxford University Press, 2006) 255, 271.

[130] Arts 11–13 TFEU.

[131] Art 9 TFEU.

[132] In fact, the origins of gender mainstreaming are at least partially derived from the experience of mainstreaming other policy objectives, such as environmental protection or the promotion of small businesses: F Beveridge and S Nott, 'Gender auditing—making the Community work for women' in T Hervey and D O'Keeffe (eds), *Sex Equality Law in the European Union* (John Wiley & Sons, 1996) 383.

3. THE INTERPRETATION OF EQUAL TREATMENT

The discussion above has chartered how equal treatment has become entrenched in the Union's constitutional lexicon. This section examines the interpretation attached to these concepts in the light of constitutionalization.

(a) The concept of equal treatment

The Court's general principle of equal treatment adopts the Aristotelian approach that those in a like situation should be treated alike.[133] This is frequently summarized in the label 'formal equal treatment'. Academic literature has extensively discussed and critiqued this concept from various angles.[134] Prominent criticisms include the weight that this approach places on identifying who is in a comparable situation. Locating the 'correct' comparator can often seem arbitrary or inconsistent, such as in the Court's judgments in *P v S and Cornwall County Council* and *Grant v South-West Trains*. The focus on the search for a comparator can often obscure a more penetrating inquiry about the cause or effects of the measure under scrutiny. For example, in *Österreichischer Gewerkschaftsbund*,[135] workers were entitled to a payment on the termination of their employment. The level of this payment varied according to length of service. In calculating length of service, periods of parental leave were not taken into account, yet periods of leave for military service were included.[136] This rule was challenged by an Austrian trade union as indirect discrimination against women, in particular, given that 98 per cent of people taking parental leave were women and compulsory military service exclusively concerned men.[137] Nevertheless, the Court of Justice held that men taking military service were not in a comparable position to women taking parental leave. It emphasized that parental leave was a voluntary choice on the part of the worker, whereas military service was, at least initially, compulsory. For the Court, the appropriate comparator was a person voluntarily taking unpaid leave for a reason other than parental leave. As this person's leave would also not be included in calculating the length of service, there was no discrimination.

Cases such as the above illustrate how the requirement of comparability can constitute a preliminary hurdle, a means of obfuscating the issues at the heart of the dispute. In *Österreichischer Gewerkschaftsbund*, the underlying question concerned the State's prioritizing of military service over child-raising, but the Court of Justice avoided stepping into such sensitive terrain by its precursor finding about the comparator. A similar tactical deployment of the comparator test can be witnessed in

---

[133] D Schiek, 'Torn between Arithmetic and Substantive Equality? Perspectives on Equality in German Labour Law' (2002) 18 IJCCLIR 149, 150.

[134] See eg Schiek (n 63 above) 303–304; S Fredman, *Discrimination Law* (Oxford University Press, 2002) 7–11.

[135] Case C-220/02 *Österreichischer Gewerkschaftsbund, Gewerkschaft der Privatangestellten v Wirtschaftskammer Österreich* [2004] ECR I-5907.

[136] There was a minimum compulsory period of leave prior to and immediately after the birth of a child. This was included in the calculation of length of service: ibid [7]–[9].

[137] ibid [24]–[25].

Maruko.[138] This case concerned a survivor's occupational pension that was only available to married couples. Mr Maruko had formed a life partnership with his same-sex partner, which was a legal status similar to, but not the same as marriage under German law. When confronted with the explosive politics that surrounds questions of family, marriage, and sexuality, the Court turned to the comparator test. It held that *if* life partners were in a comparable situation to married partners, then it would constitute direct sexual orientation discrimination to refuse Maruko access to the survivor's pension; however, the answer to this question lay within the jurisdiction of the national court.[139]

Given that *Österreichischer Gewerkschaftsbund* and *Maruko* are relatively recent cases, they suggest that the Court's outlook on equality is still heavily shaped by the concept of formal equal treatment. Indeed, in *Österreichischer Gewerkschaftsbund* the Court introduces a comparability requirement in a claim for indirect sex discrimination, whereas the requirement on the claimant to be in a comparable situation to her comparator is only a feature of the legislative definition of direct discrimination.[140] Nevertheless, signals can also be found of a willingness on the part of both the Court, and the EU legislator, to go beyond formal equal treatment. A good illustration of this trajectory can be found in relation to positive action.

In *Kalanke*, the Court adopted a narrow view of the space for positive action, emphasizing that such measures were a derogation from the prohibition of discrimination between individuals.[141] In subsequent decisions, the Court has gradually altered its rhetoric and acknowledged that equal treatment of individuals may not produce equality in practice. In *Marschall*, the Court acknowledged that 'the mere fact that a male candidate and a female candidate are equally qualified does not mean that they have the same chances', citing prejudice, stereotypes, and the unequal distribution of caring responsibilities.[142] Considering a range of positive action measures in *Badeck*, the Court acknowledged that they were 'manifestly intended to lead to an equality which is substantive rather than formal, by reducing the inequalities which may occur in practice in social life'.[143] This shift in thinking was reinforced by the amendment of the EC Treaty in 1999 to insert an express authorization for positive action:

> *With a view to ensuring full equality in practice between men and women in working life*, the principle of equal treatment shall not prevent any Member State from maintaining or adopting measures providing for specific advantages in order to make it easier for the

---

[138] Case C-267/06 *Maruko v Versorgungsanstalt der deutschen Bühnen* [2008] ECR I-1757.

[139] ibid [72].

[140] D Schiek, 'Indirect discrimination' in D Schiek, L Waddington, and M Bell (eds), *Cases, Materials and Text on National, Supranational and International Non-discrimination Law* (Hart, 2007) 323, 471.

[141] Case C-450/93 *Kalanke v Freie Hansestadt Bremen* [1995] ECR I-3051, [21].

[142] Case C-409/95 *Marschall v Land Nordrhein-Westfalen* [1997] ECR I-6363, [29]–[30].

[143] Case C-158/97 *Badeck and others* [2000] ECR I-1875, [32].

underrepresented sex to pursue a vocational activity or to prevent or compensate for disadvantages in professional careers.[144]

The key feature of this text is its construction of positive action as consistent with, even necessary for, the realization of equality. It is not presented as a derogation from an individual right, but an essential component of achieving equality. Importantly, this wording was subsequently incorporated into the Racial and Employment Equality Directives.[145]

Looking at the trend within the legislation and case law on positive action, there is an acknowledgement of the limits of formal equal treatment and the need for law to be also concerned with the achievement of substantive equality in practice. It is notable, though, that the Court has not shifted from its original position in *Kalanke* that automatic and unconditional preferential treatment at the point of selection for employment constitutes unlawful discrimination. Instead, it has emphasized the scope for positive action measures that do not involve such preferential treatment. Unhelpfully, the Charter of Fundamental Rights seems to turn back the clock in the positive action debate. Article 23 states: '[T]he principle of equality *shall not prevent* the maintenance or adoption of measures providing for specific advantages in favour of the under-represented sex' (emphasis added). The language adopted returns to the portrayal of positive action as a departure from equality, rather than an intrinsic element of its fulfilment. It is also unfortunate that the Charter only refers to positive action in the context of gender equality. In the period since it was drafted, the eastward enlargement of the Union has brought much greater visibility to the deeply rooted social disadvantage encountered by Roma communities in Europe.[146] The extent of this deprivation makes it manifest that an approach based on formal equal treatment will be inadequate in tackling Roma inequality. For example, the legacy of institutional practices of segregation in education[147] will place many Roma at an inferior position in the labour market for at least several decades. This context provides an illustration of the challenges facing the Court when eventually it has to consider the scope for positive action on grounds other than gender, and in areas other than the labour market. The history of educational segregation of Roma children, combined with other forms of institutional racism,[148] make a compelling case for not presuming that the approach taken on positive action for women in employment should be mechanically transposed to all discrimination grounds.[149]

---

[144] Emphasis added; Art 157(4) TFEU (ex Art 141(4)).

[145] Art 5, Council Directive 2000/43 (n 21 above); Art 7, Council Directive 2000/78, (n 52 above). It should be noted, however, that the definition of positive action in these Directives does not import the reference to 'measures providing for specific advantages' found in Art 157(4) TFEU.

[146] An overview is provided in: Commission, 'The situation of Roma in an enlarged European Union' (Office for the Official Publications of the European Communities, 2004).

[147] *DH and others v The Czech Republic* [GC] (2008) 47 EHRR 3.

[148] European Roma Rights Centre, 'Ambulance not on the way—the disgrace of healthcare for Roma in Europe' (Budapest: European Roma Rights Centre, 2006).

[149] O de Schutter and A Verstichel, 'Integrating the Roma into European society: time for a new initiative' in European Centre for Minority Issues, Eur Ybk of Minority Issues. Vol 4, 2004/05 (Koninklijke Brill, 2006) 429, 432.

(b) Equal treatment and diversity

The preceding discussion touches on an emerging theme within EU anti-discrimination law: the extent to which equality should be given the same interpretation when placed in the context of different discrimination grounds. As discussed in the first section of this chapter, EU legislation already provides some indication that equality is not interpreted or applied in a monolithic fashion. For example, there is the duty to provide reasonable accommodation, which only applies in respect of disability,[150] and there are various exceptions that are peculiar to specific grounds, such as the exception for employment in organizations with an ethos based on religion or belief.[151] The most far-reaching exception applies in respect of age, where there is the possibility to justify direct discrimination.[152] In *Mangold*, the Court did not attach particular weight to this distinction within the legislation. By enshrining age within the general principle of equal treatment, the Court aligned age with other discrimination grounds. This approach has encountered opposition amongst Advocates General, some of whom have queried the Court's implicit equation of age with other forms of discrimination.

On two occasions, Advocate General Mazák has robustly argued in favour of a narrow interpretation of the Employment Equality Directive as it relates to age discrimination. Both cases, *Palacios de la Villa*[153] and *Age Concern*,[154] concerned the legality of compulsory retirement upon reaching a certain age. Mazák contends that age is qualitatively different from the other grounds. In *Palacios*, he emphasizes that 'age as a criterion is a point on a scale and that, therefore, age discrimination may be graduated'.[155] This leads him to the conclusion that locating the appropriate comparator in an age discrimination case will be more difficult than in respect of sex discrimination. This is developed further in *Age Concern*, where he argues that there is:

> a genuine difference between age and the other grounds mentioned in Article 2 of the Directive. Age is not by its nature a "suspect ground", at least not so much as for example race or sex. Simple in principle to administrate, clear and transparent, age-based differentiations, age-limits and age-related measures are, quite to the contrary, widespread in law and in social and employment legislation in particular.[156]

Advocate General Geelhoed adopts a similar position in *Chacón Navas*, but extends the argument to include disability.[157] The case concerned the interpretation of the concept of 'disability' and whether this included sickness. Advocate General Geelhoed argues at some length that Article 13 EC should not be given an extensive

---

[150] Art 5, Council Directive 2000/78, (n 52 above).
[151] Art 4(2), ibid.
[152] Art 6, ibid.
[153] Case C-411/05 *Palacios de la Villa v Cortefiel Servicios SA* [2007] ECR I-8531.
[154] Case C-388/07 *The Incorporated Trustees of the National Council on Ageing (Age Concern England) v Secretary of State for Business, Enterprise and Regulatory Reform* [2009] OJ C102/6.
[155] Opinion of 15 February 2007 (n 153 above) [61].
[156] Opinion of 23 September 2008 (n 154 above) [74].
[157] Case C-13/05 *Chacón Navas v Eurest Colectividades* [2006] ECR I-6467.

interpretation. His analysis separates out age and disability from the other discrimination grounds, arguing that applying the principle of equal treatment to
these grounds could have 'potentially far-reaching economic and financial consequences'.[158] Consequently, prohibiting discrimination on these grounds should be
balanced against the flexible functioning of the labour market.[159]

The Opinions of Mazák and Geelhoed might be best described as advancing a
functional, realpolitik approach to interpreting equal treatment. In stark contrast,
Advocate General Maduro has grounded his analysis in the fundamental rights
tradition. In *Coleman*, the claimant was an employee who alleged that she had suffered
discrimination and harassment following the birth of her son, who was disabled and in
respect of whom she was the primary carer. The question arose whether an individual
who is not herself disabled could rely on the Employment Equality Directive with
regard to the prohibition of disability discrimination. Maduro began by seeking to
uncover the aims of Article 13 EC and the Employment Equality Directive, which he
defined as 'to protect the dignity and autonomy of persons belonging to those suspect
classifications'.[160] In support of his 'robust conception of equality',[161] he contended
that 'autonomy means that people must not be deprived of valuable options in areas of
fundamental importance for their lives by reference to suspect classifications'.[162]
Consequently, Article 13 EC and the Directive should be interpreted as extending to
situations where discrimination occurs against a third person closely associated with a
person belonging to a suspect classification.[163]

While a rich debate can thus be traced within the opinions of the Advocates
General, the Court remains comparatively taciturn. *Mangold* and *Kücükdeveci* remain
the clearest instances where the Court locates the Employment Equality Directive
within the framework of fundamental rights and the general principle of equal
treatment. The Court has assiduously avoided the question of whether age or disability
should be approached differently to other discrimination grounds, instead concentrating on a doctrinal interpretation of the Directive's provisions. In *Age Concern*,
it refers to the 'recognised specificity of age among the grounds of discrimination',[164]
but it then adopts a fairly rigorous interpretation of the scope for derogations under
Article 6 of the Employment Equality Directive, imposing on Member States 'the
burden of establishing to a high standard of proof the legitimacy of the aim pursued'.[165] Hence, the substantive content of its judgments does not suggest that the
Court embraces the idea that age is not a suspect ground of discrimination.[166]

In *Coleman*, the Court reached the same conclusion as Maduro, but it eschews
any theoretical discussion of dignity and autonomy. The Court opts for safer, more

---

[158] Opinion of 16 March 2006, [51].   [159] ibid [55].
[160] Case C-303/06 *Coleman v Attridge Law and Steve Law* [2008] ECR I-5603, Opinion of 31 January
2008, [10].
[161] ibid [12].   [162] ibid [11].   [163] ibid [12].
[164] *Age Concern* (n 154 above) [60].   [165] ibid [65].
[166] This is reinforced by the detailed scrutiny applied in Case C-88/08 *Hütter v Technische Universität Graz*
[2009] ECR I-5325.

traditional terrain, in particular, the need to ensure the 'effectiveness' of the protection conferred by the Directive,[167] as well as a close reading of the literal wording of the Directive.[168] The overall impression from the case law to date under the Racial and Employment Equality Directives is that the Court is not consciously ranking or prioritizing certain grounds as more suspect than others. Unsurprisingly, the Court has drawn on some of the principles already established in its gender equality case law,[169] suggesting a gradual equation of anti-discrimination law before and after Article 13 EC.

4. CONCLUSION

Compared to the position in the original Treaties, it is evident that the principle of equal treatment, in various manifestations, has undergone a gradual process of constitutionalization. This finds its roots in the Court's general principles case law, but has been latterly stamped with the authority of Treaty provisions and the prominent place of equality within the Charter of Fundamental Rights. The constitutional trajectory has been influential in releasing anti-discrimination legislation from the shackles of a market integration rationale and repositioning it within the framework of human rights protection.[170] Nevertheless, the reaction in some quarters to the decision in *Mangold* suggests there are limits to how far the Court can travel based purely on constitutional principles. The perception that the Court was giving autonomous force to the general principle of equal treatment may not tally with the actual content of the judgment, but the polemical debate which it provoked demonstrated ongoing contestation of the Court's role as a constitutional innovator.

Although equal treatment has assumed the character of a constitutional norm, its contents remain a matter of evolving negotiation. Both legislation and case law dabble with the more ambitious concept of substantive equality, but without an unambiguous commitment on either part. The Court has matured its case law on positive action in a more expansive direction, but it is inescapable that nothing in EU legislation creates any obligation on Member States to permit or take such measures. At times, the Court draws upon broader constitutional principles to enrich its interpretation of equal treatment, such as the invocation of human dignity in *P v S and Cornwall County Council*. Yet such reasoning is not commonplace and it sits alongside other decisions that seem to lack an overall vision of what the legislation is designed to achieve.[171] The terse nature of the Court's judgments is not out of character, but it leaves a navigator few theoretical signposts for how the Court will approach more complex equality

---

[167] Case C-303/06 *Coleman* (n 160 above) [51].
[168] ibid [38].
[169] eg Case C-267/06 *Maruko* (n 133 above) [60]; Case C-246/09 *Bulicke v Deutsche Büro Service GmbH* [2010] OJ C234/13.
[170] Schiek (n 63 above) 293.
[171] See eg Case C-220/02 *Österreichischer Gewerkschaftsbund* (n 135 above).

claims. Given the expanding remit of EU anti-discrimination legislation, it seems inevitable that the Court will be confronted with topical controversies, such as the wearing of religious symbols, or conflicts between discrimination grounds. Finding a satisfactory explanation of how EU law responds to these situations will demand a greater willingness to engage with the debate about what version of equality the law seeks to achieve.

D. WIDENING AND DEEPENING RECONSIDERED

In the period since the first edition of this book was published, the law relating to equal treatment has undergone a considerable transformation. The strongest feature identified was the widening of the application of the principle of equal treatment. This was most pronounced in anti-discrimination legislation in the wake of Article 13 EC, but equal treatment has also crept into immigration law and labour law. The rapid advance of legislation on equal treatment is underpinned by the progressive constitutionalization of the principle. The Charter of Fundamental Rights and revised Treaties mark a new stage in this trajectory, but their effects are still to be felt. The first part of this chapter on 'widening' found that there was a gap between equal treatment within anti-discrimination legislation and its articulation in other contexts, namely immigration and labour law. This is reinforced by the second part of the chapter. The process of constitutionalization seems directed at the personal characteristics found within Article 19 TFEU. The Charter is equivocal in its approach to the rights of third country nationals,[172] whilst there is no express reference to atypical workers.

It might have been expected that the twin processes of widening and deepening would operate in contradiction to each other. The expansion of the list of protected discrimination grounds carried the risk of diluting the concept of equality. Experience suggests that widening and deepening can in fact complement each other. The wider list of protected grounds has permitted the Union to become part of the vanguard for developing the concept of equality in international human rights law. For example, EU law has increasingly influenced the case law of the European Court of Human Rights.[173] The underlying dilemma within EU law is the extent to which equality can or should be interpreted differently according to individual discrimination grounds.[174] In this regard, there remains a risk that the process of widening could yet hinder deepening. Taking the law on positive action as an example, a uniform

---

[172] Art 15(3) states that 'nationals of third countries who are authorized to work in the territories of the Member States are entitled to working conditions equivalent to those of citizens of the Union'. This provision is not located in the equality chapter of the Charter. As discussed earlier, the Charter provision on nationality discrimination appears primarily aimed at equal treatment of EU citizens (Art 21(2)).

[173] See eg *DH and others v The Czech Republic* (n 147 above) [184]; *Bekos and Koutropoulous v Greece* (2006) 43 EHRR 2, [41].

[174] D Schiek, 'Broadening the Scope and the Norms of EU Gender Equality Law: Towards a Multidimensional Conception of Equality Law' (2005) 12 MJ 427, 448.

application of the standards developed by the Court in its gender equality case law would stifle the possibility of taking more far-reaching measures in response to specific instances of extreme inequality.

A malleable and context-sensitive concept of equality appears to be underscored by the approach found in the Charter, yet it tends to get trapped in a thicket of arguments about whether (or to what extent) the EU should set priorities in anti-discrimination law and policy. Insofar as this debate posits discrimination grounds in competition with each other, it reveals an ongoing weakness in the Union's concept of equality. Flowing from the structure of EU anti-discrimination legislation, discrimination grounds tend to be compartmentalized into isolated spheres. Academic and applied research has, though, gradually raised sensitivity to the reality of 'intersectionality',[175] in other words, the overlapping lived experience of these grounds in terms of personal identity and the ways in which discrimination is manifested. The widening process should have been fruitful terrain for law and policy to engage with inequalities linked to more than one ground. This remains a promise largely unfulfilled. Although the Racial and Employment Equality Directives make reference to gender mainstreaming and taking into account multiple discrimination as experienced by women,[176] the Commission report on the implementation of the Racial Equality Directive found that this remained 'largely untackled'.[177]

Topics such as intersectionality illustrate that, despite the rapid advancement in the law, the processes of widening and deepening are unlikely to reach a natural conclusion or to settle into a comfortable status quo. Law on equality flows from and responds to social change. This constantly throws up new complexities, which in turn demand yet further evolution, both in terms of theoretical thinking and practical solutions.

---

[175] K Crenshaw, 'Demarginalizing the Intersection of Race and Sex: A Black Feminist Critique of Anti-discrimination Doctrine, Feminist Theory, and Antiracist Politics' in A Phillips (ed), *Feminism and politics* (Oxford University Press, 1998) 314; D Schiek and V Chege, *European Union Non-Discrimination Law: Comparative Perspectives on Multidimensional Equality Law* (Routledge-Cavendish, 2009); Commission, 'Tackling multiple discrimination—practices, policies and laws' (Office of the Official Publications of the European Communities, 2007).

[176] Recital 14 and Art 17(2), Council Directive 2000/43 (n 21 above); Recital 3 and Art 19(2), Council Directive 2000/78 (n 52 above).

[177] Commission, 'The application of Directive 2000/43/EC of 29 June 2000 implementing the principle of equal treatment between persons irrespective of racial or ethnic origin' COM(2006) 643, [3.5].

21

EU 'SOCIAL' POLICY: FROM EMPLOYMENT LAW TO LABOUR MARKET REFORM

Catherine Barnard*

A. INTRODUCTION

Depending on your perspective, EU social policy is either regarded as the soft bit of EU law, an essential component of citizenship, or a vital element of the EU's single market. As we shall see, while there is an identifiable body of law which can loosely be described as 'labour' or 'social' policy, the coverage of social policy is far from comprehensive, and certainly does not represent a replication of national social policy on the EU stage. Many would argue that this is right, that social policy, of all areas, needs to be delivered close to those affected by it and so should not be a matter for the European Union at all. This raises the question, then, as to the role of, and justification for, EU-level 'social' policy, a question that has bedevilled the EU since its inception.

This chapter presents three stories about the development of EU social policy. The first, and easiest to relate, is the historical evolution of social policy where the different stages are signposted by the various Treaty amendments. It is a story of phases of great activity matched by lengthy periods of inertia (Part B). The second story concerns the contribution of the Court of Justice to the development of a distinctive EU social policy. While traditionally the Court has been seen as a supporter of the development of social rights, its true understanding of social issues has been brought into question by the controversial decisions in *Viking* and *Laval*[1] (Part C).

---

* Trinity College, Cambridge.

[1] Case C-438/05 *Viking Line ABP v The International Transport Workers' Federation, the Finnish Seaman's Union* [2007] ECR I-10779; Case C-341/05 *Laval un Partneri Ltd v Svenska Byggnadsarbetareförbundet* [2007] ECR I-11767.

The third story—for a lawyer at least—is much harder to tell because it is a story about a total reorientation of approach to regulating the labour market in the EU. It is a story that cannot be told through hard law measures on employment *law* but through a myriad of documents on employment *policy* (Part D). It is this last story which is of most relevance for the start of the new century and one that poses the most severe challenge to labour law as traditionally understood.

B. THE TRADITIONAL STORY OF THE DEVELOPMENT OF EU SOCIAL POLICY

1. THE TREATY OF ROME

(a) The Treaty provisions

When the European Economic Community (EEC) was first established in 1957, its objectives were to create a common market consisting of free internal movement of products (goods and services) and production factors (labour and capital). The view was that economic integration would in time ensure the optimum allocation of resources throughout the Union, the optimum rate of economic growth, and thus an optimum social system.[2] Consequently, the Treaty of Rome contained virtually no reference to social protection, although the Preamble did refer to the 'constant improvement of the living and working conditions of their peoples'.[3]

The Spaak Report,[4] drawn up by the foreign ministers prior to the signing of the Treaty of Rome, considered that free movement of labour was crucial to social prosperity. By allowing workers to move to find available work, they would go from areas where labour was cheap and plentiful to areas where there was demand. As a result, it was thought that wage rates would tend to rise. However, in other areas the Spaak Report envisaged only limited action to ensure the functioning of the common market. It rejected the idea of trying to harmonize the fundamental conditions of the national economy—its natural resources, its level of productivity, the significance of public burdens—considering that any harmonization might be the result of, as opposed to a condition precedent to, the operation of the common market and the economic forces which it released. In the social field this anticipated Article 117 EEC (now Article 151 TFEU (ex Article 136 EC as amended), which failed to provide any legal basis for Union-level social legislation but simply said that Member States believed that an improvement in working conditions 'will ensue not only from the functioning of the Common Market ... but also from the approximation of provisions laid down by law, regulation or administrative action'.

---

[2] M Shanks, 'Introductory Art: The Social Policy of the European Community' (1977) 14 CML Rev 375.

[3] For a fuller description, see J Kenner, *EU Employment Law: From Rome to Amsterdam and Beyond* (Hart, 2003); B Bercusson, *European Labour Law* (Cambridge University Press, 2009); P Watson, *EU Social and Employment Law: Policy and Practice in an Enlarged Europe* (Oxford University Press, 2009).

[4] Rapport des Chefs de Délégations, Comité Intergouvernemental, 21 April 1956, 19–20, 60–61.

Spaak relied heavily on the Ohlin report of ILO experts.[5] By invoking the economic theory of comparative advantage, Ohlin rejected a general role for harmonization of social policy, arguing that differences in nominal wage costs between countries did not, in themselves, pose an obstacle to economic integration because what mattered were unit labour costs, taking into account the relationship between nominal costs and productivity. Because higher costs tended to accompany higher productivity, differences between countries were less than they seemed. Ohlin also argued that the system of national exchange rates, which would be expected to reflect general prices and productivity levels within states, would cancel out the apparent advantage of low-wage states. Consequently, Ohlin argued that the market itself would ensure that conditions of competition were not distorted.

However, both Ohlin and Spaak recognized that transnational action had to be taken to correct or eliminate the effect of specific distortions which advantaged or disadvantaged certain branches of activity. By way of example, the authors cited a list of areas including working conditions of labour (such as the relationship between the salaries of men and women, working time, overtime and paid holidays), and different policies relating to credit. This argument for transnational intervention resonated with the French. At the time of the Treaty negotiations, there were important differences in the scope and content of social legislation in force in the states concerned.[6] France, in particular, had a number of rules which favoured workers, including rules permitting French workers longer paid holidays than in other states,[7] and overtime pay after fewer hours worked. France also had one of the smallest differentials between the salaries of male and female employees (7 per cent compared to 20–40 per cent in the Netherlands and in Italy).[8] This risked placing those parts of French industry employing a very large female workforce, such as textiles and electrical construction, in a weaker competitive position than identical or similar industries in other Member States employing a largely female workforce at much lower salaries.[9] This raised concerns that the additional costs borne by French industry would make French goods uncompetitive in the common market. Consequently, the French argued that an elimination of gross distortions of competition was not enough, and that it would

---

[5] International Labour Office, 'Social Aspects of European Economic Cooperation' (1956) 74 Int'l Lab Rev 99.

[6] This draws on E Ellis, *European Community Sex Equality Law* (Clarendon, 1991) 38. See also E Ellis, *European Union Anti-Discrimination Law* (Oxford University Press, 2005).

[7] ibid.

[8] M Budiner, *Le Droit de la femme a l'égalité de salaire et la Convention No. 100 de l'organisation internationale du travail* (Librairie Générale de Droit et de Jurisprudence, 1975), citing E Sullerot, *L'emploi des femmes et ses problèmes dans les Etats Membres de la Communauté Européene* (CEC, 1972) 177.

[9] Budiner (n 8 above) citing Jean-Jacques Ribas, 'L'égalité des salaires feminins et masculins dans la Communauté économique européene' (novembre 1966), Droit Social [1] and P Clair, 'L'article 119 du Traité de Rome. Le Principe de l'égalisation des salaires masculins et feminins dans la CEE', (March 1968), Droit Social 150. In addition, France had ratified ILO Convention No 100 by Law No 52–1309 of 10 December 1952 (Journal Officiel 11 December 1952). By 1957 the Convention had also been ratified by Belgium, France, Germany, and Italy, but not by Luxembourg and the Netherlands.

be necessary to assimilate the entire labour and social legislation of the Member States, so as to achieve a parity of wages and social costs.

The Germans, however, were strongly committed to keeping to a minimum the level of government interference in the area of wages and prices[10] and were most resistant to EU intervention in this area. Other Member States also considered that social policy lay at the very heart of national sovereignty,[11] and viewed it as an important vehicle to preserve 'the integrity and political stability of their respective political regimes'.[12] And so at a time of unprecedented activity at national level where workers gained new legal rights and welfare benefits, there was little pressure for harmonization at EU-level.[13]

The German approach can be explained in part by the influence of ordo-liberalism. As Joerges and Rödl explain,[14] the EU acquired a legitimacy of its own by interpreting its pertinent provisions as prescribing a law-based order committed to guaranteeing economic freedoms and protecting competition by supranational institutions. They conclude:

> The ordo-liberal European polity consists of a twofold structure: at supra-national level, it is committed to economic rationality and a system of undistorted competition, while, at national level, re-distributive (social) policies may be pursued and developed further.

A compromise was eventually reached between the French and the German positions. Articles 117 and 118 EEC (now Articles 151 and 153 TFEU as amended) on the need to improve working conditions and cooperation between states, even if textually broad, were legally shallow—at least when considered in isolation from Article 100 EEC (now Article 115 TFEU)[15]—and reflected the German preference for laissez-faire.[16] By contrast Article 119 EEC (now Article 157 TFEU) on equal pay, Article 120 EEC (now Article 158 TFEU) on paid holiday schemes, and the third Protocol on 'Certain Provisions Relating to France' on working hours and overtime[17] were specific provisions designed to

---

[10] O Kahn-Freund, 'Labour Law and Social Security' in E Stein and T Nicholson (eds), *American Enterprise in the European Common Market: A Legal Profile* (University of Michigan Law School, 1960), 300. See C Barnard, 'The Economic Objectives of Art 119' in T Hervey and D O'Keeffe (eds), *Sex Equality Law in the European Union* (Wiley, 1996).

[11] G Ross, 'The Delors' Era and Social Policy' in S Liebfried and P Pierson (eds), *European Social Policy: Between Fragmentation and Integration* (Brookings, 1995) 360.

[12] W Streeck, 'Neo-voluntarism: A New Social Policy Regime' (1995) 1 ELJ 31.

[13] For a full discussion, see B Hepple and B Veneziani, *The Transformation of Labour Law in Europe: A Comparative Study of 15 Countries 1945–2004* (Hart Publishing, 2009).

[14] C Joerges and F Rödl, 'Informal Politics, Formalised Law and the "Social Deficit" of European Integration: Reflections after the Judgments of the ECJ in *Viking* and *Laval*' (2009) 15 ELJ 1, 3–4.

[15] The legal basis for measures directly affecting 'the establishment or functioning of the Common Market'.

[16] M Forman, 'The Equal Pay Principle under Community Law' (1982) 1 LIEI 17.

[17] This provided that the Commission was to authorize France to take protective measures where the establishment of the common market did not result, by the end of the first stage, in the basic number of hours beyond which overtime was paid for and the average rate of additional payment for overtime industry not correspond to the average obtaining in France in 1956. It does not seem that France has called upon this safeguard clause—M Budiner, *Le Droit de la femme a l'égalité de salaire et la Convention No. 100 de l'organisation internationale du travail* (Librairie Générale de Droit et de Jurisprudence, 1975).

protect French industry.[18] Taken together, the provisions in the ill-named 'Social' Title of the EEC Treaty were hardly a blueprint for the development of EU employment law, let alone an EU social policy, so far short did they fall from what is traditionally regarded as social policy at national level. And in making this fundamental decision to 'decouple' the social from the economic sphere,[19] the seeds were sown for the problems that lay ahead, problems which culminated in the decisions of *Viking* and *Laval*.

(b) The market-making thesis

This brief description of why Article 119 EEC (now Article 157 TFEU) on equal pay and Article 120 (now Article 158 TFEU) on paid holiday schemes were included in the Treaty of Rome reveals that their existence can be explained in terms of market-making, not market-correcting.[20] Market-*correcting* is the more traditional justification for social policy. It means using 'political power to supersede, supplement or modify operations of the economic system in order to achieve results which the economic system would not achieve on its own, . . . guided by values other than those determined by market forces', namely social justice.[21] Yet, as we have seen, the French arguments for transnational social policy were not rooted in market-correcting but rather in terms of market-*making*. This was confirmed by Streeck who argues that the Treaty of Rome charged the Union with:

> developing a new kind of social policy, one concerned with *market making rather than market correcting*, aimed at creating an integrated European labour market and enabling it to function efficiently, rather than with correcting its outcomes in line with political standards of social justice.[22]

He argues that '[e]conomic governance through fragmented sovereignty and international relations is more suited to *market-making* by way of negative integration and efficiency enhancing regulation than to institution building and redistributive intervention, or market distortion'.

The market-making thesis comprises two limbs: first, the creation of a 'European-wide labour market',[23] by removing obstacles to the mobility of workers, and secondly (and most important for the purposes of this chapter), removing distortions to competition by seeking to harmonize costs on firms. Consequently, the provision on equal pay was included in the Treaty of Rome to impose parity of costs on the Member

---

[18] According to the French AG Dutheillet de Lamothe in Case 80/70 *Defrenne v Sabena (No 1)* [1971] ECR 445: 'It appears to be France which took the initiative, but the article [157] necessitated quite long negotiations.'

[19] F Scharpf, 'The European Social Model: Coping with the Challenges of Diversity' (2002) 40 JCMS 645.

[20] W Streeck, 'From Market Making to State Building? Reflections on the Political Economy of European Social Policy' in S Liebfried and P Pierson (eds), *European Social Policy: Between Fragmentation and Integration* (Brookings, 1995) 399.

[21] T H Marshall, *Social Policy* (Hutchinson, 1975) 15.

[22] ibid.   [23] Streeck (n 12 above) 397.

States and to prevent destructive competition. This was noted by the Court in its landmark judgment in *Defrenne (No 2)*:[24]

> Article [157] pursues a double aim. *First*,... the aim of Article [157] is to avoid a situation in which undertakings established in states which have actually implemented the principle of equal pay suffer a competitive disadvantage in intra-[Union] competition as compared with undertakings established in states which have not yet eliminated discrimination against women workers as regards pay.

However, the Court then also recognized the social dimension of the 'social' provisions:

> *Second*, this provision forms part of the social objectives of the [Union], which is not merely an economic union, but is at the same time intended, by common action to ensure social progress and seek the constant improvement of living and working conditions of their peoples... This double aim, which is at once economic and social, shows that the principle of equal pay forms part of the foundations of the [Union].

This recognition of EU social policy as serving a market-correcting, as well as a market-making, function coincided with a more general shift by the Member States in their general attitude towards the role of social policy at EU level.

2. A CHANGE OF DIRECTION

(a) The legislation

On the eve of the accession of three new Member States in 1972, the heads of government meeting in Paris issued a communiqué which stated that the Member States:

> emphasised that vigorous action in the social sphere is to them just as important as achieving Economic and Monetary Union. They consider it absolutely necessary to secure an increasing share by both sides of industry in the [Union's] economic and social decisions.[25]

This precipitated a phase of remarkable legislative activity. For example, Directives were adopted in the field of sex discrimination,[26] and the whole field of sex equality assumed a new importance as a result of judgments by the Court of Justice in the

---

[24] Case 43/75 *Defrenne v Sabena (No 2)* [1976] ECR 455 emphasis added. This point was noted, albeit somewhat obliquely, by the French AG Dutheillet de Lamothe in *Defrenne (No 1)*, the first case to consider the application of Art 157. Advancing the market-making thesis, he said that although Art 157 had a social objective it also had an economic objective 'for in creating an obstacle to any attempt at "social dumping" by means of the use of female labour less well paid than male labour, it helped to achieve one of the fundamental objectives of the common market, the establishment of a system ensuring that "competition is not distorted"'.

[25] EC Bulletin 10/1972 [6] and [19].

[26] Council Directive 75/117/EEC on equal pay ([1975] OJ L45/75), Council Directive 76/207/EEC on equal treatment ([1976] OJ L39/76). (These two Directives were repealed and replaced by Directive 2006/54 ([2006] OJ L204/23)) and Council Directive 79/7/EEC on equal treatment in social security ([1978] OJ L6/79).

Defrenne cases.[27] An action programme and a number of Directives were adopted in the field of health and safety and, in the face of rising unemployment, measures were taken to ease the impact of mass redundancies,[28] the transfer of undertakings,[29] and insolvent employers.[30] At the same time, the European Regional Development Fund[31] was introduced in order to address the problems of socio-economic convergence in the Union.

This legislation, although quite extensive, was confined to certain areas of employment law, as strictly understood, and not to the broader social sphere as originally envisaged by the 1972 communiqué. Further, this legislation had to be adopted under the general Treaty bases—Articles 100 and 235 EEC (now Articles 115 and 352 TFEU), both requiring the unanimous agreement of all the Member States. This ensured Member State control over the supranational regulation of employment rights.

(b) The market-making thesis continued?

The change of approach signalled by the heads of government in 1972 can be explained in part by reference to the social unrest in Western Europe in 1968,[32] and in part by a realization that the Union had to be seen as more than a device enabling business to exploit the common market. The Union required a human face to persuade its citizens that the social consequences of growth were being effectively tackled.[33] The adoption of the equality legislation can perhaps be justified in these terms. But most of the legislation can be explained in terms of market-making, albeit with elements of market-correcting, as the Court noted in *Commission v UK*.[34] It said that in the Directives on Collective Redundancies and Transfers[35] 'the [Union] legislature intended both to ensure comparable protection for workers' rights in the different Member States and to harmonise the costs which such protective rules entail for [Union] undertakings'.

This prompts Freedland to suggest that the evolution of EU employment law has always depended on the possibility of legitimating employment law in economic policy terms as well as social policy terms. He argues that this is a possibility which is made all

---

[27] Case 80/70 *Defrenne v Sabena (No 1)* [1971] ECR 445, Case 43/75 *Defrenne v Sabena (No 2)* [1976] ECR 455 and Case 149/77 *Defrenne v Sabena (No 3)* [1978] ECR 1365.

[28] Council Directive 75/129/EEC ([1975] OJ L48/29) now repealed and replaced by Council Directive 98/59/EC ([1998] OJ L225/16).

[29] Council Directive 77/187/EEC ([1977] OJ L61/27) now repealed and replaced by Council Directive 2001/23 ([2001] OJ L82/16).

[30] Council Directive 80/987/EEC ([1980] OJ L283/23) repealed and replaced by Council Directive 2008/94/EC ([2008] OJ L283/36).

[31] Regulation 724/75 ([1975] OJ L73/8). See now Regulation 1083/2006 ([2006] OJ L210/25).

[32] M Wise and R Gibb, *Single Market to Social Europe* (Longman, 1993) 144.

[33] Shanks (n 2 above) 378.

[34] Case C-382/92 *Commission v UK* [1994] ECR I-2435 and Case C-383/92 *Commission v UK* [1994] ECR I-2479.

[35] Council Directive 75/129/EEC ([1975] OJ L48/29) now repealed and replaced by Council Directive 98/59/EC ([1998] OJ L225/16) and Council Directive 77/187/EEC ([1977] OJ L61/27) now repealed and replaced by Council Directive 2001/23 ([2001] OJ L82/16).

the more attainable by the fact that the proponents of economic policy have felt the
need to lay claim to a social legitimation,[36] a perspective supported by the Commission
itself. For example, in its White Paper on Social Policy,[37] which in fact concerns only
labour law, the Commission said:

> Legislating for higher labour standards and employee rights has been an important part of
> the Union's achievements in the social field. The key objectives have been both to ensure
> that the creation of the single market did not result in a downward pressure on labour
> standards or create a distortion of competition, *and* to ensure that working people also
> shared in the new prosperity. The main areas of focus have been equal treatment of men
> and women, free movement of workers, health and safety, and—to a limited extent—
> labour law.[38]

In the earlier Green Paper on European Social Policy the Commission said that 'a
commitment to high social standards and to the promotion of social progress forms
an integral part of the [Treaties]. A "negative" competitiveness between Member
States would lead to social dumping, to the undermining of the consensus making
process...and to danger for the acceptability of the Union.'[39]

As we have seen with the French debate over equal pay, fears of 'social dumping'
have haunted the EU since its inception. Social dumping is the vogue, but contested,
term used to describe a variety of practices by both Member States and employers.
In essence, it concerns behaviour designed to give a competitive advantage to companies due to low labour standards[40] rather than productivity. Social dumping falls
into two categories. First, it describes deliberate attempts by *states* to adjust—usually
downwards—their labour laws in order to attract foreign investment. Companies that
move in response are said to be engaged in what we might describe as 'external' social
dumping.[41] This might in turn precipitate a race-to-the-bottom, with Member States
competing to deregulate to attract capital or at least to retain existing capital. Under
this analysis, mere differences in salary levels between states which have not been
deliberately introduced would not be seen as social dumping.

Secondly, the term social dumping is used to describe the activity of employers. It
covers two situations. On the one hand it has been used to describe the situation where
companies established in states with low wage costs win contracts in countries where
the local wage costs are considerably higher.[42] They then send their own (lower paid)

---

[36] M Freedland, 'Employment Policy' in P Davies, A Lyon-Caen, S Sciarra, and S Simitis (eds), *European Community Labour Law: Principles and Perspectives. Liber Amicorum Lord Wedderburn of Charlton* (Clarendon, 1996) 287.

[37] COM(94) 333.

[38] ibid ch III [1] emphasis added.

[39] COM(93) 551, 46.

[40] See also B Hepple, 'New Approaches to International Labour Regulation' (1997) 26 ILJ 353, 355.

[41] The Treaty rules on free movement of goods and services would allow these companies to sell their products and services back to the markets from which they have relocated. See further G Davies, '"Process and Production Method"-based Trade Restrictions in the EU' (2007–08) 10 Cam Yrbk Euro Legal Stud 69.

[42] Case C-341/05 *Laval un Partneri Ltd v Svenska Byggnadsarbetareförbundet* [2007] ECR I-11767 [103].

employees to fulfil these contracts. This could be termed 'wage dumping'. On the other hand, it describes the situation of employers moving from employing 'typical' full-time employees to atypical workers ('internal' dumping).

External social dumping inevitably leads to calls for transnational social legislation. Yet, crucially the EU has no competence over pay[43] and, as we have seen, due to the Member States' desire to protect their own sovereignty, the EU has only limited competence in respect of other types of working conditions, so its hands are severely tied. Others argue that any such legislation would be inefficient anyway.[44] It would also deprive those states of their comparative advantage—their cheaper workforce— and their vehicle for improvement.[45] So-called wage dumpers are merely taking advantage of their competitive position on the market, enabling them to offer their services to purchasers for less. These issues were fought out before the Court in *Laval* and *Rüffert*[46] in the context of the 2004 enlargement of the Central and Eastern European States (CEECs), cases which are considered in Part C below.

Despite the repeated assertion of social dumping, there is remarkably little empirical evidence on the question of whether social dumping is a myth or a reality.[47] Some of the most recent research has been carried out by Roberto Pedersini for the European Foundation for the Improvement of Living and Working Conditions, albeit that[48] his research comes with a number of caveats about the problems with the evidence on which his findings are drawn. On the one hand, he says that Foreign Direct Investment (FDI) data seem to indicate that economic actors are increasingly interested in establishing control over foreign firms located in developing, formerly peripheral, economies. This relates especially to locations in CEECs and China. Such investment flows are likely to include transfers of production capacity to these areas. Furthermore, he says survey results show a high interest in, and attention to, relocation of production among the business community.

On the other hand, Pedersini also points to the European Restructuring Monitor (ERM),[49] which suggests that cases of relocation still form a relatively small proportion of all restructuring cases. The ERM data therefore suggests that offshoring/delocalization accounts for only about 5 per cent of all redundancies. This view is supported by the Commission in its publication 'Enlargement, two years after: an economic

---

[43]   Art 153(5) TFEU.

[44]   See, for example, D Fischel, 'The "race to the bottom" revisited—reflections on recent developments in Delaware's Corporation Law' (1982) Northwestern UL Rev 913.

[45]   L Bierman and G Keim, 'On the Economic Realities of the European Social Charter and the Social Dimension of EC 1992' (1992) 2 Duke J Comp & Int'l L 49.

[46]   Case C-346/06 *Rüffert* [2008] ECR I-1989 noted by P Davies (2008) 37 ILJ 293.

[47]   This is discussed further in C Barnard, 'Social Dumping Revisited: Lessons from Delaware' (2000) 25 ELRev 57.

[48]   'Relocation of Production and Industrial Relations' (6 February 2006): <http://www.eurofound.europa. eu/eiro/2005/11/study/tn0511101s.htm>, considered in C Barnard, 'Fifty years of avoiding social dumping? The EU's economic and not so economic constitution' in M Dougan and S Currie (eds), *50 Years of the European Treaties: Looking Back and Thinking Forward* (Hart, 2009).

[49]   European Restructuring Monitor run by the European Monitoring Centre on Change (EMCC).

evaluation'.[50] Under the heading 'Fears of relocation not justified', it notes that the evidence indicates that FDI flows to the new Member States, while relevant for the recipient countries, have in fact been only a minor part of overall FDI outflows of the EU-15: within the latter, in 2004 the share of outflows to new Member States was 4 per cent against a corresponding share of 53 per cent for outflows to other Member States in the EU-15 and a 12 per cent share for flows to the US.

The Commission observes that international investment appears driven mainly by other factors, such as unit labour costs or agglomeration economies (geographical location advantages, market size, external economies, the general business environment, human capital) leading to spatial concentration. Elsewhere, the Commission notes that:

> [s]tudies confirm that relocation of companies from the old to the new Member States remains a marginal phenomenon. Moreover, Central and Eastern Europe is not the main destination for relocation, but rather Asia; it is not enlargement that mainly causes outsourcing and relocation but global competition.[51]

While the EU's hands are somewhat tied in dealing with 'social dumping' in the EU, its hands are completely tied in respect of relocation outside the EU.

3. THE SINGLE MARKET AND THE COMMUNITY SOCIAL CHARTER 1989

(a) The Treaty changes

The next major step in the Union's evolution, the Single European Act (SEA) and the single market programme, were again premised on the idea that liberalization of trade would lead to economies of scale and economic growth from which the greater number of Union citizens would benefit. Although the idea of adding a social dimension to the internal market programme was discussed, particularly by the European Parliament, the SEA eventually made few concessions to those who argued for greater social competence. The SEA did, however, extend qualified majority voting to the field of 'health and safety, particularly in respect of the working environment' (Article 118a EEC (now Article 153 TFEU as amended)), although matters 'relating to the rights and interests of employed persons' (Article 100a(2) EEC (now Article 115(2) TFEU)) still required unanimous agreement in Council. Further, the (then) Community committed itself to strengthening economic and social cohesion in the EU (Article 130a EEC (now Article 174 TFEU)) and to developing the 'dialogue between management and labour at European level', the so-called social dialogue (Article 118b EEC (now Articles 154–155 TFEU as amended)).

---

[50] <http://ec.europa.eu/economy_finance/publications/publication7548_en.pdf>.
[51] Commission, 'Myths and facts about Enlargement': <http:/ec.europa.eu/enlargement/questionsand answers/mythsen.htm>.

(b) The legislative response

Once again, the trade unions were disappointed by the absence of any clear social provisions in the Treaty. They made a powerful case that the ambitious single market programme would not succeed unless it had the support of the Union citizens and that the single market would produce negative consequences for employees: as the European market opened up uncompetitive firms would go out of business and large companies might relocate to areas of the EU where social costs were lower. In both cases unemployment would result. This prompted Jacques Delors to set out his plans for 'L'Espace Sociale Europ_ene'. He talked of:

> The creation of a vast economic area, based on market and business cooperation, is inconceivable—I would say unattainable—without some harmonization of social legislation. Our ultimate aim must be the creation of a European social area.[52]

And in so doing, he continued the process of embedding economic integration into the social dimension and thereby helped to recouple the economic and the social spheres. He was behind the adoption of the Community Charter of Fundamental Social Rights, a political declaration signed by all the Member States except Britain during the Strasbourg summit in 1989.[53] The measures to be adopted were laid down in the Social Charter Action Programme but because they were to be based on the (then) EEC Treaty they were binding on the UK.[54]

The Action Programme put forward by the Commission, when its power and prestige may have been at its highest point, proposed that forty-seven different instruments be submitted by 1 January 1993. However, these forty-seven proposals included only seventeen Directives,[55] of which ten dealt with narrow health and safety matters, such as safety of the workplace,[56] safety of work equipment,[57] safety of VDUs,[58] and manual handling of loads.[59] This contrasted unfavourably with the proposals for almost 300 Directives submitted as part of the White Paper for Completing the Internal Market.[60] Nevertheless, the Action Programme led to the enactment of important pieces of social legislation aimed at protecting individual workers, including Directives on proof of the employment contract,[61] pregnant workers,[62]

---

[52] *EC Bulletin*, 1986, 2 and 12.

[53] In 1997 the UK signed up to the Social Charter.

[54] COM(89) 568 final, 29 November 1989.

[55] Social Europe 1/90, Commission of the European Communities (Brussels, 1990) contains the full text of the Social Charter, the Action Programme, background material and comments. Reports on the progress of the implementation of the Action Programme can be found in COM(91) 511 final, summarised in ISEC/B1/92, and E Szyszczak (1992) 21 ILJ 149, and COM(93) 668 final.

[56] Council Directive 89/654/EEC, [1989] OJ L393/1.

[57] Council Directive 89/655/EEC, [1989] OJ L393/13.

[58] Council Directive 90/270/EEC, [1991] OJ L156/14.

[59] Council Directive 90/269/EEC, [1990] OJ L156/9.

[60] COM(85) 310 final.

[61] Council Directive 91/533/EEC, [1991] OJ L288/32.

[62] Council Directive 92/85/EEC, [1992] OJ L348/1.

working time,[63] young workers,[64] and posted workers.[65] Although this last Directive was seen as a social policy measure it was in fact adopted under the Treaty provisions on free movement of services. This became an issue of considerable importance in *Laval* which is considered in Part C below.[66]

(c) A case study: the Working Time Directive

What was the driving imperative behind the adoption of this legislation? As we have already seen, much rhetorical play was made of market-making and thus harmonization of costs. However, in the absence of a general power to legislate in the social field and a lack of political will, the notion of a 'level playing field' made little sense.[67] Article 118a EEC (now Article 153(4) TFEU) therefore introduced a more limited objective of the adoption of minimum standards Directives. Such Directives would create a 'floor of rights', thereby preventing a race to the bottom, while preserving Member States' rights to legislate above the floor where they chose to do so. One of the first Directives expressly adopted under this minimum standards approach, the Working Time Directive 93/104,[68] revealed just how difficult it was for the EU actually to legislate in the social domain.

Its principal opponent was the UK which was extremely hostile to any legislation in this field, partly on ideological grounds, considering that such legislation would increase labour market rigidity, and partly on historical grounds: unlike in Continental Europe, working time in the UK had traditionally been regulated through collective agreements and not through centralized legislation. To circumvent known UK opposition, the Commission seized on the new legal basis introduced by the SEA, and proposed the Directive based on Article 118a EEC (now Article 153 TFEU as amended), with its qualified majority voting. The UK abstained in Council when the Directive was put to a vote and David Hunt, the then Secretary of State for Employment, declared the Directive to be toothless. This was in part because the UK had obtained major concessions in the Directive: most (in)famously it secured the possibility for employees to sign an opt-out from the 48-hour working week. In one fell swoop, this highly controversial opt-out undermined both the market-making and market-correcting rationale of the legislation.

Even with these concessions, the British government then challenged the choice of Article 118a EEC as the legal basis,[69] arguing that since the organization of working

---

[63] Council Directive 93/104/EEC, [1993] OJ L307/18 repealed and replaced by Council Directive 2003/88, [2003] OJ L299/9.

[64] Council Directive 94/33/EEC, [1993] OJ L216/12.

[65] Council Directive 96/71/EEC, [1997] OJ L18/1.

[66] Case C-341/05 *Laval un Partneri Ltd v Svenska Byggnadsarbetareförbundet* [2007] ECR I-11767.

[67] S Deakin and F Wilkinson 'Rights v efficiency? The economic case for transnational labour standards' (1994) 23 ILJ 289.

[68] Council Directive 93/104/EEC ([1993] OJ L307/18) repealed and replaced by Council Directive 2003/88 ([2003] OJ L299/9).

[69] Case C-84/94 *UK v EU Council* [1996] ECR I-5755.

time envisaged by the Directive was intended to achieve both job creation and social policy objectives, recourse should have been had to Article 100 EEC or to Article 235 EEC (now Articles 115 and ·352 TFEU), both requiring unanimity in Council. The Court rejected the UK's arguments:

> where *the principal aim* of the measure in question is the protection of the health and safety of workers, Article 118a must be used, albeit such a measure may have ancillary effects on the establishment and functioning of the internal market.[70]

The Court then considered that the Directive was a social policy measure and not a general measure relating to job creation and reduced unemployment. It considered that health and safety was the essential objective of the Directive, albeit that it might affect employment as well, and therefore the Directive was properly adopted on the basis of Article 118a.[71] In respect of arguments based on the principle of subsidiarity the Court said:

> Once the Council has found that it is necessary to improve the existing level of protection as regards the health and safety of workers and to harmonise the conditions in this area while maintaining the improvements made, achievement of that objective through the imposition of minimum requirements necessarily presupposes [Union] wide action.[72]

Therefore the Court suggests that in the case of harmonization measures the Union should always act. However, the Court failed to interrogate the more difficult question as to why it was necessary for Union-level harmonization to occur in this field at all.

The Directive, now revised and replaced by Directive 2003/88, is striking for its complexity, its lack of clarity, and its attempt at both rigidity and flexibility. The rigidity lies in its choice of forty-eight hours as the maximum working week, eleven hours per 24-hour period as daily rest, and a maximum of eight hours as night work. Why should these particular figures be chosen as sufficient to guarantee health and safety? The lack of clarity lies in the complexity of calculating the reference periods over which average working time and rest are to be calculated, and definitions of key terms such as 'working time'.

The flexibility of the Directive[73] lies in the reference periods over which the minimum and maximum working time is calculated, the role for 'collective agreements or agreements between the two sides of industry' in setting certain standards,

---

[70] ibid [22].   [71] ibid [30].   [72] ibid [47].

[73] Other Directives contain different flexibility provisions: eg the so-called Art 13 agreements in the European Works Council Directive 94/45/EC, [1994] OJ L254/64. The Directive did not apply to enterprises which on 22 September 1996 were party to existing voluntary transnational information and consultation agreements covering the entire workforce. This offers the parties the advantage of negotiating an agreement outside the 'special negotiating body' provided by the Directive and not directly affected by the subsidiary requirements provided for in the annex. This Directive is to be repealed and replaced from 6 June 2011 by Council Directive 2009/38, [2009] OJ L122/28, but the Art 13 derogation is carried over (Art 14). See also Arts 5 and 11 of the Information and Consultation Directive 2002/14/EC, [2002] OJ L80/29. See C Barnard, 'Flexibility and social policy' in G de Búrca and J Scott (eds), *Constitutional Change in the EU: From Uniformity to Flexibility?* (Hart Publishing, 2000).

such as the duration and terms on which a rest break can be taken, and the possibility for derogations and delayed implementation. This flexibility was necessary to accommodate the diversity of industrial relations traditions. It also demonstrated the problems of harmonizing a key area of employment law at EU-level, problems exacerbated by an apparently employee-centred approach to the interpretation of substantive provisions of the Directive by the Court of Justice. For example, the Court ruled in *Jaeger*[74] that the time spent by doctors and nurses at their workplace on-call *and* on the premises of the employer (even where they could sleep in a bed provided by the employer) constituted working time. Furthermore, the time spent asleep or otherwise inactive could not count towards the rest periods because the employee must 'be able to remove himself from the working environment . . . to enable him to relax and dispel the fatigue caused by the performance of his duties'.

The cost implications of this and other rulings[75] for national health services across the EU have been enormous. These judgments have therefore resulted in more states taking advantage of the individual opt-out from the Working Time Directive (an opt-out originally seen as the exclusive preserve of the UK[76]) to ensure that they remain compliant with Union rules. Divisions between the Council and the Parliament have meant that conciliation over one of the many reform proposals has so far been unsuccessful.

4. FROM MAASTRICHT TO LISBON

(a) The Maastricht Treaty

The pressure at Maastricht to expand EU social competence was again met with stubborn resistance on the part of the UK. This led to the content of the so-called Social Chapter (the Social Policy Agreement (SPA) and the Social Policy Protocol (SPP)) being placed in a separate Protocol from which the UK secured an opt-out when the Maastricht Treaty was finally agreed. The SPA broadened the range of measures which could be decided by qualified majority vote to include information and consultation of workers, equality between men and women, and the integration of those excluded from the labour market. On the other hand, Article 2(6) SPA (now Article 153(5) TFEU) expressly excluded from the EC (and now EU's) competence 'pay, the right of association, the right to strike or the right to impose lock-outs'.

The SPA also envisaged a greater role for the Social Partners: not only would they be consulted both on the possible direction of Community and now Union action and on the content of the envisaged proposal,[77] but could also, if they chose, negotiate collective

---

[74] Case C-151/02 *Jaeger* [2004] ECR I-8389.

[75] See eg Case C-350/07 *Schultz-Hoff and Stringer* [2009] ECR I-179.

[76] Ireland also took advantage of the opt-out in the early days but then repealed its national law.

[77] Art 154(2) and (3) TFEU (ex Art 138(2) and (3) EC).

agreements[78] which could be given *erga omnes* effects by Council 'decision'.[79] Council Directive 96/34/EC on Parental Leave[80] was the first measure to be adopted via this route. This was followed by agreements on part-time work[81] and fixed-term work.[82] The social partners could not, however, reach agreement on the European Works Council Directive[83] nor on a Directive on agency work,[84] and so these measures were negotiated by the legislature in the usual way. Other agreements, such as one on teleworking[85] and another on stress at work,[86] have also been negotiated but they have been implemented not by a Directive but by national and sub-national collective agreements. These measures have enjoyed much less visibility and influence.

The significant role given to the social partners[87] formed part of the process of mobilizing a greater number of actors (including the Member States, regional and local authorities, companies through CSR, NGOs, and civil society more generally) to the cause of achieving both a social Europe[88] and the wider goals of the Lisbon strategy (see below).[89] But the more actors involved, the greater the questions about their legitimacy. This came to a head in *UEAPME*[90] where the body representing small and medium-sized undertakings (UEAPME) argued that it should have participated in the negotiation of the parental leave collective agreement, alongside the three interprofessional social partners UNICE, now Business for Europe, the employers' association, CEEP, the public sector employer's association, and ETUC, the trade union organization. In rejecting UEAPME's challenge, the General Court (then the CFI) recognized the role of the social dialogue and the contribution it makes to enhancing the legitimacy of the EU because, as the Court notes, it provides an alternative type of representative democracy.[91] Nevertheless, the judgment did force the Council and the

---

[78] Art 155(1) TFEU (ex Art 139(1) EC). See generally B Bercusson, 'Maastricht—A Fundamental Change in European Labour Law' (1992) 23 IRJ 177 and 'The Dynamic of European Labour Law after Maastricht' (1994) 23 ILJ 1; A Lo Faro, *Regulating Social Europe: Reality and Myth of Collective Bargaining in the EC Legal Order* (Hart Publishing, 2000).

[79] Art 155(2) TFEU (ex Art 139(2) EC). The term 'decision' is not used in the strict sense of Art 288 TFEU (ex Art 249 EC) but has been interpreted to mean any legally binding act, in particular Directives.

[80] Council Directive 94/55/EC, [1996] OJ L145/4. This Directive is to be repealed from 8 March 2012 by Council Directive 2010/18/EU, [2010] OJ L68/13.

[81] Council Directive 97/81/EC, [1998] OJ L14/9.

[82] Council Directive 99/70/EC, [1999] OJ L175/43.

[83] Council Directive 94/45, [1994] OJ L254/64. This Council Directive is to be repealed and replaced from 6 June 2011 by Council Directive 2009/38, [2009] OJ L122/28.

[84] Council Directive 2008/114/EC, [2008] OJ L327/9.

[85] <http://www.socialdialogue.net/en/en_cha_bestpr_framework.jsp>.

[86] <http://www.worker-participation.eu/EU-Social-Dialogue/Interprofessional-ESD/Outcomes/Framework-agreements/Framework-agreement-on-stress-at-work>.

[87] A role now formally recognized by Art 152 TFEU.

[88] See eg Commission Communication, *Social Policy Agenda* (COM(2000) 379, 14 and the Nice Presidency Conclusions, 7–9 December 2000, [27] the Commission's White Paper European Governance COM(2001) 428, 14 and Commission, *The European social dialogue, a force for innovation and change*, COM(2002) 341, 7.

[89] Luxembourg Presidency Conclusions, 22 and 23 March 2005, [6].

[90] Case T-135/96 *UEAPME* [1998] ECR II-2335.

[91] ibid [89]

Commission to scrutinize the representativity of the social partners more closely[92] as well as laying down more general criteria for those involved in the consultation process.[93]

(b) The Amsterdam Treaty

A new Labour government was elected in the UK in May 1997. This precipitated a sea change in the British approach towards the European Union. One of the first steps it took was to agree to sign up to—or opt back into—the Social Chapter. As a result, at the IGC in Amsterdam an amended chapter on social policy, incorporating and revising both Articles 117–121 EEC and the Agreement on Social Policy, was included in the EC Treaty in a new section entitled 'The Union and the Citizen' (now Titles IX and X of Part Three on Union Policies and Internal Actions). This presentational device served to highlight the social citizenship aspect of the Treaty. One of the most visible successes of the Amsterdam Treaty was the inclusion of Article 13 EC (now Article 19 TFEU) which led to the rapid adoption of the equal treatment Directive 2000/43 on race and ethnic origin[94] and the Framework Directive 2000/78.[95]

The Amsterdam Treaty also included a new Title on Employment,[96] introduced largely as a result of pressure from France and the Scandinavian countries. Article 145 TFEU (ex Article 125 EC) provides that Member States and the Union shall work towards 'developing a co-ordinated strategy for employment and particularly for promoting a skilled, trained and adaptable workforce and labour markets responsive to economic change'. Article 146 TFEU (ex Article 126 EC) requires the Member States to coordinate their policies for the promotion of employment (which is to be regarded as an issue of 'common concern')[97] within the Council, in a way consistent with the broad economic guidelines laid down within the framework of EMU, which are issued annually by the Council as part of the process of ensuring economic stability and convergence.[98] The European Council must also draw up guidelines according to Article 148 TFEU (ex Article 128 EC) which the Member States are obliged to take into account in their employment policies. Under Article 149 TFEU (ex Article 129 EC) the

---

[92] See the Social Partners' Study of 1993, Doc No V/6141/93/E. The main findings of the study can be found in COM(93) 600, Annex 3.

[93] 'General principles and minimum standards for consultation of interested parties by the Commission' COM(2002) 704.

[94] Council Directive 2000/43/EC, [2000] OJ L180/22 implementing the principle of equal treatment between persons irrespective of racial or ethnic origin.

[95] Council Directive 2000/78/EC, [2000] OJ L303/18 establishing a general framework for equal treatment in employment and occupation. See generally M Bell, *Anti-Discrimination Law and the European Union* (Oxford University Press, 2002) and his chapter in this volume.

[96] For a full consideration of this subject, see D Ashiagbor, *The European Employment Strategy* (Oxford University Press, 2006).

[97] Art 146(2) TFEU.

[98] Art 146(1) TFEU. This is now achieved through the Integrated Guidelines: see eg Council Decision 2008/618, [2008] OJ L198/47, for the years 2008–10.

Council may adopt incentive measures designed to encourage cooperation between Member States.[99]

This annual cycle of policy formation, policy implementation, and policy monitoring was formally launched at Luxembourg in November 1997 and became known as the European Employment Strategy (EES). The EES highlighted a shift in emphasis in the EU from measures protecting those in employment to addressing the high levels of unemployment in Europe. This was a direct response to the growing crisis faced by many western European states of 'welfare without work': expensive social welfare programmes unsupported by high levels of employment which risked putting Euro zone countries in breach of the budgetary commitments laid down by EMU. Thus the EES replaced the focus on demand side policies with the adoption of *supply* side policies, stimulating productivity through the creation of a favourable business environment, shorn of much red tape, and improving the quality of the workforce.[100] This new story of EU social policy is considered further in Part D below.

The inclusion of the Employment Title amounted to a recognition by the Euro zone states—largely overlooked at Maastricht—of the increased interdependencies between EU economic policy and national social policy. As Trubek and Trubek note,[101] so long as national markets are relatively closed and national budgets relatively independent, social policy is basically a domestic concern. But once nations create a common currency and join in a single market, then social policy in one country becomes relevant to other nations. Thus, the constraints and interdependencies generated by EMU pointed to the need for some form of transnational policy coordination in the field of employment. Gone were the days discussed by Ohlin when differences in productivity were reflected in the different national currencies. States in the Eurozone lost control over their currencies. The Employment Title was the EU's response. However, given the acute political sensitivities involved (the Member States have long viewed job creation as lying at the heart of national sovereignty), a new method of policy-making needed to be developed which would stimulate job creation without threatening national social, employment, and economic policies.[102] This new approach is modelled in part on the strategy which had been adopted in respect of EMU, with the Commission proposing (non-binding) guidelines which the Member States are obliged to take into account in their national reform programmes (NRPs).

Thus, in terms of regulatory technique, this new approach moved away from providing harmonized rights for individual employees through traditional command and control regulation adopted under the classic Community (Union) Method. In its stead came a new mode of governance based on coordination of action by the states,

---

[99] C Kilpatrick, 'New EU Employment Governance and Constitutionalism' in G de Búrca and J Scott (eds), *Law and Governance in the EU and the US* (Hart, 2006).

[100] V Hatzopoulos, 'A (More) Social Europe: A Political Crossroad or a Legal One-Way? Dialogues between Luxembourg and Lisbon' (2005) 42 CML Rev 1599, 1600.

[101] 'Hard and Soft Law in the Construction of Social Europe: the Role of the Open Method of Coordination' (2005) 11 ELJ 343, 345.

[102] 'The New Paradigm for Social Policy: A Virtuous Circle' (2001) 38 CML Rev 1125, 1134.

under the direction of the European Union, focusing in particular on active labour market policies such as training, and lifelong learning. The Lisbon European Council 2000 gave this new method of governance a name: the open method of coordination (OMC).

(c) The Lisbon Strategy, the Nice and Lisbon Treaties

At the Lisbon summit in March 2000[103] the Union set itself a new, ambitious, and ultimately unfeasible strategic goal to become, by 2010, 'the most competitive and dynamic knowledge-based economy in the world capable of sustainable economic growth with more and better jobs and greater social cohesion'.[104] The strategy had three mutually interdependent limbs: economic (making the EU more competitive while sustaining a stable economy), environmental (sustainable development), and social (modernizing the European social model,[105] investing in people, and combating social exclusion). This strategy was designed to enable the Union to regain 'the conditions for full employment' and to strengthen 'regional cohesion in the European Union'.

These goals were to be achieved by 'improving existing processes, introducing a new open method of coordination at all levels coupled with a stronger guiding and coordinating role for the European Council'.[106] The Presidency conclusions described the Open Method of Co-ordination (OMC) as the means of spreading best practice and achieving greater convergence towards the EU's main goals by helping Member States develop their own policies.[107] Implementation of OMC involves tools such as targets, indicators, and benchmarks, as well as the exchange of experiences, peer review, and the dissemination of good practice. In particular, the Lisbon—and subsequently Stockholm—European Councils set the EU the objective of reaching an overall employment rate of 70 per cent by 2010, an employment rate of over 60 per cent for women, and employment rate among older men and women (55–64) of 50 per cent.[108] However, in the 2005 mid-term review of the Lisbon strategy[109] it was recognized that there were significant delays in reaching these targets, and in the Lisbon relaunch – now called the Lisbon Strategy for growth and Jobs – no reference was made to the 2010 deadline.

The Nice Treaty introduced an amendment to Article 137 EC (now Article 153 TFEU) to raise the profile of OMC. What is now Article 153(2)(a) TFEU provides that the Council may 'adopt measures designed to encourage co-operation between member States...excluding any harmonization of the laws and regulations of the Member States'; the power to adopt Directives only appears in Article 153(2)(b).

The other significant innovation at Nice was the adoption of the Community (now Union) Charter of Fundamental Rights. From the perspective of this chapter, the

---

[103] Presidency Conclusions, 24 March 2000.   [104] ibid [5].
[105] See further Part D below.   [106] See n 103 above [7].
[107] Lisbon European Council, 23 and 24 March 2000 [37].
[108] Stockholm European Council, 23 and 24 March 2001 [9].
[109] <http://www.consilium.europa.eu/ueDocs/cms_Data/docs/pressData/en/ec/84335.pdf>.

significance of the Charter was that it apparently put traditional civil and political rights on the same footing as economic and social rights since, exceptionally in human rights instruments of this kind, both appeared in the same document.[110]

In fact, the main provisions relating to 'social matters' (as opposed to equality) can be found in Title IV, 'Solidarity',[111] where the Member States, especially the UK, have gone to considerable lengths to ensure that the provisions, unlike those concerning traditional civil and political rights, are not directly effective. First, the UK considers that Title IV concerns 'principles', not 'rights'. The accompanying explanations make clear that principles (unlike rights) do not 'give rise to direct claims for positive action by the Union's institutions or Member States authorities'.[112] Article 52(4)–(7), together with the explanations, was inserted into the adapted version of the Charter which was adopted to facilitate the signing of the Constitutional Treaty and then the Lisbon Treaty where Article 6(1) TEU gave legal effect to the Charter (the Charter 'shall have the same legal value as the Treaties').[113]

Secondly, if despite the drafting, the provisions in Title IV are nevertheless found to contain some rights, rather than principles, then the UK (and Poland and soon the Czech Republic) consider they may have secured an 'opt-out' from them in Protocol No 30, also adopted at Lisbon. However, the legal implications of this Protocol are much disputed, even by the UK government itself.[114]

Thirdly, any 'rights' are carefully delimited by reference to national and Union law. For example, the controversial Article 28 provides that:

---

[110] The Court has used the Charter in creative ways to steer its interpretation: see eg Case C-555/07 *Kücükdeveci*, judgment of 19 January 2010, to strike down the EU legislation Joined Cases C-92/09 and C-93/09 Volker and Schecke judgment of 9 Nov. 2010.

[111] eg Art 27 concerns information and consultation within the undertaking; Art 30 on protection in the event of unjustified dismissal and Art 31 fair and just working conditions including, in Art 31(2), 'the right to limitation of maximum working hours, to daily and weekly rest periods and to an annual period of paid leave'; and Art 33 family and professional life.

[112] This is taken from the explanations (OJ [2007] C303/35) (which themselves must be 'given due regard by the courts of the Union and of the Member States' (Art 52(7) of the Charter)). See also Art 52(5) of the Charter. The explanations provide: 'Paragraph 5 clarifies the distinction between "rights" and "principles" set out in the Charter. According to that distinction, subjective rights shall be respected, whereas principles shall be observed (Article 51(1)). Principles may be implemented through legislative or executive acts (adopted by the Union in accordance with its powers, and by the Member States only when they implement Union law); accordingly, they become significant for the Courts only when such acts are interpreted or reviewed.' Examples given of 'principles' are drawn mainly from the Solidarity Title (eg Arts 25 (rights of the elderly), 26 (integration of persons with disabilities), and 37 (environmental protection). The explanations add that '[i]n some cases, an Article of the Charter may contain both elements of a right and of a principle, e.g. Articles 23, 33 and 34.'

[113] For a discussion of the effect of the Lisbon Treaty on the field of social policy, see P Syrpis, 'The Treaty of Lisbon: Much Ado ... but about What?' (2008) 37 ILJ 219.

[114] For discussion, see C Barnard, '"The 'Opt-Out" for the UK and Poland from the Charter of Fundamental Rights: Triumph of Rhetoric over Reality?' in S Griller and J Ziller (eds), *The Lisbon Treaty: EU Constitutionalism without a Constitutional Treaty*, (SpringerWien, 2008) Cf 'Government concedes in the Court of Appeal that UK has no opt-out from the EU Charter of Fundamental Rights in the context of the *Saaedi* case' http://www.doughtystreet.co.uk/news/news_detail.cfm?iNewsID=405, so long as the Charter is considered merely to reflect existing law. See *R (on the application of NS)* [2010] EW CA Civ 990, para 7 and the reference to the CJEU in Joined Cases C-411/10 and C-493/10 *ME*.

> Workers and their employers, or their respective organisations, have, *in accordance with Union law and national laws and practices*, the right to negotiate and conclude collective agreements at the appropriate levels and, in cases of conflicts of interest, to take collective action to defend their interests, *including strike action.*[115]

It was this provision which enabled the Court to conclude in *Viking* and *Laval* that the right to strike was a 'fundamental right which forms an integral part of the general principles of [Union] law' (thereby undermining, at a stroke, much of the UK's attempts to draw the teeth of at least Article 28 of the Charter). However, the limitations on the right to strike laid down by national law, and now by Union law following *Viking* and *Laval*, have gone a long way towards undermining the substance of the right. Nevertheless, there is some hope, by trade unionists at least, that longer term, the incorporation of the Charter may have some significant impact in terms of legitimizing a more nuanced balance between social and economic rights,[116] a balance apparently called for in the phrase used in Article 3 TEU, 'a highly competitive social market economy'.[117]

5. CONCLUSIONS

The discussion in the section indicates that the development of the so-called social dimension has been spasmodic: the resulting rules represent a patchwork of European social regulation and other policies rather than a fully fledged social policy with welfare institutions and cradle-to-grave protection. It makes no provision for what is generally agreed to be the central core of social policy: social insurance, public assistance, health and welfare services, and housing policy.[118] In reality, the 'social policy' terminology masks what is in essence employment-related social policy—and an eclectic body of employment law at that. As Freedland points out, it is concerned with collective dismissals and acquired rights on transfer of undertakings, rather than with the termination of employment more generally; with particulars of the terms of the contract rather than the terms themselves; with consultation of workers' representatives on certain issues rather than with collective representation and workers' organizations as a whole; with the work-related implications of pregnancy rather than with those of maternity and parenthood more generally; and with working time and health

---

[115] Emphasis added.

[116] A view given some support by eg Advocate General Cruz Villalon in Case C-515/08 *Santos Palhota* [2010] ECR I-000, paras 51–53. See also Case C-271/08 Commission v Germany [2010] ECRJ 000.

[117] For a discussion of this term, see Ch Joerges and F Rödl, ' "Social Market Economy" as Europe's Social Model?' EUI Working Paper Law No 2004/8, 19 who argue that 'this concept contained an ordo-liberal basis which was complemented by social and societal policies, whose aims and instruments were supposed to rely on market mechanisms'. According to Working Group XI on Social Europe (CONV 516/1/03 REV 1 [17]) the objectives should refer to 'social market economy' to underline the link between the economic and social development and the efforts made to ensure greater coherence between economic and social policies.

[118] M Majone, 'The European Community: Between Social Policy and Regulation' (1993) 31 JCMS 153, 158. However, the TFEU does contain Titles on education, vocational training and youth and sport (Title XII), on culture (Title XIII), public health (Title XIV), and consumer protection (Title XV).

and safety rather than with the quality of working conditions more generally.[119] As a result, the Union has established a body of law which supplements, complements and sometimes, as we have seen, constrains existing national social policy.[120]

Nevertheless it is a sufficiently large body of law to enable the Commission to describe its content in terms of a European Social Model (ESM).[121] This social model is based around certain shared values:[122]

These include democracy and individual rights, free collective bargaining, the market economy, equality of opportunity for all and social welfare and solidarity. These values… are held together by the conviction that economic and social progress must go hand in hand. Competitiveness and solidarity have both been taken into account in building a successful Europe for the future.

The effect of the Lisbon Treaty has been to constitutionalize some of these values at Union level.[123]

The Nice Council's Social Policy Agenda 2000 took a broader approach to defining the ESM, recognizing the interplay between national and EU level delivery of social policy:[124]

The European social model, characterized in particular by systems that offer a high level of social protection, by the importance of the social dialogue and by services of general interest covering activities vital for social cohesion, is today based, beyond the diversity of the Member States' social systems, on a common core of values.

It continued:[125]

The European social model has developed over the last forty years through a substantial [Union] acquis… It now includes essential texts in numerous areas: free movement of workers, gender equality at work, health and safety of workers, working and employment conditions and, more recently, the fight against all forms of discrimination.

It also includes the agreements between the social partners in the law-making process, the Luxembourg EES, and the open method of coordination on the subject of social exclusion and greater cooperation in the field of social protection.[126] However, these

---

[119] M Freedland, 'Employment Policy' in Davies, Lyon-Caen, Sciarra, and Simitis (n 36 above) 278–279.

[120] P Pierson and S Leibfried, 'The Making of Social Policy' in Leibfried and Pierson (n 11 above) 7.

[121] See eg Commission Communication, Employment and Social Policies: a framework for investing in quality (COM(2001) 313, 5.

[122] Commission Communication, White Paper on Social Policy, COM(94) 333, [3].

[123] See Arts 2 and 3 TEU which emphasize the values of solidarity and equality. M Poiares Maduro, 'Europe's Social Self: "The Sickness Unto Death"' in J Shaw (ed), *Social Law and Policy in an evolving European Union* (Hart Publishing, 2000) 342.

[124] White Paper on Social Policy (n 122 above) [10].

[125] ibid [12].

[126] Strengthening the social dimension of the Lisbon strategy: Streamlining open coordination in the field of social protection, COM(2003) 261, [3]. Social Protection is a fundamental component of the European Model of society. It can be defined as the set of collective transfer systems which are designed to protect people against social risks.

lists make no reference to the vital role played by the European Court of Justice in fleshing out the substance of the bare bones of these texts. It is to this subject that we now turn.

C. THE ROLE OF THE COURT OF JUSTICE

1. BUTTRESSING SOCIAL RIGHTS

Any historical review of the development of EU social policy would not be complete without reference to the momentous role played by the European Court of Justice. We have already seen how the Court in the *Defrenne* cases shifted the emphasis of Article 119 EEC (now Article 157 TFEU) from a purely market-making vehicle to a vehicle with market-correcting potential. The Court also reinvigorated Article 119 EEC by insisting that it had direct effect. This highlights what Davies identifies as the Court's preoccupation, especially strong in the early years, of ensuring that those parts of Union law which were intended to govern relations between and among legal persons in day-to-day life did in fact give rise to legal rights and obligations within the judicial system of the Member States.[127] The social policy cases, with their direct impact on individuals, therefore presented the Court of Justice with the opportunity to develop important principles, such as the direct effect of directives[128] and even general principles of law.[129]

At the same time the Court showed itself willing to bolster the substantive protection provided by the social legislation. For example, it ruled that the Equal Treatment Directive 76/207 (now Directive 2006/54) prohibited discrimination against transsexuals,[130] and women on the grounds of their pregnancy,[131] and allowed 'soft quotas';[132] it recognized that Directive 77/187 (now Directive 2001/23) on transfers of undertakings could apply to contracting out,[133] even in the public sector;[134] and, perhaps most controversially, it ruled in *Barber*[135] that Article 157 TFEU required equality in respect

---

[127] P Davies, 'The European Court of Justice, National Courts, and the Member States' in Davies, Lyon-Caen, Sciarra, and Simitis (n 36 above).

[128] Case 152/84 *Marshall v Southampton Area Health Authority (No 1)* [1986] ECR 723; Case C-188/89 *Foster v British Gas* [1990] ECR I-3313.

[129] Case C-144/04 *Mangold v Rudiger Helm* [2005] ECR I-9981; Case C-555/07 *Seda Kücükdeveci v Swedex GmbH & Co. KG*, 19 January 2010. See further C Kilpatrick, 'The ECJ and Labour Law: A 2008 Retrospective' (2009) 38 ILJ 180.

[130] Case C-13/94 *P v S* [1996] ECR I-2143, but not homosexuals—Case C-249/96 *Grant v South West Trains* [1998] ECR I-621. See also Case C-267/06 *Maruko* [2008] ECR I-1757.

[131] Case C-177/88 *Dekker v Stichting Vormungscentrum voor Jong Volwassenen* [1990] ECR I-3941, Case C-32/93 *Webb v EMO Air Cargo* [1994] ECR I-3567.

[132] Cf Case C-450/93 *Kalanke v Freie Hansestadt Bremen* [1995] ECR I-3051 with Case C-409/95 *Marschall v Land Nordrhein-Westfalen* [1997] ECR I-6363.

[133] Case C-209/91 *Rask and Christensen v ISS Kantineservice* [1992] ECR I-5755. Cf Case C-13/95 *Süzen v Zehnacker Gebäudereinigung GmbH Krankenhausservice* [1997] IRLR 255.

[134] Case C-29/91 *Dr Sophie Redmond v Bartol* [1992] ECR I-3189.

[135] Case C-262/88 *Barber v Guardian Royal Exchange* [1990] ECR I-1889.

of occupational pension age, despite the derogation to Directive 86/378/EEC for equal treatment in respect of occupational pensions.

The Court also developed a second, linked area of interest—ensuring that the procedural and remedial laws of the Member States governing the enforcement of causes of action derived from Union law are effective. Once again the Court has used the social cases as the principal vehicle to develop this concept. For example, in *Johnston v RUC*[136] the Court said that the requirement of judicial control stipulated by Article 6 of the Equal Treatment Directive 76/207 (now Article 17(1) of Directive 2006/54) reflected a general principle of law so that changing an individual access to the court breached EU law. Further, in *Von Colson*[137] the Court said that the Equal Treatment Directive required that the sanction chosen by the Member State had to guarantee real and effective judicial protection.[138] In *Marshall (No 2)* the Court accepted that a limit on the total amount of compensation a tribunal could award a complainant, and the absence of any power to award interest, amounted to a breach of Article 6 of Directive 76/207 which required the award of full compensation.[139]

2. THE CHALLENGE TO SOCIAL RIGHTS POSED BY THE INTERNAL MARKET

(a) The early cases

The Court's decisions have not, of course, gone without criticism. Some condemn its activism, others its failure to see the principle of equality in its broader social context, others the substance of its decisions.[140] But perhaps most critical for the purposes of this chapter is the challenge the Court's decisions have posed to the integrity of the national system of labour and social protection.[141] This occurs when the Court has to balance the interests of national employment laws or policies with the principles of the single market.[142] In some cases the Court has striven to uphold national social regulation. For example, when interpreting Article 34 TFEU on the free movement of goods, the Court has found that national measures designed to ensure worker protection—such as legislation prohibiting employment of workers on Sunday[143] or prohibiting night work in bakeries[144]—while potentially a restriction on trade, were

---

[136] Case 222/84 *Johnston v RUC* [1986] ECR 1651.

[137] Case 14/83 *Von Colson and Kamann v Land Nordrhein-Westfalen* [1984] ECR 1509.

[138] ibid [23].

[139] Joined Cases C-6 and 9/90 *Francovich v Italian Republic* [1991] ECR I-5357.

[140] See eg H Fenwick and T Hervey, 'Sex Equality in the Single Market: New Directions for the European Court of Justice' (1995) 32 CML Rev 443.

[141] See generally B Wedderburn, 'Workers' Rights: Fact or Fake' (1991) 13 DULJ 1; P Davies, 'Market Integration and Social Policy in the Court of Justice' (1995) 24 ILJ 49.

[142] See generally P Syrpis, *EU Intervention in Domestic Labour Law*, (Oxford University Press, 2007).

[143] Case C-312/8 *Union départementale des syndicats CGT de l'Aisne v Conforama* [1991] ECR I-977 and Case C-332/89 *Criminal Proceedings against Marchandise* [1991] ECR I-1027.

[144] Case 155/80 *Oebel* [1981] ECR 1993. See generally, M Poiares Maduro, *We, the Court, The European Court of Justice and the European Economic Constitution* (Hart Publishing, 1998).

compatible with Union law. In *Rush Portuguesa*[145] the Court ruled that it was compatible with Article 56 TFEU for host states to require service providers to respect the host states' labour laws and collective agreements while their employees were working on the host state's territory.[146]

On the other hand, in *Beentjes*[147] the Court said that the exclusion of a company tendering for a contract on the grounds that it was not in a position to employ the long-term unemployed was not compatible with EU public procurement Directives. Subsequently, in *Porto di Genoa*[148] the Court said that Article 106 TFEU precluded national rules which conferred on an undertaking established in that state the exclusive right to organize dock work and require users to have recourse to a dock work company formed exclusively of national workers. Although the facts of *Porto di Genoa* were exceptional (the company was abusing its monopoly to demand payment for unrequested services, to offer selective reductions in prices, and by refusing to have recourse to modern technology), the most striking feature of the Court's judgment, as Deakin points out,[149] is the almost complete disregard shown for social arguments which could have been made in favour of the dock labour monopoly. In particular, no reference was made to the need to combat casualization of labour.

It is in this area where domestic labour market and, indeed, more general social regulation collides with European single market (de)regulation that the Court has shown itself to be least surefooted. The outcomes of the cases are unpredictable, the standards applied are unclear, and national labour protection is often undermined as a result. These conflicts came together in the most dramatic form in the *Viking* and *Laval* case law.

(b) The *Viking* and *Laval* saga

(i) The facts

Viking concerned a Finnish company wanting to reflag its vessel, the Rosella, under the Estonian flag so that it could man the ship with an Estonian crew to be paid considerably less than the existing Finnish crew. The International Transport Workers' Federation (ITF) told its affiliates to boycott the Rosella and to take other solidarity industrial action. As a result, Viking sought an injunction in the English High Court, restraining the ITF and the Finnish Seaman's Union (FSU), now threatening

---

[145] Case C-113/89 *Rush Portugesa Ltda v Office Nationale d'Immigration* [1990] ECR 1417.

[146] See also Case C-43/93 *Vander Elst v OMI* [1994] ECR I-3803 and Case C-272/94 *Criminal Proceedings against Guiot* [1994] ECR I-1905. See now Council Directive 96/71/EC on the posting of workers, [1997] OJ L18/1, discussed by P Davies, 'Posted Workers: Single Market or Protection of National Labour Law Systems?' (1997) 34 CML Rev 571.

[147] Case 31/87 *Beentjes v Minister van Landbouw en Visserij* [1988] ECR 4635. Although cf Case C-271/08 *Commission v Germany (occupational pensions)*, judgment of 15 July 2010, para 56 for a more pro-employee stance discussed in C Bernard 'Procurement Law to Enforce Labour Standards' in G Davidor and B Langille (eds), *The Idea of Labour Law* (Oxford, OUP, forthcoming).

[148] Case C-179/90 *Merci Convenzionali Porto di Genova v Siderurgica Gabrielli* [1991] ECR I-5889.

[149] S Deakin, 'Labour Law as Market Regulation: the Economic Foundations of European Social Policy' in Davies, Lyon-Caen, Sciarra, and Simitis (n 36 above) 75.

strike action, from breaching Article 49 TFEU (ex Article 43 EC) on freedom of establishment.

Laval concerned a Latvian company which won a contract to refurbish a school in Sweden using its own Latvian workers who earned about 40 per cent less than comparable Swedish workers. The Swedish construction union wanted Laval to apply the Swedish collective agreement but Laval refused, in part because the collective agreement was unclear as to how much Laval would have to pay its workers, and in part because it imposed various supplementary obligations on Laval such as paying a special building supplement to an insurance company to finance group life insurance contracts. There followed a union picket at the school site, a blockade by construction workers, and sympathy industrial action by the electricians' unions. Although this industrial action was permissible under Swedish law, Laval brought proceedings in the Swedish labour court, claiming that this action was contrary to *Union* law (in particular Article 56 TFEU (ex Article 49 EC) on freedom to provide services).

In essence, the judgments in both cases raised five issues:[150]

- Does EU (economic) law apply to the exercise of fundamental social rights, in particular the right to take industrial action?
- If it does, does EU law apply to trade unions?
- If so, does the collective action constitute a restriction on free movement?
- If it does, can it be justified?
- Is the collective act on proportionate?

We shall examine these issues in turn.

(ii) Does EU law apply?

In respect of the first question, the trade unions and certain governments argued that Union law should not apply to national social policy because the application of *Union* economic freedoms to national social policy would undermine the integrity of national law.[151] They relied, in particular, on Article 153(5) TFEU which, as we have seen, excludes Union competence in respect of, *inter alia*, the right to strike. These arguments resonated with the original settlement agreed at the time of the Treaty of Rome—that

---

[150] This section draws on the discussion in C Barnard, 'Viking and Laval: a Single Market Perspective' in K Ewing and J Hendy (eds), *The New Spectre Haunting Europe: The ECJ, Trade Union Rights and the British Government, Institute of Employment Rights* (The Institute of Employment Rights, 2009) 19. There is now a huge volume of literature on these cases. See eg (2007–08) 10 CYELS chs 17–22; P Syrpis and T Novitz, 'Economic and Social Rights in Conflict: Political and Judicial Approaches to their Reconciliation' (2008) 33 ELRev 411; J Malmberg and T Sigeman, 'Industrial Actions and EU Economic Freedoms: The Autonomous Collective Bargaining Model Curtailed by the European Court of Justice' (2008) 45 CML Rev 1115; C Kilpatrick, '*Laval's* Regulatory Conundrum: Collective Standard-setting and the Court's New Approach to Posted Workers' (2009) 34 ELRev 844. A fuller list of published work on this topic can be found at <http://www.etui.org/en/Headline-issues/Viking-Laval-Rueffert-Luxembourg/>.

[151] These arguments reflect the compromise put forward by the European Parliament to secure the adoption of the Services Directive 2006/123 ([2006] OJ L376/36) in what became Articles 1(6) and 1(7). They provide that the Directive 'does not affect' labour law or the exercise of fundamental rights, including the right 'to take industrial action in accordance with national law and practices which respect [Union] law'.

social policy was essentially a national matter—but were rejected by both the Advocates General and the Court. For example, the Court in *Viking* said that collective action fell in principle 'within the scope of Article [49]'[152] and that just because Article 153(5) excluded Union competence in respect of, *inter alia*, the right to strike, this did not mean that strike action, as a whole, fell outside the scope of Union law.[153]

This is not a surprising conclusion: in a number of areas of law (eg social security, healthcare, taxation) the Court has held that, even though Member States have the powers to organize their national systems, their action must nevertheless comply with Union law when exercising those powers.[154] Somewhat more surprisingly, the Court also refused to extend to the context of free movement[155] the principle it had recognized in *Albany*,[156] that agreements concluded in the context of collective negotiations between management and labour aimed at improving conditions of work and employment fell outside the scope of Article 101(1) TFEU which prohibits agreements restricting or distorting competition.

Finally, the Court also rejected the argument that fundamental rights, including the right to strike, fell outside Union law. Referring to its decisions in *Schmidberger*[157] and *Omega*,[158] the Court noted that fundamental rights (freedom of expression and freedom of assembly and respect for human dignity) did not fall outside the scope of the provisions of the Treaties; rather the exercise of fundamental rights had to be reconciled with the requirements relating to rights protected under the Treaties and in accordance with the principle of proportionality.[159] In other words, fundamental rights could be used to justify restrictions on free movement but were not ring-fenced from the rules on free movement.[160]

(iii) Does EU law apply to trade unions?

Having ruled that Union law in principle applied, the Court then said that Articles 49 (*Viking*) and 56 (*Laval*) could be 'relied on by a private undertaking against a trade union or an association of trade unions'.[161] While it is not surprising that the Court said that the Treaties applied to the trade unions,[162] the Court's ruling generates a particular problem for trade unions: they have now been placed in the same position as states, with the same responsibilities. Yet, unlike states, trade unions do not need to

---

[152] *Viking* (n 1 above) [37].
[153] *Viking* ibid [39]–[41]; *Laval* (n 1 above) [88].
[154] See eg Case C-158/96 *Kohll v Union des caisses de maladie* [1998] ECR I-1931, [17]-[19].
[155] ibid [51]. See also in the context of public procurement Case C-271/08 *Commission v Germany*, judgment of 15 July 2010, [45]-[6].
[156] Case C-67/96 *Albany* [1999] ECR I-5751.
[157] Case C-112/00 *Schmidberger* [2003] ECR I-5659, [77].
[158] Case C-36/02 *Omega* [2004] ECR I-9609, [36].
[159] *Viking* (n 1 above) [46]; *Laval* (n 1 above) [94].
[160] *Viking* (n 1 above) [45]; *Laval* (n 1 above) [93].
[161] *Viking* (n 1 above) [61].
[162] Case 36/74 *Walrave and Koch* [1974] ECR 1405. See D Wyatt, 'The Horizontal Effect of Articles 43 and 49' (2008) 4 Croatian Yearbook of International Law 1.

balance the interests of those losing their jobs with the interests of the citizen body as a whole in receiving cheaper services; the principal objective of trade unions is to protect the interests of their members. The invidious position that trade unions now find themselves in is exacerbated by the fact that while trade unions are subject to the same obligations as states it would be hard for them ever to be able to invoke any of the defences in Article 52 TFEU (ex Article 46 EC), such as public policy, which were drafted with states in mind. This point has particular resonance on the facts of *Laval*: as we shall see below, trade unions 'not being bodies governed by public law' could not rely on the public policy derogation in Article 3(10) of the Posted Workers' Directive.[163]

(iv) Does strike action constitute a restriction on free movement?

Having established that EU law in principle applied to the case and could be invoked by the employers against trade unions, it was a relatively easy step for the Court to find that Union law was breached. Using what is now standard single market 'market access' or 'restrictions' reasoning derived from cases like *Säger* and *Gebhard*,[164] the Advocates General and the Court concluded that the collective action constituted a restriction on free movement. So, in *Viking* the Court found a breach of Article 49 both by FSU[165] and by the ITF.[166]

For Continental labour lawyers, often from systems with a constitutionally enshrined right to strike, the Court's approach comes as something of a shock. It changes the presumption that striking is lawful subject to limitations which are narrowly construed, into a presumption that striking, at least in the context of transnational disputes, is unlawful subject to justifications which are narrowly construed. In this way the Court's stance shares more with the approach adopted by common law systems where strike action is unlawful due to the commission of an economic tort, but may be rendered lawful if the strike action falls within the four walls of a statutorily defined immunity.

The Court also found a breach of Article 56 in *Laval*. However, the added complication in this case came from the Posted Workers' Directive (PWD) 96/71[167] and, in particular, how this related to the application of Article 56 TFEU. The PWD, introduced to ensure a 'climate of fair competition',[168] lays down a 'nucleus of mandatory rules'[169] in Article 3(1) which the host state *must* apply to posted workers working in their territory. These include rules on working time, health and safety, and equality (but not general dismissal law). Most importantly for our purposes, Article 3(1) applies to pay, but only minimum rates of pay.[170] However, Article 3(1) does not cover matters such as the 'special building supplement' and the other insurance premiums employers were required to pay in Sweden under the relevant collective agreement, although Member States can, under Article 3(10), apply terms and conditions of employment on

---

[163] *Laval* (n 1 above) [84].
[164] Case C-55/94 *Gebhard* [1995] ECR I-4165 and Case C-76/90, *Säger* [1991] ECR I-4221, [712].
[165] *Viking* (n 1 above) [72].   [166] ibid [73].
[167] Council Directive [1997] OJ L18/1.   [168] Recital 5 of the Directive (n 173 above).
[169] Recital 13 of the Directive (n 173 above).   [170] *Laval* (n 1 above) [70].

matters other than those referred to in Article 3(1) in the case of so-called 'public policy provisions'. But, Member States must positively opt to rely on Article 3(10) which Sweden had not done. And, since trade unions were not a public body, they could not rely on Article 3(10), so the trade union could not apply the various insurance premiums to Laval under the Directive.[171] This highlights the predicament outlined above that trade unions are now faced with: they are treated as states for the purposes of liability but not when it comes to defences.

Article 3(7) of the PWD contains a minimum standards clause[172] which, many had thought, meant that while the Directive provided the floor, the state—always assumed to be the host state—could go further and impose higher standards, subject to the ceiling of Article 56 TFEU.[173] This was certainly the view of Advocate General Bot in *Rüffert*.[174] However, this was not the Court's understanding of Article 3(7). It said in *Laval*—and repeated in *Rüffert*[175]—that Article 3(7) applied to the situation of out-of-state service providers *voluntarily* signing a collective agreement in the host state which offered superior terms and conditions to their employees. It also covered the situation where the *home* state laws or collective agreements were more favourable and these could be applied to the posted workers.[176] It did not allow the *host* state to impose terms and conditions of employment which went 'beyond the mandatory rules [in Article 3(1)] for minimum protection'.[177] The Court thus came close to making Article 3(1) not a floor but a ceiling. And, in reaching this conclusion, the Court prevented the Swedish trade unions from relying on Article 3(7) to impose higher standards on the Latvian employer.

The Court also limited the utility of the Posted Workers' Directive to posted workers by insisting on a strict reading of Articles 3(1) and 3(8). Here the issue becomes complex. Matters listed in Article 3(1) must be laid down by:

1. law, regulation, or administrative provision; and/or

2. in respect of activities referred to in the Annex (ie all building work relating to the construction, repair, upkeep, alteration, or demolition of buildings), collective agreements or arbitration awards which have been declared universally applicable within the meaning of Article 3(8).

If they are not laid down in one of these ways, then they cannot be applied to the posted workers. The trade unions in *Laval,* and in the subsequent German case of

---

[171] ibid [83]–[84]. See also Case C-319/06 *Commission v Luxembourg* [2008] ECR I-4323.

[172] This provides: 'Paragraphs 1 to 6 shall not prevent application of terms and conditions of employment which are more favourable to workers.'

[173] See also Recital 17: 'Whereas the mandatory rules for minimum protection in force in the host state must not prevent the application of terms and conditions of employment which are more favourable to workers.'

[174] Case C-346/06 *Dirk Rüffert v Land Niedersachsen* [2008] ECR I-1989, [82]–[83].

[175] ibid [33].

[176] *Laval* (n 1 above) [81].

[177] ibid [80]. See also *Rüffert* (n 179 above) [33].

Rüffert, learned this the hard way. Since there is no *law* on the minimum wage in Sweden (or Germany)[178] (ie limb 1 does not apply), both cases focused on Article 3(8) dealing with collective agreements (ie limb 2).

Confusingly, Article 3(8) also has two paragraphs. The first deals with those systems which do have a doctrine of extension (also known as the *erga omnes* effect) of collective agreements. It explains that collective agreements, or arbitration awards which have been declared universally applicable, are those which must be observed by all undertakings in the geographical area and in the profession or industry concerned. This paragraph was at issue in *Rüffert.* Germany has a system for declaring collective agreements universally applicable. However, in the particular situation at issue, the collective agreement setting pay in the building industry had not been declared universally applicable,[179] and so the collectively agreed rules on pay rates could not be applied to the posted workers,[180] no matter that the German state law on the award of public contracts required contractors and their subcontractors to pay posted workers at least the remuneration prescribed by the collective agreement in force at the place where those services were performed.

The second paragraph of Article 3(8) deals with those systems which do not have a procedure for extending collective agreements to all workers (systems such as those in the UK and Sweden). In these situations,

Member States may, *if they so decide,* base themselves on

– collective agreements or arbitration awards which are generally applicable to all similar undertakings in the geographical area and in the profession or industry concerned, and/or
– collective agreements which have been concluded by the most representative employers' and labour organizations at national level and which are applied throughout national territory.

Once again, as with Article 3(10), the Court required Member States positively to opt for either of these possibilities.[181] Because Sweden had not taken advantage of the second paragraph of Article 3(8),[182] it could not impose on Baltic/Laval enterprise-level collective bargaining.[183]

---

[178] *Laval* (n 1 above) [8]; *Rüffert* (n 179 above) [24]. All other terms and conditions laid down by Art 3(1) of the Posted Workers Directive 96/71/EC ([1996] OJ L018) have been implemented by Swedish law: *Laval* (n 1 above) [63].

[179] *Laval* (n 1 above) [26]. This has now changed.

[180] ibid [31].

[181] Cf AG Mengozzi in *Laval* (n 1 above), especially [179]–[181]. He concludes in [187]: 'It is therefore beyond doubt, in my view, that the right to take collective action granted by Swedish law to trade unions to enable then to impose the wage conditions laid down or governed by Swedish collective agreements provides a suitable means of attaining the aim of protecting posted workers laid down in Art 3 of Council Directive 96/71.'

[182] *Laval* (n 1 above) [67].

[183] ibid [71]. By implication, therefore, the fact that the Directive did not apply meant that the Preambular paragraph in Directive 96/71, to the effect that 'this Directive is without prejudice to the law of the Member States concerning collective action to defend the interests of trades and professions', becomes irrelevant.

Three observations can be made about the Court's approach to the PWD in *Laval* and *Rüffert*. The first, and perhaps most obvious, is that the Court takes a restrictive approach to Article 3(1). In this respect, its views stand in sharp contrast to those of its Advocates General, Advocate General Bot in particular, but coincide with the arguments advanced by the Commission. A clue to understanding the Court's approach can perhaps be gained from Advocate General Mengozzi's Opinion: he says Article 3(1) is a 'derogation'[184] from the principle of home state control laid down in Article 8(2) of the Rome I Regulation on the law applicable to contractual obligations.[185] According to traditional jurisprudence, derogations must be narrowly construed.[186]

The second observation concerns the use of the Posted Workers' Directive to interpret Article 56: if the detailed terms of the Directive are not complied with to the letter, there will be a breach of Article 56[187] or, at least any breach of Article 56 cannot be justified. The interdependency between the Directive and Article 56 is confirmed in paragraph 36 of *Rüffert*, where the Court said that its interpretation of Directive 96/71 is 'confirmed by reading it in the light of Article [56 TFEU], since that Directive seeks in particular to bring about the freedom to provide services, which is one of the fundamental freedoms guaranteed by the [Treaties]'. As Deakin points out, the Directive and Article 56 are mutually reinforcing: the restrictive interpretation of the Directive is derived from Article 56 and the substance of Article 56 is derived from the Directive.[188]

The third observation concerns the phrase 'in particular' used in paragraph 36 of *Rüffert*: it is a mistake to think of the Posted Workers' Directive as a worker protection measure. Its legal basis (Articles 53(1) and 62 TFEU (ex Articles 47(2) and 55 EC)) is firmly rooted in the chapter on freedom to provide services not social policy.[189] It could, therefore, be argued that the Court has reached a careful compromise in *Laval* and *Rüffert*: posted workers will enjoy the better terms and conditions of employment in the host state but only if the host state has complied with the letter of the Directive; if it has not, then any attempt to apply the host state rules will breach both the Directive and Article 56 TFEU.

---

[184] See AG Mengozzi's Opinion in *Laval* (n 1 above) [132].

[185] Regulation 593/2008, [2008] OJ L177/6, which applies from 17 December 2009. Art. 8(2) says: 'To the extent that the law applicable to the individual employment contract has not been chosen by the parties, the contract shall be governed by the law of the country in which or, failing that, *from which* the employee habitually carries out his work in performance of the contract. *The country where the work is habitually carried out shall not be deemed to have changed if he is temporarily employed in another country.*' (Emphasis added to show the major changes from the language of the original Art 6(2)(a) of the Rome Convention.)

[186] If this reasoning is correct, then Art 3(7) and (10), as derogations to derogations, must be particularly narrowly construed.

[187] See also AG Mengozzi's Opinion in *Laval* (n 1 above) [149].

[188] See, by analogy, the Court's interpretation of the Equal Pay Directive 75/117/EEC (now Dir. 2006/54) and its relationship with Art 157 TFEU. In Case 96/80 *Jenkins v Kingsgate* [1981] ECR 911 the Court said that Art 1 'is principally designed to facilitate the practical application of the principle of equal pay outlined in Art [157] of the [Treaties] [and] in no way alters the content or scope of that principle as defined in the [Treaties]'.

[189] See also *Laval* (n 1 above) [74].

(v) Could the strike action be justified?

Having established a breach of the Treaties, the next question was whether the collective action could be justified and whether the steps taken were proportionate. Rejecting the nuanced approach proposed by Advocate General Poiares Maduro in *Viking*, the Court adopted a robust stance to the question of justification. It began by recognizing the need to reconcile and balance[190] the competing objectives of the Union: on the one hand, the completion of the internal market and, on the other, 'a policy in the social sphere'.[191] The significance of this observation lies in the fact that the Court has now confirmed just how far the EU has come from its purely economic origins in 1957 as the European *Economic* Community. Social policy is, apparently, no longer residual; it is as important as the economic policies of the Union.[192] Yet, in fact as we shall see, the reference to balance is largely rhetorical and had no substantive influence on the outcome of the decisions in *Viking* and *Laval*.

In *Viking*, the Court noted that 'the right to take collective action for the protection of workers is a legitimate interest which, in principle, justifies a restriction of one of the fundamental freedoms guaranteed by the [Treaties]' and that 'the protection of workers is one of the overriding reasons of public interest recognised by the Court'.[193] It is striking, as Novitz notes,[194] that the Court is not prepared to protect the right to strike *per se*, as it did with freedom of expression in *Schmidberger*, but will only protect industrial action which achieves a wider 'approved' purpose, namely worker protection. By implication, industrial action taken to achieve other goals (eg political strikes) may not be lawful. This highlights the limited significance of the Court's recognition of the right to strike in the earlier—and less significant—part of the judgment.

The Court of Justice gave the national court a strong steer as to whether the collective action did actually concern the protection of workers.[195] In respect of the action taken by the FSU, it said

> [E]ven if that action—aimed at protecting the *jobs and conditions of employment* of the members of that union *liable to be adversely affected* by the reflagging of the *Rosella*—could reasonably be considered to fall, at first sight, within the objective of protecting workers, such a view would no longer be tenable if it were established that the jobs or conditions of employment at issue were not jeopardised or under serious threat.[196]

This is a reference to the fact that Viking, presumably on good advice, had given an undertaking that neither it, nor companies in the same group, would 'by reason of the

---

[190] *Viking* (n 1 above) [79]; *Laval* ibid [105].
[191] *Viking* ibid [78]; *Laval* (n 1 above) [104].
[192] See also the earlier decision in Joined Cases C-270/97 and C-271/97 *Deutsche Post AG v Elisabeth Sievers and Brunhilde Schrage* [2000] ECR I-929.
[193] *Viking* (n 1 above) [77].
[194] T Novitz, 'The Right to Strike as a Human Right' (2007–08) 10 CYELS 357.
[195] *Viking* (n 1 above) [80].   [196] *Viking* ibid [81].

reflagging terminate the employment of any person employed by them'.[197] However, since the exact legal scope of the undertaking was not clear from the order for reference, 'it is for the national court to determine whether the jobs or conditions of employment of that trade union's members who are liable to be affected by the reflagging of the *Rosella* were jeopardised or under serious threat'.[198] Since the case was settled,[199] we shall never have the benefit of the national court's thoughts on this issue.

(vi) Was the strike action proportionate?

Even though the Court of Justice clearly thought that the FSU had not made out the justification, it nevertheless gave guidance on the question of proportionality, ie whether the collective action initiated by the FSU was (1) suitable for ensuring the achievement of the objective pursued, and (2) did not go beyond what was necessary to attain that objective.[200] On question (1), suitability, the Court said that 'collective action, like collective negotiations and collective agreements, may, in the particular circumstances of a case, be one of the main ways in which trade unions protect the interests of their members'.[201] This reasoning coincides with a labour lawyer's understanding of the right to strike. However, this is undermined by the Court's approach to question (2), necessity, where the Court said it is for the national court to examine whether the 'FSU did not have other means at its disposal which were less restrictive of freedom of establishment' to bring to a successful conclusion the collective negotiations entered into with Viking, and, 'whether that trade union had exhausted those means before initiating such action'.[202] Thus, the Court of Justice suggests that industrial action should be the last resort; and national courts will have to verify whether the union has exhausted all other avenues under national law before the industrial action is found proportionate. This test poses significant problems for trade

---

[197] Viking's cost savings would presumably have come from its decision not to renew short-term employment contracts and redeploying employees on equivalent terms and conditions: see question 10 referred by the national court.

[198] *Viking* (n 1 above) [83].

[199] The agreed press release of 3 March 2008 states: 'Viking Line Abp, the International Transport Workers' Federation and the Finnish Seamens' Union have today agreed to settle their dispute as to the right of the ITF and FSU to take industrial action and/or to persuade others to take industrial action to deter the reflagging of the vessel "Rosella" from the Finnish flag to the Estonian or other flag of a Member State of the European Communities and to prevent Viking from negotiating rates of pay and crew conditions other than with the FSU. These matters became the subject of legal proceedings in the Finnish courts and later became the subject of proceedings in London and before the European Court of Justice in Luxembourg in which Viking sought declaratory and injunctive relief and damages against the ITF and FSU. Accordingly all legal proceedings relating to these disputes have been discontinued. The transactions related to this settlement, which is confidential, do not adversely impact on Viking Line Abp result and have no material affect on the value of the shares of Viking Line Abp.' <http://www.itfglobal.org/press-area/index.cfm/pressdetail/1831>.

[200] *Viking* (n 1 above) [84].

[201] Citing two ECtHR decisions in support: *Syndicat national de la police belge v Belgium* Series Application 4464/70, (1975) and *Wilson, National Union of Journalists and Others v United Kingdom* Applications 30668/ 96, 30671/96 and 30678/96 EHHR 2002-V, 44.

[202] *Viking* (n 1 above) [87].

unions in the future, not least because it will make it much easier in practice for employers to obtain interim injunctions against trade unions.[203] And the threat of crippling damages for any breach of the Treaties looms large.[204]

As for *Laval*, the Court's reasoning on justification is more truncated. It recognized that 'the right to take collective action for the protection of the workers of the host State against possible social dumping may constitute an overriding reason of public interest',[205] making no reference to the contested nature of the term 'suicidal dumping'. It then added that 'blockading action by a trade union of the host Member State which is aimed at ensuring that workers posted in the framework of a transnational provision of services have their terms and conditions of employment fixed at a certain level, falls within the objective of protecting workers'.[206] Thus, the Court appears to recognize, and in principle uphold, secondary industrial action. However, because, on the facts, the obligations which the trade unions were seeking to impose on Laval/Baltic exceeded the nucleus of mandatory rules laid down in Article 3(1) of the Posted Workers' Directive, the collective action could not be justified.[207] Further, because the negotiations on pay formed 'part of a national context characterized by a lack of provisions, of any kind, which are sufficiently precise and accessible', this made it impossible or excessively difficult in practice for Laval to determine its obligations.[208] In other words, because the system lacked transparency, it could not be justified. And, since the collective action could not be justified, there was no need to consider the question of proportionality. The Court, therefore, rejected Advocate General Mengozzi's more nuanced approach to the Swedish system.[209]

(vii) Conclusions

Given the classic 'market access' structure adopted in *Viking* and *Laval*, it was inevitable that the Court would find the collective action a restriction on free movement.[210] This put the 'social' arguments on the back foot: collective action was

---

[203] See R O'Donoghue and B Carr, '*Viking* and *Laval*: From Theory to Practice' (2008–09) 11 CYELS 123.

[204] K Apps, 'Damages Claims against Trade Unions after *Viking* and *Laval*' (2009) 34 ELRev 141.

[205] *Laval* (n 1 above) [103].

[206] ibid [107].

[207] *Laval* (n 1 above) [108].

[208] ibid [110]. The Court has insisted on the requirement of transparency in other fields too eg public procurement and state aid: Case C-513/99 *Concordia Bus Finland v Helsingin jaupunki* [2002] ECR I-7213, [62]–[67] discussed by N Reich, 'Free Movement v Social Rights in an Enlarged Union: The *Viking* and *Laval* Cases before the European Court of Justice' (2008) 9 German Law Journal 125.

[209] He had suggested that if the gross wage paid by Laval (ie approx €1500 per month plus supplementary benefits) was not the same as or essentially similar to that determined in accordance with the *Byggnadsarbetareförbundet* agreement fall-back clause (which he thought was the case but could not be certain) then the collective action, insofar as it sought to impose the rate of pay provided by the *Byggnadsarbetareförbundet* agreement would not be disproportionate to the objectives of protecting workers and combating social dumping (AG Mengozzi's Opinion in *Laval* (n 1 above) [273]).

[210] Cf R O'Donoghue and B Carr, 'Dealing with *Viking* and *Laval*: from Theory to Practice' (2008–09) 11 CYELS 123.

presumptively unlawful unless the trade unions could justify it *and* show the action taken was proportionate. This is not a true case of 'balance' between the economic and the social: it is largely a victory for the economic freedoms. Further, the Court applied a strict approach to the question of justification and proportionality. As we have seen, the Court that said the right to take collective action under Union law is justified only where jobs or conditions of employment are jeopardized or under serious threat, and collective action is the last resort. These are the *Union* limits on the right to strike which are imposed in addition to any national law limits. So, while the Court has recognized the existence of the right to strike, its *exercise* is strictly controlled both by national law *and* Union law,[211] and the Union limits are stringent. The application of the existence/exercise distinction, found elsewhere in EU law,[212] leads to one of the paradoxes of the *Viking* and *Laval* judgments: cases which, for the first time, give express recognition to the right to strike as a fundamental human right, do not lead to enhanced protection of that right.

It is also remarkable that in an area of such sensitivity—national social policy and collective action in particular—the Court still insisted on applying a strict proportionality test to the trade unions, with no reference to any margin of appreciation which appears to be confined to Member States.[213] This leads to a further paradox, noted by Davies, on the application of the proportionality test to industrial action: the more the strike restricts the employer's free movement rights—and thus the more effective it is from the union's perspective—the harder it will be to justify.[214]

If the decisions in *Viking* and *Laval* essentially ensure free movement, subject to a narrow possibility of taking industrial action, then this is clearly good news for the accession states[215] and for their (posted) workers. They will continue to take advantage of their cheaper labour for so long as the wage costs remain significantly lower than in the West. They are the winners; the trade union movement and their members in the West the losers. Trade unions might take some comfort from the fact that each case was distinctive and could be explained on the basis of its facts. To a dispassionate observer, the extent and scope of the industrial action in *Viking*, especially the secondary industrial action, might seem excessive when no job losses were at stake. In *Laval*, the Court clearly took against a number of aspects of the Swedish system, in

---

[211] See also AG Mengozzi's Opinion in *Laval* (n 1 above) [80]–[82].

[212] See eg Joined Cases 56/64 and 58/64 *Consten and Grundig* [1966] ECR 299, 345.

[213] *Schmidberger* (n 157 above) [82]. For contemporary examples of the Court applying the margin of appreciation to states, see eg Case C-250/06 *United Pan-Europe Communications Belgium SA v Etat belge* [2007] ECR I-11135; Case C-244/06 *Dynamic Medien* [2008] ECR I-505, [44], and a more recent example: Joined Cases C-316/07, C-358/07 to C-360/07, C-409/07, and C-410/07 *Markus Stoss and Others v Wetteraukreis, Kulpa Automatenservice Asperg GmbH and Others v Land Baden-Württemberg*, judgment of 8 September 2010, [78]–[83]. J Sweeney, 'A "Margin of Appreciation" in the Internal Market: Lessons from the European Court of Human Rights' (2007) 34 LIEI 27.

[214] A Davies, 'One Step Forward, Two Steps Back? The *Viking* and *Laval* cases in the ECJ' (2008) 37 ILJ 126, 143.

[215] For a full discussion of the views of the new Member States, see B Bercusson, 'The Trade Union Movement and the European Union: Judgment Day' (2007) 13 ELJ 279.

particular its lack of transparency in respect of pay[216] and the Swedish government's failure to take advantage of the possibilities provided in the Directive for addressing the problem.[217] The Court, using remarkably weighted language, also objected to the fact that Laval was 'required' to negotiate with trade unions 'in order to ascertain the wages to be paid to workers and to sign the collective agreement for the building sector';[218] and that these negotiations might be of 'unspecified duration';[219] that the designated liaison office set up under the Posted Workers Directive could not help;[220] nor would the police step in to assist Laval since the blockade was lawful under Swedish law.[221] All of this resulted, in the Court's eyes at least, in Laval (and Viking) being denied access to the markets in other Member States.[222] In less exceptional circumstances, the Court might have been more sympathetic, although the subsequent rulings in *Rüffert* and *Commission v Luxembourg* may well have extinguished any glimmer of hope for trade unions that *Viking* and *Laval* were aberrant decisions.

The trade unions condemned the Court in forthright terms.[223] Addressing the European Parliament in February 2008, John Monks, General Secretary of the ETUC, said:

> So we are told that the right to strike is a fundamental right but not so fundamental as the EU's free movement provisions. This is a licence for social dumping and for unions being prevented from taking action to improve matters. Any company in a transnational dispute has the opportunity to use this judgment against union actions, alleging disproportionality.

The ETUC therefore called for the adoption of a social progress clause which would say that '[n]othing in the Treaty, and in particular neither fundamental freedoms nor competition rules shall have priority over fundamental social rights and social progress'. It added: 'In case of conflict, fundamental social rights shall take precedence.'[224]

This line may find some support from the judgment of the European Court of Human Rights in *Demir and Baykara*[225] which ruled that both a right to collective bargaining and a right to take collective action can be inferred from Article 11, the freedom of association provision of the European Convention on Human Rights. In

---

[216] *Laval* (n 1 above) [36] and [110].

[217] ibid [67]–[71].

[218] *Laval* (n 1 above) [63] and [71]. It also did not like the rigidity of the Swedish system: eg the collective agreement was for an hourly not a monthly rate [25].

[219] *Laval* ibid [100].

[220] *Laval* ibid [35].

[221] *Laval* ibid [34].

[222] The reporting judge in *Laval* was Estonian.

[223] 'Dumping social: les syndicates européens "déçus" par la Cour de Justice', lemonde.fr (8 December 2007).

[224] ETUC's Resolution adopted on 4 March 2008: <http://www.etuc.org/IMG/pdf_ETUC_Viking_Laval _resolution_070308.pdf>. Cf Report on joint work of the European social partners on the ECJ rulings in the Viking, Laval, Rüffert and Luxembourg cases, 19 March 2010: <http://www.etuc.org/IMG/pdf_Joint_report _ECJ_rulings_FINAL_ logos_19.03.10.pdf>.

[225] *Demir and Baykara v Turkey*, Application No 34503/97, 12 November 2008. See also *Enerji Yapi-Yol* (Application no. 68959/01) which confirms that the right to strike is part of Art 11.

reaching this conclusion the Court of Human Rights made wide-ranging reference to a number of international sources including the EU's Charter of Fundamental Rights and the ILO Conventions. This latter reference is of particular significance because, following a complaint by Balpa (the British Airline Pilot's Association) to the ILO's Committee of Experts on the Application of Conventions and Recommendations that the effect of *Viking* and *Laval* was to expose the unions to crippling damages if they went on strike without complying with the (unclear) terms of the judgments, the Committee observed:

> with *serious concern* the practical limitations on the effective exercise of the right to strike of the BALPA workers in this case. The Committee takes the view that the omnipresent threat of an action for damages that could bankrupt the union, possibly now in the light of the *Viking* and *Laval* judgments, creates a situation where the rights under the Convention cannot be exercised.... The Committee thus considers that the doctrine that is being articulated in these ECJ judgments is likely to have a significant restrictive effect on the exercise of the right to strike in practice in a manner contrary to the Convention.

In principle the judgment in *Demir* could have far-reaching implications for EU law. It is arguable that the Court of Justice should have regard to European human rights law when framing the extent of the four freedoms, in cases where their application involves a clash with national or EU-level social policy.[226] Article 6(2) TEU requires the EU to accede to the ECHR, which may strengthen the case for a realignment of the Court's approach, but such accession has yet to take place, and the legal difficulties presented by the prospect of accession are manyfold.

D. THE BATTLE FOR THE FUTURE SOUL OF SOCIAL POLICY

1. INTRODUCTION

Viking and *Laval* served to heighten the sense of crisis already hanging over labour law, at national and at transnational level. More books and scholarly articles have probably been written about the future of labour law than the future of any other subject.[227] Labour law is no longer seen as a good in its own right. Its detractors argue that it is a burden on competitiveness, that it creates path dependencies, that it discourages innovation. Even its supporters have been forced to advocate its benefits

---

[226] K Ewing and J Hendy, 'The Dramatic Implications of *Demir and Baykara*' (2010) 39 ILJ 2. The British courts have remained largely unmoved by the implications of the *Demir* decision: *Metrobus v Unite the Union* [2009] IRLR 851, although cf Cox J's comments in *BA v Unite (No 1)* [2009] EWHC 3541, [2010] IRLR 423.

[227] See eg C Barnard, S Deakin, and G Morris (eds), *The Future of Labour Law* (Hart, 2004); J Craig and M Lynk, *Globalization and the Future of Labour Law* (Cambridge University Press, 2006); G Davidov and B Langille, *Boundaries and Frontiers of Labour Law* (Hart Publishing, 2006).

not in social but in economic terms: that good quality labour laws help to promote productivity.[228]

The EU has been affected by this turmoil. The Commission has devoted considerable attention to the question of the future of the European Social Model. In the next section we shall tell our third and final story, a story which focuses on the cause of the crisis of labour law, the possible solutions that the EU can offer, and the form that those solutions can take.

2. THE CAUSE OF THE CRISIS

The Commission's Green Paper, 'Modernising labour law to meet the challenges of the 21st century' provides a useful diagnosis of the problem.[229] It notes that '[t]he original purpose of labour law was to offset the inherent economic and social inequality within the employment relationship. From its origins, labour law has been concerned to establish employment status as the main factor around which entitlements would be developed.' It continues that this 'traditional model reflects several key assumptions about employment status', namely:

i) permanent, full-time employment;

ii) employment relationships regulated by labour law, with the contract of employment as the pivot;

iii) the presence of a single entity employer accountable for the obligations placed upon employers;

iv) a job for life.[230]

However, the world has changed. Part of this is due to '[r]apid technological progress, increased competition stemming from globalisation, changing consumer demand and significant growth of the services sector' together with the emergence of 'just-in-time management, the shortening of the investment horizon for companies, the spread of information and communication technologies, the increasing occurrence of demand shifts'. This has led businesses to organize themselves on a more flexible basis. This flexibility is reflected in variations in 'work organisation, working hours, wages, and workforce size at different stages of the production cycle'. There are social changes too: an ageing population, higher numbers of women in the workplace, low average employment rates, high long-term unemployment, especially among the

---

[228] Commission, Social Policy as a Productive Factor (Luxembourg: OOPEC, 1996); Commission, White Paper on Social Policy COM(1994) 333, introduction [5]; 'the pursuit of high social standards should not be seen as a cost but also as a key element in the competitive formula'; Commission, Mid-term review of the Social Policy Agenda COM(2003) 312; 'A major guiding principle in the Social Policy Agenda was to strengthen the role of social policy as a productive factor. This has been extended during the past years in particular through the promotion of quality as the driving force for a thriving economy, more and better jobs and greater social cohesion.'

[229] COM(2006) 708 [5].   [230] This was added by COM(2007) 359 [3].

young, and the development of segmented labour markets where relatively protected ('insiders') and unprotected workers ('outsiders') coexist.

The question, then, is can and should the EU—and EU law in particular—respond to this challenge, and if so how? The answer to this question has been mulled over in a number of policy documents. The problem for the EU—is the age-old one—lack of competence to act, both legally and politically. The Commission noted this point in its Modernisation Green Paper:

> Responsibility for safeguarding working conditions and improving the quality of work in the Member States primarily rests on national legislation and on the efficacy of enforcement and control measures at national level. At the EU level, the social *acquis* supports and complements the actions of the Member States in this sphere.[231]

The policy documents, reflecting OMC techniques, nudge the Member States towards the changes the Commission sees necessary. The central message is 'modernization'.

3. THE MODERNIZATION AGENDA

The most high profile reference to modernization was found in the Lisbon Strategy of 2000. It required the 'European Social Model' to be modernized by 'investing in people and building an active welfare state'.[232] Inspiration was drawn from the successful Nordic model, which combines open markets and job flexibility with all the support employers need to restructure their workforce to meet changing demands. This approach is endorsed by strong trade unions because of the tripartite pact between employers, trade unions, and the state, and a generous system of social welfare to cushion the effect of change. High levels of public expenditure also produce highly educated school leavers and graduates.[233] This is combined with intensive active labour market measures and substantial investment in training.[234]

Reflecting this Nordic model, the Lisbon strategy therefore identified four elements to this process of policy modernization:

1. *education and training*: 'Europe's education and training systems need to adapt both to the demands of the knowledge society and to the need for an improved level and quality of employment';[235]

2. *more jobs*, with (unrealistic) targets set as part of the Luxembourg employment strategy, *and better jobs*, with reference to the Commission's 'quality' agenda,

---

[231] COM(2006) 708 [6].   [232] ibid [24].

[233] P Toynbee, 'The most successful society the world has ever known: The Nordic model mixes welfare and economic success, but Sweden's social democrats are at a risk from a loss of confidence', *The Guardian*, 25 October 2005, 33.

[234] COM(2006) 708 [10].   [235] ibid [35].

with 'quality as the driving force for a thriving economy...quality of work, quality in industrial relations and quality of social policy';[236]

3. *modernising social protection*: this does not mean dismantling social welfare systems, which must 'underpin the transformation to the knowledge based economy', but rather focusing on ensuring that 'work pays' (ie to ensure that social benefits do not discourage employment) and in maintaining the long-term sustainability of benefits in the face of an ageing population;[237] and

4. *promoting social inclusion*, to which the quality agenda was intended to respond. Thus, from a labour law point of view, the striking feature of the Lisbon Strategy is the absence of labour *law*. Instead, the emphasis is on improving the quality of the labour supply through active labour market policies (education and training) as well as adapting social welfare systems to ensure that they bridge 'transitions' between jobs and encourage people to return to work.

However, a plethora of labour law rules remains on national and, to a lesser extent, EU statute books and these rules are increasingly seen as outmoded. Therefore, the second element of the modernization agenda is modernizing labour law itself. As the Modernisation Green Paper points out,[238] the traditional model of the employment relationship may not prove well-suited to all workers facing 'the challenge of adapting to change and seizing the opportunities that globalisation offers'. It notes that '[o]verly protective terms and conditions can deter employers from hiring during economic upturns,' while 'alternative models of contractual relations can enhance the capacity of enterprises to foster the creativity of their whole workforce for increased competitive advantage.'[239] These alternative models of contractual relationships have proliferated: fixed term contracts, part-time contracts, on-call contracts, zero-hour contracts, contracts for workers hired through temporary employment agencies, freelance contracts.[240] Through the use of these non-standard contractual arrangements, businesses have sought to remain competitive in the globalized economy by avoiding *inter alia* the burden of compliance with employment protection rules, notice periods, and the costs of associated social security contributions.[241] Yet the flexibility that these

---

[236] COM(2000) 379 [13]. Quality of work includes better jobs and more ways of combining working life with personal life. It is based on 'high skills, fair labour standards and decent levels of occupational health and safety'. Quality of social policy implies a high level of social protection, good social services, real opportunities for all, and the guarantee of fundamental and social rights. Quality of industrial relations is determined by the capacity to build consensus on both diagnosis and ways and means of taking forward the adaptation and modernization agenda.

[237] ibid [31].

[238] COM(2006) 708 considered by S Sciarra (2007) 36 ILJ 375. See also *The Labour Lawyers and the Green Paper*: <http://www.lex.unict.it/eurolabor/news/en/doc_libroverde.pdf>. The Outcome of the public consultation can be found at COM(2007) 627.

[239] COM(2006) 708.

[240] See generally, M Freedland, 'From the Contract of Employment to the Personal Work Nexus' (2006) 35 ILJ 1.

[241] COM(2006) 708 [7]–[8].

contracts offer to employers comes at the price of insecurity for many of the individuals on such contracts. Agency workers (temps) are particular vulnerable in this respect: they are usually employed by the agency, often with self-employed status, and hired out to the user undertaking which usually has almost no legal responsibility for the individual temp. In these so-called 'triangular' situations, temps often find themselves without employment protection when the crunch comes.

The Commission's response to these challenges is through the neologism 'flexicurity',[242] a concept which is again inspired by the Nordic model. As the Commission explains in its 2007 Paper, *Towards Common Principles of Flexicurity: More and better jobs through flexibility and security*,[243] 'Flexicurity promotes a combination of flexible labour markets and adequate security.' It says flexicurity is not about deregulation, giving employers freedom to dissolve their responsibilities towards employees and giving them little security. Instead, flexicurity is about bringing people into good jobs and developing their talents. Employers have to improve their work organization to offer jobs with a future. They need to invest in their workers' skills. The Commission calls this 'internal flexicurity'. However, the Commission also recognizes that keeping the same job is not always possible. 'External flexicurity' attempts to offer safe moves for workers from one job into another, and good benefits to cover the intervening period of unemployment, if needed. This is the so-called 'lifecycle' approach to work.

In respect of security, which is meant to complement flexibility, the Commission focuses not on job security but 'employment security'. Employment security means staying in employment, within the same enterprise or in a new enterprise. It concludes: 'The philosophy behind flexicurity is that workers are more prepared to make such moves if there is a good safety net.' Once again, the emphasis is not on deregulation but on investment in employment and skills with a social safety net to catch those in transition. This, says the Commission, is the way to 'maintain and improve competitiveness whilst reinforcing the European social model'.

The Commission then proposes eight common flexicurity principles including a balance between the rights and responsibilities for employers, workers, job seekers, and public authorities; a reduction in the divide between insiders and outsiders; the promotion of internal and external flexicurity; and support for gender equality and offering possibilities to reconcile work and family life. The principles are accompanied by three 'flexicurity pathways', developed on the basis of the Member States' situations. The third is of particular relevance for the UK[244] 'where the key challenge is large

---

[242] Commission's Green Paper, Partnership for a New Organisation of Work, COM(97) 127 final; the Commission's Communication, *Modernising and Improving Social Protection in the European Union* COM (97) 102 final. See also Commission Communication; *A Concerted Action for Modernising Social Protection* COM(99) 347 and Council Conclusions on the strengthening of cooperation for modernizing and improving social protection ([2000] OJ C8/7) and *Modernising the Organisation of Work*, (COM(98) 592). See more generally J Kenner, 'New Frontiers in EU Labour Law: From Flexicurity to Flex-security' in M Dougan and S Currie (eds), *Fifty Years of the Treaty of Rome* (Hart Publishing, 2009).

[243] COM(2007) 359 [5].

[244] 'Flexicurity: Europe's Employment Solution': <http://www.euractivcom/en/socialeurope/flexicurity-europe-employment-solution/article-169840>.

skills and opportunity gaps among the population. It would promote opportunities of low-skilled people to enter into employment and develop their skills in order to obtain a sustainable position at the labour market.' However, in a rather remarkable turn-up for the books, the UK's flexible labour market which made it the social pariah in the EU for many years and the cause of so many problems in the *Working Time* case, is now held up as a model for other states to follow:[245]

> The 'targeted approach' adopted in the UK to establishing differing rights and responsi-
> bilities in employment law for 'employees' and 'workers' is an example of how categories of
> vulnerable workers involved in complex employment relationships have been given min-
> imum rights without an extension of the full range of labour law entitlements associated
> with standard work contracts.

In other words, while insiders ('employees') enjoy the full gamut of employment protection, some outsiders ('workers') enjoy the protection of at least a core of employment legislation including anti-discrimination rights, health and safety protection, and guarantees of the minimum wage.

4. THE INFLUENCE OF THE THIRD WAY AGENDA

Both the Flexicurity Agenda and the Commission's two major policy documents examining the future of social policy in the EU, *Opportunities, Access and Solidarity: towards a new social vision for 21st Century Europe* of 2007[246] and *The Renewed Social Agenda: Opportunities, Access and Solidarity* of 2008[247] are strongly imbued with 'Third Way' thinking. While there is much debate as to the meaning of the phrase 'Third Way',[248] in essence it is about creating a genuine synthesis between the state and the market. At its core lies the idea of replacing the egalitarian goal of achieving greater equality through redistributing wealth using welfare state mechanisms (ie equality of outcomes), with the goal of creating the conditions for the eradication of social exclusion (ie equality of opportunity).[249] As Collins puts it:[250]

> The objective is to provide every citizen with the necessary resources in terms of education,
> training, skills and other financial support, so that they can participate fully in the

---

[245] COM(2006) 708 [12].

[246] COM(2007) 726. These documents are fully discussed in C Barnard, 'Solidarity and the Commission's 'Renewed Social Agenda' in Y Borgmann-Prebil and M Ross, *Promoting Solidarity in the European Union* (OUP, forthcoming).

[247] COM(2008) 412: Renewed social agenda: Opportunities, access and solidarity in 21st century Europe.

[248] H Collins, 'Is there a Third Way in Labour Law?' in J Conaghan, R M Fischel and K Klare (eds), *Labour Law in an Era of Globalisation: Transformative Practices and Possibilities* (Oxford University Press, 2002) 459.

[249] Collins (n 248 above) 451. See also T Blair, writing in favour of true equality ie 'equal worth and equal opportunity', not an equality of outcome focused on incomes alone': *The Courage of our Convictions* (Fabian Society, 2002), 2 quoted in S Fredman, 'The Ideology of New Labour' in C Barnard, S Deakin, and G Morris (eds), *The Future of Labour Law: Liber Amicorum Sir Bob Hepple QC* (Hart Publishing, 2004) 14.

[250] Collins (n 248 above) 452.

opportunities afforded by a flourishing market economy. Inequalities of wealth can be tolerated provided that real equality of opportunity is available to all citizens...

There is a direct link here with Sen's capability theory,[251] namely expanding the '"capabilities" of persons to lead the kind of lives they value—and have reason to value'. He continues that these capabilities can be enhanced by public policy (eg education, training, healthcare, and a career of their choosing) but also the direction of public policy can be influenced by the effective use of participatory capabilities by the public.[252] For this reason human rights and democratic freedoms, including freedom of association and the right to participate in economic and political decision-making are so important.[253]

Collins adds that implicit in the Third Way ideal is the idea that markets produce a fair distribution of wealth for most people, and so lead to a reduction in poverty, provided that everyone has a fair opportunity to participate in the market. In contrast with pre-Third Way politics, there is no commitment on the part of the state to ensure an acceptable redistribution pattern occurs because this is 'impracticable, unafford-able, ineffective, and counter-productive owing to the problem of welfare depend-ency'.[254] Instead, individuals have the responsibility to take up the opportunities for achieving a decent standard of living that are facilitated or provided by the state. This is an aspect of what Fredman terms 'civic responsibility'[255] which is one of the hallmarks of Third Way thinking (the others being the facilitative state, equality and community, and democracy). The corollary of this civic responsibility is that if individuals fail to take advantage of the opportunities offered to them, the conse-quences rest with them, not the state (and its welfare system).

These Third Way ideas can be seen in the notions of 'Opportunities' and 'Access' which structure the Commission's *Social Vision* Communication: getting *access* to the necessary education, training, and healthcare (provided by the 'facilitative' state and/or employers) enables individuals to take advantage of the *opportunities* available to them on the market. And the market means the employment market because, according to Third Way thinking, the principal cause of social exclusion is unemployment (or at least the inability to get a decent job which the 'Quality' agenda discussed above is intended to address).

The Third Way adopts a substantive approach to the question of (equal) oppor-tunities. It recognizes that many of those currently excluded from the labour market (the young, the old, ethnic minorities, women with caring responsibilities, the dis-abled) face formal barriers to their participation, especially discriminatory barriers (hence the significance of the 'Article 13 EC' (now Article 19 TFEU) Directives on non-discrimination on the grounds of race, ethnic origin, age, sexual orientation, etc) but also substantive barriers (eg the absence of child- and elder-care as well as financial

---

[251] A Sen, *Capability as Freedom* (Oxford University Press, 1999) 18.   [252] ibid.
[253] B Hepple, 'Labour Law, inequality and global trade', Sinzheimer Lecture 2002, 10–11.
[254] ibid.   [255] Fredman (n 249 above) 14.

barriers created by the 'poverty trap'). This demonstrates a subtle but significant change of approach towards the equality Directives. They are no longer seen as combating discrimination which is seen as an evil in its own right, but they have been repositioned to service the Lisbon Agenda of active labour market policies and removing barriers to get individuals back into work. As the Commission says, its 'social vision':

> reflects an increasingly accepted view that whereas society cannot guarantee equal outcomes for its citizens, it must become much more resolute in fostering equal opportunities ... The central ambition is to achieve a wider distribution of "life chances" to allow everyone in the EU to have access to the resources services, conditions and capabilities in order to turn the theoretical equality of opportunities and active citizenship into a meaningful reality.[256]

Thus, in an unexpected twist on the market-making/market-correcting paradigm discussed in section B.1 above, the version of capabilities envisaged in the Social Vision agenda[257] is based, as Deakin and Wilkinson note, on 'the market-*creating* function of the rules of social law'.[258] They continue:

> In order to participate effectively in a market order, individuals require more than formal access to the institutions of property and contract. They need to be provided with the economic means to realize their potential: these include social guarantees of housing, education and training, as well as legal institutions which prescribe institutionalized discrimination.

Solidarity is the third leg to the *Access/Opportunities* stool: its aim is 'to foster social cohesion and social sustainability, and make sure that no individual is left behind'. The addition of 'solidarity' to the duo of opportunities and access indicates that the state, in some form, should provide a safety net for those who cannot take advantage of the opportunities available to them. In this way, the EU hopes to answer some of the criticisms of the UK's execution of Third Way principles that, if the individual does not take advantage of what is offered, the individual, not the state, suffers the consequences; there is little or no safety net. This is confirmed by the 2008 Communication where the Commission says:[259]

> Europeans share a commitment to social solidarity: between generations, regions, the better off and the less well off and wealthier and less wealthy Member States. Solidarity is part of how European society works and how Europe engages with the rest of the world. Real equality of opportunity depends on both access and solidarity. Solidarity means action to help those who are disadvantaged—who cannot reap the benefits of an open, rapidly changing society ...

---

[256] ibid. Emphasis added.

[257] See also 'Towards Common Principles of Flexicurity: More and better jobs through flexibility and security', COM(2007) 359, 14.

[258] S Deakin and F Wilkinson, *The Law for the Labour Market: Industrialization, Employment and Legal Evolution* (Oxford University Press, 2005) 348, emphasis added.

[259] COM(2008) 412 (n 247 above) [6].

However, although 'solidarity' has joined 'opportunities' and 'access' as defining features of the new social vision, it is striking just how little the word itself is actually mentioned in either the 2007 and 2008 Communications.

5. THE EU 2020 STRATEGY

The economic crisis starting in the autumn of 2008 revealed the extravagance of the aims in the Lisbon Strategy—Europe is far from being the most dynamic knowledge-based economy in the world in 2010—and the misplaced faith in the market's ability to be able to deliver social good. The crisis has wiped out any gains in economic growth and job creation which had occurred over the previous decade—GDP had fallen by 4 per cent in 2009, industrial production dropped back to the levels of the 1990s, and 23 million people (10 per cent of the active population) became unemployed. Public finances also were severely affected, with deficits at 7 per cent of GDP on average and debt levels at over 80 per cent of GDP.[260]

Does that mean that the Lisbon strategy had been a failure? Certainly, many of the criticisms of the Lisbon strategy proved justified: the goals were too ambitious, there were too many targets, the Commission had no real sanctions against defaulting states, there was a lack of commitment by a number of states to the strategy, many of which saw it as a bureaucratic exercise which had little effect on their day-to-day government, and, at a time of the largest expansion of the European Union and major Treaty reform, insufficient attention was paid both to realizing the Lisbon Strategy and communicating and promoting its benefits.

On the other hand, the shift in emphasis identified by the Lisbon strategy in fact marked a more permanent and fundamental change. Workers are no longer seen as (passive) beneficiaries of social rights; instead they are seen as having to take responsibility for updating their skills and making themselves employable. The change concretized by the Lisbon strategy fed directly into the less ambitious Europe 2020 programme adopted in March 2010. It puts forward three mutually reinforcing priorities:

- Smart growth: developing an economy based on knowledge and innovation.

- Sustainable growth: promoting a more resource efficient, greener, and more competitive economy.

- Inclusive growth: fostering a high-employment economy delivering social and territorial cohesion.

The 'Inclusive growth' priority is the direct descendant of the third limb of the Lisbon Strategy 'Modernizing the European social model' and the active labour market policies it envisages. So, the Commission says that '[i]nclusive growth means

---

[260] Commission Communication, Europe 2020. A Strategy for smart, sustainable and inclusive growth, COM(2010) 2020, 5.

empowering people through high levels of employment, investing in skills, fighting poverty and modernising labour markets, training and social protection systems' to help people anticipate and manage change, and build a cohesive society.[261] It continues that '[i]mplementing flexicurity principles and enabling people to acquire new skills to adapt to new conditions and potential career shifts will be key'. Further, in a reference to the principles underpinning the 2007 and 2008 Social Agenda, the Commission says that inclusive growth is also about 'ensuring access and opportunities for all throughout the lifecycle'.[262] The Commission also refers to the new role envisaged for equality legislation when it says that '[p]olicies to promote gender equality will be needed to increase labour force participation thus adding to growth and social cohesion.... Access to childcare facilities and care for other dependants will be important in this respect.'

The 2020 document also proposes a more limited set of targets than the Lisbon Strategy. These EU targets, which have to be translated into individualized national targets and trajectories, are still ambitious. They include 75 per cent of the population aged 20–64 to be employed; a demanding 3 per cent of the EU's GDP to be invested in R&D; the share of early school leavers to be under 10 per cent; and, according to some Eastern European states, a 'utopian' 20 million fewer people should be at risk of poverty. These targets are interrelated. As the Commission notes, better educational levels help employability and progress in increasing the employment rate helps to reduce poverty. A greater capacity for research and development as well as innovation across all sectors of the economy, combined with increased resource efficiency will improve competitiveness and foster job creation.

The Commission put forward 'seven flagship initiatives to catalyse progress under each priority theme', including 'Youth on the move' to enhance the performance of education systems and to facilitate the entry of young people to the labour market; and 'An agenda for new skills and jobs' to modernize labour markets and empower people by developing their skills throughout the lifecycle with a view to increasing labour participation and better matching labour supply and demand, including through labour mobility. Active labour market policy is clearly here to stay.

E. CONCLUSIONS

We have now reached the end of our three overlapping, inter-connected stories. It is certainly not happy ever after with the parties disappearing contentedly off into the sunset. It is not even the end because the stories continue to unfold. Are there any judgements, then, that we can make? Even with the significant changes introduced by the Lisbon strategy, and its emphasis on OMC techniques, the legacy of a European social model based on employment *rights* has not been cast aside. Sometimes these

---

[261] COM(2010) 2020, 16.   [262] ibid.

rights have been refocused and reconceptualized to fit the Lisbon story, but the rights remain. They are now buttressed by the Charter of Fundamental Rights. True, the Court's approach to the Charter and to social rights more generally in *Viking* and *Laval* was not encouraging for trade unions in this respect. On the other hand the change in approach adopted by the European Court of Human Rights, combined with the pressure from other international sources, in particular the ILO, might eventually force the Court of Justice to reconsider the balance it struck in *Viking* and *Laval*. This might suggest a new type of nesting of social rights, both vertically across a number of regimes (sub-national, national, European, and international levels) and horizontally (social partners, companies, workers). In this picture a new story might emerge of a constant contestation for the soul of social policy.

22

EMU—INTEGRATION AND DIFFERENTIATION: METAPHOR FOR EUROPEAN UNION

*Francis Snyder**

A. INTRODUCTION

Economic and monetary union (EMU) exemplifies the conjunction of integration and differentiation in the European Union (EU) today. Set in train by the founding Treaties, it was consolidated in the Maastricht Treaty, left virtually untouched by the Amsterdam and Nice Treaties, and revised, on the basis of the failed Constitutional Treaty (CT), by the Treaty of Lisbon (TL). It is a milestone in the history of European integration. Debates about EMU have often concerned the nature of European integration itself.

This chapter focuses on EMU as a type of economic regulation, with specific institutional and normative features, within the framework of EU law, and making a fundamental albeit controversial contribution to European integration.[1] It traces the legal and institutional controversies which have marked EMU since its origins. It also identifies the dynamics, achievements, and shortcomings of EMU and its role in European integration.

The central argument is that EMU is a unique conjunction of integration and differentiation and so serves as an apt metaphor for the EU as a whole. There are several strands. EMU was created mainly for political reasons. Its institutional

* Part of the research was carried out as Guest Professor, Peking University Law School. I thank Dean Zhu Suli, Professor Wu Zhipan, Professor Song Ying, and Ms Yin Ming for their support. Thanks go to Ran Yuanyi and K L Thiratakayakinant for research assistance. The usual disclaimer applies.

[1] For other approaches, see eg P de Grauwe, *Economics of Monetary Union* (8th edn, Oxford University Press, 2009); K Dyson and K Featherstone, *The Road to Maastricht* (Oxford University Press, 1999); B Eichengreen and J Frieden, *The Political Economy of European Monetary Unification* (Westview Press, 1995).

and normative shape crystallized conflicting views about the nature and purpose of European integration. It was mainly the product of a small epistemic community, which gave priority to monetary affairs. It exemplifies the approndissement of legal pluralism, or multi-site governance, characterized by interpenetration between the EU and national arenas, relations between the European Council, the Council of Economic and Finance Ministers (Ecofin), and the European Central Bank (ECB), and striking institutional and normative heterogeneity. The TL followed the CT in consolidating EMU and enhancing differentiation. Finally, EMU represents a complex compromise which is likely to perdure and possibly play an important role in international monetary governance.

The chapter consists of two main parts. The first part discusses the origins and evolution of EMU from 1950 to the 2000 Nice Treaty. It presents a chronology of the legal framework and shows how EMU reconfigured economic and monetary governance. The second part analyses the evolution of the legal framework from Nice to the TL, reasons for greater differentiation, and the impact of two contemporary challenges: the post-2007 financial crisis, and the international stage. A brief conclusion summarizes the argument.

B. ORIGINS AND EVOLUTION: 1950–2000

1. CHRONOLOGY OF THE LEGAL FRAMEWORK

(a) Origins

European monetary integration predates the EEC, but the 1957 EEC Treaty laid the foundations.[2] The intergovernmental European Payments Union (EPU) served after 1950 as a clearing house for payments and short-term credit.[3] The Rome Treaty then provided that Member States retained power over economic and monetary policy, but subject to a new legal and institutional framework. In collaboration with the Community, Member States were to coordinate their economic policies as necessary to attain the Treaty objectives.[4] They were to regard their conjunctural and exchange rate policies as matters of common concern[5] and provide for cooperation between their central banks.[6] The EEC was granted limited powers.[7] An advisory Monetary Committee was established to promote coordination.[8] Member States were progressively to abolish restrictions on domestic capital movements,[9] liberalize current

---

[2] For details, see F Snyder, 'EMU Revisited: Are We Making a Constitution? What Constitution Are We Making?' in P Craig and G de Búrca (eds), *The Evolution of EU Law* (1st edn, Oxford University Press, 1999) 417–477.

[3] Accord sur l'établissement d'une Union européenne de paiements du 19 septembre 1950 (Organisation européenne de coopération économique, 1954).

[4] Art 6(1) EEC.

[5] See EEC Treaty (Treaty of Rome), Art 103(1) (conjunctural policies) and Art 107(1) (exchange rate policies).

[6] Art 105(1) first para, EEC.   [7] See Art 103(2)–(4) and Art 107(2) EEC.

[8] Art 105(2) EEC.   [9] Art 67(1) EEC.

payments,[10] and coordinate their exchange rate policies.[11] A standstill clause applied to new exchange restrictions,[12] though specified safeguard measures could be used.[13]

In 1958 the European Investment Bank (EIB) was established.[14] In 1959 the European Monetary Agreement (EMA)[15] replaced EPU and provided rules on multilateral settlement of payments through the Basle-based Bank of International Settlements (BIS). The EEC Council issued a decision in March 1960 on coordination of national short-term economic policies.[16] Responding to demands for integration and to international monetary instability, interest in European monetary integration increased in the early 1960s. In July 1960 the Council enacted the First Capital Directive.[17] The October 1962 Commission Action Programme for the Second Stage suggested a system of fixed exchange rates with a narrow band of variation, and envisaged a full monetary union.[18] The Second Capital Directive was adopted in December 1962.[19] In June 1963, the Commission recommended strengthening monetary cooperation. Council Decisions[20] provided for a committee of central bank governors, a budgetary committee of senior national officials and Commission representatives, and consultation between Member States on specific international monetary policies.

As early as September 1964, the Commission promised to submit proposals for 'the progressive introduction of a monetary union'.[21] It linked its own political fortunes to those of the Community. However, these proposals remained mainly on paper. The main practical results were the EEC's first medium-term economic policy programme in 1967[22] and a second programme in 1968,[23] both led by the Commission in conjunction with expert committees.

(b) From the Barre Plan to the Maastricht Treaty
Political, economic, and monetary instability in the late 1960s hindered plans for European monetary integration. Nonetheless, it facilitated more limited Commission

---

[10] Art 67(2) EEC. See also Art 69 EEC.   [11] Art 70(1) EEC.

[12] Art 71, first para, EEC.   [13] Art 73(1) EEC.

[14] EEC Treaty, Protocol on the Statute of the European Investment Bank.

[15] Accord monetaire europeén du 5 aout 1955 amendé par les Protocoles additionelles Nos 2 et 3 et les Décisions prises par l'Organisation européenne de coopération économique jusqu'au 1er août 1960 (OECE, 1960).

[16] Council Decision (EEC) on coordination of the conjunctural policies of the Member States [1960] OJ L31/764.

[17] First Capital Directive, [1960] OJ L921/60.

[18] Memorandum de la Commission sur le programme d'action de la communauté pendant la deuxième étape, COM(62) 300, 107.

[19] Council Directive (EEC) 63/21, [1963] OJ L62/63.

[20] Council Decision (EEC) on cooperation between Member States in the field of international monetary relations [1964] OJ L77/1207; Council Decision (EEC) on cooperation between the central banks of the Member States of the EEC [1964] OJ L77/1206; Council Decision (EEC) on cooperation between the competent government departments of Member States in the field of budgetary policy [1964] OJ L77/1205.

[21] EEC, Official Spokesman of the Commission, 'Initiative 1964', Information Memo P-59/64 (Brussels, October 1964), 4–5.

[22] [1967] OJ 79/1513.   [23] [1969] OJ L129/1.

initiatives which aired the issues, established terms of debate, and set the agenda for the future. On 5 December 1968 the Commission announced that it would propose new means of monetary cooperation.[24] The resulting 'Barre Plan', named after Commission Vice-President Raymond Barre, recommended closer coordination of short-term economic policies, convergence of national medium-term economic policy orientations, and establishment of Community machinery for monetary cooperation.[25] Its principal concrete result was a Council Decision on the coordination of Member States' short-term economic policies.[26]

The debate revealed three enduring flashpoints.[27] First, 'monetarists' (France, Belgium, Luxembourg) gave priority to monetary union, while 'economists' (Germany, Netherlands), wanted economic union first.[28] Secondly, some countries (France, Luxembourg, Netherlands) opposed the Plan because they considered monetary union and political union to be inextricably linked, while others (Germany, Italy, Belgium) supported the Plan because economic policy coordination seemed to presage greater political integration. Finally, the debate revealed the limits of EEC competence and, correlatively, the extent of fragmented governance of economic and monetary policy. The EEC response was to encourage the creation of networks of specialized committees, an early version of 'new governance'.

On 2 December 1969, the Hague Summit agreed that a plan in stages should be elaborated to create monetary cooperation and harmonize economic policies.[29] This was the first agreement on EMU as a goal, though Member States disagreed on the means. In February 1970, Germany, Belgium, and Luxembourg submitted plans for EMU. The resulting Werner Committee, chaired by Luxembourg Prime Minister and Finance Minister Pierer Werner, proposed a full-fledged EMU by the end of the 1970s, including complete liberalization of intra-EEC capital movements, irrevocable convertibility of currencies, irrevocably fixed exchange rates, pooling of monetary reserves, and the control of monetary policy by a single European institution.[30] It adopted many proposals in the Commission's earlier Memorandum.

---

[24] ECSC, EEC, EAEC, Second General Report on the Activities of the Community 1968 (February 1969), 111.

[25] ECSC-EEC-EAEC, Secretariat General of the Commission, 'Commission Memorandum to the Council on the Co-ordination of Economic Policies and Monetary Co-operation within the Community', Supplement to *Bulletin of the European Communities*, No 3–1969 (Publishing Services of the European Communities, 1969).

[26] [1969] JO L183/41.

[27] See G G Rosenthal, *The Men Behind the Decisions: Cases in European Policy-Making* (Lexington Books, 1975) 102–105.

[28] See also I Maes, 'On the Origins of the Franco-German EMU Controversies' (2004) 17 Eur J of Land Econ 21; J Pisani-Ferry, 'Only One Bed for Two Dreams: A Critical Retrospective on the Debate over the Economic Governance of the Euro Area' (2006) 44 JCMS 823, 840.

[29] ECSC, EEC, EAEC, Third General Report on the Activities of the Community 1969 (Publishing Services of the European Communities, 1970), 50.

[30] Rapport au Conseil et à la Commission concernant la réalisation par étapes de l'union économique et monétaire dans la Communauté [1970] JO C136/1.

When Germany opposed the proposal to create a European stabilization fund, fearing that Bundesbank reserves would be used to support weak currencies, the Commission softened the plan's supranational aspects. The Council adopted decisions to strengthen economic policy coordination and to increase cooperation between central banks.[31] However, conflicting views informed the February 1971 Resolution of the Council and the Representatives of the Member States expressing support for the creation of EMU by stages,[32] including the prerequisites for a single currency and a Community organization of central banks. The Resolution lacked legal force, but this was not the main reason for its ineffectiveness, which was due instead to disagreements among Member States and the international context.

The fixed exchange rate system collapsed in Summer 1971. The European 'currency snake' was established in March 1972.[33] The April 1972 Basle Agreement provided for cooperation between Member States' central banks.[34] The 'snake' proved ineffective, and the collapse of Bretton Woods led to the collapse of the European fixed exchange rate system. In March 1973, the Council decided to leave the snake as a joint float and not to intervene concerning the dollar.[35] In fact, the Deutschmark served as anchor for the currencies of smaller EEC countries. This 'was the first concrete manifestation of the growing importance of Germany in the Community and Europe more generally'.[36]

Reflecting the increasing role of Germany, a 1974 Convergence Decision called for a high degree of economic convergence of Member States.[37] The 1974 Stability Directive was oriented toward achieving the highest possible degree of stability, full employment, and growth.[38] In 1975 the European Unit of Account (EUA) was created as a basket currency, consisting of fixed amounts of each EEC currency. It played an important role in bond markets and as a major exchange reserve in the 1980s.

A 1978 European Council Resolution established the European Monetary System (EMS) as of 1979.[39] Another 'soft law', an Agreement between Member States' Central Banks, provided operating procedures.[40] Member States could decide whether to join EMS; the UK did not join. The EMS centred on the ECU, the renamed EUA. Each EEC currency had a central rate defined in terms of the ECU. The EMS gradually established the practice that realignments were to be common decisions rather than unilateral decisions. The Basle-Nyborg Agreement of 12 September 1987[41]

---

[31] [1970] OJ C240/20.   [32] [1971] OJ C28/1.   [33] [1972] OJ C38/3.

[34] *Compendium of Community Monetary Texts* (Office for Official Publications of the European Communities, 1974) 60.

[35] Council Statement, 12 March 1973, in *Compendium of Community Monetary Texts* (n 34 above) 63.

[36] L Tsoukalis, 'Economic and Monetary Union: The Primacy of High Politics' in H Wallace and W Wallace, *Policy-Making in the European Union* (3rd edn, Oxford University Press, 1996) 282.

[37] Council Decision 74/120/EEC on the attainment of a high degree of convergence of the economic policies of the Member States of the European Economic Community [1974] OJ L63.

[38] Council Directive 74/121/EEC on stability, growth and full employment in the Community [1974] OJ L63.

[39] EC Bulletin 1978, No 12 pt 1.1.11.

[40] For a revised version, see *Compendium of Community Monetary Texts* (Office for Official Publications of the European Communities, 1989) 50.

[41] EC Bulletin 1987, No 9, 12.

consecrated an agreement of the Central Bank Governors, approved by an informal Ecofin, on instruments against monetary instability. Between 1987 and 1992 there was a strong preference against realignments, as participants sought to maintain their ERM parities against the Deutschmark.

The 1988 Third Capital Directive[42] required Member States to abolish restrictions on capital movements between EEC residents. The Commission could authorize protective measures, or in urgent cases, a Member State could take protective measures immediately and then inform other governments and the Commission.

ERM and the Third Capital Directive reduced national monetary policy powers of governments substantially. What economists often call the 'unholy trinity' illuminates the implications:

> [T]he following three things are in principle incompatible: fixed exchange rates among a set of national currencies; independent monetary policies in the countries concerned; and full mobility of capital between one and another of the countries.... Eventually one of the three things will have to give way—the exchange rate, the difference in policy, or the freedom of capital movements.[43]

By the Directive, the Member States (with limited exceptions) lost control over capital movements. With interest rates tied to that of the German Bundesbank, ERM participants lost real control of exchange rate policy. Little discretion remained for autonomous monetary policy.[44] The EMU core group lost control over exchange rates by 1997.[45]

Following the 1985 Commission's internal market White Paper,[46] and the amendment of the Treaty to include a new Chapter on Cooperation in Economic and Monetary Policy (Economic and Monetary Union),[47] France and Italy in early 1988 separately proposed the creation of a single currency and a European Central Bank.[48] In June the European Council in Hanover created a committee to make detailed proposals. The 1989 Report of the Delors Committee,[49] chaired by then Commission President Jacques Delors, envisaged EMU as a three-stage process, involving closer coordination of Member States' economic and monetary policies, establishment of

---

[42] Council Directive 88/361, [1988] OJ L178/5.

[43] J. Grahl and P Teague, 1992- The Big Market: The Future of the European Community (Lawrence & Wishart, 1990), 129. On the 'unholy trinity' in Europe from the late 1960s to the present, see K R McNamara, 'Economic Governance, Ideas and EMU: What Currency Does Policy Consensus Have Today?' (2006) 44 JCMS 803, Tables 1 and 2, at 806 and 811, respectively.

[44] C A E Goodhart, 'The Political Economy of Monetary Union' in P B Kenen (ed), *Understanding Interdependence: The Macroeconomics of the Open Economy* (Princeton University Press, 1995) 448–505, 458.

[45] W Munchau, 'Big Stride Towards EMU' *Financial Times*, 11–12 October 1997, 6.

[46] Commission of the European Communities, Completing the Internal Market: White Paper from the Commission to the European Council (Office of the Official Publications of the EC, 1985).

[47] Art 102A EEC, inserted in Title II, Part Three by Art 20 SEA.

[48] H Ungerer, *A Concise History of European Monetary Integration: From EPU to EMU* (Quorum Books, 1997) 191–192.

[49] Committee for the Study of Economic and Monetary Union (The Delors Committee), *Report on Economic and Monetary Union in the Community* (Office for Official Publications of the EC, 1989).

European Central Bank, and replacement of national currencies by a single European currency. The Madrid European Council in June 1989 decided on a first stage from 1 July 1990 to 31 December 1993.[50] The start date coincided with the entry into force of the Third Capital Directive. A second stage was to begin on 1 January 1994.[51] A third stage began on 1 January 1999[52] and continues today. Subsequent Council Decisions established a system of multilateral surveillance of economic policies[53] and amended the structure and functions of the Committee of Governors of the Central Banks.[54]

The Maastricht Treaty, which was adopted on 9 December 1991, signed on 7 February 1992, and entered into force on 1 November 1993, represented the formal legal beginning of EMU. It granted competence to the EC to establish an economic and monetary union.[55] The activities of the Member States and the Community were to include:

- the irrevocable fixing of exchange rates leading to the introduction of a single currency, the ECU;

- the definition and conduct of a single monetary policy and exchange rate policy the primary objective of both of which shall be to maintain price stability;

- and without prejudice to this objective, to support the general economic polices in the Community, in accordance with the principle of an open market economy with free competition.[56]

These activities were to comply with the principles of stable prices, sound public finances and monetary conditions, and a sustainable balance of payments.[57] With regard to economic policy, namely price stability, control of excessive budget deficits, and certain common policies, the EC's powers were limited mainly to coordination of national economic policies. Monetary policy was to be much more supranational.

The Maastricht Treaty did not adopt certain proposals of the Delors Report,[58] except in diluted form. Omitted were: transfer to the EC of decision-making power over macroeconomic management, an agreed macroeconomic framework, legally binding rules concerning economic policy, and an EC-wide fiscal policy to avoid a negative impact on the EC's peripheral regions. The Report also considered wage flexibility and labour mobility as necessary to eliminate differences in regional and national competitiveness.[59] It foresaw the possibility of additional EC financial support, based on conditionality. Community-led fiscal policy was to be achieved by

---

[50] Madrid European Council, 26–27 June 1989, Conclusions of the Presidency, *Bulletin of the European Communities No 6*, [1.1.11].

[51] Art 123(1) EC.   [52] Art 121(4) EC.

[53] Council Decision 90/41 on the progressive convergence of economic policies and performance during stage one of economic and monetary union [1990] OJ L78/23. This replaced Council Decision 74/120, [1974] OJ L63/16.

[54] Council Decision 90/42, [1990] OJ L78/25.

[55] Art 4 EC. It also set the basic normative structure for EMU in subsequent Treaties.

[56] Art 3a(2) EC.   [57] Art 3a(3) EC.

[58] See the Delors Committee Report (above n 50) 14, 18–20, 35–36 [19], [29], [30], and [59].

[59] Subsequently echoed in Commission, 'One Market, One Money' (1990) 44 Eur Economy 11.

coordination of national budgetary policies. These proposals fell by the wayside. Other aspects of EMU derived from different sources. Convergence criteria were 'merely hinted at' in the Delors Report and only agreed in the final hours at Maastricht.[60] Litigation in Germany[61] and the 1992 referenda in Denmark and France on the Maastricht Treaty stimulated widespread political debate about European integration. The Danish referendum led to the so-called 'Denmark Agreement',[62] then unique in European law.

2. RECONFIGURATION OF MONETARY AND ECONOMIC GOVERNANCE

(a) Reallocation of authority for public policy

Public policy encompasses the functions of resource allocation, stabilization, and redistribution.[63] Stabilization concerns objectives such as price stability, economic growth, and employment. It typically involves recourse to fiscal policy (taxation, public expenditure) and monetary policy (money supply, interest rates, exchange rates). Redistribution entails mainly fiscal policy.

EMU reconfigured the allocation of authority for monetary policy (see Table 22.1).

Member States transferred to the EU authority to issue currency and make monetary policy. They lost independent authority for monetary policy, though

Table 22.1 Institutional Development in Monetary Union

Stage	Regulatory Institutions	Advisory Institutions	Systemic Institutions or Arrangements
1	Committee of Governors of Central Banks of the Member States	Monetary Committee	[Council of the European Union]
2	European Monetary Institute (EMI)	Monetary Committee	[Council of the European Union]
3	European Central Bank (ECB)	Economic and Financial Committee	European System of Central Banks (ESCB); Eurosystem

Source: Based on F Snyder, 'EMU – Metaphor' (n 64 below) 97, Table 2.

---

[60] K Dyson, *Elusive Union: The Process of Economic and Monetary Union in Europe* (Longman, 1994) 146–159.

[61] *Manfred Brunner and Others v The European Union* (Cases 2 BvR 2134/92 and 2158/92 (before the 2. Senat of the *Bundesverfassungsgericht*, Federal Constitutional Court, 2nd Chamber) [1994] 1 CMLR 57.

[62] Decision of the Heads of State and Government, Meeting within the European Council, concerning Certain Problems Raised by Denmark on the Treaty on European Union, *Agence Europe*, No 5878 (15 December 1992).

[63] J M Buchanan, *The Demand and Supply of Public Goods* (Rand McNally, 1968); R A Musgrave and P Musgrave, *Public Finance in Theory and Practice* (McGraw-Hill, 1976); W Molle, *The Economics of European Integration: Theory, Practice, Policy* (Dartmouth, 1990) 27–28, adds external relations.

Table 22.2 Rules and Forms of Regulation during the Stages of EMU

Stage	Types of Rules and Forms of Regulation	
	Economic Policy	Monetary Policy
1	soft law policy coordination phased obligations	intergovernmental soft law
2	soft law phased obligations supranational surveillance	mixed 'official' soft law
3	phased obligations hard law Community framework, procedures and sanctions	hard law

Source: F Snyder, '*EMU – Metaphor*' (n 64 below) 97, Table 3.

their central banks participate in the ESCB and the Eurosystem was created by the TL.

EMU also modified EU regulatory instruments for both monetary and economic policy (see Table 22.2).

Member States retained authority for fiscal policy, but within an EU coordination framework.[64] In contrast, monetary policy involves EU legally binding measures.

EMU does not establish a strong framework for EU-wide fiscal policy. For Member States in the single currency, government instruments for dealing with economic shocks were reduced mainly to taxation, intervention in the labour market, or reliance on the market. However, for economic shocks, tax policy alone is inadequate. The EU labour market is more rigid than in comparable continental systems. If both fiscal and labour market measures prove ineffective, EMU could result in divergence, not convergence, of Eurozone economies.

(b) Monetary union

The ESCB and ECB, created on 1 June 1998, represent a complex mixture of supra-nationalism and intergovernmentalism and of 'hard law' and 'soft law'. The ESCB, comprising the ECB and the national central banks, is to conduct EU monetary policy. Its primary objective is price stability. Without prejudice to this, it must support the general economic policies in the Community and act in accordance with the principle of an open market economy with free competition.[65] Its basic tasks are to define and

---

[64] For detailed analysis, see F Snyder, 'EMU—Metaphor for European Union? Institutions, Rules and Types of Regulation' in R Dehousse (ed), *Europe After Maastricht: An Ever Closer Union?* (Law Books in Europe, 1994) 63–99.

[65] Art 105 EC and Art 2, Protocol on the Statute of the European System of Central Banks and of the European Central Bank (now Arts 127(1) and 282(2) TFEU and Art 2, ESCB/ECB Protocol).

implement EU monetary policy, conduct foreign exchange operations, hold and manage Member States' foreign reserves, and promote smooth operation of payment systems.[66]

The ECB has legal personality.[67] It comprises a President and Vice-President, an Executive Board, and a Governing Council; a General Council including the Member States not belonging to the Eurozone was added by Protocol annexed to the Maastricht Treaty.[68] The ECB is to exercise its powers independently. The EU and Member States must respect its independence.[69] The ECB can take the same acts as other institutions, except directives. It can adopt regulations to implement its tasks and in cases laid down by the Council; take decisions necessary for carrying out ESCB tasks; and give recommendations and opinions.[70] Under conditions to be laid down by the Council,[71] it may impose fines or periodic penalty payments on undertakings for failing to comply with obligations under its regulations and decisions.[72] It may institute proceedings. Its acts or omissions are subject to judicial review.[73]

The ECB alone can authorize the issue of the Euro.[74] Fixed conversion rates between the Euro and national currencies were established on 31 December 1998. The Euro replaced national currencies of the participating Member States as of 1 January 1999.[75]

---

[66] Art 105(2) EC and Art 3 ESCB/ECB Protocol (now Art 127(2) TFEU and Art 3 ESCB/ECB Protocol). See also ECB Guideline on the Eurosystem's provision of reserve management services in Euro to central banks and countries located outside the Euro area and to international organizations (ECB/2006/4, [2002] OJ L53/1). Member States cannot use overdraft facilities with the European Central or national central banks or offer debt instruments for purchase by the ECB or national central banks: Art 104(1) EC.

[67] Art 107(2) EC (see now Art 282(3) TFEU).

[68] Art 45 ESCB/ECB Protocol (see now Art 44 ESCB/ECB Protocol). The General Council is constituted as a transitional body. The Protocol provides its rules of procedure and responsibilities.

[69] Art 108 EC and Art 7 ESCB/ECB Protocol (see now Arts 130 and 282(3) TFEU and Art 7 ESCB/ECB Protocol).

[70] Art 110(1) EC and Art 34(1) ESCB/ECB Protocol (see now Art 132(1), TFEU and Art 34.1 ESCB/ECB Protocol).

[71] Council Regulation (EC) 2532/98, [1998] OJ L318/4; ECB Regulation (EC) 2157/1999 (ECB/1999/4), [1999] OJ L24/21.

[72] Art 110(3) EC (see now Art 132(3) TFEU), and Art 34.3 ESCB/ECB Protocol.

[73] Art 230 EC (see now Art 214 TFEU), and Art 35 ESCB/ECB Protocol.

[74] Art 105a(1) EC. See now Arts 128(1) and 282(3) TFEU. Euro banknotes issued by the ECB or national central banks are legal tender within the EU: Art 128(1) TFEU. See Decision of the ECB of 6 December 2001 on the issue of Euro banknotes (ECB/2001/15), [2001] OJ L337/52, as amended. Member States may issue Euro coins subject to ECB approval of the volume of the issue: Art 128(2) TFEU. So far, there are eight Euro coins, with a common design on reverse and an obverse with a different design for each Eurozone country. On counterfeit, see ECB Decision on certain conditions regarding access to the Counterfeit Monitoring System (CMS) (ECB/2001/11), [2001] OJ L337/49; Council Decision 2001/923/EC [Pericles programme], [2001] OJ L339/50, as amended, extended, and consolidated; Guideline of the European Central Bank (ECB/2003/5), [2003] OJ L78/20, extended to the 'Outs' by Council Decision 2006/850/EC, [2006] OJ L330,/30.

[75] Council Regulation (EC) No 974/98 on the introduction of the Euro, [1998] OJ L139/1, as amended and consolidated; Council Regulation (EC) No 2866/98 on the conversion rates between the Euro and the currencies of the Member States adopting the Euro, [1998] OJ L359/1 as amended and consolidated. However, even as of November 2009, prices in France are often tallied in Francs as well as Euros, and many people think of prices in French Francs.

(c) Economic policy coordination

The Maastricht Treaty required Member States to regard their economic policies as matters of common concern and to coordinate them within the Council.[76] The EU policy instruments for this purpose are multilateral surveillance using Broad Economic Policy Guidelines (BEPG), the excessive deficit procedure (EDP), and the Stability and Growth Pact (SGP). The Treaty provided the first two; the SGP was created later.

Multilateral surveillance was based on Article 99(5) of the Maastricht Treaty (now Article 121(6) TFEU). Economic policy coordination is done through Ecofin, based on BEPG drafted by the Council, approved by the European Council, then adopted by the Council as a recommendation; the Council is to inform the European Parliament.[77] On the basis of a Commission report, Ecofin monitors economic developments in Member States, taking account of reports which they submit to the Commission on their macro-economic situation, particularly inflation rates and public spending. Multilateral surveillance represents, in embryonic form, an EU economic policy-making system.

Even before Maastricht, preparing for the first stage of EMU, the Council undertook multilateral surveillance of national economic policies.[78] The Maastricht Treaty required Member States, before the second stage, to adopt convergence programmes.[79] With the third stage, such programmes were formally incorporated into the armoury of Community instruments. Member States which had accepted the Euro (the 'Ins') were required to provide 'stability programmes;' Member States which had not (or not yet) joined the Eurozone (the 'Outs') provided 'convergence programmes'. The programmes are not Community legal instruments.[80] They remain national documents, drafted by national authorities within EU guidelines.[81] They are not legally binding.

The EDP originated in the convergence criteria for entry into EMU, which were the legal expression of the economists' coronation theory postulating economic convergence as a precondition to monetary integration. They were provided by the

---

[76] Art 99 EC (now Art 121 TFEU).

[77] Most recently, see Council Recommendation on the broad economic policy guidelines for the Member States and the Community (2008–10), [2008] OJ L137/13 and Council Recommendation on the 2009 update of the BEPG and on the implementation of Member States' employment policies [2009] OJ L183/1.

[78] Council Decision 90/141/EEC, [1990] OJ L78/23.

[79] Art 109e(2)(a), second indent, EC.

[80] For all programmes and assessments, see <http://ec.europa.eu/economy_finance/sg_pact_fiscal_policy/sg_programmes9147_en.htm>.

[81] See General Secretariat of the Council and European Commission, *Economic and Monetary Union: Legal and Political Texts* (Office for Official Publications of the European Communities, 2007), 'Specifications on the Implementation of the Stability and Growth Pact and Guidelines on the Format and Content of Stability and Convergence Programmes: Section II: Guidelines on the Format and Content of Stability and Convergence Programmes' 173–193. See also A Brunila, M Buti, and D Franco (eds), *The Stability and Growth Pact: The Architecture of Fiscal Policy in EMU* (Palgrave Macmillan, 2001).

Treaty and an accompanying Protocol.[82] The Maastricht Treaty required the Commission and the EMI to report to the Council on Member States' progress towards EMU.[83] The reports formed the basis for this assessment.[84] Today the criteria still apply, as convergence criteria, to the 'Outs'.[85] For the 'Ins', only the criterion on government budgetary position is relevant. It is the basis of the EDP used to control public expenditure.

Member States are required to avoid excessive government deficits.[86] The Commission is responsible for monitoring performance.[87] It examines compliance with the following criteria:

(a) whether the ratio of the planned or actual government deficit to gross domestic product exceeds a reference value, unless

- either the ratio has declined substantially and continuously and reached a level that comes close to the reference value;
- or, alternatively, the excess over the reference value is only exceptional and temporary and the ratio remains close to the reference value;

(b) whether the ratio of government debt to gross domestic product exceeds a reference value, unless the ratio is sufficiently diminishing and approaching the reference value at a satisfactory pace.[88]

The EDP Protocol specifies reference values: 3 per cent for the ratio of planned or actual government deficit to GDP and 60 per cent for the ratio of government debt to GDP.[89] It is legally binding. However, sanctions are not automatic, and there is considerable scope for discretion.[90]

---

[82] Art 104c(2), (4) EC and Protocol on the convergence criteria referred to in Art 109j of the Treaty establishing the European Community [1992] OJ C224/121 (now Art 126(2), (14) TFEU) and Protocol on the Convergence Criteria.

[83] Art 109j(1) EC.

[84] See Art 109j(4) EC.

[85] Art 140 TFEU and Convergence Criteria Protocol.

[86] Art 126(1) TFEU ('Ins'); Art 140(1), second indent TFEU ('Outs').

[87] Art 126(2) TFEU.

[88] Art 126(2)(a),(b) [italics added to emphasize wording granting discretion].

[89] Art 1, Protocol on the excessive deficit procedure. On application, see Council Regulation (EC) 479/2009 [2009] OJ L145/1. For interpretation, see Affaire T-148/05 *Comunidad autónoma de Madrid, Madrid infraestructuras del transporte (Mintra) v Commission*, recital 2006, II-61, and Affaire C-448/07P *Ayuntamiento de Madrid, Madrid Calle 30 SA v Commission*, recital 2008, I-99.

[90] As early as 1997, the Prime Minister and Finance Minister of Luxembourg, later President of the European Council (and current President of the Eurogroup) Jean-Claude Juncker affirmed that there would not be 'strict interpretation of *criteria* but strict interpretation of *the Treaty*'. In the Treaty, he added, there is 'a margin of assessment which should be used to advantage', which does not mean 'diluting the criteria', *Agence Europe*, No 6991 (n.s.), 9/10 June 1997, 8. (emphasis added: FS)

(d) Stability and Growth Pact (SGP)

Today multilateral surveillance and EDP are the preventive and dissuasive arms, respectively, of the Stability and Growth Pact (SGP).[91] The most controversial aspect of EMU, the SGP began with a December 1995 German proposal designed to control Member States' public spending. It was intended to reassure the German public that the Euro would be as stable as the Deutschmark. The SGP was to be compatible with the Treaty, be agreed by the EU but applied only to the 'Ins', and not alter EMU entry requirements. It was an 'early warning system, based upon … existing practice'.[92]

The 1996 Dublin European Council made the crucial political decisions. It requested Ecofin to prepare a draft Resolution on SGP and to examine Commission legislative proposals on multilateral surveillance and on EDP.[93] This immediately provoked debate about 'European economic government'. French President Jacques Chirac noted a consensus among Member States about the creation of an economic policy institution to deal directly with the ECB.[94] However, Germany would not accept an economic government that might jeopardize ECB independence.[95] Commission President Santer rejected any suggestion that the Union needed 'economic government'.[96]

Agreement was reached at the Amsterdam Summit, which on 17 June 1997 adopted a Resolution on the Stability and Growth Pact[97] and a Resolution on Growth and Employment.[98] Neither was legally binding. The latter stemmed directly from French proposals. It led to a new employment Title in the Amsterdam Treaty, with the aim of implementing a coordinated employment strategy by coordinating national policies, incentive measures, and an employment committee.[99] Nevertheless, this did not provide a strong, coherent EU employment policy.

---

[91] See Brunila *et al* (n 81 above). On origins, compare M Heipertz and A Verdun, 'The Dog That Would Never Bite? What We Can Learn From the Origins of the Stability and Growth Pact' (2004) 11 JEPP 765 (German government preferences), and M Segers and F Van Esch, 'Behind the Veil of Budgetary Discipline: The Political Logic of the Budgetary Rules in EMU and the SGP' (2007) 45 JCMS 1089 (alliance between French and German financial elite).

[92] European Commission, 'Preparation of Economic and Monetary Union: A Review of the Situation,' *Europe Documents*, No 1992, 4 July 1996, 3.

[93] *Agence Europe*, No 6875 (Special Edition), 15 December 1996, 3. For further details, see Report by the ECOFIN Council to the European Council, 'The Preparations for Stage 3 of EMU', *Europe Documents*, No 2015/16, 18 December 1996.

[94] *Agence Europe*, No 6875 (Special Edition), 15 December 1996, 3.

[95] *Agence Europe*, No 6991 (n.s.), 9/10 June 1997, 6; see also *Agence Europe*, No 6992 (n.s.), Wednesday, 11 June 1997, 4–5.

[96] *Agence Europe*, No 6993 (n.s.), 12 June 1997, 2 and 6.

[97] [1997] OJ C236/1.

[98] [1997] OJ C236/3.

[99] Title VI, including Arts 125–129 EC per Amsterdam Treaty. See also Art 2 TEU per Amsterdam Treaty and Art 2 EC.

The SGP comprised the SGP Resolution and two Council Regulations which translated the Resolution more or less directly into law.[100] The measures were negotiated mainly by economists and adopted by Ecofin, but Commission and Council Legal Services were involved in drafting even before the Commission proposal.[101] Council Regulation 1466/97 concerns stability programmes and convergence programmes. Both types of programmes apply roughly analogous rules, but each requires somewhat different information. All Member States are committed to budgetary positions close to balance or in surplus (CTBOIS). Sanctions are limited to warning, recommendation (which may be made public), and report to the European Parliament. Council Regulation 1467/97, together with the EDP Protocol, establishes integrated rules for the application of Article 126 TFEU. This Article provides for sanctions, which may include report, opinion, recommendation (which may be made public), notice to take specific measures, or eventually financial sanctions. The EDP goes beyond 'naming, blaming, and shaming'. It may have dramatic effects on national policies, relations between citizens and governments, and popular perceptions of the EU. Its effectiveness is open to serious question.[102] However, the legal text does not exclude political compromise. Though legally binding, it contains open-ended terms, and the fundamental decisions are permissive in character and involve institutional discretion. Though 'hard law', the EDP is full of the permissive language of politics. The European Commission is not entitled to bring infringement proceedings against a Member State for failure to implement the Council's decision.[103]

C. EMU—FROM NICE TO LISBON: 2000–2010

1. EVOLUTION OF THE LEGAL FRAMEWORK

The Treaty of Nice (TN) followed its predecessors. However, the Treaty of Lisbon (TL) charts a new direction. It is in many ways a virtual copy of the CT, which was rejected by referenda in France and the Netherlands and never came into force.[104] Unlike the CT, however, the TL amends the existing Treaties instead of replacing them. The consolidated version of the Treaties as amended consists of two parts: the Treaty on European Union (TEU), and the Treaty on the Functioning of the European Union

---

[100] Council Regulation (EC) No 1466/97 of 7 July 1997 on the strengthening of the surveillance of budgetary positions and the surveillance of economic policies [1997] OJ L209/1, since amended; Council Regulation (EC) 1467/97 of 7 July 1997 on speeding up and clarifying the implementation of the excessive deficit procedures [1997] OJ L209/6, since amended.

[101] D Costello, 'The SGP: How Did We Get There?' in A Brunilla et al (n 81 above) 110, 134 n 13.

[102] M Artis, 'The Evolution of EMU's "Fiscal Constitution"' in J H H Weiler, I Begg, and J Peterson (eds), *Integration in an Expanding European Union: Reassessing the Fundamentals* (Blackwell Publishing, 2003) 263–266, 264, describes the use of fines in these circumstances as 'defying credibility'.

[103] Art 126(10) TFEU.

[104] F Snyder, 'Economic and Monetary Union After the Treaty of Lisbon', Table 1, Jean Monnet Conference, 'The European Community at 50: Assessing the Past, Looking Ahead', Faculty of Law, University of Macau, 27–28 May 2008. I am grateful for comments on this occasion.

(TFEU) (previously the Treaty establishing the European Community). The TEU affirms the resolve of the EU Member States 'to achieve the strengthening and the convergence of their economies and to establish an economic and monetary union including, in accordance with the provisions of this Treaty and of the Treaty on the Functioning of the European Union, a single and stable currency'.[105] The aims of the Union include the establishment of 'an economic and monetary union whose currency is the euro'.[106]

Following previous Treaties since Maastricht, the TEU makes a sharp distinction between economic policy and monetary policy.[107] Title VII TFEU contains more detailed provisions. It is divided into Chapter 1 (Articles 119–126) on economic policy and Chapter 2 (Articles 127–133) on monetary policy.

In economic policy matters, Member States are required to coordinate their economic policies 'within arrangements as determined by the Treaties, which the Union shall have competence to provide',[108] and within the Union.[109] The TL does not provide expressly that the EU has either exclusive or shared competence for economic policy. The relevant TL provisions are the result of compromise.[110] The Member States agreed on a separate category of EU competence[111] to provide arrangements for the coordination of economic policy (Article 5(1) TFEU). This category is not listed among shared competences (Article 4 TFEU) or among supporting, coordinating, and complementary actions (Article 6 TFEU). Nor is it a separate competence permitting the EU to coordinate national economic policies.[112] For this purpose, the

---

[105] Preamble, 8th recital TEU.

[106] Art 3(4) TEU.

[107] This follows from Art 4(1) and Art 3 TFEU.

[108] Art 2(3) TFEU.

[109] Art 5(1) TFEU.

[110] H Bribosia, 'Subsidiarité et répartition des compétences entre l'Union et ses États membres' and 'La politique économique et monétaire' in G Amato, H Bribosia, and B De Witte (eds), Genèse et destinée de la Constitution européenne Commentaire du Traité établissant une Constitution pour l'Europe à la lumière des travaux préparatoires et perspectives d'avenir/Genesis and Destiny of the European Constitution. Commentary on the Treaty establishing a Constitution for Europe in the light of the travaux préparatoires and future prospects (Bruylant, 2007) 389, 409–411 and 663, 673–674, respectively; and V Michel and J-P de la Rica, 'Les compétences dans le Traité établissant une Constitution pour l'Europe' in V Constantinesco, Y Gautier, and V Michel (eds), Le Traité établissant une Constitution pour l'Europe (Presses Universitaires de Strasbourg, 2004) 282–310, 292.

[111] Thus blurring any clear distinction between competence and powers.

[112] P Craig, 'The Treaty of Lisbon: Process, Architecture and Substance' (2008) 33 ELRev 137, 148 ('particular head of competence' and 'separate category of competence') and, on the CT, P Craig, 'Competence: Clarity, Conferral, Containment and Consideration,' (2004) 29 ELRev 323, 333, 337–339. Cf F-X Priollaud and D Siritzky, Le Traité de Lisbonne. Texte et commentaire Article par Article des nouveaux traités européens (TEU—TFEU) (La documentation française, 2008) 161 ('la politique économique demeure de la compétence des États membres. Toutefois, une coordination des politiques économiques...est nécessaire afin que l'Union puisse répondre aux objectifs que lui fixent les traités'). R Smits, 'The European Constitution and EMU: An Appraisal' (2005) 42 CML Rev 425, 430–431, considers the CT to have provided for shared competence for economic policy coordination.

Council is to adopt measures, in particular BEPG.[113] Special provisions apply to those Member States whose currency is the Euro.[114]

In monetary policy matters, the EU has exclusive competence for the 'Ins'. The 'Outs' retain competence concerning monetary policy.[115] The principle of free competition remains in all detailed articles concerning economic and monetary policy,[116] though following French demands it was dropped from the beginning articles of the TL. Throughout, the European Union is substituted for the European Community.

The TL promotes the ECB to the rank of a core EU institution,[117] though this was resisted by the ECB on the ground that the change might affect its independence.[118] General and detailed provisions concerning the ECB are all set out in the TFEU;[119] this differs from treatment of the European Parliament, the European Council, the Council, and the Commission, for which basic provisions are included in the TEU and detailed provisions in the TFEU. The ECB has legal personality.[120]

Basic provisions on the ECB remain on the whole the same as in the TEC, except as discussed later. However, the ECB and national central banks of the Eurozone countries, which together constitute the Eurosystem, conduct EU monetary policy.[121] As the ECJ held in 2003 concerning the applicability to the ECB of EC legislation on anti-fraud investigations,[122] the ECB has functional independence but otherwise is subject to primary and secondary EU law, including the obligation of loyal cooperation between EU institutions.[123] It is an integral part of the EU, not an autonomous sub-system. The ordinary legislative procedure, now the co-decision procedure, is extended to the modification of certain provisions of the Statutes of the ECB and of the ESCB[124] and to measures necessary for the use of the Euro as the single currency.[125] These provisions improve the power of the European Parliament.[126] There is a new

---

[113] Art 5(1) para 1 TFEU. On results and possible reforms, see S Deroose, D Hodson, and J Kuhlmann, 'The Broad Economic Policy Guidelines: Before and After the Re-launch of the Lisbon Strategy' (2008) 46 JCMS 827.

[114] Art 5(1), para 2 TFEU.

[115] Art 3(1)(c) TFEU.

[116] Arts 119(1), 120(1) and 127(1) TFEU; Art 2 ESCB/ECB Protocol.

[117] Art 13(1) TEU. See also K Kalltenhaler, *Policymaking in the European Central Bank: The Masters of Europe's Money* (Rowman & Littlefield, 2006).

[118] Opinion of the European Central Bank, [2003] OJ C229/7, pt 11.

[119] Art 13(3) TEU.

[120] Art 282(3) TFEU.

[121] Art 282(1) TFEU. See also Guideline of the European Central Bank on monetary policy instruments and procedures of the Eurosystem (ECB/2000/7), [2000] OJ L310/1, as amended.

[122] Case C-11/00 *Commission of the European Communities v European Central Bank* [2003] ECR I-07147, [135]. The ECJ followed Case 85/86 *Commission of the European Communities v Council of Governors of the European Investment Bank* [1988] ECR 1281. See also I Lianos, 'Les "autres institutions" et les organes consultatifs de l'Union' in V Constantinesco *et al* (n 110 above) 181–188, 184–186.

[123] See also M Dony, *Après la réforme de Lisbonne: Les nouveaux traités européens* (Editions de l'Université de Bruxelles, 2008), XXXVI.

[124] Art 129 TFEU.

[125] Art 133 TFEU.

[126] Cf eg Art 129(3) TFEU and Art 107(5) EC.

chapter on provisions concerning the Eurozone countries. A new Protocol consecrates the existence of the Euro Group. The TFEU also establishes an Economic and Financial Committee to promote coordination of Member States' policies;[127] the Committee is the current version of earlier institutions.

2. INSTITUTIONAL AND NORMATIVE DIFFERENTIATION

(a) 'Ins' and 'outs'

The TL enhances differentiation between Member States which have accepted the single currency and those which have not. Only 16 of the 27 Member States belong to the Eurozone.[128] The 'Ins' are Austria, Belgium, Cyprus, Finland, France, Germany, Greece, Ireland, Italy, Luxembourg, Malta, the Netherlands, Portugal, Slovenia, Slovakia, and Spain. As of 2008, the 'Ins' accounted for about 64 per cent of the EU population and more than 70 per cent of EU GDP.[129] The 'Outs' are Bulgaria, Czech Republic, Estonia, Hungary, Latvia, Lithuania, Poland, and Romania, which have already signalled their intention to adopt the Euro;[130] Denmark and the United Kingdom, which benefit from a derogation under the Treaty;[131] and Sweden, which has a de facto 'opt-out'.[132] The current EU Member States therefore comprise four different groups in relation to the Euro.

The TFEU lays down, for the first time, special provisions for the Eurozone Member States,[133] notably for reasons of legal coherence and political visibility. The Council may adopt further measures to strengthen coordination of budgetary discipline and set out specific economic guidelines, while 'ensuring that they are compatible with those adopted for the whole of the Union and are kept under surveillance'.[134] Only the 'Ins' are entitled to vote on such measures.[135] Only they are allowed to participate in the adoption by the Council of decisions establishing common positions on EMU matters

---

[127] Art 134(1) TFEU.

[128] Monaco, San Marino, and the Vatican City use the Euro as official currency and can mint coins but are not formally part of the Eurozone and are not represented on the ECB board: Monetary Agreement [2001] OJ C209/1–4 and Council Decision 1999/96/EC [1999] OJ L30/31 (Monaco); Monetary Agreement [2001] OJ L299/1 as amended and Council Decision 1999/97/EC [1999] OJ L30/33 (San Marino); Monetary Agreement [2002] OJ L142/59 as amended and Council Decision 1999/98/EC [1999] OJ L30/35 (Vatican City).

[129] E de Poncins, *Le traité de Lisbonne en 27 clés* (Editions Lignes de Repères, 2008) 245–246.

[130] A Bénassy-Quéré and E Turkisch, 'The ECB Governing Council in an Enlarged Euro Area' (2009) 47 JCMS 25 argue that enlargement will not alter fundamentally interest rate decisions of the ECB Executive Board.

[131] Protocol on Certain Provisions Relating to the United Kingdom of Great Britain and Northern Ireland; Protocol on Certain Provisions Relating to Denmark.

[132] Sweden rejected the Euro (55.9 per cent 'no', 42 per cent 'yes') in a referendum on 14 September 2003. Consequently, it has not joined the ERM, membership of which for two years is required to join the Eurozone.

[133] Title VIII, ch 4, Arts 136–138 TFEU. In a submission to the European Convention, the Commission proposed the creation of an 'Ecofin-euro area', a formal institution to take decisions and strengthen coordination for the Eurozone within the normal EC framework: see European Convention, Secretariat, Paper from the Commission, Working Group VI Economic Governance, Working Document 06, Brussels, 8 July 2002.

[134] Art 136(1) TFEU (quotation from Art 136(1)(b) TFEU).

[135] Art 136(2) TFEU.

within international financial institutions and conferences.[136] They alone participate in the Governing Council and the Executive Board of the ECB.[137] Their national central banks (NCBs) together with the ECB comprise the Eurosystem, in contrast to the broader ESCB which includes the ECB and the NCBs of both the 'Ins' and the 'Outs'.[138]

Non-Eurozone countries, known as 'Member States with a derogation,'[139] are required to ensure that their national legislation, including the status of NCBs, is compatible with the Treaties and the Statute of the ESCB and of the ECB.[140] Their NCBs participate in the ECB General Council with the Eurozone members but not in the ECB Executive Board or the Governing Council. The 'Outs' belong to the ESCB but not to the Eurosystem. They are not subject to the BEPG concerning the Eurozone, coercive means of remedying excessive deficits, the ESCB, issue of the Euro, ECB acts, measures on the use of the Euro, monetary agreements and other measures on exchange-rate policy, appointment of members of the ECB Executive Board, decisions establishing common provisions on EMU issues within international institutions and conferences, and measures to ensure unified international representation of the Eurozone.[141] Such differentiation within EMU was previously viewed as temporary.[142] The TL Euro Group Protocol includes the phrase 'pending the Euro becoming the currency of all Member States of the Union'.[143] However, at least one informed commentator considers that the UK, for example, will probably not join the Eurozone until at least 2025.[144]

(b) The Euro Group

A new Protocol on the Euro Group provides special arrangements for meetings of the finance ministers of the 'Ins'.[145] Formed at the initiative of France and Germany,[146] the Euro Group has been recognized as an informal body since the December 1997 European Council.[147] The Euro Group Protocol allows the 'Ins' to develop 'ever-closer coordination' and 'enhanced dialogue'.[148] Though now the Euro Group is recognized formally, it remains informal in its operation. It is not a formation of the Council. It prepares and lays down arrangements for Ecofin meetings. The Commission takes part in its meetings, and the ECB may be invited to do so.[149] The European Parliament does not participate. The Euro Group has a President elected for 2½ years by the 'Ins'.

---

[136] Art 138 TFEU.   [137] Art 283 TFEU.
[138] Art 282(1) TFEU; Art 1.1 ESCB/ECB Protocol.   [139] Art 139(1) TFEU.
[140] Art 131 TFEU. See also ESCB/ECB Protocol.   [141] Art 139(2) TFEU.
[142] Art 140 TFEU provides procedures for joining the Eurozone.
[143] Protocol on the Euro Group, preamble, 2nd recital.
[144] D Marsh, *The Euro: The Politics of the New Global Currency* (Yale University Press, 2009) 259.
[145] Art 137 TFEU. See Euro Group Protocol. See also U Puetter, *The Eurogroup: How a Secretive Circle of Finance Ministers Shape European Economic Governance* (Manchester University Press, 2006).
[146] See European Convention, Secretariat, Cover Note from Secretariat to The Convention, Subject: French-German contribution on Economic Governance, CONV 470/02, CONTRIB 180, Brussels, 22 December 2002.
[147] European Council, Presidency Conclusions, Luxembourg, 12–13 December 1997, pt 44.
[148] Euro Group Protocol, preamble, recitals 1 and 2, respectively.
[149] See Art 1 Euro Group Protocol.

In practice, the role of President has existed since 1 January 2005, but previously it was based only on a Council resolution and not mentioned in the Treaty.

These special provisions symbolize and consolidate increasing differentiation within EMU. The Euro Group is outside Ecofin, though acting as a preparatory forum for it. The 'Ins' meet as a special, reduced formation of Ecofin, at least in the sense that only they are entitled to vote on measures concerning the Euro.[150] This has important effects on European economic governance. Previously Ecofin dealt with economic policy coordination for all Member States.[151] The new TL provisions enable the 'Ins' to develop a kind of economic governance among themselves, stronger than that which applies among the EU-27 as a whole. At least for the 'Ins', the consecration of the Euro Group is a step toward rebalancing the institutional structure of EMU.[152]

(c) SGP Reform

SGP reform illustrates the problems of a 'one size fits all' EMU as currently constituted and exemplifies further differentiation. In November 2002 the European Commission initiated EDP against Germany.[153] On a Commission recommendation, the Council decided that Germany had an excessive deficit and made recommendations for reduction. Subsequently it decided that the German measures were effective. Later, however, the Commission considered that the measures were not appropriate. It recommended that the Council decide, under Article 104(8) EC, that the measures were inadequate and also decide, under Article 104(9) EC, to give notice to Germany to take specific deficit reduction measures.

In April 2003 the Commission initiated EDP against France. The Council, again acting on a Commission recommendation,[154] decided that France had an excessive deficit and made recommendations, including a deadline of October 2003. In October 2003 the Commission concluded that France had not taken effective action. It recommended that the Council decide, under Article 104(8) TEC, to make the determination public. Two weeks later, the Commission recommended that the Council decide, under Article 104(9), to give notice to France to take specific measures.

Ecofin met on 25 November 2003. All Member States, except France and Germany in their own cases, participated in the vote on the Commission's recommendation that the Council make its recommendation public.[155] In the vote on the Commission's recommendation that the Council should give notice to take specific measures, only Member States which had adopted the Euro participated.[156] France and Germany,

---

[150] Arts 136(2), 138(3) TFEU.   [151] Arts 98, 99, 202 EC.

[152] On the conundrum posed by the relations between the ECB, the Eurogroup, and the 'Outs' in the text of the proposed CT, see Lianos (n 110 above) 183–188. See generally Special Issue: Economic Governance in EMU Revisited (2006) 44 JCMS 669–864.

[153] On previous breaches of the SGP, see R M Lastra, *Legal Foundations of International Monetary Stability* (Oxford University Press, 2006) 265–272; S M Seyad, 'Destabilisation of the Stability and Growth Pact' (2004) 19 JIBLR 239, 242–244.

[154] The European Commission has the right of initiative in the EDP: see Art 126(3) TFEU.

[155] Pursuant to Art 104(13) EC.

[156] Pursuant to Art 104(13) EC and Art 122(3) and (5) EC.

together with Portugal and Italy, had sufficient influence to block the vote on the recommendations;[157] each voted against the imposition of measures on the other.[158] Consequently, lacking sufficient majority, neither recommendation was adopted. The Council the same day adopted similar conclusions concerning both France and Germany. It decided not to act and agreed to hold the excessive deficit procedure in abeyance for the time being, while confirming that it '[stood] ready' to take a decision under Article 104(9) if the Member State failed to act in accordance with its commitments.[159] It 'welcome[d] the public commitment' of the Member States to implement necessary measures, made recommendations 'in the light of the Commission Recommendations', recommended that the Member States end their excessive deficit situation by 2005 at the latest, invited the Member States to submit reports, without a fixed timetable, and recommended that the Commission and the Council assess the Member States' progress.[160]

The Commission then brought an application to annul the Council measures concerning Germany and France.[161] The first group of measures consisted of the Council's decisions not to adopt the instruments recommended by the Commission. The second group of measures involved Council conclusions[162] 'holding the excessive deficit procedure in abeyance, recourse to an instrument not envisaged by the Treaty and modification of the recommendations decided on by the Council under Article 104(7)'.[163]

Indicating the significance of the conflict, the case was decided by the full Court and by an expedited procedure.[164] The ECJ, using both systemic and literal interpretation, sought to uphold the letter of the law. It noted the importance of budgetary discipline as provided in the Treaty and stated that the rules should be interpreted

---

[157] P Leblond, 'The Political Stability and Growth Pact is Dead: Long Live the Economic Stability and Growth Pact' (2006) 44 JCMS 969, 973, who also describes (971) a similar procedure involving Portugal in 2002–04 and points out (975, n 8) that Italy risked being in a similar position in 2004 and 2005. After the entry into force of the TOL, only Euro Zone Member States would participate in such a vote: Art 129 TFEU.

[158] P Gerbet, 'Union économique et monétaire' in P Gerbet, G Bossuat, and T Grosbois (eds), *Dictionnaire historique de l'Europe unie* (André Versaille éditeur, 2009) 1069–1081, 1078.

[159] The unilateral commitments of France and Germany: see Opinion of AG Tizzano [68]–[76] in Case C-27/04 *Commission v Council* [2004] ECR I-6649.

[160] Case C-27/04 (n 159 above) [15]–[21], quotations from [18]–[20] respectively. Concerning recommendations to the Member State, the Council now as before acts on the basis of a Commission recommendation, compare Arts 104(7) EC and 126(7) TFEU. By contrast, in deciding whether an excessive deficit exists, the Council is now to act on the basis of a Commission proposal, not a Commission recommendation (compare Arts 104(6) EC and 126(6) TFEU), so only by unanimity could the Council change the proposal or refuse to act (see Art 250(1) EC and Art 293(1) TFEU).

[161] Case C-27/04 (n 159 above).

[162] Entitled 'Council conclusions on assessing the actions taken by the [French Republic and the Federal Republic of Germany, respectively] in response to recommendations of the Council according to Art 104(7) of the Treaty establishing the European Community and considering further measures for deficit reduction in order to remedy the situation of excessive deficit'.

[163] Art 104(7) EC.

[164] Rules of Procedure of the European Court of Justice, Art 62a.

to 'ensure [...] that they are fully effective'.[165] Both the ECJ and the Commission recognized that the Council has responsibility for ensuring budgetary discipline.[166] The ECJ then decided that Article 104 and Regulation 1467/97 provided the only rules governing the excessive deficit procedure; no alternative procedure was possible.[167] The Commission was not entitled to require the Council either to make the recommendations public or to oblige a Member State to take specific measures.[168] However, the Council could not create an alternative procedure, outside the Treaty. To do so infringed Article 104 EC and Article 9 of Council Regulation 1467/97.[169] The ECJ also concluded that the Council's conclusions were adopted by the wrong voting procedure, namely the Article 104(9) EC procedure, instead of the Article 104(7) EC procedure.[170] As the ECJ pointed out, 'where the Council has adopted recommendations under Article 104(7) EC, it cannot subsequently modify them without a fresh recommendation from the Commission since the latter has a right of initiative in the excessive deficit procedure, as the Council acknowledges'.[171]

The ECJ insisted that the Council respect the Treaty rules about its role in the decision-making procedure and hence institutional balance. Member States agreed these rules to 'tie their hands' in the highly contested domain of economic policy.[172] Now they[173] wished to reinterpret these provisions more flexibly, in a concrete situation, involving the SGP's real author, and using an act that the Council considered to be merely a 'text [...] of a political nature'.[174] The Commission deemed this a *sui generis* act[175] and the ECJ concluded that it was an act having legal effects,[176] hence susceptible of judicial review. A realistic decision, the ECJ judgment activated an implicit alliance between the ECJ and the European Commission as defenders of EC law. The ECJ wisely adopted a relatively narrow view of the judicial role, instead of venturing on the choppy seas of EU monetary politics, where the only predictable consequence would have been a loss of legitimacy for the Court.

The judgment sparked considerable controversy, even though financial markets were more concerned with the credibility of government commitments to low

---

[165] Case C-27/04 (n 159 above) [74].   [166] Case C-27/04 (n 159 above) [75].

[167] Case C-27/04 (n 159 above) [81]. In this respect, it did not follow the Opinion of the AG.

[168] Art 104(8) and (9) EC. Similarly, under Art 104(5) and (6), as early as January 2002, the Commission recommended that the Council should address an excessive deficit warning to Germany, but Ecofin refused to follow the recommendation and issued a statement saying that it considered that Germany had responded satisfactorily so the recommendation was not put to a vote.

[169] Case C-27/04 (n 159 above) [89].

[170] See Case C-27/04 (n 159 above) [95]. All Member States participate in voting under Art 104(7), whereas only members of the Eurozone participate in voting under Art 104(9).

[171] Case C-27/04 (n 159 above) [92].

[172] See F Giavazzi and M Pagano, 'The Advantage of Tying One's Hands: EMS Discipline and Central Bank Credibility' (1988) 32 EER 1055; for updating, see W Schelkle, 'The Theory and Practice of Economic Governance in EMU Revised: What Have We Learnt about Commitment and Credibility?' (2006) 44 JCMS 669.

[173] The possibility that the Member States might have sought to act as the Member States meeting in the Council, rather than as Ecofin, is legally excluded because monetary union is a matter of exclusive EC competence: see Art 4(2) EC.

[174] Case C-27/04 (n 159 above) [37].   [175] ibid [43].   [176] ibid [50].

inflation and fiscal sustainability than with what they viewed as a purely political agreement.[177] It became an important element in the SGP reform process already underway.[178] The judgment, adopted on 13 July 2004, had already been prefigured by the 19 May 2004 Opinion of Advocate General Tizzano. The European Council, meeting in Brussels on 17–18 June, adopted a Declaration on the SGP. It reiterated the importance of a rules-based system to ensure enforcement of commitments and equal treatment of all Member States and called for measures to strengthen and clarify the SGP.[179]

Citing the judgment, a Commission Communication[180] then proposed revision of the SGP. On 21 March 2005, Ecofin proposed specific reforms to the European Council, emphasizing the importance of balancing supranational coordination and national discretion and of 'keeping the rules-based framework simple, transparent and enforceable'. The 'preventive arm' of the SGP should be strengthened, and countries should adhere to the medium-term CTBOIS objective, but with more room for budgetary manoeuvre. On the EDP, Ecofin called for clarification and longer deadlines but ruled out a redefinition of the Maastricht criteria through exclusion of particular budgetary items. The European Council approved the Ecofin Report as an integral part of the revised SGP.[181]

On this basis, Ecofin adopted legislative reforms.[182] Country-specific criteria replaced the uniform CTBOIS.[183] On the EDP, the 'guiding principle' was 'prompt correction of an excessive deficit. The procedure should remain simple, transparent and equitable.'[184] The main substantive changes were, first, in determining whether an excess over reference value resulting from a severe economic downturn was exceptional, (a) strict guidance to the Commission was replaced by 'may', and (b) the statistical norm was abandoned in favour of a more flexible formula, substantially open to interpretation.[185] Secondly, the Commission report was expressly required to 'appropriately reflect' developments in national medium-term economic positions and budgetary positions and to give 'due consideration' to 'any other factors which, in the opinion of the Member State concerned' are relevant to the assessment; special consideration was to

---

[177]   Leblond (n 157 above) 969–990.

[178]   See also J-V Louis, 'The Review of the Stability and Growth Pact' (2006) 43 CML Rev 85.

[179]   Conference of the Representatives of the Governments of the Member States, IGC 2003—Meetings of Heads of State or Government, Brussels, 17–18 June 2004, D/04/3, CIG 84/04, PRES 26, 18 June 2004, Annex 7, 'Declaration on the Stability and Growth Pact, 18 June 2004. This Declaration was annexed to the draft EU Constitution as 'Declaration on Art III-184'.

[180]   Commission of the European Communities, 'Strengthening economic governance and clarifying the implementation of the Stability and Growth Pact', COM(2004) 581 final, Brussels, 3 September 2004. The Communication expressly refers (at 2) to the ECJ judgment, emphasizing that it clarified the respective roles of the Commission and the Council and confirmed the importance of a rule-based system.

[181]   See European Council, 'Conclusions', Annex 2, 22–23 March 2005.

[182]   Council Regulation (EC) 1055/2005 amending Regulation (EC) No 1466/97 [2005] OJ L174/1; Council Regulation (EC) 1056/2005 amending Regulation (EC) 1467/97 [2005] OJ L174/5.

[183]   See Council Regulation 1055/2005 (n 182 above) Art 1(1).

[184]   Council Regulation 1056/2005 (n 182 above) preamble, 5th recital.

[185]   Council Regulation 1467/97 (n 182 above) Art 2(2), as amended.

be given to budgetary efforts fostering international solidarity or achieving European policy goals, 'notably the unification of Europe'.[186] These factors were also to be taken into account in the steps leading to a decision on the existence of an excessive deficit, as well as in subsequent procedural steps.[187] The cost of implementation of pension reforms was to be taken into account.[188] Thirdly, the deadlines for Council decisions on excessive deficit and recommendations for Member State action were lengthened.[189] Fourthly, the reform gave the Council and the Member State more flexibility and clarified the procedure by insisting on the Commission's right of initiative and eventually permitting the Council to revise its earlier recommendation.[190] Fifthly, the procedure for a Council decision to give notice to a Member State to take deficit reduction measures was set out in more detail, with longer deadlines. Sixthly, the Council now could adopt a revised notice if the Member State had taken effective action and an 'unexpected adverse economic event with major unfavourable consequences for government finances' occurred after the adoption of the notice.[191] Finally, the deadline for a Council decision to take sanctions was increased from 10 months to 16 months.[192]

The reformed SGP, as its predecessor, remains a set of rules, including rules granting discretion. However, some rules have changed and the Council enjoys even greater discretion, with more room to the proportionality principle.[193] The reforms adapt the SGP to changing and very diverse national economic and political circumstances. However, they also substantially weaken supranational surveillance.[194] Indeed, there is a serious question as to how effective peer pressure can be in this sensitive policy field.[195] The reforms render complex legislation even more complicated. They diminish rather than improve the level of accountability of national and EU monetary authorities. They reveal a continuing institutional gap at the heart of EMU: the lack of adequate European economic governance.[196] Most of all they demonstrate that, in economic policy coordination, the Member States call the shots.

---

[186] ibid Art 2(3), as amended.

[187] ibid Art 2(4), (6). For an exception, ibid Art 2(6), as amended.

[188] Council Regulation 1467/97 (n 182 above) Art 2(5) and (7), as amended.

[189] ibid Art 3(3) and (4), as amended.

[190] Council Regulation 1467/97 (n 182 above) Art 3(5), as amended.

[191] ibid Art 5, as amended.

[192] ibid Art 7, as amended.

[193] See also J A Usher, 'Proportionality in the Context of Economic and Monetary Union' (2008) 35 LIEI 245.

[194] For a critical evaluation, see J Bourrinet, 'Reconnaissance et méconnaissance d'un principe. La nécessaire réforme du pacte de stabilité et de croissance (PSC)' (2005) 1 Revue des Affaires Européennes 97–104.

[195] Based on the evolution of the SGP up to 2004, D Hodson and I Maher, 'Soft Law and Sanctions: Economic Policy Co-ordination and Reform of the Stability and Growth Pact' (2004) 11 JEPP 789, argue that such soft law measures are most 'functionally suited' to circumstances of medium-term economic uncertainty.

[196] In 2004 J-V Louis, 'The Economic and Monetary Union: Law and Institutions' (2004) 41 CML Rev 575 referred (at 575) to the imbalance between economic policy and monetary policy as 'the most important problem facing the EMU now' but realistically noted (at 582) that most proponents of stronger economic governance would probably not accept the transformation of BEPG into legally binding instruments. See also I Begg, 'Hard and Soft Economic Policy Coordination under EMU: Problems, Paradoxes and Prospects,' Centre for European Studies, Harvard University, Working Paper Series No 103, 2003; J Bourrinet, *Le Pacte de stabilité et de croissance* (PUF, 2004).

3. CHALLENGES TO EMU

(a) The Post-2007 financial crisis

The post-2007 international financial crisis has been the most serious challenge to EMU so far.[197] It revealed starkly the shortcomings of the current EMU institutional structure. As early as October 2007, Ecofin adopted common principles for cross-border financial crisis management and a strategic 'roadmap' for strengthening EU arrangements for financial stability.[198] The October 2008 Brussels European Council adopted the principles of a Euro Group action plan, based essentially on the British banking rescue plan.[199] It set up an informal warning system, information exchange, and an evaluation mechanism or 'financial crisis cell'.[200]

On 29 October 2008, the Commission proposed a new EU financial architecture, specific economic measures, and a global response to the crisis.[201] The package involved strong support for the financial system from the ECB and central banks, rapid implementation of Member States' bank rescue plans, and measures to limit the spread of the crisis. It also included reinforced measures of regulation and supervision, concerning deposit guarantees and capital requirements, credit rating agencies, executive pay, derivatives, hedge funds, and private equity. The Commission also emphasized the importance of the SGP as a framework, using its flexibility in a principled way, and ensuring that deterioration of public finances was accompanied by adequate structural reforms. It also called for greater international coordination and for reforms of global financial standards and institutions. After a Euro Group draft was discussed by the European Council, the Commission on 26 November 2008 proposed a comprehensive European Economic Recovery Plan.[202] The Plan was part of the EU's contribution to international cooperation. One objective was to stabilize the banking system, ensure sufficient liquidity, and support timely, temporary, targeted, and coordinated national budgetary stimulus packages, within the framework of the SGP as revised in 2005. This was to be accompanied by structural reforms.

The Commission appointed a high-level group of financial experts, chaired by Jacques de Larosière, former governor of the Banque de France. Submitted on 25 February 2009, the de Larosière Report[203] built on earlier proposals. It urged reform of EU financial

---

[197] See also D Hodson and L Quaglia (eds), Special Issue (2009) 47 JCMS 939–1128.

[198] Council of the European Union, Council Conclusions on Enhancing the Arrangements for Financial Stability in the EU, 2822nd Economic and Financial Affairs Council Meeting, Luxembourg, 9 October 2007, Annexes I and II.

[199] See L Quaglia, 'The "British Plan" as a Pace-Setter: The Europeanization of Banking Rescue Plans in the EU?' (2009) 47 JCMS 1063.

[200] Council of the European Union, Presidency Conclusions, Brussels European Council, 15–16 October 2008, OR.fr, 14368/08, CONCL 4, Brussels, 16 October 2008.

[201] European Commission, 'From Financial Crisis to Recovery: A European Framework for Action,' COM (2008) 706 final, Brussels, 29 October 2008.

[202] A European Economic Recovery Plan, COM(2008) 800 final, Brussels, 26 November 2008.

[203] Report of the High-Level Group on Financial Supervision in the EU, chaired by Jacques de Larosière, Brussels, 25 February 2009.

architecture to create, by 2012, a European Systemic Risk Council (ESRC) under the auspices of the ECB and a European System of Financial Supervision (ESFS), consisting of national and European authorities. The ERSC would be responsible for macro-prudential oversight of the financial system, provide early risk warnings if necessary, make recommendations, and monitor implementation. The ESFS would be a network of national and European supervisory authorities to define technical supervisory standards, license and supervise EU-wide institutions, such as credit rating agencies, and mediate and arbitrate conflicts between national supervisors. The current Committee of European Supervisors ('Lamfalussy level 3 Committees') would be replaced by three new European supervisory authorities: a European Banking Authority (EBA), a European Insurance and Occupational Pensions Authority (EIOPA), and a European Securities Authority (ESA), each with legal personality and with increased responsibilities, in particular ensuring a single set of harmonized rules, licensing and supervising EU-wide institutions such as credit rating agencies, resolving disputes between national authorities, and following up and if necessary sanctioning manifest breaches of EU law. Together with representatives of national supervisory authorities and the Commission, the EBA, the EIOPA, and the ESA would be the core of the ESFS Steering Committee. The Report also recommended a review of Basil 2 banking supervision rules. In other words, the de Larosière Report did not recommend a single global or even EU-wide regulator, but rather a reconfiguration of EU financial institutions to mirror the structure of the ECB and ESCB, better coordination among EU and national regulators, improved standards, and better oversight of the EU and international financial system as a whole.

Partly on the basis of the de Larosière report, the Commission proposed wide-ranging reforms of the financial services sector.[204] In May 2009, it issued a Communication on 'European Financial Supervision'.[205] In its view, the financial crisis had revealed significant failures in financial supervision, and national models were inadequate in the face of the EU's (and international) integrated financial markets. Labelled 'a key milestone', it set out a new architecture for EU financial supervision. It supported creation of the ESRC and ESFS. The ESRC could be established as a body without legal personality on the legal basis of Article 95 TEC. It would cover the entire financial sector, including insurance. Specific responsibilities could be given to the ECB. The legal basis of the ESFS would be the EC Treaty provision 'which constitutes the specific legal basis for the policy they will be called upon to implement'.[206] This would ensure the development of a 'single rule book' on financial services in the EU. By autumn 2009, the EC had agreed[207] amendments to directives on capital

---

[204] Driving European Recovery, COM(2009) 114 final.

[205] COM(2009) 252 final [SEC(2009)715, SEC(2009)716].

[206] ibid 14.

[207] Council of the European Union, 'Financial Services: New Rules on Credit Rating Agencies, Bank Capital Requirements, Cross-Border Payments and E-Money, and A Programme to Support the Effectiveness of EU Policies' 12380/09 (Presse 234), Brussels, 27 July 2009.

requirements[208] and tighter rules on credit rating agencies.[209] A draft Directive on hedge funds, private equity and other investment funds,[210] proposals to strengthen the safety of derivatives,[211] and a proposal to regulate bonus policies for traders and managers[212] were under discussion. Further detailed legislative measures were expected as of November 2009.[213]

By Spring 2009, EU Member States had already adopted or announced financial stimulus packages, amounting in total to 400 billion Euros, or 3.3 per cent of EU GDP.[214] By September, financial stimulus measures, including automatic stabilizers, amounted to 5 per cent of EU GDP, and there were limited signs of economic improvement.[215] According to the Commission, supply-side structural measures should begin to replace short-term demand management measures; some countries, such as France, in fact pursued supply-side measures from the outset. However, there was a high cost, both financially, with public debt in the Eurozone projected to reach 100 per cent, and in terms of European integration, with each Member State adopting its own fiscal and economic policies. Consequently, it was time for a coordinated 'exit strategy' to be put in place.[216]

It is too early to assess proposed reforms, but we can draw several preliminary conclusions. First, EU-level coordination has been more effective for monetary policy than for fiscal policy.[217] Member States by and large adopted separate fiscal policies, with relatively little coordination with other Member States.[218] Secondly, policies to

---

[208] See now Directive 2009/111..../EC of the European Parliament and of the Council of 16 September 2009 Union amending Directives 2006/48/EC, 2006/49/EC and 2007/64/EC as regards banks affiliated to central institutions, certain own funds items, large exposures, supervisory arrangements, and crisis management, OJ 16.9.2009 L302/97.

[209] See now Regulation (EC)1060..../2009 of the European Parliament and the Council of 16 September 2009 on credit rating agencies, OJ 16.9.2009, L 302/1. 2008/0127 (COD), PE-CONS 3642/09, Brussels, 14 July 2009.

[210] European Commission, Proposal for a Directive of the European Parliament and of the Council on Alternative Investment Fund Managers and amending Directives 2004/39/EC and 2009/..../EC, COM(2009) 207 final, 2009/0064 (COD), [SEC(2009) 576, SEC(2009) 577], Brussels, 30 April 2009, adopted by the European Parliament on 11 November 2010 and awaiting adoption by the Council.

[211] Ensuring Efficient, Safe, and Sound Derivatives Markets: Future Policy Actions, COM(2009) 563 final. Brussels, 20 October 2009.

[212] Proposal for a Directive of the European Parliament and of the Council amending Directives 2006/48/EC and 2006/49/EC as regards trading requirements for the trading book and for re-securitizations, and the supervisory review of remuneration policies, COM(2009) XXX final, [SEC/2009)974 final, SEC(2009) 975 final].

[213] See EurActiv.com, 'Financial Regulation: The EU's Agenda' 27 October 2009.

[214] European Commission, Directorate-General for Economic and Financial Affairs, 'Economic Crisis in Europe: Causes, Consequences and Responses' European Economy 7, 2009 (provisional version).

[215] By comparison, the Chinese stimulus package launched at the end of 2008 amounted by October 2009 to 390 billion Euros (4000 billion CNY, or about 13 per cent of GDP. Chinese banks had granted loans worth 8670 billion CNY (€845 billion) during the first nine months of 2009. See Brice Pedroletti, 'La Chine est menacée de surchauffe économique' Le Monde, 24 October 2009, 1. However, automatic stabilizers are mostly absent in China.

[216] See also M Saltmarsh, 'E.C.B. faces "tricky" path to removal of bank aid' International Herald Tribune, Thursday, 3 December 2009, 16.

[217] See also L Quaglia, R Eastwood, and P Holmes, 'The Financial Turmoil and EU Policy Coordination in 2008' in N Copsey and T Haughton (eds), The JCMS Annual Review of the European Union in 2008 (Wiley-Blackwell, 2009) 63–87.

[218] [Correspondants], 'Les Vingt-Sept abordent en ordre dispersé la "sortie de crise" économique,' Le Monde, 23 October 2009, 8.

combat the financial crisis led to massive increases in public spending. Fiscal deficits were above the 3 per cent mark everywhere and were projected to be above 10 per cent of GDP in Ireland, Latvia, Spain, and the United Kingdom. Gross public debt for 2010, though differing among Member States, was projected to exceed 83 per cent of GDP in France, 98 per cent in Belgium, and 100 per cent in Italy and Greece.[219] Since 2008, the Commission has initiated the excessive deficit procedure against 10 Member States,[220] as compared to a total of 12 initiations between 2003 and 2008.[221] Thirdly, Member States argue increasingly that SGP limits are political rather than legal, flexible rather than rigid, and allow priority to be given to long-term issues. The European Commission has generally supported this viewpoint.[222] Fourthly, the crisis has raised again the question of whether the EU needs stronger European economic governance. In dealing with economic shocks, Member States are limited to national though coordinated measures, either using fiscal policy or taking advantage of a flexible SGP. Whether and how current regulatory reforms will change matters remains to be seen.

(b) EMU on the international stage

A second challenge for EMU is to ensure adequate representation of the EU, the Eurozone, and the single currency on the international monetary stage.[223] The TL does not provide for a unique representative of the EU or the Eurozone in international financial bodies.[224] In the IMF and the World Bank, the EU is represented by its Member States, though the ECB has observer status on the IMF Executive Board since

---

[219] European Commission, 'Economic Crisis in Europe,' 41, 44. See also European Commission, Directorate-General for Economic and Financial Affairs, 'Sustainability Report 2009', European Economy 9, 2009 (provisional version) 40, Table III. 1.4. On the crisis in Greece (12.7 per cent deficit, 112 per cent debt as of 10 December 2009), see A Faujas, 'La dette de la Grèce provoque une vague d'inquiétude dans toute la zone euro' Le Monde, 10 December 2009, 1–19.

[220] UK (Council Decision 2008/713/EC [2008] OJ L238/5); France (Council Decision 2009/414/EC [2009] OJ L135/19); Greece (Council Decision 2009/415/EC [2009] OJ L135/21); Ireland (Council Decision 2009/416/EC [2009] OJ L135/23); Spain (Council Decision 2009/417/EC [2009] OJ L135/25); Malta (Council Decision 2009/587/EC [2009] OJ L2002/42); Lithuania (Council Decision 2009/588/EC [2009] OJ L2002/44); Poland (Council Decision 2009/589/EC [2009] OJ L202/46); Romania (Council Decision 2009/590/EC [2009] OJ L202/48); Latvia (Council Decision 2009/591/EC, [2009] OJ L202/50).

[221] France (Council Decision 2003/487/EC [2003] OJ L165/29); Hungary (Council Decision 2004/918/EC [2004] OJ L389/27 and, on inadequacy of national measures, Council Decision 2005/843/EC [2005] OJ L314/18); Cyprus (Council Decision 2005/184/EC [2004] OJ L62/19); Netherlands (Council Decision 2005/136/EC [2004] OJ L47/26, abrogated by Council Decision 2005/729/EC [2005] OJ L274/89); Slovakia (Council Decision 2005/182/EC [2005] OJ L62/16); Poland (Council Decision 2005/183/EC [2005] OJ L62/18); Czech Republic (Council Decision 2005/185/EC [2005] OJ L62/20); Italy (Council Decision 2005/694/EC [2005] OJ L266/57); Portugal (Council Decision 2005/730/EC [2005] OJ L272/91); UK (Council Decision 2006/125/EC [2006] OJ L51/14; abrogated by Council Decision 2007/738/EC [2007] OJ L300/49).

[222] Long-Term Sustainability of Public Finances for a Recovering Economy, COM(2009) 545/3 [SEC(2009) 1354] 2.

[223] As of 2006, see R M Lastra, Legal Foundations of International Monetary Stability (Oxford University Press, 2006).

[224] Dismissed this as unrealistic by the French Finance Minister. J Mullen and A Cohen, 'ECOFIN: French Fin Min: One Euro-Zone IMF Seat Is Unrealistic' Easybourse, 6 July 2009.

1 January 1999[225] and the Commission participates as an observer in the IMF International Monetary and Financial Committee and Development Committee.[226] The ECB and the central banks of the EU Member States represent the EU on the BIS Basel Committee on Banking Supervision. The ECB represents the EU on the Financial Stability Board, established on 26–27 June 2009 to replace the Financial Stability Forum with larger membership and a broader mandate to promote international financial stability.[227] In practice, the European Commission President is a full member of the now defunct G8, whereas the rotating Council presidency and the ECB represent the EU in the G20. The Commission and the ECB represent the EU in the EU–China Financial Markets Dialogue.[228]

Logically, the 'Ins' should be represented by the Presidents of the Euro Group and the ECB,[229] but in practice the EU elides the distinction between the Euro Group and Ecofin. For the Eurozone members, the Council (Ecofin), acting on a Commission proposal and after consulting the ECB, is now competent to adopt common positions on EMU matters within international financial institutions and conferences, or to adopt appropriate measures to ensure unified representation with such institutions or conferences; only Eurozone members can take part in these votes.[230] Without prejudice to these provisions, the ECB is to decide how the ECB is to be represented with the ambit of ECB tasks, and the ECB and, subject to its approval, national central banks may participate in international monetary institutions.[231]

The Lisbon Treaty includes a legal basis for an international monetary policy on behalf of the Euro.[232] The Council, acting unanimously after consulting the ECB and the EP, can conclude formal agreements on an exchange-rate system for the Euro in relation to the currencies of third states.[233] This essentially consecrates the position of the Euro Group and the ECB. The Euro Group prepares Ecofin meetings, and only Eurozone members can vote on Euro matters. The Ecofin President may participate, without voting rights, in meetings of the ECB Governing Council and may submit motions for deliberation by the Governing Council.[234] The ECB President is to be invited to participate in Ecofin meetings when ESCB matters are discussed,[235] or when the ECB exercises its right to initiate complementary legislation.[236] The ECB

---

[225] International Monetary Fund, Press Release No 98/64, 22 December 1998. See also D-C Horng, 'The ECB's Membership in the IMF: Legal Approaches to Constitutional Challenge' (2005) 11 ELJ 802.

[226] See European Commission, Economic and Financial Affairs, 'International Economic Issues: International Institutions and Forums': <http://ec.europa.eu/economy_finance/int_economic_issues/int_economic_issues200_en.htm>.

[227] See <http://www.financialstabilityboard.org>.

[228] See F Snyder, *The European Union and China, 1949–2008: Basic Documents and Commentary* (Hart, 2009) 838–842.

[229] See also W Buiter, 'Who speaks for Europe in the G-whatever?' *Financial Times* ft.com/mavecon. 11 October 2009: <http://blogs.ft.com/maverecon/2009/10/who-speaks-for-europe-in-the-g-whatever/>.

[230] Art 138 TFEU.   [231] Art 6 ESCB/ECB Protocol.

[232] Art 219 TFEU.   [233] Art 219(1) TFEU.

[234] Art 284(1) TFEU.   [235] Art 284(2) TFEU.

[236] Art 129(4) TFEU and Art 41 ESCB/ECB Protocol.

President is invited to participate in meetings of the Euro Group,[237] informal Ecofin meetings, Ecofin itself and other bodies concerning with EU financial matters, including legislation.[238] The ECB is required to address an annual report to Ecofin.[239]

The fragmented governance structure of EMU remains an obstacle to more effective participation of the EU or the Eurozone in international financial organizations and to greater internationalization of the Euro, including expansion of its role as a reserve currency.[240] Future developments may eventually permit the Euro to be part of a new international reserve currency, as Chinese leaders have proposed.[241]

D. CONCLUSION

EMU is an apt metaphor for the EU. Compared to the past, however, both EMU and the EU have changed. The evolution of EMU before and beyond the Euro's 10th anniversary on 1 January 2009 presents an image of the increasing institutional and normative differentiation that characterizes the EU of today as compared to that of EMU's origins. EMU in the Lisbon Treaty both reflects and enhances this process. Enhanced differentiation between the 'Ins' and the 'Outs' in EMU, the consolidation of the Euro Group, and reform of the SGP are examples. A capsule summary might be 'the more integration, the more differentiation'.

The continuing debates about economic and monetary governance reflect fundamental disagreements about European integration. The evolution of EMU reveals the crucial roles played by the European Council, Ecofin, and the European Commission, as well as other monetary specialists. It also shows that an optimum institutional symmetry within EMU remains to be defined. Nonetheless, there are striking differences between the context in which EMU originated and that in which it operates today. The 2005 French and Dutch referenda on the CT called a halt to Robert Schuman's neofunctionalist dream of economic integration and political federalism. Globalization and the EU today are defined by the integration of international

---

[237] Art 2 Euro Group Protocol.

[238] For a general overview as of 2000, see European Central Bank, 'European Cooperation: Close ties with European institutions' at <http://www.ecb.int/ecb/orga/tasks/html/within-the-eu.en.html>.

[239] Art 284(3) TFEU.

[240] See also B J Cohen, 'Dollar Dominance, Euro Aspirations,' (2009) 47(4) JCMS 741–766 and from a different perspective, the interview with ECB President Jean-Claude Trichet in P-A Delhommais and A Leparmentier, 'Monnaies, bonus, déficit, G20…: M. Trichet tire les leçons de la crise' Le Monde, 18 November 2009, 1 and 14.

[241] See X Zhou [Zhou Xiaochuan], Governor of the Central Bank of China, 'Ideas about the Reform of the International Monetary System,' 23 March 2009, at <http://www.pbc.cn/detail.asp?col=4200&ID=279> ([in Chinese] or <http://news.xinhuanet.com/english/2009–03/24/content_11063193.htm> [in English]. See also X Wu (Wu Xiaoqu, Head of the Financial and Securities Research Institute, Renmin University, Beijing), 'The Future International Currency System Should be Constituted by Three or Four Kinds of Currency' Economic Information Daily, 15 May 2009 [in Chinese].

financial markets and increasingly complex relations between sites of governance, within and outside the EU.[242]

The re-emergence of China on the international stage promises to reshape international financial regulation. Relative to its main trading partners, however, the EU is at a disadvantage due partly to the current institutional shape of EMU. Today there is still no single EU market for money, or indeed for public policy on economic and monetary integration. Globalization and enlargement have enhanced previous disparities and reconfigured conflicts among EU Member States. EMU is likely to remain a fascinating albeit frustrating conjunction of integration and differentiation.

---

[242] See F Snyder, *The EU, the WTO and China: Legal Pluralism and International Trade Regulation* (Hart, 2010).

23

COMPETITION LAW MODERNIZATION: AN EVOLUTIONARY TALE?

Imelda Maher*

Modernization, a process of reform dating from the late 1990s, is the most important change in competition law in recent years[1] if not since 1958. Articulated through Regulation 1,[2] it is characterized by decentralization of enforcement to National Competition Authorities and an increasing emphasis on economic analysis. Building on the seminal work of Gerber[3] and Goyder[4] who both provide historical accounts of the development of competition law and policy up to the late 1990s, this chapter adopts an institutional perspective to examine changes in relation to the governance of the two most paradigmatic aspects of competition law—private market behaviour pertaining to restrictive agreements and the abuse of market dominance.[5] In the first

* UCD School of Law, Dublin European Institute and UCD Centre for Regulation and Governance. Thanks to Anestis Papadopoulos for comments and to participants at the Evolution of EU Law Conference, April 2009. The usual disclaimer applies.

[1] See generally S Brammer, *Co-operation between National Competition Agencies in the Enforcement of EC Competition Law* (Hart, 2009); D J Gerber, 'Two Forms of Modernization in European Competition Law' (2008) 31 Fordham Int'l LJ 1235; H Kassim and K Wright, 'Bringing Regulatory Processes back in: The Reform of EU Antitrust and Merger control' (2009) 32 WEP 738; I Maher, 'Functional and Normative Delegation to Non-Majoritarian Institutions: The Case of the European Competition Network' (2009) 7 Comparative European Politics 414; I Maher, 'Regulation and Modes of Governance in EC Competition Law: What's New in Enforcement?' (2008) 31 Fordham Int'l LJ 1713; A Riley, 'EC Antitrust Modernisation: The Commission Does Very Nicely—Thank You: Part I' (2003) 24 ECLR 604; A Riley, 'EC Antitrust Modernisation: The Commission Does Very Nicely—Thank You Part II: Between the Idea and the Reality: Decentralization under Regulation 1' (2003) 24 ECLR 657; J S Venit, 'Brave new World: The Modernization and Decentralization of Enforcement under Arts 81 and 82 of the EC Treaty' (2003) 40 CML Rev 537; S Wilks, 'Agencies, Networks, Discourses and the Trajectory of European Competition Enforcement' (2007) 3 European Competition Journal 437.

[2] Council Regulation 1/2003 of 16 December 2002 on the Implementation of the Rules on Competition laid down in Arts 81 and 82 of the Treaty, [2003] OJ L1/1 (hereinafter Regulation 1).

[3] D J Gerber, 'The Transformation of European Community Competition Law?' (1994) 35 Harv Int'l LJ 97.

[4] D Goyder, *EC Competition Law* (5th edn, Oxford University Press, 2009).

[5] Arts 101 and 102 TFEU respectively (previously Arts 81 and 82 EC).

edition, this author noted the path dependencies inherent within the governance structures of competition law within which 'progress' is constrained by institutional forms and earlier policy choices in order to explore the evolution of competition law and intellectual property rights.[6] In relation to modernization which significantly changes governance pathways in the competition sphere, it is necessary to ask if these recent changes can be explained at all in evolutionary terms given the extent to which they constitute a break from the past. While path dependencies are inherent within bureaucratic governance structures, in this instance it is not clear to what extent they constrained the new institutional forms and policy choices that characterize modernization.

The chapter falls into four sections: a brief reflection on competition policy as a policy apart; an examination of the idea of evolution; an outline of the development of competition law and policy prior to modernization; and a reflection on modernization in the evolution of competition law before concluding that while diversity is a necessary hallmark of the regime and was necessary for evolution of the law to take place, convergence may prove the most lasting outcome.

A. COMPETITION POLICY: A POLICY APART?

Ten years ago, it was categorical that competition policy could be seen as a policy apart within the Community (as it then was), mainly due to the luxury of power enjoyed by the Directorate General for Competition (DGComp[7]) manifest in its enforcement and especially its sanctioning powers. Majone's analysis[8] of the Commission as an institution with limited resources but one which has been able to increase its influence through increased regulation, did not hold true in quite the same way for the experience of DGComp which had enjoyed extensive regulatory powers since the early 1960s. Efforts to decentralize were apparent from the 1990s as concerns about lack of resources and personnel became more acute especially in the expectation that states previously members of the Soviet bloc would, within a relatively short period of time, become Member States of the EU.[9] In addition to extensive enforcement powers, the Commission also has unparalleled legislative powers in relation to the control of public undertakings and liberalization of markets.[10] However, following challenges to their exercise,[11] the liberalization process begun in the early 1990s after the

---

[6] I Maher, 'Competition Law and Intellectual Property Rights: Evolving Formalism' in P Craig and G de Búrca, *The Evolution of EU Law* (Oxford University Press, 1999) 598.

[7] Before the Kinnock reforms, known as DGIV and now known as the Department for Competition.

[8] G Majone, 'Market Integration and Regulation: Europe after 1992' (1992) 43 Metroeconomica 131.

[9] Gerber (n 1 above) 1237.

[10] See generally D Geradin (ed), The Liberalization of State Monopolies in the European Union and Beyond (Kluwer Law International, 1999).

[11] Case 188–190/80 *France, Italy and the UK v Commission* [1982] ECR 2545; Case C-202/88 *France v Commission (Terminal Equipment)* [1991] ECR I-123; Cases C-271/90, C-281/90, and 289/90 *Spain, Belgium and Italy v Commission* [1992] ECR I-5833.

introduction of the Single Act has predominantly been adopted through conventional law-making processes involving the Council and Parliament.[12]

The status of competition policy as a policy apart is now less apparent for three reasons. First, as a result of liberalization, the role of competition policy within the EU in general and the internal market in particular became more obvious. The nature of competition law as something primarily of relevance to multinational businesses changed. The privatization that followed on from the reforms of the early nineties had a direct impact on national political and employment strategies as well as on consumers' lives in ways previously unprecedented such that by the time of the French 'non' in the European Constitution referendum, the market liberalizing policies of the EU manifested in part through its competition policy, was one of the factors in securing a negative vote.[13] Secondly, the convergence of national competition laws with those of the EU in the nineties and noughties partly as a response to the opportunities and challenges of the 1992 programme and arising out of the demands prior to accession for new Member States, brought a competition law and policy discourse to the national domain—or at least created the potential for one to emerge.[14] Finally, as I have argued elsewhere,[15] decentralization of enforcement with the shift towards networks and away from hierarchy in the enforcement of competition law is separate from but in fact mirrors governance initiatives under the somewhat ill-fated Lisbon agenda[16] which is a reminder that governance in the competition sphere has significant similarities with governance means found in other European policy spheres.

Competition law and policy—in particular state aid—has come under severe pressure during the current economic crisis with the need for the Commission to agree bail-out arrangements for troubled banks bringing its regulatory role to the fore in political discussions. Lyons suggests that banks remain a special sector of the economy necessitating bail-outs and mergers.[17] Geradin, a practitioner and academic and also the former competition Commissioner, Kroes, have presented competition law as part of the

---

[12] Art 114 TFEU (previously Art 95 EC). See E Szyszczak, *The Regulation of the State in Competition Markets in the EU* (Hart, 2007) 133–138.

[13] S Seeger, 'From Referendum Euphoria to Referendum Phobia—Framing the Ratification Question' (2008) 10 EJLR 437, 445. For a discussion of the tensions underlying the liberalization process arising out of different conceptions of the role of the state in the market see, T Prosser, *The Limits of Competition Law: Markets and Public Services* (Oxford University Press, 2005) chs 6, 7, 8.

[14] This arguably is one of the best examples of Europeanization of national laws. See generally M Drahos, *Convergence of Competition Laws and Policies in the European Community* (Kluwer Law International, 2001); I Maher, 'Alignment of Competition Laws in the EC' (1996) 16 YEL 223.

[15] Maher, 'Regulation and Modes of Governance' (n 1 above).

[16] W Kok, *Facing the Challenge: The Lisbon Strategy for Growth and Employment: Report from the High Level group chaired by Wim Kok* (Official Publication of the EC; 2004); K Armstrong, I Begg, and J Zeitlin (eds), 'Governance and Constitutionalism after Lisbon' (Special Issue) (2008) 46 JCMS 413–450; D Hodson and I Maher, 'The Open Method as a New Mode of Governance. The Case of Soft Economic Policy Co-ordination' (2001) 39 JCMS 719.

[17] B Lyons, 'Competition, Bail Outs and the Economics Crisis' (CCP Working Paper 09–04) see <http://www.uea.ac.uk/polopoly_fs/1.112187!CCP09-4.pdf>.

solution to the economic crises with continuing enforcement of the anti-trust rules and active oversight of state aid essential to ensuring a stable recovery.[18]

Finally, it is still important to bear in mind those characteristics of competition law that to a greater or lesser degree still distinguish it from other areas of the law.[19] It can only be defined by reference to another discipline—economics—and economics remains fundamental to it with economic analysis a feature of case law.[20] It is a subsystem of law whose instrumental nature and mixed criminal and civil identity (depending on the enforcement methods used) means that those values of effectiveness and efficiency that characterize competition enforcement as much as other regulatory regimes, can collide or at least be in tension with values of due process that characterize other fields of law such as evidence, criminal law, and human rights.[21] It is also characterized by a strong episteme of transnational lawyers and officials with a shared vision of competition law and a common discourse framed predominantly by a consumer welfare model of competition law.[22]

B. EVOLUTION

The risk with adopting an evolutionary perspective is that of delivering a 'just so' story where the narrative, while coherent in itself, in fact has no relationship to reality.[23] This paper aims to avoid this in relation to modernization—in the first instance by setting out three fairly obvious but nonetheless important factors.

First, law changes—this is a truism. Thus writing about legal change almost begs the question. But in fact it is important to understand what changes have occurred and how in order to better understand what influences legal change. Lewis and Steinmo note that the term 'evolution' is often used simply to denote change or a connected pattern of historical events.[24] They suggest taking a closer look at evolutionary theory (or at least specific aspects of it) in order to refine this notion of change. While they are approaching the issue from a political science perspective some of their insights

---

[18] D Geradin, 'Managing the Financial Crisis in Europe: Why Competition Law is Part of the Solution, Not of the Problem' (2008) Dec issue 1 Global Competition Policy 1; N Kroes, 'Enforcement Policy and the Need for a Competitive Solution to the Crisis: Address to the Irish Centre for European Law Dublin, 17 July 2009 Speech/09/348.

[19] See generally I Maher, 'Regulating Competition' in C Parker, C Scott, N Lacey, and J Braithwaite (eds), *Regulating Law* (Oxford University Press, 2004) 192–194.

[20] D B Audretsch, W J Baumol, and A E Burke, 'Competition Policy in Dynamic Markets' (2001) 19 IJIO 613.

[21] K Yeung, *Securing Compliance* (Hart, 2004) ch 5.

[22] F van Waarden and M Drahos, 'Courts and (Epistemic) Communities in the Convergence of Competition Policies' (2002) 9 JEPP 913.

[23] The phrase comes from Rudyard Kipling's children's stories that sought to explain how certain animal characteristics—such as a spotted coat—came about by reference to particular events that occurred to one particular individual animal see R Kipling, *Just So Stories for Little Children* (Oxford University Press, 1902).

[24] O Lewis and S Steinmo, *Institutional Analysis and Evolutionary Theory*, European University Institute, 18 August 2008. See also C Zimmer, *Evolution: The Triumph of an Idea* (HarperCollins, 2001) 235 quoted in A C Hutchinson, *Evolution and the Common Law* (Cambridge University Press, 2005) 235.

are useful for a legal analysis that draws on historical institutionalism. In particular, they raise three issues that for our purposes are of particular relevance to the modernization of competition law. First, evolutionary biologists see diversity as a key driver of change.[25] This raises the question of the nature and role of diversity in the process of modernization in competition policy, given that one of the commonly understood reasons for it was the convergence of competition norms in Europe. Convergence implies similarity but does not imply uniformity. It describes a process defined in part by continuing diversity that may or may not disappear over a period of time.[26] Secondly, evolution implies gradual, path-dependent change. The modernization of competition law has many of the hallmarks of a big bang: how can we speak of evolution in that context? This is especially the case where there is punctuated equilibrium[27]—major change but without large-scale environmental shocks. One final comment: Lewis and Steinmo point out that evolutionary theory is not about prediction given that the chance of random variation is always a possibility. In fact evolution has no goal.[28] Using an evolutionary lens rather is to better understand the forces and dynamics that shape the world. So, the aim in this chapter is not to make any predictions as to the future but instead to reflect on how our understanding of the institutional framework of competition law is deepened by an evolutionary analysis.

A second obvious factor to address is that change happens but when it happens is important for a number of reasons. First, changes which may be beneficial at one time (or indeed in one geographical space), may not be so or indeed may not be possible at another time. For example, it would probably be very difficult to suggest the sort of reforms found in Regulation 1 in the deeply economically uncertain times of today when protectionism is becoming more politically attractive and competition less so than was the case when it was in fact introduced and the European and world economies were performing (relatively) well. Change may occur fortuitously at particular times and not necessarily because that was the optimal time. We cannot assume change is always an improvement because random chance (or unexpected consequences as regulatory scholars would term them) is always possible. For example it is doubtful whether the latest Treaty reforms would have been embarked on quite so enthusiastically if the difficulties of adoption were known then. Change may be possible at a certain point not necessarily because of any exogenous shock but simply because of relative stasis in the environment, combined with innovation endogenously, creating space for new ideas to be aired. *When* change occurs also affects *how* it occurs. This is especially the case in a multi-level polity like the EU where the standing of policy and policy actors within the policy arena has an impact on the duration, emphasis, nature, and outcome of negotiations.

---

[25] Lewis and Steinmo, ibid.

[26] Drahos (n 14 above) 8.

[27] See S. Krasner, 'Approaches to the State: Alternative Conceptions and Historical Dynamics' (1984) 16(2) Comparative Politics 223 at 243.

[28] Hutchinson (n 24 above) 123.

A third factor to consider in relation to evolution is that institutions matter, not because they alone determine policy but they mediate those forces (economic, political), which may shape policy.[29] The term 'institution' is not limited to organizations but extends to rules (formal and informal) and procedures which constrain and reflect the policies that they are called on to implement.[30] An institutional analysis of legal change is especially useful for an evolutionary account because it provides a conceptual framework within which to consider change. The level of responsiveness among institutions is shaped by the fact that institutions respond within their existing frameworks and values, building on existing experience—even where change is radical. In turn, future developments are shaped by earlier choices because, for example, of the costs associated with redesign, the 'paper' routes, and administrative responsibilities being clearly defined with personnel assigned at appropriate stages. Thus while providing a framework within which to focus on change, institutional analysis also focuses on the creation of pattern which limits the scope for change and removes any implicit notion of constant, inevitable, and predictable progression, instead allowing for a more prosaic consideration of how organizations, practices, and informal rules are likely to shape and limit the responses of institutions which in turn draw on internal organizational experience without necessarily adequate reference to those external events which triggered change in the first place.

Bulmer notes that this sort of historical institutionalism implies path dependency but has difficulty explaining episodes of sudden transformation (punctuated equilibrium).[31] Evolution, especially when coupled with historical institutionalism with its implication of path dependencies, does imply pattern and gradual change. However, a closer look at when and how change can occur shows that it can be episodic. The modernization process in competition law can be cast as one of sudden transformation, even allowing for the period of roughly four years between the Commission White Paper[32] on reform and the enactment of Regulation 1 with rigorous debate and negotiation in between. It is fair to say that it was unexpected, with even Mario Monti—the then Commissioner who oversaw the transformation—saying that in 2000 he would never have envisaged a new competition regime by 2003.[33] In addition,

---

[29] K Armstrong, 'Regulating the Free Movement of Goods: Institutions and Institutional Change' in J Shaw and G More (eds), *New Legal Dynamics of European Union* (Clarendon, 1995) 165.

[30] S Steinmo and K Thelen, 'Historical Institutionalism in Comparative Politics' in S Steinmo, K Thelen, and F Longstreth (eds), *Structuring Politics* (Cambridge University Press, 1992) 2–3.

[31] S Bulmer, 'Politics in Time meet the Politics of time: Historical Institutionalism and the EU Timescape' (2009) 16 JEPP 307, 308.

[32] EC Commission, White Paper on Modernization of the Rules Implementing Arts 85 and 86 of the EC Treaty, 28 April 1999.

[33] M Monti, 'New European Antitrust Regime: Implications for Multinationals, The Fall 2004 Antitrust Symposium—The New European Antitrust Regime: Implications for Multinationals—Remarks: Panel Discussion' (2005) 13 Geo Mason L Rev 269, 271. At the same time, a tone of urgency can be found in the conclusions of the House of Lords Select Committee when reviewing the reform in 2000, although at that time it was not clear how long the radical reforms proposed would take to become law and the Committee rightly expressed concerns about the problems of Commission workload and delays in its decision-making and the need to reform competition law enforcement in the light of enlargement see House of Lords Select Committee on the European Union, Reforming EC Competition Procedures, HL 33 1999/2000 15 February 2000, 145–149.

the change that has been engendered both procedurally (decentralized and directly applicable Treaty rules) and substantively (more economics-based approach) marks a major shift in the governance and approach to EC competition rules and their enforcement. Modernization thus is a critical institutional event that challenges what Bulmer describes as the fallback position of path dependence in historical institutionalism.[34] The *longue durée* of historical institutionalism lends itself to longer timeframes for evaluating the outcomes of change, their embeddedness, and their effectiveness. Evaluating that change requires a long timeframe so the emerging pathways can be properly evaluated and understood. On this basis, we are probably still too close to explain for example the puzzle of the apparent effectiveness of the European Competition Network despite its weak structural base;[35] we do not yet have enough information on how national courts are giving effect to EC competition laws;[36] the extraordinary push to encourage private enforcement actions;[37] and how the shift to a more economics-based approach can meet the challenges of these recessionary times. Nonetheless, at this seven-year juncture, a look at modernization through the evolutionary lens should help to explain the drivers of change and in particular the role of diversity as both a driver and a characteristic of the new regime.

C. THE EVOLUTION OF COMPETITION LAW AND POLICY

Competition policy has always enjoyed prominence within the EU. The preamble refers to the need for action in order to guarantee *inter alia* fair competition[38] while Article 3(g) EC listed as one of the activities of the Community the establishment of 'a system ensuring that competition in the internal market is not distorted'. This provision was removed in the most recent Treaty at the insistence of France following the negative vote in the referendum on the Constitutional Treaty.[39] However, a Protocol is attached to the Treaty indicating that the reference to the internal market in Article 3 includes a system for ensuring undistorted competition.[40] It is not clear

---

[34] Bulmer (n 31 above) 309.

[35] Wilks (2007) (n 1 above) 442.

[36] Commission Staff Working Paper accompanying the Communication from the Commission to the European Parliament and Council, Report on the Functioning of Regulation 1/2003 COM(2009) 206, final, SEC(2009) 574 final, 16, 78–89; K Wright, 'European Commission Opinions to National Courts in Antitrust Cases: Consistent Application and the Judicial-Administrative Relationship' (2008) CCP working paper 08–24 <http://www.uea.ac.uk/polopoly_fs/1.104682!ccp08–24.pdf>.

[37] EC Commission, White Paper on Damages Actions for Breach of the EC antitrust rules COM(2008) 165, 2 April 2008; EC Commission Staff Working Paper SEC(2008) 404.

[38] Preamble EC Treaty and now the Treaty on the Functioning of the EU.

[39] S Seeger, 'From Referendum Euphoria to Referendum Phobia—Framing the Ratification Question' (2008) 10 EJLR 437, 445.

[40] Protocol No 27 TEU. Art 51 TEU gives equal status to Treaty Articles and Protocols. House of Lords European Union Committee, *The Treaty of Lisbon: An Impact Assessment* 10th Report of Session 2007–08 vol 1 [9.13]–[9.18]; M Dougan, 'The Treaty of Lisbon 2007: Winning Minds not Hearts' (2008) 45 CML Rev 617, 653.

whether this political and legal fudge represents a downgrading of competition policy within the EU. What can be said is that it brings to the fore sensitivities around competition law arising out of different conceptions of the role of the state in the market,[41] sensitivities that can be lost in the technocratic discourse of competition law. The change in wording also confirms the view that while competition policy mainly remains above the political fray as a highly technocratic field enforced by (largely) independent executive agencies, Commissioner van Miert's statement that 'competition is politics' still resonates in some contexts at least.[42]

Articles 101–109 TFEU[43] elaborate on these aspirational provisions, with Articles 101 and 102 prohibiting cartels and abuse of market power, respectively. Article 103[44] requires the Council to adopt measures to clarify the functions of the Commission and Court and ensure compliance with Articles 101–102 by making provision for fines. In addition, Article 105[45] gave the Commission power to investigate infringements and propose measures to bring them to an end. This could be done through a reasoned decision which could authorize Member States to take measures, the conditions of which the Commission would determine, that would remedy the situation. Thus the Treaty itself gave the Commission a central role in enforcement.

The development of competition law was contingent on underlying policy which seeks to advance several objectives. Three objectives were identified by the Commission: to keep the market open and unified; to maintain a level of competition in the common market such that EC objectives could be achieved; and to ensure fairness in the market.[46] One of the hallmarks of modernization is the shift towards a more economics-based approach to competition law whereby competition law focuses on efficiency-orientated values. Thus market integration is no longer driving the policy to the same degree and fairness (essentially economic freedom—a core value in particular in the ordoliberal tradition which was so influential on competition law in its early years[47]), is also given less emphasis by the Commission at any rate.[48] This can be seen in the 2004 guidelines issued by the Commission on Article 101(3) where the objective of the provision is identified as the protection of competition in order to enhance consumer welfare and to ensure an efficient allocation of sources.[49] As a tool of

---

[41] See generally Prosser (n 13 above).

[42] S Wilks and L McGowan, 'Competition Policy in the European Union: Creating a Federal Agency?' in G B Doern and S Wilks (eds), *Comparative Competition Policy* (Oxford University Press, 1996) 254 quoting Commissioner van Miert.

[43] Previously Arts 81–89 EC.

[44] Previously Art 87 EC.

[45] Previously Art 89 EC.

[46] EC Commission, Ninth Report on Competition Policy at 9 and see generally T Frazer, 'Competition Policy after 1992: The Next Step' (1990) 53 MLR 609, 611.

[47] D Gerber, *Law and Competition in Twentieth Century Europe: Protecting Prometheus* (Clarendon, 1998) 233 *et seq*.

[48] For a discussion of the shifting relationship between these values see G Monti, *EC Competition Law* (Cambridge University Law, 2007) ch 2.

[49] Commission Communication, Guidelines on Art 81(3) of the Treaty, [2004] OJ C101/97 [13].

integration, competition policy was—and continues to be albeit to a lesser degree—shaped by the overall integration agenda of the EU; the nature of those subject to the competition prohibitions especially but not exclusively, large multinationals; the complex and divergent societies within which that policy is to be applied; and the institutional context within which the norms are applied. This means that even though the antitrust provisions have remained a constant in the Treaty since 1958, competition policy has changed over time, and most significantly, in the process of modernization.

David Gerber's 1994 article provided a map explaining the evolution of competition law up until that year, using a similar approach to Weiler in his seminal *Yale Law Journal* article.[50] He divides the evolution of EU law into three phases: in the first fifteen years the foundations of the competition system were established—in particular early legislation (Regulation 17[51]) secured extraordinary powers for the Commission. First, it could fine undertakings engaged in anticompetitive activities up to 10 per cent of their worldwide turnover,[52] its decisions being subject to review by the Court which can vary, reduce or cancel the fine.[53] This power remains extant and in fact the size of fines in recent years for major breaches of EC law has exceeded 1 billion Euros.[54] Second, it was given the sole power to exempt restrictive agreements that met the conditions set out in Article 101.[55] Thus the structure of that provision, where the absolute prohibition in the first paragraph is alleviated by the possibility of exemption in the third paragraph if certain conditions are met, shaped institutional relationships. The Commission, as the sole body with power to award exemptions was placed at the centre of competition policy formation and legal enforcement although it quickly became apparent that it did not have the resources that would be necessary to carry out this latter function efficiently.

Only Germany had an effective competition law at the time,[56] so other Member States were apparently willing to delegate upwards while German theory (ordoliberalism) and approach to competition law proved highly influential.[57] Given

---

[50] Gerber (n 3 above); J H H Weiler, 'The Transformation of Europe' (1991) 100 Yale LJ 2403. For a slightly different mapping of competition law see A Weitbrecht, 'From Freiburg to Chicago and Beyond—the First 50 Years of European Competition Law' (2008) 29 ECLR 81. In the first edition of this book I undertook a similar mapping exercise in relation to the development of competition law and intellectual property law see Maher (1999) (n 6 above).

[51] Reg 17/63 [1959]–[1962] OJ Sp Ed 87.

[52] ibid Regulation 17, Art 15.

[53] ibid Regulation 17, Art 17.

[54] Commission Decision 13 May 2009 COMP 37/990 Intel D(2009) 3726, final in case COMP/C3/37.990. On appeal, T-286/09, pending.

[55] ibid Regulation 17, Art 9.

[56] Brammer (n 1 above) 8. She notes that four of the then six Member States had competition laws but only France and Germany had a prohibition based regime with only Germany with an effective and sufficiently resourced Authority.

[57] S Quack and M-L Djelic, 'Adaptation, Recombination, and Reinforcement: the Story of Antitrust and Competition Law in Germany and Europe' in W Streek and K Thelen (eds), *Beyond Continuity: Instituuional Change in Advanced Political Economics* (Oxford University Press, 2005).

the importance of the German economy within Europe, such influence is hardly surprising although it was reinforced by the fact the head of DGComp, up until the Kinnock reforms, was always a German.[58] This influence may in part help to explain that it was the Germans who held out the longest on the most controversial aspect of the modernization package which was the jurisdictional divide between domestic and European competition rules.[59]

This radical delegation of powers to the Commission was followed by fifteen years of cautious enforcement while the Commission sought to educate itself, the states, and subjects of the prohibitions as to the nature and scope of the competition rules. At the same time, the prohibition on restrictive agreements in particular was interpreted very widely and in a highly legalistic fashion that underpinned the domination of legal discourse (and lawyers) in the DG. Competition law was firmly established as a motor of integration, using the anti-trust rules to break down vertical arrangements in particular which divided the market on national lines. The quality of reasoning in these cases from a competition perspective was much criticized[60] but the Court was a stout supporter of the Commission in this strict, legalistic, and integrationist approach to competition law enforcement.

The second phase identified by Gerber is that from the oil crisis to the Single European Act, although there is no clear watershed between the two phases. DGIV as it then was, consolidated its position as the engine-house of competition policy, supported by a slightly more critical Court.[61] Competition law continued to be used as a motor for integration with competition concerns particularly in relation to vertical market arrangements being underplayed. The Commission emerged from a learning phase—assisted by notification of agreements to it—by enacting a series of block exemption regulations particularly relating to vertical agreements—those between actors at different levels of the market.[62] While the notification system allowed for learning, it was simultaneously overwhelming, with the DGComp never really recovering from the initial notification of 36,000 agreements in 1963 when Regulation 17 came into force.[63] Notification triggered immunity until the date of the decision creating a major incentive to notify.[64] Block exemption regulations did not fully alleviate the problem of backlog because the approach was highly formalistic, creating a straitjacket leaving very little flexibility for firms and so limiting their capacity to fall

---

[58] See generally, M Cini, 'Norms, Culture and the Kinnock Reforms' in D Dimitrakopolos (ed), *The European Commission* (Manchester University Press, 2004); H Kassim, '"Mission Impossible", but Mission Accomplished: The Kinnock Reforms and the European Commission' (2008) 15 JEPP 648; N Kinnock, 'Accountability and Reform of Internal Control in the European Commission' (2002) 73 PQ 21.

[59] Kassim and Wright (n 1 above) 746–747.

[60] Summed up in a highly influential Article by B Hawk, see 'System Failure: Vertical Restraints and EC Competition Law' (1995) 32 CML Rev 973.

[61] See also Quack and Djelic (n 57 above) 269.

[62] Art 105(3) TFEU (formerly Art 85(3) EC).

[63] Goyder (n 4 above) 41.

[64] Regulation 17, Art 15(5).

within the exemption necessitating notification. This formalism further underlined the dominance of lawyers within DGComp.

Third, in the period after the Single Act, DGIV focused on state activity in the market-place developing rules on public procurement, state monopolies, and state aids.[65] The first Merger Regulation after a marathon of 17 years became law,[66] conferring additional powers through streamlined procedures on the Commission. The test adopted—that of creating or strengthening a dominant position—was similar to that found in German competition law underlying continuing German influence. The Court in the meantime became less activist. Faced with expanding competence and under-resourcing the Commission continued to block exempt agreements and resorted increasingly to soft law measures such as comfort letters to reduce the notification backlog which nonetheless remained a feature.[67] The post-Single Act phase was given further impetus after the Maastricht Treaty. There was an increased (but unsuccessful) emphasis on decentralization of enforcement.[68] With the realization of much of the 1992 programme, there was recognition that market integration may no longer need to be the core of policy development in areas such as competition.[69] Finally, a related development was the emerging alignment of national competition rules with Community competition rules.[70] Weitbrecht dates this third phase from the introduction of the Merger Regulation and, while acknowledging that most date the modernization process as starting in the mid-nineties, he sees it as part of this phase.[71] Nonetheless, it is helpful to distinguish between the market liberalization phase triggered by the Single Act and the later emergence of reforms in the field of anti-trust enforcement given that the political salience of the former is greater and is very loosely allied to the single market. Thus the fourth phase can be dubbed modernization.

D. MODERNIZATION

Modernization is indicative of something more than mere reform—with some commentators even dubbing this phase a revolution.[72] It is, by its very name, a process

---

[65] EC Commission, Twenty Fifth Annual Report on Competition Policy (1995) 11.

[66] Council Regulation (EC) 4064/89 of 21 December 1989 on the Control of Concentrations between Undertakings, [1989] OJ L395/1; J S Venit, 'The EEC Merger Regulation: Europe Comes of Age or Caliban's Dinner' (1990) 27 CML Rev 7. For a recent re-casting of the emergence of merger control at the European level see T Dooley, 'Incomplete Contracting, Commission Discretion and the Origins of EU Merger Control' (2009) 47 JCMS 483.

[67] On soft law measures in EC competition law see H A Cosma and R Whish, 'Soft Law in the Field of EU Competition Policy' (2003) 14 EBL Rev 125.

[68] Notice on Cooperation between National Courts and the Commission in Applying Arts 85 and 86 EEC, [1993] OJ C39/6; Notice on Coordination with National Authorities, [1997] OJ C313/3.

[69] EC Commission, Twenty Fifth Annual Report on Competition Policy (1995) 11.

[70] EC Commission 23rd Annual Report on Competition Policy (199) 81. L Laudati, 'The European Commission as Regulator: the Uncertain Pursuit of the Competitive Market' in G Majone, Regulating Europe (Routledge, 1996) 249; I Maher, 'Alignment of Competition Laws in the EC' (1996) 16 YEL 223.

[71] Weitbrecht (n 50 above).

[72] A Albors-Llorens, 'The Changing Face of EC Competition Law: Reform or Revolution?' (2002) 14 EBJ 31.

flagged by a departure from pre-existing ways of thinking and doing. At the same time, in evolutionary terms, there are path dependencies and an acknowledgement of that which has gone before. This is borne out by the discussion in the Commission White Paper that the reason reform was possible was precisely because of the experience it had developed over the previous forty years and the legal certainty available through the rich body of case law generated in that time was sufficient for a 'loosening of the reins' and a move away from a system of prior authorization.[73] The Commission claims of legal certainty were however treated with some scepticism.[74]

This phase can be dated from discussions in the mid-nineties onwards. Initially, discussions centered on the creation of an independent European competition agency separate from the Commission,[75] given that competition decisions were, and still are, taken by the College of Commissioners and not solely by the Competition Commissioner thus allowing for other policy issues to be raised when the matter is contentious.[76] The debate did not progress however. A single agency would have provided greater consistency in enforcement and ensured political independence but politically it was unattractive especially in the context of the principle of subsidiarity which was a strong part of political debate at the time, and the existence of several strong and powerful national competition authorities (NCAs), most notably in Germany.[77] Instead, in the late 1990s there was a move towards a twin-track approach of a softening of the limitations on vertical agreements moving away from the very strict rules to a more flexible approach based on a blacklist of unacceptable provisions in contracts and an explicit realization of the importance of market dominance in distribution arrangements, giving greater room for manoeuvre to firms and aligning the law with economic thinking.[78] This shift marked the formal beginning of a rebalancing of competition objectives with a move away from competition as a tool for market integration towards a greater emphasis on consumer welfare. This was a welcome reform and one achievable within the existing institutional structure for example the original 1965 Regulation allowing for the adoption of block exemptions is still a part of the *acquis*.[79]

Around the same time as the adoption of the new position on vertical agreements, another group of Commission officials promoted the adoption of a truly heretical idea—the repeal of Regulation 17 which lay at the very heart of anti-trust enforcement. The Fordham and Florence conferences in 1996 are seen as watershed moments with

---

[73] EC Commission (n 32 above).

[74] House of Lords Select Committee (n 33 above) [34]–[42].

[75] C-D Ehlermann, 'Reflections on a European Cartel Office' (1995) CML Rev 471.

[76] Laudati (n 70 above) 235.

[77] Wilks (n 1 above) 443; D Lehmkuhl, 'On Government, Governance and Judicial Review: The Case of European Competition Policy' (2008) 28 JEPP 139, 151.

[78] Regulation 2790/99, [1999] OJ L336/21. EC Commission, Green Paper on Vertical Restraints in EC Competition Policy COM(96) 721, final and EC Commission, Follow-Up to the Green Paper on Vertical restraints, [1988] OJ C365/3. R Whish, 'Regulation 1790/99: The Commission's "New Style" Block Exemption for Vertical Agreements' (2000) 37 CML Rev 887. The most recent version of the regulation is Commission Regulation 330/10, [2010] OJ L102/1 and Commission Guidelines [2010] OJ C130/1.

[79] OJ Sp Ed [1965]–[1966] 87.

criticisms from these events leading to the establishment of a hand-picked Working Group to look at the question of modernization set up by the deputy Director General of DGComp.[80] This led to the publication of the White Paper on Modernisation.[81]

1. SELF-REGULATION BY FIRMS

This proposal was based on three closely related ideas premised on the view that EC competition law was 'coming of age'.[82] First, after forty years, there was a body of law that could now be relied on by those subject to the rules. This reduced the need for the sort of close surveillance (in principle at least—honoured in the breach in practice) that pre-notification provided for. Rather than restrictive agreements being subject to scrutiny by the Commission, firms could now self-assess and decide on the basis of existing norms whether or not the agreement fell within Article 101(1) and if it did, how it needed to be modified to fall within Article 101(3). Most of these agreements were vertical and innocuous. They did not require nor need the amount of Commission time that notification required as the damage to competition was minimal. Firms now assumed the risk of compliance but that risk was relatively small. By reducing the time spent on relatively trivial vertical agreements, the Commission could turn its attention to the much more important (in competition terms) issue of cartels. These are usually horizontal agreements between competitors who cooperate with each other, eg to agree prices and/or to keep other actors out of the market. The tools used to achieve this end are information sharing and reprisals against those who fail to comply. The hallmark of such agreements is secrecy making it difficult if not impossible to detect them despite the arsenal of enforcement powers in the hands of the Commission. By changing focus away from vertical agreements to the more intractable but much more damaging cartels, DGComp would be developing a more economics-orientated competition law and deploying its limited resources where the real harm to competition arises. While efficient and effective enforcement was a driver for change, there is no doubt the Commission was also mindful of its limited resources and the strain that would be put on them by the further enlargement of the EU.[83]

2. A NEW ECONOMICS-BASED APPROACH

The second idea behind modernization was a new economics-orientated approach to competition law analysis. The focus on cartels as the 'cancer' to be removed[84] is only

---

[80] Kassim and Wright (n 1 above) 750. The annual Fordham and Florence conferences are fora where competition lawyers and policy-makers from Europe and North America gather to discuss topics of interest, leading to the publication of scholarly papers.

[81] See n 33 above.

[82] Weitbrecht (n 50 above).

[83] Albor-Llorens (n 72 above); House of Lords Select Committee (n 33 above) [98]–[102] and [142]–[144].

[84] Competition Commissioner Mario Monti referred to it as such in a speech see 'Fighting Cartels: Why and How? Address at the 3rd Nordic Competition Policy Conference' (Stockholm, 11/12 September 2000) SPEECH/00/295.

possible where there is a shift away from a pre-occupation with vertical agreements. The preoccupation with probabilities in merger regulation was also addressed through the introduction of a new substantive test emphasizing the impact on competition (significantly impedes effective competition in particular through creation or strengthening of a dominant position) rather than a pure market dominance test.[85] The General Court adopted a much stronger position on scrutiny with the Commission's nadir being the adoption of two judgments in the same week in 2002 annulling two of its merger decisions (*Tetra Laval* and *Airtours*) mainly on the basis that the economic reasoning was woeful.[86] The Commission at the press conference following the second of these decisions immediately announced that a chief economic advisor would be appointed—who would be independent of the Commission and would play devil's advocate in scrutinizing merger decisions.[87] A more economics-based approach was championed by Commissioner van Miert and his successor, Commissioner Monti, supported in particular in merger cases, by the General Court.[88] The ongoing discussions surrounding a different approach to defining and addressing abuse of market dominance is also couched very much in economic terms with one of the first steps in the process being the production of a discussion paper on market dominance by a group of economists offering blue sky thinking, at least insofar as it was not constrained by the current state of the law on Article 102.[89] The process culminated in the issuance of guidance on enforcement priorities for Article 102, indicating a shift by the Commission to a more economics-based approach.[90]

3. DECENTRALIZATION

The third idea behind modernization, and our primary focus, is that of decentralization. With firms self-assessing, the Commission was not creating a free-for-all for anticompetitive behaviour as a different enforcement mechanism other than notifica-

---

[85] Council Regulation No 139/2004 on the Control of Concentrations between Undertakings, [2004] OJ L24/22. Art 2(2). See generally, J Schmidt, 'The New ECMR: "Significant Impediment" or "Significant Improvement"' (2004) CML Rev 1555.

[86] See generally, M Clough, 'The Role of Judicial Review in Merger Control' (2003–04) 24 Northwest J Int'l L 729 on Case T-5/02 *Tetra Laval* [2002] ECR II-4071 and Case T-342/99 *Airtours* [2002] ECR II-2585.

[87] For a discussion of the role of economists in competition agencies see L Froeb, P A Pautler, and L-H Röller, 'The Economics of Organizing Economists' (3 July 2008). Vanderbilt Law and Economics Research Paper No 08–18. Available at SSRN: <http://ssrn.com/abstract=1155237>.

[88] D Hildebrand, *The Role of Economic Analysis in the EC Competition Rules* (3rd edn, Kluwer Law International, 2009) 4.

[89] Report by the EAGCP, An Economic Approach to Art 82, July 2005 <http://ec.europa.eu/competition/publications/studies/eagcp_july_21_05.pdf>. The discussion paper was in July, followed in September by a key speech from the Commissioner and then in December a working paper from the Commission see <http://europe.eu.int/comm/competition/antitrust/others/discpaper2005.pdf>.

[90] [2009] OJ C45/2. See M Kellerbauer, 'The Commission's New Enforcement Priorities in Applying Art 82 EC to Dominance Companies' Exclusionary Conduct: A Shift Towards a More Economics Approach?' (2010) 31 ECLR 175.

tion is used. Article 101(3)—the provision that can exempt restrictive agreements—has become directly applicable making it enforceable in its entirety by national competition authorities and courts.[91] This renders firms accountable (arguably) at a more appropriate national level where potentially market foreclosure behaviour—a major risk of restrictive agreements—may be more easily detectable. In other words, information asymmetries can be more appropriately addressed at national level. This is not a new idea. Article 102 and the general prohibition in Article 101 had direct effect and hence were enforceable in the national courts.[92] In 1993 the Commission had introduced a notice on cooperation with national courts in the competition sphere and followed it up in 1997 with a notice on cooperation with NCAs.[93] Both notices had little impact most notably because as soft law measures they were not binding. More fundamentally, neither the Courts nor the NCAs could apply the exemption provisions of the Treaty[94] rendering the assistance they could provide in a case severely limited. Many jurisdictions had not introduced legislation to authorize their competition authorities to apply the competition rules, such a step being required under the Treaty.[95] Experience in several Member States was extremely limited also in relation to competition law. For example even the UK did not introduce an effective competition law addressing private market behaviour until the late 1990s.[96]

In relation to national courts, it was unclear what regard was to be given to Commission decisions and to what extent parallel proceedings could continue in national courts when a matter was seized by both national courts and the Commission or the European Courts. This issue was addressed in the *Masterfoods* case where parallel proceedings had resulted in a Commission decision finding a breach of what was then Article 81 and a refusal to grant an exemption, with this decision being appealed to the General Court. In parallel, proceedings in the Irish High Court had refused to find an agreement void on the basis *inter alia* of a breach of the competition rules. This decision was appealed to the Supreme Court which made a preliminary reference to the European Court of Justice as there was a real risk of different decisions being issued by the General Court and the Irish Supreme Court—a court of last resort. The European Court held that, given the exclusive role of the Commission to grant exemptions, the Commission could not be bound by the decision of a national court and a national court could not take a decision running counter to one of the Commission, even if the Commission decision conflicted with a national judgment

---

[91] Regulation 1, Art 1(2).

[92] Cases 127/73 *BRT v SABAM* [1974] ECR 51; [1974] 2 CMLR 238; 209–213/84 *Asjes* [1986] ECR 1457.

[93] See n 68 above; R Whish, 'The Enforcement of EC Competition Law in the Domestic Court of the Member States' (1994) 15 ECLR 60.

[94] Laudati (n 70 above) 249.

[95] Art 84 EC.

[96] A MacCulloch and B Rodger, *The Competition Act: A New Era for UK Competition Law* (Hart, 2000); I Maher, 'Juridification, Codification and Sanction in UK Competition Law' (2000) 63 MLR 544.

taken at first instance. If a Commission decision was subject to appeal, national courts' duty of sincere cooperation required them to suspend their proceedings pending that appeal or to make a preliminary reference.[97] Thus the European Court underlined the pivotal and primary role of the Commission in EC competition law even in relation to national courts in the year following the publication of the White Paper at a time when debates surrounding the proposed decentralization of enforcement was intense.

(a) National courts

Thus within the new enforcement regime, national courts not only can now apply all of Article 101 and Article 102, using their own procedural rules and remedies, but have an express duty to do so where they fall within the ambit of the case.[98] This complements the enforcement role of their competition agencies, especially given their potential capacity to award damages to victims who have been subject to competition enforcement.[99] National courts are facilitated in their enhanced role through better and more direct communication with the Commission. They can ask the Commission for information or its opinion on the EU rules. The Commission can, if the coherent application of those rules requires it, submit written observations to a national court and with the court's consent, give oral evidence. Some national courts have requested this assistance.[100] And the European Court recently upheld the right of the Commission to submit written observations to a national court in proceedings flowing from an earlier Commission decision.[101] NCAs can also submit observations and act as *amicus curiae* where the court allows. In order to facilitate this dialogue between the court and enforcement agencies, the agencies can request relevant documents from the case to be forwarded to them. The corollary of this assistance is that the Member States (not the courts themselves) are to forward a copy of any Article 101 or Article 102 judgments to the Commission without delay. This obligation does not seem to have been honoured in practice in the first five years of the operation of the new regime with the Commission noting that as many as twelve Member States had not forwarded copies of any judgments.[102] While there may not have been any cases in some states, it is unlikely to be true of all of them.[103] In an effort to redress the information deficit,

---

[97] C-344/98 *Masterfoods v HB Ice Cream* [2000] ECR I-11369.

[98] Regulation 1, Art 3(1). For a discussion of the role of courts in competition law see I Maher and O Stefan, 'Competition Law in Europe: The Challenge of a Network Constitution' in D Oliver, T Prosser, and R Rawlings, *The Regulatory State: Constitutional Implications* (2010, forthcoming).

[99] Regulation 1/2003, recital 7, Arts 15 and 16.

[100] For example the Commission was asked for its opinion by the Lithuanian Supreme Court in a case decided on 16 October 2009 see ECN Brief 01/2010 at 17 and to the Paris Court of Appeal in the Pierre Fabre case where the Court has since referred the matter to the ECJ see ECN Brief 01/2010 at 17.

[101] Case C-429/07 *X BV v Inspecteur Belastingdienst* [2009] nyr; K Wright, 'European Commission Interventions as *Amicus Curiae* in National Competition Cases: The Preliminary Reference in *X BV*' (2009) 30 ECLR 309.

[102] Commission Staff Working Paper (n 36 above) [83].

[103] For a discussion of the possible reasons for non-reporting see K Wright, 'European Commission Opinions to National Courts in Antitrust Cases: Consistent Application and the Judicial-Administrative Relationship' (2008) CCP Working Paper 08–24 available at <http://wwwueaacuk/polopoly_fs/1104682! ccp08–24pdf>, 18–19.

the Commission in 2010 started to publish an ECN brief which provides information on case law as well as decisions of the NCAs at national level.[104]

The five-year review also noted that stakeholders had raised the question of uneven application of the rules in national courts.[105] The challenge of consistency, most conspicuously highlighted in the *Masterfoods* case, is still an issue for judicial enforcement of Article 101 and Article 102 even allowing for the exchanges of information and cooperation with competition authorities provided for. Regulation 1 attempted to address this by codifying the ruling on *Masterfoods* as to the binding nature of Commission decisions as well as *obiter* comments in that judgment which noted that NCAs are bound by decisions of the Commission.[106] The challenge of procedural and sanctioning autonomy remains. While early fears of forum shopping as between Member States have not materialized to any great extent, the sharp divergence in potential sanctions raises fundamental questions as to the nature of competition law and, as a result, how due process is to be met. It is difficult to talk of legal consistency when a breach of the competition rules in Ireland can lead to a criminal record and imprisonment for company officers while no criminal sanction is possible in eg Sweden.[107] Thus while the jurisdiction of national courts has been rightly (I would suggest) extended to exempt agreements and their role more clearly articulated in Regulation 1 with the judgment in *Masterfoods* paving the way, the greater formalization of the role in primary legislation has also served to cast light on the information deficit as to what is actually happening in national courts in relation to the competition rules and, even if the substantive rules are common, there is a vast range of diversity as to procedures and sanctions that belies consistency. Thus the issue remains whether the hybridity of common and divergent rules is sufficient not just for the coherence of the law but for its standing as 'good' law.

The Commission has sought to further enhance the effectiveness of the competition rules by strongly advocating private enforcement actions.[108] In doing so, it is seeking to build on the decisions of the European Court that have indicated that an individual is entitled to damages for harm suffered as a result of a breach of the competition rules.[109] The Commission suggests the adoption of a wide range of procedural measures in order to facilitate enforcement actions as well as advocating that any decision by any NCA enforcing the competition rules should constitute irrefutable proof of breach of those rules in any follow-on damages action. This clearly lends itself to legal certainty and reduces the costs of such actions while suggesting mutual recognition of EU competition decisions taken by any NCA.

---

[104] See <http://ec.europa.eu/competition/ecn/brief/index.html>.

[105] Commission Staff Working Paper (n 36 above) [270].

[106] Regulation 1, Art 16.

[107] For Ireland see s 8 Competition Act 2002 and for Sweden see Competition Act 2008 discussed in H Andersson and E Legnerfält, 'The New Swedish Competition Act' (2008) 10 ECLR 563.

[108] Commission (n 37 above).

[109] Case C-453/99 *Courage and Crehan* [2001] ECR I-6297, and Joined Cases C-295 and 298/04 *Manfredi* [2006] ECR I-6619.

In relation to enforcement of the competition rules through national courts, we do not see a big bang approach but rather a codification of an important ruling of the European Court and of its *obiter* comments clarifying the status of Commission decisions and of course, the preliminary reference procedure remains available in competition law cases. The innovation in the Regulation is to indicate that the NCA and the Commission can convey information to the national court although it is silent as to how this is actually to occur. It is for the court rules of each Member State to provide an effective mechanism for such information to be considered by a court. Unlike the competition agencies, there is no formal network of Courts with the Commission noting that such a network would sit uneasily with the important concept of judicial independence.[110] Instead, there is an informal network where matters of common concern are discussed.[111] Thus the major innovation seen for NCAs is missing in this context. What is clear is that the law is still evolving slowly in this field with gaps apparent in our knowledge of how and to what extent competition law is raised in national courts. These gaps are probably not as great as the lack of information would suggest since the amount of competition litigation may in fact be quite small despite the European Court's ruling that there is an entitlement to damages. Thus the lengthy discussions surrounding the question of private actions for damages can be viewed as the new frontier for competition law enforcement as the Commission seeks to expand the relevance of competition law for private parties and to facilitate such actions to ensure better compliance and deterrence (as well as compensation for victims). The complexity and variation of practices as well as the relative novelty of competition law in many Member States and the lack of a culture of private enforcement actions all point to an evolution that is incremental, slow, and uncertain despite the unstinting support of the European Court to the Commission and the codification of the law in Regulation 1.

(b) The European Competition Network

The major institutional innovation in the enforcement regime is the decentralization of enforcement to NCAs and their coordination through the European Competition Network (ECN). It is this innovation that appears to punctuate the long-standing equilibrium of highly centralized, highly legalized competition law enforcement heavily reliant on formal legal instruments and powers. In practice the transition to the new regime was remarkably smooth.[112] This may in part be explained by the fact that new governance techniques—in particular soft law instruments such as guidelines and

---

[110] Commission Staff Working Paper (n 36 above) 80.

[111] R Schmidbauer, 'The Institutions Involved in EC Antitrust Enforcement under Regulation 1 and the Green Paper on Damages Actions—An Overview, Critique and Outlook' (July 2006) available at SSRN <http://SSRN/com/abstract=914169>, 6; S Norberg, 'The Co-operation Between National Courts and the Commission in the Application of EC Competition Rules' (Luxembourg, 13 June 2003). Paper presented to the second conference organized by the Association of European Competition Law Judges.

[112] Communication from the Commission to the European Parliament and Council: Report on the Functioning of Regulation 1/2003 COM(2009) 206, final [7].

notices,[113] were already very well established and widespread.[114] The Network itself as a classic instrument of governance did mark a radical innovation as the allocation of cases, one of the key elements of enforcement strategy, was to be decided in a forum without legal personality with no hard rules as to how allocation was to be done and no basis on which to challenge the allocation before the European Courts with the Notice stating that decisions as to case allocation are not legally binding.[115] At the same time, an informal network of NCAs already existed and continues to exist.[116] In addition, the Advisory Committee which is consulted on Commission competition decisions before they are finalized and which consists of national representatives, has had a long-standing review function in relation to EU competition law.[117]

Nonetheless, despite these two fora and the Commission notice, prior to 2003 NCAs had played a very limited role in enforcement. The new regime explicitly and categorically empower them to apply the EU rules,[118] with all of Article 101 and Article 102 directly applicable.[119] These powers are given only limited statutory support. There is the vague obligation of close cooperation for the Commission and the NCAs with effective enforcement to be supported through the Network, itself only lightly sketched in the Regulation. Instead, as in other areas of substantive law, the detail is contained in (non-binding) guidelines.[120] Unusually, the guidelines and Regulation were accompanied by a joint statement from the Council and Commission.[121] The fact that both institutions regarded such a statement as necessary shows how radical a departure from existing institutional structures was the creation of the ECN and the concerns about adopting this form of governance technique in relation to decentralized law enforcement in the context of 28 different competition regimes with their own procedures.

Ehberlein and Newman's[122] analysis of transgovernmental networks is informative as to how and why a network like the ECN could emerge. They see these networks as having an evolutionary potential given their entrepreneurial and coalition-building

---

[113] Snyder defines soft law as rules of conduct which in principle have no legally binding force but nevertheless can have practical effects see F Snyder, 'The Effectiveness of European Community Law: Institutions, Processes, Tools and Techniques in T Daintith (ed), *Implementing EC Law in the United Kingdom: Structures for Indirect Rule* (Wiley, 1995) 64. For a discussion of soft law instruments in EU competition law see H Cosma and R Whish, 'Soft Law in the Field of EU Competition Policy' (2003) 14 EBL Rev 125.

[114] For a full treatment of this issue see Maher, 'Regulation and Modes of Governance' (n 1 above).

[115] EC Commission, Notice on Cooperation within the Network of Competition Authorities, [2004] OJ C101/43, [31].

[116] The European Competition Authorities Network consists of competition agencies from the EEA (the EU and Norway, Iceland, Liechtenstein as well as DGComp and the EFTA Surveillance Authority) and is a discussion forum.

[117] Regulation 1, Art 14.   [118] Regulation 1, Art 5.

[119] Regulation 1, recital 4, Art 1.

[120] See generally Brammer (n 1 above).

[121] Joint Statement of the Council and the Commission on the Functioning of the Network of Competition Authorities, Interinstitutional File 2000/0243(CNS) Brussels, 10 December 2002.

[122] B Eberlein and A L Newman, 'Escaping the International Governance Dilemma? Incorporated Trans-governmental Networks in the European Union (2008) 21(1) Governance 25–52.

capacity.[123] Such networks arise where there is dual delegation, ie power is delegated nationally by executives to agencies and to supranational institutions (in this instance the Commission).[124] There is some discussion in the literature as to who is the principal and agent in competition law. The Member States clearly delegated to the Union in 1958 and delegated enforcement powers more fully in 1962 in Regulation 17. Modernization can be cast as the Commission repudiating or at least re-casting that delegation.[125] They suggest that such networks emerge where there is a mix of functional interdependence and a reluctance or inability on the part of national governments to cede authority and resources to the supranational level. EU competition law is trans-jurisdictional in scope and the competition issues that arise are also frequently phenomena in several, if not all, Member States. At the same time, the Network was seen as a second best solution for ensuring consistency reflecting reluctance to delegate too much power to the combined NCAs and Commission who are obliged to work together with a relatively narrow legal base and firmly within the realm of soft law mechanisms in order to give effect to enforcement powers that are classically defined within the law.[126] Ehberlein and Newman note that transnational networks are often seen as second best as they signal a de-politicization of the field where states are unwilling to delegate upwards. However, they may be more than that as local regulators have information and resources (broadly conceived) not available at the supranational level.[127] Thus the NCAs have had powers delegated to them at the national level and so exercise some independence and can bring their direct formal authority to bear within the Network without the need to look for legislation *ex post*. In other words, they act within the shadow of hierarchy[128] and are at the high end of intensity for networks given their strong legal base and powers to share confidential information.[129]

Ehberlein and Newman suggest that such networks can only come about where two political logics are met. First, state preferences need to align in technically complex sectors.[130] Second, there has to be top-down activism by the international organization in particular to reassure states concerned about politically sensitive areas. These conditions were clearly met in relation to the Network. Competition law is a technically complex field. EU law has a very strong transnational character and it was the Commission that spearheaded the reforms. It now shares powers with both national courts and agencies that previously it had held exclusively (Article 101(3)) with the 'soft' solution of the Network as the mechanism for coordination rather than the creation of a super-agency or stronger institutional structure.

---

[123] ibid 45.

[124] ibid 26.

[125] Maher, 'Functional and Normative Delegation' (n 1 above); Wilks (n 1 above) 446, 450.

[126] Maher ibid 425.   [127] See n 122 above 45.   [128] ibid 32.

[129] A-M Slaughter, *A New World Order* (Princeton University Press, 2004) ch 4. See also, Maher, 'Regulation and Modes of Governance' (n 1 above).

[130] See n 122 above, 33.

The ECN is the primary mechanism through which the diversity (which Lewis and Steinmo identify as a key requirement for evolution[131]) inherent within the regime is managed sufficiently to ensure coherence and effectiveness in the law. There are five key factors underpinning this coherence and effectiveness. First, all the NCAs are enforcing the same substantive rules giving them a common purpose. They also retain the power to apply their own national competition rules. Thus the jurisdictional boundary between national and EU law is that if there may be an effect on inter-state trade then the EU rules apply. The constraint on the application of national law is that agreements allowed under Article 101 cannot be prohibited although stricter national rules relating to abuse of dominance can be applied.[132] Secondly, as well as sharing common substantive rules the Network is closed in nature with only twenty-eight members who have regulatory authority conferred on them both nationally and under Regulation 1, which in turn brings an authority to the work of the ECN. The NCAs and Commission have common (legal and market) dis-courses of competition[133] which in turn facilitates the emergence of a common culture. Thirdly, the legislative power to exchange confidential information be-tween members[134] creates a high trust culture. It is essential for the effective operation of any competition agency that it retains confidential information and there are no leaks. It needs sensitive business information from firms in order to carry out its investigations and the agencies in Europe have very extensive powers to seize and remove documentation. The corollary of these powers is that infor-mation is, where appropriate, kept confidential. Thus if agencies are to share information relating to investigations, they must be able to trust each other that these high standards of confidentiality will be maintained by their counterparts. Fourthly, the Commission is—on paper at least—first among equals.[135] In other words, the Network has both horizontal and vertical elements.[136] As underlined by the Court in the *France Telecom* case,[137] the Commission has the power under Regulation 1 to remove a case from an NCA.[138] This lever operates contrary to the spirit of cooperation that informs the operation of the Network and is a last resort but nonetheless an important one and especially symbolically at the time of the setting up of the Network. Finally, the Network does not simply coordinate the practicalities of enforcement. It also has a policy role where matters of common

---

[131] See n 24 above and related text.

[132] Regulation 1, Art 3. Note the constraints on the application of national law do not extend to national merger rules or national laws that predominantly pursue an objective different from that in Arts 101 and 102, see Regulation 1, Art 3(3). See Brammer (n 1 above) 69 *et seq*. There is some concern raised by stakeholders as to the potential for stricter national rules in relation to unilateral conduct see the Communication (n 122 above) [22].

[133] Wilks sees these discourses as de-politicized (n 1 above) 452.

[134] Regulation 1, Recitals 16 and 32, Arts 11 and 12.

[135] Maher, 'Regulation and Modes of Governance' (n 1 above) 519.

[136] Wilks (n 1 above) 437.

[137] Case T-339/04 *France Télécom v Commission* [2007] ECR II-521.

[138] Regulation 1, Art 11(6).

concern are discussed and proposed legal developments are discussed. This further underpins the sense of common purpose and ownership of the network and facilitates convergence in particular of procedures with the professionalism of the network an important driver for convergence (in the case of the Network particularly in relation to procedures).[139]

At the same time, the fact that the NCAs apply the EU rules within their own jurisdictions, with their own procedural rules gives them a relatively high level of autonomy. For many, Regulation 1 conferred on them new powers that they had not previously enjoyed (although additional resources did not accompany those new powers[140]), and for less well-established agencies, being members of a supranational Network headed by the very powerful and highly regarded Commission gives them leverage and standing in their domestic regimes emphasizing the independent nature of their role while also giving them access to the expertise of more experienced NCAs in a confidential environment.

There is, as the Court noted, no legislative division of competence between members.[141] Instead, the guidelines set out three presumptions that govern case allocation, the aim being that only one agency deal with a case.[142] First, the NCA first seized of a case is most likely to be well placed to deal with it. Secondly, if it is not, it will be transferred to another NCA in a timely fashion and thirdly, if more than three states are involved the Commission will assume jurisdiction.[143] An NCA is well placed if the conduct in issue has an effect in its jurisdiction; it has the powers to bring the conduct to an end; and can gather the necessary evidence to prove the conduct is anti-competitive.[144] Formally, there is no precise legal obligation on an NCA to desist in investigating a case even if another NCA is also investigating it although continuation would run counter to the requirement of mandatory cooperation. Should an NCA prove recalcitrant, then the Commission can remove a case from them.[145] However, for the Commission to take such action would constitute systemic failure and it has not happened thus far. In practice, there is little discussion on case allocation, suggesting that the guidelines work well.[146]

The Network is virtual and operates through a secure intranet in English. It has no legal personality and the secretariat is very small. The Heads of the NCAs and DGComp meet twice a year. The plenary of NCA and DGComp officials responsible

---

[139] Ehberlein and Newman (n 122 above) 36.

[140] J Fingleton, 'The Distribution and Attribution of Cases Among the Members of the Network: The perspectives of the Commission/NCAs' in C-D Ehlermann and I Atanasiu (eds), *Competition Law Annual 2002: Constructing the EU Network of Competition Authorities* (Hart, 2004).

[141] Case T-339/04 (n 137 above).

[142] Regulation 1, recital 18.

[143] Regulation 1, recital 18 and EC Commission (n 115 above) [6]–[8] and [14]. See S Brammer, 'Concurrent Jurisdiction under Regulation 1/2003 and the Issue of Case Allocation' (2005) 42 CML Rev 1383, 1385.

[144] R Smits, 'The European Competition Network: Selected Aspects' (2005) 32 LIEI 175, 179; EC Commission (n 115 above) [8].

[145] Regulation 1, Art 11(6).

[146] See generally, EC Commission, Annual Report on Competition Policy (2008) COM(2009) 374 final, 23.7 [114].

for the Network meet more frequently. Sectoral sub-groups deal with specific sectors of the economy, eg energy, transport, the liberal professions, with the number of groups varying depending on what is under discussion. There are about sixteen at the moment. As well as these sectoral sub-groups there are also Working Groups that deal with cross-cutting issues like due process and vertical agreements. They meet as (in)frequently as required. The Network has its own website on the DGComp site where the ECN brief can be accessed and statistics are provided on the cases being notified to the Network by its members.[147]

The lynchpin to the successful operation of the Network is the exchange of information.[148] This has a number of features. First, an NCA notifies the Commission when it opens an investigation and when it is about to take a decision.[149] In practice there are often informal exchanges with the Commission before formal notification. After notice of an imminent decision is made, the ECN unit in DGComp and the relevant sectoral unit review it within 30 days with informal discussion with the case handler if necessary. The notices are shared with other NCAs. Secondly, confidential information can be shared between NCAs during an investigation. However given the divergence in sanctions, information shared cannot lead to a custodial sentence or higher sanction than that allowed in the state providing the information. It can also only be used for the subject matter collected.[150] Thirdly, one NCA can ask another to carry out an inspection of premises or other fact-finding on its behalf.[151] Outside these formal mechanisms for exchange, the Network is an important forum through which members can share best practice, seek advice, and exchange views on policies. Such exchanges reinforce the sense of common purpose and culture and also mean that even though divergence of practice and procedural norms will remain a striking feature of the system, gradually it will move to one of at least informed divergence.[152] Budzinski writing about competition internationally has suggested that diversity has a value as it allows for innovation in thinking on economic theory.[153] A similar rationale can apply to law also. Thus diversity remains a challenge within the regime but it may, to some extent at least, be a strength even though it does cause some concern from a legal certainty perspective.

Enforcement of the competition rules by NCAs creates the potential for divergence in the law with NCAs having their own procedures and sanctions.[154] This risk is

---

[147] See Brammer (n 1 above) 134; Wilks (n 1 above) 440. See generally the ECN website: <http://ec.europa. eu/competition/ecn/index_en.html> and also the EC Commission, Annual Report on Competition 2006 [69].

[148] D Reichelt, 'To What Extent Does the Co-operation within the European Competition Network Protect the Rights of Undertakings?' (2005) 42 CML Rev 745 ; K Dekeyser and E De Smijter, 'The Exchange of Evidence within the ECN and how it Contributes to the European Co-operation and Co-ordination in Cartel Cases' (2005) 32 LIEI 161.

[149] Regulation 1, Art 11(3) and (4). As of the end of September 2010 NCAs had notified 1,256 investigations and 441 decisions. Clearly, not all investigations lead to formal decisions.

[150] Regulation 1, Art 12; Reichelt (n 148 above).

[151] Regulation 1, Art 22.

[152] Slaughter (n 129 above) 171.

[153] O Budzinski, 'Monoculture versus Diversity in Competition Economics' (2008) 32 Cambridge Journal of Economics 295.

[154] Riley (n 1 above); Smits (n 144 above).

exacerbated by the fact there is no definition of what an NCA is. All the Regulation says is that the Member States shall designate such an authority in such as way that the provisions of the Regulation are effectively complied with. Thus there is considerable variety as between NCAs and their powers and procedures. This is not necessarily a problem as the embeddedness of an agency within the national legal order is one of its strengths provided it is sufficiently independent from the executive to carry out its roles effectively. The European Court made it clear in Syfait that at least in relation to Article 267[155] references, it would not accept statutory statements as to independence from the executive but would examine substantively to see if an NCA was sufficiently independent to constitute a tribunal that can make a reference. In this instance, it decided that the Greek Authority was not such a tribunal because, despite the statement of independence in the legislation, the Court took the view that it was subject to Ministerial supervision and its members could be summarily dismissed or their contracts terminated.[156] The judgment did not seem to have any adverse effect on the operation of the Network—the level of independence required for a preliminary reference not being critical to the professionalism and autonomy of the NCAs. In fact, the Network has proved disciplined, generating very little adverse comment and is seen as operating well.[157]

Procedural and sanctioning variation gave rise to difficulty initially in relation to leniency programmes that give immunity from sanctions to whistleblowers in cartels. Because several Member States did not have any programme and an NCA can only offer immunity in its own jurisdiction, this undermined the effectiveness of cartel enforcement as whistleblowers were more reluctant to come forward.[158] An ECN Working Group devised a model programme and all heads of NCAs publicly committed to use their best efforts to align their own programmes with the model. This reform—again reliant on policy learning and voluntariness, has improved matters with only two jurisdictions now without a programme.[159] This shows the extent to which NCAs can coordinate their own systems to ensure better enforcement of the EU rules.

E. CONCLUSION

It is possible to examine competition law from an evolutionary perspective even if the process of change has been episodic rather than gradual. The changes wrought in relation to enforcement of EU competition rules by the Courts have yet to acquire traction in practice with the Commission continuing to debate with stakeholders how to devise an effective system of private enforcement of competition rules. The national

---

[155] Previously Art 234 EC.
[156] C-53/05 *Syfait v GlaxoSmithKline* [2005] ECR I-4609. See Maher and Stefan (n 98 above).
[157] Wilks, ibid 440 and 442; Communication (n 112 above).
[158] Brammer (n 143 above) 1408.
[159] Communication (n 112 above) [32].

courts have new powers and the relationship between the courts and the executive agencies at national and European level is also radical but in practice information on how (or if) these powers are playing out across the EU is limited suggesting that evolution in relation to judicial enforcement will remain gradual with diversity a continuing hallmark.

The creation of the ECN attracted far more attention than reforms relating to the Courts. This classic institutional form closely associated with governance methods supported by soft law measures, while drawing on techniques common in other areas of EU law and building on a tradition of soft law in the competition field, nonetheless has proved to be a radical change that has proved remarkably stable despite the wide diversity of procedures, sanctions, and practices found among its members. Radical change does not remove the importance of an institutional analysis but it does create a greater onus to explain that change in the light of the presumption of gradual path-dependence and the extent to which new institutions reflect or are a reaction to previous practice. The rapidly embedded network shows that diversity may be necessary for evolution, and ultimately that convergence born of the common culture and mission of the agencies may in the long term prove to be the most enduring outcome.

24

THE COMING OF AGE OF EU REGULATION OF NETWORK INDUSTRIES AND SERVICES OF GENERAL ECONOMIC INTEREST

Leigh Hancher* and Pierre Larouche**

A. INTRODUCTION

This chapter highlights key trends in the evolution of EU law in the period since publication of the first edition as regards the regulation of network industries and of services of general economic interest (SGEIs) more generally. We cannot and will not claim to make an exhaustive chronicle of all developments; this would be tedious and would vastly exceed the scope of this contribution.

Our aim is rather to take a more theoretical and critical view of the evolving relationships between the EU institutions, the market, and the national state, from our perspective as legal academics with an inter-disciplinary approach and with practical experience. The focus is primarily on two network sectors which have been the subject of extensive regulation—electronic communications and energy—and on the application of Article 106 TFEU to those sectors of the economy where the tensions between Community, state, and market have remained, to quote the recent Monti report, a 'persistent irritant' in the European public debate.[1]

* Professor of European Law and member of the Tilburg Law and Economics Center (TILEC), Tilburg University. Of Counsel, Allen & Overy.

** Professor of Competition Law and co-director, TILEC, Tilburg University, <pierre.larouche@uvt.nl>, papers available on SSRN. This contribution was prepared while on leave as Searle Visiting Fellow at Northwestern University, with the financial support of the Hague Institute for the Internationalization of Law (HiiL), project 100-16-503. This contribution relies on earlier work and it has benefited from the comments of many colleagues, including the participants in the 20th Anniversary Conference of CRID, held in Namur on 21 January 2010.

[1] M Monti, *A New Strategy for the single Market, at the Service of Europe's Economy and Society*, Report to the President of the European Commission, 9 May 2000, 73.

Our central claim is that over the relevant period of time, EU regulation of network industries has been—and still is—in the process of moving from one legal paradigm to another. This not merely a shift from state to market or indeed from state to Community. The process is more complex. It can only be understood by analysing both the substantive rules as well as the institutional architecture as these have evolved over the past two decades.

The first paradigm, which EU regulation is moving away from, is more traditional, static, formalistic, and self-contained (mono-disciplinary). Its hallmark is the use of legal definitions and concepts to create categories in which phenomena are placed, by way of pigeonholing or labelling, and to which consequences are attached. The underlying problems—including jurisdictional and enforcement problems—are thereby avoided. More specifically, that paradigm can be observed most clearly in instances where the law introduces a separation between two categories, whether in substance (liberalized or reserved services) or in the institutions (EU or Member State powers).

The second paradigm, towards which EU regulation is progressing, is more dynamic, integrative, and inter-disciplinary. Its hallmark is the use of general guidelines and principles (based on economic insights) to assess specific situations in a wider sectoral setting, with progressive refinement, until the point where a conclusion can be reached and consequences attached. In other words this paradigm is characterized not by separation, but rather by integration (in substance as well as institutionally). It is not mono-disciplinary or formalistic, but draws on other disciplines to inform regulatory choice as well to guide assessment of regulatory outcomes.

As this chapter will seek to explain, an analysis of the regulation of network industries, both in substantive and institutional terms, suggests that in any event EU law is shifting between a traditional formalistic pigeonholing model and a more integrative model which seeks to manage competition and not just to guarantee market access.

This in turn has generated a multi-layered institutional structure in which the interaction of Community and state is by no means hierarchical or even based on a gradual linear transfer of key powers. The substitution of state control of complex economic sectors with a centralized or 'one-stop' institutional structure based on far-reaching or maximum harmonization of *ex ante* regulation has not been the pattern of institutional reform in the network sectors.

This legal evolution is not taking place in a vacuum. Our contention is that legal formalism may be better suited to a single-minded pursuit of market opening and market access, that is to the initial task of building a single market, which drove EU policy in the 1990s. Given that the single market was all but absent in network industries, tensions were bound to arise as ambitious liberalization projects were undertaken. It would then have been appropriate to use a formalistic model to establish market opening and market access firmly amongst the legal categories and defuse tensions by turning them into classification exercises. Starting from the 2000s, however, market opening and access becomes settled as a central policy objective, and at the same time other policy objectives which had taken a backseat in the 1990s began to re-assert themselves. For instance, the need to keep the European economy competitive and innovative requires a constant stream of investment in upgrading not only electronic communications, but also energy and transport infrastructures. Environmental concerns, including sustainability and climate change, dictate that the energy and transport sectors be managed and operated differently. These changes lead to social concerns about access, inequality, and exclusion as network industries and public services undergo transformations. These concerns are not antithetic to market opening, quite to the contrary; they can probably more efficiently be addressed in an open market context. Nevertheless, we are moving from a single focus on market access and market opening to a more complex policy setting—which we term 'managed competition'. At the legal level, a formalistic paradigm may prove inadequate for managed competition, where many policy objectives intersect.

In the following pages, we will trace this process of paradigm shift, first, in relation to the substance of EU regulation of network industries, including also Article 106(2) TFEU as the central conceptual foundation for such regulation and, secondly, in relation to the institutions used for such regulation.

B. SUBSTANTIVE LAW

As far as the substance of the law is concerned, the evolution of electronic communications law (Section 1) most vividly exemplifies the tension between the two paradigms exposed above, ie the shift from a formalistic to a more integrative approach. The existing regulatory framework, has, as recognized by the Monti report,[2] been instrumental in market opening but has not yet created a single regulatory space for electronic communication. In the next section (Section 2), we will compare the evolution of energy law and the extent to which a paradigm shift has occurred here also. The challenges faced in both sectors are considerable but by no means identical. The energy market, unlike the electronic communications market, remains dominated by the presence of natural monopolies—ie the transmission system networks. Although this may indeed justify a more formalistic approach, grounded in the first paradigm, strains and cracks in the system are now evident. Both telecommunications and energy-related services and their infrastructures remain highly fragmented along national borders. Finally we will turn to certain general substantive developments under Article 106(2) TFEU (Section 3). As mentioned, this Article remains of paramount importance for non-harmonized sectors but its interplay with secondary legislation is also reflective of the gradual paradigm shift identified in this chapter.

---

[2] ibid 44.

1. ELECTRONIC COMMUNICATIONS LAW

In the run-up to liberalization, from the 1980s through the lifting of remaining monopolies in 1998, EU regulation essentially turned around the dividing line between liberalized services and reserved services which could be kept under monopoly. The original liberalization package of Directive 90/388 kept under 'reserved services' all of the infrastructure as well as 'public voice telephony'—the latter concept being defined in a very intricate fashion in order to allow, broadly speaking, fixed telecommunications services to business customers to be liberalized.[3] Even if 'public voice telephony' might sound restrictively defined, in fact more than 80 per cent of the sector as it existed at the time was left in the reserved services category. In legal terms, the road to telecommunications liberalization throughout the 1990s is a story of how the borderline between reserved and liberalized services was progressively shifted until no services were reserved any longer: first came mobile and satellite communications,[4] then cable TV networks,[5] then infrastructure used to provide liberalized services (so-called 'alternative infrastructure'),[6] and finally the removal of all remaining monopoly rights on 1 January 1998.[7] Throughout the period, the mechanics of regulation, as laid out in the various amendments to Directive 90/388[8] and in the set of parallel Directives enacted under what is now Article 114 TFEU,[9] was simple: sets of reserved and non-reserved (liberalized) services were defined, and then key regulatory issues concerning reserved services and their interface with liberalized services (interconnection, universal service) were dealt with, together with market access to the provision of liberalized services (licensing).

---

[3] Commission Directive (EEC) 90/388 on competition in the markets for telecommunications services [1990] OJ L192/10, Art 1(1).

[4] Commission Directive (EC) 94/46 amending Directive 88/301/EEC and Directive 90/388/EEC in particular with regard to satellite communications [1994] OJ L268/15.

[5] Commission Directive (EC) 95/51 amending Directive 90/388/EEC with regard to the abolition of the restrictions on the use of cable television networks for the provision of already liberalized telecommunications services [1995] OJ L256/49.

[6] Commission Directive (EC) 96/19 amending Directive 90/388/EEC with regard to the implementation of full competition in telecommunications markets [1996] OJ L74/13.

[7] ibid.

[8] Commission Dir 90/388 (n 3 above), as amended by Commission Directive 94/46 (n 4 above), Commission Directive 95/51 (n 5 above) and Commission Directive 96/19 (n 6 above).

[9] Council Directive (EEC) 90/387 on the establishment of the internal market for telecommunications services through the implementation of open network provision [1990] OJ L192/1 (as amended by EP and Council Directive (EC) 97/51 amending Council Directives 90/387/EEC and 92/44/EEC for the purpose of adaptation to a competitive environment in telecommunications [1997] OJ L295/23); Council Directive (EEC) 92/44 on the application of open network provision to leased lines [1992] OJ L165/27 (as amended by Directive 97/51); EP and Council Directive (EC) 97/33 on interconnection in Telecommunications with regard to ensuring universal service and interoperability through application of the principles of Open Network Provision (ONP) [1997] OJ L199/32; EP and Council Directive (EC) 98/10 on the application of open network provision (ONP) to voice telephony and on universal service for telecommunications in a competitive environment [1998] OJ L101/24; EP and Council Directive (EC) 97/13 on a common framework for general authorizations and individual licences in the field of telecommunications services [1997] OJ L117/15.

(a) A first step out of formalism: the ONP 1998 framework

In 1996–97, as the EU institutions debated the regulatory framework to be applied after liberalization, as of 1 January 1998, it became clear that since the reserved/non-reserved services dichotomy would vanish, regulation would have to be articulated along different lines. Fundamentally, the issue is 'why regulate?' or in other words, where to find the justification for regulation, if any, now that no special or exclusive rights remain. Broadly speaking, there are three possible answers to that question:

- *History*: regulation aims to mitigate the ongoing consequences of the 'original sin' of special or exclusive rights, in which case it will typically be targeted at firms which used to hold such rights;

- *Technology*: regulation aims to ensure that a technological system performs in line with expectations as they might have been formulated in policy. For that purpose, certain elements or features in the system might require regulation;

- *Economics*: regulation aims to ensure that the operation of market forces in a given sector produces the desired effects, as defined in policy. Regulation is then required when there is a risk of market failure, and it will be imposed following economic analysis, upon such firms and under such circumstances as are required to address that risk.

In Directive 96/19, the full liberalization Directive based on Article 106(3) TFEU, the Commission did not reflect at length on the foundation for future regulation, knowing that the provisions of the Directive would be superseded by the more extensive Open Network Provision (ONP) network then being debated in Council and Parliament.[10] It chose a decidedly historic approach, attaching regulation to 'telecommunications organizations', meaning those firms which once held special or exclusive rights.[11] Given that these firms are easily identifiable, regulation continued to be articulated around the formalistic paradigm described above.

In the course of preparing the ONP 1998 Directives,[12] the EU institutions had to take a more forward-looking approach. So the institutions were left to choose between technology and economics as the main articulation for regulation. A choice was made in favour of the latter, but it is neither clearly worked out nor applied consistently. Heavier regulation is made to rest on firms holding Significant Market Power (SMP), but SMP is defined rigidly as a 25 per cent share[13] of one of a series of pre-defined markets.[14] The content of such regulation is already determined in the Directive itself.

---

[10] As reflected in the text of Arts 4a and 4c of Commission Directive 90/388 (n 3 above) as amended by Commission Directive 96/19 (n 6 above).

[11] ibid.   [12] See n 9 above.

[13] With the possibility to stray from the 25 per cent threshold either way: Council Directive 97/33 (n 9 above) Art 4(3).

[14] These are defined peremptorily in Annex I of Council Directive 97/33, ibid, as (i) fixed public telephone network, (ii) fixed public telephone services, (iii) leased lines, as well as (iv) interconnection for mobile networks and services.

Furthermore, the ONP 1998 framework must still bear with technical definitions such as 'telecommunications network', 'telecommunications service', including 'public' networks and services, as well as 'interconnection', 'network termination point', etc.

(b) The 2002 framework as the best example of integration

The current regulatory framework for electronic communications (2002 framework)—often referred to as the 'new regulatory framework'—resulted from the review of the ONP 1998 framework. It is embodied in four Directives enacted in 2002.[15] This framework provides the best illustration so far of the integrative paradigm in the regulation of network industries in the EU.

The choice for an economics-based approach is confirmed and enshrined, as reflected in two key principles of the 2002 framework, namely *reliance on economic analysis* and *technological neutrality*.

As regards reliance on economic analysis, the 2002 framework is no longer built around a set of categories to which consequences are attached, rather it relies on economic analysis. The main component, the SMP regime, mimics competition law analysis. In a first step, markets are defined and selected for further analysis (without being pre-determined in legislation[16]). Subsequently, the degree of competition on these selected relevant markets is assessed with a view to identifying firms holding SMP. SMP is defined as dominance by another name. Thirdly, if one or more firms are found to have SMP, remedies are imposed. These remedies are chosen from a list of available remedies found in legislation;[17] however that legislation does not prescribe any specific remedy for any given case. The relationship between the 2002 framework and competition law has always been controversial. At the substantive level, the initial stance was that the 2002 framework was actually incorporating by reference key competition law concepts such as relevant market definition and dominance. Indeed the Commission seems to consider that the analysis conducted under the 2002

---

[15] EP and Council Directive (EC) 2002/19 on access to, and interconnection of, electronic communications networks and associated facilities (Access Directive) [2002] OJ L108/7; EP and Council Directive (EC) 2002/20 on the authorisation of electronic communications networks and services (Authorisation Directive) [2002] OJ L108/21; EP and Council Directive (EC) 2002/21 on a common regulatory framework for electronic communications networks and services (Framework Directive) [2002] OJ L108/33; EP and Council Directive (EC) 2002/22 on universal service and users' rights relating to electronic communications networks and services (Universal Service Directive) [2002] OJ L108/51; to which one should add Commission Directive (EC) 2002/77 on competition in the markets for electronic communications networks and services [2002] OJ L249/21.

[16] The first Recommendation on relevant markets, Commission Recommendation 2003/311 on relevant product and service markets within the electronic communications sector susceptible to ex ante regulation in accordance with Directive 2002/21/EC of the European Parliament and of the Council on a common regulatory framework for electronic communication networks and services [2003] OJ L114/45, was based on a list of markets found in Annex I to Directive 2002/21, ibid, but the second one was established without prior legislative determination: Commission Recommendation 2007/879 on relevant product and service markets within the electronic communications sector susceptible to ex ante regulation in accordance with Directive 2002/21/EC of the European Parliament and of the Council on a common regulatory framework for electronic communications networks and services [2007] OJ L344/65.

[17] Regulatory authorities can also propose other remedies, subject to Commission approval: Directive 2002/19 (n 15 above) Art 8(3).

framework has precedent value for competition law.[18] Yet at the same time the subsequent evolution has brought some distance between the two: the Recommendation on relevant markets made it clear that market selection was a crucial step in the application of the SMP regime. The 'three-criteria test' used for market selection—high and persistent barriers to entry, limited prospect for effective competition behind such barriers, comparative inefficiency of competition law—obviously entails economic analysis, but it has no equivalent in competition law.[19] It merges certain elements of relevant market and of market power analysis into a stand-alone analytical step which does capture the specificities of a network industry like electronic communications, ie the presence of high and persistent barriers to entry in some parts of the industry, essentially due to sunk costs or network effects. So in the end the 2002 framework shares with competition law the reliance on economic analysis, but it does not necessarily follow the same analytical mould. After all, the 'relevant market—market assessment—remedies' trilogy, characteristic of competition law, is not the only way to incorporate solid economic analysis into law.

The universal service regime provides another example of reliance on economic analysis. According to the Universal Service Directive,[20] Member States are not obliged to impose universal service obligations, for example if market forces would suffice to ensure that a service meeting the requirements of the definition of universal service is provided. If they determine that universal service obligations must be imposed, then the addressee of the obligations must be assessed in an open, transparent, and non-discriminatory procedure (including for instance an auction). Financial compensation on the addressee, if any, is limited to the net costs of providing universal service, and then only if that represents an unfair burden on the addressee (taking into account, for instance, the intangible benefits arising from providing universal service and the administrative costs of running a compensation mechanism). The financial compensation mechanism itself must be transparent and minimize distortion to the market.

Technological neutrality is often overlooked, yet central to the advances brought about by the 2002 framework. It is explained somewhat vaguely as 'neither impos[ing] nor discriminat[ing] in favour of the use of a particular type of technology'.[21] Technological neutrality can be defined in many ways.[22] A weak definition would not go much beyond a simple non-discrimination rule, but that would limit the added value of the principle, considering that non-discrimination is already a well-established legal

[18] See P Larouche and M de Visser, 'The Triangular Relationship between the Commission, NRAs and National Courts Revised' (2006) 64 Communications & Stratégies 124.

[19] Recommendation 2007/879 (n 16 above) [2]. In fact, it can be argued that market selection is the 'triggering factor' that is most material in the outcome, much like 'abuse' is the triggering factor in the application of Art 102 TFEU (given that dominant firms will not infringe Art 102 TFEU unless they abuse their position).

[20] Council Directive 2002/22 (n 15 above) Arts 3, 8–14.

[21] Council Directive 2002/21 (n 15 above) recital 18.

[22] I Van der Haar, *The Principle of Technological Neutrality: Connecting EC Network and Content Regulation* (2008), upon which the following discussion is based.

principle. A stronger definition would entail that the law is drafted and applied in such a way as to be sustainable over time against the background of diverse and evolving technologies, ie that the law is not tied to a specific technological model. The third and strongest definition, with a more economic underpinning, would imply that the law avoids influencing or distorting technological choices, leaving them to market forces as much as possible. The second and third definitions are mutually reinforcing and should be preferred, as they give technological neutrality its fullest meaning. In any event, just as the reliance on economic analysis shows that the EU law-makers chose to base regulation on economic justifications, the principle of technological neutrality evidences *a contrario* that the law-makers did not want to build the 2002 framework on technological categories and concepts. To be sure, some of the further implementing decisions may be open to criticism as regards technological neutrality,[23] but by and large the EU and its Member States have sought to live by that principle.

Once a choice is made in favour of economics as opposed to technology as the main justification for regulation—as enshrined in the two principles discussed above—the resulting framework will unavoidably tilt towards the second paradigm. So it can be seen that the mainstay of the 2002 framework, the SMP regime, eschews pigeonholing: the definitions of 'electronic communications networks' and 'electronic communications services', for instance, have been broadened to cover all conceivable types of networks and services provided over such networks,[24] 'interconnection' has been repositioned as a subset of access,[25] the distinction between public and non-public networks and services has been downplayed, to name but the main ones. What remains is a light regulatory framework applicable across the board to all market players, plus a heavier regime for firms holding SMP. The SMP regime does not work with pigeonholes, rather it comprises a series of guiding principles,[26] with an analytical framework,[27] and offering a choice of possible remedies.[28] Throughout, the 2002 framework relies on economic concepts and therefore takes an inter-disciplinary approach; it cannot be administered using traditional legal methods only. It is meant to be applied by a specialized National Regulatory Authority (NRA), working on the basis of a Commission recommendation indicating which markets must be reviewed.

---

[23] See for instance the continued reluctance to include broadband networks based on cable TV, on the one hand, and on ADSL, on the other hand, on the same market for the purpose of SMP analysis: Recommendation 2007/879 (n 16 above) and the Explanatory Note, C(2007) 5406 (17 December 2007) 31.

[24] This was the outcome of one of the key policy discussions which fed into the 2002 framework, concerning the convergence between the telecommunications, media and ICT sectors: see Green Paper on the Convergence of the Telecommunications, Media and Information Technology Sectors, and the Implications For Regulation, COM(97) 623 and the subsequent consultation rounds.

[25] This did not eliminate all game-playing around definitions, given that Council Directive 2002/19 (n 15 above) Art 4 extends the obligation to negotiate interconnection only to the benefit of providers of public electronic communications networks: the ECJ became entangled in this issue in Case C-227/07 *Commission v Poland* [2008] ECR I-8403.

[26] Common to the whole of the 2002 framework: Council Directive 2002/21 (n 15 above) Art 8.

[27] Council Directive 2002/21, ibid Arts 14–16.

[28] Council Directive 2002/19 (n 15 above), Arts 9–13; Council Directive 2002/22 (n 15 above) Art 17.

The Commission recommendation and the NRA decisions are reviewed periodically, ensuring that regulation evolves in tune with the sector.[29]

(c) Remaining instances of separation

Unfortunately, some remainders of the formalistic paradigm can still be found in electronic communications regulation, in the form of strict separation between two categories.

For one, the whole of EU electronic communications regulation is itself put in a box, namely that of 'networks' or 'transport' as opposed to 'content', ie what is carried on over the networks. Content regulation is expressly left outside of the 2002 framework.[30] Instead, it is covered in two Directives, the Audiovisual Media Services Directive (formerly 'Television Without Frontiers')[31] and the E-commerce Directive.[32] This creates an intricate system of pigeonholes, whereby services are supposed to fall under one and only one of the following: 'electronic communications services',[33] 'Information Society Services' (falling under the E-commerce Directive),[34] or 'audiovisual media services'.[35] Considering the rapid rate of innovation in this sector and the efforts deployed to find the 'killer application', such a pigeonholing approach can only hamper the development of the sector by forcing firms to navigate around the definitions to seek the preferred regulatory regime, instead of simply ensuring that their activities are in line with public policy objectives as they may be articulated in regulation. For instance, in the recent reform of broadcasting regulation, most energies were dedicated not to reconsidering the appropriateness and the manner of regulation in a converged environment, but rather to chisel away at the definition of 'broadcasting' (or linear) and 'on-demand' (or non-linear) audiovisual media services in order to position certain services within one or the other box, or outside of them altogether.[36] As a result of this separation between network and content (and within content between the various types of services), a key issue such as network neutrality, which involves the relationship between content providers and network operators, cannot be

---

[29] Indeed, when revising the first Recommendation on relevant markets (n 16 above), the Commission removed eleven markets from the list, to reflect the changes which took place between 2003 and 2008.

[30] Council Directive 2002/21 (n 15 above) rec 5, Arts 1(3) and 2(c).

[31] Council Directive (EEC) 89/552 on the coordination of certain provisions laid down by law, regulation or administrative action in Member States concerning the provision of audiovisual media services (Audiovisual Media Services Directive) [1989] OJ L298/23, as amended by EP and Council Directive (EC) 2007/65 amending Council Directive 89/552/EEC on the coordination of certain provisions laid down by law, regulation or administrative action in Member States concerning the pursuit of television broadcasting activities [2007] OJ L332/27.

[32] EP and Council Directive (EC) 2000/31 on certain legal aspects of information society services, in particular electronic commerce, in the Internal Market ('Directive on electronic commerce') [2000] OJ L178/1.

[33] Council Directive 2002/21 (n 15 above) Art 2(c).

[34] Council Directive 2000/31 (n 32 above) Art 2(a).

[35] Council Directive 89/552 (n 31 above) Art 1(a).

[36] ibid Art 1(a), (e) and (g), as well as Council Directive 2007/65 (n 31 above) recitals 16–25. See also Van der Haar (n 22 above).

addressed within the SMP regime, for instance.[37] It falls to be dealt with either in specific legislation or via EU competition law.

Secondly, the separation between competition law and sector-specific regulation—at the systemic level—also hampers the proper evolution of the sector. Even though sector-specific regulation and competition law are closely aligned in substance as was seen above, the mainstream opinion remains that the two realms are fundamentally different: for instance, competition law would be operating *ex post* and would aim at preserving existing competition on the market, whereas sector-specific regulation would be imposed *ex ante* and would aim to increase the level of competition on the market. In separate writing, one of us has sought to demonstrate that these distinctions cannot hold and that the two realms are largely overlapping.[38] In any event, a corollary of that mainstream opinion is that sector-specific regulation is bound to vanish, so that ultimately the sector would be policed through competition law alone. The evolution of electronic communications law in the past decade tends to show that, even if sector-specific regulation is withdrawn in certain areas, it appears in others.[39] Sector-specific regulation will accordingly not disappear any time soon. A perverse consequence of the mainstream opinion, however, is that regulatory authorities behave very expansively in seeking new regulatory endeavours, in order to stave off the sunset of regulation and their own disappearance.[40] From such a public choice perspective, then, it might have been preferable to emphasize that some regulation could remain in place, as long as it was no more than necessary and closely integrated with competition law, instead of separating the realms of competition law and regulation.

2. ENERGY

Europe's energy sector has been radically transformed from a highly monopolistic, vertically integrated, state-owned or state-controlled sector, organized on national lines and focused on national policy objectives. Although the goal of establishing a single energy market remains a complex and laborious task which is far from complete, few would disagree that the sector is now competitive, or could deny that the institutional changes that have taken place since the adoption of the first internal energy market legislation in the mid-1990s are considerable.

---

[37] F Chirico, I van der Haar, and P Larouche, 'Network Neutrality in the EU', TILEC Discussion Paper 2007-30, available on SSRN at <http://papers.ssrn.com/abstract=1018326>.

[38] See P Larouche, 'A Closer Look at Some Assumptions Underlying EC Regulation of Electronic Communications' (2002) 3 J Netw Indust 129.

[39] For instance, since the 2002 framework was enacted, regulation of mobile operators has increased, with regulatory intervention on mobile termination, international roaming, SMS termination, and international data roaming.

[40] For one, the most regarded NRA, Ofcom, has taken the habit of launching broad consultations—on the FCC model—on various topics of interest, in order to assess whether and, if so, which regulatory intervention is warranted. See in recent years the Strategic Review of Telecoms or the Next Generation Access consultation round, to name but the main ones.

The first and second 'packages' of internal energy market legislation conformed to the established approach to network sectors—to ensure market access by removing formal, national regulatory and organizational barriers which had served to privilege incumbent national energy companies. The first Directives of 1996 (electricity)[41] and 1998 (gas),[42] were framework measures, leaving substantial discretion to Member States on the speed of liberalization as well as the method to accomplish it.

Unsurprisingly, traditional market privileges enjoyed by state-dominated incumbents—including import/export rights, as well as monopolies over the production and transport of gas and electricity were removed. Ensuring access to national networks and to national markets for new players was however the principal aim of both the first and second packages. Thus a twin-track approach was first elaborated in 1996: the unbundling of the natural monopolistic functions of the 'TSOs' (transmission system operators) and the introduction of *ex ante* regulatory functions which were to be separated out from operational functions.[43] Whereas many national energy incumbents had been entrusted with wide-ranging public service obligations (PSOs) which included responsibility for maintaining energy security and reliability of supply as well as the provision of electricity and gas at low cost to all users, the adoption of the first Directives heralded the end of that golden age. Competitive, open markets would ensure security and reliability as well as consumer choice.

(a) The second regulatory package of 2003

Subsequent regulation elaborated on this twin track approach. In 2003 when the second package of internal market measures was adopted,[44] the concept of functional unbundling or separation was further elaborated upon and the Directives required further legal separation of the transmission function, so that TSOs had to create separate legal entities to operate their networks and to put in place various 'firewalls' and compliance codes to prevent covert discrimination in favour of their own production or trading subsidiaries. Distribution companies were subject only to administrative unbundling, however. A larger group of consumers, extending to all 'non-domestic' users became eligible to choose a supplier either from another Member State or from a national competitor to the local incumbent. By July 2007 all consumers were eligible to choose their suppliers. In order to protect vulnerable consumers, additional

---

[41] EP and Council Directive (EC) 96/92 concerning common rules for the internal market in electricity [1997] OJ L27/20.

[42] EP and Council Directive (EC) 98/30 concerning common rules for the internal market in natural gas [1998] OJ L204/1.

[43] See M Roggenkamp *et al* (eds), *Energy Law in Europe: National, EU and International Law and Institutions* (2nd edn, Oxford University Press, 2006).

[44] EP and Council Directive (EC) 2003/54 concerning common rules for the internal market in electricity and repealing Directive 96/92/EC [2003] OJ L176/37; EP and Council Directive (EC) 2003/55 concerning common rules for the internal market in natural gas and repealing Directive 98/30/EC [2003] OJ L176/57; EP and Council Regulation (EC) 1228/2003 on conditions for access to the network for cross-border exchanges in electricity [2003] OJ L176/1; EP and Council Regulation (EC) 1775/2005 on conditions for access to the natural gas transmission networks [2005] OJ L289/1.

regulatory concepts such as 'suppliers of last resort' and universal supply obligations were now introduced.

The second package of 2003 Directives also sharpened sectoral regulation to a certain extent. Member States now had to designate independent national regulatory authorities (NRAs). In addition, two Regulations on cross-border trade in electricity and in gas entrusted these bodies with enhanced *ex ante* powers, not just to regulate transmission access tariff methodologies and conditions, but also to address complex technical issues, such as congestion management—that is, the allocation of capacity available in the energy networks, balancing, and ancillary services. The Commission was empowered to extend and deepen this process through the Comitology procedure. This in turn has allowed for the development of a further trend: the increasing harmonization of technical or so-called non-essential measures, as well as tariff methodologies, at European level, with a concomitant decrease in national sovereignty. Economic decisions, ie on tariff rates, remain with the Member States. Thus a further layer of separation has emerged between economic and technical regulation on the one hand, and national and European energy legislation on the other. Member States continued to enjoy considerable freedom to regulate production and supply activities, however, subject only to minimal harmonization requirements. The Directives did not confer on NRAs any powers to deal with market power or its abuse; this is left to competition law. Insofar as market forces did not deliver, the remedy was to be found essentially in the application of competition law by the Commission or the national competition authorities (NCAs), as opposed to *ex ante* regulation. The activities of TSOs, pigeonholed as natural monopolies, are the main focus of harmonized *ex ante* regulation. In the 2003 Directives, TSOs are also deemed to be primarily responsible for guaranteeing security of supply as well as preferential access to the network for renewable energy. Insofar as new investments were to be undertaken by non-TSO parties, an elaborate exemption procedure was introduced to encourage the construction of cross-border infrastructure. At the same time, however, the second package failed to provide a harmonized regulatory framework to coordinate national decision-making on cross-border issues—national legislation was harmonized but trade across national borders could not benefit from any form of joint decision-making.

Indeed, that this form of pigeonholing would soon reach its inevitable limits, is illustrated by the recent *Federutility* case,[45] where the Court was required to establish the limits of the role of the Italian NRA in imposing PSOs on the liberalized gas market in the absence of effective competition. The Italian energy regulator had elected to fix 'reference prices' for the sale of gas to certain customers by way of *ex ante* regulation. First, the Court noted that the price for the supply of natural gas must, as from 1 July 2007, be determined solely by market forces, a requirement that follows from the very purpose of the total liberalization of the market for national gas. However, the Court

---

[45] Case C-265/08 *Federutility* [2010] All ER 116.

also recognized that it was apparent that Directive 2003/55 is also designed to guarantee that 'high standards' of public service are maintained and the final consumer is protected.[46] Article 3(2) expressly allows Member States to impose 'public service obligations' on gas companies, which could relate to the 'price of supply'. Secondly, the Court also confirmed that—irrespective of harmonization—Member States are entitled to define the scope of their 'public service obligations' and to take account of their own national policy objectives and national circumstances. As a result, the Court concluded that the Directive still allows Member States to assess, after 1 July 2007, whether it is necessary to impose measures to ensure that the price of the supply of natural gas to final consumers is maintained at a reasonable level. At the same time, the Court imposed several conditions in order to ensure that the national measure was also proportional. Significantly, as for the economic factors justifying intervention, the Court noted that, 'it is for the referring court to verify whether... taking account in particular of the objective of establishing a fully operational internal market for gas and of the investments necessary in order to exert effective competition in the natural gas sector... such an intervention is required'.[47] As a result, a more integrated, interdisciplinary approach would have to occur at the national level. Judicial review cannot be merely confined to assessing whether the NRA has the formal power under the Directive to act—a more complex assessment of the necessity to act is also required.

(b) The third regulatory package of 2009

The third package of measures adopted in August 2009[48] now attempts to address some of the major gaps that were evident in the first stages of gas and electricity market liberalization. First, the formalistic separation between the regulation of the network and other market and related functions is perhaps breaking down, as is evidenced in part by the two new Directives, which extend the role of the NRAs into more general market supervision, aligning their powers somewhat more closely to those of competition authorities. At the same time the so-called 'Climate Change package', adopted in 2008 gives both NRAs and TSOs important tasks in accomplishing the transition to a low-carbon economy by 2050. In accordance with the new Energy Directives, NRAs will be given an explicit mandate to promote sustainable and renewable forms of energy.[49]

Secondly, the third package provides for substantive rules and joint decision-making procedures on some cross-border issues, including tariffs and access to the network.

Thirdly, the new package provides for far-reaching unbundling and requires that TSOs should be structurally unbundled from production and supply functions. The

---

[46] *loc cit* para 20.   [47] *loc cit* para 37.

[48] EP and Council Directive (EC) 2009/72 concerning common rules for the internal market in electricity and repealing Directive 2003/54/EC [2009] OJ L211/55; EP and Council Directive (EC) 2009/73 concerning common rules for the internal market in natural gas and repealing Directive 2003/55/EC [2009] OJ L211/94.

[49] See Council Directive 2009/72 (n 48 above) Art 36, and Council Directive 2009/73 (n 48 above) Art 30.

ownership as well as the management of transmission system assets should be transferred to separate legal entities although 'lighter' unbundling regimes for vertically integrated companies are also contemplated in the light of national opposition to full structural unbundling. As a result, effective control of these assets, including decisions on future investments, is therefore now totally separated from production and supply interests.

Fourthly, technical or non-economic regulation is subject to extensive harmonization in the form of detailed regulation of a wide range of issues, including network codes, investment plans, cross-border procedures, the collection and processing of market data, and this by means of comprehensive annexes which can be updated through the Comitology procedure.

Finally, the third energy package seeks to separate national regulation from political control—NRAs must be independent not only from the industry but also from any political body. They must be fully resourced and there are strict rules on appointment and dismissal. Regulators must be appointed for a fixed minimum term of five years, renewable once.[50]

In accordance with the amended Renewable Energy Directive 2009/28, TSOs will have a pivotal role in meeting the EU's ambitious '20–20–20' targets in securing the development and priority dispatch of renewable energy across their networks. Albeit that the TSOs are expected to ensure that 20 per cent of Europe's energy supply is to consist of renewables by 2020, there is as yet little clarification as to how this task has to be realized and to what extent the Treaty rules on free movement of goods as well as the state aid regime will apply in this context.[51]

(c) Concluding remarks

Sector-specific energy legislation is not expected to be gradually phased out as markets mature and can be policed by general anti-trust law. Transmission systems are likely to remain natural monopolies, especially in the electricity sector. TSOs are now entrusted with extensive tasks, and must secure the promotion of renewables, reliability of supply, as well as adequate investment in their networks and in cross-border infrastructure. The integration of competition law concepts into the sector-specific regulation of TSOs is unlikely to serve this purpose. Rather, the trade-off is in terms of organization. A structurally unbundled TSO that is fully independent in legal and financial terms will be subject to 'lighter' regulation than the other less far-reaching options for the organization of the TSO function available under the third package.[52] If these alternative organizational forms are chosen, *ex ante* regulation is intrusive and exacting.

---

[50] See Council Directive 2009/72 (n 48 above) Art 34(5), and Council Directive 2009/73 (n 48 above) Art 38(5).

[51] EP and Council Directive (EC) 2009/28 on the promotion of the use of energy from renewable sources and amending and subsequently repealing Directives 2001/77/EC and 2003/30/EC [2009] OJ L140/16, Art 16.

[52] For a detailed discussion see E Cabau, in Ch Jones (ed), *The Internal Energy Market: The Third Liberalisation Package* (3rd edn, Claeys & Casteels, 2010).

3. SERVICES OF GENERAL ECONOMIC INTEREST AND ARTICLE 106(2) TFEU

The tension between a more formalistic and a more integrative approach can also be observed in the case law concerning Services of General Economic Interest (SGEIs) under Article 106(2) TFEU. That provision can be seen as a central conceptual foundation for sector-specific regulation in network industries, and until recently it was also a hallmark of the formalistic paradigm.

(a) Formalistic approach to special and exclusive rights

Indeed Article 106(2) TFEU lends itself easily to an interpretation along categorical lines, for two reasons.

First of all, Article 106(2) TFEU is an exception, an escape clause from the Treaty, in particular the provisions relating to the internal market or competition law. This has allowed this provision to be played up in grand debates about 'state versus market' where politics takes front stage, and therefore to antagonize—needlessly—what remains in essence one of the countless instances where conflicting public policy objectives must be reconciled. Most directives enacted on the basis of Article 114 TFEU also involve delicate balancing between the achievement of the internal market and competing policy objectives.[53]

Secondly, the concept of SGEI occupies an uneasy place in EU law, since it is an EU concept, subject to the powers of interpretation and monitoring of EU institutions, with a view to ensuring a uniform application throughout the EU, but at the same time it falls within the express province of Member States to decide which services are SGEIs.[54] The Commission (as well as the Courts) sought to solve this puzzle by professing to exert only marginal control on the way Member States organize SGEIs; on a closer look at the Commission decision practice,[55] however, one can argue that the control is more than just marginal. In any event, the concept of SGEI lends itself handily to a pigeonholing game between the Commission and the Member States.

The ECJ in recent years added an extra layer of complexity to the situation through an inconsistent approach to the line between 'economic' and 'non-economic' services, which runs through the Treaty, including through Article 106(2) TFEU. A number of cases—including core decisions under Article 106(2) TFEU such as *Höfner*,[56] *Pavlov*,[57]

---

[53] One needs only to think of the Directives concerning the harmonization of regulation in the financial sector, be it in the banking, insurance, or other financial markets.

[54] See the TFEU Protocol (No 26) on Services of General Interest [2010] OJ C83/310, as well as Art 36 of the Charter of Fundamental Rights of the EU.

[55] See for instance in public service broadcasting—where the position of Member States is further bolstered by TFEU Protocol (No 29) on the system of public broadcasting in the Member States [2010] OJ C83/312—where under the guise of marginal control, the Commission reviews the scope of the public mission of public broadcasters in great detail: Commission Communication on the application of State aid rules to public service broadcasting [2009] OJ C257/1 [43]–[49] and for a good illustration, Case E-3/05 *Financing of public broadcasting in Germany* [2007] OJ C185/1, paras 237–242.

[56] Case C-41/90 *Höfner* [1991] ECR I-1979.   [57] Case C-180/98 *Pavlov* [2000] ECR I-6451.

or *Ambulanz Glöckner*[58]—take an objective and maximalist approach, holding that any activity consisting in the offering of goods and services on a market is an economic activity, even if the activity is carried out by the public sector or under public service obligations. At the same time, other cases, such as *Poucet et Pistre*[59] and *AOK*,[60] have carved out a 'solidarity' exception via the definition of 'undertaking', or have used the definition of 'services' at Article 57 TFEU to exclude services organized by the state, such as higher education.[61] That line of case law also suggests that the state would have the power to take certain services out of the 'economic' basket through its legislative and regulatory measures, ie that the concept would be subjective. Given the uncertainty surrounding the line between 'economic' and 'non-economic' services, the Commission issued a series of policy documents concerned with an overarching concept of Services of General Interest (SGIs), which would include both SGEIs as well as those services which, while of general interest, remain non-economic and therefore fall outside of the purview of the Treaty competition and state aid rules.[62] This complex conceptual architecture was completed with the Treaty of Lisbon, which adds a Protocol on SGIs, comprising two provisions applicable to SGEIs and 'non-economic services of general interest', respectively.[63] The result can be seen in the following diagram:

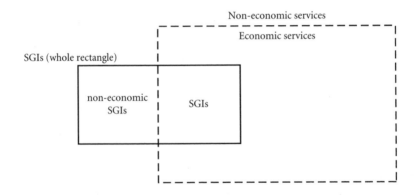

Initially, the application of Article 106(2) TFEU concerned cases of monopoly rights (and primarily, market access issues).[64] Because of the nature of monopoly rights, which must be delineated, these cases fit easily within a formalist paradigm. In the

---

[58] Case C-475/99 *Ambulanz Glöckner* [2001] ECR I-8089.
[59] Case C-159/91 *Poucet and Pistre* [1993] ECR I-637.
[60] Case C-264/01 *AOK* [2004] ECR I-2493.
[61] Case 263/86 *Humbel* [1988] ECR 5365.
[62] Green Paper on Services of General Interest, COM(2003) 270 final, White Paper on Services of General Interest, COM(2004) 374 final, Commission Communication on services of general interest, including social services of general interest: a new European commitment, COM(2007) 725 final.
[63] See n 54 above.
[64] See further, Hancher's chapter in the first edition of this volume.

original line of case law, starting with *Sacchi*,[65] the existence of the monopoly right was not challenged, but rather whether the behaviour of the holder of the right, in exercising that right, infringed the Treaty—typically Article 102 TFEU—and if so, whether Article 106(2) TFEU could apply. Starting in the late 1980s, the Commission merged Article 106(1) and (2) together to argue that the very existence of a monopoly right ran against Article 106(1) if it was not justified for a SGEI pursuant to Article 106(2). This argument underpinned the use of Article 106(3) TFEU to liberalize the telecommunications sector, and it was endorsed by the ECJ.[66] At its most elaborate, this line of argument led to a complex inquiry under Article 106(2), as seen in *Corbeau*[67] or *Glöckner*,[68] into: (i) whether the mission entrusted to the monopolist constituted an SGEI, (ii) whether the SGEI could not be profitably undertaken without the monopoly right, and (iii) whether the scope of the monopoly right was such that it delivered to the monopolist a financial stream which was sufficient to discharge the SGEI but not excessive. In theory, the second and third issues require a mix of legal and economic analysis, which echoes the integrated paradigm. But in practice, given that monopoly rights are blunt instruments, the third issue could not be answered with much precision. Since analytical accounting was not yet very developed in utilities sectors twenty years ago, the second issue was also summarily handled. This left the first issue, an issue of categorization which lent itself better to the formalistic paradigm.

(b) Public financing and the beginning of an integrative approach in *Altmark*

With the liberalization programme of the past twenty years, most large-scale monopolies in the utilities or network sectors are now removed. In the 2000s, the application of Article 106(2) shifted to another class of measures, public subsidies given to firms entrusted with a public service obligation. Initially, there was much confusion in the Commission practice and in the case law of the ECJ and the General Court,[69] having more to do with divergences on the notion of state aid at Article 107(1) TFEU than with any difficulties with Article 106(2). Two approaches emerged.[70] Under the 'state aid approach', the public subsidy given to the firm is deemed to distort competition within the meaning of Article 107(1) TFEU and therefore to constitute state aid in and of itself, even if the firm is entrusted with a public service obligation. The public service obligation can however be used to argue that the conditions of Article 106(2) TFEU are fulfilled and that an exception should be made to the prohibition of Article 107(1)

---

[65] Case 155/73 *Sacchi* [1974] ECR 409.

[66] Case C-202/88 *France v Commission* [1991] ECR I-1223 and Case C-271/90 *Spain v Commission* [1992] ECR I-5833.

[67] Case C-320/91 *Corbeau* [1993] ECR I-2533.

[68] See n 58 above.

[69] Case C-244/94 *FFSA* [1995] ECR I-4013; Case C-53/00 *Ferring* [2001] ECR I-9067; Case T-46/97 *SIC* [2000] ECR II-2125.

[70] These two approaches are best outlined in AG Jacobs' opinion in Case C-126/01 *GEMO* [2003] ECR I-13769.

TFEU.[71] In contrast, under the 'compensation approach', it is assumed that competition is distorted only if the subsidy exceeds the net extra costs imposed on the firm by the public service obligation. In other words, as long as the subsidy can be seen as compensation for these extra costs, it does not constitute state aid at all under Article 107(1) TFEU. Accordingly, Article 106(2) TFEU does not even need to be relied upon.

Matters came to a head in the pivotal *Altmark* ruling,[72] where the ECJ sought to find a compromise between the 'state aid' and 'compensation' approaches by adding to the compensation approach a number of safeguards which seemed to originate from the test used under Article 106(2) TFEU. It formulated the now-famous four *Altmark* criteria whereby a subsidy does not constitute state aid pursuant to Article 107(1) TFEU—and therefore does not need to be notified to the Commission—if:[73]

1. The recipient firm is actually required to discharge public service obligations and those obligations have been clearly defined;

2. The parameters on the basis of which the compensation is calculated have been established beforehand in an objective and transparent manner;

3. The compensation does not exceed what is necessary to cover all or part of the costs incurred in discharging the public service obligations, taking into account the relevant receipts and a reasonable profit for discharging those obligations; and

4. Where the firm which is to discharge public service obligations is not chosen in a public procurement procedure, the level of compensation has been determined on the basis of an analysis of the costs which a typical firm, well-run and adequately provided with means so as to be able to meet the necessary public service requirements, would have incurred in discharging those obligations, taking into account the relevant receipts and a reasonable profit for discharging the obligations.

In *Altmark*, the ECJ tries to push the treatment of public service obligations—certainly when it comes to those supported by subsidies—away from the formalistic paradigm inherent in Article 106(2) TFEU towards a more integrative paradigm. In essence, *Altmark* can be seen as an attempt to shift the debate away from a pigeonholing exercise, namely whether the public service mission in question constitutes an SGEI (and therefore can be used to justify limiting market access). Accordingly, the locus of the discussion is shifted to Article 107(1) TFEU, which implies that the financing of public service obligations can be accommodated from within state aid law, without the harshness and formality of a rule/exception relationship. The *Altmark* test is both more complex, since it requires greater use of economics and accounting, and more rigorous, away from the lofty discussions

---

[71] Of course, it is also possible that the aid would qualify for one of the exemptions set out under Art 107(2) and (3) TFEU and implementing legislation.

[72] Case C-280/00 *Altmark* [2003] ECR I-7747.   [73] *Altmark*, ibid [88]–[95].

on what belongs in the SGEI category. On the one hand, the concept of SGEI is evacuated—Article 106(2) TFEU does not come into play—and a vague and general idea of 'public service obligation' replaces it. Member States therefore gain some latitude as to which public service missions they want to entertain. On the other hand, the *Altmark* criteria are more severe than Article 106(2) TFEU was as regards the transparency of the public service obligation, the need to fix the rules on funding in advance, and—most importantly—the assessment of the amount of funding needed, using either a public procurement mechanism or an external efficiency benchmark. The latitude on substance is balanced with stronger procedural and financial disciplines.

Despite the daring push by the ECJ to solve the conundrum of public financing for the discharge of public service missions, that judgment left many issues open. In the seven years which have elapsed since the judgment, the most remarkable developments concern, first, the relationship between the *Altmark* test and Article 106(2) TFEU and secondly, the fourth criterion of the *Altmark* test.

(c) The relationship between *Altmark* and Article 106(2) TFEU

It is interesting to note that the Commission and the General Court—both of which preferred the 'state aid' over the 'compensation' approach before *Altmark*—seem to read *Altmark* in such a way as to bring it back into the fold of Article 106(2) TFEU. For one, the Commission, in its decision practice since 2003, seldom found that *Altmark* is applicable: typically, cases founder on the second (formula for calculating compensation known in advance) or fourth criterion, and the applicability of *Altmark* is dealt with expeditiously in a few paragraphs.[74] For example in its first decision after *Altmark*, in *BBC Digital Curriculum*,[75] the Commission held that the fourth criterion had not been met as there had been no public procurement procedure and the UK authorities had failed to provide the Commission with any information which would have allowed it to determine whether those costs could be considered as corresponding to those of a 'typical' undertaking. The Commission then went on to apply Article 106(2) to rule on the compatibility of the state aid measure. This seemed to imply that it was possible for an undertaking to receive aid that exceeded the costs of an ideal, efficient undertaking, without this resulting in overcompensation, as long as the examination was carried out under Article 106(2) TFEU. This approach has become the standard. Even though the General Court reminded the Commission to take *Altmark* seriously,[76] in practice most of the assessment continues to take place under Article 106(2) and not Article 107(1) TFEU.

---

[74] The Guidelines on state aid to public service broadcasting (n 55 above) aptly generalize this attitude when *Altmark* is mentioned and dealt with in a single paragraph [23].

[75] Case N-37/03 *BBC Digital Curriculum* [2003] OJ C271/47.

[76] Case T-266/02 *Deutsche Post AG v Commission* [2008] ECR II-1233, [74]; appeal dismissed: Case C-399/08 *Commission v Deutsche Post AG*, judgment of 2 September 2010.

Furthermore, the Commission has suggested that *Altmark* is about SGEIs, thereby further blurring the line between *Altmark* and Article 106(2) TFEU. Considering that the *Altmark* test remains entirely within Article 107(1) TFEU, it was no coincidence that the ECJ referred to 'public service obligations' rather than SGEIs, a concept found in Article 106(2) TFEU.[77] While the Commission tracked the language of *Altmark* in its policy statements, in its decision practice concerning subsidies for the roll-out of broadband networks, however, it considered that the *Altmark* criteria could only apply if the broadband project could qualify as an SGEI.[78] The latter point is subject to Commission review, whereby the definition of SGEI is further narrowed down to a concept which comes close to universal service as it is understood in secondary EU legislation, namely services which are provided to all citizens with specific availability, quality, and affordability requirements.[79] So in the end the Commission reduces the applicability of *Altmark* by introducing SGEI instead of 'public service obligation' as the ECJ intended and by narrowing SGEI down to universal service. Accordingly, most broadband cases were treated under Article 107(3)(c) TFEU instead of *Altmark* or even Article 106(2) TFEU. Most unfortunately, in *BUPA*,[80] the General Court endorsed this trend, seemingly without in-depth examination,[81] holding that 'public service obligation' as referred to in *Altmark*, means the same as SGEI within the meaning of Article 106(2) TFEU.[82] However, the Court rejects the narrow Commission reading of SGEIs as something akin to universal service.[83] Subsequent General Court cases continued to blur *Altmark* and Article 106(2) TFEU,[84] and yet other cases have underlined that the two must remain separate.[85]

(d) The efficiency of the public service firm

The fourth *Altmark* criterion—also referred to as the 'efficiency' criterion—seems to indicate that the Court requires that public services should also be organized as far as possible on market-based lines and that Member States would have to demonstrate

---

[77] Of course, one could argue that the term 'public service obligation' made sense in the specific context of *Altmark* (n 72 above) which concerned the transport sector. After all, Art 93 TFEU refers to 'public service obligations'. Yet it can be seen that, in subsequent cases, the Court continued to use 'public service obligation', even outside of the transport sector: see for instance Case C-451/03 *Servizi Ausiliari Dottori Commercialisti* [2006] ECR I-2941, [63] (provision of tax advice to individuals) or Case T-274/01 *Valmont Nederland BV* [2004] ECR II-3145, [132] (public use of a car park).

[78] Commission Guidelines for the application of State aid rules in relation to rapid deployment of broadband networks [2009] OJ C235/7, [20]–[30].

[79] This narrow reading of SGEI is put forward in the Green Paper on Services of General Interest (n 62 above).

[80] Case T-289/03 *BUPA v Commission* [2008] ECR II-81.

[81] The issue was uncontested as between the parties.

[82] ibid at recitals 162 *et seq*. The Court goes on to completely collapse the *Altmark* and Art 106(2) tests by examining, in its discussion of *Altmark* (n 72 above) the extent of the Commission review power over whether the service is an SGEI and then the actual conclusion that the service if an SGEI.

[83] ibid at recitals 186–190.

[84] See *Deutsche Post AG* (n 76 above) recitals 72–74; Case T-254/00 *Hotel Cipriani v Commission* [2008] ECR II-3269, recital 110; Case T-189/03 *ASM Brescia v Commission* [2009] ECR II-1831, recitals 124 *et seq*.

[85] Case T-354/05 *TF1 v Commission* [2009] ECR II-471, recitals 126–140.

that the most efficient operator had been selected.[86] For the Court, the optimal policy solution is a public tender entrusting the performance of the SGEI to the most efficient bidder in the market. And of course that should not only mean the national or regional market. Given that the Courts have also drawn upon the free movement rules to extend the requirements to organize some form of tender to a myriad of situations falling outside the scope of the EU public procurement regime,[87] a tender procedure would attract publicity for even the most local SGEI. At the same time, the ECJ was not prepared to stretch the limits of its own competence and require the Member States to organize tenders in all cases. Indeed to have done so might have resulted in a breach of the principle of subsidiarity (Article 5(3) TEU), especially if this had been required for areas of exclusive Member State competence, such as health care or public broadcasting. Moreover a strict requirement to hold a tender would have cast doubts on the legality of numerous existing arrangements where the operators in question had not been selected by way of a public tender.

What is of interest here is that while the introduction of the efficiency criterion opened the door to the Commission to impose a more market-based approach to public service provision, its exact degree of influence was left undefined. Rather *Altmark* raised a new set of questions—what is a typical and well-run undertaking? What are the precise benchmarks—can these also be hypothetical? And most importantly, would the efficiency test limit the freedom of the Member States to define not only the scope of their public services but also their quality? Could this fourth test provide the Commission with a vehicle for substantive 'regulation' through the application of the EU state aid regime to control the quality and not just the level of public financing for SGEIs?[88]

For instance, in *Chronopost*,[89] handed down three weeks before *Altmark*, the Court had to consider whether the Commission could and should have compared La Poste to a private operator in order to establish whether a state monopoly, La Poste, had been a source of state aid to one of its subsidiaries. The ECJ effectively acknowledged that certain services and networks do not operate on purely commercial lines. Thus, La Poste was in a very different position to that of a private operator acting under market conditions as it had been entrusted with an SGEI mission, and was the only operator on the market. The Court concluded that in the absence of any possibility of comparing La Poste with a private group of undertakings in a reserved sector, 'normal market conditions which are necessarily hypothetical, must be assessed by reference to the

---

[86] In its previous ruling in *Ferring* (n 69 above), the Court had not addressed this concept at all. Its ruling was criticized for leaving a wide discretion to Member States to finance the activities of inefficient, and invariably incumbent, firms. This would not only prevent the optimal allocation of taxpayers' money but might also allow these same firms to expand their activities into neighbouring, liberalized markets.

[87] Case C-231/03 *Coname* [2005] ECR I-7287; Case C-458/03 *Parking Brixen* [2005] ECR I-8585.

[88] See in this respect, EP and Council Regulation (EC) 1370/2007 on public passenger transport services by rail and road and repealing Regulation 1191/69 and 1107/70 [2007] OJ L315/1, recital 27. See also Case C-16/07 *Postbus-Austria* [2009] OJ L306/26, [86].

[89] Case C-83/01 P *Chronopost* [2003] ECR I-6993.

objective and verifiable elements which are available. Any assessment of a hypothetical market price would produce excessively abstract and arbitrary results ill-suited to determine any economic advantage'.[90] The correct method of assessment would have been to establish whether the price charged 'covers all the additional, variable costs incurred providing the logistical and commercial assistance, an appropriate contribution to fixed costs arising from the network and an adequate return on the capital investment in so far as it was used for [Chronopost's] competitive activity'.[91] Unfortunately the ECJ did not clarify the relationship between *Chronopost* and the fourth *Altmark* criterion in *Altmark* itself. In the meantime, several commentators have contended that *Chronopost* stands for a '*lex specialis*' which must be applied when no market exists for the services provided, and consequently no comparable operator can be found as a suitable comparator.[92]

BUPA,[93] which concerned public and private health insurance, could also be seen as a retreat from the strict approach set down in *Altmark*. There the CFI modified the efficiency criterion and held that it was not necessary to draw a comparison between the costs of the recipient and an efficient undertaking. Based on the purpose of the fourth *Altmark* criterion, the Commission was only required to satisfy itself that the compensation scheme did not entail the possibility that the compensation might result from inefficiencies on the part of the insurer subject to the scheme.

In the end, the Commission in fact applies a two-tier test, as expounded in its 2005 Community framework for state aid in the form of public service compensation.[94] It starts with a sometimes cursory examination of the four *Altmark* criteria, more often than not concluding that *Altmark* does not apply and that the subsidy in question constitutes state aid. Unless the aid is covered by one of the exemptions found in, or based on, Article 107(2) and (3) TFEU, it then proceeds to assess it under Article 106(2) TFEU, with the following steps:

- The firm receiving the subsidy is entrusted with a genuine SGEI, whereby the Commission claims to test for manifest error only.[95]

- An official act entrusts the firm with the SGEI, wherein the SGEI is specified in detail, including any compensation regime.

- The amount of compensation does not exceed what is necessary to cover the costs incurred in discharging the public service obligations, taking into account the relevant receipts and reasonable profit for discharging those obligations.

- Costs are assessed by reference to the costs of the firm in question, without benchmarking them for efficiency.

---

[90] ibid [38].   [91] ibid [40].

[92] See for example, T Mueller 'Efficiency Criteria in State Aid, (2009) European State Aid Law Quarterly vol. nr. 1, pp. 2 to 9.

[93] See n 80 above.

[94] Community framework for State aid in the form of public service compensation [2005] OJ C297/4.

[95] See n 55 above and the accompanying text.

Whilst the Commission has obviously drawn inspiration from *Altmark* in developing and refining its decision practice under Article 106(2) TFEU, it remains rather cautious as regards the fourth *Altmark* criterion. The Commission hesitates to introduce a stricter efficiency benchmark, on the *Altmark* model, in Article 106(2) TFEU. This is perhaps to be explained by the fact that the SGEI Decision, which exempts from notification any compensation measures meeting the first three criteria as further specified in its Articles 4 and 5, was in part adopted to address concerns about the retroactive effect of *Altmark*. Thus the SGEI Decision allows compensation to cover the costs of inefficient undertakings even though it provides detailed rules on entrustment, costs and revenue, and reasonable profit calculations. Furthermore it requires Member States to ensure adequate control to prevent 'over compensation', in the sense that revenues from entrusted activities should not exceed the recognized costs. A similar approach is followed in the framework.[96]

This should not prevent the Commission, though, from paying more attention to the robustness of the compensation mechanism and to its proper implementation;[97] such a supervisory task, however, is time- and labour-intensive for a thinly staffed authority like the Commission. Nevertheless, in recent broadcasting cases, the General Court has chastised the Commission for not being sufficiently rigorous in verifying the actual operation of the compensation mechanism.[98]

(e) Conclusion

Article 106(2) TFEU cannot be applied in a simple way—distinguishing a rule and an exemption to it. The formalistic paradigm, resting on a separation between the general rule that EC law applies and the exception for services falling within the SGEI category, confronts Member States with a paradox. Either they insist on their competence to decide on their public services, and they remain within the SGEI exception, subject to pressure through Commission review, or, as was done in electronic communications and energy, public service obligations—in the form of universal service—can be anchored at European level in EU legislation, so as to balance them with internal market and competition policy objectives; but then Member States have to relinquish their competence. In a way, the ECJ in *Altmark* attempted to thwart this paradox by restoring a larger Member State autonomy to define public services against closer scrutiny (through EC and national institutions) of the modalities of public financing.

So under Article 106(2) TFEU as well, the formalistic paradigm seems to be under pressure and the exact dividing line between the respective roles and rights of the Member States and those of the EC are becoming blurred. The Courts seem reluctant to confer powers on the Commission to control the quality of SGEIs—this is a matter

---

[96] For a comparison between the Art 106(2) test and the tests applied under the Decision and Framework, see Case NN-54/2009 *Financing of public hospitals in Brussels region* [2010] OJ C74/1, [167].

[97] See Case N-582/2008 *Health Insurance Intergenerational Solidarity Relief* [2009] OJ C186/2, [41]–[42] and [60].

[98] See Case T-442/03 *SIC v Commission* [2008] ECR II-1161, recitals 219–256; Case T-309/04 *TV 2/Danmark v Commission* [2008] ECR II-2935, paras 192–223.

for the Member States, and may be so even where markets are extensively regulated, as the *Federutility* case confirms. The Courts, and now the Commission, are as a result taking a tougher stance on supervisory procedures—and both *ex ante* and *ex post* controls—and demanding clearer rules and tougher sanctions.

4. CONCLUSION

The dividing lines between Community, state, and market are and remain, despite two decades of regulation, by no means clear. The creation of an internal market is certainly not a matter of elevating 'market' at the cost of either 'state' or 'Community'. Yet much of the regulation is based on inherent separations, as explained in this section, including the now obsolete separation between reserved and liberalized sectors, the separation between various steps of the production chain (production, transmission, distribution, supply in the energy sector; content and networks in the electronic communications sector), and the separation between competition law and sector-specific regulation. The most recent set of Directives have introduced more radical lines of separation, to isolate transmission systems[99] or local networks.[100] We have concluded that, looking across the substantive regulation of the sectors, there is a certain risk that there has been too much separation. Separation is no longer the remedy—it is the root of the problem. This is not merely a matter of legal conceptualism. The challenge of securing huge investments to meet the revised Lisbon objectives, to implement the Union's climate change policy, and to bridge the 'broadband divide', will not be met by insisting on the old separations of roles, concepts, and functions. In this respect, the 2002 regulatory framework for electronic communications represents the furthest reaching step away from the formalistic paradigm and towards the new integrative paradigm.

C. INSTITUTIONS

As stated in the introduction, the formalistic paradigm characterized not only the substance of the law, but also the institutions. A number of lines of separation, discussed below, threaten to infuse the implementation of the law with arcane debates on matters of competence, where institutions guard the boundaries of their jurisdictions instead of cooperating with one another to achieve public policy objectives. The

---

[99] Council Directive 2009/72 (n 48 above) Art 9; Council Directive 2009/73 (n 48 above) Art 9.

[100] Council Directive 2002/19 (n 15 above) Arts 13a and 13b as introduced by EP and Council Directive (EC) 2009/140 amending Directives 2002/21/EC on a common regulatory framework for electronic communications networks and services, 2002/19/EC on access to, and interconnection of, electronic communications networks and associated facilities, and 2002/20/EC on the authorization of electronic communications networks and services [2009] OJ L337/37. Contrary to energy regulation, separation is not compulsory in the electronic communications sector. It is one of the remedies at the disposal of NRAs and its use must be justified to the Commission.

evolution of sector-specific regulation already shows a departure from formalism towards a more integrative institutional structure (Section 1), which could serve as an inspiration for Article 106(2) TFEU (Section 2).

1. SECTOR-SPECIFIC REGULATION

While electronic communications and energy regulation might have traveled different evolutionary paths on substance, their institutional development has been more in step.

The starting point in both cases was the default institutional scheme for the enforcement of EU law, namely the reliance on Member States to implement and apply EU law in their respective jurisdictions, with various mechanisms to report to the Commission (if only about implementing measures) and the usual threat of infringement proceedings. This scheme is the institutional expression of the formalistic paradigm: EU and Member State institutions are given distinct and separate functions, with a limited amount of interaction.[101] What is more, each national jurisdiction operates in isolation from the others. Lines of separation run between the EU and national levels and between the Member States.

(a) Away from separation between EU and Member State levels
Early on, in the case of electronic communications,[102] it became clear that the default scheme would not work, if only because almost all Member States would find themselves in a conflict of interest, with a significant if not controlling interest in the former monopolist, on the one hand, and the obligation to implement EU legislation designed to introduce competition to that former monopolist, on the other hand. So the first set of Directives enacted in 1990 already provided for the creation of a 'body independent of the telecommunications organizations' to administer regulation.[103] With full liberalization, in 1998, National Regulatory Authorities (NRAs) were introduced in EU legislation, in a way which already broke the separation between EU and national institutions, in that EU legislation required that Member States endow NRAs with powers to gather information and provide for a right of appeal against NRA decisions.[104] For the first time as well, EU legislation required that NRAs be separated from the rest of the administration (if Member States have ownership or control of one of the market players).[105]

---

[101] Member States remain subject to general principles of EU law—including loyalty (now Art 4(3) TEU), effectiveness, and equivalence (the two exceptions to the principle of national procedural autonomy)—when designing and operating the national-level institutions which are meant to give effect to EU law. Within the boundaries set by these principles, Member States retain a significant amount of discretion.

[102] EU energy regulation did not deal with national regulatory authorities until the second generation of Directive in 2003.

[103] Commission Directive 90/388 (n 3 above) Art 7.

[104] Council Directive 90/387 (n 9 above) Art 5a.   [105] ibid.

EU law continued to penetrate the design and operation of Member State institutions with the 2002 framework. Provisions were added or expanded concerning the relationship of NRAs with national competition authorities, the appeal mechanisms from NRA decisions, transparency, confidentiality, information gathering, and management as well as consultations.[106] In addition, the objectives to be pursued by NRAs were set out in detail.[107] In order to ensure that NRAs would exert their powers in the EU interest, an elaborate system of supervision was put in place, whereby NRA draft decisions concerning the SMP regime are submitted to the Commission for comment; the Commission can veto alternative market definitions or SMP assessments.[108] The notion of NRA was also introduced in the second package of Energy Directives (2003), and here as well EU law dealt with a number of key organizational aspects, including tasks, powers, and resources.[109]

With the new sets of Directives in 2002 and 2003, the separation between EU and Member State institutions was breached in the other direction as well. Not only did EU law specify in greater detail how Member States organize their NRAs, but these NRAs started to play a greater role in the development of EU policy. In the electronic communications and the energy sectors, NRAs were brought together in regulatory networks, respectively, ERG and ERGEG.[110] ERG and ERGEG were created to advise the Commission, but also to bring NRAs together and to force them to look beyond their borders and take a European perspective on their respective activities. And indeed these networks soon began to conduct benchmark exercises, to form study groups, and to issue policy documents and non-binding guidelines on various regulatory topics.[111]

The creation of these regulatory networks marked a large step away from the formalistic towards the integrative paradigm: the Commission and the regulatory networks are working together as part of an enforcement community, with the Commission taking care of higher supervisory and policy-making functions, in consultation with the NRAs which deal with the day-to-day application of the law. Despite lingering issues as to legitimacy, by and large regulatory networks represent a robust

---

[106] Council Directive 2002/21 (n 15 above) Arts 3–6.

[107] ibid Art 8. In fact, this detailed statement of objectives has been criticized for its open-endedness: the objectives listed therein will often point in contradictory directions, eg the promotion of investment in infrastructure and the lowering of consumer prices.

[108] ibid Art 7. The Art 7 procedure has given rise to a large decision body, with the Commission having so far reviewed more than 1,000 draft NRA decisions (as of 1 January 2010) and issued seven veto decisions over the years.

[109] Council Directive 2003/54 (n 44 above) Art 23; Council Directive 2003/55 (n 44 above) Art 25.

[110] See Commission Decision (EC) 2002/627 establishing the European Regulators Group for Electronic Communications Networks and Services [2002] OJ L200/38 and Commission Decision (EC) 2003/796 establishing the European Regulators Group for Electricity and Gas (ERGEG) [2003] OJ L296/34.

[111] Including the massive effort of the ERG to draw up a Common Position on Remedies, ERG (06) 33 (May 2006), available at <http://berec.europa.eu>.

enforcement model for EU law, with definite advantages when compared to the traditional model or to the agency model.[112]

(b) Beyond separation along national borders

While the creation of NRAs and regulatory networks broke down the separation between EU and Member State institutions, it did not address the other separation line running through the institutions in EU regulation of network industries, namely the line running along national borders. In other service sectors where regulatory supervision has been harmonized at EU level, such as banking, insurance, or broadcasting, at least a home country supervision system was put in place, so that firms can operate throughout the EU under a single licence granted by one NRA (in the 'home country' as defined in the applicable Directive). The experience with broadcasting over the years—where stricter Member States have tried to assert jurisdiction over broadcasters established in laxer Member States—already indicates the limits of this approach. Conversely, the failure of banking supervision ahead of the current crisis shows that national authorities did not fully exert supervision over the activities of the regulated banks outside of their jurisdiction.[113] In any event, EU regulation of network industries did not even make it that far: early on, it became clear that Member States wanted to retain jurisdiction over firms operating on their respective territories.

For electronic communications, the EU institutions chose a different strategy to try to minimize regulatory burdens across the EU: instead of working with an institutional solution (home country control), a procedural solution was sought, namely making regulation (and in particular licensing requirements) as light as possible, so as to limit the regulatory burden for firms in each Member State. The 2002 framework removed any individual licence requirements at national level, replacing them with a general authorization procedure.[114] Even if the administrative requirements for market entry were reduced as much as possible, the 2002 framework contains a heavier regulatory scheme applicable to specific firms, namely firms with SMP on selected relevant markets.

In the energy sector, however, the separation running along national borders was not addressed. Although the obligations on TSOs and DSOs have been increasingly harmonized and national regulation of their activities is now the subject of detailed, technical regulation, there was no attempt to deal with the regulation of cross-border infrastructure and shared regulatory responsibilities until the adoption of the recent third package in 2009.[115]

---

[112] See the thorough study made by M de Visser, *Network-Based Governance in EC Law—The Example of EC Competition and EC Communications Law* (Hart, 2009) and S Lavrijssen and L Hancher, 'Networks on Track: From European Regulatory Networks to European Regulatory "Network Agencies" ' (2008) 34 LIEI 23.

[113] T Tridimas, Chapter 25 of this volume.

[114] 'Rights of use' must still be sought by each market player, however, in order to have access to scarce resources such as frequencies, numbers or rights of way: Council Directive 2002/20 (n 15 above) Art 5.

[115] Under Regulation 1228/2003 (n 44 above), the relevant national authorities involved had jurisdiction over cross-border infrastructure and had a duty of cooperation but remained fully entitled to take autonomous decisions.

In the light of the above, it comes as no surprise that many market players and industry observers have criticized the EU for failing to realize the internal market in network industries. The main line of criticism is that even if at a general level the substantive law is harmonized, Member States and their NRAs continue to follow diverging approaches in implementing and applying EU law to the firms active in their respective jurisdictions. As a result, firms face a regulatory patchwork across the EU. The Commission has taken these criticisms to heart; it has always insisted on a high degree of convergence among NRAs. On the other hand, it is often forgotten that, on issues where there is no obvious regulatory solution, such as for instance how to regulate Next Generation Networks so as to foster the appropriate amount of investment in new infrastructure, it can be advantageous to allow room for experimentation; in such cases, 'maverick' NRAs from smaller Member States could take the lead and follow more daring regulatory approaches, while NRAs from larger Member States would wait for a best practice to emerge.[116] In practice, such experimentation has not taken place, however.

The 2002 and 2003 Directives, as well as the second energy package already contained measures to ensure sufficient coordination and convergence amongst NRAs, including the regulatory networks mentioned above. The ERG and ERGEG, however, did not succeed in bringing about the expected level of convergence among NRAs, at least as far as the Commission was concerned. The ERG and ERGEG decided on a consensus basis, resulting in a very inter-governmental dynamic. In response to criticism, the ERG improved its internal procedures, whereas ERGEG recommended its transformation into a fully fledged independent agency.[117]

In addition to the 'voluntary' coordination taking place within the ERG and ERGEG, the Commission also has means to force the NRAs to follow its line, or even to override or sideline them. As mentioned above, within the 2002 electronic communications framework, the Commission first of all selects markets for NRAs to assess,[118] secondly issues guidelines as to how NRAs should conduct their assessment,[119] and thirdly reviews NRA draft decisions and can veto them if they would undermine the internal market or conflict with EU law.[120]

(c) The use of competition law powers

Beyond sector-specific regulation, the Commission can also intervene in NRA matters via its competition law powers; issues relating to the regulation of SMP firms (electronic communications) or large energy operators can typically be reframed as competition law issues, under Article 102 TFEU. In the 1990s, the Commission used its competition law powers against incumbents to 'convince' Member States to support

---

[116] Larouche and de Visser (n 18 above).
[117] Lavrijssen and Hancher (n 112 above).
[118] Council Directive 2002/21 (n 15 above) Art 15.   [119] ibid.
[120] ibid Art 7. See also P Larouche, 'Coordination of European and Member State Regulatory Policy—Horizontal, Vertical and Transversal Aspects' in D Geradin et al (eds), Regulation through Agencies in the EU (Edward Elgar, 2005) 164–179, also in (2004) 5 J Netw Indust 277.

telecom liberalization.[121] As regards the actions of NRAs in particular, the Commission intervened in pricing matters by fining incumbents for predatory pricing or price squeeze under Article 102 TFEU.[122] The *Deutsche Telekom* price squeeze case is particularly relevant here, since DT relied on the regulatory approval of its wholesale and retail tariffs by the German NRA to argue against the application of competition law. The Commission replied that compliance with regulation did not absolve a firm from liability under competition law, a stance confirmed by the CFI on appeal; here EU law is at variance with US law, however.[123] Finally, in one instance concerning international roaming, the Commission, dissatisfied with the way NRAs had failed to act, simply circumvented the general regulatory scheme of the 2002 regulatory framework and proposed a separate regulation.[124]

Against the backdrop of the incomplete transition from a more formalistic to a more integrative regulatory paradigm in the substantive regulation of the energy sector, as mapped out at Section 2 above, the recent use of competition law powers in the energy sector is remarkable. It had as its prelude a major sector inquiry—culminating in a comprehensive report gathering extensive data on the industry and its practices.[125] As many aspects of market structure and indeed firms' conduct are beyond the scope of the Energy Directives, competition rules have had a vital role to play to support the transition to more competitive markets. However, recent developments in the practice of the European Commission, and in particular the development of the commitment procedure on the basis of Article 9 of Regulation 1/2003[126] alongside a significant increase in fines, indicate that competition rules have an important substantive role to play, as an effective tool for market design, and can transcend the increasingly technical focus of sector-specific energy regulation outlined above.

Increasingly, the Commission is resorting to *quasi*-regulatory measures to foster competition in the EU electricity and gas markets. Unilateral commitments by the parties involved have become a standard part of the toolbox used by the Commission to restructure the European electricity and gas market and promote competition. The

---

[121] P Larouche, *Competition Law and Regulation in European Telecommunications* (Hart, 2000) ch II.

[122] Case COMP/37.451 *Deutsche Telekom AG* [2003] OJ L263/9 (upheld in Case T-271/03 *Deutsche Telekom* [2008] ECR II-477); Case COMP/38.233 *Wanadoo Interactive*, available at <http://ec.europa.eu/competition> (upheld in Case C-202/07 P *France Télécom* [2009] ECR I-2369); Case COMP/38.784 *Telefónica*, available at <http://ec.europa.eu/competition>.

[123] D Geradin, 'Limiting the Scope of Art 82 EC: What can the EU Learn from the U.S. Supreme Court's Judgment in Trinko in the Wake of Microsoft, IMS and Deutsche Telekom?' (2004) 41 CML Rev 1519; N Petit, 'Circumscribing the Scope of EC Competition Law in Network Industries? A Comparative Approach to the US Supreme Court Ruling in the Trinko Case' (2004) 5 J Netw Indust 347; P Larouche, 'Contrasting Legal Solutions and the Comparability of US and EU Experiences' in F Levêque and H Shelanski (eds), *Antitrust and Regulation in the EU and US: Legal and Economic Perspectives* (Edward Elgar, forthcoming).

[124] EP and Council Regulation (EC) 717/2007 on roaming on public mobile telephone networks within the Community [2007] OJ L171/32.

[125] Inquiry pursuant to Art 17 of Regulation (EC) No 1/2003 into the European gas and electricity sectors (Final Report) COM(2006) 851.

[126] Council Regulation (EC) 1/2003 on the implementation of the rules on competition laid down in Arts 81 and 82 of the Treaty [2003] OJ L1/1.

commitment procedure allows the Commission to accept legally binding commitments offered by defendants if is satisfied that these sufficiently address the underlying
competition problem. This procedure has the virtue of both procedural economy
and speed. It allows the Commission to bring infringement procedures to an end
without the parties being forced to concede that they have indeed breached the rules.
Confirmation and approval of this strategy in the context of merger review was given
by the General Court in the *EDP/Commission* cases.[127] Further examples can be found
in the *EDF/EnBW* and *GDF/SUEZ* merger cases.[128] Commitments should in theory be
suitable, necessary, and proportional to dealing with the underlying competition law
problem to be lawful.[129]

As of 2008 the Commission also began to accept commitments of divestiture in the
context of Article 102 TFEU cases in the German market, when first E.ON[130] and then
RWE[131] accepted to divest their transmission networks to avoid further anti-trust
scrutiny when at the same time, the German government was still strongly opposing
ownership unbundling during the negotiations on the third package. An Article 102
TFEU investigation could therefore lead to a structural remedy—the divestiture of
the essential facility. The Commission was now able to address the shortcomings of the
sector-specific legislation through '*ex post*' anti-trust control, and to realize the potential
of the commitment procedure to carry through rapid changes in the market structure.

Importantly, the commitment procedure allows the Commission to bargain liberalization outcomes directly with the incumbent, without going through the interface of
NRAs and Member States. This outcome is well illustrated in the *Svenska Kraftnet*
(SvK) decision.[132] The Commission reached the preliminary conclusion that SvK was
dominant on the Swedish electricity transmission market and may have abused its
dominant position by reducing interconnection capacity for trade between Sweden
and its neighbouring EU and EEA partners, thereby discriminating between domestic
and export electricity transmission services and segmenting the internal market.
SvK had arguably only been carrying out national policy objectives, ie maintaining
a single price area in Sweden. Nevertheless Regulation No 1228/2003 also forbade
these types of practices and it should have been open for the complainants to raise
a challenge before the national regulator. Given the apparent lack of independence
of the Swedish regulator from the government, the Commission was able to rely on
Article 102 to circumvent the national level and force SvK to accept far-reaching
commitments, including the building of new network infrastructure.

---

[127] Case T-87/05 *EDP v Commission* [2005] ECR II-3745.
[128] Case COMP/M.1853 *EDF/EnBW* [2002] OJ L59/1; Case COMP/M.4180 *Gaz de France/Suez* [2007]
OJ L88/47.
[129] Case C-441/07 *Alrosa*, judgment of 29 June 2010.
[130] Cases COMP/39.388 and COMP/39.389 *German Electricity Wholesale and Balancing Markets* [2009]
OJ 36/8.
[131] Case COMP/39.402 *RWE Gas Foreclosure* (Decision of 18 March 2009), available at <http://ec.europa.
eu/competition>.
[132] Case COMP/39.351 *Swedish Interconnectors* [2010] OJ C142/28.

(d) Increased separation between the NRA and the national legislative and executive power

Despite all of the means at the Commission's disposal to influence or even control the work of NRAs, the perceived need for more consistency across the EU led the Commission to propose the creation of regulatory agencies in both the electronic communications and energy sectors.

In order to fully understand such a proposal, it is necessary first to look at yet another line of separation running through the institutional framework, this time between the NRAs, on the one hand, and the legislature and the executive, on the other hand.

As mentioned above, the starting point for this line of separation was the potential conflict of interest arising when the state both conducts the regulation of the sector and holds a significant interest in one of the players (the incumbent).[133] In that sense, the independence of the NRA from the legislature and the executive was an extension of the separation of regulatory and operational functions.

When NRAs were originally created, most Member States were still holding a significant if not controlling share in the incumbent, so they had to give the NRA a measure of independence from the rest of the administration. Furthermore, the leading example, the British Oftel (now Ofcom), was operating largely independently. So most NRAs were created as separate authorities enjoying a measure of autonomy. Once created, these NRAs generally sought to consolidate and even increase that autonomy.

However, it soon became clear that expanding NRA autonomy beyond what is necessary to avoid conflict of interests ran into significant problems. In most Continental public law traditions, autonomous executive agencies can only be entrusted with the—presumably mechanical—implementation or application of higher ranking norms, as opposed to policy-making.[134] Indeed the delegation of norm-making power to an autonomous body would run against the separation of powers (to the extent that such norms would otherwise be set by the legislature) or against the political accountability of the executive (to the extent that such norms would otherwise be set by the executive pursuant to legislative delegation). Accordingly, NRAs could enjoy considerable autonomy as long as their tasks were limited to the mere implementation or application of law and policy. It should be apparent to the reader that the range of tasks to be performed by an NRA does not lend itself easily to formalistic categories such as 'policy-making' and 'implementation'. Rather, regulatory decisions essentially involve policy trade-offs.[135] It seems more accurate to model the regulatory

---

[133] Council Directive 90/387 (n 9 above) Art 5a; Council Directive 2002/21 (n 15 above) Art 3(2).

[134] M Thatcher, *Internationalisation and Economic Institutions; Comparing European Experiences* (Oxford University Press, 2007).

[135] For instance, short-term gains in consumer welfare from lower prices and increased competition routinely have to be weighed against longer-term gains from investments in new technologies and increased dynamic efficiency. Similarly, the interests of one category of customers often have to be balanced with those of another category.

process as a chain of decisions, each involving a further refinement in the trade-offs, always with a view to dealing with uncertainty as well as possible.

While it is not accurate to shrug off the issue as a clash between a regulatory model inspired by the common law and a Continental public law tradition,[136] it remains nevertheless the case that some theoretical foundation must be found to explain not just the existence of NRAs, but also the division of tasks between the legislature and the executive, on the one hand, and the NRA, on the other. Recent developments point towards a generalization of the conflict-of-interest rationale: in short, even if Member States have no direct interest in any of the market players, regulatory matters are high-stake games where market players will deploy considerable resources to try to influence the outcome (rent-seeking behaviour). Regulatory decisions must therefore be made in an environment which is shielded from undue influence as much as possible: this would imply transparency, independence of the decision-maker, openness, a duty to state reasons, and the possibility of review, ie the characteristics of a regulatory agency.[137] By implication, the role of the legislature and the executive would be limited to issues where there is no clear controversy among market players, i.e. issues where a decision does not immediately make winners and losers. This would explain why, in a decision chain model, the legislature and the executive can deal with the highest levels—provide guidelines and set out policy objectives—but cannot go very far down the decision chain, since very rapidly market players will begin to hold diverging views on the outcome and will engage in rent-seeking behaviour.[138] The justification just set out was put forward by the ECJ in a recent ruling which enshrined the position of the NRA via-à-vis the legislature.[139] Similarly, the recent Directives on electronic communications and energy invoke the need to avoid undue influence as a reason why the independence of NRAs should be strengthened.[140]

Of course, the more NRAs are independent towards the national legislature or executive, the more accountability becomes problematic. Many commentators argue that the NRAs are not sufficiently accountable, all the more when they act under the cloak of the ERG or ERGEG.[141] Yet a good argument can also be made that NRAs are already subject to many measures designed to ensure accountability. First of all, *ex ante*, while as is clear from the above NRAs cannot be told how to decide, the legislature and the executive have nonetheless given them some directions, ie they

---

[136] The same debate took place in common law systems when regulatory authorities were put in place, but that debate dates back from the mid-twentieth century.

[137] L Hancher, P Larouche, and S Lavrijssen, 'Principles of Good Market Governance' (2003) 4 J Netw Indust 355.

[138] This is not to say that NRAs are not vulnerable to rent-seeking behaviour as well, as public choice theory argues with regulatory capture, etc.

[139] Case C-424/07 *Commission v Germany*, 3 December 2009, in particular para 91 and the Opinion of AG Maduro at para 63. In Case C-274/08, *Commission v Sweden*, 29 October 2009, the Court also defended the position of the NRA as against the legislature, this time in the energy sector.

[140] Council Directive 2009/140 (n 100 above) recital 13 and the new Art 3a added to Council Directive 2002/21 (n 15 above); Council Directive 2009/72 (n 48 above) recitals 33–34 and Art 35.

[141] Lavrijssen and Hancher (n 115 above).

have filled in the upper echelons of the decision chain. NRAs are not told simply to act in the public interest,[142] rather they are given specific objectives,[143] their tasks are defined,[144] and their powers are also set out.[145] In the case of electronic communications, the Commission even tells them which markets to analyse and which methodology to apply.[146] Secondly, *ex post*, a number of mechanisms are in place. The NRAs are subject to the disciplines arising from good governance principles: transparency, openness, need to consult and give reasons, etc. Usually, they are also bound to file regular reports with the legislature. As outlined earlier, the Commission also has means to exert pressure on them, including through its competition law powers. Within the networks, they are also accountable towards other NRAs. Last but not least, their decisions are subject to judicial review. If accountability means that the NRA must feel that it has to answer for its actions, then NRAs are accountable; of course, they are accountable to so many principals that the incentives on NRAs might be distorted.[147]

(e) NRAs and the Commission: the creation of ACER and BEREC

In the Commission's view, inadequate political independence at national level hampers an effective and impartial application of European law. As mentioned already, the new Electronic Communications and Energy Directives adopted in 2009 reflect at least in part, a new policy direction: NRAs must now be independent, not just from industry, but increasingly from national governments, without political interference. Their ability to do so will be strengthened through the creation of the two new institutions, the Agency for the Co-ordination of Energy Regulators (ACER) and the Body of European Regulators for Electronic Communications (BEREC). The originality of ACER and BEREC compared to other agencies in the EU regulatory landscape is that they are '*network agencies*'.[148] Of necessity, multi-level governance complicates the allocation of responsibility and the accountability of these different actors from a

---

[142] As is the case with some US authorities, such as the FCC.

[143] Council Directive 2002/21 (n 15 above) Art 8.

[144] ibid.

[145] Throughout the Directives making up the 2002 framework (n 15 above).

[146] Commission guidelines on market analysis and the assessment of significant market power under the Community regulatory framework for electronic communications networks and services [2002] OJ C165/6.

[147] As was the case in *Commission v Germany* (n 140 above) where one principal (the German Parliament) disagreed with another one (the Commission) on the proper treatment of emerging markets.

[148] In terms of internal governance, ACER broadly follows the principles of the Draft Interinstitutional Agreement on the Operating Framework for the European Regulatory Agencies, COM(2005) 59 final. It comprises an Administrative Board, a Board of Regulators regrouping the NRAs and a Director. As for BEREC, even if, for institutional reasons, it is expressly not set up as a 'Community agency' within the meaning of EU law (EP and Council Regulation (EC) 1211/2009 establishing the Body of European Regulators for Electronic Communications (BEREC) and the Office [2009] OJ L337/1 Rec. 6), for the purposes of discussion here it will be treated as such. Its institutional structure is not far from the model set out in the Draft Interinstitutional Agreement either: it comprises a Board of Regulators on which NRAs sit, assisted by a Management Committee and an Administrative Manager. In comparison to ACER, BEREC leaves more power in the hands of the NRAs acting together as Board of Regulators.

political as well as a legal perspective.[149] Much of the legal and political science literature has focused on the accountability deficits of the networks themselves, but in the light of the repositioning of the regulatory networks as European network agencies, their position vis–à–vis the Commission—and the division of competences and tasks between these new agencies and the Commission itself—is an important dimension in the new institutional paradigm. Ironically, the formalistic distinction between policy-making and implementation, which undermined the position of NRAs in many Member States, is also at work at European level under the guise of the so-called *Meroni* doctrine.[150]

Regulation 713/2009 stipulates that ACER is '*to assist the regulatory authorities* [...] *in exercising, at community level, the regulatory tasks performed in the Member States and where necessary, to coordinate their action*'. Its task is to provide a framework for the cooperation of NRAs, and to complement their actions at EU level to address regulatory gaps on cross-border issues and provide greater regulatory certainty. ACER will primarily have an advisory role. Its opinions and recommendations should contribute to ensuring more coordination among TSOs and among regulators of the different Member States, spread good practices, and in particular contribute to the implementation of the new (non-binding) Community-wide ten-year network development plan, ie monitoring the work of the new European Network of Transmission System Operators (ENTSOs) for electricity and gas, a new organization also created under the third energy package. Under the third package, the powers of the Commission to adopt general technical measures through Comitology procedures are greatly extended.[151] ACER will only have an advisory role in the formulation of general binding measures. At the same time, it has limited autonomous powers to take decisions on cross-border energy infrastructure projects. The new Regulation 714/2009 modifies the allocation of regulatory powers among the NRAs who can jointly decide to delegate their power to the new ACER; in case of sustained disagreement between the NRAs involved, ACER can even take the decision itself subject, however, to Commission veto. As the ERGEG has concluded, to its regret, in reality the ENTSO has been given more important powers than the Agency itself. This is perhaps a reflection of the dominance of technical regulation in the energy sector, which has led to the inclusion of TSOs as key players in the regulatory framework. But the powers of the Agency vis-à-vis the Commission also remain weak. From a legal perspective, ACER has been conceived in strict compliance with the *Meroni* doctrine.[152] Its powers to define the terms and conditions for access and operational security of cross-border infrastructure are inherently technical and case-specific, and

---

[149] Hancher *et al* (note 112 above).

[150] Case 9/56 *Meroni* [1958] ECR 11.

[151] These now include the network codes, the certification of TSOs, rules on the provision of information, rules for the trading of electricity and lastly, rules on investment incentives for the construction of interconnector capacity.

[152] See n 151 above.

subject to close Commission scrutiny. Regulatory independence from national governments does not necessarily imply independence at the European level.

The creation of BEREC was more laborious.[153] The Commission proposal was as ambitious as in the energy sector, but in the end, as the recitals to Regulation 1211/2009 indicate, BEREC is rather a reinforced ERG. It is much less of an agency than ACER. Its governance structure is developed further than was the case with the ERG, and it is endowed with more staff (the Office).[154] It now decides by a two-thirds majority instead of consensus, which could make BEREC more efficient than ERG.[155] As with ACER, however, the relationship of BEREC with the Commission is comparatively underspecified: on the surface, BEREC is set up so as to comply with the *Meroni* doctrine, in that it is merely advising the Commission (and the NRAs), without taking any decisions, much like EMEA, for instance.[156] As the case of EMEA shows,[157] however, if BEREC ends up with a sizeable expert staff and the Commission starts to rely increasingly on its advice, then BEREC will in practice be taking decisions for the Commission, including some decisions going beyond mere implementation. In any event, if BEREC is eating away at any authority's policy-making autonomy, it is the NRA's and not the Commission's, so that no *Meroni* issue would then arise. Indeed BEREC is designed to increase 'consistency' among NRA decisions, especially as regards remedies. If the Commission retains a significant role in the matters on which it is advised by BEREC, then ultimately BEREC could serve as an additional lever to exert pressure on NRAs to fall into line.[158]

For both ACER and BEREC, the dividing lines between the practical competences of the Commission and ACER/BEREC on the one hand, and between ACER/BEREC and the NRAs on the other hand, are likely to evolve following continuous interactions in this new substantive and institutional regulatory space.

Even although the regulatory gaps on cross-border issues (in energy) and the perceived lack of consistency across borders (in electronic communications) will be

---

[153] One need only parse the various acronyms which gained currency during the legislative procedure to see that the law-making institutions were at odds: the Commission proposed a European Electronic Communications Market Authority (EECMA), whereas the Council in its common position wanted a Group of European Regulators in Telecoms (GERT), and not a Body of European Regulators in Telecoms (BERT), as found in the first reading of the EP.

[154] Regulation 1211/2009 (n 149 above) Art 6.

[155] ibid Art 4(9).

[156] T Tridimas, 'Community Agencies, Competition Law and ECSB Initiatives' (2009) YEL 216.

[157] J Pelkmans, S Labory, and G Majone, 'Better EU Regulatory Quality: Assessing current initiatives and new proposals' in G Galli and J Pelkmans, *Regulatory Reform and Competitiveness in Europe—Vol. I* (Edward Elgar, 2000) 461, 519.

[158] The pressure for 'consistency' essentially concerns remedies, since market definition and SMP designation are already subject to Commission supervision (and ultimately veto) under Council Directive 2002/21 (n 15 above) Art 7. Whether BEREC will succeed in bringing more consistency in the remedies imposed by NRAs will also depend on how the intricate review procedure of Council Directive 2002/21, Art 7a (as added by Council Directive 2009/, n 141 above) works out in practice. On the face of Art 7a, NRAs may ultimately persist with their original proposal concerning remedies, but they will face considerable pressure to follow the views of the Commission and BEREC.

incrementally reduced thanks to strengthened harmonization and cooperation at the EU level, it would be wrong to conclude that a definitive paradigm shift towards centralized powers has occurred with the creation of ACER and BEREC. Economic regulation will to a large extent remain a national competence, albeit that the NRAs should heed the European interest. Yet if European sector-specific regulation remains relatively weak and very partial in its coverage, there would appear to be some scope to 'fill in the gaps' in the current institutional architecture by resorting to a more imaginative use of *ex post* competition controls.

2. ARTICLE 106(2) TFEU

As we have explained above, in the wake of *Altmark* and the subsequent adoption of the 'Monti' package in 2005, the Commission has been confronted with the task of ensuring legal certainty for the Member States and their public service providers and at the same time ensuring sufficient flexibility to address local as well as sectoral variation in how public services are organized and operated, as well as the scope and quality of those services. This has led to some confusion as to how strictly Article 106(2) TFEU should be interpreted, and in particular its scope as an exemption to the Treaty state aid regime. As discussed above, the fourth *Altmark* criterion is not applicable in the context of Article 106(2); Member States must nevertheless ensure that public service obligations are clearly defined and entrusted through legal acts, and that the compensation for their performance is proportionate. Finally, and in accordance with the Transparency Directive,[159] cross-subsidization should be avoided through separation of accounts for PSO (or SGEI) activities from all other functions.

Yet these rules are not always easy to apply, let alone police in sectors where there is little or no harmonizing legislation and as a result, where sector-specific regulation and sector-specific regulators are not available to take up these tasks. The result is often an opaque situation at national level. The exact scope of the relevant PSO may only be inferred from a pot pourri of national as well as regional and local norms, while neither the modes nor the levels of compensation are defined *ex ante* in a transparent manner. Benchmarks for 'reasonable' levels of compensation remain elusive. *Ex post* control may be a potential substitute to avoid over-compensation, but this too is not assigned in a consistent or transparent manner. Accounting separation is not subject to harmonized rules and the failure to apply any sort of system at all is not subject to any effective sanction. Although, following the Monti Report of 2010,[160] the Commission has recently launched a consultation exercise on the possible reform of the 2005 Community Framework for state aid in the form of public service compensation and accompanying enactments,[161] its efforts to create legal certainty and preserve the necessary flexibility

---

[159] Commission Directive (EEC) 80/723 on the transparency of financial relations between Member States and public undertakings as well as on financial transparency within certain undertakings [1980] OJ L195/35, as amended.

[160] See n 1 above, 73–75.   [161] See n 94 above.

are likely to be frustrated unless it is prepared to abandon the 'market access' paradigm that has dominated its approach to date, and to embrace a more integrated paradigm which will allow not just for the development of the requisite substantive norms but also for the design of a suitable institutional architecture to supervise more closely how PSOs are entrusted, performed, and policed at national or where appropriate, regional or local level.

This has to be the correct '*quid pro quo*': if Member States are to enjoy the flexibility to deliver and organize these services in accordance with their own policy objectives, then they must at the same time be prepared to ensure the necessary level of supervision to ensure that those entrusted with such tasks do what is to be expected of them. This could mean a more pro-active role for national bodies such as courts of auditors, or even competition authorities or alternatively for specially created, de-centralized bodies, who are given a clear mandate to supervise PSOs in a transparent, independent, and democratic manner. The institutional developments in sector-specific regulation could serve as an inspiration: conceivably national authorities could be integrated in a network and placed under the supervisory powers of the Commission. It is only in this way that a true reform can succeed in integrating the aspirations of the Union and the Member States to ensure universal access to such services for European citizens with further consensus-building on the objectives of an integrated, highly competitive social market.

3. CONCLUDING REMARKS

Just as with the developments in substantive law, the dividing lines between Community, state, and market remain unclear. Although recent institutional developments have lessened the dividing lines between the EU and the national regulatory institutions, they have not resulted in a straightforward transfer of powers from Member State to the Community level. Furthermore, inherent separations remain—in particular along physical borders, so that cross-border network issues/activities are still not fully coordinated at either national or European level.

The transition to a more integrative paradigm is by no means complete. As we have argued, separation has become the root of the problem and not the remedy. It will take time to recalibrate the institutional architecture and revise the substantive rules. Given the inherent division of competences between the EU and Member States, one may also speculate on whether certain dividing lines can ever be fully eradicated.

D. CONCLUSION

We have argued in this chapter that an examination of recent trends in both substantive and institutional aspects of network regulation in two key sectors illustrates that the formalistic, 'market access' paradigm, initially relied upon by the Commission to force market access is gradually breaking down. We have explained that this paradigm is being replaced by a more integrative approach, which attempts to overcome the various separations imposed by the formalistic paradigm and which seeks to balance internal market objectives with other goals. We have traced the emergence of a more integrated institutional approach, where the dividing lines between European and national regulation are no longer clear-cut but where a choice for a more cooperative and multi-layered approach is evident. We have also argued that the substantive norms have evolved so that 'pigeonholing' of problems is no longer the dominant perspective. Instead the latest packages of regulation adopt a more integrative approach too.

We have suggested that the original assumption that informed the design and scope of early network regulation—that sector-specific rules should give way to general competition law—has not been possible to maintain. Regulation in the electronic communications sector has become more not less intensive. In spite of the introduction of structural unbundling in the energy sector, the regulation of the TSOs and transmission functions has not become 'lighter'. Indeed the TSOs must now ensure market access and reliable supply, but must also take on responsibility for additional longer term objectives, including investment, dissemination of market information, and the promotion of renewables. Their quasi-regulatory tasks sit somewhat uneasily alongside their commercial organization and objectives, especially if they are not fully unbundled from other activities and functions within a vertically integrated firm.

As the substantive norms have become more intricate, complex, and challenging, so has the institutional architecture which is now required to manage regulatory coordination across national boundaries. The Commission's role in the context of the realization of the internal market exercise in the network sectors has become far more complex as a result. We argue that in the light of our analysis of both the institutional as well as the substantial features of network regulation, the Commission has been gradually forced to accept, if reluctantly, a new role. It is no longer possible for the Commission to content itself with realizing market access or stimulating the creation of sustainable competition, or to correct market failures. The Commission's role has become one of 'managing competition' in the network sectors, alongside NRAs and NCAs.

The effective accomplishment of this task will require a further shift to a more integrative approach—at both substantive as well as institutional levels. This is equally true with respect to Article 106(2) TFEU even in the absence of sector-specific legislation. The Commission will have to ensure that it has the means at its disposal to ensure that all stakeholders involved can both subscribe to as well as meet its ambitious objectives in a complex policy setting. These objectives are, as we have explained, no longer limited to a single-minded pursuit of market access and short-term efficiencies. Instead complex policy trade-offs must be made across a multi-level institutional framework where sector-specific regulatory tools as well as competition law tools must be mobilized at Union and national level in pursuit of a careful balancing exercise. Managed competition involves managing and steering the continued interaction of 'Community, state, and market'; it is not about drawing boundaries and dividing lines, and policing the relevant spheres of competence or elaborating formalistic 'pigeonholes' so that inherent tensions between 'state versus Community' or 'state versus market' can be conveniently side-stepped. With the coming of age of EU regulation in network industries, the end of the old formalistic approach is surely inevitable.

25

EU FINANCIAL REGULATION: FEDERALIZATION, CRISIS MANAGEMENT, AND LAW REFORM

Takis Tridimas[*]

The evolution of EU financial law has been a journey towards federalization. Although the presence of the European Community in this field can be traced back to the late 1960s, it was not until the end of the 1990s that financial services law made it to the top of the political agenda. Since the launching of the Commission's Financial Services Action Plan in 1999, financial law has been one of the fastest growing areas of EU law. Whilst the principles of mutual recognition and home country control form the pivotal integration paradigm in this area, EU measures leave little room for regulatory competition and the trend is towards uniformity rather than harmonization. In quantitative terms, the EU legislative output has been impressive. This area of law has also provided a fruitful ground for regulatory experimentation. The Lamfalussy process advanced a new regulatory model which has provided for a higher degree of convergence and greater Community presence in the field of enforcement. A set of new Commission proposals launched in September 2009 takes the process of federalization a step further. They provide for a new institutional architecture, more EU powers, and the regulation of areas previously left untouched by EU, and even national, law. This chapter traces the evolution of financial legislation in EU law, explores its salient features, and examines selectively the EU's response to the financial crisis. The term 'financial law' is used to refer to securities regulation, banking, and insurance law. Developments are examined selectively and mostly by reference to securities regulation.

[*] Sir John Lubbock Professor of Banking Law at Queen Mary School of Law London and Nancy A. Patterson Distinguished Scholar and Professor, Pennsylvania State University.

There is no attempt to discuss the law of the European Central Bank or Economic and Monetary Union.[1]

A. FIVE PHASES IN THE DEVELOPMENT OF FINANCIAL LAW

Since the 1970s, the Community has embarked on an ambitious programme to harmonize the corporate and securities laws of the Member States. One may distinguish five phases in the development of this programme.

The first phase, which spanned the 1970s, focused on the harmonization of national company laws. In constitutional terms, it was characterized by the requirement of unanimity in Council decision-making, which made for slow progress. In terms of policy, it was characterized by adherence to a formal model of harmonization and the strong influence of German corporation law. The First, Second, and Third Company Law Directives[2] are prime examples of this phase. At the same time, the Council adopted the first generation of Banking and Life Assurance Directives making timid steps towards the liberalization of banking and insurance sectors.[3] The second phase began in 1979 and signalled the birth of EU capital markets law.[4] The Commission perceived harmonization of capital markets law as being more conducive to financial integration than the coordination of corporate law. The underlying policy objective was to increase the role of securities markets in corporate finance and decrease the traditional dependence of European companies on bank financing. Community intervention was based on the premise that, for securities markets to fulfil their economic function as efficient allocators of resources, it was necessary to maintain investor confidence in their integrity. Thus, an integrated securities market could not be established unless equivalent standards of investor protection were respected throughout the Community. The shift of focus from corporate to capital markets law was accompanied by a new policy in line with the Commission's White Paper on the Completion of the Internal Market.[5] Less emphasis was now placed on harmonization

---

[1] For a basic bibliography in the broader area of EU financial law, see, among others, N Moloney, *EC Securities Regulation* (2nd edn, Oxford University Press, 2008); J De Haan, S Oosterloo, and D Schoenmaker, *European Financial Markets and Institutions* (Cambridge University Press, 2009); K J Hopt and E Wymeersch (eds), *European Company and Financial Law: Text and Leading Cases* (3rd edn, Oxford University Press, 2004); G Ferrarini and E Wymeersch (eds), *Investor Protection in Europe: Regulatory Competition and Harmonisation* (Oxford University Press, 2006); E Avgouleas, *The Mechanics and Regulation of Market Abuse: A Legal and Economic* (Oxford University Press, 2005); E Ferran, *Building an EU Securities Market* (Cambridge University Press, 2004); R Lastra, *Legal Foundations of International Monetary Stability* (Oxford University Press, 2006).

[2] First Company Law Directive 68/151, [1968] OJ L65/8; Second Company Law Directive 77/91, [1977] OJ L26/1; Third Company Law Directive 78/855, [1978] OJ L295/36.

[3] See Council Directive 73/189, [1973] OJ L194/1 and Council Directive 77/780, [1977] OJ L322/30, on banking and Council Directive 79/267 on direct life assurance, [1979] OJ L63/1.

[4] This stage began with the adoption of Council Directive 79/279 on admission of securities to official stock exchange listing, [1979] OJ L66/21.

[5] COM(85) 310.

and more on the principles of mutual recognition and home country control. A distinct feature of this era was the increasing dominance of Anglo-Saxon regulatory models. Community intervention focused on harmonizing disclosure requirements for corporate issuers, the regulation of insider trading, the free movement of investment services, and the free movement of undertakings in collective investments in transferable securities (UCITS). During the 1980s, further progress was achieved towards the harmonization of company law, whilst a second generation of Banking and Insurance Directives provided for the principles of mutual recognition and home country control in those sectors.

The third phase covers the 1990s and may be considered as one of a 'new *lourder*'. The harmonization programme somewhat ran out of steam. Political priorities changed as the Community's efforts centred on the introduction of economic and monetary union. The principle of subsidiarity curbed the Commission's harmonization enthusiasm in the wider field of financial law. Furthermore, what was left on the negotiating table following the harmonization impetus of the 1980s, were key measures where strong national interests conflicted. As a result, a number of Commission proposals stalled in the light of unbridgeable divergences in national preferences. This was, for example, the case in relation to the proposed Fifth,[6] Tenth,[7] and Thirteenth Company Law Directives.[8]

The fourth phase began with the introduction of the Financial Services Action Plan (FSAP) in 1999. It was characterized by intense legislative activity and the advent of a new law-making model through the Lamfalussy process. Since the financial crisis, it may be said that we have entered a new phase, the main features of which are the following: first, the model of maximum harmonization, which was already favoured by the Lamfalussy process, is further enhanced and extended. Secondly, in contrast to the previously prevailing philosophy, EU law begins to govern not only substantive regulation but also supervision and the institutional framework of the financial services industry. Thirdly, there is a nuanced shift in objectives. Whilst earlier emphasis was placed mostly on investor protection and the promotion of financial integration, the need to avoid systemic risks and safeguard market stability now feature more prominently in the objectives of policy-making.

B. THE FINANCIAL SERVICES ACTION PLAN AND THE LAMFALUSSY PROCESS

The Financial Services Action Plan (FSAP) heralded a new area of strong EU presence in financial law. In its Communication of 28 October 1998, *Financial Services: Building*

---

[6] Proposed Fifth Directive on the structure of public limited companies (which governed the structure, powers and obligations of the organs of public companies). See proposal [1972] OJ C131/1; amended proposal [1983] OJ C240/1; new amended proposal [1991] OJ C7/1 and C321/1. The proposal was subsequently withdrawn.

[7] Tenth Directive on cross-border mergers of public companies. This was subsequently adopted as Directive 2005/65, [2005] OJ L310/28.

[8] Thirteenth Company Law Directive on Take-over Bids. The Directive was eventually adopted in 2004.

a Framework for Action,[9] the Commission identified financial services as a pivotal sector for employment expansion and economic growth in the EU and specified as a key goal the completion of a single market in financial services. The Communication was followed by FSAP[10] which laid down a framework for action and a timetable for the adoption of a series of measures to achieve three major objectives: the establishment of a single market in wholesale financial services, increasing investor protection and transparency in retail markets, and strengthening prudential supervision.

The Plan was impressive in its aspirations. Its influence in shaping financial law is as defining as the influence of the Commission's 1985 White Paper in shaping the internal market. Its significance lies not only in the adoption of Community legislation in substantive areas of law but also in precipitating the introduction of new Community methods and integration disciplines. FSAP was accompanied by the Lamfalussy Report[11] which introduced a new policy-making framework. The Report provided a strong critique of the existing harmonization attempts and decision-making processes identifying a number of key deficiencies:[12] the absence of clear and unambiguous Europe-wide regulation had impeded the implementation of the mutual recognition principle; the inconsistent implementation of Community directives prevented the operation of a level playing field and made for an inefficient regulatory system; furthermore, the lack of comprehensive Community legislation created barriers to entry. The Report considered that the existing regulatory system suffered from major shortcomings.[13] It was too slow; too rigid and thus incapable of responding speedily to market changes; it produced too much ambiguity; and failed to differentiate 'between core, enduring, essential framework principles and practical, day to day, implementing rules'.[14]

The Lamfalussy Report suggested a new four-level decision-making process. Level 1 encompasses primary legislation. It consists of Community measures adopted under the normal EC legislative procedure (ie the Council and the Parliament acting on a Commission proposal) which provide for framework principles in specific areas of substantive law. The framework principles laid down in Level 1 are concretized at Level 2 by Commission measures adopted under Comitology procedures. This is delegated legislation where the Commission acts with the assistance of two committees, the European Securities Committee (ESC) and the Committee of European Securities Regulators (CESR).[15] Level 3 provides for the elaboration of common standards for the implementation of Level 1 and Level 2 measures. The aim here is to achieve consistent and equivalent transposition of Community measures in national law. The Lamfalussy Report elevated this to a key objective as one of its main criticisms

---

[9] COM(1998) 625, available at <http://aei.pitt.edu/3353/01/000529_1.pdf>.

[10] Implementing the framework for financial markets: action plan, COM(1999) 232, available at <http://ec.europa.eu/internal_market/finances/docs/actionplan/index/action_en.pdf>.

[11] Final Report of the Committee of Wise Men on the Reg of the European Securities Markets (Lamfalussy Report), 15 February 2001, available at <http://ec.europa.eu/internal_market/securities/docs/lamfalussy/wisemen/final-report-wise-men_en.pdf>.

[12] ibid 10–12.   [13] ibid 14–15.   [14] ibid 15.   [15] ibid below.

of the previous regime was the inconsistent implementation of Community norms at national level. Under the Report, the common implementing standards at Level 3 are to be achieved through enhanced cooperation and networking among national supervisors under the auspices of CESR. Finally, Level 4 envisaged strengthened enforcement of Community law through enhanced cooperation between national supervisory authorities and more vigorous action by the Commission.

Within the context of the Lamfalussy process, CESR has played a pivotal role. This is an independent committee composed of representatives from the national securities regulators whose principal responsibilities are the following:[16] (a) to enhance cooperation between national supervisors; (b) to contribute to the common and uniform implementation and consistent application of Community legislation by issuing non-binding guidelines, recommendations, and standards; (c) to contribute to the consistent supervision and enforcement of EU measures; and (d) to act as an advisor to the Commission, in particular, in its preparation of draft measures implementing Level 1 framework measures. In practice, CESR's influence is more important than its non-binding powers might suggest. By adopting detailed guidelines specifying the way EU measures must be applied and following a 'comply or explain' approach, it places national supervisory authorities under considerable pressure and contributes to the convergence of standards throughout the EU.

A key theme which underlined the Lamfalussy Report was the distinctiveness of financial law. At a time when Member States were calling for greater use of subsidiarity and more national choice, the Report appeared to go against the policy tide advocating the federalization of securities regulation. In that respect, it contrasts sharply with the trend in competition law, an area *par excellence* of Community exclusive competence, where the Commission devolved more powers to national authorities.[17] The expansion of Community powers in the financial field, however, was perceived as justified on functional grounds. A political consensus had emerged that substantial economic benefits would be derived from the integration of the national capital markets. The establishment of a comprehensive Community regulatory regime was seen, in turn, as a *sine qua non* for that integration.

In terms of legislative output, the FSAP has been a great success. All but one[18] measure envisaged in the plan have been adopted leading to the enactment of more than fifty Level 1 and Level 2 measures.[19] In some cases, the targets set can be said to have been exceeded as legislation was adopted in areas where the Plan provided more

---

[16] Commission Decision of 6 June 2001 establishing the Committee of European Securities Regulators, [2001] OJ L191/43.

[17] Council Regulation 1/2003 on the implementation of the rules on competition laid down in Arts 81 and 82 of the Treaty, [2003] OJ L1/1.

[18] The only measure where consensus has not been reached is the proposed Fourteenth Company Law Directive on the cross-border transfer of corporate seat. The Plan had also envisaged the carrying out of a review of taxation of financial services products but no such review was in fact made.

[19] See the Commission's FSAP Evolution Chart available on <http://ec.europa.eu/internal_market/finances/docs/actionplan/index/061003_measures_en.pdf>.

abstractly for the reaching of political agreement.[20] Furthermore, the rate of implementation of the Community measures into national laws was closely monitored by
the Commission and has been very high.[21] Among the key measures adopted in
implementation of FSAP in the field of securities law are the Market Abuse Directive,[22]
the Prospectus Directive,[23] the Transparency Directive 2004/101,[24] and the Directive
in Markets in Financial Instruments (MiFiD).[25]

In 2005, the Commission issued a White Paper on Financial Services[26] in which it
outlined its priorities for the period between 2005 and 2010. The leitmotiv of the White
Paper was 'dynamic consolidation'. The Commission identified as a key objective
ensuring that Level 1 measures were followed up by Level 2 and Level 3 implementation
measures and were properly enforced. A second key objective was to provide for
enhanced supervisory cooperation and convergence in the EU. The themes of accountability and better regulation also assumed a higher place in the policy agenda. The
Commission pointed to the need for impact assessments prior to the introduction of
Community legislation and *ex post* evaluations as means of enhancing the value and
functionality of EU intervention. Impact assessments would focus on the 'costs and
benefits of proposed legislation across the broad economic, social and environmental
dimensions, and, where appropriate, the impact on financial stability, proper functioning of markets and consumer protection'.[27] *Ex post* evaluations would monitor on an
annual basis the overall state of financial integration through the Financial Integration
Monitor (FIM) report. The Commission also referred to a series of supervisory challenges.[28] It identified the need to reinforce procedures for cooperation and the exchange
of information between supervisors and, ominously, pointed out that 'co-operation in
crisis situations has to be secure'.[29] The Commission's policy plans were overtaken by
the financial crisis which brought to the fore the need for more regulation in areas
previously left untouched by EU law and precipitated calls for change in the regulatory

---

The original Plan provided for 42 measures. The Evolution Chart lists 45 measures but does not include a
host of Level 2 measures which bring the overall number to more than 50.

[20] This was, for example, the case in relation to Council Directive 2004/25 on Take-over Bids, [2004] OJ
L142/12; Regulation 2157/2001 on the European Company Statute, [2001] OJ L294/1; Council Directives 2001/
107, [2001] OJ L41/20, and 2001/108, [2001] OJ L41/35 on UCITS; and Council Directive 2002/65 on Distance
Marketing of Financial Services, [2002] OJ L271/16. Also, in some areas, the Plan did not envisage legislation
but Community action in the form of non-binding measures such as recommendations or communications.
See eg Commission Communication on E-commerce and financial services (FIN-NET), COM(2001) 66; and
Commission Report of 20 March 2000 on Retail Financial Services: Overcoming remaining Barriers—A Legal
Analysis. A measure of particular importance which was not envisaged in the original FSAP is Council
Regulation 924/2009 on cross-border payments, which seeks to eliminate differences in charges between
cross-border and internal payments in euro, [2009] OJ L266/11.

[21] See the Lamfalussy League Table, <http://ec.europa.eu/internal_market/securities/docs/transposition/
table_en.pdf>.

[22] Council Directive 2003/6, [2003] OJ L96/16.

[23] Council Directive 2003/71, [2003] OJ L345/31.

[24] Council Directive 2004/109, [2004] OJ L390/38.

[25] Council Directive 2004/39, [2004] OJ L145/1.

[26] Commission, White Paper, Financial Services Policy 2005–2010, available at <http://ec.europa.eu/
internal_market/finances/docs/white_paper/white_paper_en.pdf>.

[27] ibid 5.   [28] ibid 9.   [29] ibid 9.

architecture. In general, the Commission has been more successful in carrying out *ex post* evaluations than in performing *ex ante* impact assessments.[30]

C. TRENDS AND FEATURES OF THE HARMONIZATION PROGRAMME

The harmonization programme is pursued, first and foremost, through directives. With few exceptions,[31] Level 1 measures have taken the form of directives. By contrast, at Level 2 the Commission has acted either through directives or through regulations depending on the level of uniformity required.[32] The Community regime provides for comprehensive coverage of securities, banking, and financial law and regulates, *inter alia*, the following key areas: disclosure requirements, the regulation of market abuse, and the regulation of banks, insurance undertakings, UCITS, and financial intermediaries. Both prudential requirements and conduct of business rules are dealt with at Community level. The cornerstone of the harmonization programme is the Market in Financial Instruments Directive (MiFiD)[33] which replaces, and goes much further than, its predecessor, the Investment Services Directive.[34] MiFiD applies to investment firms, regulated markets, and multilateral trading facilities. It provides a comprehensive definition of investment services including the provision of investment advice. It introduces the suitability principle,[35] which has had major impact in the laws of the Member States, and contains detailed requirements governing authorization for investment firms, their operating conditions, and conduct of business rules. A major innovation of MiFiD is that it abolishes the concentration rule, that is, the obligation to execute orders in the stock exchange, thus allowing competition through multilateral trading facilities (MTFs) and systematic internalization.[36]

---

[30] For *ex post* assessments, see the European Financial Integration Report (EFIR) at <http://ec.europa.eu/internal_market/finances/fim/index_en.htm>.

[31] See, eg, Council Regulation 2157/2001 on the European Company Statute, [2001] OJ L294/1. The adoption of a regulation in this case was necessary to facilitate the establishment of a new corporate form governed directly by Community law and not based on the law of a Member State.

[32] Thus, Level 2 measures implementing the Market in Financial Instruments Directive (MiFiD) include both a Commission Directive 2006/73, [2006] OJ L241/26, and a Commission Regulation 1287/2006, [2006] OJ L241/1.

[33] Directive 2004/39, [2004] OJ L145/1.

[34] Directive 93/22, [1993] OJ L141/27.

[35] See MiFiD (n 32 above), Art 19(4). The suitability principle is further concretized by Level 2 measures: see Directive 2006/73, [2006] OJ L241/26, Art 35. The principle imposes an obligation on an investment firm, when providing advice, to obtain all information regarding the client's circumstances and preferences to enable it to provide advice which is suitable to the client's needs. In the absence of such information, the investment firm may not provide advice.

[36] See MiFiD (n 32 above) Art 21. Systematic internalization refers to the execution of client orders by a firm against its own books. A systematic internalizer is defined as an investment firm which, on an organized, frequent, and systematic basis, deals on own account by executing client orders outside a regulated market or a Multi-Trading Facility; see MiFiD ibid, Art 1(1)(7). Systematic internalization is without prejudice to the best execution principle, ie the obligation to execute a client's order on terms that are most favourable to the client. See MiFiD ibid, Art 21.

MiFiD establishes the single passport principle in the field of investment firms.[37] An investment firm must receive authorization by its home Member State, ie the state where its registered office is located.[38] The conditions for granting authorization are specified in the Directive. Under Article 31, once authorization has been granted by the home state, a firm is free to carry out the investment activities covered by its authorization throughout the Community either by way of provision of services or through the establishment of a branch. The host state may not require the firm to be authorized by its own authorities nor may it impose any additional requirements in respect of the matters covered by the Directive.[39] It will be noted, however, that despite the detailed provisions of MiFiD, the division of responsibilities between the home and the host state continues to be problematic.[40]

FSAP led to the repeal of a number of Directives adopted in the 1980s and the adoption of a second generation of Directives thus leading to a 'second financial law consensus'.[41] This is the first example in Community law of a wholesale amendment of a first wave of legislation thus illustrating that the Community legal order has reached a stage of some maturity.

A distinct feature of the harmonization programme is that, unlike a substantial part of national legislation in the financial field, it is not scandal-driven. A common feature of many national statutes in securities law is that they were introduced in the aftermath of fraudulent behaviour or major scandals. Remarkably, this trend of 'closing the stable doors after the horses have gone' has been as much a feature of early financial legislation as of more recent legislation in countries with highly sophisticated markets, including the United States. One need go no further than to recall the Sarbanes-Oxley Act introduced by Congress in 2002 in the aftermath of the Enron and World-Com scandals. In that respect, Community law appears to enjoy a comparative advantage. Being more detached from immediate electoral concerns, which may lead national governments to seek fast remedies in the aftermath of a scandal, the Commission has, or should have, the luxury of contemplation focusing on long-term reform. As we shall see, however, this is not necessarily the case.

---

[37] The single passport principle is provided also, among others, in relation to banks by Directive 2006/48 relating to the taking up and pursuit of the business of credit institutions, [2006] OJ L177/1, and in relation to life assurance institutions by Directive 2002/83 concerning life assurance [2002] OJ L345/1 as amended.

[38] MiFID (n 32 above) Art 5.

[39] MiFID (n 32 above), Art 31(1), second sub-para. Free movement may be exercised by the establishment of a branch or the provision of services. By contrast, if a firm wishes to establish a subsidiary in another Member State, the subsidiary is in its own right a corporate entity under the law of the host state and must receive authorization by its competent authorities before being able to carry on any investment activities. The competent authorities of the state where the subsidiary is located must consult the competent authorities of the state of the parent firm before granting authorization to the subsidiary: see MiFiD ibid, Art 60.

[40] See here, *inter alia*, the Level 3 recommendation issued by CESR for the implementation of MiFiD, The Passport under MiFiD Ref: CESR/07–337, and Commission, Internal Market and Services DG memorandum, *Supervision of Branches under MiFID*, MARKT/G/3/MV D(2007), Brussels, 18 June 2007, 2. Available at <http://ec.europa.eu/internal_market/securities/docs/isd/mifid-branches_en.pdf>.

[41] E Avgouleas, 'The New EC Financial Markets Legislation and the Emerging Regime for Capital Markets' (2004) 23 YEL 321, 327.

Following the financial crisis of Autumn 2008, the Community has reacted rapidly with a set of legislative proposals, somewhat fusing law reform and crisis management.

In some cases, directives have had an unduly long period of gestation. This has in turn lessened their importance as forces of law reform. The Take-over Bids Directive provides a prime example here. The Commission began work on the harmonization of national take-over laws in 1972 but a directive was not included in the Community statute book until 2004.[42] The same applies to insider trading. When the Commission first considered the introduction of anti-insider dealing legislation in the mid-1970s, Member States, on the whole, lacked specific and coherent regulation in the field. By the time, however, the Insider Dealing Directive was introduced in 1989,[43] a number of Member States had taken further initiatives.[44] The pace of law reform increased spectacularly in the 2000s. As already stated, FSAP was implemented speedily and it appears that the co-decision procedure has worked well.

In some cases, Community legislation crystallizes regulatory initiatives undertaken at other international or supranational fora. In that respect, the Community nature of directives may hide their true origins which may lie in supranational professional organizations, such as IOSCO, or other international groups.[45] Such 'silent' or, in some cases, express following of international initiatives raises issues of accountability and transparency as politicians appear to have little influence over the content of measures.[46] In other respects, however, EU legislation goes beyond minima proposed by international organizations. A prime example is provided by the Credit Rating Agencies Regulation[47] which introduces binding norms in lieu of the soft law approach of the IOSCO Code of Conduct for Credit Rating Agencies[48] and provides more specific requirements than that Code. Indeed, a positive aspect of the EU's prompt response to the financial crisis is that it increases its voice as a contributor to global regulatory standards and becomes a supplier rather than a recipient of policy initiatives in the international scene.

Perhaps, the most important feature of the evolution of the harmonization programme has been the trend towards centralization and maximum harmonization. In

---

[42] Directive on Take-over Bids (n 20 above).

[43] Council Directive 89/592/EEC of 13 November 1989 coordinating regulations on insider dealing, [1989] OJ L334/30.

[44] For a discussion, see T Tridimas, 'Insider Trading: European Harmonisation and National Law Reform' (1991) 40 ICLQ 919.

[45] See, eg, Directive 2002/87 on Financial Conglomerates which represented the first full transposition in the world of the recommendations on the supervision of conglomerates adopted by the G10 Group under the auspices of the Bank for International Settlements. See also Commission Regulation 1606/2002 on the application of international accounting standards.

[46] See G Bertezzolo, 'The European Union facing the global arena: standard setting bodies and financial regulation' (2009) 34 ELRev 257.

[47] Regulation 1060/2009, [2009] OJ L302/1.

[48] The International Organization of Securities Commissions (IOSCO) brings together national financial regulators. It has published a Code of Conduct Fundamentals for Credit Rating Agencies, see last version of May 2008 at <http://www.iosco.org/library/pubdocs/pdf/IOSCOPD271.pdf>.

the last decade, this trend has characterized developments especially in the field of securities regulation but has also spilled over into the fields of banking and insurance. Although there are notable exceptions,[49] the maximum harmonization trend represents the prevailing regulatory model and corresponds with the wider policy of the Commission in the field of consumer law. The process towards the federalization of securities law was set in motion by the Lamfalussy model and has been further enhanced as a result of the financial crisis. This trend towards federalization occurs at three levels: first, in terms of scope, through the introduction of Community legislation in more areas, and the gradual colonization of all aspects of capital markets law; secondly, in terms of intensity, through the establishment of new institutional arrangements and the setting up of a quasi-federal structure; and thirdly, through the gradual introduction by CESR of common implementation standards and the enhancement of Community presence in the field of enforcement.

The last aspect can be seen as part of a wider trend to place emphasis on the uniform implementation of directives and the effective supervision and enforcement of Community rules. It does not suffice for directives to find their way into the national statute book. They must also be applied in the same way by the national financial supervisors and be respected in practice. This ties in with the approach of the ECJ in the wider field of Community law as recent case law stresses the importance of 'second level enforcement', namely the need for observance of Community rules not only by the national legislatures but also by the national executive, the administration, and the courts.[50] It also ties in with the findings of various inquiries into the Equitable Life Affair which identified the lax regulatory culture of financial authorities as a key reason behind Equitable's collapse.[51]

The virtues of maximum harmonization are said to be that it increases uniformity and legal certainty; it establishes a level playing field thus avoiding a race to the bottom; it decreases transaction costs, facilitates free movement, and reduces the need for reliance on instruments of negative integration thus making outcomes less dependent on ECJ rulings; and finally, it promotes legitimacy of outcomes since they are negotiated by politicians who are accountable to their national electorates whilst internalizing national concerns in the Community decision-making process. The disadvantages, on the other hand, are said to be that it gives too much power to supranational actors who are subject to inadequate political controls; it fails in fact to facilitate free movement and reduce transaction costs since it does not do away with the need to rely on local advice; on a cost-effectiveness basis, it is less preferable than instruments of negative integration to promote free movement; it removes regulatory competition, and leads to stagnation owing to rigid amendment procedures. The

---

[49] See especially the Take Over Bids Directive (n 20 above) which far from providing a satisfactory harmonization model leaves a wide number of options to the Member States.

[50] See eg Case C-453/00 *Kühne & Heitz NV v Productschap voor Pluimvee en Eieren* [2004] ECR I-00837; Case C-129/00 *Commission v Italy* [2003] ECR I-14637.

[51] See eg the Penrose and Baird Reports on the Equitable Life collapse.

detailed discussion of these arguments is beyond the scope of this chapter.[52] Suffice it here to highlight the last two points. A consequence of the maximum harmonization model is that it leaves little margin for regulatory competition. The EU harmonization programme does not encourage either supply-side competition between regulators or demand-side arbitrage between corporate issuers or financial intermediaries. In that respect, the EU approach contrasts, to some extent, with the US model where the possibility of regulatory experimentation at state level is viewed as a virtue of federalism and informs the constitutional debate on the limits of congressional powers.[53] Furthermore, a negative aspect of maximum harmonization is that it makes law reform more difficult. Once an area is colonized by EU measures, it can only be amended by new EU norms and no longer at the national level. Thus maximum harmonization carries with it the danger of stagnation and the risk of regulators being unable to respond quickly to fast-evolving market conditions. The way to deal with this danger is, first, by ensuring that Level 1 measures contain adequate flexibility and do not provide for detailed regulation and, secondly, by providing an efficient system of delegated legislation. Whether the new procedures proposed by the Commission in the field of financial law will be able to meet these challenges remains to be seen. It is however imperative to ensure that, especially in an area as fast moving as the regulation of financial markets, the processes are sufficiently flexible to enable swift and decisive action.

The harmonization programme favours the public rather than the private enforcement of securities regulation. Directives which impose obligations on market participants typically require Member States to provide for effective, proportionate, and sufficiently dissuasive penalties for breach of their provisions. The Market Abuse Directive, for example, specifically requires Member States to adopt administrative penalties for insider trading and market manipulation whilst leaving the possibility of adoption of criminal penalties for the national laws to decide.[54] Similar provisions are included, *inter alia*, in the Prospectus Directive, the Transparency Directive, and MiFiD.[55] A journey through the national anti-insider trading laws reveals the existence of common enforcement instruments but broad variations at the level of sanctions. Out of the 29 jurisdictions, 28 impose criminal penalties, 27 have included terms of imprisonment, 24 have a variety of non pecuniary administrative sanctions, and 21 impose civil fines. The maximum term of imprisonment varies from one year in Belgium to fifteen years in Latvia. The level of a criminal fine varies from a maximum

---

[52] For a fuller discussion, see, among others, L Enriques, and M Gatti, 'The Uneasy Case for Top-Down Corporate Law Harmonization in the European Union' (2006) 27 U Pa J Int'l Econ L 939; L E Ribstein and E A O'Hara, 'Corporations and the Market for Law', U Illinois Law & Economics Research Paper No LE07–002; U Illinois L Rev (2008). Available at SSRN: <http://ssrn.com/abstract=956919>; P S Ryan, 'Will there ever be a "Delaware for Europe?"' (2005) 11 CJEL 187.

[53] See, eg, *Gonzales v Raich* 125 S Ct 2195 at 2220 per Justice O'Connor (dissenting); *New State Ice Co v Liebmann* 285 US 262, 311.

[54] Council Directive 2003/6 (n 22 above) Art 14.

[55] Prospectus Directive 2001/34, [2001] OJ L184/1, Art 25; Transparency Directive 2004/39 (n 25 above) Art 28; MiFiD, (n 32 above) Art 51. Note that the Transparency Directive also refers somewhat vaguely to civil penalties, Art 28.

of €10,000 in Belgium to a maximum of €10,000,000 in Ireland and unlimited fines in Germany and in the UK. There are wide variations also in the level of administrative sanctions that may be imposed. Thus, 21 out of 29 jurisdictions may impose administrative fines. These range from €100 in Finland to €45,000,000 in Italy and an unlimited fine in the UK.[56]

By contrast, the harmonization Directives do not typically provide for civil remedies in favour of investors. The Prospectus Directive, for example, does not seek to coordinate the rules governing liability for misstatements in prospectuses and merely provides that Member States must ensure that their laws on civil liability apply to those persons responsible for the information given in a prospectus.[57] Similarly, MiFiD and its implementing Level 2 measures articulate the standards of the suitability doctrine but leave the issue of civil liability for its breach to national laws. Whether a directive may give rise to an implied right of action remains an open question. Although this may be the case under certain conditions, the right of action would be governed by national law.[58]

By requiring the adoption of administrative penalties whilst leaving civil sanctions to national law, the EU favours in effect a public rather than a private model of securities regulation enforcement. This policy has grown out of necessity rather than out of conviction. It is easier for EU norms to require administrative rather than civil sanctions. The former are self-standing and subject to the protection of a common set of fundamental rights articulated by the ECJ and the ECtHR. Harmonization of civil sanctions, by contrast, would inevitably make inroads into national private laws and raise more complex questions. Two points may be made in this context. First, although as stated above there are wide variations in the national administrative and criminal penalties imposed, it is submitted that, on a cost-benefit analysis, harmonization of penalties should not be actively pursued by the EU. The link between coordination of national penalties and the achievement of the objectives of the coordination programme, namely the establishment of an integrated European securities market, appears too tenuous to warrant spending resources in that area. Secondly, the private model of enforcement requires perhaps more thought than it has received by policy-makers. Notably, the Commission has taken steps to encourage the private

[56] The information is taken from CESR, Report on Administrative Measures and Criminal Sanctions available in Member States under the Market Abuse Directive, CESR/07–693, February 2008, 3–4 and 9–10 (available at <http://www.cesr.eu/popup2.php?id=4975>. The 29 jurisdictions include the EU Member States plus Norway and Iceland.

[57] Council Directive 2003/71 (n 23 above) Art 6(2).

[58] Note that, in some cases, the directives refer to civil sanctions but these do not necessarily translate to rights for investors. See eg Transparency Directive 2004/39 (n 25 above) Art 28. For a rare case where a directive expressly requires the sanction of suspension or nullity of voting rights, see MiFiD, Art 10(6). The ECJ has accepted that a regulation may give rise to an implied right of action, see Case C-253/00 *Munoz Cia SA and Superior Fruitcola v Fumar Ltd and Redbridge Produce Marketing Ltd* [2002] ECR I-7289; Although directives lack horizontal direct effect, it is submitted that, in view of the principle of effectiveness, in some cases they may be able to give rise to implied rights of action depending on the specificity of their provisions and the existence of supporting provisions of national law. Note that in Case C-222/02 *Peter Paul and others* [2004] ECR I-9425, the ECJ rejected that the banking and securities law directives, as they existed before FSAP, gave to a depositor an implied right to good supervision against national supervisory authorities.

enforcement of competition law[59] and it may not be out of place to consider more seriously civil remedies for breach of securities laws.

A further feature of the harmonization programme is that the directives have generated limited case law. Whilst the ECJ has had a major impact in articulating the requirements of free movement and facilitating the liberalization of financial services, there have been few preliminary references on the interpretation of harmonization directives. In this respect, EU financial law contrasts with EU consumer or employment law where harmonization measures are heavily litigated. A number of reasons may account for this. For one thing, wholesale actors in the financial services industry prefer not to litigate. For another thing, where disputes arise between business entities, they tend to be on issues governed by contractual freedom and left untouched by Community harmonization legislation. As far as disputes involving retail investors are concerned, the dearth of litigation before the ECJ mirrors the fact that there is also little litigation at the national level. Consumers prefer to have recourse to alternative dispute resolution systems such as ombudsman services, which provide a speedier and less expensive option, albeit not necessarily one with higher chances of success. Furthermore, as already stated, Community directives rarely give rise to rights in favour of investors against issuers, banks, or financial intermediaries.[60]

The ECJ has delivered a number of judgments in enforcement proceedings against Member States but these rarely involve issues of substance. It in notable that, where references are made to the ECJ on the interpretation of EU financial legislation, they tend not to come from states with the most developed financial markets.[61] There are however reasons to suggest that the ECJ will increase its presence in this area. The sheer volume of legislation is likely to give rise to more problems of interpretation. Furthermore, the establishment of the suitability doctrine by MiFiD and its implementing directives may well give rise to disputes at the retail level. Finally, the increasing use of the copy-out technique whereby Member States incorporate directives verbatim into national law means that the text of the directive itself becomes more determinative of the interpretation of national law and therefore more likely to be material in the event of a dispute.

D. THE POST-CRISIS PHASE

In the aftermath of the financial crisis of September 2008, the Community intervened in a number of ways to contain its adverse effects. First, the Commission took urgent

---

[59] White Paper on Damages Actions for Breach of the EC antitrust rules COM(2008) 165.

[60] See n 58 above. Even where such rights arise, the lack of horizontal effect would inhibit direct reliance on a directive against a non-state actor.

[61] See eg the three references made so far on the interpretation of Directive 89/592 on Insider Trading: Case C-28/99 *Verdonck* [2001] ECR I-3399; Case C-384/02 *Grøngaard and Bang*, [2006] IRLR 214 (reference from Denmark); Case C-391/04 *Ipourgos Ikonomikon v Georgakis* [2007] ECR I-3741 (reference from Greece); and see more recently on the interpretation of Directive 2003/6 on Market Abuse, Case C-45/08 *Spector Photo Group NV v CBFA*, 23 December 2009 (reference from Belgium).

relief measures seeking to provide liquidity and rejuvenate the economy. Such crisis management measures took, in effect, the form of rewriting the state aid rulebook. Secondly, the Commission took steps to introduce or enhance existing regulation in specific fields. Finally, it put forward far-reaching proposals for redesigning the EU regulatory architecture.

1. CRISIS MANAGEMENT

When EU banks were first affected by the sub-prime mortgage lending in the US, the Commission addressed ensuing problems by reference to established rules and methodologies. It relied, in particular, on the Rescuing and Restructuring State Aid Guidelines issued under Article 87(3)(c) EC (now Article 107(3)(c) TFEU).[62] After the collapse of Lehman Brothers, however, the crisis unfolded and it became clear that there was a need for drastic action. Community intervention was precipitated by the unilateral guarantee of bank deposits announced by the Irish government on 30 September 2008. The guarantee was initially applicable only to six Irish banks and their subsidiaries located abroad but not to other EU banks operating in Ireland. This was clearly discriminatory and in patent infringement of the state aid rules of the Treaty. Following the Commission's intervention, the guarantee was extended to all EU banks with subsidiaries or branches in Ireland. The Commission noted that it was due to it its 'rapid intervention, that securing financial stability was achieved and the integrity of the Internal Market maintained at the same time'.[63] Although the Commission acted promptly and decisively, it turned necessity into virtue. The unilateral intervention by the Irish government showed that in times of crisis Member States may react somewhat atavistically, reverting to basic ideas of sovereignty. The truth is that the EU, as a constitutional arrangement of nation states, is better equipped to contribute to law reform than crisis management. The latter requires clear competence, wide executive discretion, and high expertise. In the field of financial regulation, however, the Community lacks at least the first two elements. As a result, in the aftermath of the crisis, the Commission had to fight to establish its authority.

In October 2008, the governments of the Member States agreed to implement national rescue packages for the banking sector with a view to restoring liquidity and safeguarding stability. As a result, the Commission offered guidance on the implementation of the national schemes under the state aid rules of the Treaty so as to avoid undue distortions of competition. Guidance was offered in successive

---

[62] See Guidelines on State Aid for rescuing and restructuring firms in difficulty, [2004] OJ C241/2. Art 87(3)(c) empowers the Commission to authorize aid to facilitate the development of certain economic activities or of certain economic areas, where such aid does not adversely affect trading conditions to an extent contrary to the common interest.

[63] Commission Report, State Aid Scoreboard—Spring 2009 Update—Special Edition on State Aid Interventions in the Current Financial and Economic Crisis, COM(2009) 164, 18.

documents, namely, the Banking Communication of 13 October 2008,[64] the Recapitalisation Communication of 5 December 2008,[65] and the Impaired Assets Communication of 25 February 2009.[66] Furthermore, Member States sought and obtained authorization to subsidize financial institutions in *ad hoc* cases. The detailed examination of these measures is beyond the scope of this chapter. Suffice it here to discuss the salient features of the Banking Communication of October 2008. This Communication broke with tradition as it was the first time that the Commission had authorized general aid on the basis of Article 87(3)(b) (now Article 107(3)(b) TFEU) which enables the granting of aid 'to remedy serious disturbance in the economy of a Member State'.[67] Recourse to Article 87(3)(b) was justifiable in the circumstances although it is subject to a strict proportionality requirement.[68] The financial crisis posed a systemic risk to national economies. Invoking that legal basis enabled the Member States to adopt structural measures and also to extend schemes to the entire banking sector without restricting them to banks that were in immediate financial difficulties.[69]

The Communication authorizes three kinds of state intervention in the banking sector: bank guarantee schemes, recapitalization schemes, and the controlled winding up of credit institutions.

The aid could be granted subject to compliance with a number of principles. First, eligibility for the aid must be based on objective criteria and must not be discriminatory on grounds of nationality (*non-discrimination*). All institutions incorporated in the state granting the aid, including subsidiaries of banks from other Member States, must in principle be eligible for the aid.[70] Secondly, the aid must be limited in time (*temporal scope*). This derives from the principle of proportionality: state commitments are viewed as an aberration to ordinary free market rules and must be restricted to what is necessary in order to cope with the financial turmoil. Member States must review aid schemes on a six-monthly basis and submit the results of their review to the Commission. Provided that such regular review takes place, the approval of the scheme may cover a period of up to two years.[71] This condition may well provide the litmus test of the Commission's scheme. At present, it is too early to assess

---

[64] Banking Communication, [2008] OJ C270/8.

[65] Recapitalisation Communication, [2009] OJ C10/2.

[66] Impaired Assets Communication, [2009] OJ C72/1.

[67] Art 87(3)(b) had been used only once in the 1980s in an isolated case relating to Greece.

[68] The provision can only be used to counteract a disturbance in the entire economy of a Member State: see Cases T-132/96 and T-143/96 *Freistaat Sachsen and Volkswagen AG v Commission* [1999] ECR II-3663, [167]; and Commission Decision in Case C-47/1996 *Crédit Lyonnais* [1998] OJ L221/28 pt 10.1, Commission Decision in Case C-28/2002 *Bankgesellschaft Berlin* [2005] OJ L116/1 pts 153 *et seq.*

[69] Commission Report (n 63) 10.

[70] The Communication states that the aid must be open to foreign subsidiaries 'with significant activities in that Member State': see [18]. This would permit the exclusion of a foreign subsidiary on objective grounds. Thus an aid scheme may be restricted to certain types of credit institutions or banks operating in certain sectors or subject to certain thresholds etc.

[71] ibid [24]. The Commission may approve the extension of an aid scheme beyond the two-year period if it is necessary to cope with the crisis. For latest developments, see http://europa.eu/rapid/pressReleaseAction.do?reference=MEMO/10/656&format=HTML&aged=0&language=EN&guiLanguage=en

compliance with that condition. It is important, however, to monitor the implementation and operation of the various national schemes in practice with a view to ensuring the orderly and transparent withdrawal of the state as the credit markets return to normality. One suspects that withdrawal of state support will prove a challenge at least in some Member States or, at least, in relation to certain institutions. Thirdly, state intervention must be limited in scope and clearly defined (*proportionality requirement*). The aid must be well targeted and limited to the strict minimum so as to exclude unjustified benefits for shareholders at the expense of the taxpayer and minimize negative spill-over effects for competitors.[72] Fourthly, the aid must be subject to an appropriate contribution by the beneficiary undertaking (*private sector contribution*). The *quid pro quo* for receiving a state guarantee, and thus substantially reducing market risk, is that the beneficiary institution must pay a fee to the state.[73] The difficulty here is how to determine what is appropriate remuneration for a state guarantee in circumstances where there are no comparable market benchmarks. In practice, many national aid schemes have incorporated a clawback mechanism whereby beneficiary undertakings will have to reimburse the state for the subsidies that they have received as soon as they are able to do so. Fifthly, the aid must be accompanied by behavioural rules for the beneficiaries to ensure that they do not misuse state resources to engage in aggressive market practices (*avoidance of undue distortions in competition*).[74] Such conduct of business constraints are aimed at avoiding moral hazard, ie banks taking undue risks with a view to maximizing profits on the back of a state guarantee of any potential losses. Such constraints may take the form of restrictions on advertising or even pricing and business expansion. They may also take the form of limitations on the size of the balance sheet of the beneficiary institutions, eg by reference to gross domestic product.[75] Finally, aid schemes must be accompanied by structural adjustment measures for the beneficiary sector as a whole (*structural readjustment*).[76] The underlying idea here is that government subsidies are only allowed on an exceptional basis to counteract the symptoms of the crisis and must be accompanied by long-term measures to address structural shortcomings in the organization of financial markets.

In general, the rescue packages adopted by the various Member States appear to have had the desired effect. Although retail and wholesale financial markets have moved slowly since Autumn 2008, a complete meltdown was avoided and state guarantees were crucial in providing a safety net and thus boosting consumer confidence. The national rescue measures were adopted in haste and, inevitably, they pursue a mix of economic and political objectives set by the incumbent governments. In the longer term, if the integrity of the internal market is to be safeguarded, it is imperative that the national schemes remain under close scrutiny by the Commission and that any 'spill-over' effects, ie their extension to other sectors of the economy, is avoided.

---

[72] ibid [15].   [73] ibid [26].   [74] ibid [27].
[75] ibid [27].   [76] ibid [28]–[29].

2. SUBSTANTIVE LAW REFORM

In the aftermath of the crisis, the Commission spearheaded a far-reaching programme of law reform. The Commission's response was prompt and ambitious. In November 2008, it appointed a High Level Group, chaired by Mr Jacques de Larosière, to make recommendations on how to strengthen financial markets regulation at EU level. The final Report of the de Larosière Group was presented on 25 February 2009.[77] On the basis of the Report, the Commission set out an action plan in its Communication on Driving European Recovery presented on 4 March 2009.[78] This was subsequently followed by more detailed policy plans laid down in its Communication on European Financial Supervision of 27 May 2009,[79] and an extensive and fully developed package of reform proposals was presented in September 2009.[80]

The Commission's proposals fall essentially into two categories. First, a number of proposed measures seek to regulate substantive areas of law. Secondly, the Commission proposes to overhaul the financial supervisory architecture by establishing a new pan-European regulatory framework. This section briefly examines the first while the second is examined in the subsequent section.

There is a new regulation on credit rating agencies,[81] proposed rules for hedge funds and private equity,[82] amendments to accounting rules,[83] new capital requirements,[84] and initiatives on executive pay.[85] The Commission has also focused its attention on packaged retail investment products which include investment funds, retail structured products, and insurance-based investment products.[86] The Commission considers that such products are currently subject to a fragmented regulatory framework that fails to serve investor interests and leads to regulatory arbitrage.[87] It thus

---

[77] Available at <http://ec.europa.eu/internal_market/finances/docs/de_larosiere_report_en.pdf>.

[78] COM(2009) 114, available at <http://ec.europa.eu/commission_barroso/president/pdf/press_20090304_en.pdf>.

[79] See Commission Communication on European Financial Supervision, Brussels, COM(2009) 252 final.

[80] See nn 81 to 88 and n 109 below.

[81] Regulation 1060/2009, [2009] OJ L302/1.

[82] Proposal for a Directive on Alternative Investment Fund Managers, COM(2009) 207 final.

[83] For an overview, see <http://ec.europa.eu/internal_market/accounting/news/index_en.htm>.

[84] Proposal for a Directive amending Directives 2006/48/EC and 2006/49/EC as regards capital requirements for the trading book and for re-securitizations, and the supervisory review of remuneration policies, COM(2009) 362 final.

[85] Those initiatives are mostly soft law measures in the form of recommendations and communications: see Commission Recommendation on remuneration policies in the financial services sector, COM(2009) 211 final; Commission Recommendation complementing Recommendations 2004/913/EC and 2005/162/EC as regards the regime for the remuneration of directors of listed companies, COM(2009) 3177; Communication from the Commission accompanying the above Recommendations, COM(2009) 211 final; all available at <http://ec.europa.eu/internal_market/company/directors-remun/index_en.htm>. Note also that the proposed amendments to the Capital Adequacy Directive require credit institutions to establish remuneration policies that do not reward excessive risk-taking by executives and traders.

[86] <http://ec.europa.eu/internal_market/finservices-retail/investment_products_en.htm>.

[87] See Update on Commission Work on Packaged Retail Investment Products, 16 December 2009, available at <http://ec.europa.eu/internal_market/finservices-retail/docs/investment_products/20091215_prips_en.pdf, 2.

intends to propose legislation requiring pre-contractual disclosures and rules on selling practices.[88]

One of the most important post-crisis measures adopted by the EU is the Regulation on credit rating agencies (CRAs).[89] In the aftermath of the crisis, the role of CRAs came under intense scrutiny. Among the criticisms levelled against them is that they underestimated the risks posed by complex financial products. Furthermore, the objectivity of their ratings was questioned on the ground that they operated under perverse market incentives. Given that agencies are remunerated by the very firms which they evaluate, they have an incentive to provide favourable ratings.[90] The EU Regulation provides that EU financial institutions, including banks, investment firms, insurance companies, undertakings for collective investment in transferable securities, and institutions for occupational retirement provision may use a credit rating for regulatory purposes only if it has been issued by a CRA established in the EU and registered in accordance with the provisions of the Regulation.[91] The Regulation contains provisions governing, *inter alia*, the avoidance of conflict of interests, requirements pertaining to rating analysts and CRA employees, the methodologies, models and key rating assumptions used by CRAs, and disclosure obligations. The Regulation is important for a number of reasons. It opts for a hard law, centralized approach in preference to the many soft law options considered and favoured by CESR.[92] It is EU-centric in that it requires registration of CRAs by an EU regulator despite the fact that most of the leading agencies are based in the US.[93] Finally, it departs from the home country control principle introducing a system of authorization which recognizes a role for colleges of national supervisors and CESR.[94] This paves the way for phasing in a system whereby a single passport will be granted in the future not by the home national authority but by an EU agency.

---

[88] Furthermore, the Commission is currently preparing a Directive on legal certainty of securities holding and transactions which will cover, *inter alia*, rules pertaining to the holding and disposal of securities, the exercise of investor's rights in cross-border situations, the establishment of free, EU-wide choice of issuers regarding the initial entry of their securities in central securities depositories, and safekeeping and administration of securities. See <http://ec.europa.eu/internal_market/financial-markets/securities-law/index_en.htm>.

[89] Regulation 1060/2009 (n 81 above).

[90] M Ahmed Diomande, J Heintz, and R Pollin, 'Why U.S. Financial Markets Need a Public Credit Rating Agency', The Economists' Voice, <http://www.bepress.com/ev> June 2009.

[91] Regulation 1060/2009 (n 81 above) Art 4(1).

[92] F Amtenbrink and J de Haan, 'Credit Rating Agencies in the European Union: A Critical First Assessment of the European Commission Proposal' (24 April 2009). Available at SSRN: <http://ssrn.com/abstract=1394332>.

[93] Note however that the Regulation has specific provisions on the recognition of credit ratings related to entities established or financial instruments issued in third countries and issued by third country CRAs as equivalent: see n 81 above, Art 5.

[94] See n 81 above, Arts 14–17. See now Commission Proposal for Revisions to the CRA Regulation (COM (2010) 289) which provides for the direct supervision of CRAS by the new European Securities and Markets Authority.

3. INSTITUTIONAL ARCHITECTURE

The Commission proposes the establishment of an enhanced European financial supervisory framework based on two Pillars, a European Systemic Risk Board (ESRB) and a European System of Financial Supervisors (ESFS).[95] The ESRB focuses on macro-prudential supervision. Its role is to monitor and assess potential threats to financial stability that arise from macro-economic developments and trends within the financial system as a whole.[96] The ESRB will provide early warning of emerging systemic risks and have power to issue recommendations to deal with such risks. It will analyse trends, identify imbalances in the financial system as a whole, and detect systemic risks. The ESFS, by contrast, will focus on micro-prudential supervision and its role will be to enhance the day-to-day supervision of the financial industry. It will be based on a network of national financial supervisors working together with three newly established EU authorities. This 'network approach' is intended to provide a pragmatic solution. On the one hand, it recognizes that authority for the day-to-day supervision of financial institutions lies with the national authorities since the Member States have ultimate responsibility to fund any necessary rescue plans. On the other hand, the reform package recognizes the need for coordination and for ensuring 'a balanced flow of information between home and host authorities'.[97]

At the heart of the new regulatory architecture is the replacement of the existing Level 3 committees of supervisors[98] with three new fully-fledged European Supervisory Authorities, namely, a European Banking Authority (EBA), a European Insurance and Occupational Pensions Authority (EIOPA), and a European Securities and Markets Authority (ESMA). Each of these authorities will have independent legal personality. They will take on the tasks currently performed by the Level 3 committees and, in addition, they will be allocated important decision-making, monitoring, and even quasi-regulatory functions. The objectives of the new committees will be to contribute to (a) improving the functioning of the internal market; (b) protecting depositors; (c) ensuring the integrity, efficiency, and orderly functioning of financial markets;

---

[95] These proposals were introduced in the Commission's May 2009 Communication: see above. On 24 September 2009, the Commission presented the following detailed proposals: available at <http://ec.europa.eu/internal_market/finances/committees/index_en.htm#package>. Proposal for a regulation on Community macro prudential oversight of the financial system and establishing a European Systemic Risk Board (ESRB); Proposal for a decision entrusting the European Central Bank with specific tasks concerning the functioning of the European Systemic Risk Board; Proposal for a regulation establishing a European Banking Authority (EBA); Proposal for a regulation establishing a European Insurance and Occupational Pensions Authority (EIOPA); Proposal for a regulation establishing a European Securities and Markets Authority (ESMA).

[96] May Communication (n 95 above) 3.

[97] May Communication (n 95 above) 9.

[98] Currently, there are three committees operating at Level 3 of the Lamfalussy structure. These are the Committee of European Banking Supervisors (CEBS), the Committee of European Insurance and Occupational Pensions Committee (CEIOPS), and the Committee of European Securities Regulators (CESR).

(d) safeguarding the stability of the financial system; and (e) strengthening inter-national supervisory coordination.[99]

The tasks of the proposed agencies are to develop technical standards, ensure consistent application of Community rules, take action in emergency situations, settle disputes between national supervisors, promote the smooth functioning of colleges of supervisors, promote a common supervisory culture, assess market developments, collect information, and undertake an international and advisory role.[100] Suffice to examine here briefly the first two of the above powers by reference to the proposed Regulation establishing ESMA.[101]

ESMA is intended to play a quasi-regulatory role by promoting a higher level of harmonization. It has, in particular, the power to develop 'technical standards'. In view of the limitations on the powers of Community agencies deriving from the case law of the ECJ,[102] those technical standards do not acquire binding force unless they are adopted by the Commission. The proposed regulation, however, operates a system of reverse accountability which brings the powers of ESMA very close to a regulatory competence: where the Commission decides not to endorse the standards submitted by ESMA or decides to amend them, it must provide reasons for its decision.[103] The term 'technical standards' is in itself open to interpretation. The proposals envisage that the powers of ESMA are confined to 'issues of a highly technical nature' which do not involve policy decisions and whose content is tightly framed by the Community acts adopted at Level 1.[104] However, drawing the boundaries between technical and policy matters, especially in an area as complex as financial regulation, is notoriously difficult.

One of the key new functions vested to ESMA is to ensure the consistent application of Community rules. To this end, the proposed regulation provides for an elaborate enforcement procedure which will exist alongside the Commission's enforcement powers under Article 258 TFEU (Article 226 EC). The enforcement procedure has three steps.[105] Where ESMA considers that a national supervisor does not comply with the applicable Community rules, it may investigate the matter and, if necessary, adopt a recommendation addressed to the national authority in question. Such investigations may take place either at the initiative of ESMA or upon the request of a national supervisory authority or the Commission. If the national supervisory authority does not comply with ESMA's recommendation, the Commission may adopt a decision requiring it to take specific action or abstain from an action. The national authority must then, within a strict time-limit, inform the Commission and ESMA of the steps

---

[99] Commission Proposal for a Regulation establishing a European Securities and Markets Authority, COM (2009) 503 final, 4.

[100] ibid 5 *et seq.*

[101] See n 99 above.

[102] Case 9/56 *Meroni v High Authority* [1957–58] ECR 133. For an assessment of *Meroni* especially in the field of financial law, see T Tridimas, 'Community Agencies, Competition Law and ECB Initiatives on Securities Settlement' (2009) 28 YEL 216.

[103] See proposed Regulation on EMSA (n 99 above) Art 7(1), sub-para 4.

[104] ibid 5.   [105] ibid Art 9.

that it has taken to comply with that decision. Finally, in the third stage, if the national supervisory authority fails to comply with the Commission's decision, ESMA may adopt an individual decision addressed to a specific financial institution or market participant requiring it to take the necessary action to comply with Community law. The power of ESMA is extensive and includes the power to require the entity in question to cease business.[106] The striking feature of this provision is that, in extreme cases, it enables a Community agency to bypass the national supervisor and command a specific market actor, eg a bank or investment firm.

In addition to the above tasks, ESMA will have the power to take action in emergency situations and settle disagreements between national supervisors.[107] In both cases, these powers include the power to issue individual decisions addressed to specific market participants. These powers however are subject to a so-called fiscal responsibility safeguard clause, under which decisions adopted by ESMA may not impinge on the fiscal responsibilities of the Member States.[108]

E. CONCLUSION

In the last decade, financial regulation has been one of the fastest growing areas of EU law. The most prominent feature in the development of the law has been the trend towards federalization. This has taken place through the gradual colonization of all aspects of capital markets law by EU legislation; the move from minimum to maximum harmonization; the incremental articulation of common implementation standards; and the establishment of new institutional arrangements leading to enhanced EU presence in the field of enforcement and, ultimately, a quasi-federal structure. In terms of legislative output, FSAP has been a success. Although its actual contribution in establishing an integrated EU financial market is more difficult to assess, there is little doubt that EU norms infuse a higher standard of investor protection than that previously available under many national laws.

Following the financial crisis, the EU has been actively involved in both crisis management and law reform. It is better equipped to do the second than it is to do the first. On the one hand, it lacks the two prerequisites, clear competence and wide executive discretion, that immediate intervention requires. On the other hand, being one step further than national governments from electoral pressures, it does not need to react immediately by passing scandal-driven measures and has the luxury of looking at the wider picture. In the event, the Commission acted fast by introducing a host of proposals, and one wonders whether crisis management and law reform have been fused somewhat. The Commission put forward a 'Keynesian model' of financial regulation setting investor protection and systemic stability as its key objectives. The

---

[106] ibid Art 9(6).   [107] ibid Arts 10 and 11.   [108] ibid Art 23.

new system is based on the twin Pillars of reform of financial architecture and the adoption of Community legislation in specific areas. The emphasis lies, perhaps, more in the first than in the second. There is no intention to provide for wholesale reform in substantive areas of law but to intervene selectively in areas where the normative framework proved inadequate in the light of the financial crisis. By contrast, the reform of the institutional and regulatory framework is far-reaching. The new model is based on four components: the introduction of supervisory agencies at Community level; a higher degree of harmonization through the introduction of a pan-European rulebook; greater consistency in the application of Community rules; and, finally, the transfer of direct supervisory powers over market participants to Community agencies although such transfer is limited, hesitant, and heavily conditioned. The Commission's response to the financial crisis appears to have set in motion a substantial shift in the balance of powers between national and EU regulators and opened the road for the establishment of a fully fledged system of EU federal securities regulation.[109]

---

[109] After the completion of this piece, the measures establishing the new regulatory framework have been adopted. Note, in particular, the following measures which were adopted on 24 November 2010: Regulation No 1092/2010 on European Union macro-prudential oversight of the financial system and establishing a European Systemic Risk Board, [2010] OJ L331/1; Regulation No 1093/2010 establishing the European Banking Authority, [2010] OJ L331/12; Regulation No 1094/2010 establishing the European Insurance and Occupa-tional Pensions Authority, [2010] OJ L331/48; Regulation No 1095/2010 establishing European Securities and Markets Authority, [2010] OJ L331/84; Directive 2010/78 [2010] OJ L331/120 (This measure, referred to as the 'Omnibus Directive', makes changes to existing directives in relation to the powers of the new EU supervisory agencies introduced by the above regulations); and Regulation No 1096/2010 conferring specific tasks upon the European Central Bank concerning the functioning of the European Systemic Risk Board, [2010] OJ L331/162. The new system will be operational as from 1 January 2011.

26

THE MULTI-LEVEL GOVERNANCE OF CLIMATE CHANGE

*Joanne Scott**

A. INTRODUCTION

In the first edition of this book, Damian Chalmers provided an outstanding analysis of the evolution of EU environmental law.[1] This was published over a decade ago, and before the great climate change debate had really begun.[2] The word climate does not appear, and the term carbon is used only once.[3] While this last decade has seen a range of important developments in EU environmental law,[4] none can compare with climate change either in terms of the acuteness of the problem or the political salience of the policy response.

This chapter aims to offer an overview of some key aspects of EU law and policy in relation to climate change, and to analyse and evaluate these in a multi-level govern-ance frame. This frame is especially well suited to climate change governance in view

* Professor of European Law, University College London. Many thanks to Michael Dougan, Moritz Hartmann, Mark Johnston, Maria Lee, and Richard Macrory for their valuable help and comments along the way.

[1] D Chalmers, 'Inhabitants in the Field of Environmental Law' in P Craig and G de Búrca (eds), *The Evolution of EU Law* (Oxford University Press, 1999). For another outstanding and more recent account see I von Homeyer, 'The Evolution of EU Environmental Governance' in J Scott (ed), *Environmental Protection: European Law and Governance* (Oxford University Press, 2009).

[2] Of course this is not to deny that the issue was already on the political agenda but merely that it was not yet a hot political issue outside of specialist policy circles. The Intergovernmental Panel on Climate Change published its highly influential Second Assessment Report in 1996 concluding that the balance of evidence suggests a discernible human influence on global climate. This is available at: <http://www1.ipcc.ch/pdf/climate-changes-1995/ipcc-2nd-assessment/2nd-assessment-en.pdf>.

[3] Chalmers (n 1 above) 679.

[4] See Scott (n 1 above) for a discussion of some of these, including the chapter by M Lee examining the Water Framework Directive (2000/60/EC [2000] OJ L327/1) and my chapter examining the REACH Regulation for chemicals (1907/2006/EC [2006] OJ L396/1).

of the irrefutably global nature of the challenge posed. In his recent account of the evolution of EU environmental law, von Homeyer suggests that climate change might bring about a return to a more 'top-down' approach to regulation.[5] While there is certainly some evidence of a centralizing trend, particularly in the evolution of the emissions trading regime, in general the analysis here shows a reality which is more complex. Efforts to centralize power, in favour of the EU and at the expense of the Member States, are being contested (sometimes successfully); in the European courts, by the European Parliament, and by NGOs. We see regular examples of overlapping powers, not only in relation to the EU and the Member States, but also in relation to EU and international law. Further, we see pockets of a more experimentalist approach, most notably in relation to the evolution of EU standards for the regulation of project offsets deriving from large dams. Here the establishment of the Ad Hoc Working Group has served to facilitate regulatory learning on the basis of diverse experience in the different Member States.

In terms of the evolution of EU environmental law, it may be helpful to pinpoint two key trends. Along with the move to a market-based approach to environmental protection (emissions trading), perhaps the most striking innovation in climate change law and policy is the 'out-sourcing' of responsibility for achieving emission reductions on behalf of the EU and its Member States. In critical and controversial ways, the integrity of EU law and policy in relation to climate change, and of the EU's claims to leadership in this sphere, is contingent upon the effective regulation of activities which are situated abroad. EU climate change law and policy has created an urgent demand for regulation beyond EU borders, and the question of if and how this demand can be met is a pressing, but not always visible, concern.

The EU has adopted a bewildering multitude of policies in pursuit of its greenhouse gas (GHG) emission reduction goals.[6] Alongside the high-profile Emissions Trading and Renewable Energy Directives,[7] the EU has enacted a wide range of important measures in relation to transport[8] and energy demand.[9] This chapter will examine three key measures and will analyse some of the legal questions to which they give rise. It will begin by looking at the all-important Emissions Trading Directive, turning subsequently to the introduction of EU-level CO_2 performance standards for passenger cars. It will also explore one controversial aspect of the Renewable Energy Directive, concerning the introduction of sustainability criteria for biofuels. Each of these measures raises interesting and important issues about the distribution of regulatory power in a system of multi-level governance and legal pluralism, a system

---

[5] See n 1 above, 26.

[6] The Commission helpfully identifies the most important of these in its most recent Kyoto progress report, COM(2009) 630 final. It suggests that eight policies will contribute 92 per cent of emissions savings.

[7] Directive 2003/87/EC establishing a scheme for greenhouse gas emission allowance trading [2003] OJ L275/32 and Directive 2009/28/EC on the promotion of energy from renewable sources [2009] OJ L145/16.

[8] Directive 2009/30 as regards the specification of petrol, diesel and gas-oil [2009] OJ L140/8 and Regulation 443/2009 setting emission performance standards on new passenger cars [2009] OJ L140/1.

[9] Directive 2002/91/EC on energy performance of buildings, Directive 2004/8/EC on energy co-generation, and Directive 2003/96 on energy taxation.

which includes not only the EU and its Member States, but also international organizations and international law.

By way of background, it should be recalled that the EU and its Member States are party to the Kyoto Protocol to the United Nations Framework Convention on Climate Change,[10] and that in accordance with its terms they have agreed to fulfil their emission reduction commitments jointly.[11] The EU and its Member States signed up to a greenhouse gas emission reduction commitment of 8 per cent by 2008–12,[12] and concluded a burden-sharing agreement to distribute this emission reduction burden between the Member States.[13] While certain Member States may fail to achieve their Kyoto targets, the EU as a whole is on track to achieve this goal.[14]

The EU is committed to continuing its emission reduction efforts and to this end it has recently made a unilateral commitment to reduce greenhouse gas emissions by 20 per cent by 2020.[15] This commitment forms part of a 'far-reaching package of proposals that will deliver on the European Union's ambitious commitments to fight climate change and promote renewable energy up to 2020 and beyond'.[16] Again, the burden will be unevenly distributed across the different Member States.[17]

B. EMISSIONS TRADING

The Commission issued a Green Paper in 2000 to launch a discussion on the subject of emissions trading.[18] The emergence of this new instrument for environmental

---

[10] See Council Decision 2002/358/EC approving the Kyoto Protocol on the part of the European Community (EU-15) [2002] OJ L130/1. With the exception of Cyprus and Malta, the new EU Member States have also incurred emission reduction obligations (of between 5 and 8 per cent).

[11] Kyoto Protocol, Art 3 and Council Decision 2002/358, ibid Art 2.

[12] This is relative to a 1990 baseline. The EU negotiating position for Kyoto entailed a higher level of ambition, aiming at securing a 15 per cent reduction by developed countries. See, Climate Change—The EU Approach for Kyoto, COM(97) 481 final, 1.

[13] See Annex II Council Decision 2002/358 (n 10 above). This burden-sharing agreement sanctioned wide variation between Member States, with Germany shouldering the highest emission reduction burden (–21 per cent), and Portugal the lowest burden (+27 per cent). For a further discussion see P-O Marklund and E Samakovlis, 'What is Driving the EU Burden-Sharing Agreement: Efficiency or Equity?'(2007) JEM 317–329 (concluding that both efficiency and equity played an important role in shaping this agreement).

[14] The Commission is required to publish an annual progress report under the terms of Decision 280/2004 concerning a mechanism for monitoring Community greenhouse gas emissions [2004] OJ L49/1. For the latest report see (n 6 above). According to provisional 2008 data, emissions from EU-15 have fallen 6.2 per cent compared to 1990, and emissions from EU-27 have fallen 13.6 per cent from 1990.

[15] See the climate action and renewable energy package: <http://ec.europa.eu/environment/climat/climate_action.htm>.

[16] ibid.

[17] See Decision 406/2009/EC, [2009] OJ L140/136 on the effort of Member States to reduce their greenhouse gas emission to meet the Community's greenhouse gas emission reduction commitments up to 2020. Annex II lays down the minimum contribution of each Member State. Confusingly, these reduction commitments are expressed by reference to a 2005 (rather than 1990) baseline. Note that this decision only applies to sectors not covered by the emissions trading Directive.

[18] COM(2000) 87 final. Preliminary steps were taken before this in COM(98) 353 and COM(99) 230.

protection should be viewed against the backdrop of the Commission's ill-fated attempt to introduce an energy/carbon tax.[19] On emissions trading, the Commission explained its thinking as follows:

> Emissions trading, whether domestic or international, is a scheme whereby entities such as companies are allocated allowances for their emissions. Companies that reduce their emissions by more than their allocated allowance can sell their 'surplus' to others who are not able to reach their target so easily. This trading does not undermine the environmental objective, since the overall amount of allowances is fixed. Rather, it enables cost-effective implementation of the overall target and provides incentives to invest in environmentally sound technologies.[20]

The Green Paper was issued as the EU was preparing to ratify the Kyoto Protocol which provided for the possible establishment of an international emissions trading scheme from 2008.[21] In keeping with this, the Commission stressed that '[t]here is a good case for the European Community and its Member States to prepare themselves by commencing an emission trading scheme within the Community by 2005'.[22]

Directive 2003/87 established a scheme for greenhouse gas emission allowance trading within the EU.[23] This takes the form of a cap-and-trade regime, and consequently necessitates the fixing of an overall emissions cap as well as decisions on how this is to be allocated between and within the Member States. Today, the European carbon market is by far the largest in the world, enjoying a total value of 62 billion (US $92 billion) in 2008.[24] From a standing start in 2005, the European carbon market has demonstrated impressive growth.[25]

---

[19] The Commission acknowledges that the EU has made little progress in relation to energy taxation, COM (2000) 87 final, 23. For a discussion of the Commission's doomed initiatives in relation to energy/carbon taxation see J Scott, *EC Environmental Law* (Longmans, 2008).

[20] ibid, COM(2000) 87 final, 4. For a discussion of the variety of overlapping 'discourses' which have emerged in support of emissions trading see S Bogojevic, 'Ending the Honeymoon: Deconstructing Emissions Trading Discourses' (2009) JEL 443.

[21] Kyoto Protocol, Art 17.

[22] COM(2000) 87 final (n 18 above) 4. Ironically the EU opposed the idea of including emissions trading in the Kyoto regime but compromised on this point in the face of US insistence. The inclusion of emissions trading in the Kyoto Protocol is not the only factor explaining the EU's change of heart. It has been suggested that the 'entrepreneurial behaviour of the European Commission' played an important role. See J B Skjaerset and J Wettestad, 'The Origin, Evolution and Consequences of the EU Emissions Trading System' (2009) Global Politics 101.

[23] Directive 2003/87, [2003] OJ L275/32. This was amended by the so-called 'linking Directive' 2004/101, [2004] OJ L338/18, and by a 2009 Directive which applies to emissions trading from 2013–20, 2009/29, [2009] OJ L140/63. The separate instruments and a consolidated version of the 2003 Directive is available on the Europa website: <http://ec.europa.eu/environment/climat/emission/implementation_en.htm>. These three instruments will be cited separately during this chapter, to facilitate easy understanding of when which amendments were introduced.

[24] K Capoor and P Ambrosi, *State and Trends of the Carbon Market 2009* (World Bank, 2009) 1. The global carbon market was worth 86 billion (US$126 billion) in the same year.

[25] ibid 5, amounting to 87 per cent year-on-year growth in 2008 compared to 2007.

1. SETTING THE CAP AND ALLOCATING ALLOWANCES BETWEEN MEMBER STATES

The operation of the Emissions Trading Scheme (ETS) is organized by trading phases. The first phase lasted from 2005–07, while the second phase is currently underway (2008–12). The third trading phase will start in 2013 and last for an extended period of eight years.

The first trading phase of the ETS was viewed as a 'learning by doing' phase.[26] It transpired that there was a lot to learn. During this three-year trading phase the EU-wide cap on carbon dioxide emissions was set at a level of 6,542 million tonnes (Mt) and the allowances were issued free of charge. While not apparent at the time that this figure was set, it quickly became clear that allocated emission allowances exceeded actual emissions by almost half a million tonnes.[27] When this became known, the price of carbon plunged to almost zero.

During the second and ongoing trading phase, the emissions cap is set at a level which is intended to achieve a 6.5 per cent reduction of carbon dioxide emissions.[28] While emission levels in the covered sectors decreased by 3.9 per cent in 2008 alone,[29] it is not clear how much of this decrease can be attributed to the functioning of the ETS. On the contrary, it is likely that emission levels have been 'significantly affected' by the economic downturn.[30] While the over-allocation fiasco of the first phase has not recurred, and while trading levels have remained robust, the price for allowances remains volatile and on the whole quite low (at or around 15 per tonne). Prices remain well below the level that would be required to induce significant investment in low carbon technologies.[31] One journalist likens current conditions to a 'great pollution fire sale':

Roll up for the great pollution fire sale, the ultimate chance to wreck the climate on the cheap. You sir, over there, from the power company—look at this lovely tonne of freshly made, sulphur-rich carbon dioxide. Last summer it cost an eyewatering 31 to throw up your smokestack, but in our give-away global recession sale, that's been slashed to a crazy 8.20. Dump plans for the wind turbine! Compare our offer with costly solar energy! At this low, low price you can't afford not to burn coal![32]

During both the first and the second trading phases, it fell to individual Member States to draw up National Allocation Plans (NAPs) setting out the total quantity of

[26] COM(2008) 16 final.

[27] National Audit Office, *European Emissions Trading Scheme* (National Audit Office, 2009) 21.

[28] This is relative to a 2005 baseline.

[29] The across the board decrease, including non-ETS sectors, is 1.5 per cent.

[30] GDP for EU-27 fell by 4.1 per cent in 2008.

[31] National Audit Office (n 27 above) 44. The National Audit Office point, for example, to a study which found that demonstration carbon capture and storage projects would cost in the region of 60–90 per tonne of carbon dioxide abated between 2012 and 2015.

[32] J Glover, 'A Collapsing Carbon Market Makes Mega-Pollution Cheap' in *The Guardian* (23 February 2009) at: <http://www.guardian.co.uk/commentisfree/2009/feb/23/glover-carbon-market-pollution>. It is suggested that carbon allowances need to be priced at 30–45 for renewable energy to be able to compete.

allowances they intended to issue, together with details of how these were to be distributed among installations in that state.[33] While this decentralized system has been criticized, it is also clear that it 'was probably necessary in order to get any system adopted at all'.[34] Member States were required to ensure that their NAPs (which implemented the ETS) were based on objective and transparent criteria including those listed in Annex III.[35] They were also obliged to notify these plans to the Commission which could reject the plan, or any aspect of it, on the basis of its incompatibility with the criteria in Annex III. Were the Commission to do so, the Member State concerned would be obliged to seek the approval of the Commission for any amendments subsequently proposed.

During the first trading phase, the NAPs submitted by the older Member States emerged from this process relatively unscathed.[36] The Commission proposed more stringent reductions for the newer Member States.[37] During the second phase, the Commission sought an across-the-board reduction of 10.4 per cent.[38] Again, this was unevenly split between newer and older Member States. Whereas the average reduction for the EU-15 was 4.1 per cent, this rose to 25.4 per cent for the twelve newest Member States.[39] To give a taste, the Commission proposed a cut of 56 per cent for Latvia, 48 per cent for Estonia, 47 per cent for Lithuania, and 26.7 per cent for Poland.

The robust attitude of the Commission in proposing these quite drastic cuts led to litigation before the European courts.[40] Two cases have been decided, each of which is currently subject to appeal.[41] In each of these two cases, the CFI (now the General Court) annulled the Commission Decision concluding that the NAP was not consistent with the terms of the Emissions Trading Directive, and in particular with the criteria laid down in Annex III. Underpinning the judgments of the CFI is its conclusion that

---

[33] Directive 2003/87 (n 23 above) Arts 9–11. This was subject to the proviso that during the first phase Member States were obliged to issue at least 95 per cent of allowances free of charge, and to issue at least 90 per cent of allowances free of charge during the second phase. See Art 10.

[34] Skjaerset and Wettestad (n 22 above) 119.

[35] The first of these criteria required that the total quantity of allowances issued must be consistent with a Member State's obligation to achieve its Kyoto obligations, as adjusted by the EU's internal burden-sharing agreement. See also COM(2003) 830 final, establishing guidelines on the application of the Annex III criteria.

[36] See figure 4 in the National Audit Office Report (n 27 above) 19. For four of these states, the Commission did not propose any reduction in the cap. For the other older Member States (except Luxembourg), it suggested that the proposed cap be cut by less than 10 per cent.

[37] These ranged between 12 per cent for Hungary and 55 per cent for Latvia.

[38] P Capoor and P Ambrosi, *State of the Carbon Market 2008* (World Bank, 2008) 10.

[39] ibid.

[40] Poland, Latvia, Bulgaria, Czech Republic, Estonia, Hungary, Romania, and Lithuania instituted actions before the CFI. Slovakia withdrew its case after reaching a resolution with the Commission (Case T-32/07 *Slovakia v Commission* was removed from the register of the CFI on 14 May 2007). See also Case T-188/07R concerning Poland's unsuccessful application for interim relief in respect of this application. Hungary (221/07); Bulgaria (500/07); Romania (484/07); Czech Republic (194/07); Latvia (369/07); Lithuania (368/07). Note that some of the older Member States have also challenged Commission decisions in the context of the ETS. For a full discussion see N S Ghaleigh, 'Emissions Trading Before the European Court of Justice: Market Making in Luxembourg' in D Freestone and C Streck (eds), *Legal Aspects of Carbon Trading: Kyoto, Copenhagen, and beyond* (Oxford University Press, 2009) 367–388.

[41] Case T-183/07 *Poland v Commission* and Case T-273/07 *Estonia v Commission*, 23 September 2009.

'in a Community governed by the rule of law, administrative measures must be adopted in compliance with the competences attributed to various administrative bodies'.[42] This remains the case even though global warming 'represents one of the great social, economic and environmental threats that the world currently faces',[43] and even if the findings of the court were to impact negatively on the functioning of ETS.

In each case the CFI speaks the language of constitutional law. It reminds us that Member States enjoy freedom of action as to the choice of forms and methods for implementing directives, and that in exercising its supervisory powers under the Treaty the Commission bears the burden of showing that a Member State has acted in a manner which is contrary to EU law.[44] This, the CFI insists, is necessary to ensure respect for the principle of subsidiarity which applies in the environmental domain because the EU shares competence with the Member States.[45]

The CFI's reading of the Emissions Trading Directive, and its decentralized approach, is in keeping with its emphasis upon subsidiarity. It considers that it is 'unequivocally clear' that it falls to the Member States not only to draw up a NAP but also to make a final determination regarding the level of the overall cap and the manner of its distribution.[46] The Commission, on the contrary, merely enjoys a power of review, according to which it is authorized to verify whether the NAP conforms with the terms of the Directive, and most notably with the criteria laid down in Annex III.[47]

From this starting point, it was only a short step for the CFI to condemn the Commission for having exceeded the limits of its power of review. It was deemed to have exceeded the limits of its powers, and to have failed to respect the margin of manoeuvre of the Member States, both by insisting that its own data and economic model be used in calculating the cap,[48] and by 'specifying a specific quantity of allowances, any exceeding of which is regarded as incompatible with the criteria laid down [in the 2003 Emissions Trading Directive]'.[49] As regards the latter, the

---

[42] ibid *Estonia* [49]; *Poland* [129]. Note that where precise quotations are given, these derive from the Estonian case. The precise wording of the CFI in the Polish case often differs, but where similar sentiments are expressed, the relevant paragraphs are noted.

[43] ibid *Estonia*.

[44] ibid *Estonia* [51]; *Poland* [82].

[45] ibid *Estonia* [52]; *Poland* [83].

[46] ibid *Estonia* [53]; *Poland* [85]. For an important discussion of the role of legal culture in implementing ETS see M Hartmann, 'Climate Change and Legal Culture: Implementing the EU's Emissions Trading System (on file with the author).

[47] ibid *Estonia* [54]; *Poland* [89].

[48] ibid *Estonia* [75], [79], and [90]; *Poland* [110] and [106]; where the CFI states that for the Commission to use a single method for assessing NAPs would amount to it having a 'veritable power of uniformisation' in implementing ETS and a central role in adopting NAPs, neither of which is consistent with its review powers under the Directive. It is relevant to note that in the Estonian case the CFI was also critical of the data used by the Commission, considering that the figures were not necessarily the most representative or reliable (or best available) and that sometimes they risked distorting the Commission's calculations, see eg [77] and [86]. In one particular respect, the Commission's own calculations were deemed incompatible with precise requirements imposed by EU law (ibid *Estonia* [97]).

[49] ibid *Estonia* [60]; *Poland* [123].

Commission was deemed to have effectively substituted itself for the Member States and to have rendered their powers devoid of purpose.[50]

The Commission is appealing against the judgments of the CFI on a variety of grounds. 'Most importantly, the Commission considers that the CFI has interpreted too narrowly the powers of the Commission in the NAP assessment process.'[51] It also suggests that the Court has failed to take sufficient account of the objectives underpinning the emissions trading scheme and the need to ensure equal treatment between Member States. In the meantime, the Commission prepared new decisions once again rejecting the Estonian and Polish NAPs.[52]

These judgments are clearly interesting from a multi-level governance frame. They are also practically very important. The attitude of the ECJ will bear not only upon the level of ambition underpinning the ETS during the second trading phase, but also upon the extent of Member State obligations during the third trading phase. As will be seen below, the third phase will see important changes in the mode of setting the cap and allocating allowances. Crucially though, from the point of view of these cases, the third phase cap will be set by reference to the level of allowances issued during the second phase.[53] Consequently these judgments will play a role in shaping the emissions ceiling from now until 2020 and even beyond.[54]

During the third trading phase (2013–20) the decentralized approach will be replaced by a central cap which will be set by the Commission without the involvement of the Member States. By 30 June 2010, the Commission is required to publish an EU-wide emissions cap.[55] In keeping with many other elements of the new Directive,[56] the EU is greatly empowered at the expense of the Member States.

It is interesting to speculate about the existence of a connection between the actual and threatened litigation before the European courts and this quite radical change in the governance arrangements for setting the cap. Timing is not conclusive in this respect. The first application for annulment of a Commission decision concerning a NAP was

---

[50] ibid *Estonia* [64]–[65]; *Poland* [127]–[128].

[51] 'Q&A in relation to the Commission's decision to appeal in Cases T-183/07 and T-263/07 (CFI rulings on Commission Decisions on the Polish and Estonian NAPs)' at: <http://ec.europa.eu/environment/climat/emission/pdf/qa_appeal_091203.pdf>.

[52] 'Emissions trading: Commission takes new decisions on Estonian and Polish national allocation plans for 2008–2012' at: <http://europa.eu/rapid/pressReleasesAction.do?reference=IP/09/1907&format=HTML&aged=0&language=EN&guiLanguage=en>. Once again the Commission is demanding a cut of 48 per cent from Estonia and 26.7 per cent from Poland. The Commission has since approved the Polish NAP.

[53] See Directive 2009/29/EC (n 23 above), Art 9, amending Art 9 of Directive 2003/87 (n 23 above).

[54] The Commission's stated intention is that the cap will continue to decrease on a linear basis also after 2020.

[55] ibid. Many other very important changes will be introduced at this time, including the extension of the ETS to the air transport sector and the gradual auctioning of emission allowances. See the Commission's 'Questions and Answers on the revised EU Emissions Trading System at: <http://europa.eu/rapid/pressReleasesAction.do?reference=MEMO/08/796&format=HTML&aged=0&language=EN&guiLanguage=en> for a summary of these and other changes.

[56] For example the rules for the transitional free allocation of allowances, requirements, and arrangements for auctioning allowances and rules for verification of emissions trading.

lodged in the Estonian case on 26 March 2007. This coincided with discussions in the Commission's Working Group on the review of ETS,[57] although the meeting on the theme of 'further harmonisation and increased predictability' did not convene until 21–22 May 2007.[58] This meeting put forward a 'very strong message calling for more harmonisation if not a centralized EU cap'.[59] The pending litigation was nowhere mentioned. Thus although the final Directive was adopted before the two emissions trading judgments of the CFI,[60] the lead-up to its adoption and the debates about the future shape and contours of the scheme, took place during a period when the cases were already pending before the Court. It is true that the issue of further harmonization of the cap-setting and allocation process had been raised well before the applications in question were lodged before the Court,[61] and that other convincing independent reasons for favouring increased harmonization were often cited as part of the ETS review.[62] But still, it seems almost unimaginable that the fact that one third of all Member States (nine in total) had instituted actions before the CFI challenging the legality of the Commission decisions on their NAPs, would not lead to increased awareness of the pressing need to streamline and centralize the process for determining the emissions cap.

2. THE AVAILABILITY OF PROJECT OFFSETS

The Kyoto Protocol included three 'flexibility mechanisms' intended to facilitate cost-effective implementation. This section will focus on just one of these which is known as the Clean Development Mechanism (CDM).[63] The CDM allows emission allowances (project offsets) to be generated by emission reduction projects hosted by developing countries, and for developed countries to use these to contribute to compliance with their emission reduction commitments.[64] For example, where a company in China switches from coal to biomass a certain number of carbon dioxide emissions will be saved. Where this project is recognized by the CDM Executive Board,

[57] COM(2008) 16 final, 3, noting that the group met four times for eight days between March and June 2007.

[58] For the final report of this group, see at: <http://ec.europa.eu/environment/climat/emission/pdf/070521_22_final_report_m3_tc.pdf>.

[59] ibid 3.

[60] The Directive was adopted on 23 April 2009 and the cases decided on 23 September 2009.

[61] See especially COM(2006) 676, 7–8.

[62] eg the political commitment of the European Council in March 2007 to achieve a 20–30 per cent reduction in emissions by 2020 is cited by the Commission as one such reason. It notes: 'A system based on national cap-setting does not provide sufficient guarantees that the emission reduction objectives endorsed by the European Council in March 2007 will be achieved', COM(2008) 16 final, 7.

[63] See Kyoto Protocol, Art 12. Emissions trading is one of the three mechanisms and was highlighted above. In addition to the CDM, Joint Implementation (JI) is also included. The CDM is much more significant than JI in quantitative terms. As the World Bank's latest state of the carbon market report shows (n 23 above, 1), JI is dwarfed by the CDM in terms of the volume of trading involved. In 2008 JI generated 20Mt credits, compared to 389Mt generated on the primary CDM market and 1072Mt generated in the secondary CDM market.

[64] By developing countries, I mean countries not listed as Annex I countries under the UN Framework Convention on Climate Change, or as Annex B countries under the Kyoto Protocol.

the emissions saved will be issued as 'Certified Emissions Reductions' (CERs) and they may be used by developed countries or by firms within them to contribute to compliance with their emission reduction obligations. Not to put too fine a point on it, the CDM makes it possible for developed countries to pollute more than they would otherwise be entitled to under the terms of the agreement, so long as they compensate for this by buying emission reductions in developing states. As with emissions trading more generally, the CDM is predicated on the simple principle that greenhouse gas emissions are fungible, and consequently that cost-effectiveness demands that the cheapest emission reduction opportunities should be exploited first.

In 2004 the EU adopted a 'linking Directive' which connects the CDM to the ETS (with apologies for all the acronyms!).[65] This was intended to 'increase the diversity of low-cost compliance options within the Community scheme leading to a reduction of the overall costs of compliance with the Kyoto Protocol while improving the liquidity of the Community market in greenhouse gas emissions allowances'.[66] In practice, EU buyers dominate in the CDM 'compliance market', currently enjoying a market share of more than 80 per cent.[67]

From a multi-level governance perspective, focusing largely on the relationship between the EU and its Member States, two key questions arise. First, to what extent are quantitative limits imposed on the entitlement of Member States or firms within them to use CERs to meet their ETS obligations? Secondly, where does responsibility for regulating the quality of projects yielding CERs and for ensuring the authenticity of the emissions reductions claimed rest?

Turning first to the question of quantity. In this respect, the Kyoto Protocol is noticeably vague. Parties may use CERs to 'contribute to compliance with part of their quantified emission limitation and reduction commitments'.[68] The linking Directive allows project offsets to be included in the ETS 'up to the percentage of the allocation of allowances to each installation to be specified by each Member State in its national allocation plan for that period'.[69] Due to practical difficulties, CERs were not available in the ETS during the first trading phase.[70] While the Commission took the view that a 10 per cent ceiling would be appropriate during the second trading phase, ultimately it endorsed wide variation between the Member States. It endorsed a quantitative limit on the use of project credits of 20 per cent for Spain, Lithuania, and Germany, and a limit of between 0 per cent and 17 per cent for the other Member States.[71]

---

[65] Directive 2004/101/EC (n 23 above), amending Directive 2003/87 (n 23 above).

[66] ibid recital 3.

[67] Capoor and Ambronsi (n 24 above) 33. The 'compliance market' is distinguished from the 'voluntary market' on the basis that in the former offsets are used to contribute to compliance with mandatory emission reduction targets.

[68] Kyoto Protocol, Art 12(3)(b).

[69] Directive 2004/101 (n 23 above) Art 11a(1), which relates to the first and second trading phases, amending Directive 2003/87 (n 23 above).

[70] This was due to difficulties in linking the EU emission allowance registry with its Kyoto counterpart.

[71] See National Audit Office (n 27 above) 21. See also J de Sépibus, 'Linking the Emissions Trading Scheme to JI, CDM and Post-2012 International Offsets' NCCR Working Paper 2008/18 1–29, for a full discussion of this issue and of the methodology deployed by the European Commission in working out these ceilings for project offsets.

The quantitative bottom line is that a maximum of 1,400 CERs (million tonnes) are in principle available for use in the ETS during the current trading phase. This represents more than twice the level of the emission reductions to be achieved during this phase.[72] In the event that all available offsets are used, the EU would fall well short of achieving its internal emission reduction target of 6.5 per cent. On the contrary, the National Audit Office suggests that 'maximum use of project credits in Phase II as set out in approved National Allocation Plans would result in an increase in [EU] emissions of seven per cent [compared to 2005]'.[73]

While it remains unclear how many of these CERs will in fact be used during the second phase (not least because the overall emissions cap is anyway quite generous in view of the economic downturn), unused CERs may be carried forward for use during the third phase.[74] Overall, recourse to project offsets during the second and third phases will be limited by a ceiling laid down in the 2009 Directive. This provides that up to 50 per cent of an operator's emission reduction burden for the second and third trading phases combined may be achieved through recourse to offsets of this kind.[75]

Debates about the EU's role in regulating project offsets have not been limited to questions of quantity. Even before the adoption of the linking Directive in 2004, questions of quality were placed firmly on the regulatory agenda.[76] During recent years, pressure has been mounting for the introduction of more quality controls in the European scheme. The impact assessment prepared as a prelude to the adoption of the 2009 Emissions Trading Directive, acknowledged that '[d]oubts...persist about the real emissions reduction impact of some offset projects'.[77] It suggested that in the absence of a new international agreement, 'the EU ETS needs to develop more harmonised qualitative provisions and standards on the use of offset credits to safeguard its environmental integrity'.[78] While recognizing that quality standards of this kind might increase overall emission abatement costs, it suggested that these higher costs should be seen in the light of other long-term objectives such as sustainable development. 'Higher economic efficiency in the short-term might not necessarily mean the same in the long and longer term.'[79] A report of the European Parliament similarly called for the EU to accept only Gold Standard 'type' credits,[80]

---

[72] Using the Audit Office's slightly adjusted 2005 baseline, the total abatement burden over this period amounts to 580Mt (n 27 above) 59.

[73] ibid 19.

[74] Directive 2009/29 (n 23 above) Art 11a, amending Directive 2003/87 (n 23 above).

[75] Directive 2009/29 (n 23 above) Art 11a(8), amending Directive 2003/87 (n 23 above).

[76] For an overview of these debates and a discussion of the different positions of business and environmental NGOs see Langrock and Sterk, 'Linking CDM & JI with EU Emission Allowance Scheme' (Wuppertal Institute, 2004) at: <http://www.europarl.europa.eu/comparl/envi/pdf/externalexpertise/ieep/flexible_mechanisms_brief.pdf>.

[77] SEC(2008) 52, 37.

[78] ibid 145.

[79] ibid 148.

[80] Draft Report on the proposal for a Directive of the European Parliament and of the council amending Directive 2003/87 so as to improve and extend greenhouse gas emission allowance trading system of the Community (COM(2008)0016—C6-0043/2008—2008/0013(COD)), Rapporteur Avril Doyle, 28 and 34.

namely those meeting the higher quality standards of the Gold Standard Founda-tion.[81]

The pressure on the EU to intervene more to guarantee the quality of project offsets reflects widely shared concerns about the adequacy of the international law framework for certifying and issuing CERs. While an elaborate regulatory machinery has emerged, centred on the Executive Board of the CDM, and while good-faith efforts are being made to improve it, this regulatory framework remains seriously flawed. Three types of concern have tended to dominate the debate.

First, and most important, is the issue of 'additionality' which raises the question of whether emission reductions claimed as CERs might not have occurred anyway in the absence of the CDM. It is widely accepted that 'a significant number of non-additional projects are registered',[82] and there is evidence that high-emission activities are commenced merely or primarily with a view to subsequently claiming CERs.[83] Second, concerns have been expressed about the contribution of the CDM to its sustainable development goal.[84] Certain projects have been shown to have negative social and environmental effects. Third, convincing concerns have been raised about the cost-effectiveness of certain types of project.[85]

Despite serious doubts about the adequacy of the Kyoto Protocol's regulatory framework governing the CDM, EU regulation of project offsets remains largely parasitic upon it. CERs may only be used in the ETS where these are in accordance with the UNFCC and the Kyoto Protocol, and with subsequent decisions adopted thereunder.[86] There are two exceptions to the EU's passive stance.

The first exception concerns CERs which derive from 'land use, land-use change and forestry' projects (LULUCF) which are not recognized for use in the EU emissions trading scheme.[87] The EU is committed to maintaining this exclusion until at least

---

[81] Art 11a(3)(b) Directive 2004/101 (n 23 above), amending Directive 2003/87 (n 23 above).

[82] L Schneider, *Is the CDM fulfilling its environmental and sustainable development objectives? An evalu-ation of the CDM and options for improvement* (Öko Institut, 2007), concluding that for roughly 40 per cent of projects additionality is unlikely or questionable (p. 9). See also United States Government Accountability Office, 'Lessons learned from the European Union's Emissions Trading Scheme and the Kyoto Protocol's Clean Development Mechanism' (GAO-09-151) at: <http://www.gao.gov/new.items/d09151.pdf>.

[83] M Wara and D G Victor, 'A Realistic Policy on International Carbon Offsets', Program on Energy and Sustainable Development Working Paper, No 74 (April 2008).

[84] E Boyd *et al*, 'Reforming the CDM for Sustainable Development: Lessons Learned and Policy Futures' (2009) 12 ESP 820–831.

[85] This is particularly the case for projects to capture 'industrial gases' such as HFC-23 (n 83 above).

[86] Directive 2004/101 (n 23 above) Art 11a(3)(b), amending Directive 2003/87 (n 23 above). A wide range of detailed decisions have subsequently been adopted by the Conference of the Parties. See <http://unfccc.int/resource/docs/2005/cmp1/eng/08a01.pdf>. For a good overview see Baker and McKenzie's 'CDM Rulebook' site at <http://cdmrulebook.org/3916>.

[87] Directive 2004/101 (n 23 above) Art 11a(3)(b), amending Directive 2003/87 (n 23 above). This exception remains in place for the third trading phase although Art 11a(b) of Directive 2004/101 (n 23 above) has been repealed by Directive 2009/29 (n 23 above). This is because the 2009 version of Art 11a specifies that the only offsets available during this phase are those which derive from project types eligible during the second trading phase.

2020.[88] Projects in this category result in the removal of greenhouse gases from the atmosphere through the establishment, management, or preservation of carbon sinks (in particular forests) but, as the European Commission highlighted in putting forward its proposal for the linking Directive, they result only in the temporary storage of carbon and do not drive technology development and transfer in a manner consistent with the EU's goals.[89]

The second exception concerns hydroelectric power production projects with a generating capacity of more than 20MW (large hydro projects), including dams. For this specific category of project, the EU imposes an obligation on its Member States to ensure that the relevant international criteria and guidelines, including those contained in the World Commission on Dams Report (WCD),[90] are respected during the development of CDM projects of this kind.[91] This reflects the EU's concern that Member States should avoid using credits from projects which might entail negative social or environmental impacts.[92]

From a multi-level governance perspective, the large hydro example is interesting and informative. At first, Member States were left to their own devices in interpreting and giving content to the broad objectives laid down in international standards and in designing systems and processes for promoting compliance with them. They were given autonomy to experiment in pursuit of these goals. After a period of some years, Member States came together in an informal forum to compare their interpretation of the international standards and the policies which they had put in place in pursuit of them. They were able, on this basis, to arrive at a common understanding of what these international standards require and of the decision-making procedures best capable of facilitating compliance. This led to the adoption of guidelines[93] and a compliance

[88] Note though that credits from afforestation and reforestation projects may be used by Member States to contribute to compliance with their obligations under the effort-sharing decision which applies to non-ETS covered sectors. See Decision 406/2009 (n 17 above) Art 5 for details.

[89] For a discussion of the shortcomings which led to this exclusion see COM(2003) 403 final, 10. The Commission also highlights the problems associated with accounting for and monitoring the removal of GHG by sinks, and notes that LULUCF projects are expected to be cheaper than projects involving the transfer of technologies and hence that LULUCF would operate at the expense of these more expensive projects which are nonetheless key to stabilising global levels of GHG emissions.

[90] *Dams and Development: A New Framework for Decision-Making* (Earthscan, 2000) at <http://www.unep. org/dams/WCD/report/WCD_DAMSpercent20report.pdf>. For an interesting discussion of this from a 'new governance' perspective, see A Cohen, 'Negotiation, Meet New Governance: Interests, Skills and Selves' (2008) Law and Social Inquiry 501 and also J C Nagle, 'Discounting China's CDM Dams' (2009) Loyala U Chicago Intl L Rev.

[91] Art 11b(6) Directive 2004/101 (n 23 above), amending Directive 2003/87 (n 23 above).

[92] For an overview of the difficult relationship between dams and development see the WCD report above and also J Leslie, *Deep Water: The Epic Struggle over Dams, Displaced People, and the Environment* (Picador, 2005).

[93] Guidelines on a common understanding of Art 11b(6) of Directive 2003/87EC as amended by Directive 2004/101/EC (non-paper) (17 November 2008) at <http://ec.europa.eu/environment/climat/emission/pdf/ art11b6_guide.pdf> and Compliance Report Assessing Application of Art 11b(6) of Emissions Trading Directive to Hydroelectric Project Activities Exceeding 20 MW (17 November 2008) at <http://ec.europa.eu/ environment/climat/emission/pdf/art11b6_comp_temp.pdf>. The guidelines conclude that the WCD Report can in itself be assumed to be a fair reflection of the concept of 'relevant international criteria and guidelines'.

template[94] for projects of this kind. The compliance template is stated to be based on existing UK and Swedish Compliance Reports.[95] The development of the guidelines is said to have been driven by the emergence of different interpretations of Article 11b(6) on the part of different Member States, and to be attributable to the fragmentation of the carbon market which threatened as a result.[96] The guidelines and compliance template are intended to 'give Member States confidence in accepting CERs/ERUs from projects for use in the EU ETS',[97] and as such project offsets approved by any one Member State will be accepted by all.[98]

These measures were negotiated by an Ad Hoc Working Group chaired by the European Commission and comprising representatives of the Member States. Industry actors and NGOs were also involved.[99] The results of this process are presented as taking the form of 'voluntary harmonization'.[100] It is stressed that the final decision to approve a project rests with the relevant Member State and that the guidelines do not compromise the 'sovereign authority' of each Member State.[101]

The large hydro example is interesting both in terms of process and outcome. From a process perspective, it offers a clear example of regulatory learning on the basis of diverse experience in the different Member States.[102] In a manner which is consistent with the theory of democratic experimentalism, Member State experimentation in the implementation of framework goals created opportunities to compare approaches and to identify and articulate best practice standards. Furthermore, the guidelines make it clear that the agreed guidelines and template are to be regarded as provisional and that they may be updated and amended over time.

From an outcome perspective, the guidelines and the compliance template raise questions in law. While these instruments go well beyond the regulatory demands of the CDM, it has been convincingly argued that they fall short of the standards endorsed by the WCD.[103] While a voluntary harmonization measure of this kind

---

[94] Information to demonstrate compliance is to be presented in accordance with the agreed compliance template, and in accordance with best auditing practice. Best practice is stated to involve more than a mere document review, and to require also interviews and public involvement, and site observation.

[95] UK Guidance on Approval and Authorisation to Participate in Clean Development Mechanism Project Activities (DECC, 2009), 23.

[96] Guidelines (n 93 above) 2, [4].

[97] ibid 1–2, [3].

[98] ibid 3, [7].

[99] They had the opportunity to participate in a workshop and a stakeholder meeting, and to submit written comments. The Worldwide Fund for Nature and International Rivers submitted comments to the Ad Hoc Working Group (personal email from Marzena Chodor from European Commission, 16 November 2009).

[100] See the Commission website at <http://ec.europa.eu/environment/climat/emission/ji_cdm_en.htm> where it speaks both of 'voluntary coordination' and 'voluntary harmonisation'.

[101] Guidelines (n 93 above) 1, [2] and 2, [4].

[102] The process for drafting (and revising in the future) the guidelines and template is resonant of what Sabel and Zeitlin label 'the architecture of democratic experimentalism'. See C Sabel and J Zeitlin, 'Learning from Difference: The New Architecture of Experimentalist Governance' (2009) ELJ 309.

[103] S Herz and A K Schneider, 'International Rivers' Comments on the Non-paper on a Common Understanding of Art 11b(6) of Directive 2003/87/EC as amended by Directive 2004/101/EC and the Draft Compliance Report Assessing Implementation of Art 11b(6) to Hydro-electric Projects Exceeding 20 MW' at

would not be susceptible to judicial review before the European courts, a decision by any one Member State which is based upon the agreed compliance template could be challenged before a national court. Similarly, while these voluntary standards are non-binding, Member States do have a legal obligation to comply with the requirement laid down in the 'linking Directive' to which they purport to give effect.

Before concluding this section it is necessary to look again at the legislative framework put in place to govern the third trading phase (2013–20) and to consider what implications this might have for the role of the EU in regulating the quality of project offsets. While the new Directive does not lay down additional quality standards for CERs, it does recognize that these may be made subject to additional requirements and establish mechanisms for promulgating them. Two elements are key in this respect.

First, except in relation to Least Developed Countries, and subject to the rules on the 'banking' of offsets from the second to the third trading phase, new offsets will only be available for use in the ETS where they originate in a country which is party to an international agreement on climate change or, where this does not exist, to a bilateral agreement which specifies the level of their use.[104] Any such international or bilateral agreement may also establish a 'baseline' for the use of project credits.[105] This means that they should articulate an emissions performance benchmark which will form the basis for calculating the level of availability of CERs. According to this, the only emission savings which will be deemed to be 'additional', and thus capable of generating offsets, will be those which imply a level of industrial performance which is more efficient than that implied by this baseline. The only emissions savings capable of counting as offsets would be those which go beyond the good performance rather than business-as-usual baseline. The baseline is to be determined either by reference to the level of performance required by EU law, or by reference to the performance benchmark which is to be set for the purpose of defining entitlement to free allocation of emission allowances during the third trading phase.[106]

While it is not clearly apparent from the text of the Directive, this 'baseline' idea is linked to the EU's stated intention of moving towards a 'sectoral approach' to emissions trading.[107] In a bid to come to grips with the additionality challenge, the

---

<http://www.internationalrivers.org/files/Internationalpercent20Rivers'per cent20comments.pdf>. The standards laid down in the WCD are far from clear, the report running to a total of 356 pages. For a fuller discussion of this issue and of the accountability issues to which it gives rise see J Scott, (forthcoming). 'In Legal Limbo'.

[104] Art 11a(5) Directive 2009/29 (n 23 above), amending Directive 2003/87 (n 23 above).

[105] ibid.

[106] ibid. See also Art 10a(2) which provides that the benchmark for determining the level of free allocation of allowances will be set by reference to the average performance of the 10 per cent most efficient installations in sector or subsector in the EU in the years 2007–08.

[107] The concept of a sectoral approach is not entirely clear, but in the EU version it refers to setting sectoral baselines for particular industrial sectors (for example cement), and is premised upon the idea of only allowing emissions savings which go beyond this baseline to count as CERs. See S Medina, ' "Sectoral Carbon" . . . Eh? Please Define' at <http://www.grist.org/Art/2009-05-12-sectoral-carbon-cdm-unfccc/>.

EU has highlighted its intention to design a new market instrument at a sectoral level, which would create opportunities for countries which exceed their sectoral emissions targets (as opposed to their business-as-usual targets) to sell their 'saved' emissions as offsets in the EU.[108] 'Credits would be awarded for beating reinforced ambition levels.'[109] The focus for the EU would be on 'key sectors' where emissions are rising rapidly or which form part of competitive world markets.[110]

The second mechanism laid down in the 2009 Directive which may be used to regulate the quality of project offsets during the third trading phase is found in Article 11a(9). This provides that it is open to the EU to adopt measures to 'restrict the use of specific credits from project types'. These measures would take the form of delegated legislation, to be adopted by way of the 'regulatory committee with scrutiny' procedure.[111]

The effectiveness of this regulatory mechanism will depend in part upon the legality of imposing new restrictions of this kind on project offsets which have been 'banked' and carried forward from the second trading phase.[112] This raises detailed questions of European administrative law, relating in particular to the scope of protection conferred by the principles of legal certainty and legitimate expectations.

In his discussion of these concepts, Paul Craig emphasizes the importance of distinguishing between different kinds of scenarios.[113] In particular, he distinguishes between individual representations and changes in policy, the latter arising when a 'general norm or policy choice' relied upon by an individual or group is 'replaced by a different policy choice'.[114] He points out that this 'latter type of case is especially difficult because of the obvious need for government to alter policy'.[115] In this latter situation, for a legitimate expectation to arise something more than a mere change of policy will be required, for example 'a bargain of some form between the individual and the authorities, or . . . a course of conduct or assurance on the part of the authorities which can be said to generate the legitimate expectation'.[116] That something 'more' would seem to be missing when it comes to the question of regulating 'banked' offsets during the third trading phase.

This is because the 2009 Directive spells out the possibility that policy may change in respect of the use of 'specific credits from project types', and it does not require that special consideration be given to credits which were issued during the previous trading phase, or which derive from projects registered during this earlier phase.

---

[108] COM(2009) 39 final, *Towards a Comprehensive Climate Change Agreement in Copenhagen*, 11.
[109] SEC(2009) 101 final, Annex 17, 117.
[110] ibid.
[111] See Art 5a of Decision 1999/468 [1999] OJ L184/23.
[112] Art 11a(2) and (3) Directive 2009/29 (n 23 above), amending Directive 2003/87 (n 23 above).
[113] P Craig, *European Administrative Law* (Oxford University Press, 2006) 611.
[114] ibid 635.   [115] ibid.   [116] ibid 637.

3. ETS AND MINIMUM HARMONIZATION

The Emissions Trading Directive takes Article 175 EC (now Article 192 TFEU) as its legal basis and it consequently does not preclude the adoption of more stringent protective measures by EU Member States.[117] However, the Directive requires that Member States exempt ETS-covered plants from certain regulatory requirements otherwise imposed by EU law. In particular, it prohibits Member States from including emission standards in relation to ETS-covered greenhouse gases when they issue permits under the Directive on Integrated Pollution Prevention and Control (IPPC).[118] There is currently fierce debate about the appropriateness and legality of including a prohibition of this kind in the Industrial Emissions Directive (IED), the soon to be enacted successor to IPPC.[119]

It has been argued that a prohibition on including ETS-covered gases in IPPC (or IED) permits is unlawful as it is contrary to the minimum harmonization requirement laid down in Article 176 EC (now Article 193 TFEU). According to the Worldwide Fund for Nature (WWF), a prohibition on the introduction of GHG emission standards represents 'a maximum or complete harmonisation as it excludes the possibility to use a proven regulatory tool to limit emissions'.[120]

The Commission has set forth a variety of more or less precise explanations as to why in its view this exclusion is required. It is said to be necessary to ensure the 'smooth interplay between the emissions trading scheme and the IPPC Directive',[121]

---

[117] Art 176 EC (now Art 193 TFEU).

[118] Art 26 Directive 2003/87 which states that this is the case unless such emission standards are required to ensure that no local pollution is caused. There is debate about whether emission standards of this kind could be imposed by Member States outside of the framework constituted by the IPPC Directive. For a positive conclusion in this respect see the legal opinion prepared by D Wyatt and R Macrory (9 February 2010) at <http://www.europolitique.info/pdf/gratuit_fr/269819-fr.pdf>. If this is the correct reading, leaving discretion in the hands of Member States, it would be unclear as to why the IPPC Directive did not simply give Member States the option as to whether to include greenhouse gas emission standards for ETS-covered plants and gases.

[119] COM(2007) 844 final for the proposed Industrial Emissions Directive. Late in the preparation of this chapter, the Environment Committee of the European Parliament voted to amend this proposal, changing the text to ensure that while Member States would not be obliged to introduce emission limits for ETS covered plants and gases, they would be free nonetheless to do so. Although this amendment is not included in the final version of the IED, it should nonetheless be borne in mind that still the directive takes the form of a minimum harmonization measure and that this is explicitly stated in the preamble to the new directive.

[120] WWF Letter of 21 August 2009 at <http://www.euractiv.com/29/images/WWF_letter_tcm29-184816.pdf>. In the legal opinion prepared by Wyatt and Macrory (n 118 above) the conclusion is reached that: '[i]f a provision of the IED (IPPC) were, on its true construction, to prohibit Member States from introducing ELVs [emission limit values] for CO2 for installations covered by the IPPC and ETS Directives, the result would be to prohibit national measures having the same (the reduction of CO2 emissions) as the ETS Directive, and to place obstacles in the way of individual Member States achieving a higher standard of protection from greenhouse gases than might otherwise be achieved. We cannot exclude the possibility that arguments might be made to demonstrate the compatibility of such a provision with Art 193 TFEU. But it is not immediately obvious to us how such compatibility might be convincingly demonstrated, and it is our view that at the very least there would be serious doubts as to the compatibility of such a provision with Art 193 TFEU.'

[121] COM(2001) 581 final, 9.

and to avoid 'double regulation'.[122] More concretely, the Commission argues that 'emissions trading should allow greenhouse gas emissions to vary according to the economic decisions of the operator', and that the setting of an emissions limit by the regulator would 'diminish the benefits of emissions trading because an installation would not be able to increase its greenhouse gas emissions'.[123] The Commission has recently confronted the same issue in contemplating the possibility of an extension of emissions trading to other pollutants.[124] On this occasion, it suggested that the effect of combining emissions trading with emission standards would be to diminish cost savings associated with emissions trading, resulting in an 'efficiency loss in economic terms'.[125]

Inherent in the Commission's justifications for this mandatory derogation are the seeds of a possible counter-argument in relation to Article 176 EC (now Article 193 TFEU). It is true that by pre-empting recourse to GHG emission standards, the Emissions Trading Directive has restricted the capacity of Member States to introduce more stringent protective measures. However, it would be open to the Commission to argue that this restriction is necessary to ensure the proper functioning of the ETS, and in particular its capacity to deliver in relation to its cost-effectiveness goal.[126]

An argument of this sort would raise questions of interpretation not yet directly considered by the European Court.[127] Most obviously, it would raise the question of the extent to which more stringent protective measures allowed under Article 176 EC (now Article 193 TFEU) are required to be consistent with the attainment of a directive's goals, including its cost-effectiveness as well as its environmental goal. Where consistency is required it would also fall to the court to develop criteria for managing trade-offs between different negative and positive effects and between different and sometimes competing goals. There are already signs in the existing case law of the European Court that it would be mindful of the need to evaluate the legality of more stringent protective measures by reference to a directive's underlying goals.[128] It remains to be seen which goals would be regarded as relevant to an analysis under Article 176 EC (now Article 193 TFEU), what weight would be attached to a cost-effectiveness as opposed to an environmental goal, and how the Court would seek to manage fact-intensive trade-offs of this kind.

---

[122] Recital 7 of the proposed Industrial Emissions Directive (n 119 above).

[123] Commission, 'Non-paper on synergies between the EC emissions trading proposal (COM(2001)581) and the IPPC Directive', 3 at: <http://ec.europa.eu/environment/climat/pdf/non-paper_ippc_and_et.pdf>.

[124] SEC(2007) 1679, 99–105. This refers to SO_2 and NOx.

[125] ibid 99.

[126] See Art 1, Directive 2003/87 (n 23 above).

[127] On the ECJ case law on Art 176 EC see J Jans, 'Minimum Harmonisation and the Role of the Principle of Proportionality' in M Führ, R Wahl, and P von Wilmowsky (eds), *Umweltrecht und Umweltwissenschaft: Festschrift für Eckard Rehbinder* (Schmidt Verlag, 2007) 705 and M Dougan, 'Minimum Harmonisation and the Internal Market' (2000) 37 CML Rev 853.

[128] See Case C-6/03 *Deponiezweckverband EiterKöpfe* [2005] ECR I-2753, [38]–[41] where the ECJ emphasizes that the stricter national measures in question pursue the same objective as the Directive, and follow the same policy of protecting the environment as the Directive does.

The relationship between ETS and IPPC/IED raises questions of policy as well as questions of law. The Explanatory Memorandum accompanying the proposal for the Emissions Trading Directive states that 'the quantities [of allowances] should ensure that the overall emissions of all of the participating installations would not be higher than if the emissions were to be regulated under the IPPC Directive'.[129] In contemplating an extension of the emissions trading approach to other pollutants, the discussion is likewise premised upon an assumption of functional equivalence between the different regimes.[130]

Yet it is has been suggested that there is 'no requirement to actually check the performance of emissions trading compared with IPPC',[131] and there is no evidence to suggest that the Commission has carried out any detailed comparative evaluation of this kind.[132] This is all the more surprising in view of the fact that the IPPC Directive originally required that the Commission report regularly on the effectiveness of IPPC compared to other instruments of environmental law.[133] And yet, mysteriously this important reflexivity-inducing requirement has disappeared. A careful search reveals that this requirement was excluded through recourse to the 'accelerated working method for official codification of legislative texts'.[134] In the course of this the Consultative Working Party of the Legal Services of the Commission, Council, and European Parliament offered their opinion that the proposed amendments constituted 'a straight-forward codification and did not change the substance of the existing texts'.[135] This incident raises an interesting and important point. The alteration brought about was certainly procedural. The provision removed required the Commission to report. But to say that a provision is procedural is not in itself to infer that its alteration would not impact upon the substance of the text. 'Proceduralization' is an endemic feature of EU law, and procedural norms are regularly relied upon to induce substantive effects.[136]

---

[129] COM(2001) 581 final, 13.

[130] See n 124 above.

[131] L James, 'IPPC Versus Emissions Trading', 3 at <http://www.umweltbundesamt.at/fileadmin/site/umweltthemen/industrie/IPPC_Konferenz/donnerstag_kienzl/6-_James.ppt>. There is some compelling evidence that the imposition of emission standards under the IPPC/IED regime would have a significant and positive environmental effect. See Ecofys, 'Scenarios on the Introduction of CO2 Performance Standards for the EU Power Sector' (2009) at <http://www.ecofys.com/com/publications/documents/FinalReportEcofys_EPS_Scenarios_13Jan2009.pdf>. Note once again the final comments (n 119 above) observing that the European Parliament's Environment Committee has voted to permit Member States to impose emission limits on ETS-covered firms.

[132] ibid. There are also strong doubts about the performance to date of the ETS. See: Ecofys, 'EU Climate Policy Impact in 2020' (2009) at the same web address.

[133] Original version of IPPC Directive (n 118 above) Art 16(3).

[134] CM/641145EN.doc. See Interinstitutional Agreement of 20 December 1994. Accelerated working method for official codification of legislation texts [1996] OJ C102/2. I would like to thank Mark Johnston of WWF who tracked down the relevant documents for me. He covers the debate about the relationship between ETS and IPPC regularly on his blog: <http://ccswire.blogactiv.eu/>.

[135] ibid 3. In the case of the European Parliament the matter was considered in the Committee for Legal Affairs: <http://www.europarl.europa.eu/sides/getDoc.do?pubRef=-//EP//TEXT+TA+P6-TA-2007-0239+0+DOC+XML+V0//EN>.

[136] The Environmental Impact Assessment Directive is, for example, 'merely' procedural in nature. For a discussion of the substance/procedure distinction in relation to this see J Holder, *Environmental Assessment: The Regulation of Decision-Making* (Oxford University Press, 2004), especially ch 7.

It has been suggested that one way forward in navigating the tense relationship between IPPC and ETS would be to experiment with trading but, if it underperforms, to revert to IPPC.[137] The framework for this kind of informed experimentation was originally put in place by IPPC. The re-introduction of a comparative effectiveness reporting requirement of this kind would constitute a useful and important first step.

C. CARBON DIOXIDE EMISSIONS FROM PASSENGER CARS (AND THE EU'S FREE MOVEMENT RULES)

In 2009 the EU adopted a Regulation setting emission performance standards for new passenger cars.[138] The Regulation sets the average carbon dioxide emissions for new passenger cars at 130g CO_2/km, and provides that this goal is to be achieved progressively by 2015.[139] While manufacturers must ensure that their fleet *average* meets this goal, the Regulation accepts that lower emissions from lighter vehicles may be used to compensate for higher emissions from heavier cars.[140]

The Commission originally proposed this Regulation on the basis of Article 95 EC (now Article 114 TFEU), insisting upon 'the need to ensure a level playing field for all economic actors in the internal market while at the same time ensuring a high level of protection of health and the environment'.[141] However, the legal basis was changed following a legislative resolution by the European Parliament and ultimately Article 175 EC (now Article 192 TFEU) prevailed.[142]

While the new EU performance standards for carbon emissions from passenger cars are said to be among the most ambitious in the world,[143] it remains the case that many

---

[137] See n 131 above, 1.

[138] Reg 443/2009 (n 8 above). Passenger cars account for 12 per cent of the EU's total carbon dioxide emissions. This forms part of the EU's strategy to reduce carbon emissions from passenger cars and light commercial vehicles, COM(2007) 19 final. Additional measures are to be introduced to achieve a further reduction of 10g CO_2/km (See Art 1). See also COM(2009) 593 final, setting out a proposal for a Regulation of the European Parliament and of the Council setting emission performance standards for new light commercial vehicles.

[139] Art 1, Regulation 443/2009 (n 8 above). Art 4 provides that 65 per cent of a manufacturer's cars will be taken into account in 2012, rising progressively to 100 per cent from 2015. The Regulation also establishes a more stringent target of 95g CO_2/km to be achieved from 2020. The Commission is charged with defining the 'modalities' for reaching this long-term target in a cost-effective manner (see Art 13(5)).

[140] See the formula in Annex I Regulation 443/2009 (n 8 above). For defining the emissions targets of individual cars, taking into account vehicle mass. Note also the existence of Art 7, which allows manufacturers to form a pool for the purpose of meeting their emissions targets.

[141] COM(2007) 856 final, 8.

[142] A6–0419/2008/P6-TA-PRPV(2008)0614. Note though the inclusion of recital 28 in the final version of the Regulation which states that more stringent national measures adopted pursuant to Art 176 EC (now Art 193 TFEU) should not, in consideration of the purpose of and procedures established by this Regulation, impose additional or more stringent penalties on manufacturers who fail to meet their targets under the Regulation. This offers another example of an attempt to limit Member States' powers under Art 176 EC (now Art 193 TFEU) and hence highlights a similar issue to that raised in relation to ETS and IPPC.

[143] European Commission, 'Questions and Answers on the EU Strategy to Reduce CO2 Emissions from Cars' at <http://europa.eu/rapid/pressReleasesAction.do?reference=MEMO/07/46>.

petrol and diesel cars currently available on the EU market already meet, and in many cases significantly out-perform, the 130g CO_2/km standard laid down.[144] Needless to say, this does not include 4x4 vehicles or luxury and performance cars. Add to this fact the realization that European cities are emerging as leaders in the fight against climate change,[145] and there emerges the question of how much further cities (or regions or Member States) may lawfully go in insisting on improved performance standards for passenger cars. Would it be open, for example, to the current Mayor of London (or more likely a future Mayor!) to prohibit the use in London of passenger cars which exceed the average EU emissions benchmark laid down (130g CO_2/km)?

The answer to this question depends upon the scope of the EU's free movement rules, conformity with which will always be required.[146] It seems very likely that a prohibition on the use of certain cars on the streets of London would constitute a measure with an effect equivalent to a quantitative restriction and so fall within the scope of Article 28 EC (now Article 34 TFEU). After all, 'a prohibition on the use of a product in the territory of a Member State has a considerable influence on the behaviour of consumers, which, in its turn, affects the access of that product to the market of that Member State'.[147] As such, the measure would require justification on public health or environmental grounds, and a proportionality test would be applied.[148] Regardless of how intensive a review of proportionality the European court were to engage in, and regardless of what version of proportionality it were to apply,[149] it seems almost inconceivable that the Court would choose to condemn a measure of this kind. The measure would clearly be capable of contributing to its climate change mitigation goal. Less trade-restrictive, but equally effective, alternatives would be difficult to find.[150] Even if (unusually) the Court were to apply a strong proportionality

---

[144] One straightforward way of getting some sense of this is to see which cars qualify for the £35 per year vehicle excise duty in the UK. This is available for cars which emit between 101–120g CO_2/km. Cars which emit less are exempted from paying this tax. See <http://www.parkers.co.uk/News/Road-tax/35-a-year-to-tax-cars/>. What is striking is the fact that this includes not only super-minis and minis but also some family and estate cars.

[145] eg European Commission, 'Mayors from Europe and America Join Forces to Fight Against Climate Change' (7 October 2009) at <http://europa.eu/rapid/pressReleasesAction.do?reference=IP/09/1436>.

[146] Recall again the terms of Art 176 EC (now Art 193 TFEU). It is worth noting that taxes as opposed to Regulations would be required to meet the non-discrimination/non-protectionism test set out in Art 110 TFEU (ex Art 90 EC).

[147] See Case C-110/05 *Commission v Italy* [2009] ECR I-0519, [56]. See also Case C-142/05 *Mickelsson and Roos* [2009] ECR I-4273.

[148] Public health is included in the exhaustive list of requirements laid down in Art 30 EC (now Art 36 TFEU), whereas environmental protection is recognized as a 'mandatory requirement' by the European Court. See Case C-302/86 *Commission v Denmark* [1988] ECR 4607.

[149] For an overview of the different versions of proportionality and a discussion of the varying intensity of ECJ review, see P Craig and G de Búrca, *EU Law: Texts, Cases and Materials* (4th edn, Oxford University Press, 2008) 543–551 and J Jans (n 127 above).

[150] Though bear in mind the recent tendency of the European Court to 'proceduralize' proportionality and to inquire as to whether a Member State has adequately considered the availability of less trade-restrictive alternatives. See Case C-320/03 *Commission v Austria* ECR [2005] I-09871. Labelling is an often preferred alternative for the European Court in consumer protection cases. Note though that CO_2 labelling of passenger cars has had only a limited and disappointing effect in shaping consumers' purchasing patterns when it comes to cars. For an overview see: 'Study on the effectiveness of Directive 1999//94/EC relating to the availability of consumer information on fuel economy and CO2 emissions in respect of the marketing of new passenger cars' at <http://ec.europa.eu/environment/air/transport/co2/report/final_report.pdf>.

test, it seems improbable that it would find the trade restriction caused by the measure to be excessive in the light of the contested measure's contribution to its (hugely significant) environmental goal.[151]

The main point here though is not to anticipate the conclusion of the European Court if/when confronted with a measure of this kind. It is rather to highlight the existence of environmental exceptions to the free movement rules, and to emphasize the richly contextual nature of the proportionality test which applies. When a measure is based upon Article 175 EC (now Article 192 TFEU), stricter protective measures adopted by Member States are made subject to this nuanced and eminently appropriate test. How different things could have been. Had the European Parliament not intervened, and had Article 95 EC (now Article 114 TFEU) been selected as the measure's legal base, proportionality would have been supplemented and in effect supplanted by a vastly less rational test.

Though Article 95 EC (now Article 114 TFEU) permits the adoption of both minimum and exhaustive harmonization measures,[152] the Commission's original proposal for a Regulation on carbon emissions from passenger cars was unequivocal in its pursuit of the latter:

> The targets for CO2 emissions should be harmonised to avoid differing requirements between Member States, to preserve the achievements of the internal market and ensure the free movement of passenger cars within the Community while ensuring a high level of environmental protection.[153]

It is well established by the case law of the European Court that exhaustive harmonization deprives Member States of recourse to the free movement exceptions. They can no longer rely on Article 30 EC (now Article 36 TFEU) or invoke the concept of mandatory or imperative requirements. Their regulatory room for manoeuvre is consequently much reduced. Any Member State (or region or city) wishing to *introduce* stricter standards than those laid down in an exhaustive harmonization measure will be obliged to rely on the opt-out in Article 95(5) EC (now Article 114(5) TFEU).[154] This provides that:

> ... if after the adoption by the Council or by the Commission of a harmonisation measure, a Member State deems that it is necessary to introduce national provisions based on new scientific evidence relating to the protection of the environment or the working environ-

---

[151] Recall here the conclusion of the CFI that climate change represents one of the gravest challenges facing the world. 'Strong' proportionality does not stop with the least trade-restrictive means question, but rather asks whether the trade restriction is justified given the contribution of the measure to its public interest goal.

[152] For a compelling defence of this claim, see M Dougan, 'Minimum Harmonisation after Tobacco Advertising and Laval Un Partneri' in M Bulterman *et al* (eds), *Views of European Law from the Mountain: Liber Amicorum Piet Jan Slot* (Kluwer, 2009).

[153] COM(2007) 856, 11.

[154] Art 95(4) EC (now Art 114(4) TFEU) lays down a different, and slightly more relaxed, set of circumstances in which Member States may continue to apply stricter standards already in existence before the adoption of the exhaustive harmonization measure.

ment on grounds of a problem specific to that Member State arising after the adoption of the harmonisation measure, it shall notify the Commission of the envisaged provisions, as well as the grounds for introducing them.

In addition, in deciding whether to approve the introduction of a stricter Member State measure, the Commission is required to verify that the measure does not give rise to arbitrary discrimination or a disguised restriction on trade, or create a disproportionate obstacle to the functioning of the internal market.[155] Hence, condition is piled on condition and the even the basic grounds (environment and working environment) are strictly confined.

In the context of the global problem of climate change, one particular aspect of this opt-out stands out; namely the requirement that the problem in question must be 'specific to that Member State'.[156] Where a Member State aims to address a problem which is anything other than specific to it, the introduction of stricter protective measures will not be allowed.

It was on the basis of this specificity requirement that the Court of First Instance recently upheld a Commission Decision denying a Dutch request to allow it to enforce *stricter* (than European) standards regulating diesel particulates from cars. The Court did so on the basis that any environmental problem which arises in terms which are on the whole comparable throughout the EU, and which lends itself therefore to a harmonized approach, is general and not specific. While a problem need not be unique to one Member State to count as a specific problem, there must be evidence of local particularities which distinguish the situation in that Member State. In this case, the CFI found that the Netherlands did not encounter problems significantly in excess of, or different from, those encountered in a range of other Member States.[157]

What is most striking about the specificity requirement is the way in which it privileges just one consideration, while silencing a whole host of apparently relevant concerns. A Member State measure may threaten minimal disruption to trade and yet promise to make a material contribution to resolving an environmental problem

---

[155] See Art 95(6) EC (now Art 114(6) TFEU).

[156] This requirement is somewhat resonant of the position adopted by the US Environmental Protection Agency (EPA) when denying California a waiver from the Clean Air Act to allow it to adopt state-level standards for greenhouse gas emissions from motor vehicles. In its letter to the Governor of California, the EPA emphasized that the problem of climate change is not exclusive or unique to California. Happily, the EPA subsequently changed its mind, concluding that the criteria for granting a waiver of this kind should not be read to include consideration of whether the impacts of climate change are 'compelling and extraordinary' just in California. See the various documents listed here: <http://www.epa.gov/oms/climate/ca-waiver.htm>.

[157] While the judgment of the CFI was annulled by the ECJ, the judgment of this court did not call into question the CFI's basic interpretation of Art 95(5) EC (now Art 114 TFEU). It merely admonished the CFI for failing to take relevant, more recent, data into account or to give good reasons for so doing. These more recent data demonstrated that the limits for diesel particulates had been exceeded throughout the whole territory of the Netherlands, and did not 'exclude the possibility that there was, at the date of the contested decision's adoption, a specific problem in that Member State'. See case T-182/06 Netherlands v Commission ECR [2007] 11-01983 and Case C-405/07P Netherlands v Commission ECR [2008] 1-08301.

which is both pressing and grave.[158] Yet, unless the environmental problem is specific to that Member State, still this self-evidently proportionate response would be condemned. This would remain the case regardless of the level of environmental ambition inherent in the existing EU harmonizing measure, and regardless of the EU's political appetite or capacity to contribute more. Regardless of context and consequence, specificity shuts the door firmly on national and local policy entrepreneurs.

D. RENEWABLE ENERGY: SUSTAINABILITY CRITERIA FOR BIOFUELS

Renewable energy has been on the EU agenda for more than two decades, but only recently have binding targets been set.[159] The Renewable Energy Directive establishes national targets for renewable energy as well as a specific target for renewable energy in transport.[160] While there is wide variation in the national targets set,[161] the target for renewable energy in transport is fixed at 10 per cent.[162]

Under the terms of the Renewable Energy Directive, Member States are required to adopt a national renewable energy action plan, to be submitted to the Commission by 30 June 2010.[163] While the national targets are binding, the Commission's powers are weak. It is charged with evaluating the national plans, including the adequacy of the measures envisaged by the Member State, and it may issue a recommendation as a result.[164] Member States are obliged to submit forecast documents six months before this, setting out estimates of their excess/deficit in renewable energy relative to the national target set.

---

[158] In fact in the context of climate change, even a Member State measure which threatens considerable disruption to trade may be considered to be proportionate given the CFI's acknowledgement that climate change represents one of the world's gravest threats.

[159] See especially the Commission's White Paper COM(97)599 final, Energy for the Future—Renewable Sources of Energy, which proposed an indicative target of 12 per cent by 2010.

[160] Directive 2009/28 (n 7 above). For a definition of renewable energy see Art 2(a). It includes energy from renewable non-fossil sources, including for example wind, solar, and hydropower, but excluding nuclear.

[161] ibid Annex I. The highest target is 40 per cent (Latvia, which already achieved a 32.6 per cent share in 2005). The lowest target is Malta (10 per cent, compared to a 0 per cent share in 2005). These targets are binding on Member States. However, note Art 5(2) which states that, upon request from a Member State, the Commission may decide that *force majeure* has been demonstrated, making it impossible for a Member State to meet its target. In this eventuality, the Commission shall determine what adjustments are to be made to that Member State's national target. The concept of *force majeure* is not defined.

[162] Directive 2009/28 (n 7 above) Art 3(4).

[163] ibid Arts 4(1) and 4(2). See also Commission Decision 2009/548 [2009] OJ L182/33, setting out the template to be used by Member States.

[164] Directive 2009/28 (n 7 above) Art 4(5). The intention is clearly that political pressure will play a role with the Commission being obliged to send the national plans to the European Parliament and to make the plans and any recommendations available to the public.

Though the Directive rejects the idea of establishing a fully fledged system of trading in renewable energy,[165] it does permit 'statistical transfers' of renewable energy between Member States which are in surplus or deficit relative to their national targets.[166] It also provides for the launching of joint projects between Member States, and between Member States and third countries, to allow for renewable energy generated outside the territory of one Member State to count towards compliance.[167] Joint projects of this kind may only be taken into account where the electricity has been produced by a newly constructed installation that became operational after 25 June 2009, or as a result of increased capacity of an installation that was refurbished after that date.[168] In the case of joint projects involving third countries, Member States are required to provide proof of compliance with the conditions laid down.[169] It is thus the case that, as with project offsets, the integrity of Member State compliance with national targets is to some extent contingent upon verification of compliance with conditions laid down in relation to projects which are situated abroad.

While the Renewable Energy Directive raises a host of interesting issues, the discussion here will focus on only one; namely the establishment of sustainability criteria for biofuels.[170] These are used exclusively for transport, and will be the main source of achieving compliance with the 10 per cent renewables obligation.[171] The sustainability criteria for biofuels are laid down in Article 17 of the Renewable Energy Directive, and they apply to both domestically produced and imported biofuel. While compliance with these criteria is not a precondition for biofuels being placed on the EU market, and hence biofuels may be imported even if the criteria are not met, compliance with them is required in order for biofuel to count towards attainment of EU or national renewable energy obligations or to be eligible for financial support for consumption of biofuels.[172] The introduction of these criteria is indicative of strong concerns about the authenticity of the GHG emissions savings achieved by biofuels, and about the social and environmental impact of cultivating the necessary energy

---

[165] L J Nilsson and K Ericsson, 'The Rise and Fall of GO Trading in European Renewable Energy Policy: The Role of Advocacy and Policy Framing' (2009) 37 Energy Policy 4454–4462.

[166] Directive 2009/28 (n 7 above) Art 6.

[167] ibid Arts 7 and 9.

[168] ibid Arts 7(2) and 10(2)(b). Additional conditions are also laid down in Arts 7 and 8 (joint projects between Member States) and Arts 9 and 10 (joint projects between Member States and third countries). Note especially Art 9(2)(c) which provides that joint projects eligible for compliance purposes should not have received support from a support scheme of a third country other than an investment aid granted to the installation.

[169] ibid Art 10(1)(c).

[170] See the definitions in Directive 2009/28 (n 7 above) Art 2(h) and (f). There are two main kinds of biofuel, biodiesel which is derived from sugar and starch crops and potentially in the future from trees and grasses, and bioethanol which is produced from vegetable oils and animal fats.

[171] A Swinbank, 'EU Support for Biofuels and Bioenergy: "Environmental Sustainability" Criteria and Trade Policy' (ICTSD Issue Paper No 17, 2009) 6.

[172] Directive 2009/28 (n 7 above) Art 17(1). See also Art 2(l) for the definition of 'renewable energy obligation' which refers to national support schemes for renewable energy.

crops.[173] There are concerns not only about the direct impacts of cultivating energy crops, but also about the prospect of their cultivation leading to indirect land use change, whereby food crops will be displaced by energy crops, with the food crops subsequently being grown on land of high carbon or biodiversity value such as peatlands or forest. Concerns have also been raised that the 'plantation-style' production of energy crops could jeopardize the rights of small farmers and indigenous peoples.[174]

The shape of these sustainability criteria was much debated during the legislative passage of the Renewable Energy Directive.[175] Under the leadership of a Green MEP, stricter and additional standards were proposed by the European Parliament Committee on Industry, Research and Energy, among them a range of social conditions for agricultural workers. Ultimately though, the Directive settled on four key criteria:[176]

- Sustainably produced biofuels must achieve GHG emissions savings of at least 35 per cent (rising to 50 per cent from 2018).[177]

- Sustainably produced biofuels must not derive from land enjoying high biodiversity value in January 2008.[178]

- Sustainably produced biofuels must not derive from land with high carbon stock in January 2008 where the land has subsequently lost this status.[179]

- Sustainably produced biofuel must not be obtained land that was peatland in January 2008, unless evidence is provided that the cultivation of the energy crops does not involve the drainage of previously undrained soil.[180]

The Commission also incurs wide-ranging reporting obligations in relation to a range of additional concerns including, for example, in relation to social sustainability, food prices,[181] and the impact of indirect land-use change on GHG emissions.[182]

---

[173] R Edwards et al, *Biofuels in the European Context: Facts and Uncertainties* (European Commission Joint Research Centre, 2009).

[174] Oxfam Briefing Note, 'Biofuelling Poverty: Why the EU Renewable-Fuel Target May be Disastrous for Poor People' (2007).

[175] For a meticulous account see Swinbank (n 173 above) 6–8.

[176] An additional criterion is laid down in Directive 2009/28 (n 7 above) Art 17(6) for energy crops produced inside the EU, concerning compliance with Common Agricultural Policy environmental standards.

[177] Directive 2009/28 (n 7 above) Art 17(2). The 50 per cent figure increases to 60 per cent for biofuels produced in installations which started production after the start of 2017.

[178] ibid Art 17(3). In the case of areas designated for nature conservation purposes or for the protection of rare, threatened, or endangered species, an exception applies where evidence is provided that the production of the energy crops did not interfere with the nature conservation purposes of the designation concerned.

[179] ibid Art 17(4).

[180] ibid Art 17(5).

[181] See Art 17(7) for a discussion of these concerns see Edwards (n 174 above).

[182] Directive 2009/ 28 (n 7 above) Art 19(6). See also the Commission's recent consultation paper on this theme, 'Indirect land use change—Possible elements of a policy approach preparatory draft for stakeholder/ expert comments' (2009) and the various responses received at <http://ec.europa.eu/energy/renewables/consultations/2009_07_31_iluc_pre_consultation_en.htm>.

The Renewable Energy Directive's sustainability criteria raise three issues of primary importance for the purpose of this chapter, each of which will be briefly examined. The first tracks a theme already addressed, and concerns the legal basis of the Directive and its implications for the regulatory autonomy of Member States. The second mirrors another theme previously highlighted, namely the arrangements put in place to verify compliance with legal requirements in respect of activities based abroad. The third raises a new theme, but one which is consistent with the multi-level governance focus of this chapter. This concerns the compatibility of the EU's sustainability criteria with World Trade Organization (WTO) Law.

1. THE SUSTAINABILITY CRITERIA: MINIMUM OR EXHAUSTIVE HARMONIZATION?

Though the Renewable Energy Directive rests on a dual legal basis, it expressly provides that the sustainability criteria have been adopted on the basis of Article 95 EC (now Article 114 TFEU).[183] In keeping with this, the Directive clarifies that, as far as these criteria are concerned, the Directive gives rise to exhaustive harmonization. Member States are thus precluded from introducing 'other sustainability grounds',[184] except in accordance with Article 95(5) EC (now Article 114(5) TFEU). In keeping with the earlier discussion about the regulation of passenger cars, it is clear that Member States are only permitted to introduce stricter standards in order to address a problem which is *specific* to that Member State. Insofar as the sustainability criteria apply to energy crops or biofuels imported from abroad, their goal is to contribute to the protection of the global atmosphere (by ensuring adequate GHG savings) and to help conserve biodiversity in the territory of the exporting state. For imported biofuels, these sustainability criteria seek to address problems which are external to the Member States. Consequently the practical effect of the specificity requirement is to exclude recourse to the opt-out and to shut down entirely the regulatory autonomy of Member States.

2. ENFORCING THE SUSTAINABILITY CRITERIA ABROAD

The sustainability criteria will be difficult to enforce, especially when they necessitate monitoring of land-use change abroad.[185] The Renewable Energy Directive places the burden of demonstrating compliance on the economic operator involved,[186] and it

---

[183] See recital 1, Directive 2009/28 (n 7 above) which refers to Arts 17–19, each of which is concerned with an aspect of the sustainability criteria. The other legal basis is Art 175 EC (now Art 192 TFEU).

[184] Directive 2009/28 (n 7 above) Art 17(8).

[185] See, for example, the key findings of the Cambridge Conservation Initiative Workshop which notes that 'there is an urgent need to increase the adequacy of monitoring resources such as GIS and global databases, particularly of spatially explicit information, to support robust implementation of the sustainability criteria and land use planning for biofuels. The international community must invest in making available and further developing data sets that could be used for implementing the sustainability criteria' at: <http://www.conservation.cam.ac.uk/downloads/EUBiofuelsKeyMessagesMay09.pdf>, 4.

[186] Directive 2009/28 (n 7 above) Art 18(1).

places great faith in the contribution that independent auditors can make. Member States are obliged to require that economic operators arrange for an adequate standard of independent auditing of information to be put in place, and that auditors verify that the systems used by the economic operators are accurate, reliable, and protected against fraud.[187]

While it is too early to evaluate the steps taken by the Member States and the performance of the auditors in question, experience in regulating project offsets does not bode well. In the context of the Clean Development Mechanism widespread concerns have been raised about the independence of ostensibly independent auditors whose services have been paid for by the audited firm.[188] These concerns have been recently borne out by decisions of the Executive Board to suspend two of the leading firms involved.[189] In the case of the Renewable Energy Directive, the European Commission will maintain an oversight role, as a result of its monitoring and reporting obligations,[190] and because of the powers of investigation and contestation which it enjoys.[191] Nonetheless, its resources are limited relative to the scale of the enforcement challenge involved.

3. THE SUSTAINABILITY CRITERIA AND THE WTO

Space precludes a full analysis of the implications of WTO law for the EU's biofuels regime.[192] Those familiar with the contours of WTO law will perceive in the text of the Renewable Energy Directive efforts to align the scope and application of the sustainability criteria with the multiple requirements of WTO law. The sustainability criteria apply to both domestic and imported goods.[193] They contain a range of qualifications and exceptions in a bid to ensure that they are no more trade-restrictive than their underlying objectives require.[194] Where possible, the criteria have recourse to international standards,[195] and they are cognizant of the importance of WTO-imposed due

---

[187] Directive 2009/28 (n 7 above) Art 18(3).

[188] See L Schneider and L Mohr, *An Evaluation of Designated Operational Entities (DOEs) Accredited Under the Clean Development Mechanism (CDM)* (WWF/Öko Institut, 2009) at <http://www.oeko.de/oekodoc/902/2009-020-en.pdf> (ranking the five leading auditors on a scale of A–F. The two highest-ranking firms achieved a 'D' grade).

[189] The Norwegian firm, Det Norske Veritas (DNV), was temporarily suspended in 2008 and SGS was temporarily suspended for a period during 2009.

[190] eg Directive 2009/28 (n 7 above) Art 23.

[191] ibid Art 18(3).

[192] See S Charnovitz, J Earley, and R Howse, 'An Examination in Social Standards in Biofuels Sustainability Criteria' for a full analysis albeit not one which is confined to the EU. (IPC Discussion Paper—Standards Series 2008) at <http://www.agritrade.org/SocialStandardsforBiofuels.html>.

[193] In a bid to ensure compatibility with the national treatment principle in GATT, Art III 4.

[194] See for example the qualification in the last paragraph of Art 17(3)(b) Directive 2009/28 (n 7 above). The least-trade-restrictive requirement forms part of a necessity analysis under the GATT, Art XX(b) exception and in all probability also under Art 2.2 Technical Barriers to Trade Agreement (TBT).

[195] See, for example, Art 17(3)(b)(ii) and Art 18(4) Directive 2009/28 (n 7 above). This is designed to ensure compatibility with Art 2.4 of the TBT Agreement.

process demands.[196] Procedures are put in place for regularly updating the calculation of the GHG impact of biofuels[197] and, as noted, the EU criteria operate to pre-empt the adoption of stricter standards by Member States.[198]

Yet, while the EU's sustainability criteria have clearly been designed with WTO law in mind, still they *may* be vulnerable to challenge in a number of respects. This is because the sustainability criteria exemplify a category of trade-restrictive measure which is as controversial as it is unresolved in WTO law. These criteria take the form of a measure which regulates production process rather than the intrinsic quality of the resulting good.[199] Moreover, the aim of the process-based measure is to protect the environment outside of the territory of the EU. It aims not only to promote protection of the global atmosphere but also to promote conservation of biodiversity within the territory of the exporting state.[200] While Appellate Body case law is suggestive of an interpretative approach which is broadly tolerant of measures of this sort, it has yet to address a situation in which the object of protection pursued by a trade-restrictive measure lies entirely beyond the territory of the regulating state.[201]

It is also crucial to bear in mind that WTO law has evolved in a direction which mirrors the internal market law of the EU. There is more today to the WTO than merely the GATT. Agreements such as the Technical Barriers to Trade Agreement take the WTO beyond a discrimination-based approach, providing that even non-discriminatory measures must be justified as being necessary to achieve a legitimate objective.[202] Like the parallel idea of 'mandatory requirements' in EU law,[203] the concept of a legitimate objective is broadly drawn. Nonetheless, the

---

[196] See especially Art 18(5) Directive 2009/28 (n 7 above). This is in keeping with the case law of the Appellate Body (AB) in interpreting the 'chapeau' to the GATT, Art XX exception, most notably in the *Shrimp-Turtle* case (WT/DS58/AB/R).

[197] The Commission is empowered to propose amendments in accordance with a variety of Comitology procedures. See especially Art 19 concerning the calculation of GHG savings associated with biofuels. This is reflective of the approach of the AB in the *EC—Generalised System of Preferences* case (WT/DS246/AB/R).

[198] Thereby avoiding the danger of the recurrence of an *EC—Biotech* (WT/DS291/R/Corr.1) type situation, whereby stricter Member State standards were found to amount to an EU breach of WTO law.

[199] For a very clear-sighted analysis of this category of measure see D H Regan, 'How to Think about PPMs (and Climate Change)' in T Cottier, O Nartova, and S Z Bigdeli (eds), *International Trade and the Mitigation of Climate Change* (Cambridge University Press, 2009) 97–123.

[200] For a discussion of the continuing relevance and limitations of territoriality in the context of climate change see T Cottier and S Matteotti-Berkutova, 'International Environmental Law and the Evolving Concept of 'Common Concern of Mankind'' in ibid 21–47.

[201] In *Shrimp-Turtle* (n 196 above), the AB found the existence of a 'territorial nexus' [133] between the regulating state (US) and the object of protection (turtles, some of which sometimes traverse the waters of the US).

[202] See in particular Art 2.2 TBT Agreement. Note also the definition of a technical Regulation in Annex 1.1 of the agreement. This covers Regulations concerning product characteristics or their related processes and production methods. Considerable uncertainty remains about whether this definition includes Regulations which pertain purely to how goods are produced, where production processes do not impact on the make-up or characteristics of the product in question. For a brief discussion and further references see P van den Bossche, *The Law and Policy of the World Trade Organization* (Cambridge University Press, 2008) 808–809.

[203] This concept was first outlined by the ECJ in Case 120/78 *Rewe-Zentral AG* [1979] ECR 649 (*Cassis de Dijon*). By contrast to the Treaty-based free movement exception, the list of mandatory requirements is flexible rather than fixed.

underlying necessity requirement provides an opportunity for the WTO 'courts' to 'weigh and balance' the various characteristics of a trade-restrictive measure, including the degree of trade restriction presented and the importance of its underlying goal.[204]

The broadening of the scope of international trade law to encompass even measures which do not discriminate against imported goods renders more frequent the encounters between EU and WTO law. This is clearly apparent from the cases currently pending before the WTO 'courts'. From the EU's prohibition on the importation of seal products,[205] to its ban on the use of chemical agents in cleaning poultry carcasses,[206] it is no longer enough that the EU treats others in the same way as it treats its own.

E. CONCLUSION

This chapter has focused upon the multi-level governance of climate change, illustrating how deeply contested the division of responsibilities between the different levels of governance has become. While the Commission's efforts to centralize authority have met with some success, most notably in the design of the reformed emissions trading regime, a number of actors continue to stand in its way. The Court of First Instance (General Court) found that the Commission exceeded its powers when it rejected the Polish and Estonian national allocation plans. The European Parliament prompted a change of legal basis in the Passenger Cars Regulation, thus preserving enhanced regulatory autonomy for Member States. The Worldwide Fund for Nature has been relentless in arguing that it is unlawful for the Emissions Trading Directive to deprive the Member States of authority to impose emission reduction requirements on ETS-covered industrial plants. Perhaps predictably, these battles for power are being played out in the language of constitutional law, with notions of subsidiarity, limited competence, legal basis, and minimum harmonization being called in aid.

Along with the multi-level governance dimension, there is one other feature which stands out from the preceding analysis, namely the frequency with which the EU is confronted with regulating climate change-relevant activities which are situated abroad. Be it in relation to project offsets, or joint projects for the production of renewable energy, or as a result of the introduction of sustainability criteria for biofuels, the EU's ability to meet its carbon reduction targets, and to do so in a manner which is consistent with other policy goals, depends critically upon its capacity to regulate effectively and consistently multifarious projects and activities dispersed throughout many distant parts of the world. The external dimension of the

---

[204] The AB's approach to analysing the 'necessity' requirement is set out in *Brazil—Retreaded Tyres* (WT/DS332/AB/R).

[205] *EC—Measures Prohibiting the Importation and Marketing of Seal Products* (WT/DS400/1).

[206] *EC—Certain Measures Affecting Poultry Meat and Poultry Meat Products from the United States* (WT/DS389/4).

EU's climate change policy is of increasing importance. Over the coming years, there is an urgent need for detailed empirical work which evaluates the costs and benefits of these projects and activities, and gauges the real capacity of the EU to regulate their contribution to reducing emissions, as well as their social and environmental effects.

27

CONSUMER POLICY

*Stephen Weatherill**

A. INTRODUCTION[1]

Consumer protection . . . has a bearing on what is probably the most central issue of European economic integration for it brings into very sharp relief the dialectics of open borders, protectionism, and bona fide intervention of the Member State *and/ or the European Union* to protect legitimate societal values and goals even if at the expense of interrupting the free flow of goods on which the idea of a common marketplace is postulated. To understand the problematic of consumer protection in the common market context is to understand the core issue of European market integration.[2]

Consumer policy deserves a central place in EU legal studies. So why, then, has it tended to find itself marginalized within the EU's institutions and in academic writing? The enduring reason for this relative neglect is firmly embedded in the original Treaty of Rome. A small number of trivial mentions aside, there was no focus on the notion of the 'consumer interest' in the Treaty which came into force in 1958. The implication was that the consumer was expected to be the passive beneficiary of the restructuring of European markets; integration through law was itself a form of consumer policy. Most of all, there was no explicit legislative competence conferred on the EC in the consumer field. This persisted after the Single European Act, which left consumer policy out of the list of new competences formally conferred on the EC. Only at

---

* Jacques Delors Professor of European Law and Deputy Director for European Law of the Institute of European and Comparative Law at the University of Oxford.

[1] The abbreviation 'TEU' used after a Treaty article refers to the Treaty on European Union in the version in force after 1 December 2009, while 'TFEU' refers to the Treaty on the Functioning of the European Union. 'EC' after a Treaty article refers to a provision of the European Community Treaty in the version in force until 30 November 2009; similarly, 'EU' refers to an article of the Treaty on European Union in the version in force until that date.

[2] T Bourgoignie and D Trubek, *Consumer Law, Common Markets and Federalism* (DeGruyter, 1987) vi; italicized words my addition.

Maastricht was the constitutional inhibition on the elaboration of an autonomous consumer policy removed. But even the insertion of what is now Article 169 TFEU failed to resolve the question of whether there really is (or should be) a theoretical foundation to EC intervention designed to improve the position of the consumer. Article 169 has been little employed and even today the TFEU remains barren of any sophisticated statement of the envisaged place of the consumer.

Consumer policy offers insights into how the judicial and legislative institutions of the EU are drawn into the task of elaborating regulatory policies in consequence on an inevitable dynamism whereby internal trade policy spreads beyond a one-dimensional concern for open borders. This chapter explores the rise of consumer policy as a case study in the incremental expansion of law- and policy-making at EU level.

B. MARKET INTEGRATION AND CONSUMER POLICY

Insofar as EU consumer policy is built on the assumption that an integrated market will optimize consumer welfare, then the effective application of the rules of the internal market game is a form of consumer policy. Core provisions of the Treaty guaranteeing free circulation of the factors of production, such as Articles 34, 49, and 56 TFEU, challenge market fragmentation along national lines and expand consumer choice. The Treaty competition rules fit the same pattern. They too are designed to prevent market distortion that would prejudice (ultimately) the consumer. Consumer policy is concealed, but assumed, within the structure of EU trade law.

On occasion the Court has revealed an explicit awareness of the underlying expectation of the release of consumer choice through integration. It has condemned national rules which 'crystallize given consumer habits so as to consolidate an advantage acquired by national industries concerned to comply with them'. This observation was directed at fiscal rules which favoured typical national products in *Commission v United Kingdom*,[3] where the allegation concerned tax advantages conferred on beer at the expense of wine, and at technical rules which exerted a protectionist effect in favour of typical German beers over imported products in *Commission v Germany*.[4] The consequence of finding such rules incompatible with EU trade law is that the national market undergoes deregulation, and the opportunities for out-of-state traders to penetrate new markets is enhanced. In the services sector, an example of the assumption that consumer choice underpins the Treaty rules is provided by *Commission v France*.[5] The Court found that the imposition of national licensing requirements

---

[3] Case 170/78 [1980] ECR 417, [14].
[4] Case 178/84 [1987] ECR 1227, [32].
[5] Case C-154/89 [1991] ECR I-659.

applicable to tour guides confined the pool of available guides, and that this prevented tourists taking part in organized tours from making their own selection of such services. EU law exerts a deregulatory impact, liberalizing the market in order to maximize consumer choice.

Explicit reference has been made by the Court to the consumer interest in securing free competition in accordance with what was Article 81 EC, and is now Article 101 TFEU. In *Züchner v Bayerische Vereinsbank AG*, which concerned an alleged concerted practice between banks affecting charges for cross-border transfer of funds, the Court ruled that that provision may apply where firms have abandoned competitive independence 'thus depriving their customers of any genuine opportunity to take advantage of services on more favourable terms which would be offered to them under normal conditions of competition'.[6] And, albeit that each market must be assessed on its terms, parallel trade is treated favourably in EU law because it injects new sources of supply into national markets 'which necessarily brings some benefits to the final consumer'.[7]

In these instances, the role of the consumer receives explicit acknowledgement by the Court, even though the relevant Treaty provisions are not phrased in a way that makes plain the impact on the consumer interest. The consumer is conceived as a passive beneficiary of structural change in the market. In *GB-INNO-BM v Confederation du Commerce Luxembourgeois* the Court stated: 'Free movement of goods concerns not only traders but also individuals. It requires, particularly in frontier areas, that consumers resident in one Member State may travel freely to the territory of another Member State to shop under the same conditions as the local population.'[8] But even this stirring depiction of EU trade law as a source of legal rights for the consumer actively to participate in cross-border commerce was made in the context of litigation in which a trader was able successfully to rely on what was then Article 28 EC, now Article 34 TFEU, to develop an integrated marketing strategy. Cases brought by active cross-border consumers are atypical.[9] Nevertheless, counting relevant judicial decisions is no adequate measure of a law's impact, and the post-1992 legislative adjustments have proved of significance in entitling consumers (though not commercial operators) to buy goods for private consumption duty-paid in one Member State and then to return home with them without facing a demand for extra levies. This has generated significant levels of cross-border shopping, especially in products which are taxed at materially different rates by neighbouring countries.[10]

---

[6] Case 172/80 [1981] ECR 2021, [20].

[7] Joined Cases C-468/06 to C-478/06 *Sot. Lelos kai Sia et al* [2008] ECR I-7139, [53].

[8] Case C-362/88 [1990] ECR I-667, [8].

[9] But cf Case C-372/04 *ex p Watts* [2006] ECR I-4325; and several cases concern 'consumers' of education, eg Case C-209/03 *Dany Bidar* [2005] ECR I-2119.

[10] Hence the purchase of alcoholic drinks by UK consumers in stores established for that purpose at the French Channel ports.

C. THE CONSUMER BEFORE THE COURT

1. CONSUMER CHOICE AND MARKET DEREGULATION

Before the European Court, the perception that the law of market integration is designed to serve the consumer interest has met its sharpest test in case law which has pitted the consumer interest in market integration and deregulation against the consumer interest in market regulation, albeit at national level. The former interest, deregulation/integration, is served by ruling national laws that impede cross-border trade incompatible with Articles 34/56 TFEU, whereas the latter, sustained national regulation, is served by ruling laws that impede cross-border trade compatible with Articles 34/56. In these circumstances, the Court is confronted by two competing conceptions of the consumer interest in the application of the public interest test for judging the validity of trade-restrictive technical rules which it first introduced in a sophisticated form in its 'Cassis de Dijon' ruling, Rewe Zentrale v Bundesmonopolver-waltung für Branntwein.[11] In the majority of cases that have been decided by the Court, national rules of (alleged) consumer protection have been regarded as serving a purpose of inadequate importance to override the expectations of integration through mutual recognition. The decision in 'Cassis de Dijon' itself provides a perfect example of the release of the market from rigidity caused by regulatory assumptions based on domestic cultural perceptions. German law required that liqueurs of the Cassis type be stronger than was demanded in France. The German rule did not discriminate on the basis of origin, but it exerted a protectionist effect because German products naturally tended to conform to domestic requirements, whereas imported products, following local traditions and preferences, did not. French Cassis was excluded from the German market simply as a consequence of diversity in regulatory tradition. There were no reasons based on, for example, public health protection which could justify the more rigorous German rules. Germany was therefore compelled to admit the unfamiliar French product onto its market. The assumption underpinning the decision is that it will breed a more competitive market. Whether or not (relatively) weak French Cassis thrives on the German shop shelves is a matter to be decided by private German consumers, not by German public authorities.

'Cassis de Dijon' serves as a clear illustration of the use of EU trade law to enhance consumer choice in the face of restrictive national rules of market regulation. Some more difficult cases have led the Court into a direct inquiry into whether releasing the (national) market from the grip of protective regulation will permit wider consumer choice or, the obverse, consumer confusion. A case such as Oosthoek's Uitgevers-maatschappij BV confirms that the principle of mutual recognition is not absolute:

[T]he offering of free gifts as a means of sales promotion may mislead consumers as to the real prices of certain products and distorts the conditions on which genuine

---

[11] Case 120/78 [1979] ECR 649.

competition is based. Legislation which restricts or even prohibits such commercial practices for that reason is therefore capable of contributing to consumer protection and fair trading.[12]

The Court does not insist on a lowest common denominator of regulatory protection within the EU, which carries the institutional implication that reform is the preserve of legislative activity at EU level. The Court has made explicit its view that the fact that one Member State imposes less strict rules than another does not automatically mean that the latter's rules are disproportionate and hence incompatible with EU law.[13] The Court's determination not to pursue the notion of mutual recognition of national standards to a recklessly absolute extreme is plainer still in cases where suspected health risks are at stake rather than protection of economic interests. For example, in *Eyssen* the Court ruled that Dutch rules that prohibited the use of Nisin, a preservative added to cheese, could be validly applied to exclude cheese originating in other Member States where a less serious view was taken of the equivocal scientific evidence about the safety of Nisin and where accordingly the preservative was lawfully used.[14] Such cases have typically been dealt with lately by reference to the 'precautionary principle'.[15]

2. THE 'REASONABLY CIRCUMSPECT' CONSUMER

The Court has entered an arena where difficult choices about the consumer's capacity to process information must be made. There is no homogenous consumer who is the subject of regulatory protection at national level. There are different groups of consumers, with varying levels of vulnerability. Rarely will a rule restrict trade, yet offer no conceivable element of protection. Most rules attacked via Articles 34 or 56 TFEU will protect some consumers. The European Court, in adjudicating on the validity of the measure, must balance the interests of the consumers who are thought (by national authorities) to need protection and the wider group of consumers who stand to benefit from deregulation. Yet the problem goes beyond the absence of any homogenous 'Euro-consumer' and the practical reality that markets are populated by both prudent consumers able to take advantage of market integration and gullible consumers likely to be misled by the sudden availability of new products and services. Different Member States have different priorities. 'Hard sell' in one jurisdiction may be

---

[12] Case 286/81 [1982] ECR 4575, [18]. It is not clear that the measure would today be regarded as presenting a sufficient threat to market building to cross the 'Keck threshold': Cases C-267 and C-268/91 *Bernard Keck and Daniel Mithouard* [1993] ECR I-6097.

[13] See eg Case C-294/00 *Deutsche Paracelsus Schulen* [2002] ECR I-6515; Case C-3/95, *Reisebüro Broede v Gerd Sandker* [1996] ECR I-6511.

[14] Case 53/80 [1981] ECR 4091. Cf Cases C-1 and C-176/90, *Aragonesa de Publicidad Exterior SA* [1991] ECR I-4151, where, in contrast to '*Cassis de Dijon*', public health policy was regarded as a sufficient reason for restricting the marketing of strong drink.

[15] See eg Case C-192/01 *Commission v Denmark* [2003] ECR I-9693, Case C-95/01 *John Greenham* [2004] ECR I-1333.

'unfair sell' in another. The Court is therefore called on to apply EU trade law in the context of diverse regulatory traditions.

In *Verband Sozialer Wettbewerb eV v Clinique Laboratories SNC*[16] German law prohibited the use of the name Clinique for cosmetics, because of an alleged risk that consumers would be misled into believing the products had medicinal properties. *Klinik* is a German word for hospital. The Court was unpersuaded that there was sufficient likelihood of confusion for the trade barrier to be justified. Cosmetics were not sold in outlets specializing in pharmaceutical products. Consumers in other states, with less restrictive regimes, did not encounter the alleged confusion.

In *Verein gegen Unwesen in Handel und Gewerbe Köln eV v Mars GmbH*[17] German law was also condemned as 'over-regulatory' by the Court. Mars imported ice-cream bars into Germany from France, where they were lawfully produced and packaged. As part of a Europe-wide publicity campaign, the bars were offered in wrappers marked '+10%'. The bars were indeed 10 per cent larger, though the part of the wrapper displaying the increase occupied more than 10 per cent of the total surface area. The *Landgericht*, faced with the submission that consumers might be misled about the size of the increase, granted an interim order restraining Mars, but referred questions concerning the interpretation of what was then Article 28 EC, now Article 34 TFEU, to Luxembourg. The Court pointed out that the '+10%' marking was accurate in itself. Even though it occupied a surface area exceeding 10 per cent, 'reasonably circumspect consumers' are aware that there is no necessary link between the size of markings and the size of the increase in the product. EU law was therefore to be interpreted as precluding a German prohibition of the type in question.

Insistence on the relaxation of the grip of national laws based on a conception of a consumer more gullible than the European Court will acknowledge vividly illustrates the incursion of EU law into previously sacred national territory. In *Clinique* the Court's remark that consumers in other states did not suffer from confusion invites the retort that would one not expect them to, if the issue is peculiar to the German language. In *Mars* the Court's benchmark of a 'reasonably circumspect' consumer who would not be misled by the trade practices in question leaves room for concern that the rather less alert consumers who were protected under the German regime will be misled once that system is withdrawn. *Clinique* and *Mars* illustrate the strength of the Court's impetus against 'crystallization' of consumer habits caused by national choices about market regulation. But even if one accepts that an overall improvement in consumer welfare will follow 'decrystallization' of habits consequent on the adaptation of market structures, there will be short-term costs paid by confused consumers. The European Court does not deny that some consumers will be misled by the marketing practices in question, so, one may choose to conclude, vulnerable consumers are sacrificed to the interests of self-reliant consumers in deregulation, market integration, and wider choice.

---

[16] Case C-315/92 [1994] ECR I-317.
[17] Case C-470/93 [1995] ECR I-1923.

These cases stand for the collapse of a simple divide between the Union's interest in securing market integration and the Member States' responsibility to citizens to select appropriate levels of social and economic regulation. The Court cannot avoid assessing the consumer interest, even though the Treaty provisions governing free movement omit explicit reference to the consumer. One of the finest examples of the intensely difficult choices with which the Court is presented in adjudicating on the costs and benefits of a national law which forestalls the integrative process is provided by *Drei Glocken GmbH and Gertraud Kritzinger v USL Centro-Sud and Provincia autonoma di Bolzano*.[18] This involved a challenge by a German importer to Italian rules governing types of wheat permissibly used in pasta. Advocate General Mancini, insisting that Italians like their *pasta al dente, glissant des deux côtés de la fourchette*, believed that an Italian consumer could not be adequately informed by labels about production of differently constituted pasta, given the depth of established cultural expectation in Italy. Accordingly he believed laws specifying the use of particular types of wheat should be treated as compatible with EU law despite their trade-restrictive effect. The institutional implication was made explicit by Mr Mancini: the matter should be resolved through legislative intervention, for liberalization achieved by finding the rule incompatible with the Treaty would wreck patterns of wheat production, while also causing undue consumer confusion. The Court disagreed and, adhering closely to the reasoning it adopted in 'Cassis de Dijon', regarded the Italian rules as unlawful. The Court did not seek to refute the detailed analysis presented by its Advocate General, but (by implication) treated the consumer as capable of adapting to unfamiliar products and/or regarded the damage done to (some) consumers' interests by deregulation as an insufficient reason for blocking integration. In any event, the Italian market should be freed of its regulatory constraints, leaving consumers to choose (as best they could) between a wider range of available pastas.

The majority of the Court's rulings have found national laws to be unjustified by an interest of sufficient weight to override the free movement of goods or services. The Court relies on the capacity of the consumer to process information and, on that basis, to make informed choices about available products and services as a basis for ruling against national measures that go so far as to suppress importation. The well-informed consumer serves as a lever to prise open markets sheltered by national regulation. Yet there are exceptions to these trends towards deregulation. *Oosthoek's Uitgevers-maatschappij* and *Eyssen* were mentioned above; in both cases a sufficient level of consumer prejudice was suppressed by the national rules for the Court to regard them as potentially justifiable. Similarly in *Buet v Ministère Public*[19] a restriction on door-step selling of, *inter alia*, educational material was regarded by the Court as restrictive of cross-border trade but nevertheless capable of justification as a method of protecting consumers from high-pressure sales techniques. The Court commented explicitly that the law focused on the protection of purchasers 'behind with their education and

---

[18] Case 407/85 [1988] ECR 4233.   [19] Case 382/87 [1989] ECR 1235.

seeking to catch up' and who were therefore 'particularly vulnerable'. In *A-Punkt Schmuckhandels GmbH v Claudia Schmidt* the Court was receptive to rules forbidding jewellery parties on private premises, acknowledging 'the potentially higher risk of the consumer being cheated due to a lack of information, the impossibility of comparing prices or the provision of insufficient safeguards as regards the authenticity of that jewellery and the greater psychological pressure to buy where the sale is organised in a private setting'.[20] The Court's generous approach to the permissibility of the measures in *Buet* and *Claudia Schmidt* seems to be influenced by the fact that the national regulator had already unpicked the universal category of the consumer and had chosen to protect a specific group. This was not the generalized consumer protection addressed in *Clinique, Mars*, and *Drei Glocken* which seems vulnerable to the Court's perception that most consumers are sufficiently robust and well-informed to take care of themselves in the marketplace. That is the Court's paradigm consumer—a choice that is not explicitly required by the Treaty.

D. LEGISLATIVE COMPETENCE

As mentioned in the Introduction, it was only on the entry into force of the Maastricht Treaty in 1993 that consumer protection acquired explicit recognition as a legislative competence attributed to what was then the EC. However, a string of soft law initiatives had earlier developed a framework for consumer policy once the 1972 'Paris Summit' initiated an attempt to broaden the appeal of the EC beyond economic affairs. The first Council Resolution on a preliminary programme for a consumer protection and information policy was dated 14 April 1975.[21] Point 3 of the Resolution encapsulated consumer interests in a bold statement of five rights:

  (a) the right to protection of health and safety,

  (b) the right to protection of economic interests,

  (c) the right of redress,

  (d) the right to information and education,

  (e) the right of representation (the right to be heard).

Point 4 provided an immediate reminder that, in conformity with the formal terms of the Treaty, there could be no consumer policy which existed independently of other policies. Consumer policy will be amplified 'by action under specific Community policies such as the economic, common agricultural, social, environment, transport and energy policies as well as by the approximation of laws, all of which affect the consumer's position'. Consumer policy was obliged to construct an identity in the shadow of the fundamental constitutional impediment caused by its omission from the original Treaty.

---

[20] Case C-441/04 [2006] ECR I-2093.   [21] [1975] OJ C92/1.

Despite this constitutional thin ice, the political institutions, like the Court, were gradually drawn into the evolution of a species of consumer policy. Soft law instruments—most of all Commission Communications and Council Resolutions—set out the intended place of the consumer as beneficiary of the project to complete the internal market.[22] Institutional change within the Commission established a separate Directorate-General with responsibility for consumer affairs. This was first known as DG XXIV and from 2001 as SANCO,[23] although re-arrangement in late 2009 now allocates contract and marketing matters to DG Justice, Liberty and Security, leaving SANCO to focus on health and safety matters. The scope of activity has noticeably broadened. The Commission's action plan for 1996–98[24] discusses the need to tie up the loose ends of the internal market, but also paid attention to the need to improve education and information and envisaged linkage with, *inter alia*, environmental and development policy. The Commission's Strategy to cover 2007–13, entitled 'Empowering consumers, enhancing their welfare, effectively protecting them',[25] emphasizes the benefits to the consumer of a successful internal market, while identifying three main objectives—empowering consumers, enhancing welfare, and protection from risks that consumers cannot cope with individually—and selecting five priorities— better monitoring of consumer markets and national consumer policies; better consumer protection regulation; better enforcement and redress; better informed and educated consumers; and putting consumers at the heart of other EU policies and regulation.

For fifty years consumer policy in the EU has evolved by spillover. This functional creep, largely occurring outwith the explicit parameters of the Treaty, has deprived EU consumer policy of a planned theoretical underpinning. At a constitutional level, Maastricht was a watershed, dividing pious commitments to the importance of the consumer interest expressed in soft law from the moment on 1 November 1993 when consumer policy assumed its place as a formal legislative competence recognized by the Treaty. However, in fact a bloc of measures affecting the position of the consumer had already been built up over the decades prior to the entry into force of the Maastricht Treaty. And Maastricht, though formally important as the birthplace of what are now Articles 4(2)(f), 12, and 169 TFEU which embed consumer protection in the Treaty, did not establish any grand set of guiding principles for consumer policy in the EU, nor did it accelerate legislative activity in the field. The bulk of 'EU consumer policy' remains shaped by activities underpinned by Treaty provisions which have little explicit connection with consumer protection—principally the free movement of goods and services, considered above, and harmonization policy, which now falls to be considered below.

---

[22] Especially Council Resolution concerning the future orientation of consumer policy [1986] OJ C167/1; Commission's second three-year action plan, covering 1993–95, COM(93) 378.

[23] The Directorate-General for Health and Consumer Protection: the acronym is French.

[24] COM(95) 519.

[25] COM(2007) 99, 13 March 2007.

E. HARMONIZATION POLICY

1. THE FUNCTIONS OF LEGISLATIVE HARMONIZATION

Insofar as national measures that restrict trade are judged compatible with the Treaty, the classic response is to proceed to harmonize laws in the field. The original Treaty focused on use of what is now Article 115 TFEU as a legal base, but this has been superseded in practice by a provision inserted by the Single European Act. This is Article 114 TFEU, which, prior to the entry into force of the Lisbon Treaty, was Article 95 EC. This empowers the adoption of measures to approximate provisions 'which have as their object the establishing and functioning of the internal market'. Article 114 TFEU, the former Article 95 EC, envisages adoption according to the ordinary legislative procedure. So a qualified majority vote in Council is sufficient (whereas unanimity is required under Article 115 TFEU).

Harmonization secures the realization of the objectives that underpin permitted national measures through the medium of common rules. The fact that the legislation applies across the entire territory of the Union removes the inhibition to trade consequent on national diversity. On the simplest model, twenty-seven national laws become one Union law. Where the laws subject to harmonization are consumer laws, then the fruits of the process are harmonized Union consumer laws. So the effect of harmonization is not only to accelerate integration, achieve deregulation, and serve the consumer interest in a better functioning economy but also to assert a process of re-regulation.

2. THE LIMITS OF HARMONIZATION

Article 114 TFEU is functionally broad. But it is not unlimited. Article 5 TEU declares that the Union shall act only within the limits of the competences conferred upon it by the Member States, and this statement of principle finds particular expression in relation to Article 114 TFEU in the case law of the Court. Naturally, the case law concerns the world 'pre-Lisbon', and therefore examines the use of Article 95 EC, but all relevant principles are readily translated to the world 'after Lisbon', and to the determination of the permissible scope of legislative reliance on Article 114 TFEU.

The Court, seeking to fix the limits of legislative harmonization under the Treaty, has held that 'a mere finding of disparities between national rules' is inadequate.[26] Nor is recourse to the legal base governing harmonization justified where the measure has only the incidental effect of harmonizing market conditions within the EU.[27] A connection with the achievement of the internal market foreseen by Article 26 TFEU is required.

---

[26] Cases C-154/04 and C-155/04 *Alliance for Natural Health* [2005] ECR I-6451 [28].
[27] eg Case C-209/97 *Commission v Council* [1999] ECR I-8067 [35].

That connection was missing in the case of Directive 98/43, famously annulled in the *Tobacco Advertising* case[28] in which the Court for the first time found a harmonization Directive adopted pursuant to Article 95 EC, Article 114 TFEU's predecessor, to be invalid. Subject to certain limited exceptions, the Directive prohibited all forms of advertising and sponsorship of tobacco products within the EU. It was based not only on Article 95 EC, but also on the Treaty provisions relating to establishment and services. Germany had opposed the Directive in Council but had found itself outvoted. It then brought the matter before the Court, arguing that the Directive lacked a valid legal basis. It was successful. The Court held that permitting Article 95 to be used as a general power to regulate the internal market would violate the principle that the competences of the Community are limited to those specifically conferred on it (now found in Article 5 TEU, and applicable to the wider Union). It ruled that a measure of harmonization based on Article 95 EC must genuinely have as its object the improvement of the conditions for the establishment and functioning of the internal market.

This Directive did not meet that test. The Court was persuaded that with respect to tobacco advertising in periodicals, magazines, and newspapers, where a harmonized rule on advertising would facilitate cross-border trade in such goods, the Directive was well-founded. However, the same could not be said of the prohibition of such advertising on 'posters, parasols, ashtrays and other articles used in hotels, restaurants and cafés' and in cinemas, since these prohibitions 'in no way help facilitate trade in the products concerned'.[29] The Directive, in short, went too far—beyond the process of building an internal market to which Article 95 is dedicated.

That Article 95 has limits beyond which the legislature may not tread is constitutionally banal. This is merely to apply the basic principle of conferral to the particular context of Article 95. What is, however, important and new in *Tobacco Advertising* is that the Court felt able, notwithstanding the relatively open-textured and functionally driven nature of Article 95, to find that a particular measure of legislative harmonization failed to respect its limits. As will emerge below, legislative practice today is undertaken in the shadow of *Tobacco Advertising*.

However, in subsequent rulings the Court has made plain that Article 95 EC remains a generously broad source of regulatory competence. And this now governs our understanding of the scope of harmonization post-Lisbon pursuant to Article 114 TFEU. A vivid illustration of the dynamic relationship between judicial control and legislative activity is provided by *Germany v Parliament and Council* which is the second *Tobacco Advertising* case.[30] After Directive 98/43 was annulled in *Tobacco Advertising* the legislature responded by adopting Directive 2003/33 on the harmonization of laws relating to advertising and sponsorship of tobacco products.[31] As mentioned above the Court had gone out of its way in *Tobacco Advertising* to explain

---

[28] Council Directive 98/43 [1998] OJ L213/9; Case C-376/98 *Germany v Parliament and Council* [2000] ECR I-8419.
[29] ibid [99].   [30] Case C-380/03 [2006] ECR I-11573.   [31] [2003] OJ L152/16.

what could validly be done: in particular it had approved the harmonization of rules governing tobacco advertising in magazines, periodicals, and newspapers on the basis that the adoption of common rules (in the shape of a prohibition) would promote an integrated market for press products. In Directive 2003/33 the legislature duly did precisely that—and no more. Given the congruence between the Court's identification in the earlier judgment of what could validly be achieved by way of harmonization and the content of the subsequently adopted Directive 2003/33 Germany could have had little expectation that its challenge would succeed. And the Court duly refused the application. It accepted that not only existing but also future obstacles to trade may be the subject of harmonization. 'Preventive harmonization' is valid where it addresses obstacles that are likely to emerge and where the legislation is designed to achieve that objective.[32]

3. THE CONTENT OF HARMONIZATION

As explained above, the effect of harmonization is not only to accelerate integration through the adoption of common rules but also to require that the EU choose the quality of that common (re-)regulatory regime. Harmonization of consumer law forces choices to be made about the EU's view of the function of consumer law. The Treaty recognizes this linkage between consumer policy and internal market policy. This is visible in Article 114(3) TFEU's reference to a 'high level' of (*inter alia*) consumer protection and especially in Article 12 TFEU, which stipulates that consumer protection requirements 'shall be taken into account in defining and implementing other Union policies and activities'. These provisions address the fear that harmonization may weaken established national standards, although they are insufficiently precise to go so far as to exclude the possibility that this may occur. In *Germany v Parliament and Council*[33] the Court rejected a German submission that a measure which was alleged to reduce regulatory protection in some Member States was incompatible with the objective of a high level of consumer protection. The Court observed that consumer protection is only one objective set by the Treaty and that the measure, which pursued the integration of the financial services market, was valid. It held that 'no provision of the Treaty obliges the Community legislature to adopt the highest level of protection which can be found in a particular Member State'. So, while the Court will not drive down national laws to a lowest common denominator (section 3(a) above), the legislature is not obliged to seek the highest common factor.

However, the Court accepts that provided that the conditions for recourse to Article 114 as a legal basis are fulfilled, the legislature 'cannot be prevented from

---

[32] See n 30 above [41]. See also Cases C-154/04 and C-155/04 (n 26 above); Case C-66/04 *UK v Parliament and Council* [2005] ECR I-10553. Cf M Seidel, 'Präventive Rechtsangleichung im Bereich des gemeinsamen Marktes' [2006] Europarecht 25.

[33] Case C-233/94 [1997] ECR I-2405.

relying on that legal basis on the ground that public health protection is a decisive factor in the choices to be made'.[34] Logically, then, a harmonized rule 'may consist in requiring all the Member States to authorize the marketing of the product or products concerned, subjecting such an obligation of authorisation to certain conditions, or even provisionally or definitively prohibiting the marketing of a product or products'.[35] There is plainly no objection in principle to a harmonized ban on goods—provided that the generally applicable criteria for reliance on Article 114 are met, which will typically mean that the ban must form part of a regime dealing with a wider category of products. So, to take a simple example, a harmonized ban on unsafe products opens up the market for safe products, and the matter therefore falls within the permitted scope of Article 114 TFEU.[36] This is equally applicable to consumer protection beyond the area of safety: Directive 2005/29, considered further below, bans unfair commercial practices as part of a broader régime liberalizing use of fair practices.[37]

Accordingly, just as the European Court is obliged to develop a policy on the validity of choices about how to protect the consumer despite the formal absence of any reference to the consumer in the Treaty provisions governing free movement, so too the political institutions, engaging in legislative harmonization, are forced to make choices about techniques of consumer protection that are appropriate for inclusion in EU measures, even though the relevant Treaty provisions do not offer any sophisticated elaboration of the consumer interest as such. There is no sustainable divide between the Union's interest in market integration and the role of the Member States in matters of market regulation. The fact that national public authorities have asserted a (principally) post-war commitment to legislative consumer protection has the inevitable consequence that the Union too, in pursuit of its goals of market integration and market (re-)regulation, must take consumer policy seriously.

4. MINIMUM HARMONIZATION

Mixed in to the debate about fixing the content of harmonized EU norms is the question of whether, once agreed, they must apply in common throughout all the Member States. The clear-cut notion that an EU rule pre-empts a national rule within its sphere of application did not prove sustainable at the time of the Single European Act, when Article 95 EC, Article 114 TFEU's predecessor, was inserted into the Treaty. What are now Articles 114(4) *et seq* represent responses to the fear that yielding legislative competence to the Union under a regime of qualified majority voting may cause protective standards preferred by an outvoted state to be depressed. The

---

[34] eg Cases C-154/04 and C-155/04 (n 26 above) [30]–[31].
[35] ibid [33].
[36] Directive 2001/95 on General Product Safety [2002] OJ L11/4. Cf Cases C-154/04 and C-155/04 (n 26 above); Case C-210/03 *Swedish Match* [2004] ECR I-11893.
[37] [2005] OJ L149/22.

procedures are subject to Commission management within which states may be exceptionally permitted to maintain rules that are stricter than those agreed in a harmonization measure.

However, looking beyond harmonization under the Treaty, some provisions make plain that EU legislative measures adopted pursuant to them permit any kind of stricter national rule, not simply the confined type envisaged by Article 114(4) *et seq*, provided only that the rule complies with the Treaty. This is the notion of minimum rule-making and, of direct relevance to consumer protection, it appears in Article 169(4) TFEU—as well as in Article 153(4) (social matters) and Article 193 (environmental protection). Article 114, by contrast, contains no such general concession to minimum rule-making. And although Article 4 TFEU lists both the internal market and consumer protection as areas of competence shared between the EU and the Member States, this does not solve the particular question of the extent to which legislative action pursuant to Article 114 TFEU excludes residual Member State legislative competence.

However, legislative practice reveals that much of the harmonized *acquis* pertaining to the protection of the economic interests of consumers is built on an assumption that minimum harmonization shall be the norm. Minimum Directives do not set a single rule as both floor and ceiling, but rather only a floor. Member States may maintain stricter rules, up to the ceiling set by primary law. So, for example, Directive 85/577 on 'doorstep selling'[38] contains a clause which explicitly permits Member States to apply stricter rules within its scope. In *Buet*[39] the Court ruled that although the Directive merely required that a consumer be allowed a right to cancel the contract concluded on the doorstep within a defined period, a total ban imposed by France on doorstep selling was compatible with the Directive (in view of the minimum standards clause) and, given its contribution to consumer protection, also with Article 28 EC, now Article 34 TFEU. Like Articles 114(4) *et seq*, this model reflects the notion that harmonization need not involve the automatic subordination of national choices about market regulation to the dictates of trade liberalization, although minimum harmonization is more flexible in the leeway offered to states than the relatively tightly defined provisions of Articles 114(4) *et seq*.

Pressure has been increasingly placed on the preference for minimum harmonization. Some recent Directives affecting the economic interests of consumers have been adopted as measures of maximum harmonization, thereby excluding the scope for stricter national choices within the field covered by the Directive. This is true of Directive 2005/29 concerning unfair business-to-consumer practices in the internal market, considered below.[40] The Commission has become ever more stridently insistent on the importance of switching to the maximum model as a means to secure an

---

[38] [1985] OJ L372/31.

[39] Case 382/87 (n 19 above).

[40] [2005] OJ L149/22. See also Directive 2007/64 on payment services in the internal market [2007] OJ L319/1; Directive 2008/48 on credit agreements for consumers [2008] OJ L133/66.

integrated market.[41] It has sought to address the anxiety that national autonomy is ruthlessly set aside by the maximum model by unveiling a discourse of harmonization 'targeted' at the problems that amount to the most serious blockages to the internal market.[42] It hopes thereby to allay fears of a comprehensive transfer of regulatory competence. And the Commission has assembled compelling evidence that the model of minimum harmonization leads to a fragmented pattern of laws, because Member States regularly and in very different ways take advantage of their preserved competence to apply stricter rules.[43] However, EU consumer policy is about more than merely integrating markets. The shift to maximum harmonization involves a significant choice in favour of a priority for market-making to the exclusion of local regulatory autonomy. It asserts a single notion of consumer protection when in fact consumer preferences, tastes, and capabilities differ in Europe.[44]

If the EU's consumer policy emerged in part as a sham, in the sense that harmonization was on occasion pursued politically opportunistically in circumstances where the legislation had little evident connection to the internal market, then, in the current market-driven assertion of a need for maximum harmonization, the internal market logic has returned with a vengeance. Norbert Reich's astute observation in 1992 that 'the more competences the Community is acquiring, the less exclusive will be its jurisdiction'[45] was amply borne out by inspection of the preference for minimum harmonization in the consumer law *acquis*, but today this approach is challenged both descriptively and normatively. In this matter consumer policy connects with deep questions about the proper balance of power between centralized and local rule-making in Europe.

F. DIRECTIVES IN THE AREA OF CONSUMER PROTECTION

The legislative dimension of consumer policy in the EU has been predominantly shaped through harmonization of national laws, leading to a form of (re-regulatory) consumer policy at Union level. Legislative consumer policy is in a sense a by-product of the harmonization programme, which (as we know from *Tobacco Advertising*) is

---

[41] eg EU Consumer Policy Strategy 2007–13: Empowering consumers, enhancing their welfare, effectively protecting them, COM(2007) 99 especially at 7; Green Paper on the Review of the Consumer Acquis, COM (2006) 744.

[42] eg Proposal for a Directive on Consumer Rights, COM(2008) 614; COM(2007) 99 (n 41 above) 7.

[43] eg Commission Report on implementation of Directive 97/7 on distance contracts, COM(2006) 514; Commission Communication on the implementation of Directive 99/44, COM(2007) 210.

[44] Cf T Wilhelmsson, 'The abuse of the confident consumer as a justification for EC consumer law' (2004) 27 J Consum Pol 317; S Weatherill, 'Maximum or Minimum Harmonisation—What Kind of "Europe" Do We Want?' in K Boele-Woelki and W Grosheide (eds), *The Future of European Contract Law* (2007); V Mak, 'Review of the Consumer Acquis: Towards Maximum Harmonisation?' (2009) 17 Euro Rev Priv L 55; H Micklitz and N Reich, 'Crónica de una Muerte Anunciada: the Commission Proposal for a Directive on Consumer Rights' (2009) 46 CML Rev 471.

[45] N Reich, 'Competition between Legal Orders: A New Paradigm of EC Law' (1992) 29 CML Rev 861, 895.

tied to the process of market-making, but it has also gained its own thematic shape given that (as we know from, *inter alia*, Articles 12 and 114(3) TFEU) consumer protection as a dimension of market-making is constitutionally recognized by the Treaty. The history brings its vexations. The indirect nature of consumer law-making, long concealed within the internal market programme, has deprived the pattern of a coherent theoretical underpinning. What is now Article 169 TFEU, as explained, was introduced by the Maastricht Treaty and its arrival terminated any objection to the bare fact that the EU's concern for consumer protection possesses a constitutional force. But Article 169 falls short of any sophisticated manifesto for the place of the consumer in the EU system. The new basis for legislation which it introduced, now Article 169(2)(b), has been little used,[46] and is far outstripped in importance by the traditional route of legislative harmonization. Moreover, there are institutional reasons for scepticism about the viability of treating consumer policy as distinctive. It was as late as 1995 when a separate Directorate-General within the Commission was created to take charge of Consumer Policy; and the new DG gained sufficient staff to wield real clout only as late as 1997 when its powers and resources were beefed up in the wake of the BSE 'mad cow' crisis.

Nevertheless, such flaws are not a sufficient reason for surrendering ambition to deduce a theory of consumer law. Consumer law is always a fuzzy-edged topic, at national or transnational level, for it cuts across more traditional areas of law and impinges on a broad range of regulatory policies. The absence of an institutional cutting-edge in consumer policy-making is very far from an EU-specific phenomenon; the same is true of the under-representation of consumers in policy development. Accordingly just as the Court has developed important common themes in its handling of the place of the consumer in the application of the free movement rules, so too the EU's legislative institutions have elaborated guiding themes and principles animating the *acquis* notwithstanding the textual deficiencies of the Treaty. These themes and principles will now be examined.

1. ADMINISTRATIVE CONTROLS

The shaping of advertising regulation provides a good example of how diversity in national practice causes obstacles to trade, leading to an impulse to establish a harmonized regime which in turn requires the EU to make choices about regulatory technique and content. Put another way, the fact that the Member States have (in different ways) developed views on the proper limits of advertising means unavoidably that the EU itself must make such a choice. And this involves an assessment of the capabilities of the consumer of advertising as well as the need to protect traders from unacceptable forms of commercial conduct.

The EU's first intervention in the field in 1984 dealt with misleading advertising, which was subject to a harmonized prohibition, and the scheme was subsequently

---

[46] eg Council Directive 98/6 [1998] OJ L80/27 on indication of prices offered to consumers.

extended to cover comparative advertising, which was to be permitted under defined criteria. The legislative framework is now found in Directive 2006/114, a codifying measure.[47] In the manner that one would expect post-*Tobacco Advertising*, the claim to enjoy a legislative competence to harmonize advertising rules is made with care. Recitals 2 and 5 in the preamble exhibit scrupulous attention to the limits of Article 95 EC, which is now Article 114 TFEU, asserting that advertising, a phenomenon capable of reaching beyond national borders, is impeded by variation between national rules to the detriment of the free circulation of goods and services.

The notion of 'misleading' advertising is focused on a deceptive impact which generates adverse economic consequences. Account should be taken of the perception of an average consumer of the products or services being advertised who is reasonably well informed and reasonably observant and circumspect, a phrase which readily connects with the test applied in determining whether a national measure of consumer protection survives the test presented by the free movement rules.[48] And, just as the free movement case law envisages assessment of a national measure's impact on a particular group of consumers where the measure is so targeted, so too in identifying the impact of advertising it is appropriate to determine whether it is misleading with reference to a specialist group of consumers to which it is targeted, if it is so targeted. On occasion the Court has gone so far as to give a clear steer to national courts on the threshold for finding a misleading effect. In *Procureur de la Republique v X*, a case concerning the notoriously fragmented car market, the Court insisted that prejudice be felt by a significant number of consumers before action under the Directive could be justified.[49]

The Directive envisages comparative advertising as a stimulus to more informed consumer choice and intensified competition in matters of quality. Its legitimate parameters are carefully set out in Article 4 of Directive 2006/114. It is an important feature of legislative harmonization that, once adopted, the provisions, often ambiguous, invite the Court to develop further the harmonized regime. In *Lidl Belgium v Franz Colruyt* the Court stated that 'comparative advertising helps to demonstrate objectively the merits of the various comparable products and thus stimulate competition between suppliers of goods and services to the consumer's advantage' and extracted from this the principle of interpretation that 'the conditions required of comparative advertising must be interpreted in the sense most favourable to it'.[50]

In the case of misleading advertising, Article 8 provides that Member States may apply more extensive protection than the Directive requires—so practices that are not misleading within the meaning of the Directive may be suppressed—whereas the rules

---

[47] Council Directive 2006/114 concerning misleading and comparative advertising [2006] OJ L376/21.

[48] See eg Case C-356/04 *Lidl Belgium v Franz Colruyt* [2006] ECR I-8501; Case C-220/98 *Estée Lauder* [2000] ECR I-117; Case C-44/01 *Pippig Augenoptik* [2003] ECR I-3095.

[49] Case C-373/90 [1992] ECR I-131.

[50] Case C-356/04 (n 48 above) [22]. Use of trademarks in comparative advertising is addressed in Case C-533/06 *O2 Holdings* [2008] ECR I-4231.

on comparative advertising do not permit stricter rules—so a Member State may not prevent comparative advertising which complies with the Directive's definition. As the Court has put it, the aim is 'to establish conditions under which comparative advertising is to be permitted throughout the Community'.[51]

The sensitivity of intervention in these fields should not be underestimated. Accumulated layers of national regulatory practice are challenged by harmonization. The impact is especially profound where that harmonization admits of no stricter national rules, as is true in the case of comparative advertising. Concessions occasionally emerge from the political hurly-burly. The material scope of the Directive may be tightened to allow particularly cherished national choices to survive or specific exemptions may be granted. So, for example, Article 8(4) of Directive 2006/114 allows Member States to forbid comparative advertising in the case of professional services.

Article 8(2) of Directive 2006/114 provides that it shall not apply to sectors where other EU provisions lay down specific rules. Several measures introduce extra sector-specific prohibitions. Directive 98/43 on tobacco advertising was famously annulled by the Court,[52] but nevertheless several valid Directives regulate aspects of the advertising of tobacco products. Directive 2001/37 is the source of the mandatory rules on health warnings which must be carried on the packaging of certain tobacco products.[53] The Court was persuaded that national variations in the treatment of this matter were sufficiently damaging to the functioning of the internal market for harmonization to be justified.[54] Directive 2003/33, the more narrowly drawn Directive which replaced the annulled Directive 98/43, places severe restrictions on the advertising of tobacco products in the press and other printed publications and radio broadcasting, as well as on sponsorship of events.[55] Given its contribution to removing obstacles to trade in such media, the measure was treated by the Court as a valid exercise of legislative competence, notwithstanding that public health protection was a decisive factor in the choices made.[56]

Analogous rules apply to audiovisual media services—television and other more technologically esoteric media. The logic of the harmonization programme is thematically consistent: national rules fixing the permissible scope of advertising vary, causing obstacles to trade, so in consequence common rules are required, as the Court itself accepted in *Tobacco Advertising*.[57] This then pushes the EU to make its own selection of regulatory technique. In this sector, the legislative regime, lately amended and re-labelled the Directive on Audiovisual Media Services,[58] contains

---

[51] Cf Case C-44/01 (n 48 above).
[52] Case C-376/98 (n 28 above).   [53] [2001] OJ L194/26.
[54] Case C-491/01 *R v Secretary of State ex parte BAT and Imperial Tobacco* [2002] ECR I-11543.
[55] [2003] OJ L152/16.
[56] Case C-380/03 (n 30 above) [62], [75], and [190].
[57] Case C-376/98 (n 28 above) [98].
[58] Directive 89/552 [1989] OJ L298/23, amended by Directive 97/36 [1997] OJ L202/60 and Directive 2007/65 [2007] OJ L332/27. See Special Issue of the Journal of Consumer Policy, Vol 31, March 2008 *The Consumer, the European Union and Media Law*, A Harcourt and S Weatherill (eds).

Chapter IV dealing with 'Television Advertising and Teleshopping'. It prohibits advertising of tobacco products by audiovisual communication, sponsorship, and product placement. Special provision is also made for protection of minors.

These measures demonstrate that the EU is capable of adopting a restrictive approach to commercial freedom. There is, indeed, a recognizable 'EU advertising law'. The focus on market integration distinguishes the package of rules from what one would normally expect to find in a national system, but the content reveals a clear concern to curtail the perceived pernicious effects of (in short) irresponsible advertising.

A still broader scheme has been introduced. In 2001 the Commission published a Green Paper on Consumer Protection.[59] It described the heap of diverse national laws that are relevant to the regulation of marketing practices as 'off-putting' to 'nearly all businesses but those who can afford to establish in all Member States', and, in addition, as a brake on consumer confidence. This was plainly intended to establish competence to harmonize, as well as to make the substantive case in favour of intervention. The Commission succeeded in piloting its proposal through the legislative process, to become Directive 2005/29 concerning unfair business-to-consumer practices in the internal market.[60] It displays a familiar logic. National practices controlling unfair commercial practices vary, impeding market integration, and this constitutes a basis for claiming competence to harmonize. The Directive prohibits practices which contrary to 'professional diligence' 'materially distort the economic behaviour' of an average consumer. So there is a European standard of permissible market behaviour created by this Directive. The notions of forbidden 'misleading' and 'aggressive' practice are elaborated in the body of the Directive and its Annex contains a 'black list' of practices considered unfair in all circumstances.

What scope is left for national measures that treat as unfair what is regarded as fair by the Directive? None. Directive 2005/29 is a measure of maximum harmonization. It is a floor and it is also a ceiling. The Commission has promoted this model as essential to the regeneration of EU consumer policy in the light of its contribution to the integration of markets in Europe under a common set of rules. This Directive is therefore an important example of a strong preference for a complete transfer of regulatory responsibility from Member States to the EU. This reinforces appreciation that fixing the standard of protection under the Directive has to be carefully negotiated, well understood, and effectively applied. For if a Member State considers the Directive sets too low a standard, it has nowhere to go (other than to seek to induce legislative reform at EU level): the maximum model prevents any unilateral upgrade in protection. But, as encountered above, sensitivity bubbles to the surface and it is unsurprising that the Directive reveals some scrupulous concern to confine its material scope. In particular Member States remain free to take action against commercial

---

[59] COM(2001) 531.
[60] [2005] OJ L149/22. See S Weatherill and U Bernitz (eds), *The Regulation of Unfair Commercial Practices under EC Directive 2005/29: New Rules and New Techniques* (Hart, 2007).

practices where matters of 'taste and decency' are at stake.[61] Precisely where this limit between unfair practices, regulated by the Directive, and practices designed to shock, left for treatment under national law, will fall promises to provoke litigation.

2. CONTRACT LAW AND MARKET TRANSPARENCY

Directive 2005/29 on unfair commercial practices is stated to apply 'without prejudice to contract law, and in particular to the rules on the validity, formation or effect of a contract'.[62] This statement may be read as a further instance of anxiety to insulate sensitive areas of national law from 'infection' by the harmonizing influence of the EU. Yet the assertion of a separation from contract law appears artificial and unreliable, and it is improbable that the Directive's suppression of unfair practices will not influence the way some rules of national contract law are applied, especially those pertaining to practices inducing the conclusion of an enforceable contract.[63] And in fact a batch of Directives already has a significant impact on the formation of particular consumer contracts: those concluded away from business premises ('on the doorstep'),[64] package travel,[65] timeshare,[66] consumer credit,[67] distance contracts,[68] payment services in the internal market,[69] electronic commerce,[70] and distance marketing of consumer financial services.[71]

The marketing practice subject to regulation is typically not prohibited. Instead the chosen technique involves requirements that the consumer be provided in advance with specified information about a contemplated transaction. So, for example, Directive 90/314 employs the technique of information disclosure to safeguard consumers of package travel, package holidays, and package tours. Where a brochure is made available to the consumer, it must indicate in a legible, comprehensible, and accurate manner both the price and information concerning a list of matters including transport, type of accommodation, and itinerary. The predominant concern of Directive 2008/48, harmonizing laws regulating the supply of consumer credit, is the improvement of transparency. It governs methods of advertising and a mechanism is envisaged

---

[61] Recital 7. Cf T Wilhelmsson, 'Harmonizing Unfair Commercial Practices Law: the Cultural and Social Dimensions' (2006) 44 Osgoode Hall LJ 462.

[62] Art 3(2).

[63] Cf S Whittaker, 'The Relationship of the Unfair Commercial Practices Directive to European and National Contract Laws' in Weatherill and Bernitz (n 60 above).

[64] Council Directive 85/577 [1985] OJ L372/31.

[65] Council Directive 90/314 [1990] OJ L158/59.

[66] Council Directive 2008/112 [2009] OJ L33/10, replacing with effect from February 2011 Directive 94/47.

[67] Council Directive 2008/48 [2008] OJ L133/66, replacing with effect from May 2010 Directive Council 87/102 (as amended).

[68] Council Directive 97/7 [1997] OJ L144/19 as amended by Council Directive 2007/64 [2007] OJ L319/1.

[69] Council Directive 2007/64 [2007] OJ L319/1, replacing with effect from November 2009 Council Directive 97/5.

[70] Council Directive 2000/31 [2000] OJ L178/1.

[71] Council Directive 2002/65 [2002] OJ L271/16.

for fixing a uniform method for calculating the annual percentage rate of charge. The actual cost of credit is left largely unaffected.

This regulatory technique is widespread in measures affecting protection of consumers' economic interests, although on occasion mandatory information disclosure has been employed as a technique to address health and safety issues too.[72] Information disclosure has frequently been combined with protection in the post-contractual phase, most strikingly through the prescription of a 'cooling-off' period within which the consumer is entitled to exercise a right to withdraw from an agreed deal. These procedural interventions have typically been adopted in preference to more direct checks on the content of the contract.

Here, once again, it is possible to discern a thematic choice about the character of EU consumer policy. Mandatory pre-contractual disclosure supplemented by the 'cooling-off' period suggests an emphasis on transparency and the perfecting effect on the competitive market of the attentive consumer. Much of the *acquis* rests on a paradigm of the informed consumer who is allowed to be exposed to practices that might cause harm but who is equipped with a means of protecting him- or herself. Viewed in their most favourable light, such techniques for adjusting the environment within which the bargain is struck yield a more efficient market by promoting negotiation and informed consumer choice, without substituting public decision-making about the contents of contracts for private autonomy. More intrusive controls, such as a ban on particular types of contract, diminish consumer choice. But the EU's chosen model is very far from uncontroversial and it is emphatically not neutral. The employment of such regulatory techniques assumes that the consumer is capable of processing the information provided about the deal and grasping that there is a limited opportunity to withdraw from it. There is plenty of evidence that consumers simply do not behave in this programmatically rational manner.[73] If consumers—or, more significantly, some consumers—are not so capable, the technique fails to protect consumers; the imbalance in favour of the supplier is left inadequately adjusted. So the EU measures are based on the expectation of a certain level of consumer competence in the market, failing which regulatory protection will be illusory.

These issues arise in any system of consumer law, but in the EU in particular a choice in favour of informational intervention may merely reflect a line of least political resistance, not an objective selection between regulatory options. And were the Commission's preference for maximum harmonization to prevail, these choices would be all the more significant for they would foreclose the current leeway allowed to the Member States to maintain stricter rules above the minimum standards set by most of these Directives.

---

[72] eg Council Directive 2001/37 on tobacco products (n 53 above). Cf Regulation 1830/2003 [2003] OJ L268/24 on labelling of genetically modified organisms.

[73] See eg G Howells, 'The potential and limits of consumer empowerment by information' (2005) 32 Journal of Law and Society 349; F Rischkowsky and T Döring, 'Consumer Policy in a Market Economy: Considerations from the Perspective of the Economics of Information, the New Institutional Economics as well as Behavioural Economics' (2008) 31 J Consum Pol 285.

3. CONTRACT LAW—THE SUBSTANCE OF THE TRANSACTION

Even the Directives mentioned above go some way beyond support for the consumer in the pre- and post-agreement phase. The Directive on package travel, for example, makes limited incursion into the substance of the bargain, by controlling price variation, and it also exerts an impact favourable to the consumer by extending the chain of contractual responsibility. However, a pair of more ambitious Directives go beyond contract formation and information disclosure and instead assert control over the content of the bargain. Directive 93/13 prohibits unfair terms in consumer contracts.[74] Directive 99/44 on certain aspects of the sale of consumer goods and associated guarantees imports standards of required quality into consumer contracts.[75]

A contract term is covered by Directive 93/13 only if it is not individually negotiated. Such a term shall be regarded as unfair, and consequently unenforceable, if 'contrary to the requirement of good faith, it causes a significant imbalance in the parties' rights and obligations arising under the contract, to the detriment of the consumer'. An Annex to the Directive provides an indicative 'grey' list of terms which may be regarded as unfair. This collection is thematically linked by matters which seem to be viewed by the regulator with special distaste, such as the grant of unilateral decision-making power to a supplier and lack of proportionality in the nature of the obligations undertaken. The Directive is, however, a measure of minimum harmonization. It is open to Member States to forbid terms that are permitted by the Directive. This distinguishes Directive 93/13 from Directive 2005/29 on unfair commercial practices.

It is only contracts concluded between a trader and a consumer which are subject to Directive 93/13. The Directive therefore contributes to the growth of a distinctive stream of consumer contract law within the Member States. The regulatory assumptions underpinning this Directive, and indeed much of the sweep of consumer-specific adjustments to contract law, are precisely that in modern market conditions a monolithic private law offers an inadequate basis for the efficient or fair treatment of consumer interests. Consumer contract law, like contract law affecting, *inter alia*, employment and the relationship between landlord and tenant, requires accommodation separate from the general principles of (commercial) contract law. And EU law is one element propelling the fragmentation of national private laws.

The Court has followed the interpretative lead set by the Directive. In *Oceano Grupo Editorial SA v Rocio Murciano Quintero*[76] the Court concluded that Directive 93/13 'is based on the idea that the consumer is in a weak position vis-a-vis the seller or supplier, as regards both his bargaining power and his level of knowledge'. The Directive is targeted at improving the functioning of the internal market but it also asserts a harmonized plan of consumer protection. This was not mere rhetoric. The

---

[74] [1993] OJ L95/29.   [75] [1999] OJ L171/12.
[76] Cases C-240/98 to C-244/98 [2000] ECR I-4941.

Court ruled that a national court is empowered to consider of its own motion whether a term is unfair within the meaning of the Directive. Subsequently the Court clarified in *Mostaza Claro v Centro Móvil Milenium* that this is not simply a power but in fact a duty.[77] In the same ruling the Court held that where a consumer has not pleaded the invalidity of an unfair term in the course of arbitration proceedings, but only in a subsequent action for annulment, national law must permit the matter to be re-opened—an intrusion, imperilling legal certainty, which it has expressly not required in commercial arbitration.[78] The Court accordingly gives special force to EU consumer law and, via its application by national courts, it accentuates the contours of consumer law and associated rules of civil procedure as a distinct discipline within national legal orders.

Like Directive 93/13, Directive 99/44 on certain aspects of the sale of consumer goods and associated guarantees takes Article 95 EC, Article 114 TFEU's predecessor, as its legal base.[79] Rather than require the suppression of unfair terms it instead operates in more positive vein. It provides that the seller must deliver goods to the consumer which are in conformity with the contract of sale; and that the seller shall be liable to the consumer for any lack of conformity which exists at the time the goods were delivered. This offers the consumer a basic legal guarantee of product quality which is independent of any negotiation with the seller. A framework of remedies is carefully constructed. Directive 99/44 shares with Directive 93/13 a readiness to go beyond the thematic concern for transparency and consumer information to deal instead with the content of the bargain struck between the parties.

Implementation of the Directive has presented different challenges in different Member States.[80] But it is salutary to recall that the text of the Directive may contain sufficient ambiguity to be incapable of wholly confident implementation. German law permitted the supplier to require the consumer who returns a non-conforming product and has it replaced to pay an indemnity to cover use. This, the Court concluded in *Quelle AG v Bundesverband*,[81] is not compatible with the Directive, which requires that the matter be handled free of charge. The Court placed a familiar strong interpretative emphasis on the role of the Directive as a means of strengthening consumer protection.[82] The German law found incompatible with the Directive had been comprehensively overhauled as part of the process of implementing Directive 99/44: in fact, the opportunity for a broad reform had been taken according to an appreciation that a narrow implementation of the Directive alone, alongside existing sales law, would generate an incoherent pattern.[83] At the time the assumption had

---

[77] Case C-168/05 [2006] ECR I-10421, [38]; also Case C-243/08 *Pannon GSM* [2009] ECR I-4713.

[78] Cases C-222/05 *et al van der Weerd* [2007] ECR I-4233. Cf J Jans and A Marseille, 'Annotation' (2008) 45 CML Rev 853.

[79] [1999] OJ L171/12.

[80] See Special Issue of the European Review of Private Law Vol 9, Issues 2 and 3 (2001).

[81] Case C-404/06 [2008] ECR I-2685.

[82] eg ibid [30] and [35]–[36].

[83] Cf eg S Grundmann and F Ochmann, 'German Contract Law Five Years after the Fundamental Contract Law Reform in the Schuldrechtsmodernisierung' (2007) 3 ERCL 450.

been that the requirement to pay an indemnity was compatible with the Directive. It was not, so German law now requires further amendment, although for the time being the *Bundesgerichtshof* has felt able to wrench German law by a heroic act of interpretation into conformity with the Court's stance in *Quelle*.[84] The lesson here is that compliance with EU law is a moving target.

4. TORT LAW

Directive 85/374, commonly labelled the Product Liability Directive, harmonizes laws concerning liability for defective products.[85] Article 1 declares that '[t]he producer shall be liable for damage caused by a defect in his product'. Article 6 states that a product is defective where it does not provide the safety which a person is entitled to expect.

The Directive provides another fine example of how an assumption of regulatory responsibility by the EU entails a need to select the preferred common regime against a background of national diversity. Allocation to the producer of the risk of defectiveness may be analysed as efficient and fair in the light of the producer's capacity to buy insurance and slightly increase the price, thereby to spread the costs of compensating a small number of injured consumers amongst all purchasers. By contrast, a fault-based liability system is more erratic. But the claim that a strict liability system would deter innovation and/or cause an increase in insurance premia led to the dilution of Article 1 by the inclusion of a so-called development risk defence. A producer of a defective product is able to escape liability by proving 'that the state of scientific and technical knowledge at the time when he put the product into circulation was not such as to enable the existence of the defect to be discovered'. This, then, is the balancing of producer and consumer interests: the EU had to make a choice. An option to exclude the defence was allowed, but, reflecting the influence of commercial interests relative to the consumer lobby, states have shown minimal interest in disadvantaging 'their' producers in this way. It seems that the delicate compromise struck at the time of the adoption of the original Directive is too sensitive to unpick. The Commission's latest (third) report published in September 2006 portrays the Directive as by and large satisfactory and finds no consensus favouring any particular reform.[86] It is claimed that removing the 'development risk' defence would lead to higher costs which 'would affect consumers in the long term' (p 7).

In contrast to the majority of the measures harmonizing laws governing the protection of economic interests of consumers the Product Liability Directive contains no 'minimum' formula. The only provision in Directive 85/374 which addresses its relationship with national law in the relevant field is Article 13. It stipulates that the

---

[84] VIII ZR 200/05, 26 November 2008.

[85] [1985] OJ L210/29 amended by Council Directive 99/34 [1999] OJ L141/20. See S Whittaker, *Liability for Products: English Law, French Law and European Harmonization* (Oxford University Press, 2005).

[86] COM(2006) 496. For a critical account see D Fairgrieve and G Howells, 'Rethinking Product Liability' (2007) 70 MLR 962.

Directive 'shall not affect any rights which an injured person may have according to the rules of the law of contractual or non-contractual liability or a special liability system existing at the moment when this Directive is notified'. In *María Victoria González Sánchez v Medicina Asturiana SA* the Court, faced with rights afforded to consumers under pre-existing Spanish law which were more extensive than those available under the rules introduced to transpose Directive 85/374, identified the purpose of the Directive as 'to ensure undistorted competition between traders, to facilitate the free movement of goods and to avoid differences in levels of consumer protection'.[87] It determined that accordingly Article 13 did not permit the Member States the possibility of maintaining a general system of product liability different from that provided for in the Directive. The Court's stance heavily emphasizes the function of the Directive in levelling the commercial playing field and provides a vigorous reminder that identifying the allocation of regulatory responsibility post-harmonization—of which the minimum/maximum debate is one prominent mani-festation—is highly significant in ascertaining the protective scope of national consumer law.

G. IS THIS REALLY CONSUMER POLICY?

Is this really a coherent policy on consumer protection? There are two principal objections. The first is substantive. The second is constitutional.

At a substantive level, the core allegation holds that the *acquis* is nothing more than fragments, 'a stone from Brussels here and there inserted into the edifices of national private law'.[88] The Directives mainly concern consumer contract law, but not only consumer law and not only contract law. Even the treatment of consumer contract law deals with the formation of particular contracts such as those concluded 'on the doorstep' and in the field of package travel, albeit that Directive 93/13 on unfair terms and Directive 99/44 on consumer sales stand out as more ambitious. The patchwork of measures is further distanced from any impression of plan or coherence by internal lack of congruence. The cooling-off periods are symptomatic. Far from applying a uniform period within which the consumer may withdraw, each measure eccentrically chooses a different period. Remember too that most Directives are minimum in character (although that preference is currently endangered) with the result that they do not lay down rules that are at national level complete in themselves. So perhaps 'EU consumer policy' is a label that suggests something more systematic and intelligible than is actually delivered by this odd batch of Directives.

And yet much depends on effect, not form. As a matter of simple yet irrefutable empirical observation there is a body of 'EU consumer law'. It may plausibly be regarded as a patchwork when it is compared to national law, but its presence has

---

[87] Case C-183/00 [2002] ECR I-3901 [26]; also Case C-402/03 *Skov* [2006] ECR I-199.
[88] O Remien, 'Über den Stil des Europäischen Privatrechts' 60 RabelsZ (1996) 2, 8 (my translation).

become increasingly significant in practice. And there is a degree of thematic coherence visible in the *acquis*.

The Directives do not disclose a model premised on unconditional freedom of contract. This would be unsustainable given the patterns of development in national contract laws over the course of the last century and more. So, the Commission, contributing to the debate in 2005, observed that the 'principle of freedom of contract needs to be emphasized as crucial for the process' but that 'appropriate differentiation between B2B and B2C contracts is paramount. Consumer law adjusts structural imbalances....[89] Plainly the detail demands careful attention. But the general point holds that within the shaping of EU law there is appreciation of the interests, weaknesses, and market failures to which national consumer contract law may be directed. So the content of the *acquis* is not neutral. Indeed, how could it be? The Directives harmonize national laws in the name of promoting the establishment or functioning of the market, but their incidental effect is additionally to regulate that market—or more pertinently to 're-regulate' it, in the sense that the EU is not acting as a *de novo* regulator but rather is responding to the pre-existing diverse regulatory choices among the Member States. The quality of the 're-regulatory' environment is constitutionally relevant, as is made clear by the associations between market integration and consumer protection on which Articles 12 and 114(3) TFEU insist. This deepens the interest in making sense of the thematic connections that bind together the EU's interventions into consumer law.

The academic literature accommodates a rich and energetic tussle over the nature and purpose of EU consumer law. From both descriptive and normative standpoints academic commentators have debated the weight and merits of principles and techniques that lend a degree of thematic consistency to the legislative *acquis*: information disclosure, transparency, party autonomy, inquiry into substantive unfairness, and the protection of the weaker party. Some, for sure, are sceptical that there is anything more to this than a thin veneer concealing a ruthless commitment to free(d) markets. Contestation familiar within national legal orders spills over into the evolving EU. Here, in the kneading of a dough that resists transcendent smoothness, lies the emergence of a sense of 'policy' (or perhaps 'policies') at EU level.[90] For some these threads are capable of being 'systematized' and should be so systematized, while others are conspicuously more cautious: one's preference is doubtless affected by background legal culture and education which varies across Europe.[91]

---

[89] COM(2005) 456, 6, Commission's first Annual Report on the *Acquis* Review.

[90] eg T Wilhelmsson, 'Varieties of Welfarism in European Contract Law' (2004) 10 ELJ 712; H Micklitz, 'The Relationship between National and European Consumer Policy' (2008) Yearbook of Consumer Law ch 3; J Basedow, 'Freedom of Contract in the European Union' (2008) 16 Euro Rev Priv L 901; J Davies, 'Entrenchment of New Governance in Consumer Policy Formulation: A Platform for European Consumer Citizenship Practice?' (2009) 32 J Consum Pol 245.

[91] eg contrast O Lando, 'Is Good Faith an Over-arching General Clause in the Principles of European Contract Law?' (2007) 15 Euro Rev Priv L 841 with (the more cautious) T Wilhelmsson and C Twigg-Flesner, 'Pre-contractual Information Duties in the *Acquis Communautaire*' (2006) 2 ERCL 441. Cf H Rösler, 'Auslegungsgrundsätze des Europäischen Verbraucherprivatrechts in Theorie und Praxis' RabelsZ 71 (2007) 495.

There is, however, a further reason to doubt the aptitude of the *acquis* to provide a basis for the derivation of general principles. And this engages the second principal objection to treating 'EU consumer policy' as a coherent object of study—the constitutional objection. A number of these Directives reflect the political reality that beginning with the Paris Summit in 1972 the Member States were committed to the development of consumer policy and, in the absence of any more appropriate legal basis in the Treaty, they chose to 'borrow' the market-making competence to harmonize laws to put it in place. This insincerity is well captured by Directive 85/577. Its preamble states that the practice of doorstep selling is the subject of different rules in different Member States, which is true, and then adds that 'any disparity between such legislation may directly affect the functioning of the common market', which seems far from obviously true and is left wholly unsubstantiated. Some Directives that harmonize national consumer contract law and thereby create a species of European consumer contract law were the product of a political consensus about the desirability of such a development, and were not underpinned by the constitutionally pure 'market-driven' pedigree which seems to be demanded by the relevant provisions in the Treaty.[92] One may deduce that this background undermines the quest to glue together the several elements of 'EU consumer law' with help from thematic concern(s) that would be familiar to a national lawyer.

H. THE COMMISSION'S REVIEW OF CONTRACT LAW

For both substantive and constitutional reasons there is room for scepticism about how 'coherent' EU consumer policy could and should be. The two anxieties may be connected. It could be that substantive coherence is missing precisely because there is no constitutional mandate granted to the EU to supply it. This awkward terrain would be more easily traversed were the Treaty altered to authorize the EU to develop a comprehensive consumer law or, more ambitious still, a civil code. Argument about the true political character of such a document would then be out in the open and, on an optimistic reading, fertile conditions for the nurture of a transnational civil society would be created.[93]

The Commission enjoys no such luxury. It is forced to operate within the ambiguous limits dictated by the current Treaties. And the Lisbon Treaty has changed little. Lately the Commission's principal focus has been on contract law. Even if some of the earlier Directives harmonizing rules on (consumer) contract formation could be dismissed as sector-specific, even trivial, Directive 93/13 in particular generated a heated, even hostile, debate among national private lawyers, and duly prompted the

---

[92] S Weatherill, *EU Consumer Law and Policy* (Edward Elgar, 2005) ch 3.
[93] Cf H Collins, *The European Civil Code: the Way Forward* (Cambridge University Press, 2008).

Commission to reflect more fully on the purposes of intervention in the field. Both thematic tensions—the substantive, the constitutional—are readily visible.

The Commission's July 2001 Communication on European Contract Law initiated the current decade's inquiry.[94] As a matter of substance the most potent concern in the review process has been the search for 'a significantly higher degree of coherence in European contract law', to borrow the words of one of the principal architects of the review in the Commission.[95] This, an element in the broader project of 'Better Regulation' designed to secure improved economic performance, runs like a golden thread through the review.

Two means in particular have emerged as the principal devices for improving 'coherence'. One, improving the quality of the *acquis* by ironing out internal inconsistencies within the sector-specific measures. Two, devising a 'common frame of reference' (CFR) which would set out common fundamental principles of contract law.

In February 2007 the Green Paper on the Review of the Consumer *Acquis* concluded the 'diagnostic phase' of the review, setting out the main options for reform.[96] Option I is a vertical approach, maintaining the current emphasis on sector-specific Directives. However, the unmistakable preference which emerges from the Green Paper is for Option II, which proposes a mix between vertical measures and horizontal treatment which would allow a more systematic approach involving uniform treatment of common notions and concepts across the whole field occupied by the consumer *acquis*. Quite what form this should take is to be the subject of further consultation. Option III, no legislative action, is by clear implication excluded, for it would preserve existing fragmentation and inconsistency. There is a 'need' for improvements. Moreover, maximum harmonization remains the enduringly preferred model, at least in the context of the review of the *acquis*. In the 2007 Green Paper the orthodox model of minimum harmonization is not even allowed as a possible option for the future. In October 2008, as a result of its review of the consumer *acquis*, the Commission adopted a proposal for a Directive on Consumer Rights which would replace Directives 85/577, 97/7, 93/13, and 99/44 with a 'horizontal instrument'.[97] It is constitutionally consistent and entirely unsurprising that the chosen legal base for this proposed act was Article 95 EC, Article 114 TFEU's predecessor. And the maximum model is proposed.

The draft CFR was delivered to the Commission in December 2007, and the full version of the draft was subsequently published in 2009 in six volumes containing draft rules, comments, and notes.[98] For the time being the Commission has chosen to treat this as the academic CFR and is now considering how to take the project forward

---

[94] COM(2001) 398.

[95] D Staudenmayer, 'The Place of Consumer Contract Law within the Process on European Contract Law' (2004) 27 J Consum Pol 269, 277.

[96] COM(2006) 744.

[97] COM(2008) 614.

[98] C von Bar and E Clive (eds), *Principles, Definitions and Model Rules of European Private Law: Draft Common Frame of Reference, Full Edition* (Sellier, 2009).

in a more practical (political) way, which will probably involve a shorter text and which will also require decisions about its precise legal character. Thus far the favoured metaphor has been to treat the CFR as a 'toolbox' on which courts and legislatures may draw and so of a soft law character.[99]

An unresolved tension between better law-making, focused on cleaning up the *acquis*, and an arguably much grander, perhaps alarming, vision of (ultimately) codification lurks beneath this review. Indeed there has been an impression of periodically fluctuating preferences within the Commission in the course of the current decade. But 'coherence' is the leitmotif. This seems irresistible. Who would champion incoherence?

And yet, the Commission's case that the review of the *acquis* and the promulgation of the CFR are simply devices for improving—making more 'coherent'—the quality of the regulatory environment is far from unimpeachable. Content cannot be a purely technical matter. There is an identified risk that the emphasis may be on economic growth in preference to wider distributional concerns—a priority for freedom of contract over the protection of weaker parties. This, it is argued, may subvert hard-fought adjustments in national contract law that have promoted the protection of groups such as consumers, workers, and tenants under an assumption that such economically disadvantaged parties are deprived of a genuine right of self-determination in an unregulated market.[100]

The point is that one might cheerfully champion incoherence if coherence achieved at EU level embeds political choices that one would oppose. Put another way, a coherent EU contract law may batter national law into an alarmingly incoherent shape.[101] And if that EU system follows the model of maximum harmonization, it is, as the Commission correctly contends, more 'coherent'—but the damage wrought at national level cuts still deeper. Moreover, as has been observed on several occasions, the Court's adventurous reading of EU measures may further disrupt settled national choices.[102] So there is a respectable case to be made against coherence at EU level.

As for competence, such questions are not neglected in the Commission's documentation, but they are addressed only tentatively. The July 2001 Communication, which initiated the review, calls explicitly for information on whether diversity between national contract laws 'directly or indirectly obstructs the functioning of the internal market, and if so to what extent', with a view to considering appropriate

---

[99] eg 'European Contract Law and the revision of the acquis: the way forward', COM(2004) 651, 3; Von Bar and Clive (n 98 above) 9, 23.

[100] Cf Study Group on Social Justice in European Private Law, 'Social Justice in European Contract Law: a Manifesto' (2004) 10 ELJ 653; J Rutgers and R Sefton-Green, 'Revising the Consumer Acquis: (Half) Opening the Doors of the Trojan Horse' (2008) 16 Euro Rev Priv L 427; M Hesselink, 'European Contract Law: a Matter of Consumer Protection, Citizenship, or Justice?' (2007) 15 Euro Rev Priv L 323.

[101] This anxiety may be discerned elsewhere in EU law—cf C Harlow, 'Francovich and the Problem of the Disobedient State' (1996) 2 ELJ 199, fearing the imposition of a liability system that corrupts accumulated nuance and balance at national level.

[102] eg Cases C-168/05 (n 77 above), C-404/06 (n 81 above), C-183/00 (n 87 above).

action by the EU's institutions.[103] The Commission shows itself to be actively seeking to uncover areas in which the internal market is malfunctioning because of deficiencies in the existing bloc of harmonized contract law. The mood is different from the relatively carefree attitude to competence taken in the consumer contract law Directives adopted in the 1980s. The Commission, in planning a future for EU contract law, is forced by *Tobacco Advertising* to reckon seriously with constitutional foundations. Similarly the October 2004 document on 'the way forward' makes an explicit connection between the goal of eliminating internal market barriers and review of the consumer *acquis*.[104] But it offers no extended examination of the matter. The 2007 Green Paper on the Review of the Consumer *acquis*[105] similarly identifies a 'need' for EU contract law which is embedded in an economic vision: the viable internal market must be marked by both consumer protection and competitiveness.

It is submitted that the Commission's reluctance to tackle 'competence sensitivity' aggressively is understandable. Had the Commission included an extended treatment of available legal competence in its initial 2001 Communication it would doubtless have faced the protest that it was revealing a predilection for those options which most seriously engaged the issue of competence, which are those at the more ambitious end of the scale and involve the adoption of comprehensive legislation. In order to avoid an unbalanced debate the Commission may have acted wisely in striving to maintain an open-minded focus on what is normatively desirable in the field. As the debate has developed it has become apparent that increased attention to 'softer' forms of activity—such as the common frame of reference—has in any event served to take some of the heat out of the debate. But the shadow of *Tobacco Advertising* remains visible.[106]

I. CONCLUSION

Out of an original Treaty pattern which promised little other than the indirect fruits of the process of market integration, a network of policies affecting the consumer has developed. The European Court has shaped a perception of the consumer in assessing the permissibility of national techniques of market regulation, including consumer protection, which impede the integrative process. The political institutions have been responsible for a 'soft law' framework for the development of consumer policy. Moreover, the programme of harmonization of laws has involved legislative activity in the field of consumer protection. Like environmental and cultural policy (among

---

[103] COM(2001) 398, [23]–[33] and [72].

[104] COM(2004) 651, [3].

[105] COM(2006) 744.

[106] S Weatherill, 'Constitutional Issues—How much is best left unsaid?' in S Vogenauer and S Weatherill (eds), *The Harmonisation of European Contract Law: Implications for European Private Laws, Business and Legal Practice* (Hart, 2006); M Ludwigs, 'Harmonisierung des Schuldvertragsrechts in Europa' [2006] Europarecht 370.

others) consumer policy has emerged from a combination of judicial decision-making in the area of 'negative law', soft law, and harmonization policy before finally enjoying a textually ambiguous consecration in the Treaty. This evolution is inevitable as the impact of market integration has spread into a wide range of economic and social policies pursued at national level but it has the consequence that one must work hard to identify truly coherent themes and principles. And one must reckon with 'competence sensitivity'.

But themes and principles there are. Market failure robs the consumer of an efficiently operating economy. Intransparency, for example, prompts a response through mandatory information disclosure, which has become a leitmotif of legislative policy in relation to the protection of economic interests. Concern for the possible exploitation of the economically weaker party is visible in some measures, and some pernicious practices—use of unfair terms, promotion of tobacco products, aiming advertisements at minors, exploitation though unfair commercial practices—are banned. Equally free movement law leaves space for national measures to address particular identified failings in the market, even if an obstruction to interstate trade ensues. On the other hand, the legislative vision of the consumer frequently involves an individual able to take care of him- or herself in the market by digesting and acting upon information that is mandatorily supplied and, if necessary, withdrawing from a deal on reflection after 'cooling off'. Marketing practices subject to control in this manner are not banned. They are regulated. Such legislative initiatives seek to construct an informed consumer, both confident of market conditions and inquisitive about them. And the European Court is intolerant of national measures which it concludes underestimate the ability of consumers to adapt to unfamiliar products or marketing practices.

Is this a 'consumer policy'? It is a mix of policies, frequently contested, and rarely is heard directly the voice of the consumer in its shaping. And that is characteristic of how consumer policy evolves at national level, as much as at EU level.

28

THE EVOLUTION OF CULTURAL POLICY IN THE EUROPEAN UNION

Rachael Craufurd Smith*

Ten years into the new millennium, the European Union (EU) is an established and increasingly confident player in the cultural field: its rules shape the way in which cultural goods and services are traded across the Member States; it is a major cultural patron; it has taken a high profile role in international negotiations over the preservation of cultural diversity and, at the domestic level, has recently initiated a more structured framework for dialogue and exchange on cultural matters between the Member States. These activities are now firmly rooted in the EU Treaties. A specific Article on culture, Article 167 of the Treaty on the Functioning of the European Union (TFEU), empowers the EU to 'contribute to the flowering of the cultures of the Member States' and to 'foster cooperation with third countries and the competent international organisations in the sphere of culture'.

If, however, we go back to the origins of the EU, to the fossil record as it were, we unearth some very different legal remains. The founding European Economic Community Treaty (EEC Treaty) of 1957 contained scant reference to culture: only two Articles overtly suggested that Community activity might have cultural implications. Article 36 EEC permitted Member States to restrict imports and exports in order to protect 'national treasures possessing artistic, historic and archaeological value' and on grounds of 'public morality', while Article 131 EEC enabled the Member States to extend the benefits of the Treaty to associated countries in order to further their prosperity and, in consequence, the 'economic, social and cultural development... which they desire'. Why did the EEC Treaty not explicitly provide for competence in the cultural field? The most obvious answer lies in the Treaty's title. Those who drafted the EEC Treaty, aware of the failure of more ambitious

* Senior Lecturer at the University of Edinburgh. I would like to thank Ines Sofia Oliveira, Luke Padfield, and Sean Smith for their valuable help in the preparation of this chapter.

attempts to further political integration, deliberately focused on a limited number
of key areas—inter-state trade, agriculture, transport—where state cooperation was
most likely to boost production at a time of post-war austerity.[1] From this perspective, a specific cultural mandate would have been an unnecessary and distracting
complication.

The EEC Treaty was consequently not, in any meaningful sense, intended to be
'about' culture. At best, as reflected in its approach to the associated territories,
economic prosperity was expected to create new opportunities for cultural development. Cultural development was thus premised on, not seen as itself a factor in,
economic regeneration: part of the superstructure rather than the base. This is not to
say that the architects behind the Treaty considered culture to be unimportant. On
the contrary, Konrad Adenauer, Robert Schuman, and Paul-Henri Spaak all played
a central role in the establishment in 1949 of the Council of Europe, whose founding
Treaty envisaged 'common action in economic, social, cultural, scientific, legal and
administrative matters'. Indeed, the Council's subsequent European Cultural Convention of 1954 prefigured in important respects the Article on culture that was
ultimately included in the European Community Treaty (EC) in 1992.[2] A specialized
United Nations agency, the United Nations Economic, Social and Cultural Organisation (UNESCO), had been established even earlier in 1946, with the object to
'contribute to peace and security by promoting collaboration among the nations
through education, science and culture'.[3] There were thus two major international
institutions already in place with explicit cultural remits when the EEC Treaty was
being drafted. To have included culture within the scope of the Treaty would have
seemed an unnecessary duplication of effort and could have led to inter-institutional
tensions.

The fact that there was no explicit ascription of cultural competence to the EEC in
1957 did not, however, mean that culture was excluded from the new Community's
sphere of operations. Although some Member States regarded this to be the case, the
Court of Justice in the 1968 *Italian Art Treasures* case rejected such an interpretation
of the Treaty.[4] The Commission argued that Italy's export tax on art objects, ostensibly
motivated by the desire to stem the dissipation of Italy's extensive cultural heritage to
collectors abroad, contravened Article 16 on customs duties in the EEC Treaty. Italy
argued that art works were not comparable to ordinary 'consumer goods and articles
of general use', with which the Treaty was alone concerned. The Court rejected Italy's
arguments and held it was sufficient that the art works could be valued in money
and form the subject of commercial transactions to be classified as 'goods'.[5] From a

---

[1] For a brief overview see P Craig and G de Búrca, *EU Law: Text, Cases and Materials* (4th edn, Oxford
University Press, 2008) ch 1.
[2] Art 1(b), Statute of the Council of Europe (1949) ETS 1/6/7/8/11.
[3] Art 1, Constitution of UNESCO (1945).
[4] Case 7/68 *Commission v Italy* [1968] ECR 428.   [5] ibid 49.

very early date, therefore, it was clear that Member State cultural policies, where they had an impact on trade and commercial relations, were subject to the strictures of EEC law.[6]

But even those states that did recognize the potential application of the EEC Treaty to domestic cultural policies would, in 1957, have felt fairly relaxed about its practical implications. At the time, state intervention in the cultural field was primarily concerned with the preservation and protection of traditional art forms and cultural heritage, which they had consciously sought to insulate from Community meddling by Article 36 EEC (now 36 TFEU). With regard to film and television there was considerable debate as to whether these could be categorized as art forms at all.[7] In relation to television, states such as France and Italy had established state monopolies that precluded meaningful competition, a form of market intervention accommodated by the terms of Article 90(2) EEC (now 106(2) TFEU); while technological limitations, together with linguistic and cultural differences, constrained the development of cross-border services. The common commercial policy was initially developed solely in the field of goods and it was not until the Court of Justice's Opinion 1/94 that the extension of the policy to services and intellectual property rights was confirmed.[8] Serious conflict between the Member States and the EEC in cultural affairs would initially, therefore, have seemed quite distant.

With regard to culture, the EU of 2010 thus looks a very different entity to the tightly focused EEC of 1957. And the EU of 2010 looks very different because, despite what may have been thought at its inception, the European institutions neither could, for legal reasons, nor wished, for political reasons, to ignore culture. Legal, because increasing prosperity led to an expansion in trade in cultural goods and services and, inevitably, to conflicts between domestic measures and EU law. Political, because the cultural allegiances that Europeans feel for their home states, nations, or regions can create barriers not only to European trade but also to the development of a European identity and support for the challenging process of European integration. These two distinct strands of EU engagement with culture have been present almost from the inception of the EU and are considered separately below. But before turning to these issues it is necessary to consider, briefly, what is meant by the term 'culture' and the relevance of this definitional question for the EU.

---

[6] For discussion of different Member State approaches to intervention in the cultural field see Council of Europe/ERICarts, 'Compendium of Cultural Policies and Trends in Europe, 11th edition', 2010 at <http://www.culturalpolicies.net/web.index.php>; A Littoz-Monnet, *The European Union and Culture. Between Economic Regulation and European Cultural Policy* (2007) 23–30.

[7] W Benjamin, 'The Work of Art in the Age of Mechanical Reproduction' (1936) UCLA School of Theater, Film and Television website.

[8] Opinion 1/94 *WTO* [1994] ECR I-5267, building on the 'dynamic approach' to the interpretation of Art 113 EEC in Opinion 1/78 [1979] ECR 2871, [45].

A. THE CONCEPTION OF CULTURE IN EU LAW

Neither the TFEU nor the Treaties that preceded it have attempted to define the term 'culture'. The absence of a definition is not surprising, in that culture, as an essentially contested concept, is inherently open to divergent and evolving conceptions.[9] Among these, two conceptions of culture are often contrasted. At one extreme there is the limited, yet normatively charged, conception of culture as 'artistic and intellectual work of agreed value', one that includes classical music, painting, sculpture, and literature.[10] At the other, there is the more expansive, anthropological, conception of 'distinctive ways of life'. This conception, reflected in a number of international agreements, extends well beyond the 'fine arts' to include popular and mass produced culture; pastimes such as sport, social etiquette, and modes of dress; vernacular architecture and folklore; even culinary traditions.[11] Culture in this sense can embrace such 'distinctive' practices as Nazi book burning or female circumcision: 'bad culture' as well as 'good'. In consequence, the ascription to a product or practice of the term 'cultural' should not automatically be understood as indicating that the product has a positive value or is otherwise desirable. This must be determined using other canons of evaluation, focusing, for example, on an entity or practice's aesthetic or educational value, craftsmanship, utility, social or political symbolism, authenticity, or conformity to certain fundamental human rights and ethical values.[12]

Given that the EEC Treaty did not establish specific powers relating to culture, the question of how culture should be defined would, initially at least, have seemed largely hypothetical. The reference to 'national treasures possessing artistic, historic or arch-aeological value' in Article 36 EEC did, however, indicate that a more traditional and restrictive conception would be preferred.[13] But once the Court of Justice recognized that cultural considerations could be relied on more generally to derogate from Community rights and freedoms, the definitional question began to assume greater importance.[14] In this context the broad conception of culture is problematic, in that it could enable states to justify almost any constraint on the operation of EU law, in fields as disparate as employment law or the operation of the Common Agricultural Policy.

---

[9] T Eagleton, *The Idea of Culture* (Wiley, 2000) ch 1; B De Witte, 'The Cultural Dimension of Community Law' in Academy of European Law (ed), *Collected Courses of the Academy of European Law*, Vol IV, Book 1 (1995) 229–299, 246–249; and T Ahmed and T Hervey, 'The European Union and Cultural Diversity: A Missed Opportunity?' (2003/4) 3 European Yearbook of Minority Issues 43–62.

[10] Eagleton (n 9 above) 21.

[11] The UNESCO Universal Declaration on Cultural Diversity states in its preamble that 'Culture should be regarded as the set of distinctive spiritual, material, intellectual and emotional features of society or a social group, and . . . it encompasses, in addition to art and literature, lifestyles, ways of living together, value systems, traditions and beliefs'.

[12] J H Merryman, 'The Public Interest in Cultural Property' (1989) 77 CLR 339.

[13] The Italian version of Art 36 EEC refers to a broader category of 'national heritage', see N Dafydd, 'The "not so" free movement of art and the protection of national treasures?' (2008) 14/3 National Trade Law and Regulation 49–51.

[14] See further text accompanying (n 32 below).

The EEC Treaty, for reasons discussed above, provided little, if any, guidance as to the latitude to be afforded Member States in pursuing their own cultural policies, leaving the European institutions to develop a largely implicit theory about the value of domestic cultures and how they should be accommodated within the EU's legal and political framework. In general, the Court of Justice and Commission have tended to strike down cultural measures on the grounds that they are discriminatory or disproportionate, not because the state has failed to understand what can appropriately be termed 'cultural'.[15] The Commission has, on occasion, engaged more directly with this definitional question, adopting a relatively restrictive interpretation in certain of its state aid rulings. In its *Kinderkanal and Phoenix* decision, for example, it held that television stations broadcasting educational and current affairs programmes could not be considered cultural.[16] The Commission indicated that only programmes dealing with culture in a more 'generally accepted sense' would fall within the derogation.[17] In other rulings the Commission has adopted a wide approach, accepting aid for projects of a scenic, historic, archaeological, aesthetic, architectural, engineering, artistic, or scientific nature.[18]

A concern that cultural derogations may spiral out of control and be used to support protectionist policies could explain why both the Court of Justice and Commission have at times drawn a distinction between 'culture' and the 'cultural industries'. Culture here appears to signify something akin to 'cultural content', defined in Article 4(2) of the UNESCO Convention on Cultural Diversity as the 'symbolic meaning, artistic dimension and cultural values that originate from or express cultural identities'.[19] Culture in this essentially symbolic sense can be justified on cultural grounds, while support simply for the underlying industry, or concrete manifestation on which it depends, cannot. Thus, in *FEDECINE* the Court of Justice held that discriminatory Spanish measures that promoted the theatrical distribution of national films could not be justified on cultural grounds.[20] The Court went on to note that to be legitimate the aid would, in any event, need to focus on some qualitative or content-related aspect of the good or service produced.[21] In another case concerning Spanish subsidies for the dubbing of films into the Basque language, the Commission held that the aid was directed at a specific field of commercial activity, pre-production, and consequently could not be brought within the scope of the cultural exception in Article 87(3)(d) EC (now Article 107(3)(d) TFEU).[22] Intervention had thus to be justified instead on the

---

[15] See more detailed discussion in Part B below.

[16] *Kinderkanal and Phoenix* [1999] OJ C238/3, [43].

[17] ibid and see also *State Aid in Favour of CELF* [1999] OJ L44/37.

[18] *Individual Cases of Application Based on the National Heritage Lottery Fund* [2003] OJ C/187.

[19] Convention on the Protection and Promotion of the Diversity of Cultural Expressions, UNESCO, 2005.

[20] Case 17/92 *Federación de Distribuidores Cinematográficos v Estado Español et Unión de Productores de Cine y Televisión* [1993] ECR I-2239.

[21] ibid [20]–[21].

[22] *Spain, Promotion of Movies and DVDs in Basque* [2007] OJ C/308, though note that aid was found to be justified under Art 87(3)(c) TEC (now 107(3)(c) TFEU), the Commission here relying on Art 151.4 EC (now 167(4) TFEU) to emphasize the cultural dimension of the scheme.

basis that it supported the development of 'certain economic activities' within Article 87(3)(c) EC (now Article 107(3)(c) TFEU), or not at all. This was so, even though the ultimate objective of the measure was to support a native language, accepted as a legitimate basis for a cultural derogation by the Court of Justice in the *UTECA* and *Groener* cases.[23]

The EU institutions have in fact failed to follow a consistent line here and it is possible to point to cases such as *Cinétèque* or *LIBRO* where support for a particular industry, the cinema and book publishing industries respectively, has been held in principle to be legitimate on cultural grounds.[24] States may quite rationally decide to support particular industries because of their close association with artistic innovation and creativity, or because of their symbolic importance, and consider this to be the most effective and least intrusive way of supporting a particular art form. The 'concentric circles model' of the culture industries maps onto a model similar to a circular target depending on the input from artistically creative individuals, such as writers, composers, or visual artists.[25] Industries with a high creative input, such as those at issue in *Cinétèque* and *LIBRO*, are located in the circles closest to the creative core, while those that tend to exploit existing cultural expression but do little directly to stimulate new cultural content, such as the dubbing industry, are located towards the outer edges of the model. The model may help to explain the EU institutions' greater tolerance, in certain cases, of support for specific industries, but even when a state supports a cultural industry at the centre of the model, such as original film production, *FEDECINE* suggests that states would be well advised to identify distinct creative or qualitative aspects of the product or service that is ultimately produced.

Where an institution wishes to allocate discretionary benefits or develop innovative new policies, as opposed to delimit specific obligations or exceptions to established rules, definitional precision may be much less desirable. Here, the use of open-ended, fuzzy concepts such as 'culture' can be distinctly advantageous, encouraging a dynamic process of interpretation that is responsive to social, technological, and political developments. At the national level, Member States define the term 'culture' in more or less expansive ways depending on their own particular policy agendas.[26] The absence of a formal definition of 'culture' in Article 167 TFEU affords the EU a

---

[23] Case C-222/07 *UTECA v Administración General del Estado*, judgment of the 5 March 2009 and Case 379/87 *Groener v Minister for Education* [1989] ECR 3967.

[24] Cases 60 and 61/84 *Cinétèque v Fédération National des Cinémas Français* [1985] ECR 2605 and C-531/07 *Fachverband der Buch-und Medienwirtschaft v LIBRO Handelsgesellschaft mbH*, judgment of the 30 April 2009. Although the Court in *LIBRO* held that 'measures to support books as cultural objects' could be justified under EC law, the specific measure was found to be disproportionate.

[25] D Throsby, 'The Concentric Circles Model of the Cultural Industries' (2008) 17/3 Cultural Trends 147–164. This model may also lie behind the distinction drawn between the 'cultural' and 'creative' industries in the Commission's recent Green Paper, Unlocking the Potential of Cultural and Creative Industries COM(2010) 183, 5–6.

[26] N Obuljen, 'Why We Need European Cultural Policies: the Impact of EU Enlargement on Cultural Policies in Transition Countries' (2004) at <http://www.eurocult.org>.

similarly wide margin of discretion when formulating its own cultural policy through recommendations and incentive measures.

The Commission, in this context, has taken a consistently broad approach, holding in its communication on the First Culture Programme in 1998 that 'culture is no longer restricted to "highbrow" culture (fine arts, music dance, theatre, literature). Today the concept also covers popular culture, mass produced culture, everyday culture.'[27] More recently, in its 2007 communication on 'A European Agenda for Culture in a Globalizing World', the Commission indicated its readiness to embrace all the various facets of the term, including the fine arts and broader anthropological and symbolic interpretations.[28] In this context, the Commission has committed itself to supporting the cultural and creative industries as well as culture in a more limited symbolic sense.[29]

B. THE COURT OF JUSTICE AND DOMESTIC CULTURAL POLICY

The first strand of EU engagement with culture finds its origins in the Court of Justice's refusal to exclude in principle culturally motivated regulations from the ambit of EEC law.[30] This encouraged traders to rely on the direct effect of the Treaty free movement and fiscal provisions to challenge in domestic courts regulations that protected distinct cultural practices, goods, or services from foreign competition. These regulations were either directly discriminatory or, if not overtly or in practice discriminatory, made it more costly for foreign operators to provide goods or services in the state in question. The Commission, often in parallel, initiated similar proceedings against Member States before the Court of Justice under what is now Article 258 TFEU and took action to investigate financial aid provided by States for cultural activities under what is now Article 107 TFEU. As the free movement provisions assumed an increasingly horizontal application, individuals began to rely on Community law to challenge restrictions by private individuals and organizations as well as states.[31] Initial EU engagement with culture thus took place indirectly through the application of the free trade, fiscal, and competition provisions designed to liberalize trade.

---

[27] Commission, Communication on the First European Community Framework Programme in Support of Culture (2000–04), COM(1998) 266, 3.

[28] Commission, Communication on a European Agenda for Culture in a Globalizing World, COM(2007) 242, 3.

[29] ibid 9–10.

[30] See discussion of the Italian Art Treasures Case at text accompanying (n 4 above). On those rare occasions when the Court or Commission has excluded particular categories of measure from the scope of the Treaty, the 'rules of the game', for example, in the sporting context or 'selling arrangements' in the field of goods, this has tended to complicate the legal position by creating new and contested demarcation lines.

[31] Case C 36/74 *Walrave v Union Cycliste Internationale* [1974] ECR 1405, Case C-415/93 *Union Royale Belge de Sociétés de Football v Jean-Marc Bosman* [1995] ECR I-492, *Re Joint Selling of Commercial Rights to the Champions League* [2003] OJ L291/25.

Limited recognition in the initial EEC Treaty of culture as a relevant concern clearly posed a threat to domestic cultural policies, particularly with the extension of the free movement rules to cover indistinctly as well as distinctly applicable domestic provisions.[32] In its innovative *Cassis de Dijon* ruling, the Court of Justice responded to these concerns by holding that state measures that applied without distinction to domestic and foreign goods could be justified on general interest grounds, provided the measures were proportionate.[33] The open-ended category of general interest justifications has been added to on a case by case basis over time to include such cultural considerations as the conservation of—and dissemination of knowledge regarding—the Member States' historical, cultural, and artistic heritage,[34] the promotion of the media and cultural pluralism and the maintenance of a certain level of television programme quality;[35] support for national languages and multilingualism;[36] and support for the cinema and book publishing industries.[37]

Should this wider category of cultural justifications also be available where a measure is directly discriminatory? At present Member States may not, for example, adopt policies that grant preferential entry prices to museums for their own nationals on the basis that they help to fund such institutions through their taxes, or impose quotas designed to benefit the distribution of national films over those from other EU states.[38] There are undoubtedly cases where the inability to rely on cultural justifications for directly discriminatory measures appears genuinely problematic. Thus, rather than bring international sporting competitions to a spectacular halt, the Court of Justice in *Walrave and Koch* held the requirement that only nationals could play for a national sports team to be a matter of 'purely sporting interest', and, as such, to fall outwith the scope of the Treaty.[39] And in other rulings, as in the recent *LIBRO* case, the Court appears willing to blur the line between directly and indirectly discriminatory measures, apparently countenancing the possibility that cultural justifications might be relevant even where there is direct discrimination.[40]

Despite these complications, the case for amending the law to allow a cultural derogation in the context of direct discrimination is not compelling. The decoupling of culture from nationality undoubtedly weakens the 'ownership' that certain states may wish to assert over particular cultural practices or products but it also enables those practices and products to be reinterpreted by those outside the culture itself.

---

[32] See, for example, Case 8/74 *Procureur du Roi v Dassonville* [1974] ECR 837.

[33] Case 120/78 *Rewe Zentrale v Bundesmonopolverwaltung für Branntwein* [1979] ECR 649.

[34] Cases C-180/89 *Tourist Guides Italy* [1991] ECR I-709, [20], and C-198/89 *Tourist Guides Greece* [1991] ECR I-727, [21].

[35] Case C-288/89 *Collectieve Antennevoorziening Gouda and Others* v *Commissariaat voor de Media* [1991] ECR I-4007, [22]–[23] and [27].

[36] Cases C-222/07 *UTECA* and 379/87 *Groener* (n 23 above).

[37] Cases 60 and 61/84 *Cinétèque* and C-531/07 *LIBRO* (n 24 above).

[38] See Case C-388/01 *Commission v Italy* [2003] ECR I-721 and for critical evaluation E Psychogiopoulou, *The Integration of Cultural Consideration in EU Law and Policies* (Brill, 2008) 149–150.

[39] Case C 36/74 *Walrave* (n 31 above).

[40] Case C-531/07 *LIBRO* (n 24 above) [33]–[36].

A domestic producer or artist may, of course, be better placed to reflect domestic culture in an authentic way but the EU answer to this is that what a foreign producer can offer in cultural terms should be assessed on the basis of cultural criteria, not the blunt and over-extensive criterion of nationality.

These developments have shifted the venue for consideration of cultural matters from the domestic to the European level, leading to the 'Europeanization' of cultural policy debates.[41] European scrutiny can be seen to have had both a procedural and a substantive impact on domestic cultural policies. Procedurally, EU law requires Member States to articulate and clarify the basis for their policies, support them with convincing evidence, engage in consultations with those potentially affected, and ensure that they operate in a transparent and non-discriminatory way.[42]

From a Member State perspective, providing reasons for particular cultural measures can prove unexpectedly demanding, in that the basis for the measure may have become lost over time or no longer appear particularly relevant and convincing.[43] Moreover, a practice may be important culturally simply because it is distinct, differentiating one group or society from another, rather than for any other functional or aesthetic reason. But the argument that foreign goods or services should be excluded simply because they are different was never likely to be persuasive in a legal system designed to promote the development of cross-border trade and integrated European markets. As a result, Member States have often sought to support culturally based measures on alternative grounds, such as consumer protection or public health, rather than on culture or tradition.[44] Collecting the relevant data to justify a particular policy can also be costly, while the elaboration of qualitative criteria, previously hidden behind subjective judgements, has proved to be challenging in areas such as aid for the broadcasting industry.[45]

Substantively, cultural measures have, as noted above, been challenged primarily on the basis that they curtail the free movement of goods, services, or persons or, alternatively, distort competition. Given that cultural measures often seek to afford protection to specific domestic practices or products they are frequently alleged to be discriminatory or covertly protectionist.[46] Member States are also required to respect fundamental human rights established in international agreements, signed by all

---

[41] Littoz-Monnet (n 6 above) 44–45 and 151.

[42] See, for example, Case C-250/06 *United Pan-Europe Communications Belgium SA and Others v État belge* [2007] ECR I-11135, discussed in R Craufurd Smith, 'Balancing Culture and Competition: State Support for Film and Television in European Community Law' (2007–08) 10 CYELS 35–67.

[43] H P Glenn, *Legal Traditions of the World* (2nd edn, Oxford University Press, 2000) chs 1–2. The German *Reinheitsgebot*, for example, originally introduced to prevent wheat being used for brewing rather than bread making, now serves to preserve traditional production methods and a particular quality of beer: Case 178/84 *Commission v Germany* [1987] ECR 1227.

[44] As in Case 178/84 *Commission v Germany* (n 43 above).

[45] R Craufurd Smith (n 42 above) and in relation to recent developments in Germany see W Schulz, 'The Legal Framework for Public Service Broadcasting after the German State Aid Case: Procrustean Bed or Hammock?' (2009) 2 JML 219–241, at 238–239. See also Case C-368/95 *Vereinigte Familiapress Zeitungsverlags- und vertriebs GmbH v Heinrich Bauer Verlag* [1997] ECR I-3689.

[46] Case C-353/89 *Commission v Netherlands* [1991] I-4069.

Member States, when operating within the sphere of EU law, a domain the Court of Justice has extended to situations where a Member State seeks to derogate from EU law.[47] This, coupled with the enhanced status of the Charter of Fundamental Rights of the EU and increasing emphasis on the right to non-discrimination understood in a broad sense to include discrimination on grounds of racial or ethnic origin, sexual orientation, age, and religion or belief, now affords the EU considerable scope to review domestic cultural policies on substantive grounds.[48] In addition, the principle of proportionality can be used to assess the effectiveness of a particular measure and, at its most exacting, to consider whether no less intrusive measure could have been employed to achieve the desired result.[49]

A consideration of the case law indicates that Member States have in practice been afforded considerable latitude in determining their particular cultural policy object-ives. A good example of this is the UK's scheme for film finance, reluctantly approved by the Commission even though the cultural criteria employed, such as whether the film reflects British cultural diversity, heritage, and creativity, or uses British locations, characters, and subject matter, appear designed to ensure that the films funded are produced in the UK and involve UK nationals.[50] The challenge for the Member States has consequently been not so much convincing the EU institutions that their measures pursue legitimate cultural objectives but establishing that it is necessary and propor-tionate to apply them to foreign companies or individuals wishing to access the domestic market. At the root of this problem for the Member States is the EU's preference for cultural development to be driven by consumer choice rather than government fiat, in line with internal market principles.

This preference has led the EU to gradually strip away those domestic regulations that insulate citizens from exposure to diverse foreign cultural goods and services and to restrict Member States' ability to impose their cultural preferences on other countries.[51] EU law also encourages European citizens to experience other cultures by taking advantage of the opportunities to work, study, visit, and live abroad, thereby stimulating a reappraisal of even those culturally motivated practices and regulations that are not directly threatened by EU rules. These aspects are considered in turn below.

1. EU LAW AND CULTURAL CLOSURE

The preference for consumer choice was articulated relatively early on by the Court of Justice in *Commission v UK*, which concerned a challenge to the higher rate of excise

---

[47] Case 260/89 *Elliniki Radiophonia Tiléorassi v Dimitki* [1991] ECR I-2925.
[48] As reflected in Art 10 TFEU.
[49] Case C-368/95 *Familiapress* (n 45 above).
[50] *United Kingdom, film tax incentive* [2007] OJ C/9. For a more restrictive interpretation see *Kinderkanal and Phoenix* (n 16 above).
[51] Though note impact of EU legislative initiatives, discussed at Part C below.

tax that the UK imposed on wine, an imported product, as opposed to beer.[52] Although wine in the UK was then considered something of a luxury product, the Court noted that drinking habits varied across Europe and could change over time. The UK was not permitted through its tax policies to 'crystallize consumer habits' in order to protect the domestic beer industry. The Court repeated this phrase when considering the German *Reinheitsgebot* rules, in which it held that any confusion caused by the presence of foreign beers manufactured according to different quality standards, could be met by appropriate labelling. It is important to note that the free movement provisions in the Treaty do not prevent Member States from continuing to formulate and apply culturally specific regulations, such as the *Reinheitsgebot,* to their own domestic traders.[53] But it does limit state competence in the cultural field by preventing the application of domestic rules to goods and services originating in other countries without a convincing rationale.

The preference for consumer choice also underpinned the Court's reluctance, in a series of cases in the late eighties, to allow the Netherlands to restrict the transmission of foreign television services that had been set up in Luxembourg to take advantage of Luxembourg's more relaxed advertising and content rules.[54] The Court was not convinced that it was necessary to exclude access to foreign services in order to preserve the diversity of domestic services, even though the Luxembourg services were clearly drawing advertising revenue away from the Dutch market. From an EU perspective, therefore, cultural diversity is to be framed in European rather than more insular domestic terms.

It is possible, however, to identify a number of contexts where the EU has been more accommodating of state attempts to apply domestic rules to foreign products or persons. Firstly, in *Cinétèque,* state measures designed to protect a particular art form threatened by technological and social developments were upheld, there being no indication of protectionism.[55] Secondly, where an individual or company deliberately relocates to another Member State in order to avoid the rules of the state of origin, it may be required to comply with those rules under the 'abuse of law' doctrine.[56] Thirdly, Member States remain largely free to regulate the manner in which products or services are sold within their country, for example, by imposing restrictions on Sunday trading, provided these do not operate in a discriminatory fashion.[57] Rules of this type do not directly impede access

---

[52] Case 170/78 *Commission v UK* [1980] ECR 417. A similar observation was made in Case 178/84 *Commisssion v Germany* (n 43 above) [32].

[53] As illustrated by Case 237/82 *Jongeneel Kaas v Netherlands* [1984] ECR 483.

[54] Case C-352 *Bond van Adverteerders v Netherlands* [1988] ECR 2095; Case C-288/89 *Gouda* (n 35 above); Case C-353/89 *Commission v Netherlands* (n 46 above). In a different context see Case C-368/95 *Familiapress* (n 45 above).

[55] Cases 60–61/84 *Cinétèque* (n 24 above), where cinema release was threatened by video distribution.

[56] Case 23/93 *TV10 SA* [1994] ECR I-4795, L H Hansen, 'The Development of the Circumvention Principle in the Area of Broadcasting' (1998) 2 LIEI 111.

[57] Case 145/88 *Torfaen Borough Council v B&Q plc* [1989] ECR 3851, leading to the identification of a category of 'selling arrangements' that potentially fall out with the scope of Art 34 TFEU in Case 267–268/91 *Keck and Mithouard (Criminal Proceedings Against)* [1993] ECR I-6097. Though the reasoning differs slightly across the various freedoms the general approach is the same.

to the products and thus preserve consumer choice. They also tend to protect 'external' rather than purely 'personal' preferences, that is, they relate to other people's preferences not merely one's own. For example, the preferences of those who want a quiet, non-commercial Sunday can only be realized by preventing those who want to go shopping from acting on their preferences.[58] In contrast, quality standards relate primarily to personal preferences and such preferences are not generally mutually exclusive. The German conception of beer enshrined in the *Reinheitsgebot*, for example, now competes with other 'foreign' conceptions of beer to enhance consumer choice in the German market.

The fourth, and final, category relates to rules that seek to protect values or interests that are considered of constitutional or national importance. The requirement in *Groener* that teachers in Ireland should have a basic knowledge of the Irish language sought, for example, to maintain a national language and a key aspect of Ireland's national identity.[59] Similarly, the prohibition of games involving simulated killing at issue in *Omega* has deep roots in German history and reflects the high level of importance that Article 1 of the 1949 German Basic Law ascribes to the protection of human dignity.[60] In the sensitive and controversial field of sexual morality the Court of Justice, taking its lead from the European Court of Human Rights, has also allowed Member States considerable latitude provided there is no discrimination.[61]

2. EU LAW AND CULTURAL IMPERIALISM

EU law not only prevents Member States closing their borders to foreign goods or services on cultural grounds, it also prevents them imposing their own cultural standards or expectations on operators located abroad. Thus, the Netherlands was not allowed to 'export' its broadcasting rules by requiring foreign broadcasters to adopt the same structure and system of finance as domestic broadcasters.[62] The Court noted that conditions affecting the structure of foreign broadcasting bodies could not be considered objectively necessary in order to secure media pluralism.[63]

3. EU LAW AND CULTURAL EXIT

Though still to be confirmed in the highly charged contexts of abortion or euthanasia, established principles of EU law suggest that Member States cannot legally prevent their citizens travelling abroad to receive services lawful in the state of destination but

---

[58] R Dworkin, *Taking Rights Seriously* (2nd edn, Harvard University Press, 1978) 234 and 275.

[59] Case 379/87 *Groener* (n 23 above) adopting a notably weak form of proportionality review.

[60] Case C-36/02 *Omega Spielhallen-und Automatenaufstellungs-GmbH v Oberbürgermeisterin der Bundesstadt Bonn* [2004] ECR I-9609.

[61] Case 121/85 *Conegate v Customs and Excise Commissioners* [1986] ECR 1007.

[62] Case C-288/89 *Gouda* (n 35 above).   [63] ibid [25].

which they prohibit within their jurisdiction on cultural or ethical grounds.[64] The illegality of the service in the home state does not result in the service losing its recognition as a service in EU law.[65] Similarly, measures designed to constrain the dissemination of information about the existence of goods or services available abroad have been held to be unlawful under EU law.[66] Although Advocate General Van Gerven in *SPUC v Grogan* found restrictions on the provision of information relating to foreign abortions to be within Ireland's 'considerable' margin of appreciation,[67] this must be read in the light of the European Court of Human Rights ruling in the *Open Door Counselling* case, where similar measures were held to be a disproportionate restriction on freedom of information.[68]

The ability that EU law affords EU citizens to exit their nation state and experience other ways of life in other countries, can lead to a reappraisal of their own culture and, ultimately, pressure for change internally.[69] The impact of this exposure to alternative cultures is, however, difficult to predict. On the one hand, it can lead to calls for the dismantling of restrictions 'at home' in order to allow greater scope for personal choice. In the UK, for example, the fact that the terminally ill are currently able to travel to Switzerland, though not an EU State, to be medically assisted to commit suicide has undoubtedly influenced the domestic debate as to whether existing restrictions should be relaxed.[70]

In rather happier contexts, opportunities to travel can encourage the development of a cosmopolitan outlook.[71] This may, of course, be little more than a willingness to experiment, as a consumer, with the exotic or novel but exposure to other cultures can also lead to a more fundamental shift in outlook, what Delanty terms 'critical cosmopolitanism'.[72] This embraces a 'scepticism towards the grand narratives of modern ideologies, care for other cultures and an acceptance of cultural hybridization' as well as a 'commitment to dialogue with other cultures, especially religious ones, and nomadism, as a condition of never being fully at home in cultural categories or geopolitical boundaries'.[73] The critical dimension to cosmopolitanism resonates well with

---

[64] Consider Joined Cases 286/82 and 26/83 *Graziana Luisi and Giuseppe Carbone v Ministero del Tesoro* [1984] ECR 377, [16]; Case 159/90 *SPUC v Grogan* [1991] ECR I-4685 and the UK Court of Appeal judgment *R v Human Fertilisation and Embryology Authority, ex p Blood* [1997] 2 All ER 687.

[65] For helpful examination of this area see T K Hervey and J V McHale, *Health Law and the European Union* (2004) 144–155. EU law does not, however, extend to services that are unlawful throughout the EU, Case 294/82 *Einberger* [1984] ECR 1177.

[66] Case C-362/88 *GB-INNO-BM v Confédération du commerce luxembourgeois* [1990] ECRI-667.

[67] Case 159/90 *Grogan* (n 64 above) [37].

[68] *Open Door and Dublin Well Woman v Ireland* Series A No 246-A, (1993) 15 EHRR 244.

[69] P Kurzer, *Markets and Moral Regulation: Cultural Change in the European Union* (Cambridge University Press, 2001).

[70] 'Tourism' of this type can create tensions also in the target country, see M Day, 'Polish Women Encouraged to Come to UK for "Free Abortions" on NHS', Telegraph.co.uk, 15 March 2010.

[71] F Pilcher, 'Cosmopolitan Europe' (2009) 11/1 European Societies 3–24.

[72] G Delanty, 'The Cosmopolitan Imagination: Critical Cosmopolitanism and Social Theory' (2006) 57(1) BJS 25–47.

[73] ibid 42–43.

the EU's emphasis on cross-cultural dialogue and there is some evidence that those with a more cosmopolitan outlook have a stronger sense of European identity, one less tied to concrete benefits derived from European integration and more to an awareness of social and cultural connections across Europe.[74]

On the other hand, although the opportunity for 'exit' constrains the ability of states to fully protect cultural and ethical values that they consider to be of paramount importance, it may also make it easier to maintain a hard line when protecting those values internally. Access to prohibited services, such as abortion, abroad, may reduce the risk of underground, illegal services developing at home. Exit may thus reduce the need to adopt repressive measures internally that would bring the ethical tensions behind a prohibition continually to light. Thus, Ireland has held firm to its prohibition on abortion within Ireland, yet has chosen to relax its stance on foreign travel and access to information.[75]

A final dimension to 'exit' is that it may enable entitlements to be 'reimported' on a person's return home if discontinuation of their entitlement could cause prejudice. In the case of *Stefan Grunkin*, the parents of a young German citizen relied on the citizenship and non-discrimination provisions in the EC Treaty to overturn a German prohibition on his use of the double barrelled surname, with which he had been registered at birth in Denmark.[76] Germany prohibited their citizens using such names on grounds of length and to preserve relationships between members of the extended family, but such interests were considered insufficiently compelling to override the considerable inconvenience caused through not being able to use the name with which one had been registered at birth.[77]

4. EU LAW AND THE EVOLUTION OF DOMESTIC CULTURES

EU law thus introduces an important modification to the way in which domestic cultures evolve over time: it sets in motion a process of regulatory competition, with consumers centrally placed to determine, through their economic choices, which products and, ultimately, regulatory regimes will survive. Only in a limited range of cases, where consumer choice would itself undermine the rule in question or threaten fundamental national or constitutional values, has the market been prevented from taking its course.

Although EU law is generally agnostic about the substantive cultural policies that Member States pursue, as illustrated by the Commission's approval of the UK film fund, it does have a policy regarding the *ambit* of domestic cultural policies, more specifically the use of law to insulate cultural practices from foreign alternatives.[78] This policy is given effect to through the principles of non-discrimination and

---

[74] Pilcher (n 71 above) 19.
[75] Hervey and McHale (n 65 above) 155.
[76] Case C-353/06 *Stefan Grunkin and Dorothee Regina Paul v Standesamt Niebül* [2008] ECR I-7639.
[77] ibid [30].   [78] See n 50 above.

proportionality. So although states may continue to impose culturally motivated rules on domestic traders and offer funding to promote domestic cultures, they can no longer ensure their citizens 'buy into' the particular cultural practices or lifestyles encapsulated in their own rules through a process of cultural closure.

In seeking to address the barriers to trade arising from the different cultural traditions within Europe, the EU has consequently developed what might be termed a 'meta' cultural policy: a policy about how the conflict between domestic policies should be managed as well as a policy regarding the role that law should play in this process.[79] In one sense this is no more than a working out of familiar internal market principles in the cultural field and illustrates well the expansive reach and influence of the Treaty's economic provisions. Thus, Littoz-Monnet concludes that both the Court and Commission have 'engaged in a strategy aimed at liberalising the cultural sector'.[80] But the rejection by the Court and Commission of Member State attempts to close off their citizens from alternative cultural goods and services or to afford their cultural values and traditions extraterritorial effect, may also be thought to reflect a distinct policy of cultural engagement. Rather than 'promote the diversity of its cultures' within the terms of Article 167 TFEU by simply endorsing democratically mandated policies of cultural closure, the EU can also be seen to have promoted cultural interaction in the belief that this will ultimately prove more effective in enhancing cultural diversity and innovation.

C. EU LEGISLATIVE AND FINANCIAL MEASURES: AN INDIRECT CULTURAL IMPACT

A second, indirect, strand of EU engagement with culture has been through EU legislative and financial initiatives based on Treaty articles other than the culture Article itself. Although the EU free movement provisions constrain the ability of Member States to apply their cultural regulations to foreign goods and services, certain restrictions have, as we have seen, been held to be legitimate. Given that Article 167 TFEU specifically excludes EU harmonization on cultural grounds, the EU has addressed these remaining trade barriers by recourse to Article 47 EC (now Article 53 TFEU), which allows for coordination of domestic measures to facilitate the freedom of establishment and, by virtue of Article 55 EC (now Article 62 TFEU), also freedom to provide services, and Article 95 EC (now Article 114 TFEU), which allows for the approximation of domestic laws in order to facilitate the functioning of the internal market.

Why have Member States gone along with these final incursions into their cultural jurisdiction? One reason is that legal challenges to domestic measures based on the Treaty free movement provisions created considerable uncertainty as to states'

---

[79] See Psychologiopoulou (n 38 above) especially at 145.
[80] Littoz-Monnet (n 6 above) 45 and 66.

continuing competence to regulate culturally significant fields, such as television broadcasting. Rather than remain subject to the vagaries of judicial intervention, Member States were prepared to support Commission legislative initiatives on the basis that the legislative process would enable the nature and desirability of EU intervention to be explored more broadly and would afford them at least some influence over the regulatory outcome, ideally enabling them to 'lock in' their preferred policy approach at EU level.

Littoz-Monnet notes, however, that where, as in the internal market context, legislation is adopted by the Council on the basis of qualified majority voting, individual states lose control of the policy agenda. In particular, majority voting renders it difficult for those states who wish to maintain a high level of market intervention to broker sufficient support for their preferred policy outcome in the face of opposition from more liberal states, backed by influential industry bodies.[81] She gives, by way of example, France's inability to gain sufficient support for the adoption of legally binding European programme quotas in the 1989 Television Without Frontiers Directive.[82] But it is also possible to point to cases where states *have* been able to broker a high level of protection for certain cultural interests against the wishes of a minority of states, notably in the copyright field and in relation to the artists' resale right, heavily promoted by France.[83]

Given the divergence of views among states on many cultural issues it will generally be easier and politically less divisive for Member States to agree minimum standards, typically supplemented by a provision that allows them to impose higher standards on individuals or companies established within their jurisdiction. The flexibility offered by this solution is, however, often more theoretical than real, in that states who exercise this facility will tend to place their domestic industries at a competitive disadvantage, thereby encouraging firms to relocate to more congenial regulatory environments abroad. There is evidence of 'regulatory arbitrage' occurring in the television context, with Scandinavian broadcasters establishing themselves in the UK to avoid restrictive Swedish advertising rules introduced in part to protect children from undue commercialization.[84] The abuse of law doctrine has to date proved too limited and uncertain in its operation to provide an adequate response to these

---

[81] Littoz-Monnet (n 6 above) 11–12, drawing on F W Scharpf, 'Negative and Postive Integration in the Political Economy of European Welfare States' in G Marks, F W Scharpf, P C Schmitter, and W Streeck (eds), *Governance in the European Union* (Sage, 1996) 15–39.

[82] Littoz-Monnet (n 6 above) 88–89.

[83] See Directive 2006/116 on the term of protection of copyright and related rights [2006] OJ L372/12 and Directive 2001/84 on the resale right for the benefit of the author of an original work of art [2001] OJ L272/32, discussed by C Seville, *EU Intellectual Property Law and Policy* (Edward Elgar, 2009) 38–41 and 57–60; K Graddy, N Horowitz, and S Szymanski, 'A study into the effect on the UK art market of the introduction of the artist's resale right' (IP Institute, January 2008).

[84] A J Hargreaves, 'Institution-driven Competition: the Regulation of Cross-border Broadcasting in the EU' (2007) 27/3 JPP 293–317.

concerns, though an attempt has been made to give the doctrine greater legal purchase in the Audiovisual Media Services Directive.[85]

Despite the formal competence that Member States continue to enjoy in the cultural field, the reality is, therefore, that this is highly contingent and increasingly susceptible to EU legislative intervention. Although paragraph four of Article 167 TFEU requires the EU 'to take cultural aspects into account in its action under other provisions of the Treaties, in particular in order to respect and to promote the diversity of its cultures', the examples discussed above suggest that whether or not a particular cultural interest is recognized or afforded protection at the EU level has as much to do with the ability of states to form voting alliances or broker deals than a principled evaluation of the interest's cultural value.

Rather than a simple opposition between free trade and cultural interests there may also be competing cultural interests at play. In the field of copyright, for example, major producers and distributors tend to favour a highly protective copyright regime on the basis that this encourages creativity. Consumers and a more limited category of authors, on the other hand, seek to curtail such rights on the basis that they limit access and stifle creativity. The EU has consistently prioritized cultural production over cultural dissemination, in large part due, Evangelia Psychogiopoulou suggests, to effective lobbying by authors and the copyright industries rather than principle.[86] So what steps are being, or could be, taken to ensure that more effective efforts are made to identify and evaluate competing cultural considerations during the legislative process, particularly those that do not receive backing from powerful, and vocal, economic operators?

Firstly, the Commission has started to put in place procedures to identify the full range of potential 'stakeholders' operating in the cultural field. It has also promoted greater coordination among cultural organizations in order to build their capacity, streamline discussions, and facilitate a more representative exchange of views during the policy-making and legislative processes.[87] Three civil society 'platforms' have been established to advise on the broad issues of 'interculturalism', access to culture, and the 'potential of culture as a catalyst for creativity'. These platforms are only open to non-governmental organizations representing a particular cultural sector or sectors with a transnational dimension.[88] As in many other fields, the EU has thus promoted the development of networks and sought to encourage a more European perspective through cross-border cooperation. The effectiveness of these platforms will in part depend on the participating bodies themselves but perhaps more importantly on the willingness of national governments and EU institutions to take them seriously as participators in the policy process.

---

[85] Art 4, Directive 2010/13/EU concerning the provision of audiovisual media services (Audiovisual Media Services Directive) [2010] OJ L95/1.

[86] Psychogiopoulou (n 38 above) 200.

[87] Commission (n 28 above) 11.

[88] Commission, European Agenda for Culture: Participation in the Culture Civil Society Platforms FAQ (2008) at <http://ec.europa.eu/culture/our-policy-development/doc1238-en.htm>.

Secondly, the Commission has sought to improve the quality and coverage of the information it holds on the various cultural industries. In 2000 a framework for cultural statistics was set up and, in 2009, four 'Task Forces' were established to consider methodology and enhance statistical coverage in the field.[89] Efforts have also been made to establish a clearer picture of the full extent of EU activities in this context.[90] This could facilitate synergies across the various Commission DGs in relation to culture and a more pro-active and reflective attitude to cultural issues, which, despite Article 151(4) EC (now 167(4) TFEU), have been largely absent in the past.[91]

Finally, one apparently paradoxical and controversial response would be to increase, rather than reduce, the EU's competence in the cultural field through introducing an express power to harmonize domestic rules, subject to the requirement of Council unanimity. Such a move would greatly strengthen the position of the Commission Directorate-General for Culture, Education and Youth, enabling it to take the lead in framing future EU measures with significant cultural implications. The reality, as discussed above, is that the EU has for some time been harmonizing domestic provisions in the cultural field, relying primarily on the various Treaty articles designed to facilitate completion of the internal market. Although the EU is required to take cultural matters 'into account' under Article 167(4) TFEU when acting under these heads, this imposes very little by way of practical constraint and cultural concerns have yet to be integrated into the various regulatory impact assessment procedures.[92] Moreover, Article 114 TFEU does not require the EU to afford cultural considerations a 'high level of protection' unlike health, safety, environmental, and consumer protection.

Were Article 167 TFEU to be extended in this way, it is possible that the Commission would still seek to initiate measures on the basis of, say, Article 114 TFEU (ex Article 95 EC) because of its less demanding voting requirements. Where there is more than one potential Treaty basis for action, the EU must rely on the basis which reflects the 'predominant purpose' behind the legislation.[93] If several objectives are pursued, and one cannot be said to be secondary to the other, the Court of Justice looks to see whether the Treaty itself establishes a hierarchy among the articles.[94] In relation to what is now Article 114 TFEU, the Court has concluded from the fact that the Article applies '[s]ave where otherwise provided in the Treaty' that preference should be given

---

[89] See discussion of the ESSnet-culture initiative at <http://ec.europa.eu/culture/our-policy-development/doc1577_en.htm>.

[90] See, for example, Commission Staff Working Document, 'Inventory of Community Actions in the Field of Culture' SEC(2007) 570.

[91] Psychogiopoulou (n 38 above) ch 2, especially at 129–130 and G Brown, 'Commentary, European Cultural Policy: Void or Vision?' (1999) 36 Cultural Trends 89–93.

[92] Psychogiopoulou (n 38 above).

[93] Case C-338/01 *Commission v Council* [2004] ECR I-4829, [54]–[60].

[94] D Chalmers, C Hadjiemmanuil, G Monti, and A Tomkins, *European Union Law* (Cambridge University Press, 2006) 140–144.

to any Treaty base that relates more specifically to the field in question.[95] These tests afford considerable scope for individual judgment and one might conclude that many of the existing EU measures in the cultural field were, in fact, motivated predominantly by internal market concerns. But being required to consider this issue at the outset pushes cultural considerations to the fore and it is certainly arguable that particular measures, such as those regarding the artists' resale right or the term of protection for copyright, pursue predominantly cultural objectives or are equally motivated by cultural and internal market concerns.[96]

A requirement of unanimity would, of course, make it difficult for controversial measures to be adopted, reigning back EU intervention in the cultural field. But if cultural issues are so politically sensitive that the EU has not to date been afforded competence to harmonize in the field, it should not cause undue concern that any future competence will be difficult to exercise. Alternatively, it *should* be a cause for current concern if predominantly cultural measures are being adopted on internal market grounds, enabling certain states to entrench their own preferred cultural provisions at the European level, whether of a liberal or protectionist bent. But Treaty amendment is, to say the least, unlikely given the difficult passage of the Lisbon Treaty. For states concerned at the intrusive nature of EU measures in the cultural field, the new procedures introduced by the Lisbon Treaty to facilitate monitoring of compliance with the principle of subsidiarity could provide a more promising line of resistance in the future.[97]

Despite criticisms that the EU has adopted a consistently liberal line, prioritizing trade over less easily quantifiable cultural interests, it has not been blind to the fact that competitive pressures and the operation of consumer choice can diminish as well as enhance cultural diversity. Even a liberalizing measure such as the Audiovisual Media Services Directive, contains a number of provisions that restrict competition rather than promote it. For instance, Article 14 endorses domestic measures designed to ensure that major sporting and cultural events are freely accessible to the public on television.[98] Similarly, the EU has intervened to support quality food products by offering EU-level protection for registered designations of origin, geographical indications, and for traditional speciality foods and drinks.[99] The EU in each case has rendered the pre-existing domestic schemes more effective and transparent, but Member States continue to exercise considerable control over their day-to-day operation, for example, in determining which cultural events are of major importance to their citizens. In the case of the EU food quality policy, the development of distinct European symbols for the various categories of product, stamped on the product itself,

---

[95] Case C-338/01 *Commission v Council* [2004] ECR I-4829, [59]–[60].

[96] See n 83 above.

[97] Lisbon Treaty, Protocol 2 on the application of the principles of subsidiarity and proportionality and see also Art 2 TEU.

[98] Directive 2010/13/EU (n 85 above).

[99] Council Regulation 510/2006 on the protection of geographical indications and designations of origin [2006] OJ L93/12 and Council Regulation 509/2006 on traditional specialties guaranteed OJ L93/1.

connects the 'EU brand' with some of Europe's most famous quality products, such as Parmesan cheese and 'Arbroath Smokies'. Culture is thus deployed to advertise the benefits of EU membership in Europe's shops and at the very heart of citizens' homes, on their kitchen tables.

The EU is also a major sponsor of cultural activities. By far the greatest source of funding has been the Structural Funds, which now comprise the European Regional Development Fund, the European Social Fund, and the Cohesion Fund.[100] Together, these dwarf the dedicated funds for culture and will contribute more than €6 billion between 2007 and 2013 on 'mobilising culture and creativity for regional development and job creation' across the twenty-seven Member States.[101] As this quote indicates, support is only given to cultural projects that are likely to promote economic development, notably through tourism, so that cultural organizations seeking funds will often have to rethink the relationship between their economic and cultural activities. In countries such as Greece and Italy the funds have primarily been deployed to maintain historic sites, but innovative, more contemporary initiatives have also received funding, such as the Lowry Centre and Liverpool Institute for Performing Arts in the UK.[102] Though the level of support provided by the funds has clearly been significant, it has not been without criticism.[103] Over-exposure to commercial exploitation can damage heritage sites, while 'regeneration' can lead to sterile gentrification and the loss of established communities, generating very little in terms of original cultural creativity.[104]

The Structural Funds support decentralized structures and the EU has not itself established strategic guidelines relating specifically to culture, leaving Member States considerable scope to develop their own general plans.[105] The process of project selection is then devolved again to the regional level. The direct injection of significant EU funds to the regions has greatly strengthened the position of cultural agencies working at the regional and local levels in relation to central government, particularly in unitary countries that do not have a federal structure. And this, in turn, has necessitated greater coordination across the different tiers of government—EU, national, regional. For example, long-term planning among all stakeholders is necessary where funds are provided for major infrastructure projects, such as museums, which need to be sustainable in the long term.

Apart from their impact on the relationship between regional and central tiers of government within the Member States, the Structural Funds also illustrate how

---

[100] See Commission, *Cohesion Policy 2007–13, Commentaries and Official Texts* (2007).

[101] Commission, EU Cohesion Policy—Thematic Pages 'Cohesion Policy 2007–2013: Culture' at <http://ec.europa.eu/regional_policy/themes/index_en.htm>.

[102] Brown (n 91 above) 92.

[103] G Evans and J Foord, 'European Funding of Culture: Promoting Common Culture or Regional Growth?' (1999) 36 Cultural Trends 55–87.

[104] G Evans, 'Hard-Branding the Cultural City-From Prado to Prada' (2003) 27 IJURR 417–440.

[105] Council Decision 2006/702/EC on Community Strategic Guidelines on Cohesion [2006] OJ L291/11. For further details see European Communities, *Cohesion Policy 2007–2013, Commentaries and Official Texts* (2007).

EU and Member State policies can be mutually reinforcing, with ideas passing back and forward across all levels. Thus, UK policy on the 'creative industries' has influenced the recent 'economic turn' in EU cultural policy but the injection of money from the Structural Funds in the 1990s led to an earlier shift in national cultural policy to incorporate concerns over economic regeneration and development that were largely absent from the policy agenda at that point.[106]

Funding for culture is also available from the European Agricultural Fund for Rural Development, with landscape preservation, cultural tourism, and the development of local skills and crafts all included among the Community's strategic guidelines.[107] Dedicated, though more limited, funding has been provided for the film and television industries through the various MEDIA programmes and for cultural activities linked to the EU's citizenship programmes.[108] The Lisbon Treaty has made it easier to adopt financial measures specifically for cultural objectives under Article 167 TFEU by amending the previous requirement of Council unanimity to allow qualified majority voting. This may encourage more programmes to be adopted on a cultural basis, though the practical impact of this may be lessened by the fact that Article 128(4) EC (now Article 167(4) TFEU) has since 1993 required culture to be taken 'into account' across the whole range of the EU's activities.

D. THE DEVELOPMENT OF AN EXPLICIT EU CULTURAL POLICY

Culture is both problematic for the EU and has considerable economic and political potential.[109] From an economic perspective, cultural allegiances erect barriers to trade, yet Europe's rich cultural diversity is also an extraordinary creative resource. Politically, citizens with strong national allegiances may see the transfer of powers from the nation state to the EU as undermining their own identity, yet the very existence of these allegiances suggests that cultural initiatives can be deployed instrumentally at the EU level to foster a distinct European identity and commitment to common 'European' values.[110] The Court of Justice and EU legislature have, as we have seen, developed a largely implicit policy of cultural openness, relying on the Treaty free

---

[106] Brown n 91 above. On the development of UK policy regarding the creative industries, see P Schlesinger, 'Creativity and the Experts. New Labour, Think Tanks and the Policy Process' (2009) 14/1 International Journal of Press/Politics 3–20.

[107] Council Decision 2006/144/EC on Community Strategic Guidelines for Rural Development [2006] OJ L 55/20. The fund amounts to €96 billion for 2007–2013.

[108] Decision 1718/2006/EC concerning the implementation of a programme of support for the European audiovisual sector (MEDIA 2007) [2006] OJ L327/12, providing 755 million Euro over seven years, and Decision 1904/2006/EC, establishing the programme Europe for Citizens [2006] OJ L378/32.

[109] M Sassatelli, 'European Cultural Space in the European Cities of Culture' (2008) 10/2 European Societies 225–245.

[110] R Craufurd Smith, 'From Heritage Conservation to European Identity: Article 151 and the Multi-Faceted Nature of Community Cultural Policy' (2007) 1 ELRev 48–69.

movement and fiscal provisions. What is perhaps more striking is that from the early 1970s onwards, the EEC institutions began to explore, without a mandate in the Treaty, whether cultural initiatives could be introduced explicitly to shore up popular support for European integration. The Tindemans (1975) and second Adonnino (1985) reports, for example, concluded that the Community needed to be seen to play a more positive role in people's daily lives and could do this by developing an explicit cultural dimension to its activities.[111]

Early forays in the field tended to be cautious and largely symbolic, such as the setting up of the European Community Youth Orchestra, the European Sculpture Competition and, in 1985, the European City of Culture Competition, with Athens the first capital awarded the title.[112] More ambitious initiatives, for example, to support the development of pan-European television services or inject a European dimension into the school curriculum foundered either because, as in the television context, they did not then resonate sufficiently with the public or were considered by the Member States to threaten existing national allegiances and competence.[113]

With the coming into force of Article 128 EC (now Article 167 TFEU) in 1993 the situation changed radically, empowering the EU to take direct action to 'contribute to the flowering of the cultures of the Member States, while respecting their national and regional diversity and at the same time bringing the common cultural heritage to the fore'. Intervention was, as noted above, kept in check by limiting EU action to the adoption of recommendations and incentive measures.[114] Early initiatives veered from highly focused programmes, such as Kaleidescope, Ariane, and Raphael, concerned with the performing arts, literature, and the preservation of cultural heritage respectively, to overly ambitious programmes such as Culture 2000.[115] Culture 2000, the first frame-work programme for culture, was voted an initial budget of just €167 million over five years, yet listed among its many objectives: the promotion of cultural dialogue; high-lighting cultural diversity and Europe's common cultural heritage; facilitating the transnational dissemination of culture and cultural operators; promoting creativity and innovation; and improving citizens' access to culture.[116] The combination of broad objectives and limited funds resulted in many applicants being unsuccessful, and with such a wide array of themes it was not clear what the programme added to

---

[111] L Tindemans, 'Report on European Union', (1976) 9 *Bull. EC*, supp 1/76 and P Adonnino, 'Second Report on a People's Europe' (1985) 18 *Bull. EC*, supp 7/85.

[112] R Craufurd Smith, 'Community Intervention in the Cultural Field: Continuity or Change?' in R Craufurd Smith, *Culture and European Union Law* (Oxford University Press, 2004) 22; Sassatelli (n 109 above).

[113] R Collins, *Broadcasting and Audio-visual Policy in the Single European Market* (Luton Press, 1994); T Theiler, *Political Symbolism and European Integration* (Manchester University Press, 2006).

[114] Art 167.5 TFEU.

[115] Decision 71/96, Kaleidoscope [1996] OJ L99/20; Decision 2085/97, Ariane [1997] OJ L291/26, Decision 228/97, Raphael [1997] OJ L305/31, and Decision 508/2000/EC, Culture 2000 [2000] OJ L63/1.

[116] Decision 508/2000/EC (n 116 above). See report from the Commission on the implementation of the Culture 2000 programme, COM(2008) 231 final.

existing domestic cultural policies.[117] Culture 2000 was also criticized for funding rather traditional initiatives, offering limited support for projects concerned with minority cultures or minority rights.[118]

The EU has sought to address these criticisms in the current Culture 2007 programme. The programme budget has more than doubled to €400 million, albeit now spread among twenty-seven Member States, and the programme's overarching objectives have been reduced to just three:

- transnational mobility for people working in the cultural sector;
- transnational circulation of artistic and cultural works and products; and
- intercultural dialogue.

Many of the successful projects under the present programme have a distinct contemporary feel, tackling issues such as the use of public spaces in cities or art in hospitals, and are highly innovative. There is also a marked focus on popular culture, such as folk music, cabaret, and circuses, as opposed to high art, and many projects are specifically aimed at the young.[119] This may be explained by the Commission's intention to deploy culture to foster broad support for European integration outside elite circles and particularly among the young, the EU's future citizens.[120] There are still relatively few projects organized by, or relating to, specific minorities, the Roma seeming to attract most attention, but a significant proportion address issues relating to migration, exclusion, and poverty more generally, or seek to promote EU values of cultural tolerance and respect for human rights.

If these initiatives feed into the 'bottom-up' development of a European identity, or at least sensibility, as the Commission anticipates that they will, this is likely to be in a slow and rather incremental manner, with cause and effect difficult to establish. Perhaps for this reason, the programme also allocates funding for flagship 'special actions', such as the European Capitals of Culture event, which are intended to raise the public profile of EU intervention in the cultural field and attract national attention.[121]

The Culture programmes have been designed to feed into what Michael Bruter calls the 'cultural component' of European identity, comprising a sense of belonging to a particular group, in this context a group that extends beyond national borders. But they also support, to a lesser extent, the 'civic component', which involves identification with a political structure, its values and institutions.[122] There is, of course, an overlap between the two categories, in that identification with particular values can

---

[117] Craufurd Smith (n 112 above) 70–75.

[118] Ahmed and Hervey (n 9 above).

[119] The selection results can be accessed via the Commission's culture webpage at <http://ec.europa.eu/culture/index_en.htm>. Interestingly, only a few concern the elderly.

[120] Consider Commission communication 'Making Citizenship Work: Fostering European Culture and Diversity through Programmes for Youth, Culture, Audiovisual and Civic Participation', COM(2004) 154 final.

[121] Decision 1622/2006/EC, European Capital of Culture Event for 2007 to 2019 [2006] OJ L304/1.

[122] M Bruter, 'On What Citizens Mean by Feeling "European": Perceptions of News, Symbols and Border-less-ness' (2004) 30 JEMS 21–39.

lead to a sense of group belonging and may be understood as 'cultural' in a broad sense. The picture is reversed in the EU's various citizenship initiatives, where there is a more pronounced emphasis on promoting European values and human rights, though both cultural and civic elements can be detected in initiatives such as the Citizens for Europe programme, which supports events that increase the 'peoples of Europe . . . sense of belonging to the same community, make them aware of the history, achievements and values of the European Union, involve them in intercultural dialogue and contribute to the development of their European identity'.[123]

In organizational terms, the Culture 2007 programme promotes networking among cultural organizations at the European level, requiring, in relation to specific projects, the involvement of at least three or six organizations from different states, depending on the project length. Limited grants are also available for cooperation projects with third countries. In addition, cultural organizations active in at least seven countries can obtain funding to act as 'cultural ambassadors' or to represent particular cultural interests. One potential cause for concern is the fact that organizations from the 'old' Member States, such as Italy, France, the UK, and Germany, have been more successful at securing grants under the 2007 programme than those from the 'newer' states.[124] This disparity is somewhat ameliorated, however, by the fact that organizations from the 'new' states participate in many of the projects coordinated by the 'old' states, suggesting distinct integrative and capacity building functions.[125]

The most recent stage in the EU's direct engagement with culture can be traced back to the Commission's 2007 communication on 'A European Agenda for Culture in a Globalising World'.[126] The Agenda was important not so much for proposing distinct substantive policies but for identifying overarching EU cultural objectives, designed to focus future European activity in the cultural field, and for its consideration of how the Commission's ability to formulate effective cultural policies and integrate cultural concerns into its other policies might be improved.

In terms of objectives, the Agenda emphasized the importance of preserving and protecting cultural diversity, particularly in the international field, in line with the UNESCO Convention on Cultural Diversity.[127] Culture is increasingly seen by the EU to be an important element in its external relations and, since the Agenda, it has committed additional financial resources to this field.[128] The Agenda also called for

---

[123] Decision 1904/2006/EC (n 108 above), Action 3.

[124] Statistics provided by the Education, Audiovisual and Culture Executive Agency at <http://eacea.ec. europa.eu/culture/index_en.php>.

[125] ibid.

[126] Commission communication on a European Agenda for Culture in a Globalizing World, COM(2007) 242 final.

[127] UNESCO Convention (n 19 above).

[128] Note the 'Conclusions of the Council of the European Union on the Promotion of Cultural Diversity and Intercultural Dialogue in the External Relations of the Union and its Member States', Brussels, 20 November 2008. More than one hundred million Euros have been earmarked for culture in third countries and regional cooperation since 2007: Commission Report on the Implementation of the European Agenda for Culture, COM(2010) 390.

the economic importance of the cultural and creative industries to be recognized as part of the Lisbon Strategy for economic growth, reflecting policy shifts that have already taken place in Member States such as the UK.[129] In terms of improving policy-making, the Agenda, as discussed above, envisaged a more structured dialogue with Europe's fragmented cultural organizations through the further development of networks and representative platforms; the collection of dedicated statistical information on culture; and more effective coordination within the Commission itself when dealing with cultural issues, for instance, through the inter-service group on culture.[130]

The Agenda was also important for proposing use of the open method of coordination (OMC) in the cultural field.[131] The suggestion was taken up by the Council in November 2007 and expert Working Groups have now been set up to consider such issues as how best to enhance artists' mobility and public access to culture or maximize the potential of the creative industries.[132] Given the limited resources available to both the EU and Member States in the cultural field, pooling of expertise and resources in this way offers clear advantages in terms of policy development and could facilitate greater complementarity between EU and Member State initiatives.[133] But the use of OMC in contexts where the EU could itself have acted raises concerns about representation, notably in relation to the European Parliament and Committee of the Regions, given the control that the Member States retain over the process, particularly at the early stages of policy development.[134]

An initial assessment of the practical impact of OMC in this area suggests that although it has facilitated the exchange of information and expertise among the Member States, there has been limited success in converting the policy recommendations made by the Working Groups into concrete initiatives, either at EU or national levels.[135] This is disappointing, in that a number of interesting ideas have been put forward, such as building a European network of financial institutions to provide support for the cultural and creative sectors and developing a range of think tanks, with independent academic input, to make policy proposals in economically important fields, such as copyright, where industry lobby groups have been particularly effective at directing the policy agenda.[136] OMC also

---

[129] The Department for Culture Media and Sport, for example, began to identify and evaluate the economic impact of the 'creative industries' in its *Creative Industries Mapping Document*, November 1998.

[130] See text accompanying n 87 above.

[131] See n 126 above.

[132] Council Res. on a European Agenda for Culture [2007] OJ C287/1 and Conclusions of the Council and the Representatives of the Governments of the Member States on the Work Plan for Culture 2008–2010 [2008] OJ C143/9.

[133] There is already some indication of this in the way in which the Commission and Member States initiatives cross over in the field of promoting artists mobility. For further evidence of interaction see Commission Report on the Implementation of the European Agenda for Culture (n 128 above).

[134] See 'Principles relating to the setting up and functioning of the working groups' in *Working Groups Set Up in Implementation of the Council Work Plan for Culture 2008–2010*, at <http://ec.europa.eu/culture/pdf/doc1633_en.pdf>.

[135] Commission Report on the Implementation of the European Agenda for Culture (n 128 above).

[136] See Expert Working Group on maximising the potential of Cultural and Creative Industries, in particular that of SMEs, Preliminary Report, September 2009 at 16 and 18.

offers the EU some leverage to influence policy development in areas such as the school curriculum that remain within the Member States exclusive competence.[137]

E. CONCLUSION

In its 2007 Agenda for Culture in a Globalising World, the Commission stated that the 'European Union is not just an economic process or a trading power, it is already widely—and accurately—perceived as an unprecedented and successful social and cultural project'.[138] Culture is thus seen not simply as a by-product of successful economic integration, it is now 'a project' in its own right. Increasingly, too, the Community's multi-faceted engagement with culture is presented as pursuing an overarching objective, the promotion of cultural diversity, regarded as a source of individual and social, as well as potential economic, enrichment. It is a diversity that draws on distinct domestic cultures but is no longer bounded by national borders, suggesting new and innovative ways to redraw the map of Europe.

The EU has had to follow a difficult path between, on the one hand, opening up Member States and their citizens to foreign cultural influences, spearheaded through the Treaty free movement provisions, and, on the other, leaving sufficient space for domestic and EU intervention to support specific cultures at risk in the competitive environment thereby created. In the eyes of some it has undoubtedly failed in this endeavour, the result both of a lack of genuine commitment to cultural concerns and an inappropriate institutional and legislative framework. Moreover, it is questionable whether, in straightened economic circumstances, Member States and the EU will commit the resources or display the will power to address the problems of commodification and homogenization that the market throws up. Although the EU has certainly taken steps to engage more effectively with Europe's fragmented cultural sector, this author doubts whether, without an express power to harmonize national measures in the cultural field, the EU will ever take culture seriously in those areas where EU law has arguably most cultural impact, notably in the internal market context.

The introduction of a specific culture Article in the Treaty has, however, created a space where the role that culture can, and should, play in the process of EU integration can be explored. Moreover, the current Culture 2007 programme, with its emphasis on transnational cultural exchange and intercultural dialogue, is quite distinct from national and regional initiatives with their largely inward-looking focus, as well as from the projects financed by the Structural Funds. EU cultural policy thus brings something new to the table, but limited resources and small-scale projects mean that it

---

[137] See Working Group on developing synergies with education, especially arts education, Intermediate Report, August 2009, available at <http://ec.europa.eu/culture>.
[138] Commission Communication (n 126 above) 3.

will struggle to have a concrete impact either on the development of a distinct European identity or European citizens' openness to, and tolerance of, difference.

The EU has also had an impact at the institutional level, encouraging the formation of networks among cultural organizations both within and across Member States. In countries such as the UK, for example, this has necessitated a reappraisal of how regional and national bodies cooperate in the cultural field. The introduction of the OMC in this area has stimulated further dialogue between the Member States on cultural matters, creating additional scope to enhance the synergies that exist between domestic and EU cultural policy initiatives.

EU engagement with culture has thus evolved markedly since 1957. What started off as, at best, a secondary consideration is now, at least rhetorically, at the heart of the EU's activities. With the creation of a European internal market, the EU has turned its attention to ensuring that Europe's ideological superstructure resonates with its remodelled economic base.

INDEX